Annual of German & European Law

Volume II/III
(2004/2005)

Edited by

Russell A. Miller
University of Idaho College of Law

and

Peer C. Zumbansen
Osgoode Hall Law School, York University, Toronto

Berghahn Books
NEW YORK · OXFORD

First published in 2006 by

Berghahn Books

www.berghahnbooks.com

© 2006 Russell A. Miller and Peer C. Zumbansen

All rights reserved.
Except for the quotation of short passages
for the purposes of criticism and review, no part of this book
may be reproduced in any form or by any means, electronic or
mechanical, including photocopying, recording, or any information
storage and retrieval system now known or to be invented,
without the written permission of the publisher.

Library of Congress Cataloging-in-Publication Data

A catalog record for this book is available from the Library of Congress

British Library Cataloguing-in-Publication Data

A catalogue record for this book is available
from the British Library.

Printed in the United States on acid-free paper.

ISBN 1-84545-268-2 (hardback)

Contents

Foreword   vii
Antje Wiener

SECTION I: SCHOLARLY ARTICLES

German Religious Freedoms: The Movement Toward Protection of Minorities   1
Edward J. Eberle

The Reform of the Statutory Social Welfare System and the Case Law of the *Bundesverfassungsgericht*   23
Renate Jaeger

The Learning Sovereign   45
Günter Frankenberg

Judicial Review of Administrative Agency Action: Should America Adopt the German Model?   60
Marc Chase McAllister

Preventive Detention in Comparative Perspective   89
Andrew Hammel

The Impact of Directive 1999/44/EC on German Sales Law   116
Peter Rott

European Challenges for German Law: An Analysis of the Recent Jurisprudence of the European Court of Justice on the Freedom of Establishment and its Impact on German Corporate Law and Conflict of Laws   132
Martin Schulz

On the Interpretation of Legal Precedents and of the Judgments of the European Court of Human Rights   156
Boštjan M. Zupančič

Between Citizens and Peoples: Reflections on the New European Constitutionalism   171
Sergio Dellavalle

Who Has the Right to Intra-European Social Security? From Market Citizen to European Citizens and Beyond   216
Dorte Sindbjerg Martinsen

SECTION II: FORUM: FREE MOVEMENT IN THE EU

From Persons to Citizens and Beyond: The Evolution of Personal Free Movement in the European Union 239
Nigel Foster

Freedom of Movement as a Union Citizen's Right 283
Dieter H. Scheuing

SECTION III: JURISDICTIONAL REPORTS

Report – *Bundesverfassungsgericht* (Federal Constitutional Court) – 2003 333
Felix Müller

Report – *Bundesverwaltungsgericht* (Federal Administrative Court) – 2004 354
Craig T. Smith

Report – *Bundesgerichtshof in Zivilsachen* (Federal Court of Justice, Private Law) – 2003/2004 361
Jan Stemplewitz

Report – *Bundesgerichtshof in Strafsachen* (Federal Court of Justice, Criminal Law) – 2002/2003 378
Ralph Grunewald and Christoph J.M. Safferling

Report – *Bundesarbeitsgericht* (Federal Labor Court) – 2002/2003 399
Anna L. Izzo and Friedemann F. Kiethe

Report – *Landesverfassungsgerichte* (State Constitutional Courts) – 2002 412
Christian von Coelln

Report – European Court of Justice – 2003/2004 426
Kai Peter Ziegler

Report – European Court of Human Rights – 2003/2004 445
Florian F. Hoffmann

SECTION IV: BOOK REVIEWS

Basil Markesinis and Hannes Unberath: *The German Law of Torts: A Comparative Treatise*, 4th edition 467
Bernhard Grossfeld

Peter L. Murray and Rolf Stürner: *German Civil Justice* 469
Giesela Rühl

Marcel Storme (ed.): *Procedural Laws in Europe. Towards Harmonisation* 472
Jan Bolt

Joseph A. McCahery et al. (eds.): *Corporate Governance Regimes. Convergence and Diversity*
Christin M. Forstinger: *Takeover Law in the EU and the USA*
Jennifer Payne (ed.): *English and German Law of Takeovers* 478
   Peer Zumbansen

Klaus König (ed.): *Deutsche Verwaltung an der Grenze zum 21. Jahrhundert* 493
   Markus Pöcker

Giovanna Borradori (ed.): *Philosophy in a Time of Terror. Dialogues with Jürgen Habermas and Jacques Derrida* 497
   Martti Koskenniemi

Catherine Dupré: *Importing the Law in Post-Communist Transitions* 502
   Renáta Uitz

Andreas Fahrmeir: *Citizens and Aliens – Foreigners and the Law in Britain and the German States, 1789–1870* 509
   Helene Oger

Fiona Cownie: *Legal Academics. Culture and Identity* 511
   Alexandra Kemmerer

Andreas Müller-Driver: *Grenzüberschreitende Restrukturierungen von Kapitalgesellschaften zwischen Deutschland und England* 516
   Anna L. Izzo

Jan Pieter Krahnen and Reinhard H. Schmidt (eds.): *The German Financial System* 522
   David C. Donald

Jörg Menzel: *Landesverfassungsrecht* 530
   Christian von Coelln

SECTION V:
German Federal Constitutional Court, *Teacher's Headscarf* Case
(BVerfGE 108, 282) 533

Index 553

Foreword

While the success of the *Annual of German & European Law* was acknowledged in praise of the first volume, the editors have successfully overcome an even bigger hurdle by accomplishing the compilation of this second volume. The *Annual*'s editors thus demonstrate stamina and the energy and open mind for ongoing innovation. They are to be congratulated for both, ... and more. Colleagues who lead a rather globalized, professional everyday-life, including not only frequent involvement in different cultures but also speaking, reading and writing in different languages, will appreciate the *Annual*'s achievement; especially the hard work and tremendous effort that needs to be constantly mobilized for a project that depends on making foreign language authorship available to a larger readership by translating texts, commenting on ideas, soliciting manuscripts, and encouraging critical dialogue. Interaction with different legal cultures often reveals surprises regarding writing practice, style and research focus. Thus, it is not a rare occurrence to note, for example, that for certain terms there is no easy translation. There may be too many or, indeed, too few words available in the other language. Terms and meanings are culturally contingent; they require explanation before translation into different languages or, as it were, transposition into other contexts. In addition, as Joseph Weiler quite correctly and significantly noted in his foreword to the *Annual*'s first volume, what qualifies as a "theory" for some may be considered a mere "doctrinal discussion" for others; what appears "dogmatic" to some, appears as a "specific cultural practice" when put into context. For some the "rule lies in the practice" and for others, the dogma dominates. If both the editors' efforts, not only with respect to the *Annual*, but also with respect to the *German Law Journal* (www.germanlawjournal.com), which they also founded and continue to edit, result in demystifying and rigorously scrutinizing the validity of theoretical assumptions across the boundaries between one academic culture and another, it is an achievement to be reckoned with on the international stage.

The *German Law Journal* has already brought German legal scholarship closer to an English reading audience, thus offering an important and valuable new source of information and reference to legal scholars and social scientists. The *Annual*'s additional European dimension creates opportunities for exploring broader research issues thus targeting a larger readership. This additional focus on Europe will benefit from a broader cross-cultural perspective on legal scholarship based on a more diverse range of academic experiences and traditions. The development of transnational modes of governance, changing modern constitutionalism and the future of multilateralism are some such research issues. Cross-cultural dialogue at its best will challenge so-called "universal" or Western assumptions; it will substantiate our knowledge based on debates, special issues and particular thematic and theoretical discussions. In this respect, the consistent input offered by Central and Eastern European legal scholars, with their close intellectual relationship with continental European legal scholarship is to be particularly highlighted. The renewed interaction with academic work drawn from a wider, non-English-speaking Europe offers invaluable insights into the coming debates of European and International Law. For example, engagement in scholarly debate across cultural boundaries particularly has potential to engage in a project of rigorously questioning values that are considered as lying at the core of the world of "civilised nations." After all, these particular "Western" values run the risk of becoming dangerously meaningless and evaporating into rhetoric. Their moral and institutional roots in international declarations need to be tested, compared and reassessed, so as to make sure that their commonsensical application and proliferation in policy and political discourse around the world does not undermine their potential.

Intercultural dialogue lies at the core of this publishing enterprise, which has just successfully taken its second step. If applied rigorously and consistently, this dialogue can shed some light on the paradox of building institutions within a multiversal global context by equipping them with universal certainties that have been derived from particular contexts. Thus, many of the norms political scientists are fond of considering as "universally held," such as sovereignty, citizenship, the rule of law, democracy, human rights, and minority rights, have become "essentially contested concepts" even though entrenched in international, regional and national legal texts and their provisions. The contributions to the *Annual*, especially when addressing the larger European dimension, cast a fresh light on these concepts, thus offering both authors and readership a forum for comparison, exchange and debate.

Antje Wiener
Professor of International Relations
Director, Jean Monnet Centre of Excellence
Jean Monnet Professor of European Politics
Queen's University of Belfast

SECTION I:
SCHOLARLY ARTICLES

German Religious Freedoms: The Movement Toward Protection of Minorities

Edward J. Eberle*

A. Introduction

The German *Grundgesetz* (GG – Basic Law) enumerates religious freedoms in great detail, consistent with the emphasis the 1949 charter placed on securing human dignity and human rights as the basis on which to refound a society in the aftermath of World War II. The key provision for individual freedom is article four, which protects explicitly freedoms of faith, conscience, and religious or philosophical creed (*Weltanschauung*) and provides for "[T]he undisturbed practice of religion."[1] These guarantees provide for the free exercise of religion in Germany. A host of other constitutional provisions outline the cooperative relationship between church and state that is characteristic of Germany[2] and other continental European countries, and which differs from the stricter separation of church and state traditionally mandated by the First Amendment to the United States Constitution.[3]

---

* Professor of Law, Roger Williams University School of Law Copyright 2004, by Edward J. Eberle. All rights reserved. Parts of this article appear in, Edward J. Eberle, *Free Exercise of Religion in Germany and the United States*, 78 TULANE LAW REVIEW 1023 (2004) (Copyright, *Tulane Law Review*. All rights reserved.). Use of those portions of that article is with the permission of the *Tulane Law Review*. I wish to thank Andrew Beerworth for his valuable comments and research, and Russell Miller for his valuable editorial suggestions on this article.

1 Article four of the Basic Law provides:

(1) Freedom of faith and of conscience, and freedom to profess a religious or philosophical creed [*Weltanschauung*], shall be inviolable.
(2) The undisturbed practice of religion shall be guaranteed.
(3) No person shall be compelled against his conscience to render military service involving the use of arms. Details shall be regulated by federal law.

2 The main provision in the Basic Law is article 140, which incorporates as an organic whole the provisions of the 1919 Weimar Constitution (articles 136, 137, 139 and 141). These provisions secure civil and political rights for religious actors (article 136); prohibit a state church and allow religious organizations to form bodies, regulate their own affairs, acquire and exercise legal capacity, and form public corporate bodies, including the right to levy taxes (article 137); rights to own property (article 139); provision of Sunday and other public holidays as days of rest (article 139); and rendering of spiritual care to the armed forces (article 141).

3 "Congress shall make no law respecting an establishment of religion, or prohibiting the free exercise thereof. ..." U. S. CONST. amend. I.

At the time of the framing of the Basic Law, these religious freedoms applied to an essentially homogenous population of German citizens consisting of those historically resident in Germany and Germans newly relocated from east European regions that had been ceded to Soviet forces and influence. What was then the Federal Republic of Germany – informally known as West Germany to distinguish it from its Soviet influenced cousin to the East, the *Deutscher Demokratische Republic* or *DDR* – mainly consisted of a population that was roughly split religiously between Lutheran or other Protestant Christian denominations and Roman Catholics, with a very small population of Jewish survivors who had chosen to remain in or relocate to Germany after the Holocaust. This period of relative homogeneity in population endured until the early 1960s, when the rise of the *Wirtschaftswunder* (Economic Miracle) created a great demand for labor, a demand far beyond that which the native German population could supply.

During the first fifteen years under the authority of the Basic Law, support for church and state consisted of overlapping majoritarian configurations. The main political and economic forces were Christian in orientation. In this climate of stability and homogeneity, church-state cooperation made sense and formed a comfortable fit. After all, support for the Lutheran or Roman Catholic churches overlapped with support for the majoritarian elements of society, which reinforced predominant political and cultural power. The homogeneity in religion helped form and affirm the underlying consensus on values, including the promotion of democracy, toleration, and human rights, all of which would be necessary for the refounding of German society. Church-state cooperation effectively operated, *de facto*, as an establishment of religion. This cooperative model of church and state functioned well in a society of relative religious homogeneity struggling to overcome the trauma of the Nazi nightmare. In fact, church and religious elements were one segment of German society relatively less unscathed by the Nazi experience.[4] Possessing a residue of moral stature found lacking in other public and civic institutions, religious leaders naturally were in a position to exercise influence in the building of the *Bundesrepublik Deutschland* (BRD – Federal Republic of Germany).

With the immigration of foreigners to Germany as a labor force to service the *Wirtschaftswunder*, the character of German society began to change. Initially, many foreigners were from southern Europe, especially Italy and the areas of the old Yugoslavia. The immigration, in large numbers, of non-Germans called for adjustment by the country. Yet, southern Europeans shared some similar cultural backgrounds with Germans, including common European histories, religions and cultural influences, and this helped ease the adjustment. But southern Europeans were not alone in seeking their fortunes in Germany. Muslims from Turkey also took advantage of the relaxed German policy toward immigration. The influence of Islam was a very different experience for predominately Christian and western Germany.

Today, Germany is evolving toward a pluralistic (integration of diverse groups), if not multicultural (nonintegration of diverse groups) society. Roughly eight percent of the German population is ethnically non-German.[5] The largest minority group is of Turkish

4 "The Churches did not challenge the National Socialists' claim to absolute power either. The Protestant Church in particular willingly submitted to the National Socialist state – in line with its tradition as the Church closest to the state in Germany. Only a minority of Protestant priests, who formed the Bekennende Kirche or Confessing Church, opposed this official stance. The Catholic Church was more resilient and succeeded in particular in preserving its unity as a religious community. The price it paid for this, however, was complete abstinence. Indeed, with the concordat of 20 July 1933, concluded between the German Reich and the Vatican, the Catholic Church helped significantly to enhance the standing of the National Socialist regime among the Catholic population and on the international stage." GERMAN BUNDESTAG, QUESTIONS ON GERMAN HISTORY: PATHS TO PARLIAMENTARY DEMOCRACY 268–269 (1998).
5 SEARCH EUROPE, COUNTRY GUIDE: GERMANY *at* http://searcheurope.com/countries/germany.

descent, constituting about 2.5 percent of the population.⁶ Germany has the second largest Turkish population in the world. Roughly three percent of Germany's population is Muslim.⁷ Germany is expected to become increasingly pluralistic, especially in view of declining birthrates among ethnic Germans. The need for a talented workforce will increase the demand for immigration of skilled labor.⁸ Or, at least, that will be the question for Germany: to facilitate immigration of skilled labor in order to aid Germany's ability to compete in a globalized marketplace or, alternatively, to attempt to maintain intact, as much as possible, the ethnically German nature of its population and, with that, potentially, to suffer economically in the global marketplace.

In this changing country, it is appropriate to explore the scope and range of religious freedoms, as different peoples naturally bring to a country different customs and mores. There might be many ways of measuring the strength of religious freedoms in a country. For example, one might gauge the degree to which fundamental protections of freedoms of conscience and conviction are guaranteed. A more demanding test would be to assess the degree to which a person can freely practice and exercise religious freedoms. Distinguishing between freedom of belief and freedom of religiously motivated behavior is an important attribute of western constitutional culture. On both these tests, modern Germany scores well.⁹ However, the main context in which these core religious freedoms have arisen, at least in the past, is with respect to majoritarian Christian religions and the Jewish faith. A further test of religious freedom would gauge how well the society protects the beliefs of its less-well integrated minorities or dissenters. It is relatively easy to protect the spiritual affairs of the majority because their beliefs and values tend to be reflected in society's laws and mores and the members of the cultural majority are less likely to run afoul of the status quo. In some sense, the character of a community more revealingly is displayed in how it treats those members who defy convention, stand outside the mainstream or believe in the unpopular. In fact, we might say the real value of a human right is how it protects minority groups from the overwhelming power of majoritarian groups.

In this article I will examine how well Germany protects the religious beliefs and practices of minority elements in modern German society. Gauging how Germany responds to a changing ethnic and religious population in maintaining its balance between the aspirations of individual freedom and the demands of the social order is a valuable exercise in assessing how we respond to changing forces of pluralism, globalization, terrorism and constant change.

To assess the climate of religious freedom in Germany, I concentrate on recent decisions of the *Bundesverfassungsgericht* (BVerfG – Federal Constitutional Court), interpreting and applying the religious and/or ideological protections of the Basic Law. A number of recent decisions of the Federal Constitutional Court have involved claims of constitutional violations asserted by members of minority religions or philosophical groups. These decisions include the claims of the Baha'i to autonomously run their own affairs,¹⁰ the ability of the Jehovah's Witnesses to constitute themselves as a public corporation even though they do

---

6 *Id.*
7 EDWARD J. EBERLE, DIGNITY AND LIBERTY: CONSTITUTIONAL VISIONS IN GERMANY AND THE UNITED STATES 49 (2002). GERMAN BUNDESTAG, *supra* note 4, (3.7% of German population is Muslim).
8 *See, e.g.*, Florian Becker, *The Decision of the German Constitutional Court on the Immigration Act*, 4 GERMAN LAW JOURNAL 91 (2003), *at* http://www.germanlawjournal.com/pdf/Vol04No02/PDF_Vol_04_No_02_91-106_Public_Becker.pdf.
9 For an extended examination of this topic, *see* Edward J. Eberle, *Free Exercise of Religion in Germany and the United States*, 78 TUL. L. REV. 1023 (2004).
10 BVerfGE 83, 341 (ruling that article four self-autonomy allows Baha'i religion to rule itself as it likes, even when supreme religious authorities outside Germany order affairs differently than communities within Germany).

not vote or otherwise participate in the political process,[11] the claims of a meditation society to be free from designation as a "sect" and like characterizations by the German government,[12] and the right of a Muslim, Turkish butcher to engage in ritual slaughter without the permissions typically required by law.[13] Even more recently the Federal Constitutional Court has ruled that a Muslim woman could not be denied a teaching position in public schools on account of her intention to wear a head scarf in class[14] and that a Turkish shop assistant had been wrongly dismissed for expressing a desire to wear a head scarf at work in the perfume section of a department store.[15] It is worthwhile to see how these claims of religious and/or ideological minorities fare in achieving their due under the Basic Law. Most critical is examination of Germany's treatment of people of Muslim faith, as Islam is a major religion of the world, one on the rise in Europe, but one mainly alien to European culture. The extent of religious freedom extended to Muslims is a keen test of Germany's commitment to human rights.

The scope of this study is limited: I examine three of the Federal Constitutional Court's most recent major decisions on religious freedom, *Ritual Slaughter*, *Teacher's Head Scarf* and *Jehovah's Witness*, and one involving philosophical beliefs, *OSHO*, in order to obtain a sense of the vibrancy of religious/philosophical freedoms in Germany as they pertain to minorities. I concentrate especially on cases involving claims by Muslims for religious freedoms because integration of Islam into contemporary European society is a major issue for Germany and Europe as a whole. While limited, this study is nevertheless revealing; Germany has essentially extended fundamental religious protections to religious minorities on the same terms enjoyed by the better-established and better-integrated religious communities. Germany has been more cautious with respect to newly-founded alternative religious/philosophical groups, such as the eastern meditation society at issue in *OSHO*; the group received important article four protections, but the government was also allowed to issue warnings as to its nature and aims. The difference in treatment accorded religious groups as compared to alternative groups like OSHO suggests a bifurcated model of religious/philosophical protection; religious groups enjoy more full protection, alternative philosophical, if not religious, groups, may enjoy somewhat reduced protection.

Nevertheless, there is discernible movement toward implementation of a principle of equal application of basic rights to all groups, which provide security for all citizens and people subject to Germany's domain. As an ideal, equality in application of norms serves to foster integrity of the rule of law. Commitment to the norms of the constitution, moreover, demonstrates a way by which a constitutional democracy can adjust to the influx of new citizens and peoples from diverse backgrounds, providing a way for integration of diverse communities (including religious communities) into society. In this way, the Basic Law might hold promise as an integrative force for Germany in its adjustment to a more pluralistic society.

---

11 *Jehovah's Witness*, BVerfGE 102, 370 (ruling that religion could not be denied status as public corporation on the ground its members did not vote; voting not requisite to prove loyalty to democratic order).
12 BVerfGE 105, 279; Bundesverfassungsgericht [BVerfG] [Federal Constitutional Court], 1BvR 1044/93, Aug. 12, 2002 (First Senate chamber decision).
13 BVerfG 104, 337.
14 BVerfGE 108, 282 (Muslim Teacher's Head Scarf Case).
15 Bundesverfassungsgericht [BVerfG] [Federal Constitutional Court], 1BvR 792/03, July 30, 2003 (chamber decision).

B. Ritual Slaughter

The *Ritual Slaughter*[16] case is well worth reviewing because it is one of the most recently decided major cases of the Federal Constitutional Court and because it concerns the needs of fundamentalist Islam. The influx of people of Muslim faith into Germany, and Europe more generally, has raised a set of difficult social issues as German, and European, society confront, among other issues, the question of whether diversity is best implemented through maintenance of an integrated, pluralistic or a separate, multicultural society. One problematic issue faced by these societies is the reluctance, in some cases, of people of Muslim faith to accept the norms of European society and integrate into the society on that basis. Many transplanted Muslims strive to maintain the ways of their homelands, creating friction among family generations and within European society as to the set of constitutive norms that shape life. In view of these difficulties, it pays to follow closely cases like *Ritual Slaughter*, observing how a country's highest (constitutional) court addresses such concerns.

The case concerned the claims of a Turkish citizen of Sunni Orthodox Muslim faith who worked as a butcher in Germany and sought an exemption from animal slaughter laws so he could engage in his religiously preferred method of slaughter. The butcher had lived in Germany for 20 years as the descendant of one of the many guest workers (*Gastarbeiter*) who populated Germany during its labor shortage after World War II and contributed to the *Wirtschaftswunder* of West Germany. He inherited a butcher shop from his father.[17] Free exercise rights are not confined to citizens, but apply to aliens as well. He desired to practice his craft of butchering in conformity with Muslim slaughter rites, for which he had a dedicated clientele. According to these beliefs it is necessary to slaughter animals quickly to permit the animal's blood to drain quickly and thoroughly. The Muslim rite is akin to kosher butchering (*schächten*).[18]

The problem for the butcher was that the craft of butchering, like so many aspects of German and European Union life, was heavily regulated. The German law reflected high regard for the welfare of animals, if such a thing may be said about the act of slaughtering.[19] Under the German law, animals were to be stunned first, and then killed as a way of making death as painless as possible for the slaughtered animal. The Turkish butcher refused to comply with the law, viewing it as contrary to the Muslim rites, primarily because the anesthetic might cause a constriction of blood vessels or some other effect tending to inhibit the flow of the animal's blood.[20]

The law had contemplated just such circumstances, carving out exceptions for those motivated by religion. The people contemplated by such accommodation, in fact, were Jewish and Muslim believers.[21] However, to get such an accommodation, it was necessary

---

16 BVerfGE 104, 337.
17 *Id.* at 340.
18 *Id.* at 338.
19 Germany recently incorporated into the Basic Law a provision empowering the state to protect natural foundations of life, including animal life. The provision, article 20a, provides: "Mindful also of its responsibility toward future generations, the state shall protect the natural bases of life by legislation and, in accordance with law and justice, by executive and judicial action, all within the framework of the constitutional order."
20 *See* Russell Miller, *The Constitutional Court's "Traditional Slaughter" Decision: The Muslims' Freedom of Faith and Germany's Freedom of Conscience*, 3 GERMAN LAW JOURNAL No. 2 (Feb. 1, 2002), *at* http://www.germanlawjournal.com/article.php?id=128.
21 Kosher butchering (*schächten*) was previously widely exempted from the general law in Germany requiring that animals first be stunned prior to being slaughtered. With the rise of Nazism, these exemptions were removed as part of the persecution of Jews. After World War II, there was only piece-meal, state-by-state regulation of slaughter. The federal law of 1986 at issue in the *Ritual Slaughter* case was the first national treatment of the issue in modern times. BVerfGE 104, 337 (338).

first to acquire permission from relevant religious authorities. The Turkish butcher had no such official permission.[22] Evidence indicated that prevailing Sunni opinion did not require that meat be prepared according to the slaughtering ritual practiced by the Turkish butcher.[23] Lacking official permission, German authorities and courts enjoined the butcher from practicing his craft according to his chosen creed.

The *Ritual Slaughter* case raised a number of important issues for religious freedom in Germany. First, the case is among the most recent major decisions, and thus illustrates how free exercise freedoms are conceived in contemporary Germany. Second, the case involved the practice of Islam, a growing but nonetheless minority community in relation to the predominantly Christian character of Germany. Third, the case also involved a diversity of views within the Muslim community, forcing the Federal Constitutional Court to confront a range of beliefs over what Islam is. In view of the increasingly pluralistic nature of German society, these were extremely crucial questions in need of constitutional answers.

Because enjoining his practice of his craft in his chosen way impeded his personal freedom, article two personality rights were at issue as well as article four's free exercise claims. Article two personality rights are always available as a catch-all for dimensions of personal freedom not captured by more specific basic rights.[24] Likewise, because the prohibition impacted the practice of his profession, article twelve's occupational freedoms were arguably at stake as well. However, the Federal Constitutional Court applied the plain language of article twelve to rule that occupational freedoms applied to Germans only, not aliens such as the Turkish butcher.[25] Instead, the Court transformed the occupational freedom claim into one that fit the article two personality right catch-all, the general preserve of personal freedom.[26] This move provided further evidence of the rich claim to personal freedom possible under the Basic Law.

Centrally, however, the *Ritual Slaughter* case concerned free exercise rights, and that is how the Federal Constitutional Court evaluated it. The Federal Constitutional Court cut to the chase. At issue here was the ability of the Muslim butcher to practice his creed according to his belief. The Court explained that the individual exercise of religious belief is a core manifestation of the personal vision of human existence that emanates from the

---

22 The Turkish butcher had obtained permits in the past to engage in ritual butchering. However, these permits were granted before the law went into effect and before the decision of the Federal Administrative Court enjoining the practice. Under the law, accommodations could be granted when religious authorities determined that the ritual was mandated by the religion. In this altered legal situation, officials would not grant the permit. *Id.* at 339–41.

23 *Id.* at 340–41. The Federal Administrative Court deferred to a lower administrative court ruling relying on the opinion of a Sunni expert in Cairo for its determination that the rite asserted by the Turkish butcher was not required as a matter of faith. According to this expert, Muslims consumed meat whether or not prepared pursuant to the ritual. According to the Muslim council in Germany, however, the rite was required. The Muslim Council in Germany asserted that the proper interpretation of the report of the expert from Cairo was that the rite could be dispensed with in an emergency. Muslims do not organize themselves into a hierarchical structure, which can set and manage doctrine for the whole of the religious community. The lack of organizational hierarchy makes it difficult for European countries, like Germany and France, which are accustomed to negotiating with representatives of a religion, to reach accords. Katherine Pratt Ewing, *Legislating Religious Freedom: Muslim Challenges to the Relationship between "Church" and "State" in Germany and France*, DAEDULUS, Sept. 22, 2000, at 5–6. In Germany, a representative of the religion is needed to form a public corporation, determine religious instruction in the public schools or other religious matters. Gerhard Robbers, *Religious Freedom in Germany*, 2001 BYU L. REV. 643, 657. *See, also*, Miller, *supra* note 20.

24 BVerfGE 54, 148 (153), cemented the view that article two always exists as a reserve of personal freedom to protect activities that do not fit in the more particular enunciation of freedoms in the Basic Law. For development of this idea, *see* Eberle, *supra* note 7, at 62–63.

25 BVerfGE 104, 337 (346). Instead, the Federal Constitutional Court valued the occupational freedom issue under the article two personality right catch-all.

26 *Id.*

ultimate constitutional value of human dignity. So viewed, the Court reasoned that what is important is that the personal vision prevail, not technical legal requirements. Thus, for the Federal Constitutional Court, it was less significant that the butcher had not obtained required permissions from religious authorities. More significant for the Court was the underlying religious motivation for the butcher's actions.

The Court further recognized that the preparation and consumption of meat in accordance with this Muslim rite was a central religious experience for a whole community of believers formed by the butcher and his customers. The butcher and his customers fervently believed in this ritual butchering as central to their daily lives. The Court found that it was important to recognize the religious convictions of these believers so that they might live life according to their creed, even if other Muslims believed differently. In so doing, the Court constitutionally credited a diversity of beliefs within the Muslim community.[27]

Recognition of alternative, and competing, communities of faith, within an over-arching religion, is an important principle of religious freedom. First, the principle acknowledges the validity of belief from the perspective of the believer, as compared to the body that hierarchically or organizationally stands to administer the faith. The orientation toward individual belief seems more in keeping with principles of religious freedom and individual rights. Second, providing for the possibility of competing communities of faith facilitates an open contest for multiple claims of truth and conviction to set forth their tenets, which in turn leaves the success (on earth) of any to be determined by how many adherents it can attract. Third, competition between communities of faith is, by definition, open to the new and the different. Minorities or dissenting voices thereby encounter a more hospitable environment in which they have a better chance of advancing their claims and achieving success by the strength of their creeds. This is in keeping with the origins of religion, most of which had their start in a position of dissent, gaining success later. In actualizing these facets in the *Ritual Slaughter* case, the Federal Constitutional Court has designed an approach to religious freedom that is sensitive to minorities' exercise of religious liberty. Prior jurisprudence of the Constitutional Court has primarily involved the claims of dominant religious communities, such as Christian Roman Catholics[28] or Protestants[29] or Jews,[30] and thus the Court has not had to face, head on, the unique set of claims presented in a case like *Ritual Slaughter*. In this respect, the Constitutional Court demonstrated a certain flexibility in applying core religious norms in ways that can meet the needs of emerging faiths in German society.

Facilitation of diversity of religious faith logically serves to protect religious freedom as well. Guaranteeing every person the ability to believe what they like and to act on such belief engenders broad respect for religious liberty. Vigorous religious rights will also act as a bulwark against government, as citizens will voice objection to government curtailment of liberty. In a country of diverse religious beliefs, it will be hard for any one group to impose its beliefs on another.[31] James Madison advocated diversity in

---

27 BVerfGE 104, 337 (354).
28 BVerfGE 24, 236 (Catholic youth organization could engage in used clothing and material drive, and solicit the cause in church pulpits, without running afoul of general business laws).
29 *See, e.g.*, BVerfGE 32, 98 (Blood Transfusion Case) (evangelical Christian husband relieved from criminal penalties for allowing wife to die due to loss of blood and abstinence from blood transfusion because actions were religiously motivated).
30 BVerfGE 35, 366 (cross displayed in court room must be removed in view of objection from Jewish lawyer).
31 Michael McConnell, *The Origins and Historical Understanding of Free Exercise of Religion*, 103 HARV. L. REV. 1409, 1515–16 (1990).

religious belief as security for civil rights and as security for peace and stability in a republic.³²

It was not always so in Germany. Authorities sometimes treated Islam as a threat to society because of their perception that the religion was fundamentalist, anti-democratic and hostile to human rights, especially the equality of women. Treatment of women as equal citizens represents a well-known fundamental contrast between western and Muslim society. Germans feel especially vulnerable to perceived threats to the stability of the social order in view of their history of political and economic instability during the Weimar democracy, which aided the rise of totalitarian Nazism. These perceptions may help explain authorities' reluctance to facilitate the public practice of Islam, such as the building of recognizable mosques, public broadcasting of calls to prayer through loud speakers and freedom of Muslim women and girls to cover themselves.³³ Yet, courts have also exempted Muslims from social strictures. For example, courts have allowed Muslim women and girls to wear head scarves in the classroom (unlike in France and Turkey) and exempted Muslim girls from compulsory school activities like gym and swimming classes.³⁴ These cases raise anew the pressing concern of integration of Muslims into German society.

Within this context of historical German and European treatment of Islam, the *Ritual Slaughter* case stands out in bold relief as a landmark case on religious liberty, recognizing the principle of religious equality – that liberty applies equally to majority and minority practitioners, in deed as well as in word. Similar trends are apparent with respect to Jehovah's Witnesses, as we will examine, and the Baha'i.³⁵ Each of these religions is somewhat exotic when viewed against the traditionally predominant Christian culture in Germany. Their favorable treatment attests to the growing climate of hospitality toward minority creeds and the correspondingly vigorous state of religious liberty in Germany.³⁶

---

32 "A religious sect may degenerate into a political faction in a part of the Confederacy; but the variety of sects dispersed over the entire face of it must secure the national councils against any danger from that source." THE FEDERALIST NO. 10 (James Madison). Madison repeated the idea in FEDERALIST NO. 51: "In a free government the security for civil rights must be the same as that for religious rights. It consists in the one case in the multiplicity of interests, and in the other in the multiplicity of sects." THE FEDERALIST NOS. 10, 51 (James Madison). Madison's theory for protection of religious liberty thus parallels his theory for protection of the republic against factions, as he famously developed in FEDERALIST NO. 10.

33 Ewing, *supra* note 23 at 3–4, 7–8. The experience is much the same in France. *Id.*

34 *Id. See also* Ingrid Brunk Wuerth, *Private Religious Choice in German and American Constitutional Law: Funding and Government Religious Speech*, 31 VAND. J. TRANSNAT'L L. 1127, 1200–1201 (1998).

35 BVerfGE 83, 341 (ruling that article four self-autonomy allows Baha'i religion to rule itself as it likes, even when supreme religious authorities outside Germany order affairs differently than communities within Germany).

36 In contrast to the generally liberal jurisprudential climate described here, Germany still views Scientology with suspicion, treating it as a cult and a commercial enterprise, not a religion. The German position is similar to that formerly held by the United States Internal Revenue Service, which revoked Scientology's tax exemption for a period of over 30 years because "even if religious in nature [it was operated] for the enrichment of specific private individuals." Michael Browne, *Should Germany Stop Worrying and Love the Octopus? Freedom of Religion and the Church of Scientology in Germany and the United States*, 9 IND. INT'L & COMP. L. REV. 155, 191 (1998) (citation omitted). *See also* Arthur C. Helton and Jochen Müenker, *Religion and Persecution: Should the United States Provide Refuge to German Scientologists?*, 11 INT'L J. REFUGEE L. 310, 311 (1999).

Recently, the German office of finance exempted Scientology from taxes on the basis of a treaty on double taxation with the United States. German authorities were careful to observe that the tax ruling did not imply recognition of Scientology as a religion. However, Scientology officials viewed the ruling as a first step in setting Scientology on the same plane as other religions in Germany. *Steuerbefreiung für Scientology*, FRANKFURTER ALLGEMEINE ZEITUNG, No. 29, 4 Feb. 2003, at 2; *Scientology ab sofort steuerfrei*, SPIEGEL ONLINE, 3 Feb. 2003, *at* http://www.spiegel.de/wirtschaft;0,1518,233557,00.html. Thus, some change in thinking is apparent concerning Scientology.

Similarly, the Constitutional Court's decision in *OSHO* (BVerfGE 105, 279) and later the First Senate's chamber decision in *OSHO*, Bundesverfassungsgericht [BVerfG] [Federal Constitutional Court] 1 BvR

The German principles of respect for diverse beliefs had immediate application in the case. Whether a practice is absolutely required as a matter of religious belief is less a question to be determined by religious officials. Instead, the question is to be resolved within the context of a concrete community of believers.[37] Mere subjective belief is insufficient, however, and the community must demonstrate to the court's satisfaction that the practice is required by their beliefs.[38] Given their sincerity and dedication to ritual slaughter, the Federal Constitutional Court was well satisfied that the butcher and his customers constituted a community that acted according to creed.

Posing the question in this fashion, the Federal Constitutional Court resolved it in conformity with the common pattern of its free exercise jurisprudence. Given the clash between exercise of religious freedom and the constraints of the general law, the proper resolution is recognition and respect of religious practices even if that requires accommodation of the general laws. It is improper for the state to deny legitimate religious claims just because they deviate from accepted practice.[39] In the case at hand, the general interest sacrificed to the Muslim's interest in religious freedom involved the prevention of needless cruelty to animals. Animals are accorded high respect in Germany. The purpose of the law was to recognize animals as mutually living beings, not just objects.[40] Ethical treatment was the goal. However, the Federal Constitutional Court insisted that the religious practice at issue be given fuller consideration than had been given it by the lower courts under the general balancing of interests test. The Court concluded that enforcement of the animal cruelty law would have a severe impact on the interests of the Muslim butcher. Without any exception, the butcher would not be able to practice his craft according to his creed. His customers would also have difficulty obtaining meat sanctified according to chosen ritual. Thus, the Court concluded that article two personality rights, in conjunction with the more specific protections of article four, had been violated.

1044/93, Aug. 12, 2002, also evidences a certain reluctance to accord the full panoply of article four rights to groups considered, in some way, to be on the fringe of normal religious/ideological adherents. OSHO is a meditation society that objected to being labeled a "youth sect" and other characterizations by officials. The Constitutional Court reasoned that the government was simply informing the public of the group's character and tendencies so that citizens could take appropriate actions or precautions as they saw fit. Official warnings of this sort raised no issue of the government's need to maintain neutrality in matter of church and state, a principle extrapolated from the precepts established in a case of similar import issued the same day, *Glykol*. In *Glykol*, the Court determined that official warnings that wine contained the ingredient glycol were not violations of the distributor's article twelve occupational freedoms. *Glykol*, BVerfGE 105, 252.

However, it is fair to say that official warnings that a group is a sect or a cult are likely to have negative, perhaps, chilling consequences on the ability of a group to attract or maintain adherents, thus damaging its prospects. Dietrich Murswiek, *Das Bundesverfassungsgericht und die Dogmatik mittelbarer Grundrechtseingriffe: Zu der Glykol- und der Osho-Entscheidung vom 26.6.2002*, NEUE ZEITSCHRIFT FÜR VERWALTUNGSRECHT 1, 6 (2003). In this respect, a claim for violation of article four freedoms might be plausible. *Id*. For better or worse, however, German constitutional law presently views official warnings like this as justified, and not inconsistent with the Basic Law on account of the Basic Law's commitment to positive liberty, empowering the state to act in order to safeguard citizens' rights and welfare. Whatever the merits or demerits of the doctrine, it presents quite complicated issues, well beyond this article. For careful consideration of OSHO and Glykol, and their ramnifications, see Marion Albers, *Rethinking the Doctrinal System of Fundamental Rights: New Decisions of the Federal Constitutional Court Court*, 3 GERMAN LAW JOURNAL No. 11 (2002); Murswiek, *supra*; Reinhard Ruge, *Between Law and Necessity: The Federal Constitutional Court Confirms the Right of the Federal Government to Warn the Public (In Reply to Marion Albers)*, 3 GERMAN LAW JOURNAL No. 12 (Nov. 1, 2002). For extended discussion of *OSHO*, see *infra* Section C.

37 BVerfGE 104, 337 (353–54).
38 *Id*. at 354–55.
39 *Id*. at 355.
40 *Id*. at 351.

In a sense, accommodation of the Turkish butcher was less of a leap than in previous free exercise cases of the Federal Constitutional Court.[41] The law recognized a range of exceptions from the general requirement that a person first stun animals before killing them, most of which were geared to Jewish and Muslim believers. Accommodating the butcher could as well fit within the pattern already recognized within the law.[42]

But in another sense the case did represent a leap. The Federal Constitutional Court had the prescience to recognize the inherently personal nature of the convictions at issue. The Court respected the choices of the Turkish butcher and his customers on their own terms and as they defined their belief. Recognition of such personal conviction was more important than belief as defined by religious or secular authorities. The Court's holding made validation of the personal quest for faith central. Thus, we can see that the approach of the Federal Constitutional Court is one especially sensitive to the dilemma of individual existence, including the demands of conscience.

It is worthwhile to look outside German borders, for a moment, to obtain some perspective on the nature of religious freedoms in a constitutional democracy. Looking to the United States, a long-running and alternative model of human rights, it is noteworthy that the *Ritual Slaughter* case contrasts with the state of the law in the United States regarding the process of accommodation of religion. In the United States Supreme Court decision *Employment Division, Department of Human Resources v. Smith*,[43] the Supreme Court viewed the democratic process as the main avenue for accommodation of religious belief, notwithstanding the Court's observation that minority sects would likely suffer under majoritarian rule.[44] Viewing the *Ritual Slaughter* case under this construct, one would be led to argue that democratic decision-makers had made all the accommodations they desired in the law already enacted. The Federal Administrative Court evaluated the case on this basis. Under this jurisprudence, the Turkish butcher ought to have sought political relief, not judicial relief, as in *Smith*. The Federal Constitutional Court refused to adopt this line, concluding that religious freedoms are too precious, and arguably too fragile, to be entrusted to the political process. The Federal Constitutional Court found that it is instead the core of the judicial function to safeguard these rights, especially when exercised by minorities. Minorities, more than majorities, need judicial solicitude precisely because minorities operate under laws made by majorities. Minorities are thus much more likely to run afoul of convention than majorities. In view of these concerns, the Federal Constitutional Court's decision was all the more remarkable in that it went farther than the statute in accommodating religious freedom in the polity.

Notably, German law has been stable and consistent for well over a thirty-year period,

---

41 *See, e.g.*, BVerfGE 32, 98 (evangelical Christian husband relieved from criminal penalties for allowing wife to die due to loss of blood and abstinence from blood transfusion because actions were religiously motivated); BVerfGE 24, 236 (Catholic youth organization could engage in used clothing and material drive, and solicit the cause in church pulpits, without running afoul of general business laws).

42 Moreover, the Federal Constitutional Court noted that the authorities could have given fuller consideration to the second alternative listed in the law, which granted some discretion to parties trying to fulfill the aims of the law in making death as painless and quick as possible. BVerfGE 104, 337 (353–55).

43 Employment Div., Dep't of Human Res. v. Smith, 494 U.S. 872 (1990). In *Smith*, the Court denied the free exercise claim of a Native American seeking exemption from the generally applicable controlled substance law for the sacramental use of peyote as prescribed by the Native American Church.

44 *Id.* at 890 ("It may be fairly said that leaving accommodation to the political process will place at a relative disadvantage those religious practices that are not widely engaged in, but that unavoidable consequence of democratic government must be preferred to a system in which each conscience is a law unto itself or in which judges weigh the social importance of all laws against the centrality of all religious beliefs.").

in contrast to the ebb and flow of American law, from *Sherbert v. Verner*[45] to *Smith*. Fidelity in service of basic human rights is desirable in a world undergoing severe change caused by forces like computerization, globalization, multiculturalism and terrorism. A second lesson of the *Ritual Slaughter* case is that these freedoms apply to all, minority religions as well as majority. In this respect, the case is notable in its solicitude for the Turkish minority in Germany, which has often felt like second-class citizens. Indeed, the Turkish butcher was a minority believer within a minority faith. Looking forward, the *Ritual Slaughter* case would seem to signal that Germany is prepared to deal with the demands of minorities for equal religious liberty. In these respects, Germany seems more attuned to the complexities of a pluralistic society, a likely product of globalization. By contrast, *Smith* would seem to signal the American move in an opposite direction, recognizing that minority religions will likely suffer under democratic rule while majority religions prosper.[46]

C. *Muslim Teacher's Head Scarf*

More recently, the Federal Constitutional Court rendered an important decision on the free exercise of religion, ruling five to three in a hotly contested case that an Afghani born woman of acquired German citizenship, Fereshta Ludin, could not be denied a teaching position in the public schools because of her religious conviction to wear a head scarf while performing her duties. The *Muslim Teacher's Head Scarf* case[47] is a long and complicated decision, involving a constellation of rights, including the article four religious rights of students and parents, article six parental rights, article seven educational rights and article thirty-three guarantees of equality in qualification and treatment (including with respect to religion or philosophical view) as a civil servant. All of these constitutional issues arose alongside the prospective teacher's article four free exercise rights. The *Muslim Teacher's Head Scarf* case further substantiates the Federal Constitutional Court's proactive empowerment of the free exercise of religion, especially in relation to Germany's rising minority Muslim population, and is thus in keeping with jurisprudential and social trends evident in the Court's *Ritual Slaughter* decision.

The basis for the Federal Constitutional Court's decision was that religiously compelled dress, such as the wearing of a head scarf, was a matter of the protected personal free exercise of religion, which government, therefore, could not use as a basis to deny qualification to the civil service (including public school teachers) under article thirty-three, at least in the absence of an underlying law that appropriately took into account the range of rights and considerations involved with this complicated issue.[48] In this respect, the *Muslim Teacher's Head Scarf* case underscores the continuing flowering of free exercise rights in Germany, especially with respect to minority religions such as Islam, as a major concern of the Federal Constitutional Court.[49] On this point, the *Muslim Teacher's Head Scarf* case is

---

45 Sherbert v. Verner, 374 U.S. 398 (1963) (Supreme Court applies strict scrutiny analysis to review free exercise claim of Seventh Day Adventist who claimed that she could not work on Saturdays because of her faith and accommodated her for religious reasons). In *Smith*, the Court confined the strict scrutiny regime to the unemployment context at issue in Sherbert.
46 Employment Div., Dep't of Human Res. v. Smith, 494 U.S. 872, 890 (1990).
47 BVerfGE 108, 282. *See* Matthias Mahlmann, *Religious Tolerance, Pluralist Society and the Neutrality of the State: The Federal Constitutional Court's Decision in the* Headscarf Case, 4 GERMAN LAW JOURNAL 1099 (2003), *at* http://www.germanlawjournal.com/pdf/Vol04No11/PDF_Vol_04_No_11_1099-1116_Public_Mahlmann.pdf.
48 BVerfGE 108, 282 (294).
49 BVerfGE 108, 282 (310) ("A regulation that prohibits teachers from displaying overtly their membership in a particular religious community or adherence to beliefs … is clearly in tension with especially pronounced growing diversity of religion in society.")

of a similar tenor to the *Ritual Slaughter* case and also of another recent decision in which the Court ruled that a Turkish shop assistant had been wrongly dismissed from her position in the perfume section of a department store for expressing a desire to wear a head scarf, again for religiously compelled reasons.[50] Yet, because the Federal Constitutional Court predicated its ruling on the technical point that no law undergirded authorities' decision to deny Ludin the teaching position, and further stated that a law that properly considered the relevant rights and interests at issue could result in denial of teaching positions to people wearing religiously compelled dress, the *Muslim Teacher's Head Scarf* case was a quite limited victory for religious freedom. For Ludin, however, the decision could be viewed as a victory, as the Federal Constitutional Court acknowledged her worth as a person desiring to live life according to her creed, even though the case guaranteed her no right to a position as a public school teacher.[51] Sometimes pyrrhic or "moral" victories make the fight worthwhile.

The mixed nature of the decision can perhaps best be read as a tentative attempt to resolve this contentious issue in respect to the far reaching role of Islam in Germany's western-oriented society. Integrated Muslim communities are relatively new to Germany, and more broadly Europe, and occidental society is adjusting to this new phenomenon. Many Germans are anxious about Islam, not knowing quite how to integrate people of this Middle Eastern faith and tradition into Germany's western cultural tradition. Germany is in the process of working out how Muslim minorities can express their identity in secular, western European society. Germans' multi-faceted view of Islam is particularly reflected in the numerous perceptions of what wearing a head scarf represents. Wearing a head scarf could be interpreted variously, as a political expression of Islamic fundamentalism, especially in contrast to the secular west; a cultural statement of ethnic identity expressing a longing for the distant homeland; a traditional dress that honors familial ties; a modern statement of self-determination and identity; a symbol of subordination of women to men under Islamic law; or a religious observance.[52] The Federal Constitutional Court chose the latter, valuing the dress as religiously compelled based upon Ludin's association of the head scarf with her Muslim, that is, spiritual identity.[53]

The disputed nature of the ruling left the Federal Constitutional Court open to well justified heavy criticism.[54] While it is beneficial for a constitutional democracy to engage its

---

50 BVerfG, 1 BvR 792/03 (30 July 2003) (chamber decision) (hereinafter *"Turkish Sales Clerk's Head Scarf"*).
51 In fact, Baden-Wuerttemberg has since enacted a law prohibiting the wearing of religious garb by public school teachers in classrooms. Tony Szuczka, *German State Bans Head Scarf: Law Bars Teachers from Wearing It*, COM. APPEAL (Memphis), Apr. 2, 2004, at A9. The law of Baden-Wuerttemberg is likely to be the subject of a constitutional challenge.
52 BVerfGE 108, 282 (304). The dissent viewed wearing of the head scarf as mainly a symbol of subordination of women to men and, therefore, inconsistent with the equality guarantee of article 3. *Id.* at 333–34.
53 BVerfGE 108, 282 (284–85, 294). In rejecting Ludin's application for a teaching position, school officials of Baden-Württemberg reasoned that display of a head scarf was a political symbol of cultural separation from western society as well as a religious symbol. Ludin instead valued the head scarf as an expression of her personality and of her religious faith. *Id.* at 284–85.
54 It is quite possible that the Federal Constitutional Court acted timidly out of respect for the democratic process, not wanting to substitute its judgment for democratic deliberation and decision over such a newly emerging issue as the role of Islam in German society. It is also possible the Federal Constitutional Court responded meekly in reaction to serious and sustained criticism unleashed in response to its controversial decisions in *Soldiers are Murder II*, BVerfGE 93, 266 (protected expression to call soldiers murderers) *affirming in substance*, *Soldiers are Murder I*, BVerfG NJW, 45 (1994), 2943 (chamber decision) and *Krucifix II*, BVerfGE 93, 1. (Bavarian display of crucifix in public schools declared unconstitutional in face of complaint.)
  The Federal Constitutional Court distinguished the case from *Krucifix II* on the basis that the *Muslim Teacher's Head Scarf* case involved an individual's exercise of religion (and therefore was less likely to be attributed to state sponsorship) in comparison to the state sponsorship of religion in *Krucifix II*, and on

citizens through democratic deliberation over the meaning of the constitution as much as possible, fundamental rights are not ordinarily thought to be subject to the process of democracy. In this respect, the *Muslim Teacher's Head Scarf* case approximates the line of thinking present in the Supreme Court's *Smith* decision.[55] Given the complex of rights at stake in the *Muslim Teacher's Head Scarf* case, however, there may be greater justification for caution and deference in the case as compared to *Smith*. There is some justification for a constitutional court to work in tandem with a democracy; not too far ahead, not too far behind the formation of values at work in society. Caution may be particularly well advised with respect to controversial issues, such as the role of Islam in society.

Still, while there are justifications for judicial restraint, the point of basic rights is to provide security for all people. As a guardian of the constitution, the Constitutional Court would have been better served by either enforcing, straightforwardly, Ludin's article four rights or, if this seemed too far reaching, then working out a more specific calculation as to how the constellation of rights would fit together. Either approach would have better served constitutional democracy and the stature of the Court.

The majority's recognition of the prospective teacher's free exercise rights seemed to be based on an attempt to understand the spiritual world of Muslim believers and, in this respect, we can acknowledge the Court's tolerance. Recognition of the Muslim faith acknowledges the emerging role Islam now plays in German society. In turn, these developments led the Federal Constitutional Court to reassess civil service rules and state neutrality obligations in religious affairs. The decision left unresolved how pluralism (integration of diverse groups in society) or multiculturalism (nonintegration of diverse groups within society) would change church-state relations.

Traditionally, the Basic Law has been interpreted as imposing on the state an obligation of neutrality in matters of religion. This obligation arises out of the concern that state support of particular religious/ideological views will be coercive to individuals partaking of state benefits. This principle of neutrality and corresponding posture of official restraint animates the German civil service. The German civil service is conceived as an intermediary between the state and citizens, a facilitator of citizens' rights under the positive dimension of freedom characteristic of the German constitutional order. For these reasons, civil servants are traditionally viewed as neutral agents of the legal order and, therefore, limited in their ability to exercise full basic rights in their official capacity. Proactive exercise of rights by civil servants, it is feared, would coerce or undermine citizens' exercise of their freedoms. On this view, Ludin could justifiably be denied a position as a teacher because her assertion of free exercise rights would fundamentally violate civil service norms of neutrality and restraint. This is the point the dissent argued, a point with merit.[56] After all, there either is neutrality or there is not. Once the lines have shifted or become blurred, it is hard to enforce a rule with consistency.

But the majority saw it differently. The Court concluded that requiring abstinence from religiously compelled dress out of concern that display of religious conviction would coerce students and undermine parental choice was asking too much of Ludin. The major-

---

the basis that a head scarf could be subject to multiple interpretations, only being a religious symbol when worn by a believer, in comparison to the cross, which always had the religious meaning of Christianity. BVerfGE 108, 282 (303–04). Not surprisingly, this distinction was not convincing to the dissent. *Id.* at 330. In fact, while the majority made the case for distinguishing the two decisions, the decisions were much alike. First, in both cases students had no choice but to be confronted with the symbols. Second, a teacher's display of plausibly religious dress might reasonably be attributed to state sponsorship as well, although indirectly. Third, many observers would view a headscarf as a religious symbol.

55 Employment Div., Dep't of Human Res. v. Smith, 494 U.S. 872, 890 (1990).
56 BVerfGE 108, 282 (316–25).

ity reasoned that the complainant did not totally sacrifice her religious freedoms at the school door. The Court explained that these freedoms are, fundamentally, to be determined from the perspective of the religious community of which she is a part, echoing the fundamental principle of the *Ritual Slaughter* case, namely that religious freedoms are to be judged from the perspective of the believer's community of faith.[57] The majority concluded that Ludin's community of belief viewed wearing head scarves as religiously compelled. It was, therefore, untenable to place her in a position of choosing between her religion or her job.[58]

These principles follow from the growing diversity among religions in German society and the way such diversity affects the classroom.[59] The Court explained that, rather than insulating school children, schools are precisely the place for exposure to a marketplace of ideas and beliefs.[60] The Court further explained that learning to appreciate difference, respect alternative beliefs and achieve toleration as building blocks to the integration of diverse people within society are important objectives in constitutional democracy, all of which is the legitimate mission of school's operated by the state.[61] True, overt display of religious observance in the classroom, especially controversial dress such as display of a head scarf, could create conflict between teachers and students, or among students, or among students and parents. But to the mind of the Court's majority, it was better to see whether, in fact, such conflict develops and then resolve it, as compared to presuming it will occur and prohibiting such dress out of such fear.[62]

Underlying the Federal Constitutional Court's reasoning would appear to be acknowledgment of Islam as an established and integrated religion in German society, which the Court seemed especially eager to do given Islam's minority status in Germany. The Court reasoned that Islam's status as a minority faith might give rise to a less significant risk that overt display of its observance in classrooms would coerce students. These factors seem to be an implicit basis by which the majority distinguished the *Muslim Teacher's Head Scarf* case from its earlier decision in the *Krucifix II* case.[63] There is something fundamentally different, the Court seemed to be asserting, between official accommodation of a minority belief within a majoritarian Christian culture (the *Muslim Teacher's Head Scarf* case) as compared to state sponsorship of the majority faith (the *Krucifix II* case).

Necessarily, the Federal Constitutional Court's emphasis on personal freedom and sectarian diversity, even within public classrooms, called for some reconceptualization of the role the state plays with respect to religion and, derivatively, civil service obligations. Rather than strict separation of church and state, more characteristic of the tradition in France, the Federal Constitutional Court envisioned the state role to be "not a distant, absent role ... but rather a respectful, nourishing neutrality"[64] that accords "equality to the

---

57 *Id.* at 298–99; *accord* BVerfGE 104, 337 (353–55).
58 BVerfGE 108, 282 (298–99). *Accord, Sherbert*, 374 U.S. at 404.
59 BVerfGE 108, 282 (307).
60 *Id.* at 290 ("Schools are no refuge, in which eyes are to be closed from the reality of a pluralistic society. Rather, schools have the mission to prepare youth for what they will encounter in society.").
61 *Id.* at 294–301.
62 *Id.* at 310–11. The Federal Constitutional Court reasoned that if conflicts over wearing religious garb in schools arise, then it makes sense to require proof that wearing religious garb influences students. *Id.* at 305–06. The dissent valued the situation differently, viewing display of a headscarf as fraught with such conflict. *Id.* at 325–26. *See* Lee v. Weisman, 505 U.S. 577, 588 (1992) ("The potential for divisiveness is of particular relevance here [prayer after graduation] ... because it centers around an overt religious exercise in a secondary environment where ... subtle coercive pressures exist and where the student had no real alternative which would have allowed her to avoid the fact or appearance of participation.").
63 BVerfGE 93, 1.
64 BVerfGE 108, 282 (287).

beliefs of all believers, understanding the attitudes advanced [by people] on equal terms."[65] Thus, even schools are "open for religious activity under the principle of an ... overlapping, open and respectful neutrality."[66] Concretely, in the case of Ludin, this meant that a prospective teacher could not be summarily refused a position because of a religious conviction to wear certain dress. Likewise, this more flexible principle of neutrality filtered into civil service obligations.[67]

Yet, the Federal Constitutional Court also recognized that the phenomenon of pluralism or, perhaps, multi-culturalism might result, ultimately, in a stricter separation of church and state in order to prevent discord in society.[68] Whether this would come to be would depend on how events unfolded. The contingencies at play in the issue would appear to be a factor in the Court's preference for a democratic process as the forum initially to forge some workable accommodation of the competing rights and interests at stake. In Ludin's case, the absence of such a law determined the outcome.[69] Thus, at bottom, we can see that the *Muslim Teacher's Head Scarf* case is a tentative step in determining the role of Islam in Germany. The case does not resolve definitively the issue of permissible religious garb in official forums, an additional point of contention to the Court's observers.

D. *Jehovah's Witness*

Turning away from consideration of Islam, let us now consider the religious rights of other minority groups.

Two years before the *Ritual Slaughter* case, the Federal Constitutional Court rendered another important decision concerning the scope of religious freedom enjoyed by minority sects. The *Jehovah's Witness* case[70] concerned the committed evangelical Christian group of Jehovah's Witnesses. Jehovah's Witnesses have long been considered exotic and different in the United States. A series of important Supreme Court cases[71] helped to transform the public image of the sect so that today they have gained more acceptance. But Jehovah's Witnesses are still outside the mainstream in the United States. Their status in Germany is no different. They have long been considered a fringe group and were subject to severe persecution under the Nazis and the authorities of the DDR. In these respects, Jehovah's Witnesses stand in a somewhat similar position in German society to Muslims.

The point of controversy of the case was the Jehovah's Witness's application for recognition as a public corporation under German law. Attainment of public corporate status is very important in Germany. As a public corporation, a religious group can achieve legal personality, raise taxes from among its membership using the machinery of the state, run

---

65 *Id.* at 298–99.
66 *Id.* at 290.
67 *Id.* at 298. Not surprisingly, the dissent took issue with the majority's conception of neutrality in church-state relations, and how this affected civil service obligations. *Id.* at 316–24.
68 *Id.* at 310.
69 Baden-Württemberg, the German Land at issue in the case, had considered but determined not to enact such a law. *Id.* at 300 (dissent).
70 BVerfGE 102, 370. See Peer Zumbansen, *From The Outside Looking In: The Jehovah's Witnesses' Struggle for Quasi-Public Status Under Germany's Incorporation Law*, 2 GERMAN LAW JOURNAL No. 1 (Jan. 15, 2001), at http://www.germanlawjournal.com/print.php?id=47.
71 *See, e.g.*, West Virginia State Board of Educ. v. Barnette, 319 U.S. 624 (1943) (Court holds unconstitutional state statute requiring mandatory salute and pledge of allegiance to the flag of the United States, and thereby excuses Jehovah's Witnesses from being coerced to do acts against their conscience); Cantwell v. Connecticut, 310 U.S. 296 (1940) (Jehovah's Witness within his first amendment free speech rights to walk public streets attacking organized religion, especially Catholicism, and to proselytize).

and administer extensively its affairs and work force, determine membership, and set its own rules and internal governance structure, among other matters.[72] Public religious corporations are a main way by which the church-state cooperative model in Germany is implemented. Historically, mainstream religions have predominately attained public corporate status, most notably the Roman Catholic Church, Protestant denominations and Jewish congregations. However, some minority religions and other organizations have achieved this status as well. The Seventh-Day Adventist Church, Church of Jesus Christ of Latter-Day Saints, New Apostolic Church, Mennonites and the Salvation Army are among the groups that have achieved public corporate status.[73] Other minority religions have had some difficulty achieving official recognition.[74]

Jehovah's Witnesses have historically been denied this quasi-public status and the official privileges that attend it because the sect does not allow its members to vote or participate in the democratic process. Authorities thus viewed the group as animated by values antithetical to the social order and, accordingly, a danger to society. Germany is especially sensitive to inner threats to domestic security and democracy given its history under the Weimar Republic.[75]

Because Jehovah's Witnesses did not vote or participate in the democratic process, German authorities and the administrative courts viewed the group as disloyal to the democratic order and therefore not deserving of public corporate status. This became the question of the case for the Federal Constitutional Court to resolve: what constitutional conditions were required to obtain public corporate status.

The Federal Constitutional Court's treatment of the issue was more sensitive than that of the ordinary and federal administrative courts. The Federal Constitutional Court suggested that the Jehovah's Witnesses' history of persecution and lack of official recognition might explain their skittishness about political authority and general reluctance to participate in the political process. But the Court credited deeper doctrinal reasons motivating their behavior as well. The Court recognized that Jehovah's Witnesses believe, with intense conviction, in a life and world beyond the present. They view their time on earth as temporary, as just a passing phase until they can achieve fulfillment in heaven. Based on these tenets, the Court explained that Jehovah's Witnesses view all political authority as temporary and impermanent and, at root, the devil's work.[76] Therefore, the group did not believe in any need to vote or otherwise participate in the political process. Viewed in this manner, the Court characterized the Jehovah's Witnesses' lack of participation in politics as religiously motivated, based on a desire to remain apolitical and neutral in the affairs of the world, and not as a form of hostility towards democracy or the German state.[77] Moreover, the Court noted there is no legal obligation to vote.[78] For these reasons the Court concluded that it was manifestly unfair to demand of Jehovah's Witnesses what was beyond the law.

Because the Federal Constitutional Court viewed the actions of Jehovah's Witnesses as primarily religiously motivated, denial of public corporate status was an affront to their religious belief, under article four, and could not be countenanced unless there were good reasons for such action. The Court found no good explanation forthcoming.

---

72 GRUNDGESETZ [GG] [Federal Constitution] art. 140 (incorporating WRV art. 137). BVerfGE 102, 370 (71).
73 Edward J. Eberle, *Free Exercise of Religion in Germany and the United States*, 78 TUL. L. REV. 1023, 1031 (2004) (citations omitted).
74 Scientology is the most notable failed quest to achieve constitutional status. *See* note 36.
75 To help guard against threats to the democratic social order, the Basic Law embodies the idea of a "militant democracy," which obliges the state and citizens to resist threats to the democratic social order. *See* GG art. 20 (4).
76 BVerfGE 102, 370 (397).
77 *Id.* at 380–81.
78 *Id.* at 380.

Viewing the case from this perspective, the Federal Constitutional Court found no basis for denying Jehovah's Witnesses public corporate status based on their doctrinal opposition to voting.[79] The Court recalled that the principle of official neutrality forbids the government from valuing a religion.[80] Religious tenets and their exercise are matters for the religion, not for the state.[81] It is within the autonomy of a religion to define its relationship with the state and political authorities.[82] The Court concluded that a determination not to vote fits within the province of religion.

In the view of the Federal Constitutional Court, the Jehovah's Witnesses' failure to vote did not evidence disloyalty to the social order. Placement of this condition on a group is not required by the Basic Law. Requiring more of one group than another is a violation of the equality of treatment obligatory on the state.[83] The Court reasoned that the proper focus of authorities should be on whether a group is loyal to the legal order (*Rechtstreue*).[84] The core of this duty is adherence to the norms anchored in article 79(3) of the Basic Law.[85] These norms form the essence of the German Federal Republic: commitment to human dignity and its unfolding in the ensuing catalogue of rights; the *Rechtsstaat*; and democracy.[86]

Assessing the Jehovah's Witness against this standard, the Federal Constitutional Court did not find their behavior evidenced any lack of commitment to democracy. Their actions were a better measure of this than their religious beliefs.[87] Thus, the group was not a danger to democracy and denial of public corporate status could not be made on this basis. Nevertheless, whether Jehovah's Witnesses could obtain corporate status depended on resolution of certain other questions, including investigation of whether the group mistreated children through their educational method and coerced departing adult members to remain in the fold.[88] These actions implicate other core values of the Federal Republic, including human dignity, and merited careful study before any final decision could be made.

E. *OSHO*

Finally, the Constitutional Court's treatment of government warnings about the nature and aims of an eastern oriented meditation society known as the OSHO (previously the Bhagwan) movement is worth considering.[89] *OSHO* raises the critically important issue as to what is the appropriate official role in respect of the growth of new religious or philosophical groups inspired by the new wave of religious or philosophical orientation arising from the cultural revolution of the 1960s and its aftermath. These new world groups have mainly been viewed as being on the fringe and with suspicion by the public. Not surprisingly, groups like these are often referred to as "sects" or "psycho sects" or "young

---

79 *Id.* at 394.
80 *Id.*
81 *Id.* at 394–95.
82 *Id.* at 396.
83 *Id.* at 380–81.
84 *Id.* at 379.
85 Article 79 (3), provides: "Amendments to this Basic Law affecting the division of the Federation into Laender, their participation on principle in the legislative process, or the principles laid down in Articles 1 and 20 shall be inadmissible."
86 BVerfGE 102, 370 (392).
87 *Id.* at 397–98.
88 *Id.* at 399.
89 BVerfGE 105, 279 (OSHO Case). The First Senate also evaluated aspects of *OSHO* in a chamber decision, Bundesverfassungsgericht [BVerfG] [Federal Constitutional Court] 1 BvR 1044/93, Aug. 12, 2002.

religions," as was the case here.⁹⁰ The groups have been subject to much criticism and accused of alienating members from their family and friends and manipulating them psychologically and financially.⁹¹

As a response, officials in government made a number of statements about these groups, trying to keep the public abreast of these developments and inform and warn the public about them.⁹² The government was especially concerned about the susceptibility of the young to the enticements of these groups and, accordingly, sought to inform the young and their parents about these groups.⁹³ The justification for performance of this information function came from the duty of the government to lead the state and offer guidance to social members, crystallized around the concept of *Staatsleitung*, duties flowing from the positive role of the state under the German constitutional system, according to the Constitutional Court's creative interpretation.⁹⁴

For our purposes, it is interesting to observe, first, that the OSHO group achieved article four religious/philosophical protections on account of its organization pursuant to and consistent with German constitutional principles.⁹⁵ In this respect, we can observe, again, application of article four norms on an equal, level basis. If a group fulfills the requirements for recognition as a religious/philosophical organization, it obtains the benefits due such organizations under German law. In this regard, *OSHO* is of a similar tenor to *Jehovah's Witness*; both groups reside at the fringe of society but, having made their case as to their religious/philosophical nature, meriting article four protection. Interesting for us, *OSHO*, in contrast to *Jehovah's Witness* and the other cases reviewed, was a philosophical (*weltanschaulich*), not religious organization. Of course, article four protects both forms of groups – religious or philosophical – an innovative and notable characteristic of German constitutionalism.

Vitally important to article four protection is the obligation of officials to remain neutral in religious/philosophical matters. The appropriate scope of official neutrality became a main issue of the case. At issue was a series of government statements made about religious groups, in response to parliamentary questions and a speech by the Federal Minister for Youth, Family Affairs and Health.⁹⁶ These official statements did not refer specially to the OSHO movement, but grouped them in reports under characterizations of "sect," "youth sect," a "young religion," and a "psycho sect."⁹⁷ Likewise, but more negatively, other official statements characterized OSHO as "destructive," "pseudo-religions," and manipulative.⁹⁸ The OSHO movement complained about these characterizations as violating its rights, and wanted the government to retract these statements.

Determination of the propriety of these statements called for resolution of the bounds of official neutrality in religious/philosophical issues. According to the Court, the state is justified, on account of the doctrine of *Staatsleitung*,⁹⁹ in confronting relevant issues of the day, including, if necessary, disseminating information and, where appropriate, warning the

---

90 *Id.* at 2626.
91 Albers, *supra* note 36.
92 *Id.*
93 BVerfGE 105, 279 (refers to the govt. informing youth and parents about the groups in text, the facts of the case, but subsequent cites refer to the case as cited).
94 *Id.* at 6.
95 *Id.* at 2.
96 BVerfGE 105, 279, now referring to who spoke on behalf of govt.
97 *Id.*
98 *Id.*
99 Under *Staatsleitung*, government derives the duty to lead and direct the state and society. Ordinarily, this duty includes gathering of information and passage and execution of legislation. The Court extended the concept to include also the rendering of information and warnings to departments of government and the public. BVerfGE 105, 279.

public. Members of society may not be able to obtain complete information or perspectives on issues, and the role of government is to assist them in being more fully informed.[100] Still, official rendering of information is subject to the need to maintain neutrality. Forced to work out this concept, the Court ruled that the state is not prevented from disseminating information about religious/philosophical groups to the public, and can even render critical information or facts on them, their goals or activities; state officials can critically engage in public discourse over organizations and events in society.[101] However, the state may not describe or depict these groups in a defamatory, discriminatory, distorted or inaccurate manner.[102] From this, the Court derived the important principle that article four protects against defamatory, discriminatory, distorted or inaccurate statements. In an increasingly pluralistic society, it is useful to clarify important concepts, like neutrality. All groups, majority and minority, benefit from clarity and equal application of legal norms. Society benefits as well, as neutrality helps assure peaceful coexistence between government and religion and among different religious groups.

Applying these principles, the Constitutional Court determined that official characterizations of groups, like OSHO, as "sects," "psycho sects," or "youth religions" was within the zone of official neutrality and, therefore, was permissible. However, characterizations of "destructive," "pseudo-religious," or "manipulative" were beyond the pale and exceeded the bounds of neutrality and, therefore, constituted a violation of article four.[103]

Underlying these holdings lay the Court's reconception, in part, of the concept of fundamental rights and, more particularly, how such rights might be violated.[104] Ordinarily, rights are violated by government when government undertakes some action that directly impairs a right holder's zone of protection. This could not be the case here, as government had done nothing directly against the OSHO group. Rather, what was at issue was whether statements made to others – here the Parliament and the public – could nevertheless impair the rights of OSHO. Certainly such third party statements might impact negatively on a group. For example, the statements at issue in *OSHO*, especially those that were demeaning, might influence members to quit, prospective member not to join, or people not to commit financial or personal resources to the group.[105] Recognizing this, the Court was forced to confront the doctrine of what constituted a violation of fundamental rights. Impairment of rights could occur not just in the usual case of direct official incursion against a right holder, but also in situations where facts or information directed at someone else can negatively affect a rights holder, as here.[106] We might refer to this as an indirect or mediated incursion of rights. The concept of mediated impairment of rights is a somewhat novel and innovative doctrine with important consequences for German law. It will be interesting to see how this doctrine unfolds. For now, we can recognize it as evidence of the disposition of the Constitutional Court to be flexible in applying the Basic Law to contemporary needs. We observed another illustration of this in the *Muslim Teacher's Head*

---

100 *Id.* at 6.
101 *Id.* at 3.
102 *Id.*
103 *Id.*
104 For careful examination of this theme, *see* Albers, *supra* note 36; Murswiek, *supra* note 36; Ruge, *supra* note 36.
105 BVerfGE 105, 279.
106 *Id.* In making this determination, the Constitutional Court ruled that the conventional requirement that the legislature provide a legal basis for restriction of a right (*Gesetzesvorbehalt*) could be dispensed with here on account of the duty of government to lead and direct the state and society (*Staatsleitung*). *Id.* at 5–6. Development and profliferation of new modes of communication call for new government capacities, needing to adjust to quickly changing social conditions. *Id.* at 6. These factors influenced the Court's adjustment of the *Gesetzvorbehalt*, a development with important implications for German law.

Scarf, as the Court adjusted state neutrality requirements away from a strict concept and toward a nurturing, supportive one. These adjustments bespeak a certain sensitivity and willingness to adjust to the needs of a changing society, moving toward pluralism.

OSHO is a complicated case with important consequences for German article four freedoms, consequences that will take some time to unfold and be evaluated. For now, we can say, first, that *OSHO*, like *Muslim Teacher's Head Scarf*, displays a certain sensitivity by the Court to the needs of emerging, minority dissenting groups. In *OSHO*, this entailed recognition of mediated impairments of article four rights, which allowed the OSHO group to be successful in part of its article four claim. Part of this doctrinal innovation, however, involved reconception of the doctrine of legislative authorization (*Gesetzvorbehalt*) constitutionally required to restrict rights, and it is unclear how this innovation will unfold.[107]

Second, the Court established an important component of article four freedoms that protect right holders from defamatory, discriminatory or false or distorting statements. This development fortifies the Court's commitment to equal application of norms, which benefits especially minority groups. Plausible, but arguable, was the Court's validation of official statements like "psycho sect" or "youth religion" as neutral. It might be argued, on the other hand, that such characterizations are themselves denigrating, in comparison to conventional views of religion, as a psycho sect or youth religion would seem to have the connotation as outside the mainstream and, therefore, suspicious.[108] In fact, official warnings directed at or implicating a group are hard to understand as other than a violation of the group's claim to equal treatment.[109] More important, then, is whether such incursion of rights is justified.[110] Furthermore, it seems questionable whether government should take sides at all, rendering information or warnings, in religious/philosophical matters. It seems preferable to let people themselves decide these issues. The Court would have been better served in *OSHO* by more clearly describing the appropriate relationship between neutrality and *Staatsleitung* so that its reasoning in asserting these doctrines would have been more apparent.

Third, it seems fair to say that *OSHO* represents a cautious approach to alternative, emerging religious, philosophical groups. No doubt, what to do with such groups is a difficult matter for government and society, not unlike the question of scientology[111] or Jehovah's Witnesses.[112] Certain of these groups are thought to engage in threatening conduct like exploitation, manipulation or denial of gender rights and, thus, present serious constitutional issues. Careful deliberation is necessary to resolve how to treat constitutionally such alternative groups.

OSHO would seem to suggest a model of reduced protection for groups viewed as threatening in some way. Rendering of official warnings impairs the rights of a group like OSHO. True, warnings could also be issued against other, majoritarian groups, like Roman Catholics or Protestants. But it is more likely the case that government, responding to majoritarian pressure, will warn about groups perceived to be on the fringe. The doctrines developed in *OSHO* will need to be monitored quite closely in upcoming years.

---

107 *See, e.g.*, GRUNDGESETZ [GG] [Federal Constitution] art. 19, para. 1. "Insofar as a basic right may, under this Basic Law, be restricted by or pursuant to a statute, such statute shall apply generally and not solely to an individual case. Furthermore, such statute shall name the basic right, indicating the Article concerned."
108 The Court recognized that these statements bore the imprint of the earlier age in which they were communicated, and might not be permissible in contemporary language. BVerfGE 105, 279 (OSHO Case).
109 Murswiek, *supra* note 36.
110 Even though the Constitutional Court found no incursion of rights in this situation, it obviously felt the warnings were justified under the doctrine of *Staatsleitung* it worked out. That claim is certainly disputable.
111 *See* note 36.
112 BVerfGE 102, 370.

F. Conclusion

Ritual Slaughter, Muslim Teacher's Head Scarf, and *Jehovah's Witnesses* evidence the Federal Constitutional Court's application of religious freedoms in ways that fit the needs and perspectives of marginal and minority groups. These cases called for sensitivity and understanding in assessing religious claims from the perspective of the believers, even when such practices were contrary to social convention. With respect to religious freedoms, of course, that seems totally appropriate, since religious freedoms, like all basic freedoms, are to be available to all. Naturally, a sound way to judge religious freedom is from the perspective of the believer. The faith of the believer has more to do with religion than the estimation of any supervising authority, such as a court. A court needs to determine only whether the belief is sincerely held and meaningful to the believer.

Each case called for an adjustment in thought. In the *Ritual Slaughter* case, conventional views on how to treat animals were disregarded in order to accommodate the faith of the believers. In the *Muslim Teacher's Head Scarf* case, acknowledgment of Islam called for a reconceptualization of state neutrality norms in religion and civil service obligations. In the *Jehovah's Witnesses* case, the adjustment in thought was perhaps even greater. At stake in that case was one of the cardinal principles of the German Federal Republic: the guarantee of the stability of democracy. But this seemed of less moment once the issue was properly characterized: religious conviction lie at the root of the Jehovah's Witnesses' actions; there was no real threat to the democracy.

Once the underlying claims had been identified and understood as religious, the cases fell within the normal pattern of German law: when claims of free exercise of religion are placed against the requirements of the general law, the general law must accommodate religious claims unless there is a very strong argument to the contrary. In the *Muslim Teacher's Head Scarf* case, accommodation was made, tentatively, against the general norms of civil service rules. Notable in these cases is that this general rule manifestly applies to all, including majority and minority sects. In this respect, the Federal Constitutional Court has signaled that fundamental rights apply to all on equal terms. Equality in treatment speaks to a certain strength and confidence of religious freedom in Germany today.

Equality of treatment in religious affairs is notable. Apart from the claims of Islam, Jehovah's Witnesses and the Baha'i described here, we might also observe that Jews[113] and evangelical Christians[114] have received accommodation under Germany's constitutional protections of religious freedom.

It is true that other aspects of religious/philosophical freedom in Germany have been the subject of severe criticism. Most notable has been the ongoing controversy with respect to Scientology.[115] The same might be said of *OSHO*, which produced a mixed result; rendering of article four protections benefited the group, but allowing government to issue warnings about it impaired the group.[116] OSHO would appear to suggest a different, less protective model of rights protection for alternative, emerging philosophical groups that somehow are viewed as threatening. Whether such a reduced model of protection is justifiable, on account of real or foreseeable harms or risks to persons or society,

---

113 BVerfGE 35, 366 (ruling that cross displayed in court room must be removed in view of objection from Jewish lawyer).
114 BVerfGE 32, 98 (evangelical Christian husband relieved from criminal penalties for allowing wife to die due to loss of blood and abstinence from blood transfusion because actions were religiously motivated).
115 *See* note 36.
116 BVerfGE 105, 279 (OSHO Case).

is a difficult issue that calls for careful consideration, as does Scientology, and is well beyond the scope of this article.

Notwithstanding these concerns, we should appreciate the handiwork of the Federal Constitutional Court for what it is: seeking to apply equally religious/philosophical norms to all, with some difficulties, difficulties perhaps inevitable in the complicated mix of social forces at work in early 21st century society. A look at the work of the United States Supreme Court provides some perspective on the jurisprudence of the Federal Constitutional Court. Non-Christian minority sects have never been granted an accommodation in Supreme Court case law.[117] The tolerance displayed by the Federal Constitutional Court can only help its stature as a leading model of constitutional authority.

---

117 The Supreme Court has rejected accommodations for Jews, see Goldman v. Weinberger, 475 U.S. 503 (1986), Braunfeld v. Brown, 366 U. S. 599 (1961); Muslims, see O'Lone v. Estate of Shabazz, 482 U.S. 342 (1987); and Native Americans, see Employment Div., Dep't of Human Res. v. Smith, 494 U.S. 872 (1990), Lyng v. Northwest Indian Cemetary Protective Association, 485 U.S. 439 (1988). The treatment accorded practitioners of the Santeria religion in Church of the Lukumi Babalu Aye v. City of Hialeah, 508 U.S. 520 (1993), was not an accommodation, of course, but rather discrimination under the rule of *Smith*.

The Reform of the Statutory Social Welfare System and the Case Law of the *Bundesverfassungsgericht*

Renate Jaeger*

Politically and legally, there are currently more questions than answers in the field of the statutory social welfare system. The existing clarifications under constitutional law, which I want to present from the perspective of a former Justice of the *Bundesverfassungsgericht* (German Federal Constitutional Court), with 25 years of previous experience in social welfare policy, only establish a framework within which it is hoped that politicians will make use of their creative latitude. This means that, in this context, definitive maxims cannot be expected from constitutional law.

If one does not want to limit oneself to giving answers with too narrow an outlook, one can cite many individual provisions of the *Grundgesetz* (GG – Basic Law) that provide constitutional justification for different positions, some of which may be quite contrary to each other; however, ultimately one must engage in an overall weighing process. The social welfare system cannot be inferred directly from Art. 20.1 of the *Grundgesetz*, which provides that the Federal Republic of Germany is a democratic and social federal state. The social welfare system follows directly neither from the protection of human dignity, as provided by Art. 1.1 of the *Grundgesetz*,[1] nor from the right to life and physical integrity in Art. 2.2 of the *Grundgesetz*.[2] We also speak of health care as a sector of the economy thus *ipso iure*, the right to choose freely one's occupation or profession under Art. 12 of the *Grundgesetz*,[3] the right to form associations under Art. 9 of the *Grundgesetz*,[4] and the guarantee of property under Art. 14 of the *Grundgesetz* are also implicated.[5]

Therefore, what is essential in this context is to trace constitutional guarantees, which take effect in the fabric of pension insurance and health insurance schemes. The Constitution does not prescribe a specific economic or social order but it sets seemingly conflicting parameters. On one hand, in its Articles concerning fundamental rights the Constitution protects human freedoms. On the other hand, in the pursuit of aims, which are based on the concept of the social welfare state, the Constitution assigns responsibility and funds to individual institutions within the state system.

---

* Justice of the European Court of Human Rights; formerly a Justice of the Bundesverfassungsgericht (German Federal Constitutional Court). This contribution is based on a presentation delivered at the First Cologne Social Law Convention, entitled "Solidarity–Competition–Individual Responsibility" held on 20 March 2003. The style of presentation has been maintained in the written version. The contribution was originally published in German at: Renate Jaeger, *Die Reformen in der gesetzlichen Sozialversicherung im Spiegel der Rechtsprechung*, 5 Neue Zeitschrift für Sozialrecht (NZS) 225 (2003).

1 "Human dignity shall be inviolable."
2 "Every person shall have the right to life and physical integrity. Freedom of the person shall be inviolable. These rights may be interfered with only pursuant to a law."
3 "All Germans shall have the right to freely choose their occupation or profession, their place of work, and their place of training. The practice of an occupation or profession may be regulated by or, pursuant to a law."
4 "All Germans shall have the right to form corporations and other associations."
5 "Property and the right to inheritance shall be guaranteed. Their content and limits shall be defined by the laws."

A. Continuity and Change

I.

The following reflections focus on the decisions of the *Bundesverfassungsgericht*, which have repeatedly dealt with the subject of the social welfare system. Recent decisions, and older ones, which will be presented in excerpts and in verbatim quotations, illustrate continuity and change in case-law and show that the litmus test of constitutional interpretation is whether it facilitates solutions to problems, which are appropriate to the respective conflict while, at the same time, preserving liberalism and order. Repeatedly, aspects of the public good, the content of which has changed over the years, will play a part in this discussion. The public good is a very broad concept in legal policy, which allows for numerous approaches, the concrete implementation of which is primarily entrusted to the legislature.

II.

Some preliminary remarks concerning the facts are indispensable: as compared to a living organism, the (1) *statutory pension insurance* is already beyond its expansion phase, a development that is still in store for the (2) *statutory health insurance* and possibly also for the (3) *long-term care insurance*. Each of these will be discussed in turn.

1.

The last century was characterized by the expansion of the statutory pension insurance system. More and more groups were covered by pension insurance. The workers' pension insurance was extended to salaried employees, to artisans, and to farmers. The earners of middle incomes, and above, were made compulsory members of the pension insurance when the income limit for compulsory insurance was substituted by a contribution assessment ceiling. Retraction has occurred, when specific groups of persons were split off again, but the overall demand for insurance coverage remained the same across these various groups. For example, separate pension funds were created for the members of professions, like the artists' social insurance scheme. In addition, such specific subsystems, which are of a compulsory nature, can still be understood as social security systems that are based on solidarity.

However, new ground was broken with the introduction of the so-called "Riester" pension. For the first time since the introduction of the statutory pension insurance system this scheme, was based on the assessment that part of the provision for old age must be made on a voluntary basis, albeit subsidized by the state, and no longer on a compulsory basis. Thus, after more than 100 years, what was originally established as basic insurance coverage evolved into standard-of-living insurance coverage. Interestingly, the tendency is that this will now be cut back to basic insurance coverage. This development is not justified by arguing that the poverty of society does not acknowledge anything else but rather, by the sweeping argument that non-wage labor costs are too high. Repeated over and over again, this argument has almost established a ban on thinking in a different direction. Should services in Germany really be too expensive, as compared to competing suppliers and, should unit labor costs really be too high (Germany's export success rather speaks against this) a reduction is politically desirable. However, it is difficult to convey why such a reduction must be brought about by cuts in the expenditure for the provision of old age pensions and, by abandoning the principle that half of its funding is provided by the employers. Because, deficits in the provision for old age pensions for the generation, which constitutes the working population today, will also have to be borne by the following generations, the funds required in old age will have to be provided through individual maintenance payments by the next generation or, by other tax proceeds if they are not secured under social welfare law. Unfortunately, those who today derive short-term benefit from this change – on the one hand, entrepreneurs and shareholders and, possibly on the other hand, employees whose positions may be preserved – will not at all or, only to a small extent, share these burdens, which will be shifted to the future.

2.

Since its introduction in 1883, the health insurance system has had to struggle with institutional, legal, and political problems. Among other things, challenges to the system always concerned money, e.g. the distribution of limited funds. Initially, the concern prevailed that the insured persons who definitely belonged to the low-income sector of the population could not afford certain health care services. This is the root of the principle that health care services are provided as benefits in kind. Otherwise, it was feared that physicians would refuse to accept low-income patients entitled to treatment under the statutory health insurance scheme because; they doubted that they would recover their fees payable. Attempts were made to gain physicians' support for the obligation to also or, primarily treat such patients. The relationship between physician and patient concerning treatment was therefore, legally split away from the payment relationship, e.g. from the obligation to pay on the part of the health insurance funds.

In order to operate in an economically efficient manner, the health insurance funds dispensed medical supplies and equipment themselves. They maintained hospitals and tried in every possible manner to determine the limits of what is necessary and, to influence economic efficiency. These problems accompany the discussion to this very day. The intensive debates only ceased in real times of need, e.g. during the wars and in the postwar periods on the one hand, and during times of marked prosperity, on the other hand, when the struggle for the distribution of funds continued but only the amount and the distribution of surplus was at issue. Now, both have been things of the past for 30 years. Attempts at consolidation have since determined day-to-day politics in this sector; structural changes are announced, but only rarely implemented; worldwide, keys to success are missing. In Germany, the following reasons for this can be given:

a) The revenue side of health insurance is modest for at least two reasons. First, the group of those insured is limited to persons in the medium to lower income brackets. Second, in the case of voluntarily insured persons, their entire income is not accounted for in the calculation of their contributions.
b) The health insurance scheme's expenditures have increased enormously: people live longer; advances in medicine are costly; in many areas (*e.g.* pharmaceuticals) Germany is a high-priced country; the number of physicians and of other health care providers have increased; changes in mentality have taken place (on the side of insured persons, the wish to receive as many benefits as possible free of charge, moral hazard in private health insurance, health care providers' pursuit of profit); it is difficult to give treatment to patients with multiple diseases; it is difficult to analyze processes with multiple causes; it is even more difficult to consistently influence them.

In this context, these factors must be the starting point of all assumptions.

3.

About long-term care insurance, one can almost gain the impression that it strives to catch up with the social welfare schemes, which have been in existence for a long time. It was introduced because, the gap in long-term care insurance coverage was considerable and because, the burdening of the following (sandwiched) generation was regarded as financially and factually alarming. Now that, the claims of the informed have proven true, reflections concerning the abolition of long-term care insurance have arisen namely: Such schemes create demand, they contribute to the professionalization of benefits, and thus, to a price increase and, considering the population pyramid, the percentage of those in need of long-term care will increase. Where demand increases, solidarity decreases. Precisely at a time of high unemployment, the idea of practically abolishing unemployment benefits is being contemplated. Would fire insurance companies not gladly discontinue their operations when the town is on fire? The banks have already requested that the state establish a rescue company to cover their losses. In Germany, "Ich-AG" (Me, Inc.) has been voted "Most Outrageous Word of the Year". Profits go to one's own pocket as long as everything goes well; if the risk actually occurs, it is the losers who are supposed to pay. Of course, the losers are the ones who still pay taxes in Germany. Big industry hardly does so any longer; its contribution to the public good (still) consists in taking over an equal share of the funding of the social welfare system. This contribution defies all subtleties connected with the shaping of the business structure because; it is payable where the work actually takes place.

B. The Cross-sector Components of the Different Branches of Social Welfare

Because, in social welfare there are joint cross-sector components, which allow a joint analysis, the following presentation of *Bundesverfassungsgericht* decisions cites decisions from both the health insurance and the pension insurance sectors. Under constitutional law, arguments from all sectors can be put to mutually fruitful use.

I. Contrasts between Private and Statutory Social Insurance

1.

In this context, a September 30 1987[6] decision of the Second Senate of the *Bundesverfassungsgericht*, dealing with the contrasting features of private insurance and the statutory social security system, is of fundamental importance. Here, the Second Senate concluded that the balancing of risks that characterizes private insurance only plays a subordinate role in the statutory social security system. In the statutory social security system, the principle of insurance is not abandoned altogether but it is decisively modified by introducing social aspects, which are foreign to private insurance because, the statutory insurance scheme is essentially based on the ideas of social balance and, of solidarity among its members and has always contained elements of social care and welfare. The statutory insurance scheme's priority is to promote the welfare of all its members, who form an association based on solidarity, in an approximately even manner and in a way, which gives special attention to those in need of help.

---

6 BVerfGE 76, 256 (300–306).

For the first time, this decision[7] mentioned out-of-insurance benefits (*versicherungsfremde Leistungen*) but it used this term differently than the use to which it is being put by politics today. Benefits, which the private insurance scheme regards as out-of-insurance benefits, are characteristic and typical features of statutory insurance namely, those benefits that are aimed at achieving a balance, based on solidarity, among the insured.

Only 15 years have passed since the September 1987 decision was issued. Nevertheless, today one somewhat hesitates to simply concede to it because, in the meantime, a shift in values away from solidarity and towards economic and shareholder values has taken place. Today, solidarity is a well-worn term that is used to designate the most diverse kinds of support. However, in most cases it is only verbal. In the *Bundesverfassungsgericht*'s case law, however, the term is normally still used in its conventional meaning. It is judges who still uphold the idea that Germany is not only a federal state but also, a social federal state.[8]

2.

The decision of the Second Senate was issued in 1987 although the First Senate had already placed pension claims under the protection of the guarantee of property, which is enshrined in the *Grundgesetz*.[9] This happened in 1980, when the adjustment of pension rights in the event of divorce brought about a profound change in the pension system. Acquired claims were newly allocated and divided between the divorced parties. The *Bundesverfassungsgericht* regarded this as a determination of the content and limits of property within the meaning of Art. 14.1 sentence 2 of the *Grundgesetz*, which is in principle permissible.[10] Since then, the protection of property has evolved into an important standard of constitutional review – not only as regards the allocation of rights among private individuals but also concerning their relationship to the State.

II. The Protection of Property does not Conflict with Moderate Redistribution

It is a well-known fact that this standard of review has since evolved far beyond this original holding. However, the change of standard (moving away from the principle of the social welfare state under the rule of law and the protection of public confidence, towards the guarantee of property) has promised more than it could deliver.[11] The *Bundesverfassungsgericht* has found that, in spite of the protection of property, the principle of solidarity and the social contract between the generations justifies the limitation of accrued pension rights. The essential holding of the so-called *Mothers Judgment* of July 7 1992,[12] was that Art. 14.1 of the *Grundgesetz* is not contrary to a moderate redistribution within the system.

---

7   BVerfGE 76, 256.
8   *See* Stefan Geiger, *Einigkeit und Freiheit durch Recht*, 3 DEUTSCHE RICHTERZEITUNG (DRiZ) 78 (2003).
9   BVerfGE 53, 257 (289, 295–296, 297, 298).
10 *Id.*
11 In the same line of argument, *see also* my colleague Udo Steiner, *Das Sozialversicherungsrecht in der Rechtsprechung des Bundesverfassungsgerichts*, *in* SPEYERER SOZIALRECHTSGESPRÄCHE 1991–2000, 525 (Detlef Merten ed., 2002).
12 BVerfGE 87, 1 (41).

1.

Some of these points of view have been taken up in the judgments that deal with the conversion of East German pensions after reunification. In a 1999 decision,[13] the *Bundesverfassungsgericht* held, with reference to a decision from 1985, that compulsorily insured members of the statutory insurance scheme could not expect from the outset that the provisions that regulate benefits will permanently remain unchanged.[14] The Court explained that the statutory social insurance schemes are associations established on a permanent basis and, which are based on the solidarity of their members, associations that in the course of time have to adapt to various changes. Those, who become members of associations with these characteristics, are provided, not only with the opportunities connected with such membership but also, together with other insured persons, they bear its risks. In this context, the Court held that Art. 14.1 of the *Grundgesetz* does not require a different conclusion because, the legislature has the power to give the concept of property concrete shape; the legislature determines its content and limits and in doing so, must take the social obligations that are connected with property into consideration. The Court explained that the legislature can limit pension claims and accrued pension rights, reduce benefits and, reorganize claims and accrued rights to the extent that this serves a public interest and, complies with the principle of proportionality.[15]

Thus, the pension system of the Federal Republic of Germany does not enjoy constitutional protection; it can be manipulated by the legislature.[16] This power also includes changes of acquired legal rights. This is not a new regulation, which only applies to the East German pensions; it has always applied to the Federal Republic of Germany's pension system.[17] However, the Court mitigated its holding by explaining that Art. 14.1 sentence 2 of the *Grundgesetz* does not permit any changes that incorporate losses, which are contrary to the principle of proportionality.

2.

In another 1999 ruling,[18] the *Bundesverfassungsgericht* took up, in quite conventional terms, what it had emphasized already a year before in its decision concerning survivors' pensions[19] (to which no protection of property applies). The Court concluded that, the fact that the protection provided by Art. 14 of the *Grundgesetz* does not apply here, does not mean that changes of law to the detriment of the insured persons are not subject to any effective review under constitutional law. In this case, the standards are the principle of the rule of law and, Art. 2.1 of the *Grundgesetz* (general freedom of action). First, the scope of protection secured by these constitutional provisions is affected if the legislature, when imposing compulsory membership in (and compulsory contributions to) the social welfare system, as an association under public law in so doing, considerably restricts an individuals' general freedom of action by significantly limiting his or, her economic opportunities. Second, the scope of protection is affected if the legislature considerably reduces the benefits that have been guaranteed by law to the insured, which have been financed by the

---

13   BVerfGE 100, 1.
14   BVerfGE 69, 272 (314).
15   BVerfGE 100, 1 (35–38).
16   *Id.* at 39.
17   *See* BVerfGE 53, 257 (293); BVerfGE 69, 272 (304).
18   BVerfGE 100, 59
19   BVerfGE 97, 271 (283, 286).

insured persons' contributions. In this case, the Court explained, the standard of review reduces to the principle of proportionality and, to the requirements placed on the principle of the protection of public confidence in a state under the rule of law.

III. The Legislature's Creative Latitude

All of these are clear statements. They are supposed to make the legislature aware of the creative latitude that it enjoys. The constitutional case law concerning Art. 14 of the *Grundgesetz* does not prevent the legislature from using its margin for maneuver to adapt the social welfare system of the Federal Republic of Germany to new requirements, which may emerge in a given situation. However, in doing so the legislature is called upon to abide by the principle of social justice. This principle defines an aim of the state; as such, it is a binding guideline, the concrete implementation of which is entrusted to the legislature. The principle directs the legislature's efforts and sets priorities. This, however, does not put a curb on the legislature. In times of social change, the system can be reorganized. However, the principle of social justice does not allow exclusive reliance on market mechanisms and thus, it also sets limits on private autonomy. The legislature cannot evade its responsibility by alleging that it is prevented from taking action by vested rights, which are supposedly unchangeable.

C. The Protection of Property Pursuant to Art. 14 of the Grundgesetz

The ease with which the *Bundesverfassungsgericht* has established relevant connections between older decisions and the conversion of East German pensions after reunification is due to persistent factors concerning the interpretation of the Constitution, which in this form, are not always shared by the public. The ordinary courts are also not always free from misconceptions regarding the proper interpretation of the Constitution, which is due, on the one hand, to the prevailing views of solidarity and a sense of entitlement on the other hand.

I. The Duration of Sickness Benefit Payments

For instance, through the case law of the *Bundessozialgericht* (Federal Social Court), the entitlement to sickness benefits had evolved into a permanent benefit that was paid in intervals. Those who, for whatever reasons, were not entitled to a statutory pension could, within periods of three consecutive calendar years, receive for half of each three-year period gross wage replacement benefits in the form of sickness benefits until the end of his or, her life. Under legal policy aspects, many regarded this as inappropriate. When the legislature capped, without transition, the sickness benefits to a maximum of 1 1/2 years, the *Bundessozialgericht* held that this was an infringement of the guarantee of property. In 1998, the *Bundesverfassungsgericht* rejected this view.[20]

The *Bundesverfassungsgericht* left unresolved the question whether sickness benefits even enjoy the protection of Art. 14.1 of the *Grundgesetz*. Because, there are no qualifying periods in statutory health insurance the Court found the proposed legislative change to be proportional in the case before it. This is why the relation between contributions and benefits has been considerably loosened (the decision alluded to a lack of equivalence).

---

20 BVerfGE 97, 378 (378 and 389).

The *Bundesverfassungsgericht* held that the adjustment of the system, which the legislature had performed, was constitutionally acceptable because, it had taken place for reasons of public interest and had taken the principle of proportionality into account.[21] In reality, there was no possibility for the group of persons affected to react to the amendment by autonomous dispositions. One could not rely on the old law to continue in effect and, one could not take preventive measures against a change of law. However, the remedy of an error in the system enjoys primacy over the principle of the protection of public confidence although, the confidence of those insured in the continued unchanged existence of a legal position, which had been granted for many years, must in principle, be rated highly[22] and must be taken into consideration.[23]

II. The Principle of Equivalence

Apart from the guarantee of property, the principle of equivalence between insurance contributions and possible benefits entitlements, alluded to in the *Sickness Benefits* decision,[24] is often regarded as an obstacle by politicians and scholars; it is seen as a guarantee, which ultimately flows from the Constitution and, which makes the statutory social welfare system secure from attempts at amendment. This is not the case, and this can be proved by relying on the *Bundesverfassungsgericht*'s case law. In two decisions, which mainly deal with the equivalence of benefits to contributions in health insurance the standard of review is only Art. 3 (equality before the law), rather than Art. 14 or, Art. 2.1 of the *Grundgesetz* in conjunction with the principle of proportionality.

1.

What must be mentioned above all in this context is the ruling concerning the "one-off payments" from which social welfare contributions were deducted, but in which they were not part of the basis for calculation of the wage replacement benefits.[25] The *Bundesverfassungsgericht* found that this approach only conflicts with Art. 3.1 of the *Grundgesetz* because, persons with the same annual income and the same amount of contributions, do not have the same entitlements. The Court held this in the decision of January 11 1995,[26] and also in the decision of May 24 2000,[27] which almost repeats the previous ruling. The Court explained that if the legislature established benefits, which are in fact equivalent to contributions that it must ensure all insured persons benefit equally from this approach. Herewith, I address a general problem of law making: The legislature is only free in its first step, but it must always ensure that it complies with the standard of Art. 3.1 of the *Grundgesetz*, e.g. it must ensure that it forms categories of typical cases in such a way that what is similar is treated similarly and, what is dissimilar is treated differently. The decision did not go beyond this; it does not require equivalence of benefits to contributions.

---

21 *Id.*
22 *See* BVerfGE 40, 65 (76); BVerfGE 76, 220 (245).
23 BVerfGE 97, 378 (389).
24 *Id.* at 378.
25 BVerfGE 92, 53 (68).
26 *Id.*
27 BVerfGE 102, 127 (141).

2.

Thus, the mandate given to the legislature to organize the levying of contributions to long-term care insurance in a way that takes the requirements of families into account[28] is not based ultimately on the principle of equivalence, but on an application of Art. 3.1 of the *Grundgesetz*, which takes into consideration the state's obligation under Art. 6.1 of the *Grundgesetz* to promote the family. The 2001[29] judgment also emphasizes the legislature's wide margin for maneuver concerning the amount and the manner of discharge, as required by the Constitution.

In order to ensure that the legislature's discretionary powers are maintained, the *Bundesverfassungsgericht* explicitly recognizes long-term care insurance in the form in which it has been established, which varies the amount of benefits only according to the degree of care that the person affected needs, rather than according to the prior amount in which contributions were made to the system and, also not according to the length of time for which such contributions were made.[30] This is a striking peculiarity of this newly created branch of the social welfare system to which however, the benefits of statutory health insurance correspond in one way or, another. The claim to sickness benefits (which, as a wage-replacement benefit, is the only claim that is equivalent to the contributions made) is only of marginal importance, not for the individuals' but for the health insurers' overall budget. Concerning long-term care insurance, the *Bundesverfassungsgericht* leaves the system unaffected and merely reclaims the implementation of the conclusions, which are to be drawn from this.

III. Family Insurance in the Statutory Health Insurance

Repeatedly, the issue of social security and the family gives cause for litigation. The principle of solidarity and its impact on family insurance, which is provided without additional contributions, was the subject of the oral hearing that was held on the *Bundesverfassungsgericht*'s open house in November 2002. The judgment was pronounced in February 2003.[31] The Court concluded that the legislature has creative latitude in deciding the manner in which it achieves compliance with its duty to protect marriage and the family, which has been imposed on it by the principle of social justice and by Art. 6.1 of the Grundgesetz. Insuring the children of a member of the statutory health insurance scheme, without additional contributions, is a measure of social balance, which serves to relieve the pressure on the family. However, provided that they are married to each other, it is not required that such benefits be provided irrespective of the income situation of both of the child's parents. This cannot even be requested by invoking Art. 6.1 of the *Grundgesetz*. The aspect of the need for social protection is a legitimate ground for differentiation with regard to benefits in the statutory health insurance scheme, which are determined by considerations of solidarity.

In this ruling,[32] the *Bundesverfassungsgericht* approved two distinct perspectives. First, the Court validated the view that family insurance for children presupposes that families make a contribution to the solidarity-based statutory insurance scheme, which is in line with the family's economic performance. Second, the Court confirmed the legislature's

---

28 BVerfGE 103, 242 (257).
29 *Id.*
30 *Id.*
31 BVerfGE 107, 205.
32 *Id.*

assessment that a child who is raised by married parents grows up under different, and economically more secure, circumstances than a child raised by a single parent. In actualizing these perspectives, the Courts' ruling leads to the result that it is tolerable that a law put families at a disadvantage, in specific aspects, as long as the general tendency of the law is geared towards compensating family burdens. Similarly, it is tolerable if the legal regulation partly constitutes an advantage, and partly a disadvantage to spouses if, seen as a whole, it does not result in spouses being placed at a disadvantage. To put it briefly: Systems based on solidarity – health insurance as well as the family may be regarded as such systems – do not permit the mere "taking of the pickings".

D. The Statutory Social-security Scheme v. Private Long-term Care Insurance

I. The Two-track System as a Special Feature

The special feature of the April 3 2001, judgments of the *Bundesverfassungsgericht*, concerning long-term care insurance, is that they put the two-track system of the statutory long-term care insurance scheme and, the compulsory private long-term care insurance scheme under review.[33]

1.

In principle, it was regarded as permissible to attribute different groups of persons to different insurance schemes. Mandatory attribution also satisfied constitutional law: It was within the legislature's creative latitude to divide the overall statutory long-term care insurance system into, on the one hand, a statutory long-term care insurance scheme and on the other hand, a private compulsory long-term care insurance scheme. With regard to the attribution of groups of persons to one of the two branches of insurance, the legislature had considerable room for maneuver, which however, was restricted by the principle of equality before the law and the principle of social justice. In particular, the legislature was allowed to use the following considerations as standards for delimiting the group of persons who are part of the statutory long-term care insurance scheme: Which group of persons is required for forming an association based on solidarity, and which persons need the protection of such association. Thus, the question of delimitation is answered in a manner that is consistent with former decisions of both Senates concerning pension insurance.

2.

Apart from the principles of equality before the law and of social justice, the decision[34] also invokes general freedom of action, without however, mentioning Art. 2.1 of the *Grundgesetz*. For the constitutional assessment, the grouping of persons in the health-insurance scheme is taken into account as a decisive indicator. The overall social situation justifies general compulsory insurance. An individual's social situation is decisive in considering whether he or, she will be dependent on compensation in order to ensure social balance; this is so with regard to long-term care insurance as well. The court justifies the delimita-

---

33 BVerfGE 103, 271 (287).
34 *Id.*

tion between the voluntary members of the statutory insurance scheme and, the members of the private insurance scheme by arguing that the voluntary members of the statutory insurance scheme have had the opportunity to decide between private and statutory insurance at an earlier point in time. It is even appropriate to establish a nexus to the autonomous choice between several options if people do not or, cannot consider the consequences that their decision will have much later, and if they in retrospect, would perhaps have made a different decision. Moreover, the Senate confirms, with this judgment that systemic differences between the private and the statutory insurance scheme are accepted. Peculiarities in the structure of contributions or, premiums[35] do not lead to an objection pursuant to the standard of Art. 3.1 of the *Grundgesetz*. Different contributions are merely the consequence of the fact that in the statutory insurance scheme, the contributions are income-related, and in the private insurance scheme, they are risk-related. However, at the same time, the judgment mentions , that by establishing maximum premiums, which provide insurance coverage for children without additional contributions and, by introducing a contribution ceiling of 150% for spouses as well in the private insurance scheme, the legislature has fulfilled a social mandate.

II. Compulsory Social Balance

In my opinion, this completely new aspect of a compulsory social balance in the private insurance scheme will be of considerable importance in the future.

1.

In this respect, the 2001 judgment of the *Bundesverfassungsgericht* on long-term care insurance[36] contains remarkable forecasts, which so far, have only rarely been addressed in the discussion. The *Bundesverfassungsgericht* has concluded that the generational aspect will increasingly gain importance for private insurance schemes as well, especially those organized compulsorily and nationwide. This is the case even though the amount of premiums, in principle, depends on conditions, which are different from those of the contributions to statutory insurance. Private insurance schemes rely on a system of time-related, capital-based accumulation. Meanwhile, statutory insurance schemes spend out accumulation all at once on the monthly-required benefits. In spite of this difference, similar strains on the private insurance schemes can be expected if they introduce elements of social balance, and if the consequences of the foreseeable demographic development become apparent in the private sector.

2.

This innovative approach can be conclusively justified.

To an increasing extent, the social security system rids itself of its poor risks. This development started when more and more pensioners were excluded from the pensioners' health insurance scheme; a point I will come back to in greater detail. Meanwhile, insured persons who, after a break in their membership in compulsory insurance, have again found employment where they normally would be compulsory members of health insurance are,

---

35 In the German social security system, the term *Beiträge* (contributions) is used in the context of the statutory insurance scheme, whereas the term *Prämien* (premiums) refers to the private insurance scheme.
36 BVerfGE 103, 271.

pursuant to §6.3a of the *Sozialgesetzbuch V* (Fifth Code of Social Law), excluded from health insurance at 55 years of age. Above all, this regulation affects women who, having taken a career break to raise a family, subsequently return to the workplace later in life. In the near future, it will also affect older persons who, after receiving unemployment benefits for a short time, are only entitled to social assistance payments without being members of the social security system. They are poor risks for the private insurance scheme as well, and in the long run, they will cause an increase in private insurance premiums. The same applies to pensioners. Their share among the members of the private insurance scheme will increase. The increase in premiums will be accelerated by the fact that, in §257.2a of the *Sozialgesetzbuch V*, private health insurance companies are encouraged to introduce a special contribution rate for this group of persons.

In the final analysis, the health insurance scheme is a national insurance scheme, which is divided into a private and a statutory part, just like long-term care insurance. However, the legislature did not have to establish a compulsory private health insurance scheme because; experience shows that almost all people insure their risk of disease on their own initiative. This is an elementary risk, which arouses a fundamental need to insure against it; the legislature is aware of the mental urge to cover such a risk.

Individuals, whom the legislature exclude from statutory health insurance in spite of their bad economic circumstances must therefore, be provided a possibility to take out a health insurance contract with a private insurance company under acceptable conditions. This can be facilitated by an incentive system. Health insurance companies, who want to gain young members with high wages and salaries, must be organized in such a way that the employers subsidize the contributions. Such subsidies, however, must be paid only if the health insurance companies offer a standard contribution rate for pensioners and those over 55 years of age, whose benefits correspond to the *Sozialgesetzbuch V*. The premiums may not be calculated in accordance with the risk and the age of entry; an approach, which is foreign to the private insurance companies' scheme. Instead, the premiums are to be limited to the average maximum contribution in the statutory health insurance scheme and, may only levy an additional premium for spouses to the maximum amount of 50 percent. Insurance companies that want to remain in business will be forced to offer such a premium rate. For older insured persons, private health insurance coverage at the cost of the maximum contribution to the statutory health insurance for one person, and at one and a half of such contribution for a married couple, is obviously, an attractive offer, even if the benefits are lowered to the level provided by the statutory health insurance scheme. What will result from this outcome, particularly with a view to the economic performance of the private health-insurance scheme, and the allegedly efficient manner in which it manages its premiums? Someone who takes out a private health insurance policy at age 30 will have to pay dearly for his low initial premium in the last 20 years of his life; frequently, he will be forced to lower his personal insurance level.

3.

It becomes apparent that in the private insurance scheme marked elements of redistribution on the basis of solidarity have been established; they include a risk structure compensation scheme, which is timidly referred to as "peak compensation" (*Spitzenausgleich*) (§257.2b of the *Sozialgesetzbuch V*), e.g. the insurance companies equalize the losses caused by pensioners. Unnoticed by the public, private health insurance is becoming more and more similar to statutory health insurance. However, it is still praised as the solution to the statutory scheme's poor financial position – a contradiction, which can be solved neither legally nor politically.

At the same time, such an exclusion of poor risks from the statutory health insurance scheme results in a rise of private health insurance premiums. The burden of the premiums that remains in spite of the elements of solidarity, and which at any rate, corresponds to a high-income earner's contributions to the statutory health insurance scheme, can carry the risk, for persons with a low overall income, that their health insurance premium alone can make them dependent on social assistance payments. In such a situation, the municipalities will make an appeal for further redistribution based on solidarity, and the private insurance companies will no longer be in a position to distance themselves from such an appeal. Ultimately, in order to avoid too great an increase in the employer's contributions, it is the taxpayer to whom this appeal is addressed.

III. Minimum Contributions for Self-employed Persons are Compatible with the Constitution

At any rate, in acknowledging that only a sound financial endowment can guarantee insurance coverage irrespective of whether, it is provided by the statutory social security scheme or, by private insurance companies, the *Bundesverfassungsgericht* has approved the minimum contributions for self-employed persons, the introduction of which was supposed to ward off poor risks in the statutory health insurance scheme.[37] The public interests that were manifested in the streamlining of the system, and in the adaptation of the position of the self-employed to that of the employees, took primacy over the individual's interest in maintaining his or, her vested rights, which are worthy of protection. The protection of public confidence is only possible within the system and not outside it.

In addition, this serves as an example, which shows that structural changes are possible in health insurance. If, through practical experience, imbalances in the statutory system are detected, and become visible, the legislature can take countermeasures without being prevented from doing so by the Constitution.

E. Pensioners' Health Insurance

Fundamental statements regarding the creation of efficient associations in the area of social security, and the limits that the protection of public confidence in a state under the rule of law set on the legislature's intention to make use of its creative latitude, can be found in the *Bundesverfassungsgericht* decision of 15 March 2000, which concerns the limitation of access to pensioners' health insurance.[38]

Under review in the decision was a law that changed pensioner's access to health insurance for the worse. Prior to the enactment of the law, in order to stay in the system during old age, pensioners had to prove that compulsory contributions had been paid for at least half the entire period of coverage; after the enactment of the law, they were already excluded if they missed the contributory period for compulsory insurance required over their entire working lives, by ten percent in the second half of their working lives. This meant that if someone transgressed the, relatively low, compulsory insurance income limit on health insurance for two years, this was sufficient for the person to be excluded, upon his or, her retirement, from advantageous compulsory membership in the statutory health insurance scheme. This change in law did not stand up to review under constitutional law.

---

37 BVerfGE 103, 392 (397).
38 BVerfGE 102, 68 (87, 96).

I. Obligation of Uninterrupted Membership before Retirement is Unconstitutional

The regulation did not meet the requirements of the rule of law. Instead, it simply amended an older regulation, pursuant to which, pensioners benefited from the old law providing they had made a timely filing, to the effect that their plans for their lives had turned out to be in vain.

Admittedly, it is true that no one who observes the legislature's activity in the field of social security can rely on the continued existence of laws. Nevertheless, ultimate limits do exist. If the legislature, by explicitly setting time limits, promises to keep a specific regulation in force for a specific period of time, it is prevented from, so to speak, terminating this promise without notice. However, the wording of the judgment is very cautious in this respect and, it also suggests that the situation may be different in the case of a sufficiently important public interest.[39] A sufficiently important public interest cannot be substantiated by stating the expectation of higher contributions or, lower benefits. In this context, purely financial interests, which often determine the legislature's action and, which are regarded as compelling and of paramount importance by legislature do not, under constitutional aspects, always convince the *Bundesverfassungsgericht* in Karlsruhe.

II. The Exclusion from the Pensioners' Statutory Health Insurance Scheme is not Justified

In its substantive part, the decision[40] describes the situation of the compulsorily insured persons and the change that results if, due to a very short break, a long compulsorily insured working life ends with an exclusion from the pensioners' health insurance. The change imposed on the system requires justification yet, justification cannot be provided.

1.

An indication of the appropriateness of the limits is whether, the change follows the overall principles that guide the legislature when establishing compulsory insurance. In this respect, the legislature focuses on the one hand, on the individual's need for protection[41] and takes into account, on the other hand, that the solidarity-based association of insured persons must be endowed with sufficient funds, and additionally remain so. Pursuant to the categorization provided by the law, compulsory insurance includes, at any rate, those groups of persons who due to their low incomes need coverage in the case of illness. This coverage must be achieved by obliging these groups to join the statutory health insurance scheme. In the view of the legislature, those whose annual remuneration is above the ceiling established by the law, no longer need such coverage. This assessment is not fundamentally called into question under constitutional law. To the degree, that health insurance covers risks it at the same time, protects the public from taking recourse to social assistance payments in the case of illness.

---

39   *Id.* at 68, 98.
40   BVerfGE 102, 68.
41   This line of argument is already followed by the Federal Constitutional Court. *See* BVerfGE 29, 221 (235); BVerfGE 44, 70 (94).

2.

As opposed to this, provisions concerning voluntary insurance pursue the aim of opening the statutory health insurance scheme to persons who are not in the same, but in a similar situation, and who are in less need of protection. If these individuals' need for protection typically were to remain less pressing when they reach retirement age or, if other factually convincing reasons existed, one could accept that pensioners remain excluded from compulsory insurance; even when they previously exceeded the income limit only for a short time. This, however, has not been established; it has not even been alleged in the opinions expressed in the proceedings. The need for protection during retirement age does not cease if the pensioner exceeds the income limit for merely a few years. On average, pensions are about DM 2,000[42] lower than the respective ceiling for annual remuneration. There are no statistics, which prove that pensioners, on average, receive income that approximates this amount from other sources (company pensions, property). After a long, compulsorily insured working life, pensioners normally remain in need of protection even if they have exceeded the contribution assessment ceiling for some years.

The *Bundesverfassungsgericht* regards another systemic argument as important. People who voluntarily remained members of the statutory insurance scheme, and whose annual remuneration exceeded the ceiling for a short time have, in their working lives, shouldered a considerable share of the costs caused by the previous generation of pensioners through their contributions to health insurance and also, to pension insurance. Through redistribution between the young and the old, and between high and low income earners on the basis of solidarity, they definitely have, through their health insurance contributions, contributed a considerable share to the pensioners' health insurance because generally, pensioners cause considerable costs and only make low contributions; e.g. they constitute a bad risk. The gainfully employed however, have also supported the health insurance scheme by their pension insurance contributions because, until 1983, the pension insurance scheme made a contribution to the health insurance scheme with lump sums in the amount of 11.7% of the pensions and afterwards, paid subsidies to each pensioner's contributions in addition to the pension.

Here, the *Bundesverfassungsgericht* recalls the fact that the transfer of payments from other insurers is not made by anonymous institutions or, corporations under public law, but by the compulsorily insured contributors who are associated within them; e.g. by the working generation. These are parts of contributions, which are not used to fund the risk that is insured in the respective branch but to quietly and covertly fund other risks, in this case, that of the health insurance scheme. In the constitutional assessment, the shifting that the legislature performs is brought back to its original essence. The working generation funds the health insurance scheme, not only by the contribution that is directly levied, but also always by its pension contribution.[43]

III. Options for Subsequent Improvement have been Left Open

In this decision on the pensioners' health insurance scheme,[44] the *Bundesverfassungsgericht*, for lack of better insight of its own, has left all options for subsequent improvement open to the legislature. The latter however, has not found the strength to subject compulsorily

---

42 The order was issued before the Euro conversion.
43 In this context, indirect funding through the unemployment insurance is just not mentioned; however, the same applies to it.
44 BVerGE 102, 68.

insured persons to payments, which are in line with their actual economic performance and, which take all types of income into account. Instead, it has remedied cases of hardship and has caused decreases in revenue, on the side of the statutory health insurance funds, which have resulted, even now, in enormous deficits.

Meanwhile, these deficits have led to the enactment of the *Beitragssatzsicherungsgesetz* (Act Securing the Stability of Contribution Rates), which caused the most diverse groups of providers of benefits and services in the health care sector to take to the streets, to write letters to newspaper editors, and of course, to bring temporary injunction proceedings before the *Bundesverfassungsgericht*. The temporary injunction proceedings were unsuccessful.[45] It is true that the facts submitted substantiated that drastic changes for the worse had taken place for the professional groups affected, but they did not substantiate risks to the public good. The constitutional complaints, on which the temporary injunction proceedings are based, are still pending; above all, it is an open question whether, the law required the approval of the *Bundesrat* (the upper house of the German parliament).

The members of the professional groups in question however, are not at all interested in these legal issues. With their statements, they substantiate that they expect the statutory health insurance scheme to guarantee them an income that is commensurate with their status in life. Whoever, is admitted to the lists of physicians eligible to provide services under the statutory health insurance scheme – the *Bundesverfassungsgericht* has banned a restriction of access[46] – whoever, establishes himself or, herself as a pharmacist – the *Bundesverfassungsgericht* has enforced the freedom of establishment[47] – believes that he or, she is entitled to receive an adequate income from the system. Concerning this question, the *Bundesverfassungsgericht* has not yet taken a definitive stand. However, its decision regarding the fixed reimbursement rates for pharmaceuticals[48] (e.g. a ceiling for the prices of certain groups of similar pharmaceuticals), and the grounds on which the motions for a temporary injunction against the *Beitragssatzsicherungsgesetz* were denied, do permit some conclusions.

F. Unavoidable Effects on the Interested Parties in the Health Care Sector

So far, the *Bundesverfassungsgericht* decisions, which have been presented, have referred to corrections, adjustments, and changes within the statutory insurance scheme. In a very few decisions, however, the *Bundesverfassungsgericht* has also dealt with the relationship of the statutory and the private health-insurance schemes *vis-à-vis* third parties and, with the unavoidable effects on the providers of benefits and services and, on the participants in the health care market.

I. Private Insurance Companies' Occupational Freedom

The decision concerning long-term care insurance has already been mentioned,[49] which reminds us, by means of a quotation, of the legislature's creative latitude. This, with regard to an appropriate delimitation of the group of insured persons, with a view towards establishing a solidarity-based association of insured persons endowed with sufficient funds.[50]

---

45 BVerfGE 106, 351; BVerfGE 106, 359; BVerfGE 106, 369.
46 BVerfGE 11, 30.
47 BVerfGE 7, 377.
48 BVerfGE 106, 275.
49 BVerfGE 103, 271; BVerfG 103, 197 (221).
50 BVerfGE 44, 70.

1.

In this context, case law is based on a 1977 decision on the new establishment of a special health insurance scheme for self-employed farmers.[51] In 1977, constitutional review took the situation of private insurance companies into account, but not in such a way, that a balance would have had to be achieved between the insured persons' interests and the legislature's social policy aims *vis-à-vis* the consolidated legal positions or, even constitutional rights, of private insurance companies. At that time, the reasoning concerning private insurance companies merely served the aim of justification in relationship to the standard of Art. 3.1 of the *Grundgesetz* because, compulsory insurance had not been extended to all farmers without exception; this had been regarded as permissible.[52] In this respect, the unequal treatment of the group of persons affected, for once, does not find its justification in the different position and the different circumstances of these individuals themselves, but in the consideration of economic interests of third parties affected, e.g. the private insurance companies. Under constitutional law, this is an argument, which has been very strongly toned down; it does not permit the conclusion that constitutional law provides for the so-called "peace line" between statutory and private health insurance, as is often mentioned in politics.

2.

It is true that the insurance companies' occupational freedom is undoubtedly affected when the public-law sector is expanded. For instance, this has happened, and still happens, in the field of pension insurance through the introduction of pension funds for the members of the professions, and through the abolition of the compulsory insurance income limit in 1968.[53] However, it is also the consequence of new delimitations under the statutory health insurance scheme of the group of individuals who are compulsorily insured.

II. Limits of Creative Latitude

The standard that applies when examining the legislature's creative latitude is possibly, the one that the *Bundesverfassungsgericht* found in its decision on public gambling establishments.[54] Pursuant to this decision, restrictions are also permissible concerning access to an occupation or, a profession if they pursue important public interests, and if they respect the principle of proportionality. It will always be possible to regard social security, in this case health insurance coverage at affordable conditions, as a public interest of paramount importance. There are also a sufficient number of statements in *Bundesverfassungsgericht* decisions, which set forth that this public interest, of paramount importance, justifies numerous restrictions on the part of those insured; e.g. disappointed confidences,[55] reduction of benefits, restrictions of the freedom to practice or, even to choose an occupation.[56] With a view to the insurance companies, nothing different applies.

---

51 *Id.*
52 *Id.* at 70 and 90.
53 BVerfGE 23, 221 (237, 241).
54 BVerfGE 102, 197.
55 BVerfGE 100, 138
56 BVerfGE 78, 179.

III. On "National Insurance"

Moreover, it seems quite doubtful whether, the private insurance companies' freedom to practice an occupation or, profession is affected if the statutory social insurance is organized as insurance for all inhabitants. The freedom to choose an occupation or, profession would be affected if such a project would mean the end of their economic existence. All experience speaks against such an assumption.

On the one hand, a national insurance exists in several European states (Switzerland, Netherlands, and Austria). In addition, in these states, private insurance companies definitely still have their area of activity. On the other hand, a comparable reorganization took place in the field of the life insurance companies in Germany, 35 years ago, without this pushing the life insurance companies to the margins. As of January 1 1968, compulsory insurance in the salaried employees' insurance scheme was introduced for all salaried employees, e.g. also for high-income earners. There were transitional arrangements for those who were 50 years or older or, had taken out a so-called exempting life insurance, which provided full coverage for old age and for spousal survivors and, for which the premiums paid were at least as high as the contributions that would have been paid in the salaried employees' pension insurance scheme.

1.

The abolition of freedom of insurance was not challenged by the life insurance companies before the *Bundesverfassungsgericht* but rather, by those salaried employees who had not taken out sufficient exempting life insurance contracts, and instead invoked inter alias, their existing company pensions and property.[57] Salaried employees, with a higher income, assumed that they were deprived of the choice between the numerous types of provision for old age, and that they could no longer act in accordance with their own degree of responsibility and foresight. Here, the complainants put forward that the encroachment upon general freedom of action, which was to be measured against the standard of Art. 2.1 of the *Grundgesetz*, was disproportionate, and that a factual reason for the amendment was not apparent; salaried employees who earned more than DM 21,600 a year could ensure sufficient insurance coverage themselves. They further argued that the change in law carried the idea of social assistance too far and, it was in line with the image of the total welfare state. Moreover, they stated that, the argument that the inclusion of this group of persons strengthened solidarity was not convincing. Due to their relatively small number of members, this might be appropriate in the case of pension funds, which were reserved for the professions but this had no effect in mass insurance.

Accordingly, in order to belong to the group of top earners, a monthly gross income of less than €1,000 was sufficient 35 years ago. Today, the contribution assessment ceiling is five times this number. Those who, at that time, received earnings up to that amount need not, yet today, become a pensioner. How can anyone be expected to calculate his or, her adequate provision for old age if such a shift of reference values occurs in the span of one working life? Anyone who would promise a 30-year-old today that he or, she will receive his or, her present gross income as a pension, would promise, provided that the present circumstances are projected to the future, a pension in the amount of 20 percent of the beginning salaries that can then be achieved. These figures are able to shed a more realistic light

---

57 BVerfGE 76, 256.

on the question of possible individual responsibility and, on the necessity of solidarity in the area of long-term provision.

The constitutional complaints that challenged the extension of compulsory insurance in the salaried employees' insurance scheme were unsuccessful.[58] The *Bundesverfassungsgericht* emphasized the legislature's wide margin for maneuver and compared the interests of the individuals, who are not only burdened by the system, but also obtain advantages from it, with the more important overall public interests, which above all, take into account the risk increases that go along with increased life expectancy. The *Bundesverfassungsgericht* held that the considerably high number of voluntary members of statutory health insurance proved that higher income earners also take an interest in the statutory social insurance scheme. The *Bundesverfassungsgericht* concluded that, due to the contribution assessment ceiling, the individual still had enough economic margins for maneuver to seek and to acquire other, e.g. complementary, forms of social security.

2.

In the same manner, the *Bundesverfassungsgericht* had previously approved the establishment of pension funds for the members of the professions (in this case, physicians) with the resulting restriction of freedom of those who were covered by them.[59] This decision was issued in 1960, when the public was still aware that sharp declines in property were possible, although at that time, such awareness was not due to the sharp drop of stock market quotations but due to the loss of property after World War I or, alternatively to the currency reform or, to the destruction of assets in the World Wars. According to the *Bundesverfassungsgericht*, this forced many physicians to practice their profession until very late in life irrespective of whether they were still fully able to do so. The Court held that the overcrowding of the profession was a consequence of this conduct and this prevented young physicians from establishing themselves in a timely manner. A collective provision for old age could prevent this:

> General objections raised by the opponents of a compulsory insurance scheme, such as for instance, that they are incompatible with a liberal economic system, that they exaggerate the idea of the social welfare state, that the aspired aim could have been achieved by other means, cannot be accepted here; they misjudge the fact that in the area of conflict, which is fundamental and cannot be eliminated, between the protection of the freedom of the individual and the requirements of the system of a social welfare state, a wide margin for maneuver remains for the legislature, within which it is called upon to determine the extent and the nature of the acts of encroachment upon freedom that are necessary, or at least acceptable, in the interest of the common good.[60]

A view that goes back far in time substantiates, with verbatim quotations,[61] the *Bundesverfassungsgericht*'s continuity in its fundamental line of argument. At the same time, how-

---

58 BVerfGE 29, 221 (235).
59 BVerfGE 10, 354 (363); BVerfGE 12, 319 (323–324).
60 *Id.* at 354, 369, 370.
61 "It may be observed that it is not for the *Bundesverfassungsgericht* to decide whether the establishment of such institutions is desirable, expedient, or even necessary from the point of view of social policy. Instead, the important question is merely whether the legislature if it decides to take such a measure exceeds the boundary set for it by the Basic Law ... This applies here no more than in the case that was decided earlier. In the case of a legal regulation that is constitutionally unobjectionable, it is irrelevant whether those affected by the regulation or only a majority of them agree with it as the complainant thinks." BVerfGE 12, 319 (323, 324).

IV. Delimitation between Entrepreneurial Freedom and the Guarantee of Social Security

1.

For the first time, in its decision concerning the calculation of required hospital facilities, the *Bundesverfassungsgericht* made a delimitation of entrepreneurial freedom as against the guarantee of social security.[62] At first consideration, the *Krankenhausfinanzierungsgesetz* (Hospital Funding Act) was geared towards securing the economic position of hospitals. An economically sound hospital sector, as a prerequisite to the provision of health care services, tailored to the needs of the population and supplied at socially acceptable costs, was accepted as a public interest of overriding importance. Efficient hospital care tailored to the needs of the population was regarded as an inalienable part of health care. However, the social aspect of the burden of costs in health care was also given considerable weight. These standards of weighing are in line with a conventional pattern of reasoning from the *Bundesverfassungsgericht*.

Each time the *Bundesverfassungsgericht* invokes, as justification, the stability of the statutory health insurance scheme as a public interest of paramount importance, the Court puts forward a multifunctional argument that can carry weight *vis-à-vis* those insured, and also *vis-à-vis* the providers of benefits and services or, possible competitors in the private insurance system. The stability of the statutory health insurance scheme is a public interest with many different aspects; as an overall concept, it stands for the aim of factually guaranteeing, for the economically less well to do as well, full access to medical care, hospital care, pharmaceuticals, medical devices and other therapeutic facilities at financially affordable conditions. This general line of reasoning is open to many argumentative critiques.

The margin for assessment of whether, where, and how, it will perform acts of encroachment remains with the legislature. This is based on the *Bundesverfassungsgericht*'s insight that, even in regard to the regulation of complex circumstances, it has no better source of knowledge than the legislature because, the Constitution does not provide any specific directions to this effect. The social system is neither predetermined, nor embodied, by the Constitution. In the case of complex matters, it cannot be proved that the aims pursued by the legislature can be achieved in their entirety by a means, which affects the interests of individual parties concerned, in a less incisive manner. The individual who is burdened always sees only the encroachment that affects him or, her however, an encroachment, which affects others, is not a less pointed means.

2.

The beginnings of this view can be found in a decision from 1999,[63] which is outside social security law and, which concerns the fee for professional providers of advisory care. This line of reasoning was extended, in particular with a view to the field of health insurance, in March 2001,[64] in the decision about the age limit for admission to the lists of physicians

---

62 *See* BVerfGE 82, 209 (229).
63 BVerfGE 100, 331 (348, 349).
64 BVerfGE 103, 172.

eligible to provide services under the statutory health insurance scheme. This decision gives a relatively brief status report on the statutory and the private health insurance schemes; the development, which included decades of consolidation efforts, is outlined below. The outcome under constitutional law, as is laid down in the reasoning, reads as follows:

> Apart from the provision of health care services for the population, to which the *Bundesverfassungsgericht* has referred, in consistent case law, as a public interest of special importance,[65] the aspect of cost carries considerable weight for legislative decisions especially in the health care sector. Admittedly, the stability of the statutory health-insurance scheme is of high importance for the public good.[66] If the provision of health care services for the population is supposed to be achieved with the help of a social security system, the financing of such system also constitutes a public interest of overriding importance and, the parliament can take this interest as a guideline for the shaping of the system and for the steering of the service providers' behavior that goes with it.... To the extent that the legislature strives to ensure the provision of health care services for the population through a statutory health insurance scheme, the legislature must, in this context, reconcile different, sometimes opposed, legal positions and public interests of many groups of persons...

* * *

> Purpose and intensity of the encroachment must always be in a reasonable proportion to one another (*c.f.* BVerfGE, vol. 101, 331, 347). In areas in which a very general objective is pursued by a great variety of measures, which affect different legal positions of various subjects of fundamental rights, the assessment of the proportion is determined by the extent to which the restriction affects the respective individual. If the legislature pursues a complex aim like the financial stability of the statutory health insurance scheme by various means, the fact that the persons affected by a specific measure see greater potential for cost-cutting elsewhere does not make the challenged measure unsuitable. Also a specific measure cannot be regarded as unnecessary because, other measures exist within the system that would burden other persons less. Neither is a single measure disproportionate merely because, it does not place an equal burden on all persons affected by its terms.[67]

3.

This means that the Constitution, and not politics, decides the right way to provide adequate health care for the population. In a legal system that is bound by the principles of social justice, the legislature may not abandon this aim. It can however, pursue it by altogether different means. None of the groups involved are entitled to demand that the system, as it has existed to date, remain unchanged. There is no constitutional provision, which guarantees that opportunities of earning an income are maintained. A balance of the conflicting interests must be achieved in the political sphere.

It is exactly this fundamental statement regarding the legislature's creative latitude that is confirmed in the December 17 2002, judgment of the *Bundesverfassungsgericht* concerning the fixed reimbursement rates for pharmaceuticals.[68] The decision places particular emphasis on the fact that, in the health care sector as well, market elements can be strengthened. With reference to previous case law, the Court states the following:

---

65 *See* BVerfGE 78, 179 (192).
66 *See* BVerfGE 70, 1 (30); BVerfGE 82, 209 (230).
67 *Id.* at 172,183.
68 BVerfGE 106, 275.

Competitors have no claim, based on fundamental rights, to have conditions of competition remain the same for them. In particular, fundamental rights do not guarantee a claim to success in competition or, a claim to secure future opportunities for earning an income. While it is true that entrepreneurs can fix their prices, neither the market, nor the Constitution, guarantee that they will find customers who are willing to buy at such prices. The scope of protection of Art. 12.1 of the *Grundgesetz* (freedom of occupation) is not affected because statutes, which, for instance, limit the statutory health insurance scheme's spectrum of benefits and services, have factual market consequences for producers. Even though, the economic consequences can be considerable, the effect of these unavoidable consequences is not that they regulate access to an occupation or, a profession within the meaning of the *Bundesverfassungsgericht*'s case law. Moreover, the decision contains an explicit encouragement to the legislature to ensure more transparency in the field of the intricate health insurance law, as well, so that economic conduct on the part of the actors involved will become possible, "There is no entitlement resulting from Art. 12.1 of the *Grundgesetz* that demands that conditions be maintained, which due to missing transparency, make sales success possible as against competitors."

G. Outlook

Whatever reforms the legislature may implement, in accordance with or, contrary to pressure group interests, they will always have to take the *Bundesverfassungsgericht*'s case law into consideration because; reforms cannot be implemented without considerable cuts that affect the numerous groups who are part of the system. The groups will try to find "their right" in Karlsruhe. It is for the legislature to establish a balance between individual liberty rights, the state's duties to protect, and the fabric of interests, which are hidden behind public interests. The *Bundesverfassungsgericht* will probably, only in very few cases, conduct an isolated constitutional assessment of individual cost containment measures in the health care sector and, reject them as unconstitutional against the standards of equality before the law, the freedom to practice an occupation or profession or, general freedom of action. This is due to the fact that the legislature, as a general rule, bundles measures that are to the detriment of many of the parties involved, e.g. of the providers of benefits and services, of those insured and of the contributors, in order to maintain the operability of the statutory health insurance system.

Due, not only to the obligations under constitutional law to protect life and physical integrity, but also in the interest of a society's cohesion, politics must succeed in providing a good health care system at acceptable prices. In this context, that system appears most viable that most effectively takes into account the decision-making mechanisms, which take effect within the human psyche. In this context, it appears logical that the existing system will repeatedly be improved on. The human being is a being that can adapt to new basic premises. Therefore, the preconditions of the decision-making processes change with the respective framework conditions. Every change of law solves problems while, at the same time, sowing the seeds for new ones.

At the end of the day, the legislature's margin for maneuver, as measured against the standard of the Constitution, is very wide whereas it is very narrow when measured against social reality.

The Learning Sovereign

Günter Frankenberg*

A. A Note on Sovereignty

Constitutions of democratic republics legitimize political government with an appeal to the sovereignty of the people. The people, and no one other than the people, are solely responsible for all generally binding laws and decisions. For a long time, or to be somewhat more exact, for a little over 200 years, since the great democratic revolutions marked the dawn of the modern constitutional age, the continental idea of a sovereign people has suffered from a lack of distance to its antithesis, the sovereignty of the absolutist monarch. The shadow of this opposition stretched over the semantic and theoretical efforts to develop a concept of a sovereign people that held the *summa protestas* or final power of decision. In these teachings, theories and images, the people, from whom all governing authority derives and to whom, by means of a legitimation chain of command, all power returns, play a peculiarly static and monolithic role. This gave room to the impression that a democratic society of active citizens is only incorporated in a different manner and can still be symbolically represented as a body or *body politic* like the early modern or absolutist society of subjects (*Untertanen*).

The backwards-oriented theory of a constitution, describing the constitution as a concrete order rather than a frame of reference for societal conflicts, confirms the validity of this impression. This theory is supported, with wider reaching consequences, by a series of decisions of the German Federal Constitutional Court (FCC). In its decision not to grant foreigners the right to vote,[1] the Court, in viewing the people as a homogeneous political body, opened a semantic and normative connection between today's constitution and the absolutist past. It is only fair, however, to point out that, according to a different line of reasoning by the Court, this past has no information in store for us. This alternative line of reasoning is not based on an incorporated but rather on an internally differentiated, pluralist society.

This reasoning was set forward in the *Lüth* decision, elaborated in the *Brokdorf* decision and is still evident in the decisions concerning the sit-in protests.[2] It conceives more or less carefully of the politically active citizens as individuals or as members of associations, and connects the interpretation of the freedoms of communication to the presence of a

---

* Professor of Public Law, Comparative Public Law and Philosophy of Law, Johann Wolfgang Goethe-University, Frankfurt, Germany. Email: frankenberg@jur.uni-frankfurt.de.
1 See only the Federal Constitutional Court's decisions on municipal voting rights for foreigners, published in BVerfGE 83, 37 and in BVerfGE 83, 60. The problem of sovereignty and homogenity is addressed in the decision on the Maastricht Treaty, published in BVerfGE 89, 155 (182). Some of the critique of these rulings is collected in DEMOKRATIE UND GRUNDGESETZ (KRITISCHE JUSTIZ ED., 2000).
2 BVerfGE 7, 198 (Lüth Case) and BVerfGE 69, 315 (Brokdorf Case) and concerning the problem whether sit-in demonstrations are to be qualified as duress in accordance with §240 StGB: BVerfGE 73, 206 and BVerfGE 82, 236; Bundesverfassungsgericht (BVerfG), 54 NEUE JURISTISCHE WOCHENZEITSCHRIFT (NJW) 1031 (2002).

constitution guaranteeing fundamental rights that is not solely set upon defending rights against encroachments by the government but by means of the *status activus* and the *status constituens* also guarantees the status and creative possibilities of active citizens.[3] Regardless of what one might criticize relative to the individual decisions, they open up a new and more modern perspective on sovereignty: This normative construction confers the final power of decision jointly to the plurality of constitutionally empowered citizens.

I would like to bridge the contradiction, which both senates of the FCC have run into, with the metaphor of the "learning sovereign" and the therein-implied orientation to the future. I shall try to illustrate this venture by using the example of the most precarious and corroded[4] instrument for protecting the constitution – the banning of political parties as provided for in Art. 21 II Basic Law. Paradoxically, this reveals quite clearly the remnants of a past that many would like to finally see disappear. I intend to make use of the fact that past events only end grammatically, not historically.

B. About the Learning of the Sovereign

In the beginning there is the thesis that the people or rather the population from which, according to the constitution, emanates all governing power is a "learning sovereign."[5] We as shareholders of sovereignty think we know what a sovereign "is." With respect to the past, we also have a clear picture of sovereignty. Summarizing inherited doctrine, the sovereign is he who has the last word. Let me suggest a slight modification: Sovereign is he who learns while speaking the last word.

In this context, learning has two meanings: First, the modern agency of sovereignty *must* learn. The sovereign is – as a learning god going to elementary school – constantly dependent upon new information, forced to taking the necessary precautions so that the horizon remain open for new information. Thus, learning has a self-critical and at the same time normative meaning, that radically separates the democratic from the pre-democratic or anti-democratic sovereign. The latter was never constitutionally obliged to learn; at best, political wisdom dictated that he not turn a deaf ear to new experiences. This duty to learn, which may be characterized as democratic self-constraint, destroys the myth of omniscience and undermines any claim of privileged access to knowledge. A Sovereign is he who knows that he does not know it all and is therefore open to what has yet to be heard. It is openness to essential learning experiences that guarantees the principle of a democratic republic together with the constitutional freedoms of political communication. The republican principle is to guarantee transparency and publicity of learning. The principle of democracy is to grant all those concerned, especially minorities, access to the forums where these learning processes may take place. The freedoms of communication support and implement both principles, or in other words, they create opportunities for learning.

Second, a democratic sovereign can, or more precisely *may* learn, which literally and not only theoretically separates him from an absolutist sovereign. Empirically this means that the sovereign is capable of learning. From a normative perspective, this means he is able to represent the past and to draw conclusions for the future. The fact that certain learning experiences lead to practical consequences confers legitimacy on regulations that limit the freedom of communication and organization, thereby excluding certain experiences. Such

---

3 The concept of the *status constituens* was introduced by Erhard Denninger, STAATSRECHT 1, (1973).
4 *See* CLAUS LEGGEWIE & HORST MEIER, REPUBLIKSCHUTZ (1995).
5 I took the term, not the concept, for the learning sovereign from HAUCKE BRUNKHORST, SOLIDARITÄT UNTER FREMDEN 119 (1997) and HAUCKE BRUNKHORST, DEMOKRATIE UND DIFFERENZ 199 (1994).

regulations are especially precarious and require justification. Whether or not they are also contradictory will be addressed later.

The preliminary conclusion would be the following: the sovereignty of the people is doubly encoded democratically. It has an empirical and a normative component. The normative component is again doubly encoded as the obligation *and* the right to learn. There is also a second preliminary conclusion we may draw: when sovereignty is connected to the idea of a learning process the formerly monolithic-rigid entity becomes fluid and temporalised, and the risk of premature cut-off and thus invalid learning experiences comes to the fore. A democratic society cannot protect itself from the risks of learning and from experiments with uncertain results, nor is there any insurance against the risks of "wrong" learning processes. Due to its obligation to future-oriented learning, it has to take all the possible procedural and institutional precautions that provide for a high level of openness. Regardless of possible and likely objections, the following three principles may be considered *prima facie* as such precautionary measures: the binding of encroachments on fundamental rights to the provison of legality, the principle of proportionality, and the so-called party privilege (*Parteienprivileg*), which reserves the power to ban a party to the FCC.

C. Restrained and Unrestrained Democracy

The thoughts on people's sovereignty outlined above fit seamlessly in a concept of democracy with at least two different layers of meaning as *restrained* and *unrestrained* forms of political self-determination. One might say that democracy is doubly encoded. The philosophical and political-theoretical reading deals with democracy as a *universal* principle expressing as "the rule of the people" or "self-government" the idea of a collectively autonomous disposal of the common affairs. Democracy is thus connected with political autonomy and the freedom to conduct or participate in political experiments; this is what we refer to as democratic experimentalism. Disregarding its origin in the Anglo-European tradition, this connotation of democracy as a temporally and territorialy *unrestrained* principle, has spread worldwide and was adopted, as it appears by all constitutions. No society organized as a state can afford to write a constitution without reference to democracy. Even the former socialist dictatorships of the unasked proletariat called themselves "people's democracies."

Translations of the theoretical universalism of democracy into constitutional law are not only to be found at the national level, but also in supranational and international law. It is instructive to look at the European Convention on Human Rights, which allows for limitations of human rights as long as they are "necessary for a democratic society." The Amsterdam version of the European Union Treaty sets forth in Art. 6 that the Union is "founded on the principles of liberty, democracy, respect for human rights and fundamental freedoms, and the rule of law," opening up the "union of states" for criticism of the democratic deficits of its institutions.

These two examples refer to the second definition or the "particular" definition of democracy as a self-declaration and self-description of a society framed in time and space and defined politically and culturally. When we talk about "the constitutional democracy of the German Basic Law" or "American democracy," we refer to a contextualized or *restrained* democracy. Every society expresses its own idea of democracy by way of its constitution. It appropriates the universal principle and tailors it to its particular needs through the very act of writing the constitution, as well as through all the subsequent constitutional interpretations and changes as they pertain to democracy. Constitutionalizations operate on two levels: Rhetorically, they refer to the universal principle, while at the same time they lend "democracy" a concrete form through specific rules, procedures and institutions. As a result, no constitution – not even the German Basic Law – implements the universal principle as we know it from Rousseau, Kant and Locke; instead, it proposes a more or less context-sensitive translation, implementation and integration. One might say this or that particular aspect of the German constitutional democracy contradicts this or that theory of democracy. Or in other words: the German constitutional democracy lags behind the promises of the universal principle according to which all people concerned should be able to have a direct say in all matters that affect them. Remarks like these are trivial, however, because constitutions do not apply philosophical-political theories and theorems one-to-one, but rather specific – *restrained* – ideas of democracy, which also applies to "republic" and "the rule of law" (*Rechtsstaat*). Vulgo: Every society opts for the form of democracy it considers correct, fitting or tolerable.

Does that strip democracy of any normative content leading beyond the historical-social or political-cultural horizon? Must democracy fall victim to particularity through the act of writing a constitution? The answer is: No. Every declaration of democracy, regardless of however particular it might be, unavoidably takes its cues from the universal form, thereby gaining its special dignity. Democratic semantics and grammar cannot be had without the philosophical-political background. Whoever speaks of democracy gets entangled in its unrestrained meaning. When people stand up for democracy they fight for the possibility to achieve unrestrained democracy in a specific historical-social context.

Two virtues of this double character are: First, it initially grants the political architects and builders, whether they are the elite, social movements, the civil society or contingent majorities, a certain and necessary prerogative and creative licence and allows them to take into consideration – as did Montesquieu – the history, mentality and distribution of power etc.[6] Second, this double nature generates a *practice of justification*. The political architects and builders are clearly forced to justify limitations of democracy as legitimate. The rhetorics of democracy bear an inherent and at the same time overarching normative tendency that unfolds through a justificatory constraint. As a result the double code allows observers as well as participants to check and see whether and to what extent, a society through its self-declaration of democracy has oriented itself to the universal principle, and what contradictions they may have created in the process of constituition making. The greater the distance between democratic universalism and democratic particularism or, in other words, the greater the distance between Rousseau's idea of self-government and a people's democracy, the more reference to democracy turns out to be sheer ideology, mostly a tactic or rhetorical loan motivated by foreign and domestic politics, which invites activists to protest and intellectuals to criticize. The universal unrestrained principle of democracy remains, in specific democratical contexts, the guiding regulatory idea and the background of every normative criticism.

D. Libertarian and Protectionist Democracy

The gloomiest and longest lasting learning experience for the German people was and is the liquidation of the first republic by the Nazi terror regime and its horrific macro-crimes. From these experiences the sovereign as writer of the constitution, supervised by the occupation powers, was entitled to draw normative conclusions without violating the code of democratic decision-making power and constraints. The constitutional Framers of

---

6 Montesquieu's "contextualization" addresses the conditions of legislative work in THE SPIRIT OF LAWS.

1949 had the right to contextualize the abstract democratic principle historically and politically, without being accused of having acted in a self-contradictory way.

It is, however, too soon to assume that the constitutional installation of a "militant democracy" with its constitutional and sub-constitutional clauses is simply the product of a historical learning process and therefore a legitimate restriction free from all criticism. More than anything the teachings and practices of a "militant democracy" should be questioned whether and to what degree they betray the principle of general self-defermination and cut off political learning experiences and experiments vital to the future orientation of democracy. This questioning will be applied to the practice of banning political parties in the Federal Republic of Germany, and the theoretical and dogmatic arguments used to justify this practice. (I will refer to arguments and distrinctions set forth in the Federal Parliament's brief to ban the neo-Nazi party NPD, developed by Wolfgang Löwer and me, which were further carried out by Peter Niesen.[7])

The banning of political parties clearly falls under Otto Kirchheimer's definition of political justice.[8] Equally clearly, party bans affect central prerequisites of democratic self-determination. To be more specific, they directly restrict the freedom of political organization and, indirectly, the freedom of political communication, namely the right to assemble and to free speech: parties declared unconstitutional are dissolved. As a rule, their assets are confiscated. Furthermore, they are prohibited from forming substitute organizations (*Ersatzorganisationen*).[9] Their programs and propaganda are stripped of the protection and premiums of legality. Consequently, a party ban has to set in motion the constraint of justification outlined above. This constraint is illustrated by the overwhelming amount of constitutional literature concerning Art. 21 II Basic Law which provides that, "Parties that, by reason of their aims or the behavior of their adherents seek to undermine or abolish the free democratic basic order or to endanger the existence of the Federal Republic of Germany shall be unconstitutional."[10]

The relevant literature can easily be divided into two camps, differing in matters of principle due to their contrary views as to the legal admissibilty of regulations concerning political freedom, in particular the formation and organization of political parties. Accordingly we need to differentiate between two legal regimes: the *libertarian* regime based on the principle of non-interference (*Nichteinmischung*), which is critical of "militancy" and the *protectionist regime* which raises no prinicipled objections against such militancy. It is obvious that these two regimes have different effects on societal learning processes and democratic experimentalism. The libertarian regime leans toward an unconditional preference for opeaness, accepting that "coincidence is worthy to decide our destiny" (Richard Rorty). The protectionists want to avoid too risky or otherwise unacceptable coincidences.

---

7   See Peter Niesen, *Anti-Extremism, Negative Republicanism, Civic Morality: Three Paradigms for Reflecting Past Injustice in Germany and Italy*, 3 GERMAN LAW JOURNAL 7 (2001) *available at* http://www.german-lawjournal.com/article.php?id=164; and *in* 1 ANNUAL OF GERMAN AND EUROPEAN LAW 2003 81–112 (Russell Miller & Peer Zumbansen eds., 2004). *See also, id., Äußerungsfreiheit und kultureller Pluralismus*, *in* ÜBERSETZUNG ALS MEDIUM DES KULTURVERSTEHENS UND DER SOZIALEN INTEGRATION (Joachim Renn, Jürgen Straub & Shingo Shimada eds, 2002).

8   OTTO KIRCHHEIMER, POLITISCHE JUSTIZ 186 (1981).

9   The consequences of a party ban are regulated in Art. 21 Abs. 2 und 3 GG – the applicable provisions of the law on political parties (§§32 *et seq.*) and of the Law on the Federal Constitutional Court (§46 Abs. 3 GG).

10 Jörn Ipsen, *Art. 21 GG, in* GRUNDGESETZ KOMMENTAR, margin number 850 (Michael Sachs ed., 2nd ed., 1999); Wolfgang Streinz, *Art. 21, in* KOMMENTAR ZUM GRUNDGESETZ, margin number 212 (Herrmann v. Mangoldt, Friedrich Klein & Christian Starck eds., 4th ed., 2000); Hans H. Klein, *Art. 21 GG, in* KOMMENTAR ZUM GRUNDGESETZ, margin number 485 (Theodor Maunz et al. eds., 2001); Christoph Gusy, *Art. 21 GG, in* ALTERNATIV-KOMMENTAR ZUM GRUNDGESETZ (AK-GG), margin number 113 (Erhard Denninger et al. eds., 3rd ed., 2001) with further references.

The libertarian regime commands the charm of radicality and a pure tolerance, that accepts wisdom as well as foolishness. It holds on to these virtues, however, only in the realm of free speech. The general freedom to act (*allgemeine Handlungsfreiheit*) expressed in Art. 2 Basic Law cannot be held as a democratic reference freedom on its own because of its indeterminate applicatory scope. Instead, it receives special support from the democratic principle only in specific manifestations that are specially regulated, such as the right to assemble or the forming of associations.

Consequently, libertarians are entangled in an endless debate over the question which statements or opinions are "just words,"[11] and where the realm of actions begins that may be confronted with the "prohibition of violence" (*Gewaltverbot*)[12] and finally how to define violence without compromising the libertarian dogma.[13] Furthermore, protagonists of the libertarian position have to deal with the question of how they plan to protect minorities whose realistic chance of becoming the majority should somehow legitimize majority rule. As a result the libertarian position runs into trouble in two constellations: First, when forced to deal with a power which has monopolized the media and employs well-honed manipulative strategies for the purpose of general disinformation. The noble principle of non-interference clearly favors the status quo of power distribution to the detriment of manipulated and outvoted minorities. Second, the libertarian paradigm is in trouble in situations with third party effect (*Drittwirkungssituationen*) calling for the government to prevent minorities from being bombarded with defamatory, offensive or derogatory statements from the majority or other social groups. Protecting the state's honor may be rejected with relatively little argumentative effort because it openly violates the priciples of a libertarian position. However, the burden of justification increases dramatically, for example, in the case of pornography or racist statements[14] that might be qualified as actions after all. Furthermore, we confront this issue in light of the problem whether and how the psychological integrity of people, in particular holocaust survivors, should be protected from retraumatization through public statements and actions. In these cases it does not suffice to refer, with a generous liberal gesture, to the inadmissible "chilling effect" that encroachments on free speech have, given that these forms and contents of public communication are purposefully designed to silence the addressees of hatred and threat, and to force them out of the public sphere. As distinct from a libertarian regime, protectionists introduce cognitive criteria and normative limits, in order to fence in the unpredictability of democratic experiments. Protectionism claims that the ideal of absolute and formal freedom is empty. Therefore it turns to the prerequisites of the possibility to learn through communication and to free oneself from the powers that be. Thus protectionism reveals itself as a critique of the administered society entrenched in power relations. Protectionism removes public statements from the exclusive domain of civil-societal controversy insofar as it introduces a modicum of inevitable governmental

---

11   CATHERINE MACKINNON, ONLY WORDS (1983); ("NUR WORTE", 1994).
12   However, the prohibtion of violence does not provide us with specific criteria. That is illustrated by the previously cited decisions of the BVerfG to the sit-in demonstrations and the accompanying literature, also compare Josef Brink & Rainer Keller, *Politische Freiheit und strafrechtlicher Gewaltbegriff*, 16 KRITISCHE JUSTIZ 107 (1983).
13   For the applicable case law from the U.S. Supreme Court compare the analysis from GÜNTER FRANKENBERG & ULRICH RÖDEL, VON DER VOLKSSOUVERÄNITÄT ZUM MINDERHEITENSCHUTZ chapter II (1981). Concerning the rulings of the BVerfG to Art. 5 Abs. 1 GG *see* Dieter Grimm, *Die Meinungsfreiheit in der Rechtsprechung des Bundesverfassungsgerichts*, 48 NJW 1687 (1995). As to the differences between actions and words, *see* Herbert Marcuse, *Repressive Toleranz*, *in* KRITIK DER REINEN TOLERANZ, 91 (Robert Paul Wolff et al. eds., 1967).
14   The proliferation of "hate-speech" is exemplarly documented in the almost 80-page hate catalogue on the internet: http://www.hatedirectory.com.

control, and if necessary, censorship. The problems and dangers associated with this position are apparent and cannot be resolved by simply referring, in a justifying gesture, to "repressive tolerance,"[15] the need for democratic self-control or the unavoidable paternalism according to the slogan: "Nip things in the bud." The center of the problem seems to be where to draw the line between interventions concerned with democracy and promoting self-determination on the one side and arbitrary-authoritarian measure which undermine self-determination on the other. The greatest danger is produced by the inherent dynamic and the disciplining effects of any governmental control system that are then reduced by legal doctrine to an "abuse" of power.

The restrained democracy of the German Basic Law testifies to a preference for protectionism. Other constitutions, notably the French, transfer their protectionism to the sub-constitutional laws allowing so-called "minus-measures" against parties, organizations and individuals. The German constitutional democracy reveals its restraint as "militant" quite openly and institutionally in the Articles 9 II (outlawing associations), 18 (forfeiture of basic rights), and 21 II (party ban). Along these lines a more generalized and somewhat hidden type of protectionism may be located in the provision of legality, for example allowing restrictions of free speech by "general laws" (Art. 5 II Basic Law), or the exclusion of non-peaceful demonstrations from the constitutional protection of the right to assemble (Art. 8 I Basic Law). This generalized protectionism leads to a casuistry of the allowable that may be uneasily steered to the libertarian pole on the grounds of a preference for freedom. This type of preference is revealed by the heavy criticism of the "ultra-liberal" decisions of the FCC regarding free speech[16] or its labeling of the freedoms of communication as "preferred freedoms."[17] This libertarian preference, however has been negated by §130 III of the German Criminal Code (StGB) which makes punishable[18] the approval, denial or the playing down of racial persecution as incitement to hatred and violence against minorities. One may find this criminal provision politically correct. Its defense of a historical truth is, in any case, an act of sin against the libertarian regime. Even protectionism has trouble justifying this provision as long as the need to provide for public peace is taken to be the protected public good. The fact that the protection of minorities as a possible legitimate justifaction is not mentioned in §130 StGB will be referred to later.

The same applies to the overlapping concept as well as the individual instruments of a "militant democracy." They have protectionism written on their foreheads. However, the text of the "militant democracy" in the German constitution is not easily readable. It was, and remains, as a complete concept and in its different expressions, equally in need of interpretation and remains contested.[19] Unavoidably, each interpretation shifts the direction and limits of protectionism and indicates its tolerance for social learning processes thus influencing its own need for substantiation and legitimacy as an expression of a

---

15 Marcuse, *Repressive Toleranz*, in KRITIK DER REINEN TOLERANZ 91 (Robert Paul Wolff et al. eds., 1967). See also Jean Paul Sartre, *Vorwort zu Frantz Fanon*, in DIE VERDAMMTEN DIESER ERDE (1968).
16 Besides BVerfGE 7, 167 (Lüth Case), BVerfGE 93, 266 and Bundesverfassungsgericht (BVerfG), 47 NEUE JURISTISCHE WOCHENSCHRIFT (NJW) 2413 (1994), as tolerance limits for free speech, are cases in point.
17 This concept temporally played a role in the rulings of the U.S. Supreme Court. GÜNTER FRANKENBERG & ULRICH RÖDEL, VON DER VOLKSSOUVERÄNITÄT ZUM MINDERHEITENSCHUTZ 151 (1981).
18 For an incisive criticism see Sebastian Cobler, *Das Gesetz gegen die „Auschwitzlüge" – Anmerkungen zu einem rechtspolitischen Ablasshandel*, 18 KRITISCHE JUSTIZ 159 (1985).
19 In general Horst Dreier, *Grenzen demokratischer Freiheit im Verfassungsstaat*, 49 JURISTENZEITUNG 741 (1994) with further references. Concerning *Abwehrbereitschaft*: Erhard Denninger, *Der Schutz der Verfassung*, in HANDBUCH DES VERFASSUNGSRECHTS, 1293 (Ernst Benda et al. eds., 1983); Hans H. Klein, *Art. 21 II GG*, in KOMMENTAR ZUM GRUNDGESETZ, margin number 485 (Theodor Maunz et al. eds., 2001).

restrained democracy. With regard to the institutions and the practice of the "militant democracy" in Germany one may discern three prominent patterns, or paradigms, of interpretation and justification.[20] Each paradigm aims to protect different goods and is quided by different ideas of danger prevention.

E. Anti-Extremism as a Secondary Constitution

In order to exclude extremist organizations or actions from the realm of constitutional protection, one is prone to undertake an act of violence. One must define and occupy the constitutional point-zero and mark it either implicitly or explicitly as the norm and its immediate action environment as normality, thereby labeling extremists as appearances of unacceptable political deviance, and/or criminal delinquency. Criticism of this type of normal construction has never played a noteworthy role in Germany. This applies to the party bans of the 1950s,[21] the controversial anti-extremism decrees of 1972 and the *Berufsverbote* (occupational bans) they triggered in the 1970s and early 1980s,[22] as well as to the prohibition of organizations based on Art. 9 II Basic Law which clearly outnumber the party bans.[23] Always in the forefront has been the democracy – and rule of law – based criticism of the defense mechanisms and their application, describing this practice a "secondary constitution."[24] The reason that the normalizing power of definition was overseen, is most likely due to the fact that anti-extremism in the Federal Republic has always been combined with an anti-totalitarian rationale. This rationale reduces the center of defining power not to normality, but – compared with totalitarian regimes quite plausibly – to liberality.

Even if the primary background for the acceptance of the entire concept of a "militant democracy" in the early Federal Republic was the shock triggered by the destruction of the Weimar Republic, the discussions of the Herrenchiemsee Convention reveal two recognizable impulses. The liberal democratic fundamental order was to be protected from "what we know from before and from 'over there' (a reference to the territory beyond the Iron Curtain)."[25] It is quite obvious that the totalitarian theories[26] of National-Socialism and Stalinism in connection with the constellation of the Cold War paved the way for an – not original but soon dominant – understanding of a democracy prepared to defend itself against extremist movements and therefore "restrained" political order.

Above all, the instrument of a party ban was originally[27] designed as a weapon, or to put it less militantly: a barrier against the rise of organized totalitarianism.[28] By way of

---

20 The structure of these paradigms is explained in Niesen, *supra* note 7.
21 For details *see* HORST MEIER, PARTEIVERBOTE UND DEMOKRATISCHE REPUBLIK. ZUR INTERPRETATIONEN UND KRITIK VON ART. 21 ABS. 2 DES GRUNDGESETZES (1993).
22 References and criticism *in* ERHARD DENNINGER, FREIHEITLICHE DEMOKRATISCHE GRUNDORDNUNG (1977); Günter Frankenberg, *Angst im Rechtsstaat*, 10 KRITISCHE JUSTIZ 353 (1977); Thomas Blanke & Günter Frankenberg, *Zur Kritik und Praxis des Radikalenerlasses*, 12 KRITISCHE JUSTIZ 45 (1979).
23 Wolfgang Löwer, *Art. 9 GG*, *in* 1 GRUNDGESETZ-KOMMENTAR, margin number 36 (Ingo von Münch & Philip Kunig eds., 5th ed., 2000).
24 HELMUT RIDDER, DIE SOZIALE ORDNUNG DES GRUNDGESETZES 54 (1975).
25 Günter Dürig, *Art. 18 GG*, *in* KOMMENTAR ZUM GRUNDGESETZ, margin number 48 (Theodor Maunz & Günther Dürig eds., 1st ed., 1958).
26 The classic version was developed by HANNAH ARENDT, ELEMENTE UND URSPRÜNGE TOTALER HERRSCHAFT (1985). Also influential is CARL J. FRIEDRICH (ed.), TOTALITÄRE DIKTATUR (1957).
27 The original concept called for a "militant," later referred to as *"streitbare"* or *"abwehrbereite"* democracy from Karl Loewenstein, *Militant Democracy and Fundamental Rights*, XXXI AMERICAN POLITICAL SCIENCE REVIEW, 417 and 638 (1937).
28 In the KPD decision the BVerfG makes reference to "totalitarian parties", against whom "a neutral position is no longer possible" (BVerfGE 5, 85 (137)).

confirmation, one may refer to the symmetry of the proposals of the Federal Government in 1951 to ban the Nazi-SRP and the KPD (Communist Party). The symmetry, however, appears in a slightly different light when one takes into account newer research[29] and the decisions of the FCC. This research allows for the conclusion that the Adenauer administration did not just propose the ban of the SRP as a cover for their real intention, the ban of the KPD, but was an attempt to get rid of political groups that might endanger the concept of silent integration of former national-socialists into the new republic according to a pattern of "disposal of the past" (*Entsorgung der Vergangenheit*).[30] The unequal length of the proceedings and the resistance of the Court to issue a ban against the KPD limits the credibility of the symmetry theory.

However, the justification of protectionism does not hinge upon strict symmetry: far more decisive is the direction given to the party bans under the anti-extremist paradigm. It serves to secure the free democratic order against fascist or Stalinist infiltration and adds this instrument to the arsenal of political risk prevention. Anti-extremism protects the integrity or stability of the liberal system and its constitutive principles and institutions. The orientation toward stability may be inferred from most of the defining elements put forth by the FCC in the SRP decision and characterizing the free democratic fundamental order, namely: sovereignty of the people; separation of powers; governmental accountability; lawfulness of the administration; independence of the courts; party pluralism; and equal opportunity of the parties, with a right to form and exercise an opposition.[31] The "order" is to be understood as based upon the sovereignty of the people, governed by the rule of law and practiced within the framework of pluralist parliamentary and party democracy.

This anti-extremist "system" logic led to an extensive restraint on democracy that the Federal Constitutional Court in its SRP decision recognized and labeled as a result of a learning process: "The framers of the German constitution were faced with the question, could they implement these conclusions [of a liberal democratic state – G.F.] in pure form, or *having just learned from the recent past, must they set some kind of limit.*"[32] In the decision banning the Communist Party, the Court also held that the position of the Constitution on political parties can only be understood with regard to the background of experience in the fight against this totalitarian system,[33] referring to the system of National-Socialism. The Court affirmed the need to draw a line by pointing to the value restraint of the political order, which in the case of a "position fundamentally hostile to democracy" may trigger the ban.

The anti-extremist logic of the 1950s carried with it a problem that the FCC in its SRP decision easily avoided. Given the members, program, and party structure continuity, there was enough evidence to verify the "essential likeness"[34] of the SRP to Hitler's NSDAP. The problem can be described like this: According to the internal logic of democracy – its self-restraint – only a danger to the democratic order, that is, a verifiable threat to the universal core, may legitimately lead to the exclusion of a party from constitutional protection. Who reads "danger" as an unwritten defining element into Art. 21 II Basic Law, faces a structural political dilemma: a party ban which takes effect too soon would – for want of a threat to stability – be unnecessary, even improper; waiting too long, on the other hand.

---

29 Norbert Frei, Vergangenheitspolitik 343 (1996). For a different interpretation *see* Helmut Ridder, Die soziale Ordnung des Grundgesetzes 54 (1975) and Ridder, Zur Ideologie der streitbaren Demokratie (1979).
30 Helmut Dubiel & Günter Frankenberg, *Entsorgung der Vergangenheit*, Die Zeit 12 (18 March 1983).
31 BVerfGE 2, 1 (12).
32 BVerfGE 2, 1 (11) (emphasis added).
33 BVerfGE 5, 85 (138).
34 BVerfGE 2, 1 (69).

would lead to a situation in which a ban against a powerful party, in light of the strength of its supporters and its representation in parliament, would literally be dangerous and could no longer be implemented.[35] Either way, an argument based on Art.21 II Basic Law would have no grounding.

Followers of the system logic have labeled the justification problem as a self-contradiction, paradox or dilemma from the beginning,[36] some even calling Art.21 II Basic Law "unconstitutional constitutional law".[37] The FCC was able to circumvent this problem in the SRP decision with the "essential likeness" argument. This road was blocked in the KPD decision. The court combined the values of the political order with an "actively combative, aggressive" and therefore unconstitutional stance over against "the inviolable fundamental values of the democratic order",[38] and added as a new criterion a *logical danger*: The party to be banned "must plan to encroach upon the functioning of this system, and *when left to run its course* seek to abolish this system".[39] The deciding factor is "the political orientation" of the party. If allowed to follow this course, its actions would lead to the upheaval of the system. A party can therefore "be unconstitutional in accordance with Art. 21 II Basic Law even when a reasonable assessment determines that it has no chance of realizing its unconstitutional plans at any foreseeable time in the future".[40] "For the Court the goals or ideas that the party plans to achieve during its political legitimacy remain the decisive factors."[41] Logical, if perhaps not plausible, within the scope of anti-extremist system logic, the FCC in the KPD decision spread out the Marxist-Leninist goals over nearly 50 pages, stated their incompatibility with the free democratic system and then explained through 180 pages the Marxist-Leninist and therefore unconstitutional goals of the KPD.[42] Abounding in words and quotes the Court undertook the attempt, damned to failure, to avoid the prerequisites of the anti-extremist logic. The protection of the system is shifted forward hyper-preventively into an area, in which one can no longer refer to a tangible danger to the universal core elements of democracy.

While prematurely cut-off learning processes may be understandable in the founding era of the Federal Republic, these justifications lose all striking power in a consolidated and comparatively upheaval-resistant democracy.[43]

---

35 Rudolf Schuster, *Relegalisierung der KPD oder Illegalisierung der NPD?*, 23 JURISTENZEITUNG 413, 420 (1968); FRANK STOLLBERG, DIE VERFASSUNGSRECHTLICHEN GRUNDLAGEN DES PARTEIENVERBOTS 26 (1976).

36 Beginning with the "father" of the concept LOEWENSTEIN, MILITANT DEMOCRACY AND FUNDAMENTAL RIGHTS 417 (1937), continuing *in* ALTERNATIV-KOMMENTAR ZUM GRUNDGESETZ (AK-GG) margin number 1424 (1st ed. 1984) and on to Ulrich K. Preuß, *Die empfindsame Demokratie – Über die inneren Grenzen eines Parteiverbots in der Gesellschaft der Individuen*, FRANKFURTER ALLGEMEINE ZEITUNG, Aug. 22, 2000, at 51.

37 See BVerfGE 5, 85 (137).

38 BVerfGE 5, 85 (head note 5 and 133, 138).

39 BVerfGE 5, 85 (141) (emphasis added).

40 BVerfGE 5, 85 (143).

41 BVerfGE 5, 85 (146).

42 For critique: Wolfgang Abendroth, *Das KPD-Urteil des Bundesverfassungsgerichts. Ein Beitrag zum Problem der richterlichen Interpretation von Rechtsgrundsätzen der Verfassung im demokratischen Staat*, in ANTAGONISTISCHE GESELLSCHAFT UND DEMOKRATIE 139, 146 (Wolfgang Abendroth ed., 1967); HORST MEIER, PARTEIVERBOTE UND DEMOKRATISCHE REPUBLIK, ZUR INTERPRETATIONEN UND KRITIK VON ART. 21 ABS. 2 DES GRUNDGESETZES 72 (1993).

43 This is also the tenor of the current criticism of party bans. *See* DAS BUNDESVERFASSUNGSGERICHT. GESCHICHTE – AUFGABE – RECHTSPRECHUNG 51 (Jutta Limbach ed., 2000) or Horst Meier, *Ob eine konkrete Gefahr besteht, ist belanglos – Kritik der Verbotsanträge gegen die NPD*, 29 LEVIATHAN 439 (2001) (below cited after CLAUS LEGGEWIE & HORST MEIER, VERBOT DER NPD 14, 2002), who consequently refers to the paradigm of the 1950s while seeing the state, state power, or public order endangered.

F. Negative Republicanism as an Anti-Constitution

In the 1990s, a change of paradigms took place relative to the "militant democracy," which was characterized in Germany by a transition from anti-extremism to anti-National-Socialism. This transition changed the aim and perspective of "militancy:" It confronted organized attempts to re-install a National-Socialist "people's community" (*Volksgemeinschaft*), denying them the premiums of legality. The goal is now to prevent the resurrection of an overcome historical system of injustice. This paradigm draws its legitimacy from the collective historical experience of society. Its designation as "negative republicanism"[44] has three connotations: first, the historical embedding and restraint of democracy that, second, refers to a specific learning experience and, third, enforces a restriction of the access to the public sphere, which is to say a limitation of the republican principle. In the German context, this argument for "militancy" lends the constitution the character of an anti-Nazi constitution.[45] In other contexts one might think of an anti-Franco (in Spain), anti-apartheid (in South Africa) or anti-Stalinist (in the former state socialist societies).

The FCC hinted at this concept, which contrary to anti-extremism identifies a specific adversary and expresses an anti-fascist particularity, in its SRP decision: "It is beyond doubt that the former NSDAP according to its development, if it existed today, would be unconstitutional pursuant to Art. 21 II Basic Law; the experiences with this very party were the very cause for the creation of Art. 21 II Basic Law."[46] However, this first move toward a "negative republicanism" was not further developed in the 1950s.

A more recent approach of negative republicanism argues *de lege ferenda*: Art. 21 II Basic Law needs to be rewritten, along the line of a corresponding clause in the Italian Constitution of 1947, namely Art. XII of the transitional and final provisions, as an "anti-fascist barrier:" "A clear political decision is overdue: either one considers neo-Nazis to be of negligible size, and therefore has to accept their outrageous freedom – and has to grant police protection to parades of swastikas or one suppresses any trace of neo-Nazi politics with a rigorous statutory exemption."[47] According to Leggewie and Meier such an "unbalanced, anti-Nazi basic order constitutes a breach of the democratic constitution and of the danger-oriented protection of the republic." The term "breach" indicates that the authors consider their option as undemocratic and unconstitutional. With their stability-oriented concept of danger they operate more over within the frame work of an anti-extremist logic and follow only intuitively and not systematically to limit the republican principle.

A second approach takes up the idea of "essential likeness" (*Wesensverwandtschaft*), giving the idea of a "militant democracy" a new turn through a systematic interpretation of the constitution in connection with the idea of the learning sovereign.[48] On the grounds

---

44 This item was taken from Peter Niesen, *supra* note 7. For a related concept of negative universalism, *see* Klaus Günther, *The Legacies of Injustice and Fear: A European Approach to Human Rights and their Effects on Political Culture*, *in* THE EU AND HUMAN RIGHTS 117, 125 (Philip Alston ed., 1999).

45 *See also* Karl-Heinz Ladeur, *Art. 139*, *in* ALTERNATIVKOMMENTAR ZUM GRUNDGESETZ II (Erhard Denninger et al. eds., 1st ed., 1989).

46 BVerfGE 2, 1 (70). This line of argumentation is continued by the of the *Bundesverwaltungsgericht* (Federal Administrative Court) in regard to the banning of organizations pursuant to Art. 9 Abs. 2 GG: BVerwG, 48 NJW 2505 (1995), BVerwG, 16 NEUE ZEITSCHRIFT FÜR VERWALTUNGSRECHT 66 (1997); *see also* BVerwGE 61, 194, 197.

47 CLAUS LEGGEWIE & HORST MEIER, REPUBLIKSCHUTZ 308, 319 (1995); HORST MEIER, PARTEIVERBOTE UND DEMOKRATISCHE REPUBLIK 20, 363 (1993) refers to an "anti-national-socialistic exemption," which is "justified by the recent German history."

48 Günter Frankenberg & Wolfgang Löwer, *Antragsschriftsatz des Deutschen Bundestages vom 29.03.2001 – Innenausschuss des Deutschen Bundestages*, AUSSCHUSSDRUCKSACHE 14. WP NR. 434 (below cited as VERBOTSANTRAG BT).

of normative considerations, democratic experimentalism is limited to the extent that new experiments in National-Socialism are no longer tolerated. The democratic sovereign, one may infer, has come to the conclusion based on the singularity of the crimes committed by the National-Socialist terror regime that, should it reappear, regardless of its particular form, there is no further requirement for learning. Neo-Nazi organizations, whether they are clubs, associations, paramilitary groups or political parties, are confronted with the presumption that with their operative program and practice they enter upon a criminal inheritance and therefore have nothing, absolutely nothing to contribute to a future-oriented democracy. That is why it is justified to restrict their access to the public sphere. Due to the temporal distance to National-Socialism and its criminal singularity, the second approach of anti-National-Socialism is faced with the problem of laying down precise criteria for the affinity of the new National-Socialism to the old version so as, on the one hand, to avoid being anachronistic and therefore empty and useless, and on the other, to avoid cutting off necessary learning processes too early which, in other words, means not to stab democracy in the back.[49] "Essential likeness," definitely a problematic concept, requires strong proof of a structural, programmatic, strategic and rhetorical affinity that is evident in the daily practices of a party. This proof can only be furnished by a cross-check which verifies that the differences between neo-Nazis and Nazis are the result of a different temporal and political context, hence can be overlooked without eliminating the similarity and comparability of the programmatic and tactical-strategic core elements as well as their political practice, rhetoric and traditionalism.[50]

The problem of negative republicanism is obvious: The license to erect a barrier against the organized renaissance of any historical experience would grant a society and its constitutional élite the power to translate any unpleasant memory into a party ban. In order to prevent negative republicanism from getting out of control, learning experiences, to justify a precarious exclusion to the principle of democracy, must be qualified according to the weight of the injustice done. In the German context, the singularity of the Nazi crimes takes on a legitimizing and restrictive meaning.

Singularity refers not only to the incomparability of what happened but also, to what Jürgen Habermas called the specific responsibility demanded from the German people.[51] The sheer empiricism of the past experience is connected with a normative tie: The moral and legal responsibility for this negative historical experience of suffering can never be delegated by any German sovereign. Hence a sovereign assuming this historical responsibility does not act inconsistently, *per se*, when he abridges the rights of neo-Nazis to free communication and organization. It would be more accurate to say that in order to live up to the responsibility placed upon him by an exceptional crime, he creates a specific exemption tailored precisely to an experienced and evidently unjust regime which resists arbitrary generalization. As a result, Art. 21 II Basic Law would have to be restrictively interpreted in the context of constitutional provisions designed to guarantee the discontinuity of the NS regime; and it would function as a renewal of the bond of the sovereign to a singular historical experience, not only to the moral but, more importantly, to the legal responsibility.

---

49 Therefore Horst Meier accused the applicants in the NPD case of not having sufficiently displayed that, while keeping a safe distance to his propagated "anti-National-Socialist order" – Horst Meier, "*Ob eine konkrete Gefahr besteht, ist belanglos.*" – *Kritik der Verbotsanträge gegen die NPD*, in VERBOT DER NPD 14 (Claus Leggewie & Horst Meier eds., 2002).
50 VERBOTSANTRAG BT, 91–183.
51 Jürgen Habermas, *Vom öffentlichen Gebrauch der Historie*, in EINE ART SCHADENSABWICKLUNG 144 (Jürgen Habermas ed., 1997). Peter Niesen pointed out to me the differentiated meaning of the importance of unjustness: Niesen, *supra* note 7.

The anti-National-Socialist paradigm leads to a dramatic change of perspective on "militancy" and to an exchange of the protected good. The defense is aimed, in the German context, at prohibiting the revival of the Nazi regime of injustice, regardless of the guise under which it should reappear. Not that the stability of the system is to be protected but there is a responsibility founded upon historical experience justifying prevention of an abstract danger. Within the bounds of this paradigm, the victims and survivors are at least indirectly protected, too. They are joined by many other groups singled out for persecution by a more "modern" neo-Nazism. Thus, negative republicanism must deal with the problem of differentiating between foe images which update the old Nazi ideology and those which transgress the historical bounds and therefore the limits of the paradigm. As long as the exclusive, ethnically founded *Volksgemeinschaft* operates as the core ideology, all aliens (*Fremdvölkische*) join the Jews and the political opposition ("the system") and fall under and within the bounds of the paradigm.

G. Constitution of a Civil Society

The third paradigm leaves the abstract and preventive protection of the system behind and moves beyond the historical orientation and responsibility. The "civil society" paradigm seeks to secure the agonal democracy – more commonly referred to as the culture of democratic conflicts and democratic life-forms. As a result, organized attempts come into view that severely violate the fundamental rules of conflict: thus parties that, first, "go for it all" and know no retraints to their methods of conflict, i.e. resort to violence, and, second, label their opponents as "enemies," re-designating democratic debate as civil war and denying their "enemies" any human right, thereby – and not only verbally – leaving the horizontal plane of a "society of equality."

This paradigm has a broader scope, raising significantly the danger of generalization. It does, however, focus on the fundamental conditions under a which a civil society resolves its conflicts and thus, in return, ensures a restrictive application.[52] It does not fall back on anti-extremism but emphasizes the first element of the FCC's "classic" definition of a free democratic order – the respect for human rights. Along with the culture of democratic conflicts this paradigm seeks to protect libertarian forms of conflict resolution and egalitarian relationships of recognition as guaranteed by human rights. Hence the paradigm of civil society has a moral basis and is geared toward integration.

The constitutional starting point of the paradigm of civil society and its integration through conflict is the reciprocal obligation, embedded in the democratic principle, to defend the integrity of democratic procedures and institutions in order to protect the legitimate interests of minorities. An endangerment to the interests of minorities does not begin with a political upheaval but rather earlier, with movements and organizations succeeding in intimidating groups and individuals or driving them out of certain areas, or threatening them that, if given the power, their right to exist (not only) in the public realm will be liquidated. Whoever aims to create "areas of fear" and "nationally liberated zones" (liberated from certain minorities), whoever publicly and systematically persecutes even terrorizes those who think, live or simply look differently, violates democratic life-forms and drastically denies the very civil acceptance one owes in a democracy even to opponents.

This version of "militancy" protects the *minima moralia et legalia* of a democracy, without demanding that the democratic system as a whole be in danger. What matters is not a

---

52 In detail: Günter Frankenberg, *Zur Rolle der Verfassung im Prozess der Integration*, in INTEGRATION DURCH VERFASSUNG 43 (Hans Vorländer ed., 2002).

danger to the system but a threat of violation of people in a minority situation. The civil society paradigm does not claim that a ban covers all political necessities. It merely limits the freedom of action of proven anti-democratic organizations specialized on declaring others as enemies, to the benefit of threatened minorities.

Those who consider this conception as too moral or as constitutionally too restrictive must be reminded that democracy is not to be had free of charge or normatively in "a state of nature". Societies, notably the Federal Republic, have committed themselves at the international, supranational and national levels to defend a certain standard of human rights and protect minorities that have been or are being discriminated against and persecuted.

Moreover, *legitimate* majority rule implies that minorities enjoy a modicum of protection. Thus, much to the dismay of liberal democrats, these societies have prescribed themselves a particular form of protectionism. Whoever thinks party bans are automatically a contradiction, a paradox or a dilemma of democracy reveals that he reduces democracy to the principle of political autonomy and at the same time refuses to admit that democracy is normatively far more complex. Democracy does not only refer to the relationship of a society to itself, its self-determination and future orientation but also concerns its relationship to minorities, especially foreigners, to gender relations, to future generations, and to its natural environment. The paradigm is based on the premise that this normatively and institutionally complex entity can only endure and develop upon a minimal willingness of the citizens to accept one another as equals.[53] It combines tolerance with the principle of reciprocal recognition. Recognition demands that each individual recognize himself or herself in the other and grant the other equal rights and equal participation in the democratic life-forms.

A self-declared democracy must develop an increased sensitivity for outbreaks of violence, hate, racism, and antisemitism. When and to what extent an intervention is adequate is outlined by a script that is well-defined by the principle of subsidiarity, rules of graduated tolerance and reciprocal recognition. First come discussion and enlightenment, self-healing and self-help, like the somewhat pathetically named "uprising of the decent" (*Aufstand der Anständigen*), democratic self-control and soft social-educational interventions. Without further discussion this can be conceded to the critics of bans[54] and prohibitions. However, where genuine civil relief is not available or simply insufficient, the civil society paradigm proposes an individual or collective liability for organizations in the form of criminal sanctions, specifically regarding serious violations of the democratic way of life. If the democratic argument is ineffective and the daily contempt, persecution and violations are organized and carried out under the cover of legality, more extensive constitutional sanctions in the form of organization or party bans cannot be ruled out. Who may demand that an anti-semitic or racist intimidation propaganda and/or methods of persecution not be accepted and demand that they be curbed early on? And who can do so with a gesture of "comfortable radicality," as part of the unpleasant but tolerable democratic normality? It seems clear that it should neither be the system nor the majority of those not affected, as they can be recognizd as the ones who would seem to dictate the tenor of opportunist as well as principled critics of bans.[55] Instead, only the the victims should be in the position to demand a ban.

---

53 Ulrich K. Preuß, *Die empfindsame Demokratie – Über die inneren Grenzen eines Parteiverbots in der Gesellschaft der Individuen*, 194 FRANKFURTER ALLGEMEINE ZEITUNG 51 (22 August 2000). For a critical reading, see Karl-Heinz Ladeur, *Die Rechten und das Recht – eine Warnung vor der Zivilgesellschaft*, in VERBOT DER NPD 120 (Claus Leggewie & Horst Meier eds., 2002).
54 Especially the papers by Dieter Grimm and Wolf-Dieter Narr *in* VERBOT DER NPD (Claus Leggewie & Horst Meier eds., 2002).
55 *E.g.* Horst Meier, *Ob eine konkrete Gefahr besteht, ist belanglos*, in VERBOT DER NPD 14, and especially 23, 24 and 27 (Claus Leggewie & Horst Meier eds., 2002).

Surely finding the right measure and choosing the right point in time for the appropriate intervention, is again a question of *trial* and *error* which brings us back to where we began: the learning sovereign who has a right to commit errors but who, at the same time, also has the obligation to avoid serious mistakes wherever possible. One of the avoidable mistakes seems to be taking a danger or a risk seriously only when it directly affects the majority.

Judicial Review of Administrative Agency Action: Should America Adopt the German Model?

Marc Chase McAllister[*]

"For only by making comparison can we distinguish ourselves from others and discover who we are, in order to become all that we are meant to be."[1]

A. Introduction

A major challenge facing legal systems today is how the civil law and common law traditions will react to the general increase in legislation and administration in order to retain the legitimacy of their respective legal orders.[2] As one commentator recently stated, "one cannot have a modern public administration and still preserve the rule of law *without* evolving administrative law in the full sense including *judicial* control ... ."[3] Perhaps the most important tools for confronting this challenge are the structures of judicial review – both in terms of physical court systems and substantive court doctrine – already in place in any given country.

Ernst Benda, the former President of Germany's *Bundesverfassungsgericht* (BVerfG – Federal Constitutional Court) recently noted, "man's dignity is no[w] endangered by ... the complexities of modern life, by the potential invasion of an ever-present welfare state into almost all aspects of private life ... ."[4] This notion, which was repeated almost verbatim in May 2003 by Justice Dieter Grimm of the Federal Constitutional Court,[5] recognizes that administrative law is not simply an isolated body of rules dealing with the operation of the administration, but also concerns the ordering of society in line with its overall objectives. Therefore, it is vital for a given country to adopt a system of administration that is effective and efficient without sacrificing the constitutional rights of its

---

[*] The author received his Jurisdoctorate (J.D.) from the University of Notre Dame Law School in South Bend, Indiana, graduating with honors. He also received a Bachelor of Arts (B.A.) from DePauw University, graduating with honors as a member of Phi Beta Kappa. He clerked for Judge Charles Wilson of the Eleventh Circuit Court of Appeals, and is currently employed as an Associate Professor of Law at Western State University College of Law in Fullerton, California. The author would like to thank the following individuals for their support and guidance in preparing this article: Professor Russell Miller, Associate Professor of Law, University of Idaho College of Law; Professor Paolo G. Carozza, Associate Professor of Law, University of Notre Dame Law School; and Keith Alexander, friend and respected colleague.

1 THOMAS MANN, JOSEPH IN EGYPT, *translated in* DAVID P. CURRIE, THE CONSTITUTION OF THE FEDERAL REPUBLIC OF GERMANY (1995).
2 *See* MARY ANN GLENDON ET AL., COMPARATIVE LEGAL TRADITIONS: TEXT, MATERIALS AND CASES 249 (2nd ed. 1994).
3 MAHENDRA P. SINGH, GERMAN ADMINISTRATIVE LAW IN COMMON LAW PERSPECTIVE X (2001) (emphasis in original).
4 DONALD P. KOMMERS, THE CONSTITUTIONAL JURISPRUDENCE OF THE FEDERAL REPUBLIC OF GERMANY 326 (1997) (citing "Fundamental Rights: A Comparative Analysis" (Lecture presented at the Center for Contemporary German Studies, Johns Hopkins University, Washington, D.C., September 23, 1987)).
5 *See* Morag Goodwin & Peer Zumbansen, *American and European Constitutionalism Compared: A Conference Report from the UNIDEM Conference in Gottingen, May 23–24, 2003*, *in* 4 GERMAN L.J. 620 (2003), *at* http://www.germanlawjournal.com.

citizens.⁶ This article compares the German and American systems of administrative adjudication in light of this desired end.

This article briefly addresses the initial stages of administrative activity, namely – rulemaking and its enforcement by agencies. The article, however, focuses primarily on the second stage of administrative activity – judicial review of agency rulemaking and adjudication. Focusing on this stage, the article compares the structures and procedures of judicial review of administrative agency action in Germany and the United States.

A comparison of Germany and the United States is particularly appropriate for several reasons. First, there is much that these two countries have in common. They are two of the world's strongest constitutional democracies,⁷ and both are liberal states especially committed to the protection of individual rights and freedoms.⁸ Second, their highest courts are arguably among the world's most powerful domestic judicial bodies.⁹ Because of their power and prestige, other national courts often invoke the decisions of both high courts.¹⁰ Finally, each country has enjoyed several decades to reach an optimal interplay between the roles of the various governmental bodies involved in administration, including the appropriate level of deference that courts are to afford agency actions. Each country's system of administrative law is therefore highly relevant to the world community today, and each should continue to serve as a model for developing and transitional states.

Section B of this article discusses the rise of the administrative state in America, and suggests that America may soon face a crisis in its ability to handle the everyday task of administration. Section C details Germany's system of judicial review of agency action. Section D then examines the major historical and ideological factors that have shaped the German and American systems of judicial review of administrative action. Finally, the last two sections, E and F, conclude by comparing both systems in light of their effectiveness in promoting certain core judicial values. In these final two sections, I argue that, as compared to the United States, Germany's unique administrative court system is better able to adapt to the rising demands of administrative law upon the judiciary in the modern administrative state. Specifically, I argue that Germany's system of judicial review is more likely to produce accurate and consistent results across litigants, while protecting basic rights to a greater degree than in America by subjecting powerful administrative agencies to greater judicial control. Thus, I argue that, following Germany's lead, America should adopt a separate hierarchy of Article III courts to handle all federal administrative law disputes.

B. American Administrative Law System

I. The Rise of Administrative Agencies in America

Literally hundreds of federal agencies exist today.¹¹ Indeed, statutes broadly define federal agencies as "each authority of the Government of the United States, whether or not it is

---

6 See SINGH, *supra* note 3, at 5.
7 See Donald P. Kommers, *Foreword* to EDWARD J. EBERLE, DIGNITY AND LIBERTY: CONSTITUTIONAL VISIONS IN GERMANY AND THE UNITED STATES, at xii (2002). As of 2002, for example, the United States economy was the largest in the world, while Germany's economy was the fourth largest. See EDWARD J. EBERLE, DIGNITY AND LIBERTY: CONSTITUTIONAL VISIONS IN GERMANY AND THE UNITED STATES 4 (2002).
8 See EBERLE, *supra* note 7, at 4 (stating, "the Constitution [of the United States] and the *Grundgesetz* (GG – Basic Law or Constitution) are the two leading charter documents in the world").
9 See Kommers, *supra* note 7, at xii. *See also* KOMMERS, *supra* note 4, at 15–16 (recounting the Constitutional Court's increase in prestige and influence from its inception in 1951 through 1968).
10 See Kommers, *supra* note 7, at xii.
11 A directory of existing federal agencies is available at http://www.lib.lsu.edu/gov/alpha (last visited June 2005).

within or subject to review by another agency."[12] Thus, federal agencies currently include[13] well-known organizations such as the Federal Trade Commission[14] and the newly-created Department of Homeland Security,[15] but also lesser known agencies like the Bureau of Arms Control[16] and the Postal Rate Commission.[17]

The rise of the modern administrative state in America was a direct result of the Depression and the New Deal measures enacted to combat it.[18] The significant increase in administration that occurred during the Roosevelt administration, however, did not come without judicial resistance. Initially, the United States Supreme Court vigorously opposed broad delegation of legislative authority from Congress to unelected administrative agencies,[19] as demonstrated in cases such as *Schechter Poultry Corp. v. United States*[20] and *Carter v. Carter Coal Company*.[21] New Dealers, however, believed that the judiciary should defer to agency decisions.[22] Accordingly, President Roosevelt responded to the Court's decisions with his proposal to "pack" the Court by appointing an additional Justice for every member who had reached the age of 70 and had been on the Court for at least ten years.[23] Not by coincidence, six Supreme Court Justices fit these criteria at the time of Roosevelt's proposal – exactly those justices who had been striking down New Deal legislation.[24]

Arguably in response to President Roosevelt's proposed action,[25] the Supreme Court

---

12 *See* 5 U.S.C. § 551(1) (2005). The statute specifically exempts from this definition the Congress, federal courts, the governments of the territories or possessions of the United States, and the government of the District of Columbia. *See id.*
13 *See* http://www.lib.lsu.edu/gov/alpha (last visited June 2005) (listing all current federal agencies).
14 President Woodrow Wilson signed the FTC Act into law on September 26, 1914. *See* http://www.ftc.gov (last visited June 2005). *See also* 15 U.S.C. § 41, *et seq.*
15 *See* 6 U.S.C. § 101, *et seq.*
16 *See* http://www.state.gov/t/ac (last visited June 2005).
17 *See* http://www.prc.gov/main.asp (last visited June 2005).
18 *See* W. Michael Gillette, *Administrative Law Judges, Judicial Independence, and Judicial Review: Qui Custodiet Ipsos Custodes?* 20 J. NAT'L ASSOC. ADMIN. L. JUDGES 95, 96 (2000); *see also* Peter Marra, *Have Administrative Agencies Abandoned Reasonability?*, 6 SETON HALL CONST. L.J. 763, 769 (1996) (noting that the first administrative agency was created in 1789 and its purpose was to "estimate the duties payable" on imports and to perform other related duties, but that it was not until the 1930's that the number of agencies began to grow toward its current level).
19 Both the Constitution and fundamental democratic principles limit the ability of Congress to delegate law-making powers to administrative agencies. *See* U.S. CONST. Art. I, § 1 (stating, "[a]ll legislative Powers herein granted shall be vested in ... Congress"); see also Peter H. Aronson et al., *A Theory on Legislative Delegation*, 68 CORNELL L. REV. 1, 2–5 (discussing John Locke's contractarian view that the legislature cannot delegate its legislative authority without undermining the foundation of that authority). For an overview of the Supreme Court's application of the nondelegation doctrine prior to the 1930s, *see* David A. Herrman, *To Delegate or Not to Delegate – That is the Preemption: The Lack of Political Accountability in Administrative Preemption Defies Federalism Constraints on Governmental Power*, 28 PAC. L.J. 1157, 1173–1176 (1997).
20 Schechter Poultry Corp. v. United States, 295 U.S. 495 (1935) (striking down part of the National Industrial Recovery Act (NIRA) as applied to the Schechter Poultry Corporation on the basis that Schechter's activities had no direct effect on interstate commerce; portion of statute struck down authorized the President to adopt "codes of fair competition" for various trades or industries regulating such items as minimum wages and prices).
21 Carter v. Carter Coal Company, 298 U.S. 238 (1936) (striking down the Bituminous Coal Conservation Act of 1935, which had set maximum hours and minimum wages for workers in coal mines, on basis that Act was not a valid use of the commerce power).
22 *See* Reuel E. Schiller, *Enlarging the Administrative Polity: Administrative Law and the Changing Definition of Pluralism, 1945–1970*, 53 VAND. L. REV. 1389, 1403–04 (2000).
23 *See generally* William E. Leuchtenburg, *FDR's Court-Packing Plan: A Second Life, A Second Death*, 1985 DUKE L.J. 673 (1983) (providing an excellent historical background of FDR's Court-Packing Plan and its aftermath).
24 *See* GERALD GUNTHER & KATHLEEN SULLIVAN, CONSTITUTIONAL LAW 183–84 (13th ed. 1997).
25 *See* Gillette, *supra* note 18, at 96. *See also* Aranson, *supra* note 19, at 10 (arguing that the total absence of cases invaliding legislation under the nondelegation doctrine since the time of the New Deal line of cases

changed course and ruled that it was perfectly constitutional for Congress to delegate extensive rulemaking authority to administrative agencies.[26] Since that time, as Congress has become increasingly burdened by the volume of work and level of expertise necessary to enact a sufficient body of positive law for our modern society, it has doled out ever more rulemaking power to administrative agencies.[27] The Supreme Court, meanwhile, has held fast to its position that Congress enjoys almost unlimited power to delegate such rulemaking authority.[28]

II. Executive Review of Agency Decisions

The expansion of administrative law resulting from the Depression led to the need for institutional checks on agency action. Over the past seventy years, those checks have come, in varying degrees, from the judiciary, Congress,[29] and the executive.[30] The recent trend in America is toward greater executive review and less judicial review.[31] Indeed, from the early days of the Reagan administration, the executive branch, not the judiciary, has been responsible for most meaningful regulatory review in America. This policy favoring greater executive review continued, and actually expanded, during the Clinton administration.[32]

Executive review of administrative agency action takes place both prospectively and retroactively. Prior to rule adoption, agencies must meet certain criteria and procedural rules, such as submitting a cost-benefit analysis of the proposed regulation to the executive

---

reveals a temporary judicial hostility toward the New Deal). *But see* PHILIP BOBBIT, CONSTITUTIONAL FATE: THEORY OF THE CONSTITUTION, 27–30 (1982) (arguing that the "real crisis in constitutional law" that occurred between 1932 and 1937 was not, in fact, the Supreme Court's frustration of New Deal legislation, but rather the attempted resolution of "the tension between legal realism, which held that there were no discernible, non-formal legal rules of any significance, and the American faith in law, which depended on political conflict being transmuted into legal conflict when issues of constitutional importance were involved.").

26 *See* Gillette, *supra* note 18, at 96. The Supreme Court changed course in *NLRB v. Jones & Laughlin Steel Corp.*, 301 U.S. 1 (1937), ruling in favor of the validity of the NLRA and substantially relaxing the required nexus between the intrastate activity being regulated and interstate commerce.
27 *See* J.B. Ruhl, *Complexity Theory as a Paradigm for the Dynamical Law-and-Society System: A Wake-Up Call for Legal Reductionism and the Modern Administrative State*, 45 DUKE L.J. 849, 923 (1996) (noting that "[i]t would be impractical to expect Congress to make all the substantive regulatory decisions necessary to run the law-and-society system"); K. DAVIS, ADMINISTRATIVE LAW TREATISE § 3:3, 152–56 (2d ed. 1980) (noting that, due to the eclectic areas of law Congress must regulate and the limited time available, it is virtually impossible for Congress to formulate standards for every legal issue).
28 *See* Gillette, *supra* note 18, at 98. *See also* Herrman, *supra* note 19, at 1177–78 (discussing the Supreme Court's extremely limited application of the nondelegation doctrine since the 1930s).
29 Congress has always held significant power to influence agency actions, especially in its ability to control agency budgets and by its power to adopt statutes overriding undesirable agency rules. *See* David B. Spence, *Administrative Law and Agency Policy-Making: Rethinking the Positive Theory of Political Control*, 14 YALE J. ON REG. 407, 416 (1997).
30 In 1995, Professors Richard Pildes and Cass Sunstein noted that "[p]residential oversight of the regulatory process, though relatively new, has become a permanent part of the institutional design of American government." *See* Richard Pildes & Cass R. Sunstein, *Reinventing the Regulatory State*, 62 U. CHI. L. REV. 1, 15 (1995).
31 *See* James F. Blumstein, *Regulatory Review by the Executive Office of the President: An Overview and Policy Analysis of Current Issues*, 51 DUKE L.J. 851, 851–55 (2001) (arguing in favor of centralized presidential review of agency regulatory activity).
32 The Clinton administration's Executive Order 12,866 retained the Reagan–Bush centralized presidential regulatory review structure. *See id.* at 853, 867. According to Elena Kagan, "presidential control of administration, in critical respects, expanded dramatically during the Clinton years, making the regulatory activity of the executive branch agencies more and more an extension of the President's own policy and political agenda." Elena Kagan, *Presidential Administration*, 114 HARV. L. REV. 2245, 2248 (2001).

and to Congress.[33] In addition, prior to rule promulgation, the President can use his power of appointment to indirectly control agency policymaking by, for example, placing political appointees sharing a similar ideology in key agency positions.[34] At the back end, the executive, through the Office of Management and Budget (OMB) and its Office of Information and Regulatory Affairs (OIRA), may review any final rule and monitor agency compliance with the general requirements for rule promulgation.[35]

III. Judicial Review and Chevron Deference

American courts play a significant role in reviewing agency action because not all agencies are subject to Presidential review.[36] In addition, regardless of the agency, judicial review is necessary in the event that an individual litigant wishes to challenge a particular agency decision and he or she feels that the political process leading to the election of the President[37] will not adequately resolve the concern.[38] In such highly personalized rulings, involving, for example, an agency's decision whether to deport a particular resident alien,[39] both the President and Congress are highly unlikely to enter the review arena. In such cases, the courts seem particularly well suited to guard against arbitrary or unjust agency action.

Before a litigant may seek review of agency action in the courts, he must first exhaust his available remedies within the particular agency.[40] In America, special administrative adjudicators, referred to as administrative law judges (ALJs), often handle the first stage of individual challenges to agency decisions.[41] Such adjudicators are, in fact, necessary to

---

33 *See* 5 U.S.C. § 801 (2003) (setting forth requirements that must be met before an agency rule may take effect, including the submission of a cost-benefit analysis of the proposed rule to the Comptroller General).
34 *See* Spence, *supra* note 29, at 419–20 (noting the existence of both Presidential and Congressional ex ante controls, but concluding that "most scholars [have] ascribed greater ex ante control to the President than to Congress."). Spence questions the extent to which the President's appointment power actually influences agency policymaking: "Theoretically, presidentially appointed agency administrators can control the agency's policy-making agenda; however, whether that power can be translated into a tool of influence for the President is uncertain. Absent ongoing communication between the President and the administrator, the administrator can do the President's bidding in the agency policy-making process only if the administrator shares the President's ideology." *See id.* at 430–31.
35 *See* Blumstein, *supra* note 31, at 867–70. *See also* http://www.reginfo.gov/public/do/eoPackageMain (last visited July 2005) (containing information about current and recent regulatory reviews).
36 Independent agencies, such as the Federal Communications Communication, are statutorily granted decision-making autonomy by Congress, and therefore are not subject to centralized regulatory review through the Executive's Office of Information and Regulatory Affairs (OIRA). *See* Blumstein, *supra* note 31, at 876. But note that the Clinton Administration, for the first time, subjected independent agencies to Presidential oversight. *See id.* at 867–68.
37 *See* Chevron U.S.A. Inc. v. Natural Resources Defense Council, 467 U.S. 837, 865 (1984) (noting that "[w]hile agencies are not directly accountable to the people, the Chief Executive is, and it is entirely appropriate for this political branch of the Government to make ... policy choices").
38 *See, e.g.*, Barnhart v. Walton, 535 U.S. 212 (2002) (involving judicial review of Social Security Administration's denial of an individual claimant's application for disability insurance benefits based on the Administration's unfavorable interpretation of the statutory definition of "disability").
39 Courts often review agency deportation determinations. *See, e.g.*, Adefemi v. Ashcroft, 386 F.3d 1022 (11th Cir. 2004) (in affirming decision of Board of Immigration Appeals that alien was deportable on basis of firearms offense, court applied the "substantial evidence test," viewing the record evidence in the light most favorable to the agency's decision and drawing all reasonable inferences in favor of that decision).
40 *See, e.g.*, 42 U.S.C. § 405(g) ("Any individual, after any final decision of the Commissioner of Social Security made after a hearing ... may obtain a review of such decision by a civil action commenced within sixty days ...."). *See also* Bowen v. City of New York, 476 U.S. 467, 471–72 (1986).
41 *See* Linda G. Mills, *A Calculus for Bias: How Malingering Females and Dependent Housewives Fare in the Social Security Disability System*, 16 HARVARD WOMEN'S L.J. 211 (1993) (citing Committee on Ways and Means, U.S. House of Representatives, Overview of Entitlement Programs, 1991 Green Book,

assist agencies in handling the increase in litigation that flows out of their expanded rulemaking role.[42] A federal ALJ is an employee of a federal agency who holds hearings for an agency,[43] is assured of tenure and freedom from agency input,[44] and is generally subject to the Code of Judicial Conduct.[45]

Ordinary state and federal appellate courts review both agency rulemaking and agency adjudication. Both types of appeals, however, are marked by a high degree of deference. First, with respect to judicial review of individualized adjudications (such as, for example, judicial review of an agency's deportability determination),[46] courts generally ask whether the agency's decision is "supported by reasonable, substantial, and probative evidence on the record considered as a whole."[47] Such decisions are reversed only where the evidence presented on the side of reversal is such that "a reasonable factfinder would have to conclude" against the agency's decision.[48]

Second, with respect to judicial review of agency rulemaking,[49] *Chevron U.S.A. Inc. v. Natural Resources Defense Council*[50] dictates that courts are to apply the following test: (1) if Congress has expressly given the agency authority to elucidate a statutory provision through regulations, then such legislative regulations are given controlling weight "unless . . . arbitrary, capricious, or manifestly contrary to the statute;" alternatively, (2) if Congress's statute is either silent or ambiguous with respect to the issue in question, then the court must simply ask whether the agency's interpretation is based on a "permissible construction" of the statute; in such cases, the court may not substitute its own construction of a statutory provision for a "reasonable interpretation" made by the agency.[51] While the Supreme Court recently limited the impact of *Chevron* in a narrow set of delegations,[52]

Background Material and Data on Programs Within the Jurisdiction of the Committee on Ways and Means, at 59 (1991)) (noting that in 1990, the Social Security Administration processed approximately 1.5 million applications for disability, and Social Security ALJ's heard 270,000 appeals – a figure roughly equivalent to the number of cases on the civil dockets of the nation's federal district courts).

42 See Gillette, *supra* note 18, at 98.
43 See 5 U.S.C. § 3105 ("[e]ach [federal] agency shall appoint as many administrative law judges as are necessary . . . .").
44 See Butz v. Economou, 438 U.S. 478, 512 (1978) (noting that "the Administrative Procedure Act contains a number of provisions designed to guarantee the independence of hearing examiners"); *see also* 5 U.S.C. § 554(d)(2) (setting forth rule that a hearing examiner "may not ... be responsible to or subject to the supervision or direction of an employee or agent engaged in the performance of investigative or prosecuting functions for an agency").
45 See Ronnie A. Yoder, *The Role of the Administrative Law Judge*, 22 J. OF THE NAT'L ASSOC. OF ADMIN. LAW JUDGES 321, 324 (2002).
46 See, e.g., Adefemi v. Ashcroft, 386 F.3d 1022 (11th Cir. 2004) (in affirming decision of Board of Immigration Appeals that alien was deportable on basis of firearms offense, court applied the "substantial evidence test," viewing the record evidence in the light most favorable to the agency's decision and drawing all reasonable inferences in favor of that decision); *see also* Reyes-Rodriguez v. Ashcroft, 2005 WL 79096 (9th Cir. 2005) (unpublished) (denying alien's petition for review of an order of the Board of Immigration Appeals which had affirmed an IJ's denial of his application for asylum and withholding of removal).
47 See I.N.S. v. Elias-Zacarias, 502 U.S. 478, 481 (1992) (citing 8 U.S.C. § 1105a(a)(4)).
48 See *id.*; *see also* 5 U.S.C. § 706(2)(A), (E) (requiring that, except where *de novo* judicial review is appropriate, courts reviewing agency action are to limit substantive review to the question of whether the agency's decision was either "arbitrary [or] capricious" or "unsupported by substantial evidence.").
49 For a discussion of what types of agency rules and regulations actually constitute "rulemaking," see United States v. Mead Corp., 533 U.S. 218 (2001); *see also* Peter L. Strauss, *The Rulemaking Continuum*, 41 DUKE L.J. 1463 (1992).
50 Chevron U.S.A. Inc. v. Natural Resources Defense Council, 467 U.S. 837 (1984).
51 *Id.*, at 843–44.
52 In *United States v. Mead Corp.*, 533 U.S. 218 (2001), the Supreme Court considered exactly what level of deference is to be afforded an informal tariff classification ruling letter issued by the United States Customs Services, where such ruling was issued outside the notice and comment procedures set forth in 5 U.S.C. § 553. See *id.* at 226–27. The Court concluded that the Customs ruling at issue did not qualify for *Chevron* deference, *id.* at 226–27, and therefore remanded the case for a determination as to whether it

today, in the case of express delegations of rulemaking authority by Congress and in some instances of implied delegation, the highly deferential *Chevron* rule still applies.

In effect, *Chevron* instructs the judiciary to set aside its traditional function to "say what the law is"[53] – a function embodied in the courts' *de novo* review of most legal determinations – and to instead defer to the agency's presumed expertise.[54] Indeed, a reviewing court will only invalidate an agency regulation if it is "arbitrary, capricious, or manifestly contrary to the [delegating] statute."[55] Such extreme deference has its advantages. The *Chevron* Court, for example, justified this standard by noting that agencies have greater expertise in their respective fields. Judges, the argument goes, typically have less specialized knowledge than agencies and should defer to the "experts."[56]

There is no doubt that agencies often have a better grasp on their particular field of regulation than do the courts; however, it is precisely for this reason that courts should review agency decisions *more* carefully. An agency, by firmly setting its sights on the pursuit and effectuation of its chosen policy, may disregard how its actions affect specific individuals or groups. At this point, a neutral and detached judge – rather than one arguably influenced by the agency itself – is needed to ensure that individual rights are not trampled upon.

A related justification offered by the *Chevron* Court is that administrative agencies, not the courts, should be engaged in the business of formulating policy.[57] While admirable in theory,[58] this justification can only go so far, as it ignores the reality that the Supreme

---

deserved some deference under *Skidmore*. *See id.* at 238–39; *see also* Fed. Election Comm'n v. Nat'l Rifle Ass'n of America, 254 F.3d 173, 184 (D.C. Cir. 2001) (holding that relatively informal agency interpretations such as those in opinion letters, policy statements, agency manuals, and enforcement guidelines, do not warrant *Chevron* deference but instead are entitled to respect under *Skidmore*). Thus, the majority in *Mead* held that, in the case of an express delegation by Congress – i.e., where Congress either provides an agency with the power to engage in formal adjudication or in notice and comment rulemaking – "any ensuing regulation is binding in the courts unless procedurally defective, arbitrary or capricious in substance, or manifestly contrary to the statute." *Mead Corp.*, 533 U.S. at 227 (citing *Chevron*, 467 U.S. at 822). In the case of *no* express delegation (and where the Court does not imply a delegation for the agency "to speak with the force of law,"), however, reviewing courts are to consider the specialized technical expertise and the well-reasoned views of agencies implementing a statute as guidance for courts "facing questions the agencies have already answered." *Id.* at 227.

53 *See* Marbury v. Madison, 1 Cranch 137 (1803) (establishing the proposition that "[i]t is emphatically the province and duty of the judicial department to say what the law is."); *see also* Plaut v. Spendthrift Farm, Inc., 514 U.S. 211 (1995) ("Article III establishes a 'judicial department' with the 'province and duty ... to say what the law is' in particular cases and controversies. [citation omitted]. The Framers crafted this charter with an expressed understanding that it gives the Federal Judiciary the power, not merely to rule on cases, but to decide them conclusively, subject to review only by superior courts in the Article III hierarchy.").

54 In *Chevron* itself, the Supreme Court scolded the Court of Appeals for adopting a "static judicial definition of the term [at issue] when it had decided that Congress itself had not commanded that definition." *See Chevron*, 467 U.S. at 842. Indeed, not until 1999, in *AT&T Corp. v. Iowa Utilities Board*, 525 U.S. 366 (1999), did the Supreme Court for the first time invalidate an agency interpretation under the second step of the *Chevron* test. *See* Lisa Schultz Bressman, *Schechter Poultry at the Millenium: A Delegation Doctrine for the Administrative State*, 109 YALE L.J. 1399, 1399–1400 (2000).

55 *Chevron*, 467 U.S. at 844. This rule applies even if Congress has only *implicitly* delegated legislative power to an agency on a particular question. *Id.* For additional rules regulating the scope of judicial review for agency action in America, *see* 5 U.S.C. § 706 (2003).

56 *See, e.g.*, Skidmore v. Swift & Co., 323 U.S. 134, 139 (1944) (noting that agencies formulate policy "in pursuance of official duty [and] based upon more specialized experience and broader investigations and information than is likely to come to a judge in a particular case"); *see also Mead Corp.*, 533 U.S. at 227 ("[T]he well-reasoned views of the agencies implementing a statute 'constitute a body of experience and informed judgment to which courts and litigants may properly resort for guidance.'") (citations omitted).

57 *See Chevron*, 467 U.S. at 843, 864 ("policy arguments are more properly addressed to legislators or administrators, not to judges").

58 In a political system based on majority rule (i.e., a representative democracy), such policy decisions would arguably fall more properly within the scope of the legislature, as its actions, in theory, reflect majority opinion more accurately than those of the less politically accountable judiciary. *See, e.g.*, ALEXANDER M.

Court often makes policy decisions.[59] The Court's abortion jurisprudence is one rather striking example of the judicial determination of a controversial political issue.[60] The Court's significant role in bringing an end to segregation is another powerful example.[61] Rather than framing the debate as "which branch is best suited to *formulate policy*," the *Chevron* Court could have simply asked "which branch is best suited to *define the abstract meaning of statutes*," especially where (as in *Chevron*), Congress has not spoken to the precise issue in question. Framed this way, the courts, not politically appointed agencies, are arguably better suited to the task.[62]

Prior to *Chevron*, the Supreme Court had adopted varying standards for review of agency decisions, from extreme deference on the one hand to *de novo* review on the other.[63] From the mid-1940s to the end of the 1950s, judicial review of administrative action was marked by a high degree of deference, reflecting the notion that the state formed public policy only in response to interest groups who were fully capable of representing the interests of all American citizens.[64] Beginning in the 1960s, however, with rising concern over agency

---

BICKEL, THE LEAST DANGEROUS BRANCH: THE SUPREME COURT AT THE BAR OF POLITICS, at 3–5 (1962) In discussing which branch of government should decide "issue[s] of policy," Bickel declared, "[T]o leave the matter to the legislature is to leave it ultimately to the people at the polls. In this view the people as the principal would set the limits of the power that they have delegated to their agent [in the Constitution]." Bickel later noted that "judicial review is a deviant institution in the American democracy," arguing that while "one may infer that judicial review ... may have ways of being responsive [to the wishes of the governed], ... nothing can finally depreciate the central function that is assigned in democratic theory and practice to the electoral process; nor can it be denied that the policy-making power of representative institutions, born of the electoral process, is the distinguishing characteristic of the system. Judicial review works counter to this characteristic." *Id.* at 18–19.

59 Incidentally, the same can be said of Germany's Constitutional Court. Constitutional Court Justice Deiter Grimm has opined, "[C]onstitutional courts inevitably cross the line between law and politics" because "the constitution does not offer an unambiguous and complete standard for [reviewing the validity of legislation]." *See* KOMMERS, *supra* note 4, at 44 (citing CONSTITUTIONAL REVIEW AND LEGISLATION: AN INTERNATIONAL COMPARISON 169 (Christine Landfried, ed., 1988).

60 *See, e.g.*, Roe v. Wade, 410 U.S. 113, 163–64 (1971) (dividing pregnancy into three trimesters and adopting different standards for permissible state regulation of abortion in each phase); Planned Parenthood of S.E. Pa. v. Casey, 505 U.S. 833, 873–74 (1992) (abandoning Roe's trimester framework and holding that before viability the state may not place an "undue burden" on the woman's right to choose whether to have an abortion). *See also* Donald P. Kommers, *The Constitutional Law of Abortion in Germany: Should Americans Pay Attention?* 10 J. CONTEMP. HEALTH L. & POL'Y 1, 2 (1993) (arguing that the key American and German abortion cases "were extraordinary assertions of judicial power").

61 *See, e.g.*, Brown v. Board of Education, 347 U.S. 483 (1954). *See also* Michael W. Combs & Gwendolyn M. Combs, *Revisiting Brown v. Board of Education: A Cultural, Historical-Legal, and Political Perspective*, 47 HOWARD L.J. 627 (2004) (analyzing the ways in which *Brown v. Board of Education* has transformed American culture). *See generally* MARK V. TUSHNET, MAKING CIVIL RIGHTS LAW: THURGOOD MARSHALL AND THE SUPREME COURT, 1936–1961 (1994) (analyzing the legal struggles employed in the courts to achieve civil rights for African-Americans).

62 *See, e.g.*, BICKEL, *supra* note 58, at 25–27 (arguing that "courts have certain capacities for dealing with matters of principle that legislatures and executives do not possess," and that "questions of principle never carry the same aspect for the [courts] as they did for the legislature or the executive. Statutes, after all, deal typically with abstract or dimly foreseen problems. The courts[,] [however,] are concerned with the flesh and blood of an actual case."). *But see Chevron*, 467 U.S. at 865–66 ("it is entirely appropriate for [the executive] branch of the Government to ... resolv[e] the competing interests which Congress itself either inadvertently did not resolve, or intentionally left to be resolved by the agency charged with the administration of the statute in light of everyday realities").

63 *See* United States v. Mead Corp., 533 U.S. 218, 228 (2001) ("The fair measure of deference to an agency administering its own statute has been understood to vary with circumstances, and courts have looked to the degree of the agency's care, its consistency, formality, and relative expertness, and to the persuasiveness of the agency's position. The approach has produced a spectrum of judicial responses, from great respect at one end, to near indifference at the other.") (internal citations omitted).

64 *See* Schiller, *supra* note 22, at 1400–01.

capture[65] and a surge in legal liberalism,[66] courts began to review agency action with less deference.[67] In the mid-1960s, the Court reversed its previous position and established *de novo* review of administrative decisions.[68] Under its new "hard look doctrine," the Court instructed lower courts to review agency action to ensure that the agency had "taken a 'hard look' at the salient problems" and that it had "genuinely engaged in reasoned decision-making."[69] Such scrutiny involved a detailed look at the factors considered by the agency in reaching its decision.[70] This relatively intense review of agency decisions dominated through the 1970s. By the end of that decade, however, the Supreme Court began to move back toward greater deference of agency action, a move which culminated in its *Chevron* decision.[71]

Oregon Supreme Court Justice W. Michael Gillette argues that *Chevron* sanctioned judges to take the attitude, "[w]hew, the U.S. Supreme Court says it is okay just to sort of wash our hands of this responsibility [of judicial review of administrative agency decisions], and that feels good, so let's do it."[72] While *Chevron* does not specifically make mention of efficiency concerns, to the extent that goals of efficiency and economy, perhaps due to the judiciary's lack of time and resources, were the motivating force behind the Supreme Court's reluctance to provide for more meaningful judicial review of a substantial body of rules and regulations,[73] the problem is correctable and should be addressed.[74] Heavy judicial workloads, perceived inefficiency, and lack of resources simply do not provide the judiciary with a valid excuse to abandon its duty to protect the rights of citizens[75] against

---

65 "Agency capture" occurs when an agency favors the concerns of the industry it regulates, which is well-represented by its trade groups and lawyers, over the interests of the general public, which is often unrepresented. *See* RICHARD J. PIERCE, JR., ET AL., ADMINISTRATIVE LAW AND PROCESS § 1.7.2 (2d ed. 1992).

66 "Legal liberalism" is based on the premise that the judiciary is the institution most capable of protecting the rights of individuals. *See* Schiller, *supra* note 22, at 1450.

67 *See id.* at 1417.

68 *See id.* at 1421.

69 *See* Kleppe v. Sierra Club, 427 U.S. 390, 410 n. 21 (1976). Though courts had been applying the "hard look" doctrine since the mid-1960's, the doctrine got its name from a 1970 case, *Greater Boston Television Corp. v. FCC. See* Greater Boston Television Corp. v. FCC, 444 F.2d 841, 851 (D.C. Cir. 1970).

70 *See, e.g.*, Citizens to Preserve Overton Park v. Volpe, 401 U.S. 402, 415 (1971) (subjecting agency action to "a thorough, probing, in-depth review" and "consider[ing] whether the [agency's] decision was based on a consideration of the relevant factors").

71 *See* Schiller, *supra* note 22, at 1421–28 (detailing the level of deference employed by various federal courts between the time of the emergence of the hard look doctrine in the mid-1960s, which ushered in "the pinnacle of judicial involvement in the administrative process," through the late 1970s).

72 *See* Gillette, *supra* note 18, at 104.

73 Supreme Court Justice Stephen Breyer has noted,

> A judge can do little more in [administrative law] case[s] than read the record and ask if the result is reasonable. The records are lengthy and the number of such cases vast. Given the enormous judicial workload, ... these cases are prime candidates for delegation. In run of the mill cases, a law clerk or an administrative staff member may be assigned initial responsibility for checking the record for "problems;" the individual judge's decision thus becomes an "institutional" decision. The time needed to conduct a thorough review in all (or many) such cases is simply lacking.

See Stephen Breyer, *Symposium: The Legacy of the New Deal: Problems and Possibilities in the Administrative State (Part 2)*, 92 YALE L.J. 1614, 1616–17 (1983).

74 For why this problem should be corrected, *see* Gillette, *supra* note 18, at 102–113 (arguing that "*Chevron* changed the balance of power between private citizens and agencies, without incorporating or giving us any reason to expect that the other checks on the agency, in the absence of particular judicial scrutiny, would step in to take their place.").

75 *See, e.g.*, Bowen v. Gilliard, 483 U.S. 587, 628 (1987) (noting that "concern for program efficiency ... cannot in itself ... provide a purpose sufficiently important to justify an infringement on fundamental constitutional rights. If it could, its reach would be limitless, for it is probably more efficient in most cases for Government to operate without regard to the obstacles of the Constitution than to attend to them. Nonetheless, 'the Constitution recognizes higher values than speed and efficiency.'") (citation omitted); *see also* Shapiro v. Thompson, 394 U.S. 618, 633 (1969) ("[t]he saving of welfare costs cannot justify an otherwise invidious classification" under equal protection analysis).

unchecked governmental action.[76] The German system of administrative adjudication presents an effective and established model to fulfill this task.

IV. The Rising Volume of Administrative Law in America

In America today, administrative regulations impact nearly every American citizen on a daily basis. Indeed, the current volume of administrative law in America is immense.[77] In 1957, Supreme Court Justice Felix Frankfurter wrote, "[r]eview of administrative action ... constitutes the largest category of the court's work, comprising one-third of the total cases decided on the merits;"[78] and by the early 1980s, there were more cases decided for just one federal agency – the Social Security Administration – than cases decided in all the traditional court systems of the United States combined.[79] Thus, in 1997, Seventh Circuit Court of Appeals Justice Diane Wood observed that "the judicial role in the administrative state ... permanently and profoundly changed the business of the courts."[80]

This trend toward increasing administration will likely continue. Seventh Circuit Chief Justice Richard Posner, for example, notes that any perceived deregulation of the American economy has been matched by the rise of new agencies including those concerned with health and safety,[81] environmental amenities,[82] discrimination, and retirement and disability.[83] The recent creation of the Department of Homeland Security is a noteworthy example.[84]

Strong economic and theoretical arguments support the notion that the volume of administrative law will only continue to grow.[85] J.B. Ruhl argues that the law, as a complex

---

76 Chief Judge of the Seventh Circuit Court of Appeals, Richard Posner, has highlighted the dangers of unfettered agency discretion. He describes agencies as "political captives and instruments" that often cater to powerful interest groups. See Richard A. Posner, *The Rise and Fall of Administrative Law*, 72 CHI.-KENT L.REV. 953, 955–56 (1997).
77 See Jerry L. Anderson, *The Environmental Revolution at Twenty-Five*, 26 RUTGERS L.J. 395, 413 (1995) (reporting that the "EPA alone published almost 3500 pages of proposed and final regulations ... during the first six months of 1994," and that just the federal agencies with environmental jurisdiction collectively produce over 35 pages of new or proposed regulations every working day); see also RICHARD A. EPSTEIN, SIMPLE RULES FOR A COMPLEX WORLD 7 (1997) (noting that the annual pages of the Federal Register have grown in number from 2,411 in 1936 to 67,716 in 1991; the annual pages of the Federal Reporter have grown from 6,138 to 49,907 during the same period; and the annual Federal Supplement pages have grown from 5,179 to 42,727 during the same time).
78 Felix Frankfurter, *The Supreme Court in the Mirror of Justices*, 105 U. PA. L. REV. 781, 793 (1957).
79 See Gillette, supra note 18, at 100 (citing BERNARD SCHWARTZ, ADMINISTRATIVE LAW 25–26 (2nd ed. 1983)); see also John Holmes, *In Praise of the ALJ System*, 21 ADMIN. & REG. L. NEWS 3 (1996) (noting that in 1996, there were approximately 1,335 federal ALJs of which 1,082 were employed with the Social Security Administration; in contrast, in 1947, the federal government only employed 196 ALJ's); see generally Mary Ann Glendon, *The Sources of Law in a Changing Legal Order*, 17 CREIGHTON L. REV. 663, 665–84 (1984) ("Despite sporadic and modest attempts at deregulation, as more areas of public concern are identified, such as protection of the environment or health and safety in the workplace, the scope of administrative law continues to expand. Today, ... the laws that have the most direct impact on the lives of most people ... are the predominantly administrative bodies of tax law, social security law, public assistance law, housing law, immigration and naturalization law ... .").
80 See Diane P. Wood. *Generalist Judges in a Specialized World*, 50 SMU L. REV. 1755, 1758 (1997).
81 Examples include the National Highway Transportation Safety Administration, the Department of Labor's Benefits Review Board, and the Occupational Safety and Health Administration. See Posner, supra note 76, at 956.
82 The Environmental Protection Agency has increased its administrative activities, as have other agencies such as the Army Corps of Engineers. See id.
83 See id. at 956–57.
84 See 6 U.S.C. § 101, et seq.
85 See Ruhl, supra note 27, at 883–886 (describing the interaction of law and society through analogy to dynamical systems and stating: "The sheer numbers of environmental regulations and regulated entities lead to the possibility of intricate interactions at levels far below the surface of what we believe we are reg-

dynamical system, can be characterized as an "arrow of irreversibility" – that is, its "evolutionary processes cannot be put into reverse ... ."[86] According to Ruhl, complexity theory confirms three features of America's legal structure: first, as demonstrated by the vast increase of administrative law since World War II,[87] social systems tend towards increasing use of complex structures to solve both internal and external problems; second, although at first complex structures enhance adaptive behavior in society with increasing investment and structural complexity, a society's further investment eventually leads to decreasing marginal benefits; finally, at the point where the cost of investing further exceeds the problem-solving benefits of a complex system, the system becomes vulnerable of collapsing into a simpler mode of behavior through deconstruction.[88] Ruhl notes that "history provides no examples of societies in which structural complexity of law is high and the number of groups is high [as in America and Germany], but the distribution of population across groups is even and the level of inequality is low."[89] As a result, he suggests that as America continues its struggle to erase inequalities in society, it will add more and more legal rules. The recent increase in environmental law regulation provides a striking example of this trend.[90] Thus, in Ruhl's opinion, in the coming decades America can expect to see a greater complexity of, and reliance upon, administrative law.[91]

As noted by J.B. Ruhl, administrative law tends to increase in scope like a snowball that grows larger as it proceeds downhill.[92] An increase in demand for judicial review of administrative decision-making will inevitably attend such an increase in regulation.[93] Basil Markesinis notes, "more administration inevitably brings more maladministration and more rights generate a greater willingness to assert them."[94] A variety of solutions exist to more effectively review administrative agency action. However, as argued in the final two

---

ulating. Those interactions, in turn, lead to emergent behaviors that we perceive as yet more issues for regulation, and the cycle continues." Thus, according to Ruhl, we are left with "a law-and-society system that requires adding one statutory component after another, seemingly ad infinitum, to combat one emergent behavior pattern after another ... .").

86 See J.B. Ruhl & Harold J. Ruhl, Jr., *The Arrow of the Law in Modern Administrative States: Using Complexity Theory to Reveal the Dminishing Returns and Increasing Risks the Burgeoning of Law Poses to Society*, 30 U.C. DAVIS L. REV. 405, 409–10 (1997). In describing the law as behaving like an arrow, Ruhl draws heavily from Oliver Wendell Holmes, who argued that changes in law followed a "path" dictated by many prior choices along the way. *Id.* at 414–15.
87 See EBERLE, *supra* note 7, at 24.
88 See Ruhl, *supra* note 86, at 411.
89 See *id.* at 456.
90 Ruhl illustrates his point by invoking the "brownfields" problem. Ruhl notes that the brownfields problem itself was actually created by prior legislation and that, rather than repealing that prior legislation, the government simply responded with the passage of even more rules and regulations. *See id.* at 465. Ruhl argues,

While investment in legal structure as a strategy unquestionably has solved many problems of environmental degradation, it also has spawned large new regulatory bureaucracies, breathtakingly complicated regulatory schemes, masses of specialized legal and engineering consultants, new curriculums in law and engineering schools, new technologies and methodologies, and so on. Thus, problem solving through increasing structural complexity in the style of modern environmental law requires additional investment in the infrastructure of the modern administrative state. Environmental law is but one example of the approach that becomes the default position of the modern administrative state generally.

Id. at 460.
91 *See id.* at 460.
92 *See* Ruhl, *supra* note 27, at 911 (arguing that "the administrative state responds to the surprises of dynamical system behavior by producing more rules exhibiting increasingly abstract complicatedness").
93 *See* Gillette, *supra* note 18, at 113.
94 BASIL S. MARKESINIS, *Learning From and Learning in Europe*, in FOREIGN LAW AND COMPARATIVE METHODOLOGY: A SUBJECT AND A THESIS 163, 192 (1997).

sections of this article, the best solution – in terms of its ability to curtail agency power and to promote consistent and accurate judicial decisions – is to adopt a separate system of administrative adjudication similar to that utilized in Germany.

C. Judicial Review of Administrative Law in Germany

As in America, Germany has experienced a similar rise in administrative activity. This section details how the German judiciary has responded to this increase in administration while protecting its citizens against state abuses.

I. Scope of Agency Rulemaking Power in Germany

German administrative law is divided into "general" and "particular" administrative law. General administrative law is the counterpart of administrative law in the United States. It encompasses rules, general principles, concepts, and legal institutions applicable to all administrative activities, as well as how decisions of administrative authorities are challenged, and how duties are enforced, in the courts.[95] As in the United States, all levels of government – federal, state, and local – are responsible for producing administrative law, and each level of government is subject to constitutional requirements in its performance of that duty.[96]

Two general types of legislation may result from a direct delegation by Parliament to the executive – executive legislation, known as "statutory orders;" and laws stemming from delegation to autonomous bodies, referred to as "bylaws."[97] The executive's rulemaking power, however, is restrained by two basic features of German law: (1) constitutional limitations upon the legislature's initial power to delegate its lawmaking authority; and (2) in the event of an attempted delegation, rather strict limitations upon the scope of such delegations.

With respect to the first restraint, the executive may exercise only those legislative powers specifically delegated to it by the legislature.[98] In contrast to the United States,[99] where Congress enjoys the nearly unlimited right to delegate rulemaking power to agencies (notwithstanding the nondelegation doctrine),[100] the *Bundestag*'s (German Parliament) actual power to delegate lawmaking ability is extremely limited. This limitation is expressed in Article 80 of the *Grundgesetz* (GG – Basic Law or Constitution), making it a fundamental part of the German legal order.[101]

---

95 *See* SINGH, *supra* note 3, at 5–6; *see also* NIGEL G. FOSTER, GERMAN LEGAL SYSTEM & LAWS 172 (1996).
96 *See* FOSTER, *supra* note 95, at 170–71 (citing GRUNDGESETZ [GG] [Constitution] art. 80).
97 Bylaws are subordinate legislation made by the juristic bodies assigned by the state for that purpose, such as communes, universities, professional bodies, broadcasting establishments, and the German Federal Bank. Legislative authorization is always necessary for making bylaws. Municipalities have been given general authority to issue bylaws under Article 28(2) of the *Grundgesetz* (Basic Law). *See* SINGH, *supra* note 3, at 57. Bylaws are subject to judicial review in the same manner that statutory orders are. *See id.* at 59.
98 *See id.* 41.
99 *See id.* at 41–2. Notably, the French Constitution expressly provides that the executive has inherent powers to legislate through regulations with respect to all matters not specifically assigned to the legislature. *See id.* at 41 (citing Articles 34 and 37 of the Constitution of France).
100 *See supra* notes 20–29 and accompanying text.
101 Article 80(1) of the *Grundgesetz* (Basic Law) declares, "The Federal Government, a Federal Minister, or the Land governments may be authorized by a law to issue statutory instruments. The content, purpose, and scope of the authority conferred shall be specified in the law. Each statutory instrument shall contain a statement of its legal basis." GRUNDGESETZ [GG] [Constitution], Article 80(1), *reprinted at* http://www.iuscomp.org/gla/statutes/GG.htm#80. The grounding of this limitation within the Basic Law is significant, as it seeks to prevent the failings of the Weimar Republic from reoccurring. During the Third

With respect to the second restraint – limitations upon actual delegations – the delegating legislation must clearly define the "content, purpose, and scope" of the executive's resulting legislation.[102] In the *Equalization of Tax Liability Case*, the Federal Constitutional Court elaborated upon the "content, purpose, and scope" requirement:

> [T]he authorization must be so exactly definite that the citizen is able to foresee initially from it and not from the statutory orders only made under it, the requirements of law which he is expected to observe or satisfy.[103]

In subsequent cases, the Constitutional Court further clarified that the particular policy decision at issue must be made by the legislature and incorporated into the enabling legislation.[104] This is in contrast to America, where agencies routinely make policy choices.[105]

II. Germany's Administrative Court System

As a social welfare state,[106] perhaps the most fundamental purpose of Germany's administrative court system is to affirmatively protect and defend the rights of the individual against administrative excesses.[107] To better accomplish this objective, Germany utilizes a separate system of courts to settle administrative disputes. These courts enjoy their own hierarchy independent from courts with other jurisdictions.[108] Thus, the decisions of these tribunals are final within the hierarchy and may not be questioned by other courts (with the exception that matters of constitutional law arising out of such cases are typically reviewed by the separate constitutional courts).[109]

Unlike in France and in America where administrative tribunals are a part of the executive branch,[110] the German administrative courts are fully integrated into the judicial branch.[111] This feature is grounded in the Basic Law and in federal statutes. The opening provision of Germany's 1960 Administrative Courts Act, for example, specifically declares that administrative adjudication is to be exercised by courts independent of, and separate

---

Reich, the legislature almost completely abdicated its lawmaking power by authorizing the executive to make not only ordinary laws but also laws having the effect of amending the Constitution – a move which led to an extreme concentration of power in the hands of the executive. The Basic Law attempts to preclude this concentration of power from reoccurring. See SINGH, *supra* note 3, at 41–42.

102 See GRUNDGESETZ [GG] [Constitution] art. 80(1) ("The Federal Government, a Federal Minister or the *Land* governments may be empowered by law to issue statutory orders. The content, purpose, and scope of that power shall be specified in the law."), *reprinted in* KOMMERS, *supra* note 4, at 516. [Note: This article utilizes Kommers' translation of the Basic Law unless specifically noted otherwise]. *See also* BVerfGE 1, 14 (60) (stating, "It must be determined in each case whether the contents, purpose and scope of the authorization to make statutory orders are sufficiently defined or explained. The authorization fails to satisfy the required limitations if it is so indefinite that the cases in which and the propensity to which it can be used and the contents of the statutory orders that can be made on its basis could not be foreseen."). *See also* SINGH, *supra* note 3, at 43–47 (analyzing the 'content, purpose, and scope' provision).
103 SINGH, *supra* note 3, at 47 (emphasis added) (citing BVerfGE 7, 282 (302)).
104 *See id.* at 47 (citing BVerfGE 58, 257 (277); BVerfGE 78, 349 (272)).
105 *See* Chevron U.S.A. Inc. v. Natural Resources Defense Council, 467 U.S. 837, 865 (1984) (noting that "[w]hile agencies are not directly accountable to the people, the Chief Executive is, and it is entirely appropriate for this political branch of the Government to make ... policy choices").
106 *See* GRUNDGESETZ [GG] [Constitution] art. 20(1) ("The Federal Republic of Germany is a democratic and social federal state.").
107 *See* SINGH, *supra* note 3, at 191.
108 *See id.* at 183.
109 *See id.* at 184.
110 *See id.* at 183.
111 *See id.* at 7–8.

from, the administrative authorities.[112] This separation fulfills both the Basic Law's demand for the separation of powers as set forth in Article 20(2), as well as the requirements of Article 92,[113] which vests judicial power solely in the judiciary.[114]

As a part of the judicial branch, German administrative courts constitute one of the five independent branches of the German judiciary. The other four branches are the ordinary (civil and criminal) courts, labor courts, fiscal courts, and social courts.[115] Each branch consists of a federal court of last instance, specified in the Basic Law as the *Bundesverwaltungsgericht* (Federal Administrative Court), *Bundesarbeitsgericht* (Federal Labor Court), *Bundesfinanzgericht* (Federal Finance Court), *Bundessozialgericht* (Federal Social Court), and *Bundesgerichtshof* (Federal Court of Justice).[116] The five branches of the German judiciary enjoy equal status; no branch is superior or inferior to another.[117] Germany also has a separate Federal Constitutional Court (*Bundesverfassungsgericht*), whose primary task is to interpret the Basic Law and to rule on the constitutionality of the Federal and Land laws.[118] Relative to American federal courts, each of these last-instance courts is staffed by a large number of judges; there are, for example, 125 judges serving on the Federal Court of Justice alone.[119]

Beneath each of the federal last-instance courts is a hierarchy of earlier instances. Administrative courts retain this three-step hierarchy, and consist of (1) the lower administrative courts (first-instance courts), followed by (2) the higher administrative courts (appellate courts),[120] and finally (3) the Federal Administrative Court.

Each *Bundesland* (federal state) determines the number of lower administrative courts based upon the size and judicial needs of the particular *Land*.[121] Depending on the level of demand for the court's services, a particular lower administrative court can employ as many panels as are necessary.[122] Indeed, the possible number of panels is unlimited,[123] enabling Germany to accommodate an increased demand for administrative adjudication by simply adding more judges to its pre-existing framework. Each panel deals with rather specific matters within the realm of administration, such as law and order, commerce and industry, asylum law, and education.[124]

---

112 The Code of Administrative Court Procedure (*Verwaltungsgerichtsordnung*, 21 January 1961 (VwGO)), initially enacted in 1960 and amended in 1991 and 1997, is the Federal law dealing with the constitution, jurisdiction, powers, and procedure of the German administrative courts. See SINGH, *supra* note 3, at 187 n. 5.
113 Article 92 of the Basic Law declares, "Judicial power shall be vested in the judges; it shall be exercised by the Federal Constitutional Court, by the federal courts provided for in this Basic Law, and by the courts of the Lander." See GRUNDGESETZ [GG] [Constitution] art. 92.
114 See SINGH, *supra* note 3, at 190.
115 See KOMMERS, *supra* note 4, at 3.
116 See id.
117 See SINGH, *supra* note 3, at 184.
118 See id. For a general overview of centralized and decentralized systems of judicial review, see MAURO CAPPELLETTI & WILLIAM COHEN, COMPARATIVE CONSTITUTIONAL LAW 73–90 (1979).
119 See KOMMERS, *supra* note 4, at 3. Indeed, in 1998, Germany employed roughly one judge for every 4,000 German residents, while during that same year the United States employed just one judge for every 10,000 American citizens. See Russell Miller, *Judicial Selection Controversy at the Federal Court of Justice*, 2 GERMAN LAW JOURNAL 8, ¶ 19 (May 2001), at http://www.germanlawjournal.com/past_issues.php?id=69.
120 See SINGH, *supra* note 3, at 187.
121 See id. at 187.
122 See id.
123 See id.
124 See id.

The German administrative judiciary itself is marked by three key features: (1) the participation of lay judges, (2) the independence of German judges,[125] and (3) the use of preset panels. Each of these features is discussed below.

First, as noted, lay judges play an integral role in the German administrative judiciary at the first-instance level of the hierarchy,[126] where professional and lay judges together judge the merits, apply the law, and determine the remedy or sentence.[127] Lay judges generally serve four year terms, participate in up to twelve panels per year, and are paid expenses and a small fee.[128] The current participation of lay judges in Germany's overall judiciary is substantial; for example, the criminal courts alone employ nearly 40,000 lay judges.[129]

Second, as in the American federal courts, the independence of administrative law judges is ensured through the grant of life tenure to all professional administrative court judges, which arguably assures judges freedom from political pressure.[130] To further ensure independence, German administrative law judges are prohibited from engaging in legislative or executive work and may not serve as a consultant for either branch.[131]

Finally, unlike the American federal courts of appeal, judicial panels are not randomly created and assigned to given cases. Instead, judicial panels are constituted well in advance to entertain particular types of disputes, regardless of the specific parties or case.[132] This requirement reflects the mandate of Article 101(1) of the Basic Law, which establishes that "[n]o one may be deprived of the jurisdiction of his lawful judge." The above two features, taken together, ensure that German administrative law judges are free from influence from other branches of government and that judicial panels are not tampered with in a given case.[133] Theoretically, this ensures the equal treatment of all litigants. When coupled with the relatively high level of consistent case outcomes (due to the high degree of specialization among administrative law panels),[134] the result is a relatively efficient and just system of adjudication.

III. Judicial Review of Administrative Agency Action in Germany

An administrative decision, whether it comes from the executive or an agency, has a binding effect and is directly enforceable.[135] The decision, however, is suspended if an injured party files a complaint against it.[136] As in the United States, a complainant must first file a

---

125 *See* GRUNDGESETZ [GG] [Constitution] art. 97(1) ("Judges shall be independent and subject only to the law."). Section 25 of the German Judiciary Act of 1972, like article 97(1) of the Basic Law, reiterates that a judge is independent and subject only to the law. *See* SINGH, *supra* note 3, at 194.
126 *See* FOSTER, *supra* note 95, 106. *See also* SINGH, *supra* note 3, at 188, 195 (noting that any German citizen who is at least thirty years of age, has lived within the judicial district of the court at issue, and who does not suffer from any legal disqualification may be appointed as an administrative court lay judge).
127 *See* FOSTER, *supra* note 95, at 106.
128 *See id.*
129 *See id.*
130 German judges, however, are subject to imposed retirement requirements. For example, administrative judges with life tenure may continue in office only until the completion of sixty-eight years in the Federal Administrative Court and sixty-five years in the higher and lower administrative courts. *See* SINGH, *supra* note 3, at 193. In addition, as in America, German judges are subject to possible impeachment in the event that a judge infringes either the Basic Law or particular Land constitution. *See id.* at 192.
131 *See* SINGH, *supra* note 3, at 190.
132 *See id.* at 188.
133 To further ensure that panels are not manipulated in any given case, the actual membership of the panels and the allocation of business to them is open to the public for review. *See id.*
134 *Id.* at 188.
135 *See* FOSTER, *supra* note 95, at 174 (citing *Verwaltungsverfahrensgesetz* [VwVfG] [Administrative Law Code], May 25, 1976, BGBl. I at 1253, § 43).
136 *See id.*

complaint with the particular agency at issue before he may seek review in the courts.[137] Upon receipt of a complaint, the agency must either issue a formal reply or forward the matter to the higher administrative agency, which must then issue a reply, provide reasons for its decision, and list available remedies.[138] Pursuant to the authority vested in Article 19(4) of the Basic Law (which generally provides citizens with the right to seek judicial review),[139] if the complainant wishes, he can appeal the agency's decision in court within one month of receipt of the formal reply.[140] Proceedings before the administrative courts are less formal than those of the regular civil courts. Written briefs, for example, are not required.[141]

Like other German courts, the administrative courts hear two types of complaints – direct and indirect. Indirect review is similar to review in common law countries. Indirect review occurs when an individual challenges the validity of an administrative decision in the course of enforcement proceedings against him.[142] On the other hand, no actual case is required to initiate direct judicial review proceedings (also referred to as abstract judicial review).[143] Under direct review, a litigant may challenge the validity of a particular law immediately after it comes into force without waiting for what Americans call an actual "case or controversy."[144]

On questions of a non-constitutional nature, standing is liberally construed. For example, the Federal Administrative Court has permitted anyone whose private interests were taken into account in the approval of a building plan to challenge a bylaw relating to the plan even though his legally protected interests were not actually infringed by the action.[145] By providing for abstract review and by liberalizing standing requirements, German courts provide greater access for individuals to test the validity of administrative acts than their American counterparts.[146]

With respect to the substance of administrative appeals, German litigants may challenge the legality of an administrative decision on one of three grounds – competence, procedure, and substance.[147] Lack of competence can be asserted if the decision concerns a power

---

137 *See id.* (citing *Verwaltungsgerichtsordnung* [VwGO] [Code of Administrative Procedure], Jan. 21, 1960, BGBl. I at 17, § 68).
138 *See id.* Under certain circumstances, the authority itself may withdraw or revoke lawful or unlawful decisions without judicial review. *See* VwVfG §§ 48–49.
139 Article 19(4) of the Basic Law declares, "Should any person's right be violated by public authority, recourse to the court shall be open to him." GRUNDGESETZ [GG] [Constitution] art. 19(4).
140 *See* FOSTER, *supra* note 95, at 174.
141 *See id.* at 174–75.
142 *See id.* at 175.
143 *See id.*
144 *See* SINGH, *supra* note 3, at 51.
145 *See id.* at 53 (citing BVerwGE 59, 87). In contrast, in order to satisfy American standing requirements, a party must be injured, and the party's injury must be "concrete and particularized." *See* McConnell v. Federal Election Com'n, 540 U.S. 93, 227 (2003) ("to satisfy our standing requirements, a plaintiff's alleged injury must be an invasion of a concrete and particularized legally protected interest.") (citing Lujan v. Defenders of Wildlife, 504 U.S. 555, 560 (1992)). The *Lujan* Court clarified, "[b]y particularized, we mean that the injury must affect the plaintiff in a personal and individual way." *Id.* at 561 n. 1.
146 *Cf.* Lujan, 504 U.S. at 560–61:

[O]ur cases have established that the irreducible constitutional minimum of standing contains three elements. First, the plaintiff must have suffered an 'injury in fact' – an invasion of a legally protected interest which is (a) concrete and particularized, and (b) "actual or imminent, not 'conjectural' or 'hypothetical[.]'" Second, there must be a causal connection between the injury and the conduct complained of – the injury has to be 'fairly ... trace[able] to the challenged action of the defendant. ... Third, it must be 'likely,' as opposed to merely 'speculative,' that the injury will be 'redressed by a favorable decision.'"

147 *See* Foster, *supra* note 95, at 175 (citing VwVfG § 44).

belonging to some other governmental authority.[148] A decision may be challenged on procedural grounds if the issuing authority has failed to follow the particular rule promulgation requirements set forth in the Basic Law, *Land* constitution, or enabling law.[149] Finally, a substantive challenge may be brought where the administrative rule conflicts with a substantive provision of the Basic Law or *Land* constitution or where the administrative rule goes beyond the substantive scope of the enabling legislation.[150] If any of the above challenges are successful, the court will declare the decision null and void, stripping it of all legal effect.[151]

Various forms of relief are available to a challenger. For example, an injured party may seek to annul a decision within one month of the decision's publication.[152] Alternatively, similar to the writ of mandamus in America,[153] a litigant may request that the court direct an authority to make an administrative decision it has failed to make.[154] Finally, a litigant may seek a declaration as to the nature of the relationship between the applicant and an authority.[155] Monetary damages, however, may only be obtained in the civil, not the administrative, courts.[156]

D. Accounting for Differences Between the American and German Systems of Administrative Law

Before addressing whether America may realistically borrow features of Germany's legal system, it is important to examine the social, economic, and historical underpinnings of each country's unique system. One comparativist recently noted,

> The essential key for an appreciation of a legal culture lies in an unraveling of the cognitive structure that characterizes that culture. The aim must be to try to define the frame of perception and understanding of a legal community so as to explicate how a community thinks about the law and why it thinks about the law in the way it does.[157]

This section thus details significant cultural similarities and differences between the United States and Germany, focusing specifically on those that have contributed to the development of each administrative law system.

The political and legal systems of the United States and Germany share several important similarities. First, both the United States and the Federal Republic of Germany are

---

148 *See id.*
149 *See* SINGH, *supra* note 3, at 54. Specifically, an executive administrative order may be invalidated on procedural grounds if the issuing authority fails to observe the requirement of citing the basis of the statutory order; if it fails to take the consent of the Bundesrat in cases where such consent is required under Article 80(2); if the statutory order is either not signed or not published in accordance with the provisions of Article 82(1); or if someone has participated in its promulgation who was not authorized to do so under the enabling legislation. *Id.* at 56.
150 *See id.*
151 *See* FOSTER, *supra* note 95, at 175–76.
152 *See id.* at 176 (citing VwGO §42, para. 1).
153 *See, e.g.*, Board of Comm'rs of Knox County v. Aspinwall, 65 U.S. 376 (1860) (noting that mandamus may be utilized to compel a person, corporation, public functionary, or tribunal to perform some duty required by law, where the party seeking relief has no other legal remedy and the duty sought to be enforced is clear and indisputable). *But see* FED. R. CIV. P. 81(b) (abolishing the formal writ of mandamus and stating that such relief may be obtained by an appropriate motion made pursuant to the Federal Rules of Civil Procedure).
154 *See* FOSTER, *supra* note 95, at 177.
155 *See id.* at 177 (citing VwGO §43).
156 *See id.* at 176–77.
157 Pierre Legrand, *European Legal Systems Are Not Converging*, 45 INT'L & COMP. L.Q. 55, 60 (1996).

federal states, as both are divided into three sets of administrative authorities – federal, state, and municipal.[158] Another key similarity is that both countries are marked by a separation of the three major branches of government – legislature, executive, and judiciary.[159] These two factors serve to decentralize governmental power in each country. These factors, however, have shaped German and American administrative law in different ways.

In America, there is a clear, formal separation between the three branches of the federal government.[160] Germany, however, has opted to follow the French model of separation of powers rather than the common law conception of the doctrine.[161] In Germany, there is no formal separation between the executive and the legislature.[162] All members of the executive – the Chancellor and the ministers – are usually also members of the legislature. Only the German judiciary is truly separate from the other branches, as no judge may be a member of the other branches.[163]

Historical events and pressures have also led to major differences between German and American administrative law. Since 1952, German administrative courts have been completely separate from the rest of the German judiciary.[164] This was not always so. As far back as 1495, the highest German courts of general jurisdiction also had jurisdiction to entertain complaints against the administration.[165] However, rulers who did not wish to submit to the jurisdiction of these courts eventually removed administrative matters from the jurisdiction of the ordinary courts and vested them in administrative panels.[166] The administrative panels thus became responsible for supervising administrative efficiency, while the regular courts entertained individual complaints against the state.[167] This separation remains today, as only the regular civil courts may provide monetary damages to individual litigants, while the German administrative courts deal solely in matters of administration.[168] Meanwhile, in England and the United States, the common law courts have always exercised jurisdiction in all matters affecting the rights of an individual.[169]

The separation of administrative adjudication from German courts of general jurisdiction was also influenced by the distinction between public law and private law long recognized in Germany but not in England.[170] This distinction, arising from Roman law, encompasses the belief that ordinary courts are unsuitable for dealing with public law matters.[171]

---

158 See U.S. CONST. amend. X (establishing that "[t]he powers not delegated to the United States … nor prohibited by it to the States, are reserved to the States respectively, or to the people"). See also SINGH, supra note 3, at 33 (citing GRUNDGESETZ [GG] [Constitution] art. 20(1)).
159 See U.S. CONST. art. I, § 1 (establishing the legislative power), art. II, § 1 (establishing the executive power), and art. III, § 1 (establishing the judicial power). See also GRUNDGESETZ [GG] [Constitution] art. 20(2) ("all state authority … shall be exercised … by specific legislative, executive, and judicial organs").
160 See SINGH, supra note 3, at 14.
161 For example, the executive (i.e. the Chancellor and ministers) initiates most of the legislative measures and may be authorized to legislate through statutory orders; in addition, all legislation requires the President's assent. See SINGH, supra note 3, at 15–16. See also KOMMERS, supra note 95, at 115–17.
162 See SINGH, supra note 3, at 15–16. See also KOMMERS, supra note 4, at 116–17.
163 See SINGH, supra note 3, at 16–17.
164 After World War II, the framers of Germany's new Constitution envisaged a Federal Administrative Court modeled after the pre-Hitler Prussian system of administration. This system was adopted on September 23, 1952. See SINGH, supra note 3 at 24–25.
165 See id. at 21.
166 See id.
167 See id.
168 See id.
169 See id.
170 See id. at 17 (citing BVerfGE 10, 200 (217); BVerfGE 14, 56 (68); BVerfGE 18, 172 (183); and BVerfG NEUE JURISTISCHE WOCHENSCHRIFT [NJW] 34 (1981), 912).
171 See id. at 191.

Germany's administrative law system has also been shaped by two fundamental constitutional values – the *Rechtstaat* (rule of law) and the *Demokratie Prinzip* (democratic order).[172] The *Rechtstaat* grew out of the participation of German citizens in lawmaking from the middle of the nineteenth century onward, a move which established the supremacy of law over the state and which resulted in the inability of the administration to interfere with the rights of citizens without the authority of law.[173] Today, the German emphasis on the rule of law generally, and on upholding the Basic Law's enumeration of individual rights more specifically, is reflected in the right of German citizens to obtain judicial relief from infringement of individual rights by any public authority. This right to judicial relief is a fundamental one, specifically enumerated in the Basic Law.[174]

Germany's commitment to the *Demokratie Prinzip* (democracy) similarly reflects the notion that administration must garner its legitimacy from democratic processes. To increase democratic accountability, this principle dictates that every minister is a representative of his people and that all administrative decisions are made only by the departments within the specific hierarchy at issue.[175] The German principle of democracy is significant in the instant comparison in that it partially accounts for Germany's decision to keep normal judicial functions separate from administrative review functions.[176]

Another key difference between these two countries that also helps to account for their differing conceptions of administration is that Germany, unlike America, is a *Sozialstaat* (social welfare state).[177] In contrast to a liberal or individualistic state such as America, which is primarily concerned with protecting individual rights through non-interference by the state, the social state seeks to restructure the existing social order with the goal of removing any social and economic inequalities.[178] Such readjustment often requires direct and proactive state interference.[179] Pursuant to the requirements of socialism, when carrying out acts of administration, both the German administration and reviewing courts have an affirmative obligation to consider and promote social welfare.[180] In contrast, courts reviewing agency action in America serve as mere "watchman" over the administration with the singular purpose of ensuring that the particular agency acts within the law's bounds.[181] Because the goal of the American judiciary is to ensure that administrative agencies simply act within the

---

172 See GRUNDGESETZ [GG] [Constitution] art. 20(1), art. 20(3). *See also* KOMMERS, *supra* note 4, at 36–37 (analyzing these two German conceptions).
173 See KOMMERS, *supra* note 4, at 36–37. *See also* GG art. 20(3).
174 See GG art. 19(4).
175 See SINGH, *supra* note 3, at 13–14.
176 See id.
177 See GG art. 20(1) ("The Federal Republic of Germany is a democratic and social federal state.").
178 See, e.g., KOMMERS, *supra* note 4, at 37 (noting that "[the fundamental system of] values [embodied in the German Constitution] and the concept of justice … may trump liberty when they come into conflict. Under the United States Constitution, on the other hand, liberty would win over what the Germans have come to understand as values as well as over the unwritten constitutional principles that the term 'justice' implies.").
179 See SINGH, *supra* note 3, at 18–19. But note that the degree to which the German government is obligated to provide for its citizens' basic needs is a matter of debate in Germany. As Donald Kommers explains, "[w]hether particular policies such as family allowances or educational benefits are constitutionally required by the principle of the social welfare state is a matter of dispute among constitutional scholars." KOMMERS, *supra* note 4, at 35.
180 See SINGH, *supra* note 3, at 19.
181 See id. at 191. Singh observes, "if we look at the literature on administrative law in the common law system we get an impression as if the primary, if not the only, concern of administrative law is legal control of the administration." *Id.* at 3. *See also* Chevron U.S.A. Inc. v. Natural Resources Defense Council, 467 U.S. 837, 843–44 (1984) (stating that in the case of an express delegation to an agency to elucidate a specific statutory provision through the enactment of regulations, "[s]uch … regulations are given controlling weight unless they are arbitrary, capricious, or *manifestly contrary to the statute*") (emphasis added).

bounds of law, rather than to compete with the agency in setting policy, it is perhaps structurally sound for American courts to give great deference to administrative agency action.

In short, the distinctions between the German and American conceptions of separate powers, the two countries' relative levels of judicial specialization, their differing conceptions of democracy, and the differing roles of government in the social state versus the liberal state, are critical as they necessarily alter the nature of judicial review in each country. Thus, any comparison between the two countries' systems of administration must be cognizant of these and other fundamental differences.

E. The German and American Systems of Administrative Law Compared

Now that the German and American systems of administrative law have been viewed through the lenses of their respective social, political, and legal orders, a critical evaluation of their relative strengths and weaknesses can be made. This section identifies those parts of the American and German systems of judicial review that ensure agency fidelity to the rule of law and that make optimal use of judicial resources. This section thus compares each system's ability to produce accurate and consistent results while also protecting basic rights and ensuring democratic accountability.

I. Accuracy, Consistency, and Fairness

The ordering of German courts by relatively narrow subject matters arguably provides a significant advantage over American courts. Because individual German judges deal only with rather specific legal claims, the German court structure ensures greater specialization than does the American system. As compared to common law judges of general jurisdiction, such specialization ensures greater judicial expertise, creates a greater likelihood of consistent and accurate case outcomes, and ultimately leads to a more efficient justice system.[182] As Seventh Circuit Chief Judge Richard Posner stated so succinctly, "[t]here are ... plenty of interesting questions of administrative law. But if I am right, they can be answered well only by administrative lawyers ... ."[183]

Other aspects of the German judiciary create a greater likelihood of consistent case outcomes. In Germany, only a panel of judges constituted in advance to rule on particular types of disputes tries and decides a given case, without regard to the parties. Thus, disputes are not decided by a panel of judges assigned by chance, as in America's Federal Courts of Appeal. This simple structural arrangement arguably guarantees greater consistency and assures more equal treatment of similarly-situated litigants (both across jurisdictions and across panels).[184]

---

182 Seventh Circuit Court of Appeals Judge Diane Wood notes the many advantages of specialization:

> [S]pecialization has its advantages. It can enhance efficiency; it would ensure that the adjudicators were knowledgeable in the subject matters presented to them; and it might increase uniformity of result across the country (as the example of the Federal Circuit's patent jurisdiction suggests). If these results came about, they would represent real gains for the system.

Wood, *supra* note 80, at 1766. Judge Wood admits that, as a generalist judge, "there is a risk of winding up 'a mile wide and an inch deep' when it comes to legal expertise – jack of all trades but master of none.'" *Id.* at 1756.
183 *See* Posner, *supra* note 76, at 963 (emphasis added).
184 *See* SINGH, *supra* note 3, at 188. *See also* Ahmed E. Taha, *How Panels Affect Judges: Evidence From United States District Courts*, 39 U. RICH. L. REV. 1235 (2005) (noting empirical studies that indicate that when a judge is part of a panel of judges, the judge's decision is often greatly affected by the other members of the panel).

As compared to the American dual court system, the unique state and federal balance of the German judiciary also arguably leads to more consistent outcomes. In Germany, all trial and intermediate appellate courts are *Land* courts, while all federal courts serve as courts of last resort. In contrast, the United States utilizes two separate court systems – one that rules primarily on matters of federal law and the other that may rule on both state and federal matters.[185] Under Germany's arrangement, *all* legal issues arising from the lower state courts are reviewable by the federal courts, whereas in America, federal courts may only review federal law matters arising out of an appeal from a state court decision.[186] The German structure thus ensures that variations among German states will be ironed out at the federal level.[187] In contrast, in the United States, the outcome of a particular case often turns on whether the litigation occurs in state or federal court;[188] this possibility, in itself, creates a costly and highly inefficient incentive for forum shopping, which further brings an element of inefficiency to a system already plagued by inconsistency.[189]

For a variety of reasons, the German system of administrative law also arguably leads to a greater protection of individual rights than does America's system. First, standing to challenge administrative acts in Germany is much broader than in America, thereby providing greater access for individuals to challenge the validity of unlawful administrative acts.[190] Similarly, the mere availability of abstract judicial review in Germany creates an additional incentive for agencies to enact rules and regulations that will hold up under judicial scrutiny.[191] This, in turn, arguably leads to regulations that are more protective of individual rights. Finally, because the German executive's discretion in promulgating legislation is more limited than in America, an arguably greater percentage of German legislation is enacted under democratic processes, which in itself is more likely to lead to a greater protection of individual rights. When these factors are combined, the result is that Germany's administrative law system provides a greater likelihood that individual rights will be protected than does America's.

---

185 See SINGH, *supra* note 3, at 183.
186 *See, e.g.*, Coleman v. Thompson, 501 U.S. 722, 729 (1991) ("Because this Court has no power to review a state law determination that is sufficient to support the judgment, resolution of any independent federal ground for the decision could not affect the judgment and would therefore be advisory.").
187 Interestingly, Eleventh Circuit Court of Appeals Judge William Pryor characterizes German states as "little more than convenient districts for the administration of the federal government's policies … ." William H. Pryor, Jr., *Madison's Double Security: In Defense of Federalism, The Separation of Powers, and the Rehnquist Court*, 53 ALA. L. REV. 1167, 1172–73 (2002).
188 *See, e.g.*, Murdock v. City of Memphis, 87 U.S. 590, 638 (1874) (holding that "[t]he claim of right here … is one to be determined by the general principles of equity jurisprudence [i.e. not a Federal claim], and is unaffected by anything found in the Constitution, laws, or treaties of the United States. Whether decided well or otherwise by the State court, we have no authority to inquire. … [T]he judgment of the Supreme Court of Tennessee must be affirmed.").
189 *See* Susan Block-Lieb, *The Costs of a Non-Article III Bankruptcy Court System*, 72 AM. BANKR. L.J. 529, 565 (1998) (proposing the creation of a uniform Article III bankruptcy court system in part because of the "jurisdictional ills" that currently afflict the federal bankruptcy courts).
190 *See, e.g.*, Lujan v. Defenders of Wildlife, 504 U.S. 555, 560–61 (1992) (setting forth three requirements for standing: (1) that the plaintiff suffered an injury in fact, or an invasion of a legally protected interest that is "concrete and particularized;" (2) the injury has to be "fairly traceable to the challenged action of the defendant, and not the result of the independent action of some third party not before the court;" and (3) it must be "likely," as opposed to "speculative," that the injury will be "redressed by a favorable decision.").
191 *See* SINGH, *supra* note 3, at 53.

II. Democratic Accountability

Experience shows that American agencies may become caterers to powerful interest groups.[192] This danger is almost inevitable given the concentration of executive, legislative, and judicial powers in any particular American agency, the extreme deference to agency action given by reviewing courts, and the greater ability of American agencies to set policy vis-à-vis their German counterparts.

As discussed in Section C-IV above, in Germany, constitutional principles of democracy and the rule of law require administrative agencies to refrain from making policy decisions.[193] This feature inevitably leads to greater democratic accountability in lawmaking. In the words of Mahendra Singh,

> [T]he legislature's competence to delegate its powers has been expressly admitted in the German law ... [German courts, however], would not let [legislative delegations] go to the extent that the boundaries of the administrative powers that may be exercised under such delegation become judicially indeterminable. That is a great safeguard against the misuse of administrative powers.
> ...
> [These safeguards] are an express reminder to the legislature and the executive that the law making function must primarily be performed by the people's representatives in the legislature assisted [only] in matters of detail by the administration. ... This is a major assurance for democracy and the rule of law.[194]

While the American executive branch is gaining greater powers of rulemaking and judicial review, these two stages of administration have remained clearly separate in Germany. In Germany, the initial stage of lawmaking is primarily performed by Parliament,[195] whereas the German administrative courts enjoy sovereignty over the review stage. Thus, the German administrative law system arguably better separates the two broad powers of legislation and review than does the American system.

In addition to their powers of legislation and review, federal agencies in America also enjoy substantial executive powers. One commentator recently noted the danger inherent in the concentration of legislative, executive, and judicial functions in American agencies, arguing,

> [I]nsofar as administrative agencies now exercise a substantial amount of the legislative power of the United States, and insofar as these agencies are under far greater control by the President than by Congress, and insofar as federal judges are far more likely to enforce original legislative deals than agencies controlled by the President are, the effect of decisions such as *Chadha* and *Chevron* that curtail federal judicial review of agency determinations is to displace legislative power into the executive branch [which contravenes the goal of the Constitution] to lodge the legislative and executive powers in different branches.[196]

Cynthia Farina argues that the President, not the judiciary, is "uniquely situated to bring to the messy and expensive sprawl of regulatory programs the sorely needed qualities of coordination, technocratic efficiency, and managerial rationality."[197] James Blumstein

---

192 See Posner, *supra* note 76, at 956.
193 See SINGH, *supra* note 3, at 47 (emphasis added) (citing *Equalization of Tax Liability Case*, BVerfGE 7, 282 (302) (citing BverfGE 58, 257 (277); BVerfGE 78, 349 (272)) *supra* note 104 and accompanying text.
194 See SINGH, *supra* note 3, at 60–61.
195 See SINGH, *supra* note 3, at 15.
196 Posner, *supra* note 76, at 960. But see Cynthia Farina, *Undoing the New Deal Through the New Presidentialism*, 22 HARV. J.L. & PUB. POL'Y 227 (1998) (arguing that most regulation falls under the exercise of "executive power," which, under Article II, may legitimately take place only under the control of the President of the Untied States).
197 See id. at 228.

asserts a similar view, arguing that centralized presidential regulatory review is necessary "to encourage accountability to the administration."[198] Farina and Blumstein, however, are concerned only with a narrow slice of the agency review pie – coordination among the various federal agencies. When, in the exercise of its authority, one agency substantially affects the interests of another agency, some mechanism for coordination across agencies is indeed needed.[199] I do not challenge the assertion that the President is well situated to centralize and coordinate this process. I argue instead that, because agencies often represent the concentration of all three powers of government in the hands of one body, that body should be subject to greater judicial control as in Germany.

Farina recognizes this separation of powers problem, but ultimately backs away from the problem without proposing a viable solution. Farina argues that by placing the regulatory enterprise squarely in line with Article II, "[t]he regulatory state can go forward with its constitutional identity crisis finally resolved."[200] While such a solution may be effective in resolving the purported identity crisis of federal agencies, it altogether ignores America's clear preference for diffusing power among the various branches. Deep systematic problems emerge when the three unique functions of rulemaking, judicial review, and execution are consolidated in the hands of a single branch.[201] Yet, the Clinton administration's Executive Order 12,866 changed the nature of centralized presidential regulatory review by declaring that such review is aimed at making agency regulations "consistent with . . . the President's priorities," as opposed to "consistent with the Constitution," or "consistent with the will of the people."[202] In the area of administration, it seems that America has forgotten James Madison's warning that "ambition must be made to counteract ambition."[203]

The American Constitution reflects a general skepticism about humanity's ability to reject the possibility of despotic power.[204] The German Basic Law, on the other hand, with its emphasis on the objective dimension of rights, envisions a sort of partnership between state and citizen under which human potential may be fully maximized.[205] Given America's

---

198 Blumstein, *supra* note 31, at 885. Blumstein's position is clear: "I contend that important values are served by centralized presidential regulatory review, and that those values are consistent with our traditional understanding of how the agency rulemaking process works both in theory and in practice." *Id.* at 856.
199 *See id.* at 878.
200 Farina, *supra* note 196, at 228–29.
201 Legal scholarship is replete with arguments for and against a strict application of the separation of powers doctrine (i.e., as between the branches of the federal government, and as between the federal government versus the states), particularly with regard to today's modern welfare state. *See generally* Thomas O. Sargentich, *The Contemporary Debate About Legislative-Executive Separation of Powers*, 72 CORNELL L. REV. 430 (1987) (analyzing the various conceptions of the separation of powers doctrine). For an argument in favor of the continued adherence to James Madison's "double security" conception of separation of powers, *see* Pryor, *supra* note 187, at 1181–82 (concluding, "True to Madison's vision of competitive federalism, the Rehnquist Court has exercised the power of judicial review to remedy the abuse of power by both the states and the federal government. The Court has properly left the Calhoun/Wallace perspective of States' Rights dormant and instead challenged the National Statist vision of cooperative federalism with a restoration of Madison's double security. There lies the promise of liberty."). For an argument in favor of a more flexible and pragmatic approach to the separation of powers concept, *see* Dean Alfange, Jr., *The Supreme Court and the Separation of Powers: A Welcome Return to Normalcy?*, 58 GEO. WASH. L. REV. 668, 670 (1990) (arguing that "[t]o insist upon the maintenance of an absolute separation merely for the sake of doctrinal purity could severely hinder the quest for 'a workable government' with no appreciable gain for the cause of liberty of efficiency.").
202 *See* Blumstein, *supra* note 31, at 853.
203 THE FEDERALIST No. 51 (James Madison).
204 As Edward Eberle notes, "Americans are by nature skeptical about the existence and use of government power. Thus, it seems appropriate that the American conception of rights lacks any claim to government action." EBERLE, *supra* note 7, at 26.
205 *See id.* at 25.

historic emphasis on securing individual liberty by limiting governmental power, it is both ironic and troubling that America's system of review of administrative acts arguably permits a greater intrusion into liberty than does Germany's. The following quote from Germany's Federal Constitutional Court is particularly striking because it is a statement one would rather expect from the United States Supreme Court:

> The doctrine of ... separation of powers serves the division of political power and accountability as well as control of the power wielder; its object is to ensure the correctness of the state decisions, which means they should be taken by that organ which according to its organization, composition, capacity and procedures best satisfies the prerequisites to deal with them, and it intends at the overall moderation of the state power.[206]

In short, with the potential for American agencies to become political captives, and with a limited ability for individuals to challenge agency action in court, administration in America does not line up well with the nation's core principles of democracy and limited government. If these troubling characteristics of American administration continue, and if American administrative law as a whole continues to expand, the entire American administrative system will become vulnerable of losing its legitimacy among the American people.

F. Solutions

I. Greater Judicial Review of Agency Action in America

To dispose of the immense number of challenges to agency decisions and lighten court dockets, American courts could simply deter appeals of administrative disputes by providing greater deference to agency decisions. This approach, however, is structurally undesirable because it ignores the need to review agency action and it would likely lead to legitimate appeals being handled (at least preliminarily) by staff attorney offices rather than appointed judges.[207] Alternatively, American courts could limit judicial review of agency determinations by narrowing standing and justiciability, but this approach also ignores the need to hold agencies accountable for their actions, often made possible only through individual complaints.[208] Courts might instead impose various procedural requirements that would cause regulatory action to take on significantly legislative dimensions, such as requiring agencies to explain and justify their actions on normative and technocratic grounds, or requiring agencies to collect substantial amounts of data before acting.[209] Such requirements would help ensure that agencies stay within certain bounds to avoid the possibility of arbitrary action. In addition, courts could choose not to defer to agency action, but instead adopt a variety of short-cut procedures, such as alternative dispute

---

206 SINGH, *supra* note 3, at 18 (citing BVerfGE 68, 1 (86)).
207 *See* Donald P. Ubell, *Report on Central Staff Attorneys' Offices in the United States Courts of Appeals*, 87 F.R.D. 253 (1980) (discussing the role and use of staff attorneys' offices in the United States Courts of Appeal).
208 *See, e.g.*, Lujan v. Defenders of Wildlife, 504 U.S. 555, 560–61 (1992) (setting forth three requirements of standing: (1) that the plaintiff suffered an injury in fact, or an invasion of a legally protected interest that is "concrete and particularized;" (2) the injury has to be "fairly traceable to the challenged action of the defendant, and not the result of the independent action of some third party not before the court;" and (3) it must be "likely," as opposed to "speculative," that the injury will be "redressed by a favorable decision."); *see also* Heckler v. Chaney, 470 U.S. 821 (1985) (reviewability); Block v. Community Nutrition Inst., 467 U.S. 340 (1984) (reviewability).
209 *See* Farina, *supra* note 196, at 233.

resolution techniques, to more efficiently review agency actions.[210] Finally, courts could simply wash their hands of this responsibility, placing trust in the other branches to fully police agency rulemaking.[211] Over time, American courts have, in fact, resorted to all of these practices in varying degrees.

A better approach would be to simply increase both the size and efficiency of the judiciary by creating a separate system of administrative courts similar to that in Germany. This approach is more desirable than those described above because it better advances the values of consistency, accuracy, and democratic accountability. This approach would also better disperse governmental power among the various branches. Further, courts of general jurisdiction would undoubtedly benefit from the reduced workload. In addition, a separate administrative court system would likely lead to more intense review of agency action, which, in turn, would create greater accountability and care in the initial rule promulgation process. Finally, creating an entirely separate set of administrative courts with its own independent hierarchy, as in Germany, would moot several of the arguments commonly advanced by those opposing an increase in the size of the judiciary. For example, the argument that increasing the number of American judges would make it more difficult to maintain consistent laws carries much less force when judges are added to an entirely new court system rather than a preexisting one.[212] By channeling administrative matters into a small and specialized court system, consistency concerns no longer carry much weight.

Thus, following Germany's lead, I would propose the creation of a new federal administrative court system – one deriving its power from Article III of the United States Constitution rather than Article I.[213] This proposed system would consist of both trial and appellate courts[214] dealing only in administrative matters, with possible final review by the United States Supreme Court. Trial courts would employ a mix of professional and lay judges. Lay judges would be selected based upon their expertise in particular fields of regulation and would be assigned to cases concerning only their respective areas; for example, a judge expert in environmental matters would be assigned to a panel of judges dealing only in those matters. The use of such expert lay judges would arguably increase accuracy, thereby leading to a more efficient system (due to a lower appellate court reversal rate).[215]

---

210 As one commentator recently noted, "there is no longer any doubt that alternative dispute resolution (ADR) in administrative practice is here to stay. Whether through refined settlement rules, negotiation, mediation, or other processes, these mechanisms are required because they are accepted by the polity. ADR exists in administrative law because command-and-control regulation costs too much, [and] takes too long." Andrew F. Popper, *Administrative Law in the 21st Century*, 49 ADMIN. L. REV. 187, 187–88 (1997).

211 The Congressional Review Act (CRA) of 1996 formally attempted to do just that. The CRA established a procedure whereby Congress can review virtually all federal agency rules. This system has largely failed. Between April 1996 and the fall of 1999, for example, while over 15,000 rules were became effective and subject to review by Congress, only eight joint resolutions of disapproval were introduced in Congress, and not one of these passed either House. *See* Morton Rosenberg, *Whatever Happened to Congressional Review of Agency Rulemaking? A Brief Overview, Assessment, and Proposal for Reform*, 51 ADMIN. L. REV. 1051, 1052 (1999).

212 *See* Posner, *supra* note 76, at 953.

213 Article III provides, "The judicial Power of the United States, shall be vested in one supreme Court, and in such inferior Courts as the Congress may from time to time ordain and establish." U.S. CONST. art. III, § 1.

214 *See, e.g.*, 28 U.S.C. § 158(b)(1) (1994) (requiring, as part of the Bankruptcy Reform Act of 1994, for judicial councils within a federal circuit to consider establishing a bankruptcy appellate panel to decide bankruptcy appeals in cases where a party does not opt-out).

215 *See* Judge James F. Holderman, *Judicial Patent Specialization: A View From the Trial Bench*, 2002 U. ILL. J.L. TECH. & POL'Y 425 (2002) (arguing for the creation of a specialized trial court for patent cases in part because empirical studies reveal that district courts improperly construe patent term claims in 33% of cases appealed to the Federal Circuit; also noting that "when [...] trial judges are not accurate, the cost of enforcing patent rights goes up"); *see also* Arti K. Rai, *Specialized Trial Courts: Concentrating Expertise on*

Further, the grounding of this court in Article III rather than Article I would more closely follow Germany's approach and would guarantee equal status to all members of the judiciary through life tenure and salary protections.[216]

The notion of creating separate court systems is not a novel idea. The federal bankruptcy court system is just one of many examples of successful, specialized court systems,[217] and almost every American state has implemented specialized courts in the areas of family law, wills and probate, and small claims.[218] Because common law courts have already been moving toward greater specialization of judicial expertise,[219] a move toward a separate system of administrative courts is not as radical as it may seem.[220] Indeed, in 1990, the Federal Courts Study Committee recommended a similar court system for the resolution of federal tax disputes. The Committee would have retained the Article I Tax Court and restricted all initial tax litigation to that court, and would have established an Article III appellate division with exclusive jurisdiction over appeals in federal income, estate, and gift tax cases.[221]

Similarly, Lloyd D. George, Chief Judge of the United States District Court for the District of Nevada, has argued for the establishment of a bankruptcy court system employing Article III judges in the bankruptcy appellate division and non-Article III judges in the trial division.[222] According to Judge George, the advantages of such a system would include the elimination of a costly dual-appellate system, which currently allows a bankruptcy litigant "two bites at the apple" by providing for appeal to the district court

---

Fact, 17 BERKELEY TECH. L.J. 877, 896–97 (2002) (arguing that because trial courts decide issues of fact while appellate courts are primarily involved with developing the law, expert judges are more appropriate at the trial level).

216 For a related argument as to why it would be beneficial to convert the Article I bankruptcy courts into Article III courts, *see* Susan Block-Lieb, *The Costs of a Non-Article III Bankruptcy Court System*, 72 AM. BANKR. L.J. 529 (1998). *See also* Pacemaker Diagnostic Clinic of America v. Instromedix, 725 F.2d 537, 541 (9th Cir. 1984) (en banc) ("The attributes of Article III judges, permanency in office and the right to an undiminished compensation, are as essential to the independence of the judiciary now as they were when the Constitution was framed. In addition to the unimpeached precedent supporting this proposition, our own experience attests to the substance and reality of the guarantees. A separate and independent judiciary, and the guarantees that assure it, are present constitutional necessities, not relics of antique ideas.") (citations omitted). But *see* Wood, *supra* note 80, at 1766–68 (arguing against specialization of Article III judges).

217 *See* Cost Containment Strategy for the Federal Judiciary: 2005 and Beyond. Report of the Executive Committee, Judicial Conference of the United States, Aug. 12, 2004, at 25 (reporting that bankruptcy courts greatly improved productivity from 1994 through 2003; for example, during this time period, the number of bankruptcy filings nearly doubled while staffing levels remained constant, the number of deputy clerks per 1,000 bankruptcy cases dropped from 5.8 in 1994 to 3.1 in 2003, and the bankruptcy courts improved their case-processing times by an average of 40 percent saving more than $1 billion).

218 *See* Wood, *supra* note 80, at 1763 (noting that "[r]ecently, some states have been experimenting more boldly with specialized tribunals, and the early reports appear to be positive").

219 *See id.* at 1761–1765 (discussing the move toward greater judicial specialization in various state court systems).

220 *See generally* Block-Lieb, *supra* note 189 (proposing the creation of an Article III bankruptcy court system); *see also* Christopher F. Carlton, *Greasing the Squeaky Wheels of Justice: Designing the Bankruptcy Courts of the Twenty-First Century*, 14 BYU J. PUB. L. 37, 45–51 (1999) (same); John Pegram, *Should There be a U.S. Trial Court With a Specialization in Patent Litigation?*, 82 J. PAT. & TRADEMARK OFF. SOC'Y 766 (2000) (arguing for the creation of a specialized trial court for patent cases). But *see* Vern Countryman, *Scrambling to Define Bankruptcy Jurisdiction: The Chief Justice, The Judicial Conference, and The Legislative Process*, 22 HARV. J. ON LEGIS. 1, 9 (1985) (noting the concern of various federal judges that the creation of an Article III bankruptcy court system would diminish the prestige of the Article III federal district courts).

221 *See* Wood, *supra* note 80, at 1766.

222 *See* Lloyd D. George, *From Orphan to Maturity: The Development of the Bankruptcy System During L. Ralph Mecham's Tenure as Director of the Administrative Office of the United States Courts*, 44 AM. U. L. REV. 1491 (1995).

and allowing a second appeal to the circuit court. Other advantages include the development of uniform laws with precedential value within the circuits,[223] in contrast to the current non-binding nature of decisions by the bankruptcy appellate panels upon those courts.[224]

Richard Posner has also proposed a solution for handling the incredible volume of administrative law which is, at its core, quite similar to the German system of administrative review. Posner has argued that, rather than standardizing administrative law judge decisions by creating consistent and uniform procedures like the federal sentencing guidelines, America should instead "strengthen the appellate review process within the administrative agencies in order to reduce the burden of appellate review on the federal courts."[225] At its core, Posner's proposal can be interpreted as an argument favoring the creation of an independent system of judicial review of agency decisions that is separate from the regular federal courts. This too would further Posner's goal – to "reduce the burden of appellate review on the federal courts."[226]

II. Why Judicial Review?

In response to this proposal, one might argue that America's current system of executive review is protection enough against potential abuse by administrative agencies. Thus, in order to accept my proposal, one must first accept that it is desirable for the judiciary to review the acts of agencies. Supreme Court Justice Antonin Scalia has argued that judicial review exists only for protecting individual rights, not to ensure agency fidelity to law. Under Scalia's view, an agency's choice of which regulations to adopt is essentially a political choice, and should be accepted by a reviewing court as *per se* legitimate.[227] This position, however, is flawed for a variety of reasons.

First, administrative agencies are not purely executive in nature; instead, their functions and duties often cross over into the field of legislation, where it is well settled in American jurisprudence that judicial review is both necessary and proper.[228]

Second, Scalia's view that courts must never review policy decisions implies that any judicial review of agency decisions is simply a waste of precious judicial time and resources. While it is true that reviewing the decisions of another branch of government often results in a loss of resources – as most lower court decisions are ultimately affirmed – this alone does not justify abandoning the process altogether. America's system of government is

---

223 *See id.* at 1500–1501.
224 *See id.*
225 *See* Posner, *supra* note 76, at 961.
226 *See id.* The American Corporate Counsel Association Board of Directors' recommendation of June 13, 1996 urged the several states to create separate business courts, arguing that "[b]usiness courts will ease pressure on overcrowded state court systems." *See* Wood, *supra* note 80, at 1764. Some states, including New York, Wisconsin, and Illinois, have followed that advice by creating such specialized courts. *See id.*
227 *See* Gillette, *supra* note 18, at 105. Justice Scalia has expressed this view in various judicial opinions. *See, e.g.,* United States v. Mead Corp., 533 U.S. 218, 239 (2001) (Scalia, J., dissenting) (arguing generally that the Supreme Court's decision in Mead Corp. is unwise and declaring: "in an era when federal statutory law administered by federal agencies is pervasive, and when the ambiguities (intended or unintended) that those statutes contain are innumerable, totality-of-the-circumstances *Skidmore* deference is a recipe for uncertainty, unpredictability, and endless litigation. [For the Court] [t]o condemn a vast body of agency action to that regime ... is irresponsible.").
228 *See* Marbury v. Madison, 1 Cranch 137 (1803) (establishing the fundamental proposition that where a conflict between a constitutional provision and a congressional statute exists, the courts have the authority and the duty to declare the statute unconstitutional); *see also Cooper v. Aaron*, 358 U.S. 1 (1958) (stating that "the federal judiciary is supreme in the exposition of the law of the Constitution" and that the Supreme Court's interpretation of the Constitution is binding on state officers).

one *intentionally* designed to be inefficient, as reflected in the requirements of checks and balances and separation of powers. More than two hundred years of experience confirms that this foundational concept should not be abandoned now. As Edward Eberle recently noted, "[t]his separation of power reflected the great insight of [James] Madison over human nature. People, when in power, could not be trusted over the long term to rule with wisdom and disinterest for the common good of all."[229] Similarly, writing in 1971, Federal Circuit Judge David Bazelon warned that "[t]o protect the [] [fundamental] interests [of life, health, and liberty] from administrative arbitrariness, it is necessary . . . to insist on strict judicial scrutiny of administrative action . . . [f]or judicial review alone can correct only the most egregious abuses."[230]

Finally, strong structural arguments exist in favor of judicial review, even when one views agencies as purely executive in nature. Because agencies exist for the purpose of carrying out the law, judicial review is needed to ensure that agencies stay within the law's bounds.[231] Review by the executive itself is insufficient because such review tends to be based on the changing standards of the current President, not the more permanent ones embodied in the Constitution.[232] Accordingly, a meaningful system of review free from undue political influence is needed, and the judiciary is particularly well suited for such task.

III. Practical Concerns

One could argue that, even if Germany's system of judicial review of agency action is normatively desirable, it is simply not a practical solution for the American judiciary. Indeed, such a proposal would require a tremendous commitment of national resources. While it is certainly true that such a system would be costly, practicality and efficiency should not trump the protection of individual rights and freedoms through adequate checks upon agency action. Again, the words of James Madison are instructive, "[t]he great security against a gradual concentration of the several powers in the same department consists in giving to those who administer each department the necessary constitutional means, and personal motives, to resist encroachments of the others."[233]

One might also argue that judges are ill-equipped to handle these types of appeals. As Supreme Court Justice Stephen Breyer has noted,

> A judge can do little more in [administrative law] case[s] than read the record and ask if the result is reasonable. The records are lengthy and the number of such cases vast. Given the enormous judicial workload, ... these cases are prime candidates for delegation. In run of the mill cases, a law clerk or an administrative staff member may be assigned initial responsibility for checking the record for "problems;" the individual judge's decision thus becomes an "institutional" decision. The time needed to conduct a thorough review in all (or many) such cases is simply lacking.[234]

While Justice Breyer's concerns are certainly valid ones, his concerns are more directly applicable to proposed solutions that would increase the number of administrative appeals handled by the existing federal court system. Justice Breyer's arguments, in fact, support

---

229 EBERLE, *supra* note 7, at 14.
230 *See* Environmental Defense Fund, Inc. v. Ruckelshaus, 439 F.2d 584, 597–98 (D.C. Cir. 1971).
231 *See* Gillette, *supra* note 18, at 106.
232 Recall that the Clinton administration's Executive Order 12,866 changed the nature of centralized presidential regulatory review by declaring that review is aimed at making agency regulations "consistent with ... the President's priorities." Blumstein, *supra* note 31, at 853.
233 Farina, *supra* note 196, at 235–36 (quoting THE FEDERALIST NO. 51 (James Madison), at 321–22).
234 *See* Breyer, *supra* note 73, at 1616–17.

my proposal. It is precisely because the time needed to conduct a thorough review in such cases is lacking, and precisely because law clerks handle most such reviews, that America should create a separate court system staffed with competent administrative judges. Not only would this system ensure greater review of agency action generally, it would also ensure lengthier and therefore arguably more accurate review of the cases already handled by the overburdened federal courts.

Finally, one could argue that Congress should not encroach upon executive review by creating a set of courts to supersede that system. To the extent that the executive can unilaterally seize power to review agency rulemaking, as President Regan did through his controversial Executive Order 12,291,[235] then Congress could, pursuant to Article III, §1, create a line of courts to take over such review. Constitutionally, Congress would have just as much, if not more, justification for doing so.[236]

G. Conclusion

The steady replacement of outdated administrative agencies with new ones and the lessons of complexity theory reveal that administrative law in America may continue to increase in volume and in scope over the coming decades. Because administrative agencies engage in lawmaking processes, some form of institutional check upon their activities is necessary to ensure that agencies do not run roughshod over individual rights and liberties. Such review of legislative activities has traditionally been performed by the courts. However, the trend in America is toward less judicial review through greater deference, combined with greater executive review of agency action. I argue that the judiciary is better suited to perform this vital task, and that to accommodate such review, America should adopt a separate system of administrative courts similar to the German model. This proposed solution is more desirable than alternative ones in that it better promotes consistent and accurate case outcomes, democratic accountability, and limited governmental power.

---

235 *See* Blumstein, *supra* note 31, at 859–60 (explaining that President Reagan's Executive Order 12,291, establishing a process of centralized presidential regulatory oversight of agency rulemaking, "stunned" top agency officials, and that "[l]ike Athena, born from the head of Zeus, the executive order [had] sprung full-grown from the senior managers of President Reagan's team.").

236 "The judicial Power of the United States, shall be vested in one Supreme Court, and in such inferior Courts as the Congress may from time to time ordain and establish." U.S. CONST. art. I, § 1.

Preventive Detention in Comparative Perspective

Andrew Hammel*

A. Introduction

Wilfried Sabasch has spent most of his life in psychiatric institutions. In 1971, when he was 17, he was sent to a secure psychiatric facility in Wiesenhof, Germany after he sexually assaulted a woman by throwing her to the ground and pulling down her underwear.[1] Clinicians described him as "sexually abnormal" and seriously mentally ill, and repeatedly obtained court permission to extend Sabasch's confinement.[2] Year after year, according to Sabasch, the authorities seized on one pretext or another to extend his confinement, even though he had committed only minor rule infractions.[3] They justified his continued detention by pointing to these infractions and asserting that he was too *schwachsinnig* (feeble-minded) to be released.[4] After 30 years, Sabasch interested a local lawyer in his case, and the lawyer in turn interested a large German newsweekly, *stern*.[5] *stern* hired a prominent forensic psychiatrist, Dr. Johann Glatzel of the University of Mainz, to evaluate Sabasch.[6]

Glatzel interviewed Sabasch for twenty minutes, and studied his file for two hours and 40 minutes.[7] Glatzel's conclusions were clear. Sabasch was no longer a danger, and "must be released, now."[8] *stern* asked anxiously: "Can it be that people in this country, even today, can simply be locked away?"[9] "Yes," answered Glatzel, "The Sabasch case is an example of how people can simply disappear forever into such institutions."[10] After the local court arranged for two more evaluations, which also concluded that Sabasch was no longer a considerable threat, he was released from confinement on April 24, 2002.[11] He became a minor media sensation.[12] Shortly thereafter, however, Sabasch was arrested on suspicion of having sexually assaulted and robbed a twenty-year-old woman in Uetersen, Germany, a crime to which he confessed.[13] The expert witness assigned to evaluate him for the trial of this crime concluded that he suffered under reduced criminal culpability as to the sexual assault, and should therefore be required to undergo yet more treatment in a secure

---

* Lecturer in Anglo-American Common Law, Heinrich-Heine-Universität, Düsseldorf, Germany (ahammel@post.harvard.edu). All translations of German sources in this Article are by the author, unless otherwise noted.
1 Günter Handlögten, *Lasst Diesen Mann Frei!*, STERN, Mar. 8, 2001, at 228.
2 Sabine Rückert, *Wird Er Es Wieder Tun?*, DIE ZEIT, Feb. 13, 2003, at 11.
3 Handlögten, *supra* note 1, at 228. *But see* Gisela Friedrichsen, *Kein Mörder sitzt so lange*, DER SPIEGEL, March 10, 2003, at 54 (noting several attacks on women perpetrated by Sabasch during his confinement).
4 Friedrichsen, *supra* note 3, at 54.
5 *Id.*, 56.
6 Handlögten, *supra* note 1, at 228.
7 Friedrichsen, *supra* note 3, at 56.
8 Rückert, *supra* note 2 at 12.
9 Handlögten, *supra* note 1 at 228.
10 *Id.*
11 Friedrichsen, *supra* note 3 at 56.
12 *Id.*
13 Rückert, *supra* note 2 at 12.

psychiatric facility.[14] Sabasch was eventually sentenced to 10 years in prison for the new crimes – followed by yet another indefinite confinement in a mental hospital.[15]

The Sabasch case, and others like it, are symptomatic of a perceived rise in persistent violent criminality – especially of a sexual nature – in Germany.[16] Several German states, beginning with Baden-Württemburg,[17] responded to the public concern by enacting laws permitting authorities to detain certain prisoners who are felt to pose a severe risk of recidivism after they have served the entire term of their prison sentences. Four states followed Baden-Württemburg's lead, with Bavaria passing a virtually identical law, and Thuringia, Saxony-Anhalt, and Lower Saxony passing largely similar laws.[18] After the state laws were struck down on federalism grounds by the German Federal Constitutional Court, the German federal government proposed and passed a similar law in 2004.[19]

These laws are the latest response to an age-old problem: how should a state respond to public pressure to protect society from criminals who appear to present a continuing danger of violence, even as they approach the end of the prison sentence imposed for their prior crimes?[20] Is there a coherent philosophy of punishment which can justify imposing punishment not for defined prior crimes, but for potential future ones?[21] Where does detention for the purposes of continued therapy end, and confinement for the purposes of punishment begin?

The German laws invite comparative study in how two modern legal systems have approached the same problem, highlighting the fact that these concerns are universal. In the early 1990s, many American states enacted laws allowing for the continued post-sentence confinement of so-called "sexual predators."[22] The laws provoked great controversy,

---

14 Friedrichsen, *supra* note 3 at 57. After several conflicting messages from Sabasch's public defender concerning whether they would accept the expert's recommendation, the judge declared a mistrial. *Id.*
15 Claus Hornung, *Schwachsinn erheblichen Grades*, DIE WELT, May 16, 2003, at 10.
16 *See, e.g.*, Tatjana Hörnle, *Penal Law and Sexuality: Recent Reforms in German Criminal Law*, 3 BUFF. CRIM. L. REV. 639, 643 (2000) (asserting that, in the late 1990s, an insistent media focus on sex crimes against youths in Germany had created an atmosphere of "public indignation" based on "widespread fears which lacked a rational, scientific basis").
17 Gesetz über die Unterbringung besonders rückfallgefährdeter Straftäter [Law Concerning the Treatment of Especially Recidivism-Prone Criminals], Mar. 14, 2001, GBl. BW. at 188.
18 The citations for the relevant state laws are as follows: Niedersachsen (Lower Saxony), Oct. 2003, NdsGVBl. at 368; Thüringen (Thuringia), Mar. 2003, ThürGVBl. at 195); Sachsen-Anhalt (Saxony-Anhalt), Mar. 2002, GVBl. LSA. at 80); Bayern (Bavaria), Dec. 2001, GVBl. LB. at 978).
19 BVerfGE 109, 190.
20 *See, e.g.*, C.L. TEN, CRIME, GUILT AND PUNISHMENT: A PHILOSOPHICAL INTRODUCTION 134 (Oxford ed., 1987) (noting that the modern trend toward shorter, determinate prison sentences had spurred extensive debate surrounding the question of whether traditional criminal sentences should be supplemented by a period of therapeutic post-sentence confinement for "dangerous offenders who are still likely to commit grave offences after serving ... shorter sentences").
21 TEN, *supra* note 20, (those who take a utilitarian approach to matters of crime and punishment would have "no problem imposing a protective sentence on an offender if we are certain that this would prevent him from committing a serious offence.") *Id.* at 135 *and also* (those who favor a more retributivist approach, in which punishment for a crime is tied to a finding of personal responsibility for a specific criminal act, tend to express skepticism concerning preventive detention, as it results result in treatment similar to punishment which is not linked to the offenders' personal moral responsibility for a crime.) *Id.* at 136–38. The debate is still quite lively. *Compare, e.g.*, Alexander D. Brooks, *The Constitutionality and Morality of Civilly Committing Violent Sexual Predators*, 15 U. PUGET SOUND L. REV. 709, 753 (1992) (arguing that preventive detention is permissible given that a mistaken decision to release a dangerous prisoner is "much less harmful" than a mistaken decision to confine him) *with* John Q. LaFond, *Washington's Sexually Violent Predator Law: A Deliberate Misuse of the Therapeutic State for Social Control*, 15 U. PUGET SOUND L. REV. 655, 698–99 (1992) (describing Brook's reasoning as "worthy of George Orwell's 1984").
22 For a detailed discussion of the law passed in Washington State and citations to similar statutes, *see infra*, section D.I.

but were eventually upheld, in modified form, against all constitutional challenges.[23] The purpose and basic outline of the German and American laws are quite similar. However, as this Article will demonstrate, the constitutional and cultural background against which the laws were enacted differs markedly.

This article will provide review of recent developments in Germany, beginning with a presentation of the Bavarian law. The article will then assess the reception of the laws by scholarly commentators, practitioners, and courts, and describe the recent decision of the German Federal Constitutional Court which struck down the Bavarian law on federalism grounds. Next, the new federal law will be considered. The article will then turn to the treatment of the issue in the United States, considering the so-called "Sexual Predator Civil Commitment" statutes passed by many American states in the early 1990s, and analyzing American court decisions upholding the laws. Finally, the article will describe how each legal system negotiates the gray zone between punishment and therapy, and how the differing American and German conceptions of the purpose of confinement influenced the constitutional fate of the respective bills.

B. The Bavarian State Law

I. Overview of the Bavarian Law for the Treatment of Especially Recidivism-Prone Dangerous Criminals

Bavaria passed the *Gesetz zur Unterbringung von besonders rückfallgefährdeten hochgefährlichen Straftätern* [*BayStrUBG*] [Law for the Treatment of Especially Recidivism-Prone Dangerous Criminals] in December of 2001.[24] The law applies only to certain persons (hereinafter "proposed detainees") who are currently serving a criminal sentence in a *Justizvollzugsamt* (correctional facility).[25] The law specifies that the prison authorities, during the detainee's confinement, may file a petition with the local court seeking an order to permit an extension of confinement.[26] Such an extension may be ordered,

> because of facts that have occurred after the prisoner's conviction, it may be assumed that the detainee[27] poses a significant present danger to the life, bodily integrity, personal freedom, or sexual autonomy of others, in particular because while serving his sentence, he persistently refused cooperation in reaching the goals of punishment according to Sec. 2 of the *Strafvollzugsgesetz* [StVollzG] [Law for the Execution of Criminal Sentences[28]], namely by refusing or breaking off psychological or social therapy intended to reduce recidivism.[29]

The prison must file the petition promptly after becoming aware of the relevant

---

23 For a summary and analysis of two major recent Supreme Court decisions on preventive detention *see infra*, section D.II.
24 Gesetz zur Unterbringung von besonders rückfallgefährdeten hochgefährlichen Straftätern [BayStrUBG] [Law for the Treatment of Especially Recidivism-Prone Dangerous Criminals] Dec. 2001, GVBl. Bayern at 450-5-I.
25 *Id.* Art. 1 § 1.
26 *Id.* Art. 4 § 1.
27 The German original, "*Betroffene*", is more accurately translated as "the affected party." I have elected to translate it as "detainee" for consistency and clarity.
28 *See* § 2 StVollzG describes the purpose of incarceration. The *Strafvollzugsgesetz* has no precise counterpart in the common-law legal world. It is a comprehensive German federal law that sets out the purpose and nature of corrective sanctions in German law, and sets out in extreme detail regulations for the operation of correctional facilities. For a fuller discussion of paragraph 2 of the *Strafvollzugsgesetz*, *see infra*, section E.II.b.
29 Art. I § 1 BayStrUBG.

circumstances.[30] The petition may be filed at the earliest two years before the completion of the detainee's sentence.[31] The court shall convene a hearing and order testimony from at least two *Sachverständiger* (expert witnesses).[32] At least one of these witnesses must be neither involved in the treatment of the detainee nor regularly employed by a prison.[33] The hearing shall be public, and the expert witnesses are to testify and are subject to questioning by all participants.[34]

If the Court orders an extension of confinement, it shall be carried out pursuant to Sections 129 to 135 of the *Strafvollzugsgesetz*, which governs "preventive detention."[35] This detention, the law makes clear, is to be served in facilities distinct from those designed for ordinary incarcerated criminals.[36] The period of detention can either be limited if the court finds that the danger posed by the prisoner will be limited,[37] or indefinite.[38] The Court ordering the detention is to review the detainee's case on its own motion every two years.[39] The detainee is further entitled to file petitions to have his continued confinement reviewed more frequently – up to once per year.[40]

Any order of confinement under the law may be suspended or cancelled if the prisoner becomes subject to confinement on grounds of mental illness,[41] or if he is already subject to or will become subject to "normal" preventive detention under the *Maßregel der Besserung und Sicherung* (Reform and Prevention Measures).[42] These laws, which represent a category of alternative or supplemental sanctions that are declared to be non-punitive in nature, may be imposed in addition to or instead of a prison sentence.[43]

Although the Reform and Prevention Measures have long given German courts the power to order an offender held in preventive detention after his actual prison sentence is complete, they were traditionally only able to do so by entering a required finding *at the time they impose the prison sentence*,[44] thereby giving the offender warning that he may face additional incarceration after the term of his sentence is over. The new laws, by contrast, permit a judge to order detention *while* a prisoner is serving his prison sentence, even when no mention of possible post-sentence detention had been made by the court that fixed the original prison sentence. To distinguish the new state and federal laws, which all share this property, from the previously-existing detention laws, the new laws will be referred to as "subsequent detention laws."

---

30 *Id.* Art. 4 § 1.
31 *Id.*
32 *Id.* Art. 4 § 2.
33 *Id.* Art. 4 § 2.
34 *Id.* Art. 4 § 3.
35 *Id.* Art. 6.
36 *See* § 140 (1) StVollzG: "Treatment of those subject to preventive detention shall be carried out in separate correctional facilities or in separate departments of facilities intended for the incarceration of prisoners."
37 Art. 2 § 1 BayStrUBG.
38 *Id.* Art. 2 § 2.
39 *Id.* Art. 5 § 1.
40 *Id.* Art. 5 § 2.
41 *Id.* Art. 1 § 2.
42 *Id.* Art. 1 § 3.
43 *See* GÜNTHER KAISER, KRIMINOLOGIE 440 (10th ed., 1997) ("[The Reform and Prevention Measures] are criminal sanctions which, according to the intention of the legislator, are not to be regarded as having a punitive character.")
44 For a discussion of the history of German preventive-detention laws *see, supra*, section E.II.3.

II. The BayStrUBG Applied: The Case of Albert Haidn

A 2003 article in the German weekly broadsheet *Die Zeit* profiled Albert Haidn.[45] In 1999 Haidn was tried for raping the twelve-year-old daughter of his girlfriend.[46] The assaults had actually occurred, according to the victim, some 17 years prior.[47] At trial, Haidn strongly protested his innocence and claimed he was the victim of an act of revenge.[48] He was nevertheless convicted.[49] Taking into account a head injury and stroke which diminished Haidn's *Schuldfähigkeit* (criminal responsibility),[50] the Passau District Court sentenced him to three years and six months' imprisonment, with no provision for potential post-sentence preventive detention.[51]

Haidn's strong protestations of innocence worked against him during his confinement. He refused sex offender therapy because, in his words, "I never raped anyone."[52] The mental health professionals responsible for Haidn's care viewed his denial of guilt as a failure to acknowledge and develop insight into the psychiatric problems that led to his offenses, leading to their conclusion: "At this time, a valid prognosis cannot be formed. Because Haidn considers himself innocent, he is not open to therapeutic measures."[53] The prison in which he was incarcerated sought a subsequent preventive detention order, which was in due course granted.[54] "Nasty surprise for Haidn," the article's author concluded. "[H]e cannot leave prison, even though he has completed his three-and-a-half-year sentence. He will remain behind bars perhaps for the rest of his life: possibly ten years, possibly twenty, who knows?"[55] As will shortly be seen, Haidn continued his fight against confinement by filing a complaint with the Federal Constitutional Court.

C. Reaction to the German Detention Laws among the Defense Bar, Commentators, and Courts

I. A Chilly Reception among Defenders and Scholars

A report from a session about the subsequent detention laws held during an annual nationwide gathering of criminal defense attorneys reported widespread opposition to the laws.[56] When the State Secretary of Saxony-Anhalt spoke in defense of her state's version of the legislation, she came in for "harsh criticism."[57] The laws encountered a calmer, but no less negative, reception among commentators. The opinion of most scholarly commentators is that the

---

45 Rückert, *supra* note 2, at 11.
46 *Id.*
47 *Id.*
48 *Id.*
49 *Id.*
50 *Id.* § 21 of the *Strafgesetzbuch* (Penal Code) permits a court to reduce a defendant's sentence based on mental disability that reduces his ability to conform to the law.
51 *Id.*
52 *Id.*
53 *Id.* Although the article gives no reason to suspect Haidn's conviction was anything but orderly, the prospect of professions of innocence being used to justify confinement might appear troubling. It is notable that the Federal Constitutional Court, in striking down the BayStrUBG on other grounds, expressly criticized the law for placing exaggerated emphasis on an offender's attitude toward therapy during his confinement. *See supra*, Section C.II.
54 *Id.*
55 *Id.*
56 Antje Kramm & Esther Noske, *Konflikt und Konsens beim 26. Strafverteidigertag*, ZEITSCHRIFT FÜR RECHTSPOLITIK (ZRP) Nr. 4, 174 at 176 (2002).
57 *Id.*

detention laws suffered from multiple grave constitutional deficiencies. The most immediate problem is the relative legislative competence of the federal government and the states. In a review of a major German journal devoted to criminal law, the author noted an "overwhelming" scholarly consensus that the laws are unconstitutional on the grounds that they exceed the legislative jurisdiction of the States."[58] In the major German weekly review of legal events, Judge Dr. Reinhard Müller-Metz of the Regional Appeals Court of Frankfurt-am-Main, faults the laws primarily on procedural grounds, in that they failed to accord the proposed detainee procedural rights commensurate to the seriousness of the deprivation of liberty.[59]

II. The Federal Constitutional Court Rules

The objections to the laws on grounds of legislative competence were fully endorsed by the Federal Constitutional Court. Two detainees, Albert Haidn[60] from Bavaria and another detainee from Saxony-Anhalt, filed constitutional complaints against the laws.[61] In a decision published on February 10, 2004, a five-justice majority of the eight-member Second Senate of the Court struck down the laws on grounds of legislative competence.[62]

Whether, the States had the legislative competence to pass the laws, the Court held, depended on whether, the laws belonged to the domain of *Polizeirecht* (roughly, local police law). Here, the Court defined *Polizeirecht* as "regulations that [relate to] the maintenance of public order and security" which, so long as they do not intrude on the federal legislative sphere, "fall under the jurisdiction of state legislation."[63] Traditional criminal legislation, by contrast, falls under the exclusive legislative competence of the federal government: "The legislative competence of the federal government in criminal law according to Art. 74.1(1) of the Basic Law goes back to the ... Reich Constitution of 1871 and the 1919 Weimar Constitution."[64] Further, the historical analysis confirmed for the majority that "preventive reactions in response to a criminal act" had always been considered part of the criminal law.[65] The preventive detention laws were classically matters of criminal law, the majority held, because they "are triggered by a criminal act, are valid solely as against offenders, and obtain their objective justification from a particular criminal act."[66]

---

58 Thomas Ullenbruch, *Nachträgliche Sicherheitsverwahrung – Fragen über Fragen*, NEUE ZEITUNG FÜR STRAFRECHT (NStZ) 466, 468 (2002).
59 *See* Dr. Reinhard Müller-Metz, *Nachträgliche Sicherungsverwahrung – ein Irrweg der Kriminalpolitik*, 56 NEUE JURISTISCHE WOCHENSCHRIFT (NJW) 3173, 3174 (2003).
60 Although Haidn is not identified by name in the Federal Constitutional Court's decision, the similarities between the facts of his case and the facts set out in the opinion are unmistakable.
61 "According to Article 93 (1) [4a] of the Basic Law, any person may enter a complaint of unconstitutionality if one of his or her fundamental substantive or procedural rights has been violated by 'public authority.'" DONALD P. KOMMERS, THE CONSTITUTIONAL JURISPRUDENCE OF THE FEDERAL REPUBLIC OF GERMANY 14 (2d ed., 1997) (although the Federal Constitutional Court grants review to less than one percent of the constitutional complaints it receives, "such complaints result in some of its most significant decisions and make up about 55 percent of its published opinions."). *Id.* at 15. The procedures for such complaints are set out in §§ 90–95 of the Bundesverfassungsgerichtgesetz (Federal Constitutional Court Act).
62 *Bundesverfassungsgericht* (BVerfG), *Fehlende Länderkompetenz zur Regelung der Straftätrerunterbringung* (Lack of State Legislative Competence to Regulate the Treatment of Offenders), NJW (2004) 750. Opinions of the Federal Constitutional Court are published in the main German legal weekly, the *Neue Juristische Wochenschrift* (NJW), before they appear in the official reporter, *Entscheidungen des Bundesverfassungsgerichts* (Decisions of the Federal Constitutional Court, abbreviated BVerfGE). Because this opinion does not yet have an official citation to the Court's own reporter series, the NJW citation will be used. German court cases are referred to not by name but by subject matter.
63 *Id.* at 752.
64 *Id.* at 751.
65 *Id.*
66 *Id.*

The majority went beyond the relatively uncontroversial question of legislative competence (as to which the Court's decision was unanimous)[67] to determine whether the laws impermissibly infringed the defendants' rights. This review on the merits was necessary owing to the choice of remedies available to the Court when it strikes down a law as unconstitutional. It may either declare the law immediately void (*nichtig*), or simply declare the law incompatible (*unvereinbar*) with the Basic Law, in which case it may remain in effect for a short time while the legislator contemplates revisions.[68] The latter option is permissible, the Court noted, when "the immediate invalidity of the objectionable norm would remove the basis for the paramount protection of the common good, and a weighing of the affected basic right reveals, that the [legislation's] encroachment on the basic right can be accepted for a transitional period."[69]

At the start, the majority recognized that the state laws constituted a severe infringement of the detainees' right to liberty.[70] This infringement could be legitimized only if it were shown to be proportional to the danger posed by the detainee; that is, if it is shown that the "conditions and the form of the limitation on freedom is strictly connected to the narrow goal of protecting the public safety."[71] The majority found that the number of persons affected by the laws was very limited, and the State's interest critical:

> The experiences the states have had with the treatment laws up to now has shown that there are actually a few prisoners who, at the time of their sentencing, did not satisfy the legal or factual prerequisites for potential post-sentence detention – but who at the time of their release from prison appear to be extremely dangerous. Despite the uncertainty inherent in any prognosis, experts and judges have come to the conclusion, in rare and exceptional cases, that there is so much certainty of the dangerousness of certain offenders that further detention appears necessary for the protection of others.[72]

The majority thus decided to permit the laws to remain in force for a transitional period, to give the federal legislature time to decide on a response to the Court's decision.[73]

Nevertheless, the majority was not content to permit the laws to be applied in their current form during the transitional period. The importance of the detainees' right to personal freedom, and the limited legitimacy of the application of an unconstitutional law during a transition period, required that the invasion of the detainees' right to personal freedom be as limited as possible.[74] In their current form, the majority held, the laws do not serve this purpose. The majority noted that the mere fact that the detainees are being confined based on a prediction of their future conduct is not, in itself, objectionable: "Prognoses always carry with them the risk of error, but are at the same time unavoidable."[75] However, the

---

67 *Id.* at 759.
68 *Id.* at 757. "When held to be "nichtig", the statute immediately ceases to operate; when declared "unvereinbar", the statute or legal norm is held to be unconstitutional but not void, and it remains in force during a transition period pending its correction by the legislature, a decisional mode that has the sanction of law and ... is an option the court frequently exercises." KOMMERS, *supra* note 61, at 53 (footnote omitted).
69 *Id.* The translation is literal. The complex syntax is typical of opinions from the Federal Constitutional Court. See KOMMERS, *supra* note 61, at xvii (Federal Constitutional Court decisions are "complex, and philosophically profound," but are often marked by "convoluted and repetitious prose").
70 *Id.* Art. 2.2 of the Basic Law provides: "Everybody has the right to life and physical integrity. Personal freedom is inviolable. These rights may not be encroached upon save pursuant to a law." Basic Law of the Federal Republic of Germany 13 (Press and Information Office of the Federal Republic of Germany 1994).
71 Lack of State Legislative Competence, NJW (2004) 750 (757).
72 *Id.*
73 *Id.*
74 *Id.* at 758.
75 *Id.* The Federal Constitutional Court is not alone in its pragmatic approach to the necessity of future-dangerousness predictions in the modern legal system. *Compare, e.g.,* Barefoot v. Estelle, 463 U.S. 880, 896 (1983) (United States Supreme Court approves constitutionality of death penalty sentencing scheme

Court explicitly criticized the fact that the current laws focused their assessment of the defender's dangerousness far too much on his decision to refuse treatment while incarcerated.[76] The only constitutionally acceptable basis for continued confinement, the majority held, was a *Gesamtwürdigung* (comprehensive evaluation) of the offenders' overall status.[77] Existing detention orders, the majority held, must be re-evaluated according to this criterion without delay.[78]

In a lengthy and influential dissent, Judges Broß, Osterloh and Gerhardt criticized the majority's decision to permit the laws to remain in force.[79] According to the dissenters, such a decision could only be justified when (1) the immediate invalidation of the laws would threaten the constitutional order more than their temporary maintenance for a transition period; and when (2) the Federal Constitutional Court in fact has the authority to permit the laws to continue in force.[80] According to the dissent, neither condition was fulfilled in this case.[81] The only constitutional value that could possibly have justified permitting these laws to remain in force, argue the dissenters, is the *Untermaßverbot*, which requires the state to implement minimum basic measures for the protection of rights guaranteed by the Basic Law.[82] The *Untermaßverbot* only comes into play, however, when the measures the state has taken to protect the constitutional right (here, the general public's right to safety from dangerous offenders), are "totally inadequate" to the task.[83]

Such was not the case here, the dissent observed, given the ready availability of other sanctions and procedures for limiting the dangers posed by released detainees.[84] In any event, the dissenters observed, the immediate invalidation of the laws in the relevant federal States would only reinstate the legal situation that existed before the laws were passed, in which the federal legislature had not perceived such a gaping hole in public protection that a new federal law was needed to fill it.[85] In conclusion, the dissenters observed, the state laws clearly violated the principle of the rule of law in that they attached new adverse consequences to criminal proceedings that "have already been dealt with and belong to the past."[86] If the federal government were considering passing a similar law on its own, the court warned, it would have to deal squarely with such constitutional objections.[87]

---

which relies on a prediction of the offender's future dangerousness, commenting that predictions of future dangerousness were so prevalent and necessary in the justice system that holding them unconstitutional would be "somewhat like ... disinvent[ing] the wheel.")

76 *Id.* at 758.
77 *Id.* The Court cited its earlier decision in the case of *Treatment in a Psychiatric Hospital*, BVerfGE 70, 297, in which the Court had attempted to balance the right of personal freedom against a citizens' right to liberty. The Psychiatric Hospital case emphasized that a deprivation of a citizen's liberty on grounds of his potential dangerousness can only be based on a thorough examination by an expert which takes into account, among other factors, "his state of health, his behavior during confinement, the effects of the treatment [he has received], the conditions of his life, and the circumstances and measures which could positively influence his life circumstances after his release from treatment." *Id.* at 307–08.
78 *Id.* at 759
79 *Id.* at 759–61.
80 *Id.* at 760.
81 *Id.*
82 *Id.* The leading case describing the Untermaßverbot is the *Abortion II Case*, BVerfGE 88, 203, in which the Federal Constitutional Court ruled that a proposed federal abortion law passed in 1992 provided insufficient protection to the right to life of the fetus. For an English translation of the most important parts of the decision and a brief historical commentary, *see* KOMMERS, *supra* note 61, at 349–56.
83 BVerfG, NEUE JURISTISCHE WOCHENSCHRIFT (NJW), 57 (2004), 750 (760).
84 *Id.* The dissenters mentioned the possibility of observation by the police, restraining orders, monitoring by social service agencies, and psychiatric confinement for dangerous offenders who display mental illness. *Id.*
85 *Id.*
86 *Id.* at 761.
87 *Id.*

The tone of the dissenting opinion, which accused the majority of ignoring basic principles of the rule of law, was uncompromising. Other commentators were no less concerned. As noted by Professors Dünkel and van Zyl Smit,[88] the majority's decision to permit detentions to continue under the laws, earned the Court outraged public criticism in an editorial entitled "Appalled at the Federal Constitutional Court,"[89] written by Eberhard Foth, a former judge of the German High Court. Foth declared the Federal Constitutional Court's decision "criminal" and urged prosecutors to investigate whether the judges, in authorizing continued confinement of detainees without a legal basis, might themselves have violated Section 239 of the Penal Code, making it a crime if someone "locks up a human being or otherwise deprives him of his liberty."[90]

III. The Federal Government Responds

Despite the powerful dissent and skeptical reception of the Federal Constitutional Court's decision, the governing coalition, through Justice Minister Brigitte Zypries, lost little time replacing the invalidated state laws with a federal counterpart. On March 10, 2004, Minister Zypries introduced proposed legislation to create a new regime permitting extended detention on the federal level.[91] The proposal was passed by both houses of the federal legislature and became law on July 29, 2004.[92] It adds a new section 66b to the Penal Code entitled *Nachträgliche Anordnung der Unterbringung in der Sicherungsverwahrung* (Subsequent Ordering of Treatment in Preventive Detention). Those who may be eligible for subsequent detention are defined as follows:

> When, after sentencing for a crime against life, bodily integrity, personal freedom, or sexual self-determination ... before the end of the execution of the prison sentence facts become recognizable that indicate a considerable danger from the prisoner for the general public, the court may order [subsequently to the original sentencing] treatment in preventive detention, if a complete evaluation of the prisoner, his crimes, and further his development during prison confinement reveal, that with high probability he will commit serious crimes, through which the victims will be seriously psychologically or bodily injured, and if the other conditions of Section 66 of the Criminal Code are met.[93]

Dr. Jörg Kinzig, a leading authority on preventive detention, summarizes how the new definition is to be read in the context of the existing legal framework: "The formal conditions for subsequently-ordered preventive detention ... are thus essentially that the person to be detained subsequently is serving a sentence of a minimum of 2 or 3 years, exhibits certain previous crimes or previous prison sentences, or has been (formerly) sentenced to prison for 3 crimes with a certain minimum level of punishment. For sexual crimes, in particular, the required conditions are further reduced, to the commission of only 2 crimes."[94] The definition of those to whom the law applies, Kinzig notes, closely tracked language found in the Federal Constitutional Court's decision striking down the state laws,

---

88 Frieder Dünkel & Dirk van Zyl Smit, *Preventive Detention of Dangerous Offenders Re-examined: A Comment on Two Decisions of the German Federal Constitutional Court*, 5 GERMAN LAW JOURNAL 619, 631 (2004) at http://www.germanlawjournal.com/pdf/.Vol05No06/PDF_Vol_05_No_06_619–637_Public_Duenkel_van_Zyl_Smit.pdf.
89 R. Eberhard Foth, *Entsetzt über Bundesverfassungsgericht*, FRANKFURTER RUNDSCHAU, Feb. 25, 2004, at 14.
90 *Id.* The translation of § 239 StGB is provided by the German Federal Ministry of Justice, and is *available at* http://www.iuscomp.org/gla/statutes/StGB.htm#239.
91 *Available at* http://www.bmj.bund.de/media/archive/617.pdf.
92 2004 (BGBl I. S. 838).
93 *See* § 66b(1) StGB.
94 Dr. Jörg Kinzig, *Umfassender Schutz vor dem gefährlichen Straftäter?*, NEUE ZEITSCHRIFT FÜR STRAFRECHT (NStZ) 655, 657 (2004).

although Kinzig doubts the Federal Constitutional Court intended to create any sort of formal standard in its decision.[95] Also of note is the fact that the federal law omits any mention of the prospective detainee's negative attitude toward treatment, a factor which the Federal Constitutional Court singled out for criticism.[96]

To Kinzig, the most important features of this new definition include the fact that the law does not require the ordering court to determine that the proposed detainee has a tendency to commit crimes (which was "always required to order traditional preventive detention") and the phrase "high probability" in reference to the likelihood of the defendant committing future crimes, which it is not found elsewhere in the Penal Code.[97] Further, Kinzig notes, the new federal law goes further than the state laws which it replaced in that it permits a construction that allows subsequent preventive detention to be ordered against (1) those who have been found criminally non-culpable and sent to psychiatric hospitals; and (2) to first-time criminals, even ones who are young adults.[98] With this last step, Kinzig observes, the federal legislature gave up a 50-year legislative and judicial tradition of caution in the application of preventive detention to adolescents (*Heranwachsende*) and young adults.[99]

Kinzig views the new law as raising serious constitutional questions. The gravest, according to Kinzig, is raised by the possibility of first-time offenders being affected: "The fact that until now at least two previous crimes were required to justify ordering perhaps the most severe sanction known to the criminal law was well-grounded. Only then, if at all, would there be a satisfactory (negative) legal biography to form the indispensable basis for a valid prognosis."[100] Especially given the recent emphasis of the Federal Constitutional Court on the need for invasions of the defendant's liberty to be based on an extremely thorough investigation of the defendant's background, the use of preventive detention against first-time offenders appeared especially problematic.[101] Kinzig, citing the dissenting opinion from the Federal Constitutional Court's decision, argues that the retroactive effect of the new law violates the principle of the rule of law, which can only be violated in a state of emergency. In light of the many other ways of controlling dangerous persons available under German law, Kinzig argues, it cannot be serious maintained that the danger posed by a few dangerous criminals constitutes a state of emergency.[102]

---

95 *Id.* at 656.
96 *See* Lack of State Legislative Competence, NEUE JURISTISCHE WOCHENSCHRIFT (NJW) 750, 758 (2004). A recent court decision dissolving a lower court's order of subsequent detention proposed an extremely narrow reading of the new § 66a StGB. Subsequent detention can be ordered only when the court relies primarily on facts which (1) have come to light only since the detainee began serving his prison sentence; (2) which indicate that the detainee has grown more dangerous during confinement; and (3) which go beyond the detainee's mere failure to participate in resocialization programs. Oberlandesgericht (Regional Appeals Court) Koblenz, NEUE ZEITSCHRIFT FÜR STRAFRECHT (NStZ) 97 (2005).
97 *Id.* at 657–58.
98 *Id.* at 658. An adolescent, as defined by Section 1(2) of the Jugendgerichtgesetz (Youth Court Law, abbreviated JGG) is a person who is eighteen years of age but not yet 21. § 106(2) JGG specifically forbids the court to order preventive detention against adolescents. Kinzig observes that courts, for their part, themselves were cautious in ordering preventive detention even against young adults over 21, citing a study showing that of the over 800 persons being detained in preventive detention in West Germany between 1963 and 1967, not one was under 25. Kinzig, *Umfassender Schutz? supra* note 94, at 658 *quoting* ULRICH GUMMEL, JUNGTÄTERVERWAHRUNG: DIE UNTERBRINGUNG IN EINER SOZIALTHERAPEUTISCHEN ANSTALT ALS MAßREGEL GEGEN GEFÄHRDETE JUNGTÄTER 30 (1972).
99 *Id.*
100 *Id.* at 659.
101 *Id.*
102 *Id. quoting* Lack of State Legislative Competence, NEUE JURISTISCHE WOCHENSCHRIFT (NJW) 750, 761 (2004), *and also* Frieder Dünkel, *Sicherheitsverwahrung (erneut) auf dem Prüfstand*, NEUE KRIMINALPOLITIK 42 (2004) (arguing that the new § 66(b) "unquestionably violates the violation on retroactive legislation").

D. America's New Experiment with Preventive Detention

In Germany, the critical constitutional questions posed by the subsequent detention laws have yet to be squarely addressed. In the United States, however, similar questions have already been decided – albeit by narrow margins, and with a similar degree of controversy.

Beginning with the State of Washington in 1990,[103] many American states have passed laws intended to permit the confinement of persons thought to pose an imminent danger of committing serious sex offenses.[104] Often called "sexual predator" or "sexual psychopath" laws, they represent an attempt to update an earlier set of detention regimes that had fallen out of favor in the mid-1970s to take into account modern notions of due process.[105] As in Germany, the main impetus for these laws was public outrage over high-profile instances of sex criminals being released from prison only to commit new offenses.[106] Many legislative packages passed in the wake of such instances bore the name of the victim. In New Jersey, for instance, the law was popularly known as "Megan's Law," after the seven-year-old victim of a rape/murder committed by a previously convicted offender.[107]

I. Washington State Ushers in a New Era of Preventive Detention

The Washington statute, called the Community Protection Act (CPA), bears closer examination, since it was the first in the nation, and served as the model for many later

---

103 WASH. REV. CODE ANN. §§ 71.09.010-.120 (1992 & Supp. 1995).
104 Other states that have passed similar detention laws include Florida, Illinois, Iowa, Missouri, New Jersey, South Carolina, Texas, Virginia, and North Dakota. *See, e.g.,* FLA. STAT. ANN. §§ 394.910-.931 (West 2002 & Supp. 2004); 725 ILL. COMP. STAT. ANN. §§ 207/1–207/99 (West 2002 & Supp. 2004); IOWA CODE ANN. §§ 229A.1–.16 (West 2000 & Supp. 2003); MO. ANN. STAT. §§ 632.483–.513 (West 2000 & Supp. 2004); N.J. STAT. ANN. §§ 30:4-27.24 to -27.38 (West Supp. 2004); S.C. CODE ANN. §§ 44-48-10 to -170 (Law. Co-op. 2002); TEX. HEALTH & SAFETY CODE ANN. §§ 841.001-.150 (Vernon 2003 & Supp. 2004); VA. CODE ANN. §§ 37.1-70.1 to 70.19 (Michie Supp. 2003); N.D. Cent. Code §§ 25-03.3-01 to .3-23 (2002)). More states can be expected to pass similar laws in the coming years, given that "thirty-eight states, the District of Columbia, and three territories" signed an amicus brief before the United States Supreme Court arguing for the validity and constitutionality of such laws in the first case to address challenges to them. Grant H. Morris, *Mental Disorder and the Civil/Criminal Distinction,* 41 SAN DIEGO L. REV. 1177 at 1190 n. 86 (2004).
105 In 1940, the United States Supreme Court upheld a Minnesota law providing for the confinement of "psychopathic personalities," which the statute defined as a person who displays "'emotional instability, or impulsiveness of behavior, or lack of customary standards of good judgment, or failure to appreciate the consequences of his acts, or a combination of any such conditions, as to render such person irresponsible for his conduct with respect to sexual matters and thereby dangerous to other persons." Minnesota ex rel. Pearson v. Probate Court of Ramsey County, 309 U.S. 270, 272 (1940). The Court rejected facial due-process challenge to the law's procedures. *Id.* 276-77.

   In the following decades, the older generation of laws fell into disuse, as the Supreme Court's strengthened due-process protections for civil commitment proceedings raised doubts about their constitutionality. *See generally* Andrew Horwitz, *Sexual Psychopath Legislation: Is There Anywhere to Go but Backwards?*, 57 U. PITT. L. REV. 35, 38–48 (1995) (noting that during historical review of treatment of the issue in the American states, over 30 states had passed such legislation by 1970, but that in the 1970s the states began "repealing their statutes in droves" owing to doubts about their effectiveness and constitutionality).
106 *See, e.g.,* Laura Mansnerus, *Questions Rise Over Imprisoning Sex Offenders Past Their Terms,* NEW YORK TIMES, Nov. 17, 2003, at A1 ("In 1998 New Jersey – like other states reacting to murders by sex offenders with previous convictions – authorized the commitment of anyone who has served time for a sex crime and is found to have a 'mental abnormality or personality disorder' that makes him likely to commit another crime.")
107 Mansnerus, *supra* note 106, at 1.

enactments.[108] The broad outlines of the statute are similar to the German federal law. To extend the detention of an offender who is serving or has fulfilled his or her sentence, the local district attorney must file a petition for confinement under the law.[109] Four groups of people are eligible for extended confinement: adults and juveniles serving a prison sentence in "total confinement" for a "sexually violent offense," those who have been found incompetent to stand trial for a sexually violent offense, and those who have been found not guilty of such an offense by reason of insanity.[110]

A proceeding[111] is then convened to determine whether there is probable cause to believe that the person, is a "sexually violent predator" (SVP) which the law defines as a person "who has been convicted of or charged with a crime of sexual violence and who suffers from a mental abnormality or personality disorder which makes the person likely to engage in predatory acts of sexual violence."[112] If probable cause is found, the person is transferred to a facility for evaluation,[113] and the court schedules a trial to determine, beyond a reasonable doubt, whether the person is an SVP.[114] The accused SVP has the right to an attorney and a jury, if he so wishes, but remains "confined in a secure facility" during the trial.[115] If committed as an SVP, the person has the right to treatment, and to no less frequent than yearly review of whether he should continue to be labeled an SVP, and "whether conditional release to a less restrictive alternative is in the best interest of the person and conditions can be imposed that would adequately protect the community."[116]

II. First Constitutional Challenges to the New SVP Laws

Andre Brigham Young and Vance Cunningham, both of whom had long histories of criminal sexual violence and had been confined pursuant to Washington's SVP law, filed constitutional challenges on a variety of grounds, including substantive due process.[117] In order

---

108 *See, e.g.*, Kelly A. McCaffrey, *The Civil Commitment of Sexually Violent Predators in Kansas: A Modern Law for Modern Times*, 42 U. KAN. L. REV. 887, 889 (1994) (observing that a task force of the Kansas legislature decided to pass a law modeled on Washington's law after the Washington Supreme Court upheld the Washington Community Protection Act). After the United States Supreme Court, in turn, upheld Kansas' act against constitutional challenges in Kansas v. Hendricks, 521 U.S. 346 (1997), many passed laws "mimic[king]" the Kansas statute, "to avoid constitutional problems." Morris *supra* note 104, at 1190.
109 WASH. REV. CODE § 71.09.030 (West 2001).
110 *Id.* § 71.09.025(1)(a)(i)–(iv)
111 *Id.* § 71.09.030(1).
112 *Id.* § 71.09.020(1).
113 *Id.* § 71.09.040(4).
114 *Id.* § 71.09.060(1).
115 *Id.* § 71.09.050 (1)–(3).
116 *Id.* § 71.09.070, 71.09.080(2).
117 Substantive due process, in American constitutional law, denotes the idea that the promise of "due process" of law to every citizen not only requires the government to afford procedures adequate to protect a citizens' interest before depriving that citizen of liberty or property, but also places certain absolute substantive limits on the government's ability to intrude on citizens' "exercise of their liberty under the Due Process Clause of the Fourteenth Amendment to the [United States] Constitution" no matter what procedural protections the government affords. Lawrence v. Texas, 539 U.S. 558, 564 (2003) (holding that substantive due process protection prevented the government from criminalizing private consensual sex acts between homosexuals).

The doctrine of substantive due process, which has also been invoked by the United States Supreme Court to prevent the government from banning abortion and contraception, is controversial among American constitutional scholars. *Compare* JOHN HART ELY, DEMOCRACY AND DISTRUST 18 (1980) (disputing notion that idea of due process of law has a substantive component and arguing that term "substantive due process" is "a contradiction in terms – sort of like green pastel redness.") *with* I LAURENCE H. TRIBE, AMERICAN CONSTITUTIONAL LAW § 8–1 1333 (3rd ed. 2000) (arguing that there is a "reasonable historical argument" that phrase "due process of law" was intended to include a substantive component).

to confine a person in a mental health care facility, substantive due process requires a state to demonstrate that the person suffers from a mental illness *and* that he presents a danger to himself or others.[118] The SVP laws, however, concededly permitted sexually violent predators to be confined only upon a showing that they had some mental abnormality, even if this did not equate to a recognized, serious mental illness. The Preamble to the Washington Community Protection Act, for instance, notes that the law applies to a "small but extremely dangerous group of sexually violent predators ... who do not have a mental disease or defect that renders them appropriate for existing involuntary treatment."[119] Rather, the legislature found, these persons have "personality disorders and/or mental abnormalities which are unamenable to existing mental illness treatment modalities and [which] render them likely to engage in sexually violent behavior."[120]

The second group of constitutional complaints characterized the laws as punitive rather than therapeutic. Under this view, the laws authorize retroactive punishment of the offender (in violation of the *ex post facto* clause of the United States Constitution[121]) and multiple punishments of the offender for the same offense (in violation of the U.S. Constitution's prohibition on double jeopardy, made applicable to the states through its incorporation into the Fourteenth Amendment[122]).

The Washington Supreme Court, by a narrow majority, upheld the laws in In re *Young*.[123] The critical question, noted the majority, was whether the laws were criminal or civil in nature.[124] The majority explained that if the laws were found to inflict a criminal punishment, they would likely be invalid under both the Double Jeopardy and *ex post facto* Clauses, because they would punish an offender for crimes for which he had already been punished or for a "status" (that of being an SVP) that was not illegal when the defendant had it.[125]

The majority first acknowledged that the legislature had labeled the laws civil commitment statutes.[126] However, the majority observed, U.S. Supreme Court precedent required it to look beyond the legislature's characterization to the "actual impact" of the laws, to determine whether they were punitive in their nature, regardless of the legislature's

---

118 Allen v. Illinois, 478 U.S. 364, 370–71 (1986). For commentary on the decision, *see* Edward P. Richards, *The Jurisprudence of Prevention: The Right of Societal Self-Defense Against Dangerous Individuals*, 16 HASTINGS CONST. L. Q. 329, 372–75, 392 (1989) (arguing that *Allen*, which held protections relevant to criminal trials inapplicable to proceedings to commit an individual as a "sexually dangerous person," along with other decisions, "substantially erode" citizen's civil liberties.)
119 WASH. REV. CODE § 71.09.010.
120 *Id*.
121 *See* U.S. CONST. Art. I, § 10, cl. 1 ("[n]o State shall ... pass ... any ex post facto Law."). Justice Salmon P. Chase, in an early and influential interpretation of the ex post facto Clause, held that it forbade "1st. Every law that makes an action done before the passing of the law, and which was innocent when done, criminal; and punishes such action. 2d. Every law that aggravates a crime, or makes it greater than it was, when committed. 3d. Every law that changes the punishment, and inflicts a greater punishment, than the law annexed to the crime, when committed[; and] 4th. Every law that alters the legal rules of evidence, and receives less, or different, testimony, than the law required at the time of the commission of the offense, in order to convict the offender." Calder v. Bull, 3 Dall. 386, 390, 1 L.Ed. 648 (1798) (*seriatim*, Chase, J.) (*emphasis deleted*). For a more recent account of the history and interpretation of the Clause, *see* Rogers v. Tennessee, 532 U.S. 451, 456–62 (2001).
122 The phrase Double Jeopardy refers to the Fifth Amendment to the United States Constitution, which forbids any person to be "twice put in jeopardy of life or limb" for the "same offence." Although the Amendments to the United States Constitution expressly limit only the conduct of the federal government, the United States Supreme Court has held that the Due Process Clause of the Fourteenth Amendment requires the States also to respect the Constitutional prohibition on double jeopardy. Benton v. Maryland, 395 U.S. 784 (1969).
123 In re Young, 857 P.2d 989, 993 (Wash. 1993).
124 *Id*. 996.
125 *Id*. 996–97.
126 *Id*. 996.

characterization of them.[127] The majority applied the U.S. Supreme Court's definitive test, which calls for inquiry into,

> [w]hether the sanction involves an affirmative disability or restraint, whether it has historically been regarded as a punishment, whether it comes into play only on a finding of *scienter*, whether its operation will promote the traditional aims of punishment – retribution and deterrence, whether the behavior to which it applies is already a crime, whether an alternative purpose to which it may rationally be connected is assignable for it, and whether it appears excessive in relation to the alternative purpose assigned. ...[128]

Applying this test, the majority of the Washington Supreme Court held that the detention under the SVP laws did not constitute a criminal punishment.[129] The majority concluded that the SVP extended confinement provisions served the "civil commitment goals of incapacitation and treatment" rather than punitive goals. The majority also underscored the fact that the decision to commit is based not on proof of a criminal state of mind, but rather of "a mental abnormality or personality disorder."[130]

The majority of the Washington Supreme Court then turned to the question of whether the SVP laws satisfied the "substantive due process" requirement for constitutional civil commitment, which permits this grave intrusion into a citizen's rights only upon proof that he is mentally ill and dangerous.[131] The majority found that the danger presented by the detainees was clear from their record of serious sex crimes.[132] The detainees also argued that they could not be confined because they were not mentally ill, a finding required for civil commitment under the Supreme Court's substantive due process precedents.

The detainees noted that they had only been diagnosed with personality disorders – generally considered to be ingrained behavior patterns resistant to conventional psychiatric treatment – rather than more serious mental illnesses with a recognized biochemical basis, such as depression or schizophrenia. How could they be legitimately confined for "treatment" of their "illness," the detainees asked, when the very preamble to the law classified their conditions as "unamenable to existing treatment modalities"? The majority took what might be called a pragmatic approach, reasoning that "the mere fact that an illness is difficult to treat does not mean it is not an illness" and that, in any event, that there actually appeared to be some treatment modalities that offered some promise.[133]

After thus upholding the laws against the most fundamental constitutional challenges, the majority discerned various procedural problems with the laws, including the failure to require a finding that the relatively drastic remedy of confinement in a secure facility was the least restrictive means of protecting the public.[134] The Court remanded the two cases for new proceedings necessary to remedy these flaws.[135]

One dissenting judge, joined by two concurring colleagues, would have gone farther. Calling the statute a "well-intentioned attempt by the legislature to keep sex predators off the streets," the dissenters nevertheless criticized it for setting up an "Orwellian 'dangerousness court', a technique of social control fundamentally incompatible with our system of ordered liberty."[136] Quoting from an *amicus curiae* brief from the Washington State

---

127 *Id.* 997.
128 Kennedy v. Mendoza-Martinez, 372 U.S. 144, 168–69 (1963).
129 *Id.* 997–99.
130 *Id.* 998.
131 *Id.* 1000 *quoting* Addington v. Texas, 441 U.S. 418, 426 (1979).
132 *Id.* 994–96.
133 *Id.* 1003–04.
134 *Id.* 1012.
135 *Id.* 1018.
136 *Id.* 1019 (Johnson, J., *dissenting*).

Psychiatric Association opposing the law, the dissenter argued that "the term 'mental abnormality' has no clinically significant meaning and no recognized diagnostic use," and therefore, cannot serve as a Constitutional basis for the deprivation of a citizen's freedom.[137]

III. The United States Supreme Court Rules

The various SVP laws also provoked disputes over the proper interpretation of the United States Constitution in other state supreme courts,[138] prompting the United States Supreme Court to intervene by granting *certiorari* to decide a case arising under Kansas' SVP law. The Kansas Supreme Court had struck down that state's law on the grounds that the statute's "precommitment condition of a 'mental abnormality' did not satisfy what the court perceived to be the 'substantive' due process requirement that, involuntary civil commitment must be predicated on a finding of 'mental illness.'"[139]

The Supreme Court disagreed. It first reaffirmed a state's power to order the "forcible civil detainment of people who are unable to control their behavior ... provided the confinement takes place pursuant to proper procedures and evidentiary standards."[140] The Court then addressed Hendricks' claim that the term "mental abnormality," as used in the statute, was too vague. While conceding that a state may only justly deprive a citizen of freedom (as a matter of civil law) upon a showing that his dangerousness is caused by mental illness, the Court nonetheless concluded that it had never attempted to define what a mental illness was, and doubted that this was possible with the level of precision Hendricks requested.[141] The Court noted that it had previously upheld commitment statutes that defined mental illness in terms of a mental disorder that renders an individual unable "to control his dangerousness," and held this showing sufficed to justify a civil detention order.[142] Drawing on its arguments that the laws represented a therapeutic intervention, the Court turned aside the petitioners' *ex post facto* and double-jeopardy complaints, holding that the statutes did not explicitly or, covertly inflict any criminal punishment.[143]

The Supreme Court again addressed the Kansas statute in *Kansas v. Crane*,[144] a case which grew out of Kansas prosecutors' failed attempt to confine Michael Crane, a sex offender who had been diagnosed with exhibitionism and an antisocial personality disorder. The Kansas Supreme Court had overturned Crane's confinement order, holding the State had failed to satisfy *Hendricks*' requirement that the State must demonstrate that the individual to be confined lacks control over his behavior.[145] The State of Kansas appealed to the U.S. Supreme Court, claiming that the Kansas Supreme Court had read *Hendricks* too narrowly. In fact, argued the prosecutors, the Kansas statute could be applied to anyone whose personality "makes [him] likely to engage in repeat acts of sexual violence,"[146]

---

137 *Id.* 1021.
138 *See, e.g.*, Matter of Linehan, 557 N.W.2d 171 (1996) (*aff'g* over two dissenting opinions, constitutionality of Minnesota version of SVP statute); In re Matter of *D.C.*, 656 A.2d 861 (N.J. 1995) (*striking down* retroactive application of New Jersey SVP statute over one dissent), *rev'd*, 679 A.2d 634 (1996); In re Care and Treatment of Hendricks, 912 P.2d 129 (1996) (*striking down*, over four dissenting opinions and one concurrence, Kansas Sexually Violent Predator Act).
139 Kansas v. Hendricks, 521 U.S. 346, 350 (1997) *quoting* In re *Hendricks*, 912 P.2d at 138.
140 *Id.* 357 (citations omitted).
141 *Id.* For a review of the various tests that have been proposed for legal insanity in the United States and England *see* WAYNE R. LAFAVE, CRIMINAL LAW § 4.2, at 339–42 (2000).
142 *Id.* 360.
143 *Id.* 360–70.
144 534 U.S. 407 (2001).
145 *See* In re *Crane*, 7 P.3d 285, 287 (2000).
146 KAN. STAT. ANN. §§ 59–29a02(a), (b) (2000 Cum. Supp.).

regardless of whether he is able to control his behavior or not.[147] Crane, for his part, defended the Kansas Supreme Court's interpretation of *Hendricks*, and argued that he could not be confined, since no showing had been made that he lacked any control over his exhibitionist impulses.[148]

The Supreme Court chose the middle ground between the parties' positions. The lack-of-control requirement imposed by *Hendricks*, the Court emphasized, was necessary to the statutory scheme's constitutionality because it distinguished individuals with some sort of mental disorder from ordinary criminals who are "more properly dealt with exclusively through criminal proceedings."[149] This distinction, the Court held, was necessary to its conclusion that the statute was primarily a therapeutic, civil measure rather than a criminal sanction.[150] Nevertheless, the Court held that the Kansas Supreme Court had interpreted *Hendricks* incorrectly when it suggested that the State must prove an offender lacked *any* control over his behavior. To justify a commitment under the SVPA, the Court explained,

> there must [only] be proof of serious difficulty in controlling behavior. And this, when viewed in light of such features of the case as the nature of the psychiatric diagnosis, and the severity of the mental abnormality itself, must be sufficient to distinguish the dangerous sexual offender whose serious mental illness, abnormality, or disorder subjects him to civil commitment from the dangerous but typical recidivist convicted in an ordinary criminal case.[151]

The Court acknowledged this might be a "less precise standard" than many of the parties desired.[152] However, the Court reasoned that psychiatry is a developing science and that the legal system and the mental health system view symptoms of mental abnormality from very different perspectives.[153] When addressing the interplay between constitutional standards and psychiatric diagnoses, the Court noted, it prefers to "provide constitutional guidance" not by defining precise criteria but rather "by proceeding deliberately and contextually, elaborating generally stated constitutional standards and objectives as specific circumstances require."[154] The Court remanded the case to the Kansas Supreme Court for further proceedings in light of its opinion.[155]

Justice Scalia dissented, joined by Justice Thomas, the author of the majority opinion in *Hendricks*. In their view, the majority had seized on *Hendricks*' discussion of the "volitional control" element of the Kansas SVPA's definition of a mental disorder as some kind of talisman.[156] Justice Scalia argued that the Kansas statute, as upheld by the United States Supreme Court, permitted confinement when the State prove two things: that (1) the defendant had a mental disorder; and (2) the disorder made him likely to commit future acts of sexual violence.[157] Although the Hendricks Court had *mentioned* the offender's lack of ability to control his impulses, Scalia argued, the Court had in no way intended to add an additional "lack of volitional control" element to the definition given in the Kansas statute. Under Scalia's view, the Kansas statute approved detention upon a *mere* showing

---

147 *Id.* 416 (*citing* definition found in KAN. STAT. ANN. §§ 59–29a02(a), (b) (2000 Cum. Supp.)).
148 *Id.* 412.
149 *Id. quoting* Kansas v. Hendricks, 521 U.S. at 360.
150 *Id.* 413.
151 *Id.* 413.
152 *Id.*
153 *Id.* 413–14. For a thorough discussion of the complex interplay between medical diagnoses of mental disorders and legal definitions of insanity and incompetency *see* NORVAL MORRIS, MADNESS AND THE CRIMINAL LAW (1982).
154 *Id.* 414.
155 *Id.* 415.
156 *Id.* 419–20.
157 *Id.* 422.

that one had a mental disorder and would commit future acts of sexual violence, full stop, and the question whether one could control one's behavior was irrelevant.

It was also unnecessary, continued Scalia: some lack of ability to control one's behavior can always be inferred from the two statutory findings, and therefore need not expressly be made by the jury that orders confinement.[158] To Justice Scalia's mind, the majority's restrictive interpretation of the SVPA also undermined the Act's evident purpose – to protect the public from dangerous sexual predators. He commented, with characteristic verve: "[i]t is obvious that a person may be able to exercise volition and yet be unfit to turn loose upon society. The man who has a will of steel, but who delusionally believes that every woman he meets is inviting crude sexual advances, is surely a dangerous sexual predator."[159]

E. Comparative Observations: Federalism and the Geography of the Civil/Criminal Divide in Germany and the United States

At first, the similarities of the American and German approaches (as exemplified by the German federal statute and the Washington SVP law) stand out: both start by isolating offenders who have already demonstrated a tendency to commit violent crimes;[160] both provide for adversarial proceedings that lead to commitment,[161] and both demand that a high standard of proof be satisfied. From this common starting point, however, differences emerge that can be placed in two categories: (1) structural/constitutional and (2) cultural (what, in German, might be called *kriminalpolitisch*).

I. Two Visions of Federalism

Under German federalism, "the bulk of the legislative power is vested in the federal government."[162] Article 74 of the Basic Law lists twenty-eight general subject areas in which both the federal and state governments have "concurrent" legislative authority. Article 72(1) of the Basic Law permits the states to legislate in these areas only "as long as, and to the extent that, the federation does not exercise its right to legislate."[163] The federal government, in turn, is called upon to use its legislative power only when necessary to regulate effectively and ensure a basic level of uniformity in living conditions.[164]

Although the structure of German federalism is difficult to summarize,[165] the situation in the specific area of criminal law is considered fairly straightforward. The German federal government has passed three comprehensive sets of regulations in the area of substantive criminal law: (the *Strafgesetzbuch*), criminal procedure (the *Strafprozessordnung*),

---

158 *Id.* 420.
159 *Id.* 422.
160 *Compare* Strafgesetzbuch [StGB] [Penal Code] § 66(b)(1) (limiting scope of law to person who has committed a crime of violence crime) *with* WASH. REV. CODE §§ 71.09.020(7), 71.09.030 (limiting scope of law to individuals who have committed a sexually violent offense and who are "[l]ikely to engage in predatory acts of sexual violence").
161 *Compare* Strafprozessordnung [StPO] [Criminal Procedure Code] § 275a(2) (providing that the procedure for determining whether a person should be subject to subsequent detention will proceed according to §§ 213–275 StPO, which govern ordinary criminal trials) *with* WASH. REV. CODE § 71.09.050 (providing defendant with right to assistance of counsel, expert assistance, and a jury).
162 KOMMERS, *supra* note 61, at 75.
163 *Id.* 76 (translation in KOMMERS).
164 *Id.* (discussing GRUNDGESETZ [GG] [Basic Law] art. 72(2)).
165 For a thorough treatment, including English translations of the major Federal Constitutional Court decisions, *see* KOMMERS, *supra* note, 61 at 61–114.

and the structuring and administration of criminal penalties (the *Strafvollzugsgesetz*). Under the German version of what might be called constitutional pre-emption, these three federal laws have left precious little room for the individual states to devise their own answers to the most fundamental questions of criminal and penal law.[166]

By contrast, the United States Supreme Court has observed that "[i]t goes without saying that preventing and dealing with crime is much more the business of the States than it is of the Federal Government, and ... we should not lightly construe the Constitution so as to intrude upon the administration of justice by the individual States."[167] The Supreme Court can regulate a state's substantive criminal law only when its application violates specific Constitutional guarantees of fairness or due process.[168] Diversity is prized; in fact the Supreme Court has referred to the States as "laboratories" in which various potential solutions to criminal-procedure issues can be tried and evaluated.[169] Further, the jurisdiction of state and federal law is independent: even when the federal government passes a law criminalizing conduct that is also illegal under state law, authorities can, under the doctrine of dual sovereignty, elect to prosecute the offender under federal law, state law, or both.[170]

II. Two Visions of Corrections: Rehabilitation in American and German Criminal Justice Policy

A more fundamental difference between the two legal cultures will arguably, play a much larger role in future developments in America and Germany, as regards these extended detention provisions. However similar the intent of the American and German legislators who passed preventive detention laws, they operate in two surprisingly different legal landscapes shaped by different basic assumptions about how the government should respond to criminal offenses.

1. America: "Nothing Works," and the Civil-Criminal Divide

The American jurisprudence concerning SVP laws focuses on the civil/criminal distinction; that is, the distinction between imprisonment as a response to crime, and (civil)

---

166 *See* Lack of State Legislative Competence, NJW (2004), 750 (751) (although "criminal law" is a field of "concurrent competence" between the federal and state governments according to the § 74(1) of the Basic Law, German constitutional history shows that criminal law has always been thought to be a matter for federal regulation, and the postwar German federal government has exercised broad regulatory powers in the area of criminal law, making traditional criminal law solely a matter for federal regulation).
167 Patterson v. New York, 432 U.S. 197, 201 (1977).
168 *See, e.g.*, Medina v. California, 505 U.S. 437, 443 (1992) ("In the field of criminal law, we have recognized that '[b]eyond the specific guarantees [of fairness in criminal procedure] enumerated in the Bill of Rights, the Due Process Clause has limited operation.") *quoting* Dowling v. United States, 493 U.S. 342, 352 (1990); Spencer v. Texas, 385 U.S. 554, 564 (1967) (the Constitution "has never been thought [to] establish th[e Supreme] Court as a rule-making organ for the promulgation of state rules of criminal procedure").
169 Justice Louis Brandeis of the United States Supreme Court once famously remarked that "[i]t is one of the happy incidents of the federal system that a single courageous State may, if its citizens choose, serve as a laboratory; and try novel social and economic experiments without risk to the rest of the country." New State Ice Co. v. Liebmann, 285 U.S. 262, 311 (1932).
170 Two successive prosecutions by the federal government or, one particular state for the same crime would violate the United States Constitution's Double Jeopardy clause. The doctrine does not, however prevent successive prosecutions by different sovereigns (such as the federal government and the government of a State) for the same crime because "'[a]n offence, in its legal signification, means the transgression of a law.' Consequently, when the same act transgresses the laws of two sovereigns, 'it cannot be truly averred that the offender has been twice punished for the same offence; but only that by one act he has committed two offences, for each of which he is justly punishable.'" Heath v. Alabama, 474 U.S. 82, 85 (1985) *quoting* Moore v. Illinois, 14 How. 13, 19–20 (1852).

confinement justified by therapeutic motives. To understand the clarity of the distinction, it is helpful to look at the uneasy junction between the civil and criminal: the insanity defense. The American legal system recognizes insanity as an exculpating factor only in the smallest class of most egregious cases,[171] which results in large numbers of seriously mentally ill individuals being sent to ordinary prisons.[172]

Scholars tend to identify two reasons for this state of affairs. First, the definition of legal insanity in many American states became more restrictive after the notorious 1982 insanity acquittal[173] of John Hinckley, Jr., after his trial for his attempt to assassinate President Reagan, the definition of criminal insanity was further by the federal government and many state governments.[174] The federal government, for its part, eliminated any chance for an offender to be acquitted by reason of insanity unless he could prove that at the time of the crime mental illness rendered him "unable to appreciate the nature and quality or the wrongfulness of his acts."[175]

Further, cynical jurors who may act on the unwarranted belief that the insanity defense is widely abused will apply this fairly restrictive legal standard. After a thorough comparison of public perceptions of the insanity defense to reality, Professor Michael Perlin concluded:

> [I]t is taken as common wisdom that the insanity defense is an abused, over-pleaded and over-accepted loophole used as a last-gasp plea solely in grisly murder cases to thwart the death penalty; that most successful pleaders are not truly mentally ill; that most acquittals follow sharply contested "battles of the experts"; and that most successful pleaders are sent for short stays to civil hospitals. Each of these myths has been clearly, definitively, and empirically disproven, yet they remain powerful, and show no sign of abating. Even when the inaccuracies of public perceptions are demonstrated by contrary data, the public remains resistent [sic] to change.[176]

---

171 *See* Anne C. Gresham, *The Insanity Plea: A Futile Defense for Serial Killers*, 17 LAW & PSYCHOL. REV. 193, 198 (1993) (reporting that the defendant formally enters a defense of not guilty by reason of insanity in fewer than one percent of all American criminal cases, and that that "chances are very slim" that the plea will be successful).

172 *See* Jeffrey L. Kirchmeier, *A Tear in the Eye of the Law: Mitigating Factors and the Progression Toward a Disease Theory of Criminal Justice*, 83 OR. L. REV. 631, 690 (2004) (observing that the large increase in incarceration rates and decrease in mental hospital populations signifies a trend toward incarceration as a way of dealing with the mentally ill and citing studies and articles demonstrating large population of mentally ill inmates in American prisons); HUMAN RIGHTS WATCH, ILL-EQUIPPED: U.S. PRISONS AND OFFENDERS WITH MENTAL ILLNESS 17–19 (2003) *available at* http://www.hrw.org/reports/2003/usa1003/ usa1003.pdf (collecting sources that estimate that as many as 20–40 percent of American prisoners have serious mental illnesses, and that in fact there are more seriously mentally ill people in prison than in ordinary mental hospitals).

173 Walter Isaacson, *Insanity On All Counts*, TIME, 5 July 1982, at 22 (reporting that on June 21, 1982, John Hinckley was acquitted by reason of insanity on all counts relating to his attempted assassination of President Reagan).

174 In 1987, scholars completed a comprehensive review of reforms to state-law insanity defenses carried out between 1978 and 1985. Lisa Callahan et al., *Insanity Defense Reform in the United States – Post-Hinckley*, 11 MENTAL & PHYSICAL DISABILITY L. REPORT 54 (1987). The authors observed that, during the period under study, which covered the Hinckley assassination attempt, thirteen states either abolished the defense or adopted one of the following four kinds of reforms: "(1) changes in the test of insanity or in the entering of the plea; (2) addition of the GBMI [guilty but mentally ill] option; (3) changes in the burden and/or standard of proof; (4) changes in trial procedures; and (5) changes in commitment and release procedures." *Id.* 54–55. The scholars hypothesized that many reforms were likely to have been responses to the Hinckley verdict, but that others were likely prompted by unrelated factors. *Id.* at 58.

175 18 U.S.C. § 17(a) (2002). For a description of the effect of the Hinckley acquittal on the development of the insanity defense in the United States, *see* Jessie Manchester, *Beyond Accommodation: Reconstructing The Insanity Defense To Provide An Adequate Remedy For Postpartum Psychotic Women*, 93 J. CRIM. L. & CRIMINOLOGY 713, 735–38 (2003).

176 Michael L. Perlin, *Unpacking the Myths: The Symbolism Mythology of Insanity Defense Jurisprudence*, 40 CASE W. R. L. REV. 599, 707–08 (1989/1990) (footnotes omitted).

If a defendant with a mental illness insufficient to support an insanity acquittal is convicted as an ordinary criminal, he will be sent to a state prison. There, the level of individualized care and therapy he get vary wildly from state to state, and may be minimal indeed: the American prison population has quadrupled in the last 30 years,[177] and "[f]unding for correctional programs has not kept pace with population growth, which has led to a reduction in the number of programs aimed at helping prisoners, such as general literacy and higher education programs, in most state prison systems."[178]

The lack of attention to funding for correctional is, in turn, related to the existence of the school of thought in American criminology and sociology known by the catchphrase "nothing works."[179] Prompted by an article published in the 1974 *Public Interest* which critically assessed the results of then-existing rehabilitation programs, the idea that nothing works to rehabilitate criminals rapidly permeated American legal culture. To quote one 1991 review of American criminal justice policy:

> In less than two decades, almost everyone involved in the criminal justice system has rejected the rehabilitative ideal, described less than twenty years ago as the predominant justification of punishment. By the mid-1980s, a major criminal law treatise concluded that "retribution ... 'is suddenly being seen by thinkers of all political persuasions as perhaps the strongest ground ... upon which to base a system of punishment.'"[180]

This atmosphere helped create the climate that led to the passage of the 1984 of the Federal Sentencing Guidelines. Congress replaced the former flexible sentencing regime, which was "based on concepts of the offender's possible, indeed probable, rehabilitation," with a new system of rigid "guidelines" intended to ensure a fundamental consistency of sentences across geographical reasons.[181] Congress also explicitly jettisoned the idea of rehabilitation as a goal of imprisonment.[182]

Thus, in the United States, the system sorts virtually all persons who have violated the law into a negligible "mentally ill" group and the great mass that can be characterized as an "ordinary criminal" group, and there is a substantial difference in the treatment those groups receive. Oversimplification should be avoided: there are movements in the United States to recognize the frequent influence of mental illness on criminal behavior, and to

---

177 Sasha Abramsky, Hard Time Blues: How Politics Built a Prison Nation xii (2002) (reporting statistic and arguing that "by the mid-1990s ... the politics around crime and drug abuse had been largely reduced to a battle of sound bites: who could successfully communicate their toughness to voters clamoring for harsher punishments").
178 Sarah Lawrence et al., Urban Institute Justice Policy Center, The Practice and Promise of Prison Programming 3 (2002) *available at* http://www.urban.org/UploadedPDF/410493_PrisonProgramming.pdf *citing* James Austin & John Irwin, It's About Time: America's Imprisonment Binge (2001) and Paul Van Slambrouck, *Push to Expand Book-Learning Behind Bars*, Christian Science Monitor, 15 September 2000, at 3.
179 The phrase is a rhetorical answer to the questions posed by Robert Martinson in an influential article published in 1974. *See What Works? Questions and Answers About Prison Reform*, The Public Interest, Spring 1974, at 22–54. Martinson, after reviewing reports of rehabilitation programs conducted between 1948 and 1967, concluded: "With few and isolated exceptions, the rehabilitative efforts that have been reported so far have had no appreciable effects on recidivism." *Id.* at 25 (emphasis removed).
180 Michael Vitiello, *Reconsidering Rehabilitation*, 65 Tul. L. Rev. 1011, 1012–1013 (1991) (footnotes omitted) *quoting* Wayne LaFave & Austin W. Scott, Criminal Law 26 (2d ed. 1986); *quoting* Martin R. Gardner, *The Renaissance of Retribution – An Examination of Doing Justice*, 1976 Wis. L. Rev. 781, 784.
181 Mistretta v. United States, 488 U.S. 361, 363 (1989).
182 *See id.* at 367 (noting that 1984 Sentencing Guidelines "reject[ed] imprisonment as a means of promoting rehabilitation" and announced that federal incarceration should henceforth serve "retributive, educational, deterrent, and incapacitative goals" (citing 28 U.S.C. § 994(k) & 18 U.S.C. § 3553(a)(2)).

integrate some form of mental health treatment into the correctional regime.[183] But it is fair to say that these efforts have not yet revolutionized the landscape.

Thus, there remains a clear conceptual distinction between the mad and the bad in American law. Indeed, one of the reasons the sexual predator laws have posed so many difficulties in the United States is that they create a third class of law breakers who are only "somewhat" mentally ill and who receive treatment of a nature and quality somewhere "in between" that accorded to a prisoner and that accorded to a lawbreaker who has been judged legally insane. The commensurability of this new definition of offender with the stark discontinuity between the mentally ill/criminal distinction is still a matter of open debate.[184]

2. Germany: Therapy and Resocialization on a Continuum

The policy landscape in Germany is very different. It is possible for criminals to be found not responsible for their actions by reason of insanity under Section 20 of the *Strafgesetzbuch*.[185] However, the assessment of an offenders's *Schuldfähigkeit* (criminal culpability) is assessed pursuant to Section 21, which permits the reduction of any penalty upon a showing that a mental disorder of any kind "substantially diminished" the offender's ability "to appreciate the wrongfulness of the act or to act in accordance with such appreciation."[186]

For convicts with reduced criminal responsibility (and in certain other cases), German law has established the above-discussed Reform and Prevention Measures, which may involve confinement, but are officially intended only to resocialize and rehabilitate offenders.[187] Sometimes called the "second track" of correctional sanctions,[188] these measures apply to two groups of people. The first group includes those "against whom no accusation of criminal responsibility can be lodged (for example, because of a mental illness), but

---

183 Perhaps the best-known conceptual movement in this direction is so-called "therapeutic jurisprudence," which asks the question whether "a particular legal rule, either presently in effect or proposed, [is] therapeutic or antitherapeutic to patients (and perhaps to society as a whole." DAVID V. WEXLER & BRUCE J. WINICK, THERAPEUTIC JURISPRUDENCE, Introduction at x (1992). Later in the volume, Wexler suggests that the "creative application of substantive criminal law doctrine ... can shape prosecutorial policies that ought to motivate persons with dangerous disabilities and disorders to follow a therapeutically appropriate path." David B. Wexler, *Inducing Therapeutic Compliance Through the Criminal Law*, in THERAPEUTIC JURISPRUDENCE, *supra* at 187.
184 *Compare, e.g.*, Morris *supra* note 104, at 1192–94 (arguing that concept of sexually-violent predator does violence to existing conceptual categories of who is deserving of punishment and who is deserving of treatment) and *see, e.g.*, Kyron Huigens, *Dignity and Desert in Punishment Theory*, 27 HARV. J. L. & PUB. POL'Y 33, 37–38 (2003) *and c.f.* Christopher Slobogin, *A Jurisprudence of Dangerousness*, 98 NW. U. L. REV. 1 (2003) (also criticizing conceptual incoherence of SVP laws because of their ambivalence concerning the mental illness requirement, but defending a limited regime of preventive detention based on dangerousness).
185 *See* § 20 StGb: "Whoever upon commission of the act is incapable of appreciating the wrongfulness of the act or acting in accordance with such appreciation due to a pathological emotional disorder, profound consciousness disorder, mental defect or any other serious emotional abnormality, acts without guilt." (translation provided by the German Federal Justice Ministry; *available at* http://www.iuscomp.org/gla/statutes/StGB.htm#20).
186 *See* § 21 StGB (translation provided by the German Federal Justice Ministry; *available at* http://www.iuscomp.org/gla/statutes/StGB.htm#21)
187 *See* §§ 61–72 of the StGB set out the legal framework governing the Reform and Prevention Measures.
188 *See, e.g., Verfassungsmäßigkeit des Wegfalls der Höchstdauer der erstmaligen Sicherungsverwahrung* (Constitutionality of Removal of Time Limit on First-Time Preventive Detention), NJW (2004), 739 (744) (Federal Constitutional Court, Feb. 5, 2004) (referring to the "two-track sanction system" created by the Penal Code) (case title translated by author).

who can be assumed to present a risk of committing further illegal acts in the future."[189] The second group includes those "as to whom a punishment oriented along criminal lines will be insufficient to avert the danger of further crimes."[190]

Even when prisoners are adjudged criminally responsible and sent to prison, their confinement will often have a very strong therapeutic component.[191] Germany has, significantly, declined to recognize punishment and retribution as an *official* goal of correctional intervention. Section 2 of the *Strafvollzugsgesetz* sets out the principal aim of the execution of sentences: "While serving his penal sentence, the prisoner should become capable of leading a socially responsible life without further criminal acts. (Goal behind the execution of sentences). The imposition of a prison sentence also serves to protect the public from further crimes."

This completely retribution-free, rehabilitation-oriented construction of the goal of correctional enforcement was no accident; rather it resulted from a legislative process in which notions of retribution and punishment, as such, were expressly excluded from the official definition of the goals of correctional intervention.[192] The decision to exclude the more traditional "general" goals of criminal punishment, such as general deterrence, atonement, and retribution, has obviously not met with universal acclaim. However, later attempts to integrate these more traditional goals into the *Strafvollzugsgesetz* have been universally rebuffed.[193]

This orientation, in turn, profoundly influences the correctional ideology. As one commentator puts it: "The *Vollzugsziel* [goal of confinement] is the polestar and yardstick for a multitude of decisions in the framing of correctional policy. It influences not only the legal position of the prisoner but also the organization, personnel structure, and spatial arrangement of the correctional facility. The *Vollzugsziel* is 'the most important program target for that which takes places in the correctional facility.'"[194] The everyday administration of German prisons is thus overwhelmingly focused on preparing prisoners for their ultimate release. This is accomplished not only through a variety of vocational and career training programs,[195] but also through a minute regulation of the everyday life of prisoners, which is intended to enhance their sense of personal responsibility, integrate them into the modern social state, and increase their ability to effectively organize their time and manage their relationships.

3. Reconciling Preventive Detention with the Rule of Law: Two Models

Both the German and American systems of preventive detention end up at largely the same point: a small fraction of particularly dangerous offenders can now be singled out and kept

---

189 BERND-DIETER MEIER, STRAFRECHTLICHE SANKTIONEN §5.1.1.1 217 (2001).
190 *Id.*
191 For a thorough exploration of the goal of resocialization and its implementation in the criminal justice system, *see* MICHAEL WALTER, STRAFVOLLZUG 269–291 (1999).
192 *See* GUENTHER KAISER ET AL., STRAFVOLLZUG: EIN LEHRBUCH § 4, 82–85 (1982) (describing history of European conceptions of the remedial purpose of punishment and the immediate history of the adoption of the current German formulation). The authors maintain: "Resocialization is the exclusive goal of punishment, not just one goal among others. The 'protection of the public from further crimes' is simply another task that imprisonment should 'also' serve." *Id.* at 85.
193 *See* ERNST-PETER HARTWIG, DER EINFLUß DER "ALLGEMEINEN" STRAFZWECKE IM STRAFVOLLZUG 7–8 (1995).
194 GÜNTHER KAISER & HEINZ SCHÖCH, STRAFVOLLZUG §6.1.1 230 (5th ed., 2002).
195 For a non-academic look at everyday life in a German prison, *see* Hinter Gittern, *Der Alltag im Knast*, available at www.zdf.de/ZDFde/inhalt/31/0,1872,2035039,00.html (describing strict regimentation of life behind bars for Germany's 60,000 prisoners, and noting extensive variety of vocational, educational, sports and social activities available to them).

in prison-like conditions indefinitely. The legal predicates of lawful confinement are also similar. First, the procedures leading to the confinement must be sufficiently reliable and selective. Second, detainees must be held under conditions at least somewhat different from ordinary prisoners. Third, they must be given regular opportunities to demonstrate their readiness for release. Each regime can be seen as the attempt of a highly developed legal system to reconcile preventive confinement with a legal order that traditionally strictly limits governmental intrusion into personal freedom.

However, the United States and Germany use subtly different rationales for extending the confinement past the end of the prisoner's official prison sentenceand these rationales, in turn, highlight important differences. The United States Supreme Court's due process jurisprudence, as well as its recognition of a rigid distinction between confinement for criminal punishment and confinement for psychiatric therapy, forced lawmakers to at least attach a label of *some* sort of treatable mental abnormality to the offenders who were to be detained. Despite the lawmakers' best efforts, however, the detention laws simply do not map well onto the conceptual landscape of American criminal justice. Commentators have attacked the curious, unwieldy hybrid of therapy and incapacitation.[196] Even those who defend a limited form of preventive detention, such as Professor Christopher Slobogin, find the apparent need to require a finding of mental illness to be a hindrance: "If a person wants to commit serious crime so badly that he is willing to be deprived of liberty or suffer similarly serious consequences for it, then he should be eligible for preventive detention, whether the desire stems from mental illness, subliminal 'drives,' or cold calculation."[197]

Seen from a purely conceptual point of view, Germany's detention laws are a better fit for the German penal system. First, the subsequent detention laws fit into the frame of the existing system of preventive detention, which was first proposed in 1909, and enacted into German law in 1933 by the then-new National Socialist regime.[198] Although often attended by controversy,[199] the notion that the State has the power to detain certain

---

196 See Slobogin, *supra* note 184, at 3 (summarizing arguments of American opponents of preventive detention).
197 Slobogin, *supra* note 184, at 42. According to Slobogin, a model of detention which jettisoned the psychotherapeutic rationale and simply focused on detaining persons who were highly dangerous and "undeterrable" – but not necessarily mentally ill – can be defended within the context of the American political and jurisprudential landscape. *Id.* at 43–48, 61–62 (defining concept of undeterrability, and arguing that authorizing preventive detention for a very limited subgroup of undeterrable offenders might reduce the pressure on American government officials to rely excessively on lengthening criminal sanctions as a response to perceived dangers).
198 JÖRG KINZIG, DIE SICHERUNGSVERWAHRUNG AUF DEM PRÜFSTAND 7–29 (1996). Kinzig's detailed study provides a thorough historical and empirical evaluation of the legal institution of preventive detention in Germany.
199 The institution of preventive detention has been repeatedly criticized, especially by legal scholars of the left. The High Court of the German Democratic Republic (popularly known as East Germany), for instance, abolished the preventive detention laws it inherited in 1952, arguing that the definition of career criminal or habitual criminal in the existing law is "as a reflection of the notion of the criminal type, 'fascistic in content' [and] that 'democratic criminal law' has recognized the 'class nature of crime' and therefore rejects the concept of a 'criminal type' and also 'habitual criminal.'" *Id.* at 23–24 quoting Oberlandesgericht [OLG – Higher Regional Court] NEUE JUSTIZ [NJ] 54 (1953).
  Commentary in West Germany tended to accept the basic idea of preventive detention, but stressed that its character as a very last resort (ultima ratio) was critical, and that much work was required to integrate it into the framework of basic human rights established by the German Basic Law. *See id.* at 29–36 (noting that preventive detention was originally thought to be justified by purely utilitarian considerations, but that especially after World War II, legal scholars sought to justify the institution with reference to its potential to reform the offender and through a recognition that the significant invasion of the offender's right to freedom could only be justified by clear proof of the severe threat he might pose to society).
  Kinzig also details his own and others' commentary on the more practical problems with the

offenders, past the end of their prison sentences, based solely on a carefully-reasoned prediction of their future dangerousness, has become a widely-accepted component of the German legal landscape.

The existing legal landscape, moreover, freed the German legislator from any duty to require a finding of mental illness on the part of those to be detained. This was made particularly clear in the February 5 decision of the Federal Constitutional Court in the case of *Verfassungsmäßigkeit des Wegfalls der Höchstdauer der erstmaligen Sicherungsverwahrung* (Constitutionality of Abolition of Maximum Time Limit on First-Time Preventive Detention),[200] which upheld the retroactive application of the removal of the 10-year limit on preventive detention orders under the pre-existing preventive detention law.[201] There, the court acknowledged that the detainee-petitioner had no serious mental illnesses.[202] The conclusion was that he was just very dangerous, and that was enough to constitutionally justify his continued preventive detention. To the extent that his further confinement needed to be justified on therapeutic grounds, the Court was easily able to draw upon the more fluid line between criminal and civil confinement in Germany: preventive detention, the Court noted, was not a conventional criminal punishment but a reform measure, which by law was defined as therapeutic and resocializing.[203] To the extent the preventive deten-

---

implementation of the preventive detention law in Chapter 5 of his study. The points include difficulty forming an accurate prognosis of an offenders' dangerousness, the prevalence of false positives, psychiatrists' limited competence to predict future dangerousness, the vagueness and irrelevance of the statutory terminology defining a criminal "tendency" and "serious crimes." *Id.* at 79–107. Kinzig notes also that empirical research has indicated troubling differences in the extent to which various West German courts have resorted to preventive detention. *Id.* at 107–08.

200 *See* NJW (2004), 739. The German case-title is provided by the editors of the NJW; the English translation is provided by the author.

201 More specifically, the February 5 decision upheld the indefinite confinement of an offender, even though when the original order authorizing post-sentence confinement was handed down in his particular case, the law imposed a 10-year limit on post-sentence preventive detention. *See* Dünkel & van Zyl Smit, *supra* note 88, at 4–8 for an insightful analysis of this decision.

202 *See* BVerfG, 2 BvR 2029/01, para. 53 (Although petitioner's detention was taking place in a psychiatric hospital, the court conceded that "it is no longer to be assumed that the petitioner is psychiatrically ill. He does, however, display histrionic personality traits, which appear to be embedded in a pronounced problem of narcissism".) The Federal Constitutional Court's own citation form is used here, because this description of the individual complainant does not appear in the portions of the opinion printed in the NJW, whose reprints usually concentrate on the legal reasoning employed by the Court. The decision in full may be found at the Federal Constitutional Court's website: http://www.bverfg.de/entscheidungen/rs20040205_2bvr202901.html.

Although there is no mention of German detention law in Professor Slobogin's recent article, it is interesting to note the striking parallels between his detention regime – in which detention would be limited to a small class of highly dangerous "undeterrable" offenders, regardless of whether they are mentally ill or not, and the outlines of the existing German system of preventive detention, which similarly uses a reliable prediction of dangerousness as justification for commitment. *See* Slobogin, *supra* note 184, at 48 (criticizing limitation of detention to the mentally ill because, regardless of the detainee's mental illness, "the state should not be precluded from preventively detaining truly undeterrable individuals in some type of facility, if they meet the [dangerousness] prediction criterion"). Slobogin's proposal that the proof of the defendant's future dangerousness must become ever clearer the longer his detention persists also finds a remarkable parallel in the Federal Constitutional Court's jurisprudence. *Compare id.* at 52 ("Although each new commitment [of the detainee] need not be preceded by a new anti-social act …, it should be permitted only upon increasingly more stringent proof of dangerousness. … At some point, however, release should be required simply because the requisite certainty level demanded by the proportionality principle has become so high it cannot be met by any type of evidence.") *with* Constitutionality of Removal of Time Limit, NJW (2004), 739 (742) (in order to acknowledge the importance of the detainee's right to freedom and its ever-growing injury through prolonged detention, "the longer the treatment in preventive detention lasts, the stricter the conditions that must be satisfied to demonstrate the appropriateness of the denial of the detainee's freedom").

203 *See* Constitutionality of Removal of Time Limit, NJW (2004), 739 (745–46).

tion had to be justified by some kind of mental or social deficit, the detainee was already being offered treatment for it.[204]

Thus, the special status of the reform measures neatly solved two conceptual problems at once, at least in the eyes of the Court. First, since preventive detention was not criminal in nature, a preventive detention order could not possibly violate the German constitutional principles forbidding double criminal punishments for the same offense, or punishment for an act that was not a crime when it was committed.[205] Second, preventive detention was part of the reform measures, which served solely therapeutic and rehabilitative purposes.[206] Therefore, to the extent that the constitutionality of preventive detention depended on it having a therapeutic character distinct from criminal punishment,[207] this therapeutic character was inherent in the nature of the detention scheme itself.[208]

Unlike the United States Supreme Court in *Crane*, the German Court had no need to grapple with the distinction – if there is one – between "the dangerous sexual offender [with a] serious mental illness, abnormality or disorder," who may be indefinitely imprisoned past the authorized term of confinement and the "dangerous but typical recidivist convicted in an ordinary criminal case," who must be released at the end of his officially-imposed prison sentence.[209] And, *Crane* and *Hendricks* are hardly the only times the Supreme Court has been forced by American constitutional doctrine to ponder these imponderables.[210]

F. Conclusion

The remaining question is, of course, whether having preventive-detention laws is desirable.[211] It is not hard to understand why democratic governments respond to severe pressure to protect their citizens from offenders who have given every indication of posing a

---

204 *Id.* at 741 (observing that most secure facilities provide special privileges to preventive-detention detainees based on the non-punitive nature of their confinement, and that the detainees were generally offered "therapeutic, employment, and training opportunities" that most of them took advantage of).
205 *Id.* at 744–47. It should be noted that the prisoner in the February 5 decision was not challenging preventive detention as such; he was challenging the fact that he was not released from detention after 10 years, in accordance with the legal regime in existence when his detention was originally ordered.
206 Id at 745 ("Prison sentences and preventive detention pursue fundamentally different goals.")
207 *See id.* at 741 (although constitutional requirements required preventive detention to be more than mere "warehousing" (*Verwahrvollzug*) of criminals, actual psychiatric therapy was not required so long as detainees were subjected to program of resocialization designed to make possible their eventual release).
208 Throughout its history, preventive detention has been challenged by German scholars as little more than imprisonment in a slightly different form. See KINZIG, *supra* note 198, at 117–21. *See also* Joachim Käppner, *Außer wegsperren machen die nichts*, SÜDDEUTSCHE ZEITUNG, 5 February 2004 (reporting one detainee's complaint: "The resocialization here is so small, you don't even *see* it anymore. They're not doing anything except locking us up.") *available at* http://www.sueddeutsche.de/panorama/artikel/131/26105/
209 Kansas v. Crane, 534 U.S. 407, 413 (2001).
210 For instance, Foucha v. Louisiana, 504 U.S. 71 (1992), involved Kevin Foucha, who had been acquitted of a crime because of insanity. He was locked in a secure psychiatric facility, and was denied release from the facility because he appeared to be dangerous and because he suffered "antisocial personality disorder." The Supreme Court explicitly found Foucha's future dangerous an insufficient ground for his further confinement, and ruled that the diagnosis of antisocial personality disorder was insufficient on medical grounds to permit his future confinement, since antisocial personality disorder is "a condition that is not a mental disease and that is untreatable." *Id.* at 75.
211 For arguments in favor of the general idea of focusing the attention of the criminal justice system on especially violent offenders, including by means of authorizing post-sentence preventive confinement for them, *see* JEAN FLOUD & WARREN YOUNG, DANGEROUSNESS & CRIMINAL JUSTICE (1981) and Slobogin, *supra* note 184.

considerable future danger of violence.[212] As the Federal Constitutional Court argued, techniques of violence prediction, while still admittedly crude, have improved recently.[213] Even given the inevitable incidence of false positives, preventive detention, when carefully regulated and targeted against the most serious offenders, could surely prevent numerous crimes.

Can this consequentialist argument justify an "acceptable" level of intrusion into a particular detainee's right to return to society after he has served the prison sentence handed down in accordance with law? I have previously argued that it cannot.[214] In my view, the attempts of the high courts of Germany and the United States to reconcile subsequently-imposed preventive detention with the rule of law fall short. As one reads the respective decisions, it is hard to avoid the impression that definitions and categories are being stretched beyond recognition in order to fit the notion of subsequent preventive detention into the legal landscape. The American courts never satisfactorily answer the question why the State is permitted to take away someone's freedom to treat them for a mental condition that is neither an illness nor treatable. If we lock up a person only until he can be healed of his tendencies, and simultaneously declare that his tendencies cannot be healed by any available method, shouldn't we simply admit that we are locking him up for the foreseeable future, and perhaps his entire life? As one commentator recently pointed out, of the more than 500 people committed to "therapy" under California's SVP law in the first nine years of its existence, only two had been released again into the community.[215]

Nor, does the Federal Constitutional Court's reasoning come across as particularly convincing. In the February 5 decision, the Court holds that "ordinary" preventive detention is *not* criminal punishment, even though it may well be carried out within a prison,[216] and is ordered as part of the State's reaction to a criminal act.[217] This line of reasoning, of course, exempts preventive detention from the constitutional regulations that attend criminal punishments. Five days later, however, the same Court holds that the state-level subsequent preventive detention laws must be considered a part of the criminal law. The Court justified these seemingly contradictory outcomes with an exceptionally nuanced exploration of the distinction between the goals and justification of criminal punishment on the one hand, and the Reform and Prevention Measures, on the other.

Reasonable minds, however, may differ on the question of whether this conceptual distinction is robust enough to remove the punitive character from what is, in essence, a sen-

---

212 For an argument that American and German political culture differ in ways that affect the ability of ordinary citizens to demand longer prison sentences, *see* Michael Tonry, *Why Aren't German Penal Policies Harsher and Imprisonment Rates Higher?*, 5 GERMAN LAW JOURNAL 1187, 1204–05 (2004) at http://www.germanlawjournal.com/pdf/.Vol05No10/PDF_Vol_05_No_10_1187–1206_Public_Tonry.pdf). Tonry notes that Germany has largely been an exception to a trend of increasingly harsh penal policy in Western Europe and North America, and suggests this fact is explained by (1) less widespread public support for a harshly punitive penal policy in German as compared to countries like the United States and Britain, (2) the fact that the German public tend to trust unelected elites to form and implement criminal justice policy; and (3) the relatively widespread consensus among these influential elites in favor of a penal policy favoring resocialization and rehabilitation. *Id.*
213 Constitutionality of Abolition of Time Limit, NJW (2004), 739 (742) (arguing that improvements in the state of knowledge concerning habitual criminals had "considerably improved" the ability to render reliable prognoses of future dangerousness).
214 *See* Andrew Hammel, *The Importance of Being Insane: Sexual Predator Civil Commitment Laws and the Idea of Sex Crimes as Insane Acts*, 32 HOUS. L. REV. 775 (1995).
215 Morris, *supra* note 104, at 1209.
216 Constitutionality of Abolition of Time Limit, NJW (2004), 739 (744) (arguing that it was not inappropriate for preventive detention to occur in secure facilities pursuant to the "regulations for general criminal incarceration," given that both preventive detention and criminal punishment relied on the removal of personal freedom to achieve their purportedly different ends).
217 *Id.*

tence of potentially lifelong confinement in a prison. Confronted with the nice distinctions employed by both the German and American courts in their efforts to uphold preventive detention, one recalls H.L.A. Hart's acerbic commentary on German preventive-detention laws: "Certainly the prisoner who after serving a three-year sentence is told that his punishment is over but that a seven-year period of preventive detention awaits him, and that this is a 'measure' of social protection, not a punishment, might think he was being tormented by a barren piece of conceptualism – though he might not express himself in that way."[218]

---

218 H.L.A. HART, PUNISHMENT AND RESPONSIBILITY: ESSAYS IN THE PHILOSOPHY OF LAW 166–67 (1968) (criticizing as "somewhat metaphysical" and "artificial" the Continental "'double-track'" system, which specifies that prison sentences are punishment imposed for the offense, but preventive detention is simply a "'measure' orientated to the criminal's character and the needs of society").

The Impact of Directive 1999/44/EC on German Sales Law

Peter Rott*

The implementation of Directive 1999/44/EC has turned German sales law on its head and has led to a major reform of the general contract law. Old problems have been solved, and new ones created. Academics and practitioners have commented widely on the reform, and their perceptions range from fundamental opposition to strong enthusiasm. This article attempts to give an impression of the significance of these changes for German sales law and of the most controversially debated issues under the new law. It also deals with the acceptance of the new provisions with their European origin by academics and by the courts that had already ample opportunity to engage with the new provisions.

A. A Brief History of German Sales Law

The *Bürgerliches Gesetzbuch* (BGB, German Civil Code) was adopted in 1895 and the provisions on sales remained largely unchanged prior to the implementation of the Consumer Sales Directive 1999/44/EC. Previously, only one major attempt to modernize contract law was made.[1] In 1979, the former Minister of Justice commissioned a study on the reform of German contract law. On the basis of this study,[2] a Commission on Contract Law Reform was established that produced an impressive report.[3] While the proposals by this Commission were never enacted, they were of considerable influence when it came to the implementation of Directive 1999/44/EC.

Conceptually, German sales law was still based on Roman law and therefore out of date. At the same time, German sales law, and German law of obligations in general, deviated largely from modern international doctrine, as embedded in the Convention on the International Sale of Goods (CISG).[4] Legal practice had remedied many problems.

---

* Junior Professor for Private Law with a focus on European Private Law, University of Bremen. This article builds upon Peter Rott, *German sales law two years after the implementation of Directive 1999/44/EC*, 3 GERMAN LAW JOURNAL [GLJ] 237 (2004), *available at* http://www.germanlawjournal.com. Email: rott@uni-bremen.de.
1 *See also* HANS SCHULTE-NÖLKE, THE NEW GERMAN LAW OF OBLIGATIONS: AN INTRODUCTION (2002) *at* http://www.iuscomp.org/gla/literature/schulte-noelke.htm.
2 The report on sales law was produced by Ulrich Huber in GUTACHTEN UND VORSCHLÄGE ZUR ÜBERARBEITUNG DES SCHULDRECHTS, vol. 1, 647 (*Bundesministerium der Justiz* [Federal Ministry of Justice – BMJ] ed., 1981).
3 ABSCHLUßBERICHT DER KOMMISSION ZUR ÜBERARBEITUNG DES SCHULDRECHTS [FINAL REPORT OF THE COMMISSION ON THE REFORM OF THE LAW OF OBLIGATIONS] (BMJ ed., 1992).
4 For an account, *see* Stefan Grundmann, *European Sales Law – Reform and Adoption of International Models in German Sales Law*, 9 EUROPEAN REVIEW OF PRIVATE LAW [ERPL] 239 (2001).

Consequently, the 'black letter law' no longer reflected legal practice.[5] A few examples illustrate the need for reform.

First, German law of obligations drew a sharp distinction between remedies for impossibility of performance, delayed performance, and the breach of ancillary duties. On top of this, it provided for special rules for bad performance, for example, of the seller's duty under a sales contract. In sales law, the right to specific performance ceased to exist once the specified good was delivered, irrespective of whether or not the good was in conformity with the contract. From the moment of delivery, a special warranty regime took over that deviated largely from the general rules on breach of contract ("warranty theory" or *Gewährleistungstheorie*). In some respects, this special warranty regime was advantageous for the buyer relative to his or her rights under general contract law, especially in allowing immediate rescission of the contract. On the other hand, one of its most problematic features was its short limitation period of only six months, rather than a period of up to thirty years that applied otherwise. This difference led to great difficulties in practice, in particular regarding the question of whether goods delivered were defective (*peius*), with the consequence of a six month limitation period, or completely different (*aliud*), with the consequence of a thirty year limitation period for the delivery of the goods the parties had agreed upon.[6] Similarly, the distinction between defects and misrepresentation became enormously important, in particular in the context of the sale of enterprises, since – again – the limitation period for misrepresentation was thirty years.[7] This difference in limitation periods also necessitated a distinction between defects of goods and the breach of ancillary duties, such as correct instructions[8] or appropriate packaging,[9] and between defects of goods and consequential damage (*Mangelfolgeschaden*).[10] Finally, the short limitation periods led courts to apply tort law in certain cases where products were destroyed due to a defect of a component (*weiterfressender Schaden*) since tort law provided for a longer limitation period of three years from the time the purchaser was aware of the damage, with a maximum period of ten years.[11] It seems fair to say that these court decisions were sometimes arbitrary,[12] and that their focus on the individual case did not serve legal certainty well.

Second, the previous law of sales focused on the sale of specifically determined items,

---

5 See Andreas Heldrich, *Ein zeitgemäßes Gesicht für unser Schuldrecht*, 54 NEUE JURISTISCHE WOCHENSCHRIFT [NJW] 2521, 2522 (2001). For a proponent of this initiative see Jan Wilhelm, *Schuldrechtsreform 2001*, 56 JURISTENZEITUNG [JZ] 861 (2001), and Holger Altmeppen, *Schadensersatz wegen Pflichtverletzung*, 54 DER BETRIEB [DB] 1131 (2001); the latter with a reply by Stefan Lorenz, *Schadensersatz wegen Pflichtverletzung – ein Beispiel für die Überhastung der Kritik an der Schuldrechtsreform*, 56 JURISTENZEITUNG [JZ] 742, 745 (2001).

6 See, e.g., Grundmann, *supra* note 4, at 249; Stefan Lorenz, *Aliud, peius und indebitum im neuen Kaufrecht*, 43 JURISTISCHE SCHULUNG [JuS] 36 (2003). On the famous example of the delivery of winter wheat seed instead of summer wheat seed, decided by the BGH in 1967, NEUE JURISTISCHE WOCHENSCHRIFT [NJW] 640 (1968), see SCHULTE-NÖLKE, *supra* note 1.

7 See, e.g., Gert Brüggemeier, *Das neue Kaufrecht des Bürgerlichen Gesetzbuches*, 56 WERTPAPIER-MITTEILUNGEN [WM] 1376, 1379 (2002); Christiane Brors, *Zu den Konkurrenzen im neuen Kaufgewährleistungsrecht*, 56 WERTPAPIER-MITTEILUNGEN [WM] 1780, 1784 (2002).

8 See 47 ENTSCHEIDUNGEN DES BUNDESGERICHTSHOFES IN ZIVILSACHEN [BGHZ] 47, 312 (1967).

9 See 66 BGHZ 208 (1977); 87 BGHZ 88 (1984). See also Grundmann, *supra* note 4, at 249; Brüggemeier, *supra* note 7, at 1378.

10 On this issue, see André Janssen, *Die Zukunft des weiterfressenden Mangels nach der Schuldrechtsmodernisierung*, 18 VERBRAUCHER UND RECHT [VuR] 60 (2003).

11 See, in particular, Bundesgerichtshof [BGH], 45 NEUE JURISTISCHE WOCHENSCHRIFT [NJW] 1678 (1992); Bundesgerichtshof [BGH], 51 NEUE JURISTISCHE WOCHENSCHRIFT [NJW] 2282 (1998).

12 See also Markus Krajewski, *The New German Law of Obligations*, 14 EUROPEAN BUSINESS LAW REVIEW [EBLR] 201, 203 (2003).

and consequently on the remedies of rescission (*Wandelung*) and reduction of price.[13] Only in the case of goods described in a general manner (generic goods), was replacement an available remedy. The remedy of repair was not provided by the BGB, but was usually effected in practice by agreement. The remedy of *Wandelung* was regulated in a very antiquated fashion. In theory, it was only available upon agreement between purchaser and seller. Thus, a purchaser who wished to rescind the contract would have had to sue the seller for agreement to the rescission first. If the seller then failed to return the purchase price, the purchaser would have to sue him again. Fortunately, courts avoided this strange consequence that was, nevertheless, laid down in the BGB.

Third, German sales law was somewhat restrictive with regard to the relevant characteristics of the subject matter of the sale. Although German courts followed, in principle, a subjective approach under which the necessary quality of goods is determined by agreement between the parties, they were reluctant to consider descriptions of the goods that were made in public statements of either the seller or a third party.[14] Moreover, it was difficult to enforce statements about characteristics of the goods beyond their physical appearance and quality, such as the good reputation of a guest-house.[15]

Outside the scope of the Directive, one should note that German sales law provided for different regimes for defects in quality and defects in the legal status of goods.[16] Another much criticized feature was the previous outdated regime for damages in sales law. Under the previous § 463 BGB, the purchaser could only claim damages if either the seller had guaranteed specific characteristics of the goods or if he had acted fraudulently. In cases of pure negligence, no such claim was granted.

Finally, with respect to the law of obligations in general, courts developed an immense body of case-law that was not visible in the BGB. Prime examples were the rules on breach of ancillary duties (*positive Vertragsverletzung*) and on breach of pre-contractual obligations (*culpa in contrahendo*). Such absence of important rules did not serve well the idea of a complete codification that the BGB aimed for.

B. The Implementation Debate and Process

It became clear at a very early stage that Germany, unlike other Member States, would not create an additional body of consumer sales law that would be separate from sales law in general.[17] Rather, the doctrinal underpinning of the sales law of the BGB was adjusted to

---

13 See the critique by Gert Brüggemeier, *Zur Reform des deutschen Kaufrechts – Herausforderungen durch die EG–Verbrauchsgüterkaufrichtlinie*, 55 JURISTENZEITUNG [JZ] 529, 531 (2000).
14 See, e.g., Karl-Nikolaus Peifer, *Die Haftung des Verkäufers für Werbeangaben*, JURISTISCHE RUNDSCHAU [JR] 265 (2001); Simone Jorden & Michael Lehmann, *Verbrauchsgüterkauf und Schuldrechtsmodernisierung*, 56 JURISTENZEITUNG [JZ] 952, 954 (2001). The view expressed by Grundmann, *supra* note 4, at 246, seems overly optimistic.
15 See Bundesgerichtshof [BGH], 45 NEUE JURISTISCHE WOCHENSCHRIFT [NJW] 2564, 2565 (1992). See also Carola Glinski & Peter Rott, *Umweltfreundliches und ethisches Kaufverhalten im harmonisierten Kaufrecht*, 14 EUROPÄISCHE ZEITSCHRIFT FÜR WIRTSCHAFTSRECHT [EuZW] 649, 650 (2003), concerning statements on environmentally sound or ethical production.
16 Whether or not defects in the legal status of goods are subject to Directive 1999/44/EC is being discussed controversially in Germany. For an inclusion of defects in the legal status, see Grundmann, *supra* note 4, at 250.
17 See Grundmann, *supra* note 4, at 242. One of the reasons was that consumer sales contracts account for the vast majority of sales contracts anyway, see Christian Schubel, *Schuldrechtsreform: Perspektivenwechsel im Bürgerlichen Recht und AGB-Kontrolle für den Handelskauf*, 56 JURISTENZEITUNG [JZ] 1113, 1115 (2001). Previous special rules for the sale of animals were abolished, see Harm Peter Westermann, *Das neue Kaufrecht*, 55 NEUE JURISTISCHE WOCHENSCHRIFT [NJW] 241, 252 (2002).

Directive 1999/44/EC and the CISG, while some specific elements of the Directive were only reserved to consumer sales contracts. However, the main focus of the discussions was on the question of whether this provided an opportunity to modernize major parts of contract law and to integrate the consumer-specific legislation, hitherto adopted in a piecemeal fashion to implement the various measures of EC consumer law, into the BGB.[18] There were numerous supporters for both solutions;[19] more than 200 German professors signed a manifesto that favored a narrow approach to implementation, restricted to sales law only.

In contrast, the former Minister of Justice, Herta Däubler-Gmelin, and the responsible official in the Ministry of Justice, Jürgen Schmidt-Räntsch, decided to renew the project of the 1980s and to reform contract law drastically.[20] Apart from the general need for reform, this decision was taken with an eye to the EC Commission's considerations to create a whole EC Contract Code. Instead of merely reacting to the development at EC level, the German Ministry of Justice intended to be at the forefront of contract law reform, and to introduce new rules that might be capable of serving as a model for EC legislation. In a process that was unprecedented in its openness and transparency,[21] the Ministry of Justice published a Consultation Paper in August 2000. This Consultation Paper was followed by intense discussion that included expert groups of government officials, academics and lobby groups, and also academic conferences. In May 2001, a bill was laid before Parliament[22] that was largely based on the expert groups' reports.[23]

The outcome of this process was a complete reform not only of consumer sales law and sales law in general but also of the law of limitation periods, of the consequences of breach of contract, of the law of services, of credit law, and also of some fields of consumer law.[24]

Most importantly, a harmonized regime for all types of breach of contract was introduced, with merely a few additional rules for cases of impossibility of performance and for delayed performance. Case-law on *positive Vertragsverletzung* and *culpa in contrahendo* was codified.[25] Most consumer law, including the rules on unfair contract terms, doorstep selling, distance selling, time-sharing and consumer credits, was integrated into the BGB.[26] The normal limitation period was shortened from thirty years to three years, beginning at the year in which the claimant gained knowledge of the grounds of his claim and of his debtor.[27]

---

18 On the latter, see, e.g., Wulf-Henning Roth, *Europäischer Verbraucherschutz und BGB*, 56 JURISTENZEITUNG [JZ] 475 (2001).

19 In favor of a restrictive implementation see, e.g., Wolfgang Ernst & Beate Gsell, *Kaufrechtsrichtlinie und BGB*, 21 ZEITSCHRIFT FÜR WIRTSCHAFTSRECHT [ZIP] 1410 (2000).

20 *See, in particular*, Herta Däubler-Gmelin, *Die Entscheidung für die so genannte Große Lösung bei der Schuldrechtsreform*, 54 NEUE JURISTISCHE WOCHENSCHRIFT [NJW] 2281 (2001).

21 For an appraisal, see Claus-Wilhelm Canaris, *Die Reform des Rechts der Leistungsstörungen*, 56 JURISTENZEITUNG [JZ] 499, 524 (2001).

22 BUNDESTAGSDRUCKSACHE [Printings of the Federal Parliament – BTDrucks] 14/6040.

23 For a description of this process, see Grundmann, *supra* note 4, at 241.

24 For a brief overview in English, see Peter Schlechtriem, *The German Act to Modernize the Law of Obligations in the Context of Common Principles and Structures of the Law of Obligations in Europe*, 2 OXFORD UNIVERSITY COMPARATIVE LAW FORUM (2002) at http://ouclf.iumscomp.org.; SCHULTE-NÖLKE, *supra* note 1; Krajewski, *supra* note 12.

25 For details, see Canaris, *supra* note 21; Daniel Zimmer, *Das neue Recht der Leistungsstörungen*, 55 NEUE JURISTISCHE WOCHENSCHRIFT [NJW] 684 (2002); Johann Kindl, *Das Recht der Leistungsstörungen nach dem Schuldrechtsmodernisierungsgesetz*, 56 WERTPAPIER-MITTEILUNGEN [WM] 1313 (2002); Dieter Medicus, *Die Leistungsstörungen im neuen Schuldrecht*, 43 JURISTISCHE SCHULUNG [JuS] 521 (2003).

26 For details, see VERBRAUCHERSCHUTZ UND SCHULDRECHTSMODERNISIERUNG (Micklitz et al. eds., 2001).

27 For details, see Detlef Leenen, *Die Neuregelung der Verjährung*, 56 JURISTENZEITUNG [JZ] 552 (2001); Heinz-Peter Mansel, *Die Neuregelung des Verjährungsrechts*, 55 NEUE JURISTISCHE WOCHENSCHRIFT [NJW] 89 (2002).

Following the reform of sales law, the law of services was also reformed in order to adjust the two regimes.[28] Credit law was also modernized since the credit law provisions of the BGB had almost completely lost their relevance in practice.[29]

The sales law reform extends to all sales contracts except for those that are covered by the CISG.[30] The concept of conformity as laid down in Art. 2 of the Directive and the remedies that are provided in Art. 3 of the Directive now apply broadly. Merely the seller's redress, Art. 4, the reversal of the burden of proof, Art. 5 (3), some features of the consumer guarantee, Art. 6, and the mandatory nature of the rules, Art. 8 (1), were reserved to consumer sales contracts. At the same time, only a few rules of the Commercial Code that apply exclusively to commercial contracts have survived the reform.[31]

C. The Implementation in Detail

Generally speaking, the new German sales law is in line with the requirements of Directive 1999/44/EC.[32] For linguistic reasons,[33] the legislature has changed most of the wording of the relevant provisions but emphasized that the new law has, of course, to be interpreted in light of the Directive.[34]

I. Relevance of the Distinction Between Consumer Sales Contracts and Other Sales Contracts

1. Exclusively applicable provisions and mandatory nature

The distinction between consumer and non-consumer sales contracts is, of course, relevant insofar as there are a few rules that apply exclusively to consumer sales contracts as defined in § 474 BGB. Beyond that, the new sales law is only mandatory as far as consumer sales contracts are concerned, according to § 475 BGB, while the provisions can be deviated from by agreement in non-consumer sales contracts. Whether or not a sales contract is a consumer sales contract depends on the particular circumstances. Lower instance courts decided that a dentist who sold her old car that she used for private and for business purposes was dealing as a consumer since she had no special knowledge of cars.[35]

---

28 For details, see Herbert Roth, *Die Reform des Werkvertragsrechts*, 56 JURISTENZEITUNG [JZ] 543 (2001); Jörg Schudnagies, *Das Werkvertragsrecht nach der Schuldrechtsreform*, 55 NEUE JURISTISCHE WOCHENSCHRIFT [NJW] 396 (2002).
29 For details, see Peter O. Mülbert, *Die Auswirkungen der Schuldrechtsmodernisierung im Recht des "Bürgerlichen" Darlehensvertrags*, 56 WERTPAPIER-MITTEILUNGEN [WM] 465 (2002); Udo Reifner, *Schuldrechtsmodernisierung und Verbraucherschutz bei Finanzdienstleistungen*, 13 ZEITSCHRIFT FÜR BANKRECHT UND BANKWIRTSCHAFT [ZBB] 193 (2001).
30 Previous special rules for the sale of animals were abolished. For the rules on animals under the new sales law see, e.g., Sascha Brückner and Antje Böhme, *Neues Kaufrecht – Wann ist ein Tier "gebraucht"?*, 56 MONATSSCHRIFT FÜR DEUTSCHES RECHT [MDR] 1406 (2002).
31 See, e.g., Gerd Müller, *Zu den Folgen des Rügeversäumnisses i. S. d. § 377 HGB*, 23 ZEITSCHRIFT FÜR WIRTSCHAFTSRECHT [ZIP] 1178 (2002).
32 For an overview see, e.g., Brüggemeier, *supra* note 7, at 1376; Westermann, *supra* note 17, at 241; Thomas Zerres, *Das neue Sachmängelrecht beim Kauf*, 17 VERBRAUCHER UND RECHT [VuR] 3 (2002).
33 See the heavy critique by Heinrich Honsell, *Die EU-Richtlinie über den Verbrauchsgüterkauf und ihre Umsetzung ins BGB*, 56 JURISTENZEITUNG [JZ] 278, 279 (2001).
34 An English translation of the relevant provisions by Geoffrey Thomas & Gerhard Dannemann is available at the webpage of the German Law Archive *at* http://www.iuscomp.org/gla.
35 See LG Frankfurt a.M., 19 NEUE JURISTISCHE WOCHENSCHRIFT – RECHTSPRECHUNGSREPORT [NJW-RR] 1208 (2004); AG Bad Homburg, 19 NEUE JURISTISCHE WOCHENSCHRIFT – RECHTSPRECHUNGSREPORT [NJW-RR] 345 (2004).

Thus, in other sales contracts, exclusion clauses are still permitted to a certain extent, provided that they do not violate the law on unfair contract terms. The effects of this distinction between consumer sales and others can already be felt in the context of second-hand cars. These contracts appear to make up the bulk of the case-law applying the new sales law. Since exclusion clauses are no longer allowed, the focus is on means of avoiding liability. One such way is that second-hand car traders formally act as mere agents for private owners of cars.[36] Consequently, the sale is not a consumer sale but a sales contract between private persons in which liability for defects can be excluded.[37] In a judgment of January 2005, the *Bundesgerichtshof* (BGH, German Supreme Court) took a different approach on such agency contracts: In general, the construction is legitimate and takes the sale out of the consumer sales provisions. However, in the individual case, consumer sales law provisions may be circumvented. The relevant criterion is the economic risk of the sale. If the trader guarantees the private seller of the car a fixed sum that is deducted from the purchase price for the new car, the trader is the true seller of the car. If instead the economic risk lies with the previous owner of the old car, the latter is the true seller.[38]

More problems are raised by contract clauses in which the purchaser confirms to be a trader.[39] This latter construction, however, does not hold once the trader is aware of the fact that the purchaser is a consumer, since the consumer's rights cannot be negotiated away by his negating being a consumer.[40] On the other hand, the BGH recently held that a consumer who claimed to be a trader because the seller did not wish to sell to consumers had lost his consumer rights.[41]

2. Principles of Interpretation

The new sales law provisions are intended as the implementation of Directive 1999/44/EC, and therefore they have to be interpreted in the light of this Directive. However, through the extension of most of the provisions of the Directive to sales law in general, the question arose as to whether sales law has to be interpreted in this way now.[42] While no case-law is available yet on this particular issue, most German authors support this view, and case-law on doorstep selling law also points into this direction. The government has made it clear in its proposal for the new sales law that all sales law should follow identical rules and principles. By definition, this must mean the principles of EC consumer sales law,[43] and for reasons of legal certainty this makes perfect sense. A similar principle was recently accepted by the BGH in the famous *Heininger* case on doorstep selling law. The European Court of Justice (ECJ) had decided that the period of withdrawal cannot expire if the

---

36 See Markus Müller, *Die Umgehung des Rechts des Verbrauchsgüterkaufs im Gebrauchtwagenhandel*, 56 NEUE JURISTISCHE WOCHENSCHRIFT [NJW] 1975, 1978 (2003). The agency model was very popular from 1970 to 1990 for reasons of tax law, see Jens-Hinrich Binder, *Die Inzahlungnahme gebrauchter Sachen vor und nach der Schuldrechtsreform am Beispiel des Autokaufs „Alt gegen Neu"*, 56 NEUE JURISTISCHE WOCHENSCHRIFT [NJW] 393, 394 (2003).
37 See Amtsgericht Rheda-Wiedenbrück, 72 DEUTSCHES AUTORECHT [DAR] 120, 121 (2003). For the opposing view, see Brüggemeier, *supra* note 13, at 532, who proposes to declare such contracts as consumer sales.
38 See Bundesgerichtshof, 58 NEUE JURISTISCHE WOCHENSCHRIFT [NJW] 1039 (2005). See also Oberlandesgericht (OLG) Stuttgart, 57 NEUE JURISTISCHE WOCHENSCHRIFT [NJW] 2169 (2004).
39 See Müller, *supra* note 36, at 1979.
40 See Amtsgericht Zeven, 72 DEUTSCHES AUTORECHT [DAR] 379 (2003).
41 See Bundesgerichtshof, 58 NEUE JURISTISCHE WOCHENSCHRIFT [NJW] 1045 (2005).
42 See, e.g., Hans Christoph Grigoleit & Carsten Herresthal, *Grundlagen der Sachmängelhaftung im Kaufrecht*, 58 JURISTENZEITUNG [JZ] 118, 119 (2003).
43 See BTDrucks 14/6040, 208. See also Claus-Wilhelm Canaris, *Die Nacherfüllung durch Lieferung einer mangelfreien Sache beim Stückkauf*, 58 JURISTENZEITUNG [JZ] 831, 837 (2003).

trader has not informed the consumer of his right to withdrawal.⁴⁴ The *Heininger* case, however, did not fall into the scope of application of the Directive at all because the contract was not concluded in one of the situations set out in Art. 1 of Directive 85/577/EEC. Instead, it came under the broader scope of application of the German implementation in § 1 of the old Doorstep Selling Act.⁴⁵ Thus, from an EC law point of view, there was no need to follow the ruling of the ECJ in that particular case.⁴⁶ Nevertheless, the BGH pointed out that one cannot assume without question that the German legislature intended to create different rules and to allow divergent interpretation of the same German provision, depending on whether the present case comes under the scope of application of both German and EC law or merely under the extended German rules.⁴⁷ In conclusion, all German sales law should now be interpreted in the light of Directive 1999/44/EC.

3. Frame of Reference for the Control of Standard Terms in Commercial Sales Contracts

Since the new sales law is merely mandatory for consumer sales contracts, contracting parties can agree on reduced protection of the purchaser in other sales contracts, particularly commercial sales contracts. This is very often achieved by the use of standard terms. In German law, such standard terms in business contracts are subject to a general fairness test which is, of course, less strict than in consumer contracts but has hitherto applied similar principles.⁴⁸ For example, the BGH held that a clause that allowed rescission of the contract only after three failed attempts to repair the goods was void,⁴⁹ a judgment that was clearly inspired by case-law on consumer sales contracts.⁵⁰ Now the rules on consumer sales that stem from Directive 1999/44/EC have become a model for the regulation of sales law in general, and there is good reason to believe that they will also serve as a frame of reference for the control of standard terms in non-consumer sales contracts.⁵¹ In fact, this would appear to make perfect sense since most of these new provisions equally or similarly appear in the CISG which is designed for the needs of commercial sales.⁵²

---

44 Case C-481/99 Georg und Helga Heininger v. Bayerische Hypo- und Vereinsbank AG, 2001 E.C.R. I-9945. This judgment has received wide attention in Germany. Follow-up preliminary proceedings, brought by the Landesgericht Bochum, 56 NEUE JURISTISCHE WOCHENSCHRIFT [NJW] 2612 (2003), and by the Oberlandesgericht Bremen, 25 ZEITSCHRIFT FÜR WIRTSCHAFTSRECHT [ZIP] 1253 (2004) are still pending. *See also* Peter Rott, *Gemeinschaftsrechtliche Vorgaben für die Rückabwicklung von Haustürgeschäften*, 18 VERBRAUCHER UND RECHT [VuR] 409 (2003).
45 The Doorstep Selling Act (*Haustürwiderrufsgesetz*) has been integrated in §§ 312 ff and 355 ff of the Bürgerliches Gesetzbuch [BGB] [Civil Code], *see, e.g.*, the commentary by Peter Rott *in* DAS NEUE SCHULDRECHT (Wolfhard Kohte et al., 2003).
46 *See also* Grigoleit & Herresthal, *supra* note 42, at 119; Christian Bärenz, *Die Auslegung der überschießenden Umsetzung von Richtlinien am Beispiel des Gesetzes zur Modernisierung des Schuldrechts*, 56 DER BETRIEB [DB] 375 (2003).
47 Bundesgerichtshof, 55 DER BETRIEB [DB] 1262 (2002), with a positive comment by Peter Ulmer, *Anmerkung*, 23 ZEITSCHRIFT FÜR WIRTSCHAFTSRECHT [ZIP] 1080, 1082 (2002). *See also* the critique by Mathias Habersack & Christian Mayer, *Der Widerruf von Haustürgeschäften nach der "Heininger"- Entscheidung des EuGH*, 56 WERTPAPIER-MITTEILUNGEN [WM] 253 (2002).
48 *See, e.g.*, 60 BGHZ, 377, 380 (1973).
49 Bundesgerichtshof, 19 ZEITSCHRIFT FÜR WIRTSCHAFTSRECHT [ZIP] 70 (1998).
50 *See* Schubel, *supra* note 17, at 1115.
51 For more detailed discussion, *see* Schubel, *supra* note 17, at 1113; Westermann, *supra* note 17, at 242.
52 *See, in particular*, Grundmann, *supra* note 4, at 245.

II. Conformity

Under the new § 433 para. 1 s. 2 BGB, the seller has to deliver goods which are in conformity with the contract. This formula marks the shift from the old "warranty theory" to the "performance theory" (*Erfüllungstheorie*) that the CISG and Directive 1999/44/EC follow, namely that the seller only performs if he delivers goods which are in conformity with the contract.[53]

Section 434 para. 1 BGB implements Art. 2 (2), (4) and (5) of the Directive, whereas Art. 2 (3) has found its equivalent in § 442 BGB. Under § 434 para. 1 BGB, the goods as delivered are free from defects as to quality if, upon the passing of the risk, the goods are of the standard of quality agreed in the contract. If the quality has not been agreed expressly, the goods are free from defects as to quality (1) if they are fit for the use specified in the contract and, otherwise, (2) if they are fit for the normal use and their quality is such as is usual in items of the same kind and can be expected by virtue of their nature. For the purposes of the latter, the normal condition includes features which the purchaser may expect by virtue of public statements concerning the goods' features that are made by the seller, the producer or persons assisting him, in particular in advertisements or in connection with labeling, unless the seller was not aware of the statement nor ought to have been aware of it, or at the time of the conclusion of the contract it had been corrected by equivalent means, or it could not influence the decision to purchase the item.[54] § 434 para. 2 BGB relates to assembly and instruction defects.[55] Again, it must be emphasized that the relevance of public statements and of assembly and instruction defects apply to sales law in general, despite considerable resistance of traders during the implementation process.[56] From an EC law perspective, the only criticism may relate to the fact that § 434 BGB, unlike Art. 2 (2)(a) of the Directive, does not mention models and samples *expressis verbis* so that § 434 para. 1 BGB lacks transparency in this respect.[57]

Importantly, the German legislature has also harmonized the regime for non-conformity, for delivery of an *aliud*, and for the delivery for the wrong quantity, § 434 para. 3 BGB.[58] This was done explicitly with a view to Art. 35 CISG, and it has solved a number of problems of the previous sales law.

In contrast, the legal consequences of the breach of ancillary duties other than installing goods or providing installation instructions have not been clarified in the implementation process. Thus, such breach could still come under the general rules on breach and therefore under the longer limitation period of three years. However, there are also scholars who propose to take assembly and corresponding instructions as *pars pro toto* for other ancillary duties, such as appropriate packaging, and to bring all those ancillary duties under

---

53 *See, e.g.*, Dietmar Boerner, *Kaufrechtliche Sachmängelhaftung und Schuldrechtsreform*, 22 ZEITSCHRIFT FÜR WIRTSCHAFTSRECHT [ZIP] 2264, 2265 (2001); Brüggemeier, *supra* note 7, at 1377.
54 *See* on this issue Susanne Augenhofer, *Bedeutung von Werbeaussagen – sowohl des Verkäufers als auch des Herstellers – für die Begründung von Gewährleistungsrechten*, 123 JURISTISCHE BLÄTTER [JBl.] 82 (2001); Michael Lehmann, *Die Haftung für Werbeangaben nach neuem Schuldrecht*, 55 DER BETRIEB [DB] 1090 (2002); Frank Weiler, *Haftung für Werbeangaben nach neuem Kaufrecht*, 56 WERTPAPIER-MITTEILUNGEN [WM] 1784 (2002); Friedrich Bernreuther, *Sachmangelhaftung und Werbung*, 57 MONATSSCHRIFT FÜR DEUTSCHES RECHT [MDR] 63 (2003); Glinski & Rott, *supra* note 15, at 649.
55 For details, *see* Jan Stoppel, *Die Rechte des Käufers nach Lieferung einer mangelhaften Montageanleitung*, 18 VERBRAUCHER UND RECHT [VuR] 176 (2003).
56 For support for this extension, *see* Jorden & Lehmann, *supra* note 14, at 955.
57 *See* Beate Gsell, *Kaufrechtsrichtlinie und Schuldrechtsmodernisierung*, 56 JURISTENZEITUNG [JZ] 65, 66 (2001).
58 For details, *see* Lorenz, *supra* note 6, at 36. Indeed, some German authors argue that Art. 2 (1) of Directive 1999/44/EC requires the inclusion of the delivery of an *aliud* and of too low quantities, *see* Jorden & Lehmann, *supra* note 14, at 952.

the sales law regime. With respect to packaging, this would also mean following Art. 35 (1) CISG.[59] There is no judgment by a court on this issue at present.

The new § 434 BGB arguably has broadened the concept of conformity with the contract with regard to the non-physical properties of the sold good. One example is a case decided by the *Landgericht* (LG, Regional Court) *Ellwangen*. The court held that one of the defects of the Volkswagen car at stake was that it had been manufactured in the Republic of South Africa whereas it was sold as manufactured in the EC.[60] Clearly, the place of manufacture does not as such have an impact on the physical quality of a product. Thus, under previous German sales law, courts would have been highly unlikely to regard a product as being defective for that reason. Nevertheless, consumers may put value to the place of manufacture. Under Art. 2 of the Directive, any characteristics of the goods that the parties agree upon appear to be relevant, including those that are not physically connected with the goods in question, and indeed, the *LG Ellwangen* seems to have adopted this approach under the new § 434 BGB, thereby explicitly declaring the case-law of the BGH under the old sales law no longer relevant. In contrast, the *Oberlandesgericht* (OLG, Higher Regional Court) *Hamm* held that the mere fact that a Renault car was not produced by Renault in France but by Matra in Italy, did not affect its conformity with the contract, although this had an impact on the market value of the car. The court explicitly referred to pre-reform case-law by the BGH.[61]

A highly controversial issue is the extent to which the required quality can be lowered below the usual standard by agreement, for example by defining a car as "wreck".[62] A majority of authors support such a possibility as important for maintaining party autonomy in sales law.[63] However, there must also be limitations in order to prevent traders from circumventing the protection of the consumer.[64] Courts have already rejected such descriptions if they were in obvious contradiction with the protocol on the specific defects of the car.[65] It is certainly safer, from a trader's perspective, to name the defects of a second-hand car so that the consumer is aware of them and liability is excluded under § 442 BGB.[66]

The presumption of non-conformity during the first six months after delivery of Art. 5(3) of the Directive merely applies to consumer sales contracts, § 476 BGB. This provision has been subject to some debate as well. In particular, its application to second-hand cars has been the subject of some controversy. Scholars have argued that the reversed burden of proof in consumer sales law of § 476 BGB does not apply to second-hand cars, due

---

59 *See* Grundmann, *supra* note 4, at 250; Brüggemeier, *supra* note 7, at 1378.
60 Landgericht Ellwangen, 18 NEUE JURISTISCHE WOCHENSCHRIFT – RECHTSPRECHUNGSREPORT [NJW-RR] 517 (2003).
61 Due to the mentioned difference in value, the court held a pre-contractual information obligation to be violated, *see* Oberlandesgericht Hamm, 18 NEUE JURISTISCHE WOCHENSCHRIFT – RECHTSPRECHUNGSREPORT [NJW-RR] 1360 (2003), with a critical comment by Volker Emmerich, *Anmerkung*, 44 JURISTISCHE SCHULUNG [JuS] 163 (2004).
62 Which may cause a conflict with waste law, *see, e.g.*, Müller, *supra* note 36, at 1978.
63 *See, e.g.*, Grundmann, *supra* note 4, at 247; Müller, *supra* note 36, at 1976. *See also* SCHULTE-NÖLKE, *supra* note 1, at III. 3.
64 On the relationship between interpretation of the contract and the prohibition of circumventing the law, under § 475 para. 1 s. 2 BGB, *see* Müller, *supra* note 36, at 1975.
65 *See* Oberlandesgericht Oldenburg, 73 DEUTSCHES AUTORECHT [DAR], 92 (2004), and Amtsgericht Marsberg, 72 DEUTSCHES AUTORECHT [DAR] 322 (2003): The description as *Bastlerfahrzeug* (kit car) was held void under § 475 para. 1 s. 1 BGB because the car was supposed to be admitted to public roads. *See also* Amtsgericht Zeven, 72 DEUTSCHES AUTORECHT [DAR] 379 (2003): The description as *Schrottauto* (wreck) was held irrelevant with a view to an otherwise positive description of the car.
66 *See* Christian Kesseler, *Der Kauf gebrauchter Waren nach dem Diskussionsentwurf eines Schuldrechtsmodernisierungsgesetzes*, 34 ZEITSCHRIFT FÜR RECHTSPOLITIK [ZRP] 70, 71 (2001).

to their very nature as being used.[67] This opinion was rejected by several courts in cases where cars had defects that were not due to the long-term use of the car. For example, in a case decided by the *OLG Köln*,[68] a ten-year-old Porsche had a very untypical engine-defect. The defect came to light one day after delivery, when the purchaser had driven the Porsche for 700 km. Explicitly referring to Directive 1999/44/EC, the *OLG Köln* held that § 476 BGB applies, in principle, to second-hand goods as much as to new goods. A restriction may only be made where defects arise from normal use[69] but certainly not for rare defects such as that in the stated case.[70]

Other issues of § 476 BGB have been considered by the BGH. In a judgment of April 2004, the BGH made it clear that the burden of proof only relates to the time aspect but not the defect as such. In the instant case, a belt in the engine had torn. The consumer claimed that the belt had been defective, whereas the trader claimed that a mistake by the consumer – changing into a lower gear at high speed – was responsible for the defect. The BGH held that the consumer had to prove that the belt had been defective as such before § 476 BGB could apply.[71] In another judgment of November 2004, the BGH held that § 476 BGB was not excluded by the fact that a third party had installed the goods, a garden pool, which turned out to be defective a few days later.[72]

III. Remedies

Section 437 BGB offers the purchaser of a defective good a variety of remedies: § 437 no. 1 BGB grants the right to repeat performance, a notion that includes replacement and repair, while § 437 no. 2 BGB mentions the rights to rescission and reduction of price. In addition to that, the purchaser can claim damages, § 437 no. 3 BGB. In contrast, unlike in contracts of works and services, the purchaser does not have the right to remedy defects himself and then seek compensation for expenses incurred afterwards.[73] Although not immediately obvious, the German legislator has maintained the hierarchy of remedies as provided for by Directive 1999/44/EC.[74] The system of remedies is now the same for defects in the legal status, § 435 BGB.

1. "Second Performance"

Under § 439 para. 1 BGB, the purchaser can claim replacement and repair. The seller is liable for all expenses related to the second performance, in particular transportation, labor and material costs, § 439 para. 2 BGB. If the seller delivers another item to the purchaser, he can claim return of the defective item he first delivered, § 439 para. 4 BGB. In addition,

---

67 *See, e.g.*, Kurt Reinking, *Die Haftung des Autoverkäufers für Sach- und Rechtsmängel nach neuem Recht*, 71 DEUTSCHES AUTORECHT [DAR] 15, 23 (2002).
68 Oberlandesgericht Köln, 3 ZEITSCHRIFT FÜR DAS GESAMTE SCHULDRECHT [ZGS] 40 (2004).
69 *See, e.g.*, Landgericht Dessau, 72 DEUTSCHES AUTORECHT [DAR] 119 (2003); Amtsgericht Offenbach, 72 DEUTSCHES AUTORECHT [DAR] 178 (2003).
70 *See also* Amtsgericht Marsberg, 72 DEUTSCHES AUTORECHT [DAR] 322 (2003); Amtsgericht Zeven, 72 DEUTSCHES AUTORECHT [DAR] 379 (2003) (Catalytic Converter Case).
71 Bundesgerichtshof, 25 ZEITSCHRIFT FÜR WIRTSCHAFTSRECHT [ZIP] 1368 (2004).
72 Bundesgerichtshof, 58 DER BETRIEB [DB] 1005 (2005).
73 *See, e.g.*, Schubel, *supra* note 17, at 1116; Brüggemeier, *supra* note 7, at 1379. This was confirmed by the Amtsgericht Kempen, 57 MONATSSCHRIFT FÜR DEUTSCHES RECHT [MDR] 1406 (2003).
74 *See* Jorden & Lehmann, *supra* note 14, at 957. For a discussion as to whether or not Member States are allowed to deviate from this hierarchy, *see* Peter Rott, *Minimum harmonisation for the completion of the internal market? – The example of Directive 1999/44/EC*, 40 COMMON MARKET LAW REVIEW [CMLREV] 1107 (2003).

the consumer, according to the legislature, has to pay for using the replaced good, and consequently to pay a certain amount of money in order to obtain the good that is in conformity with the contract – a clear breach of Art. 3 (2) of the Directive.[75] In a recent judgment, the *OLG Nürnberg* has explicitly turned against the legislature and interpreted § 439 para. 4 BGB in such a way that the consumer was under no obligation to pay for the use of the defective good.[76]

If replacement or repair is impossible, the seller will be automatically discharged of this duty, § 275 para. 1 BGB. Here, the change of focus from the sale of specific goods to generic goods becomes apparent. This was confirmed in a judgment of 13 December 2002 by the *LG Ellwangen*.[77] A consumer had bought a new Volkswagen Golf that he had chosen from a selection of cars of the same state at the trader's yard. Since the car was not in conformity with the contract, the question arose as to whether the consumer had the right to rescind the contract or whether he could merely claim a replacement which the trader offered. Under the old law, replacement was impossible since the trader only owed the one car that was specified in the contract. In contrast, in line with the majority of academic writing on this issue,[78] the *LG Ellwangen* held that replacement was the correct remedy. This opinion was shared by the *OLG Braunschweig* in a case where a Seat car that had already been registered and that had been driven for 10 km was sold.[79] The decision was welcomed by the majority of academic writing.[80]

If, however, replacement and/or repair is possible but merely at disproportionate expense, the seller can reject either, § 439 para. 3 BGB. What exactly is disproportionate is an important point of discussion in German literature. It was proposed to allow rejection completely once the costs make up 150% of the total value of the goods. The *OLG Braunschweig* has clarified in a recent judgment that the costs for replacement or repair must be compared not to the purchase price but to the objective value of the goods. Thus, the fact that goods were sold at a reduced price, for example, during a promotional period, does not impact on the assessment of whether replacement or repair are disproportionate.[81] It is clear that repair is not disproportionate merely because the seller does not have his own repair facilities.[82] This was confirmed by the *Amtsgericht* (AG, District Court) *Kempen* in a decision of August 2003.[83]

Furthermore, the seller can reject replacement or repair if the other remedy is cheaper

---

75 For details, see Peter Rott, *Austausch der fehlerhaften Kaufsache nur bei Herausgabe von Nutzungen?*, 59 BETRIEBS-BERATER [BB] 2478 (2004). See also Beate Gsell, *Nutzungsentschädigung bei kaufrechtlicher Nacherfüllung?*, 56 NEUE JURISTISCHE WOCHENSCHRIFT [NJW] 1969 (2003); Christoph Woitkewitsch, *Nutzungsersatzanspruch bei Ersatzlieferung?*, 20 VERBRAUCHER UND RECHT [VuR] 1 (2005).
76 See Oberlandesgericht Nürnberg, 58 NEUE JURISTISCHE WOCHENSCHRIFT [NJW] 3000 (2005).
77 Landgericht Ellwangen, 18 NEUE JURISTISCHE WOCHENSCHRIFT – RECHTSPRECHUNGSREPORT [NJW-RR] 517 (2003).
78 See, e.g., Georg Bitter & Eva Meidt, *Nacherfüllungsrecht und Nacherfüllungspflicht des Verkäufers im neuen Schuldrecht*, 22 ZEITSCHRIFT FÜR WIRTSCHAFTSRECHT [ZIP] 2114, 2119. For the opposing view, see Lorenz, supra note 5, 744; id., *Rücktritt, Minderung und Schadensersatz wegen Sachmängeln im neuen Kaufrecht: Was hat der Verkäufer zu vertreten?*, 55 NEUE JURISTISCHE WOCHENSCHRIFT [NJW] 2497 (2002); Andreas Thier, *Aliud- und Minus-Lieferung im neuen Kaufrecht des Bürgerlichen Gesetzbuches*, 203 ARCHIV FÜR DIE CIVILISTISCHE PRAXIS [AcP] 399, 403 (2003).
79 See Oberlandesgericht Braunschweig, 56 NEUE JURISTISCHE WOCHENSCHRIFT [NJW] 1053, 1054 (2003).
80 See Canaris, supra note 43, at 831; Sebastian Pammler, *Zum Ersatzlieferungsanspruch beim Stückkauf*, 56 NEUE JURISTISCHE WOCHENSCHRIFT [NJW] 1992 (2003).
81 See Oberlandesgericht Braunschweig, 56 NEUE JURISTISCHE WOCHENSCHRIFT [NJW] 1053, 1054 (2003).
82 See Bitter & Meidt, supra note 78, at 2122; against the explanations by the German government, BTDrucks 14/6040, 232, and Harm Peter Westermann, *Das neue Kaufrecht einschließlich des Verbrauchsgüterkaufs*, 56 JURISTENZEITUNG [JZ] 530, 535 (2001).
83 See Amtsgericht Kempen, 57 MONATSSCHRIFT FÜR DEUTSCHES RECHT [MDR] 1406 (2006), with a comment by Arnold Dötsch.

and the purchaser is not seriously disadvantaged by the choice. For the choice between replacement and repair, a 10 percent limit was suggested.[84] Therefore, the costs of replacement are calculated by deducting the remaining value of the returned good from the costs for the delivery of a new good.[85] Apart from this, the sheer number of defects can tip the balance towards replacement. In one case, a new car had eight different defects, and later on further defects became apparent. The *LG Münster* that called the car a "lemon" held that it was unacceptable for the consumer to hope for the success of repair but that he could claim replacement.[86] The lack of conformity was considered "minor" in terms of Art. 3 (5) of the Directive, as implemented in § 323 par. 5 BGB, when the costs for repair were only 2 to 3 percent of the purchase price.[87]

2. Rescission

The purchaser can rescind the contract after having unsuccessfully set a reasonable period of time for second performance, § 440 s. 1 BGB. This rule implicitly contains the hierarchy of remedies set out in Art. 3 of the Directive. Exceptions apply where the seller refuses to perform again, or where he rejects replacement and repair in accordance with § 439 para. 3 BGB, or if replacement and repair have failed or are unacceptable to the purchaser. Failure of repair was clearly defined in § 440 s. 2 BGB: Repair has failed after two failed attempts unless the nature of the defect or the circumstances indicate otherwise.[88] This latter rule appears to be rather generous for the seller; perhaps even too generous when compared to Art. 3 (3) of the Directive. In fact, the leading academic opinion with respect to failure of repair under the CISG merely accepts one attempt by the seller.[89]

The above-mentioned obligation to set a reasonable period of time might be a second flaw of the German implementation with respect to remedies since Directive 1999/44/EC implies that such a time-limit exists even without notice.[90] It has been argued that this rule is not in breach of the Directive since the disadvantage of having to set a time-limit is compensated by the advantage of legal certainty.[91] Others find compensation in a specific interpretation of § 440 BGB in the light of Art. 3 of the Directive. They argue that replacement or repair that takes too long can be regarded as failed even though no period has been set. This latter solution, however, appears to be too uncertain for the consumer.[92]

3. Reduction of Price

Under the same conditions under which he can rescind the contract, the purchaser may declare a reduction of price, § 441 para. 1 BGB. Technically, he can do that by unilateral

---

84 *See* Bitter & Meidt, *supra* note 78, at 2122.
85 *See* Oberlandesgericht Braunschweig, 56 Neue Juristische Wochenschrift [NJW] 1053–1054 (2003); Landgericht Münster, 73 Deutsches Autorecht [DAR] 226 (2004).
86 *See* Landgericht Münster, 73 Deutsches Autorecht [DAR] 228 (2004).
87 *See* Oberlandesgericht Düsseldorf, 73 Deutsches Autorecht [DAR] 392 (2004).
88 Some authors doubt that this rule is in line with Directive 1999/44/EC, taking into consideration that Art. 48 CISG is usually interpreted as allowing only one such attempt. *See* Brigitta Jud, *Die Rangordnung der Gewährleistungsbehelfe*, Jahrbuch der Gesellschaft Junger Zivilrechtswissenschaftler [JbJZivRWiss] 205, 218 (2001).
89 *See* Grundmann, *supra* note 4, at 253.
90 *See* Ernst & Gsell, *supra* note 19, at 1418; Rolf Knütel, *Zur Schuldrechtsreform*, 54 Neue Juristische Wochenschrift [NJW] 2519 (2001).
91 *See* Jud, *supra* note 88, at 215.
92 *See, in particular,* Case C-144/99, Commission v. The Netherlands, 2001 E.C.R. I-3541, concerning Directive 93/13/EEC. *See also* the transparency requirement of Art. 9 of Directive 1999/44/EC.

declaration that lowers the purchase price. If the purchaser has already paid the higher price that the parties had agreed upon he can claim return of the difference, § 441 para. 4 BGB. In § 441 para. 3 BGB, the German legislator has specified how to calculate the reduction of price: The purchase price is reduced in the ratio to which the value of the item free of defects would, at the time of the conclusion of the contract, have had to the actual value. Where necessary, the price reduction is to be estimated.

4. Damages

In addition to this, the purchaser can claim damages. The previous extremely restrictive regime has been given up. However, in contrast to Art. 74 CISG, German sales law has maintained a fault-based system for damages even though the rules of the CISG have been adopted for a number of other issues.[93] At least, the purchaser's situation was improved by imposing the burden of proof on the seller, § 280 para. 1 s. 2 BGB. It should, however, be noted that in normal distribution chains the seller is under no obligation *vis-à-vis* the purchaser to examine goods that he merely passes on to him. Therefore, he will usually not be negligent if he sells goods that are not in conformity with the contract.[94]

5. Self-Help

Interestingly, unlike contracts of work and materials, the purchaser does not have the explicit right to remedy defects himself and then seek compensation for expenses incurred afterwards. This has been a highly controversial issue under the new German sales law. In a number of cases, the consumer had his car repaired by a third person and then passed the bill on to the seller who of course refused to pay. The question then was whether or not the seller at least had to pay for his saved expenses. A similar rule, § 326 par. 2 s. 2 BGB, exists in the general part of the German law of obligations. A number of authors had argued that this rule should be applied directly or by analogy to sales law since the consumer would otherwise lose out completely, and the seller would be better off than he deserves. The BGH rejected this approach in February 2005, predominantly with the formal argument that the legislator had introduced the right to self-help in the law on contracts for services but deliberately not in sales law. Moreover, the BGH referred to the intention of the Directive always to give the seller a second chance.[95]

IV. Limitation Periods

Limitation periods were at the center of the implementation debate. As mentioned above, previous German sales law only granted a six months warranty. The 1980s Law Commission had proposed a three year period, and this proposal was resurrected during the course of the implementation debate. This solution was supported by the fact that a

---

93 For details and critique, *see* Brüggemeier, *supra* note 13, at 535; *id., supra* note 7, at 1382.
94 *See also* Brüggemeier, *supra* note 7, at 1383.
95 *See* Bundesgerichtshof, 78 NEUE JURISTISCHE WOCHENSCHRIFT [NJW] 1348 (2005). *See also* Landgericht Gießen, 73 DEUTSCHES AUTORECHT [DAR] 454 (2004); Amtsgericht Kempen, 57 MONATSSCHRIFT FÜR DEUTSCHES RECHT [MDR] 1406 (2006); Martin Tonner, *Ansprüche des Käufers bei Selbstvornahme der Mängelbeseitigung*, 60 VERBRAUCHER UND RECHT [VuR] 207 (2005).

three year limitation period was introduced into German contract law anyway, replacing the previous period of thirty years.[96] Thus, the harmonization of limitation periods across the law of obligations could have put an end to the remaining problems related to the distinction between defects and the violation of pre-contractual information obligations, and it could have also made unnecessary the much criticized case-law on damages for the destruction of goods due to a defect of a component.[97]

Nevertheless, in the end the legislator followed Art. 5 of the Directive. Thus, the limitation period in sales law is two years now, § 438 para. 1 no. 1 BGB. For second-hand goods, the two years period applies, in principle, as well. However, the contracting parties can agree to a period of no less than one year, § 475 para. 2 BGB. For claims for damages, the limitation period of two years can be reduced by agreement as well, § 475 para. 3 BGB. Of course, the control of standard terms remains in place with respect to such reduction.

A notification period has never formed part of German sales law and was not introduced in the course of the implementation of the Directive. Whether or not parties can agree to such a notification period is discussed controversially in German literature.[98] Recently, the *Landgericht Hamburg* declared a standard term void under which customers were supposed to notify obvious defects of delivered goods immediately after delivery. The trader thereby tried to improve his position *vis-à-vis* the transportation company[99] but the clause could also be interpreted in such a way that a consumer might lose his rights if he does not notify obvious defects immediately. The court held that such a clause violated § 475 para. 1 BGB according to which a consumer cannot waive his rights conferred by the new consumer sales law. According to the *LG Hamburg*, Art. 5 (2) of the Directive only allowed a notification period of at least two months from the time the consumer gained knowledge of the non-conformity of the good with the contract. Even with obvious defects, such knowledge is not guaranteed.[100]

V. Redress

The rules on the seller's redress that implement Art. 4 of the Directive[101] exclusively apply to consumer sales in the terms of § 474 BGB. German law grants the final seller remedies only against his supplier, not against the producer. This has been criticized, in particular, with respect to cases where the final seller is held liable for public statements made by the producer, without being given the right to bring a direct claim against the producer.[102]

§ 478 para. 1 BGB applies to cases where the consumer has rescinded the contract or has claimed a price reduction, whereas § 478 para. 2 BGB covers expenses made for repairing or replacing consumer goods. The redress chain ends with the producer of the final product. The suppliers of components included in the finished product are not included.[103] The

---

96 *See, e.g.*, Grundmann, *supra* note 4, at 256.
97 *See supra*, at A. The future of this case-law is now unclear, *see* Brüggemeier, *supra* note 7, at 1384; Janssen, *supra* note 10, at 60; Bernhard Klose, *Das neue Kaufrecht und der weiterfressende Schaden*, 57 MONATSSCHRIFT FÜR DEUTSCHES RECHT [MDR] 1215 (2003).
98 *See* the overview by Carsten Fröhlisch, *Anmerkung*, 20 COMPUTER UND RECHT [CR] 141, 142 (2004).
99 *See* Fröhlisch, *supra* note 98, at 142.
100 *See* Landgericht Hamburg, 20 COMPUTER UND RECHT [CR] 136, 138 (2004).
101 On the requirements of Art. 4, *see* Martin Schmidt-Kessel, *Der Rückgriff des Letztverkäufers*, 55 ÖSTERREICHISCHE JURISTEN-ZEITUNG [ÖJZ] 668 (2000).
102 *See* Boerner, *supra* note 53, at 2266.
103 *See* Peter Mankowski, *Ein Zulieferer ist kein Lieferant*, 55 DER BETRIEB [DB] 2419 (2002). For a discussion of the related problems of the producer, *see* Annemarie Matusche-Beckmann, *Unternehmerregress im neuen Kaufrecht: Rechtsprobleme in der Praxis*, 57 BETRIEBS-BERATER [BB] 2561, 2564 (2002).

presumption of non-conformity within the six months applies to the final seller as well, § 478 para. 3 BGB. This means that the final seller (the retailer) is not left with the burden of proof of a defect in the relationship with his supplier while – in the relationship with the consumer – there is a presumption of a non-defective good at the time of delivery. Also, under § 479 para. 2 BGB the limitation period for redress claims only expires two months after the final seller has fulfilled the consumer's claims, which may be some time after the normal limitation period of two years after delivery has expired.

With respect to the final seller's expenses related to the consumer's claims, the situation is somewhat unclear. The wording of § 478 para. 1 and 2 BGB is very broad and covers all the final seller's expenses, including, for example, expenses for the examination of the good, and even lawyers' fees.[104] Some dispute has arisen about the recoverability of the expenses for the handling of consumers' claims, such as expenses for employing staff that deals with complaints.[105] These expenses may exceed the value of the consumer's claims by far.[106] Therefore, some authors suggest that the wording of § 478 para. 1 and 2 BGB was a mistake by the legislator that should be rectified by a narrow interpretation of these provisions.[107]

The rules are not fully mandatory. Instead, § 478 para. 4 BGB offers the traders the possibility of agreeing on different solutions provided that the final seller is, in an overall perspective, adequately compensated for the loss of his right to redress under § 478 para. 1 and 2 BGB in each individual case. The reason for such flexibility is that the producer may be the person that has to bear the consequences of non-conformity in the end. At the same time, he has, in principle, no influence on the compensation of the consumer by the final seller. Instead, he has to compensate the final seller for whatever expenses the final seller had.[108] Therefore, it was suggested that the producer could establish an after-sales services network that is available, free of charge, to the final seller. Or, a lump-sum agreement could be made that draws on experience made with a certain product.[109] Some authors have even raised the idea of avoiding the redress regime of § 478 BGB by selling goods through foreign subsidiaries.[110]

A major point of critique is that in the case of dual-use goods such as cars, computer equipment etc., the final seller decides *a posteriori* the legal relationship with his supplier. If he sells such goods to a consumer, §§ 478 and 479 BGB apply, and may have implications on the contractual relationship with his supplier. If he sells such goods to a trader as final purchaser, his supplier's liability will be significantly reduced. This creates some uncertainty in the contractual relationship between the final seller and his supplier.[111]

VI. Consumer Guarantees

Consumer guarantees are regulated in §§ 443 and 477 BGB. German implementation codifies previous case-law and follows Art. 6 of the Directive but does not make use of the option of specific language requirements as allowed by Art. 6 (4).

---

104 See Stefan Ernst, *Gewährleistungsrecht – Ersatzansprüche des Verkäufers gegen den Hersteller auf Grund von Mangelfolgeschäden*, 57 MONATSSCHRIFT FÜR DEUTSCHES RECHT [MDR] 4, 5 (2003).
105 See Claudius Marx, *Handlingkosten im Unternehmerrückgriff*, 57 BETRIEBS-BERATER [BB] 2566 (2002).
106 For details, see Jens Böhle, *Teleologische Reduktion beim Rückgriff in der Lieferkette*, 56 NEUE JURISTISCHE WOCHENSCHRIFT [NJW] 3680 (2003).
107 See, e.g., Böhle, *supra* note 106, at 3680.
108 See Böhle, *supra* note 106, at 3681.
109 See BTDrucks 14/6040, 249. For more details, see Schubel, *supra* note 17, at 1118; Jens Matthes, *Der Herstellerregress nach § 478 in Allgemeinen Geschäftsbedingungen – ausgewählte Probleme*, 55 NEUE JURISTISCHE WOCHENSCHRIFT [NJW] 2505 (2002); Ernst, *supra* note 104, at 7.
110 See Matthes, *supra* note 109, at 2508.
111 See Matusche-Beckmann, *supra* note 103, at 2563.

D. Conclusion

Overall, the new German sales law is a huge step towards modernization and towards simplification in practice. The enthusiasm for the new provisions is not shared by all academics. There are those writers who try to read old concepts into the new provisions of the BGB,[112] partly ignoring their European origin. However, the majority of writers welcome the reform and use the European origins of the new provisions in order to escape the constraints that were set by a hundred years of case-law on sales law. On the whole, one dares to say that the initial resistance has faded and that academics fully engage with the new sales law regime, though not without occasionally criticizing the legislator heavily for perceived flaws of the new law.

Also, courts appear to be generally positive about the reform, although again, one can find decisions that stick to the old case-law of the BGH. Certainly, the German implementation of Directive 1999/44/EC is not entirely beyond doubt, and it is suspected that a number of questions will have to be decided by the ECJ.[113] Still, it was a courageous and laudable attempt to deviate from piece-meal solutions and to create a new, coherent codification of sales law and its wider legal environment.[114]

More generally, the Consumer Sales Directive has achieved a breakthrough in German academia and practice in demonstrating an importance of EC private law for day-to-day practice that was hitherto underestimated. With all necessary caution, German academics and practitioners now noticeably engage with EC private law at a far earlier stage.

---

112 *See, e.g.*, the analysis of § 434 BGB by Grigoleit & Herresthal, *supra* note 42, at 123.
113 At the same time, one should not overestimate the role of the ECJ in interpreting the Directive. In particular, with a view to the interpretation of the manifold general clauses that describe the conformity and the remedies system of the Directive, the ECJ might prove to be reluctant and try to avoid becoming the highest instance to decide a multitude of individual cases. *See* Peter Rott, *What is the Role of the ECJ in EC Private Law? – A Comment on the ECJ judgments in Océano Grupo, Freiburger Kommunalbauten, Leitner and Veedfald*, 1 HANSE LAW REVIEW 6 (2005), *available at* http://www.hanselawreview.org.
114 *See also* Westermann, *supra* note 17, at 253.

European Challenges for German Law: An Analysis of the Recent Jurisprudence of the European Court of Justice on the Freedom of Establishment and its Impact on German Corporate Law and Conflict of Laws

Martin Schulz[*]

Introduction

Recent landmark decisions of the European Court of Justice (ECJ) on the freedom of establishment (granted under Articles 43, 48 of the EC Treaty) have challenged some traditional principles of German corporate conflict of laws and German corporate law in general. These decisions, rendered between June 2001 and July 2003, have caused a paradigm shift in German conflict of laws for corporations.[1] As will be highlighted, several important decisions of Germany's *Bundesgerichtshof* (Federal Court of Justice) during the relevant period of time may well be linked to this development (e.g. concerning the private law partnership (*Gesellschaft bürgerlichen Rechts* or *GbR*),[2] the doctrine of piercing the corporate veil (*Durchgriffshaftung*)[3] and the use of shelf companies (*Vorrats- und Mantelgesellschaften*)).[4] At the outset, I will briefly describe the context of European law and the problems created by Germany's so-called "real seat" doctrine (*Sitztheorie*), which, until recent ECJ decisions, had been almost unanimously applied by the courts to

---

[*] Dr. jur. (University of Frankfurt); LL.M. (Yale). Attorney at Law and Knowledge Management Lawyer, Freshfields Bruckhaus Deringer, Frankfurt am Main, and Lecturer in Law at Marburg University. Email: martin.schulz@freshfields.com. The author wishes to thank Peer Zumbansen, York University, Toronto, Canada for many helpful comments.

1 For a description of this paradigm shift *see, e.g.*, Ulrich Forsthoff & Martin Schulz, *Gläubigerschutz bei EU-Auslandsgesellschaften*, in GRENZÜBERSCHREITENDE GESELLSCHAFTEN – PRAXISHANDBUCH FÜR AUSLÄNDISCHE KAPITALGESELLSCHAFTEN MIT SITZ IM INLAND 432 (Thomas Bücker & Heribert Hirte eds., 2005); Otto Sandrock, *Was ist erreicht? Was bleibt zu tun? Eine Kollisions- und Materiellrechtliche Bilanz*, in DEUTSCHES GESELLSCHAFTSRECHT IM WETTBEWERB DER RECHTSORDNUNGEN 33 (Otto Sandrock & Christoph F. Wetzler eds., 2004); Gebhard Rehm, *Völker- und Europarechtliche Vorgaben für die Bestimmung des Gesellschaftsstatuts*, in AUSLÄNDISCHE KAPITALGESELLSCHAFTEN IM DEUTSCHEN RECHT 44 (Horst Eidenmüller ed., 2004); MARCUS LUTTER (ED.), EUROPÄISCHE AUSLANDSGESELLSCHAFTEN IN DEUTSCHLAND (Marcus Lutter ed., 2005); Erich Schanze & Andreas Jüttner, *Die Entscheidung für Pluralität: Kollisionsrecht und Gesellschaftsrecht nach der EuGH-Entscheidung "Inspire Art"*, 48 DIE AKTIENGESELLSCHAFT (AG) 661 (2003); Hans-Peter Westermann, *Die GmbH in der nationalen und internationalen Konkurrenz der Rechtsformen*, 96 GMBHRUNDSCHAU (GMBHR) 4, 6, 11 (2005); Holger Altmeppen & Jan Wilhelm, *Gegen die Hysterie um die Niederlassungsfreiheit der Scheinauslandsgesellschaften*, 57 DER BETRIEB (DB) 1083 sub II (2004) with extensive references to the current German debate.

2 *See* BGHZ 149, 10, NJW (2001) 3622.

3 *See* BGHZ 149, 10; NJW (2001) 3622; BGHZ 150, 61; NJW (2002) 1803; BGHZ 151, 181, NJW (2002), 3024.

4 *See* Bundesgerichtshof (BGH), NEUE ZEITSCHRIFT FÜR GESELLSCHAFTSRECHT (NZG) 170 (2003); BGH, ZEITSCHRIFT FÜR WIRTSCHAFTSRECHT (ZIP) 1698 (2003).

cross-border corporate issues.[5] After analyzing the relevant ECJ decisions and their impact on German law, I will conclude with some remarks on the prospects of German company law reform and the further harmonization of competing legal systems within the European Union.

A. Two Incompatible Principles: Freedom of Establishment and Germany's "Real Seat" Doctrine

I. The Ideal of the Common Market

The European Union was formed to create a common market enabling the free exchange of goods, services and capital among its member states.[6] To achieve this goal, the EC Treaty includes such fundamental rights as the free movement of goods, the freedom of movement of persons, services and capital and the freedom of establishment.[7] The freedom of establishment (Art. 43, 48 EC Treaty) is granted not only to the member states' citizens, but also to companies formed in accordance with the law of one member state and having their registered office, center of administration or principal place of business within the community.[8] Due to the ever-increasing exchange of goods, services and capital within the European common market, many companies are engaged in cross-border activities.[9] However, despite this increased cross-border movement, the unrestricted exchange of goods, services and capital has not yet been achieved. One reason lies in the differences between the member states' legal systems. Efforts to harmonize the law have been only partially successful. The fact that member states' conflict of laws rules that determine the applicable law in cross-border cases have, on the whole, been neither assimilated nor harmonized, further complicates matters.[10] Consequently, companies still face numerous problems when engaged in cross-border activities in the common market. Until the recent ECJ jurisprudence, the activities of foreign companies in Germany had traditionally been restricted by a specific German conflict of laws doctrine, the so-called "real seat" theory (*Sitztheorie*).

---

5 *See* Bundesgerichtshof (BGH), DER BETRIEB (DB) 1114, 1115 (2000) (Überseering Case); further references in Martin Schulz & Peter Sester, *Höchstrichterliche Harmonisierung der Kollisionsregeln im Europäischen Gesellschaftsrecht: Durchbruch der Gründungstheorie nach "Überseering"*, 13 EUROPÄISCHES WIRTSCHAFTS- UND STEUERRECHT (EWS) 545, 547 (2002).
6 *See, e.g.*, Julius von Staudinger & Bernd von Hoffmann, *Vorbem. zu Art. 38 ff. EGBGB, in* BGB No. 8 (13th ed., 2001). *See also* MARTIN SCHULZ, VERFASSUNGSRECHTLICHE VORGABEN FÜR DAS KOLLISIONSRECHT IN EINEM GEMEINSAMEN MARKT 184 (2000).
7 *See* von Staudinger & von Hoffmann, *supra* note 6..
8 *See* Treaty Establishing the European Community, Nov. 10, 1997, 1997 O.J. (C 340) art. 48 [hereinafter EC Treaty].
9 *See* Horst Eidenmüller & Gebhard M. Rehm, *Gesellschafts- und zivilrechtliche Folgeprobleme der Sitztheorie*, 26 ZEITSCHRIFT FÜR UNTERNEHMENS- UND GESELLSCHAFTSRECHT (ZGR) 89 (1997); Ulrich Haas, *Die Betätigungsfreiheit ausländischer Kapitalgesellschaften im Inland*, 50 DER BETRIEB (DB) 150 (1997).
10 In the area of corporate law, attempts to reach agreement on the mutual recognition of companies and legal persons has failed, *see* Eddy Wymeersch, *Company Law in Europe and European Company Law, in* 1ST EUROPEAN JURISTS FORUM 87, 90 (2001). A directive on the cross-border transfer of a company's domicile has been drafted but not yet passed. The European Commission has just presented: *Commission Proposal for a Directive on Cross-Border Mergers of Companies*, COM (2003) 703 final – 2003/0277 (COD); however, large areas of corporate law have not yet been assimilated or harmonized, *see* MATHIAS HABERSACK, EUROPÄISCHES GESELLSCHAFTSRECHT 47 (2nd ed., 2003); Harald Halbhuber, *National Doctrinal Structures and European Company Law*, 38 COMMON MARKET LAW REVIEW, 1385, 1405 (2001).

II. German Conflict of Laws regarding Corporations

With regard to the legal framework of cross-border activities, there are still no unified conflict rules for corporations at the European level,[11] and Germany has not yet passed any conflict of laws rules on this matter either. Previous attempts to create common conflict of laws rules for corporations have failed; accordingly, this area is, to a great extent, still regulated by each member state.[12]

As with most civil law systems, the German legal system is mainly characterized by codified rules. In turn, conflict of laws questions are generally codified in the German Introductory Law of the Civil Code (EGBGB). However, this code contains neither provisions for cross-border corporate law questions, nor specific provisions determining the applicable law for companies moving headquarters between states. The answers to these questions have been left for the courts and legal commentators to determine. In the controversy surrounding the appropriate legal regime for cross-border corporate issues, two competing doctrines dominate the debate.[13]

The so-called "incorporation" theory (*Gründungstheorie*) holds that the legal system of the jurisdiction in which the company's founders choose to incorporate determines the law applicable to the corporation.[14] Under the "incorporation" theory, a company effectively established in one state is generally recognized in every other state, exceptions where public policy reasons ("ordre public", Art. 6 *EGBGB*) justify the application of domestic law to foreign companies.[15]

In contrast, under the so-called "real seat" theory (*Sitztheorie*), the applicable law for corporations is determined by the legal system of the place where the company has its actual head office or center of administration (*tatsächlicher Verwaltungssitz, real seat*).[16] This place is usually defined as the place where fundamental management decisions are put into practice.[17] Although this somewhat artificial approach has often caused practical problems, in particular with regard to multi-national corporations operating in more than one state, the German courts traditionally applied the "real seat" theory to corporate law cases with

---

11 See Wulf-Henning Roth, E. I No. 91, in HANDBUCH DES EU-WIRTSCHAFTSRECHTS (Manfred A. Dauses ed., 2002).
12 Roth, *supra* note 11, at Nos. 90 and 91; *see also* UWE EYLES, DAS NIEDERLASSUNGSRECHT DER KAPITALGESELLSCHAFTEN IN DER EUROPÄISCHEN GEMEINSCHAFT 313 (1990); VIOLA KRUSE, SITZVERLEGUNG VON KAPITALGESELLSCHAFTEN INNERHALB DER EG 5 (1997); Otto Sandrock, *Sitztheorie, Überlagerungstheorie und der EWG-Vertrag: Wasser, Öl und Feuer*, 35 RECHT DER INTERNATIONALEN WIRTSCHAFT (RIW) 505 (1989).
13 *See* Andreas Spahlinger, *Deutsches Internationales Gesellschaftsrecht*, in INTERNATIONALES GESELLSCHAFTSRECHT IN DER PRAXIS 7 (Andreas Spahlinger & Gerhard Wegen eds., 2005); Peter Kindler, *Internationales Handels- und Gesellschaftsrecht*, in MÜNCHENER KOMMENTAR No. 258 (11th ed., 1999); HELMUT GROTHE, DIE AUSLÄNDISCHE KAPITALGESELLSCHAFT & CO., 18 (1989); VIOLA KRUSE, *supra* note 12, at 6; DOMINIK SCHNICHELS, REICHWEITE DER NIEDERLASSUNGSFREIHEIT 144 (1995); MAX HACHENBURG & PETER BEHRENS, *Introduction*, in GMBHG No. 108 (2002); JULIUS VON STAUDINGER & BERNHARD GROSSFELD, INTERNATIONALES GESELLSCHAFTSRECHT No. 15, 22 (1998); DANIEL ZIMMER, INTERNATIONALES GESELLSCHAFTSRECHT 28 (1996).
14 *See* WOLFRAM BECHTEL, UMZUG VON KAPITALGESELLSCHAFTEN UNTER DER SITZTHEORIE 9 (1999); HACHENBURG & BEHRENS, *supra* note 13, at No. 125; Peter Kindler, *supra* note 13, at No. 265; DANIEL ZIMMER, *supra* note 13, at 28; HELMUT GROTHE, *supra* note 13, at 28; Brigitte Knobbe-Keuk, *Umzug von Gesellschaften in Europa*, 154 ZEITSCHRIFT FÜR DAS GESAMTE HANDELSRECHT UND WIRTSCHAFTSRECHT (ZHR) 325, 326 (1990).
15 *See* Brigitte Knobbe-Keuk, *supra* note 14, at 327.
16 The "real seat" theory (*Sitztheorie*) has been traditionally followed by the German courts and literature, *see* Peter Kindler, *supra* note 13, at No. 264, 312 (with reference to German case law); KARSTEN SCHMIDT, GESELLSCHAFTSRECHT 26 (4th ed., 2002); JULIUS VON STAUDINGER & BERNHARD GROSSFELD, *supra* note 13, at No. 17, 22.
17 BGHZ 97, 269 (272) and Peter Kindler, *supra* note 13, at No. 316.

foreign elements.[18] Until the *Centros* judgment of the ECJ in 1999, this theory also had widespread support in German legal literature.[19]

III. Devastating Effects of the Traditional "Real Seat" Theory

Applying the "real seat" theory to companies from other member states had long been criticized as being both incompatible with the freedom of establishment (Art. 43, 48 EC Treaty), doctrine of proportionality and as an inappropriate treatment of foreign legal systems in the Single European Market.[20] Historically, the "real seat" theory was intended to prevent foreign companies from operating in the German domestic market.[21] Thus, advocates of the "real seat" theory welcomed the restriction on foreign companies in Germany as an "automatic sanction."[22]

More specifically, under this theory, a company's legal capacity to sue and be sued before the German courts is determined by the company's "real seat." In Germany, the application of the "real seat" theory dictates that a company has legal capacity only if its "real seat" is *in* the state of its incorporation. Since a company established in another member state will hardly ever have fulfilled the mandatory German requirements for incorporation (such as notarization of the articles of a *GmbH*[23]), foreign companies have been treated as lacking legal capacity.[24] This denial of legal capacity meant that the company could not acquire rights or be a party to legal proceedings in Germany. Additionally, in such circumstances, the shareholders' limitation on liability was disregarded and the shareholders could have potentially been held personally liable.[25] Since the "real seat" theory was traditionally used as a means of rejecting foreign companies and laws, its devastating effects on non-German corporations cannot be seen as merely accidental.[26]

IV. Transforming Foreign Corporations into German Partnerships

To avoid these devastating effects, the Second Senate of the *Bundesgerichtshof* (Federal Court of Justice), in July 2002,[27] applied a modified form of the "real seat" theory to foreign corporations by using some new principles developed in its case law on private law partnerships (*Gesellschaften bürgerlichen Rechts* or *GbR*). The following brief outline of the new case law on private law partnerships will be helpful to illuminate this modified application of the "real seat" theory.

---

18 BGH, 21 March 1986, V ZR 10/85, BGHZ 97, 269 (272), 32 RIW (1986) 822 and Peter Kindler, *supra* note 13, at No. 316. See also Ulrich Forsthoff, *Mobilität von Gesellschaften im Binnenmarkt*, in GRENZÜBERSCHREITENDE GESELLSCHAFTEN – PRAXISHANDBUCH FÜR AUSLÄNDISCHE KAPITALGESELLSCHAFTEN MIT SITZ IM INLAND 50 (Thomas Bücker & Heribert Hirte eds., 2005).
19 See Peter Kindler, *Niederlassungsfreiheit für Scheinauslandsgesellschaften?* NEUE JURISTISCHE WOCHENSCHRIFT (NJW) 1996 (1999); Kindler, *supra* note 13, at No. 371; Holger Altmeppen & Jan Wilhelm, *supra* note 1, at 1083.
20 See Brigitte Knobbe-Keuk, *supra* note 14, at 325.
21 See JULIUS VON STAUDINGER & BERNHARD GROßFELD, *supra* note 13, at No. 38, 43.
22 See JULIUS VON STAUDINGER & BERNHARD GROßFELD, *supra* note 13, at No. 38, 43.
23 See § 2 GmbHG.
24 See, e.g., BGHZ 97, 269. See also Peter Behrens, *Die Umstrukturierung von Unternehmen durch Sitzverlegung oder Fusion über die Grenze im Licht der Niederlassungsfreiheit im europäischen Binnenmarkt (Art. 52 und 58 EWGV)*, 23 ZGR (1994) 1, 8; UWE EYLES, *supra* note 12, at 313, 314; HELMUT GROTHE, *supra* note 13, at 159–160; DOMINIK SCHNICHELS, *supra* note 13, at 149, 150.
25 See UWE EYLES, *supra* note 12, at 313; VIOLA KRUSE, *supra* note 12, at 38; DOMINIK SCHNICHELS, *supra* note 13, at 143, 149.
26 See JULIUS VON STAUDINGER & BERNHARD GROßFELD, *supra* note 13, at No. 38, 43.
27 See BGHZ 151, 204.

1. Specifics of Private Law Partnerships and Recent Case Law

In contrast to the German stock corporation (*Aktiengesellschaft*, or *AG*) and the German limited liability company (*Gesellschaft mit beschränkter Haftung*, or *GmbH*), the *GbR* is an association of persons without corporate organization. According to the statutory concept the *GbR* does not have the status of a corporation as a separate legal entity. The *GbR* is established by the conclusion of a partnership agreement by at least two partners who want to pursue any legal purpose. However, if the partners intend to pursue a commercial business, this partnership will be treated as a commercial partnership (*Offene Handelsgesellschaft*, *OHG* or *Kommanditgesellschaft*, *KG*) in which the partners undertake to pursue a common purpose. A *GbR* is characterized by its partners' unlimited liability for its debts. The assets of the *GbR* belong to all partners jointly and all partners are jointly and severally liable for any liabilities of the *GbR*. Therefore, a *GbR* was typically not considered a separate legal entity. According to the traditional view, the *GbR* could not itself be held liable and could not sue or be sued in legal proceedings.

Beginning in 2001, several landmark decisions of the *Bundesgerichtshof* fundamentally changed this traditional regime. In essence, the *Bundesgerichtshof* has treated the private law partnership here as a legal entity quite similar to the commercial partnership (which has the capacity to sue and be sued). Furthermore, the court has applied the liability regime for partners of a commercial partnership *mutatis mutandis* to partners of a private law partnership.

As mentioned above, in its decision of January 29, 2001,[28] the *Bundesgerichtshof* acknowledged the capacity of a *GbR* to sue and be sued in private proceedings. Furthermore, the court applied the liability rules for partners of German commercial partnerships (*OHG*, *KG*) to partners of a private law partnership (*GbR*). The extension of these liability rules means that, for claims against that partnership, creditors may hold partners of a private law partnership personally liable.

With its decision of February 24, 2002,[29] the *Bundesgerichtshof* further extended the liability of the private law partnership by maintaining that damages caused by the managing directors have to be compensated by the civil law partnership. The court emphasized that partners of a private law partnership are personally and jointly liable for the liabilities of that partnership.

In another landmark decision of April 7, 2003,[30] the *Bundesgerichtshof* held that a new partner of a private law partnership may be held liable for obligations that arose even before he joined the private law partnership. With this decision, the Court thus further expanded the personal liability of partners of a private law partnership by analogizing them to partners of a commercial law partnership.

2. Applying the New Principles of Private Law Partnerships to Foreign Corporations

In an attempt to save the "real seat" doctrine, the Second Senate of the Bundesgerichtshof, in its decision of July 1, 2002, explicitly referred to the above-mentioned case law on private partnerships when considering the treatment of a Jersey-based company in the

---

28 *See* BGHZ 146, 341. For a succinct description of the characteristics of private law partnerships prior to this case law, *see* DIETER BEINERT, CORPORATE ACQUISITIONS AND MERGERS IN GERMANY 3 (1991).
29 *See* BGHZ 154, 88; *see also* Wolfram Waldner, *Anwendung des § 31 BGB auf die GbR – der vorletzte Schritt auf dem Weg zur OHG*, 6 NEUE ZEITSCHRIFT FÜR GESELLSCHAFTSRECHT (NZG) 620 (2003).
30 *See* BGHZ 154, 370.

German courts.³¹ Applying the "real seat" theory the Second Senate held that the Jersey-based company could not be recognized as a corporation under German law. However, the devastating effect of denial of the company's legal capacity, which had usually been the outcome of applying the "real seat" theory, was avoided because, in the view of the Second Senate, the Jersey-based company could be treated as a German private law partnership. Thus, according to the new conceptualization of private law partnerships, the capacity of this Jersey-based private law partnership to sue and be sued in the German courts was acknowledged.

By deciding to treat the Jersey-based company in this manner, the Second Senate avoided stirring the controversy of whether the application of the "real seat" doctrine to corporations established in other EU member states violates the freedom of establishment. Treating the Jersey-based company as a German partnership had the advantages that this foreign company was granted the capacity to sue and be sued in the German courts. However, it also had the obvious disadvantage that the Jersey-based company's shareholders could be held personally liable. In effect, the shareholders of the limited liability company founded under Jersey law were now being treated as partners of a *GbR* with unlimited liability under German law. As I will explain, given recent ECJ decisions this effect of the modified form of the "real seat" doctrine still makes it incompatible with the freedom of establishment.³²

B. Recent ECJ Decisions on the Freedom of Establishment: from *Centros* to *Inspire Art*

Having long been criticized as being incompatible with the freedom of establishment under the EC Treaty, the "real seat" theory came under heavy attack following the ECJ's decision in the *Centros* case in 1999.

I. The ECJ's Judgment in Centros

The *Centros*³³ case concerned a Danish couple living in Denmark who had set up a private limited company, Centros Ltd, in England. In contrast to the requirements under Danish law, under English law this type of company did not require a minimum paid-up share capital. Centros Ltd did not conduct any business at its registered office in England, but operated its business exclusively in Denmark. When the director of the company applied for

---

31 See BGHZ, 151, 204. This decision could be seen as a last attempt to save the "real seat" doctrine, *see* Martin Schulz & Peter Sester, *Höchstrichterliche Harmonisierung der Kollisionsregeln im Europäischen Gesellschaftsrecht: Durchbruch der Gründungstheorie nach "Überseering"*, 13 EUROPÄISCHE WIRTSCHAFTS- UND STEUERRECHT (EWS) 545 (2002); Walter Bayer, *Die EuGH-Entscheidung "Inspire Art" und die deutsche GmbH im Wettbewerb der europäischen Rechtsordnungen*, 58 BETRIEBS-BERATER (BB) 2357, 2361 (2003).

32 See Martin Schulz, *(Schein-)Auslandsgesellschaften in Europa – Ein Schein-Problem?* 56 NEUE JURISTISCHE WOCHENSCHRIFT (NJW) 2705, 2706 (2003); Horst Eidenmüller, *Wettbewerb der Gesellschaftsrechte in Europa*, 23 ZEITSCHRIFT FÜR WIRTSCHAFTRECHT (ZIP) 2233, 2238 (2002), 2240; Erich Schanze & Andreas Jüttner, *Anerkennung und Kontrolle ausländischer Gesellschaften – Rechtslage und Perspektiven nach der Überseering-Entscheidung des EuGH*, DIE AKTIENGESELLSCHAFT (AG) 30, 35 (2003); Ulrich Forsthoff, *EuGH fördert Vielfalt im Gesellschaftsrecht*, 55 DER BETRIEB (DB) 2471, 2474 (2002).

33 Case C-212/97, Centros Ltd., 1999 ECR, I-1493. For an English analysis of *Centros*, see, *e.g.*, Wulf-Henning Roth, *From Centros to Überseering: Free Movement of Companies, Private International Law, and Community Law*, 52 INTERNATIONAL AND COMPARATIVE LAW QUARTERLY 177 (2003); Mathias Siems, *Convergence, Competition, Centros and Conflicts of Law: European company law in the 21st century*, 27 EUROPEAN LAW REVIEW (E.L.REV.) 47 (2002).

registration of a branch office of Centros Ltd in Denmark, the Danish authorities denied the registration on the basis that Centros Ltd was attempting to circumvent the relevant Danish provisions regarding minimum share capital. More specifically, in support of the denial of the application, it was argued that Centros Ltd intended to establish its head office, and not merely a branch office, in Denmark. Referring to its effective formation under English law, Centros Ltd took legal action against this decision. Centros Ltd claimed that, under Articles 52 and 58 EC Treaty (now Articles 43 and 48 EC Treaty), it was entitled to set up a branch office in Denmark[34] under the principles of freedom of establishment.

When the case came before the ECJ, the court decided that:

> A member state which refuses the registration of a branch office of a company which has been validly set up in another member state in which it has its registered office, but at which it does not conduct any business activities, violates Articles 52 and 58 of the EC Treaty (now Articles 43 and 48 EC) if the branch office enables the company to carry out its entire business activities in the state in which the branch office is set up without setting up a company there and thus avoiding the law there regarding the setting up of companies, which makes higher demands on the payment of a minimum share capital.[35]

In the ECJ's opinion, the fact that Centros Ltd had been set up in England solely to circumvent the mandatory minimum share capital requirements in Denmark, did not affect its right to make use of the freedom of establishment principles to set up a Danish branch office.[36] Consequently, the ECJ regarded the refusal of registration by the Danish authorities as an unjustifiable restriction on the freedom of establishment.[37] According to the ECJ, freedom of establishment may, in certain circumstances, be restricted by national regulations. However, any national restriction must pass a test developed by the court. Examining possible justifications for the refusal of the Danish authorities (e.g. the protection of creditors), the ECJ noted specifically that it did not constitute an abuse of the freedom of establishment if a citizen who wished to set up a company did so in the member state where the company law would allow him the greatest freedom.[38]

The ECJ thus left open the possibility of "incorporation law-shopping" according to the preferences of the founders of a company.[39] This endorsement of the right to choose the applicable law for corporations could be seen as an outright rejection of any national legal barriers to the freedom of establishment, such as Germany's "real seat" theory. However, some German commentators dismissed the relevance of this decision for German conflict of laws, given the fact that *Centros* involved a branch office (instead of the inter-member state relocation of a company's "seat") and that the UK and Denmark both adhered to the "incorporation" theory in contrast to Germany's reliance on the "real seat" theory.[40] Even the German courts did not appear particularly impressed by the *Centros* verdict and continued to adhere to the "real seat" theory.[41]

---

34 Case C-212/97, Centros Ltd., 1999 ECR-I-1488.
35 Case C-212/97, Centros Ltd., 1999 ECR-I-1497.
36 Case C-212/97, Centros Ltd., 1999 ECR-I-1491.
37 Case C-212/97, Centros Ltd., 1999 ECR-I-1496, 1497.
38 Case C-212/97, Centros Ltd., 1999 ECR-I-1493.
39 *See* Eva-Maria Kieniger, *Niederlassungsfreiheit als Rechtswahlfreiheit*, 28 ZEITSCHRIFT FÜR UNTERNEHMENS- UND GESELLSCHAFTSRECHT (ZGR) 724, 747 (1999).
40 *See* Peter Kindler, *supra* note 19, at 1996 and Kindler, *Münchener Kommentar*, *supra* note 13, at No. 371.
41 *See, e.g.*, Oberlandesgericht Düsseldorf, 4 NEUE ZEITSCHRIFT FÜR GESELLSCHAFTSRECHT (NZG) 506 (2001); Oberlandesgericht Hamm, 4 NEUE ZEITSCHRIFT FÜR GESELLSCHAFTSRECHT (NZG) 562 (2001). *See also* Ulrich Forsthoff, *supra* note 18, at 51.

II. The ECJ's Judgment in Überseering

Such disregard for the impact of EC law will no longer be possible, since Germany's "real seat" theory itself came under the scrutiny of the ECJ in the *Überseering* case.

1. Facts

Überseering B.V., a Dutch company with the corporate form of a *Beslooten Vennootschap* (*B.V.*), comparable to a German private limited company (*GmbH*), had been effectively incorporated in the Netherlands. It brought claims before a German court for building defects arising from a building contract with a *GmbH*. In 1992, the German *GmbH* had entered into a building contract with Überseering B.V. that obliged the *GmbH* to renovate specific buildings on land owned by Überseering B.V. in Düsseldorf. By the end of 1994, two German citizens had acquired the shares of Überseering B.V. and proceeded to manage its business from Germany. When Überseering B.V. sued the German *GmbH*, the German courts dismissed the action. In accordance with the "real seat" theory, Überseering B.V. was found to be a foreign company not validly formed and registered under German law and, thus, lacking the legal capacity to be party to legal proceedings.

In contrast to *Centros*, this case obviously concerned the compatibility of the "real seat" theory with the EC law. When on March 30, 2000 the case came to appeal before the Seventh Senate of Germany's *Bundesgerichtshof*, it referred the following questions to the ECJ:[42]

(1) Should Articles 34 and 48 EC Treaty be interpreted to mean that because of the freedom of establishment of companies, the legal capacity of a company validly incorporated under the law of one member state cannot be determined according to the law of another state to which the company has moved its actual center of administration and where, under the law of that second state, the company may no longer bring legal proceedings there in respect of claims under a contract?
(2) If the ECJ's answer to the above question is affirmative, does the freedom of establishment of companies (Articles 43 and 48 EC Treaty) require a company's legal capacity to be a party to legal proceedings to be determined according to the law of the state where the company is incorporated?

Under Article 234 EC, the ECJ has jurisdiction to give preliminary rulings concerning the interpretation of the EC Treaty if such a question is raised before a court of a member state. If such a question is raised in a pending case, the member state's court of last instance has to bring the matter before the ECJ.[43]

In its referral to the ECJ, the *Bundesgerichtshof* defended the "real seat" theory by holding that the legal capacity of a company incorporated under the law of another member state did not continue with that company's relocation to Germany. The establishment of the "real seat" in Germany would result in the foreign incorporated company losing its legal capacity.[44] The *Bundesgerichtshof* justified its endorsement of the "real seat" theory primarily by arguing against the "incorporation" theory. Application of the "incorporation" theory permits the shareholders of a company to choose a legal system best suited to their needs when choosing the place of incorporation. In the opinion of the *Bundesgerichtshof*, this ability to choose a favorable jurisdiction is the decisive disadvantage of

---
42 Bundesgerichtshof, 21 ZEITSCHRIFT FÜR WIRTSCHAFTSRECHT (ZIP) 967 (2000).
43 *See, e.g.*, TREVOR HARTLEY, THE FOUNDATIONS OF EUROPEAN COMMUNITY LAW 258 (4th ed., 1998).
44 Bundesgerichtshof, 21 ZEITSCHRIFT FÜR WIRTSCHAFTSRECHT (ZIP) 967 (2000).

using the "incorporation" theory. While favoring shareholders, the system under which choice of the less onerous law is possible neglects the interests of third parties and of the member state in which the company has and operates its "real seat" (*Sitzstaat*).[45] Conversely, the "real seat" theory ensures that the provisions protecting the interests of third parties cannot be circumvented by incorporation in another state. Permitting such a simple evasion of rules under the "incorporation" theory would lead to a "race between legal systems," wherein the legal system with the weakest protection for third parties would inevitably prevail ("race to the bottom"[46]). In the view of the *Bundesgerichtshof*, company creditors in particular needed the kind of protection German law provides, with its detailed rules and regulations regarding a company's capital. In addition, especially with regard to groups of companies, the controlled companies and their minority shareholders require, and can rely on, various provisions protecting them under the German law applicable to groups of companies. Finally, the German provisions dealing with employee rights should not be circumvented, since comparable rights do not exist in all the other member states of the European Union.[47] Thus, the *Bundesgerichtshof* fully endorsed the "real seat" theory.

2. The ECJ's Opinion

The ECJ rejected this approach and decided that Überseering B.V.'s legal capacity must be recognized by the German courts.

a) Scope of the Freedom of Establishment

In its decision, the ECJ first rejected the view that the question of transferring a company's seat from one member state to another could be left to legislative measures, such as mutual conventions among the member states based on Article 293 of the EC Treaty. In the ECJ's view, the fact that no such convention (nor any other European-wide regulation on the transfer of a company's seat between member states) had been passed,[48] had little effect on the applicability of the freedom of establishment. Thus, the ECJ clarified that the scope of the freedom of establishment does not depend on the progress of European legislation with regard to transferring a company's seat between member states. It thereby rejected the German government's argument that Articles 43 and 48 EC Treaty had been included in the EC Treaty with full knowledge of the differences between member states' company law and with the intention of letting national law prevail as long as no harmonization of the law was achieved.[49]

The ECJ asserted that the freedom of establishment cannot depend on the conclusion of agreements within the scope of Article 293 EC Treaty.[50] Independent of such agreements, companies within the protective scope of Articles 43 and 48 EC Treaty (such as

---

45 *Id.*
46 *See* Bundesgerichtshof, 21 ZEITSCHRIFT FÜR WIRTSCHAFTSRECHT (ZIP) 967 (2000).
47 *Id.*
48 *See* Ulrich Forsthoff, *supra* note 18, at 51.
49 *See* Case C-208/00, Überseering, 2002, *available at*: http://www.curia.eu.int/en/content/jurisp, where the English version of the judgment can be retrieved under "Case law" indicating the above-mentioned case number. This line of thought had already been rejected by the Advocate General in his final submission to the ECJ. The Advocate General Colomer had argued that Article 293 EC Treaty (dealing with the harmonization of member states' law) did not contain any proviso of legislative competence vested in the member states. Instead, Article 293 EC Treaty should simply be regarded as a warning to the member states to eliminate the problems that arise (as a result of the different legal systems of the member states in the area of reciprocal recognition of companies) in the case of a cross-border relocation and merger.
50 *Id.*

Überseering B.V.) have the right to carry on their business in any member state.[51] Freedom of establishment necessitates recognition of these companies by all the member states in which they wish to do business[52] and cannot depend on the question of whether the member states have reached agreement on the mutual recognition of companies.[53]

The ECJ explicitly distinguished this case from the *Daily Mail* decision of 1988. In *Daily Mail*,[54] the ECJ had held that the EC Treaty had accepted the differences of the various national conflict of law rules and left resolution of related problems to future harmonization efforts of the member states. The *Daily Mail* case centered on a tax dispute between the English company Daily Mail and General Trust plc (Daily Mail) and the British Inland Revenue. Daily Mail wanted to move its "real seat" to the Netherlands in order to avoid British corporation tax. The British Inland Revenue rejected the application for the relocation of the company. Daily Mail brought an action in the English courts, arguing that the decision was a violation of Articles 52 and 58 EC (now Articles 43 and 48 EC Treaty). The English High Court of Justice referred the case to the ECJ. The ECJ held that the requirement for approval by the British Inland Revenue was consistent with the freedom of establishment. "As of the current status of Community law," the ECJ reasoned in 1988, "a company that is formed in accordance with the laws of a member state will not have the right to relocate to another state. The solution to difficulties arising from cross-border activities of companies should be left to legislation by the member states."[55]

In *Überseering*, however, the facts were different than those surrounding *Daily Mail*, since *Überseering* concerned an entering, and not an exiting of a company into another member state.[56] Correspondingly, the ECJ distinguished *Daily Mail* on the basis that *Daily Mail* concerned the relocation of an English company which had its "real seat" in England and wanted to relocate to another member state ("exiting scenario" or *Wegzug*) whereas *Überseering* concerned a company that moved its headquarters into Germany ("entering scenario" or *Zuzug*).

b) The German Courts' Denial of Überseering B.V.'s Legal Capacity

After the ECJ had established that in this "entering" scenario Überseering B.V. was profiting from its freedom of establishment, the court went on to deal with the question of possible restrictions on this freedom under national (in this case German) law. The ECJ determined that the most severe restriction on the freedom of establishment was actually constituted by the German courts themselves. Their refusal to recognize the legal capacity of Überseering B.V., which had been validly incorporated under Dutch law, led to a "negation of the freedom of establishment."[57]

The ECJ subsequently assessed whether this severe restriction of the freedom of establishment could be justified by the reasons put forward in the referral of the *Bundesgerichtshof*. This option was ultimately rejected. According to the ECJ, restrictions on the freedom of establishment may be justified only in specific circumstances, e.g. for the protection of overriding interests such as the protection of creditors, minority shareholders, employees or the tax authorities.[58] However, these interests may not justify the denial of a company's legal capacity, where that company has already been duly incorporated in one member state and

---

51 *Id.*
52 *Id.*
53 *Id.*
54 Case C-81/87, Daily Mail, ECR 1988, 5512.
55 Case C-81/87, Daily Mail, ECR 1988, 5512.
56 *See* hereto the discussion in Norbert Horn, NEUE JURISTISCHE WOCHENSCHRIFT (NJW) 893, 895, 897 (2004).
57 *See* Case C-208/00, Überseering, 2002, *available at* http://www.curia.eu.int/en/content/jurisp.
58 *See* Case C-208/00, Überseering, 2002, *available at* http://www.curia.eu.int/en/content/jurisp.

is domiciled in another. Such a denial would be tantamount to an outright negation of the freedom of establishment granted to companies by Articles 43 and 48 EC Treaty.[59]

When the case was referred back to the *Bundesgerichtshof*, the Seventh Senate followed the ECJ's binding guidelines and held that Überseering B.V. had the capacity to sue in the German courts.[60] Furthermore, the Seventh Senate of the *Bundesgerichtshof* emphasized that Überseering B.V. did not sue as a German partnership, but as a B.V. (i.e. a Dutch limited liability company) under Dutch law. In the opinion of the Seventh Senate, Überseering B.V. therefore had to be recognized as such and could not be re-qualified as a German partnership with unlimited liability of its partners.

Thus, the Seventh Senate of the *Bundesgerichtshof* explicitly distinguished the modified version of the "real seat" doctrine developed by the Second Senate and held that treating corporations from other member states as German partnerships would also violate the freedom of establishment.[61]

3. Analysis

a) The "Real Seat" Theory as a Violation of the Freedom of Establishment

In its *Überseering* judgment of November 5, 2002[62] the ECJ scrutinized the "real seat" theory and ruled that, where a company validly formed and domiciled in one member state moves its center of administration to another member state, Articles 43 and 48 of the EC Treaty preclude that subsequent member state from denying the company's legal capacity. Articles 43 and 48 of the EC Treaty require that member state to recognize the legal capacity of such a company, including its ability to be a party to legal proceedings, to be the same as enjoyed under the law of its state of incorporation.

Following the ECJ's *Daily Mail* and *Centros* decisions, *Überseering* is another landmark decision on the impact of the freedom of establishment (Articles 43 and 48 EC Treaty) on the member states' choice of law for corporations. In *Überseering* the ECJ has clearly rejected the "real seat" theory.[63] Furthermore, the legal consequences of denying the legal capacity of companies incorporated in other member states, and the resulting need for foreign companies to re-incorporate themselves under German law, have been held to be in clear violation of the freedom of establishment (Articles 43 and 48 EC Treaty).

---

59 *See* Case C-208/00, Überseering, 2002, *id.*
60 Bundesgerichtshof, 57 NEUE JURISTISCHE WOCHENSCHRIFT (NJW) 1461 (2003). For an analysis of this decision, *see* Martin Schulz, *supra* note 32, at 2705.
61 Bundesgerichtshof, 57 NEUE JURISTISCHE WOCHENSCHRIFT (NJW) 1461 (2003). *See also* Ulrich Forsthoff, *supra* note 32, at 2705, pointing out that the liability regime of a corporation is part of its identity under the law of incorporation which is protected under Articles 43, 48 EC Treaty.
62 Case C-208/00, Überseering, 2002, *available at* http://www.curia.eu.int/en/content/jurisp.
63 With a few exceptions, like Peter Kindler, *Auf dem Weg zur Europäischen Briefkastengesellschaft? – Die „Überseering"-Entscheidung des EuGH und das Internationale Privatrecht*, 56 NEUE JURISTISCHE WOCHENSCHRIFT (NJW) 1073 (2003), the *Überseering* Decision has been strongly approved of in the German literature. *See, e.g.,* Schulz & Sester, *supra* note 5, at 545; Ulrich Forsthoff, *supra* note 32, at 2471; Eidenmüller, *supra* note 32, at 2233; Schanze & Jüttner, *supra* note 32, at 30; Peter Behrens, *Das Internationale Gesellschaftsrecht nach dem Überseering-Urteil des EuGH und den Schlussanträgen zu Inspire Art*, 23 PRAXIS DES INTERNATIONALEN PRIVAT- UND VERFAHRENSRECHTS (IPRAX) 193 (2003); Peter Behrens, *Gemeinschaftsrechtliche Grenzen der Anwendung inländischen Gesellschaftsrechts auf Auslandsgesellschaften nach Inspire Art*, 24 PRAXIS DES INTERNATIONALEN PRIVAT- UND VERFAHRENSRECHTS (IPRAX) 20 (2004); Daniel Zimmer, *Wie es Euch Gefällt? Offene Fragen nach dem Überseering-Urteil des EuGH*, 58 BETRIEBSBERATER (BB) 1 (2003); Marcus Lutter, *„Überseering" und die Folgen*, 58 BETRIEBSBERATER (BB) 7 (2003); Otto Sandrock, *Die Schrumpfung der Überlagerungstheorie – zu den zwingenden Vorschriften des deutschen Sitzrechts, die ein fremdes Gründungsstatut überlagern können*, 102 ZEITSCHRIFT FÜR VERGLEICHENDE RECHTSWISSENSCHAFT (ZVGLRWISS) 447 (2003).

Moreover, the ECJ repeatedly emphasized that the plaintiff (i.e. Überseering B.V.) was asserting its claim to freedom of establishment in Germany as a company validly set up under the laws of the Netherlands.[64] Referring to this part of the decision, many commentators agree that the freedom of establishment includes the protection of a company's identity defined by the law of its place of incorporation. This protection of identity covers the company's structure, including the question of shareholders' liability.[65]

b) European Law Guidelines for National Restrictions on the Freedom of Establishment

Since the ECJ considered the denial of Überseering B.V.'s capacity to sue under the "real seat" theory to be a negation of the freedom of establishment, it was no longer necessary to examine whether such restriction on the freedom of establishment could be justified. However, the ECJ conceded in *Überseering* that overriding general interests such as the protection of creditors, minority shareholders, employees, and even tax authorities, may, in certain circumstances and subject to certain conditions, justify restrictions on the freedom of establishment.[66] The ECJ emphasized that such interests cannot justify denying the legal capacity of a company properly incorporated in another member state where it has a registered office. Such a measure would be tantamount to an outright negation of the freedom of establishment conferred on companies by Articles 43 and 48 EC.[67]

Although the ECJ did not need to give any detailed comments on the permissibility of national restrictions in *Überseering*, it referred to some general guidelines developed in previous case law. According to the guidelines developed in the *Gebhard*[68] case, all national measures which restrict fundamental freedoms, such as the freedom of establishment, must satisfy the following four conditions:

- they must be used in a non-discriminatory manner;
- they must be justified by imperative general interests;
- they must be suitable for securing the objective which they pursue; and
- they must not go beyond what is necessary in order to attain the objective.

These principles apply not only to national restrictions on the so-called "secondary" freedom of establishment (i.e. concerning the establishment of branch offices as in *Centros* and in *Inspire Art*), but also to national restrictions on the primary freedom of establishment (i.e. the relocation of a company to another member state as in "*Überseering*"). All national regulations (including national conflict of laws) must satisfy the above-mentioned requirements where they lead to a restriction of fundamental freedoms.[69] There can be no priority of national (conflict of laws) rules over EC law. On the contrary, all national regulations, including the national conflict of laws, violate the freedom of establishment if they do not satisfy the requirements for a justification of member state limitations on fundamental freedoms.[70] This conclusion stems from the supremacy of EC law over national law.

---

64 *See* Case C-208/00, Überseering, 2002, *available at* http://www.curia.eu.int/en/content/jurisp at subsection 80, 81.
65 *See* Schulz, *supra* note 32, at 2707; Lutter, *supra* note 63, at 9; Harald Kallmeyer, *Tragweite des Überseering-Urteils des EuGH vom 5.11.2002 zur grenzüberschreitenden Sitzverlegung*, 55 DER BETRIEB (DB) 2521 (2002); Ulrich Forsthoff, *supra* note 32, at 2477.
66 *See* Überseering, *supra* note 64, at para. 92.
67 *See* Überseering, *supra* note 64, at para. 93.
68 Case C-55/94, Gebhard, 1995 ECR I-4165, 4168.
69 *See* Schulz & Sester, *supra* note 5, at 549.
70 For a detailed discussion of European law guidelines for national restrictions resulting from member state conflict of laws, *see* SCHULZ, *supra* note 6, at 123, 154.

III. The ECJ's Judgment in Inspire Art

In *Inspire Art*,[71] the most recent decision discussed here, the ECJ has confirmed and extended the position taken in the *Centros* and *Überseering* decisions.

Inspire Art Ltd was incorporated in the UK in 2000 as a private company limited by shares, with a registered office in Folkestone, United Kingdom. The company was engaged in art dealing and its business was conducted primarily (if not exclusively) through its branch office in the Netherlands. The founders of the company made no secret of the fact that one of the reasons they incorporated in the UK was to circumvent the more onerous Dutch incorporation requirements, especially with respect to minimum share capital requirements. Another reason was the lower cost of incorporation in the United Kingdom.

Given that all of the company's business was done in the Netherlands, the Amsterdam Commercial Register sought the registration of the branch office as a "formal foreign company" (*wet op de formeel buitenlandse vennootschappen*) pursuant to the Dutch law on formal foreign companies,[72] arguing that there was no real nexus between the company and its country of incorporation. Apart from the company having to add the words "formal foreign company" to its name, the application of the Dutch law on foreign companies results in additional disclosure requirements and triggers certain mandatory Dutch corporate rules, such as minimum share capital and potential joint and several liability of the directors for breach of duty. Given its UK incorporation, Inspire Art Ltd would not otherwise be subjected to these rules and requirements.

Inspire Art Ltd objected to the additional requirements, which the Amsterdam Commercial Register sought to impose, on the grounds that this request was in breach of the freedom of establishment provisions enshrined in Articles 43 and 48 of the EU Treaty. In accordance with Art. 234 EC, the Amsterdam Commercial Register referred the matter to the ECJ for decision.

In its decision, the ECJ first found that several provisions of the Dutch law on formal foreign companies imposed more extensive disclosure obligations for branches than those for companies regulated under the 11th directive[73] and, therefore, constituted a violation

---

71 Case C-167/01, Inspire Art Ltd, 2003, *available at* http://www.curia.eu.int/en/content/jurisp. Again, with the exception of Peter Kindler, *"Inspire Art" – Aus Luxemburg nichts Neues zum internationalen Gesellschaftsrecht*, 6 NEUE ZEITSCHRIFT FÜR GESELLSCHAFTSRECHT (NZG) 1086 (2003), the decision has been strongly approved of in the German literature and is considered to be in line with *Centros* and *Überseering, see, e.g.,* Martin Schulz & Alexander Dörrbecker, *Neues zur Rechtswahlfreiheit im europäischen Gesellschaftsrecht*, 57 BETRIEB UND WIRTSCHAFT (BuW) 990 (2003); Schanze & Jüttner, *supra* note 1, at 661; Horst Eidenmüller, *Mobilität und Restrukturierung von Unternehmen im Binnenmarkt*, JURISTENZEITUNG (JZ) 24 (2004); Bayer, *supra* note 31, at 2357; Holger Altmeppen, *Schutz vor "europäischen" Kapitalgesellschaften*, 57 NEUE JURISTISCHE WOCHENSCHRIFT (NJW) 97 (2004); Volker Geyrhalter & Peggy Gänßler, *"Inspire Art" – Briefkastengesellschaften "on the Move"*, 41 DEUTSCHES STEUERRECHT (DStR) 2167 (2003); Stefan Leible & Jochen Hoffmann, *Wie inspiriert ist "Inspire Art"?*, EUROPÄISCHE ZEITSCHRIFT FÜR WIRTSCHAFTSRECHT (EuZW) 677 (2003); Hildegard Ziemons, *Freie Bahn für den Umzug von Gesellschaften nach Inspire Art?!*, 24 ZEITSCHRIFT FÜR WIRTSCHAFTSRECHT (ZIP) 1913 (2003); Daniel Zimmer, *Nach "Inspire Art": Grenzenlose Gestaltungsfreiheit für deutsche Unternehmen?*, 56 NEUE JURISTISCHE WOCHENSCHRIFT (NJW) 3585 (2003). See also Christian Kersting & Clemens Phillip Schindler, *The ECJ's Inspire Art decision of 30 September 2003 and its effects on practice*, 4 GERMAN LAW JOURNAL 12 (2003) at 1277, *available at* http://www.germanlawjournal.com.
72 *Wet op de Formeel Buitenlandse Vennottschappen* (Law on Formally Foreign Companies) of 17 December 1997 (Staatsblad 1997 No 697, "the WFBV").
73 Council Directive 89/666/EWG, 1989, O.J. (L395/36).

of European law. With regard to the Dutch minimum share capital requirements and joint and several liability of directors for breach of duty, the ECJ examined whether these provisions could be justified under the exceptions of Article 46 of EC Treaty such as public policy, public security, or public health reasons. The court denied that such matters fell within one of the listed exceptions. The ECJ next examined whether Dutch law could pass the general guidelines for national restrictions of the freedom of establishment. However, the purported protection of creditors by the Dutch authorities was not regarded as a persuasive argument. In the court's view, creditors were aware from the outset that Inspire Art Ltd was a company incorporated in the UK and that therefore they did not enjoy the same protections as they would have were they dealing with a Dutch registered company.

Significantly, the Court held that it was irrelevant that the company was incorporated in the UK specifically in order to enjoy the incorporation advantages available there, even if its founders always intended that its business be carried on exclusively in the Netherlands.

In *Inspire Art* the ECJ again held that companies have the right to decide freely both on the jurisdiction in which they wish to incorporate (i.e. "freedom of establishment"), and on the ability to relocate their business activity within the EU without restriction. In addition, the court held that it is irrelevant that the choice of jurisdiction is made specifically to circumvent the incorporation requirements of a particular jurisdiction or to benefit from those of another. The ECJ also held that it does not matter that the business activity of a company is concentrated in a jurisdiction other than the one in which it is incorporated.

C. Consequences for German Conflict of Laws and German Company Law

I. Incompatibility of the "Real Seat" Theory with European Law

Following the ECJ's decisions in *Centros*, *Überseering* and *Inspire Art*, most commentators now agree that the "real seat" theory may no longer be applied to companies established in other member states that move their "seat" into Germany.[74]

Important elements of the ECJ's guidelines on national restrictions of the freedom of establishment are the suitability of restrictions for the objective sought and the proportionality of these restrictions (i.e. that they do not go beyond what is necessary to attain such objective).[75] Due to the general "chilling" effect that prevents foreign companies from moving their seat to Germany, the "real seat" theory clearly violates these two principles. The "real seat" theory does not provide for an examination of whether the need for protection in a given case arises, or whether such needs could be realized by means less draconian than the denial of the foreign company's legal capacity.[76] In addition, the "real seat" theory completely disregards the extent to which the legitimate need for protection can be met using similar mechanisms in foreign law, i.e. the law of the place of incorporation.[77]

---

74 *See, e.g.*, Ulrich Forsthoff & Martin Schulz, *supra* note 1, at 432; PALANDT & HELDRICH, BGB (63rd ed., 2004), Anhang zu Art. 12 EGBGB Rn. 6 and 9 with further references; Peter Ulmer, *Gläubigerschutz bei Scheinauslandsgesellschaften – zum Verhältnis zwischen gläubigerschutzendem nationalem Gesellschafts-, Delikts- und Insolvenzrecht und der EG-Niederlassungsfreiheit*, 57 NEUE JURISTISCHE WOCHENSCHRIFT (NJW) 1201, 1208 (2004); Schulz & Sester, *supra* note 5, at 552; Walter Bayer, 58 BETRIEBS-BERATER (BB) 2357, 2363 (2003); Daniel Zimmer, 56 NEUE JURISTISCHE WOCHENSCHRIFT (NJW) 3585, 3587 (2003); Marc-Philippe Weller, 23 PRAXIS DES INTERNATIONALEN PRIVAT- UND VERFAHRENSRECHTS (IPRax) 324, 328 (2003); Peter Behrens, 24 PRAXIS DES INTERNATIONALEN PRIVAT- UND VERFAHRENSRECHTS (IPRax) 20, 25 (2004); Horst Eidenmüller & Gebhard Rehm, *Niederlassungsfreiheit versus Schutz des inländischen Rechtsverkehrs: Konturen des Europäischen Internationalen Gesellschaftsrechts*, 33 ZGR 159, 160 (2004).
75 *See* Case C-55/94, Gebhard, 1995 ECR I-4168.
76 *See* MARTIN SCHULZ, *supra* note 6, at 172.
77 *See* Schulz & Sester, *supra* note 5, at 549.

The freedom of establishment and the mutual respect of the legal systems of the individual member states demand that the legal systems of other member states be treated equally.[78]

After *Centros*, *Überseering* and *Inspire Art*, the "real seat" theory can no longer be applied to companies from other member states. The legal capacity and legal identity of a company validly established in another EU member state must be recognized in Germany. Nevertheless, the precise scope of the applicability of national law to companies formed in other EU member states is still unclear. It remains to be seen to what extent national rules protecting vital interests of creditors and employees can still be applied to foreign companies moving into Germany.

II. Legitimate Scope of Application of German Law – Some Unresolved Questions

1. Scope of the ECJ's Decisions

a) Different Standards for "Entering" and "Exiting" Scenarios?

In *Centros*, *Überseering* and *Inspire Art*, the ECJ dealt with "entering scenarios." In each case the member state to which a company had moved its business activities (either through relocating its "real seat," as in *Überseering*, or through operating a branch, as in *Centros* and *Inspire Art*) was required to recognise the foreign entity validly established under the law of its place of incorporation. On the other hand, in *Überseering* the ECJ confirmed that a state is free to impose restrictions on companies established in its territory which want to move into another member state ("exiting scenario").[79] It seems therefore that the ECJ does not apply the same guidelines for "exiting scenarios" as those developed in *Centros*, *Überseering* and *Inspire Art* for "entering scenarios". This has been criticized, with some commentators asserting that since both scenarios are covered by the freedom of establishment, the same legal standards should apply.[80] However, this issue might be settled after the ECJ's decision in the case of *Hughes de Lasteyrie du Saillant*. In that case, the ECJ decided upon the conformity of certain French tax provisions regarding the change of fiscal residence from one member state to another. The ECJ held that the taxation of a natural person moving to another member state constitutes a violation of the freedom of establishment.[81] It remains to be seen, however, whether the ECJ will apply the same principles to companies being involved in "exiting scenarios" and will treat them in the same way as natural persons.

Another unresolved question concerns the remaining scope of national law (e.g. with regard to the protection of creditors, employees, and minority shareholders) that may be legitimately applied to companies from other EU member states relocating their seat to or operating a branch or subsidiary in Germany. Even after *Inspire Art*, there is no unrestricted freedom to choose a favorable corporate jurisdiction in Europe.[82] The ECJ has

---

78 See Otto Sandrock, *Sitzrecht contra Savigny? Zum angeblichen Chaos im internationalen Gesellschaftsrecht*; 59 BETRIEBSBERATER (BB) 897 (2005); SCHULZ, *supra* note 6, at 195.

79 For a critical analysis of this distinction *see, e.g.*, Schulz & Dörrbecker, *supra* note 71, at 994 with further references; Behrens, *supra* note 63, at 26.

80 *See* Schulz & Dörbecker, *supra* note 71, at 994; Schulz & Sester, *supra* note 5, at 550; *see also* Wulf-Henning Roth, *Die Wegzugsfreiheit für Gesellschaften*, in EUROPÄISCHE AUSLANDSGESELLSCHAFTEN IN DEUTSCHLAND (Marcus Lutter ed., 2005) 379, 402; Ziemons, *supra* note 71, at 1919.

81 Hughes de Casteyrie du Saillant, Opinion of Advocate General Jean Mischo vom 13.03.2003, Rs. C-9/02, *available at* http://www.curia.eu.int/jurisp.

82 *See* Schanze & Jüttner, *supra* note 1, at 666.

repeatedly emphasized that there might be legitimate national restrictions on the freedom of establishment. In *Überseering*, the ECJ held that:

> It cannot be ruled out that pressing reasons of public interest, such as protecting the interests of the creditor, the minority shareholder, the employee or also the treasury, can justify restrictions on the freedom of establishment in certain circumstances and under certain conditions.[83]

However, all these rules must fulfill the strict European law guidelines described above, which the ECJ developed for any national restrictions on fundamental freedoms.

2. Protection of Creditors – an Ongoing Controversy

Opinions vary in the current debate on the impact of *Inspire Art* on German law as to whether and to what extent specific German creditor protection rules may be applied to companies formed in other member states.[84] Very few court decisions have been published so far on this question.[85] While some courts have applied the law of the place of incorporation, others have taken the view that German creditor protection rules could be applied.[86] The *Bundesgerichtshof* generally tends to be quite strict with regard to the application of German capital protection rules. The court has repeatedly emphasized its endorsement of the German capital protection rules and has even expanded this concept in some recent decisions on the use of shelf companies.

a) German Capital Protection Rules – Still Valid or Outdated?

The application of the German "real seat" theory to foreign companies has regularly been justified by the need to protect the company's creditors. One traditional form of German creditor protection can be found in the rules on the initial supply of a mandatory minimum capital when the company is established.[87] Although these rules have not prevented the vulnerability of German *GmbH*s to insolvency and their effectiveness with regard to creditor protection has been the subject of some controversy,[88] the *Bundesgerichtshof* still considers these rules to be an essential part of creditor protection and has also just extended

---

83 See Case C-208/00, Überseering, 2002, *supra* note 64.
84 See Forsthoff & Schulz, *supra* note 1, at 432; Holger Fleischer, *Kapitalschutz und Durchgriffshaftung bei Auslandsgesellschaften*, in EUROPÄISCHE AUSLANDSGESELLSCHAFTEN IN DEUTSCHLAND (Marcus Lutter ed., 2005) 49; Eidenmüller & Rehm, *supra* note 74, at 161, 181; Gerald Spindler & Olaf Berner, *Der Gläubigerschutz im Gesellschaftsrecht nach Inspire Art*, 50 RIW 7 (2004); Bayer, *supra* note 31, at 2364; Zimmer, *supra* note 71, at 3587; Walter Paefgen, *Auslandsgesellschaften und Durchsetzung deutscher Schutzinteressen nach "Überseering"*, 56 DER BETRIEB (DB) 487 (2003); Alexander Schumann, *Die englische Limited mit Verwaltungssitz in Deutschland: Kapitalaufbringung, Kapitalerhaltung und Haftung bei Insolvenz*, 57 DER BETRIEB (DB) 743, 745 (2004); Peter Behrens, *supra* note 63, at 25; Altmeppen, *supra* note 71, at 97; Altmeppen & Wihelm, *supra* note 1, at 1083 sub II with extensive references to the current German debate.
85 See Landesgericht Hannover, NEUE ZEITSCHRIFT FÜR GESELLSCHAFTSGERICHT (NZG) 1072 (2003); Amtsgericht Hamburg-Altona in an unpublished Decision dated 3 April 2003 (317 C-614/02)
86 See Landesgericht Hannover, NEUE ZEITSCHRIFT FÜR GESELLSCHAFTSGERICHT (NZG) 1072 (2003); Amtsgericht Hamburg-Altona in an unpublished Decision dated 3 April 2003 (317 C-614/02); Amtsgericht Hamburg, ZEITSCHRIFT FÜR WIRTSCHAFTSRECHT (ZIP) 1008, 1009 (2003); Landesgericht Stuttgart, NEUE JURISTISCHE WOCHENSCHRIFT-RECHTSPRECHUNGSREPORT (NJW-RR) 463, 466 (2002), both of the latter decisions were, however, published before the ECJ's decision in *Inspire Art*.
87 See Friedrich Kübler, *The Rules of Capital under Pressure of the Securities Markets*, in CAPITAL MARKETS AND COMPANY LAW (Klaus J. Hopt & Eddy Wymeersch eds., 2003). For a description of different forms of creditor protection under German law in general *see*, *e.g.*, Altmeppen, *supra* note71, at 100; more substantially, *see* HOLGER ALTMEPPEN & GÜNTHER H. ROTH, GMBHG § 30 (4th ed., 2003).
88 See Sandrock, *supra* note 63, at 470 with further references; *see also* Halbhuber, *supra* note 10, at 1417.

them to shelf companies. In its decisions of December 9, 2002 and July 7, 2003,[89] the *Bundesgerichtshof* has, *inter alia*, applied the minimum capital rules *mutatis mutandis* to shelf limited liability companies (*Vorrats-GmbH*) as well as to so-called dormant companies (*Mantelgesellschaften*). In contrast to shelf companies established for later use, e.g. by a purchaser of the shelf company, a dormant company is one that has already been active in the past but subsequently lain dormant before later resuming its commercial activity. In the decisions mentioned above,[90] the *Bundesgerichtshof* has tightened the requirements for both shelf and dormant companies, thus extending the applicability of the rules on the formation of limited liability companies, including the rules on the initial supply of capital. Although the Limited Liability Companies Act (*GmbHG*) prescribes that the relevant commercial register has to evaluate the minimum share capital only upon the company's initial registration (§ 7 *GmbHG*), the *Bundesgerichtshof* has now held that there is a necessity for a renewed control of minimum capital requirements in cases of "economic new formation" (*wirtschaftliche Neugründung*), i.e. when a shelf company is commercially activated. This "economic new formation" typically takes place when the relevant amendments to the articles of association are registered following the acquisition of the shelf or dormant company by a purchaser. The crucial factor for such control by the registration court is the renewed affirmation by all the managing directors, who have been newly appointed after acquisition of the shelf company by the purchaser, that the statutorily-prescribed share capital contributions have been paid. In the event that the managing directors either do not give this affirmation or do not give it in the required form, the registration of the requested changes to the articles of association may be rejected. This additional requirement diminishes the time-saving advantage of using a shelf company as opposed to the tedious registration process of a newly-formed *GmbH*. In the future, the tightened restrictions on the use of a shelf *GmbH* may lead to delays, making quicker registrations of "economic formations" (as opposed to new formations of *GmbH*) rather doubtful.

Furthermore, the *Bundesgerichtshof* has confirmed that the strict statutory rules applying to the formation of a limited liability company in general also apply to the use of shelf companies. This expansion includes the rules on liabilities incurred by the founders in respect of the company prior to formal registration (*Gründerhaftung*). For corporate practice, this inclusion means that substantial liability risks remain with the purchasers of a shelf *GmbH* up until registration of the "economic formation" of the shelf company, which typically involves changes of the company's name, business object, and directors. The potential liability of the purchaser of a shelf company during the registration of changes to the articles of association also diminishes the purported advantage of using a shelf company instead of a newly formed *GmbH*. Thus, the recent case law has clearly reduced the perceived benefits of using a shelf or dormant company instead of an altogether new formation of a *GmbH*.

These new restrictions for the use of shelf companies have been criticized as an unnecessary burden on corporate practice.[91] The court's approach on this matter also contrasts

---

89 BGHZ 153, 158; BGHZ 155, 318.
90 BGHZ 153, 158; BGHZ 155, 318.
91 *See, e.g.*, Martin Schulz, *Registergerichtliche Kontrolle bei der Verwendung einer Vorrats-GmbH*, 57 BETRIEB UND WIRTSCHAFT (BuW) 331, 336 (2003); Martin Heidenhain, *Anwendung der Gründungsvorschriften des GmbH-Gesetzes auf die wirtschaftliche Neugründung einer Gesellschaft*, 6 NEUE ZEITSCHRIFT FÜR GESELLSCHAFTSRECHT (NZG) 1051 (2003); Holger Altmeppen, *Zur Verwendung eines "alten" GmbH-Mantels*, 56 DER BETRIEB (DB) 2050 (2003); Harald Kallmeyer, *Ist die Wiederbelebung einer Mantel-GmbH wirklich strenger zu behandeln als der Formwechsel einer AG in eine GmbH?*, 56 DER BETRIEB (DB) 2583 (2003); Bernhard Schaub, *Vorratsgesellschaften vor dem Aus?*, 56 NEUE JURISTISCHE WOCHENSCHRIFT (NJW) 2125, 2130 (2003); Karsten Schmidt, *Vorratsgründung, Mantelkauf und Mantelverwendung*, 57 NEUE JURISTISCHE WOCHENSCHRIFT (NJW) 1345 (2004).

with the new opportunities to choose a favorable law. Given that minimum capital is not statutorily prescribed in all European member states, the new obligations for the use of shelf and dormant companies can be avoided under the new ECJ jurisprudence on the freedom of establishment by forming a limited liability company in a state such as England and later moving its headquarters to Germany.[92] As discussed below, however, such a strategy does not leave local creditors of companies "moving in" from jurisdictions without minimum capital rules completely without protection.

b) "Piercing the Corporate Veil" – a New Form developed by the *Bundesgerichtshof* and its Applicability to EU Companies

As indicated above, the effectiveness of the German concept of minimum capital has long been controversial on account of its alleged benefit for creditor protection.[93] Furthermore, in the current debate on German corporate law reform, some commentators argue for reducing or even abandoning the minimum capital requirements of the *GmbH* in order to keep the *GmbH* structure attractive in the emerging European competition of corporate forms (*see infra*, section III).[94] Regardless of the outcome of this debate it should be noted, however, that creditor protection can obviously also be achieved by other means.[95] For example, the doctrine of "piercing the corporate veil," may in many cases provide a functional equivalent to the rules for the supply and maintenance of capital. In fact, the *Bundesgerichtshof* has recently developed a new form of "piercing the corporate veil" in support of creditor protection described as "liability due to interference leading to the destruction of the *GmbH*'s corporate existence" (*Haftung wegen existenzvernichtenden Eingriffs*).[96] Whether this new form of "piercing the corporate veil" may be applied to companies formed in other member states and operating in Germany remains a controversy.[97] Some argue that following the recent ECJ jurisprudence one would principally have to apply only the liability rules (including rules on "piercing the corporate veil") of the place of incorporation.[98] Others argue that creditor protection under this new form of "piercing the corporate veil" will also be extended to foreign companies despite the ECJ decisions in *Überseering* and *Inspire Art*.[99] Before commenting on this controversial question, let me briefly outline the new form of "piercing the corporate veil" developed by the *Bundesgerichtshof*. Since there is no statute which specifically provides for piercing of the corporate veil, the relevant principles have been developed by the courts on a case-by-case basis. In some recent decisions, the Bundesgerichtshof has further elaborated the German concept of piercing the corporate veil in a new sub-group of

---

92 See Peter O. Mülbert, *Zukunft der Kapitalaufbringung/Kapitalerhaltung*, 2 DER KONZERN 151 (2004).
93 See Barbara Grunewald & Ulrich Noack, *Zur Zukunft des Kapitalsystems der GmbH – Die Ein-Euro-GmbH in Deutschland*, 96 GMBHRUNDSCHAU (GMBHR) 189 (2005); Mülbert, *supra* note 92, at 151; Sandrock, *supra* note 71, at 470, Halbhuber, *supra* note 10, at 1417.
94 See, e.g., Wienand Meilicke, *Die Niederlassungsfreiheit nach „Überseering"*, 94 GMBHRUNDSCHAU (GMBHR) 793, 808 (2003); Grunwald & Noack, *supra* note 93, at 189.
95 See Altmeppen, *supra* note 71, at 100.
96 See Holger Altmeppen, *in* HOLGER ALTMEPPEN & GÜNTHER H. ROTH, GMBHG (4th ed., 2003), § 13, annotations 22–27.
97 See, e.g., Forsthoff & Schulz, *supra* note 1, at 451. See also Fleischer, *supra* note 84, at 49 with further references; MARC-PHILIPPE WELLER, EUROPÄISCHE RECHTSFORMWAHLFREIHEIT UND GESELLSCHAFTERHAFTUNG 123 (2005).
98 See Spindler & Berner, *supra* note 84, at 11. See also Forsthoff & Schulz, *supra* note 1, at 462.
99 See Altmeppen, *supra* note 71, at 101, 104; Marc-Philippe Weller, *Scheinauslandsgesellschaften nach Centros, Überseering und Inspire Art: Ein neues Anwendungsfeld für die Existenzvernichtung*, 22 PRAXIS DES INTERNATIONALEN PRIVAT- UND VERFAHRENSRECHTS (IPRAX) 207, 210 (2003); Günter H. Roth, *Gläubigerschutz durch Existenzschutz*, 6 NEUE ZEITSCHRIFT FÜR GESELLSCHAFTSRECHT (NZG) 1081, 1085 (2003).

cases dealing with a shareholder's destructive interference in the company (*existenzvernichtender Eingriff*).[100]

Broadly speaking, the new concept developed by the *Bundesgerichtshof* is based on the idea that a shareholder may not abuse the fact of the separate corporate personality of the *GmbH* or the attendant privilege of limited liability. The *Bundesgerichtshof* presumes such an abuse when, for example, a shareholder interferes with the *GmbH* in a manner which considerably impairs the *GmbH*'s ability to meet its obligations towards its creditors. A shareholder who has committed such an abuse may not claim the privilege of limited liability and, consequently, may be held directly liable vis-à-vis the *GmbH*'s creditors if (i) the *GmbH*'s ability to meet its obligations cannot be restored by shareholder repayments pursuant to the German share capital maintenance rules (§§ 30 ff. *GmbHG*), and (ii) as a consequence of such interference by the shareholder, the creditors of the *GmbH* cannot successfully claim satisfaction from the *GmbH* because of insufficient assets. Since the latter prerequisite will typically only be met when a *GmbH* is insolvent, this shareholder liability concept has been described as "liability due to interference leading to the destruction of the GmbH's corporate existence" (*Haftung wegen existenzvernichtenden Eingriffs*).[101]

In essence, shareholder liability under this concept is only triggered if, as a consequence of the shareholder's interference, the *GmbH* is not able to fulfill its obligations towards its creditors. Examples of interference include, for example, the transfer of material assets from the company to a shareholder, allocating the risks or losses of a certain business operation to a certain group company while at the same time allocating all of the opportunities, benefits or profits to another group company, cash-management within a group of companies depriving the subsidiary of the liquidity necessary to meet its obligations, and measures in connection with the integration into a group of companies (e.g. transfer of material business operations to other group companies or upstream guarantees).

However, since this new form of "piercing the corporate veil" is designed as a narrow exception, its application is restricted to interferences involving risks and disadvantages for the *GmbH* which, from an ex ante point of view, are clearly disproportionate to the potential opportunities, profits or benefits to be gained, and are therefore highly likely to result in the destruction of the *GmbH*. Whether, and to what extent, a subjective element is also required, is not quite clear from the court decisions cited above. At present, there are no decisions of the Federal Court of Justice determining the requirements in more detail.

With regard to the protection of the company's creditors after *Überseering* and *Inspire Art*, one would have to look primarily at the law of the place of incorporation.[102] If that law contains adequate rules on the protection of the company's creditors, the application of other national creditor protection rules would not pass the test of the ECJ, since such application would not be necessary.[103] However, the ECJ has again emphasized in *Inspire*

---

100 This concept was originally developed in the *"Bremer Vulkan"* judgment of September 17, 2001, 22 ZIP (2001) 1874, and further elaborated in the decision dated February 25, 2002, 23 ZIP (2002) 848 and in the *"KBV"* judgment of June 24, 2002, 22 ZIP (2002) 1578. For analysis of this jurisprudence, *see, e.g.*, Roth, *supra* note 99, at 1081; Hans-Peter Westermann, *Haftungsrisiken eines "beherrschenden" GmbH-Gesellschafters*, 5 NEUE ZEITSCHRIFT FÜR GESELLSCHAFTSRECHT (NZG) 1129 (2002); Peer Zumbansen, *Liability Within Corporate Groups ("Bremer Vulkan"): Federal Court of Justice Attempts the Overhaul*, 3 GERMAN LAW JOURNAL (1 January 2002), *available at* http://www.germanlawjournal.com.
101 *See* Altmeppen, *supra* note 96.
102 *See* Eidenmüller & Rehm, *supra* note 74, at 161, 181; Spindler & Berner, *supra* note 84, at 7; Bayer, *supra* note 31, at 2364; Zimmer, *supra* note 71, at 3587; Paefgen, *supra* note 84, at 487; Schumann, *supra* note 84, at 745; Behrens, *supra* note 63, at 25. *See also* Forsthoff & Schulz, *supra* note 1, at 439, 456, 467.
103 *See* Forsthoff & Schulz, *supra* note 1, at 439, 456, 467; Schulz & Sester, *supra* note 5, at 549; Eidenmüller & Rehm, *supra* note 74, at 161, 181.

Art that a member state is entitled to take measures designed to prevent the company from "improperly or fraudulently taking advantage of provisions of community law."[104] Although the ECJ has not yet given a more precise definition, a fact pattern constituting a destruction of the company's existence (*existenzvernichtender Eingriff*) might also be considered as an abuse of the freedom of establishment.[105] Thus, it seems likely that, in cases of fraud and abuse under national law, e.g. fact patterns revealing an intentional damage to the company's creditors, for example by deliberately using insolvent foreign companies, the German doctrine of "piercing the corporate veil" might be legitimately applied to companies established in other EU member states.[106] It remains to be seen whether the ECJ will consider such cases of abusive behavior under German law also as an abuse of the freedom of establishment.

3. Co-determination of Employees

Problems with respect to the recognition of foreign companies in Germany also arise from Germany's unique regulation of employees' participation in corporate governance. Depending on the size of the German company, its supervisory board must partly consist of representatives of the workforce. This specific German concept of workers' co-determination faces enormous problems when applied to foreign companies not having a supervisory board as part of their corporate governance structure. Even if one takes into account that the co-determination regulation is considered part of Germany's mandatory public policy,[107] there are serious doubts as to whether German co-determination rules can be implemented in foreign companies. Such a move would result in a fundamental change of the foreign company's structure and would therefore be incompatible with the ECJ's judgment in *Überseering*.[108] Furthermore, forcing a foreign company to establish a domestic subsidiary with a co-determined supervisory board (instead of moving its domicile to Germany) would appear to be equally incompatible with the freedom of establishment,[109] since forced relocation under the "real seat" theory was one of the leading arguments of the ECJ for rejecting possible grounds for restricting the freedom of establishment in *Überseering*. Most commentators therefore agree that the application of the German rules on workers' co-determination in supervisory boards to companies formed in other member states would be incompatible with the freedom of establishment.[110]

---

104 *See* Case C-167/01, Inspire Art Ltd, 2003, *available at* http://www.curia.eu.int/en/content/jurisp, at 136.
105 *See* Zimmer, *supra* note 71, at 3588; Weller, *supra* note 99, at 210; Roth, *supra* note 99, at 1085.
106 For a detailed discussion of such cases, *see* Forsthoff & Schulz, *supra* note 1, at 462.
107 *See* references at Sandrock, *supra* note 63, at 486.
108 *Id.*, *see also* Schanze & Jüttner, *supra* note 1, at 668; Schulz & Dörrbecker, *supra* note 71, at 994.
109 *See* Peter Ulmer, *Schutzinstrumente gegen die Gefahren aus der Geschäftstätigkeit inländischer Zweigniederlassungen von Kapitalgesellschaften mit fiktivem Auslandssitz*, 54 JURISTENZEITUNG (JZ) 663 (1999).
110 *See* Zimmer, *supra* note 71, at 3590; Martin Veit & Joachim Wichert, *Unternehmerische Mitbestimmung bei europäischen Kapitalgesellschaften mit Verwaltungssitz in Deutschland nach "Überseering" und "Inspire Art"*, 49 DIE AKTIENGESELLSCHAFT (AG) 14 (2004); Thomas Müller-Bonnani, *Unternehmensmitbestimmung nach "Überseering" und "Inspire Art"*, 94 GMBHRUNDSCHAU (GMBHR) 1235 (2003); Schanze & Jüttner, *supra* note 1, at 668; Schulz & Dörrbecker, *supra* note 71, at 994.

4. Protection of Minority Shareholders

As far as the protection of the minority shareholders is concerned, it has already been pointed out that this concept generally cannot justify a restriction on the freedom of establishment.[111] Becoming a shareholder of a foreign company is basically an individual decision of (minority) shareholders. With respect to their relationship with the company and other shareholders, their rights are embedded in the articles of association and the laws according to which the company was established. This special link of company law to rules and regulations for the protection of minority shareholders would mean encroaching on the autonomous decision of each individual shareholder. The fact that the "real seat" of the foreign company is in Germany does not justify this encroachment. The position of a shareholder who holds shares in a company governed by foreign law is not altered by the fact that the company is domiciled abroad, so in this respect there is no causal link to the "real seat."

In summary, none of the above interests of creditors, employees or minority shareholders can justify the severe restrictions on the freedom of establishment for foreign corporations resulting from the "real seat" theory.

III. Inspire Art as an Inspiration for German Company Law Reform

The recent ECJ decisions have stirred up the debate on whether German company law, especially the strict rules on minimum capital, should be reformed. Many commentators consider the recent ECJ's jurisprudence to be not only an attack on the traditional German "real seat" doctrine, but also to be an opportunity for a general reform of German corporate law and of the German Limited Liability Company (*GmbH*) in particular.[112] The *GmbH* is still the most popular German corporate form[113] and is also frequently used by foreign companies doing business in Germany. The legal framework for the *GmbH* is more flexible compared to that of the German stock corporation (*Aktiengesellschaft* or *AG*), another popular German corporate form which also allows the general exclusion of personal liability of its shareholders. In contrast to the statutory regime for the *AG*, the *GmbH-Gesetz* leaves considerable room for flexibility in the articles of association with regard to the relationship of the shareholders between themselves.[114] Apart from some mandatory requirements, the articles of association (as well as subsequent amendments), can be tailored to the needs of the shareholders[115] regarding their relationships with each

---

111 *See* Knobbe-Keuk, *supra* note 14, at 346; *see also* Sandrock, *supra* note 63, at 481, pointing out that national protective rules for minority shareholders may legitimately be applied to foreign companies in exceptional circumstances.
112 *See, e.g.*, Grunewald & Noack, *supra* note 93, at 189; Uwe Blaurock, *Mindestkapital und Haftung bei der GmbH*, in FESTSCHRIFT FÜR THOMAS RAISER (Rüdiger Damm ed., 2005), 3; Bayer, *supra* note 31, at 2366; Wilhelm Haarmann, *Die Überseering-Entscheidung – Ein Anstoß zur Entrümpelung und Flexibilisierung des deutschen Gesellschaftsrechts?*, 58 BB (2003) 1; Wienand Meilicke, *Die Niederlassungsfreiheit nach „Überseering"*, 94 GMBHRUNDSCHAU (GMBHR) 793, 807 (2003). *See also* Heribert Hirte, *Der Anfang vom Ende der GmbH droht*, FRANKFURTER ALLGEMEINE ZEITUNG, 22 January 2003, 19 suggesting, among others, that minimum capital requirements for the *GmbH* should be abolished and that the scope of workers' codetermination rules should be diminished; *see also* Ulrich Noack, *Das GmbH-Recht braucht eine Runderneuerung*, FRANKFURTER ALLGEMEINE ZEITUNG, 26 November 2003, 25.
113 *See* WIRTH, ARNOLD & GREEN, CORPORATE LAW IN GERMANY (2004) p. 4, pointing out that, presently, there are more than 800,000 *GmbHs* in Germany, whereas the number of *AGs* (stock corporations) is below 6000.
114 *See* Lutz Michalski, *GmbH-Gesetz* (2002), SYST. DARST. 1, No. 27.
115 Pursuant to section 3 *GmbH-Gesetz* the articles of association must contain the company name and its registered office (*Sitz*), the objects of the company, the amount of the share capital and the amount each shareholder has to contribute to the share capital (share capital contribution).

other. Last but not least, the *GmbH* is also quite frequently used as an all-purpose vehicle within groups of companies where the parent company can directly influence the management of the subsidiary. In contrast to the *AG*, the shareholders of a *GmbH* have more power to influence the management of the *GmbH*, for example by giving binding instructions to the managing directors even in the day to day management of the affairs of the company.

For these reasons, the *GmbH* is still an attractive company form, especially for small and medium-sized businesses. According to some commentators, the *GmbH* can even remain attractive in the emerging European competition of company forms resulting from the expanded options under the freedom of establishment, provided that the legal framework for the *GmbH* is modernized and deregulated.[116] Thus, *Inspire Art* might indeed offer an incentive for German corporate law reform.

IV. Company Law Developments in the EU: Towards a "Race to the Bottom" or a "Race to the Top"?

Finally, it is interesting to consider the long term effects of the ECJ's decisions in *Centros*, *Überseering*, and *Inspire Art* on the further assimilation and harmonization policies of member states' law in the European Union. In Germany, the "real seat" theory was often defended on the basis that it prevents a negative competition of laws ("race to the bottom"), since it eliminates the freedom to choose a favorable jurisdiction for incorporation. According to this view, under a competition of legal systems, the legal system with the weakest protection of third party interests would prevail. In this respect, reference was often made to U.S. company law, where the "incorporation" theory has long been used and companies enjoy a virtually unrestricted freedom of establishment.[117]

When describing this phenomenon, German commentators often allege that, due to the "incorporation" theory, a downward race of legal systems has taken place in U.S. law.[118] However, this generalization finds much less approval in the U.S.A. than in Germany.[119] Given the success story of Delaware, the most popular state for the incorporation of American companies, such skepticism could not be proved by way of empirical investigation.[120] To the contrary, the bleak prospect of a "race to the bottom" has been confronted

---

116 *See, e.g.*, Bayer, *supra* note 31, at 2366; Hirte, *supra* note 112, at 19.
117 *See, e.g.*, Uwe Blaurock, *Europäisches und deutsches Gesellschaftsrecht – Bilanz und Perspektiven eines Anpassungsprozesses*, 6 ZEITSCHRIFT FÜR EUROPÄISCHES PRIVATRECHT (ZEuP) (1998), 460, 462; Kindler, *supra* note 13; SCHULZ, *supra* note 6, at 198; from an American perspective *see, e.g.*, David Charny, *Competition among Jurisdictions in Formulating Corporate Law Rules: An American Perspective on the "Race to the Bottom" in the European Communities*, 32 HARVARD INTERNATIONAL LAW JOURNAL (1991), 423; Terence L. Blackburn, *The Unification of Corporate Laws: the United States, the European Community and the Race to Laxity*, 3 GEO. MASON INDEP. L. REV. (1994), 1.
118 *See, e.g.*, Blaurock, *supra* note 112, at 6; ZEuP (1998), 460, 462; Kindler, *supra* note 13. See also Bundesgerichtshof, 21 ZEITSCHRIFT FÜR WIRTSCHAFTSRECHT (ZIP) 967 (2000) (defending the "real seat" theory when referring the *Überseering* case to the ECJ).
119 *See, e.g.*, Roberta Romano, *The State Competition Debate in Corporate Law*, 8 CARDOZO LAW REVIEW (1987), 709; Roberta Romano, *Law as a Product: Some Pieces of the Incorporation Puzzle*, J. L. EC. & ORG. (1985) 225; FRANK H. EASTERBROOK & DANIEL R. FISCHEL, THE ECONOMIC STRUCTURE OF CORPORATE LAW 212 (1996); Daniel R. Fischel, *The "Race to the bottom" revisited: Reflections on recent developments in Delaware's Corporation Law*, 76 NORTHWESTERN UNIVERSITY LAW REVIEW (1982), 913; Ralph K. Winter, *State Law, Shareholder Protection, and the Theory of the Corporation*, 25 THE JOURNAL OF LEGAL STUDIES (1977), 251. For a recent account of Delaware's popularity as a place of incorporation, *see* Katharina Kort, *Anleger erhalten mehr Rechte im Unternehmer-Paradies Delaware*, HANDELSBLATT, 13 November 2002, B3.
120 *See, e.g.*, Fischel, *supra* note 119, at 913; Winter, *supra* note 119, at 251; Peter Dodd & Richard Leftwich, *The Market for Corporate Charters: "Unhealthy Competition" versus Federal Regulation*, 53 J. BUS. 259 (1980).

by several commentators with the bright vision of a "race to the top".[121] For various reasons, Delaware law is considered to be a driving force for progress in U.S. corporate law. Delaware offers a simple and unbureaucratic incorporation process and, with its "Court of Chancery", Delaware has established a court system with specialized judges for company law disputes. The Delaware Court of Chancery and the Delaware Supreme Court have developed special expertise in the area of company law and have created a comprehensive pool of precedents based on numerous corporate law decisions.[122] This specialization and the expertise of the Delaware judiciary ensures legal stability and, in the case of legal disputes, enables an analysis of the risks of litigation and results in faster legal proceedings in Delaware compared to those in other federal states.[123] Thus, the negative opinion of U.S. developments held by some German commentators seems unjustified.

A closer look at the U.S.A. reveals that we do not need to be afraid of a "race to the bottom" as a result of the recent ECJ jurisprudence on the freedom of establishment. Furthermore, within Europe, it seems unlikely that a competition of legal systems will occur on the same scale as in the U.S.A., as the conditions for a market of company laws in Europe are different: the company laws of the member states are still only partially harmonized and, in contrast to the U.S.A., there is no common language and culture in Europe which would facilitate a competition of legal systems.[124] In addition, within its guidelines for national measures, the ECJ leaves room for the legitimate application of national law thereby preventing an unrestricted freedom of establishment. These European law guidelines may ultimately serve as a safeguard against a "race to the bottom." On the other hand, *Centros*, *Überseering* and *Inspire Art* may lead to some positive competition of European company laws and may force member states to compare and assimilate their rules to those of other member states.[125]

D. Summary

The recent decision of the ECJ in *Inspire Art* confirms the line of reasoning of the court developed in *Centros* and *Überseering*. The ECJ has extended its general guidelines for national restrictions of fundamental freedoms under the EC Treaty to the freedom of establishment applied to cross-border corporate activities. Thus, a company established in one member state has to be generally recognized in all other member states. As has been shown, the recent jurisprudence of the ECJ has a great impact on German conflict of laws as well as German corporate law. Given the effect of preventing companies established under foreign law from operating in Germany in their original form, the traditional "real

---

121 See, e.g., Romano, *supra* note 119, at 709; Romano, *supra* note 119, at 225; EASTERBROOK & FISCHEL, *supra* note 119, at 212; Fischel, *supra* note 119, at 913; Winter, *supra* note 119, at 251.
122 See, e.g., Romano, *supra* note 119, at 709; Romano, *supra* note 119, at 225; Fischel, *supra* note 119, at 913; Winter, *supra* note 119, at 251. See also Brent Hatzis-Schoch, *Die Bedeutung von Delaware für das US-amerikanische Gesellschaftsrecht*, 38 RIW (1992) 539, 542.
123 See Hatzis-Schoch, *id.*
124 In the area of corporate law, attempts to reach agreement on the mutual recognition of companies and legal persons has failed, see Wymeersch, *supra* note 10; HABERSACK, *supra* note 10; Halbhuber, *supra* note 10.
125 For a positive view on the overall effects of the competition among European legal systems from a German perspective, see, e.g., Friedrich Kübler, *Rechtsbildung durch Gesetzgebungswettbewerb? Überlegungen zur Angleichung und Entwicklung des Gesellschaftsrechts in der Europäischen Gemeinschaft*, 77 KRITISCHE VIERTELJAHRESSCHRIFT FÜR GESETZGEBUNG UND RECHTSWISSENSCHAFT (KritV) (1994), 79. See also Siems, *supra* note 33. See also Horst Eidenmüller, *Theorien zur Bestimmung des Gesellschaftsstatuts und Wettbewerb der Gesellschaftsrechte*, in AUSLÄNDISCHE KAPITALGESELLSCHAFTEN IM DEUTSCHEN RECHT (Horst Eidenmüller ed., 2004) 8.

seat" doctrine is incompatible with the freedom of establishment. Generally, companies from other EU member states now have to be recognized. However, in anticipation of future decisions of the ECJ, some problems, such as the residual scope of applicability of the law of the member state in which the company operates and has its "real seat," remain unresolved. On the one hand, the ECJ has emphasized in *Überseering* that a company formed in one member state has to be recognized as such, i.e. in its identity under the place of incorporation (e.g. as a Dutch *B.V.*). Consequently, all other member states would have to respect the original corporate structure defined by the place of incorporation. The national rules which interfere with such structure, such as, for example, the application of German co-determination rules to companies without supervisory boards, will be incompatible with articles 43 and 48 of EC Treaty.[126] On the other hand, the ECJ has again confirmed in *Inspire Art* that certain national restrictions on the freedom of establishment remain legitimate to protect overriding interests, e.g. those of creditors or employees. Thus, foreign companies will obviously remain subject to national rules in the jurisdiction of their domicile to some extent, as long as those rules pass the strict guidelines developed by the ECJ. The uncertainty of the applicable scope of such national rules remains subject to future decisions of the ECJ.

However, with its recent jurisprudence on the freedom of establishment, the ECJ has clearly broadened the options for choosing a favourable law in the European Union. As the example of the United States shows, the competition of legal systems resulting from such free choice of company forms need not necessarily lead to negative results. Furthermore, where German legislators manage to keep them attractive, German corporate forms need not lose such competition. In the case of the *GmbH*, legislators would do well to implement some of the reforms suggested by many commentators. The ECJ has already stimulated German corporate law reform and created incentives for the further assimilation and harmonization of EU corporate law.

---

126 *See* Thomas Müller-Bonanni, *Mitbestimmung*, in GRENZÜBERSCHREITENDE GESELLSCHAFTEN – PRAXISHANDBUCH FÜR AUSLÄNDISCHE KAPITALGESELLSCHAFTEN MIT SITZ IM INLAND (Thomas Bücker & Heribert Hirte eds., 2005) 389, 394 with further references to the extensive German literature on this issue.

On the Interpretation of Legal Precedents and of the Judgments of the European Court of Human Rights

Boštjan M. Zupančič*

A. Introduction

Built into the above title are two classical jurisprudential suggestions: the concept of *"a judgment"* and the doctrine of *"legal interpretation."*

In principle, however, a judgment is not something that would need, or even should need, to be interpreted. Quite the contrary! A concrete *inter partes* judgment itself – and especially so in the European legal tradition – must interpret the abstract legal norm.[1] By definition, therefore, the judgment should be plain and clear and should require no interpretation at all.

Moreover, a judgment that lends itself to different interpretations, a judgment that has a range of possible meanings, that is ambiguous – may be difficult or impossible to execute. The purpose of a judgment, because it is meant to put a definite end to a legal controversy – is to be executed, not interpreted. This derives from the need for legal certainty and security.[2] The finality of a judgment, any judgment, is reflected in the Roman Law maxim: *res judicata pro veritate habetur*, i.e. an irrefutable presumption (sometimes as a fiction) is established precisely in order to prevent further interpretation both of the judgment and of the truth concerning the underlying historical event.

What I have just said, however, is also a fiction. The cause of the abstract-to-concrete teaching concerning a pyramid of legal acts originated in the wake of the 1789 French Revolution and its overreaction to the arbitrariness of aristocratic justice in the *ancien*

---

* Boštjan M. Zupančič, dipl. iur. (Lab.), LL.M. and S.J.D. (Harvard), Professor of Law (U.S. and Slovenia), former Justice of the Constitutional Court of Slovenia, former Vice-Chairman of the U.N. Committee against Torture, since 1998 Judge of the European Court of Human Rights in Strasbourg. E-Mail: bostjan.zupancic@echr.coe.int. The perspective is author's own; it does not necessarily reflect the views of the European Court of Human Rights. Copyright © 2004 by B.M. Zupančič.

1 See Rekvényi v. Hungary, App. No. 25390/94 para 34 (Eur. Ct. H.R., 1999) *available at* http://cmiskp.echr.coe.int/tkp197/portal.asp?sessionId=3375411&skin=hudoc-en&action=request. "[M]any laws are inevitably couched in terms which, to a greater or lesser extent, are vague and whose interpretation and application are questions of practice (*see* Sunday Times v. United Kingdom, App. No. 6538/74 31 (Eur. Ct. H.R., 1979) *available at* http://cmiskp.echr.coe.int/tkp197/portal.asp?sessionId=3375613&skin=hudoc-en&action=request, and the Kokkinakis v. Greece, App. No. 14307/88 19 (Eur. Ct. H.R., 1993) *available at* http://cmiskp.echr.coe.int/tkp197/portal.asp?sessionId=3375637&skin=hudoc-en&action=request). The role of adjudication vested in the courts is precisely to dissipate such interpretational doubts as remain (*see, mutatis mutandis*, Cantoni v. France, App. No. 17862/91 1628 (Eur. Ct. H.R. 1996) *available at* http://cmiskp.echr.coe.int/tkp197/portal.asp?sessionId=3375652&skin=hudoc-en&action=request). [emphasis added] *See*, *infra* notes 16 and 47.

2 Here, the need for legal certainty and security is *retrospective*; it concerns a past historical event (a conflict) that must be irrevocably settled, resolved, determined. As we shall see, the doctrine of precedents deals with the *prospective* need for legal certainty and security. The need for the interpretation of the judgments of the European Court of Human Rights derives from the need to foresee its decisions.

régime.³ Even with Hans Kelsen – the originator of the idea of constitutional courts – the postulate, which Montesquieu, Beccaria and other Enlightenment writers have called for, is still very much alive. The strictest possible division of labour between the legislative and the judicial branches, along with the less and less realistic Cartesian distinction between what is abstract (legal norms) and what is concrete (their interpretation and their application) – is still distinctly present.

According to this way of thinking, only the legislative branch is entitled to produce abstract legal acts, with the concession that they possibly require interpretation by the judges.⁴

The judges are entitled to generate only concrete and executable legal decisions. Only the abstract legal acts produced by the legislative branch have an *erga omnes* effect. The decisions of the courts have a limited *inter partes* effect. We have a relic of this unrealistic and misleading idea in article 46 (1) of the European Convention of Human Rights which reads as follows:

Article 46 – Binding force and execution of judgments
(1) The High Contracting Parties undertake to abide by the final judgment of the Court *in any case to which they are parties*.⁵

If it were true that the judgments of the European Court of Human Rights had the strictly limited *inter partes* effect, there would be no need to interpret their abstract *erga omnes* effect. Only insofar as these judgments *de facto* do have an *erga omnes* binding force the need for an interpretation of their meaning, significance and importance arises in the first place.

In the nineteenth century, the enlightened despots of Continental Europe, from Napoleon in France to Frederic the Great in Germany, Leopold of Tuscany in Italy, Catherine the Great in Russia, Maria Theresa and her son Joseph II in Austria – endeavored to produce completely self-sufficient and self-referential normative systems that would make the interpretation of the abstract provisions in the code utterly superfluous. Under the penalty of the forfeiture of all property, for example, Frederic II in his Prussian *Landesgericht* proscribed all interpretation of his Code's provisions. In this, as in other things, the Enlightened Despots followed Napoleon's example.⁶ In today's language we would say that in their codifications they attempted to create a self-referential virtual reality.

3   CAPPELLETTI & COHEN, COMPARATIVE CONSTITUTIONAL LAW, CASES AND MATERIALS (1979).
4   Consequently, the word "interpretation" has acquired a meaning so extensive in Continental law that it goes far beyond simple explanation, construction, or elucidation of an abstract legal norm. In German language the jurists use the more accurate word *"Konkretisierung"* in order to denote the mental process, which goes from the abstract to concrete. In French legal philosophy and elsewhere the word "interpretation" has long been a catchword covering everything creative that judges do to find solutions to real problems that they are faced with. All things considered, the notion of "interpretation" also represents an attenuation of creative legal process, i.e. an unconscious reduction of it to mere elucidation. This is how the Continental legal professions have internalized Montesquieu's categorical appeal that a judge be a mere *"bouche de la loi."* (MONTESQUIEU, DE L'ESPRIT DES LOIS, [Spirit of the Law] vol. XI. 6 (1748)). By contrast, in the judgments of the Anglo-Saxon legal system the occurrence of the words such as "interpretation", "construction" etc., is far less common.
5   Emphasis added. *But see*, Vienna Convention on the Law of Treaties, art. 31, May 22, 1969, 1155 U.N.T.S. 331, available at http://www.un.org/law/ilc/texts/treatfra.htm. *General rule of interpretation*, par. 3(b): *There shall be taken into account, together with the context: (b) any subsequent practice in the application of the treaty which establishes the agreement of the parties regarding its interpretation*. See, *infra*, note 39.
6   Deuteronomy 4:2. *You shall not add to the word that I speak to you, neither shall you take away from it: keep the commandments of the Lord your God which I command you*. See, Perelman, L'interprétation juridique, XVII *in* ARCHIVES DE PHILOSOPHIE DU DROIT 29, 33 (1972).

At the outset, this attempt to completely restate and to codify the hitherto empirically accumulated practical judicial wisdom from Roman law onwards – for Napoleon was deeply influenced by Justinian' *Corpus Juris Civilis* – represented a revolution in legal thinking.

Today, however, this same mentality and its internalized residual values represent an obstructive denial of the autonomy of the judicial branch of power. This historically noxious denial of respect for the judicial branch is an integral part of our Continental political and legal tradition.[7] Demonstrably, this imbalance is, in terms of re-establishing the checks and balances between the three branches of power, a matter *par excellence* to be corrected by today's Continental constitutional courts.

Since there was no check on the arbitrariness of the legislative and especially of the executive branch of power, this uncalled for denial of the power of the judicial branch and the concomitant denial of the autonomy of legal decision-making was and still is destructive of the rule of law. As long as the Constitution is a cloud-hidden abstract tip of the Kelsenian legal pyramid, its provisions cannot be directly litigated. The Constitution, albeit the virtual source of all abstract and concrete legal acts, thus remains the remote and unapproachable queen bee of the legal system.

As a consequence, constitutional provisions cannot be directly invoked and neither the legislative nor the executive branch in their possibly arbitrary exercise of power could be directly challenged in court. Insofar as the rule of law is indispensable for political stability, because it infuses reasoned judgment into politicized divisions and schisms of democratic political life – the function now exercised primarily by the constitutional courts, is truly essential.

The absence of constitutional litigation damaged the whole Continental European history between 1789 and today. In the aftermath of the horrors of World War II, the establishment of the European Court of Human Rights was an act of regret and contrition on the one hand and an act of hope and attempted redemption on the other hand. Perhaps the founding fathers of the European Convention on Human Rights thought that the power of the judicial branch and of the rule of law imposed by it could have stopped Hitler and Mussolini in their tracks?[8] That I do not know, but I do know that Milošević in Yugoslavia could have been stopped, had the Constitutional Court in Belgrade enjoyed the powers and the respect it unfortunately did not.[9]

In any event, the immediate litigation of the Convention's provisions in Strasbourg, where all three branches of state power turn into one defendant, represents a clear break with the tradition, pursuant to which the ultimate abstract legal acts (Convention or the national Constitution) were not available to the individual citizen for direct litigation.[10] In

---

7   In reality, of course, most of the judgments at least of the higher courts have always had an erga omnes effect. In French the word *"la jurisprudence"* connotes just that. But the legal systems still pretend that the lower courts are not bound by the decisions of the higher courts. This denial of an obvious reality derives from the somewhat fictitious division of labour between the legislative and judicial branches. In France, for example, this derives from the historically laden fear of the "government of the judges" (*"le gouvernement des juges"*).
8   To the best of my knowledge, this has never been explored in depth. Wherefrom, in 1945, the assumption that the rule of law is the best antidote for the totalitarian rule? On the other hand, this assumption is an integral part of American constitutional law.
9   In retrospective this is not an entirely unrealistic supposition. But the judges' traditional self-perception and their lack of courage proved to be determinative.
10 As the *travaux préparatoires* clearly demonstrate, the remedies available to the European Court of Human Rights according to Article 41 of the Convention have been watered down from the initial (directly binding) nature of the Court's judgments to the pecuniary "just satisfaction." European Convention on Human Rights, Nov. 4, 1959, 213 U.N.T.S. 221 *available at* http://www.hri.org/docs/ECHR50.html.

terms of constitutional law, the analogue to the individual application in Strasbourg, clearly, is the individual constitutional complaint (*Verfassungsbeschwerde* in Germany, *certiorari* in the United States, *amparo* in Spain, etc.). For this reason, too, the individual domestic constitutional complaint is, from the point of view of domestic constitutional law, the best preventive device. It resolves the problematic cases at home rather than authorizing their submission in the European Court of Human Rights in Strasbourg.

Clearly, much of what I said above has to do with power. On the one hand the refusal of the executive branch, even today, to share its prerogatives with the legislative and especially with the judicial branches of power, is a symptom both of the atrophy of the rule of law as well as of the deterioration of democratic political stability. On the other hand, one must keep in mind the dialectical relationship between the power of logic that is the rule of law and the logic of power that is the domestic law and order.[11]

In the language of today's constitutional law we speak of separation of powers, of checks and balances between the three powers, of their mutual control. The word "power," here, refers to the power to interpret and to the power to command respect for this interpretation.

The Constitution is a social contract binding on all three branches of power as well as on the on the people. The European Convention is a contract binding on the member states. In essence, every contract is an articulation and fixation of an agreement. This articulation and this fixation are arrived at through the use of words. These words are the contract's form whereas the underlying agreement is its substance. The purpose of an articulation of an agreement is to prevent and to remedy, in case they do arise, future disagreements.

Needless to say, at the time of disagreement there is no more agreement between the parties. The substance of the past agreement is irretrievably gone. However, its form, i.e. the verbal articulation of the past agreement, remains on paper. This metamorphosis of an agreement into a disagreement and this permanence of form in view of the evanescence (impermanence) of substance are at the center of the rule of law and of everything legal.

The re-infusion of meaningful substance into the form is the creative enterprise of judges resolving real conflicts in the real world. It is thus absurd to suppose, as did the Enlightened Despots of nineteenth-century Europe, either that legal interpretation is superfluous or that it can be purely mechanical and syllogistic. What we call "Law," is the accumulated practical interpretive wisdom of generations of judges and other jurists. The real genesis of Roman law proves this. It was the judges in Beirut in the fifth century B.C. who crafted it and not Justinian in the sixth century A.D.

In other words, the notion of legal interpretation has an immense semantic overload ranging from simple formal logic and exegesis to the invocation of what modern philosophers call the hermeneutic pyramid.

When interpreting the judgments of the European Court of Human Rights we should keep this in mind.

---

11 The Turkish cases concerning the wearing of the *foulard* are a good example of the so-called *margins of appreciation* accorded to the State by the European Court of Human Rights. In terms of comparative constitutional law, these margins of appreciation are analogous to the U.S. Supreme Court's *doctrine of fundamentality* where the federal court will (in accordance with the XIVth Amendment) limit itself to the violations of the fundamental constitutional provisions leaving the rest to state supreme courts. This also implies that the federal instance imposes only the fundamental (minimal) standards of constitutional rights.

B. The Doctrine of Precedents

Imagine an urban landscaping architect in the process of drawing-up the map of a middle-sized park in the center of a town. He sits at his drawing board; he is trying to decide where to place the trees, the bushes, the benches on which people could sit etc. In addition, he must decide where to draw the pathway corridors, which people will use while choosing destinations within the park or while simply trying to get across the park, from one part of the town to another. A typical architect will work out a symmetrical design that looks good from above, the bird's-eye-view perspective, i.e. from the viewpoint of the drawing board. He will then present the plan to the local authorities and since they, too, will only look at the blueprint or a *maquette*, it will probably please them.

There is, however, an alternative empirical way of devising the plan for the park. It is less elegant and neat, but it is effective and functional. A less authoritarian or pretentious and more practical architect, who has the good of the people at heart, will propose to local authorities initially not to foresee any pathways and corridors at all. He will say, *"I suggest if you will, that initially we simply plant grass all over the park and let the people themselves crisscross the park with their own irregular paths, trails, passageways, and shortcuts. Only when these paths become obvious, we shall reinforce and strengthen them. Thus we shall know for certain that these corridors across the park will truly serve the best interests of the local people."*

This wonderful parable comes from Lon L. Fuller, the famous Harvard legal philosopher. The story is authentic and it concerns the making of Cambridge Common, a park in the middle of Cambridge, Massachusetts. If you happen to visit the place, make sure to inspect the park. From the frog's perspective it is not at all obvious that the paths, now of course paved, are irregular.

In terms of comparative law, the parable stands for the comparison between the European synthetic and deductive Cartesian rationality[12] in law on the one hand and the empirical, analytic muddling-through case-by-case approach of the Anglo-Saxon legal tradition. The latter has not developed any sophisticated legal doctrine regarding the interpretation of judicial precedents. Usually they enunciate only two basic rules.

The first rule is that *like cases should be decided alike*.

The second rule is that the precedent is binding only insofar as the ruling (the holding) and the *ratio decidendi* of a judgment derives from the *underlying facts of the case*. The rest is *obiter dicta*.

However, the misleadingly simple principle according to which "like cases should be decided alike" does represent a radical break with the syllogistic logic, to which we as Continental lawyers are accustomed. It is based on *lateral* reasoning by means of finding similarity between cases and applying analogy. The Continental legal reasoning adheres to *vertical* logical subsumption.[13]

Reasoning by logical subsumption of concrete facts under a major premise is based on

---

12 *See* e.g., Erazim Kohak, *Quest of Qualitative Rationality*, Kira Conference 2000 (2000), at http://www.kira.org/kss2000abstracts.html. "Western thought in the twentieth century has worked itself into a dead end by assuming that the only alternatives available to it were those of a technical, solely quantitative rationality which excludes questions of value and meaning from scholarly consideration (so called "Cartesian rationality," better represented by writers like Reichenbach in his `Rise of Scientific Philosophy') or, alternately an irrationalism which surrenders all claim to critical reason (as in Heidegger or more recently in various post-modernists)."

13 Of course, this is a very schematic and overstated way of presenting the differences. The intention is to present two Weberian "ideal types" in order to explain the issue of interpretation of judgments. If the differences were as important as presented here, no fruitful dialogue between those who come from two different legal systems would be possible. The fascinating aspect of the European Court of Human Rights in Strasbourg is precisely the facility with which the legal discourse develops between judges coming from different legal traditions.

an abstract – not concrete! – concordance; it presupposes a strict vertical distinction between the abstract and the concrete. The principles of legality, legal certainty (*lex clara, lex certa*) etc. express the faith placed in predetermined legal outcomes (legal determinism), i.e. the central faith placed in the rule of law rather than in the arbitrariness of man.[14]

Yet this mode of legal reasoning, too, requires different modes of interpretation: the interpretation of words (concepts), grammatical, systemic, historical and above all teleological, i.e. the interpretation of the legislature's purpose. The need for interpretation, and especially for the teleological interpretation, proves that the vertical syllogistic mode of reasoning based on the concordance between the abstract and the concrete is not as predetermined as most would like to believe.[15] Besides, it leads into legal formalism and it often collides with common sense: *summum jus, summa injuria* ...

Needless to say, for constitutional courts and other courts of last instance this mode of reasoning turns out to be almost completely useless, because in these instances the judges must often deal with the subsumption of concrete facts under the most abstract norm. The case-law of the European Court of Human rights testifies to this, i.e. to the need to fill in the enormous gap between an abstract meaning of a norm of the Convention and the facts of a concrete case.[16] Half a century ago, of course, the Court was faced with this open

---

14 Ideologically and socio-psychologically, the essence of the rule of law is mistrust, i.e. skepticism concerning the power placed in a fellow man. It is probably fair to say that this distrust, which typically leads to the doctrine of checks and balances, i.e. the mutual blocking of reciprocal power in constitutional law, is now a central feature of Western democratic political and legal ideology. It is encapsulated in Lord Acton's maxim: *"Power tends to corrupt, and absolute power corrupts absolutely."*

15 *See*, Refah Partisi and others v. Turkey, App. No. 41340/98, 41342/98, 41343/98 and 41344/98 para 57 (Eur. Ct. H.R. 2003) *available at* http://cmiskp.echr.coe.int/tkp197/portal.asp?sessionId=3375746&skin=hudoc-en&action=request. "As regards the accessibility of the provisions in issue and the foreseeability of their effects, the Court reiterates that the expression 'prescribed by law' requires firstly that the impugned measure should have a basis in domestic law. It also refers to the quality of the law in question, requiring that it be accessible to the persons concerned and formulated with sufficient precision to enable them – if need be, with appropriate advice – to foresee, to a degree that is reasonable in the circumstances, the consequences which a given action may entail. *Experience shows, however, that it is impossible to attain absolute precision in the framing of laws, particularly in fields in which the situation changes according to the evolving views of society. A law which confers a discretion is not in itself inconsistent with this requirement, provided that the scope of the discretion and the manner of its exercise are indicated with sufficient clarity, having regard to the legitimate aim in question, to give the individual adequate protection against arbitrary interference.*" [emphasis added]

16 *See, e.g.*, Rekvényi v. Hungary, App. No. 25390/94 para 34 (Eur. Ct. H.R., 1999) *available at* http://cmiskp.echr.coe.int/tkp197/portal.asp?sessionId=3375411&skin=hudoc-en&action=request. "According to the Court's well-established case-law, one of the requirements flowing from the expression 'prescribed by law' is foreseeability. Thus, a norm cannot be regarded as a "law" unless it is formulated with sufficient precision to enable the citizen to regulate his conduct: he must be able – if need be with appropriate advice – to foresee, to a degree that is reasonable in the circumstances, the consequences which a given action may entail. Those consequences need not be foreseeable with absolute certainty: experience shows this to be unattainable. Again, whilst certainty is highly desirable, it may bring in its train excessive rigidity and the law must be able to keep pace with changing circumstances. Accordingly, many laws are inevitably couched in terms which, to a greater or lesser extent, are vague and whose interpretation and application are questions of practice (*see* Sunday Times v. United Kingdom, App. No. 6538/74 31 (Eur. Ct. H.R., 1979) *available at* http://cmiskp.echr.coe.int/tkp197/portal.asp?sessionId=3375613&skin=hudoc-en&action=request, and the Kokkinakis v. Greece, App. No. 14307/88 19 (Eur. Ct. H.R., 1993) *available at* http://cmiskp.echr.coe.int/tkp197/portal.asp?sessionId=3375637&skin=hudoc-en&action=request). The role of adjudication vested in the courts is precisely to dissipate such interpretational doubts as remain (*see, mutatis mutandis*, Cantoni v. France, App. No. 17862/91 1628 (Eur. Ct. H.R. 1996) *available at* http://cmiskp.echr.coe.int/tkp197/portal.asp?sessionId=3375652&skin=hudoc-en&action=request). The level of precision required of domestic legislation – which cannot in any case provide for every eventuality – depends to a considerable degree on the content of the instrument in question, the field it is designed to cover and the number and status of those to whom it is addressed (*see* Vogt v. Germany, App. No. 17851/91 24 (Eur. Ct.H.R. 1995) *available at* http://cmiskp.echr.coe.int/tkp197/portal.asp?sessionId=3376317&skin=hudoc-en&action=request). Because of the general nature of constitutional provisions, the level of precision required of them may be lower than for other legislation."

space; it filled in the intermediate layers of case-law. The real substance of the Convention now lies in this casuistic jurisprudence. This then generates the need for interpretation of the Court's case-law – rather than the abstract provisions of the Convention itself.

Let us now consider the alternative lateral mode of legal reasoning by case analogy formerly characteristic only of the Anglo-Saxon legal system. For reasons which we have spelled out, this mode of reasoning is slowly gaining ground both in domestic constitutional law as well as in the international law of human rights.

In principle, the choice of the precedent case similar to the case at hand depends on the criteria of similarity. In terms of formal logic, this may mean – if only we choose the right criteria of similarity for the comparison – that any case is similar to any other case and as the French say *la comparaison n'est pas raison*. In formal logical terms, therefore, the level of legal predetermination may seem to be very low indeed.[17]

In turn, this implies the need for a higher level of trust placed in the judiciary, their competence, the judicial self-restraint, their discernment *et cetera*. This indispensable need for the credibility of the judiciary is now coming to the forefront in Continental legal systems that have accorded precedent-creating power to their constitutional courts.[18] Clearly, the balance of power between the three branches has swung in the direction of the judiciary.

In reality, however, the legal reasoning by analogy need not be – and generally is not – any less predetermined than the deductive Continental reasoning by abstract syllogism.

In the case-law system of precedents there are several features that make legal reasoning very transparent. The judgments are published and fed into the collective memory.[19] Should the reasoning of the judges be intellectually dishonest, their judgments are there for the academics and lay public to scrutinize and criticize. Of course, this criticism mostly regards the judgments of constitutional, supreme and international courts whose generally binding pronouncements receive the highest level of attention. Besides, the publication of separate dissenting (and even concurring) opinions will draw the attention to the weak points in the reasoning of the majority.

More importantly, the lateral comparison and the search for similarity between the case at hand and the appropriate precedent is not abstract and fuzzy. In the European Court of Human Rights we deal with hundreds of the so-called clone cases in which the factual pattern is practically identical. Then there are cases which are similar, but not identical and in which the continuation of established jurisprudence does not present a problem.

---

17 There is some truth to this, which is why in the 1970's the United States have adopted the now famous Model Penal Code [MPC], probably the most advanced criminal code with an extremely sophisticated system of interlocking rules, doctrines and principles. In criminal law, where the required level of predetermination is the highest in any legal system (principle of legality, art. 7 of the European Convention on Human Rights) the reasoning by analogy is least suitable. Moreover, due to the jury's unexplained verdict the possibility of an appeal based on substantive criminal law's principle of legality is strictly limited, i.e. most appeals proceed narrowly on procedural grounds. This has left the *substantive* – as opposed to *procedural* – criminal law in an underdeveloped state and had made the MPC codification inevitable. The codification itself went far beyond simple restatement and drew heavily on Continental legal theory. The lesson to be learned from this is that the case-law approach has its own serious disadvantages.
18 For example, this socio-political development is rapidly progressing in some former Communist countries (Slovenia, Check Republic, Slovakia, Hungary etc.) where there has been, some twelve years ago, a sudden reversal to the rule of law. The unquestionable respect for the decisions of the constitutional courts has become an ideological canon that the politicians do not dare to disobey.
19 Formerly, the choice of judgments to be published was made by private law reporters (in England and also in the United States). Today, practically all the judgments are fed into Lexis, Westlaw, and the HUDOC of the European Court of Human Rights. Internet made all this legal material widely available. The legal search machines also make the retrieval of relevant cases far easier, i.e. legal search for the relevant case-law is now completely overhauled.

On the other hand, the Court is well aware when faced with a new issue and when the need arises for establishing a new precedent.

In jurisprudence concerning Turkey a good example of this is the following procedural problem. The six-months rule concerning the filing of an application with the European Court of Human Rights[20] presupposes that the date of the final domestic decision is clear. Usually, the period of six months commences when the last domestic decision is delivered to the applicant. In countries where the decision is not sent by registered mail (Turkey, Italy etc.) but is simply deposited in the registry of the Court of Cassation there may be doubts concerning the exact beginning of the running of the preclusive six months period. In criminal cases the appellant is already in prison and he may be precluded from both finding out that there has been a decision as well as from getting hold of it. If he has a lawyer, he is at his mercy; if he does not have one he may fail to notice the judgment altogether.

Then there are the leading cases of *Akuş v. Turkey* and *Aka v. Turkey*[21] to which many fully analogous cases followed suit. In all of these cases the basis for calculating the additional loss ought to have been the rate of inflation and not the rate of statutory interest for delay. There is little or no problem of interpretation in such cases because the factual situations are classical and clear-cut and because the ruling in both leading cases is clear. Still, such a clear ruling could not be directly deduced from the abstract norm of Protocol I, art. (1),[22] i.e. the cases themselves represent an interpretation of this provision.

Similarly, there have been a number of identical cases following the judgment in the leading cases of *Kalaç c. Turquie*.[23]

All of these cases represent good illustrations of clear interpretation. In all three cases there is a key paragraph of the leading judgment that is easy to discern. Yet, in all three cases further theoretical interpretation may be made. For example, in *Kalaç c. Turquie* it could be said that the judgment of the European Court of Human Rights relied on the *prior consent* of Mr. Kalaç which made the limitations placed on his freedom of religious expression acceptable. A legal theorist, for example, could question just how far such an implicit consent could go in order to justify the limitations placed on constitutional and

---

20 European Convention on Human Rights, Nov. 4, 1950, 213 U.N.T.S. 221, art. 35, *available at* http://www.hri.org/docs/ECHR50.html – *Admissibility criteria*. (1) The Court may only deal with the matter after all domestic remedies have been exhausted, according to the generally recognised rules of international law, and *within period of six months from the date on which the final decision was taken*.
21 In Akkus v. Turkey, App. No. 19263/92 (Eur. Ct. H.R. 1997), Mrs. Akkus sought a ruling that the basis for calculating the additional loss should be the rate of inflation and not the rate of statutory interest for delay. In Aka v. Turkey, App. No. 19639/92 (Eur. Ct. H.R. 1998), the case concerned the fact that statutory interest for delay had been insufficient to compensate for high monetary depreciation during periods of more than four and five years respectively between dates proceedings for additional compensation had been brought and dates sums awarded were actually paid.
22 European Convention on Human Rights, Nov. 4, 1950, 213 U.N.T.S. 221, art. 1, *available at* http://www.hri.org/docs/ECHR50.html. – *Protection of property*. (1) *Every natural or legal person is entitled to the peaceful enjoyment of his possessions. No one shall be deprived of his possessions except in the public interest and subject to the conditions provided for by law and by the general principles of international law. The preceding provisions shall not, however, in any way impair the right of a State to enforce such laws as it deems necessary to control the use of property in accordance with the general interest or to secure the payment of taxes or other contributions or penalties.*
23 Kalac v. Turkey, App. No. 20704/92 para. 28 (Eur. Ct. H.R. 1997) *available at* http://cmiskp.echr.coe.int/tkp197/portal.asp?sessionId=3376408&skin=hudoc-en&action=request "En embrassant une carrière militaire, M. Kalaç se pliait, de son plein gré, au système de discipline militaire. Ce système implique, par nature, la possibilité d'apporter à certains droits et libertés des membres des forces armées des limitations ne pouvant être imposées aux civils (arrêt *Engel et autres c. Pays-Bas* du 8 juin 1976, série A n° 22, p. 24, par. 57). Les Etats peuvent adopter pour leurs armées des règlements disciplinaires interdisant tel ou tel comportement, notamment une attitude qui va à 'encontre de l'ordre établi répondant aux nécessités du service militaire."

human rights.[24] Such further theoretical interpretation, needless to say, is precious because it represents valuable feedback to the courts (national as well international) and contributes decisively to the further development of jurisprudence. However, this kind of creative interpretation should be seen as different from the narrower interpretation concerning the binding nature of a specific precedent.

Of course, there are several issues on the periphery of the established jurisprudence, e.g. concerning euthanasia,[25] the right to know the identity of your parents,[26] environmental issues,[27] the substantive and procedural criteria for torture,[28] positive obligation of the state concerning the protection of life,[29] the nature of parole (conditional release),[30] and the obligation of the state to restitute *in integrum the status quo ante*.[31]

Here the question of interpretation cannot be generalised. Typically, in *Selmouni v. France* the Court itself undertook to clarify its criteria (for torture), i.e. it undertook its own authoritative interpretation. In *Scozzari and Giunta v. Italy*, on the other hand, the Court's own interpretation of article 41[32] makes the interpretation of art. 41 for the Court's addressees more difficult. Only time will show whether the States will in the future (and in what cases) be required to restitute in integrum the situation that has led to violation of the Convention. However, the effect of *Pretty v. U.K.* is clear, i.e. that the issue of euthanasia is not *ratione materiae* under the Convention. This does not require any further interpretation. For different reasons (the so-called margin of appreciation) the effect is perhaps similar concerning the right of the adopted person to find out the identity of his or her parents.

Yet the Court's reasoning (and many dissenting opinions) in *Odievre v. France* leave the possibility open that in the future (and in a different legislative framework) the decision of the Court might be different. That, too, is very difficult to interpret solely on the basis

---

24 In terms of comparative constitutional law, *see* South Dakota v. Neville, 459 U.S. 553, 103 S.Ct. 916, 74 L.Ed.2d 748 and Schmerber v. California, 384 U.S. 747 (1966).
25 Pretty v. United Kingdom, App. No. 2346/02 56 (Eur. Ct. H.R. 2002) *available at* http://cmiskp.echr.coe.int/tkp197/portal.asp?sessionId=3376423&skin=hudoc-en&action=request "The Court therefore concludes that no positive obligation arises under Article 3 of the Convention to require the respondent State either to give an undertaking not to prosecute the applicant's husband if he assisted her to commit suicide or to provide a lawful opportunity for any other form of assisted suicide. There has, accordingly, been no violation of this provision."
26 Odièvre v. France, App. No. 42326/98 (Eur. Ct. H.R. 2003) *available at* http://cmiskp.echr.coe.int/tkp197/portal.asp?sessionId=3376437&skin=hudoc-en&action=request.
27 Hatton and Others v. United Kingdom, App. No. 36022/97 (Eur. Ct. H.R. 2003) *available at* http://cmiskp.echr.coe.int/tkp197/portal.asp?sessionId=3376452&skin=hudoc-en&action=request.
28 Selmouni v. France, App. No. 25803/94 (Eur. Ct. H.R. 1999) *available at* http://cmiskp.echr.coe.int/tkp197/portal.asp?sessionId=3376458&skin=hudoc-en&action=request; Al-Adsani v. United Kingdom, App. No. 35763/97 (Eur. Ct. H.R. 2001) *available at* http://cmiskp.echr.coe.int/tkp197/portal.asp?sessionId=3376464&skin=hudoc-en&action=request.
29 Calvelli and Ciglio v. Italy, App. No. 32967/96 (Eur. Ct. H.R. 2002) *available at* http://cmiskp.echr.coe.int/tkp197/portal.asp?sessionId=3376467&skin=hudoc-en&action=request.
30 Ezeh and Connors v. United Kingdom, App. No. 39665/98 and 40086/98 (Eur. Ct. H.R. 2003) *available at* http://cmiskp.echr.coe.int/tkp197/portal.asp?sessionId=3376470&skin=hudoc-en&action=request.
31 Scozzari and Giunta v. Italy, App. No. 39221/98 and 41963/98 (Eur. Ct. H.R. 2000) *available at* http://cmiskp.echr.coe.int/tkp197/portal.asp?sessionId=3376473&skin=hudoc-en&action=request.
32 European Convention on Human Rights, Nov. 4, 1950, 213 U.N.T.S. 221, art. 41, *available at* http://www.hri.org/docs/ECHR50.html. – *Just satisfaction*. If the Court finds that there has been a violation of the Convention or the protocols thereto, and if the internal law of the High Contracting Party concerned allows only partial separation to be made, the Court shall, if necessary, afford just satisfaction to the injured party.
"[U]nder Article 41 of the Convention the purpose of awarding sums by way of just satisfaction is to provide reparation solely for damage suffered by those concerned to the extent that such events constitute a consequence of the violation *that cannot otherwise be remedied*." *Scozzari and Giunta* App. No. 39221/98 at para 250 (2000).

of the judgment in question.³³ Most probably it is impossible to cite or invent a rule of interpretation that would enable someone in Turkey or elsewhere to say with certainty whether the anonymity of delivery would, or would not, be sustained in the European Court of Human Rights in Strasbourg.

C. How to Read and Interpret the Judgment

The practical question on the receiving end of this jurisprudence, however, is how to interpret the cases coming from Strasbourg. Here, instead of advising as to any firm rules of interpretation I would first point out simply how to *read* a case.

If we subject any precedent to a legal analysis we should pay attention to three principal legal aspects: *the facts* that affect the specific realistic configuration in which the decision is taken; *the issue*, which transposes these facts into a legal context and transforms them into a juridical question to be resolved; and *the holding (ruling)* of the court, which presumably resolves the question and takes a clear stand on the issue.³⁴

Each judgment of the European Court of Human Rights is divided into three principal sections. The first one is entitled *"The Facts,"* the second one *"The Law"* whereas the so-called *"Operative Part"* at the end represents the implemental ruling of the Court. Compared to the Anglo-American tradition in which the judges write the judgments themselves (or are assisted in doing so by their personal law clerks) and where there are no prescribed rules as to the structure of the judgments, the decisions of the European Court of Human Rights are highly structured and therefore comparatively transparent and explainable. The renowned quality of these judgments derives from both from their characteristic structure and from the constant endeavor of the Court to make them comprehensive and concise. The writing of each major judgment, usually delivered by the Grand Chamber of seventeen judges, is supervised by a *comité de rédaction* composed of several judges. The Court's deliberations before the vote are in fact mostly dedicated to the final

---

33 Odièvre v. France, App. No. 42326/98, para 49, 38 Eur. H.R. Rep. 43 (2004) (ECHR) [decided Feb. 13, 2003].
"Par ailleurs, le système mis en place par la France récemment, s'il conserve le principe de l'admission de l'accouchement sous X, renforce la possibilité de lever le secret de l'identité qui existait au demeurant à tout moment avant l'adoption de la loi du 22 janvier 2002. La nouvelle loi facilitera la recherche des origines biologiques grâce à la mise en place d'un conseil national de l'accès aux origines personnelles, organe indépendant, composé de magistrats, de représentants d'associations concernées par l'objet de la loi et de professionnels ayant une bonne connaissance pratique des enjeux de la question. D'application immédiate, elle peut désormais permettre à la requérante de solliciter la réversibilité du secret de l'identité de sa mère sous réserve de l'accord de celle-ci de manière à assurer équitablement la conciliation entre la protection de cette dernière et la demande légitime de la requérante, et il n'est même pas exclu, encore que cela soit peu probable, que, grâce au nouveau conseil institué par le législateur, la requérante puisse obtenir ce qu'elle recherche.
La législation française tente ainsi d'atteindre un équilibre et une proportionnalité suffisante entre les intérêts en cause. La Cour observe à cet égard que les Etats doivent pouvoir choisir les moyens qu'ils estiment les plus adaptés au but de la conciliation ainsi recherchée. Au total, la Cour estime que la France n'a pas excédé la marge d'appréciation qui doit lui être reconnue en raison du caractère complexe et délicat de la question que soulève le secret des origines au regard du droit de chacun à son histoire, du choix des parents biologiques, du lien familial existant et des parents adoptifs."
34 The schematic division into *facts*, *issue* and *ruling*, however, may be misleading – and especially so to one who is not used to contextual legal research, case analysis etc. Especially important is not to take too literally the distinction between the facts and the issue of the case. One must keep in mind that the facts *per se* do not exist. The facts only become real when seen through a particular legal prism. We cannot go deeper into this here, but we can paraphrase Hobbes in his famous saying: *"Civil laws ceasing, facts also cease."* THOMAS HOBBES, LEVIATHAN, chapter 28, para 3 (1651) *available at* http://etext.library.adelaide.edu.au/h/h68l/chapter27.html.

reading and editing of the judgment. The text of the opinion is supposed to reflect the contributions of the judges in the decisive first deliberations, which take place immediately after the public audience (in cases where there is one).

The deliberations of the judges of the Court concerning a particular case could be seen as being of three kinds. The procedural considerations concern the admissibility of the case and the discussion of the procedurally relevant occurrences, sometimes last-minute submissions and events during the public audience. The substantive discourse itself concerns two major aspects. The first one concerns the extant case-law and the discussion of parallels between the case at hand along with the possibly applicable precedents.

The second aspect of the substantive discourse concerns what the French call *la qualification du cas*. Here, the case's legal nature is characterised and typified in the general legal discourse which goes far beyond the discussion of similarities between the precedents and the case at hand. Different legal notions that are part of our shared legal culture are discussed, weighed and reflected upon. I would venture to say that it is this juristic discourse which represents the real substance of the Court's deliberations.

In the "Law" part of every judgment there is usually one key paragraph and in it one or more key sentences. I am not referring to the *inter partes* purpose of the judgment, which is taken care of in the final operative part. Clearly, in order to understand the *erga omnes* effect of the decision, since this will apply to all future similar cases, one must look for the extant grounds of the decision.

On the other hand, the interpretation of precedents is *contextual*.[35] Because the meaning of the judgment's holding (ruling) – often encapsulated in the key sentence or paragraph of the judgment – depends both on the facts and the implied juridical comprehension of the case, the key sentence can never be separated from the case as a whole (*ratio decidendi*).[36]

The doctrine of precedents tells us that the holding (ruling) of the case carries only insofar as the facts of the case will allow it.[37] When it is said that like cases must be decided alike, this also means that the holding of a case cannot be elevated to a general principle detached from its specific facts. When a new case comes along, in other words, the applicability of a principle, doctrine or rule established in a precedent will in principle apply only if the facts of the case are identical, similar, analogous etc.

One way of understanding this is to compare the usefulness e.g. of Michele de Salvia's book[38] with a casebook containing the leading cases of the European Court of Human Rights. De Salvia's book is an excellent *aide mémoire* for somebody already acquainted with the hundreds of judgments of the Court, i.e. with their factual and juridical context. For a novice, however, a much better method is to read the select key cases in their complex entirety.

---

35   See Vienna Convention on the Law of Treaties, *supra* note 5. In the *Vienna Convention on the Law of Treaties*, 1969, article31, paras. 2 and 3, the word "context" applies to the *normative* surroundings of a particular legal concept (word). In. 3(b), however, there is a reference to "subsequent practice in the application of the treaty." Of course, the *case-law* contextuality is very different from the *normative* contextuality, which the drafters of the Vienna Convention on the Law of Treaties must have intended.
36   Perelman, *supra* note 6 at 36, citing DIGESTAE, L. XVII, 1 *"Non ex regula jus sumatur sed ex jure quod est regula fiat:* `Il ne suffit pas de connaître les règles de droit. Une des principales tâches de l'interprétation juridique est de trouver des solutions aux conflits entre les règles, en hiérarchisant les valeurs que ces règles doivent protéger. C'est comme on le sait, cette fine hiérarchisation des droits constitutionnels qui a été et qui continue à être une des tâches principales de la Cour Suprême des Etats-Unis.'"
37   In principle the ruling (holding) of a case is just that (a ruling, a holding) only insofar as it resolves the specific problem presented by the case's fact pattern. The rest is *obiter dictum* (pl. *obiter dicta*). *Obiter dicta* may have a pedagogical meaning and effect – a message sent to lower courts – but they neither binding on its own source (the court producing the precedent) nor upon the lower courts.
38   MICHELE DE SILVA ENGEL AND NORBERT PAUL, COMPENDIUM DE LA CEDH (1998).

Another way to explain the contextuality of the case law is to ask whether the current jurisprudence of the European Court of Human Rights could be restated i.e. codified, in a concise system of rules, doctrines and precedents. This would only be possible to a very limited extent or not at all. Why? The standard answer would be, among other things, as the Court itself has so often emphasized in its decisions, that the Convention is a "living instrument."[39] Very rarely, the Court, and only if there are *compelling reasons* to do so, will change its case law and explicitly reverse itself on a previous standpoint.[40]

More likely, however, is that a new fact pattern in a new case will call for a new or less ambiguous legal approach in resolving the case.[41] What is happening, therefore, is not so much the reversal of preceding case law as its further differentiation. New nuances of decision making are brought into play when new legal issues are singled out and new precedents (principles, doctrines, rules) established concerning the finer distinctions between previously undifferentiated legal issues. A specific new legal issue is sorted out, voted upon and decided. Thereafter, the standpoint thus taken applies to other similar cases, i.e. if and when they do arrive. I would venture to say that this, rather than the self-reversal of previously established rules, is the real meaning of the incantation formula used by the Court, according to which the Convention is not a static but a dynamic, living instrument of the law on human rights. In this fashion the Court – mostly through its Grand Chamber compositions of 17 judges – interprets the Convention and creates new precedents.

A question might be raised as to this quasi-legislative creativity of the Court in Strasbourg. Yet today, fortunately, this question originating in the traditional and ideologically overloaded division of labor between the legislative and judicial branches – along with the unrealistic (to put it mildly) and epistemologically untenable "Cartesian" line of separation between the abstract and the concrete – is for the most part technically outdated and ideologically obsolete. Of course, in Continental Europe the transcendence of this dialectic between the abstract and the concrete[42] is mostly transpiring *via* empirical case-by-case creative problem solving by the constitutional and international courts.[43]

---

39 The phrase appears in thirty judgments (in English language).
40 In constitutional law (discrimination cases) the notion of "compelling reasons" evokes the strictest possible criteria of assessment. *See, e.g.*, Equality Foundation of Greater Cincinnati, Inc. v. Cincinnati, 54 F. 3d 261, 267 (6th Cir. 1995) "The law will be upheld only if it is suitably tailored to serve a *compelling* state interest."
41 Typical examples are Comingersoll v. Portugal, App. No. 35382/97 (Eur. Ct. H.R., 2000) *available at* http://cmiskp.echr.coe.int/tkp197/portal.asp?sessionId=3388777&skin=hudoc-en&action=request, Selmouni v. France, App. No. 25803/94 (Eur. Ct. H.R., 1999) *available at* http://cmiskp.echr.coe.int/tkp197/portal.asp?sessionId=3388780&skin=hudoc-en&action=request.
42 *See*, more extensively, ROBERTO UNGER, KNOWLEDGE AND POLITICS 88–100 (1975). Unger speaks of the "antinomy of rules and values", i.e. of the dialectic in which the clear rules of law are established and fixed in order to take the place of fuzzy values –, but are constantly informed by them (via teleological interpretation). In constitutional and in the international law of human rights this antinomy is of special concern. Since values come into play in concrete cases they tend to have an impact on abstract precedents.
43 From the point of view of systems analysis, the legal system is – just like human consciousness – an arrangement of interconnected feedback channels. These feedback channels feed the experiences deriving from the real cases that the system deals with, back into the legal system's memory. In this way the system further develops its know-how, differentiates its problem-solving approaches and is capable of learning from its own experiences. Legal system is thus a virtual reality (legal culture) with more or less contact with the actual and factual social, political etc. reality of the nation (or of the international community). The significant difference between the traditional Continental legal system and the emerging precedent empirical feedback (traditional in the Anglo-Saxon legal systems) of the constitutional courts lies precisely in the immediacy and the magnitude of the system's self-learning capacity. In other words, the system is better able to maintain its contact with reality, which increases the adequacy and the social relevance of these responses. The main obstacle to the advancement of this beneficial process may be political but in large measure the barriers also derive from the internalized attitude of the jurists, lawyers, judges etc.

To academic constitutionalists and to constitutional court judges the process is familiar. This is especially so in countries where the citizens may file individual constitutional complaints (*Verfassungsbeschwerde* in Germany, *amparo* in Spain, *certiorari* in the United States etc.), because the individual constitutional complaint is largely analogous to the application (*requête*) in the European Court of Human Rights. From the point of view of the state signatory of the Convention, this *in concreto* judicial review is also the best domestic screening device.

Because constitutional rights stand for a far larger circle of rights than human rights – the latter establish only the *minimal* standards for 43 signatories of the Convention and apply to roughly 800 million people from Iceland in the West to Russia in the East, from Norway in the North, to Turkey in the South, *in concreto* judicial scrutiny – when fair and independent – is a superior domestic remedy. When efficacious, it must be used before the case ever comes to the Court in Strasbourg, whose jurisdiction is international and thus subsidiary (supplementary, auxiliary, ancillary) to domestic legal remedies to be previously exhausted.

D. Conclusion

The interpretation of a judgment of the European Court of Human Rights is no different from the interpretation of any other precedent-setting judgment delivered by other courts. In the last analysis, the only difference obtains from the perception of the binding nature of the superior court judgments.

Because the judges of the lower courts know that the judgments of the higher courts are at least *de facto* binding on them, these judges – even in countries with the Continental legal tradition – read and interpret judgments delivered by the higher (supreme and constitutional) courts. They know that effectively their independence *vis-à-vis* the higher courts is an ideological fiction. If they were to believe it, they would be reversed over and over again. Thus, for example, the jurisprudence of the *Cour de cassation*, although it is not formally binding on the lower courts, is a *de facto* source of French law.

From the point of view of the lower court, the art of reading the judgment as well as of interpreting its relevance as a precedent, and its impact, is admittedly less clear-cut than the art of interpreting an abstract norm issued by the legislature. At worst, it amounts to a speculation about the outcome of the case were the parties to file an appeal leading the court of appeal decide the case anew.[44]

A case filed with the European Court of Human Rights (an application, a *requête*) may be inadmissible for a number of reasons: *ratione materiae*, because the substance of the case does not fall under the Convention; or *ratione temporis*, because the event occurred before the coming into force of the Convention, because it was filed more than six months after the last decision of the domestic highest instance, because domestic remedies have not been exhausted, etc. But these are procedural criteria that do not lend themselves to much interpretation.[45]

From the point of view of the Constitutional court, these procedural reasons are not interesting. In the *in camera* deliberations of a national constitutional or supreme court,

---

44 Of course, concerning ordinary domestic cases we do keep in mind that the grounds for appeal may be limited, may concern only purely legal issues, the absolutely essential procedural violations etc. Nevertheless, we are aware that these distinctions are relative and not as clear-cut as imagined.
45 Still, of the 97.3 percent of the rejected applications filed with the European Court of Human Rights, except those that are found to be "manifestly unfounded," most are declared inadmissible for these procedural reasons.

the real issue is whether the European Court of Human Rights will reverse their decision. Here, the practical issue is not so much the in-depth interpretation of the relevant case of the European Court of Human Rights, as is the simple awareness that such a resemblance (analogy) between the case dealt with by the domestic court and a specific precedent of the European Court of Human Rights – exists in the first place. If the domestic court is aware of the similarity between the domestic case to be decided and the specific European precedent, the situation for the domestic court is pretty predictable.[46]

In principle, although the precedents of the European Court of Human Rights are only *de facto* binding on the State signatory of the Convention, the first instance courts and all the courts of appeal ought to apply the Convention (as interpreted by the European Court of Human Rights). Both from the point of view of the protection of human rights as well as in terms of procedural economy in the domestic legal system this would be the ideal state of affairs.

One, however, realizes that this is necessarily a long term assimilation process – also due to language and other cultural communication barriers.

Moreover, a stance taken by the European Court of Human Rights on a particular legal issue is always taken *via* the specific case and *vis-à-vis* a specific domestic legal system: British, French, German, Russian, Swedish, Turkish, etc. Only rarely does the Court pronounce an abstract ruling that may be directly applied in the domestic legal systems of all states signatories of the Convention.[47]

At the current stage of development, therefore, there exist three needs for interpretation. *First*, the ruling of the European Court of Human Rights must be abstracted from the differential specifics of the particular case and the specific domestic legal system. *Second*, the meaning of the ruling must be meaningfully transposed into the situation of the domestic legal system. *Third*, the ruling must be applied to the specific domestic case at hand. Clearly, this is best done by the domestic court of last resort – ideally, by the constitutional court applying the precedent in the *in concreto* judicial review. Here, the practical advice of the European Court of Human Rights is that each of the national courts of last instance should have at least one senior jurist who is intimately acquainted with the case law of the European Court of Human Rights.[48]

Once the domestic court of last instance establishes a similarity between the case at hand and the specific precedent of the European Court of Human Rights, the question arises whether the distinguishing characteristics of the domestic case set it apart from the precedent delivered by the European Court of Human Rights. From the point of view of the domestic court, this "differential diagnosis" of the borderline case is perhaps one of the most difficult aspects of interpretation. It presupposes the full cognizance of the case law context in which the specific precedent is being perceived.

46 Again, this predictability – we are referring to *sécurité juridique* – is lateral (based on analogical reasoning), rather than vertical (based on syllogistic reasoning). Yet, lateral reasoning looking for similarities proceeds to finding a common major premise to both cases. Once found, this major premise is likely to be much more specific than the one derived from a remote major premise. In consequence, the predictability and *sécurité juridique* are commensurably increased.
47 Such was the case in Selmouni v. France, App. No. 25803/94 (Eur. Ct. H.R., 1999) *available at* http://cmiskp.echr.coe.int/tkp197/portal.asp?sessionId=3411047&skin=hudoc-en&action=request, (concerning the definition of torture as per Art. 3 of the Convention). Another example may be Commingersol v. Portugal, App. No. 35382/97 (Eur. Ct. H.R., 2000) *available at* http://cmiskp.echr.coe.int/tkp197/portal.asp?sessionId=3411074&skin=hudoc-en&action=request, (concerning the standing of corporations and perhaps other legal persons to claim non-pecuniary damage).
48 Of course, the Internet site of the European Court of Human Rights – http://www.echr.coe.int – has the search machine capable of retrieving the judgments dealing with a certain issue. However, in order to be able to use this search machine one must be able to configure the specific idiomatic combination of words (both in English and in French languages) that evoke the relevant series of judgments and admissibility decisions.

Given that the applicability of a precedent is sometimes debatable even in the European Court of Human Rights itself, it might be difficult for the domestic court clearly to distinguish the applicability of one precedent as opposed to another – or none at all.[49] At the current stage of national assimilation of international human rights law it is perhaps not realistic to expect of all the States signatories of the Convention, i.e. of their courts of last resort, the capability of making this differential diagnosis, although, of course, the British House of Lords, the French *Cour de Cassation* or the German *Bundesverfassungsgericht* in Karlsruhe, the Dutch Supreme Court and others will occasionally do just this. Naturally, the arguments proffered in their discussions of the applicability of the specific precedent are taken into account by the European Court of Human Rights and they may be wholly persuasive.

Here, it becomes apparent in what way the European Court of Human Rights is – despite all the formalistic arguments to the contrary – an international constitutional court with the power of *in concreto* judicial review and with the *de facto erga omnes* effect of its judgments.[50]

---

49 *See, e.g.*, Hatton v. U.K., App. No. 36022/97 (Eur. Ct. H.R., 2003) *available at* http://cmiskp.echr.coe.int/tkp197/portal.asp?sessionId=3411097&skin=hudoc-en&action=request, as well as Ezeh and Connors v. U.K., App. No. 39665/98 and 40086/98 (Eur. Ct. H.R., 2003) *available at* http://cmiskp.echr.coe.int/tkp197/portal.asp?sessionId=3411106&skin=hudoc-en&action=request, and especially the appended dissenting opinions.

50 More specifically on that question in, Zupančič, *Droit Constitutionnel Et Jurisprudence De La Cour Européenne Des Droits De L'Homme, Tentative de synthèse*, 2001 ANNUAIRE DE DROIT CONSTITUTIONNEL 14 (2001).

Between Citizens and Peoples: Reflections on the New European Constitutionalism

Sergio Dellavalle*

A. The Democratic Foundation of the Public Power in the European Union by the Sole Reference to the "Peoples of the Member States"

This article is primarily concerned with the question how the democratic legitimacy of the European public power can be fully assured. Before I turn to that issue I would like to address two assumptions which form the backdrop to the entire analysis, but which are better considered independent of that context.

I. First Assumption: A Well-intended Legitimacy of Public Power Must be Democratic

By beginning my reflections with this assertion, I do not intend silently to pass over the alternative ways of legitimizing public power that some important scholars have proposed in the last decade, precisely with reference to the legitimacy problems of European political integration and efforts to seek a solution to its specific shortcomings.[1]

One of the most interesting of these "post-democratic" proposals[2] typifies the core concept of a quite common position among scholars.[3] That position denies citizens the recourse to procedures by which they can consciously participate, according to the notion of autonomy, in the elaboration of the rules they have to follow. Alternative proposals would resort to so-called "technocratic-utilitarian" or "formal-juridical" legitimization. "Technocratic-utilitarian" legitimacy is understood as "the capability to assure the functioning of the social system ... and the satisfaction of the needs of the individuals [in a society]."[4] "Formal-juridical" legitimacy, on the other hand, guarantees respect for the rules of the legal system in force.[5]

---

* Marie-Curie Fellow and Co-director of the research project on the "Philosophy of International Law" at the Max-Planck-Institute for Comparative Public Law and International Law at Heidelberg; Assistant Professor at the Faculty of Law of the University of Turin (Italy).

   1 Among the most significant examples: Armin von Bogdandy, *The European Union as a Supranational Federation*, 6 COLUM. J. OF EUR. L. 27, 44 (2000); A. v. Bogdandy, *L'unione sovranazionale come forma di potere politico*, 10 TEORIA POLITICA 133, 146 (1994); A. v. Bogdandy, *Supranationale Union als neuer Herrschaftstypus*, 16 INTEGRATION 210, 219 (1993); FRITZ WILHELM SCHARPF, GOVERNING IN EUROPE: EFFECTIVE AND DEMOCRATIC? (1999); Joseph H. H. Weiler, *Problems of Legitimacy in Post 1992 Europe*, 46 AUSSENWIRTSCHAFT 411, 433 (1991).
   2 Bogdandy, *L'unione sovranazionale*, *supra* note 1.
   3 *See* Markus Jachtenfuchs & Beate Kohler-Koch, *Regieren im dynamischen Mehrebenensystem*, in EUROPÄISCHE INTEGRATION, 15 (Markus Jachtenfuchs & Beate Kohler-Koch eds., 1996); Giandomenico Majone, *Europe's "Democratic Deficit": The Question of Standards*, 4 EUR. L J. 5 (1998).
   4 Bogdandy, *L'unione sovranazionale*, *supra* note 1, at 146.
   5 *Id.*

Undoubtedly, a system's ability to provide society with sound governance solutions, as well as a high degree of rationality and certainty regarding the rule of law, are non-replaceable pillars of an acceptable public power and essential conditions of the system's legitimacy.[6] Nevertheless, some important arguments lead to the conviction that these facets of democratic governance cannot, when taken alone, be seen as sufficient for establishing democratic legitimacy. Indeed, it seems clear that they are themselves grounded in a deeper basis, i.e. on the participation of the citizens. The first argument recalls the classical principle that *volenti non fit iniuria*: only the control by the citizens as well as their participation can ensure that the rulers will not turn into an autonomous caste and the legitimate power into an autocracy.[7] Second, the legitimization "by silent consensus" presupposes and consolidates a certain ethical regression of the citizenry, i.e. their decline from the status of conscious members of the society who are able to make an original contribution to the normative principles of the polity in which they live, to a mass of passive subjects, sometimes patient and sometimes rather treacherous, but never really participating and creatively cooperating.[8] Finally, the political and normative system can be seen as firm and solid only if it remains permeable to the stimulus originating from the evolution of civil society, the best conveyer of which is still to be found in the democratic process.[9] When social conflicts cannot find a proper expression in political proposals, after fermenting unresolved for some time, they may emerge explosively, with disruptive effects on the social and political order as a whole.[10] These arguments simply should not be ignored in an attempt to articulate a quick-fix solution for the legitimacy shortcomings of the European political and juridical system. Policies that effectively manage the social and economic problems and which promote certainty with respect to the rule of law must be understood as essential elements of the legitimacy of political power, but only on the condition that they can be linked to civic participation. They cannot, alone, serve as substitutes for this.

II. Second Assumption: To be Effectively Democratic the Legitimization of Public Power Should Provide for Adequate Instruments to Assure the Real Participation of Citizens in the Political Process

We should not forget that "democracy" does not translate directly into "parliamentarianism." The range of action of every individual in democratic life should not be restricted to the right of putting his or her vote into the ballot box. Instead, the full range of democratic action must be guaranteed by rules which allow a continuous osmosis between the structures of power and the demands of the civil society.[11] Only in this way can the élitarian essence of power be weakened, according to the democratic principle, and be brought

---

6 It is significant, on this point, that also most authors who eminently emphasize the centrality of the principle of legitimacy and autonomy acknowledge the importance of the efficacy of law, failing which merely formal democratic rules cannot work. For two pre-eminent examples, among many others, see HANS KELSEN, VOM WESEN UND WERT DER DEMOKRATIE (1929); NORBERTO BOBBIO, IL FUTURO DELLA DEMOCRAZIA (1984); JÜRGEN HABERMAS, FAKTIZITÄT UND GELTUNG (1992).
7 IMMANUEL KANT, DIE METHAPHYSIK DER SITTEN (1797), RECHTSLEHRE, § 46; KELSEN, *supra* note 6, at 98.
8 CHARLES TAYLOR, PHILOSOPHY AND THE HUMAN SCIENCES 211(1985); HABERMAS, *supra* note 6, at 349.
9 HABERMAS, *supra* note 6, at 399.
10 This may have been, to a high degree of certainty, the situation in Eastern Europe behind the iron curtain (*see* PETER CIPKOWSKI, REVOLUTION IN EASTERN EUROPE (1991)), but it can have been also the reason – quite in a less dramatic way – of the 1968 student protest era in reaction to the conservatism and stasis of the 1950s and 1960s (*see* MARK KURLANSKY, 1968: THE YEAR THAT ROCKED THE WORLD (2003)).
11 Actual participation is, in fact, a pre-condition of a every well-intended concept of democracy (thus, apart from the idea of a "national" democracy which is rather a populistic variant of the authoritarian governmental form; *see* CARL SCHMITT, VERFASSUNGSLEHRE 223 (1928), 223). On the different concepts of democracy, *see* DAVID HELD, MODELS OF DEMOCRACY (1987).

nearer to the governed themselves, an ongoing process which distinguishes the democratic form of government from autocratic and aristocratic traditions.[12]

An adequate discussion of this second assumption would presuppose a sufficiently profound inquiry into: (1) the standards associated with a well-intended guarantee of political rights; (2) the electoral system which should be seen as the most preferable in general or at least in a concrete context; and (3) the institutional methods of giving civil society a full and fair opportunity to express itself, even beyond the electoral moment. Surely, these are important questions which, nevertheless, would draw us away from the focus of the article, which consists in verifying whether the conditions exist for a democratic legitimization of the public power of the Union. More specifically, this article will consider how such legitimization could be enhanced, as a fundamental criterion of public power itself, in a Constitutional Treaty which aims to serve as the re-foundation of European integration. Therefore, I will largely pass over the problems connected with the concrete procedures of the legitimization process, dealing with them only as far as they are necessary for a more correct understanding of the solutions proposed in response to the article's focus.

III. Democratic Legitimacy, Public Power and Sovereignty

As an answer to the requirement that democratic legitimacy must be based on civic engagement, a principle that is central to the democratic idea (particularly as it has been formulated in the first assumption presented above), democratic states have traditionally inserted into the Preamble or into an article of their constitutions a formulation which explicitly states that public power exists only as far as it has been legitimated by the community of the citizens who are subject to it. The first significant example of this in modern times was the Constitution of the United States of America (1787), which, in its Preamble, provides for the community of citizens. The framers of the American constitution formulated this element with the phrase "We the People," which establishes the citizenry as the essential element as well as constituent power of the new polity and as the fundament of an order governed by justice and committed to "domestic tranquility ... general welfare" and to securing "the blessings of liberty to ourselves and our posterity."[13]

In Western Europe, during the two centuries of the modern constitutional history that followed the American constitutional experiment, three main patterns have been developed which have characterized – with only a few exceptions[14] – the commitment to democracy fixed by the constitution in almost all countries belonging to the Union. Only a few months after the Constitution of the United States went into effect, it fell to the French Revolution to produce the oldest and best known of the European constitutions fitting into the first of these three patterns, the most relevant characteristic of which consists in the identification of democratic legitimacy with the sovereignty of the nation. Article 3 of the *Déclaration des droits de l'homme et du citoyen* (1789) provides for "the principle of all

---

12 HANS KELSEN, GENERAL THEORY OF LAW AND STATE (1945); NORBERTO BOBBIO, STATO, GOVERNO, SOCIETÀ. PER UNA TEORIA GENERALE DELLA POLITICA 129 (1985).
13 U.S. CONST. pmbl.
14 Some member states of the EU do not provide in their constitutions for an explicit derivation of all public power from the citizens. These states are, first, the United Kingdom which does not have a Constitution in a proper sense, then Denmark, the Constitution of which mentions only the legislative power of the *King in Parliament*, and the Netherlands, where the Constitution is limited to the definition of the Parliament as representative of the people (art. 50). Yet, in these cases the lack of a clear normative commitment to the democratic power of the citizens did not have any negative consequence on the political role of the Parliament, the relevance of which has been much more the very core of the democratic substance of these traditions – a situation, nevertheless, that we can not find in a similar way (as we will see later) in the EU.

sovereignty," which resides "essentially in the Nation."[15] One of the two remaining patterns, both of which are of decidedly more recent vintage than the French constitution, is embodied in the Italian Constitution (1948). The Italian text concisely asserts in art. 1, para. 2, that "the sovereignty belongs to the people."[16] In this second example from among the three European patterns we also have a reference to sovereignty, but linked to the "people" and not the nation.[17] The third and most successful of the three European patterns – successful in the sense that it is also present in the greatest number of constitutions of the member states of the EU – is that which we find in the German *Grundgesetz* (GG – Basic Law or Constitution) (1949) with its synthetic and pregnant formulation: "all state authority is derived from the people."[18] The advantage of this formulation is that it does not presuppose any reference to historically important, but quite inflexible concepts like "nation"[19] or "sovereignty,"[20] which only can be applied to the present context of political relations with difficulty, inside as well as outside the context of single states. It should be noted that the constitutions of the new member states of the EU include provisions which can be traced back to one of these three European patterns, although the pattern characterized by the German constitution enjoys priority here as well.[21]

Although the democratic commitment was expressed *de facto* in all member states of the

---

15 *Déclaration des droits de l'homme et du citoyen* [The Declaration of the Rights of Men and Citizens] art. 3 (1789). Substantially identical to the French model are the formulations in the constitutions of Belgium (art. 33, para. 1) and Luxembourg (art. 32, para. 1).
16 COSTITUZIONE DELLA REPUBBLICA ITALIANA [Constitution], art. 1, para. 2. (1948).
17 Near to the Italian model are the constitutions of Portugal (art. 3, para. 1) and Spain (art. 1, para. 2).
18 The German Constitution, art. 20, para. 2. (F.R.G.) is identical to the formulations of the Constitution of Austria (art. 1), and very similar to those of Finland (chapter 1, section 2, para. 1), Greece (art. 1, para. 3) and Sweden (art. 1, para. 1). Analogous in its substance, furthermore, the provision of the Constitution of Ireland, although in this last case also a reference to God is present (art. 6, para. 1).
19 On the shortcomings deriving from the use of a nation-based concept of the "people" as the fundament of democratic legitimacy, *see infra*, C.
20 The concept of "sovereignty" was first introduced in modern times to express the absolute power of the monarch, i.e. a power which should not be bound by limitations and conditions (*see* JEAN BODIN, SIX LIVRES DE LA RÉPUBLIQUE Livre I, Chap. VIII and X (1579)). As a consequence of the revolutions of the late eighteenth century this understanding of power was then transmitted, quite unchanged, from the monarch to the "people" or "nation" (*see* Declaration of the Rights of Men, *supra* note 15). Though very important for the meaning of legitimacy, this transmission did not question the claim of any sovereign power not to be limited within its home sphere of influence. Only the external use of force could represent a limitation, however a factual, not a legal one. Therefore, the conception of the absolute sovereignty was essentially linked to the idea of supremacy of domestic public law over international law which, first, was largely at disposal of the will of the single countries, and second was not allowed to claim any authority on their domestic policies. Following a universalistic humanitarian approach and the acknowledgment that the societies and the interests of the single countries were becoming more and more interconnected, a vision was drawn where international law was charged with the role to "humanise" inter-state relationships (*see* MARTTI KOSKENNIEMI, THE GENTLE CIVILIZER OF NATION (2001)). The most radical development of this attitude culminated in the theory of the supremacy of international law, challenging explicitly the notion of absolute sovereignty (*see* HANS KELSEN, REINE RECHTSLEHRE 129 (1934)). Since then, the overcoming of sovereignty has becoming an essential aspect of the legal evolution both in domestic as well as in international law. On this issue, *see* CHRISTIAN TOMUSCHAT, INTERNATIONAL LAW: ENSURING THE SURVIVAL OF MANKIND ON THE EVE OF A NEW CENTURY (1999); JÜRGEN HABERMAS, DER GESPALTENE WESTEN 113 (2004); Anne-Marie Slaughter, *A Liberal Theory of International Law*, 94 AMERICAN SOCIETY OF INTERNATIONAL LAW 240 (2000); GLOBAL LAW WITHOUT A STATE (Gunther Teubner ed., 1997).
21 Near to the German model are the provisions in the constitutions of Estonia (art. 1, para. 1), Latvia (chapter 1, art. 2), Hungary (chapter 1, art. 2, para. 2) and Slovenia (chapter 1, art. 3, para. 2). Interesting are the formulations in the constitution of Slovakia, where the reference is not to the "people", but to the "citizens" (chapter 1, art. 2, para. 1: "State power is derived from citizens"), and of the Czech Republic, with a Preamble which mentions the "citizens" and the chapter 1, art. 2, para. 1, that provides for the "people" to be the origin of state power, according to the tradition referring to the German Basic Law. On the other side, the constitution of Lithuania (chapter 1, art. 2) follows the Italian pattern and that of Poland (chapter 1, art. 4, para. 1) the French one. To some extent specific are the constitutions of Malta (which

EU by a constitutional provision concerning the origin of the public power from the will of the people, until the Treaty of Nice of December 2000 no similar proposition had been introduced into the Treaties founding the European Union and the European Communities. Consequently, the fundamental law of the Union is still lacking an adequate normative statement establishing the citizenry as the democratic control over the public institutions of the Union. At first, this gap was understandable because the Communities had their source within the frame of international law and as such were supposed to be seen as organizations based on covenants between sovereign states.[22] In so far as the competencies exercised by the central institutions of the Union (particularly of the European Community) were the direct emanation of the sovereignty of the member states, there was no reason to raise the question of a specific legitimization of European public power because, apparently, this power did not exist as such.[23] To be sure, some aspects of the European project that went beyond the traditional nature of a covenant between sovereign states were present in the Treaties from the very beginning.[24] For example, it has been pointed out[25] that the Treaties provided for the perpetuity[26] of the communities they founded.[27] Moreover, as regards the amending procedure,

---

concentrates, following the British tradition, particularly on the procedures of the representative institutions) and of Cyprus (aiming rather at ethnic balance).

22 In this sense, Hans Peter Ipsen qualified the Communities as "associations aiming at functional integration", characterised by a limited "frame of intervention" and no eminently political goals (HANS PETER IPSEN, EUROPÄISCHES GEMEINSCHAFTSRECHT, 1972). Though weakened, this claim has not totally disappeared from the doctrine (see Josef Isensee, *Integrationsziel Europastaat?*, in FESTSCHRIFT FÜR ULRICH EVERLING, 567, 583, (Ole Due, Marcus Lutter, & Jürgen Schwarze eds., 1995)). For a contrary opinion, better reflecting the evolution of the last decades, see ARMIN VON BOGDANDY, SUPRANATIONALER FÖDERALISMUS ALS WIRKLICHKEIT UND IDEE EINER NEUEN HERRSCHAFTSFORM 22 (1999).

23 On the member states as "masters of the Treaties" ("Herren der Verträge"), see Ulrich Everling, *Zur Stellung der Mitgliedstaaten der Europäischen Union als "Herren der Verträge"*, in RECHT ZWISCHEN UMBRUCH AND BEWAHRUNG 1161 (Ulrich Beyerlin et al. eds., 1995).

24 At the very beginning of the legal history of European integration stands the Treaty of the European Coal and Steel Community (ECSC), or Treaty of Paris (signed April 18, 1951; effective July 25, 1952; expired July 23, 2002; not published). But the most important step of this first phase of legal integration was taken by the signature of the Treaties of Rome, March 25, 1957, 298 U.N.T.S. 11, which founded the European Economic Community and the Euratom (see note 27). The first three Treaties were amended several times: first by the "Merger Treaty" which gave to the Communities common institutions (Apr. 4, 1965, 1967 O.J. (152)); then by the Treaty Amending Certain Budgetary Provisions stating that the Communities should have own resources (Apr. 22, 1970, 1971; 1971 O.J. (L 2)); the Treaty Amending Certain Financial Provisions that gave to the Parliament first significant competencies (July 22, 1975, 1977 O.J. (L 359); see infra, D, I); the Single European Act (quoted infra as SEA), the first major reform of the Treaties, extending the areas of qualified majority voting in the Council and increasing the role of the European Parliament by the introduction of the cooperation procedure (Feb. 17, 1986, 1987 O.J. (L 169)); the Treaty on European Union (Maastricht Treaty) which brought the three original Communities together under the umbrella of the European Union, institutionalised cooperation in the fields of foreign policy, defence, police and justice, and introduced the codecision procedure (Feb. 7, 1992, 1992 O.J. (C 191)); the Treaty of Amsterdam bringing further the reform of the Maastricht Treaty (October 2, 1997; 1997 O.J. (C 340)); and at last the Treaty of Nice dealing above all with the composition of Commission and Parliament as well as with the weighting of votes in the Council (Feb. 6, 2001, 2001 O.J. (C 80)). The Treaty of Nice contains the most recent amendments to the TEU and the EC Treaty (see note 27).

25 Bogdandy, *L'unione sovranazionale*, supra note 1, at 138; Augusto Barbera, *Esiste una "costituzione europea"?* 20 QUADERNI COSTITUZIONALI 59, 60 (2000).

26 Significantly, perpetuity has been outlined traditionally as one of the most important insignia of sovereign power (see BODIN, supra note 20).

27 See Treaty Establishing the European Economic Community, art 240, 298 U.N.T.S. 11 (TEEC); Treaty Establishing the European Atomic Energy Community (Euratom), art. 208, available at http://europa.eu.int/abc/obj/treaties/en/entoc38.htm. The provision stating that the "Treaty is concluded for an unlimited period" has been then taken over by the Maastricht Treaty and inserted into both the Treaty on European Union, art. 51 O.J. (C 224/1) (1992), (cit. infra as TEU); and the Treaty Establishing the European Community, Nov. 10 1997, art 312, 1997 O.J. (C 340/1), available at http://europa.eu.int/abc/obj/treaties/en/entoc05.htm (cit. infra as TEC), amending the former TEEC.

the Treaties bound the member states in such a way that their sovereignty had to be considered quite limited,[28] and even a common denunciation has not been provided for by law.[29] On the other side, a sophisticated and pervasive system of jurisdiction based on the European Court of Justice in Luxembourg, entrusted with broad competencies and characterized by a strong will favoring the integration process,[30] as well as – since the Maastricht Treaty – an ambitious and precisely articulated provision aiming at preventing serious breaches of the fundamental values of the Union by member states and inflicting severe sanction upon the occurrence of such breaches,[31] make even a unilateral denunciation according to the Vienna Convention on the Law of Treaties[32] hardly sustainable from a legal point of view.[33] Finally, the Treaties created supranational institutions like the Commission, the European Parliament, and the Court of Justice.[34] All of these entities are quite beyond the traditions of international law, partially referring as they do to constitutional essentials.[35]

Nonetheless, these elements were too weak to justify a more profound reflection on the essence of the power embodied in the European institutions. Yet, the situation changed dramatically during the next decades with the emergence of a number of principles: the priority of Community law and the immediate enforceable validity of the Community regulations in the member states;[36] the introduction by the Single European Act (1987)[37] of the qualified majority vote in the Council;[38] the extension of parliamentary competencies;[39] the insertion by the Maastricht Treaty (1992) of fields like foreign policy, defense, justice and home affairs into the matters over which the Union has at least some competencies of intervention;[40] the transfer of monetary and financial sovereignty – also introduced by the

---

28 Bogdandy, *L'unione sovranazionale, supra* note 1, at 138, with reference to the art. 236 of the Treaty Establishing the European Economic Community. According to the Treaties now in force, *see* TEU, *supra* note 27, at art. 48.
29 *See* note 25.
30 JOSEPH H. H. WEILER, THE CONSTITUTION OF EUROPE 19 (1999).
31 TEU, *supra* note 27, at art. 6 and following.
32 *Convention on the Law of Treaties*, 22 May 1969, 1155 U.N.T.S. 331, art. 60.
33 On the other side, it has also been claimed that the member states of the Communities and then of the Union maintain, in opposition to the situation within federal states, a right of secession (Ipsen, *supra* note 22, at 575). Supporters of this interpretation admit themselves, however, that such a step would be "against the Treaties" (*id.*), thus a decision relying exclusively on the monopole of the use of force, and not on law. The underlying contradiction of this vision can be eventually referred to a Schmittian understanding of legality, where law is, first, the expression of a quite homogeneous and pre-existent nation, and second essentially linked to the factual possibility of using force. It is almost superfluous to say that European integration is a project growing on a totally different – to be precise: on an opposite – tradition. *See infra*, C.
34 To be precise, these institutions were constituted by the TEEC and then extended to the other Communities by the Treaty of Brussels (Merger Treaty, *supra* note 24).
35 This is evident for the European Parliament but also for a large part of the role played by the Court of Justice. On the function of the Court of Justice as a (partial) constitutional court, *see* Gil Carlos Rodriguez Iglesias, *Der Gerichtshof der Europäischen Gemienschaften als Verfassungsgericht*, 27 EUROPA-RECHT 225 (1992).
36 WEILER, *supra* note 30, with reference to the case law.
37 *See infra*, B, II, 1.
38 Up to the Treaty of Nice, "Council" was officially used for that institution which the Constitutional Treaty names "Council of Ministers," since the other "Council" – namely the "European," composed by the Heads of state or government – was not seen as an institution of the Union in the proper sense of the word. Few mentions are made on it in the TEC, *supra* note 27, at art. 11, para. 2; art. 99, para. 2; art. 113, para. 3; art. 128, para 1, 2, and 5, while in the TEU its function is specified – but not, as I said, as an "official" institution, TEU, *supra* note 27, at art. 4, 7, 13, 17, 23 and 40.
39 *See infra*, D, I.
40 On the pillar structure, also introduced by the Maastricht Treaty, see the discussion in note 110.

Maastricht Treaty – from the member states to the institutions of the Union;[41] and the establishment of structures like Europol[42] and Eurojust.[43] This accretion of authority by the Union has significantly consolidated European integration, raising, now with urgent priority, the question whether the normative articulation of the democratic principle in the Treaties founding the Union is sufficient and satisfactory. This is the often regretted democratic deficit of the Union, which is not just a vaguely eurosceptical slogan but much more the ascertainment of a shortcoming that gives rise to justified concern.[44] Once defining a constitution as a document grounding, defining, organizing, and limiting a public power that claims to have an autonomous range of application,[45] a not dissimilar public power has grown in the Union, which no longer can be exhaustively identified with the sovereignty of the member states, thus giving rise to the constitutional debate regarding Europe, i.e. the claim that the European Union needs a constitution not only in the material, but also in a rather formal, traditional and – one could say – even proper sense of the word.[46]

However, even before the official start of the discussion on a new constitution for Europe, the political class of the Union has shown signs of an initial awareness of the problem of a "democratic deficit" as well as of the impact that it could have on the citizens. In fact, on a recent occasion there was discussion of inserting a provision into the Union's normative framework that would have made its fundamental law analogous to the formulations that can be found in many constitutions of the member states. In particular, during the work of the Convention entrusted with the elaboration of a Charter of Fundamental Rights[47] a proposal was advanced on March 20, 2000 which, along with the formulation of

41 The single currency (the euro) was introduced on January 1, 2002. It may be useful to remember that only twelve member states have adopted it: Germany, France, Italy, Netherlands, Belgium, Luxembourg, Spain, Ireland, Portugal, Greece, Finland, and Austria. Although the introduction of the euro can be seen as a success, during the last years there has been a growing difficult by many of the member states adopting the single currency to comply with the deficit restriction provided for by the Stability and Growth Pact (July 7, 1997). *See*, on this issue: SVEN FRIEDL, DIE EUROPÄISCHE WIRTSCHAFTS- UND WÄHRUNGSUNION (2003); JÜRGEN STARK, DIE ZUKUNFT DES STABILITÄTSPAKTES (2004); Benjamin Angel, *Le pacte de stabilité est-il mort?* 145 REVUE DU MARCHÉ COMMUN ET DE L'UNION EUROPÉENNE 476 (2004); Rudolf Streinz, *Totgesagte leben länger – oder doch nicht?*, 57 NEUE JURISTISCHE WOCHENSCHRIFT [NJW] 1553 (2004).
42 TEU, *supra* note 27, at art. 29, art. 30, and art. 31.
43 TEU, *supra* note 27, at art. 29, and art. 30.
44 Within the vast collection of commentary highlighting and treating Europe's "democratic deficit" we have very different positions, expressing quite diverging opinions. On the one side, there are authors who deny the very existence of a "democratic deficit" in the European Union: moving from the assumption that the Union cannot be claimed to be legitimated through the same institutions and procedures as the nation-states since it would lack a homogeneous "people" (*see infra*, C), they argue that the legitimacy deriving from the outcomes of the European integration, or from the legitimating procedures within the member states (for example, the ratification processes) has to be seen as sufficient. *See* Manfred Zuleeg, *Demokratie ohne Volk oder Demokratie der Völker? – Zur Demokratiefähigkeit der Europäischen Union*, *in* EUROPÄISCHE DEMOKRATIE 11 (Josef Drexl et al., eds., 1999); MARCEL KAUFMANN, EUROPÄISCHE INTEGRATION UND DEMOKRATIEPRINZIP (1997); SCHARPF, *supra* note 1; Majone, *supra* note 3. On the other side, we have the scholars who insist on the unsustainability of the present situation. For two opposite solutions to the herewith identified problem, *see* Dieter Grimm, *Braucht Europa eine Verfassung?*, 50 JURISTENZEITUNG 581 (1995); JÜRGEN HABERMAS, DIE EINBEZIEHUNG DES ANDEREN 185 (1996).
45 MARIO DOGLIANI, INTRODUZIONE AL DIRITTO COSTITUZIONALE (1994).
46 For a critique of this claim, *see* JOSEPH H. H. WEILER, FEDERALISM AND CONSTITUTIONALISM: EUROPE'S SONDERWEG (2000) (Jean Monnet Working Paper).
47 Reacting to the lack of an "official" catalogue of the fundamental rights within the basic law of the Union – although the Court of Justice already dealt with the human rights issues since the late 1960s (*see* note 304) – the European summits of Cologne and Tampere decided to entrust a Convention ad hoc, composed by members appointed by the governments of the member states, the European Parliament, the national parliaments and the Commission, with the drawing up of a Charter of Fundamental Rights of the European Union. *See* Presidency Conclusions, Cologne European Council 150/99 REV 1, 44, 45 Annex IV; Presidency Conclusions, Tampere European Council, SN 200/99, Annex. The document delivered by

several political rights, would have provided in art. A, para. 1 the same principle stated in the *Grundgesetz*, namely that "all state authority is derived from the people."[48] This proposal was not a surprise considering that the Union, intending to subject its institutions to the criteria of democratic legitimization, could be expected – simply from a logical point of view – to introduce such a provision into the Charter. To the contrary, while para. 2 of the same art. A of the Convention document dated March 20, 2000,[49] reproducing art. 6 TEU, found its way into the Preamble of the Charter[50] we do not find anything in the text finally approved by the Convention and then by the member states that attributes the origins of European public power to the will of the people. In other words, not even this declaratory assertion, so important in defining the quality of democratic power in contrast with any other source of political authority, could survive the transition from the draft of the Convention to the drawing up of the final text. Instead of the invocation of the "people of the Union," the approved version of the Charter included a mention of the "European peoples" which, "in creating an ever closer union among them, are resolved to share a peaceful future based on common values."[51]

Continuing a tradition already consolidated in the Treaties,[52] the authors of the Charter did not want to postulate, as a foundation for European public authority, a political entity with no historical sedimentation, like the "people of the citizens of the Union." Instead, they preferred the exclusive recourse to the will of the *peoples* (in the plural) of the member states. For their own part, the participants at the second Convention – entitled "on the future of Europe" – charged with the task of drawing up the draft of the Constitutional

---

the Convention was then approved and proclaimed by Council, European Parliament and Commission at the Nice European Council meeting, but never included into the Treaties in force. See Presidency Conclusions, Nice European Council Meeting, SN 400/00 2; Charter of Fundamental Rights of the European Union, Solemn Proclamation, 2000 O.J. (C 364/01). Yet, it was later included, without any modifications, into the Constitutional Treaty as its Part II; *see* Treaty establishing a Constitution for Europe, 2004 O.J. (C 310/01), Part II: The Charter of Fundamental Rights of the Union (quoted infra as Constitutional Treaty). Therefore, the articles of the Charter will be mostly quoted hereinafter with reference to the Constitutional Treaty.

48 Draft of the Charter of Fundamental Rights of the Union 4170/00, Convent 17, art. A, para. 1, *at* http://register.consilium.eu.int/pdf/en/00/st04/04170en0.pdf.
49 "The Union is founded on the principles of liberty, democracy, respect for human rights and fundamental freedoms, and the rule of law, principles which are common to the Member States," *id.*, at art. A, 2.
50 "Conscious of its spiritual and moral heritage, the Union is founded on the indivisible, universal values of human dignity, freedom, equality and solidarity; it is based on the principles of democracy and the rule of law" Constitutional Treaty, *supra* note 47 at prmbl., para.2; Charter of Fundamental Rights, *supra* note 47, at prmbl., para 2). On the reference to common values within the Constitutional Treaty, *see infra*, D, II.
51 Constitutional Treaty, *supra* note 47, at Part II: Charter of Fundamental Rights, prmbl., para. 1.
52 The TEC mentions the peoples of Europe in the Preamble, yet not as a founding element of the Community, but rather as addresses of the common policies of the member states, represented by their highest executive offices. Among these policies: the laying of "the foundations of an ever closer union among the peoples of Europe" (para. 1), "the constant improvements of the living and working conditions" (para. 3), the pooling of the resources "to preserve and strengthen peace and liberty" (para. 8), the promotion of the development of "the highest possible level of knowledge" (para. 9). The "peoples" (but in this case "of the states", and not "of Europe") are mentioned also in the art. 189 and 190 of the TEC, where the European Parliament is said to be composed of the representatives of these peoples. Inspired by the same principles is also the Preamble of the TEU, which at para. 12 repeats the reference to the "ever closer union among the peoples of Europe," along with the addition of several other objectives, nevertheless yet intended in the sense of policies which are to be lavished on the peoples, not autonomously decided by them (more correctly, by the citizens) and adequately legitimated at supranational level. As we will see, this is a not only formal, but rather substantial deficit. Compared with the formulations in TEC and TEU, even the Preamble of the Charter of Fundamental Rights, in spite of its above mentioned limits, went further saying that "the peoples of Europe … are resolved to share a peaceful future …" Constitutional Treaty, *supra* note 47, at Part II: The Charter of Fundamental Rights, prmbl., para. 1 [emphasis added].

Treaty which is the main object of the present analysis,[53] dared to do even less than their predecessors, failing altogether to conceive a concrete proposal concerning the introduction of a statement on the democratic origin of public power into the Constitutional Treaty. Apart from the contingent reasons, arising out of the political context, that can explain the option of the European would-be Framers for the less courageous solution over the decades, two consistent, logically, and systematically relevant justifications should be recalled here and then verified in their solidity:

(a) The option to favor the legitimization of the European public power by invoking the "peoples of Europe" and not the "European people" (meaning the community of the citizens of the Union) could have been produced by the fact that such a shift was not *necessary*. In other words, either no European public power exists which would require proper legitimization at the European level, or the democratic legitimacy of the European institutions as well as their decisions is adequately guaranteed by the participation of the member states in the decisional procedures of the Union, in particular through the actions at the European level of the democratically elected executives of the member states, controlled in turn by the national parliaments as representations of their respective peoples (*infra*, B.).

(b) The second justification for avoiding a normative formulation of the notion of a "European people" could consist, eventually, in a conceptual deficit, namely in the difficulty in formulating this idea in a coherent way, without falling into self-contradictory assumptions and irresolvable theoretical as well as practical problems (*infra*, C.).

B. The Necessity of Taking Recourse to the "European People" (as the Community of the Citizens of the Union) as Foundation of the Legitimacy of the European Public Power

Let us consider separately the two possible justifications identified above for avoiding the recourse to the "European people" as the legitimizing democratic source of the public power of the Union, always comparing both aspects: on the one side, the situation consolidated up to the Treaty of Nice; on the other side, the proposals formulated in the "Treaty establishing a Constitution for Europe" drawn up by the Convention on the Future of Europe and submitted to the President of the European Council in July 2003,[54] approved (with some – not irrelevant – modifications) by the Inter-Governmental Conference in June 2004,[55] and finally signed in Rome by the heads of state and government on October 29, 2004.[56] First, I will examine the claim that the invocation of the "European people" is not necessary to secure the democratic legitimacy of European public power. In this case, however, one must distinguish between two variants of the argument: the first one denying the very existence, in the Union, of a public power in the proper sense of the word; the second one asserting that the Union's power is already adequately legitimated by the democratic procedures within the member states.

---

53 The convening of a "Convention on the Future of Europe" was decided at the Laeken summit in December 2001. *See* Presidency Conclusions – Laeken Declaration on the Future of the European Union, European Council Meeting in Laeken Dec. 14–15, 2001, SN 300/1/01 Rev 1, Annex I. Its composition followed the same patterns as the first Convention, with representatives of the governments of the member states, of the European Parliament, of the national parliaments and of the Commission.
54 Preliminary Draft Treaty Establishing a Constitution for Europe, European Convention 850/03, *available at* http://european-convention.eu.int/docs/Treaty/cv00850.en03.pdf.
55 Presidency Conclusions – Brussels European Council. 17 and 18 June 2004, 10679/2/04, I, 4 and following.
56 For further information, *see* http://europa.eu.int/scadplus/cig2004/index_en.htm.

I. The Consolidation of the European Public Power: the Question of Competencies

I have already mentioned above that the European public power was steadily consolidated during the decades following the establishment of the Communities and then of the Union. This evolution had already led to a situation, within the *acquis communnautaire* consolidated by the Treaty of Nice, which demanded a specifically European legitimization of an emerging public power that had been growing beyond the sovereign authority of the member states.[57] Meeting that demand, the European Council stated at its summit in Laeken (December 2001) its intention to establish a second Convention entrusted to draft a Constitution for Europe, aiming to replace the existing Treaties.[58] In the purposes of the European Council, the Constitutional Treaty that would result from the works of the Convention and from the following Inter-Governmental Conference should explicitly deliver a response to the "democratic challenge facing Europe,"[59] i.e. to the citizens' call "for a clear, open, effective, democratically controlled Community approach."[60]

Considering the modifications introduced by the Constitutional Treaty and concentrating on the issue of legitimacy, it has to be stressed, that at first a new or at least renewed democratic legitimization at a specifically European level should be seen as superfluous if we could conclude that those modifications establish again – at least to a great extent – the *status quo ante*, annulling the existing nucleus of public power in the Union and giving back its competencies to the member states. In other words, any discussion about the ways to legitimate the European public power through the Union's institutions would become a waste of time if we could ascertain the dismantling of the Union's competencies.[61] Thus, we should start by verifying whether this "roll-back" has really been accomplished by the Constitutional Treaty.

In fact, during the preparatory phase of the Convention requests were raised in favor of a return of many (according to the more moderate positions: of some) competencies to the member states. This appeal was justified with the principle of subsidiarity, or even with the argument that such devolution would result in better democratic legitimacy for the Union's now narrower range of competencies.[62] In the mandate of the Convention the eventuality was mentioned – but just as one of the possible outcomes of the Convention – that the simplification as well as a new settlement of the division of competencies between the Union and the member states might "lead ... to restoring tasks to the member states."[63] Furthermore, in the report on the plenary meeting of March 21 and 22, 2002 we read the explanation, referring to the position expressed by some members of the

---

57 For the different positions, *see* the literature collected in GUSTAVO ZAGREBELSKY ET AL., eds. DIRITTI E COSTITUZIONE NELL'UNIONE EUROPEA (2003).
58 *See also* note 53 and following.
59 Presidency Conclusions – Laeken Declaration on the Future of the European Union, European Council Meeting in Laeken Dec. 14–15, 2001, SN 300/1/01 Rev 1, Annex I 19.
60 *Id.*, at 21.
61 In fact, particularly after the Maastricht Treaty claims arose among scholars that the transmission of competencies provided for by the establishment of the European Union had to be considered as a constitutional breach from the point of view of the nation-states traditions and constitutional exegesis. Especially in Germany, the debate led to some estreme positions. As an example, *see* PETER M. HUBER, MAASTRICHT – EIN STAATSSTREICH? (1993); Karl Albrecht Schachtschneider, *Die existentielle Staatlichkeit der Völker Europas und die staatliche Integration der Europäischen Union*, *in* DIE EUROPÄISCHE UNION ALS RECHTSGEMEINSCHAFT 75 (Wolfgang Blomeyer & Karl Albrecht Schachtschneider eds., 1995).
62 Presidency Conclusions – Laeken Declaration on the Future of the European Union, European Council Meeting in Laeken Dec. 14–15, 2001, SN 300/1/01 Rev 1, Annex I 19.; Note on the Plenary Meeting, Brussels, Mar. 21–22, 2002, European Convention 14/02.
63 Presidency Conclusions – Laeken Declaration on the Future of the European Union, European Council Meeting in Laeken Dec. 14–15, 2001, SN 300/1/01 Rev 1, Annex I 21.

Convention, that "reducing Europe's powers and limiting the *acquis communautaire* to areas where it could bring real added value would lend Europe greater legitimacy."[64]

In the course of the later work of the Convention, the leadership, with respect to the most radical proponents of restoring the greatest possible sovereignty to the nation-states, was taken up by Working Group V (WG V) on Complementary Competencies.[65] Starting from the conviction, however widely shared, that the Treaties lacked clarity on the division of competences,[66] Working Group V raised in its final report a harsh criticism of the past, present, and potential future transfer of competences from the member-states to the Union. In particular, the proposals supported by the WG V included:[67] the amendment (or the cancellation) of the reference throughout the Treaties, to an "ever closer union;"[68] the detailed enumeration of the competencies of the Union as a bulwark against their future enlargement; the specification of the principle providing for the respect of national identity;[69] the preference for the intergovernmental method and against co-decision and majority vote in the Council; and the reformulation of art. 308 TEC.[70] At first, none of the WG V proposals were supported by the Convention.[71] In fact, in the report on the plenary discussion concerning the results of the work of WG V, a final judgement was reported, the tenor of which is unusually harsh: "the plenary debate had shown that a large majority of members [of the Convention] did not agree with the approach adopted in the report and that the Presidium would subsequently consider the matter in the light of the various points arising from the debate."[72]

So much more surprising, then, is the fact that some of the ideas of the WG V eventually reappeared, albeit in a less radical fashion, in the final Constitutional Treaty. First, one does not find in the final text any reference to the "ever closer union," except in the Preamble of the Charter of Fundamental Rights, where the oft-quoted formulation appears,

---

64 Note on the Plenary Meeting, Brussels, Mar. 21–22, 2002, European Convention 14/02 3.
65 The Convention established several Working Groups (WG) on the most sensible issues: WG I on "Subsidiarity"; WG II on "Charter"; WG III on "Legal Personality"; WG IV on "National Parliaments"; WG V on "Complementary Competence"; WG VI on "Economic Governance"; WG VII on "External Relations"; WG VIII on "Defense"; WG IX on "Simplification of Legislative Procedures and Instruments"; WG X on "Area of Freedom, Security and Justice"; WG XI on "Social Europe". On the mandates of the Working Groups, *see* European Convention 71/02 (WG I); European Convention 72/02 (WG II); European Convention 73/02 (WG III); European Convention 74/02 (WG IV); European Convention 75/02 (WG V); European Convention 76/02 (WG VI); European Convention 206/02 (WGs VII-X); European Convention 421/02 (WG XI). On the composition of the Working Groups, *see* European Convention 77/02 (WGs I–VI); European Convention 243/02 (WG VII-X); European Convention 445/1/02 (WG XI). The final reports can be found under: European Convention 286/02 (WG I); European Convention 354/02 (WG II); European Convention 305/02 (WG III); European Convention 353/02 (WG IV); European Convention 375/1/02 Rev 1 (WG V); European Convention 357/02 (WG VI); European Convention 459/02 (WG VII); European Convention 461/02 (WG VIII); European Convention 424/02 (WG IX); European Convention 426/02 (WG X); European Convention 516/1/03 Rev 1 (WG XI).
66 Explicit is the remark of the deficit in the discussion paper on competencies, preparing the debate in the Convention on this issue: Discussion Paper – Delimitation of competence between the European Union and the Member States, European Convention 47/02 3 (May 15, 2002).
67 Final Report of the Working Group on Complementary Competencies, European Convention 375/1/02 2, 5, 10, 11, 12, 14.
68 TEU, *supra* note 47, at prmbl., art 1, para. 2; TEC, *supra* note 47, at prmbl.
69 This principle had to comprehend, among other issues, the definition of citizenship, the territory, the national defence including the organization of the armed forces, tax and redistribution policies, the welfare system, the education as well as health and culture, Final Report of the Working Group on Complementary Competencies, European Convention 375/1/02, 11.
70 Art. 308 (ex art. 235) TEC is the so-called "elastic clause" of the Community. on which has been based the doctrine of the "implied powers," elaborated and maintained by the Court of Justice since 1970s. WEILER, *supra* note 30, at 22 and 23.
71 Summary Report of the Plenary Session, Brussels, Nov. 7–8, 2002, European Convention 400/02, 12.
72 *Id.* at 14.

and which was inserted verbatim as Part II of the Constitutional Treaty.[73] Then, for the first time, the concept of the "conferral" of competencies[74] appears in the fundamental law of the Union, in order to make clear that the competences of the Union derive from the sovereignty of the member states and, therefore, can not be extended *motu proprio* by the Union itself.[75] Furthermore, while the application of co-decision has been consolidated, and although the definition of the national identity, albeit cumbersome, do not fulfil the most extreme anti-integrationalist claims,[76] the "flexibility clause" was amended to significantly limit its range of application and consequently also its function. Indeed, the version of the Constitution approved by the Convention and signed by the governments asserts that "provisions adopted on the basis of this Article may not entail harmonisation of member states' laws or regulations in cases where the Constitution excludes such harmonisation."[77] Moreover, this exclusion of harmonization, and with it the neutralization of the principle of the "implied powers," is provided for in many, not insignificant areas, including: the measures needed to combat discrimination;[78] the intervention in favour of the cooperation between the member states in the social policies;[79] the measures to provide incentives and support with a view to promoting the integration of third-country nationals residing legally in the territories of the member states;[80] to prevent crime;[81] to protect and improve human health;[82] the measures to incentivize actions supporting culture;[83] the fields of tourism,[84] industry,[85] education, youth and sport,[86] vocational training,[87] civil protection,[88] and administrative cooperation.[89]

Notwithstanding the extent of the limitation imposed on the "flexibility clause," these constitutional shifts taken alone, are not sufficient to support the thesis that the reduction of the competencies of the Union eviscerate the need for normatizing the democratic legitimacy of European public power. In other words, the amendment of the "flexibility clause" does not reach so far, on its own, to say that the public power of the Union has become too insignificant to require specific legitimization. In fact, the discourse on the legitimacy of public power in the Union would be a useless pastime only if it could be demonstrated that the introduction into the Constitutional Treaty of some proposals coming from the WG V is further supported by the Constitution's strengthening of the areas of exclusive intervention by the member states, and its substantial weakening of those

---

73 Constitutional Treaty, *supra* note 47, at Part II: The Charter of Fundamental Rights, prmbl., para. 1.
74 *Id.* at art. I-11, para. 1–2. In the French and German version of the Constitutional Treaty the concept of "conferral" is expressed, respectively, by *attribution* and *begrenzte Einzelermächtigung*.
75 On the concept of "conferral," *see* Paul P. Craig, *Competence: Clarity, Conferral, Containment and Consideration*, 29 Eur. L. Rev. 323 (2004).
76 Constitutional Treaty, *supra* note 47, at art. I-5, para. 1.
77 *Id.* at art. I-18, para. 3., and art. III-315, para. 6, specifies that "the exercise of the competences conferred by this Article in the field of commercial policy shall not affect the delimitation of competences between the Union and the member states, and shall not lead to harmonisation of legislative or regulatory provisions of member states insofar as the Constitution excludes such harmonisation."
78 *Id.* at art. III-124, para. 2.
79 *Id.* at art. III-210, para. 2, a).
80 *Id.* at art. III-267, para. 4.
81 *Id.* at art. III-272 (limitation not included into the Draft of the Constitutional Treaty approved by the Convention).
82 *Id.* at art. III-278, para. 5.
83 *Id.* at art. III-280, para. 5, a).
84 *Id.* at art. III-281, para. 2.
85 *Id.* at art. III-279, para. 3.
86 *Id.* at art. III-282, para. 3, a).
87 *Id.* at art. III-283, para. 3, a).
88 *Id.* at art. III-284, para. 2.
89 *Id.* at art. III-285, para. 2.

areas where the Union has some kind of competencies. All of this would seek to underscore the claim that the Constitutional Treaty makes significant modifications to the competence structure, giving an advantage of the member states.

With regard to these claims it must be specified, above all, that the Constitutional Treaty does not enumerate explicitly the competences of the member states, referring instead to the principles of subsidiarity and "conferral" (as discussed above), and stating that "competences not conferred upon the Union in the Constitution remain with the member states."[90] Only the specification of the competences of the Union, therefore, can help us to settle the question of an eventual shifting of the line of demarcation between Brussels and the nation-states. On the question of competencies the Constitutional Treaty certainly introduces a significant clarification in comparison with the normative situation up to Nice. In particular, the competencies attributed to the European institutions are here divided in three sections: (a) the exclusive competences of the Union;[91] (b) the shared competences;[92] and (c) the competence "to carry out actions to support, coordinate or supplement the actions of the member states."[93]

The competencies of the first class, which are exclusive to the Union unless the Union itself authorizes the member states to engage these subjects, comprehend a very small number of fields: (a) monetary police for the states of the euro zone; (b) common commercial policy; (c) customs union; (d) the conservation of marine biological resources under the common fishery policy; (e) the establishing of the competition rules necessary for the functioning of the internal market; and (f) the conclusion of international agreements when provided for in a legislative act of the Union.[94] Albeit not introducing any substantial modification to the situation consolidated in the Treaties up to Nice,[95] the listing of the exclusive competences included in the Constitutional Treaty may be interpreted – at least by the supporters of a "closer" European integration – as something negative, namely as a kind of stagnation, particularly when compared to the more progressive proposals presented to the Convention. Just to recall one of the most interesting and advanced suggestions that was submitted during the preliminary work of the Convention, the Lamassoure Report of the European Parliament recommended the extension of the

---

90 *Id.* at art. I-11, para. 2. Similar was the proposal formulated in the Lamassoure Report of the European Parliament, which suggested not to list the exclusive competences of the member states, implying that all areas for which the Constitutional Treaty would not provide otherwise belong to the member states Parlement européen, Commission des Affaires Constitutionnelles, *Rapport sur la délimitation des compétences entre l'Union et les États membres (Rapport Lamassoure)*, PE 204.376, § 4.3.2, 20. Besides, the same formulation of the final Constitutional Treaty approved by the Convention and signed by the member states was already included in the art. 8, para. 1, of the Preliminary Draft of the 28th of October 2002, Preliminary Draft Constitutional Treaty, Oct 28, 2002, European Convention 369/02.

91 Constitutional Treaty, *supra* note 47, at art. I-12, para. 1, and art. I-13.

92 *Id.* at art. I-12, para. 2, and art. I-14.

93 *Id.* at art. I-12, para. 5, and art. I-17 ("areas of supporting, coordinating or complementary actions"). Initially, it had been proposed to define these competencies as "complementary". The present definition – different from the original proposal – is derived from an idea of the WG V which had suggested not to use the term "complementary competencies," preferring that of "supporting measures," in order to express a kind of "re-investiture," albeit of limited extension, of the member states. See Final Report of the Working Group on Complementary Competencies, European Convention 375/1/02, 1. The Convention censured also in this case the suggestion of the WG V, arguing that the new definition would "not make clear that the reference was to areas in which the Union was empowered to act," Summary Report of the Plenary Session, Brussels, Nov. 7–8, 2002, European Convention 400/02, 12. Nonetheless, the proposal of the WG V had been introduced in the Preliminary Draft, Preliminary Draft Constitutional Treaty, *supra* note 90, at art. 12. Therefore, the final Constitutional Treaty can bee seen as a kind of compromise since the reference to the "competence" of the Union has been maintained while the adjective qualifying it was modified.

94 Constitutional Treaty, *supra* note 47, at art. I-13.

95 Description of the Current System for the Delimitation of Competence between the European Union and the Member States, European Convention 17/02, 3.

exclusive competencies to include: (a) the identification of the objectives as well as the management of the common foreign and defence policy; (b) the legal foundation of the common area of freedom and security; and (c) the budgetary provisions for the Union.[96] Nevertheless, in spite of the limited results achieved in the Constitutional Treaty and the disappointment that these shortcomings might spread among the supporters of an "ever closer" European Union, it is difficult to affirm the claim that the Constitutional Treaty so substantially reduces the exclusive competences of the Union that a discussion of the need for legitimizing European public power would become irrelevant.

This is especially not the case in the fields which fall under the so-called "shared competences." First, it is quite interesting to see how this second class of competencies are defined. Art. I-12, para. 2, of the Constitutional Treaty, which specifies that in the areas of shared competence "the member states shall exercise their competence to the extent that the Union has not exercised, or has decided to cease exercising, its competence," gives to the Union a potentially wide scope. In this case, the text signed by the member states takes up both the proposal of the Lamassoure Report[97] as well as art. 72, para. 1, of the German *Grundgesetz*, which states that "on matters within the concurrent legislative power the *Länder* shall have power to legislate so long as and to the extent that the Federation has not exercised its legislative power by enacting a law."[98] The Constitutional Treaty's adoption of this German provision differs only in that it employs a different qualifying adjective: "shared" and not "concurrent."[99] Rooted in a deep tradition of state centralism,[100] this provision led, at least in the first decade after the introduction of the Basic Law, to a development towards a "unitarian federal state."[101] Surely, in spite of the provision in art. I-12, para. 2, of the Constitutional Treaty this is not going to be the destiny of the European Union, which is characterized by an undoubtedly higher level of plurality. Nevertheless, the Constitutional Treaty lacks, for its part, a similar juridical antidote against centralization, which was introduced into the German Basic Law on the intervention of the Allies.[102] Indeed, the German Basic Law states, within the same article quoted above, that "the Federation has the right to legislate where (1) a matter cannot be effectively regulated by the legislation of individual *Länder*, or (2) regulation by a *Land* might prejudice the interests of other *Länder* or the country as a whole, or (3) the maintenance of legal and economic unity, especially uniform living conditions beyond the territory of any one *Land*, calls for Federal legislation."[103] The Constitutional Treaty has no similar provision as a specification of its definition of shared competencies.

96 *Rapport Lamassoure*, *supra* note 90, at 10. With respect to the extension of the competencies of the Union to the areas of foreign policy, defence and justice the opinion expressed by the Convention in its plenary meeting was quite positive, although it would go too far to interpret this attitude as an approval by the majority of its members to the introduction of particularly ticklish fields among the exclusive competencies, Note on the Plenary Meeting, Brussels, Apr. 15–16, 2002, European Convention 40/02, 3. Partially discordant were the positions expressed on the eventual introduction of an autonomous tax arrangement by the Union (*id.* at 4). The WG IX did not adopt a definite position regarding the question of the financial competence, only forwarding some quite reasonable proposals concerning the budgetary procedure, Final Report of the Working Group on Simplification, European Convention 424/02, 18.
97 *Rapport Lamassoure*, *supra* note 90, at 10.
98 GRUNDGESETZ [GG][Constitution], art. 72, para. 1.
99 Also the German version of the Constitutional Treaty speaks – curiously – of "geteilter (shared) Zuständigkeit," but not for example the Italian translation where the wording is "competenze concorrenti."
100 Markus Rau, *Subsidiarity and Judicial Review in German Federalism: The Decision of the Federal Constitutional Courtin the Geriatric Nursing Act Case*, 4 GERMAN LAW JOURNAL 223, 227 (2003).
101 KONRAD HESSE, DER UNITARISCHE BUNDESSTAAT (1962); Rau, *supra* note 100, at 228.
102 CHRISTOPH NEUMEYER, DER WEG ZUR NEUEN ERFORDERLICHKEITSKLAUSEL FÜR DIE KONKURRIERENDEN GESETZGEBUNG DES BUNDES (1999); Rau, *supra* note 100, at 227.
103 GRUNDGESETZ [GG][Constitution], art. 72, para. 2. This provision indeed was claimed to be re-activated by many scholars since the 1960s, specifically in order to contain the centralizing tendency. *See* Rau, *supra* note 100, at 227.

It is difficult to say, at present, which consequences this lack of restraint could have on the delimitation of competencies between Union and member states: this will depend on political and social evolution as well as on the interpretation that the scholarship will elaborate on the issue. However, what can be claimed now, albeit provisionally, is that the Constitutional Treaty does not impose any direct limitation[104] on the Union's legislative actors as regards matters of shared competence.[105] Therefore, it will be in any case arduous to oppose at the normative level, given a favourable political background, the further penetration of the Union into fields which are quite significant for the nation-states and their understanding of sovereignty.

The second point that can be drawn from the Constitutional Treaty's mapping of shared competences, which favours an interpretation of the work of the Constitutional Convention as an endorsement of an "ever closer" integration, involves the gravity of the fields included in this class of competences. The Union, pursuant to their classification as "shared competences," will have a right to intervene over a dramatic range of concerns, some of which have hitherto been seen largely as the sole province of the nation-state: from the internal market to the justice; from agriculture and fisheries to transport; and including energy policy; social policy; economic, social and territorial cohesion; environmental policy; consumer protection and public health (though limited to the "common safety concerns").[106] Furthermore, the provision that "the Union shall share competence with the member states where the Constitution confers on it a competence which does not relate to the areas referred to in Articles 13 and 17,"[107] evidences the fact that the areas listed in para. 2 are merely, as it is explicitly said, the "principal" subjects of shared competence, but not the exclusive range of fields which are potentially subject to concurrent legislation. Finally, it has to be underlined that the fundamental nature of the fields identified as being among those principally subject to shared competences (in particular, justice, energy, social policy and public health) suggests, at least potentially, a far-reaching change in the European legal system, a change which could have as its consequence the overcoming of the traditional selfishness deeply rooted in the sovereignty of the nation-states.[108]

---

104 As a "direct limitation" I understand here a restraint *directly* imposed to the range of legislative intervention of the Union in matters of shared competence. Yet, a kind of *indirect* limitation could be seen in the provision of the Constitutional Treaty stating that "the union shall respect the equality of Member States before the constitution as well as their national identities, inherent in their fundamental structures, political and constitutional, inclusive of regional and local self-government. It shall respect their essential State functions, including ensuring the territorial integrity of the State, maintaining law and order and safeguarding national security. Constitutional Treaty, *supra* note 47, at art. I-5, para. 1.

105 On this point, it has also to be reminded that the Constitutional Treaty does not limit the legislation concerning matters of shared competence to mere "framework laws", which would necessarily give to the member states a broader autonomy. In fact, while the "European law" (or "regulation," in concordance with the wording of the Treaties up to Nice) has immediate validity within the member states, excluding any differentiation between them and, therefore, potentially overruling their legislative sovereignty on these matters, the European framework law, albeit "binding, as to the result to be achieved, upon each Member state to which it is addressed, ... shall leave to the national authorities the choice of form and methods" Constitutional Treaty, *supra* note 47, at art. I-33, para. 1. *See also* Presidency Conclusions – Laeken Declaration on the Future of the European Union, European Council Meeting in Laeken Dec. 14–15, 2001, SN 300/1/01 Rev 1, Annex I, 22 where framework legislation was defined as the instrument which "affords the member states more room for manoeuvre in achieving policy objectives."

106 *Id.* at art. I-14, para. 2.

107 Constitutional Treaty, *supra* note 47, at art. I-14, para. 1.

108 With regard to social policy and public health the first wording of the Constitutional Treaty was even more courageous, lacking the limitations of the final text. *See* Draft of Articles 1–16 of the Constitutional Treaty, European Convention 528/03.

It is necessary to pause and reflect on the field of freedom, security and justice, which is probably the most important of the matters to be made subject to shared competence.[109] Rather than constituting an enlargement of the Union's competencies, this is a matter of shifting some areas subject to the Union's intervention, within a general aim pursued by the Constitutional Treaty to overcome the "pillar" structure.[110] The reframing of the area of freedom, security and justice is also part of an attempt to abandon the intergovernmental approach characterizing the provisions of the Treaties up to Nice under Title VI TEU[111] and, partially, under Part III, Title IV TEC,[112] in favour of the "Community method" including the majority vote in the Council and codecision of the European Parliament.[113] In fact, following the suggestion of Working Group X on Freedom, Security and Justice,[114] the Convention has extended the legislative procedure now called "ordinary" (which, like the old "communitarian method," provides for majority vote and codecision)[115] to the matters included in Part III, Title IV TEC, i.e. asylum, refugees, displaced persons, immigration, visas, judicial cooperation in civil matters.[116] Even in the area of judicial cooperation in criminal matters, which until the Treaty of Nice fell under Title VI TEU, the ordinary legislative procedure becomes the rule and shall be applied to several new fields.[117]

This integrative movement notwithstanding, in the field of judicial cooperation (both civil and criminal), as well as in the police cooperation,[118] some core spheres are expected to remain under the unanimity rule in the Council. In these cases, the European Parliament is merely to be consulted or may be called upon to give its consent. The limitation concerns civil judicial cooperation in family law,[119] and the following aspects of criminal law: any specific aspect of criminal procedure which may go beyond those already listed in the Constitutional Treaty;[120] the extension of the areas of crime in which the Union has a

---

109 Indeed, the supreme control of jurisdiction was always seen, from the very introduction of the concept of sovereignty, as one of its core attributes. *See* Bodin, *supra* note 20, at Livre I, Chap. X, 159.
110 From the Maastricht Treaty until the Treaty of Nice the Union has consisted of three "pillars": the Communities, the Common Foreign and Security Policy (Title V TEU) and the Police and judicial Cooperation in Criminal Matters (Title VI TEU). Along with the adoption of a single legal personality for the Union, the Constitutional Treaty provides for the unification of the "pillars." *See* Constitutional Treaty, *supra* note 47, at art. I-7. The unification of the pillars was also suggested in the Lamassoure Report. *Rapport Lamassoure*, *supra* note 90, at 8. On the proposals of the WG III, *see Final Report of the Working Group on Legal Personality*, Conv 305/02, 6.
111 Title VI TEU comprehends provisions concerning "police and judicial cooperation in criminal matters." *See* TEU, *supra* note 47, at art. 29 and following articles.
112 Part III, Title IV of the TEC comprehends provisions on "visa, asylum, immigration and other policies related to free movement of persons." *See* TEC, *supra* note 47, at art. 61 and following articles.
113 Concerning in general the TEU, the Constitutional Treaty introduces, at least as a matter of principle, in every area the Community method (with majority vote in the Council and co-decision of the European Parliament) as "ordinary legislative procedure." *See* Constitutional Treaty, *supra* note 47, at art. I-34. Doing so, it overcomes – always on principle – the intergovernmental cooperation which was – as well as it is at present, and will also be until the Constitutional Treaty will eventually enter into force – the rule within the second and third "pillar" of the TEU. *See* note 110. Nonetheless, this reform would not imply that the "ordinary legislative procedure" will be in force for all matters on which the Union has competence: in some areas, reportedly central to the interests of the member states, derogations of the ordinary procedure will continue to exist – actually at a large extent, as we are going to see.
114 Final Report of the Working Group on Freedom, Security and Justice, European Convention 426/02, 3.
115 Constitutional Treaty, *supra* note 47. at art. III-396.
116 *Id.* at art. III-257 and following articles.
117 *Id.* at art. III-270 and following articles.
118 *Id.* at art. III-275 and following articles.
119 *Id.* at art. III-269, para. 3 (with consultation of the Parliament); nonetheless the article provides for the possibility that, following the same procedure, the Council may adopt a decision on proposal of the Commission "determining those aspects of family law with cross-border implications may be the subject of acts adopted by the ordinary legislative procedure." *Id.*).
120 *Id.*, art. III-270, para. 2, d (the consent of the Parliament is required).

shared competence;[121] and the establishment of a European Public Prosecutor's Office.[122] In the area of police cooperation the Constitutional Treaty provides for derogations from the application of the ordinary legislative procedure in the case of the establishment of "measures concerning operational cooperation" between police authorities of different member states,[123] as well as for the specification of the conditions under which police authorities from a member state "may operate in the territory of another member state in liaison and in agreement with the authorities of that state."[124] No doubt, these restrictions were introduced into the Constitutional Treaty to ensure the control of the national governments within fields perceived as particularly significant for national identity and the interests of the member states. The result, of course, is to make European public power thinner at these points.

The last category of competencies of the Union refers to "supporting, coordinating or complementary" actions, including areas such as education, culture, industry, tourism, administrative cooperation, civil protection and health (excluding security questions of cross-border relevance).[125] Here, the Union's intervention can only complete that of the member states, "without thereby superseding their competence in these areas," nor providing for any "harmonization of member states' laws or regulations."[126]

The Constitutional Treaty introduces, beside the three "official" categories of European competencies, a number of surreptitious categories, which are not systematically integrated into the rationalisation of the constitutional structure as a whole. For example, the Constitutional Treaty provides that "the member states shall coordinate their economic and employment policies within arrangements as determined by Part III, which the Union shall have the competence to provide."[127] The Constitutional Treaty also provides that the Union shall have the authority "to define and implement a common foreign and security policy, including the progressive framing of a common defence policy."[128] Neither of these particular competences can be easily inserted into one of the three "official" categories outlined above. Furthermore, the Constitutional Treaty adds a quite curious kind of "parallel" competence, applied to "research, technological development and space,"[129] as well as to "the areas of development cooperation and humanitarian aid."[130] This last surreptitious category, though presented in the Constitutional Treaty as part of the shared competencies (second category competence), is distinguished from them by the caveat that "the

---

121 *Id.*, art. III-271, para. 1 (the consent of the Parliament is required).
122 *Id.*, art. III-274, para. 1 (the consent of the Parliament is required).
123 *Id.*, art. III-275, para. 3 (with consultation of the Parliament).
124 *Id.*, art. III-277 (with consultation of the Parliament). Quite similar suggestions concerning the areas of derogation from the ordinary legislative procedure were made by the WG X. Final Report of the Working Group on Freedom, Security and Justice, European Convention 426/02, 7.
125 Constitutional Treaty, *supra* note 47, at art. I-17. At first, also social policy and research were proposed to be included into this category of competences. Yet, at the plenary meeting of the Convention criticism was raised against this proposal. Summary Report of the Plenary Session, Brussels, Nov. 7–8, 2002, European Convention 400/02, 13. Furthermore, in the final version of the Constitutional Treaty a limitative provision has been cancelled which was included in the Draft by the Convention, this provision stating that "legally binding acts adopted by the Union on the basis of the provisions specific to these areas in Part III may not entail harmonisation of member states' laws or regulations." Constitutional Treaty Establishing a Constitution for Europe, Jul 18, 2003, European Convention 850/03, art. I-16, para. 3.
126 Constitutional Treaty, *supra* note 47, at art. I-12, para. 5.
127 Constitutional Treaty, *supra* note 47, at art. I-12, para. 3, with implicit reference to the open method of coordination. The Draft Treaty approved by the Convention rather pointed out the competence of the Union, which was put on the first place, before referring to the coordinating action by the member states, Draft Treaty establishing a Constitution for Europe, European Convention 850/03, art. I-11, para. 3.
128 Constitutional Treaty, *supra* note 47, at art. I-12, para. 4.
129 *Id.* at art. I-14, para. 3.
130 *Id.* at art. I-14, para. 4.

[Union's] exercise of that competence may not result in member states being prevented from exercising theirs."[131] While it can be presumed that these three surreptitious competencies will raise some problems for juridical exegesis, it is on the other side already the case that they partially undermine the rationalising attempted by the Treaty with regard to the reallocation of competencies between Union and member states, which was one of the most important reasons to undertake the constitutional procedure in the first place.[132]

Among the three competencies not framed into the system, the most ticklish is certainly that concerning the common foreign and defence policy. In both of these areas some changes have been introduced. Starting with foreign policy, the Constitutional Treaty creates the office of the Union Minister for Foreign Affairs, who should be appointed by the European Council, acting by a qualified majority and with the agreement of the President of the Commission, but without any involvement of the Parliament.[133] This new office merges the present functions of the High Representative (TEU) and of the Commissioner for External Relations (TEC).[134] The new Minister of Foreign Affairs will still serve in this dual capacity. One the one hand, in pursuing the common foreign and security policy of the Union, the Minister for Foreign Affairs is accountable to the European Council.[135] On the other hand, as regards the handling of those subjects of external relations within the competence of the Commission, the Minister of Foreign Affairs will be responsible to the European Parliament like any other Commissioner.[136] This Solomonesque arrangement makes the actions of this new office perfectly subject to the governments of the member states, preventing a "breakthrough" of the Community method into these areas.[137]

The intergovernmental aim is also embodied in the unanimity required for the decision of the European Council in identifying "the strategic interests and objectives of the Union."[138] The institutions devoted to protecting the supranational dimension have been here marginalized: while the Commission has no role at all, the Parliament obtained only the quite modest guarantee that it would be regularly consulted on and kept informed of the evolution of initiatives concerned with foreign policy.[139] The Constitutional Treaty also requires unanimity as regards the decisions of the Council of Ministers putting into effect the strategic interests and objectives identified by the European Council, as well as react-

---

131 *Id.* at art. I-14, para. 3–4.
132 The "better division and definition of competence in the European Union" was already outlined in the *Laeken Declaration* as one of the chief justifications (more precisely as the first of those listed) for the constitutional effort. *See* Presidency Conclusions – Laeken Declaration on the Future of the European Union, European Council Meeting in Laeken Dec. 14–15, 2001, SN 300/1/01 Rev 1, Annex I, 21.
133 Constitutional Treaty, *supra* note 47, at art. I-28, para. 1.
134 The proposal of this merger was made, among others, by the Commission for External Relations, Human Rights and Common Security and Defence Policy of the European Parliament, *Rapport Lamassoure, supra* note 90, at § 6, 29, and resumed later by the Commission, Communication from the Commission. A Project for the European Union, European Convention 229/02, 18, as well as by the WG III, Final Report of the Working Group on Legal Personality, European Convention 305/02, 8, and VII, Final Report of the Working Group on External Actions, European Convention 459/02, 5, 19. Nevertheless, as regards the appointment procedure the WG VII suggested to require also the consent of the Parliament.
135 Constitutional Treaty, *supra* note 47, at art. I-28, para. 1–2.
136 *Id.* at art. I-28, para. 4.
137 According to the hypothesis of the Commission, the Union Minister for Foreign Affairs should have been accountable for all his activities to the Parliament. Romano Prodi, *La nuova struttura istituzionale dell'Unione*, Speech before the European Parliament, 4 (Dec. 5, 2002). Besides, quite on the issue of the merger of the offices of the High Representative and of the Commissioner for External Relations the Convention expressed some doubts, deriving from the fear that the (intergovernmental) specificity of the foreign policy would get lost, Summary Report on the Plenary Session, Brussels, Dec. 20, 2002, European Convention 473/02, 7.
138 Constitutional Treaty, *supra* note 47, at art. III-293, para. 1.
139 *Id.* at art. I-40, para. 6 and para. 8; art. I-41, para. 8; and art. III-304, para. 1.

ing to an international situation requiring operational action by the Union.[140] In these cases, in order to avoid the vetoing of any initiative by a single member state, the Treaty provides for an "opting out" clause pursuant to which every state may abstain in a vote, which exempts the abstaining state from any obligation to apply the decision (without prejudice to the general commitment to loyalty towards the Union).[141] If the abstention does not involve at least a third of the member states representing at least a third of the population of the Union, the decision shall be adopted in despite the reservations of a potentially significant bloc of member states.[142] This clause does not seem likely to stave off the intergovernmental method in the field of foreign policy. The effectiveness of a common foreign policy could be seriously at risk. Even the article concerning the coordination of the position of member states in international organisation and at international conferences[143] does not imply, given its weak binding effect, any transfer of competencies to the Union in order to capitalize on its single, international legal personality.[144] The Constitutional Treaty's reiteration of provisions obliging the member states (one could debate whether "exhorting" or "inviting" them better characterizes the intent of the Framers) to solidarity and compliance with the acts adopted by the Union[145] also seems unlikely to stem the priority each member state can be expected to give to its national interests in deliberations on matters of foreign policy.

An analysis of the provisions concerning the common defence policy leads to similar conclusions. On this point, convergence has proven particularly difficult because of the different strategic posture of each member state, which is necessarily related to their distinct histories, resources and military alliances (this being especially true as between the countries that are members of NATO and those that are neutral).[146] As with foreign policy, decisions on common strategic or defence missions must be adopted unanimously by the Council of Ministers.[147] The Commission is totally excluded from the process[148] and the Parliament merely has to be consulted.[149] Like the provisions on foreign policy, those on defence also seek to avoid the likely paralysis on common defence initiatives resulting from the required unanimity. Here, the Constitutional Treaty authorizes willing member states to establish closer cooperation in defence matters,[150] while obliging all member states to give "aid and assistance by all the means in their power" to other member states which may be victims of armed aggression on their territory.[151] The intergovernmental emphasis

---

140 *Id.* at art. III-300, para. 1.
141 *Id.*
142 *Id.*
143 *Id.* at art. III-305.
144 *Id.* at art. I-7. On the necessity to give to the Union a single voice in the international organisations, *see* the proposals of the WGs III and VII. Final Report of the Working Group on Legal Personality, European Convention 305/02, 11; Final Report of the Working Group on External Actions, European Convention 459/02, 31.
145 Constitutional Treaty, *supra* note 47, at art. I-16, para. 2; art. III-294, para. 2.
146 As stressed in the final report of the WG VIII, Final Report of the Working Group on Defence, European Convention 461/02, 10.
147 Constitutional Treaty, *supra* note 47 at art. I-41, para. 4.
148 The Commission may be involved, "where appropriate," if the use of Union instruments is required (*id.*, at art. I-41, para. 4).
149 *Id.*, at art. I-41, para. 8.
150 *Id.*, at art. I-41, para. 6, and art. III-312.
151 *Id.*, at art. I-41, para. 7. The Draft Treaty approved by the Convention limited the obligation to provide aid to the member states participating to a closer defence co-operation, Draft Treaty establishing a Constitution for Europe, European Convention 850/03, art. I-40, para. 7. This limitation took into consideration the exhortation by the WG VIII to respect the neutrality of some of the member states, Final Report of the Working Group on Defence, European Convention 461/02, 20.

in the field of defence and security hardly seems mitigated by the Constitutional Treaty's creation of a European Defence Agency.[152]

This pass over the issue of competence suggests that neither the supporters of the strengthening of the national sovereignty nor those promoting an "ever closer union" can claim to be fully satisfied with the results. On the one hand, the modification of the flexibility clause sets a quite clear limitation on the potential self-attribution of competencies by the Union, with the attendant cost in efficiency. On the other hand, the Constitutional Treaty defines a range of the Union's shared competencies that is, to some extent, broader than that which exists under the Treaty of Nice. In some strategic areas intergovernmental governance still prevails; on other matters the Community method, i.e. the majority vote in the Council of Ministers and the co-decision of the Parliament, has been consolidated as the ordinary legislative procedure. In other words, although the Treaty does not stand for a remarkable step forward on the path to European integration, it would also be unjustified to say that a real roll-back on the Union's competencies has occurred.

There is no reason to believe that European public power will be dismantled by the Constitutional Treaty such that a discussion of the democratic legitimacy of the power is no longer necessary. To the contrary, as a consequence of a remarkable range (in both quantity and quality) of provisions consolidating the Union's authority that were forwarded by the Convention and approved by the member states, reports of the death of European public power can be said to be greatly exaggerated. Therefore, the herewith consolidated European public power should not – and actually will not – forego a specific discussion of its own legitimization.

II. The Gap in the Legitimization-chain Leading from the Democratically Legitimated Powers of the Member States to the Competences of the Union

Even if I have succeeded in the preceding section to establish that a nucleus of public power persists at the Union level, the claim that such authority suffers from a democratic deficit must still overcome the argument that European public power is wholly legitimized by the control of the member states, via their domestically legitimized institutions, over the exercise of this power. Two responses seem to merit consideration. First, it can be disputed that the member states actually exercise authority over the European public power. In fact, it is possible that the member states (and their citizens) have transferred competences to instances which bind them but which are not properly controlled by them anymore, no more by the intergovernmental method than by the Community method. Second, it is necessary to evaluate whether, even if the member states are said to control the European public power, their domestic democratic legitimacy is effectively attributable upwards to the actions of the Union by way of a so-call "legitimization-chain."[153] The assumptions that (a) the European public power is controlled by the member states; and that (b) the acting of the national governments at the European level is legitimated by the democratic procedures within the member states are at the center of the argument, which I intend to consider now, that no gap exists between the Union's exercise of its competencies and the control over that power asserted by the democratically legitimated member states.

In fact, if it could be demonstrated that the democratically legitimated national institutions of the member states have such thoroughgoing control over the exercise of the

---

152 Constitutional Treaty, *supra* note 47, at art. I-41, para. 3, and art. III-311, following the proposal of the WG VIII, Final Report of the Working Group on Defence, European Convention 461/02, 22.
153 *See* Zuleeg, *supra* note 44; KAUFMANN, *supra* note 44.

Union's competencies (and that they are able to implement this control effectively), then it might be incorrect to speak of a European public power in the proper sense that requires its own legitimacy. Thus, the very assertion of a domestic basis for the legitimacy of European public power, taken to the extreme, poses an existential challenge to the idea of a specific European public power. This would render superfluous the discussion of the concept of a "European people" as the community of the citizens of the Union – and as one of the foundations of the specific legitimacy of the European public power.

Nevertheless, at least two considerations lead to the conviction that the legitimization-chain, which should pass from the nation-states to the institutions of the Union, has been irreparably weakened by so much so that it shows evident signs of collapse. This matter of fact, already present in the normative system in force under the Treaty of Nice, has not been changed by the Constitutional Treaty.

1. Legitimacy Problems Arising from the Majority Vote in the Council of Ministers

At the very beginning of European integration, the Treaty of Rome[154] already provided for the adoption of simple and qualified majority voting in the decision procedures of the Council of Ministers, after a transitional period. The Council is, of course, the Community institution charged with the highest legislative power. However, as this rule should have come into force, France opposed the transition, bringing about a crisis which was then resolved, albeit in an unsatisfactory fashion, by the Luxembourg Accord (1966) stating that "each and every member state," invoking vital national interest, "could veto Community proposed legislation."[155] Therefore, under the conditions imposed by the Luxembourg Accord the Council actually exercised its authority solely on the basis of unanimity. This unquestionable limitation on efficiency guaranteed, otherwise, the full democratic legitimacy of its deliberations. In fact, given the European Parliament's insignificant – or rather nonexistent role – in the decision-making procedures of the Council of Ministers, the only effective legitimacy could be derived from the political participation of European citizens *within* the member states. Thus, the factual implementation of Council's procedural rules excluding majority voting among representatives in the supranational institutions was seen as a guarantee of the sovereignty of the national civic communities and the establishment of the legitimization-chain passing from the nationals of every member state to the Community institutions.

The situation changed dramatically with the Single European Act of 1987, which provided for the reintroduction of the majority voting in the Council while adopting "the measures for the approximation of the provisions laid down by law, regulation or administrative action in Member States which have as their object the establishment and functioning of the internal market."[156] Although limited to the measures establishing the internal market, the amendment developed an extraordinary effect, particularly if seen in synergy with art. 8a TEEC stating the centrality of the establishment of the internal market.[157] This way, the decision procedures of the Community were becoming more effective, but certainly less legitimated as well. The range of the competencies where majority voting in the Council should be applied has been then progressively extended, from Treaty to Treaty, to include many of the areas under Union control, although,

---

154 See note 24 and note 27.
155 WEILER, *supra* note 30, at 30. The text of the Luxembourg Accord can be found in K.R. SIMMONDS ED., ENCYCLOPEDIA OF EUROPEAN COMMUNITY LAW, vol. B2, para. B10–336 (1974).
156 Single European Act Feb. 17, 1986, 1987 O.J. (L 169), art. 18, introducing art. 100a into the TEEC.
157 *Id.*, at art. 14. See WEILER, *supra* note 30, at 70.

significantly, not all of them. The transition was justified by arguments for the improved efficiency of the Council and the necessity to avoid indiscriminate vetoes that could have threatened the desired progress of European integration. Problems concerning the democratic legitimacy of the Community arose because a gap was opened, for the first time so clearly, between the legitimating procedures at the national level, the only legitimating procedures at that time, and the institutions of the Community.[158] The European Treaty-Framers reacted to this newly emerging deficit by increasing the competences of the European Parliament, in particular by creating first the cooperation procedure with the Single European Act and then the co-decision procedure with the Maastricht Treaty, which nevertheless could only partially counterbalance the alienation of citizens from the European legislative process.[159]

On this point it has to be outlined that the situation created by the amendments introduced by the Single European Act placed Community law in a position outside the traditional international law. The fact that decisions could be taken by majority voting within the most important institution was not unusual for international law, but what was unusual was the range of the decisions themselves. They were specified in TEEC, and had the at least implicit possibility to extend the competencies of the Community according to the implied powers provided for in art. 18 of the Single European Act (introducing art. 100a into the TEEC). This way, the Council was empowered to "create" new law, immediately binding within all member states, even without a consensus among all of them. A situation indeed not just atypical, but also – and much more – characterized, as it has been already said, by an uncertain legitimacy. Moreover, it may be reminded that the resort to majority voting within assemblies, councils or executive boards of international organizations is far away from being free from criticism. Rather, an intense discussion has arisen on how the legitimacy of the decision-making process could be enhanced, giving a firmer foundation for the application of the majority rule.[160]

Partially leaving the field of international law, Community law approached the constitutional tradition. Within this range it could try to find another reason – possibly a more consistent one – for justifying the majority rule in the Council. In fact, majority voting is the norm in all parliamentary assemblies, although no one objects to a lack of legitimacy in that context. However, the majority principle is accepted within the representative assemblies of nation-states because two assumptions are operating here, which are lacking

---

158 The problem was particularly stressed, among others, by Weiler, *supra* note 1.
159 The reason of the only partial success, or rather: of the partial failure, of the strengthening of the competences of the European Parliament depends on the half-hearted measures taken by the Treaty-Framers, leaving the Parliament for a long time in a subordinate role. See *infra*, D, I.
160 Just to remember the most important case, many interesting contributions on the reform of the Charter of the United Nations concentrate on the necessity to better qualify the organisation with regard to its democratic legitimacy. *See*, for just two examples among many: DAVID HELD, DEMOCRACY AND THE GLOBAL ORDER (1995); DANIELE ARCHIBUGI & DAVID HELD EDS., COSMOPOLITAN DEMOCRACY. AN AGENDA FOR A NEW WORLD ORDER (1995). Similar discussions can be found also for other international organizations, like the IMF, the World Bank, or the WTO. Going back to the United Nations, however, the resort to majority voting can also be justified, on principle, referring to interests common to the whole mankind (Charter of Fundamental Rights, *supra* note 47, at prmbl.), creating this way a kind of shared substrate on which decisions can be taken for the sake of all. On the recourse to humankind as the fundament of the constitutionalization of international law, see TOMUSCHAT, *supra* note 20. On the Charter of the United Nations as a constitutional document, *see* James Crawford, *The Charter of the United Nations as a Constitution*, *in* THE CHANGING CONSTITUTION OF THE UNITED NATIONS 3 (Hazel Fox ed., 1997); BARDO FASSBENDER, UN SECURITY COUNCIL REFORM AND THE RIGHT OF VETO. A CONSTITUTIONAL PERSPECTIVE (1998). On legitimacy in international law, see THOMAS M. FRANCK, THE POWER OF LEGITIMACY AMONG NATIONS (1990); THOMAS M. FRANCK, FAIRNESS IN INTERNATIONAL LAW AND INSTITUTIONS (1995); Gregory H. Fox & Brad R. Roth, *Democracy and International Law*, 27 REV. OF INT'L STUD. 327 (2001).

at the level of the European Union. First, in nation-states one assumes the juridical fiction of a single "people," so that the decisions adopted by representatives in the name of this people, even by majority vote, can be better justified in a claim to bind all citizens.[161] Second, national parliaments, as institutions empowered to deliberate and decide by a majority, are regularly elected as a whole body by the peoples they represent. As already noted, the European Union is lacking on both assumptions. No fiction of a "European people" has been accepted, at least up to the Treaty of Nice and the *Charter of Fundamental Rights*,[162] and the Council, as its highest legislative institution, is not constituted by a general election of the whole community of the citizens of the Union. As a consequence, the citizens of a member state, which is outvoted by a majority procedure in the Council, are condemned to a passive condition without any chance to influence the composition of the Council as a whole. They only have the possibility of influencing the action of their national government, which has been placed in a marginal position by its dissenting vote in the Council. To compound the matter, they are unlikely to feel the loyalty and solidarity central to a national "people," which could grow from an ambitiously shaped European citizenship and would form the connections which ease the blow of being on the losing end of a policy debate.

Even the argument that such a situation of specific "impotence" would be the rule within the Chambers of Regions or of States in the institutional architecture of federations, without generating any particular deficit of legitimacy, cannot be applied to the situation of the Union. In the case of the Chambers of Regions or of States it is always presupposed, that a "federal people" does exist, at least as a juridical fiction. This "people" elects in its unity and as a whole its representatives to the other Chamber of the parliament, appointed to cooperate – mostly with broader competencies – with the Chamber of Regions or of States in its legislative function. At the level of the Union this role should be played by the European Parliament, which, given the normative situation up to the Treaty of Nice, is far too subordinate to the Council to fulfil this ambitious task.[163]

Having identified the problem, it is necessary to see now how the Constitutional Treaty addresses it. It must be recalled, above all, that the Treaty of Amsterdam still provided for unanimity in the Council in many significant areas, including the fields into which European competencies were expanded by the TUE: foreign policy, defence, and cooperation in criminal matters.[164] Unanimity remained the rule for a significant number of traditional areas of competence of the TEC as well: measures to combat discrimination;[165] the free movement of the citizens of the Union;[166] the measures to strengthen the rights related to Union citizenship;[167] provisions limiting the free movement of capital to or from third countries;[168] immigration and asylum policy;[169] decisions stating that aid or subsidization granted by a member state is compatible with the internal market;[170] tax harmonisation as far as it is necessary for the functioning of the internal market;[171] the approximation

---

161 Kelsen, *supra* note 6, at 14.
162 See *supra*, A.
163 See *infra*, D, I.
164 The following lists of matters has not to be understood as complete, but only as an attempt at making clear how relevant were (and still are) the areas in which the unanimity of the Council was (or still is) required.
165 Treaty Establishing the European Community, *supra* note 27, at art. 13. (Version incorporating the amendments made by the Treaty of Amsterdam).
166 *Id.*, at art. 18, para. 2.
167 *Id.*, at art. 22.
168 *Id.*, at art. 57, para. 2.
169 *Id.*, at art. 61 and following.
170 *Id.*, at art. 88, para. 2.
171 *Id.*, at art. 93.

of the legislation of the member states as directly affecting the establishment or functioning of the internal market;[172] measures to replace the Protocol on the excessive deficit procedure;[173] some provisions regarding the competences of the European Central Bank;[174] measures on an exchange-rate system for the European currency in relation to the currencies of third states;[175] the social security of the citizens of the Union as well as of third-country nationals legally residing in Community territory;[176] measures concerning migrant workers (particularly their social security);[177] provisions on industry;[178] provisions on culture;[179] actions taken outside the Structural Funds aiming at social and economic cohesion;[180] provisions on tasks and organisation of the Structural Funds;[181] fiscal and planning measures concerning environmental protection and energy;[182] some aspects of the economic cooperation with third countries;[183] rules and procedures for the association of overseas countries and territories;[184] the establishment of common measures for the election of the members of the European Parliament[185] and concerning the condition regulating their performances and duties;[186] the composition of several European institutions;[187] provisions relating to the system governing the resources of the Community;[188] and the flexibility clause.[189]

The Treaty of Nice extended the application of the qualified majority vote to several of these fields:[190] to some provisions concerning the free movement of persons, specifically those related to the status of asylum seekers, refugees and displaced persons[191] (but with the exception of the provisions regarding identity documents, residence permits or provisions on social protection of the citizens of the Union);[192] to certain areas of the economic and monetary policy;[193] partially to the social security of the workers of the Union or from third-countries;[194] to the provisions concerning industry;[195] to objectives and organisation

---

172 *Id.*, at art. 94.
173 *Id.*, at art. 104, para. 14.
174 *Id.*, at art. 105, para. 6.
175 *Id.*, at art. 111, para. 1 and 4.
176 *Id.*, at art. 137 and art. 139.
177 *Id.*, at art. 144.
178 *Id.*, at art. 157.
179 *Id.*, at art. 151.
180 *Id.*, at art. 159.
181 *Id.*, at art. 161.
182 *Id.*, at art. 175, para. 2.
183 *Id.*, at art. 181a, para. 2.
184 *Id.*, at art. 186 and art. 187.
185 *Id.*, at art. 190, para. 4.
186 *Id.*, at art. 190, para. 5.
187 So for the European Court of Justice, *id.*, at art. 221 and following, the Economic and Social Committee, *id.*, at art. 258, and the Committee of the Regions, *id.*, at art. 263.
188 *Id.*, at art. 269.
189 *Id.*, at art. 308.
190 However, the Treaty of Nice limited also, in at least one case, the application of the majority vote rule. *See* the article on international agreements where unanimity is required when it is also the case for the adoption of internal rules, Treaty Establishing the European Community, Dec. 12, 2002, art 133, para. 5, 2002 O.J. (C 325/33) (Consolidated version incorporating the amendments made by the Treaty of Nice), compared to the former version where this limitation was not present, Treaty Establishing the European Community, Oct. 2, 1997, art. 133, para. 4, 1997 O.J. C 340/1 (Version incorporating the amendments made by the Treaty of Amsterdam).
191 Treaty Establishing the European Community, Dec. 12, 2002, art. 67, para. 5, 2002 O.J. C 325/33 (Consolidated version incorporating the amendments made by the Treaty of Nice).
192 *Id.*, at art. 18, para. 3.
193 *Id.*, at art. 100 and art. 111, para. 4.
194 *Id.*, at art. 137, para. 2–3, with reference also to art. 139 and art. 144.
195 *Id.*, at art. 157.

of the Structural Funds;[196] and to the provisions regulating performances and duties of the members of the European Parliament.[197] In spite of these amendments, the partial reform introduced by the Treaty of Nice in favour of majority rule in the Council has been considered rather quantitative than qualitative,[198] since in all the remaining above mentioned matters unanimity was still required and majority rule was not yet declared to be the ordinary procedure of the Council.

During the discussion on the new Constitutional Treaty radical proposals were forwarded aiming at a general abolition of unanimity in the Council of Ministers,[199] but they were not sufficiently backed by the Convention. Nevertheless, the Constitutional Treaty introduces the important reform desired by the supporters of the integration but which they failed to obtain in the Treaty of Nice. Indeed, the Constitutional Treaty provides that qualified majority voting is to be one of the essential elements of the "legislative procedure" which is now called "ordinary."[200] Thus, it becomes the rule and it is not merely one procedure among others.[201]

Exceptions to the rule require a well motivated justification.[202] This does not mean that the Constitutional Treaty would not provide for a large number of these exceptions, in order to ensure to some extent the intergovernmental dimension of European policies.[203] The intergovernmental character, under the Constitutional Treaty, of the areas of justice, foreign policy and defence has already been taken into consideration.[204] Further more, all the above mentioned matters which were excluded by the TEC from applying the majority vote[205] have also been actually included into the Constitutional Treaty, with only few marginal, i.e. essentially formal modifications.[206] Unanimity is also required for fields where the Constitutional Treaty is aiming to reach a more precise regulation than within the former

---

196 *Id.*, at art. 159 and art. 161.
197 *Id.*, at art. 190, para. 5. The provisions concerning the taxation of the present or former MEPs still requires, however, unanimity within the Council (*id.*, at art. 190, para 5).
198 This was the largely shared opinion on the extension of the application of the majority rule by the Treaty of Nice expressed by Romano Prodi, President of the European Commission, Speech at the European Parliament (Dec. 12, 2000) *available at* http://www.eic.ac.cy/EN/Prodi12Dec00.htm.
199 Communication from the Commission. A Project for the European Union, European Convention 229/02, 8. The proposal was later confirmed, Prodi, *supra* note 137, at 3; Communication from the Commission on the Institutional Architecture – For the European Union. Peace, Freedom, Solidarity, European Convention 448/02, 6.
200 Constitutional Treaty, *supra* note 47 at, art. I-34 and art. III-396, following the proposal of the WG IX, Final Report of the Working Group on Simplification, European Convention 424/02, 14.
201 Constitutional Treaty, *supra* note 47, at art. I-23, para. 3.
202 Constitutional Treaty, *supra* note 47, at art. I-34, para. 2 and following.
203 Also in this case the list does not pretend to be exhaustive.
204 *Supra* at B, I.
205 A partial exception is given by the articles containing the provisions on culture: while on principle the unanimity rule has been substituted by the qualified majority procedure, Constitutional Treaty, *supra* note 47, at art. III-280, para. 5; compared to Treaty Establishing the European Community, *supra* note 191, at art. 157, in detail the sovereignty of the nation-states should not be superseded. Constitutional Treaty, *supra* note 47, at art. III-280, para. 5: "excluding any harmonization of the laws and regulation of the member states." *See also*, *id.*, at III-315, para. 4. Indeed, culture has been coherently inserted into the Constitutional Treaty only as an area of "supporting, coordinating or complementary action" *id.*, at art. I-17.
206 For a better orientation within the complex structure of the Constitutional Treaty and for an easier comparison to the former Treaties, these areas comprehend: the application of the flexibility clause, Constitutional Treaty, *supra* note 47, at art. I-18, para. 1; provisions relating to the system of own resources of the Union, *id.*, at art. I-54, para. 3, and art. I-55, para. 4; measures to combat discrimination, *id.*, at art. III-124, para. 1; measures related to passports, similar documents and provisions on social security or protection of the citizens of the Union, *id.*, at art. III-125, para. 2; measures concerning the right of Union citizens to vote and to stand as a candidate in municipal or European elections in their member state of residence without being a national of this state, *id.*, at art. III-126; provisions extending the rights related to Union citizenship, *id.*, at art. III-129; the limitation of the free movement of capital to or from third countries, *id.*, at art. III-157, para. 3; this matter has now been integrated by a provision, not present in the former Treaties, concerning the

Treaties,[207] where it has to regulate the transition from the former to the new order,[208] or where competencies originally entrusted to the European Council have been passed to the Council of Ministers.[209] In some other cases, the principle of unanimity in Council of Ministers voting can be directly referred to elements of the functioning of the Union which the Constitutional Treaty derives originally from the intergovernmental essence of the TEU. This is the case for matters like the admission of new member states,[210] the suspension of the membership rights,[211] and the authorization to proceed with and regulating enhanced cooperation.[212] Similar are the cases in which the European Council is the European institution that shall act by unanimity, namely when deciding on a change of the composition of the European Parliament,[213] on the composition of the Commission,[214] as well as on the extension of the qualified majority vote procedure in the Council of Ministers (applying a simplified revision procedure, i.e. without any amendment of the Constitutional Treaty, but excluding decisions with military implications or in the area of defence).[215] Finally, we have in the Constitutional Treaty some provisions in which the application of the unanimity rule in Council of Ministers voting is even more severe (however in a soft fashion) than in the TEC.[216]

approval by the Council, also requiring unanimity, of the adoption of restrictive tax measures provided by a member state against one or more third countries; *see id.*, at art. III-158, para. 4; decisions stating that aid or subsidization granted by a member state is compatible with the internal market, *id.*, at art. III-168, para. 2; tax harmonisation as far as it is necessary for the functioning of the internal market, *id.*, at art. III-171; the approximation of the legislation of the member states as directly affecting the establishment or functioning of the internal market, *id.*, at art. III-173; measures to replace the Protocol on the excessive deficit procedure, *id.*, at art. III-184, para. 13; some provisions regarding the competences of the European Central Bank, *id.*, art. III-185, para. 6 – provision not included into the Draft Treaty approved by the Convention; some areas concerning the protection of workers, *id.*, at art. III-210, para. 3, and art. III-212, para. 2; fiscal and planning measures concerning environmental protection and energy, *id.*, at art. III-234, para. 2, and art. III-256, para. 3 – provision not included into the Draft Treaty approved by the Convention; rules and procedures for the association of overseas countries and territories, *id.*, at art. III-291; international agreements when unanimity is required for the adoption of internal rules, *id.*, at art. III-315, para. 4; measures on an exchange-rate system for the European currency in relation to the currencies of third states, *id.*, at art. III-326, para. 1; the establishment of common measures for the election of the members of the European Parliament, *id.*, at art. III-330, para. 1; rules concerning the taxation of MEPs, *id.*, at art. III-330, para. 2; the composition of several European institutions, *id.*, at art. III-354 and following, art. III-386, and art. III-389.

207 This is the case for following areas: the establishment of language arrangements for the European intellectual property rights, *id.*, at art. III-176; agreements in the field of trade in cultural and audiovisual services implying risks for the cultural and linguistic diversity within the Union, *id.*, at art. III-315, para. 4; trade in social, education and health services if seriously disruptive of the national organisation of such services, *id.*, at art. III-315, para. 4.

208 So in the article concerning the first provisions on the structural and cohesion funds following the Constitutional Treaty has been signed, *id.*, at III-223, para. 2 – this provision has been slightly modified with respect to the Draft Treaty approved by the Convention – *see* Draft Constitutional Treaty, European Convention 850/03 art. III-119, para. 2.

209 *See* the provision regulating the amendment of the Statute of the European Investment Bank, Constitutional Treaty, *supra* note 47, at art. III-393; compared to Treaty Establishing the European Community, *supra* note 191, at art. 266 (before and after the Treaty of Nice).

210 Constitutional Treaty, *supra* note 47, at art. I-58, para. 2.

211 *Id.*, at art. I-59, para. 2.

212 *Id.*, at art. III-419, para. 2; III-420, para. 2 (these provisions were not included into the Draft Treaty approved by the Convention, but are already present, with few differences, in the TEU, art. 23 and following). On enhanced cooperation *see* also the following articles.

213 *Id.*, at art. I-20, para. 2.

214 *Id.*, at art. I-26, para. 6 (provision not included into the Draft Treaty approved by the Convention).

215 *Id.*, at art. IV-444, para. 1.

216 This is the case for the provisions concerning: the introduction of the euro in further countries after a period of derogation, Constitutional Treaty, *supra* note 47, at art. III-198, para. 3; *see* Treaty Establishing the European Community, *supra* note 191, at art. 122), and some aspects of the economic cooperation with third countries, Constitutional Treaty, *supra* note 47, at art. III-325, para. 8; *see* Treaty Establishing the European Community, *supra* note 137, at art. 181a, para. 2.

When compared with the Treaties of Amsterdam and Nice, the list of the matters with regard to which the Constitutional Treaty requires unanimity in the Council of Ministers reveals very little substantial change. In other words, the Constitutional Treaty consolidates the *acquis communautaire*, maintaining – perhaps reinforcing – the danger that the bond to unanimity might be too tight and frequent to make efficient policies possible in a Union with twenty-five or more member states. As regards the question of legitimacy, it is necessary clearly to distinguish between the matters where unanimity is required and those for which qualified majority is the rule. Concerning the latter, as I have already noted, the only possible solution is to resort to the "people of citizens of the Union" taking recourse to its representative institution, namely the European Parliament. I will take up the role of the Parliament in more detail later.[217] It will be sufficient here to anticipate that, in so far as areas requiring qualified majority in the Council exclude the co-decision by the Parliament, the democratic legitimacy simply cannot be seen as guaranteed.[218] To the contrary, in all matters where the Treaty on the European Community consolidated after Nice provides for the co-decision of the Parliament[219] the democratic legitimacy was actually guaranteed[220] even before the discussion on the Constitutional Treaty had begun.

---

217 See *infra*, D, I.
218 In the version of the TEC incorporating the Amendments made by the Treaty of Amsterdam this was the case for several – quite non marginal – fields, in particular: art. 11, para. 2 (authorization to establish closer cooperation – with consultation of the Parliament); art. 14, para. 3 (measures to establish the internal market); art. 26 (fixing of common customs tariff); art. 37, para. 2–3 (common agricultural policy); art. 47 (limitation of the right of establishment); art. 49 (extension of the freedom to provide services to nationals of third countries); art. 52, para. 1 (liberalization of specific services – with consultation of the Parliament); art. 57, para. 2, art. 59, and art. 60, para. 2 (some aspects of the free movement of capital with third countries); art. 64, para 2 (adoption of restrictive measures concerning the inflow of nationals of third countries); art. 67, para. 3 (visa policy – with consultation of the Parliament); art. 75, para. 3 (abolition of discrimination in the area of transport); art. 80, para. 2 (adoption of provision on sea and air transport); art. 83, para. 1 (some measures to guarantee the freedom of the common market – with consultation of the Parliament); art. 87, para. 3, e), and art. 89 (the specification of the categories of aid granted by member states non compatible with the common market – with consultation of the Parliament); art. 92 (the introduction of specific tax charges); art. 96 (provisions removing distortions of the competition within the common market); art. 99, para. 2, and 4 (the definition of the guidelines of the economic policies); art. 100, para. 2 (aid to member states in difficulties because of natural disasters); art. 104, para. 6 (decision on the existence of an excessive deficit); art. 104, para. 14 (rules on the application of the excessive deficit procedure); art. 107, para. 6 (provisions referred to in the Statute of the ESCB – with consultation of the Parliament); art. 111, para 1–4 (establishment of a exchange-rate system in relation to the currencies of third countries); art. 114 (composition of the Economic and Financial Committee); art. 117, para. 6 (conditions for the consultation of the European Monetary Institute – with consultation of the Parliament); art. 119, para. 2–3 (assistance to a member state in difficulties as regards its balance of payments); art. 120, para. 3 (provisions on protective measures by a member state); art. 121, para. 2–4, art. 122, para. 1–2, and 5 (measures on economic and monetary union); art. 128, para. 2, and 4 (drawing up of guidelines on employment policies); art. 132, para. 1 (aid for exports to third countries); art. 133, para. 4 (measures on common commercial policy), art. 139, para. 2 (agreements on social provisions); art. 166, para. 4, and art. 172 (research programmes – with consultation of the Parliament); art. 210, art. 247, para. 8, and art. 258 (determination of salaries, allowances and pensions of the members of the Commission, of the Court of Justice, of the Court of Auditors, and of the Economic and Social Committee); art. 300, para. 1, and art. 301 (signing of international agreements); art. 309, para. 2–3 (suspenction of the rights deriving from the Treaty). Very significantly, the Treaty of Nice has strengthened the European Parliament only as regards the matter regulated by art. 11, para. 2. For the rest, nothing has been changed, so that the legitimacy deficit referred to the here mentioned provisions remains unchanged.
219 Treaty Establishing the European Community, *supra* note 137, at art. 251.
220 This can be said, although with some limitations, also for the matters where the residual procedure of cooperation (according to art. 252 TEC) applies. The cooperation procedure has been made residual by the Treaty of Amsterdam which, in comparison with the provisions of the Maastricht Treaty, extended the application of art. 251 TEC to over twenty further areas, limiting the procedure of cooperation to less than a half dozen of areas. These residual areas, however, were not further reduced by the Treaty of Nice which did not introduce any change on this issue.

Nevertheless, this factual dimension, positively legitimating the public power of the Union, has not been in conformity, up to Nice, with the normative principles laid down in the Treaties since the European Parliament was still defined as the assembly of the "representative of the peoples of the states,"[221] and as such it could not be seen as acting in the common interest of the citizens of the Union. This, of course, is the precise role that could justify the minority's respect of majority rule in the Council. The question regarding the matters subject to unanimity raises different concerns. In fact, the decisions of the ministers of the national governments acting as members of the Council can be considered democratically legitimated only if they undergo an adequate control by the representative assemblies of the country from which every single minister comes. This last point requires the consideration of the role played by national parliaments in the European architecture, which will be the main issue of the next section.

2. The Role of National Parliaments in the Legitimization of the European Public Power

Assuming that the European public power ought to obtain its legitimization – totally or partially – within the nation-states and through their democratic procedures, the logical consequence will be that the representative institutions of the citizens in the member states, namely the national parliaments, should be adequately involved in the political life of the Union.[222] More precisely, this involvement should be so well shaped that it might allow them to take on the difficult task of investing the Union's institutions with full democratic legitimacy.[223] But the lack of sound mechanisms actualizing this claim, up through the Treaty of Nice,[224] has given rise to justified discontent for some time. According to the fundamental law of the Union, in force until the new Constitutional Treaty enters into force, and in particular Protocol No. 9 added to the TEC by the Treaty of Amsterdam, the role of the national parliaments in the institutional architecture of the Community is limited to the provision that they should receive all Commission documents, which in the case of proposals for legislation is done indirectly, i.e. passing through the national governments.[225] Moreover, parliamentary control of the activity of the ministers of the national governments within the Council has been left totally to the rules laid down by national laws. In those cases where this control is insufficient we have, because of the priority and immediate validity of Union laws, an implicit transition of competencies from the legislative to the executive power.

The discontent concerning the lack of involvement of national parliaments was expressed in the conclusive declaration of the European Council in Laeken of December 15, 2001,[226] which established the *Convention on the Future of Europe* charged with the drawing up of a Constitutional Treaty. In the mandate for the Convention, among the issues it would deal with, it was recognized:

---

221 Treaty Establishing the European Community, *supra* note 137, at art. 189.
222 Final Report of Working Group IV on the Role of National Parliaments, European Convention 253/02.
223 On the role hitherto played effectively by the national parliaments within the European architecture, see PHILIP NORTON ED., NATIONAL PARLIAMENTS AND THE EUROPEAN UNION (1996); RICHARD S. KATZ ED., THE EUROPEAN PARLIAMENT, THE NATIONAL PARLIAMENTS, AND EUROPEAN INTEGRATION (1999); ANDREAS MAURER ED., NATIONAL PARLIAMENTS ON THEIR WAYS TO EUROPE: LOSERS OR LATECOMERS? (2001); PETER M. HUBER, NATIONAL PARLIAMENTS AND THE LAW-MAKING PROCESS OF THE EUROPEAN UNION (2002); PHILIPP DANN, PARLAMENTE IM EXEKUTIVFÖDERALISMUS (2004).
224 On this issue, see Discussion Paper – The Role of National Parliaments in the European Architecture, European Convention 67/02.
225 Treaty Establishing the European Community, *supra* note 191, at art. I-1 and I-2, Protocol (9).
226 Presidency Conclusions – Laeken Declaration on the Future of the European Union, European Council Meeting in Laeken Dec. 14–15, 2001, SN 300/1/01 Rev 1, Annex I, 19.

a second question, which also relates to democratic legitimacy, involves the role of national parliaments. Should they be represented in a new institution, alongside the Council and the European Parliament? Should they have a role in areas of European action in which the European Parliament has no competence? Should they focus on the division of competence between Union and member states, for example through preliminary checking of compliance with the principle of subsidiarity?[227]

After the role of national parliaments had been discussed superficially at an early plenary meeting,[228] the issue was handed over to Working Group IV, which had been explicitly established to this end and the conclusions of which were later widely accepted by the Convention.[229] Having rejected the hypothesis of the establishment of a new institution *ad hoc* consisting of representatives of the national parliaments, which had been proposed both in the above mentioned mandate of the Laeken Council as well as in preliminary texts,[230] the changes introduced by the Constitutional Treaty concentrate above all on the procedures through which the national parliaments can better take part in framing the Union's policies.[231] These procedural provisions have been drawn up in two Protocols, the first of them on the role of national parliaments in the European Union,[232] the second on the application of the principles of subsidiarity and proportionality.[233] The first Protocol states in particular that all legislative documents have to be forwarded by the Commission "directly" to the national parliaments,[234] and not, as provided for in the Protocol No. 9 TEC, to the national governments in order that they be handed over to the parliaments.[235] At this point – as specified in the second Protocol – every Chamber of the national parliaments may present, within six weeks from the transmission of the proposal, "a reasoned opinion stating why it considers that the draft in question does not comply with the principle of subsidiarity."[236] If at least one third of the national parliaments express such an opinion, the Commission must review the proposal.[237] After this procedure, the

---

227 *Id.*, at 23.
228 *See*, in particular, Note on the Plenary Meeting, Brussels, Apr. 15–16, 2002, European Convention 40/02 7; Note on the Plenary Meeting, Brussels, May 23–24, 2002, European Convention 60/02 7.
229 Summary Report of the Plenary Session, Brussels, Oct. 28–29, 2002, European Convention 378/02. Also the Commission agreed with the proposals, Communication from the Commission on the Institutional Architecture, For the European Union. Peace, Freedom, Solidarity. European Convention 448/02 19.
230 Discussion Paper – The Role of National Parliaments in the European Architecture, European Convention 67/02, 12. This notwithstanding, the art. 19 of the Preliminary Draft provided for "the possibility of establishing a Congress of the Peoples of Europe," presumably conceived as representative institution of the national parliaments, Preliminary Draft Constitutional Treaty, *supra* note 90, 3 and 13. However, the proposal was not inserted later into the Constitutional Treaty.
231 For an overview of the modifications introduced by the Constitutional Treaty, see The Role of National Parliaments in the Draft Constitution, European Convention 738/03.
232 Constitutional Treaty, Dec. 16, 2004, 2004 O.J. (C 310/01), Protocols and Annexes, A. Protocols, Protocol No.1: Protocol on the Role of Member States' National Parliaments in the European Union.
233 Constitutional Treaty, *supra* note 232, at Protocols and Annexes, A. Protocols, Protocol No.2: Protocol on the Application of the Principles of Subsidiarity and Proportionality.
234 Constitutional Treaty, *supra* note 232, at Protocol on the Role of Member States' National Parliaments in the European Union, art. 1. Further rules are added concerning the obligations by the Union's institutions to directly inform the national parliaments, *id.*, at art. 2.
235 Discussion Paper – The Role of National Parliaments in the European Architecture, European Convention 67/02 3.
236 Constitutional Treaty, *supra* note 232, at Protocol on the Application of the Principles of Subsidiarity and Proportionality, art. 6. *See also*, *id.*, at Protocol on the Role of Member States' National Parliaments in the European Union, art. 3.
237 The rule applies for a quarter of the national parliaments if the proposal regards art. III-264 of the Constitutional Treaty, on the area of freedom, security and justice, *id.*, at Protocol on the Application of the Principles of Subsidiarity and Proportionality, art. 7). Every member state has two votes, both for the one Chamber in the countries with unicameral parliamentary system, one for each Chamber in the states with bicameral system, *id.*

Commission as well as the other institutions and bodies of the Union are authorized to maintain their position, but only delivering further arguments for it.[238] Finally, the Court of Justice "shall have jurisdiction in actions on grounds of infringement of the principle of subsidiarity."[239] But such review is requested by the governments of the member states on behalf of and not by the national parliaments themselves.[240]

Turning to the control national parliaments exercise over the activities of members of the national governments in the Council of Ministers, Working Group IV acknowledged that this issue belongs essentially to each national constitutional system, but proposed that minimum standards should be established at Union level.[241] Largely in fulfilment of this aim, the Constitutional Treaty provides for the Commission to be obliged – as mentioned above – to directly transmit to the national parliaments the documents related to legislative initiatives.[242] Officially, this provision ensures "that all national parliaments have the earliest possible access to documents,"[243] unofficially it can also prevent an eventual attempt by national governments to keep their own parliaments partially or totally uninformed about the details of European initiatives. Furthermore, the Constitutional Treaty requires that the Council of Ministers "shall meet in public ... when considering and voting on a draft legislative act."[244] The most innovative aspect of the Constitutional Treaty, as regards this matter, consists in the provision that "member states are represented in the European Council by their Heads of state or government and in the Council by their governments, themselves democratically accountable either to their national parliaments, or to their citizens."[245] Thus, for the first time the democratic accountability of national representatives within the European institutions has been acknowledged as an objective that has to be ensured by the fundamental law of the Union.

Surely, the provisions of the Constitutional Treaty here briefly presented can guarantee that the national parliaments attain relevance within the European institutional architecture which was unknown before. No less certainly, this newfound engagement on the part of national parliaments cannot adequately legitimize the European public power. Three considerations, in particular, suggest caution:

(a) The first one refers to the essence of the role of national parliaments. In fact, their task consists in the protection of their national interests against abuses of power by European institutions, concerning particularly the infringement of the principles of subsidiarity and proportionality. Indeed, this is also the aim of the rules included in the Constitutional Treaty. However, European public power can violate the rights of the citizens not only in their status as nationals of a member state, but also, and maybe

---

238 *Id.*, at art. 7.
239 *Id.*, at art. 8.
240 *Id.* Actions before the Court of Justice may also be brought by the Committee of the Regions, but only "against European legislative acts for the adoption of which the Constitution provides that it be consulted," *id.*
241 The control by the national parliaments of the national ministers within the Council should happen, however, rather in an informal way, i.e. by a "code of conduct" agreed upon by the national parliaments, and not by a specific provision within the Constitutional Treaty, Final Report of Working Group IV on the Role of National Parliaments, European Convention 253/02 5.
242 *See*, Constitutional Treaty *supra*, note 234.
243 Final Report of the Working Group on the Role of National Parliaments, European Convention 353/02 6.
244 Constitutional Treaty, *supra* note 232, at art. I-50, para. 2, following the proposals of the WG IV, Final Report of the Working Group on the Role of National Parliaments, European Convention 353/02 3. Remarkably, this provision goes beyond the conclusions of the European Council of Seville, which stated that the meetings of the Council of Ministers should be opened to the public opinion only when issues are discussed for which the codecision procedure is required, Conclusions de la Présidence, Conseil Européen de Séville, Jun. 21–22, 2002, all. II, § 10 and following.
245 Constitutional Treaty, *supra* note 232, at art. I-46, para. 2.

rather, in so far as they are citizens of the Union.[246] With regard to Union citizenship, however, the new provisions introduced by the Constitutional Treaty on the role of national parliaments do not provide protection because the function of protecting the Union's citizens does not belong in reality, and cannot belong as a matter of principle, to national instances. Protection from European public power must emanate from European institutions.

(b) Secondly, the intervention of the national parliaments in the legislative procedures of the Union is limited with regard to its object and to its temporality. Its main object consists in monitoring that respect be paid to the principles of subsidiarity and proportionality. The timing of its effect is limited to control *ex ante* and *ex post*. All further aspects of the legislative procedure remain outside the competencies of the national parliaments. This is not very surprising; European legislation needs, above all, European legislators.

(c) Finally, though recognizing the courage expressed in the mandate for minimum standards concerning the democratic control of the members of the national executives acting in the European Council or in the Council of Ministers, at least one reservation arises as regards the effectiveness of the measure. In fact, it is not easy to imagine, and it is not made clear by the Treaty, how the constitutional principle of minimum standards, albeit valid, could be implemented through effective rules and praxis.

Any attempt to analyze the hypothesis that the legitimization of European public power can derive from the national parliaments of the member states reveals, notwithstanding the validity of some new provisions introduced by the Constitutional Treaty, that there is no convincingly comprehensive solution to the problems that plague the claim for a definitive role for the national parliaments. Even Working Group IV underlined in its final report that its proposals were not aiming at raising a competition between the national parliaments and the European Parliament: "each had its distinct role but both shared the common objective of bringing the EU closer to citizens and thus contributing to enhancing the democratic legitimacy of the Union."[247] Therefore, even those who pressed – undoubtedly with positive results – for the institutional role of the national parliaments as the real source of democratic legitimacy of European institutions, must acknowledge that this source of legitimacy cannot be anything but: (1) national democratic legitimacy deriving from the parliaments of each member state and manifesting itself at the European level through control over the activities of the nation's ministers in the Council as well as by participating in some aspects of European legislation; and (2) a second, wholly separate wellspring of democratic legitimacy, which must be explicitly European and therefore must derive from the citizens of the Union, both directly participating in the European political life as well as represented by the Parliament in Strasbourg.

C. The Concept of the "People of the Citizens of the Union"

The preceding paragraphs have established that European public power exists and that it cannot be adequately legitimated by the domestic democratic procedures of the member states. In particular, the European Council in almost all its functions as well as the Council of Ministers in many of its competencies seems to be free, at least to a considerable extent,

---

246 This should be the main reason, in fact, why the Charter of Fundamental Rights has been first proclaimed and then introduced into the Constitutional Treaty. See Louis Favoreu, *I garanti dei diritti fondamentali europei*, in DIRITTI E COSTITUZIONE NELL'UNIONE EUROPEA 247 (Gustavo Zagrebelsky et al., eds., 2003).
247 Final Report of the Working Group on the Role of National Parliaments, European Convention 353/02 2.

of the democratic accountability to the national parliaments. Given these conditions, the only way to resolve the Union's democratic deficit must be in the recourse to the "European people," i.e. to the community of the citizens of the Union as a distinctly European foundation for the democratic legitimacy of the Union's institutions.[248] On the contrary, in spite of the striking necessity of such a recourse, the fundamental law of the Union, even including the Treaty of Nice, has lacked it.

Once it is established that the reason for this is not the absence of a democratic deficit, it becomes necessary to consider the second motivation given by the European would-be Framers for having renounced any reference to a "European people" in the Treaties. This secondary justification asserts the impossibility of formulating the notion of a "European people" in a coherent, i.e. non-self-contradictory manner. In other words, even admitting that the recourse to a "European people" may be opportune or quite desirable, it would not be acceptable not only because such a people presently does not exist, but also and principally because the concept presupposes that categories which exclusively suit national realities would have to be applied to the European context. This is the so-called "no demos thesis," largely diffused in scholarship and public opinion alike: in so far as Europe can not be conceived as anything but a community of peoples, the very idea of a single European people would be in conflict with its very preconditions.[249] Moreover, even if this idea could be realized, for these critics it would not be desirable.[250] But the widespread acceptance of this critique does not make it true. Instead, it gives rise to a couple of questions. First, one might ask whether the thesis is really so self-evident that the European citizens, because of *vis major*, cannot define themselves as a "people" and therefore qualify themselves as the constituent power of the Union's constitution. And second, on the contrary, one might ask whether a characterization of the people as well as of the constituent power is not conceivable, which may be compatible with the specificity of the European condition.

The answer to these questions depends on the way one interprets the concept of a "people."[251] In this matter two traditions stand in opposition to one another, both referring to one of the components of the classical dichotomy in political thought known as "holism" and "individualism."[252] The first way to define a "people" is that which finds expression in

---

248 This certainly need not be seen as the only foundation, but can operate in synergy with the representative institutions of the member states.
249 Among many other scholars, *see* Josef Isensee, *Nachwort Europa – die politische Erfindung eines Erdteils, in* EUROPA ALS POLITISCHE IDEE UND ALS RECHTLICHE FORM 103 (Paul Kirchhof et al., eds., 1993); Paul Kirchhof, *Der deutsche Staat im Prozeß der europäischen Integration, in* HANDBUCH DES STAATSRECHTS DER BUNDESREPUBLIK DEUTSCHLAND. BAND VII. NORMATIVITÄT UND SCHUTZ DER VERFASSUNG – INTERNATIONALE BEZIEHUNGEN 855 (Josef Isensee & Paul Kirchhof eds., 1992); M. Rainer Lepsius, *Nationalstaat oder Nationalitätenstaat als Modell für die Weiterentwicklung der Europäischen Gemeinschaft, in* STAATSWERDUNG EUROPAS? OPTIONEN FÜR EINE EUROPÄISCHE UNION 19 (Rudolf Wildenmann eds., 1991); Grimm, *supra* note 44; SCHARPF, *supra* note 1; Jachtenfuchs & Kohler-Koch, *supra* note 3; Majone, *supra* note 3.
250 For the criticism relying upon the idea of the nation-state (*see* note 249) the perspective of a Europe united on the fundament of a single *demos* is not desirable since it would jeopardize the social and political cohesion of the historically consolidated nations, for the "liberal" authors the danger of such a vision consists rather in the annihilation of the pluralism inherent to the Community project. Its most significant innovation should be seen in the "multiple *demoi*" (which means the contemporary and non-contradictory belonging of every European citizen to a plurality of social and cultural groups) which the Community project decisively contributes to establish, as well as in the "constitutional tolerance" which characterizes the political and juridical life within the Union. Both principles would be at stake if the idea of the creation of a new unitarian "people of Europe" should prevail. *See*, WEILER, *supra* note 30, at 344; WEILER, *supra* note 46.
251 In more detail, S. DELLAVALLE, UNA COSTITUZIONE SENZA POPOLO? (2002).
252 NORBERTO BOBBIO, L'ETÀ DEI DIRITTI 45, 121 (1990).

nation-states: the "people" is here identified with the *nation*,[253] seen as a pre-political social entity which is grounded as a totality (or as an *holon*, according to the ancient Greek terminology) – at least in the intentions of the upholders of this ideology – on an objective substrate, preceding in its origins and axiologically prior to the will, the rights and the interests of the individuals.[254] In this tradition, the nation is understood as a reality, organically based on a common *substance*, made of shared language, customs, culture, way of life, history and frequently strengthened, more or less explicitly, by a shared "blood."[255] The "people" is thus despoiled of its eminently political character, of its constructivist nature, becoming the *ethnos*, the ancestral tribe as source of a visceral identity which pretends to imbue the whole social life of the polity, from the public sphere to the individual habits, and against which any purpose of supranational integration is condemned to end in failure. It would be worth asking, indeed, whether such a "people" has ever really existed in modern nation-states,[256] or, even admitting that it was once a reality in a more or less distant past, whether the transition to a more properly political form of coexistence should not be identified as one of the most significant moments of human progress,[257] namely as one of the indispensable premises of the change from the *status naturae* to the *societas civilis*.

In any event it is evident that no "people" with these characteristics can be specified in the Union at the present time, nor it is likely that such a "people-building" will occur in the immediate future (wholly apart from the fact that many European citizens would not like this evolution). Therefore, anyone – either scholar or interested citizen – who adopts the holistic approach to the issue of a "people" as the origin of the democratic legitimization of public power, must come to the conclusion that the Union should build its legitimacy on the nation-states, namely on the only political entities which possess, or pretend to possess, a "people" in the substantial sense of the term. Thus, the democratic legitimization of European public power could only be possible through indirect means, i.e. resorting to institutions of the member states, which brings us back, nevertheless, to the difficulties identified in the precedent paragraphs.[258]

There is, however, another way, which consists of the identification of a "people" with the community of individuals willing to build a political society, a polity which subjects them to a shared public power. This is the individualistic understanding of "people," according to which the normative nucleus of the political and juridical system must be identified in the individuals with their rights and interests.[259] Here, the highest value is not

---

253 The literature on the concept of nation is extremely vast. Just to give some references, for the idea of nation and nationalism, included its different interpretations, see EUGEN LEMBERG, NATIONALISMUS 2 (1964); HANS KOHN, DIE IDEE DES NATIONALISMUS: URSPRUNG UND GESCHICHTE BIS ZUR FRANZÖSISCHEN REVOLUTION (1962); BOYD C. SHAFER, NATIONALISM. MYTH AND REALITY (1955). On the difference between nationalism and patriotism, see LOUIS L. SNYDER, THE MEANING OF NATIONALISM (1968); LOUIS L. SNYDER, VARIETIES OF NATIONALISM: A COMPARATIVE STUDY (1976). Arguing the substantial origin of nations, see ANTHONY D. SMITH, THE ETHNIC ORIGINS OF NATIONS (1986). Sustaining, to the contrary, their political construction, see JOHN BREUILLY, NATIONALISM AND THE STATE (1982); ERNEST GELLNER, NATIONS AND NATIONALISM (1983); ERIC J. HOBSBAWM, NATION AND NATIONALISM SINCE 1780 (1990).
254 BOBBIO, *supra* note 252.
255 This conception goes back to ADAM MÜLLER, ELEMENTE DER STAATSKUNST (1809). For a more recent reproposal of it, *see* SMITH, *supra* note 253.
256 *See* BREUILLY, *supra* note 253; GELLNER, *supra* note 253; HOBSBAWM, *supra* note 253.
257 HABERMAS, *supra* note 44, at 138.
258 Isensee, supta note 22, 579; Kirchhof, *supra* note 249, at 876; KAUFMANN, *supra* note 44, 534; Dieter Grimm, *Il significato della stesura di un catalogo europeo die diritti fondamentali nell'ottica della critica dell'ipotesi di una Costituzione europea*, in DIRITTI E COSTITUTIONE NELL'UNIONE EUROPEA 5, 15 (Gustavo Zagrebelsky et al., eds., 2003).
259 Norberto Bobbio, *Il modello giusnaturalistico*, in SOCIETÀ E STATO NELLA FILOSOFIA POLITICA MODERNA 15, 34 (Norberto Bobbio & Michelangelo Bovero eds., 1979), with references, in particular, to the works of Thomas Hobbes, John Locke, Jean-Jacques Rousseau, and Immanuel Kant.

the whole of the social body with its tendency to self-preservation but rather the reasonable will of the individuals living together in a freely organized society.[260] Starting from this point of view, even the specification of a "people of the Union" becomes a resolvable problem: if "people" means the community of individuals subject to a specific public power – and not nationals who belongs to a pre-constituted body and share with it and with each other the deepest aspects of their socio-psychological and existential identity – then, such a reality can be identified also for the Union, namely in the *totality of its citizens*. In light of these considerations, the concept of a "people of the Union" or "European people," often invoked in the preceding paragraphs, must be understood as "the totality of the citizens," and not as a substantial entity, rooted in a pre-political substrate.

Undoubtedly, the individualistic paradigm also implies the risk of some unpleasant and problematic consequences. In particular, it may lead to reductionism in the interpretation of the concept of citizenship, which may come to be seen as merely the right to freely move in the market.[261] In the discussion on European integration this could mean that citizens are of value exclusively as men and women acting in the market, whose rights and duties are exclusively and essentially deducible from the so-called "four freedoms" (of movement of persons, capital, goods and services).[262] Conceived in this way, the idea of the "citizenship of the Union" can scarcely ensure the democratic legitimacy of the European institutions. First because this legitimacy is nearly irrelevant from the point of view of the social philosophy of the free market economy, and second because individuals whose ethical and political dimension has been reduced to action in the market are not capable of delivering an eminently extra-economic output.[263] In order to avoid this impasse, we must overcome even the narrowly individualistic perspective, arriving at a third paradigm, called *communicative*,[264] in which the political interaction among individuals does not aim at their merely egoistic interest but produces, already through its existence and development, a pool of shared values deeply influencing the identity of every member of the polity.[265] Particularly, the communicative approach to the social and political world has the advantage of giving a way for a solid anchoring, through political interaction, of the ethical foundation affecting an entire society. The well-balanced discussion concerning how we can deal, as a society of free and equal citizens, with common issues has an axiopoietic

---

260 The contractualist theory of state has been re-vitalized in the 20th century especially by John Rawls. *See* JOHN RAWLS, A THEORY OF JUSTICE (1972); JOHN RAWLS, POLITICAL LIBERALISM (1993).

261 Ernst Joachim Mestmäcker, *Der Kampf ums Recht in der offenen Gesellschaft*, 20 RECHTSTHEORIE 273 (1989); Ernst Joachim Mestmäcker, *On the Legitimacy of European Law*, 58 RABELS ZEITSCHRIFT FÜR AUSLÄNDISCHES UND INTERNATIONALES PRIVATRECHT 615 (1994).

262 Already the Treaty of Rome established in the TEEC the four freedoms under *Part Two: Foundations of the Community*, the "free movement of goods" (Title I, art. 9 and following articles), and the "free movement of persons, services and capital" (Title III, art. 48 and following articles).

263 See the above discussed weakening of the concept of legitimacy with regards to European public power, *see* A, I.

264 JÜRGEN HABERMAS, THEORIE DES KOMMUNIKATIVEN HANDELNS 2 (1981). On this matter it must be pointed out that the "theory of communicative action" has little to do with that trend of the recent political philosophy usually called "communitarianism." While the latter presupposes historically consolidated common values as the fundament of political societies, Habermas' theory assumes that shared values origin first from the open, best-argument-oriented interaction among citizens, all and everyone of them aiming to achieve a non-prejudicial solution to common issues. For an overview of the approach of the communitarian political philosophy, *see* ALASDAIR MACINTYRE, AFTER VIRTUE (1981); Charles Taylor, *Cross-Purposes: The Liberal-Communitarian Debate*, *in* LIBERALISM AND THE MORAL LIFE 159 (Nancy L. Rosenblum ed., 1989); CHARLES TAYLOR, SOURCES OF THE SELF: THE MAKING OF THE MODERN IDENTITY (1994). For Habermas' criticism, *see* HABERMAS, *supra* note 6, at 324.

265 HABERMAS, *supra* note 44, at 237. Similar the claim of Rawls, albeit stressing more the issue of the common historical and cultural tradition as a necessary background of the political interaction, in: John Rawls, *Justice as Fairness: Political not Metaphysical*, 14 PHIL. AND PUB. AFF. 223 (1985).

dimension in so far as it distils values, i.e. ethically over-shaped patterns of interaction, on which the democratic life is grounded.[266] The structure of a well-intended democratic legitimacy emerges from the virtuous circle of the implementation of just and valid procedures for the discussion and deliberation of public issues, which in turn leads to the building of shared values.

It would be too involved to discuss here, even partially, the complicated problems surrounding the holism-individualism dichotomy and to closely examine the reasons for the transition to a third approach.[267] Thus, concerning the relationship of this last paradigm with the two former paradigms, it should be noted summarily that the communicative understanding of politics and society assumes the protection of individual interests and rights to an undiminished extent, especially when compared to the individualistic paradigm, while enriching the understanding of politics and society with a degree of the stronger reference to the ethical dimension of social life captured by the holistic paradigm. Even treating these issues in these summary terms, what must be emphasized here, given the main issue of inquiry to this article, is the fallacy inherent in the thesis that a "European people" would be unthinkable in itself or, at least, presupposes an unlikely evolution of European society which would nonetheless take a long time to unfold. The response to this fallacy must be that if the "people" understood in a post-ethnical and fully democratic sense coincides with the community of citizens there is no conceptually relevant reason – admitting, obviously, that a political discourse on common issues can develop in Europe – why a "people of the citizens of the Union" cannot exist. Furthermore, if a "people of the citizens of Europe" can be conceived of, it is evident that it ought to play a central role in legitimating the distinctly European public power to which it is subject.

D. Bringing Closer Citizenry and European Institution: A Difficult Task Between Active Political Commitment and Common Identity

Once it is verified that in order to guarantee an adequate democratic legitimacy to the European public power the recourse to the citizens of the Union is both necessary (*supra*, B) and conceptually coherent (*supra*, C), two ways of bringing that citizenry closer to the institutions governing it at Union level must be examined. The first consists in the strengthening of the political representation and participation of an active citizenry, the second in the enhancement or even creation of a shared identity.

I. The Progressive Revaluation of the Role of the European Parliament

For several years after its establishment, the European Parliament had only a consultative function[268] in fulfilment of the principle that democratic legitimacy and parliamentary control in an organization based on international law are adequately assured by each nation's national parliament. Since, with decisions taken in 1970 and 1975,[269] it was decided that the Community should have its own resources, it was also necessary that the European representative assembly would play a specific role within the procedure of budget approval.

---

266 HABERMAS, *supra* note 6, at 349.
267 *See* DELLAVALLE, *supra* note 251, at 206.
268 In accordance with the Treaty Establishing the European Economic Community (1957).
269 *See*, respectively, the Treaty Amending Certain Budgetary Provisions, Jan. 2, 1971, 1970 O.J. (L 2); and the Treaty Amending Certain Financial Provisions, Dec. 13, 1977, 1975 O.J. (L 359) of 31 December 1977. *See* note 24.

Therefore, it was admitted that the Community, once made partially autonomous from the member states, needed to be provided with parliamentary control and endowed with its own competencies. Nevertheless, these were tightly limited to the right of the Parliament to enter into negotiations with the Council on matters concerning the budget, thus excluding any other area. In the subsequent decades, however, the relevance of the European Parliament within the legislative process of the Community progressively increased even beyond the question of the Community's resources. The first step was the introduction by the Single European Act (1987) of the principle of consent and, even more important, of the cooperation procedure. Yet, the matters affected by the first principle were few, and the cooperation procedure was not able to guarantee an equal dignity to the Parliament when compared with the Council because the parliamentary assembly was not endowed, according to the herewith provided rules, with the possibility to finally veto the Council decisions.[270]

An eminently larger impact was achieved by the second step, i.e. by the co-decision procedure, which was formulated for the first time in the Maastricht Treaty (1992). Among all decision procedures provided by the Treaties (consultation, assent, cooperation, and co-decision) only this last one guarantees that the Parliament be in a position of comparable strength with the other institutions of the Community involved in the legislative process, giving to it the right to eventually reject even a unanimous position expressed by the traditionally mightiest of them, namely the Council.[271] With the Treaties of Amsterdam the co-decision procedure was extended to a broader range of areas,[272] but nevertheless, significantly, not to all. Indeed, as noted above, the Treaties up to Nice provide for a large number of fields where unanimity within the Council is required (i.e. which do not apply art. 251 TEC),[273] in which the Parliament is either not involved, or its mere consultation (as well as, in the most favourable but rare cases, its consent) is required. Moreover, which is even more negative for the implementation of the democratic legitimization of the European public power, we have in the Treaties up to Nice an impressively wide range of areas in which binding decisions can be taken, as well as legislative acts can be passed, by the Council according to the qualified majority vote procedure without the check of external participation (co-decision, cooperation, or even only assent) by the Parliament.[274] Last but not least, in the cases where the co-decision procedure guarantees to a large extent the parliamentary legitimization of the public power of the Union, this democratic legitimacy – implicitly conceded "in the name of the European people" – has not been coupled with the necessary amendments of its normative foundation in the fundamental law. In the Treaties up to Nice there is no reference to the citizens of the Union as the basis of the democratic legitimacy and the Parliament of Strasbourg itself is defined as the representation of the peoples of the states (and not of the "European citizens").[275]

The very beginning of the article has already pointed out how deeply the normative definition of democratic legitimacy has suffered from neglect within the Treaties,[276] and that this has lasted up to the Treaty of Nice. Yet, precisely on this issue some important changes have been finally introduced by the Constitutional Treaty. The first one consists in the already noted transformation of the art. 251 TEC into the "ordinary legislative procedure," which states that "European laws and framework laws shall be adopted, on the basis of

---

270 This shortcoming remains at present time, yet within a limited field of application, in art. 252 TEC.
271 TEC, *supra* note 25, at art. 251, para. 2, b), and para 4–6.
272 *See supra* note 220.
273 *See supra* B, II, 1.
274 *See supra* note 218.
275 *See supra* note 221.
276 *See supra*, A.

proposals from the Commission, jointly by the European Parliament and the Council".[277] According to this provision, the previous co-decision procedure would be placed, for the first time officially, in a clearly pre-eminent position, ceasing to be only one legislative procedure among others. Yet, the most innovative aspect – at least at the political and cultural (we could even say: philosophical), if not juridical, level – has to be identified elsewhere, namely in the new definition of the "identity" of the Parliament, as well as in the reference to the citizens of the Union as the basis of the democratic legitimacy of the European institutions and decisions. For the very first time the European Parliament has been defined in the Constitutional Treaty as the institutional representation of the citizens "at Union level,"[278] which prefigures, albeit implicitly, the idea of a unitary whole of the European citizenry as a co-foundation of the Union. This hypothesis is corroborated by art. I-1, para. 1, which states: "reflecting the will of the citizens and States of Europe to build a common future, this Constitution establishes the European Union." This is a relatively clear expression of the twofold foundation of the Union's democratic legitimacy.[279] However, this courageous innovation is immediately counterbalanced, in the same article, by the statement that only the member states may confer competencies upon the Union.[280] Thus, through the restrictive principle of the exclusive conferral of competencies by the member states, any autonomous initiative of the Union seeking to enlarge its own competencies is excluded. Furthermore, this provision also denies what the Constitutional Treaty has just asserted, namely that the community of the citizens of the Union might bring their will to bear. Of course in the most cases this is to be articulated jointly with the interests expressed by the governments of the member states, but in some circumstances and to some extent it is to be formulated independently. In a different context, to make the question even more complicated, it is just this right of the citizens of the Union, as a whole, to express their will that is explicitly recognised through the provision that opens the way for the citizens themselves, for the first time at the European level, to invite the Commission (albeit not to oblige it) to submit a legislative proposal.[281] This provision outlines, quite interestingly, a frame for the expression of an active citizenry even beyond the representative institutions and parliamentary procedures.

Notwithstanding the relevance of the changes introduced by the Constitutional Treaty, providing it is ratified by all member states, the Parliament is still lacking some of the fundamental prerogatives of an assembly that aims to serve as the representation of

---

277 Constitutional Treaty, *supra* note 232, at art. I-34, para. 1, and art. III-396, following the proposals of the WG IX, Final Report of the Working Group on Simplification, European Convention 424/02, 15. The idea of generalizing the co-decision procedure had been presented also by the Commission, Communication from the Commission – A Project for the European Union, European Convention 229/02, 27; Communication from the Commission on the Institutional Architecture – For the European Union. Peace, Freedom, Solidarity, European Convention 448/02, 16; Prodi, *supra* at note 137, 3.

278 Constitutional Treaty, *supra* note 232, at art. I-46, para. 2. In the same direction goes also the rule aiming at making the procedures uniform for the election of the European Parliament in the member states (*id.*, at art. III-330, para. 1). The proposal was pleaded by the Commission, Communication from the Commission on the Institutional Architecture – For the European Union. Peace, Freedom, Solidarity, European Convention 448/02, 16.

279 In the final report of the WG IX we read that "the democratic legitimacy of the Union is founded on its states and peoples, and consequently an act of a legislative nature must always come from the bodies which represent those states and peoples, namely the Council and the Parliament," Final Report of the Working Group on Simplification, European Convention 424/02, 2. Yet, the twofold legitimization would not introduce anything unprecedented in the constitutional history: just to remember the most famous case, the Constitution of the United States of America mentions both the unitary federal people (in the Preamble), and the peoples of the states (art. 1, section 2, as well as in the 17th amendment).

280 Constitutional Treaty, *supra* note 232, at art. I-1, para. 1, "this Constitution establishes the European Union, on which the Member States confer competences to attain objectives they have in common."

281 *Id.*, at art. I-47, para. 4.

citizens empowered with real autonomy. Just to mention a few examples of these shortcomings, the Parliament: has no right to bring a legislative initiative;[282] does not play any role in the election of the President of the European Council;[283] can not propose the candidate for the Presidency of the Commission;[284] nor the Minister for Foreign Affairs;[285] and has neither autonomy nor equal dignity with the Council of Ministers as regards the financial resources of the Union.[286] Furthermore, even if the art. I-34, para. 1, of the Constitutional Treaty accords, on principle, an equal dignity to the Parliament and the Council of Ministers within the ordinary legislation, an impressive number of further articles provide for many exceptions to the ordinary legislative procedure,[287] namely in areas where mere consent[288] or even only consultation[289] of the European Parliament are

282 *Id.*, at art. I-34.
283 *Id.*, at art. I-22.
284 *Id.*, at art. I-27.
285 *Id.*, at art. I-28.
286 *Id.*, at art. I-54. More favourable to the Parliament were the proposals of the WG IX, Final Report of the Working Group on Simplification, European Convention 424/02, 19, and of the Commission, Communication from the Commission, A Project for the European Union, European Convention 229/02, 31; Communication from the Commission on the Institutional Architecture – For the European Union. Peace, Freedom, Solidarity, European Convention 448/02, 15; Prodi, *supra* note 137, 3.
287 During the debate in the Commission the conviction consolidated that "exceptions [to the co-decision procedure] would continue to exist for various reasons," Summary Report on the Plenary Session, Brussels, Dec. 5–6, 2002, European Convention 449/02, 5, 9.
288 The consent of the Parliament is required: for the application of the flexibility clause, Constitutional Treaty, *supra* note 232, at art. I-18, para. 1; the modification, on initiative of the Parliament itself, of the rules concerning its composition, *id.*, at art. I-20, para. 2; the implementing measures of the Union's own resources system, *id.*, at art. I-54, para. 4; the adoption of the multiannual financial framework, *id.*, at art. I-55, para. 2; the adoption of measures against discrimination, *id.*, at art. III-124, para. 1; the addition of new rights connected to the Union citizenship, *id.*, at art. III-129; the first measures concerning structural and cohesion funds after the Constitutional Treaty having been signed by the member states, *id.*, at art. III-223, para. 2; the extension of the judicial cooperation in criminal matters (*id.*, art. III-270 and following); the establishment of the necessary measures for the election of the European Parliament in accordance with a uniform procedure, *id.*, at art. III-330, para. 1; the beginning of an enhanced cooperation, *id.*, at art. III-419, para. 1.
289 The Constitutional Treaty provides for the mere consultation with regard to: the measures concerning passports and comparable documents, as well as social protection, related to the right of Union's citizens to free movement, *id.*, at art. III-125, para. 2; the determination of the detailed arrangements for exercising the right for every Union citizen "to vote and to stand as a candidate in municipal elections and elections to the European Parliament in their member state of residence without being a national of that state," *id.*, at art. III-126; measures to secure diplomatic protection of Union's citizens, *id.*, at art. III-127; the adoption of measures in order to restrict the free movement of capital with third countries, *id.*, at art. III-157, para. 3; some rules concerning competition and aids granted by member states, *id.*, at art. III-161 and following, and at art. III-167 and following; some fiscal provisions, *id.*, at art. III-171; the approximation of national legislation directly affecting the establishment or functioning of the internal market, *id.*, at art. III-173; the establishment of language arrangements for the European instruments for the European intellectual property rights, *id.*, at art. III-176; several measures concerning the economic and financial policies, *id.*, at art. III-183 and following, and at art. III-198, para. 2; guidelines concerning the coordination of the national employment policies, *id.*, at art. III-206, para. 2, and at III-208; some matters related to the social protection of workers, *id.*, at art. III-210, para. 3, as well as to the protection of the environment, *id.*, at art. III-234, para. 2; the establishment of a Social Protection Committee, *id.*, at art. III-217; measures to avoid discrimination in the field of transport within the Union, *id.*, at art. III-240, para. 3; the financing of research, *id.*, at art. III-251, para. 3, and at art. III-253; fiscal measures regarding energy policies, *id.*, at art. III-256, para. 3; the area of freedom, security and justice, *id.*, at art. III-263, art. III-266, para. 3, art. III-269, para. 3, art. III-275, para. 3, and art. III-277; provisions concerning the association of the overseas countries and territories, *id.*, at art. III-291; the organisation of the European External Action Service, *id.*, at art. III-296, para. 3; the replacement of a vacancy within the Commission during the legislature period, *id.*, at art. III-348, para. 2; the appointment of the members of the European Central Bank, *id.*, at art. III-382, para. 2, and of the Court of Auditors, *id.*, at art. III-385, para. 2; the amendment of the Statute of the European Investment Bank, *id.*, at art. III-393; some measures referring to the establishment of enhanced cooperation, *id.*, at art. III-421, and art. III-422, para. 2; rules concerning the application of the Constitution in the overseas territories, *id.*, at art. III-424.

required.²⁹⁰ Certainly, these matters are anything but insignificant, reaching so far to involve to a great extent the Union's competencies. The role of the Parliament is quite subordinate in matters of foreign and security policy,²⁹¹ in which only the consultation of the Parliament is required of the Minister for Foreign Affairs,²⁹² while for some typologies of international agreements the parliamentary assent is necessary.²⁹³

Moreover, it is interesting to note the second-rate function the Parliament would serve within any future procedure for the amendment of the Constitution It would have only the right to bring in proposals, to be consulted as regards the establishment of a new Convention as well as to send its representatives to an *ad hoc* assembly.²⁹⁴ Notably, the Parliament lacks the prerogative to autonomously initiate the amendment procedure, which is given exclusively to the European Council, as well as to express its binding assent (or veto) on the final results.²⁹⁵ These restrictions are the more significant because they affect the institution which officially represents the citizens of the Union, who are thus excluded from the fundamental function to decide upon the basic law which governs their civic life. We have an analogous limitation in that the European citizens are not allowed to deliberate on the normative premises of their very definition, namely on the provisions that lay down the conditions, the fulfillment of which leads to the attainment of the citizenship of the Union. Indeed, according to the wording of art. I-10, para. 1, "every national of a member state shall be a citizen of the Union," such that the "citizenship of the Union shall be additional to national citizenship and shall not replace it." In so far as the laying down of the conditions for national citizenship is left exclusively to the member states, the community of the citizens of the Union is not allowed to determine, through its representative institution or anyway else, the criteria of its own composition – a strange limitation, indeed, for a citizenship which is now thought to be democratically participating and autonomous in the full sense of the word.

In order to meet, at least implicitly, the shortcomings of democratic representation at the Union level, the Constitutional Treaty introduces the "principle of participatory democracy" which provides for the institutions of the Union "to give citizens and representative associations the opportunity to make known and publicly exchange their views in all areas of Union action,"²⁹⁶ and to "maintain an open, transparent and regular dialogue with representative associations and civil society,"²⁹⁷ as well as for the Commission to "carry out broad consultations with parties concerned in order to ensure that the Union's actions are coherent and transparent."²⁹⁸ Notwithstanding the relevance of these new steps towards a broader conception of democratic legitimacy, and although the European Parliament has been claimed, certainly with some good reasons, to play a substantially different role, at least at a descriptive level, compared to the parliamentary assemblies within

---

290 In the proposal of the WG IX, on the contrary, the consultation was limited to technical fields and the consent to some kinds of international agreements. *See* Final Report of the Working Group on Simplification, European Convention 424/02, 16.
291 Constitutional Treaty, *supra* note 232, at art. III-292 and following.
292 *Id.*, at art. III-304, para. 1, and art. III-313, para. 3, with reference to the establishment of specific procedures guaranteeing rapid access to the Union budget in order to finance initiatives.
293 *Id.*, at art. III-325, para. 6, a), and b). This article provides for the specification of the cases in which only the consultation of the Parliament is required, and of those in which, on the contrary, its consent is necessary. The mere consultation is also required for the agreements fixing the exchange rates for the euro in relation to the currencies of third countries, *id.*, at art. III-326, para. 1.
294 *Id.*, at art. IV-443.
295 *Id.*
296 *Id.*, at art. I-47, para. 1.
297 *Id.*, at art. I-47, para. 2.
298 *Id.*, at art. I-47, para. 3. Para. 4 of the same article provides for the citizens, as already mentioned, to bring in a legislative proposal (*see supra*, note 281).

the nation-states,[299] from a normative point of view the legitimacy deficit deriving from the refusal to endow it with appropriate competences cannot be counterbalanced by attempts to a inevitably incomplete participative democracy. The partial substitution of representative with participative legitimacy is a difficult issue for itself – albeit surely not a senseless goal – which should not be introduced under suspicion that its task, actually, is to make a legitimacy-indifferent program shallowly more attractive for the citizens.

II. Common Values and Shared Identity

I have already claimed – as the second assumption informing the analysis presented in this article[300] – that the legitimization of public power must provide, if it is to be effectively democratic, for adequate institutional procedures in order to guarantee the participation of the citizens. The restrictions included in the Constitutional Treaty and here briefly examined represent, however, a consistent violation of this principle and thus a problematic limitation of the instruments that the Treaty makes available in order to ensure the democratic legitimacy of the public power hereby established. Curiously, these limitations go hand-in-hand with a significant number of provisions that aim at specifying, for the first time in such a pervasive way, the ethical content of the Union as well as its collective identity. Strengthening the ethical content of a polity means that the values on which it is grounded and which determine at the same time its peculiar identity shall be specified and distinguished from those belonging to other communities. In fact, although the debate on the presumable common European identity is not new,[301] it could never fully persuade the scholars.[302] Nor could this idea reach further than to build the first clusters of a political identification with the Union on the background of the traditional cultural and national belonging, which is nevertheless a great success in a continent divided for centuries by sanguinary wars and hatred.[303] Moreover, which is more important for our analysis, the question of a common European identity did not enter significantly into the Treaties for a long time. The pragmatic – and we could also say value-free – character of the ECSC, EURATOM, and ECC Treaty is not quite surprising, given the pre-eminent role played at the beginning of the institutional European integration by economic (not political) purposes and functional (not constitutional) proceeding.[304]

The situation changed in a relevant way with the Maastricht Treaty, and specifically with the Treaty on the European Union. Here, already in the Preamble, we find references to "attachment to the principles of liberty, democracy and respect for human rights and fun-

---

299 On the peculiar nature of the European Parliament and its structural inadequacy to play the same role as the national assemblies at the level of the member states, see DANN, *supra* note 223. However, precisely the theory of an "executive federalism", claimed by Dann, raises the question how an appropriate legitimacy can be guaranteed under the modified constellation.
300 See *supra*, A, II.
301 EDGAR MORIN, PENSER L'EUROPE (1987).
302 For two examples for skepticism towards the claim of a common European identity, justified in quite opposite ways, see Anthony D. Smith, *National Identity and European Unity*, in THE QUESTION OF EUROPE 318 (Peter Gowan & P. Anderson eds., 1997) (1992); HABERMAS, *supra* note 44, at 185.
303 On the fluidity of social identities, with particular reference to the European integration, see ORIETTA ANGELUCCI, ZUR ÖKOLOGIE EINER EUROPÄISCHEN IDENTITÄT (2003).
304 Yet, as a consequence of some provisions of the ECC Treaty could be developed an ethically relevant doctrine of human right, as it was pursued at a very early stage of the European integration by the European Court of Justice. See WEILER, *supra* note 30, 23. Nevertheless this doctrine, as the product of the case law within a system largely influenced by the continental tradition, stays still at margin of the Treaties as the fundamental law of the European integration, endowed with the important function of integrating them, but without any possibility to substantially overcome their indifference to ethical contents.

damental freedoms and of the rule of law,"[305] as well as to "fundamental social rights,"[306] "solidarity between their peoples,"[307] "economic and social progress,"[308] and "sustainable development."[309] Moreover, in the paragraph concerning the objective of implementing "a common foreign and security policy," the Preamble explicitly underlines the task of "reinforcing the European identity and its independence in order to promote peace, security and progress in Europe and in the world."[310] Some of these values – specifically, "liberty, democracy, respect for human rights and fundamental freedoms, and the rule of law"– are then reminded in art. 6, which defines them as the principles founding the Union and "common to the member states." Also the realisation of a common area of freedom, security and justice aims, at least implicitly, at delimiting a shared territory and citizenry to be jointly protected in its common values founding the social and political life.[311] Thus the Maastricht Treaty, establishing the European Union, creates, though in a very cautious way, a first nucleus of a shared identity based on common values, clearly beyond the typical fundaments of international law agreements but also actually uncommitted to the principles of a really active citizenship.[312]

Although claiming a core of shared values, the Treaties up to Amsterdam were missing a fundamental element of an ethically ambitious constitutional document, namely a declaration of fundamental rights. As has already been recalled,[313] this deficit has been partially removed by the Charter of Fundamental Rights (2000). Consistent to its task, the Charter points out in its Preamble that "the peoples of Europe ... are resolved to share a peaceful future based on common values."[314] Immediately below, the values are listed which derive from the "spiritual and moral heritage" of the Union: human dignity, freedom, equality, solidarity, democracy, and the rule of law[315] – the same values that form the titles under which the rights proclaimed by the Charter and guaranteed by the Union are gathered in the following articles.[316]

Since the Charter has been introduced into the Constitutional Treaty as its Part II, we find also here the same list of values. Yet, this is not the only reference to values within the Constitutional Treaty. Rather, we have to deal here with a real proliferation of value catalogues. Apart from the catalogue contained in Part II and derived from the Charter, the Constitutional Treaty returns to the issue in two separate contexts, albeit with some different accentuations. This happens first within its own Preamble, the first paragraph of which includes a reference to "the universal values of the inviolable and inalienable rights of the human person, freedom, democracy, equality and the rule of law."[317] Compared to the list of the Charter we miss the recall to solidarity, i.e. to the title that comprehends

---

305 TEU, *supra* note 27, at prmbl, para. 3.
306 *Id.*, at prmbl, para. 4.
307 *Id.*, at prmbl, para. 5.
308 *Id.*, at prmbl, para. 8.
309 *Id.*
310 *Id.*, at prmbl, para. 10.
311 The claim has been raised, albeit referring to the Treaty of Amsterdam, BOGDANDY, *supra* note 22, at 30.
312 This lack of commitment is testified, first, by the above mentioned competence deficits of the European Parliament, second by the fact that the political rights guaranteed by the Maastricht Treaty were – and are up to the Treaty of Nice – clearly insufficient if compared to the constitutional traditions of the member states.
313 *See supra* note 47.
314 Constitutional Treaty, *supra* note 232, at Part II: The Charter of Fundamental Rights of the Union, prmble, para. 1.
315 *Id.*, at para. 2.
316 To be precise, "democracy" and "the rule of law" are substituted as "Titles" by "citizens' rights" and "justice," which nevertheless does not change in any way the meaning of the concepts.
317 Constitutional Treaty, *supra* note 232, at prmbl, para. 1.

most of the social rights. This lack is partially overcome within the second paragraph in which the Preamble of the Constitutional Treaty refers, albeit not describing them as "values," to the protection of "the weakest and most deprived," as well as to "culture, learning and social progress," to "the democratic and transparent nature of its public life," and to "peace, justice and solidarity throughout the world."[318]

Moreover, the Constitutional Treaty returns to the question at the beginning of its first Part, listing once again the most important values: "respect for human dignity, freedom, democracy, equality, the rule of law and respect for human rights, including the rights of persons belonging to minorities."[319] In this way, largely the same values declared in the first paragraph of the Preamble are here simply repeated, although with the addition (maybe only a politically motivated redundancy) of the last two references. However, this article of Part I is then integrated by a specification which could rather complicate a coherent understanding of the issue: "These values are common to the member states in a society in which pluralism, non-discrimination, tolerance, justice, solidarity and equality between women and men prevail."[320] Some questions arise from this proliferation of values catalogues: Why does solidarity disappear from the main catalogues in the Preamble and in Part I of the Constitutional Treaty only to reappear, then, not just in the Preamble of the Charter, but also within the specification of the article of Part I? Is this only a casualty, or does it bear on a more profound intention? And should the specifications introduced both in the Preamble and in the article of Part I only be an attempt to a better description of premises and consequences of the centrality of the core values? Or should they rather try to introduce a kind of hierarchy between more or less important ethical principles? The clearing of these questions will be part of the exegetic work of lawyers and scholars. Here, it should be only emphasised that the proliferation of the value catalogues can be hardly seen as a contribution to the conceptual coherence of the project.

Furthermore, to make its ethical pregnancy even more evident, the Constitutional Treaty also specifies the objectives of the Union as implicitly contrasting with those pursued by other polities, in particular by the United States.[321] It refers to the common destiny of the peoples of Europe,[322] as well as to the "independence and integrity" of the Union;[323] and introduces for the Union the most important symbols of the sovereign identity (flag, anthem, motto, currency and May 9 as "Europe day").[324] If compared with the shortcomings concerning the institutions of the concrete political interaction, the doubt arises that the rhetoric on common values and identity could not be but a shield to hide the lack of a real democratisation of the European civic life. In fact, democratic constitutions mostly forego to specify formally the values of the polity that they ground, seeing their concrete determination as a consequence of the actual protection of the rights they proclaim, as well as of the ethical content embodied within the procedures of political participation and the practices of social life.[325] Therefore, the underlining of shared symbols and ethical content in the Constitutional Treaty – for the first time so insistent – may be seen as the attempt to create a kind of *communitas europaea*, failing to support the main way of bringing the citizens closer to the Union's institution, i.e. the recognition of full political and institutional competencies to its citizenry.

---

318 *Id.*, at prmbl, para. 2.
319 *Id.*, at art. I-2.
320 *Id.*
321 *Id.*, at art. I-3 and, with reference to the foreign policy, art. III-292.
322 *Id.*, at prmbl, para. 3.
323 *Id.*, at art. III-292, para. 2, a).
324 *Id.*, at art. I-8.
325 JÜRGEN HABERMAS, DIE POSTNATIONALE KONSTELLATION 171 (1998).

E. Conclusions

At the end of the enquiry, a summary of the results is in order, with some final remarks to consider.

(a) A nucleus of public power has consolidated in the European Union, which is not made uncertain in its essential aspects through the partial reorganisation of the competences introduced by the Constitutional Treaty.
(b) European public power can not be adequately legitimated by the democratic institutions of the nation-states. In order that the decisions adopted at the Union level, in particular by the European Council and the Council of Ministers, can be seen as fully legitimated, inevitably it becomes necessary to consider a specifically European source of legitimacy, which shall not substitute but integrate the legitimization deriving from the member states.
(c) This source can not be anything but the community of citizens of the Union. As far as the concept of "people" is meant in a post-ethnic sense, nothing stands against the identification of a unitary political and juridical subject for the Union, once it is ensured that the historically rooted cultural diversity is maintained. Indeed, the Constitutional Treaty for the first time timidly mentions the citizens of the Union as a source of the democratic legitimacy of the public power.
(d) The democratic activity of the "people" as a community of citizens expresses itself, under conditions of transparency, in participatory and representative (namely through the European Parliament) forms. The Constitutional Treaty introduces some important changes on these issues. Particularly interesting on the question of participation are the provisions committing the European institutions to transparency[326] and guaranteeing the public access to documents.[327] On the other side, concerning representation, co-decision is advanced to the status of "ordinary legislative procedure."
(e) Notwithstanding the foregoing, several deficits still remain. Particularly in the areas where no involvement of the Parliament of Strasbourg is required – or even just an insufficient involvement – a creeping transition of competences from the legislative to the executive power is occurring, with the consequence that the worrying democratic deficit will further consolidate, maybe even increase as new areas fall under the Union's competence. Under these premises, the strengthening of the participative democracy can only be understood as an important integration of representation, not as its substitute.
(f) To implement democratic rights adequately, the status of political citizenship ought to be correctly defined. Even on this issue, the Constitutional Treaty is still insufficient with regard both to the rules concerning the rights conferred by Union citizenship, as well as to the conditions of its acquisition. With respect to the status of Union citizenship it has to be admitted, first, that the replacement of the national citizenships through the Union's is not a desirable goal – at least for most Union citizens. Second, merely flanking traditional national citizenship with Union citizenship endowed with an autonomous status, i.e. conferred autonomously by the Union's institutions, would hardly bring a real increase of prerogatives to the Union citizens since a relevant number of important rights, related to the national citizenship, would still depend exclusively on the decisions of the member states. Thus, several arguments can be brought

---

326 Constitutional Treaty, *supra* note 232, at art. I-50, para. 1.
327 *Id.*, at art. I-50, para. 3–4, art. II-102 and art. III-399. On the proposal that documents of relevant public interest should be placed on the internet, *see* WEILER, *supra* note 30, 351.

for the maintaining of the principle now in force, stating that European citizenship derives from the national ones. Nevertheless, this solution has an evident shortcoming consisting in the fact that an institutions that is relevant at the European level, namely the Union citizenship, is defined solely by national instances, which gives rise to an incoherence on principle as well as to a significant risk of inequality within a legal framework pretending to be homogeneous. To avoid both deficits, it is necessary that the European legislator promotes a harmonization of the criteria for the concession of the citizenship by the nation-states which takes into consideration the shared dimension of the issue without cancelling the peculiar tradition of every single country.[328]

(g) At present time, the Union citizen residing in a member state that is not the one that he/she is national of, is a privileged foreigner, nevertheless a foreigner indeed. Yet, if the fundamental role of the Union citizenship within the European institutional system is expected to be fully recognised, it is indispensable that every Union citizen has unlimited access to the political and social rights in all member states in which he/she may reside without being a national of them, once admitted a reasonable period of suspense between the acquisition of the legal residence and the full exercise of the rights. Also in this case the European legislator should not elude its responsibility. While it is true that through the power increase of the European Parliament the Union citizens are allowed to express their will, participating in the deliberative process of the whole polity and even the social rights are more and more protected at supranational level,[329] nevertheless the right to free movement on Union territory has to be fully recognised also with respect to the political and social issues within the member states (above all, because these are alleged to maintain relevant competences, particularly in social and, in a broad sense, political matters).

(h) Beside significant deficits concerning the democratic participation, the Constitutional Treaty contains for the first time a consistent appeal to the alleged European identity. However, a solid democratic identity of a polity ought to be grounded rather on the active participation, and not on the rhetoric of belonging.

Synthetically, the Constitutional Treaty, if seen from the point of view of the democratic legitimization of the public power, shows lights and shades. Although it is difficult to be totally satisfied with the results, the criticism I have asserted in this article does not justify the radical refusal of the text as a whole. Rather, it is only one reason more – let me say it not just as a scholar, but also as a European citizen – for continuing the scientific and political commitment to a further improvement of the normative basis underlying the civic life of the Union. This is important to be underlined precisely in the current difficult phase of the ratification process, after the negative outcome of the people's consultation in France and the Netherlands, and with the Constitutional Treaty facing an uncertain future. In fact, as far as we can foresee at the present time, this could even end in failure since its entering into force presupposes the unanimous ratification by all member states.[330]

Whatever the future evolution may be, the difficulties that the Constitutional Treaty is finding on its way to ratification is already opening a crisis of the European constitutional process, with three possible scenarios that can be imagined. According to the first one, we would have a sudden or, more likely, creeping roll-back of the European integration process. The member states would put their chance again on national policies and, case by

---

328 RAINER BAUBÖCK, CITIZENSHIP AND NATIONAL IDENTITIES IN THE EUROPEAN UNION, Jean Monnet Working Paper Series (1997).
329 Interesting, in this respect, is the "Grzelczyk"-sentence by the Court of Justice, dated September 20, 2001. Case C-184/99, Grzelczyk, [2001] E.C.R. I-6193 (2001).
330 Constitutional Treaty, *supra* note 232, at art. IV-447.

case, on intergovernmental cooperation, while their peoples could get back to the illusion to control political processes as long as they are contained within national borders. This way, the marginalization of Europe would go hand-in-hand with a powerless national enclosure, where the illusionary democratic legitimization of public power at national level, for its part, could not go actually so far as public power already reaches, namely beyond the borderlines of nation-states.

Following the second scenario, things would largely remain as they are, with the present Treaties in force as they were consolidated by the Treaty of Nice and no immediate perspective to fulfil the constitutional process by the adoption of a more coherent and far-going document as the basic law of the Union. Given this case, it is almost superfluous to point out that no problem would be met adequately this way, not even the question of a proper democratic legitimacy of public power. But if the European constitutional process really falls into a crisis, we have also a third scenario – may be less probable, nevertheless more ambitious in its premises as well as in its possible outcomes. In this case, a large debate should start among European peoples and Union's citizens on what they want to be in a political sense, whether they have common interests and perhaps values, and how they imagine to fulfil the first and realize the second ones together. This path may be long and sometimes uncomfortable – however, if the European peoples want to continue shaping their history and keeping alive the principle of democratic legitimization, then they won't have any alternative.

Who Has the Right to Intra-European Social Security? From Market Citizens to European Citizens and Beyond

Dorte Sindbjerg Martinsen*

A. Introduction

This article traces the process of how the personal scope of Regulation 1408/71,[1] coordinating social security rights across European borders, has been defined and extended over time. The article examines the legal–political dialogue, cultivating a process, which for more than four decades has questioned and settled the scope of "who has a right to intra-European social security." This process departed from the notion of Community worker "stricto sensu," i.e. the market citizen[2] and has recently been substantively reformed and extended to encompass all European citizens with the adoption of Regulation 883/2004.[3] Furthermore, third-country nationals have recently been included in the personal scope.[4] This evolution, thus apparently decouples the right to coordinated social security from a communitarian conception of welfare.

The Council adopted Regulation 1408/71 in 1971 as a Community instrument to realize the aim of the free movement of workers.[5] The regulation was approved using the legal basis of the Rome Treaty's (hereinafter Treaty) article 51 (now article 42), which required unanimity. Unanimity has been maintained as the procedural rule, which indeed has conditioned the incremental development of the regulation. The history of the regulation, however, dates back long before 1971 to one of the Community's first major legislative pieces, Regulation no. 3/58,[6] and before that to bilateral agreements between present

---

* Assistant Professor, University of Copenhagen, Institute of Political Science. For correspondence: dm@ifs.ku.dk.
1 Council Regulation 1408/71, The Application of Social Security Schemes to Employed Persons, Self-Employed Persons, and Members of Their Families Moving within the Community, 1971 O.J. (L 149) (EEC Treaty).
2 The concept of 'market citizen,' as it is used here, refers to the one exercising economic activity. Among others, a market citizen is the worker '*stricto sensu*,' i.e. the one with a contract of employment. The European market citizen is one production factor among three others; goods, services and capital, whose free movement is one of the constituting pillars of the internal market. In the following analysis, 'market citizen' is used as a contrast to 'European citizen.' The former refers to a status where market participation releases rights. As a contrast, the latter has rights without necessarily being an active market participant. *See* M. EVERSON, THE LEGACY OF THE MARKET CITIZEN, IN NEW LEGAL DYNAMICS OF EUROPEAN UNION 72, 84 (J. Shaw & G. More eds., 1995).
3 Council Regulation 883/2004, The Coordination of Social Security Systems, 2004 O.J. (L 166) 1–123 (Treaty Establishing the European Community, Nov. 10, 1997, O.J. (C 340) 3 (EC Treaty).
4 Third-country nationals are covered by Council Regulation 859/2003, 2003 O.J. (L 124) (EC Treaty).
5 Since the coming into force of the Agreement on the European Economic Area of 1 January 1994, the regulation applies to the nationals from Norway, Iceland and Liechtenstein. This paper will, however, not distinguish between European Union (EU) and EEA nationals, but simply refer to the rights of EU or European citizens.
6 Council Regulation 3/58, 1958 O.J. (146).

member states.⁷ Regulation 1408/71, in addition to inheriting certain principles and coordinating methods, also inherited a broad interpretation of 'worker' as well as a most extensive material scope.⁸ Since then, principles and substance have been extended on the basis of Regulation 1408's own premises and its Treaty base. The coordination system institutionalized by Regulation 1408 has been viewed as the most advanced social policy achievement of the EU, and as the most comprehensive system of access to cross-border health care in international social law.⁹ The regulation prescribes that migrants included in the personal scope have equal social security rights within the material scope of the regulation when settling in another member state as the nationals of that state, as they have a right to export defined social security rights if deciding to reside in another member state. The regulation thus prohibits national legislation, which discriminates against migrants from other member states, as it partly prohibits territorial principles formulated in national social security legislation.

The following examination of the extension of Regulation 1408's personal scope demonstrates how an inter-institutional dynamic of supranational and intergovernmental actions and reactions integrates the 'less likely' policy field of social security.¹⁰ Within a general discussion on European integration, the case of social security arguably represents a "less likely case" of integration, since decisions on the content and scope of social security policies have traditionally been regarded as a national prerogative, carried out by the national welfare state. By coordinating social security rights, the Community has conditioned the member states' autonomy to define to whom social security rights shall be granted as well as where.

The article is divided into three parts, focusing individually on the institutional actors of Court, Commission and Council, whose actions and reactions nonetheless overlap, intertwined as they are. In fact, regarding the recurring discussion in political science and law-in-context,¹¹ a specific analysis of the question 'who has the right to intra European social security' demonstrates that the Court, the Commission and the Council of Ministers participate in a dialogue, which compromises the autonomy and position of each of them. This dialogue reflects changes in preferences over time, as well as transformations in the reading of the Community's objectives and competences.

---

7   J. HOLLOWAY, SOCIAL POLICY HARMONISATION IN THE EUROPEAN COMMUNITY (1981).
8   Council Regulation 883/2004, The Coordination of the Social Security Systems, 2004 O.J. (L 166), has extended the material scope so that it currently covers (a) sickness benefits; (b) maternity and equivalent paternity benefits; (c) invalidity benefits; (d) old-age benefits; (e) survivors benefits; (f) benefits in respect of accident at work and occupational diseases; (g) death grants; (h) unemployment benefits; (i) pre-retirement benefits; (j) family benefits.
9   E. EICHENHOFER, SOZIALRECHT DER EUROPÄISCHEN UNION 227 (2001); IMPLICATIONS OF RECENT JURISPRUDENCE ON THE COORDINATION OF HEALTH CARE PROTECTIONS SYSTEMS (2000) (Summary Report produced for the European Commission Directorate-General for Employment and Social Affairs).
10 See H. Eckstein, *Case Study and Theory in Political Science*, in STRATEGIES OF INQUIRY 79 (Greenstein & Polsby eds., 1975), for a discussion of the strategic-theoretical purpose of choosing between a "most likely" and a "least likely" case.
11 See K. Alter, *Who are the "Masters of the Treaty?" European Governments and the European Court of Justice*, 52 INT'L. ORG. 121 (1998); A.-M. Burley & W. Mattli, *Europe Before the Court: A Political Theory of Legal Integration*, 47 INT'L. ORG. 41 (1993); G. Garrett et al., *The European Court of Justice, National Governments, and Legal Integration in the European Union*, 52 INT'L. ORG. 149 (1998); A. Moravcsik, *Preferences and Power in the European Community: A Liberal Intergovernmentalist Approach*, 4 J. OF COMMON MKT. STUD. 473, 31 (1993); M. POLLACK, THE ENGINES OF EUROPEAN INTEGRATION: DELEGATION, AGENCY, AND AGENDA SETTING IN THE EU (2003); A. Stone Sweet & T.L. Brunell, *Constructing a Supranational Constitution: Dispute Resolution and Governance in the European Community*, 92 AM. POLI. SCI. REV. 63 (1998); J. Weiler, *Journey to an Unknown Destination: A Retrospective and Prospective of the European Court of Justice in the Arena of Political Integration*, 31 J. OF COMMON MKT. STUD. 417 (1993); J. Weiler, *A Quiet Revolution – The European Court of Justice and Its Interlocutors*, 26 COMP. POLI. STUD. 510 (1994), among many others.

The first section focuses on the role of the *Court* and its historical definitions for 'employed persons.' It also considers the purpose of the Regulation's predecessor and its Treaty base. The second section analyses the agenda set by the *Commission*, which, by continuously linking intra-European social security to the free movement of persons and Union citizenship, as well as to the stated political commitment to treat non-Community nationals equally, argued that the Regulation should be extended to all persons, irrespective of economic activity and nationality. The third section turns to the reactions by the *Council* and individual member states and analyzes how the negotiations on a generalized personal scope evolve, and how the Court's ruling – by what appears as political choice rather than judicial conviction – finally settles the matter and paves the way for a political compromise, formally entitling legally residing third-country nationals to intra European social security, and extending rights to all European citizens.

The integration of social security rights in Europe has been one of small subtle steps. However, aggregated over time, the individual steps towards 'more Europe' constitute a historical move from rights granted to market citizens, narrowly defined, to a European citizenship right and beyond. Alongside that process, the political and judicial perception of Community objectives and competences has gradually changed.

B. The Historical Setting of a Personal Scope

The personal scope of Regulation 1408 has been extended incrementally through judicial interpretations by the Court, Commission proposals and the Council's codification thereof. The current personal scope has been under definition since the adoption of Regulation 1408's predecessor, Regulation no. 3, in 1958 and has been incrementally expanded to the point where, by April 2004, the Regulation has been extended to *all European citizens*.

In this first section, the article examines how an independent social security conceptualization of employed person developed from the judicial activism of the Court, and how Regulation 1408 inherited the personal scope from its predecessor Regulation No. 3, but subsequently extended it far beyond that. First, the article briefly sketches the current personal scope of Regulation 883/2004. Second, it analyzes the historical definition of 'employed person' based on Regulation No. 3. In the third part, the article presents a discussion of the inclusion of self-employed persons in early case law, while part four analyses the later Council codification thereof.

I. Who Is Included in the Personal Scope?

April 2004 marks the perhaps most remarkable extension of Regulation 1408/71's personal scope, and thus temporarily closes the long-running history of defining those with a right to cross border social security. With the adoption of Regulation 883/2004, the right to coordinated social security has been extended to *all nationals* of member states covered by the social security legislation of a member state.[12] This means, that not only employed workers, self-employed workers, civil servants, students and pensioners but also *non-active persons* are to be protected from the coordination rules. Furthermore, as of 1 June 2003, *nationals from third countries* as well as their family members and survivors, if they are legal residents in the territory of a Member State and if they have moved between member

---

12 The new Regulation will not enter into force before its implementing Regulation is adopted by the Council, *see Commission Proposal to Amend the Current Implementing Regulation 574/72*, COM (2006) 16 final.

states, are covered by the Regulation. Although, on it's face the inclusion of third-country nationals marks another, significant, step towards a generalized personal scope irrespective of nationality, the practical rights of third-country nationals are much more restricted, since they lack the underlying right of free movement.

By extending the personal scope to *European citizens*, the regulation has definitively broken its established link with the exercise of an economic activity. Over the years, the litigation of the Court of Justice has, however, compromised the link between work activity and rights according to the regulation, among other cases by extending the rights of family members;[13] by denying that employment status depends on the hours spent on the work-activity[14] and by declaring that the migrant's family has an individual right to equal treatment.[15] The successive case law of the Court has thus taken the personal scope far beyond its original meaning.

II. The Historical Definition of "Employed Person"

The distinctiveness of the concept of worker in Regulation 1408 was established through clusters of case law, and subsequently codified by the Council. The historical process establishing the Community's social security meaning of worker, started from the same place as the 'worker' in Regulation 1612[16] and in the Treaty's article 48 (now article 39), with a more traditional understanding of 'wage-earner.'[17] The concept, however, gradually developed its own meaning and scope through case law and the Council's codification of it.

In one of the first social security cases *Hoekstra*,[18] the Court interpreted the personal scope in Regulation No. 3 quite broadly, presumably applying it far beyond what the authors of the regulation could have imagined.[19] In the *Hoekstra* case, the Court emphasized that since Regulation No. 3 was adopted on the basis of article 51 of the Treaty, the meaning of 'wage-earner' depended on the scope of this Treaty provision. Included in the Treaty's chapter on workers and placed in Title III on free movement of persons, services, and capital, situated in part two of the Treaty, describing its foundations, the Court interpreted the aim of article 51 to be

> "The establishment of as *complete a freedom of movement of workers as possible* [emphasis added], which thus forms part of the "foundations" of the community, therefore constitutes the principal objective of article 51 and thereby conditions the interpretation of the regulations adopted in implementation of that article."[20]

---

13 Case 7/75, Mr. and Mrs. Fracas v. Belgian State, 1975 E.C.R. 679.
14 Case C-2/89, Bestuur van de Sociale Verzekeringsbank v. G.J. Kits van Heijningen, 1990 E.C.R. I-1755.
15 Case C-308/93,Bestuur van de Sociale Verzekeringsbank v. J.M. Cabanis-Issarte, 1996 E.C.R. I-2097.
16 Council Regulation 1612/68, Freedom of Movement of Workers within the Community, 1968 O.J. (L 257) 2 (EC Treaty).
17 *See, e.g.*, Persons with a contract of employment.
18 *See* Case 75/63, Mrs. Hoekstra (née Unger) v. Bestuur der Cont. Bedrijfsvereniging voor Detailhandel en Ambachten, 1964 E.C.R. 177 (where Mrs. Hoekstra (born Hungarian) was residing in the Netherlands and had been compulsorily insured against sickness as a person with a contract of employment. When she stopped working, she remained voluntarily insured. While visiting her parents in Germany, Mrs Hoekstra fell ill, and after her return to the Netherlands, she applied for her medical treatment costs to be reimbursed. She was however, denied reimbursement with reference to a provision in the Dutch law, according to which the voluntarily insured could not have the costs of medical treatment reimbursed when treated outside the borders of the Netherlands).
19 S. Van Raepenbusch, *Persons Covered by Regulation No. 1408/71 (EEC) and European Citizenship: From Migrant Worker to European Citizen*, *in* 25 YEARS OF REGULATION NO. 1408/71 (EEC) ON SOCIAL SECURITY FOR MIGRANT WORKERS – PAST EXPERIENCES, PRESENT PROBLEMS AND FUTURE PERSPECTIVES 71 (1997).
20 Case 75/63, Mrs. Hoekstra née Unger v. Bestuur der Cont. Bedrijfsvereniging voor Detailhandel en Ambachten, 1964 E.C.R. 177 (summary of the judgment).

The objective to establish "as complete a freedom of movement of workers as possible" meant that the term 'wage-earner' could not be defined by national legislation alone. The objectives of the Treaty would not be achieved if the concept was, "unilaterally fixed and modified by national law."[21] The preliminary questions of the case furthermore addressed the question whether the term 'wage-earner' covered a person such as Mrs. Hoekstra, who was no longer in active employment, but still covered by the social security scheme for employed persons, and whose movement was motivated by leisure. The Court answered that the concept 'wage-earner or assimilated workers' referred to "all those who, as such and under whatever description, are covered by the different national systems of social security."[22] The Court thus clarified that it was the attachment to a social security scheme for wage earners that linked a person to the Community regulation. This conception even covered those who no longer held active employment, but continued to be voluntarily insured in a social security scheme for wage earners.[23] Thus, the concept did not restrict protection to those in active employment. Also, the motives of the movement were treated as irrelevant, since Regulation No. 3 did not only cover movements for work reasons, but also for leisure, such as Mrs. Hoekstra desire to stay with her parents in Germany.

Since one of its first social security cases, the Court has stretched the personal scope through a teleological interpretation, where the aim and spirit of the Treaty have been decisive for the conceptual borders of 'wage-earner.' Subsequent case law repeated that the reasons motivating movements were irrelevant as long as the person moving was covered by a social security scheme for wage earners.[24]

III. Judicial Anticipation – Bringing in the Self-Employed

The case law on the scope of Regulation No. 3 developed a broad definition of worker, clarifying that the actual nature of the work was irrelevant.[25] The definition went far beyond the written text of the regulation, extending the personal scope to practically everyone insured under a social security scheme for wage earners.[26] When adopting Regulation 1408, the same extended scope was codified in Article 1 (a), defining a worker merely by his attachment to a relevant social security scheme.

Two years after Regulation 1408 was approved, the United Kingdom, Ireland, and Denmark joined the Community, and with this first enlargement, the *acquis communautaire* was to be applied to the residence-based social security models of the new members. The application was by no means straightforward, one reason being that the residence-based model did not have distinct schemes for workers on the one hand and other categories of persons on the other. The problem with applying institutionalized rules to different social security traditions became evident in the European Court of Justice Case *Brack*, on which both the United Kingdom and Denmark submitted observations.[27]

In the *Brack* case, the Court was asked whether a British national who had been an employed person 17 years previous, but was self-employed at the time of the actual

---

21 *Id.*
22 *Id.*
23 *See* HOLLOWAY, *supra* note 7, at 168.
24 *See* Case 44/65, Hessische Knappschaft v. Maison Singer et Fils, 1965 E.C.R. 1191.
25 R. Cornelissen, *25 Years of Regulation No. 1408/71 (EEC) – Its Achievements and its Limits*, in 25 YEARS OF REGULATION NO. 1408/71 (EEC) ON SOCIAL SECURITY FOR MIGRANT WORKERS – PAST EXPERIENCES, PRESENT PROBLEMS AND FUTURE PERSPECTIVES 27, 42 (1997).
26 *See* Van Rapenbusch, *supra* note 19, at 75.
27 Case 17/76, M. L. E. Brack, Widow of R. J. Brack v. Insurance Officer, 1976 E.C.R. 1429.

incident, had a right to cash sickness benefits for a period of illness in France.[28] Mr Brack had been insured under the British national insurance scheme both as an employed and as a self-employed person. The observation submitted by the British government provided a description of the development of its social security legislation, which initially covered only narrowly defined classes of workers, but gradually had been extended to other classes. The general scheme did not draw a distinction between those regarded as wage-earning workers and those belonging to other categories.

In the Danish observation, the government drew attention to the fact that the legislation of the three new member states differed on important aspects, covering either all persons resident in the territory of the competent state or the entire national population irrespective of employment. The Danish government found it unacceptable that the regulation should also apply to self-employed persons who had formerly been workers. Such an extension of the personal scope would according to the Danish government, "... bring about an unreasonable extension of the area of application of the regulation in that *most nationals of the Member States have been workers at one time or another*" (emphasis added).[29]

In this specific case, the Court did not consider the institutional objections put forward in the observations submitted by the United Kingdom and Denmark, but referred instead to the historical logic of Regulation 1408/71. In the same way as Regulation No. 3, Regulation 1408/71 must be interpreted in light of the spirit and the objectives of the Treaty. With reference to the historical case-law on Regulation No. 3, the Court stressed that the evolution of the Community rules on social security reflected the development in the social law of member states, where more personal categories have been covered by social security schemes:

> ... it must be borne in mind that, as the Court has previously held, the Community rules on social security "follow a general tendency of the social law of Member States to extend the benefits of social security in favour of new categories of persons by reasons of identical risks."[30]

Since Mr. Brack was still insured under the social security scheme for employed persons, the Court found that he enjoyed the rights to sickness cash benefits despite falling ill outside of British territory. Though Brack had been self-employed for most of his working life, and was so when he fell ill in France, he retained the full rights provided for in Regulation 1408/71.

In the *Brack* case, the European Court of Justice granted intra-European social security rights to the self-employed, five years before the Council adopted the amended Regulation 1390/81, which definitively included this category.

---

28 *See id.* (Where Mr Brack, a British national, is residing in Britain and insured under the British national insurance scheme 9 years as an employed person, and thereafter 17 years as a self-employed person. In September 1974, Brack went on holiday in France where he fell ill and received immediate treatment. By the end of October 1974, he returned to the United Kingdom and claimed cash sickness benefits for the period when he was ill in France. The claim was refused by the British insurance officer due to the relevant national Act, according to which "a person shall be disqualified for receiving any benefit ... for any period during which that person ... is absent from Great Britain ..." (Section 49 (1) of the British National Insurance Act of 1965)).
29 Case 17/76, M.L.E. Brack, Widow of R.J. Brack v. Insurance Officer, 1976 E.C.R. 1429.
30 *See id.* at para. 20 (Where the Court referenced Case 19/68, Giovanni de Cicco v. Landesversicherungsanstalt Schwaben, 1968 E.C.R. 473 and Case 23/71, Michel Janssen v. Landsbond der christelijke mutualiteiten, 1971 E.C.R. 864).

IV. Council Codification and Further Interpretation

A key feature throughout the historical development of co-ordinated social security has been continuous work to amend the regulation. The high number of proposed amendments suggests that from the Commission's point of view, co-ordinated social security was never really sufficient or up-to-date.

When the Commission began its revision of Regulation No. 3 in 1964, it initially envisioned that the self-employed would be included in the personal scope.[31] However, the proposal was later withdrawn on the argument that including the self-employed would add too much technical complexity to the regulation.[32]

In light of the case law interpretations of the personal scope, the Commission proposed in December 1977 that the self-employed should be included.[33] The proposal was subsequently amended and re-proposed to the Council in October 1978.[34] At the same time, the "Administrative Commission"[35] suggested extending the applicable scope to include all persons covered by a social security scheme of a member state, regardless of their employment status.[36] However, the latter idea remained pending until the beginning of the 1990's when it was re-vitalized in light of the three residence directives.[37]

Envisioned as early as 1964, the self-employed and their family members were finally included in the personal scope by amended Regulation 1390/81, adopted in May 1981.[38] In the explanatory memorandum, the extension of the scope of application was justified by the fact that free movement of persons is not confined to employed persons, and in the framework of the freedom of establishment and the freedom to supply services, Regulation 1408 should include the self-employed as well. The explanatory memorandum further reasoned that since Regulation 1408 already covered certain categories of self-employed persons, it should for the sake of equity be extended to all self-employed persons.

Whereas the inclusion of the self-employed in the co-ordinating framework was deemed necessary for attaining one of the Community objectives, the Treaty did not provide a specific legal basis for this purpose. Since the Treaty's article 51 could not be used as a legal basis for any extension of social security rules beyond workers, the self-employed were brought within the regulatory scope on the legal basis of article 235 (now article 308). The

---

31 See Van Rapenbusch, *supra* note 19, at 71.
32 See HOLLOWAY, *supra* note 7, at 296.
33 Proposed to Council, 31 December 1977 Question No. 2 De M. Klepsch a la Commission: Relations Commerciales Avec les Pays de l'este, 1978 O.J. (C 14) 9.
34 Proposed to Council, 28 September 1987, 1987 O.J. (C 246) 2.
35 The Administrative Commission on Social Security for Migrant Workers is attached to the Commission and consists of a government representative from each member state and a representative from the Commission. The tasks of the Administrative Commission are, among others, to deal with administrative and interpretive questions regarding the regulation, to develop cooperation between the member states in social security matters and to submit suggestions for amendments to the Commission on the basis of the more practical insight of its members.
36 D. Pieters, *Towards a Radical Simplification of the Social Security Co-ordination*, in PROSPECTS OF SOCIAL SECURITY CO-ORDINATION 117, 205 (P. Schoukens ed., 1997).
37 See Van Rapenbusch, *supra* note 19, at 80. The three Residence Directives are: Council Directive 90/364, The Right of Residence, 1990 O.J. (L 180) 26 (EEC Treaty); Council Directive 90/365, The Right of Residence for Employees and Self-Employed Persons who have Ceased their Occupational Activity, 1990 O.J. (L 180) 28 (EEC Treaty); and Council Directive 90/366, The Right of Residence for Students, 1990 O.J. (L 180) (EEC Treaty). The Court did however, not accept Article 235 as a Treaty basis for students and annulled the Directive in 1992. The Directive was subsequently amended to Council Directive 93/96, 1993 O.J. (L 317) 59 (EEC Treaty).
38 Council Regulation 1390/81, The Application of Social Security Schemes to Employed Persons, Self-Employed Persons and Their Families Moving within the Community, 1981 O.J. (L 143) (extending to self-employed persons and members of their families Council Reg. No. 1408/71) (EC Treaty).

Council hereby agreed that the Community objectives went beyond the strict meaning of article 51. The total Treaty basis for the inclusion of self-employed thus consisted of articles 2, 7, 51 and 235.

Despite its inclusion, the meaning of 'self-employed' was not immediately elaborated on, and had to be clarified through another legal dispute. In the *van Roosmalen* case, the Court was asked whether a Roman Catholic priest fell within the definition of self-employed.[39] In its judgment, the Court emphasized that Regulation 1390 was adopted to achieve the same objectives as Regulation 1408, and therefore self-employed were entitled to the same level of protection as employed persons. The term 'self-employed' had a wide meaning as well.[40] Despite a somewhat non-standard kind of self-employment, a person engaged in work such as van Roosmalen's fell within the personal scope of the regulation, because like "employed person" "self-employed" was to be interpreted according to the objective of the Treaty's article 51,

> With regard to the interpretation of the expression "self-employed person", it must first be pointed out that initially the provisions of Regulation no 1408/71, adopted for the implementation of Article 51 of the Treaty, applied only to those who were covered by the term "employed person". According to the established case law of the court, "employed person" is a term of Community law rather than national law and must be interpreted broadly, having regard to the objective of Article 51, which is to contribute towards the establishment of the greatest possible freedom of movement for migrant workers, an objective which is one of the foundations of the Community.[41]

The Court reasoned its interpretation, by referring to previous case law, and the logic of the argument closely resembled that used in the early judgments on Regulation No. 3. The teleological interpretation of the Court defined the concept of self-employed broadly.

V. In the Light of the Treaty Spirit – Dynamic Aims and Means

The personal scope of both Regulation No. 3 and its descendant Regulation 1408 extended incrementally due to a teleological interpretation by the Court and the Council's acceptance and codification of it. The Court cultivated a distinct social security notion of 'worker,' which from its earliest interpretations covered more than just those in active employment, such as individuals with personal reasons and those moving for leisure. The first cases justified the broad interpretation on the basis of Article 51 of the Treaty itself. The principal objective of Article 51 was not simply to guarantee migrant workers social

---

39 *See* Case 300/84, A.J.M. van Roosmalen v. Bestuur van de Bedrijfsvereniging voor de Gezondheid, Geestelijke en Maatschappelijke Belangen, 1986 E.C.R. 3097 (where Van Roosmalen was a priest of Dutch nationality who always worked outside of the geographical borders of the Community. Already at the age of 22, he moved to Belgium to continue his studies. After becoming a priest, he was sent to Belgian Congo (Zaire), where he remained for 25 years, only interrupted by three years on leave, which he spent with his parents in the Netherlands. During his stay in Zaire, he was supported by his parishioners, but was at the same time voluntarily insured in the Netherlands. However, he did not pay income tax to the Dutch state while residing in Zaire. In January 1981, he became work incapable and returned to Europe. He settled temporarily in the Netherlands and received invalidity benefit here. In June 1982, he established himself in Belgium, and since he no longer fulfilled the residence requirement in the Dutch law, the competent institution decided to suspend his benefit. The preliminary reference to the European Court of Justice questioned whether van Roosmalen fell within the personal scope of the regulation and whether the residence requirement in national law was compatible with Community law).
40 R. Cornelissen, *The Principle of Territoriality and the Community Regulations on Social Security (Regulations 1408/71 and 574/72)*, 33 COMMON MKT. L. R. 439, 443 (1996).
41 *See* Case 300/84, A.J.M. van Roosmalen v. Bestuur van de Bedrijfsvereniging voor de Gezondheid, Geestelijke en Maatschappelijke Belangen, 1986 E.C.R. 3097 at para. 18.

security, but also to promote the greatest possible freedom of movement for workers. Interpretations followed the guiding light of the Treaty spirit. After the adoption of Regulation 1408, the Court anticipated the imminent inclusion of the self-employed, once again justified as being in keeping with the spirit of the Treaty. Five years later, the Council adopted the regulation amendment, which finally covered the self-employed. However, no matter how broadly the aims of the Treaty's article 51 were constructed, it could not be used as the legal basis of any extension beyond workers. Adopting Regulation 1390/81 required article 235 (now article 308) as the other Treaty basis. In this way, the member states accepted that the purpose of Regulation 1408 was beyond promoting the free movement of *workers*. The adoption illustrates that the Community objective with Regulation 1408 and the Treaty's article 51 in conjunction with articles 235, 2 and 7 was by no means a given, but was still open to further interpretation. With self-employed persons included under the umbrella, the Court continued its broad definition of the personal scope, whereby the line of reasoning in previous case-law served as grounds for new conclusions. Since 'employed persons' was understood broadly, 'self-employed' had to be as well.

The development of the personal scope from Regulation No. 3 through the first two decades of Regulation 1408's institutional existence left only students, non-active persons, and third-country nationals without co-ordinated social security rights. These excluded groups were subsequently incorporated into new proposals formulated by the Commission and considered by the Council.

C. Proposing a Generalized Personal Scope

Until the 1990s, the personal scope of Regulation 1408 was extended mainly through the jurisprudence of the Court and the Council's 1981 adoption of the extension to the self-employed. The 1990's were the decade when the Commission re-challenged the status quo of the regulation, and initiated a dialogue with member states on the future personal scope of the regulation through proposals and recommendations. According to the Commission, a personal scope restricted to the market citizen would be inadequate. Instead, it should include all European citizens as well as legally residing third-country nationals. By putting the latter on the agenda, the Commission went beyond a communitarian conception of social protection.

This section focuses on the Commission's position as initiator, and it analyses the way in which it managed, through proposals and recommendations, to set an agenda that proved the insufficiency of Regulation 1408's personal scope. As later negotiations demonstrate, the Commission pursued its agenda by coupling key issues. European citizenship and the free movement of persons were invoked as strong arguments for extending co-ordination of social security rights to all Community nationals. The moral obligation and the political commitment to improve the legal status of third-country nationals became arguments for including persons who were not member states nationals. Below, the analysis first illustrates how a 'People's Europe' developed into a citizenship argument, and how Commission recommendations were used as a means to substantiate the need to extend Regulation 1408. Second, it explains how the Commission initiated its dialogue with the member states concerning the extension of the regulatory scope beyond European citizens, and also how the Commission initially interpreted the scope and limits of the Treaty basis so as to justify an extension to third-country nationals.

I. A People's Europe – Proposing New Value to European Citizenship

The adoption of the three residence directives in 1990 revived the idea dating back to the late seventies that Regulation 1408 should be extended to all member states' citizens. In December 1991, the Commission presented a proposal to extend the regulation to all Community citizens insured in a member state.[42] The proposal was reasoned according to the new general right of residence, and found "indispensable in the context of the social dimension of the internal market and a People's Europe."[43]

However, it soon became clear that the member states were far from prepared to grant any such radical extension of the personal scope. The Commission therefore had a long way to go to gain support for its proposal. The soft-law tool of recommendations was used to emphasize how 'the peoples of Europe' merited equal rights. European citizenship was brought in as a new dimension of European integration.[44] In the Communication, *Modernizing and Improving Social Protection in the European Union*[45] the Commission argued: "The original dimension of European integration, i.e. a common market allowing and fostering free movement of workers, has been enriched by a new *concept*, namely that of *European citizenship*. The personal scope of Regulation 1408/71 should be adapted accordingly."[46]

Soft-law communications on the free movement of persons continued in 1997, and also dealt with the instrument of Regulation 1408. By Commission mandate, a high-level panel on the free movement of persons was set up to identify the "obstacles which confront European citizens seeking to exercise their rights to move freely and to work within the Union."[47] The report was motivated by the Commission's recognition that of the four fundamental freedoms of the single market, the least progress had been made on the free movement of persons. The Commission argued that even though free movement was an institutionalized right, it was not yet a practicable fact for the European people. The report confirmed the Commission's line of reasoning according to which exercise of free movement was argued to constitute an essential means leading to other Union objectives,

> The effectiveness of the right to move freely would contribute not only to attaining the objectives of the single market but also bringing the Community closer to the goal of an *"ever closer union among the peoples of Europe"* envisaged in the original treaties, which gave form to the Communities and, subsequently, to the European Union.[48]

The high-level panel pointed out the incompleteness of Regulation 1408 as one of the obstacles to free movement. Its personal scope was held to be inadequate, given the many changes that had occurred since its adoption, particularly the adoption of the three residence directives. The panel found it both logical and essential to extend the scope to cover all persons entitled to move freely within the Union.

The panel's recommendations were later followed up in *An Action Plan on the Free Movement of Workers*. In this document, the Commission stressed that free movement had

---

42 *Commission Proposal to Extend the Regulation to all Community Citizens Insured in a Member State*, at 1, COM (1991) 528 final (Dec. 13, 1991).
43 *See id.* at 3.
44 *See* Cornelissen, *supra* note 40, at 30.
45 *Commission Proposal for Modernizing and Improving Social Protection in the European Union*, at 1, COM (1997) 102 final (Mar. 12, 1997).
46 Improving Social Protection in the European Union, at 16, COM (1997) 102 final.
47 *See Commission Report of The High Level Panel on the Free Movement of Persons* (Mar. 18, 1997), *available at* http://europa.eu.int/comm/internal_market/citizens/index_en.htm.
48 *See id.* at 94 (emphasis added).

to be seen in a new perspective. The Commission expected that due to demographic changes and the changed nature of working life, free movement would become much more important over the next 10–20 years than it had been for the last 30 years.[49] Although the *acquis communautaire* was identified as the starting point for reinforcing free movement, it contained "serious flaws and lacunae."[50] Once again, the Commission identified the right of free movement as a substantial part of European citizenship,

> Moreover, following the report of the High Level Panel, which also concerns free movement of persons who are not exercising an economic activity, the Commission has already announced its intention to present in 1998 proposals to simplify and enhance the existing secondary legislation with a view to drawing all consequences in order *to give full value to citizenship of the Union*.[51]

II. Proposals, Recommendations and a Partial Adoption

The proposals and recommendations set forth by the Commission in the 1990s introduced and reinforced new perspectives on the co-ordination of social security rights. Whereas the institutional aim in the 1970s and 1980s had been to more efficiently allocate production factors, by the 1990s, the goal of cultural integration among the 'peoples of Europe' had been added among the economic objectives of the single market.

However, the proposal of a generalized personal scope made no headway until the late 1990s. During the Austrian presidency in the autumn of 1998, a compromise was formulated that proposed a separate extension of the personal scope to students. The strategy of the Commission and the Austrian presidency was to isolate the more controversial part of COM (91) 528 on the extension to non-active persons and special schemes for civil servants, and thereby accelerate the Council's approval of the inclusion of students.[52] Furthermore, the compromise was made possible by proposing a separate material scope for students. The proposal held students outside of the regulation's provision on social pension, and the material impact of the extended personal scope was thus reduced.[53] Since students had already been granted the right to medical treatment outside of their home country,[54] the inclusion only meant access to cross-border family benefits. On this background, the Council adopted Regulation 307/99 in February 1999.[55]

III. Beyond European Citizenship – Preparing for the Extension to Third-country Nationals

At the same time "European citizenship" was introduced as the new justification for an extension of Regulation 1408's personal scope, the Commission also suggested that the regulation be extended to legally residing third-country nationals. It thus presented a

---

49 *Commission Presentation on An Action Plan on the Free Movement of Workers*, at 8, COM (97) 586 final (Nov. 13, 1997) [hereinafter Plan on Free Movement of Workers].
50 *Id.* at 5.
51 *Id.* at 9 (emphasis added).
52 Informative Note from the Danish Ministry of Labour to the European Committee of the Danish Parliament, Supp. 47, 15 (Oct. 19 1998).
53 Interview with Employment and Social Affairs, Danish Government (Sept. 12 2001).
54 *See* Council Regulation 3095/95, 1995 O.J. (L 335), (EC Treaty) (where the right to cross-border medical treatment had been granted to all insured member state citizens, thus including students).
55 Council Regulation 307/1999, 1999 O.J. (L 80), (EC Treaty) *amending* Council Reg. 1408/71 (EEC Treaty).

notion of European citizenship independent of the exclusion of a third part and hereby challenged a traditional communitarian perception of co-ordinated social security rights with rights assigned exclusively to nationals of the Community. By placing the rights of third-country nationals on the agenda, the Commission introduced an amplified comprehension of Regulation 1408's purpose, arguing that although non-Community nationals do not enjoy any rights of free movement under Community law, they should still enjoy the social protection of Regulation 1408. The questions of whether and how to ensure the co-ordination of social security rights for third-country nationals launched a long drawn out legal and political dispute, in which legal questions became political and vice versa. Indeed, this dispute exemplifies the degree to which law and politics may become intertwined.

The background behind the Commission's initiative was the fact that even though third-country nationals are not entitled to free movement under Community law, they may, due to international law or bilateral agreements, enjoy the right to move between member states.[56] Due to their exclusion from Regulation 1408/71, they risked losing any social security entitlements they had accrued via regular contributions to a member state's social security scheme, if they left that member state for another.[57]

On these grounds, the Commission opened the discussion in 1993, questioning whether it was still justifiable to exclude third-country nationals from the protection offered by Regulation 1408.[58] The Belgian chair posed the question to member state representatives at an informal Council in Charleroi in November 1993. However, the meeting did not mobilize sufficient support for a general extension of Regulation 1408 beyond Community citizens. The meeting nevertheless suggested that a limited extension granting third-country nationals a right to intra European health care, as regulated under Article 22 of Regulation 1408/71, might be supported.[59] On this basis, the Commission announced its intention to extent Article 22 to third-country nationals as a first step.[60] Furthermore, at the Portuguese colloquium in November 1994, the Commission presented its long-term intentions to extend the whole scope of Regulation 1408 to non-Community nationals legally residing in the Union. The member states' delegates attending were told that such an extension would not only satisfy a moral obligation, but that it would also introduce a legal and administrative simplification.[61] Even though granting third-country nationals a right to health care benefits would only be an initial and very limited extension of Regulation 1408, the proposal was vetoed by the United Kingdom when finally presented to the Council in November 1995. As part of the same negotiations, the Council adopted Regulation 3095/95, which extended Regulation 1408/71's Article 22 to all member states' nationals insured in a social security scheme.

This initial Council refusal did not however discourage the Commission from proceeding with its long-term intention. In the recommendation that suggested free movement and Regulation 1408 be brought in line with European citizenship, the Commission also insisted that Regulation 1408 overall should be extended to third-country nationals.[62] The Commission obliged itself to present a separate proposal in 1997 concerning

---

56 Interview with Employment and Social Affairs, Danish Government (Sept. 13 2001).
57 S. Roberts, "*Our View has not Changed*" *The UK's Response to the Proposal to Extend the Co-ordination of Social Security to Third Country Nationals*, 2 EURO. J. OF SOC. SECURITY 189, 190 (2000).
58 *Commission Green Paper on Options for the Union*, COM (1993) 551 final (Nov. 17, 1993).
59 See Roberts, *supra* note 57 at 192.
60 *Commission White Paper on a Way Forward for the Union*, COM (1994) 333 final (July 27, 1994).
61 See Roberts, *supra* note 57 at 192.
62 Improving Social Protection in the European Union, at 17, COM (1997) 102 final.

Regulation 1408's extension to non-Community nationals with legal residence in the Union.[63]

IV. The First Separate Proposal on Third-country Nationals

Within the normative framework of the *European Year Against Racism* in 1997, the Commission came up with its announced separate proposal on an extension of Regulation 1408 to third-country nationals, legally residing and insured in one of the member states.[64] The rather extensive explanatory memorandum of COM (97) 561, amounting to no less than eight pages, indicates that the proposal might have been controversial on several points.

The Commission pointed out that third-country nationals suffered from a "muddied legal situation," where rights were by no means uniform and each individual case could be considered through a "multiplicity of protection levels."[65] Some might be covered by Regulation 1408 as refugees or stateless persons, some as family members, others through an agreement between the Community and a specific third country, and yet others by individual bilateral or multilateral agreements. A remaining group of third-country nationals might not benefit from any social security protection at all, if they move within the Community. This complexity was identified as harmful to individuals and the source of administrative difficulties when deciding specific rights. The Commission noted that third-country nationals contribute to the social security systems of member states, just as Community nationals do.

The Commission did not find that Regulation 1408's requirement to be "nationals of one of the Member States" precluded an extension of the regulation to third-country nationals. It emphasized that the nationality requirement was not an absolute, and indeed was set aside in the cases of family members and survivors, refugees and stateless persons, and persons from the EEA member countries.[66]

V. The Scope and Limits of the Treaty – the Reach of Community Competence?

The issue of nationality underlies the long argumentation in proposal COM (97) 561 on its Treaty basis. Traditionally, Regulation 1408 had been formulated as an instrument to promote the free movement of workers, and according to article 48 (now article 39) of the Treaty, only Community workers enjoy the right to free movement. A key point in the long-running dispute on the potential inclusion of non-communitarian nationals in Regulation 1408 was the question of whether article 51 (now article 42) of the Treaty was inextricably bound to article 48, and thus dependant on the nationality requirement of the latter. According to the Commission, this was not the case. Article 51 and Regulation 1408 had gained instrumental value, not solely as a means of promoting free movement, but also as instruments of social protection,

> Regulation (EEC) No Regulation 1408/71 is not just geared to the free movement of workers *but also constitutes an instrument of social protection*. For applying the Regulation, the crucial element is *not* exercise of the right to freedom of movement *but the fact that the person concerned is insured under a social security scheme*. The *purpose* is to maintain social protection

---

63 Plan on Free Movement of Workers, *supra* note 49, at 12.
64 Commission Proposal on the Extension of Regulation 1408 to Third Country Nationals, Legally Residing and Insured in One of the Member States, at 5, COM (1997) 561 final (Nov. 12, 1997).
65 *See id.* at 5.
66 *See id.* at 4.

for persons moving within the Community for whatever reason. In line with the task devolving on the Community under Article 2 of the EC Treaty, the *aim is to provide a high level of social protection*.[67]

To support its interpretation, the Commission pointed out that Regulation 1408 also regulated cases where the person concerned might not have exercised his right to free movement for workers, but where a problem of social security arose due to a cross-border situation.[68] Furthermore, it substantiated its viewpoint with the historical fact that Regulation No. 3 was adopted on the basis of article 51 ten years before the right to free movement for workers actually came into force in 1968 with Regulation 1612/68 and Council Directive 68/360.

Referring to the extension of the regulation to the self-employed, the Commission suggested that in so far as article 51 was not a sufficient legal basis on which to include third-country nationals, article 235 could be added with the objective of attaining 'a high level of social protection' stated as a Community task in the Treaty's article 2.

Despite the various arguments listed by the Commission, member states remained deadlocked on the issue, and it was left unresolved for years. One political concern put forward by the United Kingdom was that although the proposal emphasized that third-country nationals were not granted any right of free movement under Community law,[69] it still remained unclear whether non-community nationals would be entitled to the social protection of the regulation without having moved between member states. Regulation 1408's article 3, stating equal treatment, in conjunction with Article 2 of COM (97) 561 could be understood as if the regulation covered non-Community nationals moving from a third country directly into a member state, and who had only been subject to the legislation of one member state.[70] The UK thus feared that Community law could oblige member states to treat third-country nationals equally to their own nationals on the basis of Regulation 1408/71, without their having moved across Community borders.

Directly or indirectly, the major disagreement hampering negotiations in the Council was the question of the appropriate Treaty basis and the scope and limits of Community competences. On the one hand, the Commission held that Regulation 1408 had become an instrument of social policy even when free movement had not been exercised. It did not find that the use of Articles 42 and 308 as based on the Treaty required the personal category addressed to also allow the right to free movement. On the other hand, a minority of member governments, i.e. the UK, Denmark and Ireland, maintained that Articles 42 and 308 did not together constitute an appropriate Treaty basis.[71] Behind these reservations was a political conviction that since the Treaty conferred free movement on Community citizens only, the task formulated in the Treaty's Article 2, to promote a high level of social protection equally, applied only to citizens of the Community. These member governments thus found that the primary law of the Community did not contain any competence to extend the personal scope of Regulation 1408/71 beyond Community nationals. Such

---

67 See id. at 8 (emphasis added).
68 The Commission emphasized that Article 10 of the Regulation makes it possible for a person to export benefits to a member state in which he may never have worked, that Article 22 enables persons temporarily staying in another member state to receive health care, and that Article 73 ensures family benefits to family members who reside in another member state.
69 See Extension of Regulation 1408 to Third Country Nationals, *supra* note 64, COM (97) 561 final at 7.
70 See Roberts, *supra* note 57, at 194.
71 Proposal for a European Parliament and Council Regulation on the Extension to Third Country Nationals of Regulation (EEC) No. 1408/71 on the Application of Social Security Schemes to Employed Persons, to Self-Employed Persons and to Members of Their Families Moving Within the Community. Council Doc. 12831/99 (Nov. 12, 1999) (European Council Documents referenced in this piece are available by request at: http://ue.eu.int/cms3_fo/showPage.asp?id=854&lang=en&mode=g).

an extension would fundamentally extend the Community's objectives and thus require a Treaty amendment.[72]

VI. Proposing New Borders of a Personal Scope

In the 1990s, the Commission formulated its agenda for the future personal scope of Regulation 1408. The Commission found Regulation 1408 outdated and incongruous with the Union's development from economic community to political union with rights granted on citizenship. The argument so far seemed to replicate traditional communitarian reasoning for granting rights, where social rights strengthen the link between the political centre and its citizens. However, the Commission's agenda went beyond such limitations and aimed at including all persons with legal residence in the geographical territory of the Community, independent of the exercise of economic activity and nationality.

The Commission did not find that it would be beyond the scope of the Treaty, and thus the competence of the Community, to extend Regulation 1408's personal scope to third-country nationals legally residing in a member state. This viewpoint was widely supported, although opposed by the minority of the United Kingdom, Ireland and Denmark. Although the Amsterdam Treaty and the Tampere conclusions gave new momentum to ease rigid positions, the disagreement on Community competences and the appropriate Treaty basis continued until case law of the Court in 2001 came to settle the matter, as shall be demonstrated below.

D. Negotiating a Generalized Personal Scope

The following analysis will be presented in four stages and concerns the negotiations on the personal scope. First, this article examines the reform proposed by the Commission to simplify and modernize Regulation 1408, and how that proposal was initially negotiated in the Council. Second, the article discusses how the political question of inclusion of third-country nationals turned into a legal search for the correct Treaty basis. Third, it describes the case law solution that emerged out of that legal search. Finally, in the fourth part, the article analyzes how the *Khalil* judgment brought about a breakthrough in negotiations, and how the original Commission proposal was split in two whereby negotiations on the rights of European citizens were held separate from those of third-country nationals. After a decade of negotiations and political-judicial dispute, legally residing third-country nationals have finally been granted a right to intra-European social security in 14 member states, with Denmark as the exception. However, without the right of free movement, the extension is primarily of an abstract and symbolic value rather than enforceable in practical terms, as will be argued below. Furthermore, intra-European social security has finally become a substantial right attached to European citizenship.

I. Modernisation and Simplification Proposed and Negotiated

With no appreciable progress on the separate proposal concerning third-country nationals, the Commission presented its long announced proposal to simplify and modernize Regulation 1408 by late December 1998, as had been politically mandated at the Edinburgh

---

72 See Roberts, *supra* note 57, at 195.

Council in 1992.[73] The six years between mandate and proposal had been used for detailed discussions in the "Administrative Commission" as well as seminars held in each individual member state, followed by careful drafting.[74] The aim of the proposal was twofold; to *simplify* and *modernize* Regulation 1408.

The Edinburgh Council recognized the need to simplify the regulation at the highest political level. The Commission in its various communications, arguing that, over the years, the instrumental value of the regulation had decreased by its overwhelming complexity, followed up the political mandate. The requirement of unanimity had repeatedly hindered major reforms, and the consensus procedure had established a practice whereby a strong political pressure in favour of an exception to the main rule was met by adding an annex.[75] However, the practice of adding exceptions had created a situation where very important aspects of the regulation were found in annexes and not the main text.[76] Within this procedural context the regulation's complexity had gradually been fortified by;[77] 1) the many exceptions from the main rules formulated in the annexes; 2) the case law interpretations on how to read the regulatory text, distancing the literal text from the correct interpretation; and 3) the lack of memoranda explaining the rationale of the individual provisions, whereby administrative institutions and the Court of Justice of the European Communities had to continuously interpret the actual content of the article. The result was that rights and obligations could not be read directly from the text, but had to be 'translated' on the basis of detailed knowledge of the extensive annexed text and established case law as well as national administrative practices.

With simplification as one ambitious purpose, the proposal furthermore aimed at modernizing Regulation 1408. The negotiations on modernisation highlighted several sensitive political issues. Among other issues, modernisation meant an amended personal scope. As originally proposed, the regulation was meant to "apply to all persons who are or have been covered by the social security legislation of any of the Member States."[78] This formulation meant that 'persons' would be covered irrespective of their economic status *and* of their nationality. Hereby Regulation 1408 would come to include non-active persons, students with no separate substantive scope, and third-country nationals. By including non-active persons and non-community nationals, the original proposal addressed the two main controversial aspects of the previous proposals COM (91) 528 and (97) 561.

In the explanatory memorandum, the former aim of the regulation – to promote free movement of *workers* – had now been replaced by the aim of giving "real and tangible value" to the free movement of *persons*,

> Community legislation on social security is a *sine qua non* for exercising the right to *free movement of persons*. Only by ensuring that persons moving within the Community do not suffer disadvantages in their social security rights will this freedom guaranteed by the Treaty be of real and tangible value.[79]

From the outset, the Council in principle agreed to simplify the regulation.[80] Negotiations,

---

73 *Commission Proposal for a Council Regulation on Coordination of Social Security Systems*, at 1, COM (1998) 779 final (Dec. 21, 1998) (EC Treaty).
74 Interview with German Federal Ministry of Labour and Social Affairs (Sept. 19, 2001).
75 Interview with Danish Government Employment and Social Affairs (Sept. 12, 2001).
76 Interview with Danish Ministry of Social Affairs (Nov. 8, 2002).
77 F. Pennings, *The European Commission Proposal to Simplify Regulation 1408/71*, 3 EURO. J. OF SOC. SECURITY 45–47 (2001).
78 *See Commission Proposal for a Council Regulation on Coordination of Social Security Systems, supra* note 73, at 4.
79 *See id.* at 1 (emphasis added).
80 Interview with Danish Government Employment and Social Affairs (Sept. 13, 2001).

initiated during the German presidency in the first half of 1999 continued during the Finnish, Portuguese and French presidencies, but without noticeable result.[81] The real crux of the matter appeared to be the politically sensitive parts of the proposal.[82] The inclusion of third-country nationals was controversial from the beginning, Denmark and the United Kingdom held strong reservations about such a policy.[83] In addition, the inclusion of non-active persons caused some trouble, and, furthermore, the extension of the material scope delayed negotiations.[84]

II. Searching for a Legal Basis – Third-country Nationals Readdressed

The Treaty of Amsterdam had introduced important changes in the primary law premises for negotiating modernisation and simplification. The Amsterdam Treaty amendments made Title IV on *Visas, Asylum, Immigration and other Policies related to the Free Movement of Persons* and article 63 a possible Treaty basis upon which to extend Regulation 1408 to non-Community nationals. Furthermore, the Treaty of Amsterdam had amended article 42, still requiring unanimity, but granting the European Parliament co-decision. The future negotiations on modernisation and simplifications thus counted an extra veto-player.

In addition to this, the European Council of Tampere of October 15 and 16, 1999 subjected the status of third-country nationals to renewed political attention, and the member states politically committed themselves to work for a treatment more equal to that of Community nationals. Based on the Tampere conclusions, the Commission's proposal to include non-Community nationals in the personal scope of Regulation 1408 should have gained sufficient momentum for progress. Despite the fact that the Tampere conclusions mandated the Commission and the Finnish presidency to proceed with the work, the dispute on the legal basis continued to block any progress. Whereas the qualified majority of 12 member states were in favour of adopting the proposal on the basis of articles 42 and 308, as suggested by the Commission, the United Kingdom and Ireland were not, and instead argued that after the Amsterdam Treaty came into force in May 1999, the appropriate legal basis was the new article 63(4). Denmark announced that it would accept neither article 42 in conjunction with 308 nor 63(4) as legal bases for extending Regulation 1408 beyond community nationals, and repeated its political problem with the extension as such.[85]

Denmark, the United Kingdom and Ireland opposed the use of the legal base that had traditionally, been used for extensions of Regulation 1408. Relying on Article 63(4) as a legal base, however, meant that all three member states could stay outside the extension of Regulation 1408. Under the Protocol on the position of the United Kingdom and Ireland, the two member states must opt in to participate in Title IV of the Treaty. Furthermore, the Protocol on the Danish position excludes Denmark from participating in Title IV. Examining the positions of the three states, it becomes clear that their reservations were motivated differently. Both the United Kingdom and Ireland saw article 42 as limited to

---

81 Interview with Danish Permanent Representation (Dec. 18, 2002).
82 See Pennings, *supra* note 77, at 45.
83 See Roberts, *supra* note 57; Proposal for a Council Regulation on the Extension to Third-Country Nationals of Regulation No. 1408/71 (EEC) on the Application of Social Security Schemes to Employed Persons, Self-Employed Persons and to Members of Their Families Moving Within the Community, Council Doc. 8807/99 (June 1, 1999).
84 Interview with Danish Government Employment and Social Affairs (Sept. 12, 2001).
85 Proposal for a Council Regulation on the Extension to Third Country Nationals of Regulation No. 1408/71 (EEC) on the Application of Social Security Schemes to Employed Persons, Self-Employed Persons and to Members of Their Families Moving Within the Community, Council Doc. 12831/99 (Nov. 12, 1999).

European Union nationals. Despite this reservation, Ireland emphasized, as early as November 1999, that it was a question of the appropriate legal basis and that it would choose to "opt in" on the basis of article 63.4. In addition, the United Kingdom stressed that its problem was purely a legal one, and that, politically, it supported the extension.[86]

From the outset, Denmark refused the traditional legal basis as well as the new one, and politically opposed any extension of Regulation 1408 to third-country nationals.[87] However, a few months after the coming into force of the Amsterdam Treaty, Article 63(4) was examined and rendered a sufficient legal basis by the Council's legal service.[88] On this background, Denmark consented to examine the use of 63(4), and two years later finally accepted it.[89] The Danish position changed as negotiations proceeded. Denmark finally decided to change its foot-dragging and isolated position. However, due to the Danish opt-out, such a change of position was politically free of charge.

Together, the Amsterdam Treaty and the Tampere conclusions offered a legal alternative and a political mandate. Regardless of the momentum this supposedly gave to the negotiations on the inclusion of third-country nationals in Regulation 1408, the negotiations did not progress in the Council for the next two years. During that time, the Commission initiated improvements on the general status of non-community nationals, for example by proposing a partial free movement for long-term residents, mandated by the Tampere conclusions.[90]

Among other issues, the question of third-country nationals had pushed proposal COM (1998) 779 into a deadlock of political and legal reservations. Facing the improbability of a political break-through, the Commission and the Council awaited a legal clarification of the dispute, which they assumed would occur with the *Khalil* case.[91]

III. The Case Law Solution of a Political Problem

On October 11, 2001, the Court decided in the Joined Cases C-95/99 to C-98/99 and C-180/99 (Khalil and others).[92] The concrete cases concerned whether Community law, as

---

86 *Id.*
87 Proposal for European Parliament and Council Regulation on the Extension to Third-Country Nationals of Regulation No. 1408/71 (EEC) on the Application of Social Security Schemes to Employed Persons, Self-Employed Persons and to Members of Their Families Moving Within the Community, Council Doc. No. 12830/99 (Sept. 11, 1999).
88 Proposal for a Council Regulation on the Extension to Third-Country Nationals of Regulation No. 1408/71 (EEC) on the Application of Social Security Schemes to Employed Persons, Self-Employed Persons and to Members of Their Families Moving Within the Community, Council Doc. No. 11043/99 (Sept. 17, 1999).
89 Proposal for European Parliament and Council Regulation on the Extension to Third-Country Nationals of Regulation No. 1408/71 (EEC) on the Application of Social Security Schemes to Employed Persons, Self-Employed Persons and to Members of Their Families Moving Within the Community, Council Doc. No. 13186/99 (Nov. 22, 1999); Proposal for a Regulation of the European Parliament and of the Council on the Coordination of Social Security Systems – Parameters with a View to Modernizing Regulation No. 1408/71 (EEC), Council Doc. No. 13027/01 (Oct. 23, 2001).
90 *Commission Proposal for a Council Directive Concerning the Status of Third Country Nationals who are Long Term Residents*, COM (2001) 127 final (Mar. 13, 2001).
91 Interview with Danish Government Employment and Social Affairs (Sept. 13, 2001); Proposal for a Regulation of the European Parliament and of the Council on the Coordination of Social Security Systems – Parameters with a View to Modernizing Regulation No. 1408/71 (EEC), Council Doc. No. 12296/01 (Sept. 28, 2001).
92 *See* Joined Cases, Case C-95/99 Mervet Khalil, 2001 E.C.R. I-7413; Case C-98/99 Issa Chaaban, 2001 E.C.R. I-7413; Case C-97/99 Hassan Osseilli v. Bundesanstalt für Arbeit, 2001 E.C.R. I-7413; Case C-98/99 Mohamad Nasser v. Landeshauptstadt Stuttgart, 2001 E.C.R. I-7413; Case C-180/99 Meriem Addou v. Land Nordrhein-Westfalen, 2001 E.C.R. I-7413 (where all cases concerned third-country nationals regarded as stateless persons under German law. In four of the cases, child benefit had been stopped, because only foreigners possessing a residence permit are entitled to child benefit under the new version ((entered into

stated in Regulation 1408/71, entitled stateless persons to the German child benefit and child raising allowance. German law[93] made foreigners' entitlement to family benefits dependent on their possession of a residence permit. Although not asked directly, the Court laid the preliminary reference out as if to examine whether it was valid to include stateless persons, refugees and their family members in the personal scope of Regulation 1408/71 on the Treaty basis of article 42, although they were not Community nationals. In this examination, the case became relevant to the question of whether article 42 could be used as the legal base for the extension of Regulation 1408 to third-country nationals, or whether the article was limited to granting rights to European Union nationals, since only they are entitled to free movement under Community law. The Court found that the inclusion of stateless persons and refugees had to be considered in its historical context. The original inclusion of stateless persons and refugees took place in a historical context of international and European agreements, signed by the six original member states, in which the Geneva Convention, the European interim agreements and the New York Convention formulated the norm to grant equal treatment to these groups of persons. The European convention on social security of 1957,[94] which to a large extent was replicated in Regulation no. 3, was prepared in this context and granted the principle of equal treatment not only to the nationals of the contracting parties but to stateless persons and refugees as well.[95] Regulation 1408 later inherited both the personal scope of Regulation No. 3 and its embedded norm. On the basis of these historical considerations, the Court answered, on the first question, that its examination had not pointed to any factors making Regulation 1408's inclusion of stateless persons and refugees invalid.[96]

The second question put forward by the referring German Court asked the Court whether stateless persons and refugees could rely on the rights granted by Regulation 1408 if they had moved to a member state directly from a third country, i.e. if they might rely on the protection of Regulation 1408 without having moved within the Community. The Court's answer to the second question was fairly short. The ECJ referred to established case law under which it had concluded that article 42 of the Treaty and the equal treatment provision of Regulation 1408 did not apply to situations, which happen only within the same member state.[97] For the same reason, the Court concluded that stateless persons and refugees could not rely on Regulation 1408 if all aspects of their situations referred to one and the same member state.[98] The Court thereby affirmed that the regulation could only be invoked when a Community cross-border movement had taken place.

---

force on 1 January 1994)) on the Federal Law on Child Benefit. The family has not been granted asylum. In the fifth case, child raising allowance had been refused, since Mrs Addou did not possess any residence permit, which is a requirement under the Federal Law on Child-Raising Allowance).

93 Bundeskindergeldgesetz [BKGG] [Federal Law on Child Benefit] Nov. 10, 1995, BGBl. I at 1250; Bundeserziehungsgeldgesetz [BErzGG] [Federal Law on Child-Raising Allowance], July 12, 2001, BGB1. I at 3358.
94 The European Convention on Social Security was signed by the six member states of the European Coal and Steel Community on Dec. 9, 1957. The convention was however, never ratified.
95 *See* Joined Cases C-95/99-98/99; C-180/99, 2001 E.C.R. I-7413, Judgment of the Full Court at 39 paras. 50, 51 (Oct. 11 2001).
96 *Id.* Para. 58
97 *See* Joined Cases, Case C-95/99 Mervet Khalil, 2001 E.C.R. I-7413; Case C-98/99 Issa Chaaban, 2001 E.C.R. I-7413; Case C-97/99 Hassan Osseilli v. Bundesanstalt für Arbeit, 2001 E.C.R. I-7413; Case C-98/99 Mohamad Nasser v. Landeshauptstadt Stuttgart, 2001 E.C.R. I-7413; Case C-180/99 Meriem Addou v. Land Nordrhein-Westfalen, 2001 E.C.R. I-7413 (where among other cases, the Court referred to Case C-153/91,Camille Petit v. Office National des Pensions (ONP), 1992 E.C.R. I-4973).
98 *See* Joined Cases, Case C-95/99 Mervet Khalil, 2001 E.C.R. I-7413; Case C-98/99 Issa Chaaban, 2001 E.C.R. I-7413; Case C-97/99 Hassan Osseilli v. Bundesanstalt für Arbeit, 2001 E.C.R. I-7413; Case C-98/99 Mohamad Nasser v. Landeshauptstadt Stuttgart, 2001 E.C.R. I-7413; Case C-180/99 Meriem Addou v. Land Nordrhein-Westfalen, 2001 E.C.R. I-7413; Judgment para. 72.

IV. Proposal Split in Two

On the basis of the *Khalil* judgment, the Council resumed its discussions on the appropriate legal base for including non-Community nationals in Regulation 1408. Compared with previous considerations on the legal matter, its quick decision on the matter after *Khalil* stands out remarkably. At the Employment and Social Policy Council, December 3, 2001, the Council stated that in light of the *Khalil* judgment, article 42 did not appear to be the appropriate legal basis for extending Regulation 1408 to third-country nationals. At the same meeting, the Council instead agreed on the possibility of using article 63(4) as an alternative legal basis.[99] The case law decision had thus transformed a 12–15 majority in favour of the traditional legal basis of Regulation 1408/71 to a unanimous rejection of that same basis and an agreement on the new article 63(4).

Furthermore, at the same meeting the Council adopted a text subdividing proposal COM (1998) 779 into 12 parameters, each dealing with individual modernisation and simplification topics that had been mandated at the Stockholm European Council in March the same year.[100]

The second parameter dealt with the personal scope. It stated that the personal scope should be extended to all European nationals and pointed out that,

> The application of coordination to all insured *persons* also meets the need to adapt it [Regulation 1408/71] to the development of free movement within the Union, which has changed from a right in favour of *workers only to a right and a reality for all European citizens*.[101]

At the same time, the parameter on the personal scope concluded that the negotiations on third-country nationals should be carried out independently. Hereby the original proposal COM (1998) 779 had been split in two.

By its quick actions, the Commission seemed to have left out all doubts about article 63 as the correct Treaty base for the inclusion of third-country nationals. Only 2 months after the decisive Council meeting, the Commission presented its second separate proposal on third-country nationals, COM (2002) 59,[102] with the sole purpose of extending Regulation 1408 to cover non-community nationals as well. However, the argumentation in the explanatory memorandum had changed. The fact that the Commission viewed social protection as the other objective of Regulation 1408 had been omitted, and instead it was stressed that, in light of the Amsterdam Treaty and the recent case law of *Khalil*, the question of the Treaty basis had been re-examined with the conclusion that article 63(4) appeared to be the appropriate one.

By submitting to the new Treaty basis, the Commission clearly compromised its original intentions, which was to clarify a "muddied legal situation" for third-country nationals. As part of the Treaty's Title IV, the UK and Ireland had to 'opt in' to participate, whereas Denmark remained outside of the Community cooperation on visas, asylum and immigration policies. The proposal therefore accepted a continuation of "multiple protection levels" by allowing variable consent.

---

99 Proposal for a Regulation of the European Parliament and of the Council on the Coordination of Social Security Systems Extension of Regulation No, 1408/71 (EEC) to Third-Country Nationals, Council Conclusions on the Legal Basis, Council Doc. No. 15056/01 (Dec. 6, 2001).

100 Stockholm Presidency Conclusions of March 23–24, 2001 at § V, point 33 *available at* http://www.eu2001.se/static/pdf/conclusions/conclusions_eng.PDF

101 Proposal for a Regulation of the European Parliament and of the Council on the Coordination of Social Security Systems – Parameters for the Modernisation of Regulation No. 1408/71 (EEC), Council Doc. No. 15045/01 (Dec. 6, 2001) (emphasis added).

102 *Commission Proposal for a Council Regulation Extending the Provisions of Regulation 1408/71 (EEC Treaty) to Nationals of Third Countries who are not Already Covered by these Provisions Solely on the Ground of their Nationality*, COM (2002) 59 final (Feb. 6, 2002).

The threat of vast complexity with three member states not coordinating social security rights for third-country nationals was, however, reduced, when the United Kingdom and Ireland in May 2002 announced their 'opt in' on the adoption and application of proposal COM (2002) 59.[103] The UK, which had opposed the extension of Regulation 1408 to third-country nationals from the first proposal on, had finally changed its position.[104]

Even though the *Khalil* judgment apparently silenced all disagreements between member states and the Commission on the legal basis, the European Parliament did not immediately accept this sudden conciliation. In the Parliament's report on proposal COM (2002) 59, it noted that it fully supported the original proposal, which had now been "withdrawn by the Commission under pressure from the Council," and that it, "… is not convinced by the argument the Commission is now using, to the effect that it is compelled by the Khalil and others judgment (case C-95/99) to use a different legal basis."[105]

However, even though the proposal based on article 63(4) reduced the Parliament's competence from co-decision to mere consultation, the Parliament chose to behave pragmatically and allow the Council to "strike while the iron is hot." The Parliament reporter recommended that the proposal be accepted by the Parliament and thus prioritized political results over "legal hair-splitting." The Parliament should,

> not indulge in legal hair-splitting which might impede the rapid resolution of the matter at issue. Particularly since agreement now seems to have been reached in the Council on this proposal, the proverb 'strike while the iron is hot' seems to apply more than ever.[106]

Proposal COM (2002) 59 was finally adopted by the Council on May 15, 2003.[107] Having been on the agenda as far back as 1993, legally residing third-country nationals were finally included within the personal scope of Regulation 1408/71.

About one year after, and precisely two days before enlargement, the Council adopted Regulation 883/2004, which definitively extended the right to intra-European social security to all, "nationals of a Member State, stateless persons and refugees residing in a Member State who are or have been subject to the legislation of one or more Member States, as well as to the members of their families and to their survivors." The reformed Regulation confirms that European citizenship has a material and social dimension.

V. Negotiating the Borders of a Personal Scope

The process of extending social security across European borders has been shaped through judicial activism, the persistence of the Commission and through political reluctance and compromise. This extension to all European citizens marks a historical move from a privilege held only by market citizens to a right reflecting Union citizenship.

All the same, before generalizing Regulation 1408's personal scope to Community nationals, the Council adopted its extension to third-country nationals. At first sight, the adoption of Regulation 859/2003 seems to be a radical move towards a more egalitarian

---

103 Proposal for a Council Regulation Extending the Provisions of Regulation No. 1408/71 (EEC) to Nationals of Third Countries Who are not Already Covered by These Provisions Solely on the Ground of Their Nationality, Council Doc. No. 8482/02 (May 2, 2002).
104 *See* Roberts, *supra* note 57, for a detailed description of the traditional position of the UK.
105 Report from the European Parliament Committee on Employment and Social Affairs of 5 Nov. 2002, Eur. Parl. Doc. No. A5-0369 (Nov. 21, 2002).
106 *Id.*
107 *See* Council Regulation 859/2003 , 2003 O.J. (L 124) (EC Treaty) (extending provisions of Council Reg. 1408/71 (EEC Treaty); Council Reg. 574/72 (EEC Treaty) to nationals of third countries who are not already covered by those provisions solely on the ground of their nationality).

clarification of "who has a right to intra-European social security," disregarding a communitarian conception of welfare.

However, there are decisive objections, which mean that the adoption is not a straightforward application of equal treatment between Community and non-Community nationals. In fact, these objections mean that equal treatment of third-country nationals in cross border social security matters remains merely an idea rather than a fact of life.

Legally residing third-country nationals do not enjoy the right to free movement according to Community law. On the contrary, Regulation 859/2003 emphasizes that the application of Regulation 1408/71 does not give third-country nationals, "any entitlement to enter, to stay or to reside in a Member State or to have access to its labour market." Furthermore, the regulation sets out explicitly that Regulation 1408/71 is, "not applicable in a situation which is confined in all respects within a single Member State." Only the significantly reduced number of Non-Community nationals who, due to international law or bilateral agreements, move between member states will, therefore, be able to practice their newly granted rights. Thus the right to intra-European social security appears rather meaningless, since third-country nationals lack the underlying right of free movement.[108] That will, however, be partly changed when the member states finally implement the Directive granting a partial free movement for long-term residents from third countries.[109]

Furthermore, as noted by the European Parliament, it is not entirely clear how the *Khalil* judgment came to settle the dispute on the Treaty basis. In fact, the settlement of the matter appears to be based on the need to mask a pragmatic and rather dubious political choice by the neutrality of law. The *Khalil* judgment did not say that article 42 is inextricably bound to article 39 of the Treaty and thus to its nationality requirement. The answer to the second question, that Regulation 1408/71 cannot be invoked if no movement between member states has taken place, could be argued to simply be an affirmation of precedent and not a statement tying the Treaty's article 42 to the right to exercise free movement. The Court did not conclude Community nationality to be an absolute premise for inclusion in the personal scope of Regulation 1408/71 on the basis of the Treaty's article 42. On the contrary, it made a contextual analysis, referring to international law, and concluded that the context and political commitment at the time when Regulation No. 3 was formulated and adopted made it a natural choice to include refugees and stateless persons in Regulation 1408's personal scope. The question is whether a similar contextual argument, referring to the European Convention of Human Rights, the Charter of Fundamental Rights of the European Union and the Tampere conclusions, would not in the year 2003 be of sufficient validity to justify the inclusion of legally residing third-country nationals in the personal scope of Regulation 1408/71 on the basis of the Treaty's articles 42 and 308. However, in the end that seems to have depended on the existence of a contemporaneous political commitment.

E. Concluding Remarks

The personal scope of "who has the right to intra-European social security" has been under debate and negotiation for more than four decades. With worker *"stricto sensu"* as the point of departure for a generalized personal scope including the non-active European citizen as

---

108 S. Peers, *Joined Cases C-95/99 to 98/99, Mervett Khalil and others v. Bundesanstalt für Arbeit and Landeshauphtstadt Stuttgart and Case C-180/99, Meriem Addou v. Land Nordrhein-Westfalen, Judgment of the Full Court of 11 October 2001 [2001] E.C.R. I-7413*, 39 COMMON MKT. L. R. 1395 (2002).
109 Council Directive 2003/109, The Status of Third Country Nationals who are Long-Term Residents, 2004 O.J. (L 016) 44–53 (EC Treaty) (the date of transposition is set for Jan. 23, 2006).

well as legally residing third-country nationals, a specific integration story is depicted in which intra European rights are extended on the basis of flexible concepts and a dynamic perception of the Community's objectives and competences.

It is the interaction between the Court, the Commission and the Council, which moves the process. This study demonstrates that the inter-institutional relation modifies individual positions and preferences as time unfolds.

From the outset, the judicial activism of the Court amplified the meaning of 'employed persons' and interpreted the aim of the legal basis in the most extensive way. When the Council later brought in the self-employed, it merely codified what the Court, had already ruled, and the member states unanimously agreed that the aim of Regulation 1408 went even further than what could be based on the most extensive reading of the Treaty's article 51. The Treaty's article 235 (now article 308) became the additional legal basis to achieve new policy aims. The agenda-setting capacity of the Commission once more assured that the collective perception of aims and means did not stagnate. European citizenship became the next key concept, substantiating new need for reform and further energizing the process. Proposing the generalisation of the personal scope of Regulation 1408 to all European citizens was not a departure from established reasoning, since Community nationals enjoy the underlying right of free movement. That was, however, not the case with third-country nationals. By proposing that non-Community nationals be included in Regulation 1408's personal scope, the Commission attempted to introduce a path-breaking understanding of the regulatory aim, where the decisive factor was no longer to exercise the right of free movement but to be insured under a social security scheme. The full consequences of such a break remain speculative, but were hypothesized by the government of the United Kingdom and vetoed against this background. The intense dispute concerning the appropriate legal basis for including third-country nationals can be interpreted as both a Commission defeat and as an example of successful mediation. On the one hand, the Commission and the large majority of member states were finally forced to accept the Treaty's article 63(4) legal basis. The final choice of legal basis shows that under the unanimity rule, the minority prevails. On the other hand, the Commission managed by compromising its own and twelve member states' initial preferences to put an end to a long-lasting controversy and achieve the desired political result. In the end, such an outcome transcends a negotiating process characterized by political and legal reluctance. The practical effect of the political result depends on the future inter-institutional actions and reactions, and whether new and subtle steps of integration gradually grant free movement right to third-country nationals. For European citizens, on the other hand, intra European social security and free movement have been launched as integral parts of European citizenship – a conception which departed as a mere symbol without substantial meaning.

SECTION II:
FORUM: FREE MOVEMENTS IN THE EU

From Persons to Citizens and Beyond: The Evolution of Personal Free Movement in the European Union

Nigel Foster*

A. Introduction

The European Community's (EC) legal regime for the free movement of persons has developed considerably since the European Economic Community was founded in 1957. It is not just the original personal scope of the legislation that has been expanded, by both additional statutory law and judicial interpretation; the consequences for the Community and national legal regimes are also much greater than that which may have been anticipated by the Member States. They have learned that areas of law once thought to be entirely within the national legal jurisdiction and indeed, even protected by Community law Directives may now also be subject to Community law because the significance of the personal free movement legal regime as developed is being exposed, largely through the case law of the European Court of Justice (ECJ). Hence, the boundary between EC and national law has been changed in favour of EC law, and this change has been given even greater impetus recently by the ECJ's far reaching interpretations of the concept of European Citizenship, which when first introduced appeared to be rather toothless.[1]

In this article, I shall consider the original regime for the free movement of persons in order to outline the scope of the law at the start of the Community's life. Then I will consider how this has been developed and expanded both by new legislative provisions and by judicial interpretation, the latter however, restricted to a few decisions in which the ECJ has made its strongest and clearest marks. The introduction of general directives on free movement and the concept of European citizenship, which extended free movement rights beyond their original economic base, will be considered. It is at this stage that closer attention will be given to the ECJ's interpretation of these new provisions because of the further

---

* Professor of European Law, Buckingham Law School, Buckingham University. With thanks to my former colleague Dr. Jo Hunt for valuable comments on an earlier version and to Emily Cartwright, former Cardiff Law School research assistant for valuable assistance. This text was originally completed in January 2004, revised in January 2005, and proofed in January 2006.

1 Particularly because at first it was unclear as to whether Article 18 could have direct effects and thus be able to be pleaded as a directly enforceable Community law right before the national courts. See M. Everson, *The Legacy of the Market Citizen*, in NEW LEGAL DYNAMICS OF THE EUROPEAN UNION 73 (J. Shaw & G. More eds., 1995); or H.U. Jessurun D'Oliviera, *Union Citizenship: Pie in the Sky?*, in A CITIZEN'S EUROPE (A. Rosas & E. Antola eds., 1995).

consequences these cases have had for other rights within both the EC and national legal orders. Indeed, the development of the concept of citizenship and the rights it now conveys throws into sharp relief the rights or lack of them that other lawful inhabitants of the EU enjoy. In particular, the legal position and rights of Third Country Nationals[2] within the EC, both as family members of European Union (EU) workers/citizens and in their own right. The case law of the ECJ has also had an impact on the changing concept of the "wholly internal rule" (that is, a situation ostensibly not involving EC law). Additionally, I will consider how these expanded citizenship rights have already had an unexpected impact on areas of national law such as social and welfare law so that a kind of legal boundary-shifting may be taking place which goes beyond the strict legislative competences of the Community. However, it will be noted that new Directives to some extent have already confirmed existing case law and further legislative proposals are in the pipeline,[3] which would, if enacted, expressly take EC law, in some instances, in the very direction that has already been anticipated by the ECJ's case law and resolve some of these long lingering inequalities in the enjoyment of personal free movement rights by TCNs in the Community legal order.

B. The Original Legal Basis for the Free Movement of Persons

Any investigation as to the original regime must, of course, refer to the EEC Treaty as first enacted.[4] However, it is also useful to try to discover just what the founding fathers had in mind when first considering the free movement of persons because these original reasons and intentions are useful in determining whether the framework law to be provided was to be liberally or strictly applied.[5] Whilst it became clear after the first cases were decided that the ECJ was going to liberally interpret Treaty rights,[6] this fate does not seem predetermined by the language of the original Treaty Articles.[7] It is right, therefore, to pose the question of whether the free movement of persons was, as originally conceived, just a necessary appendage to the free movement of goods and capital in order to complete the

---

2 Hereinafter referred to as TCNs, although sometimes the term "Denizens" is used as an alternative, not however, so comprehensively or so clearly accepted as TCNs.
3 Council Directive 03/86 of 22 September 2003 on the right to family reunification (2003 O.J. (L 251/12)), Council Directive 04/38 on the rights of Citizens and their family members to move and reside within the Territory of the Member States (2004 O.J. (L158/77)), Council Directive 03/109 on the status of TCNs who are long term residents (2003 O.J. (L16/14)). There are in addition the proposals: The proposed Posting of TCNs abroad Commission Directive 00/43 271 final (2000 O.J. (C311/197)) but as of the beginning of 2005, this has not progressed any further. The proposed Entry and residence rights of TCNs Commission Directive 01/44 386 final (2001 O.J. (C332/248)) which has been subject to an EP opinion ((COM (2001) 386 – C5-0447/2001 – 2001/0154(CNS))) and is discussed at the end of this article. There is also Council Directive 04/114 of 13 December 2004 on the conditions of admission of third-country nationals for the purposes of studies, pupil exchange, unremunerated training or voluntary service. (2004 O.J. (L375/12)) but which enters into force only in 2007.
4 Treaty Establishing the European Economic Community, March 25, 1957, 298 UNTS 3 [hereinafter EEC Treaty].
5 See I. WARD, A CRITICAL INTRODUCTION TO EUROPEAN LAW 100–101 (2nd ed. 2003), and J. BENGOEXEA, THE LEGAL REASONING OF THE EUROPEAN COURT OF JUSTICE: TOWARDS A EUROPEAN JURISPRUDENCE (1993). See also American literature on original intent as an appropriate method for constitutional interpretation especially P. BOBBIT, CONSTITUTIONAL FATE: THEORY OF CONSTITUTION (1982); and the following papers: Dennis Patterson, *Symposium on Philip Bobbitt's Constitutional Interpretation: Wittgenstein and Constitutional Theory*, 72 TEX. L. REV. 1837 (1994), V. Kesavan & M. Stokes Paulsen, *The Interpretive Force of the Constitution's Secret Drafting History*, 91 GEO. L.J. 1113 (2003).
6 *See, e.g.*, the comments in J. STEINER & L. WOODS, TEXTBOOK ON EC LAW 543 (8th ed. 2003).
7 *See* WARD, *supra* note 5, 93–101; S. DOUGLAS-SCOTT, CONSTITUTIONAL LAW OF THE EUROPEAN UNION 207–224 (2002).

freedom of the factors of production for economic/capitalist development. In other words, whether the development of economic activities and the balanced expansion and accelerated raising of the standard of living referred to in the preamble of the Treaty would be realisable unless capital could also take advantage of freely moveable labour without border restrictions. It is well documented that the ideals for the Community were high,[8] as can be seen by looking at the original Treaty preambles.[9] However, these ideals did not indicate the extent of the rights of unrestricted movement that Community nationals were to enjoy. The legal regime as first laid down in the Treaty provided in Article 3 for "(c) the abolition, as between Member States, of obstacles to freedom of movement for persons, services and capital" as one of the activities in support of the general task set out in Article 2. Articles 48 to 66 (now 39 to 55) provided the broad rights to move to take up an economic activity either as a worker or a self-employed person and not to be discriminated against whilst doing so in comparison with nationals.[10]

---

8 See, inter alia, on this theme: J. & N. FOSTER, TEXT, CASES AND MATERIALS ON EUROPEAN UNION LAW 34 (4th ed. 2003); WARD, supra note 5, at 38; or P. CRAIG AND G. DE BURCA, EU LAW, TEXT, CASES AND MATERIALS 3 (3rd ed. 2003).

9 Article 2: The Community shall have as its task, by establishing a common Market and progressively approximating the economic policies of Member States, to promote throughout the Community a harmonious development of economic activities, a continuous and balanced expansion, an increase in stability, an accelerated raising of the standard of living and closer relations between the states belonging to it.

10 Article 48 (now 39) (1): "Freedom of movement for workers shall be secured within the Community by the end of the transitional period at the latest." This was planned to be 12 years after the entry into force of the treaty and hence the end of 1969, but which ended on June 30, 1968.

Art. 48 (now 39) (2) required the abolition of any discrimination based on nationality to secure the freedom of movement for nationals of the Member States. This was to apply particularly in respect of employment, remuneration and other conditions of work and employment.

Art. 48 (now 39) (3) described in broad outlines, the rights of workers but subjected those rights to the limitations on grounds of public policy, public security or public health. Later amplified in Council Directive 64/221, 1964 O.J. (L850/64) 117.

The rights as listed are:

(a) to accept offers of employment actually made;
(b) to move freely within the Territory of Member States for this purpose;
(c) to stay in the Member State for the purpose of employment in accordance with the provisions governing the employment of nationals of that State laid down by law, regulation of administrative action;
(d) to remain in the territory of a Member State after having been employed in that State, subject to conditions which shall be embodied in implementing regulations to be drawn up by the Commission.

These were finally produced in 1970, Council Regulation 1251/70, 1970 O.J. (L142/24) 402. Article 48 (now 39) (4) provided that "The provisions of this Article shall not apply to employment in the public service." Article 52 (now 43) set out that

> Within the framework of the provisions set out below, restrictions on the freedom of establishment of nationals of a Member State in the territory of another Member State shall be abolished by progressive stages in the course of the transitional period. Such progressive abolition shall also apply to the restrictions on the setting up of agencies, branches or subsidiaries by nationals of any Member State established in the territory of any Member State. Freedom of establishment shall include the right to take up and pursue activities as self-employed persons and to set up and manage undertakings, in particular companies or firms within the meaning of the second paragraph of Article 58.

Article 59 (now 49) states:

> Within the framework of the provisions set out below, restrictions on freedom to provide services within the Community shall be progressively abolished during the transitional period in respect of nationals of Member States who are established in a State of the Community other than that of the person for whom the services are intended.

Article 60 (now 50) states:

> Services shall be considered to be "services" within the meaning of this Treaty where they are normally provided for remuneration, in so far as they are not governed by the provisions relating to freedom

These articles have barely changed since 1957 with the exception of removing the references to the transitional period. Thus, free movement of persons as set out in the Treaty of 1957 should have been secured by 1968. However, as originally provided, the Treaty Articles were concerned only with the narrow rights of workers and other economically active nationals within the EEC. Free movement of persons was restricted to the pursuit of those engaged in an economic activity in another Member State and the rights were perceived as a form of support for the common market and economic progress in the Community,[11] a view that was also acknowledged by the Commission in its early documentation, albeit qualifying that view in the light of the way in which the rights were developed.[12] The economic link is also to be found in the second preamble to Regulation 1612/68,[13] which gave the following as one of the reasons for achieving the objectives of Article 48 and 49 (now 39 and 40): "the early establishment of the customs union."[14] Thus, whilst in support of the economic aims of the EC, rights were granted which provided free movement for economically active member state nationals.

The rules were designed to apply to those in the labour market who wished to move to another Member State and who first had been offered a contract of employment. In addition, the self-employed who also wished to move were protected.[15] These rights, however, were not taken up in large numbers by western Europeans residing in the original six Member States, with the exception of Italians moving to Germany, which, for the most part, involved short-term and not permanent relocation.[16] Hence, the view was quickly

> of movement for goods, capital and persons.
> "Services" shall in particular include:
> (a) activities of an industrial character;
> (b) activities of a commercial character;
> (c) activities of craftsmen;
> (d) activities of the professions.
> Without prejudice to the provision of the Chapter relating to the right of establishment, the person providing a service may, in order to do so, temporarily pursue his activity in the State where the service is provided, under the dame conditions as are imposed by that State on its own nationals.

11 "The founding Treaties do not purport to establish an absolute freedom of migration in a general sense. They confine themselves to the movement of persons as an economic factor of production of the commodities envisaged by each Treaty" (D. LASOK, THE LAW OF THE ECONOMY IN THE EUROPEAN COMMUNITIES 92 (1980)); "The EEC does not give the right of free movement to everyone, but only to certain categories of persons – workers, self-employed persons and providers of services. The absence of a general right of free movement, and the consequent categorization of the person who benefit from it, is one of the basic features of the Community law on this subject. ... If we just look at the EEC Treaty, especially if we concern ourselves only with the Treaty in its original form, the economic viewpoint predominates. ... One can conclude, therefore, that the authors of the EEC Treaty regarded the Community as predominantly an economic organisation" (GREEN ET AL., THE LEGAL FOUNDATIONS OF THE SINGLE EUROPEAN MARKET 92 (1991)); "The rules of the Treaty on freedom of movement deal with three aspects of life in the Community which all serve to make the Community more mobile and to put its manpower, trading and professional skills and its financial resources to more rational use for the benefit of the Community as a whole" (K. LIPSTEIN, THE LAW OF THE EUROPEAN ECONOMIC COMMUNITY 84 (1974)); "It should be clear however that the objective of free movement of workers is mainly economic and closely linked with free movement of goods, rather than social" (P.S.R.F. MATHIJSEN, A GUIDE TO EUROPEAN COMMUNITY LAW 49 (1972)).
12 "Even if initially the free movement of persons was mainly an economic matter, concerning only workers, the concept has gradually expanded to allow any citizen of the Union to move and stay freely within the Member States" *available at* http://europa.eu.int/comm/archives/abc/cit2_en.htm.
13 Council Regulation 1612/68 (1968 O.J. (L 257/2)).
14 *Id.*
15 As provided by Arts. 52 and 59 EEC Treaty (now Arts. 43 and 49).
16 Most employment migration was from outside of the EC Member states. *See, inter alia*, K. Foster, *The Free Movement of Workers, in* THE LAW OF THE COMMON MARKET 170, 179–180, (B.A. Wortley ed., 1974), "Some studies have been undertaken of the trend and pattern of migration within the Community. One study (Yannopoulos, 1969), based on the years 1958 to 1965 inclusive, reveals the following facts. The

formed that, regardless of the original intentions, free movement rights were not being used, as originally intended, as an instrument of encouraging economic progress but were really being used as individual social rights by member state nationals.[17] By the time the first legislative expansion of the rights had been carried out, the view was clearly that the rights had this dual purpose and effect.[18] That the original provisions did little to facilitate free movement of persons does not mean that the rights themselves were toothless. Perhaps the initial but continuing minimal impact of the rights on migration of labour can be attributed to a system of domestic preferences built into the regime. For example, until 1961, Member States could maintain a priority for national workers,[19] and then up to 1965, Member States needed only accept other Member State workers if no nationals had applied for the vacancy within three weeks.[20] After 1965, Member States could insist that potential host workers first notify employment authorities.[21] Finally, Member States could rely on escape clauses that allowed them to suspend Treaty provisions in favour of nationals where national or local interests required it.[22] Thus, in reality, it was not until the ECJ was able to give clear expression to the rights or until clarifying secondary legislation was enacted to complete the treaty promises that the rights themselves started to take on meaning. The regime as first conceived and executed was rather limited and was of limited attraction to workers.[23] It has to be acknowledged, however, that the new EC regime was better than the previous situation in which Member States rigorously controlled the right of aliens to enter the country and even more so where they were regarded as a threat to national employment interests.[24]

> number of work permits granted for the first time to foreign workers (intra-Community migration) rose from 156,000 in 1958 to 305,000 in 1965. In 1965 80 per cent of all permits issued in respect of intra-Community migration were for movement to West Germany. Italy was the main provider of migrant labour – between 1958 and 1965 the Italian percentage of total Community workers migrating ranged from 75 per cent to 83 per cent" (SWANN, THE ECONOMICS OF THE COMMON MARKET 148 (1981)).
>
> 17 "In a Recommendation and Opinion of July 1962, 1962 J.O. (2118), the Commission argued that this freedom was not concerned with traditional notions of emigration and immigration. These notions assumed that individuals migrated because they were unable to secure satisfactory living standards in their own countries. The Community, however, sought to ensure uniformly high living standards throughout its territory. The problems of depressed areas of high unemployment should be remedied through investments in those areas rather than though emigration. In effect capital should be moved to the unemployed rather than vice versa. ... Consequently, in the context of the Community the traditional motive for migration would cease to exist..." "Therefore, the freedom of movement in Community law represented a considerable expansion of personal freedom" (A. Evans, *European Citizenship*, 45 MOD. L. REV. 497, 499 (1982)).
> 18 "On the one hand, the free movement of manpower as a factor of production is essential to the undertaking which has to decide upon the location for a place of business which is most favourable from the economic viewpoint and upon the way in which the factor of production consisting of capital is utilized. On the other hand it offers economic and social advantages both to the worker and to the provider of services" (COMMISSION OF THE EUROPEAN COMMUNITIES, THIRTY YEARS OF COMMUNITY LAW 285 (1981)). D. WYATT & A. DASHWOOD, THE SUBSTANTIVE LAW OF THE EC 162 (1987), in the mid 1970s, noted "It is significant that the macroeconomic objectives of the Community are placed second to the personal rights of the Community worker to improve his standard of life by the exercise of rights by Art. 48 (now 39)."
> 19 The original Art. 49 (d) EEC Treaty.
> 20 Governed by Commission Regulation 15/61 (1961 J.O. (1073)).
> 21 Commission Regulation 38/64, 1964 J.O. (965).
> 22 For details of the transitional period, *see* K. Lewin, *The Free Movement of Workers*, 2 COMMON MKT. L. REV. 300 (1964), and H. ter Heide, *The Free Movement of Workers in the Final Phase*, 6 COMMON MKT. L. REV. 466 (1970).
> 23 The scope of basic rights of freedom of movement within the Community "is closely linked to the notion of labour as a factor of production in the liberalization designed to create a common market. Article 48 does not address the reality that such rights to cross borders will hardly be taken up unless migrants also enjoy associated rights ..." (S. WEATHERILL & P. BEAUMONT, EC LAW 485 (1993)).
> 24 *See further*, Lipstein, *supra* note 11, 84 and K. Lewin, *supra* note 22, in which the transition of completely free labour movement prior to the first world war to the hermetically sealed national borders of the inter wars years which virtually halted labour movement, is outlined.

Whilst these statutory developments were taking place, the ECJ began to play, and continues to play today, a significant role in determining the meaning of the rights provided in the Treaty. For example, the ECJ defined and expanded the concept of a "worker" in a manner that favoured a community interpretation over a series of judgments. This expansion applied the concept beyond those who were actually economically active, i.e. from those in full-time work or self employment, giving protection instead to those who were only active part-time, or who were looking for work or (in certain circumstances) were in training or full-time education.[25] Furthermore, the ECJ has interpreted the public service exception as allowing the Member States under Article 39 (4) very restrictively to exclude from the scope of the article many of the occupations claimed by the Member States as being part of the public service and, thus, excluded from the scope of the free movement provisions.[26]

Overall, the situation in respect of free movement of persons prior to 1968 was that the rights existed effectively on paper only. In any event, there was little demand for free movement within the original Member States with the exception of the labour migration from Italy to Germany. Confronted with this record, something more had to be provided to encourage free movement.

C. The Expansion of the Rights Under Secondary EC Legislation

The first legislative interventions were enacted both to facilitate the original rights provided and secondly to provide genuinely new rights, particularly when it came to members of the Member State national's family. The Commission itself has explained the evolution of the regime:

> The first steps towards the freedom of movement for workers were taken in 1961 and 1964, with the adoption of Council Regulations,[27] which were subsequently replaced by Council Regulation No 1612/68 of 15 October 1968 on freedom of movement for workers within the Community. This third regulation contained the definitive provisions for freedom of movement for workers and their families. It is stated in the recitals of the regulation that freedom of movement constitutes a fundamental right of workers and at the same time one of the means which helps to satisfy the requirements of the economies of the Member States and afford workers the opportunity to improve their living and working conditions, thus promoting upward social mobility.[28]

This legislation not only helped further define the basic Treaty rights but also added to them quite significantly. As noted by Stephen Weatherill and Paul Beaumont in 1993, it is

---

25 *See, inter alia*, Case 75/63, Hoekstra v. BBDA (aka Ungar v Bestuur) 1964 E.C.R. 177; Case 61/65 Vaassen-Goebbels, 1966 E.C.R. 377; Case 53/81, Levin v. The Minister of State for Justice, 1982 E.C.R. 1035; Case 139/85, Kempf v. Staats Secretaria van Justitie, 1986 E.C.R. 1741; Case 66/85, Lawrie-Blum v. Land Baden-Würtemberg, 1986 E.C.R. 2121; Case C-292/89, Antonissen, 1991 E.C.R. I-745; Case 39/86, Lair v. Universität Hannover, 1988 E.C.R. 3161; and Case C-357/89, VJM Raulin v. Netherlands Ministry of Education and Science, 1992 E.C.R. I-1027.
26 Case 152/73, Sotgui v Deutsche Bundespost, 1974 E.C.R. 153; Case 149/79, Commission v. Belgium, 1980 E.C.R. 3881; Case 307/84, Commission v. French Republic, 1986 E.C.R. 1734 (nurses); Case 66/85, Lawrie-Blum v. Land Baden-Würtemberg, 1986 E.C.R. 2121 (trainee secondary school teachers); Case C-4/91, Bleis v. Ministry of Education, 1991 E.C.R. I-5627 (secondary school teachers); Cases C-259/91 & C-331-2/91, Allue and Others v. University of Venice and Others, 1993 E.C.R. 1-4309 (foreign language lecturers).
27 Commission Regulation 15/61 (1961 J.O. (1073)) and Commission Regulation 38/64 (1964 J.O. (965)).
28 Freedom of movement for persons in the European Community – European Documentation. Periodical 3/1982 22.

only with the addition of associated rights to the basic rights of free movement that the basic rights themselves become more attractive.[29] And indeed, without the generous interpretation by the ECJ of the rights contained in the secondary legislation, those rights would, quite simply, be less extensive. Judicial interpretation has also served to support and considerably widen these rights by providing a narrow interpretation of what Member States can lawfully do under the exceptions and thus supporting the continued freedom of movement of persons as much as possible. One or two examples will be considered following a brief outline of the relevant provisions.[30]

The rights outlined in Article 39 (ex 48) of the Treaty were amplified and supplemented most importantly by three measures: Directive 64/221, Regulation 1612/68, and Directive 68/360.[31] In essence, these measures secured the freedom of movement for workers as originally perceived in the treaty. In particular, concern had been expressed about the rights of citizens to move and the Member States' ability to deny them entry under the grounds listed in Article 48 (now 39) (3).[32] Hence, amongst the measures introduced in the batch of secondary legislative provisions authorized by EC Treaty, Articles 49, 54 and 63 (now 40, 44 and 52), were closer definitions of what the Member States could do under the broad policy grounds of public policy, public security, and public health. Directive 64/221 details the exclusions and restrictions allowed the Member States on those grounds under Art. 39 (3). These grounds are also specifically repeated in the Directive 68/360 Art. 10, excusing Member States from the provisions of that directive. Directive 64/221 thus seeks to clarify the extent of the discretion given to the Member States under the Treaty. The scope of the Directive is given under Art. 2 (1) and includes all measures taken by the Member States to exclude EC nationals on the basis of public health, public policy, and public security. The latter two overlap to such an extent that they can be regarded in practice as a single category. Public health as a justification for exclusion is established by Directive 64/221, Art. 4(1) and the annex to the Directive[33] and is relatively straightforward.

Article 2 (2) provides that an exception to the principle of free movement cannot be invoked to serve economic ends, in other words to offset localized or even national difficulties in specific industries or areas of the country.

---

29 "Article 48 does not address the reality that such rights to cross borders will hardly be taken up unless migrants also enjoy associated rights…" (STEPHEN WEATHERHILL & PAUL BEAUMONT, EC LAW 485 (1993)).

30 This case law has now been summarized in a Commission Communication on Directive 64/221 (COM (1999) 372).

31 Council Directives 64/221 (1964 O.J. (L850/64) 117); Council Directive 68/360 (1968 O.J. (L257/13) 485); and Council Regulation 1612/68 (1968 O.J. (L257/2) 475). But see also Council Directive 73/148 (1973 O.J. (L172/14)); Council Directive 75/34 (1975 O.J. (L14/10)); and Council Regulation 1251/70 (1970 O.J. (L142/24) 402) now replaced by Directive 2004/38, 2004 O.J. (L158/77).

32 See F. Wooldridge, *Free Movement of EEC Nationals: The Limitation based on Public Policy and Public Security*, 2 EUR. L REV. 190 (1977); E. Guild, *Security of Residence and Expulsion of Foreigners: European Community Law*, in SECURITY OF RESIDENCE AND EXPULSION: PROTECTION OF ALIENS IN EUROPE 68 (Guild and Minderhoud eds. 2000).

33 Annex to Commission Directive 64/221
A. Diseases which might endanger public health:
1. Diseases subject to quarantine listed in International Health Regulation No. 2 of the World Health Organisation of 25 May 1951;
2. Tuberculosis of the respiratory system in an active state or showing a tendency to develop;
3. Syphilis;
4. Other infectious diseases or contagious parasitic diseases if they are the subject of provisions for the protection of nationals of the host country.
B. Diseases and disabilities which might threaten public policy or public security:
1. Drug addiction;
2. Profound mental disturbance; manifest conditions of psychotic disturbance with agitation, delirium, hallucinations or confusion.

Article 3 (1) provides that measures adopted on public policy or security must be based on personal conduct. In the case of *Bonsignore*,[34] an Italian national faced deportation as a general preventative measure after conviction for accidentally but fatally shooting his brother in a firearms accident. The ECJ held

> that measures adopted on grounds of public policy and for the maintenance of public security against the nationals of Member States of the Community cannot be justified on grounds extraneous to the individual case, ... that "only" the "personal conduct" of those affected by the measures is to be regarded as determinative. As departures from the rules concerning the free movement of persons constitute exceptions which must be strictly construed, the concept of "personal conduct" expresses the requirement that a deportation order may only be made for breaches of the peace and public security which might be committed by the individual affected.[35]

In *Adoui and Cornaille*,[36] French prostitutes facing expulsion from Belgium on public policy grounds could not be denied residence on the basis of their personal conduct when similar conduct on the part of nationals did not attract similar repressive measures to combat such behaviour.

Article 3 (2) provides that previous criminal convictions shall not of themselves constitute grounds for expulsion. The *Bouchereau* case[37] had held that public policy measures could only be invoked where conduct and criminal convictions were a genuine and sufficiently serious threat affecting one of the fundamental interests of society. In the case of *Donatella Calfa*,[38] a Greek rule of automatic life expulsion from Greek Territory was applied following conviction of certain offences. As an exemption, the ECJ held that it must be interpreted restrictively and where a person has been convicted, expulsion could only be based on personal conduct outside of the conviction itself but in any event, a life ban was disproportionate.[39]

Article 3 (3) provides that the expiry of an ID or a passport is no justification for expulsion and a series of cases have made it clear that failures in obtaining or renewing the appropriate paperwork required by national authorities constitute no valid grounds to support expulsion or the adoption of excessively restrictive measures against those taking advantage of free movement such that the measures would have the effect of discouraging free movement or making it unattractive.[40] Such considerations also overlap with failures to comply with the paperwork regime allowed under Directive 68/360, which will be discussed below.

Directive 64/221 has also provided a number of procedural rights which further support free movement by providing for non-discriminatory rights of appeal, rights to remain to hear the appeal result, to be given reasons for deportation and judicial review of decisions.[41]

---

34 Case 67/74, Bonsignore v. Oberstadtdirektor of the City of Cologne, 1975 E.C.R. 297.
35 *Id.* at 488, para. 6.
36 Cases 115-116/81, Adoui and Cornauille v Belgian State, 1982 E.C.R. 1665.
37 Case 30/77, R v. Bouchereau, 1977 E.C.R. 1999.
38 Case C-348/96, Donatella Calfa, 1999 E.C.R. I-111.
39 *Id.*, paras. 27–28.
40 *See, inter alia,* Case 159/79, R v. Pieck, 1980 E.C.R. 2171; Case C-344/95, Commission v. Belgium, 1997 E.C.R. I-1035; Case 118/75, Italy v. Watson and Belmann, 1976 E.C.R. 1185.
41 *See, inter alia,* Cases 115–116/81, Adoui and Cornaille v. Belgian State, 1982 E.C.R. 1665; Case C-175/94, Gallagher, 1995 E.C.R. I-4253; Case 98/79, Pecastcaing v. Belgium, 1980 E.C.R. 691. Note that Commission Directive 64/221 will be has been replaced by Council Directive 04/38, considered below, which must be transposed by Member States by April 30, 2006. Article 25 of the Directive will replace the provisions of Directive 64/221 concerned with the public policy, public security or public health grounds for refusal of entry or deportation and consolidates both the previous statutory law and the case law of the ECJ. Article 25 (2) requires that measures taken on grounds of public policy or public security shall

Directive 68/360 provides for workers to leave one Member State and enter the territory of another and prescribes the entry formalities a Member States may impose, in particular, the rules regarding the issue and withdrawal of residence permits. It applies to workers only and not to the self employed for whom Directive 73/148 applies. Cases arising under the Directive have also sought to eradicate unnecessary restrictions on free movement.[42] This directive opened the way for workers to enter a country to seek work without having pre-arranged employment and with it a Community myth arose that the period that was sanctioned within the minutes of the Directive was a maximum period of three months because this was the period during which newly unemployed EC nationals could claim unemployment benefits whilst seeking work under Regulation 1408/71.[43] The belief in the three-month period was later de-bunked by the ECJ in the *Antonisson* case,[44] which urged six months as the minimum period under Community law during which a person could remain in the Member State to look for work. Notably, the ECJ based this right on the Treaty itself and not Directive 68/360.[45]

Of all of the examples of the earlier legislation, Regulation 1612/68 has certainly proved to be the most supportive of free movement, particularly in the way that Article 7 of the Regulation has been interpreted by the ECJ. The Regulation details access to employment and rights for workers and more importantly, as far as an extension of the rights is concerned, introduced the rights of free movement for members of the workers' family.[46]

Articles 1 and 2 provide the right of nationals of Member States to take up an activity of an employed person in another Member State under the same rules as a national, that is,

---

comply with the principle of proportionality and shall be based exclusively on the personal conduct of the individual concerned. This provision repeats that previous criminal convictions shall not, in themselves, constitute grounds for taking such measures. It further provides that the personal conduct of the individual concerned must represent a "genuine, present and sufficiently serious threat affecting one of the fundamental interests of society" which was a phrase taken form the case law, noted above. Justifications that are isolated from the particulars of the case or that rely on considerations of general prevention shall not be accepted. Personal conduct may not be considered a sufficiently serious threat unless the Member State concerned takes serious enforcement measures against the same conduct on the part of its own nationals. Furthermore, in Article 26 the Member States are now required to take a number of factors into consideration, including how long the individuals concerned have resided within its territory, their age, state of health, family and economic situation, and social and cultural integration into the host Member State, and the extent of the links with their country of origin, before taking the decision to remove an EU citizen or a member of his or her family. Removal decisions cannot be taken against Union citizens or family members, irrespective of nationality, who have the right of permanent residence within its territory or against family members who are minors.

42 *See, inter alia*, Case 48/75, Procureur du Roi v. Royer, 1976 E.C.R. 497; Case 118/75, Watson & Belmann, 1976 E.C.R. 1185; Case 157/79, R v. Pieck, 1980 E.C.R. 2171; Case C-265/88, Messner, 1989 E.C.R. 4209; Case C-344/95, Commission v. Belgium, 1997 E.C.R. I-1035; Case C-459/99, Mouvement contre le racisme, l'antisémitisme et la xénophobie ASBL (MRAX) v. Belgian State, 2002 E.C.R. I-6591.
43 Art. 69, 1971 O.J. (L 149)
44 Case C-292/89, Antonissen, 1991 E.C.R. I-745.
45 Notably, this has been revised in that there will be a three month condition free period when the new Council Directive 04/38 comes into force. *See* Art. 6 (1) (2004 O.J. (L158/77)). The period, though may be extended beyond three months where the Union Citizen has sufficient resources for themselves and their family members so as not to become a burden on the social assistance system of the host Member State. The six month job search period following involuntary unemployment is now confirmed in Article 7 which expressly states that the status of worker is retained during this period. On a general note, although the new Directive, which replaces previous legislation, formally only comes into force on April 30, 2006, the existing law, much of which is case law, remains in force until that date.
46 Rights, supposedly taken for granted in respect of the original Treaty Articles, although not express prior to Council Regulation 1612/68. *See* K. Foster, *The Free Movement of Workers, in* THE LAW OF THE COMMON MARKET 170, 172 (B.A. Wortley ed., 1974).

without discrimination. Article 5 of the Regulation obliges Member States to give the same assistance to other EC nationals as their own when seeking employment.

Whilst economically active persons received confirmation that their rights extended to matters such as tax and social advantages, vocational training, trade union membership and housing rights and benefits,[47] the most significant provision introduced by the first expansion of the rights was in respect of the members of the family of the EC worker or self-employed person desiring to move. This was made even more significant by the fact that these additional rights (of free movement, to take up employment or to take up education or vocational training) applied also to non-EC members of the EC worker's[48] family, that is, to TCNs.

Regulation 1612/68, Art. 7 (1) reflects Art. 12 of the EC treaty and prohibits discrimination against workers on the grounds of nationality, but specifically mentions terms and conditions of employment, dismissal and, where relevant, reinstatement. Regulation 1612/68, Art. 7 (2), is a provision with extremely wide scope. It refers specifically to equality in social and tax advantages, which also apply to the family of workers and has received close attention from the ECJ.

Article 10 extends the above rights to a spouse and descendants and ascendants. The descendants can be any nationality and includes those under 21 and adult children over 21 where they are dependent on the worker.[49]

Article 11 entitles the spouse and children of an entitled worker to take up any activity as an employed person and Article 12 provides that the children of a national of a Member State shall be admitted to the general educational, apprenticeship and vocational training courses under the same conditions as nationals.

The secondary legislation, particularly as interpreted by the ECJ, provided valuable support rights for those wishing to work in another Member State, making possible the realization of the bare rights contained in the Treaty Articles. Before some of this case law is reviewed, I will consider here the new directive which consolidates much of the aforesaid provisions.

D. The Contributions of the ECJ

It has been noted, in an examination of one of the many reports that had been sanctioned in the 1950s and 1960s to see how the Communities could be developed further, that the

> Spaak Report described workers as one of the economic factors of production for which mobility was necessary in order to achieve an integrated economy. ... It becomes apparent, however, that although the primary objectives of the Treaty are economic, the general approach of the ECJ in interpreting the relevant provisions has been to endow them with a human rather than a purely functional economic aspect.[50]

---

47 Council Regulation 1612/68, Arts. 7–9 (1968 O.J. (L 257)).
48 From now on the term worker will also include the term "and self employed person", as the secondary legislation, even where not applying expressly to the self employed has nevertheless been applied without distinction to workers and self-employed by the ECJ, *see*, *e.g.*, Case 63/86 Commission v. Italy (social housing), 1989 E.C.R. 1461. The term person cannot yet be used as this right to move just as a person rather than an economically active person was not yet established.
49 Council Regulation 1612/68, Art. 10 (1968 O.J. (L 257)). "1. The following shall, irrespective of their nationality, have the right to install themselves with a worker who is a national of one Member State and who is employed in the territory of another Member State:
   (a) his spouse and their descendants who are under the age of 21 years or are dependants;
   (b) dependent relatives in the ascending line of the worker and his spouse."
50 INSTITUTIONS AND POLICIES OF THE EUROPEAN COMMUNITY 110 (J. Lodge ed., 1983).

Thus, it was not just the new legislation that moved matters along, but that this legislative expansion was accompanied and complemented by significant judgments of the ECJ that declared the sometimes surprisingly extensive scope of the legislation. A few examples of this line of jurisprudence are discussed here.

In *Fiorini a.k.a. Christini v SNCF*,[51] a reduced fare entitlement was claimed by the widow of an Italian SNCF worker. Widows of French workers were allowed such a family entitlement but it was denied to the Italian. The SNCF claimed that since it was not express in the contract of employment, it was not available to foreign workers. The ECJ was asked if this was the kind of "social advantage" protected by Art. 7 and it held that Art. 7 applies to all advantages, not just those limited to the terms of an employment contract. It therefore applies to the family of an EC worker in the same way as the right would apply to nationals.

In *O.N.E. v Deak*,[52] an unemployed Hungarian national living with his mother, an Italian national working in Belgium, was refused special unemployment benefits for non-nationals on the basis that no agreement for such benefits existed between Belgium and Hungary. The ECJ held that special unemployment benefits were a "social advantage" within the meaning of Art. 7 and that Deak, regardless of nationality, could derive rights as the descendant of a worker. The ECJ reasoned that, otherwise, a worker might be hindered from moving because of the financial difficulties that might result from the discrimination to which his or her descendants might be subject.

In *Castelli v ONPTS*,[53] the Italian mother of a retired Italian worker in Belgium claimed an old age pension. Mrs. Castelli herself had never worked in Belgium; therefore her claim was based on her status as a member of her son's family. The Belgian authorities refused to pay on the grounds that she was not Belgian and they did not have a reciprocal agreement with Italy. The ECJ held Mrs. Castelli was entitled to install herself with her son under Art. 10 of Regulation 1612/68. She was also entitled to remain after her son's retirement and had a right to the pension under Art. 7.

In *Mutsch*,[54] a Luxembourg national living in a German speaking commune in Belgium was denied the use of the German language before a court, a right granted to the Belgium German minority. The ECJ held that right was a "social advantage" under Article 7 (2) despite there being no link to a contract of employment.

Article 7 (2) has even been interpreted to include a grant to cover funeral expenses in the case of *O'Flynn*.[55]

Article 7 of the Regulation has thus been revealed by the ECJ to have a very wide scope. It is, of course, debatable whether these social advantages do in fact figure highly in a worker's original decision to move to another Member State to take up or find work. This debate should bear in mind the facts of these cases, that is, the dependents who received protection have mostly followed an initial migrant. The ECJ, however, seems not to be taking any chances that the ability of the dependants to receive various rights in the form of social assistance is a significant factor in the decision of the worker to move in the first place.

In a judgment concerned with Articles 7 and 10 of the Regulation, the ECJ was required to consider whether the term "spouse" included the co-habiting partner in *Netherlands v Reed*.[56] Ms. Reed applied for a residence permit in Holland claiming her right to remain was

---

51 Case 32/75, Fiorini a.k.a. Christini v. S.N.C.F., 1975 E.C.R. 1085.
52 Case 94/84, O.N.E. v. Deak, 1985 E.C.R. 1873.
53 Case 261/83, Castelli v. O.N.P.T.S., 1984 E.C.R. 3199.
54 Case 137/84, 1985 E.C.R. 2681.
55 Case C-237/94, 1996 E.C.R. I-2617.
56 Case 59/85, The Netherlands v. Reed, 1986 E.C.R. 1283.

based on her co-habitation with a UK national working in the Netherlands. The Dutch Government refused to recognize this. The ECJ was aware that provisions of national laws regarding the legal rights of co-habiting partners could be quite varied. It was unable to overcome the clear intention of Art. 10, which referred to a "relationship based on marriage."[57] The ECJ instead invoked the "social advantages" guaranteed under Art. 7 of the Regulation and concluded that they include the companionship of a co-habiting partner, which could contribute to integration in the host country. Where such relationships amongst nationals were accorded legal advantages under national law, these could not be denied to nationals of other Member States without being discriminatory and thus breaching Arts. 7 & 48 (now 12 and 39) of the Treaty. This is a somewhat convoluted decision but it did support free movement in the case at hand. The co-habiting partner is not protected in his or her own right, but the companionship he or she provides is recognized as one of the advantages to which workers are entitled.[58]

The right to take up any activity under Art. 11 has also been interpreted widely and has been interpreted to include *any* activity or profession, providing the appropriate qualifications and formalities are observed.[59]

The rights of a spouse are not dependent on residence with the protected worker. In *Diatta v Land Berlin*,[60] Mrs. Diatta, a Senegalese citizen, was married to a Frenchman living and working in Berlin. She obtained work in Berlin but shortly thereafter the couple separated. Upon application to extend her residence permit, the German authorities refused on the ground that she was no longer "a member of the family" for the purposes of Regulation 1612/68. The ECJ ruled that the rights under 1612/68 were not contingent on how or where members of the family lived. Therefore a permanent common family dwelling cannot be implied as a condition of the rights granted under Regulation 1612/68. Article 11, which entitles the spouse and children of an entitled worker to take up any activity as an employed person, was also affirmed in the case of *Diatta v Land Berlin* in favour of Mrs. Diatta.[61]

In the case of *Gaal*,[62] the ECJ extended the right under Article 12 to a migrant worker's independent child who was over the age of 21. Gaal was the Belgian son of a Belgium national who had worked in Germany but who had since died. Gaal was attending university and applied for a grant to undertake an eight-month period of study in the UK, which was refused on the grounds that he was over 21 and was not dependant and therefore no longer eligible for protection as a descendant of an EC worker. The ECJ held that Gaal still fell within the personal scope of Article 12 of the Regulation because the definition of a child was not subject to the same definition applied to that concept in Articles 10 and 11. Article 12, the ECJ explained, extends to all forms of education including university

---

57 Council Regulation 1612/68, Art. 10 (1968 O.J. (L 257)), "1. The following shall, irrespective of their nationality, have the right to install themselves with a worker who is a national of one of the Member State and who is employed in the territory of another Member State: (a) his spouse ..." (O.J. Sp. Ed. 1968 (L272/2) 475).

58 Hence then, the case merely supports the well established right in EC law not to be discriminated on the grounds of nationality. Of course, in some countries co-habitees are not afforded the same rights as married couples. The reasoning of the Court has been carried over into Article 2 (2) (b) of the new Council Directive 04/38 in respect of same sex partner rights. Where national law supports this, EC law will demand that other Community nationals are equally treated and where national law does not support such right, EC law cannot impose them on Member States. *See* text at notes 68 below.

59 *See, e.g.,* Case 131/85, Emir Gül v. Regierungspräsident Düsseldorf, 1989 E.C.R. 1363 (especially at paras. 2–5 in which the ECJ held that this right includes the right of workers' spouses to access to employment also under the same conditions as nationals of the host state).

60 Case 267/83, Diatta v. Land Berlin, 1985 E.C.R. 567.

61 *Id.*, at 167.

62 Case 7/94, Gaal, 1995 E.C.R. I-1031.

education and must include older children no longer dependant on their parents. The case was, however, decided on the basis that the child must have lived at some time with the protected parent whilst the parent was an EC worker; this factual matrix provided the nexus appropriate for Art. 12 protection.

Free movement for the self-employed was facilitated painfully slowly by the enactment of a number of sectoral directives,[63] until the slow progress in this direction was highlighted by judicial pronouncements from the ECJ.[64] These decisions enabled the Court to promote the rights to establish and provide services in a host state without discrimination or the imposition of unnecessary requirements and without having to wait for the enactment of directives for each and every profession. Instead, general directives were enacted applicable over a range of professions[65] to make movement easier to realize.

The earlier legislation and the significant and extensive interpretations of it by the ECJ did a great deal to eliminate most of the restrictions and disincentives for economically active nationals of EC Member States and members of their family to move freely to another Member State. This considerably advanced the original provisions and aims of the EC Treaty. Much of this case law was recognized and incorporated into a consolidating Directive of most of this earlier legislation, which although postdating a number of other developments in Community law, will be dealt with next as it concerns the same rights just considered.

E. The New Directive 2004/38

The new Directive 2004/38[66] has replaced most of the existing directives and parts of Regulation 1612/68 on the free movement of persons and brings together the rules concerning the right of citizens of the Union and their family members to move and reside freely within the territory of the Member States. It also reflects the case law developments which have taken place. The Directive enters into force on April 30, 2006 and will cover both workers and the self-employed. The directive both clarifies and extends the definition of who should be regarded a member of the family or a person otherwise provided with rights derived from an economically active EU citizen, in order to permit that person to establish permanent rights of residence after a certain period.[67] The Directive also tightens the definition of the circumstances whereby the Member States can refuse entry or deport persons on the grounds of public policy and public security.

---

63 Mathijsen notes that "Since 1963 (to 1972) 39 directives concerning the freedom of establishment and freedom to supply services were adopted by the Council" *Id.*, at 54.
64 Case 2/74, Reyners v. Belgian State, 1974 E.C.R. 631 (establishment). The Court of Justice held that the prohibition of discrimination under Art. 52 (now 43) was directly effective and declared that nationality could be no barrier to appropriately qualified lawyers entering a country to practise. The Directives were simply to facilitate free movement and not to establish it, which had already been done by the Treaty by end of the initial transition period of the Communities (1969). The ECJ decided similarly for the provision of services in Case 33/74, Van Binsbergen, 1974 E.C.R. 1299.
65 Council Directive 89/48 The Mutual Recognition of Diplomas (1989 O.J. (L19/16)); Council Directive 92/51 The second Directive on Mutual Recognition (1992 O.J. (L209/29)); and more recently Council Directive 1999/42 of the European Parliament and of the Council of 7 June 1999 establishing a mechanism for the recognition of qualifications in respect of the professional activities covered by the Directives on liberalisation and transitional measures and supplementing the general systems for the recognition of qualifications (1999 O.J. (L201/77)).
66 Council Directive 04/38 on the rights of Citizens and their family members to move and reside within the Territory of the Member States (2004 O.J. (L158/77) 11).
67 The Directive therefore also concerns the rights of TCN family members and will also be referred to in the section J below which discusses the rights foundation of TCNs in Community law.

Article 2 of the Directive provides that as well as including spouses as before, the status of partners will be equated with that of spouses in those Member States which recognize such a registered or attestable stable relationship.[68] Article 2 (c) considerably widens the definition of the family in providing that members of the family include the direct descendants and ascendants of the spouse as well as a partner. It should be noted, however, that some of the amendments proposed by the European Parliament with regards to providing the same residence rights for same sex partners were not taken up by the Commission, which felt that it could not make a proposal that would require some Member States to make amendments to national family law, an area which does not fall within the Community's legislative jurisdiction.[69]

Article 3 provides rights of entry and residence for any other family members not within the definitions in Article 2 who, in the country from which they have come, are dependent or are of the household of the Union citizen having the primary right of residence. This broader category is also open where there are serious health or humanitarian issues to consider requiring the personal care by the Union citizen.

The right to enter, travel and reside in a host Member State for a period of up to six months by an EU citizen and his or her family is not restricted to the economically active but is open to any EU citizen without any other conditions, other than the requirement of a valid identity and/or visa document.[70] The financial self-sufficiency requirements in the general free movement directives are not applied during the initial three-month period, but the right to reside for a period of more than three months is made conditional on: being engaged in a gainful activity, being self-employed, or self-sufficiency coupled with comprehensive health insurance coverage. Temporary unemployment does not remove the employed or self-employed status.[71] Whilst the period is not specified, previous case law[72] and Article 7 (3) (d) provides that six months would be the limit after which the favoured status would then be lost. Whether the host Member State would then be entitled to deport the citizen concerned is doubtful in view of the case law under citizenship that will be considered below and in the light of the more restrictive grounds for deportation outlined in Articles 27–28 of the Directive.

With the aim of preserving the rights of family members who acquire them, Article 12 provides that the Union citizen's death or departure from the host Member State shall not affect the right of residence of his or her family members who are nationals of a Member State. In a similar vein, Article 13 provides that divorce, annulment of marriage, or termination of the partnership or relationship referred to in point 2(b) of Article 2 shall

---

68　This proposal is therefore in line with the case law of the ECJ in the *Reed* cases considered at note 56 below.
69　*See* for some of the background discussion on this and other points, Second report from the Commission on citizenship of the Union COM (1997) 0230 final, Communication from the Commission to the European Parliament and the Council on the Follow-Up to the Recommendations of the High-Level Panel of the Free-Movement of Persons, COM (1998) 0403 and in particular, the amended proposal COM (2003) 0199 at section 3.2 which discusses the amendments proposed by the European Parliament and the responses of the European Commission. In respect of EU family policies or the previous lack of them *see*, *inter alia*, E. Caracciolo di Torella & A. Masselot, *Under construction: EU family law*, 29 EUR. L. REV. 32–51 (2004); N. Lowe, *The growing influence of the European Union on international family law – a view from the boundary*, 56 CURRENT LEGAL PROBLEMS (2003) 439–480, N. Foster, *Family and welfare rights in Europe: the impact of recent European Court of Justice decisions in the area of the free movement of persons*, 25 J. OF SOC. WELFARE AND FAMILY L. 291–303 (2003), C. McGlynn, *A Family Law for the European Union*, in SOCIAL LAW AND POLICY IN THE EUROPEAN UNION (J. Shaw ed. 2000); C. McGlynn, *Families and the European Charter of Fundamental Rights: Progressive Change of Entrenching the Status Quo?* 26 EUR. L. REV. 582 (2001).
70　*See* Council Directive 04/38 on the rights of Citizens and their family members to move and reside within the Territory of the Member States, Art. 5–6 (2004 O.J. (L158/77).
71　*Id.*, Article 7.
72　Antonissen, *see*, *supra* notes 44 and 217.

not affect the right of residence of a Union citizen's family members regardless of country of origin. Non-Union nationals are, however, subject to the requirement that the marriage or partnership had lasted at least two years, with one of those years spent in the host state, or where the spouse or partner has custody of family children, or where an exception is warranted by particularly difficult circumstances.[73]

As is so often the case in Community law making, the Directive is based on both a general concern for the revision of the law and on the case law of the ECJ, which has often advanced the law ahead of formal legislative change.[74] Legislation then plays catch-up with the judge-made law and it can be observed that once a new proposal is published, further cases are decided, often along the lines of the proposed new law, as seems to be the position with the cases considered in the sections following. Some of the Articles discussed have, to some extent, already been achieved by that case law.[75] However, the extent to which the ECJ reacts to the writing on the wall in advance of legislative enactments in order to reach its conclusions in cases is not measured here.[76] It certainly seems to be the case, however, that the leap-frogging of legislative proposals, case law, legislation and case law again, is a positive dynamic in the development of EC law and thus individual citizenship, family and welfare rights.

In recognition and support of the view that those who work in a country and their family acquire more than just a temporary right to remain in the country whilst that work or economic activity continues, Article 16 provides that Union citizens who have resided legally for a continuous period of five years in the host Member State shall have the right of permanent residence there and that continuity of residence shall not be affected by temporary absences not exceeding a total of six months during a year or by longer absences not exceeding twelve months necessitated by important reasons such as compulsory military service, serious illness, pregnancy and childbirth, study or vocational training, or a work assignment in another Member State or a third country. Paragraph 1 shall apply also to family members who are not nationals of a Member State and have resided with the Union citizen in the host Member State for five years.

The new consolidating Directive will certainly clarify the law in this area and supplement the existing rights. Whilst the right of permanent residence appears new, in reality it merely reflects the existing situation for many union citizens and families who have chosen to live in another Member State but who previously could have obtained this right under the rules of national law only.

The next development to be considered is the provision of rights of free movement that were not based on the economic activity of an EC national.

F. The General Free Movement Directives

The next extension to personal free movement rights was facilitated by the enactment of three general free movement Directives,[77] which provided rights of residence as a right for

---

73 This reflects the positions reached by the ECJ in cases such as Baumbast and Akrich, considered below at notes 108 and 145.
74 *See generally* DOUGLAS-SCOTT, *supra* note 7, at 207–224.
75 In particular those concerned with the meaning of citizenship and family and welfare law rights. *See id.*, especially at p. 215
76 T. Tridimas, *The Court of Justice and Judicial Activism*, 22 EUR. L. REV. 199 (1997); U. Everling, *The ECJ as a Decision Making Authority*, 82 MICH. L. REV. 1294 (1994).
77 Council Directive 90/364 (1990 O.J. (L180/26)); Council Directive 90/365 (1990 O.J. (L180/28)); and Council Directive 93/96 (1993 O.J. (L317/59)).

nationals of the Member States and their families to reside in a host Member State regardless of economic activity. The first Directive, applied in respect of any persons who could support themselves whilst in the host state, has been termed the "playboy Directive" to suggest that only the financially self-sufficient would be able to take advantage of it. Under Directive 90/364, Member States are required to grant the right of residence to nationals of Member States who do not otherwise qualify for this right under other provisions of Community law, and to members of their families. This general grant of residence can be limited only by the requirements that the non-national and the members of his or her family demonstrate that they are covered by health insurance in respect of all risks arising in the host Member State and that the non-national demonstrates sufficient resources to avoid becoming a burden on the social security system of the host Member State during their period of residence (Art. 1).

In a similar manner, Directive 90/365 grants the right of residence to employees and self-employed persons who have ceased their occupational activity. Directive 93/96 provides similar rights for students to attend an educational establishment to get vocational training.

These Directives provide residual rights in that they need only be relied on by persons wishing to move to another country if they are unable to obtain a right to move and reside in the host state in any other way, that is, through derived rights as a member of the family of a worker who has moved to the host state or through retirement after a period of work in the host state. The provisions of Directive 64/221 also apply to persons taking advantage of these Directives.

The three Directives seemed to have little impact in providing a general right of free movement for all and, as formulated, do not provide an unconditional right to move and reside in another Member State. Furthermore, there have only been a few cases in which these Directives have been considered and these have added nothing of any fundamental importance to the rights provided. Some of these cases simultaneously considered the citizenship provisions thus shifting the focus of attention away from the provisions of the Directives themselves.[78] In the case law, the ECJ has confirmed that Member States may ask for evidence of self-sufficiency but cannot dictate the nature and content of that evidence.[79] And, whilst Article 4 appears to limit the right to remain whilst the conditions of Article 1 continue to be fulfilled, in *Grzelczyk*[80] the ECJ held that it may be possible to make a claim on the social funds of a Member State provided that the burden on the state is not unreasonable. "Unreasonable" was the qualifying word used in the preamble to the Directives rather than simply "burden," which appeared in the Article itself.[81] In other words, a reasonable burden on the state, particularly if temporary in nature, would be acceptable. The ECJ has also held that the requirement of insurance coverage for all risks did not have to include emergency insurance. The ECJ found in the *Baumbast* case that

---

[78] And of these few cases, those which pay most attention to the Directives and the limitations contained within them are those which also are concerned with later developments in Community law, most notably citizenship but also TCN rights and wholly internal situations. The main reason for this coincidence is also noted in the text that the Directives were barely in force (June 1992 for 90/364 and 90/365 and indeed December 1993 for 93/96) when the Treaty of European Union entered into force (November 1993) and introduced the citizenship articles. Hence then, a number of these cases will be revisited in subsequent sections of this article.

[79] Case C-424/98, Commission v. Italy, 2000 E.C.R. I-4001.

[80] Case C-184/99, Rudy Grzelczyk v. Centre public d'aide sociale d'Ottignies-Louvain-la-Neuve, 2001 E.C.R. I-6193.

[81] Article 4: The right of residence shall remain for as long as beneficiaries of that right fulfil the conditions laid down in Article 1. Council Directive 93/96 (1993 O.J. (L317/59)).

emergency insurance provided by the Member State also extended to EC migrant workers.[82]

Apart from these few cases, the Directives have thus done little of substance to expand the free movement of persons and they were overtaken rather quickly by other legislative changes, potentially of far greater significance.

G. The Treaty of European Union & European Citizenship

The Treaty of European Union signed at Maastricht formalized the concept of European citizenship[83] and added a small section to the EC Treaty.[84] However, it was not immediately obvious what the true scope of European citizenship would be and the effect of EU citizenship on free movement is only now becoming clearer as a result of subsequent ECJ judgments.

The EC Treaty provides under Art. 17 that "citizenship of the Union is hereby established. Every person holding the nationality of a Member State shall be a citizen of the Union." Furthermore Art. 18 provides that "Every citizen of the Union shall have the right to move and reside freely within the territory of the Member States, subject to the limitations and conditions laid down in this Treaty and by the measures adopted to give it effect." Thus, the right of free movement now provided by the Treaty, under the citizenship guarantees, remove the "economic activity" requirement of the previous free movement regime. This is the case in spite of the fact that the original reason for providing for the lawful presence of a non-national in another Member State may have been to promote migration for labour and education/training. It must also be noted that the right of residence under Art. 18 is still subject to the limitations and conditions laid down in the Treaty and by the measures adopted to give it effect, in other words, limitations already in existence and future implementing measures.

What is meant by European Union citizenship?[85] Firstly, any definition of Union

---

82 Case C-413/99, Baumbast v. Secretary of State for the Home Department, 2002 E.C.R. I-7091.
83 Formalized because there has been plenty of discussion in the past about the development of European Citizenship, see, e.g., A. Durand, *European Citizenship*, 4 EUR. L. REV. 3 (1979); A. Evans, *European Citizenship*, 45 MOD. L. REV. 497 (1982).
84 The Maastricht Treaty introduced into the EC Treaty, Articles 17 and 18.
 ARTICLE 17 (ex Article 8).
 1. Citizenship of the Union is hereby established. Every person holding the nationality of a Member State shall be a citizen of the Union. Citizenship of the Union shall complement and not replace national citizenship.
 2. Citizens of the Union shall enjoy the rights conferred by this Treaty and shall be subject to the duties imposed thereby.
 ARTICLE 18 (ex Article 8a)
 1. Every citizen of the Union shall have the right to move and reside freely within the territory of the Member States, subject to the limitations and conditions laid down in this Treaty and by the measures adopted to give it effect.
85 There is a wealth of material which has sought to reach conclusions on what this is and indeed whether there can be a clear concept of European citizenship. See, inter alia, Durand, supra note 83; Evans, supra note 83; A Castro Oliviera, *Workers and other Persons: Step by Step from Movement to Citizenship*, 39 COMMON MKT. L. REV. 77 (2002); C. Jacqueson, *Union citizenship and the Court of Justice: something new under the sun? Towards social citizenship*, 27 EUR. L. REV. 260 (2002). (See also NYU Jean Monnet papers. N. Reich, *The European Constitution and New Member Countries: The Constitutional Relevance of Free Movement and Citizenship*, Revised paper of the Annual Lecture 2004 at the Centre for European, Comparative and International Law (CECIL), Department of Law, University of Sheffield, on February 26, 2004, at http://www.shef.ac.uk/law/research/cecil/docs/citizenshipnewmembercountriesrev.pdf. J. D'Oliveira, *Union Citizenship-Metaphor or Source of Rights?* 7 ELJ 4 (2001); S. O'Leary, *Flesh on the bones of EU citizenship*, 24 EUR. L. REV., 68–79 (1999); S. O'LEARY, THE EVOLVING CONCEPT OF COMMUNITY

Citizenship inevitably must depend on the present 25 Member States' definitions of nationality.

Declaration No. 2 on Nationality attached to the Maastricht Treaty provides that nationality shall be settled solely by reference to the national law of the Member State concerned and this was upheld in the *Manjit Kaur* case,[86] in which the ECJ held that it is for each Member State to lay down the conditions for the acquisition and loss of nationality.[87] Therefore the UK could exclude a UK overseas citizen from its territory without violating Community law. This has had the result that there can be no Community definition of European Citizenship established by the ECJ's jurisprudence; the concept can only be determined by an examination of the collective definitions of national citizenship from all of the Member States. Thus, if a person is a national of a Member State, then Articles 17 and 18 apply. A suggestion has been advanced that "a deprival of nationality will undoubtedly be in breach of Article 17 (2) as it will at the same time deprive the person of his or her Union Citizenship and the rights attached thereto."[88] Without judicial support for such a suggestion, and indeed, the fact that that ECJ was given the opportunity to decide that issue in the *Manjit Kaur* case but chose not to, it is difficult to see how the agreed Declaration of the Member States can be circumvented. Indeed, in the *Chen* case,[89] the ECJ confirmed that the decision about nationality is purely for each Member State to decide and is thus beyond legal challenge by the law of another Member State or Community law.

So, just what do these rights provide? Can they be read alone? We know from Article 18 that the right of free movement is subject to restrictions, but it does not expressly state in the relevant Articles which restrictions actually apply. The question remains whether the three public provisos of health, policy and security should apply. Arguably, with now some judicial support for this view, this would appear to be the case, in which case Directive 2004/38 will also apply to the rights.[90] Situations wholly internal to the Member States and any application to TCNs in the Member States appeared to be excluded from the scope of the provisions of citizenship introduced by the Treaty of Maastricht.[91] However, as the following discussion reveals, these Articles and their importance have been given fairly extensive consideration by the ECJ, which has liberally construed them and applied them in situations to benefit persons not initially considered as coming within their ambit.

CITIZENSHIP (1996), S. Douglas-Scott, *In search of Union citizenship*, 18 Y.B. OF EUR. LAW 29–65 (1998); J. Shaw, *The many pasts and futures of citizenship in the European Union*, 22 EUR. L. REV. 554–572 (1997); R. W. Davis, *Citizenship of the Union ... rights for all?*, 27 EUR. L. REV. 121–137 (2002).

86 Case C-192/99, The Queen v. Secretary of State for the Home Department, *ex parte* Manjit Kaur, 2001 E.C.R. I-1237.
87 "As the Court held in paragraph 10 of Micheletti and Others, cited above (Case C-368/90 Micheletti and Others 1992 E.C.R. I-4239), under international law, it is for each Member State, having due regard to Community law, to lay down the conditions for the acquisition and loss of nationality." Case C-192/99, The Queen v. Secretary of State for the Home Department, ex parte Manjit Kaur, 2001 E.C.R. I-1237, at para. 19.
88 C. Jacqueson, *Union citizenship and the Court of Justice: Something New Under the Sun? Towards Social Citizenship*, 27 EUR. L. REV. 260, 262 (2002).
89 Kunqian Catherine Zhu and Man Lavette Chen v. Secretary of State for the Home Department, 2004 E.C.R. I-9925, at paras. 44–45.
90 *See, e.g.*, Case C-482/01 and C-493/01 Orfanopoulos v. Germany, 2004 E.C.R. I-5257 (in which Directive 64/221 was considered by the ECJ as a limitation to the right provided by Art. 18 EC).
91 Both of these areas will be considered below.

H. Case Law on the Citizenship Articles

The first mention of the citizenship articles appeared in the case *Skanavi and Chyssanthakopoulos*.[92] The ECJ, whilst considering Article 18, would not grant it primary status with other Articles granting free movement and residence in host states. Later, in *Criminal Proceedings v. Bickel & Franz*,[93] the independent status of Article 18 appeared to be increased, although not to an overriding Community law right but to one which could be pleaded in support of other rights, in this case to support the argument that the refusal to allow Germans the use of German in the courts of Italy's South Tirol region would be contrary to Article 12, which guaranteed Italian citizens of Austrian extract in South Tirol the right to use German. After all, these German-speaking Italians had entered Italy lawfully under the terms of Article 59 EC.[94] This case itself supports the conclusion that, in some way, the citizenship rights were rights which could be used in a limited manner to support and supplement other rights.

In *María Martínez Sala v. Freistaat Bayern*,[95] Sala, a Spanish national who had worked in Germany for many years, lost her job but remained in Germany and received social assistance from 1989. Her residence permit expired but the German authorities supplied her with certificates stating she had applied for an extension to her permit. Nonetheless, authorities refused her a child allowance because she did not have a valid residence permit, which she claimed was contrary to Art. 12 because German nationals were not subject to the same condition. Although, in the case, Sala's actual status as a worker was not determined, the ECJ held that she was lawfully resident in Germany. Sala thus came within the personal scope of Treaty citizenship and the Court concluded that Art. 8 (2) (now 18) acted to attach other rights, including the right to be protected against discrimination under Art. 12. The ECJ further concluded that this, in turn, applied to a right within the material scope of the treaty such as the child allowance claimed in the case on an equal basis with nationals.[96]

In *Criminal Proceedings v. Florus Wijsenbeek*,[97] a Dutch MEP refused to show his passport and state his nationality on entry to Holland and was prosecuted for that failure. He claimed that the rights under Arts. 7a and 8a EC Treaty (now Arts. 14 and 18) had direct effect and that he could rely on them when refusing to establish his nationality at the border. The ECJ held that even if they respected the right of free movement, Member States still had the right to carry out border checks. The ECJ was not, however, able to declare that those Articles provided a direct right to free movement in their own right and unattached to any other Community right to free movement.

In *Grzelczyk*,[98] a French national who studied and worked on a part-time basis to help support himself for three years in Belgium applied at the beginning of his fourth and final year of study to the CPAS for payment of the *minimex*, a non-contributory minimum subsistence allowance. The CPAS granted Mr. Grzelczyk the *minimex* but then later denied this on the basis that he was not Belgian, presenting a case of clear discrimination on the grounds

---

92 Case C–193/94, Skanavi and Chyssanthakopoulos, 1996 E.C.R. I–929.
93 Case C-274/96, Criminal Proceedings v. Bickel & Franz, 1998 E.C.R. I-7637.
94 *Id.*, para 15 of the judgment. See for comment on the case *Bulterman*, Mielle, COMMON MKT. L. REV. 1325–1334 (1999) *or* Barry Doherty, IRISH J. OF EUR. L. 70–83 (1999); C. J. M. Safferling, AM. J. INT'L L. 155–159 (2000).
95 Case C–85/96, María Martínez Sala v. Freistaat Bayern, 1998 E.C.R. I-2691.
96 *Id.*, at para. 63.
97 Case C–378/97, Criminal Proceedings v. Florus Wijsenbeek, 1999 E.C.R. I 6207.
98 Case C–184/99, Rudy Grzelczyk v. Centre public d'aide sociale d'Ottignies-Louvain-la-Neuve, 2001 E.C.R. I-6193.

of nationality. This case did not turn on Grzelczyk's status as a worker. Instead, the ECJ held that the citizenship rights require that union citizens be treated equally. Previously, students who worked just for the purpose of their studies were not entitled to non-contributory benefits.[99] The ECJ distinguished this previous case by emphasizing the new citizenship provisions and by claiming that the new EU competences over education, albeit limited, allowed it to hold that Articles 12 and 17 precluded discrimination in the granting of a non-contributory social benefits to union citizens where they are lawfully resident, even though not economically active. The Court did consider Directive 93/96, under which Grzelczyk entered Belgium and which made his residence conditional on the fact that he not become a burden on the host state's finances. Relying on the sixth recital of the preamble to Directive 93/96,[100] the ECJ found that this condition required only that the migrant not become an "unreasonable burden," the interpretation of which the Court held to be a matter for the Member State.[101] So, instead of accepting a blanket exclusion or restriction on the citizenship rights of anyone who is a "burden," it is now only possible to exclude those who represent an "unreasonable burden," which is a quite different matter and category.[102] The decision leaves open the question who should define reasonableness in similar circumstances. Is it a matter for the ECJ or the Member States? Presumably, in line with the ECJs' comments in *Grzelczyk*, this would be within the Member States' courts' discretion.[103]

D'Hoop[104] involved a Belgian national who had studied in France. She was refused a Belgian "tide-over" allowance granted to students who are between their studies and employment because she had studied in another Member State and not Belgium. The ECJ held that the tide-over allowance was a "social advantage" under Article 7 (2) of Regulation 1612/68 but that receipt of the allowance could be conditioned on the applicant's participation in the employment market or obtaining a derived right in some way. D'Hoop's parents had remained in Belgium; therefore, according to the facts, she had obtained no rights of her own in Belgium because she was not a worker whilst in France, nor did she have derived rights from her parents. The ECJ referred to the EU's new competence in education, particularly to its mandate to encourage mobility of students and teachers,[105] and it cited *Grzelczyk*,[106] in holding that it would be incompatible with the right of free movement to expose a citizen to discrimination for having taken advantage of the right. The ECJ explained:

> Such inequality of treatment is contrary to the principles which underpin the status of citizen of the Union, that is, the guarantee of the same treatment in law in the exercise of the citizen's freedom to move. The condition at issue could be justified only if it were based on objective considerations independent of the nationality of the persons concerned and were proportionate to the legitimate aim of the national provisions.[107]

---

99 *See* Case 197/86, Brown v. Secretary of State for Scotland, 1988 E.C.R. 3205.
100 Council Directive 93/96 (1993 O.J. (L317/59)).
101 Case C-184/99, Rudy Grzelczyk v. Centre public d'aide sociale d'Ottignies-Louvain-la-Neuve, 2001 E.C.R. I-6193, paras. 38–46.
102 *See* text above at E and *see* M. Dougan & E. Spaventa, *Educating Rudy and the non English patient: a double bill on residency rights under Article 18 EC*, 28 EUR. L. REV. 699–712 (2003); D. Martin, 4 EUR. J. OF MIGRATION AND L. 136–144 (2002).
103 Case C-184/99, Rudy Grzelczyk v. Centre public d'aide sociale d'Ottignies-Louvain-la-Neuve, 2001 E.C.R. I-6193, paras. 42–46.
104 Case C-224/98, Marie-Nathalie D'Hoop v. Office national de l'emploi, 2002 E.C.R. I-6191.
105 Articles 3 (1) (q) and 149 (2) EC.
106 Case C-184/99, Rudy Grzelczyk v. Centre public d'aide sociale d'Ottignies-Louvain-la-Neuve, 2001 E.C.R. I-6193, para. 31.
107 Case C-224/98, Marie-Nathalie D'Hoop v. Office national de l'emploi, 2002 E.C.R. I-6191, paras. 35–36.

The Belgian authorities offered no objective considerations. Thus, the ECJ concluded that the limitation on the places of education which qualify for the tide-over allowance went beyond what is necessary to attain the objective pursued.

In the *Baumbast* case,[108] Mr. Baumbast was self employed in the UK, where he resided with his Colombian wife and two children, one Colombian and one with dual Colombian-German nationality who were being educated in the UK. He then became employed by a German company and worked outside the EU whereas the family remained in the UK. Their residence permits were not renewed, however, and Mrs. Baumbast and the children faced deportation. The case was referred to the ECJ, which in reaching a judgment, interpreted Regulation 1612/68 in the light of Article 8 of the ECHR[109] and identified it as one of the fundamental rights recognized by Community law. The ECJ emphasized the right of children of EU nationals under Regulation 1612/68 to continue their education even if the worker, from whom their rights derived, was no longer working. The ECJ further held that the text of the Treaty requires the continued enjoyment of the privileges of EU citizenship even if the activity upon which a citizen of the Union has lawfully established him or herself in another Member State as an "employed person" come to an end. Then, in the most important statement from the judgment, the ECJ held that Baumbast's right to stay under Article 18 (1) is conferred directly on every citizen of the Union by a clear and precise provision of the EC Treaty. The Court reasoned that, purely as a national of a Member State, and consequently a citizen of the Union, Mr. Baumbast had the right to rely on Article 18(1) EC.

The Court then considered Directive 90/364 and the facts that Baumbast and family were not a burden on UK social security and had German insurance coverage, albeit not for emergency treatment, although the Court noted that this was provided as a matter of course in the UK. The Court held: "The answer to the first part of the third question must therefore be that a citizen of the European Union who no longer enjoys a right of residence as a migrant worker in the host Member State can, as a citizen of the Union, enjoy there a right of residence by direct application of Article 18(1) EC."[110]

In *Trojani*,[111] which is a case where the status of the applicant is actually unclear and left to the national court to determine,[112] the ECJ held that even if not coming within Articles 43 and 49 (the economically active) or, on the facts, unable to qualify as a worker for the purposes of Article 39, Trojani nevertheless had the direct right of residence granted by Article 18. And, although subject to the restrictions allowed by Art. 18, the national authorities must be sure that any such restrictions are applied in conformity with

---

108 Case C-413/99, Baumbast v. Secretary of State for the Home Department, 2002 E.C.R. I-7091.
109 Providing for respect for family life.
110 Case C-413/99, Baumbast v. Secretary of State for the Home Department, 2002 E.C.R. I-7091, para 94.
111 Case C-456/02 Trojani v. Centre public d'aide sociale de Bruxelles (CPAS) 2004 E.C.R. nyr, [2004] 3 C.M.L.R. 38, [2004] All E.R. (EC) 1065.
112 The facts of this case resemble and overlap two previous cases in Community law (Case 196/87 Steymann v. Staatssecretaris van Justitie 1988 E.C.R. 6159 and Case 344/87 Bettray v. Staatssecretaris Van Justitie, 1989 E.C.R. 1621). In the first, a person who received payment in kind from a social institution was capable of having the status of a worker but in the second, employment within a social services rehabilitation scheme was held not to constitute "real and genuine activity" required for the status of worker under Community law and thus not entitled as such. In *Trojani*, Trojani had secured accommodation in a Salvation Army hostel, where in return for board and lodging and some pocket money he undertook various jobs for about 30 hours a week as part of a personal socio-occupational reintegration programme, thus straddling both previous cases in terms of fact and potentially causing the ECJ difficulties in categorizing Trojani for the purposes of Community law. On the other hand, avoiding any definitive statement of which category a person should be placed has probably allowed the Court to develop the law on citizenship further than other wise possible. *See*, for example, the consideration of the status of Sala and Grzelczyk in those cases.

Community law principles, especially proportionality. However, where such EU citizens are in possession of a residence permit, they are thus entitled, according to Art. 12 EC, to social assistance on the same basis as nationals.[113]

The case of *Chen*[114] increases the sanctity of European citizenship yet further. In a case, which also involves a consideration of TCN rights and family rights within the EU legal order and will enter into those discussions below, the EU citizen concerned is Catherine, the newly born daughter of a Chinese national, Mrs. Chen, who was visiting the UK with her husband and who went to Belfast to give birth to Catherine. Under Irish law,[115] any person born in any part of the island of Ireland can acquire Irish nationality and Catherine was subsequently issued with an Irish Passport. It is noted as a matter of record by the ECJ that this factual situation was deliberately engineered in order for the child to get EU citizenship so that the parents could subsequently acquire a right to reside in the UK. The parents are financially self-sufficient with full private medical insurance but their application for UK long-term residence permits was rejected. Chen appealed against that decision and a reference was made to the ECJ. In support of their right to remain in the UK, rights under Directive 73/148[116] for the receipt of services, Directive 90/364 for self-financed movement and generally Art. 18 EC were pleaded. The UK and Ireland contended that no Community law rights should arise as there had been no movement and Catherine was not exercising any Community law rights. The ECJ held that Directive 73/148 does not provide long term residence rights but simply rights to receive services on a short term basis, and was, thus, not a foundation for any rights in this case. With regard to the argument put forward by the UK that the actions of the parties were an abuse of Community law rights, the ECJ held that it was up to each Member State to determine nationality and once those rules had been satisfied that other Member States could not question the rights under Community law that arose as a consequence. In other words, the conferral of Irish nationality and thus EU citizenship was beyond challenge in the UK and that Community law, in particular Article 18 EC and Directive 90/364, thus applied. The ECJ concluded that Article 18 EC and Council Directive 90/364 confer a right to reside for an indefinite period on a young minor who is a national of a Member State and who is covered by appropriate sickness insurance and is in the care of a parent who is a third-country national having sufficient resources for that minor not to become a burden on the public finances of the host Member State. "In such circumstances, those same provisions allow a parent who is that minor's primary carer to reside with the child in the host Member State."[117]

The *Chen* decision is clearly an extremely liberal decision on the part of the ECJ but very disturbing for the UK and other Member States who have to accept rights of TCNs in similar circumstances, although they must be self-sufficient and not a burden on the host state. Nevertheless, the decision provides rights of residence to TCNs based on Art. 18 EC and could hardly have been envisaged when Art. 18 was first introduced into the Community legal order.

There has been some sign that the ECJ is prepared to draw a line on just how thin the connection to the host state can be before Art. 18 and consequent rights are triggered. In

---

113 Case C-456/02 Trojani v. Centre public d'aide sociale de Bruxelles (CPAS) 2004 E.C.R. nyr, [2004] 3 C.M.L.R. 38, [2004] All E.R. (EC) 1065, para. 46.
114 Kunqian Catherine Zhu and Man Lavette Chen v Secretary of State for the Home Department, 2004 E.C.R. I-9925.
115 Section 6(1) of the Irish Nationality and Citizenship Act of 1956.
116 Council Directive 73/148 (1973 O.J. (L172/14)).
117 Kunqian Catherine Zhu and Man Lavette Chen v Secretary of State for the Home Department, 2004 E.C.R. I-9925.

Collins,[118] decided before *Chen*, the ECJ followed the AG in deciding that the applicant did not have a genuine link with the UK. Collins, American born but with dual American and Irish nationality, had worked part-time in the UK in 1980 and 1981. He returned to the UK in 1998 and whilst looking for work applied for a jobseeker's allowance which was refused by the UK authorities on the grounds that he was not habitually resident in the UK. Collins claimed his previous stay and work in the UK entitled him as a worker to all the benefits that such status conveys. On this point, the ECJ held that whilst Collins may have had the status of a worker in the UK in 1981, any link with the later job search was effectively broken by the intervening 17 years. In the absence of a sufficiently close connection to the UK employment market, Collins was to be regarded as any other national of a Member State looking for a job in the host Member State and therefore was not to be regarded as a worker for the purposes of EC law.[119] The second claim in support of the right to stay and to the allowance, based on Directive 68/360, was also rejected as the rights under Directive 68/360 are available to established workers only. Any right to stay and seek work stems not from the Directive itself but from the Treaty, Article 39.[120] Thus the case turned on whether Collins had the right to the job seekers' allowance, which, according to the ECJ, was clearly within the scope of the Treaty.[121] It was argued that its denial on the basis of a lack of habitual residence, to an EU citizen lawfully in the UK, was indirectly discriminatory contrary to Art. 12 EC because, although also applicable to UK nationals, it could be far more easily met by them. The Court then emphasized the importance of the citizenship rights and equal treatment in the Community legal order but held that a difference in treatment could be objectively justified and that the insistence of a genuine link by the Member State between the person seeking work and the employment market of that State and that this might be determined by laying down a minimum time period. The ECJ, thus, held that Art. 17 did not go as far as to prohibit the UK from insisting that an entitlement to a benefit is conditional on a residence requirement.

Whilst the ECJ in the Collins case did not specifically mention Art. 18 in its judgment and referred instead to Article 17, which provides for citizenship rather than the rights it establishes, it is clear that any other rights stemming from citizenship must do so from Article 18. The case nevertheless adds to the body of law on citizenship.

What is the overall view of the right of free movement in light of this line of cases? One view is that there has been no further expansion and that existing rights have now found a Treaty expression rather than being based on secondary Community law.[122]

It is, however, worthwhile to take stock of the jurisprudence. Article 18 (1) has been declared to be directly effective and it can be activated in favour of EU citizens in a variety of ways. First, the force of Article 18(1) can be reached *via* exhausted free movement rights, i.e. those once enjoyed by a Member State national and which gained him or her lawful entrance and residence in the host state when exercised but which no longer are or can be relied upon because of changed circumstances (as in the *Baumbast* case). Second, the force of Article 18(1) can be reached by movement into another Member State in order to receive services (as in the *D'Hoop* case), this cross border movement then serves as the "economic activity" triggering the general rights of citizenship (Article 17). In

---

118 Brian Francis Collins v. Secretary of State for Work and Pensions 2004 E.C.R. I- nyr, [2004] 2 COMMON MKT L. REV. 8.
119 *Id.*, at paras. 28–33.
120 *Id.*, at paras. 36–44.
121 *Id.*, at para. 45.
122 "Thus citizenship only deals with the codification of existing rights with the proviso that non-economically active persons are granted a right to move and reside directly by provisions of primary law and not be secondary law as was the case before 1993.' Jacqueson, *supra* note 85, at 263.

both cases, Articles 17 and 18 then give rise to other rights, the most notable is the right under Article 12 not to be discriminated against on the grounds of nationality. Whilst the right of residence under Article 18 continues, according to the ECJ, to be restricted by the previously issued Directives, Articles 17 and 18 now seem to state that, where Union citizens are lawfully resident in a host state, they cannot be subjected to discrimination as regards social benefits, including non-contributory benefits.[123] Hence the status of the person, i.e., whether a worker or self-employed person is no longer an important factor in determining a right to move and reside in a host state. Furthermore, once lawfully residing in another Member State, citizens will be entitled to be treated without discrimination as compared with nationals, presumably but arguably, in all matters. So, lawful residence but not necessarily economic activity will trigger citizenship rights, the most important of which are not the political rights contained in Art. 19 but the general right to be free of discrimination and to be treated on equal terms as nationals, including, most importantly, social assistance rights. Finally, in the *Chen* case the assumption of citizenship of one of the Member States of the EU will, even without any cross-border movement, justify further rights of residence also for members of the person's family. From *Collins* we know that Art. 18 will not, however, prohibit the application of nationals rules imposing objectively justified conditions on the granting of other rights and benefits to EU citizens.

Just how far can Community law and the ECJ go, particularly with the right to receive services as the trigger for a citizenship right? The right to receive services is not an express treaty-based right, but it is mentioned in Directive 64/221, Article 1 and acknowledged in many ECJ cases.[124] A myriad of technical questions remain. For example, is an unemployed tourist on holiday entitled to receive services? If so, do these activate Art. 18 citizenship rights? Again, if so, does this then trigger the general right of equal treatment, i.e. to get needed benefits on the same basis as nationals, if, for the sake of argument, he or she runs short of money whilst on holiday? Presently under Community law, there is no clear answer. I do know that if I were in need of social support, I would rather receive it on the Greek island of Santorini or in the Algarve or Menorca, or southern Italy. I suspect that the Greek, Portuguese, Spanish or Italian authorities would argue that I am not entitled to such support. To a thus far, limited extent, the *Collins* case has drawn some sort of a line in the further extension of these rights in that Member States are able to impose residence requirements on the uptake of additional rights by EU citizens where there is no other real and genuine link to the Member State.[125] Whether this judgement will influence future development of EU rights or whether it will be restricted to the narrower concept of the employment market of the Member State remains to be seen.

Free movement and citizenship have now, as developed by the ECJ's jurisprudence, had a dramatic affect on EU and non-EU citizens' rights and their families. There is, however, another aspect of the changing relationship between what falls within the EU jurisdiction and Member states' jurisdiction and this so called "wholly internal rule" whereby the legal question ostensibly under EC law arises entirely within the home state of the Community national, and is thus in reality not a question of EU law at all but a question to be resolved by the application of national law. Also, the legal position and rights of Third Country Nationals (TCNs) within the EC has received both judicial and critical attention. Citizenship has also brought in its train other consequences on equal rights within the EC

---

123 Which will be considered in more detail below.
124 *See, inter alia*, Case 286/82, Luisi v. Ministero del Tesauro 1984 E.C.R. 377.
125 Thus there appears to be some curb on the feared spectre of benefit tourism, *see* Davies, *The high water point of free movement of persons: ending benefit tourism and rescuing welfare*, 26 J. OF SOC. WELFARE AND FAMILY L. 211–222 (2004).

I. The Wholly Internal Rule: No Freedom Without Movement?

It has been recognized that EC law sometimes engenders reverse discrimination internally against nationals of Member States in relation to other EC nationals who have moved there and benefit from EC law.[126] This problem is highlighted in the EC where strict professional rules continue to apply to nationals established and providing services. However, these protections have sometimes been found by the ECJ to be unsuitable or inappropriate for application to EC lawyers providing services temporarily in the host state. This was the holding of the ECJ regarding the restriction on areas of practice for lawyers in Germany in the *Commission v. Germany (Lawyers)* case.[127] The consequence of the Court's ruling was that German lawyers could still be restricted in the geographical areas in which they could practise,[128] but because this was an entirely internal matter of the application of national rules to nationals without EC law being invoked in any way, the ECJ could not and would not interfere in what was perceived as being a wholly internal matter. Indeed, this conclusion would be supported by the argument that the ECJ should refuse to accept references from national courts which implicate wholly internal matters.[129] That is to say, no question of Community law arises in such wholly internal matters and therefore there should be no need for a reference of the case to the ECJ. For example, in *R. v. Saunders*,[130] a criminal sanction imposed a mobility restriction on Saunders that was applicable within the UK only and was claimed by Saunders to be contrary to Article 48 (now 39). The ECJ held that no factor connected the situation with Community law. Hence, the provisions on the free movement of workers cannot be applied to situations which are wholly internal to a Member State. The Saunders case can be compared with *Rutili v. France*[131] to demonstrate the difference when Community law applies. In that case a French restriction on the Italian national Rutili's freedom to enter certain departments of France was regarded as contrary to both the Treaty and Community secondary legislation. The ECJ held that Article 48(3) (now 39) derogations may be imposed only in respect of the whole of the national territory.

The cases discussed below much more clearly illustrate how the wholly internal rule appears to give rise to reverse discrimination because nationals or those lawfully resident in the Member State in question are denied rights upon which EU nationals from other Member States are able to rely.

In *Morson and Jhanjan*,[132] the applicants, both Surinamese nationals, claimed the right to stay in Holland where their Dutch national children were working. It was held by the ECJ that there was no application of Community law to the wholly internal situation where national workers had not worked in any other Member State. In the case itself, because

---

126 Of the recent literature, see N. Shuibine, *Free Movement of Persons and the Wholly Internal Rule: Time to Move On?*, 39 COMMON MKT. L. REV. 731 (2003).
127 Case 427/85, EC Commission v. Germany: Re Lawyers' Services, 1988 E.C.R. 1123.
128 Note now, however, that the restriction known in German as the *Lokalisierungsgebot* has now been removed. Gesetz zur Neuordnung des Berufsrechts der Rechtsanwälte und der Patentanwälte, Sept. 2, 1994, BGBl. I, at 2278.
129 S. van den Bogaert, *Not a Wholly Internal Situation*, 25 EUR. L. REV. 554 (2000).
130 Case 175/78, R v. Saunders, 1979 E.C.R. 1129.
131 Case 36/75, Rutili v. Minister of Interior, 1975 E.C.R. 1219.
132 Cases 35 and 36/82, Morson and Jhanjan v. Netherlands, 1982 E.C.R. 3723.

there was no movement from one Member State to another, Community law did not apply.[133] Movement from a third country does not qualify. This was confirmed in *Land Nordrhein-Westfalen v. Uecker and Jacquet*,[134] which concerned two TCNs seeking to avail themselves of Community law as spouses of German nationals in Germany. The case was deemed to be wholly internal and thus not within the scope of application of EC law. However, if both cases had involved Spanish nationals moving to either Holland or Germany, they would be have been allowed to take TCN spouses or relatives with them.

Of late, there appears to be some softening of the wholly internal rule. Some cases look wholly internal but, because some prior cross-border movement is involved, Community law rights have been found to apply against the home state. The amount of movement deemed necessary to exempt a situation from the wholly internal rule to permit the application of EC law appears to be shrinking.

In *Surinder Singh*,[135] for example, an Indian spouse of a British national was able to use EC law to derive a right of residence in the UK on the basis of the fact that the spouse had previously exercised the right of free movement by providing services in another Member State prior to then re-establishing himself in the UK. In *Scholz*,[136] as another example of the Court's effort to close the gap opened by the wholly internal rule, the ECJ held that a border worker who continues to live in his or her home state and is just employed in another state but who crosses the border to work triggers Community rights which can be claimed within the home state.

The ECJ's erosion of the wholly internal rule continued in the *Carpenter* case,[137] in which a Philippine national claimed a right of residence in the UK with her British spouse on the grounds that he provided services from time to time in other Member States. The case is similar to the *Singh* case, except that Mrs. Carpenter had not left UK soil whilst services were being provided by her husband both from the UK and travelling to other Member States. The argument put forward by the applicants was that, if Mrs. Carpenter had also gone to another Member State, both she and her husband would have rights of residence and the right to work in the other host EU states. However, she chose to stay put to look after the children and thus assist her husband in providing services in other Member States. With regard to her lack of movement, the EC Commission regarded the case as a wholly internal matter for determination by the Member State and thus exclusively subject to its law. The ECJ referred to the EC secondary legislation including Regulation 1612/68 which, strictly, does not apply to the provision of services. It does, however, provide rules protecting the family life of nationals of the Member States in order to eliminate obstacles to the exercise of the fundamental freedoms guaranteed by the Treaty. The Court concluded:

> It is clear that the separation of Mr. and Mrs. Carpenter would be detrimental to their family life and, therefore, to the conditions under which Mr. Carpenter exercises a fundamental freedom. That freedom could not be fully effective if Mr. Carpenter were to be deterred from exercising it by obstacles raised in his country of origin to the entry and residence of his spouse.[138]

---

133 But *see* the discussion of *Chen*, following.
134 Cases 64 and 65/96, Land Nordrhein-Westfalen v. Uecker and Jacquet, 1997 E.C.R. I-3171 (particularly para. 24).
135 Case C-370/90, R v. Immigration Appeal Tribunal & Surinder Singh, ex parte Secretary of State for the Home Department, 1992 E.C.R. I-4265.
136 Case 419/92, Scholz v. Opera Universitaria de Cagliari and Cinzia Porcedda, 1994 E.C.R. I-505.
137 Case C-60/00, Carpenter v. Secretary of State for the Home Department, 2002 E.C.R. I-6279.
138 *Id.*, at para. 39.

The ECJ considered that the rights could be subjected to objective restrictions, but held that such restrictions must comply with fundamental rights. Thus the Court held that

> the decision to deport Mrs. Carpenter constitutes an interference with the exercise by Mr. Carpenter of his right to respect for his family life within the meaning of Article 8 of the Convention for the Protection of Human Rights and Fundamental Freedoms … (and) … does not strike a fair balance between the competing interests, that is, on the one hand, the right of Mr. Carpenter to respect for his family life, and, on the other hand, the maintenance of public order and public safety.[139]

The ECJ noted that the marriage appeared genuine, that there were no official complaints against Mrs. Carpenter and that she had in fact looked after the children while her husband was providing services in other Member States. The Court held that Article 49 EC, read in the light of the fundamental right to respect for family life, ensures the right of residence of a TCN in the Member State of his or her spouse if the spouse is the provider of services in other Member States.[140]

In *Angonese*,[141] an Italian citizen applied for a job in Italy but was refused entry to the selection process as he did not have the appropriate local authority certificate of bilingualism, despite being accepted by the local court as perfectly bilingual and possessing certificates of language study from the University of Vienna where he had studied. The Italian Government and defendant bank argued that the matter was wholly internal and had no connection with Community law and the Advocate General agreed.[142] The ECJ did not address this issue in ruling in favour of Angonese and held that the "requirement to provide evidence of his linguistic knowledge exclusively by means of one particular diploma, such as the Certificate, issued only in one particular province of a Member State, constitutes discrimination on grounds of nationality contrary to Article 48 (now 39) of the EC Treaty."[143] Whilst there had been some movement in this case, in that Mr. Angonese had studied in Austria, the only economic activity was the receipt of educational services. These technical points were simply not discussed by the Court. The Advocate General, on the other hand, was of the clear opinion that the study abroad, which was the factor triggering Community law rights, was too remote from the post for which Mr. Angonese had applied and could not be characterized as satisfaction of requirements of the post advertised.[144]

The case *Akrich*[145] raised some important questions in respect of the scope of the *Singh* judgment, previously considered, in particular whether a situation which would otherwise be wholly internal can be deliberately engineered to become one with a Community context.[146] The case involves a Moroccan who, after both lawful and unlawful attempts to enter and remain in the UK, married a UK national after which the couple moved to Ireland for

---

139 *Id.*, at paras. 41 and 43.
140 *Id.*, at paras. 45–6.
141 Case C-281/98, Angonese v. Cassa di Risparmio di Bolzano SpA, 2000 E.C.R. I-4139.
142 *See id.*, paragraph 44 of the AG's opinion in which the AG considered that Angonese as a national of that Member State who has never exercised an economic activity elsewhere in the Community and whose studies in another Member State have no connection either with the nature of the vacant post or with the languages in question was not indirectly discriminated against.
143 *Id.*, at para. 45.
144 It is on the opinions of the Advocates General specifically relating to the connection to the state of the person concerned that it can be observed the rudiments of legal reasoning which will allow the ECJ to claw back the extent of citizenship rights if the conclusion is reached that the to much is being demanded of EC law or that the claim does relate to matter still within the discretion of nationals law. This development is discussed further below and briefly in the concluding remarks of this article.
145 Case C-109/01, Secretary of State for the Home Department v. Hacene Akrich, 2003 E.C.R. I-9607.
146 Arguably so in the case of *Chen* also, but for different reasons. Refer to the discussion following.

a short period expressly in order to take advantage of EC law rights and in particular the judgment in *Singh*, to be able to return to the UK and take advantage of Community law rights. The Secretary of State considered that Mr. and Mrs. Akrich's move to Ireland was no more than a temporary absence deliberately designed to manufacture a right of residence for Mr. Akrich on his return to the United Kingdom and thereby to evade the provisions of the United Kingdom's national legislation, and that Mrs. Akrich had not been genuinely exercising rights under the EC Treaty as a worker in another Member State.

The ECJ was asked, amongst other questions, whether an engineered situation to evade national immigration laws was an abuse of Community law rights and if so whether the UK authorities could lawfully refuse entry.

The ECJ held that the motive for going to Ireland is not relevant to the status of a worker nor the decision to return to the home state. The ECJ held that Art. 10 of the Regulation applies to TCNs only if they are lawfully resident in a Member States before they can move to another one to take advantage of the rights provided by the Regulation. It is not applicable where a marriage of convenience has been arranged to circumvent a Member State's laws. Therefore, if the marriage is genuine, despite a lack of lawful residence, Member States should pay regard to Art. 8 ECHR. This judgement does not provide a full answer and the main question that is left to the Member State is to determine whether the marriage was genuine or not.

In the *Chen* case, discussed above,[147] in spite of the fact that the baby daughter was born in the UK and had not moved to or from any other Member State, or indeed not even from a third country state, and her parents as carers, wished that she remain in the UK, thus ruling out the intention to move to another Member State, the ECJ rejected the argument put forward by the UK, that the matter was wholly internal. The ECJ held:

> The Irish and United Kingdom Governments' contention that a person in Catherine's situation cannot claim the benefit of the provisions of Community law on free movement of persons and residence simply because that person has never moved from one Member State to another Member State must be rejected at the outset. The situation of a national of a Member State who was born in the host Member State and has not made use of the right to freedom of movement cannot, for that reason alone, be assimilated to a purely internal situation, thereby depriving that national of the benefit in the host Member State of the provisions of Community law on freedom of movement and of residence.[148]

Thus the conferral of Irish nationality and, thus, EU citizenship relieved the requirement of cross-border movement to trigger Community law rights.

In light of the above case law, it is suggested that a factual circumstance, which on the face of it appears to be wholly internal, may cease to be wholly internal and thus be subject to EC law, provided that there has been some previous movement into another Member State or if services have been provided in another Member State. Also, it is argued that the movement needed to trigger EC law can be the receipt of services rather than the provision of services; thus, it is possible to passively, rather than actively, engage in an economic activity. Furthermore, it can be suggested that the movement can also be metaphysical, that is, the receipt of services over the telephone or, more probable these days, over the Internet. Of course, such an interpretation raises the question, not yet decided by the ECJ and certainly not expressly provided for by any EC legislation, whether receiving services in such a manner is within the concept of engaging in an economic activity? If the

---

147 Kunqian Catherine Zhu and Man Lavette Chen v Secretary of State for the Home Department, 2004 E.C.R. I-9925.
148 *Id.* at paras. 18–19.

simple receipt of services, irrespective of the manner of delivery of these services, triggers the application of EC law, then it could be argued that potentially any receipt of services will do, regardless of how minimal.[149] And finally, according to the *Chen* case, neither movement nor an intention to move is necessary, if national citizenship is conferred on an individual, who then automatically enjoys European citizenship.

However, stepping back slightly from this possible development in the state of EC law, we could draw, by analogy, on the case law of the ECJ on the concept of a worker and suggest that any qualifying activities would have to be "effective and genuine activities, to the exclusion of activities on such a small scale as to be regarded as purely marginal and ancillary."[150] In other words, an economically determined level of activity could be set, below which EC rights would not be triggered for the reason that the services received were marginal. The establishment of such a threshold is not, however, without its difficulties. A start nonetheless appears to have been made in a slightly different manner by the Advocates General in the *Carpenter*, *Angonese* and *Collins* cases by the imposition of a sufficiently close interest test and to a limited extent, taken up by the ECJ in the *Collins* case by the recognition that Member States my objectively justify an indirect discrimination by the imposition of a residence requirement.[151]

In the next section, concerned with TCNs, there have been further developments in the scope of EC law.

J. The Treatment and Free Movement of Third Country Nationals (TCNs)[152]

Basically and originally, nationals from third countries lawfully or unlawfully resident in a Member State were not a concern of the EC and originally neither Treaties nor secondary legislation made any reference to them. However, since the 1960s Community law has increasingly both indirectly and specifically provided for TCNs.[153] Thus, historically, all independent TCNs resident in Member States who are not members of a EU Citizens' family obtained no rights under Community law to reside in the EU or move from country to country.[154] Their rights were entirely a matter for national law regulation and as such, those who stopped being a family member as a result of divorce but who had perhaps lived many years in the host state, would simply lose their rights under Community law.[155] It became apparent that these persons also required legislative protection. Furthermore, the wider social and economic significance of these lawful residents in the EU becomes clear

---

149 Telephoning advice or sex lines where the provider resides in another EU Member State? Downloading products or advice packages over the internet which server is based in another Member State?
150 Case 53/81, Levin v. Staatssecretaris van Justitie, 1982 E.C.R. 1035, para. 17.
151 *See* comments at notes 137 and 141 and the discussion of *Collins* at note 118.
152 Here we are only concerned with independent TCNs and not those seeking rights as family members of EU citizens, who have been dealt with above. *See* article text at section C. Note also in respect of family members who are not nationals of a Member State Article 16 of the new Directive 2004/38 provides that the family members of a Union citizen to whom Articles 12(2) and 13(2) apply shall acquire the right of permanent residence after residing legally for a continuous period of four years in the host Member State.
153 Until EC Secondary law for the free movement of workers was enacted which provided entry rights for members of the family also, the entry and rights of the TCNs was entirely a matter for national regulation. *See* text and notes at 3 and 66 above and the increasing list of measures now providing TCNs with rights as discussed in the text below.
154 *See, e.g.*, E. Guild, *Security of Residence and Expulsion of Foreigners: European Community Law*, in SECURITY OF RESIDENCE AND EXPULSION: PROTECTION OF ALIENS IN EUROPE (E. Guild & P. Minderhoud eds., 2000), S. Peers, *Towards Equality: Actual and Potential Rights of Third Country Nationals in the European Union*, 33 COMMON MKT L. REV. 7 (1996).
155 *See* Case 267/83, Diatta v. Land Berlin, 1985 E.C.R. 567.

if the statistics are considered. TCNs, according to estimates,[156] comprised 4% of the EU population in 2000 of the then 15 Member States of the EU, a figure which translated then to roughly 13 million TCNs lawfully resident in the EU. There is little doubt that that figure has risen significantly since the expansion of the EU to 25 Member States in 2004.[157] This means that there are a significant number of lawfully resident persons in the EU who do not share the same rights, especially those rights of free movement, as EU citizens.

Also, there is another important factor to take into account when considering how TCNs are or should be treated in the EU. According to population growth figures, or figures demonstrating a shrinking population, the slight increases in population in the UK and in the EU overall, arise more from net migration into the Member States than from births.[158] Decreasing populations, or those experiencing only very slow growth, are not generally regarded to be good for economic expansion.[159] Hence, in the absence of natural population growth, the EU requires inward migration to keep the economy buoyant. Interestingly, the 10 acceding Member States also showed an overall population decrease in 2003.[160] If the economic studies are to be taken seriously, then, far from resisting inward migration from outside the EU by setting up barriers or quotas, the Member States should actively be encouraging immigration. Indeed, a lot of attention has been directed to the immigration policies and the Schengen agreement[161] regarding the entry and visa regulation of TCNs, but less attention has been paid to the free movement rights of those already in the EU. Although, after some considerable delay, some action is now slowly being taken.[162] Previously, the ECJ had made clear in the case *Mr. and Mrs. Richard Meade*,[163] that the Treaty articles on free movement of workers apply solely to EU nationals and not, therefore, to TCNs.

---

156 *See* European Commission report (EC COM (1994) 23, Annex I, 22) putting the figure on non-EC nationals working in the EU in the early 1990s at 10 million.
157 Although it is too early for any confirmed statistics to have been recorded in relation to the position in the EU25.
158 UK Home Office Online Report 25/03, at http://www.homeoffice.gov.uk/rds/pdfs2/rdsolr2503.pdf European Foundation for the Improvement of Living and Working Conditions "Migration trends in an enlarged Europe" 94 (2004), at www.eurofound.eu.int/publications/EF03109.htm.
159 C. Turner, *Fortress Europe Lowers its Drawbridge But What Protection for Third Country Nationals*, 85 EU FOCUS 2–4, (2001); D. L. Wiesen, *The Economic Effect of Population Decline: A Subject for Study*, available at http://alum.mit.edu/ne/whatmatters/200311/; N. Myers, *Europe's Population Decline: Problem or Opportunity?* (Oxford, UK, 2004), available at http://www.popco.org/press/articles/2004-1-myers.html; M. Sircelj, *The European Population Committee's Recent Demographic Studies and their Relevance for Social Cohesion*, Statistical Office, Slovenia, Council of Europe, European Population Committee, Directorate General III — Social Cohesion, F-67075 Strasbourg, Council of Europe, March 2002, ISSN 1683-2663, http://www.coe.int/t/e/social_cohesion/population/No_2_The_European_Population_Committee%92s_Recent_Demographic_Studies.pdf; H. Stalford, *The Impact of Enlargement on Free Movement: A Critique of Transitional Periods*, Paper delivered at the Third Meeting of the UACES Study Group on the Evolving EU Migration Law and Policy, The University of Liverpool, Dec. 5, 2003.
160 In 2003, more than three quarters of the increase in the EU's population came from cross external-border migration. The natural population growth in the EU (live births minus deaths) is expected to decrease from +309 000 in 2002 to +294 000 in 2003, and net migration should be also down, from +1 260 000 in 2002 to +983 000 in 2003. On the other hand, and despite net migration (+0.4‰), the population fell by 0.8‰ in the Acceding Countries, due to a negative natural growth of 1.2‰. Eurostat, Statistics in focus, Population and social conditions, 1/2004, "First demographic estimates for 2003". Eurostat News Release 105/2004, August 31, 2004.
161 And now incorporated as Protocol 2 to the Final Act of the Amsterdam Treaty O.J. 1997 C340. Refer to S. Peers, *Building Fortress Europe: The Development of EU Migration Law*, 35 COMMON MKT. L. REV. 1235 (1998).
162 *See, e.g.*, the New Directive 03/109 and a comprehensive article on this by S. Peers, *Implementing Equality? The Directive on Long Term Resident Third Country Nationals*, 29 EUR. L. REV. 437–460 (2004).
163 Case 238/83, Mr. and Mrs. Richard Meade, 1984 E.C.R. 2631.

Whilst it might have been the case in the past that the treatment of TCNs by the European Community was expected to be below the standards of treatment of EU citizens as observed in some comments,[164] this is no longer regarded as being acceptable and more recently both the ECJ has been addressing the rights of TCNs in case law and the European Union Institutions have also addressed this issue by the enactment of new secondary legislation with further proposals in the pipeline.[165] Whilst at first there was no Treaty base in the EC Treaty for such legislation and such measures could be brought under the intergovernmental third pillar of the Treaty on European Union only, the Treaty of Amsterdam established a new section in the EC Treaty in 1999, which has become the legislative base for measures concerned with TCNs.[166] Indeed the European Council which took place in Tampere, Finland in 1999, called for the fair treatment of TCNs residing legally in the EU and that the legal status and rights should be brought as near as possible to EU citizens' rights.

The first of the exceptions to the absence of measures relating to TCNs were the various association and co-operation agreements with countries such as Turkey, Algeria and Morocco,[167] under the European Economic Area[168] and, as another example, Switzerland.[169] The problem with these agreements though, is that they vary considerably in the rights accorded to the TCNs and the status of a particular TCN depends on the countries with whom the EU has concluded agreements. The agreements with Turkey and Switzerland assimilate the rights of workers from these countries most closely to the rights of EU workers.[170]

Second, TCNs may form part of the workforce of workers of a company established in the EU which sends workers abroad to complete a contract in another Member State. In *Vander Elst*,[171] for example, the Court confirmed that nationals of third countries also have the right of free movement within the context of the right of free movement of companies that are established within the EU. This exception to the exclusion of EC protection of TNCs is contingent on the fact that the non-EU nationals are part of the legal labour force of the company established in the home Member State and that the employer provides services in another Member State; but they do not provide a right to cross an internal EU border but simply to move around in the State where services are being provided but do not extend to establishment.[172]

---

164 "If the Community is to have an area without internal frontiers, it becomes progressively absurd that non-Community nationals established in the Community should not be afforded the protection of Community law. If third country nationals work and reside in the Community, as they will in increasing numbers, thereby contributing to the achievement of the aims of the EEC Treaty, the Community has a duty to come to terms with the phenomenon. To entrust competence in this area to the Member States at this stage of European Integration only recalls and reinforces a statist view of Community law which is inappropriate in this area." (D. O'Keefe, *The Free Movement of Persons and the Single Market*, 17 EUR. L. REV. 3 (1992).) "More notorious still is the continued refusal to extend the right of free movement to non-EC migrants. Indeed, the whole issue of non-EC migration reveals a very familiar and very regrettable underside to the supposedly new Europe." (WARD, A CRITICAL INTRODUCTION TO EUROPEAN LAW 149 (1996)). See also P. Oliver, *Non-Community Nationals and the Treaty of Rome*, 5 Y.B. OF EUR. L. 57–92 (1985).
165 Refer to note 3 above.
166 Title IV. Visas, Asylum, Immigration and other Policies related to Free Movement of Persons. Article 61 (b) EC Treaty.
167 Turkey (1963 J.O. (L3867)); Algeria (1978 O.J. (L263/1)); Morocco (1978 O.J. (L264/1)) and up to an estimated 30 association and co-operation agreements, *see* Turner, *supra* note 158.
168 EEA (1997 O.J. (L1/1)).
169 (2000 O.J. (L114/6)).
170 For details, *see* A. MacGregor & G. Blanke, *Free Movement of persons within the EU: current entitlements of EU Citizens and Third Country Nationals – A Comparative Overview*, 8 INT'L TRADE LAW AND REGULATION 173, 189–191 (2002).
171 Case C-43/93, Vander Elst v Office des Migrations Internationales, 1994 E.C.R. I-3803.
172 *See also* Case C-113/89, Rush Portuguesa, 1990 E.C.R. I-1417.

There has now been more extensive legislative intervention in this area with further proposals made still in the pipeline. Regulation 1091/2001[173] was enacted, which provides limited rights of free movement for those TCNs in the EU on a long-stay visa. TCNs may also be helped by the new Directive 2000/43,[174] which prohibits discrimination based on race, however, Article 3 (2) of the Directive states that it is without prejudice to the provisions and conditions relating to the entry and residence of TCNs and to any treatment which arises from the legal status of TCNs. So, whilst it may prevent unequal treatment in the country of residence, it is unlikely to provide an independent right of free movement either into the EU or between Member States.

Specifically, addressing the situation of divided families with TCN family members, the Institutions have enacted Directive 2003/86,[175] which provides that lawfully resident TCNs in Member States may apply to have their family join them from a third country providing they are self sufficient and have been in the Member State for a year or more. Furthermore, Article 3 requires that they must have a reasonable prospect of remaining longer. The definition of "family" has been restrictively drawn and Member States retain much discretion in deciding whether to grant an application.[176] The Directive does not apply to the UK, Ireland and Denmark which have opted out of these sections of the Treaty.[177]

A Directive has been enacted concerning the status of TCNs who are long-term residents in a Member State.[178] This Directive provides TCNs who have been lawfully resident in the EU for a minimum of five years to apply for and acquire a certain status which entitles them to long term residence in the host state and limited rights of movement within the EU. These rights are subject to the public policy and security derogations, self sufficiency and sickness insurance requirements and quotas and restrictions on movements imposed by other secondary states. The Directive extends to core family members as defined by the re-unification Directive, but these may not be admitted by a second EU state. Indeed whilst the Directive does provide new rights for TCNs, it only does so without prejudice to all the other legislative provisions already providing rights and is subject to interpretation by the Member States which may dilute some of its provisions. It comes into force on January 23, 2006,[179] and is nevertheless a welcome, if in the end a somewhat modest, improvement.

Finally, there is also Council Directive 2004/114[180] of December 13, 2004 on the conditions of admission of third-country nationals for the purposes of studies, pupil exchange, unremunerated training or voluntary service but which enters into force only in 2007.

So whilst some progress has been made by legislation thus far enacted, a number of proposals affecting the rights of TCNs remain very firmly in the pipeline. And some rights have already been recognized or confirmed by the ECJ. Both of these aspects will be considered next.

The earliest proposed change stems from 1986, following an amendment made by the Single European Act[181] to Article 59(2) (now 49) of the original EEC Treaty to permit the Community to extend freedom of services to TCNs. It provides that the Council may

---

173 (2001 O.J. (L150/4)).
174 (2000 O.J. (L180/22)).
175 (2003 O.J. (L251/12)).
176 For full details, see J. APAP & S. CARRERA, TOWARDS AN PROACTIVE IMMIGRATION POLICY FOR THE EU? (Centre for Eur. Policy Studies Working Doc. no. 198, December 2003) at http://www.ceps.be.
177 See the protocols attached to the Treaty of European Union and the amended EC Treaty.
178 Council Directive 03/109 (2004 O.J. (L16/44)).
179 For a detailed review of the Directive, see S. Peers, *Implementing Equality? The Directive on Long Term Resident Third Country Nationals*, 29 EUR. L. REV. 437–460 (2004).
180 Council Directive 04/114 (2004 O.J. (L375/12)).
181 Article 16 (3) SEA (1997 O.J. (L169)).

extend the provisions of the Chapter to nationals of a third country who provide services and who are established within the Community. After many years of lying dormant, a proposal has finally been made, although it is far from being enacted.[182] It proposes, without going so far as to allow TCNs to establish in another Member State, to provide a limited freedom of movement to provide services, outside of the transport services industry; but did not include the freedom to move to receive services in other Member States.[183]

There is a proposed directive[184] to harmonize the entry and residence rights of TCNs, which concerns common conditions of entry and residence for TCNs who seek paid employment, or self-employment, within the EU. This is intended primarily to harmonize work and residence permit rights and should not be confused with the Regulation already passed on residence permits for TCNs, which merely harmonizes the format of the permit.[185] A further proposal would, if enacted, provide limited travel rights for periods of three months but up to six months within the Schengen area providing the entering TCNs are self sufficient and possess comprehensive medical and sickness insurance.[186]

A proposed posting of a TCN abroad Directive[187] seeks to confirm the right of the free movement of TCNs to move to other Member States for specific contracts only to supplement the present Directive relating to EU citizens[188] and to confirm the ECJ case law approving the right of TCNs to carry out work as employees in another Member State.[189] As of the beginning of 2005, this proposal has not progressed any further since amended in 2000.

Finally, within this subsection, the Constitutional Treaty, which incorporates the European Charter of Fundamental Rights, provides for a number of rights which are available to all persons within the EC rather than just to citizens, although there is a section, Title V, which reserves some rights, such as the right to vote and freedom of labour, for citizens. However, in line with some of the new secondary legislation discussed above, the Charter also provides under Article II-105 (2) that: "Freedom of Movement and of residence may be granted to nationals of third countries legally resident in the territory of a Member State."[190]

Turning now to the case law involving TCN rights, the *Baumbast* case[191] concerns R., an American woman, who was held by the ECJ to have a right of residence under Community law, which enabled her to resist an attempt to deport her. R. moved to the UK with her then-husband, a French national who had obtained work in the UK. They were later divorced and, in line with the jurisprudence of the *Reed* and *Diatta* cases,[192] R. lost her own legal right to remain in the host state under Article 10 of Regulation 1612/68. R. and her children nevertheless remained in the UK, but, whilst the children were granted indefinite leave to remain, R. was not. The UK authorities wanted to deport her and by necessity her

---

182 *See* COM (2000) 271 final (2000 O.J. (C311/197)). However, there has been no further action on this since May 8, 2000 when an amended proposal was sent to the European Parliament. The document has subsequently expired; *see* Commission Document 51999PC0003(02).
183 COM (2000) 271 final (2000 O.J. (C311/197)). Articles 1–2.
184 COM (2001) 386 final (2001 O.J. C332/248) which has been subject to an EP opinion C5-0447/2001 - 2001/0154(CNS) O.J. C E/2004/43/230 but has not moved any further since 12/02/2003.
185 Council Regulation 1030/2002 (2002 O.J. (L157/1)).
186 *See* COM (2001) 388 final.
187 COM (2000) 271 final (2000 O.J. C311/197)).
188 Council Directive 96/71 (1996 O.J. (L18/1)).
189 *See* notes 171 and 172 above.
190 This possibility is further acknowledged in Article III-265 in the section on Policies on Border Checks, Asylum and Immigration.
191 Case C-413/99, Baumbast v. Secretary of State for the Home Department, 2002 E.C.R. I-7091.
192 *See supra* notes 56 and 60.

children who remained the children of an EU national no longer working in the UK. The ECJ held that Regulation 1612/68 "must be interpreted as entitling the parent who is the primary carer of those children, irrespective of his nationality, to reside with them in order to facilitate the exercise of that right notwithstanding the fact that the parents have meanwhile divorced."[193] The fact that only one parent is a citizen of the Union and that parent has ceased to be a migrant worker in the host Member State and that the children are not themselves citizens of the Union are irrelevant in this regard. Hence, there is an implied right within Article 12 of the Regulation that the child of a migrant worker can pursue his or her education in the host Member State and that that child has the right to be accompanied by the person who is the primary care-giver. Furthermore, that person is permitted to reside with the child in that Member State during his or her studies.[194] According to the ECJ, to refuse to grant permission to remain to a parent who is the primary care-giver of the child exercising the right to pursue his or her studies in the host Member State infringes that right.[195]

The *Akrich* case[196] suggests that even in the case of initial unlawful residence, a TCN may acquire Community law rights, even where the situation was deliberately engineered, provided that a marriage to a EU citizen was genuine. However, the determination of genuineness was a matter for the national authorities. If the marriage was found to be not genuine, then EC law rights would not be available.

The *Chen* case[197] also serves as a clear demonstration that, where fundamental rights such as citizenship and family relationships are present, TCNs will be afforded rights under Community law in a situation that is not immediately obvious and indeed might appear positively generous. TCNs' rights derive from EU citizens, very often children, or because, irrespective of nationality, are descendant children of EU workers. They provide TCNs, who would otherwise possess no rights under EC law, with rights to remain and reside in the EU. Indeed, the baby Catherine Chen, on acquisition of Irish nationality, obtained far greater rights than TCNs who have been resident in a Member State for very many years.

This seemingly generous treatment of TCNs, where personal free movement rights appear to be transferred to them by reason of the fundamental importance of the family and family life as guaranteed by the ECHR, supports the view that further legislative intervention in support of the rights of TCNs who have been resident in a EU Member State for a long time is required. However, in the opposite direction such generous leads us on to consider further two areas of law. Court of Justice judgments have also had a profound if not a concerning impact on national legal systems, in particular in areas which are not typically considered to be fertile ground for EC law due to a lack of clear assignment of competence to the EU over these fields by the Treaties. The fear has arisen that ECJ decisions in these areas so closely to the heart of state financial expenditure will encourage so-called "benefit tourism." This is taken to be where individuals with little or no real connection to the host state are able to move lawfully to another Member State as EU Citizens or as members of the family of EU citizens and claim social benefits that will then

---

193 Case C-413/99, Baumbast v. Secretary of State for the Home Department, 2002 E.C.R. I-7091, para. 75.
194 The presumption must then be that once the children have completed their education, at whatever age (*see* Case 7/94, Gaal, 1995 E.C.R. I-1031), R will then loose the right to remain in the EU unless rescued by any of the new Directives providing rights in favour of TCNs as discussed in this article.
195 *See*, Case C-413/99, Baumbast v. Secretary of State for the Home Department, 2002 E.C.R. I-7091, para. 73
196 Considered in more detail at note 145 above.
197 *See* Kunqian Catherine Zhu and Man Lavette Chen v. Secretary of State for the Home Department, 2004 E.C.R. I-9925.

in turn undermine both the division of legal competences between the Union and Member States and the social security systems of the Member States.[198] Whilst there is a genuine Community interest in social matters, the problem is that the case law may not yet have achieved an acceptable balance of interests.

Even before the proposals for further law reform and development affecting family rights of EU citizens were put forward by the Commission,[199] and provisions now contained in the consolidating and replacement Directive on free movement of persons rights,[200] ECJ case law had already made significant strides towards establishing similar rights. Whilst the ECJ may have been influenced by the proposals even before they were enacted into binding law, they did not contribute directly to the Court's reasoning. In the following cases, the Court had already considerably expanded the scope of welfare and social benefits and also the protection of families as matters related to and indeed stemming from rights of free movement.

K. Welfare and Family Rights: The Impact of Recent European Court of Justice Decisions[201]

The welfare and family rights provided and protected by Community law have been incrementally advanced over the years.[202] However, the recent judgments of the ECJ, which have arisen under the citizenship provisions, are not just concerned with the scope and meaning of the term "citizenship", but also evidence the ECJ's assertive approach to upholding welfare and family rights through its interpretation of EC law, also by reference to the European Convention of Human Rights. Indeed, the Court's interpretation of citizenship rights appears to contradict the general free movement Directives by extending the welfare benefits rights of EU citizens who, pursuant to the Directives, were not supposed to be a burden on the host Member State. Indeed such developments seem even to raise the question whether the ECJ has gone too far and has encroached on the competences of the Member States,[203] competences that have not been signed over to the EU. The developments suggest that the Community, at least the ECJ, is more concerned with the welfare rights of EU citizens and the sanctity of their family than it is with Member States' concerns about the possible drain on national resources posed by welfare claims from citizens of other Member States or the claims to a right of residence by TCNs.

---

198 See R.C.A. White, *Residence, Benefit Entitlement and Community Law*, 12 J. OF SOC. SECURITY L. 10–25 (2005); and G. Davies, *The High Water Point of Free Movement of Persons: Ending Benefit Tourism and Rescuing Welfare*, 26 J. OF SOC. WELFARE AND FAMILY L. 211–222 (2004).
199 Communication from the Commission to the European Parliament and to the Council on the follow-up to the recommendations of the High-Level Panel on the Free Movement of Persons (COM(98) 403 final).
200 Council Directive 04/38 (2004 O.J. (L158/77)).
201 See of the more recent articles: N. Reich & S. Harbacevica, *Citizenship and Family on Trial: A Fairly Optimistic Overview of Recent Court Practice with regard to Free Movement of Persons*, 40 COMMON MKT. L. REV. 615 (2003).
202 Leading case law includes: Case 261/83, Castelli v. O.N.P.T.S., 1984 E.C.R. 3199; Case 267/83, Diatta v. Land Berlin, 1985 E.C.R. 567; Case 94/84, O.N.E. v. Deak, 1985 E.C.R. 1873; Case 59/85, The Netherlands v. Reed, 1986 E.C.R. 1283; Case 316/85, Centre public d'aide sociale de Courcelles v. Marie-Christine Lebon, 1987 E.C.R. 2811; Case C-370/90, R v. Immigration Appeal Tribunal & Surinder Singh, ex parte Secretary of State for the Home Department, 1992 E.C.R. I-4265.
203 Refer to White, *supra* note 198, Davies, *supra* note 198 and J. Meulman & H. De Waele, *Funding the Life of Brian: Jobseekers, Welfare Shopping and the Frontiers of European Citizenship*, 31, LEGAL ISSUES OF ECON. INTEGRATION 275–288 (2004).

In the previously discussed *Sala* case,[204] Sala's right to rely on Treaty citizenship triggered other rights, including most importantly, Article 12 (the right not to be discriminated against according to nationality). This, in consequence, included the right to receive, on equal terms, social welfare benefits including the non-contributory child allowance, the subject matter of the case. Similarly, in *Grzelczyk*,[205] the ECJ held that the new citizenship provisions and new EU competences for education, albeit limited,[206] led to the result that Articles 12 and 17 preclude discrimination as regards the grant of a non-contributory social benefits to Union citizens where they are lawfully resident, even though not economically active. In the third of the cases dealing with a form of welfare benefit, *D'Hoop*,[207] the ECJ held that it would be incompatible with the right of freedom of movement if a citizen, who had taken advantage of free movement, were then subjected to discrimination as a consequence of the exercise of that right. The Court held:

> Such inequality of treatment is contrary to the principles which underpin the status of citizen of the Union, that is, the guarantee of the same treatment in law in the exercise of the citizen's freedom to move. The condition at issue could be justified only if it were based on objective considerations independent of the nationality of the persons concerned and were proportionate to the legitimate aim of the national provisions.[208]

This can easily be interpreted as meaning that citizenship rights, which have now been held to be directly effective,[209] and which are not dependent upon previous economic treaty rights,[210] also provide now the right to equal treatment under Article 12. According to the ECJ, the right of residence under Article 18 still continues to be subject to the potential restrictions inherent in the Directives previously issued.[211] Articles 17 and 18, on the other hand, appear, according to the ECJ, to ensure that Union citizens cannot be discriminated against in social welfare benefits, including non-contributory ones, provided the Union's citizens are lawfully resident in the host state. Hence, for the moment it would seem that the right to any welfare benefit is dependant on being a lawfully resident EU citizen in the host state.

To get a clearer view of the extent of this incursion into national law competences we need to return to two more recent cases, considered above.

In the *Collins* case[212] Collins entered the UK on an Irish Passport to seek work and whilst doing so, claimed an income-based jobseeker's allowance on the strength of 10 months part-time work from 1980–81. The UK authorities refused the benefit as he was not habitually resident in the UK. Collins claimed that this was discrimination as nationals were advantaged by automatically satisfying the time period required whereas other

---

204 Case C-85/96, María Martínez Sala v. Freistaat Bayern, 1998 E.C.R. I-2691.
205 Case C-184/99, Rudy Grzelczyk v Centre public d'aide sociale d'Ottignies-Louvain-la-Neuve, 2001 E.C.R. I-6193.
206 Articles 3 (1) (q) and 149 (2) EC.
207 Case C-224/98, Marie-Nathalie D'Hoop v. Office national de l'emploi, 2002 E.C.R. I-6191; see A. Iliopoulou & H. Toner, *A New Approach to Discrimination Against Free Movers? D'Hoop v. Office National de l'Emploi*, EUR. L. REV. 389 (2003).
208 Case C-224/98, Marie-Nathalie D'Hoop v. Office national de l'emploi, 2002 E.C.R. I-6191, paras. 35–36.
209 *See* Case C-413/99, Baumbast v. Secretary of State for the Home Department, 2002 E.C.R. I-7091.
210 *See also* Case C-224/98, Marie-Nathalie D'Hoop v. Office national de l'emploi, 2002 E.C.R. I-6191, paras. 27–30.
211 Art. 18 provides that it can be restricted by other EU/EC laws issued or to be issued, but that even where there was a clear restriction not to be a burden contained in Dir 93/96 in the *Grzelcyzk* case, the ECJ was able, with support of the looser language in the preamble, to arrive at a judgment which opened the door for Grzelcyzk to get a benefit from the state.
212 Brian Francis Collins v. Secretary of State for Work and Pensions 2004 E.C.R. I- nyr, [2004] 2 C.M.L.R. 8.

Community nationals would have to fulfil this extra requirement. The AG and the Court, in agreement, concluded that he did not have the status any longer of a worker and was therefore not entitled to all the rights provided for in the secondary legislation. The AG considered that Member States have a right to require a period of habitual residence and was of the view that Collins had not demonstrated the required affinity with the UK. The AG thus distinguished Collins' situation from both *Sala* and *Grzelcyzk* and gave the opinion that a required period of residence to show a connection with a state was acceptable under Community law and that Collins had not fulfilled this requirement and, thus, must fail in his. He concluded in paragraph 77 (3) that "Community law as it now stands does not require that an income-based social security benefit, intended for jobseekers, be provided to a citizen of the Union who enters the territory of a Member State with the purpose of seeking employment while lacking any connection with the State or link with the domestic employment market." Whilst the Court emphasized the importance of the citizenship rights and equal treatment in the Community legal order, it held that a difference in treatment could be objectively justified. An insistence of a genuine link by the Member State between the person seeking work and the employment market of that State, which might be determined by laying down a minimum time period was acceptable. The ECJ thus held that Art. 17 did not goes as far as to prohibit the UK from insisting that an entitlement to a benefit is conditional on a residence requirement. As was noted in essence by Davies (2004),[213] the Court has stepped back from allowing the spectre of welfare tourism to haunt the Member States and thus allow for a more pragmatic exploration of the rights which citizenship encapsulates.

In *Trojani*,[214] the ECJ confirmed the position in the *Grzelczyk* case by holding that, where a EU citizen is a lawful resident and in possession of a resident permit, they have a right to equal treatment under Article 12 EC and thus the rights to any national allowance on the same basis as nationals. Whilst the Member State may remove him or her within the limits of EC law, it may not do so as an automatic consequence of the fact that he or she demands social assistance. This seems once more to support the view that Member States must treat EU-citizens equally once they become lawful residents, even if they do not have sufficient means to support themselves; this is again in seeming contrast to the Directives which provide limits to the citizenship rights of Articles 17 and 18 EC Treaty.[215]

A clearly important matter that requires clarification is a precise definition of what is meant by "lawful residence" as this is thus far missing in EC law, and is arguably as important as the Member State's ability to determine state citizenship because it enables all other rights to flow from it.[216] With only the judgments of the ECJ in *Sala*, *Grzelczyk*, *Chen*, *Collins* and *Trojani*, it is suggested that, provided an EU citizen had a lawful right to enter or indeed even be in the host state in the first place and has not done anything to endanger

---

213 Refer to White, *supra* note 198; Davies, *supra* note 198; and Meulman & De Waele, *supra* note 203.
214 Case C-456/02 Trojani v. Centre public d'aide sociale de Bruxelles (CPAS) 2004 E.C.R. nyr, [2004] 3 C.M.L.R. 38, [2004] All E.R. (EC) 1065.
215 Council Directive 90/364 (1990 O.J. (L180/26)); Council Directive 90/365 (1990 O.J. (L180/28)); and Council Directive 93/96 (1993 O.J. (L317/59)). There is, however, the forthcoming case of Bidar (Case C-209/03, opinion of the AG, November 11, 2004) dealing with a claim for financial assistance for study. The AG opined that as a result of Community developments in the area of education, assistance with maintenance costs for students attending university courses either in the form of subsidized loans or grants no longer falls outside the scope of the application of the EC Treaty for the purposes of Article 12 EC. This means that provided there is a real link and that the student is lawfully resident in the host state, the state authorities cannot deny assistance on the grounds of nationality. This case may really set the cat amongst the pigeons if the AGs opinion is followed by the ECJ.
216 H. Oger, *"Residence" as the new additional inclusive criterion for citizenship*, WEB J. OF CURRENT LEGAL ISSUES 5 (2003), *at* http://webjcli.ncl.ac.uk/.

his or her residence subsequently, the right to remain and not to be discriminated against continues. Exploring this further, is it possible to say that the absence of a designation of unlawful residence is the equivalent of lawful residence? Certainly we know from the case law that, provided the person concerned has done nothing to justify deportation, they must continue to be lawfully resident and are thus entitled to the rights provided by EU citizenship.[217]

In *Grzelczyk*, the ECJ held that its judgment

> does not, however, prevent a Member State from taking the view that a student who has recourse to social assistance no longer fulfils the conditions of his right of residence or from taking measures, within the limits imposed by Community law, either to withdraw his residence permit or not to renew it. Nevertheless, in no case may such measures have the automatic consequence that a student who is a national of another Member State requiring recourse to the host Member State's social assistance system is required to leave as a matter of fact.[218]

This would seem to suggest that, if a Member State does decide to withdraw the status of lawful residence, the Member State would be entitled to deport the claimant. However, such a decision is subject to the proportionality standard[219] and the review of the ECJ.[220]

As far as welfare rights entitlement is concerned, it would seem now that the economic status of the person, that is, whether worker or self-employed, is no longer an important factor. Providing that there is movement in some way, even back to the home state or continued lawful residence in the host state, EU citizens will be entitled to be free of discrimination as compared to nationals in all matters. The welfare rights cases considered here have dealt specifically with EU citizens but could equally be extended to cover non-EU nationals if and when cases dealing with family members arise. Take for example the family rights discussed following, where the cases are concerned, for the most part, with non-EU citizens. These cases, in which a greater respect for family life has emerged, are also a product of the move from regarding free movement rights in the EC legal order as wholly dependant on the pursuit of an economic activity to recognizing rights which are based on citizenship, lawful residence and fundamental freedoms. Nevertheless, it is the evolution of the free movement rights that have led to these possibilities to extend family and welfare rights.

In turning now to family law developments, in trying to reach a just solution in *Carpenter v. Secretary of State for the Home Department*,[221] the Advocate General took the view that the matter was not wholly internal as argued by the UK but that instead Mrs. Carpenter was covered by Directive 73/148,[222] which provides rights to move and reside in

---

217 For this review of the right of Member States to determine whether EU citizens can or can not remain in the UK, *see* Case 159/79, R. v. Pieck, 1980 E.C.R. 2171; and Case C-292/89, Antonissen, 1991 E.C.R. I-745 (in which respectively the ECJ held that deportation of Pieck would be disproportionate and thus contrary to EC law, whereas Antonissen could be deported). Hence, it would seem that previous cases law provides us with a workable model of how we decide lawful residence. Only a deportation that could be condoned by the ECJ would remove lawful residence.

218 Case C-184/99, Rudy Grzelczyk v. Centre public d'aide sociale d'Ottignies-Louvain-la-Neuve, 2001 E.C.R. I-6193, at paras 42–3.

219 For a brief discussion of the standard of proportionality in the EU legal order, *see* J. TILLOTSON & N. FOSTER, *supra* note 8, 239–241; DOUGLAS-SCOTT, *supra* note 7, 373–374; N. EMILOU, THE PRINCIPLE OF PROPORTIONALITY IN EUROPEAN LAW (1996).

220 *See, inter alia*, Case 178/84, Commission v. Germany (Re Purity Requirements for Beer), 1998 E.C.R. 1227, Case C-131/93, Commission v. Germany, 1994 E.C.R. I-3303, Case C-44/94, R v. Minister of Agriculture, Fisheries and Food, *ex parte* National Federation of Fishermen's Organisations, 1994 E.C.R. I-3115.

221 Case C-60/00, Carpenter v. Secretary of State for the Home Department, 2002 E.C.R. I-6279.

222 Council Directive 73/148 (1973 O.J. (L172/14)).

a host Member State in terms similar to those provided for in Directive 68/360 for workers and the self-employed and their spouses. However, the AG did not address the fact that there was no movement to reside in the host state by Mrs. Carpenter, but looked instead for a connection with the Member State, which would then activate the application of Community law, in this case Directive 73/148. It would appear from its judgment, that the ECJ was not impressed with all the views of the Commission or the AG.[223] The ECJ instead referred to Article 49 EC and Regulation 1612/68, although the latter, if read strictly, does not apply to the provision of services. These provisions, according to the ECJ, provide rules protecting the family life of nationals of the Member States in order to eliminate obstacles to the exercise of the fundamental freedoms guaranteed by the Treaty. The Court held:

> It is clear that the separation of Mr. and Mrs. Carpenter would be detrimental to their family life and, therefore, to the conditions under which Mr. Carpenter exercises a fundamental freedom. That freedom could not be fully effective if Mr. Carpenter were to be deterred from exercising it by obstacles raised in his country of origin to the entry and residence of his spouse.[224]

The ECJ considered that the rights of residence could be subjected to objective restrictions,[225] but held that any such restrictions must comply with fundamental rights and that

> the decision to deport Mrs. Carpenter constitutes an interference with the exercise by Mr. Carpenter of his right to respect for his family life within the meaning of Article 8 of the Convention for the Protection of Human Rights and Fundamental Freedoms and does not strike a fair balance between the competing interests, that is, on the one hand, the right of Mr. Carpenter to respect for his family life, and, on the other hand, the maintenance of public order and public safety.[226]

The ECJ noted that the marriage appeared genuine, that there were no official complaints against Mrs. Carpenter and that she looked after the children while her husband was providing services. The Court thus held that Article 49 EC, read in the light of the fundamental right to respect for family life, is to be interpreted as precluding a refusal, by a Member State, of the right of residence to a TNC who is the spouse of a citizen of that Member State who provides services to recipients established in other Member States.[227] Apart from promoting the protection of family life within the Community legal order, the *Carpenter* case also confirms that TCNs gain derivative rights from those providing services, despite the absence in this area of law of an equivalent of Regulation 1612/68. The new Directive 2004/38, considered above, has remedied this previous lack of legislation.[228]

Quite rightly, commentators have questioned[229] where the limits of Community law should be in cases similar to *Carpenter*. These dangers were foreseen by the Advocates

---

223 Although the theme of connection to the state was also put forward by the AGs in the Angonese case (discussed at note 142 above), and in Case C-138/02, Collins and Secretary of State for Work and Pensions and in this latter case, discussed in the text below, actually taken up by the ECJ as a way of pulling back from the interpretation by the ECJ which would seem to open up all benefits equally to all EU citizens.
224 Case C-60/00, Carpenter v. Secretary of State for the Home Department, 2002 E.C.R. I-6279, para. 39.
225 Arguably, but not expressly stated, of the type found in Art. 39 (3) and Directive 64/221.
226 Case C-60/00, Carpenter v. Secretary of State for the Home Department, 2002 E.C.R. I-6279, paras. 42–3.
227 *Id.*, at paras. 45–6.
228 See recital 4 of the preamble Council Directive 04/38 (2004 O.J. (L158/77)).
229 See an extended case note by S. Acierno, *The Carpenter Judgment: Fundamental Rights and the Limits of the Community Legal Order*, 28 EUR. L. REV. 398 (2003); C. Tomuschat, COMMON MKT. L. REV. 449 (2000); and S. FRIES & J. SHAW, CITIZENSHIP OF THE UNION: FIRST STEPS IN THE EUROPEAN COURT OF JUSTICE EUROPEAN PUBLIC LAW 533 (1988).

General in the *Carpenter*, *Angonese* and *Collins* cases. It may be questioned whether it is now at all necessary to travel in order to provide services, given that the ECJ has already held that services include the provision of telephone services[230] and could easily therefore include the provision of services over the internet and possibly even the receipt of services over the internet as a sufficiently strong cross-border element needed to trigger EC law rights in the areas of family and welfare law.[231] Indeed, in *Chen*, considered above, there was no movement at all merely the acquisition of nationality which automatically conferred EU citizenship on the baby which in turn led to the right of a non-EU national family member carer to remain in the UK.

Returning to the *Baumbast* case,[232] we already knew that the status of a worker is not necessarily lost if a worker ceased work,[233] but the case did not focus on this aspect, particularly because the Immigration Adjudicator had decided already that the family of Mr. Baumbast enjoyed an independent right of residence under Article 12 of Regulation 1612/68. It is also settled law, according to the Court, that rights enjoyed by members of a Community worker's family under Regulation 1612/68 can, in certain circumstances, continue to exist even after the employment relationship has ended.[234] The question raised by the Immigration Appeal Tribunal concerned, essentially, the status of both the non-EU parent and the no-longer-working EU national. The UK and German governments argued against the decision of the Immigration Adjudicator. They argued that Community law did not confer on the TCN spouse of an EU citizen a right of residence derived from the children's right to be educated. In this case also, the ECJ relied on Article 8 of the ECHR in justifying its interpretation of Regulation 1612/68 that emphasized the right of children of EU nationals to continue their education even if the worker, from whom their rights derived, was no longer working in the host state. The ECJ held further that the text of the Treaty does not permit the conclusion that citizens of the Union who have lawfully established themselves in another Member State as an employed person are deprived, where that activity comes to an end, of the rights that are conferred on them by virtue of that citizenship.[235]

The *Baumbast* case also highlights the support of the ECJ for family rights. As discussed above, the UK authorities wanted to deport R., but because the children had a right to remain and to pursue their education under the best possible conditions in the host Member State, the ECJ reasoned that this necessarily implies that that child has the right to be accompanied by the person who is his or her primary care-giver and, accordingly, that that person is able to reside with the child in that Member State during his or her studies. To refuse to grant permission to remain to a parent who is the primary care-giver of the child exercising his or her right to pursue studies in the host Member State infringes that right.[236] The EC Commission argued against such an interpretation but the ECJ held that Regulation 1612/68, interpreted in the light of Art. 8 ECHR, entitled

> the parent who is the primary carer of those children, irrespective of nationality, to reside with them in order to facilitate the exercise of that right notwithstanding the fact that the parents have meanwhile divorced. The fact that only one parent is a citizen of the Union and that

---

230 Case C-384/93, Alpine Investments BV v. Minister of Finance, 1995 E.C.R. I-1141.
231 For example, would the receipt of advice from a professional in another Member State over the internet be sufficient to help a TCN family member assert residence rights in any of the Member States?
232 Case C-413/99, Baumbast v. Secretary of State for the Home Department, 2002 E.C.R. I-7091.
233 *See* cases Case 75/63, Hoekstra v. BBDA (aka Ungar v Bestuur), 1964 E.C.R. 177; Case C-292/89, Antonissen, 1991 E.C.R. I-745; Case 39/86, Lair v. Universität Hannover, 1988 E.C.R. 3161.
234 *See* Cases 389 & 390/87, Echternach and Moritz, 1989 E.C.R. 723, paragraph 21; and Case C-85/96, Martínez Sala, 1998 E.C.R. I-2691, paragraph 32.
235 Case C-413/99, Baumbast v. Secretary of State for the Home Department, 2002 E.C.R. I-7091, para. 83.
236 *Id.* at para. 73.

parent has ceased to be a migrant worker in the host Member State and that the children are not themselves citizens of the Union are irrelevant in this regard.[237]

This derived right stems not directly from the worker but from the children of the worker, who are themselves recipients of derived rights. This could be termed "indirect derived rights."

A further case which provides express support for family life by the ECJ and thus now the EC legal order is *MRAX*,[238] which involves the challenge by an interest group to the Belgian authorities' application of Community law in respect of the visa requirements for TCN family members. Certainly, according to Art. 3 of Directive 68/360,[239] Member States are entitled to demand a visa from the TCN family members. The ECJ reasoned, however, that it is apparent, in particular from the Council Regulations and Directives on freedom of movement for employed and self-employed persons within the Community, that the Community law maker has recognized the importance of ensuring protection for the family life of nationals of the Member States within the recognition and application of fundamental freedoms guaranteed by the Treaty.[240] In this light, the ECJ concluded that it is, in any event, disproportionate and therefore prohibited to send back a TCN married to a national of a Member State, even if the TCN is not in possession of a valid visa. The Court found that this protection applies where the TCN is able to prove his or her identity and the existence of conjugal ties. Furthermore, the Court emphasized that there should not be evidence to establish that the TCN represents a risk to the requirements of public policy, public security or public health within the meaning of Article 10 of Directive 68/360 and Article 8 of Directive 73/148.[241]

Then, in what was a quite strange interpretation of the requirements of EC legislation, the ECJ held that "While Article 4(3) of Directive 68/360 and Article 6 of Directive 73/148 authorize the Member States to demand, for the purpose of issue of a residence permit, production of the document with which the person concerned entered their territory, they do not lay down that that document must still be valid."[242] It seems to me that, if a Member State is permitted to demand a visa, it is not unreasonable to expect the visa to be valid. This judgment may have been easier to accept if it had been cast in the same terms as the residence permit requirements arising out of cases such as *Pieck*,[243] whereby the permits themselves merely constitute evidence of a right and not the right itself. The Court held that the decision to expel based on the lack of a valid residence permit or the failure to possess a residence permit at all was disproportionate and thus contrary to Community law. The requirement to possess a valid visa could be viewed in the same light. The Court did, however, follow the reasoning in the case of *Giagounidis*,[244] in which the ECJ held that Member States are obliged to grant the right of residence within their territory to the workers referred to in Article 1 of Directive 68/360, that is, workers who can produce either a valid identity card or a valid passport, regardless of the document with which they entered their territory. Consequently, the ECJ held,

---

237 *Id.* at para. 75.
238 Case C-459/99, Mouvement contre le racisme, l'antisémitisme et la xénophobie ASBL (MRAX) v Belgian State, 2002 E.C.R. I-6591.
239 From 2006 to be found in Article 5 of Council Directive 04/38 (2004 O.J. (L158/77)).
240 *Id.* at para. 53.
241 *Id.* at para. 61, but *see* now Article 27–33 of Council Directive 04/38 (2004 O.J. (L158/77)).
242 *Id.* at para. 89.
243 Case 159/79, R v. Pieck, 1980 E.C.R. 2171.
244 Case C-376/89, Giagounidis, 1991 E.C.R. I-1069.

a Member State cannot make issue of a residence permit under Directives 68/360 and 73/148 conditional upon production of a valid visa. Furthermore, the ECJ held, an order of expulsion from national territory on the sole ground that a visa has expired would constitute a sanction manifestly disproportionate to the gravity of the breach of the national provisions concerning the control of aliens.[245]

Hence, the right to family life protected by Art. 8 ECHR has been instrumental in achieving far-reaching judgments on the rights of family members of Community citizens, creating a sphere of protection clearly beyond any strict interpretation of Community law rights.[246]

The *Chen* case also affirms the ECJ support of the family, without this time feeling the need to rely on the ECHR for support. The ECJ concluded that Article 18 EC and Council Directive 90/364 confer a right to reside for an indefinite period on a young minor who is a national of a Member State and who is covered by appropriate sickness insurance and is in the care of a parent who is a TCN having sufficient resources for that minor not to become a burden on the public finances of the host Member State in that State. "In such circumstances, those same provisions allow a parent who is that minor's primary carer to reside with the child in the host Member State."[247]

It is clear, as a result of this case law, that, in combination, Articles 18 and 12 EC,[248] the latter already a well established fundamental right in the Community legal order, emerge as providing even stronger rights for EU citizens. If Article 12 applies, as it appears to do in the above case law, then, as a matter of right, it opens the door to protection against discrimination regardless of the subject matter, including all areas outside of the Treaties. That is, once lawfully residing in a host state, EU citizens should not be discriminated against regardless of whether the subject matter of treatment is one which comes four square within the competences assigned to the EU by the treaties or is in reality a matter still within the jurisdiction of the Member States, such as in the areas of welfare and family law rights as in the above case law.[249]

L. Conclusions

After a slow start and limited application, the right of free movement was opened up by secondary legislation that was regarded as being necessary to give meaning to the bare Treaty rights themselves. Furthermore, both the Treaty Articles and the provisions of the secondary legislation were subject to generous and often far reaching interpretations by the ECJ. It must be noted, however, that the rights provided by this regime were not employed in a way that helped promote the economies of the European Community and Member States at the macro level by the mass migration of workers from one Member State to another. Instead, the rights were assumed by individuals alone and consequently

---

245 Case C-459/99, Mouvement contre le racisme, l'antisémitisme et la xénophobie ASBL (MRAX) v. Belgian State, 2002 E.C.R. I-6591, para. 90 of the judgement.
246 The *Chen* judgment also supports this view although not directly addressing the issue again, the ECJ referred to the judgment in the *Baumbast* case, see Kunqian Catherine Zhu and Man Lavette Chen v. Secretary of State for the Home Department, 2004 E.C.R. I-9925, at para. 45.
247 *Id.* at paras. 44–47.
248 Article 12 provides: Within the scope of application of this Treaty, and without prejudice to any special provisions contained therein, any discrimination on grounds of nationality shall be prohibited.
249 Tax law is another area reserved to the Member States but it would not surprise me if cases reached the national courts and were then referred to the ECJ where discriminatory tax rules or a refusal to grant certain tax benefits to EU citizens arose. This would clearly be a battle ground between the EU and the Member States.

on a small scale. The secondary legislation and continued liberal interpretation of it by the ECJ opened up free movement for persons in the EC and their families and it is argued that, because families were granted derived rights from the workers to work and obtain various social benefits, these aspects helped further remove the disincentives in moving to a new country in order to engage in an economic activity. The next major step was to allow for free movement of persons not dependant on economic activity and three Directives were enacted, soon followed by Treaty amendments, which provided for general free movement and citizenship respectively. But, according to the letter of these laws, these rights were subject to conditions that the persons so moving would be self-sufficient and would not be a financial burden on the host state. More recent case law, which also continues to consider the scope of the previous legislation, also reveals the scope of the new regime and has provided some interesting results. In particular, these results have raised further questions as to where the boundary of EC laws now ends. EU nationals can claim non-contributory benefits and be a burden on the state, albeit a reasonable one only. TCNs derive rights from their family members where the family members are either the children of EU citizens or EU citizens themselves, including newborn babies, as in the *Chen* case. Even more interesting, a TCN's justification for residing and drawing benefits in a Member State can be based upon non-EU national children, as in the case of R. EU nationals and TCN family members can derive rights in situations previously regarded as wholly internal or where the degree of movement or activity appears to be minimal or, indeed, non-existent, once again, as in *Chen*. Where citizenship rights are established through lawful residence, Article 12 EC applies. The limit of the range of rights to which this applies is far from clear. Whether it should apply to rule out all discrimination against host EU citizens in comparison with nationals in all areas of the law is the burning question left open by the present development of the law. The *Collins* case appears thus far[250] to be the only decision which provides the Member States with some discretion to be able to refuse the granting of certain allowances but only if objectively justifiable.

Thus, the above case law, new legislation and further new legislative proposals lead to this suggested state of the law: if you are an EU citizen lawfully resident in another Member State you do not have to be economically active to be entitled to equal treatment including, for example, equal treatment in non-contributory welfare benefits on the same basis as nationals. In addition, if you are a national having returned to your home EU state after receiving services in another EU Member State, you and members of your family or your spouse's or partner's family, who are or who are not EU citizens, will be entitled to reside with you and also obtain benefits on the same basis as nationals. It would seem that EU citizens who do not move at any time to another Member State to receive or provide services are the only ones unable to obtain these welfare and family rights unless equivalent rights are provided under national law or if any member of the family becomes a national of another Member State. Particularly with regards to the rights of TCNs who are

---

250 The fcase of Bidar (Case C-209/03, The Queen (on the application of Dany Bidar) v. London Borough of Ealing and Secretary of State for Education and Skills, 2005 E.C.R. I-2119) dealing with a claim for financial assistance for study presented the ECJ with an opportunity to either follow or ignore the opinion of the AG. The AG considered that as a result of Community developments in the area of education, assistance with maintenance costs for students attending university courses either in the form of subsidized loans or grants no longer falls outside the scope of the application of the EC Treaty for the purposes of Article 12 EC. This means that provided there is a real link and that the student is lawfully resident in the host state, the state authorities cannot deny assistance on the grounds of nationality. The question of the real link was the turning point on which the ECJ decided that the UK could not discriminate against Bidar under Art. 12 EC.

lawfully resident in the Member States, Community law developments in free movement and citizenship have helped add pressure for the reform.[251]

Hence, there is an understandable concern[252] that EC law now means EU citizens who have established lawful residence in a host state will have equal rights to the full spectrum of contributory and non-contributory social benefits and that, as such, the spectre of "benefit tourism" had effectively been raised, whereby EU nationals can roam the Member States in search of the "good life." Certainly, if this were the effect of the rulings, the Member States would understandably argue it was not something they had agreed to and that EC law was overriding national laws in the absence of an express agreement to that effect. There may be a possible backlash, resulting from the conclusion that the ECJ has gone too far and that free movement and citizenship rights need to be qualified. There is evidence that this might be the case within the opinions of the Advocates General in the *Carpenter*, *Angonese* and *Collins* cases, although in the first two cases, the opinions were not taken up by the ECJ but in the *Collins* case the ECJ handed back some discretion to the Member States and may follow this in future. This would be a way of restricting or indeed preventing so called benefit tourism. An additional factor that may be lurking in the background and fuelling these concerns is the awareness of the recent expansion of the number of Member states. There was widespread fear and concern of further demands being placed on the 15 old Member States when the 10 new Member States joined in May 2004.[253] This concern was particularly underscored by the transition periods established under the Accession Treaties which have been taken up by most Member States which will delay the free movement provisions applying universally and without exception in the enlarged EU for an initial two-year period.[254]

It is clear that the legal regime regulating the free movement of persons has come a long way from the near empty and little used original Treaty provision for it. It is ironic that, at the present stage of the evolution of free movement rights, the concern is whether those rights have now actually gone too far and encroached too much on areas of the Member States own national laws than is universally acceptable. However, as is often the case with the Community's very dynamic system of law, the burning questions we are left with will only be answered by either the ECJ in future cases or by the intervention of the Member States. The Constitutional Treaty though, presently undergoing the long slow process of ratification by all 25 Member States, will not disturb this regime in any significant way, therefore it will be by secondary legislation or court judgments only that the law develops further or is restrained.

---

251 Refer to the preamble and recitals in Council Directive 04/38 (2004 O.J. (L158/77)).
252 *See*, White, *supra* note 198; Davies, *supra* note 198; and Meulman & De Waele, *supra* note 203.
253 The informed prognosis was far from being so bleak. *See, inter alia*, The impact of EU enlargement on migration flows: Home Office Online Report 25/03 at http://www.homeoffice.gov.uk/rds/pdfs2/ rdsolr2503.pdf, European Foundation for the Improvement of Living and Working Conditions, Migration Trends in an Enlarged Europe 94 (2004) *at* www.eurofound.eu.int/publications/EF03109.htm. Since May 1, 2004, when the new Member States joined, there has not been any reports evidencing a flood of labour to the 15 old EU States.
254 Although it is possible this can be extended following reviews to five years and then further to seven years if difficulties are experienced by any or all of the 15 pre-enlargement Member States. For full details of the enlargement *see* http://europa.eu.int/comm/enlargement/negotiations/pdf/negotiations_report_to_ep.pdf. The Accession Treaty *available at* http://europa.eu.int/comm/enlargement/negotiations/treaty_of_accession_2003/index.htm.

Freedom of Movement as a Union Citizen's Right

Dieter H. Scheuing*

A. Introduction

The free movement of Union citizens within the European Union has gained great importance and continues to do so. This is true, in particular, when looking at aspects dealing with non-discrimination. In 1993, when the Maastricht Treaty entered into force, such a development could not have been expected. Of course, being a basic right of the newly created Union citizenship, the free movement of all Union citizens within the entire area of the European Union was obviously indispensable. A Union citizenship lacking such a guarantee of Union-wide mobility for every Union Citizen would not even have merited its name. Thus, it was only natural for the general right for every Union citizen to move and reside freely within the territory of all Member States to be enshrined as the first Union citizen's right in Article 8a of the European Community Treaty (EC Treaty), immediately following the introduction of Union citizenship for all Member States' nationals in Article 8 EC Treaty.

I. The Initially Unobstrusive Character of the General Right of Free Movement

This Article 8a EC Treaty, however, was not a step into entirely new ground. Prior to this, European Community law had contained market-related rights of free movement for nationals of the Member States. Furthermore, complementary rights of free movement without any linkage to the internal market had been created through residence directives and through the jurisprudence of the Court of Justice of the European Communities (ECJ). In addition, the wording of Article 8a of the Treaty had been formulated rather obscurely. Therefore, it could be argued that this new Treaty-based guarantee of free movement did not bring about any substantial changes, but should merely be seen as a confirmation of the status quo.[1]

---

* Jean Monnet Professor of European Law, University of Würzburg. Email: scheuing@jura.uni-wuerzburg.de. This essay is a revised and updated version (January 2005) of an article originally published in German as *Freizügigkeit als Unionsbürgerrecht*, EUROPARECHT 744 (2003). It further developes ideas first laid down in the author's contribution to RAUM UND RECHT. FESTSCHRIFT 600 JAHRE WÜRZBURGER JURISTENFAKULTÄT (H. Dreier, H. Forkel & K. Laubenthal eds., 2002). The author owes many thanks to A. Kemmerer for her help in the preparation of this English version.

1 *See, e.g.*, D. O'Keeffe, *Union Citizenship, in* LEGAL ISSUES OF THE MAASTRICHT TREATY 87, 94 (D. O'Keeffe & P.M. Twomey eds., 1994); H.U. Jessurun d'Oliveira, *European Citizenship: Its Meaning, Its Potential, in* EUROPE AFTER MAASTRICHT. AN EVER CLOSER UNION? 126, 135 (R. Dehousse ed., 1994); A.P. VAN DER MEI, FREE MOVEMENT OF PERSONS WITHIN THE EUROPEAN COMMUNITY 46 (2003).

II. The Innovative Dynamics of the General Right of Free Movement

Despite this, in cases before the Court reference was soon made to the general right of free movement in Article 8a EC Treaty. For some time the Court was reluctant to take a position regarding the scope and content of this new Treaty provision. However, in its more recent jurisprudence, the ECJ recognized Article 8a EC Treaty (now, following amendment, Article 18 EC) as an independent guarantee with far-reaching scope that had significant potential for further development.[2] It has become a fundamental freedom for all Union citizens, forming part of their basic legal rights.[3] Furthermore, a variety of changes in the relevant EU primary and secondary law are taking shape.

III. Structure of this Essay

All these developments shall be studied hereafter. Firstly, in section B the content of the market-related rights of free movement shall be examined. Against this backdrop, the general right of free movement of all Union citizens shall be discussed in greater detail in section C. Finally, in section D some further developments will be briefly outlined.

IV. Definitions and Delimitations

In this essay the notion "free movement" will be used as a general term for the twofold right "to move and reside freely" as enshrined in Article 18 EC (formerly Article 8a EC Treaty). This terminology is also employed, for example, in Article 11 (1) of the German Basic Law (*Grundgesetz*) and in Article 2 of the Fourth Protocol to the European Convention on Human Rights. In comparison, the European Union law contains a wider as well as – more recently – a narrower notion of "free movement". A wider notion of free movement can be found in Article 39 (1) EC, where the "freedom of movement for workers" not only encompasses their right to move and reside freely within the territory of other Member States, but also, first and foremost, their right to take up employment in other Member States.[4] In contrast, the European Charter of Fundamental Rights as well as the Treaty establishing a Constitution for Europe now adopt a significantly narrowed wording. There, the "free movement" is only and exclusively to be understood as the right to move freely, with the right to reside freely as a distinct right.[5] In the context of the following discussion, however, the notion "free movement" shall encompass the right to move freely as well as the right to reside freely. The main thrust of the argument lies here: while the notion encompasses both these alternatives, it is also limited to these two.

---

2 *See, in particular,* E.C.J. Case C-85/96 of 12 May 1998, E.C.R. 1998, I-2691 – *Martínez Sala*; E.C.J. Case C-184/99 of 20 September 2001, E.C.R. 2001, I-6193 – *Grzelczyk*; E.C.J. Case C-224/98 of 11 July 2002, E.C.R. 2002, I-6191 – *D'Hoop*; E.C.J. Case C-413/99 of 17 September 2002, E.C.R. 2002, I-7091 – *Baumbast*; E.C.J. Case C-224/02 of 29 April 2004, E.C.R. 2004, I-5763 – *Pusa*; E.C.J. Case C-456/02 of 7 September 2004, E.C.R. 2004, I-7573 – *Trojani*.

3 *See, explicitly, e.g.,* E.C.J. Case C-357/98 of 9 November 2000, E.C.R. 2000, I-9265 para. 25 – *Yiadom*; E.C.J. Case C-224/98 of 11 July 2002, E.C.R. 2002, I-6191 para. 29 – *D'Hoop*; E.C.J. Case C-224/02 of 29 April 2004, E.C.R. 2004, I-5763 paras. 16 *et seq.* – *Pusa*.

4 Referring to an even wider notion, the heading of Title III of the Third Part of the EC Treaty encompasses under "free movement of persons" even the self-employed persons' right of establishment.

5 Article 45 of the Charter of Fundamental Rights of the European Union, O.J. EC 2000 L 364, 1, and Article II-105 (1) of the Treaty establishing a Constitution for Europe, O.J. EC 2004 C 310, 1; as to the – inconsequent – simultaneous retention of wider notions of "free movement" *see* Article 52 (2) of the Charter and the headline to Articles III-133 *et seq.* of the Treaty establishing a Constitution for Europe.

Finally, free movement will only be examined in this work in so far as it is to be enjoyed by Union citizens; a consideration of questions relating to third country nationals and stateless persons would go beyond the scope of this paper.[6]

B. Market-related Rights of Free Movement

Some fundamental freedoms first of the common market, now of the internal market encompass free movement rights for nationals of the Member States.

I. Common Features of these Free Movement Rights

Three common features of these free movement rights should be highlighted here.

1. Free Movement Rights as Indispensable Elements of the Fundamental Freedoms of the Internal Market

From the beginning, free movement of persons has formed a central part of the common market.[7] Indeed, a common market, as well as now the internal market, cannot be imagined without the unhindered geographical mobility of its "market citizens"[8] in the Community-wide market. Therefore, European Community law has granted various special rights for Member States' nationals, allowing them to move and reside freely within the whole Community in order to pursue economic activities.

2. Free Movement Rights as Egalitarian Elements of the Fundamental Freedoms of the Internal Market

However, if a Member State's national makes use of such a right and moves to another Member State, he or she stays there not solely as an economic factor, but also as a human being with all his or her needs, fragilities and weaknesses. Therefore, he or she must not be treated in an ambiguous manner: in one respect welcomed as an economically promising achiever and consumer, protected by the Treaty's fundamental freedoms, and in another respect unwelcome as an alien. Indeed, he or she should be granted as far as possible a treatment no less favorable than that accorded to that State's own nationals. This should be reflected in the special guarantees for free movement enshrined in the market-related fundamental freedoms. In furtherance of this topic, the following subsections deal with the jurisprudence of the ECJ as well as the European Community's legislation as they relate to the various fundamental freedoms involved in the free movement of persons and their rights to equal treatment.

---

6 On this topic, *see, e.g.,* S. Magiera, *in* KOMMENTAR ZUR CHARTA DER GRUNDRECHTE DER EUROPÄISCHEN UNION (J. Meyer ed., 2003), Article 45 paras. 16 *et seq.*

7 *See* J. Bourrinet, *Vers une citoyenneté européenne. Aspects économiques*, REVUE DU MARCHÉ COMMUN ET DE L'UNION EUROPÉENNE 772, 774 (1992).

8 This notion of *"Marktbürger"* was coined in 1963 by H.P. Ipsen, *see id., in* LÜNEBURGER SYMPOSION FÜR HANS PETER IPSEN ZUR FEIER DES 80. GEBURTSTAGES 94 (G. Nicolaysen & H. Quaritsch eds., 1988). It underlines the fact that from 1958 on Community law has directly conferred far-reaching rights on nationals of the Member States, but for a long time only rights of a market-related nature.

3. Free Movement Rights as Subordinate Elements of the Fundamental Freedoms of the Internal Market

However, it must be borne in mind that free movement of persons in the sense indicated above has solely a subordinate function in conjunction with fundamental freedoms of the internal market. What is decisive here is the further-reaching economic goal which the fundamental freedoms in question are designed to serve, this being the facilitation of cross-border economic activities. The geographic mobility of persons wishing to pursue such activities is only a precondition in this context. Thus, free movement in the mere sense of a right to cross-border movement and residence constitutes, in the context of market-related freedoms, nothing more than a corollary[9] or accompanying right.[10]

II. The Free Movement of Workers

The "free movement of workers" guaranteed as a fundamental freedom by the Treaty in Article 39 EC (initially Article 48 of the European Economic Community Treaty, EEC Treaty) means the right of Member States' nationals to work in other Member States as employed persons. This right was and is exercised by millions of migrant EC workers throughout Europe. Hence, it has been fleshed out and further developed by Community legislation and the Court's jurisprudence on a large scale. For the purposes of this analysis, this comprehensive guarantee will be viewed as containing three aspects of particular interest touching free movement as understood in the narrow sense of mere geographic mobility: 1. the residential status, 2. the public policy proviso and 3. equality of treatment.

1. The Residential Status

The fact that guaranteed residence for migrant EC workers in the Member State of their employment is a precondition for their economic activity in that State is so obvious that from the beginning a right of residence was explicitly laid down in Article 48 EEC Treaty (now, following amendment, Article 39 EC).[11]

a) The Residential Status as a Treaty-based Right

Hence, the right of migrant EC workers to reside in the Member State of their employment flows directly from Treaty law. In this way, it cannot be considered terminologically correct in relation to Treaty law that secondary Community law still requires a "Residence Permit for a National of a Member State", valid for at least five years from the date of issue and unrestrictedly renewable.[12] These secondary law provisions merely give substance to rights which are inherent or express in the Treaty itself. For this reason the requirement for a residence permit can only be understood as a requirement for a declaratory proof of

---

9 With a view to the freedom of establishment (as enshrined in the Europe Agreement with the Czech Republic), see E.C.J. Case 257/99 of 27 September 2001, E.C.R. 2001, I-6557 para. 50 – *Barkoci and Malik*.
10 See U. Becker, *Freizügigkeit in der EU – auf dem Weg vom Begleitrecht zur Bürgerfreiheit*, EUROPARECHT (EuR) 522 *et seq.* (1999).
11 Article 48 (3) lit. c EEC Treaty (now, following amendment, Article 39 (3) lit c EC).
12 Article 4 (2) of Council Directive 68/360/EEC of 15 October 1968 on the abolition of restrictions on movement and residence within the Community for workers of Member States and their families, O.J. EC 1968 L 257, 13. This situation will change when the new Directive 2004/38/EC will have replaced the Directive 68/360/EEC with effect from 30 April 2006, *see infra* note 243.

an already existing right of residence.[13] Breaches of corresponding declaration and registration formalities by migrant EC workers may be sanctioned by the Member States on the condition that these States prescribe similar formalities to their own nationals. The national authorities are then entitled to impose sanctions on migrant EC workers comparable to those imposed on nationals for infringement of the provisions of such formalities.[14] Imprisonment or even expulsion of migrant EC workers, however, must never be imposed as sanctions in this context.[15]

b) Extensions of the Residential Status

The Treaty grants migrant EC workers not only the right to reside within another Member State for the purpose of actual employment, but also for seeking work during a period of at least six months.[16] Furthermore, secondary law protects the right of a worker to remain in the territory of a Member State in the event of temporary incapacity to work or involuntary unemployment[17] as well as, through its continuing effect following the termination of working life, in the event of retirement or permanent incapacity to work.[18] In these respects, the free movement of workers extends beyond a purely economic perspective.

c) Benefits for Family Members

The latter is also true with regard to the family members of migrant EC workers including those members who are not nationals of a Member State. While the Treaty still ignores these people, secondary law has granted them from very early on a complementary right to reside in the migrant workers' host State.[19] In taking such an approach, European Community law has recognized that a migrant EC worker enters the Member State of his or her employment not only as a mobile unit of production, but as a human being with social relations and needs. Without this legal acceptance of the worker's family members in the host State, a national of a Member State might not even be willing or able to leave his or her country of origin in order to be employed in another Member State.

2. The Public Policy Proviso

Freedom of movement for workers is granted, according to Article 39 (3) EC, "subject to limitations justified on grounds of public policy, public security or public health". However, the absence of such grounds must not be regarded as a condition precedent to the acquisition of the right of entry and residence. The clause only provides the option, in

---

13 E.C.J. Case C-48/75 of 8 April 1976, E.C.R. 1976, 497 paras. 31/33 – *Royer*; E.C.J. Case 8/77 of 14 July 1977, E.C.R. 1977, 1495 para. 8 – *Sagulo, Brenca and Bakhouche*.
14 E.C.J. Case C-24/97 of 30 April 1998, E.C.R. 1998, I-2133 paras. 13 *et seq.* – *Commission v Germany* (penalties in the event of failure to comply with the obligation to hold a residence permit).
15 E.C.J. Case C-48/75 of 8 April 1976, E.C.R. 1976, 497 paras. 38 *et seq.* – *Royer*; E.C.J. Case 157/79 of 3 July 1980, E.C.R. 1980, 2171 paras. 18 *et seq.* – *Pieck*.
16 Article 48 (3) lit. b EEC Treaty (now, following amendment, Article 39 (3) lit. b EC); E.C.J. Case C-292/89 of 26 February 1991, E.C.R. 1991, I-745 – *Antonissen*.
17 Article 7 (1) of Directive 68/360/EEC (*supra*, note 12).
18 Article 48 (3) lit. d EEC Treaty (now, following amendment, Article 39 (3) lit. d EC) and Commission Regulation 1251/70/EEC of 29 June 1970 on the right of workers to remain in the territory of a Member State after having been employed in that State, O.J. EC 1970 No. 142, 24.
19 Article 10 of Council Regulation (EEC) No. 1612/68 of 15 October 1968 on freedom of movement of workers within the Community, O.J. EC 1968 No. 257, 2, with subsequent amendments; Article 1 of Regulation (EC) No. 1251/70 (*supra*, note 18). *See*, recently, E.C.J. Case C-109/01 of 23 September 2003, E.C.R. 2003, I-9607 paras. 48 *et seq.* – *Akrich*.

individual cases where there is sufficient justification, of imposing restrictions on the exercise of the rights of entry and residence directly conferred by the Treaty.[20] These restrictions *vis-à-vis* nationals of other Member States can consist in measures which the Member States could not apply to their own nationals, inasmuch as they have no authority *vis-à-vis* the latter to deny them access to the national territory, to expel them from the national territory or to limit their rights of entry and residence to a mere part of the national territory.[21]

Hence, the true degree of free movement enjoyed by migrant EC workers depends on how this public policy proviso is actually interpreted and applied. The Court has stated:

> In so far as it may justify certain restrictions on the free movement of persons subject to Community law, recourse by a national authority to the concept of public policy presupposes, in any event, the existence, in addition to the perturbation of the social order which any infringement of the law involves, of a genuine and sufficiently serious threat to the requirements of public policy affecting one of the fundamental interests of society.[22]

Therefore, while accepting that the Member States will retain a certain discretion,[23] the Court has interpreted this derogation to the principle of free movement narrowly. Moreover, the scope of the public policy proviso has been further defined in secondary legislation. Grounds of public policy, security or health shall not be invoked by Member States in restricting rights of free movement to serve economic ends (such as, for example, to secure jobs for nationals or to protect the national public finances from foreign covetousness). Measures taken shall be based exclusively on the personal conduct of the individual concerned, and criminal convictions shall not in themselves constitute grounds for the taking of such public policy measures by Member States.[24] Consequently, the public policy proviso can only be used as a last resort in cases of serious threat to the protected interests and cannot otherwise take away a worker's right of free movement within the Union.

3. Equality of Treatment

The free movement of workers also requires that migrant EC workers not be treated as second-class persons in other legal fields.

a) The Non-discrimination Clause

Therefore, Article 39 (2) EC provides a comprehensive prohibition of discrimination against migrant EC workers on grounds of nationality. This prohibition has been further elaborated in secondary law and is taken very seriously by the ECJ. Accordingly, Community law prohibits not only direct discrimination based on nationality, but also all

---

20 E.C.J. Case 48/75 of 8 April 8, E.C.R. 1976, 497 para. 29 – *Royer*; E.C.J. Case 157/79 of 3 July 1980, E.C.R. 1980, 2171 para. 9 – *Pieck*; E.C.J. Case 321/87 of 27 April 1989, E.C.R. 1989, 997 para. 10 – *Commission v Belgium* (border controls).
21 *See* E.C.J. Cases C-65/95 and 111/95 of 17 June 1997, E.C.R. 1997, I-3343 para. 28 – *Shingara and Radiom*; E.C.J. Case C-100/01 of 26 November 2002, E.C.R. 2002, I-10931 paras. 40 *et seq.* – *Olazabal*, see F. Chaltiel, *L'ordre public devant la Cour de justice des Communautés européennes. A propos de l'arrêt Olazabal du 26 novembre 2002*, REVUE DU MARCHÉ COMMUN ET DE L'UNION EUROPÉENNE 2003, 120 *et seq.*
22 E.C.J. Case 30/77 of 27 October 1977, E.C.R. 1977, 1999 paras. 33/35 – *Bouchereau*.
23 E.C.J. Case 36/75 of 28 October 1975, E.C.R. 1975, 1219 paras. 26/28 – *Rutili*.
24 Article 2 (2) and Article 3 (1) and (2) of Council Directive (EEC) 64/221 of 25 February 1964 on the coordination of special measures concerning the movement and residence of foreign nationals which are justified on grounds of public policy, public security or public health, O.J. EC 1964, 850. On these requirements recently, *see* E.C.J. Cases C-482/01 and C-493/01 of 29 April 2004, E.C.R. 2004, I-5257 – *Orfanopoulos and Oliveri*.

covert or indirect forms of discrimination which, by the application of other criteria of differentiation (e.g. place of origin or residence), result in giving preference to national workers over migrant EC workers.[25] Even national legislation on a jobseeker's allowance can make entitlement to such an allowance conditional on a residence requirement only to a very limited extent.[26] Moreover, a migrant EC worker must not suffer from a reduction in ability to obtain social benefits from his or her State of origin as a result of having exercised his or her right to free movement instead of remaining in this State.[27]

b) Social and Tax Advantages

Furthermore, migrant EC workers enjoy not only a right to equal working conditions, but also a right to "the same social and tax advantages as national workers".[28] This right goes beyond the special rules in the field of social security designed to provide freedom of movement for workers.[29] It has been held even to cover public payments which, though not addressed explicitly to workers, actually benefit national workers, when the extension of these payments to migrant EC workers seems suitable to facilitate the cross-border mobility of workers in the Community. This includes social assistance as well as interest-free "childbirth loans" granted to low-income families in order to stimulate the birth rate of the population.[30]

c) Danger of Abusive Claims for Student Grants

Moreover, the Court has ruled that educational grants for students can be considered "social advantages" for workers. Accordingly, nationals of a Member State who decide to pursue university studies in another Member State following employment in that State are entitled to student grants and other social advantages on an equal footing with nationals of the host State. This entitlement derives from their previous status as migrant EC workers.[31] However, because the notion of "worker" in Article 39 EC does not require a minimum duration of employment in the host state,[32] there is an obvious danger of people becoming employed for short time periods in the host Member State in order to qualify for student grants.

The ECJ seeks to preclude such abuse in a twofold manner. Firstly, if the worker has voluntarily left employment in order to take up a course of full-time study, the Court requires that there be a link (i.e. a substantive continuity) between the previous employment and the course of study now undertaken.[33] Secondly, the Court has established that

---

25 E.C.J. Case 152/73 of 12 February 1974, E.C.R. 1974, 153, paras. 11–13 – *Sotgiu*; E.C.J. Case C-326/90 of 10 November 1992, E.C.R. 1992, I-5517 – *Commission v Belgium* (Residence Requirement); E.C.J. Case C-350/96 of 7 May 1998, 1998 E.C.R. I-2521 para. 29 – *Clean Car Autoservice*; E.C.J. Case C-290/00 of 18 April 2002, E.C.R. 2002, I-3567 para. 38 – *Duchon*.
26 E.C.J. Case C-138/02 of 23 March 2004, E.C.R. 2004, I-2703 para. 72 – *Collins*.
27 E.C.J. Case 10/90 of 7 March 1991, E.C.R. 1991, I-1119 para. 18 – *Masgio*; Article 3 (1) of Council Regulation (EEC) 1408/71 on the application of social security schemes to employed persons and their families moving within the Community, O.J. EC 1971 L 149, 2.
28 Article 7 (2) of Regulation (EEC) 1612/68 (*supra*, note 19).
29 See, e.g., Art. 42 EC and the Council Regulation (EEC) No. 1408/71 of 14 June 1971 on the application of social security schemes to employed persons and their families moving within the Community, O.J. EC 1971 L 149, 2, with subsequent amendments.
30 E.C.J. Case 122/84 of 27 March 1985, E.C.R. 1985, 1027 – *Scrivner*; E.C.J. Case 68/81 of 14 January 1982, E.C.R. 1982, 33 – *Reina*.
31 E.C.J. Case 39/86 of 21 June 1988, E.C.R. 1988, 3161 – *Lair*.
32 E.C.J. Case 249/83 of 27 March 1985, E.C.R. 1985, 973 – *Hoeckx*; E.C.J. Case 157/84 of 6 June 1985, E.C.R. 1985, 1739 – *Frascogna I*.
33 E.C.J. Case 39/86 of 21 June 1988, E.C.R. 1988, 3161 para. 37 – *Lair*; E.C.J. Case C-413/01 of 6 November 2003 (not yet published in E.C.R.) para. 35 – *Ninni-Orasche*.

a migrant EC worker's entitlement to a student grant will be denied if it can be established on the basis of objective evidence that the worker has entered a foreign Member State for the sole purpose of enjoying, after a very short period of occupational activity, the benefit of a student grant in that State. In these circumstances the occupational activity is only a subordinate transition stage leading to the studies the migrant worker actually wishes to undertake. It would constitute an abuse to found a claim for a student grant on such a "merely ancillary" employment relationship.[34]

d) Prohibition of Discrimination against Family Members

Finally, secondary legislation prohibits discrimination against workers' family members and ensures there are no barriers to their freedom of movement.[35] In particular, children of migrant EC workers residing in the host State are entitled to the same educational grants for secondary school and university education as children of nationals of the host State. Where grants are available to the children of nationals to enable them to study abroad, these grants must also be made available to the children of migrant EC workers, even if their studies abroad are to be undertaken in the Member States of which the migrant EC workers are citizens.[36]

e) Assessment

In an overall assessment, it becomes clear that the free movement of workers is an area of law which has been highly developed. Its scope exceeds by far the securing of mere physical cross-border mobility and aims at the full integration of migrant EC workers and their families in the social structure of the host countries.

III. The Free Movement of Persons as Part of the Right of Establishment

Parallel to the free movement of workers provided for in Article 39 EC, the freedom of establishment pursuant to Article 43 EC (initially Article 52 EEC Treaty) forms a basic guarantee which allows for permanent self-employed economic activity of Member States' nationals through fixed infrastructures in other Member States. This freedom necessarily encompasses rights of the self-employed Union citizens to move and reside freely.[37] Hence, the ECJ held that, even in the absence of an explicit reference in Article 43 EC to these rights, they could be invoked as directly effective Treaty-based rights by Member States' nationals seeking to exercise their rights of establishment as self-employed persons in another Member State.[38] The free movement of their family members is ensured through

---

34 E.C.J. Case 39/86 of 21 June 1988, E.C.R. 1988, 3161 para. 43 – *Lair*; E.C.J. Case 197/86 of 21 June 1988, E.C.R. 1988, 3205 para. 27 – *Brown*; E.C.J. Case C-413/01 of 6 November 2003 (not yet published in E.C.R.) paras. 36 and 47 – *Ninni-Orasche*.
35 Articles 10 *et seq.* of Regulation (EEC) No. 1612/68 (*supra*, note 19). E.C.J. Case 32/75 of 30 September 1975, E.C.R. 1975, 1085 – *Cristini*; E.C.J. Case 256/86 of 9 July 1987, E.C.R. 1987, 3431 para. 9 – *Frascogna II*.
36 Article 12 of Regulation (EEC) 1612/68 (*supra*, note 19); E.C.J. Case 9/74 of 3 July 1974, E.C.R. 1974, 773 – *Casagrande*; E.C.J. Cases 389/87 and 390/87 of 15 March 1989, E.C.R. 1989, 723 paras. 33 *et seq.* – *Echternach und Moritz*; E.C.J. Case C-308/89 of 13 October 1990, E.C.R. 1990, I-4185 – *di Leo*; *see also* E.C.J. Case C-3/90 of 26 February 1992, E.C.R. 1992, I-1071 – *Bernini*.
37 *See, e.g.*, M. Schlag, *in* EU-KOMMENTAR (J. Schwarze ed., 2000), Article 43 EC para. 50 *et seq.*; A. Scheuer, *in* EU- UND EG-VERTRAG. KOMMENTAR (C.O. Lenz & K.-D. Borchardt eds., 3rd ed., 2003), Article 43 para. 15; F. WEISS & F. WOOLRIDGE, FREE MOVEMENT OF PERSONS WITHIN THE EUROPEAN COMMUNITY 49 (2002).
38 E.C.J. Case C-48/75 of 8 April 1976, E.C.R. 1976, 497 paras. 19/23 – *Royer*; E.C.J. Case 118/75 of 7 July 1976, E.C.R. 1976, 1185 paras. 11/12 – *Watson and Belmann*. *See also* Council Directive (EEC) 73/148 of

complementary secondary legislation.[39] There is also a public policy proviso[40] which corresponds to the proviso applicable in the context of the free movement of workers and construed in a similar way.[41]

Moreover, the principle of equal treatment, which is formulated in Article 43 (2) EC explicitly as a principle of equal treatment of nationals of the host Member State and self-employed nationals of other Member States, is also applicable in this context. This provision even opens up access to leisure activities as "a corollary to that freedom of movement".[42] Therefore, the right to register a vessel other than a fishing vessel (for example, a pleasure craft) must not be limited to nationals of the host State, but must be extended to self-employed nationals of other Member States established in that State.[43] If a national of one Member State, who pursues an activity as a self-employed person in another Member State, has children, they can invoke the principle of non-discrimination laid down in Article 43 (2) EC (initially Article 52 (2) EEC Treaty) to obtain study grants under the same conditions as are applicable to children of nationals of the host State.[44]

IV. The Free Movement of Persons as Part of the Freedom to Provide Services

The freedom to provide services, covered by Article 49 EC (initially Article 59 EEC Treaty), means the freedom for self-employed nationals of a Member State occasionally to exercise remunerated economic activities in another Member State without establishing themselves there permanently, in so far as these activities are not governed by other fundamental freedoms of the internal market. As far as the freedom to provide services implies the crossing of Member State borders within the European Union by persons pursuing an economic activity, this fundamental freedom also must encompass a right to free movement. This does not apply when only services as such cross Member State borders as can be the case, for example, with insurance or telecommunications services.[45] However, such a right to free movement of persons is required when persons have to cross Member State borders in order either to provide or to receive services in another Member State.

1. Free Movement of Service Providers

Under Article 49 (1) EC, self-employed nationals of Member States are granted the right personally to provide services in other Member States. Hence, even though the Treaty does not explicitly mention, in that context, rights to move and reside freely, the Court rightly

---

21 March 1973 on the abolition of restrictions on movement and residence within the Community for nationals of Member States with regard to establishment and the provision of services, O.J. EC 1973 L 172, 14.

39 Directive (EEC) 73/148 (*supra* note 38). E.C.J. Case C-370/90 of 7 July 1992, E.C.R. 1992, I-4265 paras. 17 *et seq.* – *Singh*.
40 Article 46 (1) EC; Directive (EEC) 64/221 (*supra* note 24).
41 E.C.J. Cases 115 and 116/81 of 18 May 1982, E.C.R. 1982, 1665 paras. 5 *et seq.* – *Adoui und Cornuaille*.
42 Sic E.C.J. Case C-334/94 of 7 March 1996, E.C.R. 1996, I-1307 para. 21 – *Commission v France* (registration of vessels), and E.C.J. Case C-151/96 of 12 June 1997, E.C.R. 1997, I-3327 para. 13 – *Commission v Ireland* (registration of vessels).
43 E.C.J. Case C-334/94 of 7 March 1996, E.C.R. 1996, I-1307 – *Commission v France* (registration of vessels), and E.C.J. Case C-151/96 of 12 June 1997, E.C.R. 1997, I-3327 – *Commission v Ireland* (registration of vesseis).
44 E.C.J. Case C-337/97 of 8 June 1999, E.C.R. 1999, I-3289 paras. 27 *et seq.* – *Meeusen*.
45 As to this kind of services, *see, e.g.*, M. Holoubek, *in* EU-KOMMENTAR (J. Schwarze ed., 2000), Article 49 EGV paras. 52 *et seq.*; W. Kluth, *in* KOMMENTAR ZUM EU-VERTRAG UND EG-VERTRAG (C. Calliess & M. Ruffert eds., 2nd ed., 2002), Article 50 EC Treaty para. 29.

held that this Treaty provision contains such rights for service providers and that they are Treaty-based rights having direct effect.[46] These rights include the service provider's right to provide staffing, i.e. to send his or her employees to another Member State, in order to implement the provision of the services in question.[47]

2. Free Movement of Service Recipients

Furthermore, the ECJ has widened the scope of the freedom to provide services by stating that this freedom also covers cases in which a Member State's national goes to another Member State to receive a service there, for example a surgery in the host State. Thus, the Court affirmed a directly effective Treaty-based freedom of movement for recipients of services which is in particular exercised by legions of tourists, having recourse to hotel lodging and numerous other services in other Member States.[48]

3. Limitations

However, the freedom of movement for service providers as well as for service recipients is limited to the temporary cross-border pursuit of economic activities.[49] Consequently, a national of a Member State who takes up permanent residence in another Member State in order to provide or receive services there, is not covered by the guarantee of free movement of services.[50] In such cases this person may be able to provide or to receive services through rights contained in the freedom of establishment or the free movement of workers, though. For the rest, once a Member State restriction on the freedom to provide services is found to exist, it is open to the Member State to justify the restriction on grounds of public policy, security, or health, similar to the other fundamental freedoms discussed above.

Through Article 55 EC, those derogations set out in Article 46 (1) EC are also applicable to the freedom to provide services.[51] However, in cases concerning this freedom, since it is not the transfer of a person's main residence into a foreign Member State which is at stake, the Member States may enjoy here, when applying the public policy clause, a slightly wider discretion than is seen in cases concerning the free movement of workers or the right of establishment. Nevertheless, the Court has held that the public policy proviso does not allow a Member State to expel for life from its territory nationals of other Member States found guilty on that territory of offences related to drugs, be they

---

46 E.C.J. Case 48/75 of 8 April 1976, E.C.R. 1976, 497 paras. 19, 23, 50 et seq. – *Royer*; E.C.J. Case C-363/89 of 5 February 1991, E.C.R. 1991, I-273 para. 9 – *Roux*. Rather far-reaching, however, the Court's characterisation of the deportation order for a service provider's third-country national spouse, expelled from the provider's State of origin and residence, as constituting a violation of his right freely to provide services, in: E.C.J. Case C-60/00 of 11 July 2002, E.C.R. 2002, I-6279 – *Carpenter*; on this case see S. Puth, *Die unendliche Weite der Grundfreiheiten des EG-Vertrags*, EuR 2002, 860, 865 et seq.

47 E.C.J. Case C-113/89 of 27 March 1990, E.C.R. 1990, I-1417 – *Rush Portuguesa*; E.C.J. Case C-43/93 of 9 August 1994, E.C.R. 1994, I-3803 – *Vander Elst*.

48 E.C.J. Cases 286/82 and 26/83 of 31 January 1984, E.C.R. 1984, 377 para. 10 – *Luisi and Carbone*; E.C.J. Case C-68/98 of 30 May 1991, E.C.R. 1991, I-2637 para. 10 – *Commission v Netherlands* (border controls); E.C.J. Case C-274/96 of 24 November 1998, E.C.R. 1998, I-7637 para. 15 – *Bickel and Franz*.

49 See Article 50 (3) EC.

50 E.C.J. Case 196/87 of 5 October 1988, E.C.R. 1988, 6159 para. 17 – *Steymann*; E.C.J. Case C-456/02 of 7 September 2004, E.C.R. 2004, I-7573 para. 28 – *Trojani*; E.C.J. Case C-200/02 of 19 October 2004, E.C.R. 2004, I-9923 para 22 – *Zhu and Chen*.

51 Article 55 in conjunction with Article 46 (1) EC. As to secondary law, e.g. the Directive (EEC) 64/221 (*supra*, note 24) and the Directive (EEC) 73/148 (*supra* note 38) encompass explicitly the provision of services.

recipients of services (tourists), migrant EC workers or self-employed persons exercising their right of establishment.[52]

4. Equality of Treatment

Finally, the principle of equal treatment, expressly laid down in Article 50 (3) EC with regard to service providers, also covers recipients of services. This principle even guarantees to service recipients, as far as is useful for the actual exercise of their right to receive services, equal access to social housing and reduced-rate mortgage loans in the host State.[53]

Furthermore, in cases only loosely linked with the enjoyment of services, the Court additionally cites the general prohibition, contained in Article 12 EC (initially Article 7 EEC Treaty; later on Article 6 EC Treaty), against discrimination on grounds of nationality within the scope of application of the Treaty.[54] Hence, the ECJ assumes that the Treaty applies to nationals of a Member State who travel to another Member State in exercise of their right to receive services. These people can invoke a right to equal treatment on par with nationals of the host State – even without actually receiving services. Consequently, the host State must protect them from violent crime on the same basis as its own nationals. If they are victims of a crime, as it happened to the British national Cowan in Paris, they are entitled to the same State compensation for criminal injury as is available to nationals. The Court's reasoning which leads to this finding is formulated in rather general terms: "When Community law guarantees a natural person the freedom to go to another Member State, the protection of that person from harm in the Member State in question, on the same basis as that of nationals and persons residing there, is a corollary of that freedom of movement."[55]

5. Beginning Merger of Specific Rights of Free Movement into a General Right of Free Movement

In the Court's ruling in *Cowan*, one may easily discover a tendency to treat these specific guarantees of free movement as practically congruent. This tendency can also be found in numerous other decisions on aspects of free movement contained in the fundamental freedoms of the internal market. The Court often refers to several or even all fundamental freedoms of the internal market which have aspects of free movement (as well as to the relevant secondary law).[56] Sometimes the Court even emphasizes explicitly that exact classi-

---

52 E.C.J. Case C-348/96 of 19 January 1999, E.C.R. 1999, I-11 para. 29 – *Calfa*. See, regarding workers' freedom of movement and freedom of establishment, E.C.J. Case 115 and 116/81 of 18 May 1982, E.C.R. 1982, 1665 para. 12 – *Adoui and Cornuaille*; E.C.J. Cases C-65/95 and C-111/95 of 17 June 1997, E.C.R. 1997, I-3343 paras. 39 et seq. – *Shingara and Radiom*.
53 E.C.J. Case C-305/87 of 30 May 1989, E.C.R. para. 24 – *Commission v Greece* (real estate property); E.C.J. Case 63/86 of 14 January 1988, E.C.R. 1988, 29 – *Commission v Italy* (social housing and reduced-rate mortgage loans).
54 *See*, recently, E.C.J. Case C-388/01 of 16 January 2003, E.C.R. 2003, I-721 para. 12 – *Commission v Italy* (admission to museums).
55 E.C.J. Case 186/87 of 3 February 1989, E.C.R. 1989, 195 para. 17 – *Cowan*.
56 *See, e.g.* E.C.J. Case 48/75 of 8 April 1976, E.C.R. 1976, 497 paras. 19 et seq. and 50 et seq. – *Royer*; E.C.J. Case 16/78 of 28 November 1978, E.C.R. 1978, 2293 para. 8 – *Choquet*; E.C.J. Case C-363/89 of 5 February 1991, E.C.R. 1991, I-273 para. 9 – *Roux*; E.C.J. Case C-68/98 of 30 May 1991, E.C.R. 1991, I-2637 para. 10 – *Commission v Netherlands* (border controls); E.C.J. Case C-24/97 of 30 April 1998, E.C.R. 1998, I-2133 para. 11 – *Commission v Germany* (sanctions in the event of failure to comply with the obligation to hold a residence permit); E.C.J. Case C-348/96 of 19 January 1999, E.C.R. 1999, I-11 para. 18 – *Calfa*; E.C.J. Case C-337/97 of 8 June 1999, E.C.R. 1999, I-3289 – *Meeusen*.

fication is irrelevant for its ruling.[57] Here can be seen, although still retaining a certain market-relation, the beginnings of the merger of specific guarantees of free movement into a general right of free movement.

C. The General Right of Free Movement

Since 1993, the primary law has contained, through Article 8a EC Treaty (now, following amendment, Article 18 EC) a provision which has been formulated from the outset as a general right to free movement. Prior to analyzing this Treaty provision in detail, its prefigurations, emerging from two converging strands of legal development, will be examined. These two developments, which have been of crucial importance in the creation of Article 8a EC Treaty (now, following amendment, Article 18 EC), will be presented in sections I and II. Firstly, in section I the introduction of non-market-related rights to free movement through secondary legislation will be retraced. Section II will then deal with the shaping of an education-related right to free movement through the Court's jurisprudence. Following this, the genesis of the general right of free movement will be recalled in section III, after which the direct effect of the general right of free movement will be discussed in Section IV. Section V will look at relations between the general right of free movement and other guarantees of free movement in Community law. Section VI will point out limitation possibilities, and finally section VII will focus on the equality of treatment.

I. The Introduction of Non-market-related Rights of Free Movement in Secondary Law

As early as 1977, the European Parliament expressed a demand for a "right to residence for all citizens of the Community".[58] This demand originated from the intention to complement the common market with a "Citizens' Europe". As a result, in 1979 the Commission proposed the introduction of a general right of residence laid down in one single directive.[59] However, this proposed legislation never came into existence. Instead, a series of three directives based on Article 235 EC Treaty (now, following amendment, Article 308 EC) were enacted in 1990 to confer rights of residence on a number of residual categories of persons who are not economically active (pensioners, students, other nationals of the Member States not covered otherwise by residence rights as well as their respective family members).

This series of directives in its entirety practically filled the *lacunae* regarding rights to free movement left by the fundamental freedoms of the internal market.[60] The fact that those *lacunae* consisted of the lack of non-market-related rights to free movement may also explain a peculiarity which can be found in all three residence directives. As "filling the gap" meant not a further shaping of existing rights laid down in primary law, but

---

57 E.C.J. Case C-363/89 of 5 February 1991, E.C.R. 1991, I-273 para. 23 – *Roux*.
58 Point 3 j of the Resolution of the European Parliament of 16 November 1977 on the attribution of special rights to the citizens of the European Community, in application of the decisions taken at the Paris Summit of December 1974 (Point 11 of the Final Communiqué), O.J. EC 1977 C 299, 26. See R. Bieber, *"Besondere Rechte" für die Bürger der Europäischen Gemeinschaften*, Europäische Grundrechte Zeitschrift (EuGRZ) 203, 206 (1978).
59 Commission Proposal for a Council Directive on a right of residence for nationals of Member States in the territory of another Member State (COM(79)215 final), O.J. EC 1979 C 207, 14.
60 Council Directive (EEC) 90/365 of 28 June 1990 on the right of residence for employees and self-employed persons who have ceased their occupational activity, O.J. EC 1990 L 180, 28; Council Directive (EEC) 90/366 of 28 June 1990 on the right of residence for students, O.J. EC 1990 L 180, 30; Council Directive (EEC) 90/364 of 28 June 1990 on the right of residence, O.J. EC 1990 L 180, 26.

rather the constituent introduction of new rights to free movement through secondary legislation, the meaning and scope of these new residence rights could freely be defined. On this point, Member States with high standards of social welfare were concerned that their social assistance systems could become overburdened as a result of granting an unrestricted right of residence to all nationals of the Member States, including migrants from Member States whose systems of social welfare were less generous. Therefore, in order to prevent "social welfare tourism", a social cover proviso was inserted into all three residence directives. Accordingly, the Member States granted non-market-related rights of movement and residence to nationals of other Member States "provided that they themselves and the members of their families (...) are covered by sickness insurance in respect of all risks in the host Member State and have sufficient resources to avoid becoming a burden on the social assistance system of the host Member State during their period of residence".[61]

In the course of events following this, the students' directive was declared void by the ECJ because it was enacted on the basis of an improper Treaty provision. However, the Court stated that the effects of the directive annulled were provisionally to remain in force.[62] The students' directive was again enacted in 1993, without any substantive change, but henceforth based on Article 7 (2) EC Treaty (now, following amendment, Article 12 (2) EC) which the Court had held to be the proper Treaty provision.[63] Furthermore, the implementation of the three directives caused problems leading up to Court proceedings. In two rulings, the ECJ found Germany and Italy to be in breach of their obligations under Community law.[64]

II. The Shaping of an Education-related Right of Free Movement in Primary Law

The ECJ developed additionally an education-related right of free movement in the framework of primary Community law which was based on the general prohibition of discrimination on grounds of nationality within the scope of application of the Treaty, laid down in Article 7 EC Treaty (now, following amendment, Article 12 EC). At issue was the question of access to vocational training in Member States' public educational institutions by nationals of other Member States who could not claim market-related rights of free movement (e.g., as migrant EC workers or children of such workers).[65] In those cases, the freedom to receive services could not be invoked as long as no remuneration was charged for vocational training offered by public educational institutions.[66]

The ECJ decided, based on rather generally formulated Treaty provisions on vocational training (initially Article 128 EEC Treaty; now, following amendment, Article 149

---

61 Article 1(1) of Directive 90/364 (*supra* note 60); similarly Article 1(1) of Directive 90/365 (*supra* note 60) and Article 1(1) of Directive 90/366 (*supra* note 60).
62 E.C.J. Case C-295/90 of 7 July 1992, E.C.R. 1992, I-4193 – *European Parliament v Council* (students' directive). See, e.g., R. Kampf, *Die "richtige" Rechtsgrundlage der Richtlinie über das Aufenthaltsrecht der Studenten*, EuR 1990, 393 et seq.; E. Klein & A. Haratsch, *Das Aufenthaltsrecht der Studenten, die Unionsbürgerschaft und intertemporales Gemeinschaftsrecht*, JURISTISCHE SCHULUNG (JuS) 7 et seq. (1995).
63 Council Directive (EEC) 93/96 of 29 October 1993 on the right of residence for students, O.J. EC 1993 L 317, 59.
64 E.C.J. Case C-96/95 of 20 March 1997, E.C.R. 1997, I-1653 – *Commission v Germany* (residence directive); E.C.J. Case 424/98 of 25 May 2000, E.C.R. 2000, I-4001 – *Commission v Italy* (residence directive). See also Report from the Commission to the Council and the European Parliament on the implementation of Directives 90/364, 90/365 and 93/96 – (right of residence), COM(99)0127 final; G. de Búrca, *Report on the further development of citizenship in the European Union*, in REFERATE FÜR DEN 1. EUROPÄISCHEN JURISTENTAG NÜRNBERG 2001, 2001, 39, 55.
65 On these aspects of market-related guarantees of free movement, see *supra* notes 31, 36 and 44.
66 E.C.J. Case 263/86 of 27 September 1988, E.C.R. 1988, 5365 paras. 16 et seq. – *Humbel*.

et seq. EC), that the conditions of access to vocational training fall within the scope of application of the Treaty. Therefore it would be contrary to Article 7 EC Treaty (now, following amendment, Article 12 EC) to charge nationals of other Member States a specific enrolment fee for access to vocational training which nationals of the host State were not required to pay.[67] Furthermore, the Court held, still based on the principle of non-discrimination enshrined in Article 7 EC Treaty, that a national of a Member State who has been admitted to a vocational training course in another Member State must have a right of residence in that State for the duration of the course.[68] Thus, the Court derived from existing primary law an implicit education-related right of free movement.

However, the Court added immediately, probably with the intention of keeping its judgment in line with the directive on the right of residence for students enacted in 1990, that the host Member State could impose conditions "deriving from the legitimate interests of the Member State", such as requirements that the person provide for his or her own maintenance costs and health insurance.[69] The Court also placed another limit – notwithstanding certain inconsequencies.[70] According to the Court this education-related right of free movement did not require that grants available to nationals of the host State to cover their basic needs also be made available to nationals of other Member States. In distinction from the workers' freedom of movement, the education-related right of free movement would only provide a right to equal treatment in so far as the educational grants were meant to cover enrolment fees.[71]

III. The Genesis of the General Right of Free Movement

The legal developments, which have been described above, prepared the ground for the introduction of a general right of free movement into primary Community law. Indeed, in the course of the negotiations leading up to the Maastricht Treaty, the Commission[72] as well as the Spanish Government[73] submitted proposals concerning such a right. The insertion of a general right of free movement into the EC Treaty in the context of the issues discussed above would be in one respect an appropriate synthesis of previous developments, and in another respect a conspicuous furnishing of the newly introduced Union citizenship with a basic right. This right would, through the use of suitable wording including explicit restrictions, not develop unwanted innovative dynamics.

1. The Basic Guarantee

The Member States finally agreed upon the following formulation which was laid down in Article 8a (1) EC and which entered into force on 1 November 1993:

---

67 E.C.J. Case 293/83 of 13 February 1985, E.C.R. 1985, 593 – *Gravier*; E.C.J. Case 24/86 of 2 February 1988, E.C.R. 1988, 379 para. 24 – *Blaizot*.
68 E.C.J. Case C-357/89 of 26 February 1992, E.C.R. 1992, I-1027 para. 34 – *Raulin*; E.C.J. Case 295/90 of 7 July 1992, E.C.R. 1992, I-4193 para. 15 – *European Parliament v Council* (students' right of residence). See also E. Klein & A. Haratsch, *Neuere Entwicklungen des Rechts der Europäischen Gemeinschaften. 2. Teil*, DIE ÖFFENTLICHE VERWALTUNG (DÖV) 133, 134 (1994); VAN DER MEI, FREE MOVEMENT (*supra* note 1), 371 *et seq*.
69 E.C.J. Case C-357/89 of 26 February 1992, E.C.R. 1992, I-1027 para. 39 – *Raulin*. See also Klein & Haratsch, *supra* note 62, 11.
70 On their subsequent correction, *see infra* note 219.
71 E.C.J. Case C-39/86 of 21 June 1988, E.C.R. 1988, 3161 paras. 14 *et seq.* – *Lair*; E.C.J. Case C-357/89 of 26 February 1992, E.C.R. 1992, I-1027 para. 28 – *Raulin*.
72 *See* the Commission's statement of 21 October 1990, Bull. EC, Annex 2/91, 69 (91).
73 *See* the proposal of 21 February 1991, submitted by the Spanish Delegation, *cited in* E. A. MARIAS (ED.), EUROPEAN CITIZENSHIP 141, 143 (1994).

Every citizen of the Union shall have the right to move and reside freely within the territory of the Member States, subject to the limitations and conditions laid down in this Treaty and by the measures adopted to give it effect.[74]

This provision has remained unchanged, but is now Article 18 (1) EC.

2. The Authorization to adopt Secondary Law

In addition, in Article 8a (2) EC Treaty (now, following amendment, Article 18 (2) EC) the Council has been authorized to adopt provisions "with a view to facilitating the exercise of the rights referred to in paragraph 1". The Maastricht Treaty initially had granted this authorization unconditionally. However, since the entering-into-force of the Nice Treaty on February 1, 2003 the Council's right to adopt such provisions has been limited to situations where action by the Community is necessary to ensure free movement for Union citizens and the necessary powers cannot be found in the Treaty.

3. Changes to Procedure for Adopting Secondary Law

The procedure for adopting such secondary law also underwent changes. The Maastricht Treaty had required, as necessary procedural steps, a Commission proposal, an approval by the European Parliament and a unanimous vote by the Council. In the Amsterdam Treaty, the co-decision procedure was declared applicable to the participation of the European Parliament, while the Council still had to act unanimously. The Nice Treaty has abolished that requirement of unanimity, and the rules on the co-decision procedure in Article 251 EC are now to be applied throughout.[75]

4. Exclusions from the Authorization

However, the Nice Treaty has limited the scope of the legal basis for secondary legislation on Union citizens' free movement by explicitly excluding two fields. According to the new paragraph 3, Article 18 (2) EC shall not apply to provisions on passports, identity cards, residence permits or any other such document or – as Denmark had urged[76] – to provisions on social security or social protection.[77]

---

74 French wording: "Tout citoyen de l'Union a le droit de circuler et de séjourner librement sur le territoire des États membres, sous réserve des limitations et conditions prévues par le présent traité et par les dispositions prises pour son application." German wording: "Jeder Unionsbürger hat das Recht, sich im Hoheitsgebiet der Mitgliedstaaten vorbehaltlich der in diesem Vertrag und in den Durchführungsvorschriften vorgesehenen Beschränkungen und Bedingungen frei zu bewegen und aufzuhalten."
75 English wording of the actual Article 18 (2) EC: "If action by the Community should prove necessary to attain this objective and this Treaty has not provided the necessary powers, the Council may adopt provisions with a view to facilitating the exercise of the rights referred to in paragraph 1. The Council shall act in accordance with the procedure referred to in Article 251." French wording of the actual Article 18(2) EC: "Si une action de la Communauté apparaît nécessaire pour atteindre cet objectif, et sauf si le présent traité a prévu des pouvoirs à cet effet, le Conseil peut arrêter des dispositions visant à faciliter l'exercice des droits visés au paragraphe 1. Il statue conformément à la procédure visée à l'article 251." German wording of the actual Article 18 (2) EC: "Erscheint zur Erreichung dieses Ziels ein Tätigwerden der Gemeinschaft erforderlich und sieht dieser Vertrag hierfür keine Befugnisse vor, so kann der Rat Vorschriften erlassen, mit denen die Ausübung der Rechte nach Absatz 1 erleichtert wird. Er beschließt gemäß dem Verfahren des Artikels 251."
76 See K.H. FISCHER, DER VERTRAG VON NIZZA 111 (2001).
77 English wording of Article 18 (3) EC: "Paragraph 2 shall not apply to provisions on passports, identity cards, residence permits or any other such document or to provisions on social security or social protection." French wording of Article 18 (3) EC: "Le paragraphe 2 ne s'applique pas aux dispositions concernant

IV. The Direct Effect of the General Right of Free Movement

One of the numerous questions related to the interpretation of Article 18 EC (formerly Art. 8a EC Treaty) is the problem of direct effect of this general right of free movement.[78]

1. Arguments against Direct Effect of the General Right of Free Movement

Despite the fact that the direct effect of the general right of free movement seems obvious at first glance, there have been some critical voices questioning that effect. It was indeed argued that the condition contained in Article 18 (1) EC (formerly Article 8a (1) EC Treaty) which states that the right to move and reside freely within the territory of the Member States is "subject to the limitations and conditions laid down in this Treaty and by the measures adopted to give it effect" gives sufficient grounds for denying direct effect to Article 18 (1) EC (formerly Article 8a (1) EC Treaty) as this provision clearly refers to secondary law and therefore the general right of free movement would only exist as enshrined in secondary law.[79] Such an interpretation would also be in accordance with the historical intent of the Maastricht Intergovernmental Conference.[80] Furthermore, Article 18 (1) EC (formerly Article 8a (1) EC Treaty) would only function to consolidate the three directives in primary law. Looked at in this way, its direct effect would not be required. Such direct effect would by no means ameliorate the legal status of Union citizens as the meaning and scope of Article 18 (1) EC (formerly Article 8a (1) EC Treaty) would be congruent with the meaning and scope of the three residence directives.[81]

2. Arguments in Favor of Direct Effect of the General Right of Free Movement

In contrast, more convincing is the position that Article 18 (1) EC (formerly Article 8a (1) EC Treaty) contains a directly effective right which may be invoked by individuals.[82]

---

les passeports, les cartes d'identité, les titres de séjour ou tout autre document assimilé, ni aux dispositions concernant la sécurité sociale ou la protection sociale." German wording of Article 18 (3) EC: "Absatz 2 gilt nicht für Vorschriften betreffend Pässe, Personalausweise, Aufenthaltstitel oder diesen gleichgestellte Dokumente und auch nicht für Vorschriften betreffend die soziale Sicherheit oder den sozialen Schutz."

78 As far as Community law has direct effect, national administrations and courts must apply it as the law of the land and individuals can invoke it to that end.

79 Also in this sense, see W. Kaufmann-Bühler *in* EG-VERTRAG. KOMMENTAR (C.O. Lenz ed., 2nd ed., 1999), Article 18 para. 1 and, apparently, K. Hailbronner, *Diskriminierungsverbot, Unionsbürgerschaft und gleicher Zugang zu Sozialleistungen*, 64 ZEITSCHRIFT FÜR AUSLÄNDISCHES ÖFFENTLICHES RECHT UND VÖLKERRECHT (ZaöRV) 603, 606, 612 (2004). In *Baumbast*, the British Government and the German Government presented the same argumentation, see E.C.J. Case C-413/99 of 17 September 2002, E.C.R. 2002, I-7091 para. 78 – *Baumbast*. However, W. Kaufmann-Bühler abandoned this position following the E.C.J. judgment in the *Baumbast* case; see W. Kaufmann-Bühler *in* EU- UND EG-VERTRAG. KOMMENTAR (C.O. Lenz & K.-D. Borchardt eds., 3rd ed., 2003), Article 18 para. 1.

80 See M. Degen, *Die Unionsbürgerschaft nach dem Vertrag über die europäische Union unter besonderer Berücksichtigung des Wahlrechts*, DÖV 1993, 749, 752.

81 See M. Pechstein & A. Bunk, *Das Aufenthaltsrecht als Auffangrecht. Die fehlende unmittelbare Anwendbarkeit sowie die Reichweite des Art. 8a Abs. 1 EGV*, EuGRZ 1997, 547 et seq.

82 In the same sense Advocate General A. La Pergola in his Opinion of 1 July 1997 on the *Martínez Sala* case, E.C.R. 1998, I-2694 para. 18; Advocate General G. Cosmas in his Opinion of 16 March 1999 on *Wijsenbeek*, E.C.R. 1999, I-6209 paras. 79 et seq.; Advocate General S. Alber in his Opinion of 28 September 2000 in *Grzelczyk*, E.C.R. 2001, I-6197 para. 120; Advocate General L.A. Geelhoed in his Opinion of 5 July 2001 on the *Baumbast* case, E.C.R. 2002, I-7094 paras. 101 et seq. See, furthermore, e.g. K.-D. Borchardt, *Der sozialrechtliche Gehalt der Unionsbürgerschaft*, NEUE JURISTISCHE WOCHENSCHRIFT (NJW) 2057, 2060 (2000); C. Closa, *Citizenship of the Union and Nationality of Member States*, 32 COMMON MARKET LAW REVIEW (CML.REV.) 487, 495 et seq. (1995); P. Fischer, *Die Unionsbürgerschaft. Ein*

This can be seen as true in one respect because of the schematic context in which that right to move and reside freely is placed in the Treaty. It appears as the first of the rights ascribed to citizens of the Union, immediately after the establishment of Union citizenship by Article 17 EC (formerly Art. 8 EC Treaty) with its final reference to "the rights conferred by this Treaty (...) and the duties imposed thereby". But, above all, the exact wording of Article 18 EC should be noted. In paragraph 1, Union citizens are said to enjoy the right to move and reside freely. There is no mention of Union citizens enjoying this right merely through secondary law. Moreover, paragraph 2 then provides for the adoption of provisions for the purpose of facilitating the exercise of "the rights referred to in paragraph 1". Under such circumstances, the reservation in favor of "limitations and conditions laid down in this Treaty and by the measures to give it effect" – which, significantly, in languages other than German appears after the guarantee of free movement[83] – must not be interpreted as referring only to the future creation of a general right of free movement. It should rather be understood as functioning to allow for limitations of this right as already conferred on Union citizens by the Treaty itself.

Therefore the existence of this general right of free movement is neither subject to the enactment of corresponding secondary legislation, nor subject to implementation by Member States. The clause in question only signifies that Community institutions as well as Member States can limit the exercise of the general right of free movement to some extent. While it is true that as a consequence of this reservation clause the restrictions contained in the three residence directives must still be considered as being of continuing relevance,[84] the added Treaty provision must be seen as having an impact on this relevance of the directives. Therefore the legal situation as given previously has not remained entirely unchanged. It must be assumed that the inclusion of the general right of free movement of Union citizens into the Treaty, far from being a mere stylistic exercise without any consequences, has legal significance through its enhancement and generalization of the legal protection of free movement. Article 18 (1) EC (formerly Article 8a (1) EC Treaty) is to be interpreted as securing in itself the general right of free movement of all Union citizens, who may invoke that directly effective Treaty provision alone without having made any previous or complementary reference to secondary legislation in this field.

3. History of the Court's Recognition of Direct Effect of the General Right of Free Movement

Against the backdrop of these findings, it can hardly be understood why the ECJ refused for a long time to take a stand on the question of direct effect of the general right to free movement. Admittedly, Article 8a EC Treaty (now, following amendment, Article 18 EC)

---

neues Konzept im Völker- und Europarecht, in STAAT UND RECHT. FESTSCHRIFT FÜR GÜNTHER WINKLER (H. Haller, C. Kopetzki & R. Novak et al. eds., 1997), 237, 255 et seq.; M. Haag, in KOMMENTAR ZUM VERTRAG ÜBER DIE EUROPÄISCHE UNION UND ZUR GRÜNDUNG DER EUROPÄISCHEN GEMEINSCHAFT, VOL. 1 (H. v. d. Groeben & J. Schwarze eds., 6th ed., 2003), Article 18 EC para. 7; A. Hatje, in EU-KOMMENTAR (J. Schwarze ed., 2000), Article 18 EC para. 5; M. Hilf, in DAS RECHT DER EUROPÄISCHEN UNION. KOMMENTAR (E. Grabitz & M. Hilf eds., Stand August 2003), Article 18 EC para. 1; S. Kadelbach, Unionsbürgerschaft, in EUROPÄISCHES VERFASSUNGSRECHT (A. v. Bogdandy ed., 2003), 539, 553; W. Kluth, in KOMMENTAR ZU EU-VERTRAG UND EG-VERTRAG (C. Calliess & M. Ruffert eds., 2nd ed., 2002), Article 18 EC Treaty para. 9; N. KOTALAKIDIS, VON DER NATIONALEN STAATSANGEHÖRIGKEIT ZUR UNIONS-BÜRGERSCHAFT 153 et seq., 164 (2000); I. Pernice, in GRUNDGESETZ-KOMMENTAR, BD. 1 (H. Dreier ed., 2nd ed. 2004), Article 11 para. 5. Initially doubtful Klein & Haratsch, supra note 68, 134 with note 24; but then affirmative, see Klein & Haratsch, supra note 62, 11 et seq.

83 See supra note 74.
84 See infra note 123.

played a role in the Court's jurisprudence shortly after being enacted. However, until recently the Court only mentioned this article in situations where it was interpreting secondary law or where it was applying the general principle of non-discrimination enshrined in Article 6 EC Treaty (now, following amendment, Article 12 EC) which unquestionably has direct effect. Only after a rather long and uneven period of jurisprudential development has the ECJ become ready to attribute specific weight to, and recognize the true importance of, Article 8a (1) EC Treaty (now, following amendment Article 18 (1) EC).

a) First judgments

In the early period of its interpretation of Article 8a (1) EC Treaty (now, following amendment Article 18 (1) EC), the Court showed great reluctance to give importance to this Article. In *Skanavi* and in *Calfa*, the Court plainly declared that it would not be required to discuss the questions raised with regard to Article 8a EC Treaty, as market-related rights to free movement were applicable instead in this case.[85] However, in the period between both these decisions the Court, in *Bickel* and *Franz*, made reference not only to the right to move and reside freely in Article 59 EC Treaty (now, following amendment, Article 49 EC), but also to Article 8a EC Treaty (now, following amendment, Article 18 EC) and in its subsequent argumentation did not make any distinction between both guarantees in this case.[86]

b) *Martínez Sala*

In its important judgment in *Martínez Sala*, the Court still avoided expressing an opinion on the direct effect of Article 8a (1) EC Treaty (now, following amendment, Article 18 (1) EC), notwithstanding a detailed exposition on that point given in the Opinion of Advocate General La Pergola who had, in accordance with the Commission, strongly pleaded the provision's direct effect.[87]

As the European Convention on Social and Medical Assistance, concluded under the auspices of the Council of Europe, already gave the Spanish national Ms Martínez Sala a right to stay in Germany, the ECJ concluded that it was not necessary to examine her possible right of residence by virtue of Article 8a EC Treaty. The Court decided that it was sufficient, for the purpose of applying the general prohibition against discrimination, to state that a Union citizen, lawfully residing in another Member State, falls within the scope of application of the Treaty provisions on Union citizenship *ratione personae*.[88] In mentioning such Treaty provisions, however, the Court must have meant Article 8a (1) EC Treaty. Nevertheless, if this was the Court's meaning, it was then illogical to set aside all questions concerning the existence of a right of residence based on this Treaty provision and to take recourse instead to the prohibition of repatriation derived from the European Convention on Social and Medical Assistance. For the Court to have been legally correct, the prohibition of repatriation should have been considered only in the context of possible restrictions to Ms Martínez Sala's right of residence as derived from Article 8a (1) EC Treaty. Although the Court's reasoning is therefore not convincing,[89] the judgment is still beneficial in terms of its substantive result, that being the right of Ms Martínez Sala to receive a child-raising allowance in Germany.

---

85 E.C.J. Case C-193/94 of 29 February 1996, E.C.R. 1996, I-929 para. 22 – *Skanavi*; E.C.J. Case C-348/96 of 19 January 1999, E.C.R. 1999, 11 para. 30 – *Calfa*. See also E.C.J. Case C-100/01 of 26 November 2002, E.C.R. 2002, I-10981 para. 26 – *Olazabal*.
86 E.C.J. Case C-274/96 of 24 November 1998, E.C.R. 1998, I-7637 para. 15 – *Bickel and Franz*.
87 See Advocate General A. La Pergola in his Opinion of 1 July 1997 on *Martínez Sala*, E.C.R. 1998, I-2694 paras. 15 and 18.
88 E.C.J. Case C-85/96 of 12 May 1998, E.C.R. 1998, I-2691 paras. 60 *et seq*. – *Martínez Sala*.
89 See *infra* at note 197.

c) *Wijsenbeek*

In the *Wijsenbeek* case, the Court had to decide whether Member States could still require Union citizens to present a passport or an identity card when crossing borders between Member States. Still reluctant to give direct effect to Article 8a (1) EC Treaty (now, following amendment, Article 18 (1) EC) the ECJ stated that "even if, under ... Article 8a of the Treaty, nationals of the Member States did have an unconditional right to move freely within the territory of the Member States", the Member States still retained the right, at least in the legal situation present at the time, to carry out identity checks at the internal frontiers of the Community. The purpose of the identity checks was to establish whether the persons concerned were nationals of a Member State, thus having the right to move freely within the territory of the Member States, or nationals of a non-member country, not having that right.[90] The Court mentioned that Article 8a of the Treaty "confers" on citizens of the Union the right to move and reside freely in the territory of the Member States, but at the same time it emphasized that this right is "subject to the limitations and conditions laid down in the Treaty and by the measures to give it effect".[91]

d) *Kaba I*, *Yiadom* and *Elsen*

In *Kaba I*, the Court ruled that a certain discrimination against workers' family members was acceptable under Community law, referring in its judgment to a similarly vague twofold characterization of Article 8a EC Treaty as it had done in *Wijsenbeek*.[92] However, in its judgment in *Yiadom* the Court decided, in contrast to its previous decisions, that the freedom of movement as enshrined in Article 8a (1) EC Treaty (now, following amendment, Article 18 (1) EC) is a "fundamental freedom", which has to be interpreted broadly in favor of Union citizens. For this reason procedural guarantees as laid down in Directive (EEC) 64/221 must be broadly interpreted in favor of Union citizens who have made use of that fundamental freedom.[93]

Furthermore, in *Elsen* the ECJ underlined the fact that Union citizens who have transferred their residence to another Member State while continuing to work in their country of origin, "have exercised their right to move and reside freely in the Member States, as guaranteed in Article 8a of the EC Treaty". Therefore, when granting an old-age pension, the competent institution of a Member State is required to take into account, as though they had been completed in national territory, periods devoted to child-rearing which have been completed in another Member State by a person who, at the time the child was born, was a frontier worker employed in the territory of the first Member State (i.e. his or her State of origin) while residing in the territory of the second Member State.[94]

e) *Grzelczyk*

In a similar way the Court stressed in the *Grzelczyk* case, referring to a formulation made by Advocate General La Pergola in his opinion in *Martínez Sala*, that Union citizenship is "destined to be the fundamental status of nationals of the Member States".[95] This includes, according to the Court, the exercise of "the right to move and reside freely in another

---

90 E.C.J. Case C-378/97 of 21 September 1999, E.C.R. 1999, I-6207 para. 43 – *Wijsenbeek*.
91 E.C.J. Case C-378/97 of 21 September 1999, E.C.R. 1999, I-6207 para. 41 – *Wijsenbeek*.
92 E.C.J. Case C-356/98 of 11 April 2000, E.C.R. 2000, I-2623 para. 30 – *Kaba I*; confirmed in: E.C.J. Case C-466/00 of 6 March 2003, E.C.R. 2003, I-2219 para. 46 – *Kaba II*.
93 E.C.J. Case C-357/98 of 9 November 2000, E.C.R. 2000, I-9265 paras. 23 *et seq*. – *Yiadom*.
94 E.C.J. Case C-135/99 of 23 November 2000, E.C.R. 2000, I-10409 paras. 34 *et seq*. – *Elsen*.
95 *See* Advocate General A. La Pergola in his Opinion of 1 July 1997 on *Martínez Sala*, Slg. 1998, I-2694, 2703 para. 18.

Member State, as conferred by Article 8a of the Treaty". Therefore a student lawfully residing in a Member State other than the Member State of origin is to be treated equally with nationals of the host State in terms of non-contributory social benefits.[96]

f) *Baumbast*

The breakthrough regarding direct effect, however, was not reached until the Court's decision in the *Baumbast* case. Mr. Baumbast, a German national, pursued economic activities in the United Kingdom, initially as a worker and then as head of his own company. However, after the company failed and he was unable to obtain a sufficiently well-paid job in the United Kingdom, he worked for German companies in China and Lesotho, but continued to reside in the United Kingdom. The Secretary of State as the competent authority in the United Kingdom refused to renew Mr Baumbast's residence permit. That refusal was brought before the Immigration Adjudicator. Since Mr Baumbast had taken up work for German companies in third countries, he could no longer invoke to his benefit the free movement of workers clause in Article 39 EC nor the right of establishment in Article 43 EC in order to remain as a resident of the United Kingdom.

However, the Court decided that a right of residence in the United Kingdom, based on Community law, could be derived from the free movement of Union citizens as laid down in Article 18 (1) EC. In this judgment the ECJ finally affirmed that the right to reside within the territory of the Member States under Article 18 (1) EC is a right conferred directly on every citizen of the Union by a clear and precise provision of the Treaty. Admittedly, this residency right is conferred subject to the limitations and conditions laid down in the Treaty and by the measures adopted to give it effect. However, all these restrictions are open to judicial review in respect of the general right to move and reside freely within the territory of the Member States. Consequently, as in the case of the free movement of workers,[97] any limitations and conditions imposed on that right do not prevent Article 18 (1) EC from directly conferring rights on individuals which can be invoked before national courts and which these courts must protect.[98]

g) *Trojani*

Since *Baumbast*, direct effect of Article 18 (1) EC seems to be taken for granted by the Court. Therefore, when judging in *Trojani* an impoverished French national's demand for social assistance in Belgium, the Court limited itself to recall "that the right to reside in the territory of the Member States is conferred directly on every citizen of the Union by Article 18 (1) EC (…) Mr Trojani therefore has the right to rely on that provision of the Treaty simply as a citizen of the Union."[99]

h) *Zhu and Chen*

In similar words the ECJ affirmed still more recently in *Zhu and Chen* the right of the Irish minor Catherine Zhu to reside in the United Kingdom: "As regards the right to reside in the territory of the Member States provided for in Article 18 (1) EC, it must be observed

---

96 E.C.J. Case C-184/99 of 20 September 2001, E.C.R. 2001, I-6193 paras. 31, 33 and 46 – *Grzelczyk*.
97 *See supra* note 20.
98 E.C.J. Case C-413/99 of 17 September 2002, E.C.R. 2002, I-7091 paras. 84 *et seq.* – *Baumbast*; affirmative e.g. S. Bode, case note on *"Baumbast"*, EUROPÄISCHE ZEITSCHRIFT FÜR WIRTSCHAFTSRECHT (EuZW) 767, 768 (2002); N.Reich & S. Harbacevica, *Citizenship and family on trial: A fairly optimistic overview of recent court practice with regard to free movement of persons*, CML.REV. 615, 628 (2003).
99 E.C.J. Case C-456/02 of 7 September 2004, E.C.R. 2004, I-7573 para. 31 – *Trojani*.

that that right is granted directly to every citizen of the Union by a clear and precise provision of the Treaty. Purely as a national of a Member State, and therefore as a citizen of the Union, Catherine is entitled to rely on Article 18 (1) EC."[100]

i) Conclusion

Obviously, there was no easy way for the Court to take an affirmative position on the direct effect of Article 18 (1) ECJ (formerly Article 8a (1) EC Treaty). As has been seen through the discussion of the case law above, however, the Court now has deliberately affirmed this direct effect.

V. The Relations between the General Right of Free Movement and Other Guarantees of Free Movement in Community Law

Article 18 EC's relations to other guarantees of free movement under Community law can be studied on both the level of primary law, which will be discussed in section 1, and on the level of secondary law, which will be examined in section 2.

1. Relations to Other Guarantees of Free Movement in Primary Law

Although Article 18 EC (formerly Article 8a EC Treaty) does not include in its wording a reservation for other guarantees of free movement in primary law, the aforementioned developments show clearly that, while this Treaty provision is to be seen as creating a new right of free movement, this new right should not be viewed as a substitute for already existing and accepted rights. It should be seen merely as a complement to those rights.

a) The General Right of Free Movement as *Lex Generalis*

Consequently, other guarantees of free movement enshrined in primary law are to be regarded as leges speciales. Their applicability therefore precludes application of Article 18 EC (formerly Article 8a EC Treaty), the latter constituting the *lex generalis* in the field of free movement.[101] This interpretation finds support in the wording of the competence provision for secondary legislation in Article 18 (2) EC as re-formulated by the Nice Treaty. This provision is stated to apply only if action by the Community is necessary to ensure free movement and the Treaty has not provided the necessary powers. Hence, other Treaty-based competence provisions which exist to ensure free movement such as market-related competence provisions in the framework of the internal market's fundamental freedoms enjoy priority. For the rest, the specific Treaty provisions designed to ensure free movement cover wide areas, as already demonstrated above. Therefore, one could easily be led to assume that Article 18 EC has merely a subsidiary function, namely to provide legal

---

100 E.C.J. Case C-200/02 of 19 October 2004, E.C.R. 2004, I-9923 para 26 – *Zhu and Chen*.
101 *See also* the E.C.J. in its judgments *Skanavi* and *Calfa*, *supra* note 85; furthermore E.C.J. Case C-100/01 of 26 November 2002, E.C.R. 2002, I-10981 para. 26 – *Olazabal*. *See also, e.g.*, Y. Gautier, *in* TRAITÉ SUR L'UNION EUROPÉENNE. COMMENTAIRE (V. Constantinesco, R. Kovar & D. Simon eds., 1995), Article 8 A. C.E. para 4; M. Haag, *in* DIE EUROPÄISCHE UNION. EUROPARECHT UND POLITIK (R. Bieber, A. Epiney & M. Haag, 6th ed., 2005), 67; Hatje, *supra* note 82, Article 18 para. 12; Hilf, *supra* note 82, Article 18 EC para. 5; S. Kadelbach, *Die europäischen Bürgerrechte*, *in* EUROPÄISCHE GRUNDRECHTE UND GRUNDFREIHEITEN (D. Ehlers ed., 2003), 467, 478; Kluth, *supra* note 82, Article 18 EC Treaty para. 10; KOTALAKIDIS, *supra* note 82, 158; Magiera, *supra* note 6, Article 45 para. 5; W. Obwexer, case note on *Grzelczyk*, EuZW 2002, 56; Pechstein & Bunk, *supra* note 81, 547, 553; S. Staeglich, *Rechte und Pflichten aus der Unionsbürgerschaft*, ZEITSCHRIFT FÜR EUROPARECHTLICHE STUDIEN (ZEuS) 485, 512 (2003).

coverage for pensioners and students as well as for "playboys and vagrants". Upon closer inspection, however, such an assumption proves to be unfounded.

b) Replacement of Other Rights of Free Movement in Primary Law

Firstly, certain primary law guarantees of free movement, previously developed by the ECJ in order to legally protect Union citizens, have now been made superfluous by the explicit provision contained in Article 18 EC.

In *Grzelczyk* and *Bickel and Franz* the Court seems already to have drawn such consequences. Indeed, in contrast to its decision in *Raulin*,[102] where the Court based itself on an implicit, education-related freedom of movement, the Court in *Grzelczyk* explicitly and exclusively relied on Article 8a EC Treaty (now, following amendment, Art. 18 EC)[103] to give a student the right of residence in Belgium to pursue vocational training. Furthermore, the ECJ stressed in *Bickel and Franz*, although still in an abstract manner, that both the Austrian Mr. Bickel and the German Mr. Franz were covered by the freedom to receive services when entering the Province of Bolzano. Even so, Article 8a (1) EC Treaty is cited in the case in its full wording. The subsequent deduction of the right of both defendants to use the German language throughout judicial proceedings in the Province of Bolzano also appears to be based more on Article 8a EC Treaty than on Article 59 EC (now, following amendment, Article 49 EC).[104] Thus, while up until now the extensive interpretation of Article 59 EC Treaty (now, following amendment, Article 49) has given almost unlimited freedom of movement to travelers and tourists,[105] *Bickel and Franz* could indicate a trend to abandon this interpretation.[106]

c) Avoidance of Problems resulting from Recourse to Specific Rights of Free Movement in Primary Law

Secondly, the guarantees of free movement will often be congruent, whether derived from the fundamental freedoms of the internal market or from Article 18 EC. In such cases, it may be best to refer exclusively to Article 18 EC and to avoid in this way unnecessary investigation of the economic activities pursued and the related problems of delimitation between the various fundamental freedoms of the internal market. The ECJ seems to have taken the first steps towards such an abridged approach already through its decision in *Elsen*, where it based the claim to equal treatment concerning periods devoted to child-rearing primarily on Article 8a EC Treaty (now, following amendment, Article 18 EC). Articles 48 and 52 EC Treaty (now, following amendment, Article 39 and 42 EC) were only briefly mentioned *in obiter*.[107]

---

102 See *supra* note 68. As to the impossibility still to derive the right of residence from the directive on the right of residence for students, *infra* note 114.
103 E.C.J. Case C-184/99 of 20 September 2001, E.C.R. 2001, I-6193 para. 33 – *Grzelczyk*. As to the replacement of the previous right of residence for students by Article 18 EC, *see also* Becker, *supra* note 10, 531; apparently in the same sense Klein & Haratsch, *supra* note 62, 11 *et seq*.
104 E.C.J. Case C-274/96 of 24 November 1998, E.C.R. 1998, I-7637 paras. 15 *et seq*. – *Bickel and Franz*.
105 *See also supra* note 48, and Advocate General A. Trabucchi in his Opinion of 2 June 1976 in *Watson und Belmann*, E.C.R. 1976, 1201 (1203); furthermore N. REICH, BÜRGERRECHTE IN DER EUROPÄISCHEN UNION 196 (1999).
106 Apparently in the same sense M. Bulterman, case note on *Bickel and Franz*, CML.REV. 36, 1999, 1325, 1334; P. Hilpold, *Unionsbürgerschaft und Sprachenrechte in der EU*, JURISTISCHE BLÄTTER 2000, 93, 97; *see, in general, also* T. OPPERMANN, EUROPARECHT (2nd ed., 1999), para. 1595. *But see*, more recently, E.C.J. Case C-60/00 of 11 July 2002, E.C.R. 2002, I-6279 – *Carpenter*; in this case, however, was the right of a provider (and not of a recipient) of services at issue, and this decision should be seen as an individual ruling anyway.
107 E.C.J. Case C-135/99 of 23 November 2000, E.C.R. 2000, I-10409 paras. 33 *et seq*. – *Elsen*.

d) The General Right of Free Movement as a Potential Main Right of Free Movement in Primary Law

Accordingly, in many cases where the free movement of persons is at issue, argumentation can mainly or exclusively make use of Article 18 EC for reasons of simplification. For example, when deciding a question on lawful residence, it is sufficient for a positive answer, from the perspective of Article 18 EC, to state that a Union citizen is staying in another Member State without having been subjected to individual measures of denial or termination of residence.[108] It does no more matter, then, whether or not the Union citizen has taken up, interrupted or terminated an economic activity in the host State and whether or not a market-related guarantee of free movement could therefore apply.[109] There is also no difference in the case of a decision involving the determination of the legality of measures being used to deny or to end residence on public policy grounds.[110]

Thus, it is only necessary still exceptionally to refer to specific primary law rights of free movement and to shoulder the corresponding burden of additional argumentation in those cases where the protection given by these rights goes beyond the one provided for by the general right of free movement in Article 18 EC.[111] A situation like this would occur, for example, in the event of a migrant EC worker claiming social advantages which are made available by the host State only to workers and not to other citizens of the Union, or when it is necessary to establish the illegality of a measure being used to deny or terminate residence of a citizen of the Union on grounds of insufficient resources since, in contrast to the general right of free movement, market-related rights of free movement do not cover this requirement. Under such circumstances and conditions Article 18 EC may, while remaining from a legalistic point of view a mere *lex generalis* in relation to other guarantees of free movement contained in primary law, in fact gradually change from a subsidiary guarantee into the main right of free movement enshrined in the EC Treaty.

2. Relations to Guarantees of Free Movement in Secondary Law

When Article 8a EC Treaty (now, following amendment, article 18 EC) entered into force, it changed the three residence directives of 1990/1993[112] significantly, if not in their

---

108 See *infra* at note 125.
109 In similar cases, German administrative courts limited themselves to find that individuals enjoyed the status of Union citizens and the right of residence which can be derived from that status (without further discussion of respective special market-related guarantees of free movement), see the decisions of the *Verwaltungsgericht Karlsruhe* of 21 June 1999 (12 K 871/99) and of the *Verwaltungsgericht Stuttgart* of 20 November 2001 (6 K 1307/01), both cited in F. Wenger, *Die Unionsbürgerschaft als aufenthaltsrechtlicher "Hebel"?*, NEUE ZEITSCHRIFT FÜR VERWALTUNGSRECHT (NVwZ) 1342, notes 3 and 5 (2002). Similarly, the *Bundesverwaltungsgericht* examined the conformity of the requirement of German men liable for military service to seek permission before traveling abroad according to § 3 (2) *Wehrpflichtgesetz* (WPflG) with Community law exclusively by making reference to Article 18 (1) EC, but not (as well) to special market-related guarantees of free movement, see BVerwG Case 6 C.30.98 of 10 November 1999, ENTSCHEIDUNG DES BUNDESVERWALTUNGSGERICHT (BVerwGE) 110, 40 (53 *et seq.*); this may, however, be due to the fact that in the actual case postgraduate PhD studies of a young German in the United Kingdom were concerned; furthermore, the Court referred in its reasoning to the somewhat misleading formulation by M. Haag *in* KOMMENTAR ZUM EU-/EG-VERTRAG, VOL. 1 (H. v.d. Groeben, J. Thiesing & C.-D. Ehlermann eds., 5th ed., 1997), Article 8a EC para. 4 (this formulation is maintained by the same author *in supra* note 82, Article 18 para. 6), according to whom Article 8a EC Treaty (now, following amendment, Article 18 EC) as a political fundamental freedom overrules the right of residence based on economically-inspired rights of residence; but, as should be noted, Haag corrects that statement still in the same paragraph of his commentary in order to emphasize the supremacy of special Treaty-based rights of free movement.
110 See E.C.J., Cases C-482/01 and C-493/01 of 29 April 2004 (not yet published in E.C.R.) para. 71 – *Orfanopoulos and Oliveri*.
111 See also R. STREINZ, EUROPARECHT (6th ed., 2003), para. 655.
112 See *supra* notes 60 and 63.

wording, then in their meaning and scope. Since Article 18 EC grants Union citizens a comprehensive freedom of movement with direct effect,[113] and this freedom of movement ranks higher than secondary law guarantees of free movement, the three directives have lost their previous function of establishing rights of residence for Union citizens.[114]

The directives however still function to limit residence rights. Indeed, Article 8a EC Treaty (now, following amendment, Article 18 EC) states that the right to move and reside freely is subject to limitations and conditions laid down "by the measures adopted to give it effect". Therefore this Article on the one hand maintains the restrictive clauses in the directives and on the other hand profoundly alters their objective. The directives now operate as restrictions on the right of free movement deriving from Article 18 EC. Since these directives are secondary law restrictions, they cannot challenge a legal guarantee based on primary law. Hence, they cannot impair the coming into existence of the right of free movement, but rather can only affect its exercise (by Union citizens, within the scope of the directives). The residence directives can now only be used as the legal basis for measures of limitation in individual cases.[115] Furthermore, Article 18 (2) EC prohibits the tightening up of the restrictions contained in the three residence directives.[116] Indeed, the legislative competence contained therein only allows the adoption of secondary law provisions for the purpose of facilitating the exercise of the rights of free movement through further liberalization.[117]

VI. Limitation Possibilities

1. In General

The guarantee of free movement for all Union citizens including minors[118] provided for in Article 18 (1) EC is subject, as laid down in the clause incorporated into this Treaty provision, "to the limitations and conditions laid down in this Treaty and by the measures to give it effect". This limitation clause still allows for restrictions on the free movement of foreign Union citizens in primary and secondary law. However, since it operates to create an exception to the principle of free movement for all Union citizens within the territory of the Member States, this clause is to be interpreted and handled in a narrow sense.

a) Primary Law-based Limitations on Free Movement

As far as primary Community law-based restrictions on free movement are concerned, the limitation clause in Article 18 (1) EC can only be understood as referring to the public

---

113 See *supra* at note 98.
114 Only for a Union citizen's family members being third country nationals or stateless persons are these directives still of constitutive importance regarding the right of residence.
115 See Advocate General A. La Pergola in his Opinion on *Martínez Sala* of 1 July 1997, E.C.R. 1998, I-2694 para. 18. See also E.C.J. Case C-456/02 of 7 September 2004, E.C.R. 2004, I-7573 para. 46 – *Trojani*. See, moreover, Haag, *supra* note 82, Article 18 EC, para. 16; Hilf, *supra* note 82, Article 18 EC, para. 12; R. Höfler, *Europa auf dem Weg zu einer sozialen Union? Die EuGH-Rechtsprechung zu unionsrechtlichen Ansprüchen auf Sozialhilfe*, NVwZ 2002, 1206, 1207; KOTALAKIDIS, *supra* note 82, 171; Magiera, *supra* note 6, Article 45 para. 6; C. Tomuschat, *Staatsbürgerschaft – Unionsbürgerschaft – Weltbürgerschaft*, in EUROPÄISCHE DEMOKRATIE (J. Drexl, K.F. Kreuzer, D.H. Scheuing & U. Sieber eds., 1999), 73, 78.
116 See, e.g., Haag, *supra* note 82, Article 18 EC, para. 17; Hatje, *supra* note 82, Article 18 EC para. 13; W. Kaufmann Bühler *in* EU- UND EG-VERTRAG. KOMMENTAR (C.O. Lenz & K.-D. Borchardt eds., 3rd ed., 2003), Article 18 para. 7; H. ROTHFUCHS, DIE TRADITIONELLEN PERSONENVERKEHRSFREIHEITEN DES EG-VERTRAGES UND DAS AUFENTHALTSRECHT DER UNIONSBÜRGER 218 (1999).
117 Therefore wrong Kluth, *supra* note 82, Article 18 EC, para. 14.
118 See E.C.J. Case C-200/02 of 19 October 2004, E.C.R. 2004, I-9923 para 20 – *Zhu and Chen*.

policy provisos which are part of all Treaty provisions on market-related rights of free movement. This results from the failure of the Treaty itself to lay down any specific limitations on, and conditions to, the right of free movement as provided for in Article 18 (1) EC.

b) Secondary Law-based Limitations on Free Movement

With regard to restrictions on free movement based on secondary Community law, it is worth mentioning that for a long time no measure has been adopted which would have given effect to the general right of free movement as provided for in Article 18 (1) EC (formerly Article 8a EC Treaty).[119] As discussed above, no such measure could include new restrictions anyway.[120] Article 18 (2) EC only allows for the adoption of relevant secondary legislation provided that this legislation consists exclusively of provisions "with a view to facilitating the exercise of the rights referred to in paragraph 1". Therefore, the comprehensive free movement directive finally enacted in 2004 on the basis, among others, of Article 18 EC,[121] was unable to impose new limitations on the general right of free movement. It could only uphold, as it has done to a certain extent, existing secondary law restrictions.[122]

Thus, when Article 18 (1) EC refers nevertheless to limitations and conditions laid down in secondary law, this can only be understood as a reference to the restrictions on free movement which were already part of the three residence directives prior to the entering-into-force of Article 8a EC Treaty (now, following amendment, Article 18 EC).[123] Accordingly, in addition to the public policy proviso contained in these directives, but applicable already as a primary law-based limitation, the conditions dealing with sickness insurance and sufficient resources which are provided for in all three residence directives remain applicable.[124]

c) Common Features of these Limitations

The public policy proviso and the clause on sickness insurance and sufficient resources are similar in that when they apply, they do not automatically render the right of free

---

119 But, on the proposal for a directive submitted by the Commission in 2001 and amended in 2003, see *infra* notes 240 and 241.
120 See already *supra* notes 116 and 117.
121 Directive 2004/38/EC of the European Parliament and of the Council of 29 April 2004 on the right of citizens of the Union to move and reside freely within the territory of the Member States amending Regulation (EEC) No 1612/68 and repealing Directives 64/221/EEC, 68/360/EEC, 72/194/EEC, 73/148/EEC, 75/35/EEC, 90/364/EEC, 90/365/EEC and 93/96/EEC, O.J. EU 2004 L 158, 77; corrigendum O.J. EU 2004 L 229, 35.
122 See *infra* notes 244 *et seq.*
123 The same conclusions were drawn by the Court in E.C.J. Case C-184/99 of 20 September 2001, E.C.R. 2001, I-6193 paras. 37 *et seq.* – *Grzelczyk*; E.C.J. Case C-413/99 of 17 September 2002, E.C.R. 2002, I-7091 para. 87 – *Baumbast*; see, furthermore, Closa, *supra* note 82, 496; Gautier, *supra* note 101, Article 8 A C.E. para. 5; Hilf, *supra* note 82, Article 18 EC para. 10; H.G. Fischer, *Die Unionsbürgerschaft*, EuZW 1992, 566, 568; P. Fischer, *supra* note 82, 255; Kadelbach, *supra* note 82, 553 *et seq.*; Klein & Haratsch, *supra* note 62, 12; KOTALAKIDIS, *supra* note 82, 171 *et seq.*; P. Letzner, *Sozialhilfe für Student aus anderem Mitgliedstaat*, JuS 118 (2003); Magiera, *supra* note 6, Article 45 para. 12; J. Martínez Soria, *Die Unionsbürgerschaft und der Zugang zu sozialen Vergünstigungen*, JURISTENZEITUNG (JZ) 643, 647 (2002); Obwexer, *supra* note 101, 57; Reich & Harbacevica, *supra* note 98, 629; ROTHFUCHS, *supra* note 116, 201 *et seq.*; M. SCHWEITZER & W. HUMMER, EUROPARECHT (5th ed., 1996), para. 820 with note 11; Staeglich, *supra* note 101, 511. A different view seems to hold: V. Constantinesco, *La citoyenneté de l'Union*, in VOM BINNENMARKT ZUR EUROPÄISCHEN UNION (J. Schwarze ed., 1993), 25, 30; restrictive also Advocate General G. Cosmas in his Opinion of 16 March 1999 on *Wijsenbeek*, E.C.R. 1999, I-6209 paras. 91 *et seq.*
124 E.C.J. Case C-456/02 of 7 September 2004, E.C.R. 2004, I-7573 para. 33 – *Trojani*.

movement under Article 18 (1) EC null and void. Rather, the existence of the relevant conditions means only that Member States can adopt restrictive measures with constituent effect in individual cases, provided that further legitimacy requirements such as the proportionality principle are observed. Until such measures have been adopted, the person concerned continues to legitimately exercise his or her right to free movement under Article 18 EC.[125]

d) Additional Limitation Issues

An additional restriction imposed specifically on non-nationals is laid down in the students' directive. Foreign Union citizens do not have the right to demand maintenance grants for students from the host Member State. However, the further validity and scope of this exclusion clause still needs to be clarified. There is also the question of whether the right to cross-border mobility in Article 18 EC, which Union citizens can invoke even against their own State of origin,[126] cannot be made subject to Member State restrictions which are applicable to both national and foreign Union citizens.

2. The Public Policy Proviso

The reference made in Article 18 (1) EC to "limitations and conditions laid down in this Treaty and by the measures adopted to give it effect", is, as already stated above, primarily to be understood as a reference to the public policy clauses contained in all Treaty provisions on market-related guarantees of free movement.[127] This reference also applies to the public policy clauses of the three residence directives[128] as well as to Directives (EEC) No. 64/221[129] and 2004/38/EC[130] in so far as they operate to shape public policy aspects. It thus becomes clear that, even in the scope of the right to free movement under Article 18 (1) EC, the traditional public policy proviso remains valid.[131] However, the proviso applies only in truly severe and grave situations and therefore Union citizens still enjoy a high level of residence security in other Member States.[132]

Concerning the general right of free movement, the ECJ had to deal with the application of the public policy proviso in *Yiadom*, where the expulsion of a Dutch national from the

---

125 *See, e.g.*, E.C.J. Case C-456/02 of 7 September 2004, E.C.R. 2004, I-7573 para. 45 – *Trojani*. *See also* E.C.J. Case 184/99 of 20 September 2001, E.C.R. 2001, I-6193 paras. 42 *et seq.* – *Grzelczyk*, and the references already given – in the context of the free movement of workers – *supra* at note 20. *See* furthermore, Bode, *supra* note 98, 768; Borchardt, *supra* note 82, 2060.
126 *See, e.g.*, Haag, *supra* note 82, Article 18 EC para. 9; Hatje, *supra* note 82, Article 18 EC para. 6; N. Reich, *The European Constitution and New Member Countries: The Constitutional Relevance of Free Movement and Citizenship*, Annual Lecture 2004 at the Centre for European, Comparative and International Law (CECIL), Department of Law, University of Sheffield/UK, 26 February 2004, 10; J. Wouters, *European Citizenship and the Case-Law of the Court of Justice of the European Communities on the Free Movement of Persons*, *in* EUROPEAN CITIZENSHIP (E.A. Marias ed., 1994), 25, 49 *et seq*. *See* further, regarding the *causa Habsburg*, P. Fischer, *supra* note 82, 257 *et seq*.
127 Articles 39 (3), 46 (1) and 55 EC.
128 Article 2 (2) para. 3 of Directive (EEC) 90/364, *supra* note 60; Article 2 (2) para. 3 of Directive (EEC) 90/365, *supra* note 60; Article 2 (2) para. 3 of Directive (EEC) 93/96, *supra* note 63.
129 *See supra* note 24.
130 *See supra* note 121.
131 *See also, e.g.*, Becker, *supra* note 10, 530; Gautier, *supra* note 101, Article 8 A C.E. para. 5; Hilf, *supra* note 82, Article 18 EC para. 10; Kadelbach, *supra* note 82, 554; Kluth, *supra* note 82, Article 18 EC para. 12; KOTALAKIDIS, *supra* note 82, 164; O'Keeffe, *supra* note 1, 93; ROTHFUCHS, *supra* note 116, 200 *et seq.*; SCHWEITZER & HUMMER, *supra* note 123, para. 820 with note 10; Staeglich, *supra* note 101, 510 and 512.
132 Tomuschat, *supra* note 115, 78. *See also supra* notes 20 *et seq.*, 40 and 51.

United Kingdom as a public policy measure was at issue. The Court was correct in deciding that legal protection against such measures, made available under Directive (EEC) No. 64/221, in the light of Article 8a (1) EC Treaty (now, following amendment, Article 18 (1) EC) had a wide scope and therefore could be invoked to the benefit of Ms Yiadom.[133]

In *Orfanopoulos and Oliveri*[134] the Court considered it as possible that Mr Oliveri, an Italian national who had lived in Germany since his birth, could rely for his residence in Germany on no other Community law provision than Article 18 (1) EC. He had committed numerous offences in Germany including thefts and illegal sale of narcotics and had therefore been the subject of an expulsion order. In the Court's view, Directive (EEC) No. 64/221 precludes national legislation requiring automatic expulsion in such cases without any account being taken of the personal conduct of the offender or of the danger which that person represents for public policy. The directive also precludes a national practice whereby the national courts may not take into consideration, in reviewing the lawfulness of the expulsion, factual matters that may have occurred after the final decision of the competent authorities and which may point to the cessation or the substantial diminution of the present threat for public policy.

It is still worth mentioning a case in which the German *Bundesverwaltungsgericht* (Federal Administrative Court) had to decide the validity of the legal obligation which required German men liable for military service to seek permission from public authorities before leaving Germany. The *Bundesverwaltungsgericht* used Article 18 (1) EC as a yardstick in examining this restriction and held in its convincing decision that "public security", in so far as it relates to the public policy proviso, also encompasses external security. The legal obligation in question was therefore held to be a legitimate restriction of free movement under Article 18 (1) EC.[135]

3. The Social Cover Proviso

Because of the reference made in Article 18 (1) EC to the "limitations and conditions laid down (...) by the measures adopted to give it effect", freedom of movement of Union citizens outside of market-related guarantees of free movement is subject to conditions requiring these citizens to have sickness insurance and sufficient resources as laid down in all three residence directives.[136] This clause will be hereafter referred to as the "social cover proviso". Its aim becomes clear when it is considered in the light of the different levels of social standards in existence in the Member States. It should prevent the migration of

---

133 E.C.J. Case C-357/98 of 9 November 2000, E.C.R. 2000, I-9265 – *Yiadom*.
134 E.C.J., Cases C-482/01 and C-493/01 of 29 April 2004 (not yet published in E.C.R.) – *Orfanopoulos and Oliveri*.
135 In that sense the Court's secondary reasoning in BVerwG, Case 6 C 30/98 of 10 November 1999, BVerwGE 110, 40 (57 *et seq.*); not convincing is, however, the primary reasoning in this case (54 *et seq.*), according to which Article 18 (1) EC does not apply to restrictions of the right of free movement of a purely security policy-nature.
136 This proviso is to be found in Article 1 (1) of Directive (EEC) 90/364 (*supra* note 60), in Article 1(1) of Directive (EEC) 90/365 (*supra* note 60) as well as in Article 1(1) of Directive (EEC) 93/96 (*supra* note 63); as far as students are concerned, they only have to assure, according to the latter directive, the relevant national authority that they have resources sufficient to avoid becoming a burden on the social assistance system of the host Member State during their stay, whereas no specific amount of financial resources nor evidence by specific documents is required, see E.C.J. Case C-424/98 of 25 February 2000, E.C.R. 2000, I-4001 paras. 20 *et seq.* and 44 *et seq.* – *Commission v Italy* (requirement of sufficient resources); E.C.J. Case C-184/99 of 20 September 2001, E.C.R. 2001, I-6193 para. 40 – *Grzelczyk*. The social cover proviso is partially upheld in Directive 2004/38/EC, *see infra* note 246.

Union citizens between Member States for the sole purpose of obtaining social benefits in Member States with higher standards of social welfare.[137]

a) The Proviso Interpreted as an Initial Limitation

From this point of view, it seems possible to consider only an initial lack of social cover as a valid ground for denying a Union citizen the right of residence in a Member State. It would then not be allowed to regard the subsequent ceasing of social cover as a ground for expulsion. Such an approach would avoid the practical difficulties which result from the need of a permanent administrative control instead of a punctual control which operates only upon entrance to the Member State's territory. This approach would also comply with the Court's jurisprudence on the housing requirement in Regulation No. 1612/68[138] regarding the free movement of workers. This secondary law requirement for appropriate family housing has been interpreted by the Court in the light of the workers' freedom of movement as laid down in primary Community law. In its interpretation, the Court held that the housing requirement is only relevant at the time of admission of the migrant EC worker's family members to the territory of the host State. In contrast, the continuing availability of appropriate family housing cannot be made a precondition for the continuing residence of the family members in the host State.[139]

b) The Proviso Interpreted as a Permanent Limitation

However, it should be noted that unlike Regulation No. 1612/68 mentioned above, the three residence directives expressly make the continuing exercise of the right of residence subordinate to the continuing existence of social cover during the entire duration of residence in the host State.[140] Hence, even in the situation where a non-national citizen of the Union subsequently loses social cover, the host State will still be entitled to adopt appropriate measures to terminate this person's residence. Yet it can rightly be questioned whether such a fragile "residence under revocation proviso" is compatible with the ever increasing importance of free movement as a fundamental right of Union citizens. It might well be that the scope and meaning of the social cover proviso laid down in secondary legislation before the entering-into-force of Article 8a EC (now, following amendment, Article 18 EC) could and should now be interpreted in a way consistent with this new Treaty provision.

c) The Role of the European Convention on Social and Medical Assistance

In consideration of possible answers to that question, the provisions of the European Convention on Social and Medical Assistance should be taken into account. This convention, which came into force before the establishment of the European Economic Community, is not binding on the EU/EC. However most EU Member States have acceded to it. The convention can therefore be seen as an expression of common basic values. It obliges each contracting State to ensure that nationals of the other contracting States, who are lawfully present in its territory and who are without sufficient resources, are able to procure, on terms of equality with and on the same conditions as that State's own nationals, social and medical assistance provided for by national legislation. No

---

137 *See also supra* note 61.
138 Article 10 (3) of Regulation (EEC) 1612/68 (*supra* note 19).
139 E.C.J. Case 249/86 of 18 May 1989, E.C.R. 1989, 1263 – *Commission v Germany* (housing requirements).
140 Article 3 of Directive (EEC) 90/364 (*supra* note 60); Article 3 of Directive (EEC) 90/365 (*supra* note 60); Article 4 of Directive (EEC) 93/96 (*supra* note 63).

contracting State in whose territory a national of another contracting State is lawfully resident, is allowed to repatriate that national on the sole ground that he or she is in need of assistance.[141] The European Convention on Social and Medical Assistance therefore calls for a minimum of solidarity. This obligation should be respected even more in the framework of the EU/EC, where the Member States' nationals are interconnected through the far stronger bond of common Union citizenship.

d) The Non-limitation of Market-related Rights of Free Movement by a Social Cover Proviso

It is also worth noting that none of the market-related guarantees of free movement in Community law are subject to a social cover proviso. The fact that the approach chosen here is different from that used in relation to the general right to free movement is usually justified on the ground that Union citizens exercising market-related guarantees of free movement contribute economically to the host State. Therefore their claims to solidarity in case of necessity should be granted on an equal footing with those of nationals of the host State. However, the cross-border migration of Union citizens, when not pursuing economic activities in the host State, would be something completely different.[142]

One objection to this economically based argument is that the free movement of workers, including their right to equal treatment with nationals of the host Member State as far as social advantages are concerned, does not depend on their producing a minimum economic value or on their being employed for a minimum period in the host State.[143] Therefore, the free movement of workers as guaranteed by the Treaty is also applicable if from the beginning a Union citizen, taking up residence in a Member State other than his or her State of origin, needs financial support from public authorities to complement his or her income from employment in the host State.[144]

e) The Doubtfulness of Distinguishing between Market-related and Non-market-related Rights of Free Movement in this Context

Moreover, the exercise of market-related free movement cannot always be clearly distinguished from the exercise of non-market-related free movement. For this reason the application of fundamentally different residence regimes, depending on affirmation or rejection of a relationship with the market, cannot be justified. Uncertainties arise above all in situations where a Union citizen has taken up economic activities in another Member State, but has been subsequently prevented from continuing these activities. For example, in the cases *Martínez Sala*, *Grzelczyk* and *Trojani* it was questionable whether or not Ms Martínez Sala, Mr. Grzelczyk and Mr. Trojani could invoke a right to equal treatment with nationals of the host State in terms of the social advantages at issue based on the grounds of their having been previously employed or still being employed in the host State.[145]

---

141 Article 1 and Article 6 lit. a of the European Convention on Social an Medical Assistance of 11 December 1953 (BGBl. 1956 II, 564).
142 *See, e.g.* C. Tomuschat, case note on *Martínez Sala*, CML.Rev. 37, 2000, 449, 453 *et seq.*
143 *See, e.g.*, E.C.J. Case C-53/81 of 23 March 1982, E.C.R. 1982, 1035 – *Levin*, and Advocate General G. Slynn in his Opinion of 17 September 1987 on *Lair*, E.C.R. 1988, 3179 (3185). *See also supra* note 32.
144 E.C.J. Case 139/85 of 3 June 1986, E.C.R. 1986, 1741 – *Kempf.*
145 *See* Advocate General A. La Pergola in his Opinion of 1 July 1997 on *Martínez Sala*, E.C.R. 1998, I-2694 paras. 10 *et seq.*; Advocate General S. Alber in his Opinion of 28 September 2000 on *Grzelczyk*, E.C.R. 2001, I-6197 paras. 65 *et seq.*, as well as A. Iliopoulou & H. Toner, case note on *Grzelczyk*, CML.Rev. 39 (2002), 609, 612 *et seq.*; Letzner, *supra* note 123, 121; R. Streinz, case note on *Grzelczyk*, JuS 2002, 387; E.C.J. Case C-456/02 of 7 September 2004, E.C.R. 2004, I-7573 paras. 13 *et seq.* – *Trojani.*

Moreover, the problem of abuse of the right to free movement through the exercise of this freedom exclusively in order to enjoy social advantages has been identified and discussed in the Court's jurisprudence regarding the free movement of workers. In so far as the access to general systems of student grants was concerned, the Court found a solution to the problem of abuse through the denial of access to such advantages in cases where employment appears to be only a subordinate transition stage on the way to the commencement of studies.[146] It seems reasonable to also apply this solution to the interpretation of the social cover proviso under Article 18 EC.

f) Reduction of the Social Cover Proviso to a Mere Exception Clause

After all, in the light of the concept of Union citizenship, it would be viable to interpret the secondary law-based social cover proviso consistent with primary law in order to reduce this proviso to a mere exception clause aimed at the prevention of abuse until a European Social Union is established.[147] Such an abuse can be assumed if it can be proven, on the basis of objective evidence, that a Union citizen is exercising the right of free movement under Article 18 EC exclusively in order to benefit from social advantages provided under the law of the host State.[148] This would clearly be the case if a Union citizen, without sickness insurance and without sufficient resources, moved to another Member State simply in order to get access to social assistance there, with no intention of ever pursuing an economic activity. An abuse might also be provable in a case where social cover existed at the moment when the Union citizen moved to the host State, but was subsequently lost, causing the Union citizen to then seek access to social assistance in the host State. However, the sole fact of a person claiming social assistance in such a situation cannot automatically be regarded as an abuse. Instead, the concrete circumstances of each case will have to be considered, especially the reasons for the loss of social cover. This understanding of the social cover proviso will allow the legitimate needs and expectancies of Union citizens exercising their right of free movement to be taken seriously, while at the same time preventing the host State from becoming a victim of greedy and unlimited "social welfare tourism".[149]

g) The Court's Rulings

In its rulings the ECJ shows a tendency to have the social cover proviso interpreted and applied as such a mere exception clause.

i) *Martínez Sala*

In the *Martínez Sala* case, the Court still circumvented the problem discussed above by adjudicating in substance – though inconsequently[150] – to Ms Martínez Sala the child-raising allowance at issue as a social advantage for workers,[151] thereby evading any discussion of the social cover proviso.[152]

---

146 See *supra* note 34.
147 See *already* Borchardt, *supra* note 82, 2060.
148 For a description of the abuse of rights, see E.C.J. Case 39/86 of 21 June 1988, E.C.R. 1988, 3161 para. 43 – *Lair*.
149 See K.-D. Borchardt, *Kosten, nichts als Kosten?*, EuZW 2001, 321.
150 See *infra* note 197.
151 This can also be said as to the qualification of the child-raising allowance as family benefit covered by Regulation (EEC) 1408/71 (*supra* note 27); see E.C.J. Case C-85/86 of 12 May 1998, E.C.R. 1998, I-2691 paras. 35 *et seq.* – *Martínez Sala*.
152 E.C.J. Case C-85/86 of 12 May 1998, E.C.R. 1998, I-2691 paras. 57 *et seq.* – *Martínez Sala*.

ii) *Grzelczyk*

In *Grzelczyk*, the ECJ could no longer avoid ruling on the social cover proviso.[153] The French student Rudy Grzelczyk had saved himself the costs of maintenance, accommodation and tuition during the first three years of his studies in physical education at the University of Louvain-la-Neuve in Belgium by taking on various minor jobs and by obtaining credit facilities. However, at the beginning of his fourth and final year of study, which involved the writing of a dissertation and the completion of a qualifying period of practical training, he applied to a Belgian Public Social Assistance Center for payment of social assistance. This social assistance, the so-called minimex (minimum subsistence allowance), which Belgian nationals in his situation would have had the right to claim, was initially granted to Mr. Grzelczyk, but then revoked on the ground of his French nationality.

As it was not clear to the ECJ whether or not Mr Grzelczyk had taken up employment covered by the free movement of workers during his three initial years of study, the Court examined the case instead as one in which employment could not be established. Therefore only Article 8a EC Treaty (now, following amendment, Article 18 EC) in conjunction with Article 6 EC Treaty (now, following amendment, Article 12 EC) and the students' directive could be applied. The ECJ affirmed a right of access to the minimum subsistence allowance on an equal footing with nationals of the host State. This will be examined in more detail below in the discussion of the principle of equal treatment with nationals of the host State.[154] Whether that right of access to minimum subsistence was compatible with the social cover proviso under the students' directive, was also a problem. In so far, the ECJ made clear that when a Union citizen is residing in a foreign Member State under Article 18 EC and subsequently loses sufficient resources with which to maintain himself or herself, this does not mean that his or her right of residence will automatically cease to exist. In the case of such a loss, the host State is only entitled to adopt measures to terminate the Union citizen's residence. Until such measures are adopted, the Union citizen still remains a lawful resident of the host State.

Furthermore the ECJ has clearly restricted the Member States' competence to adopt measures to terminate a Union citizen's residence for lack of social cover. The Court recognized that the directive in question does not only require the initial, but also the continuing, existence of social cover. Therefore, it would be possible for a host State, in the case of subsequent recourse to social assistance by a student who is a national of another Member State, to consider measures for terminating the lawful residence of this student. Such measures, however, could only be taken "within the limits imposed by Community law", and they could never be an automatic consequence of recourse to social assistance.

Instead, it should be noted that, according to the preambles to all three residence directives, the aim of the social cover proviso is merely to avoid unreasonably burdening the public finances of the host Member State through abusive claims by foreign Union citizens. Thus, a certain degree of financial solidarity between the nationals of the host Member State and the residing nationals of other Member States is necessary, particularly if the difficulties encountered by a beneficiary of the right of residence are temporary. Furthermore, it should be taken into account that a student's financial position may change with the passage of time for reasons beyond his control.[155]

---

153 E.C.J. Case C-184/99 of 20 September 2001, E.C.R. 2001, I-6193 – *Grzelczyk*.
154 *See infra* note 219.
155 E.C.J. Case C-184/99 of 20 September 2001, E.C.R. 2001, I-6193 paras. 42 *et seq.* – *Grzelczyk*. The differentiated reasoning of the Court justifies by no means a critical statement according to which Union citizenship after Grzelczyk would have become a Damokles sword threatening the national systems of social security, *but see* Höfler, *supra* note 115, 1206. *See*, in contrast, the rather prudent answer given by Parliamentary Secretary of State W.-M. Catenhusen (Federal Ministry for Education and Research) on 1 November 2001,

iii) *Baumbast*

In the *Baumbast* case, the Court further held that the social cover proviso must be applied "in compliance with the limits imposed by Community law and in accordance with the general principles of that law, in particular the principle of proportionality".[156] Mr. Baumbast, however, had sufficient resources and comprehensive sickness insurance in Germany. He had been living in the United Kingdom already for several years without ever having become a burden on the public finances of the host Member State. Under such circumstances, the termination of Mr. Baumbast's right to reside in the United Kingdom under Article 18 (1) EC on the – possibly even unfounded – ground that his sickness insurance did not cover an emergency treatment given in the United Kingdom would have amounted to disproportionate interference with the exercise of his right.[157]

iv) *Trojani*

In *Trojani*, the Court resumed its general explanations on the necessary compliance with Community law including the principle of proportionality.[158] However, in its view, it was not disproportionate to deny a right of residence in Belgium to the French national Trojani, who had moved from France to Belgium as a non-economic migrant without sufficient resources and who had then asked for social assistance in Belgium. In these circumstances Belgium would in principle have been justified, within the limits imposed by Community law, to take a measure to remove Mr Trojani from Belgian territory, although recourse to the social assistance system of the host State may not automatically entail such a measure. Instead, Belgium had given Mr Trojani a five-year residence permit. Consequently, during the legal existence of this permit, Belgium was bound to grant Mr Trojani social assistance on an equal footing with Belgian nationals. Belgium's refusal of such assistance could not be based on the social cover proviso and was incompatible with Community law.

v) *Zhu and Chen*

Finally, in *Zhu and Chen*, it was clear for the ECJ from the order for reference that the four-year-old Irish national Catherine Zhu wanting to reside in the United Kingdom had both sickness insurance and sufficient resources, provided by her Chinese mother. However, the issue was whether the social cover proviso required a Union citizen, when moving to another Member State, to possess sufficient resources personally.

The Court stressed that the free movement of persons had to be interpreted broadly and all limitations to this fundamental principle narrowly. Since the social cover proviso did not contain any express requirement as to the origin of the sufficient resources, a request for the personal origin of the sufficient resources would add to that condition without being necessary for the protection of the public finances of the host State. Such a requirement would therefore constitute a disproportionate interference with the exercise of the fundamental right of free movement upheld by Article 18 EC. Instead, it would suffice for the minor citizen of the Union to be covered by appropriate sickness insurance and

---

responding to the Member of the Bundestag M. Böttcher's question for the consequences of the *Grzelczyk* decision concerning educational grants for students in Germany. Secretary of State Catenhusen emphasized that only such students lawfully residing in Germany are concerned who, notwithstanding their initially proven secure financial situation, are temporarily and involuntarily facing a situation of financial needs, BUNDESTAGS-DRUCKSACHE (BT-DRS.) 14/7414, 34 (35). Similarly VAN DER MEI, *supra* note 1, 150.

156 E.C.J. Case C-413/99 of 17 September 2002, E.C.R. 2002, I-7091 para. 91 – *Baumbast*; resumed in E.C.J. Case C-456/02 of 7 September 2004, E.C.R. 2004, I-7573 para. 34 – *Trojani*.
157 E.C.J. Case C-413/99 of 17 September 2002, E.C.R. 2002, I-7091 paras. 92 *et seq.* – *Baumbast*.
158 E.C.J. Case C-456/02 of 7 September 2004, E.C.R. 2004, I-7573 para 34 – *Trojani*.

to be in the care of a parent who is a third-country national having sufficient resources for that minor not to become a burden on the public finances of the host Member State.[159] For the rest, the Court did not consider it as abusive that the child's Chinese mother deliberately had taken up residence in the island of Ireland when she was about six months pregnant in order to enable the child she was expecting to acquire Irish nationality. On the contrary, this was legally making use of the existing Irish nationality legislation.[160]

vi) Conclusion

In summing up all these considerations of the Court, it becomes clear indeed that the function of the social cover proviso is not to comprehensively ban foreign Union citizens from seeking access to social benefits in a host Member State, but rather merely to provide a Member State with measures which it can use to deny or terminate lawful residence in cases of abuse.

4. The Exclusion of Maintenance Grants for Students

By referring to the measures adopted to give effect to the free movement of Union citizens, Article 18 (1) EC (formerly Article 8a (1) EC Treaty) seems also to confirm the applicability of the provision laid down in the students' directive according to which foreign students benefiting from the right of residence shall not be entitled to claim student maintenance grants from the host Member State.[161] However, the students' directive only provides that an entitlement to such student grants shall not be established by "this directive". Hence, the directive does not affect the primary and secondary law which ensures access to Member States' systems of study grants on the basis of the free movement of workers and the right of establishment.[162] The directive provision in question only refers to students from other Member States who are not already otherwise entitled to residence and financial support. These students, though granted a right of residence, shall not enjoy a parallel entitlement to student maintenance grants provided by the host Member State.

a) The Problem

With the entering-into-force of Article 8a EC Treaty (now, following amendment, Article 18 EC) the students' directive lost its function of conferring a special right of residence on students from other Member States who were not otherwise covered by a residence right. Since then, the right of residence enjoyed by these students has flowed from the directly applicable Article 8a EC Treaty (now, following amendment, Article 18 EC).[163] This leads to the question of how far these changes in primary law have had an impact on the exclusion of foreign students from maintenance grants as laid down in secondary law.

b) Arguments against the Validity of the Exclusion Clause

As the students' directive's preamble confirms, the exclusion clause was originally based on the ECJ's previous restrictive jurisprudence. The Court had stated that public assistance given to students for maintenance and training fell outside the scope of application

---

159 See E.C.J. Case C-200/02 of 19 October 2004, E.C.R. 2004, I-9923 paras 28 *et seq.* and 47 – *Zhu and Chen*.
160 See E.C.J. Case C-200/02 of 19 October 2004, E.C.R. 2004, I-9923 paras 11 and 36 *et seq.* – *Zhu and Chen*.
161 Article 3 of Council Directive (EEC) 93/96 of 29 October 1993 on the right of residence for students, O.J. EC 1993 L 317, 59.
162 See *supra* notes 31, 36 and 44.
163 See E.C.J. Case C-413/99 of 17 September 2002, E.C.R. 2002, I-7091 paras. 84 *et seq.* – *Baumbast*.

of the Treaty as referred to in the former Article 7 EEC Treaty (later on Article 6 EC Treaty; now, following amendment, Article 12 EC). Therefore foreign students were only entitled to the payment of host State grants intended to cover charges for vocational training, such as registration and tuition fees.[164] This jurisprudence, which was not very convincing,[165] has been overruled by the Court. In *Grzelczyk*, the Court stated that since the entering-into-force of the Maastricht Treaty, a Union citizen pursuing university studies in a Member State other than his or her State of origin can also claim, on the basis of the general prohibition of discrimination on grounds of nationality laid down in the Treaty, equal treatment by the host State regarding grants intended to cover maintenance and training costs.[166]

Under such circumstances the directive clause excluding foreign students from maintenance grants could be regarded as being obsolete. When looked at from a legal point of view, it could be stated that against the backdrop of the nowadays primary law-based right of foreign students to eligibility for maintenance grants, the secondary law clause excluding the establishment of such a right by "this directive" remains without legal content. This finding can also be supported by other elements of the Court's ruling in *Grzelczyk*. Admittedly, the Court emphasized in this case that the reference to secondary law as contained in Art 18 (1) EC still allows for exceptions to the prohibition of discrimination on grounds of nationality.[167] Furthermore, the Court considered the social cover proviso contained in the students' directive as one of these legitimate exceptions. But the proviso is seen by the Court as entitling the host Member State, while observing the proportionality principle, to take measures to deny or terminate the lawful residence of foreign Union citizens. It does not, however, give the host State the right to exclude these citizens from social benefits during lawful residence. The ECJ only in addition underlined that, according to its wording, the directive does not by itself establish any entitlement to maintenance grants provided by the host Member State. The judgment also indicates that Mr. Grzelczyk, though a French national, was entitled to the Belgian minimum subsistence allowance because a Belgian national in his situation would have been granted such social assistance. The Court held, moreover, that measures terminating Mr. Grzelczyk's residence would have been disproportionate to the situation and therefore would have breached Community law.

c) Arguments in Favor of the Validity of the Exclusion Clause

On the other hand, it can be argued that unconditionally opening the Member States' systems of study grants for the benefit of all Union citizens who are entitled to free movement under Article 18 (1) EC, would constitute a far-reaching legal change. This change should therefore, if actually intended, have been made more explicit in the Treaty and in the Court's jurisprudence than has so far been the case. Moreover, in *Grzelczyk* a specific maintenance grant for students was not at issue (and therefore neither was the applicability of the exclusion clause for maintenance grants), but rather the issue was the right of a Belgian national to a general social benefit (and the relation of this right to the social cover

---

164 Recital 7 of Council Directive (EC) 93/96 of 29 October 1993 on the right of residence for students, O.J. EC 1993 L 317, 59. E.C.J. Case 39/86 of 21 June 1988, E.C.R. 1988, 3161 paras. 14 *et seq.* – *Lair*; E.C.J. Case 197/86 of 21 June 1988, E.C.R. 1988, 3205 para. 27 – *Brown*; E.C.J. Case C-357/89 of 26 February 1992, E.C.R. 1992, I-1027 para. 28 – *Raulin*.
165 See *infra* note 217.
166 E.C.J. Case C-184/99 of 20 September 2001, E.C.R. 2001, I-6193 paras. 34 *et seq.* – *Grzelczyk*.
167 Also to the following explanations, see E.C.J. Case C-184/99 of 20 September 2001, E.C.R. 2001, I-6193 paras. 37 *et seq.* – *Grzelczyk*.

proviso).[168] Furthermore, the directive excluding foreign students from maintenance grants was originally intended to complement the new right of residence as laid down in secondary law. One can argue that when Article 8a EC Treaty (now, following amendment, Article 18 EC) made this right of residence a part of primary law, the exclusion clause did not become obsolete, but rather underwent a functional change in the same way as did the social cover proviso. It can now be regarded as a legitimate secondary law restriction on the right of residence as laid down in primary law in Article 18 (1) EC and therefore as a restriction to student grant claims based on that provision (in conjunction with Article 12 EC).[169]

d) The Limited Applicability of the Exclusion Clause

Even if one accepts the latter interpretation, though, the exclusion clause will still not function to preclude foreign students entirely from accessing maintenance grants provided by the host Member State. The reason for this is that when interpreting this secondary law clause one has to take into account two factors. Firstly, one has to consider primary law as represented by the concept of full social integration of all foreign Union citizens who have exercised their right of free movement under Article 18 (1) EC (in conjunction with Article 12 EC) as well as by the general principles of Community law, in particular the principle of proportionality.[170] Secondly, it must be remembered that the exclusion clause is only intended to protect the host Member State's public finances from "an unreasonable burden" as expressed in the preamble to the students' directive.[171]

The resulting interpretation of the exclusion clause should make clear that this clause, in so far as it operates to deny unlimited access to Member States' systems of study grants to Union citizens entitled to free movement under Article 18 (1) EC, can only preclude individual entitlements to these grants if the principle of exclusion is put into question. In this sense, the exclusion clause and the social cover proviso both serve to prevent the abuse of Treaty rights, pending the establishment of a European Social Union. Accordingly, Union citizens who intend to study in another Member State and who lack sufficient resources to do this cannot simply claim student maintenance grants which the host Member State has reserved for its own nationals. This is all the more true for Union citizens who possess sufficient resources to pay for their studies in another Member State.

However, the exclusion clause does not apply to cases in which neither a circumvention of the general exclusion of foreign Union citizens from maintenance grants nor another abuse can be proven. Whether the public aid is formally labeled as social assistance or as a maintenance grant is not decisive.[172] If Mr. Grzelczyk had, instead of applying to Belgian authorities for social assistance,[173] applied for a provisional maintenance grant for students

---

168 See Iliopoulou & Toner, *supra* note 145, 619; Martínez Soria, *supra* note 123, 648.
169 With this conclusion, e.g., Iliopoulou & Toner, *supra* note 145, 616.
170 See E.C.J. Case C-184/99 of 20 September 2001, E.C.R. 2001, I-6193 paras. 42 *et seq*. – *Grzelczyk*; E.C.J. Case C-413/99 of 17 September 2002, E.C.R. 2002, I-7091 para. 91 – *Baumbast*. See furthermore *infra* note 214.
171 Recital 6 of Council Directive (EC) 93/96 of 29 October 1993 on the right of residence for students, O.J. EC 1993 L 317, 59. On that formula, the Court based its reasoning that the directive recognizes a "certain degree of financial solidarity" among nationals of the host Member State and nationals of other Member States, see E.C.J. Case C-184/99 of 20 September 2001, E.C.R. 2001, I-6193 para. 44 – *Grzelczyk*. See also the E.C.J.'s jurisprudence emphasizing that financial reasons can justify a restriction of fundamental freedoms only in exceptional cases where a Member State's public finances are at grave risk: E.C.J. Case C-120/95 of 28 April 1998, E.C.R. 1998, I-1831 para. 39 – *Decker*; E.C.J. Case C-158/96 of 28 April 1998, E.C.R. 1998, I-1931 para. 41 – *Kohll*.
172 In this sense, VAN DER MEI, *supra* note 1, 380 *et seq*. A dissenting position seems to present Martínez Soria (*supra* note 123), 649.
173 See E.C.J. Case 184/99 of 20 September 2001, E.C.R. 2001, I-6193 paras. 8 *et seq*. – *Grzelczyk*.

which would have been given to a Belgian student in his situation, he would still have been acknowledged as having the right to such a grant. Similarly, if the Italian spouse of an Austrian national has lived in Austria for a couple of years before applying for an Austrian grant to complete a course of studies at an Austrian university, she could not be denied access to student grants simply on the ground that the Austrian grant system is only available to Austrian nationals.[174]

5. Legitimate Barriers

The prohibition of all forms of discrimination on grounds of nationality is modified through the public policy proviso, the social cover proviso and the exclusion of maintenance grants for students, which each allow in exceptional cases restrictions on free movement to the disadvantage of foreign Union citizens. In addition, it should be examined whether Article 18 EC encompasses also a prohibition of non-discriminatory limitations of free movement, modified by an unwritten limitation proviso.[175]

a) The Possibility of a Prohibition of Non-discriminatory Limitations of Free Movement, modified by an Unwritten Limitation Proviso

Such a construction could be inspired by the ECJ's jurisprudence on the fundamental freedoms of the internal market. Indeed, the Court considers each of these freedoms to not only contain a prohibition on discrimination by Member States, but also a prohibition of non-discriminatory limitations. This latter prohibition does not have absolute validity, but is modified by an unwritten limitation proviso according to which "national measures liable to hinder or make less attractive the exercise of fundamental freedoms guaranteed by the Treaty must fulfill four conditions: they must be applied in a non-discriminatory manner; they must be justified by imperative requirements in the general interest; they must be suitable for securing the attainment of the objective which they pursue; and they must not go beyond what is necessary in order to attain it".[176] It seems reasonable to assume that the same rules must apply to the general right of free movement.[177]

b) The Court's Rulings

Four judgments of the ECJ have relevance to the matter in hand.

i) *Wijsenbeek*

The *Wijsenbeek* case raised the question of a possible "transfer" of the said concept into the framework of the freedom of movement as laid down in Article 18 EC. The Court had to rule on whether border controls by Member States on Union citizens traveling between Member States still were compatible with Community law. Mr. Wijsenbeek, a Dutch national, had refused, when returning from Strasbourg to the Netherlands through

---

174 The same conclusion was drawn for such a constellation by Advocate General L. A. Geelhoed in his Opinion of 27 February 2003 on *Ninni-Orasche*, Case C-413/01 (not yet published in E.C.R.). Not convincing is, however, this Advocate General's underlying reasoning; he stated the continuing effect of the exclusion clause, but "corrected" his finding by taking into account the rights laid down in Article 17 EC in conjunction with Article 12 EC. The E.C.J. limited itself in its judgment to questions concerning the free movement of workers, *see* E.C.J. Case C-413/01 of 6 November 2003 (not yet published in E.C.R.) – *Ninni-Orasche*.
175 In this sense, e.g., Obwexer, *supra* note 101, 58; more reluctant S. Bode, case note on *D'Hoop*, EuZW 637, 638 (2002).
176 E.C.J. Case C-55/94 of 30 November 1995, E.C.R. 1995, I-4165 para. 37 – *Gebhard*.
177 *See also* H. TONER, PARTNERSHIP RIGHTS, FREE MOVEMENT AND EU LAW (2004), 216 *et seq.*

Rotterdam airport, to present his passport or identity card to the Dutch police officer responsible for border controls. Therefore he was accused of having breached his obligation, as laid down in Dutch law, of establishing his Dutch nationality by presenting his passport or identity card when encountering the border control.

Article 8a EC (now, following amendment, Article 18 EC) seemed a rather obvious choice as a benchmark for testing the legality of the Dutch border controls in question. This provision covers all Union citizens – hence, nationals as well – when exercising their rights to free movement and cross border mobility.[178] The ECJ considered the Dutch obligation requiring people to establish, under threat of criminal penalties, their nationality upon entry into the Dutch territory as being in compliance with Community law. This decision was based on the reasoning that as long as specific Community rules on the control of people at the external frontiers of the European Union did not exist, the Member States retained the right to carry out identity checks at the internal frontiers of the Community, which included the right to require persons to present a valid identity card or passport. These procedures were deemed necessary in order to allow Member States to establish whether a person who wished to exercise freedom of movement was a national of a Member State, thus having the right to move freely within the territory of the Member States, or a national of a non-member country not having that right. Consequently, the Member States still remain competent to impose penalties in cases of check refusals, provided that these penalties be proportionate and comparable to those which apply to similar national infringements.[179]

These considerations of the Court are perfectly reasonable as to their result. However, the ECJ has left open the question of their relation to Article 8a EC Treaty (now, following amendment, Article 18 EC), other than that there was an interference with the right to move freely.[180] The public policy proviso was not applicable here as it only authorizes individual measures against foreign citizens of the Union on serious grounds.[181] It appears, however, legitimate to interpret Article 8a EC (now, following amendment, Article 18 EC) as also being a general prohibition of non-discriminatory limitations subject to an unwritten limitation proviso.[182] From such a perspective, it is possible to justify the reasoning of the Court as well as the decision reached.[183]

In substance, the Court in *Wijsenbeek* may therefore have interpreted Article 8a EC (now, following amendment, Article 18 EC) in this way, even if this is not expressly declared in the judgment. The parallels which can be drawn to the "four freedoms" of the

---

178 See *supra* note 126. A different conclusion may be drawn for the mobility of a Member State's nationals within the territory of that Member State, see Hilf, *supra* note 82, Article 18 EC para. 1; C. Jacqueson, *Union citizenship and the Court of Justice: something new unter the sun? Towards social citizenship*, 27 EUROPEAN LAW REVIEW (E.L.REV). 260, 279 (2002); Kadelbach, *supra* note 101, 480; Magiera, *supra* note 6, Article 45 para. 19. *See also* E.C.J. Cases C-64/96 and C-65/96 of 5 June 1997, E.C.R. 1997, I-3171 paras. 16 and 23 – *Uecker und Jacquet*.
179 E.C.J. Case C-378/99 of 21 September 1999, E.C.R. 1999, I-6207 para. 45 – *Wijsenbeek*.
180 This has also rightly been emphasized by Advocate General G. Cosmas in his Opinion of 16 March 1999 on *Wijsenbeek*, E.C.R. 1999, I-6209 paras. 99 *et seq.* Of another opinion is Kluth, *supra* note 82, Article 18 EC para. 4.
181 See *supra* notes 20, 22 and 132. *See*, furthermore, Directive (EEC) 64/221 (*supra* note 24) and, more recently, Articles 27 *et seq.* of Directive 2004/38/EC (*infra* note 243). However, Hatje, *supra* note 82, Article 18 EC para. 11, states that an unwritten limitation clause would be applicable in such cases.
182 Apparently in that sense also K. Füßer, *Grundrecht auf wirtschaftliche Freizügigkeit und Art. 8a EGV als Auffangbeschränkungsverbot des Gemeinschaftsrechts*, DÖV 1999, 96, 101 *et seq.*; M. Zuleeg, *Die Einwirkung des Europäischen Gemeinschaftsrechts auf die deutsche Pflegeversicherung*, DEUTSCHES VERWALTUNGSBLATT (DVBl.) 445, 448 (1997); rather unclear Kluth, *supra* note 82, Article 18 EC paras. 5, 11 *et seq.*
183 Consequently, Advocate General G. Cosmas based his Opinion of 16 March 1999 on *Wijsenbeek* explicitly on the Court's jurisprudence on the fundamental freedoms of the internal market, see E.C.R. 1999, I-6209 paras. 105 and 118.

internal market also would explain why in *Wijsenbeek* the Court only affirmed the legitimacy of identity checks based on national law as long as specific Community rules governing controls over persons at the external frontiers of the European Union had not yet entered into force. Indeed, according to the Court's jurisprudence, the Member States lose their regulating power in the area of the "four freedoms" only when definite secondary EC legislation is enacted.[184]

ii) *Elsen*, *D'Hoop* and *Pusa*

Also in the Court's subsequent decisions in *Elsen*, *D'Hoop* and *Pusa* the issue was not direct or indirect discrimination against foreign Union citizens, but rather disadvantages inflicted by Member States on their own nationals who had exercised their right to reside freely in other Member States, as guaranteed under Article 8a EC Treaty (now, after amendment, Article 18 EC).[185] In deciding in these three cases that the general right of free movement had been violated or could have been violated, it was obvious that the Court considered Article 18 EC as also constituting a prohibition of non-discriminatory limitations. In *D'Hoop* and *Pusa*, the Court even held Article 18 EC to be one of the "fundamental freedoms" of the internal market.[186] In keeping with its jurisprudence on the scope of the fundamental freedoms of the internal market, the Court considered that when Member States' regulations make free movement under Article 18 EC less attractive and when such restrictions cannot be justified on objective grounds, those regulations are a violation of that fundamental freedom.[187]

VII. Equality of Treatment

The principle according to which Union citizens exercising their right of free movement must be treated on an equal footing with nationals of the host Member State is of great importance not only as far as market-related rights of free movement are concerned, but also in cases where the general right of free movement is at stake. As Article 18 EC covers foreign and national Union citizens alike, it is also relevant in a situation where a national of a Member State exercising his or her right of residence in a foreign Member State incurs disadvantages in comparison to other nationals of the home State who have remained "immobile".[188]

1. The Court's Rulings

In such circumstances it is not surprising that in its case law on Article 8a EC Treaty (now, after amendment, Article 18 EC) the ECJ often had to deal with equality problems.

---

184 *See, e.g.*, E.C.J. Case 120/78 of 20 February 1979, E.C.R. 1979, 649 para. 8 – *Rewe* (Cassis de Dijon); E.C.J. Case 298/87 of 14 July 1988, E.C.R. 1988, 4489 para. 15 – *Smanor*; E.C.J. Case C-193/94 of 29 February 1996, E.C.R. 1996, I-929 paras. 24 *et seq.* – *Skanavi*.
185 E.C.J. Case C-135/99 of 23 November 2000, E.C.R. 2000, I-10409 – *Elsen*; E.C.J. Case C/224/98 of 11 July 2002, E.C.R. 2002, I-6191 – *D'Hoop*.
186 *See* already E.C.J. Case C-357/98 of 9 November 2000, E.C.R. 2000, I-9265 para. 25 – *Yiadom*.
187 E.C.J. Case C-224/98 of 11 July 2002, E.C.R. 2002, I-6191 paras. 29 *et seq.* – *D'Hoop*; E.C.J. Case C-224/02 of 29 April 2004, E.C.R. 2004, I-5763 para 20 – *Pusa*.
188 *See supra* notes 126 and 178.

a) Equal Treatment

In a number of cases the Court chose to insist on equal treatment. In *Bickel and Franz*, the Court decided, based on the principle of equal treatment, that German-speaking foreign Union citizens, exercising their right of free movement, have the same right to use the German language in court proceedings before courts in the Italian Province of Bolzano as do German-speaking Italians of that Province.[189] Furthermore, the Court stated in *Elsen* that the German Federal Insurance Institute for Employees was not allowed to treat a German national having resided in another Member State for a certain period less favorably than other German nationals having remained in Germany all the time. The Insurance Institute thus had to take into account, when calculating Ms Elsen's old-age pension, the child-rearing periods completed while Ms Elsen was residing in a foreign Member State.[190]

According to the Court's judgment in *D'Hoop*, Belgium could not simply turn down Ms D'Hoop, who was a Belgian national having made an application for a tideover allowance, on the grounds that she had exercised her right of free movement and completed her secondary education in France.[191] In *Pusa* the ECJ stressed that this Finnish national should not be penalized by Finnish legislation, in the determination of the attachable part of his Finnish pension, for having moved from Finland to Spain upon retirement.[192] Finally, in *Martínez Sala*, *Grzelczyk* and *Trojani*, the Court gave foreign Union citizens, who had exercised their right of free movement, the same entitlement to social benefits as was available to nationals in similar circumstances.[193]

b) Unequal Treatment

On the other hand, the Court derived from the principle of equality not only the concept that comparable situations must not be treated differently, but also that different situations must not be treated in the same way. Therefore, in *Garcia Avello*, a case concerning the application for a change of surname made for two children with dual (Spanish and Belgian) nationality residing in Belgium, the ECJ found that by virtue of difficulties specific to their situation such Union citizens may assert their right to be treated in a manner different to that in which persons having only Belgian nationality would be treated in the same situation. Consequently, the Belgian administrative authority in question had to grant the application enabling the two children to bear the surname to which they were entitled according to Spanish law and tradition.[194]

c) The Court's Reasoning in *Martínez Sala*

Concerning in particular the Court's ruling in *Martínez Sala*, it should be stressed that, while this ruling can be welcomed in substance, the line of argumentation concerning equal treatment is not convincing. The Spanish national María Martínez Sala, who was resident in Germany, but not pursuing economic activities at the time in question, applied after the birth of her second child for a child-raising allowance pursuant to the German *Bundeserziehungsgeldgesetz* (BErzGG). Her application was rejected on the ground that she did

---

189 E.C.J. Case C-274/96 of 24 November 1998, E.C.R. 1998, I-7637 paras. 20 *et seq*. – *Bickel and Franz*.
190 E.C.J. Case C-135/99 of 23 November 2000, E.C.R. 2000, I-10409 – *Elsen*. For a similar constellation in the context of the free movement of workers, *see supra* note 27.
191 E.C.J. Case C-224/98 of 11 July 2002, E.C.R. 2002, I-6191 – *D'Hoop*.
192 E.C.J. Case C-224/02 of 29 April 2004, E.C.R. 2004, I-5763 – *Pusa*.
193 E.C.J. Case C-85/96 of 12 May 1998, E.C.R. 1998, I-2691 – *Martínez Sala*; E.C.J. Case C-184/99 of 20 September 2001, E.C.R. 2001, I-6193 – *Grzelczyk*; E.C.J. Case C-456/02 of 7 September 2004, E.C.R. 2004, I-7573 – *Trojani*.
194 E.C.J. Case C-148/02 of 2 October 2003, E.C.R. 2003, I-11613 paras. 31, 37 and 45 – *Garcia Avello*.

not have a formal residence permit as required by the BErzGG in cases of applications by non-nationals. Although the legitimacy of her stay in Germany, which was covered by the European Convention on Social and Medical Assistance, was undisputed, the German authorities had refused to provide her with a formal residence permit.

The Court correctly held that the child-raising allowance was a social advantage for workers which fell within the scope of application of the Treaty *ratione materiae*. Ms Martínez Sala, as a Union citizen lawfully residing in a Member State other than her State of origin, fell within the scope of application of the Treaty *ratione personae*.[195] The Court then simply argued, through reference to the general prohibition of discrimination on grounds of nationality, that the national law of a Member State, in cases comparable to the case of Ms Martínez Sala, must not operate to restrict child-raising allowances to persons who are able to present a residence permit, if this law requires nationals to only be in residence within the Member State, and not also to be able to prove their residential status.[196]

This conclusion was wrong in so far as the only obligation that could be deduced from the reasoning in the case (child-raising allowance as social advantage for workers) was an obligation for the Member State equally to treat national workers and workers having the nationality of other Member States when granting child-raising allowances. In contrast to this, the ECJ based this part of its judgment on the assumption that Ms Martínez Sala could not qualify as a worker.[197] To be consequent, the ECJ would first have had to explain that under German law Germans who did not qualify as workers and who were in the same situation as Ms Martínez Sala would also have been entitled to receive the child-raising allowance. The Court could then have discussed the question of equal treatment. However one should not conclude from the sole fact that the Court's judgment does not contain any precise explanations on this point that, according to the ECJ, all national social advantages for workers should now be granted not only to migrant EC workers from other Member States, but also to all non-national Union citizens lawfully residing in the host Member State and not pursuing economic activities.[198] Had the Court intended to make this far-reaching step through its judgment in *Martínez Sala*, it would have had to engage in more compelling reasoning and more detailed argumentation than it did.

2. The Legal Construction of the Equality of Treatment

It should be emphasized that the legal construction of the principle of equal treatment as chosen by the ECJ in most of the cases examined here, is distinct from the concept used in the context of market-related rights. In the case of the latter, the principle of equal treatment flows from special prohibitions against discrimination contained in the fundamental freedoms themselves.[199] Hence, the principle of equal treatment appears to be an integral part of these market-related guarantees of free movement.[200]

a) The Detour via the General Principle of Non-discrimination

In contrast, in the cases *Bickel and Franz* and *Grzelczyk* the Court affirmed the applicability of the principle of equal treatment to free movement under Article 8a EC (now, after

---

195 *See supra* note 88.
196 E.C.J. Case C-85/96 of 12 May 1998, E.C.R. 1998, I-2691 paras. 57 *et seq.* – *Martínez Sala*.
197 *See also* Becker, *supra* note 10, 532; Borchardt, *supra* note 82, 2058; Iliopoulou & Toner, *supra* note 145, 615: "rather obscure"; Jacqueson, *supra* note 178, 265; Tomuschat, *supra* note 142, 452.
198 *But see* Jacqueson, *supra* note 178, 267.
199 Articles 39 (2), 52 (2) and 50 (3) EC.
200 *See supra* notes 25 *et seq.*, 42 *et seq.* and 53 *et seq.*

amendment, Article 18 EC) by making a detour via Article 6 EC Treaty (initially Article 7 EEC Treaty; now, after amendment, Article 12 EC). Starting from this general principle of non-discrimination, the Court first established in both cases discrimination based on grounds of nationality. Article 6 EC Treaty (initially Article 7 EEC Treaty; now, after amendment, Article 12 EC), however, prohibits direct or indirect discrimination only within the scope of application of the Treaty, meaning in situations governed by Community law. Therefore, the Court declared in both cases that the exercise of the right of free movement under Article 8a EC Treaty (now, following amendment, Article 18 EC) was a situation governed by Community law.[201]

The Court's protracted reasoning in justifying the application of the principle of equal treatment in the context of Article 8a EC Treaty (now, following amendment, Article 18 EC) may have been due to the fact that the wording of Article 8a EC Treaty, in contrast to the wording of the present Articles 39, 43 and 50 EC, does not expressly include a prohibition of discrimination. Moreover, Article 6 EC Treaty (initially Article 7 EEC Treaty; now, after amendment, Article 12 EC) is a provision with recognized direct effect.[202] For this reason the question of the eventual direct effect of Article 8a EC Treaty (now, following amendment, Article 18 EC) could in such cases be set aside. As far as *Martínez Sala* is concerned, the Court also based in that case the right to equal treatment on Article 6 EC Treaty (initially Article 7 EEC Treaty; now, after amendment, Article 12 EC). There was, however, no other possibility, since the Court erroneously referred in its reasoning not to Ms Martínez Sala's right of free movement, but to the fact that her continuing residence in Germany was tolerated due to the European Convention on Social and Medical Assistance.[203] Still in the case of Mr. Trojani, the Court, though expressly recognizing direct effect to Article 18 (1) EC, had recourse to Article 12 EC in order to establish this French national's equal right to social assistance in Belgium.[204]

b) The Principle of Equal Treatment as a Necessary Component of the General Right of Free Movement

One could argue that what actually counts is the applicability of the principle of equal treatment in the context of Article 18 EC (formerly Article 8a EC Treaty), with the legal construction justifying such applicability being more or less irrelevant. But it may well be that the detour via Article 6 EC Treaty which occurred in *Martínez Sala* led the ECJ to adopt a reasoning that reflects the meaning and scope of the principle of equal treatment in too vague a manner.[205] Moreover, Articles 12 and 18 EC (formerly Article 6 and Article 8a EC Treaty) being two disparate topics, their conjunction could be seen as merely an accident.

In any case it seems preferable to understand the principle of equal treatment as a necessary component of the general right of free movement itself and to then derive from Article 18 EC Treaty an unwritten requirement of equal treatment which governs the general right of free movement.[206] The necessity of this approach becomes obvious if one

---

201 E.C.J. Case C-274/96 of 24 November 1998, E.C.R. 1998, I-7637 paras. 14 *et seq.* – *Bickel und Franz*; E.C.J. Case C-184/99 of 20 September 2001, E.C.R. 2001, I-6193 para. 33 – *Grzelczyk*. A similar approach can be found in E.C.J. Case C-148/02 of 2 October 2003, E.C.R. 2003, I-11613 paras. 24 and 29 – *Garcia Avello*.
202 *See, e.g.*, E.C.J. Case C-293/83 of 13 February 1985, E.C.R. 1985, 593 – *Gravier*; C.O. Lenz *in* EU- UND EG-VERTRAG. KOMMENTAR (C.O. Lenz & K.-D. Borchardt eds., 3rd ed., 2003), Article 12 para. 8.
203 *See supra* note 89.
204 E.C.J. Case C-456/02 of 7 September 2004, E.C.R. 2004, I-7573 paras. 39 *et seq.* – *Trojani*.
205 *See supra* note 197.
206 Similarly Borchardt, *supra* note 82, 2059; Zuleeg, *supra* note 182, 448. An opposite position is taken by M. Rossi, case note on *Grzelczyk*, JZ 351, 352 *et. seq.* (2002); similarly, as far as social advantages are concerned, S. Bode, *Von der Freizügigkeit zur sozialen Gleichstellung aller Unionsbürger?* EuZW 552, 556 (2003).

realizes that Article 8a EC Treaty (now, following amendment, Article 18 EC) must be interpreted as prohibiting not only direct and indirect discrimination against foreign Union citizens, but also a treatment less favorable of national Union citizens who have exercised their right to reside in another Member State when compared to the treatment of nationals who have not exercised that right. In cases of this latter kind, where no discrimination of foreigners is at issue, no reference whatsoever can be made to Article 6 EC Treaty (initially Article 7 EEC Treaty; now, after amendment, Article 12 EC).

Therefore, the ECJ was correct in not referring in *Elsen* to the general prohibition in Article 12 EC of discriminations on grounds of nationality. The Court instead derived Ms Elsen's right from an inherent prohibition of unequal treatment contained in Article 8a EC Treaty itself.[207] In the *D'Hoop* case the Court also showed such an understanding of the principle of equal treatment. A Belgian national's application for a tideover allowance had been turned down by the Belgian authorities on the ground that Ms D'Hoop had completed her secondary education in France. Without making any reference to Article 6 EC Treaty (initially Article 7 EEC Treaty; now, after amendment, Article 12 EC) the Court emphasized that this unequal treatment "is contrary to the principles which underpin the status of citizen of the Union, that is, the guarantee of the same treatment in law in the exercise of the citizen's freedom to move."[208]

The same approach was imperative in the *Pusa* case.[209] Upon retirement, Mr. Pusa, a Finnish national, had left his country of origin and settled in Spain. He then was placed at a disadvantage by Finnish legislation simply because he had moved to Spain. Indeed, according to the Finnish legislation, the attachable part of his Finnish pension had to be calculated in a manner less favorable for him than it would have had to be calculated if he had continued to reside in Finland. The Court held in *Pusa* that no Union citizen should be penalized by national legislation for having exercised his or her general right of free movement. Therefore Community law in principle precluded the Finnish legislation at stake. This judgment is to be seen as confirming that the principle of equal treatment is a necessary component of the general right of free movement itself.

3. Equal Treatment and Article 18 (3) EC

It should be noted that the principle of equal treatment as discussed here, whether based on Article 18 EC itself or on Article 12 EC as well, has in any event the character of primary law. This is to be taken into account in assessing the impact of the amendment of Article 18 EC through paragraph 3 according to the Nice Treaty.[210] This amendment has indeed not repealed the primary law-based right of Union citizens, having exercised their right of free movement, to receive equal treatment as far as social advantages provided by national authorities are concerned. It has simply limited the power to enact secondary law in the field of the general right of free movement by establishing that no provisions on social security or social protection can be enacted on the basis of Article 18 (2) EC. However, the Treaty establishing a Constitution for Europe, once entered into force, will undo this limitation.[211]

---

207 E.C.J. Case C-135/99 of 23 November 2000, E.C.R. 2000, I-10409 para. 34 – *Elsen*.
208 E.C.J. Case C-224/98 of 11 July 2002, E.C.R. 2002, I-6191 para. 35 – *D'Hoop*. Advocate General L. A. Geelhoed had, however, in his Opinion of 21 February 2002 on *D'Hoop* proposed a solution on the basis of Article 12 EC, *see* E.C.R. 2002, I-6194.
209 E.C.J. Case C-224/02 of 29 April 2004, E.C.R. 2004, I-5763 – *Pusa*.
210 *See supra* note 77.
211 *See* Article III-125 (2) of the Treaty establishing a Constitution for Europe, O.J. EU 2004 C 310, 1.

4. Lawful Residence as a Prerequisite for Equal Treatment

The right to equal treatment only applies to cases of lawful residence. Therefore, foreign Union citizens cannot invoke the principle of equal treatment linked to the general right of free movement in situations where legitimate restrictions on the freedom of movement (such as the public policy proviso, the social cover proviso or the exclusion of maintenance grants for students) enable Member States to take discriminating measures against foreign Union citizens, and such measures have indeed been taken. From that perspective, and in contrast to fears caused by the Court's recent jurisprudence, it is safe to say that there is not an overly large danger of a massive threat to public finances in the host Member States due to equal treatment in the field of the general right of free movement.[212] The right of free movement as laid down in Article 18 (1) EC is still subject to considerable restrictions. Thus, it is not likely that additional burdens on Member States' public finances will exceed reasonable limits.[213] When lawful residence ends following a legitimate measure, taken by the host Member State, to deny or terminate the residence, the Union citizen can no longer invoke a right to equal treatment based on his or her right of residence.

5. The Principle of Equal Treatment as a Means of Social Integration

It must be noted that, as a consequence of the right to equal treatment, Article 18 EC (formerly Article 8a EC Treaty) requires not only that a person be allowed to be physically present in the host Member State, but also that he or she be fully integrated into the social fabric of that State.[214] "Half way solutions" are not in compliance with that requirement. The Treaty does not authorize the host Member State to recognize the right of residence of a Union citizen exercising his or her right of free movement, while denying or restricting that Union citizen's access to social benefits provided by that State. This has become clear in the Court's recent jurisprudence. Hence, a Union citizen like Ms Martínez Sala, legitimately residing in another Member State, can apply for social benefits in the host Member State under the same conditions as nationals in a similar situation.[215]

As far as students are concerned the Court at first, probably out of fear of transgressing the threshold of acceptance, developed a compromise solution. A Union citizen enrolled in a course of studies in another Member State could apply for grants to cover registration and tuition fees, but not for assistance in covering maintenance needs, even though this assistance could in a similar situation be obtained by national students.[216] The reason given by the Court for this restriction – that assistance given to students for maintenance would as a matter of social and educational policy fall outside the scope of application of Community law[217] – was not convincing. The Court already had made clear in previous decisions that lack of competence on the part of the Community to regulate cer-

---

212 *See*, nevertheless, *e.g.*, Höfler, *supra* note 115, 1206; Iliopoulou & Toner, *supra* note 145, 620; Rossi, *supra* note 206, 353.
213 *See supra* note 155.
214 *See* Borchardt, *supra* note 82, 2060; U. Everling, *Auf dem Weg zu einem europäischen Bürger?*, *in* BÜRGER UND EUROPA 49, 54 (R. Hrbek ed., 1994); Hilf, *supra* note 82, Article 18 EC para. 7; KOTALAKIDIS, *supra* note 82, 154 *et seq.*; Magiera, *supra* note 6, Article 45 para. 9; Pechstein & Bunk, *supra* note 81, 547, 552 *et seq.*; Staeglich, *supra* note 101, 515. Too restrictive Kluth, *supra* note 82, Article 18 EC para. 5. For a basically different approach *see* Hailbronner, *supra* note 79.
215 E.C.J. Case C-85/96 of 12 May 1998, E.C.R. 1998, I-2691 paras. 61 *et seq.* – *Martínez Sala*.
216 *See* references at *supra* note 71.
217 E.C.J. Case C-39/86 of 21 June 1988, E.C.R. 1988, 3161 para. 15 – *Lair*.

tain policy areas did not relieve the Member States of their obligation to respect Community law in these areas.[218]

In *Grzelczyk*, the Court explicitly declared that as a result of changes in Community law its former compromise solution was outdated. The Court affirmed the right of students, who are exercising their right of free movement, to equal treatment with regard to access to assistance for maintenance in the host Member State.[219] Moreover, the useful effect of Article 18 EC implies that a minor Union citizen taking up residence in another Member State is entitled to be accompanied by the primary caregiver parent. However, that parent, if he or she is a third-country national, must be in a position to reside with the child in the host Member State for the duration of such residence.[220]

Finally, the right of a Union citizen to residence and equal treatment under Article 18 EC (in conjunction with Article 12 EC) does not automatically become suspended or even obsolete at the moment when the host Member State becomes entitled to take measures to terminate that citizen's residence on the basis of the public policy proviso or of the social cover proviso. The right to equal treatment ceases only when such measures have actually been taken.[221] Until then, the citizen remains a lawful resident of the host Member State with a right to full equal treatment during the entirety of his or her lawful residence in that State. Therefore Belgium could have questioned the French national Trojani's right to reside in a hostel of the Salvation Army in Brussels as a non-economic migrant without sufficient resources. However, since Belgium provided Mr. Trojani with a five years residence permit, it was not allowed to refuse to grant Mr. Trojani social assistance without also revoking his residence permit.[222] In this sense, a "small" or "temporarily diminished" right of free movement cannot exist within the framework of Article 18 EC (formerly Article 8a EC Treaty). The supremacy of the right to free movement as laid down in primary law has to be respected.

6. Political Rights of Union Citizens exercising their Right of Free Movement

Finally, it should be highlighted that it follows from the requirement of full equal treatment of foreign Union citizens, exercising their right of free movement, in the host Member State that these citizens basically must have the same political rights as nationals of that State. Therefore, these foreign Union citizens have rights to freedom of assembly, to freedom of association and to freedom of expression in the host State.[223] However, as far as the rights to vote and to run as a candidate in elections are concerned, the EC Treaty contains specific provisions which confirm and place limits on such activities. Article 19 EC specifically establishes the right of a Union citizen residing in a foreign Member State to vote and to run as a candidate in municipal elections and in elections to the European

---

218 E.C.J. Case 9/74 of 3 July 1974, E.C.R. 1974, 773 para. 6 – *Casagrande*. See also Advocate General G. Slynn in his Opinion of 17 September 1987 on *Lair*, E.C.R. 1988, 3179 (3188). *See*, furthermore, Jacqueson, *supra* note 178, 271 *et seq.*
219 E.C.J. Case C-184/99 of 20 September 2001, E.C.R. 2001, I-6193 paras. 34 *et seq.* – *Grzelczyk*.
220 *See* E.C.J. Case C-200/02 of 19 October 2004, E.C.R. 2004, I-9923 para 45 – *Zhu and Chen*.
221 E.C.J. Case C-184/99 of 20 September 2001, E.C.R. 2001, I-6193 para. 42 – *Grzelczyk*. E.C.J. Case C-456/02 of 7 September 2004, E.C.R. 2004, I-7573 paras. 40 and 45 – *Trojani*. See also Borchardt, *supra* note 82, 2060. As to the specific problem of the exclusion of maintenance grants for foreign students by the students' directive, *see supra* notes 161 *et seq.*
222 E.C.J. Case C-456/02 of 7 September 2004, E.C.R. 2004, I-7573 – *Trojani*. For a different view concerning the equality of treatment *see* Advocate General L. A. Geelhoed in his Opinion of 19 February 2004 on *Trojani* (not yet published in E.C.R.).
223 *See*, *e.g.*, U. Everling, *supra* note 214, 54; KOTALAKIDIS, *supra* note 82, 156; *also* Magiera, *supra* note 6, Article 45 para. 9.

Parliament taking place in the host Member State. At the same time, these Treaty provisions must be understood as allowing for further reaching electoral rights, for example the right to vote and to run as a candidate in elections to regional parliaments or to the national Parliament of the host Member State, only after corresponding amendments to the Treaty.[224]

D. Outlook on Further Developments

By introducing Article 8a into Treaty law (effective from 1 November 1993) and thereby highlighting free movement as the "most important feature of Union citizenship",[225] the Maastricht Treaty has opened up the right of free movement in Community law to further development. In the meantime, as outlined above, the EJC has handed down significant jurisprudence which reveals new perspectives on the matter. In this regard, granted that suitable cases occur, further developments can certainly be expected. However, instead of speculating about future court rulings, it is more useful at this point still to mention some further developments resulting from newly formulated provisions in primary and secondary law.

I. Further Developments of the General Right of Free Movement in Primary Law as Found in the Charter of Fundamental Rights of the European Union

A first step towards a reformulation of the general right of free movement in primary law was taken by the "Charter of Fundamental Rights of the European Union", solemnly proclaimed as a non-binding text by the European Parliament, the Council and the Commission on 7 December 2000 in Nice.[226] This Charter provided in its Chapter on Citizens' Rights under the heading "Freedom of Movement and of Residence" a general right of free movement in the following words:

> Every citizen of the Union has the right to move and reside freely within the territory of the Member States.[227]

The intention was, that if the Charter would become a binding instrument in primary law, this new fundamental right of free movement would not repeal or supersede Article 18 EC, but constitute an additional guarantee of free movement.[228] The *status quo* would not be changed, though. For the Charter rights congruent with existing Treaty rights should continue to be exercised under the conditions and within the limits of these existing Treaty rights.[229] The following commentary from the European Fundamental Rights Convention's Presidency confirms that the new fundamental right to free movement contained in the Charter should not create substantial changes:

---

224 See also KOTALAKIDIS, *supra* note 82, 157; Obwexer, case note, *supra* note 101, 57.
225 See the Commission's characterisation of Article 8 a EC Treaty in its Second report from the Commission on citizenship of the Union of 27 May 1997, COM(97)230 final, 19.
226 O.J. EC 2000 C 364, 1.
227 Article 45 (1) of the Charter (*supra* note 226). French wording: "Tout citoyen ou toute citoyenne de l'Union a le droit de circuler et de séjourner librement sur le territoire des États membres." German wording: "Die Unionsbürgerinnen und Unionsbürger haben das Recht, sich im Hoheitsgebiet der Mitgliedstaaten frei zu bewegen und aufzuhalten."
228 Article 45 (1) of the Charter has then been resumed unaltered in Article I-10 (2) and in Article II-105 (1) of the Treaty establishing a Constitution for Europe (*infra* note 233).
229 Article 52 (2) of the Charter (*supra* note 226); resumed, with some technical adaptations, in Article II-112 (2) of the Treaty establishing a Constitution for Europe (*infra* note 233).

The right guaranteed in paragraph 1 is the same right as guaranteed in Article 18 EC. Pursuant to Article 52 (2) it shall be exercised under the conditions and within the limits laid down in the Treaty.[230]

It remains unclear what relationship should exist, according to the Charter, between the old and new general right of free movement on one side and that fundamental right of the Charter to social security and social assistance on the other side which provides that "everyone residing and moving legally within the European Union is entitled to social security benefits and social advantages in accordance with Union law and national laws and practices".[231] This provision covers third-country nationals and stateless persons.[232] However in so far as it encompasses as well the right of Union citizens to equal treatment in social matters when exercising their general right of free movement, it could be regarded as *lex specialis* precluding recourse to Article 18 EC in these respects. Even then, it could be assumed that the present standard regarding equal treatment in social matters of Unions citizens, exercising their general right of free movement, should neither be exceeded nor reduced through the introduction of this special guarantee in the Charter. Therefore, no substantial changes would result from that provision either.

II. Further Developments of the General Right of Free Movement in Primary Law as Found in the Treaty establishing a Constitution for Europe

The Treaty establishing a Constitution for Europe, signed on 29 October 2004 and now open to ratification in the Member States,[233] contains a restatement of the general right of free movement for Union citizens based on the preparatory works by the European Fundamental Rights Convention[234] and by the European Constitutional Convention.[235]

1. Positioning of Relevant Rules in Different Parts of the Constitution

First of all, the Constitutional Treaty (CT) integrates the Charter of Fundamental Rights with its guarantee of free movement for Union citizens to form Part II of the new European Constitution.[236] However, Union citizenship and some Union citizens' rights such as the free movement of Union citizens were deemed important enough to be already mentioned in Part I.[237] In order to avoid overcomplication of the provisions in Part I, provisions on the competency to enact relevant secondary law were transferred to Part III, which deals with the policies and functioning of the Union.[238] As a result, the free movement of Union citizens is mentioned in three different parts of the Constitutional Treaty.

---

230 Cited, e.g., in EuGRZ 2000, 559, 567. See also Magiera, *supra* note 6, Article 45 para. 3.
231 Article 34 (2) of the Charter (*supra* note 226); resumed unaltered in Article II- 94 (2) of the Treaty establishing a Constitution for Europe (*infra* note 233).
232 See E. Riedel, *in* KOMMENTAR ZUR CHARTA DER GRUNDRECHTE DER EUROPÄISCHEN UNION (J. Meyer ed., 2003), Article 34 para. 19 *et seq.*
233 O.J. EU 2004 C 310, 1 *et seq.*
234 See the Charter of Fundamental Rights of the European Union, solemnly proclaimed on 7 December 2000, O.J. EC 2000 C 364, 1.
235 See the Draft Treaty establishing a Constitution for Europe, submitted by the European Constitutional Convention on 18 July 2003, O.J. EU 2003 C 169, 1.
236 Charter: Articles II-61 to II-114 CT; Freedom of Movement and of Residence: Art. II-105 CT.
237 Article I-10 CT.
238 Article III-125 CT.

2. The Double Guarantee

The general right of free movement can be found in Article I-10 (2) CT as well as – in the same wording – in Article II-105 (1) CT. According to these provisions, Union citizens shall have "the right to move and reside freely within the territory of the Member States". If the Constitution enters into force, this new and equivalent double guarantee will express the fundamental character and the direct effect of the general right of free movement in a far clearer way than the somewhat obscure wording of the present Article 18 EC.

3. Limitation Possibilities

The possibilities of limiting the general right of free movement are laid down in Article I-10 (2) CT in a uniform formula, applicable to all Union Citizens' rights listed there. Accordingly, these rights, including the general right of free movement, "shall be exercised in accordance with the conditions and limits defined by the Constitution and by the measures adopted to give it effect". The limitation clause in the present Article 18 (1) EC has obviously been used as a model for this clause. Hence, in this respect no substantial changes will occur upon the entering-into-force of the Constitution. This is also true as far as the parallel guarantee of freedom of movement for Union citizens in Article II-105 (1) CT is concerned. Indeed, for parallel guarantees such as this one, Article II-112 (2) CT declares that limitation provisions found outside of the Charter in other parts of the Constitution are applicable: "Rights recognised by this Charter for which provision is made in other Parts of the Constitution shall be exercised under the conditions and within the limits defined by these relevant Parts." As far as the general right of free movement is concerned, this provision is to be read as creating a comprehensive reference to possible limitations based on Article I-10 (2) CT. Limitations on the general right of free movement can therefore be based exclusively on Article I-10 (2) CT. As discussed above, that provision will not bring about changes in the status quo.

4. Authorization to adopt Secondary Law

Provisions dealing with the enactment of relevant secondary legislation can be found in Article III-125 CT. This article contains the following paragraphs concerned with enacting secondary law:

> 1. If action by the Union should prove necessary to facilitate the exercise of the right, referred to in Article I-10(2)(a), of every Union citizen to move and reside freely and the Constitution has not provided the necessary powers, European laws or framework laws may establish measures for that purpose.
> 2. For the same purposes as those referred to in paragraph 1 and if the Constitution has not provided the necessary powers, a European law or framework law of the Council may establish measures concerning passports, identity cards, residence permits or any other such document and measures concerning social security or social protection. The Council shall act unanimously after consulting the European Parliament.

In this regard, as far as the new formulation of legislative powers in the aforementioned paragraph 1 is concerned, the entering-into-force of the Constitution will only bring about technical adjustments and not change the *status quo*. However, the authorization to enact legislation contained in paragraph 2 represents a change in substance. The Nice Treaty, by adding paragraph 3 to Article 18 EC, has explicitly excluded the enactment of such secondary law on the basis of Article 18 (2) EC. Therefore it is understandable, though regrettable, that the Constitutional Treaty – while reintroducing such an authorization in the free movement context – provides an inadequate legislative procedure which requires unanimity in the Council and a simple consultation of the European Parliament.

5. Relation to the Fundamental Right to Social Security and Social Assistance

The Treaty establishing a Constitution for Europe includes the fundamental right to social security and social assistance, as already contained in the Charter of Fundamental Rights, in an unaltered form. Hence, it is not necessary to deal with it here again.[239]

III. Further Developments of the General Right of Free Movement in Secondary Law

The relevant secondary law is undergoing major changes due to the enactment of a new directive.

1. Preparation of a Comprehensive New Directive

In May 2001, the Commission adopted a proposal for a comprehensive new directive designed to streamline the existing secondary law arrangements which deal with the exercise of the rights of free movement by Union citizens.[240] This proposal was submitted to the Council in July 2001. The Commission amended its proposal in April 2003 in the light of the outcome of the European Parliament's first reading.[241] The Council then reached a common position in December 2003.[242] The directive was finally enacted in April 2004.

2. The Directive 2004/38/EC

The new Directive 2004/38/EC of the European Parliament and the Council of April 29, 2004 on the right of citizens of the Union to move and reside freely within the territory of the Member States[243] is to be transposed into national law by April 30, 2006. With effect from that date the nine directives on the free movement of Union citizens currently in force will be replaced by the new comprehensive directive.[244] This new directive is based

---

239 *See* Article II-94 (2) CT and *supra* note 233.
240 Commission Proposal of 23 May 2001 for a European Parliament and Council Directive on the right of citizens of the Union and their family members to move and reside freely within the territory of the Member States, COM(01)257 final – COD 2001/0111, O.J. EC 2001 C 270, 150; this proposal had been announced already in 1993, *see* Report from the Commission on the Citizenship of the Union of 21 December 1993, COM(93)702 final, 5. *See also* Toner, *supra* note 177, 60 *et seq.*
241 Amended Commission Proposal of 15 April 2003 for a Directive of the European Parliament and of the Council on the right of citizens of the Union and their family members to move and reside freely within the territory of the Member States (presented by the Commission pursuant to Article 250 (2) of the EC Treaty), COM(03)199 final – COD 2001/0111.
242 Common Position (EC) No 6/2004 adopted by the Council on 5 December 2003 with a view to adopting Directive 2004/.../EC of the European Parliament and of the Council of ... on the right of citizens of the Union and their family members to move and reside freely within the territory of the Member States, O.J. EU 2004 C 54 E, 12.
243 Directive 2004/38/EC of the European Parliament and of the Council of 29 April 2004 on the right of citizens of the Union to move and reside freely within the territory of the Member States amending Regulation (EEC) No 1612/68 and repealing Directives 64/221/EEC, 68/360/EEC, 72/194/EEC, 73/148/EEC, 75/35/EEC, 90/364/EEC, 90/365/EEC and 93/96/EEC, O.J. EU 2004 L 158, 77; corrigendum O.J. EU 2004 L 229, 35.

cumulatively on Articles 12, 18, 40, 44 and 52 EC. It shall bring the general right of free movement into line with the market-related rights of free movement, and in so doing will simplify the free movement of persons and make it more accessible.

The applicable provisions will operate on the basis of the duration of the Union citizen's residence in another Member State. Three cumulative periods are to be differentiated: a first period of residence up to three months, a following period of four years and nine months and then a period of more than five years.

During the first period it shall suffice for cross-border mobility, as it suffices now, that Union citizens are in possession of valid identity cards or passports.[245]

During the second period, the purpose of a person's residence will continue to be relevant. Thus, during this period, there will still be a difference between market-related and non-market-related rights of free movement. Union citizens who are not economic migrants shall still be required to have social cover (sickness insurance and sufficient resources) and the host Member State can ask them to provide evidence that they are fulfilling this condition.[246] However, Member States may not lay down a fixed amount which they regard as "sufficient resources", but they must take into account the personal situation of the person concerned.[247] Moreover, an expulsion measure shall not be the automatic consequence of a Union citizen's or his or her family member's recourse to the social assistance system of the host Member State.[248]

The main innovation can be found in the third period. If a Union citizen has resided legally and continuously for five years in the host Member State, he or she shall have the right of permanent residence regardless of the purpose of his or her residence or whether or not he or she has social cover.[249] Moreover, the directive shall, apart from introducing more precise conditions regarding the public policy proviso,[250] also lay down a general principle of equal treatment for Union citizens exercising their right of free movement.[251] However, the host Member State will in all cases not be obliged to confer entitlement to social assistance during the first three months nor to grant maintenance aid for studies prior to acquisition of the right of permanent residence.[252] Furthermore, the proposed advantages shall not only be granted to Union citizens, but also to their family members including registered partners (if the legislation of the host Member State treats registered partnerships as equivalent to marriage).[253]

3. Assessment

The details of this new directive cannot be discussed here. For an overall assessment one should stress that the directive could have promoted the free movement of Union citizens much more than it has done. The original proposal of the Commission had been far more ambitious than the directive finally voted. But even in this reduced version, the directive, once transposed, will be a useful development. By streamlining different strands of development concerning the free movement of persons, by simplifying and facilitating the exer-

---

244 Articles 38 and 40 of Directive 2004/38/EC (*supra* note 243).
245 Article 6 of Directive 2004/38/EC (*supra* note 243).
246 Article 7 of Directive 2004/38/EC (*supra* note 243).
247 Article 8 (IV) of Directive 2004/38/EC (*supra* note 243).
248 Article 14 (3) of Directive 2004/38/EC (*supra* note 243).
249 Article 16 of Directive 2004/38/EC (*supra* note 243).
250 Article 27 *et seq.* of Directive 2004/38/EC (*supra* note 243).
251 Article 24 (1) of Directive 2004/38/EC (*supra* note 243).
252 Article 24 (2) of Directive 2004/38/EC (*supra* note 243).
253 Article 2 of Directive 2004/38/EC (*supra* note 243).

cise of this freedom and by ultimately giving Union citizens, who have exercised their right of free movement for a satisfactory period of time, a "right of permanent residence", the directive will strengthen the freedom of movement as a fundamental Union citizens' right.

IV. Conclusion

All in all, in the near future several technical changes can be expected in primary law concerning the general right of free movement. It is still not foreseeable that there will be substantial developments on this level. However, in secondary law, the comprehensive directive will foster that progressive integration of Union citizens in other Member States which is an outstanding expression of, and at the same time further motivation for, the development of an ever closer European Union.

SECTION III:
JURISDICTIONAL REPORTS

Report – *Bundesverfassungsgericht* (Federal Constitutional Court) – 2003

Felix Müller*

A. Introduction

This report will review a small selection of significant decisions handed down by the *Bundesverfassungsgericht* (*BVerfG* – German Federal Constitutional Court) in 2003.[1] It is not the purpose of this report to give a comprehensive overview of the Constitutional Court's vast jurisprudence, which comprises several thousand decisions every year.[2] Instead, the report focuses on a small number of decisions that have attracted attention because of their significant impact on political, social and jurisprudential life in Germany.[3] The political and social dimensions of the selected decisions are closely related to Germany's history and comprise aspects of international military engagement as well as questions of how to adapt the legal system to changed social and political reality.

First, the Federal Constitutional Court's *NPD Party Ban* case will be discussed.[4] In this case the Court was petitioned to declare the right wing *Nationaldemokratische Partei Deutschlands* (NPD – National Democratic Party of Germany) unconstitutional and therefore banned. Second, the Court's decision on the constitutionality of the participation of German soldiers in a NATO AWACS mission in Turkey in the course of the war against Iraq will be considered.[5] Third, the report will then take up the Court's decision in the *Headscarf* case (*Kopftuchentscheidung*),[6] in which the Court addressed the question whether a Muslim female teacher is entitled to wear a headscarf in the classroom as an expression of her religious convictions. Finally, the report concludes with a consideration of the Court's treatment of a constitutional complaint brought by a Yemeni citizen who challenged his extradition to the United States of America for criminal prosecution on terrorism charges.[7]

---

* Felix Müller is academic assistant at the Chair for Constitutional Law and Law of the European Union, Prof. Dr. Gabriele Britz, Justus-Liebig-Universität Giessen, Germany.
  1 *See* Donald Kommers, The Constitutional Jurisprudence of the Federal Republic of Germany (2nd ed., 1997), for an introduction to the function and jurisprudence of the Federal Constitutional Court.
  2 *See* http://www.bverfg.de/texte/deutsch/organisation/statistik_2002/A-I-2.html (Federal Constitutional Court statistics).
  3 *See* http://www.bverfg.de/cgi-bin/link.pl?entsheidungen (Federal Constitutional Court decisions).
  4 Bundesverfassungsgericht (BVerfGE) 107, 339.
  5 BVerfGE 108, 34.
  6 BVerfGE 108, 282.
  7 BVerfGE 109, 38.

B. The *NPD Party Ban* Case (BVerfGE 107, 339)

One of the most prominent decisions of the Federal Constitutional Court in 2003 was the *NPD Party Ban* case.[8] The case was of great importance because proceedings to ban a political party are very rare;[9] rightly so, considering the significance a political ban has for a democratic system.[10] The Federal Constitutional Court has banned a political party on only two occasions. In 1952, the Court declared the neo-fascist *Sozialistische Reichspartei* (SRP – Socialist Party of the German Reich) to be unconstitutional.[11] In 1955, the *Kommunistische Partei Deutschlands* (KPD – Communist Party of Germany) was banned and prohibited by the Federal Constitutional Court.[12] Moreover, interest in the *NPD Party Ban* case was surely stirred by the relationship between the beliefs and ideology of the NPD and Germany's National Socialist past, and the meaningful connection between those themes and the reunification of East and West Germany.[13]

The unexpected turn in the *NPD Party Ban* proceedings, triggered by last minute revelations that the NPD had been infiltrated by state supported confidential informers, also attracted a lot of attention and led to considerable scholarly debate on the procedural and substantive prerequisites of a party ban.[14]

I. Statement of the Facts

A number of xenophobic attacks on foreigners and minorities in 2000 caused a stir in Germany.[15] Although not proven beyond a doubt, those incidents were attributed to right wing and neo-Nazi groups.[16] In the course of the following debate on racism and anti-

---

8 Jörn Ipsen, *Das Ende des NPD-Verbotsverfahrens*, 2003 JURISTENZEITUNG (JZ) 485; Lars Oliver Michaelis, *Einstellung des NPD-Verbotsverfahrens*, 2003 NEUE ZEITSCHRIFT FÜR VERWALTUNGSRECHT (NVwZ) 943; Alexander Hanebeck & Felix Hanschmann, *Ein konstruiertes Dilemma zum Verbot der NPD – und seine Umgehung*, 2002 ZEITSCHRIFT FÜR PARLAMENTSFRAGEN (ZParl) 196; Michael Sachs, *Einstellung des NPD-Verbotsverfahrens*, 2003 JURISTISCHE SCHULUNG (JuS) 809; Alexander Hanebeck, *FCC Suspends Hearing in NPD Party Ban Case*, 3 GERMAN LAW JOURNAL 2 (2002) available at http://www.germanlawjournal.com; Jörn Ipsen, *Rechtsfragen des NPD-Verbots*, 2002 NEUE JURISTISCHE WOCHENSCHRIFT (NJW) 866; Martin Morlok, *Parteiverbot als Verfassungsschutz – Ein unauflösbarer Widerspruch?*, 2001 NEUE JURISTISCHE WOCHENSCHRIFT (NJW) 2931; Ingo von Münch, *Der Aufstand der Anständigen*, 2001 NEUE JURISTISCHE WOCHENSCHRIFT (NJW) 728.

9 It had been more than fifty years since the Court's prior party ban proceedings. However, in 1994 the Federal Constitutional Court handed down two motions by the *Bundesregierung* (Federal Government) in which the *Bundesregierung* requested the court to declare two political organizations unconstitutional since those organizations were not political parties, but associations according to GRUNDGESETZ [GG] [Constitution] art. 9 para. 1, which could be prohibited by the Federal Government itself pursuant to GG art. 9 para. 2; *see* (1994) Bundesverfassungsgericht (BVerfGE) 91, 262; *see also* (1994) BverfGE 91, 276; HARTMUT BAUER, 1 GRUNDGESETZ KOMMENTAR (2nd ed., 2004); GG art. 9 para. 19.

10 *See* RUDOLF STREINZ, 2 BONNER GRUNDGESETZ (Mangoldt et al. eds., 4th ed., 2000); GG art. 21 para. 212, *see* MORLOK ET AL., 2 GRUNDGESETZ KOMMENTAR (Dreier ed., 1998); GG art. 21 para. 135; PHILIP KUNIG, 2 GRUNDGESETZ-KOMMENTAR (Kunig & Muench eds., 5th ed. 2001); GG art. 21 para. 72.

11 BVerfGE 2, 1.

12 BVerfGE 5, 85.

13 Ingo von Münch, *supra* note 8.

14 Jörn Ipsen, *Das Ende des NPD-Verbotsverfahrens*, *supra* note 8; Lars Oliver Michaelis, *supra* note 8; Michael Sachs, *supra* note 8; Jörn Ipsen, Rechtsfragen des NPD-Verbots, *supra* note 8; Martin Morlok, *supra* note 8; Ingo von Münch, *supra* note 8; Thilo Rensmann, *Procedural Fairness in a Militant Democracy: The "Uprising of the Decent" Fails Before the Federal Constitutional Court*, 4 GERMAN LAW JOURNAL 11 (2003), available at http://www.germanlawjournal.com .

15 For a detailed description of the backgrounds, *see* Thilo Rensmann, *supra* note 14, para. 6, *available at* http://www.germanlawjournal.com.

16 Ingo von Münch, *supra* note 8.

Semitism, which took place as a result of the attacks, the right wing *Nationaldemokratische Partei Deutschlands* (NPD – National Democratic Party of Germany) came under increasing public scrutiny.[17] In an unprecedented move the *Bundesregierung* (Federal Government), the Bundestag (Federal Parliament) and the *Bundesrat* (Federal Council of the States) jointly filed applications requesting that the Federal Constitutional Court declare the NPD unconstitutional, and as a consequence, that it's dissolution be ordered.[18] These institutional applicants argued that the NPD, which had enjoyed considerable political success in the late 1960s, but which was without any political importance today,[19] was a radical organization seeking to undermine and abolish the free democratic order.[20] Moreover, the applicants asserted that the NPD, by its nature, was a fascist, anti-Semitic and racist political party, which aims at undermining Germany's pluralistic society.[21]

The Court's preliminary rulings favoured the applicants. The Federal Constitutional Court ruled that the motions by the *Bundesregierung*, the *Bundestag* and the *Bundesrat* were admissible and not patently unfounded,[22] and the Court scheduled a full hearing on the applications for February 2002.[23] Shortly after scheduling the hearing, however, the Court gave the public notice that the hearing had to be suspended because the Court had discovered facts that raised serious legal questions.[24] More precisely, the Court had been informed only a few days before the hearing was to commence that there were so-called *V-Leute* (confidential informers) of the federal agency for internal security, and the agencies for internal security of the *Länder* (federal states), among the witnesses and serving as high-ranking officials of the NPD.[25] The Court found it of the gravest significance that the applications, at least partly, relied on statements of NPD officials who were also acting as informers for, and agents of the federal and states agencies for internal security.

The hearing was postponed to October 2002, at which time, the Court undertook to determine how and to what extent the NPD had been infiltrated, influenced and controlled by state informants. During the hearing it became clear that approximately 15% of the members of the NPD executive board were supervised and paid by federal or state agencies for internal security.[26] The applicants acknowledged that the NPD had been observed by confidential informers but argued that at no time had these informants exercised control over or, instructed the NPD leadership.[27] The NPD officials, defending against the applications seeking a ban on the party, countered by arguing that the political party had acted under the sway of the state supported secret services.[28] The NPD argued that the Federal Constitutional Court could not establish that the NPD was unconstitutional in light of the fact that confidential informers, which were controlled by the state

---

17 Thilo Rensmann, *supra* note 14, para. 6, *available at* http://www.germanlawjournal.com.
18 In the two prior party ban proceedings each application was solely filed by the Federal Government, See Entscheidungen des Bundesverfassungsgerichts (BVerfGE), (1952) 2 BVerfGE 1 *and* (1955) BVerfGE 5, 85. However, in the NPD party ban proceeding, all entitled constitutional bodies jointly filed applications to express their resoluteness against neo-fascist tendencies, see BVerfGE 107, 339; Thilo Rensmann, *supra* note 14, *available at* http://www.germanlawjournal.com.
19 *See* BverfGE 107, 341 (the enumeration of election results).
20 BVerfGE 107, 342.
21 *Id.*
22 BVerfGE 104, 63.
23 *Id.*
24 BVerfGE 104, 370.
25 *See* Alexander Hanebeck, *supra* note 8; Jörn Ipsen, *Rechtsfragen des NPD-Verbots*, *supra* note 8; Alexander Hanebeck & Felix Hanschmann, *supra* note 8, for further information.
26 BVerfGE 107, 350.
27 BVerfGE 107, 346.
28 BVerfGE 107, 349.

agencies, had foisted the questionable content of its platform upon the party.[29] Therefore, rather than squarely confronting the substantive allegations of unconstitutionality the Court instead, was called upon to decide whether the proceedings against the NPD could be continued, despite the revelation that members of the NPD had acted as government informers before and even during the proceedings.

II. The Ruling of the Federal Constitutional Court

The objections to the potential governmental influence over the NPD could not be overcome. Therefore, the Federal Constitutional Court, with its decision of March 18, 2003, dismissed the applications of the three government institutions and discontinued the proceedings against the NPD.

Because the applications were dismissed for procedural reasons, (and not the substantive question of the constitutionality of the NPD's activities and ideology), the Federal Constitutional Court began its decision with an exposition of §15 para. 4 of the *Bundesverfassungsgerichtsgesetz* (BVerfGG – Federal Constitutional Court Act). Pursuant to § 15 para. 4 of the BVerfGG, any decision with negative consequences for the respondent, in a proceeding to prohibit and dissolve a political party, requires a two-thirds majority.[30] This means that six of the senate's eight judges have to agree in order for the Court to reach a decision that negatively affects the respondent. In the context of the procedural question with which the Court was confronted, the negative action requiring this two-thirds majority would have been the decision to allow the party ban proceedings to go forward. But, a minority of three judges had already expressed the conviction that the mere presence of confidential informers among the NPD leadership constituted an absolute impediment to the continuation of the proceedings.[31] The remaining five judges, a simple majority, took the contrary view, concluding that the mere possibility that the state had exercised influence or, control over the NPD ought not serve as an obstacle to the continuation of the proceedings.[32] As a consequence of this failure to reach a consensus among two-thirds of the judges on the question posed, the Court felt itself obliged to dismiss the motion.[33] Section 15 para. 4 of the BVerfGG, and a minority of three judges, tipped the scales in the *NPD Party Ban* case in favour of the NPD.

The minority and the majority agreed that political parties in general enjoy the special protection of the state because of their significant role in a democracy.[34] In the shared portion of the Court's decisions, the Court explained that the role of political parties within the constitutional order is laid down in art. 21 of the Basic Law. Art. 21 para. 1 of the Basic Law entrusts political parties with the function of participating in the formation of the political will of the people.[35] However, the constitution provides that political parties who by reason of their aims or, the behaviour of their adherents seek to undermine or abolish the free democratic order or, to endanger the existence of the Federal Republic of Germany shall be considered unconstitutional.[36] Nonetheless, the full Court emphasized that political parties accused of seeking to undermine the free democratic basic order

---

29 BVerfGE 107, 352.
30 *See* Zierlein at §15 para. 43 BUNDESVERFASSUNGSGERICHTSGESETZ (Umbach & Clemens eds.,1992).
31 BVerfGE 107, 360.
32 BVerfGE 107, 356.
33 *Id.*
34 BVerfGE 107, 358.
35 *See* RUDOLF STREINZ, *supra* note 10; GG art. 21 para. 1; *see* MARTIN MORLOK, *supra* note 10; GG art. 21 para. 19, PHILIP KUNIG, *supra* note 10; GG art. 21 para.11.
36 GG art. 21, para. 2.

remain entitled to the full protection of the political rights guaranteed by the Basic Law until such time as the Federal Constitutional Court pronounces them banned from political life.[37] Unlike political or social associations, which only enjoy protection under art. 9 para. 1 of the Basic Law and can be prohibited by the executive branch, political parties are entitled to greater constitutional protection and cannot be prohibited by the executive branch.[38] To rule on the question whether a political party is unconstitutional is thus, the exclusive right of the Federal Constitutional Court.[39] In the present case, a procedural subtlety of the Court's governing statute would prevent the Court from reaching the substantive question whether the NPD actually sought to undermine or abolish the free democratic basic order.

The decisive minority of three judges held that the influential control of the confidential informants over the NPD was an absolute and irredeemable impediment to any further proceedings.[40] With reference to the principles of fairness and due process, the minority judges stated the opinion that the discontinuation of the proceedings was the only equitable and proportional outcome for this case.[41] The minority judges acknowledged that political parties could be observed by governmental agencies.[42] To monitor and to observe political parties is, the minority judges explained, the only way to find out whether a political party actually seeks to undermine or abolish the free democratic order or, to endanger the existence of the Federal Republic of Germany. In spite of this, the three judges concluded that the goals of such monitoring could also be achieved by observing publications of political parties by examining their political programs, and by scrutinizing their gatherings and assemblies.[43] Confidential informers among high-ranking officials of a political party, on the other hand, have the tendency to influence and to affect the political party's autonomy and decision-making.[44] The presence of informers among the executive board of the NPD, the minority of the Court concluded, inevitably caused the possibility of an influential government control over the NPD.[45]

Furthermore, even if the NPD had acted the same without the influence of the informers among its officials, the minority judges expressed doubts that the party ban proceedings themselves could be freed of any taint caused by the behaviour of the informers.[46] In particular, the fact that the applicants had referred to, and relied upon statements made by confidential informers to prove the unconstitutionality of the NPD, was considered incompatible with the principles of fairness and due process.[47] The minority judges urged that all informers who had infiltrated a political party should be withdrawn before any party ban motion could be filed against this party.[48] This was regarded as a fundamental question of fairness, since the right to defend oneself effectively on the basis of a freely chosen procedural strategy could not be guaranteed, as long as the respondent itself had

---

37 Thilo Rensmann, *supra* note 14, para. 4 *available at* http://www.germanlawjournal.com .
38 Rudolf Streinz, *supra* note 10; GG art. 21 para. 215, Philip Kunig, *supra* note 10; GG art. 21 para. 87.
39 *See* GG art. 21 para. 2 (which provides that the Federal Constitutional Court shall rule on the question of whether a political party is unconstitutional), GG art. 21 para. 3 (pursuant to which details shall be regulated by federal laws). Consequently, *Bundesverfassungsgerichtsgesetz* (Federal Constitutional Court Act) § 13 (2), §§ 43–47 deal with questions of a party ban.
40 BVerfGE 107, 377.
41 The principle of fairness and due process is not explicitly laid down in the GRUNDGESETZ (Federal Constitution) (GG) however, it can be deduced from GG art. 20 para. 3.
42 BVerfGE 107, 365.
43 BVerfGE 107, 366.
44 BVerfGE 107, 366 (367).
45 BVerfGE 107, 360.
46 BVerfGE 107, 373.
47 *Id.*
48 BVerfGE 107, 369.

been infiltrated with informers who could inform the applicants of the party's litigation strategy.[49]

Finally, the minority judges concluded that the presence of informers among the officials of a political party being subjected to party ban proceedings before the Federal Constitutional Court infringed the fundamental principles of fairness and due process because, it was impossible to remove all traces of doubt regarding the extent of the influence and control the confidential informers exercised over the NPD.[50] Thus, the minority judges inferred, and by preventing the Court from achieving a two-thirds majority on the issue, they also determined that the proceeding had to be discontinued.[51]

In this strange procedural situation, the majority was required to dissent from this conclusion, arguing that the surveillance to which the NPD was subjected by the governmental agencies before, and even during the proceeding, could not be considered an absolute impediment to the continuation of the proceedings.[52] The dissenting majority held that despite the presence of informers among the executive board of the NPD there was no evidence, and not even an indication, that the NPD's decision-making was substantially influenced by government control.[53] The majority judges stressed that the requirements of due process and the principle of fairness could be met if those statements and political decisions by the NPD, which clearly could be attributed to or were caused by confidential informers, were not taken into account.[54]

III. Recent Developments

After the attempt to ban the NPD ended when, in March, 2003, the Federal Constitutional Court refused to hear the case, the NPD garnered national attention and concern after winning 9.2 percent of the vote in the state elections of Saxony in September, 2004, by capitalizing on discontent in the economically struggling state with the Federal Government's drive to cut social programs. The NPD provoked renewed outrage when its twelve delegates walked out of Saxony's state parliament in January 2005, before a moment of silence to mark the 60th anniversary of the liberalization of the Auschwitz concentration camp.[55] Moreover, the NPD announced a march in Berlin on the 60th anniversary day of Nazi-Germany's defeat in World War II and made plans to hold a rally at the Brandenburger Tor, one of Berlin's best-known monuments, a block away from a new national Holocaust memorial.[56] With the regional rise of the NPD and their provocations, politicians have publicly worried that the party will damage Germany's international reputation, which has been steadily changing in the generations since World War II. Moreover, the president of the Federal Constitutional Court, Hans Jürgen Papier, announced in the media that the 2003 ruling did not preclude future attempts to outlaw the NPD and that a ban of the far-right party in the future should not be ruled out.[57] As a consequence, the Federal

---

49 BVerfGE 107, 378.
50 *Id.*
51 *Id.*
52 BVerfGE 107, 378 (379).
53 BVerfGE 107, 381.
54 BVerfGE 107, 382.
55 *NPD-Eklat im Sächsischen Landtag*, FRANKFURTER ALLGEMEINE ZEITUNG, Jan. 22, 2005, at 1.
56 *Brüllende Parlamentsfeinde. Wie die NPD versucht, die sächsische Volksvertretung für ihre extremistischen und revisionistischen Absichten zu benutzen*, FRANKFURTER ALLGEMEINE ZEITUNG, Jan. 25, 2005, at 3.
57 *Wink aus Karlsruhe für NPD-Verbot*, FRANKFURTER RUNDSCHAU, Jan. 31, 2005; *Verfassungsrichter werben für neues NPD-Verfahren*, FINANCIAL TIMES DEUTSCHLAND, Jan. 31, 2005, at 9; FRANKFURTER ALLGEMEINE ZEITUNG, Jan. 2, 2005, at 1.

Government considered the initiation of a new application requesting that the Federal Constitutional Court declare the NPD unconstitutional, and called on all democrats to join in a political struggle against neo-fascist activities.[58]

C. AWACS Mission (BVerfGE 108, 34)

With a March 23, 2003, decision,[59] the Federal Constitutional Court added another aspect to its jurisprudence regarding the participation of German soldiers in foreign military missions.[60] The specific legal question before the Court was whether, the participation of German soldiers in NATO missions required the assent of the *Bundestag* (Federal Parliament).[61] The Federal Constitutional Court had held recently that German force deployments, justified by a change in NATO's Strategic Concept, did not require the assent of the parliament.[62] In the present case, however, the Court was confronted with the parliamentary involvement in the engagement of German soldiers within the NATO mission in Turkey during the war against Iraq in 2003.[63]

I. Statement of the Facts

In February 2003, Turkey requested military support from NATO member states pursuant to Article 4 of the NATO Treaty, claiming that it felt threatened by Iraqi military forces in the face of an imminent gulf war.[64] On February 19, 2003, the Defence Planning Committee authorized NATO to send AWACS (Airborne Warning and Control System) aircrafts to Turkey.[65] The AWACS planes are a special aircraft equipped with radar systems capable of detecting air traffic over longer distances and at lower levels.[66] Moreover, AWACS planes serve as a strategic system and provide essential air surveillance and early warning capability in military operations.[67]

As part of the deployment of Alliance defensive assistance to Turkey, NATO AWACS units began patrolling Turkish airspace on February 26, 2003, in order to repulse potential attacks of Iraqi missiles or armed forces.[68] Their mission was to monitor Turkish airspace

---

58 *NPD-Verbot wird wieder diskutiert*, SÜDDEUTSCHE ZEITUNG, Jan. 31, 2005, at 1; *Schroeder in Call to Oppose Nazis*, FINANCIAL TIMES, Jan. 26, 2005, at 8.
59 BverfGE 108, 34; BverfG, 2 BvQ 18/03, Mar. 25, 2003, *available at* http://www.bverfg.de.
60 BVerfG, 2 BvE 6/99, Nov. 22, 2001, (NATO Strategic Concept); (AWACS/Somalia) BVerfGE 90, 286, Andreas L. Paulus, *Quo vadis Democratic Control? The Afghanistan Decision of the Bundestag and the Decision of the Federal Constitutional Court in the NATO Strategic Concept Case*, 3 GERMAN LAW JOURNAL 1 (2002) *available at* http://www.germanlawjournal.com; Hans Heinrich Rupp, *AWACS-Einsätze und die Rechte des Bundestages*, 2003 JURISTENZEITUNG (JZ) 899; Martin Nolte, *Der AWACS-Einsatz in der Türkei zwischen Parlamentsvorbehaltung und Regierungsverantwortung*, 2003 NEUE JURISTISCHE WOCHENSCHRIFT (NJW) 2359; Andreas Fischer-Lescano, *Konstitutiver Parlamentsvorbehalt: Wann ist ein AWACS-Einsatz ein "Einsatz bewaffneter Streitkräfte"?*, 2003 NEUE ZEITSCHRIFT FÜR VERWALTUNGSRECHT (NVwZ) 1474.
61 BVerfGE 108, 34, Andreas Fischer-Lescano, *supra* note 60.
62 BVerfG, 2 BvE 6/99, 22 Nov., 2001, (NATO Strategic Concept); Michael Sachs, *Beteiligungsrechte des Bundestages bei Fortentwicklung des strategischen Konzepts der NATO*, 2002 JURISTISCHE SCHULUNG (JuS) 807; Heiko Sauer, *Die NATO und das Verfassungsrecht: neues Konzept – alte Fragen*, 2002 ZEITSCHRIFT FÜR AUSLÄNDISCHES ÖFFENTLICHES RECHT UND VÖLKERRECHT (ZaÖRV) 317.
63 Hans Heinrich Rupp, *supra* note 60; Martin Nolte, *supra* note 60.
64 BVerfGE 108, 35.
65 *See also* http://www.nato.int.
66 *Id.*
67 *See* NATO Airborne Early Warning and Control Force E-3A Component Website *available at* http://www.e3a.nato.int/.
68 *See* http://www.nato.int/docu/update/2003/02-february/e0226a.htm.

and provide early warning for defensive purposes.[69] The AWACS planes were manned by multinational crews from NATO countries, with one third of the AWACS crews consisting of German soldiers.[70]

The *Freie Demokratische Partei* (FDP – Free Democratic Party), a parliamentary faction, notified the *Bundeskanzler* (Chancellor) on March 14, 2003 that the party believed that the participation of German soldiers in the AWACS mission in Turkey required the assent of the *Bundestag*.[71] As the FDP saw it, the AWACS mission in Turkey was not a mere routine deployment of NATO forces, but the indirect participation of German soldiers in the broader military conflict surrounding Iraq in the spring of 2003. As a result, the FDP insisted upon *Bundestag* approval of the AWACS mission, as required by the constitution.[72] When the Chancellor refused to submit the AWACS mission to a vote of the Federal Parliament, and after the U.S.-led military conflict in Iraq had begun on March 20, 2003, the FDP requested that the *Bundestag* pass a resolution calling on the Federal Government to put the AWACS mission to a vote of the Federal Parliament.[73] After the *Bundestag* voted against the FDP's proposed resolution, the party's parliamentary faction petitioned the Federal Constitutional Court for a temporary injunction to prevent German participation in the NATO mission.[74] The party's parliamentary faction enjoys the right to pursue such actions before the Court as part of the Court's *Organstreit* (disputes between high federal organs) jurisdiction.[75]

II. The Ruling of the Federal Constitutional Court

In a March 25, 2003, decision the Federal Constitutional Court dismissed the FDP's motion for a preliminary injunction. Beginning with a comment on temporary injunctions, the Court emphasized that § 32 of the Federal Constitutional Court Act obliged the court to use its emergency power to intervene with deliberation and great care.[76] The Court concluded that, in light of these terms, the granting of a temporary injunction must remain the exception, limited to those cases in which the reasons for the application are so severe as to make the Court's intervention necessary to head off serious violations of the constitution.[77] The Federal Constitutional Court accentuated that it would not grant a temporary injunction where the case at issue could also be clarified in a proceeding on the merits without running the risk of violating constitutional rights.[78] Therefore, the Court refused to initiate a temporary injunction.[79]

---

69 BVerfGE 108, 35.
70 *Id.*
71 *Id.*
72 *See* (AWACS/Somalia) BVerfGE 90, 286; Andreas L. Paulus, *supra* note 60; Hans Heinrich Rupp, *supra* note 60; Martin Nolte, *supra* note 60; Andreas Fischer-Lescano, *supra* note 60.
73 BVerfGE 108, 36.
74 *See* BVerfGE 108, 36; Bundesverfassungsgerichtsgesetz (BVerfGG) (Federal Constitutional Court Act) § 32 provides that the Federal Constitutional Court may provisionally deal with a matter by means of a temporary injunction, if this is urgently needed to avert serious detriments, ward off imminent force or for any other important reason for the common good, *see* Andreas Maurer, *The Federal Constitutional Court's Emergency Power to Intervene: Provisional Measures Pursuant to Article 32 of the Federal Constitutional Court Act*, 2 GERMAN LAW JOURNAL 13 (2001), *available at* http://www.germanlawjournal.com.
75 GRUNDGESETZ [GG] (Basic Law) art. 93, para. 1, No. 1; Bundesverfassungsgerichtsgesetz (BVerfGG) (Federal Constitutional Court Act) § 13 No. 5.
76 BVerfGE 108, 41.
77 *Id.*
78 BVerfGE 108, 43.
79 However, it is notable that the FDP did not initiate the principle proceeding according to GG art. 93 para. 1 No. 1, but solely relied on the provisional proceeding as enshrined in Federal Constitutional Court Act. (BVerfGG) § 32, BVerfGE 108, 36 (41).

However, the Court refrained from prejudicing the prospects of a proceeding on the merits, which had not been initiated by the FDP and, which therefore, was not yet pending before the court.[80] In spite of this, the Federal Constitutional Court recalled its earlier AWACS decision in which it had already addressed the question whether a foreign military mission of German soldiers required the assent of the Federal Parliament.[81] In its earlier decision, the Court concluded that the federal government was obliged by the constitution to seek prior approval from the Parliament as a basis for the deployment and participation of German soldiers in military missions abroad.[82] Put differently, the court had ruled that the Federal Parliament had to consent to the deployment of German troops before they were to be sent on a foreign military mission.[83]

In the case at hand, however, the Federal Government argued that the AWACS mission in Turkey was a routine deployment of NATO forces rather than a military engagement of German soldiers in a military conflict.[84] Consequently, the Federal Government took the view that any assent of the Federal Parliament was superfluous. The Federal Constitutional Court responded to this line of argument by concluding that nowadays, where wars take place without a formal declaration of war, any involvement in military conflicts is to be equated with a military engagement.[85] Therefore, the Court intimated that any participation of German soldiers in foreign military missions is only admissible with the proviso that the deployment finds the prior approval of the Parliament.[86] Still, the Federal Constitutional Court left it open as to whether the AWACS mission in Turkey actually was a deployment of German troops, which necessitated the assent of the *Bundestag*. The Court underlined that it was conceivable that the present AWACS mission required the assent of the Federal Parliament.[87] However, the Court held that this question would not be addressed in the pending preliminary injunction proceeding, but only in the proceedings on the merits, which had not yet been initiated.[88] In this regard, the Federal Constitutional Court enumerated several questions to be addressed in a proceeding on the merits. Among others, the Court would confront the question how to determine the threshold between a mere participation in a routine NATO mission and an indirect involvement in a military conflict in cases like the one under review.[89] Moreover, the Court noted that in a proceeding on the merits it was worth considering whether participation in a routine NATO mission, which gradually bore the risk of becoming an embroilment in a military conflict, also required the assent of the *Bundestag*.[90]

Although the Court voiced grave doubts, a final decision on this issue was shifted to the principle proceeding and thus, to a later point in time. The Federal Constitutional Court emphasized that the highly controversial subject of the participation of German soldiers in the AWACS mission in Turkey could not be addressed in a preliminary proceeding seeking a temporary injunction at a time where the U.S.A. and the United Kingdom, two

---

80 BVerfGE 108, 43.
81 BVerfGE 90, 286.
82 BVerfGE 90, 286 (381). The Federal Constitutional Court (BverfG) deduced the constitutional obligation to request a previous consent of the parliament from GG art. 115a, para. 5; GG art. 115b; GG art. 115l, para. 3 and GG art. 87(a), para. 3, *see* Jarass & Pieroth, GRUNDGESETZ (7th ed. 2004); GG art. 87(a) para. 11, *see* Ondolf Rojahn, *in* 2 GRUNDGESETZ-KOMMENTAR (Münch & Kunig eds., 5th ed. 2001); GG art. 24, para. 93.
83 Heiko Sauer, *supra* note 62; Andreas Fischer-Lescano, *supra* note 60.
84 BVerfGE 108, 36.
85 BVerfGE 108, 43.
86 *Id.*
87 BVerfGE 108, 42.
88 BVerfGE 108, 43.
89 BVerfGE 108, 34.
90 *Id.*

prominent NATO Parties, were at war.[91] By dismissing the FDP's motion, the Court moved to ensure the Federal Government's capacity to act without limitation in its foreign policy, particularly in troubled political times.[92]

III. Prospects for Future Military Missions

Military as well as humanitarian engagement of German troops in international operations remains contested.[93] German participation in military missions is mainly opposed in light of historical backgrounds whereas humanitarian engagement of German soldiers in foreign countries is criticized for lack of necessary equipment. Indeed, the structure as well as training and equipment of Germany's armed forces are predominantly aimed at national defence and are not fully operational in terms of participation in international missions.[94] Besides the fact that the armed forces have to be restructured and modernized to face the challenges of changed geo-strategic tasks, international military engagement remains controversial for legal and political reasons. It is still under discussion if there are constitutional limits to the participation of German soldiers in military missions,[95] in particular if such missions violate international law.[96] Therefore, it is to be expected that future military engagement of German soldiers in international operations will likewise be challenged before the Federal Constitutional Court.

D. The "Headscarf Decision" (BVerfGE 108, 282)

In its *Headscarf* case the Federal Constitutional Court dealt with the issue of religious freedom for a Muslim teacher. The Court was called upon to address the question whether a female Muslim teacher is entitled to wear a headscarf in the classroom as an expression of her religious convictions. This matter is crucial in regard of the neutrality of the state in religious concerns. In other words, the decision takes up the tense relationship between religious fundamental rights for civil servants, on the one hand, and the neutrality of the state, on the other hand. The present case, however, involved a conflict that could not have been foreseen when the constitution was drafted half a century ago and when Germany had only a small population of non-Christian immigrants.[97] The Federal Constitutional Court's finding, and the liberal manner in which it dealt with the apparent conflict, provoked vehement protest and attracted considerable public and academic attention.[98]

---

91 BVerfGE 108, 44.
92 BVerfGE 108, 45; BVerfGE 33, 197; BVerfGE 83, 173.
93 Rafael Biermann, *Der Deutsche Bundestag und die Auslandseinsätze der Bundeswehr*, 2004 ZEITSCHRIFT FÜR PARLAMENTSFRAGEN (ZParl) 605; Martin Limpert, *Auslandseinsatz der Bundeswehr*, 2002 TÜBINGER SCHRIFTEN ZUM STAATS- UND VERWALTUNGSRECHT Bd. 67, Berlin; Michael Wild, *Verfassungsrechtliche Möglichkeiten und Grenzen für Auslandseinsätze der Bundeswehr*, 2000 DIE ÖFFENTLICHE VERWALTUNG (DÖV) 622, Florian Schröder, *Ein Entsendegesetz für Auslandseinsätze der Bundeswehr*, 2004 JURISTISCHE ARBEITSBLÄTTER (JA) 853, Michael Brenner & Daniel Hahn, *Bundeswehr und Auslandseinsätze*, 2001 JURISTISCHE SCHULUNG (JuS) 729, Günter Krings & Christian Burkiczak, *Bedingt abwehrbereit?*, 2002 DIE ÖFFENTLICHE VERWALTUNG (DÖV) 501.
94 Günter Krings & Christian Burkiczak, *supra* note 93.
95 Martin Limpert, *supra* note 93; Michael Wild, *supra* note 93; Florian Schröder, *supra* note 93; Michael Brenner & Daniel Hahn, *supra* note 93.
96 See GG art. 26 (stipulating that acts tending towards, and undertaken with, intent to disturb the peaceful relations between nations, especially to prepare for a war of aggression, shall be unconstitutional).
97 See http://www.destatis.de/basis/e/bevoe/bevoetab5.htm (statistics on religious affiliation).
98 Christine Langenfeld & Sarah Mohsen, *The Teacher Headscarf Case*, INT'L J. CONST. L. 86 (2005); Oliver Gerstenberg, *Freedom of Conscience in Public Schools*, INT'L J. CONST. L. 94 (2005); Matthias Mahlmann,

However, the Court did not cut the Gordian knot. On the contrary, the Federal Constitutional Court left it to the parliaments of the *Länder* (Federal States) to individually solve the conflict between the religious rights of teachers, the religious rights of students, and the neutrality of the state.[99]

I. Statement of the Facts

The complainant, born in Afghanistan in 1972 but residing in Germany since 1987, was naturalized as a German citizen in 1995.[100] She is a devout Muslim. After she had successfully taken her university exam and had gone through her probationary period as a teacher, she applied for a teaching post. However, local school officials turned her down for a teaching position because of her insistence on wearing a headscarf at all times.[101] The complainant appealed this administrative decision to the administrative courts. She argued that the decision to deny her civil servant status because of her insistence on wearing a headscarf violated her fundamental right of religious freedom.[102] The complainant considered the headscarf a religious sign of piety for women in Islam. Nonetheless, the administrative courts, comprising the *Verwaltungsgericht Stuttgart* (lower administrative court of Stuttgart),[103] the *Verwaltungsgerichtshof Mannheim* (higher administrative court of Mannheim)[104] and the *Bundesverwaltungsgericht* (federal administrative court),[105] confirmed the administrative decision of the school officials and dismissed her complaint. The administrative courts reasoned that allowing a teacher to wear a headscarf in the classroom would violate the public school system's obligation to maintain neutrality on political and religious affairs.[106] In the view of the administrative courts, Muslim teachers are not suited to working in German schools if they insist on wearing a headscarf during class.[107] Moreover, the headscarf was regarded as a symbol for a distinct interpretation of a religion that is abused as an excuse for violence and oppression by some of its proponents. After the complainant had exhausted all legal remedies in the ordinary courts, she filed a constitutional complaint maintaining that her religious freedom, as enshrined in art. 4 paras.1 and 2 of the Basic Law, was being infringed.

Religious Tolerance, Pluralist Society and the Neutrality of the State: The Federal Constitutional Court's Decision in the Headscarf Case, 4 GERMAN LAW JOURNAL 11 (2003), *available at* http://www.germanlawjournal.com; Ute Sacksofsky, *Die Kopftuch-Entscheidung: von der religiösen zur föderalen Vielfalt*, 2003 NEUE JURISTISCHE WOCHENSCHRIFT (NJW) 3297; Karl-Hermann Kästner, *Darf eine muslimische Lehrerin im Unterricht das Kopftuch tragen?*, 2003 JURISTENZEITUNG (JZ) 1164; Hans Michael Heinig & Martin Morlok, *Von Schafen und Kopftüchern*, 2003 JURISTENZEITUNG 2003 (JZ) 777; Gabriele Britz, *Das verfassungsrechtliche Dilemma doppelter Fremdheit: Islamische Bekleidungsvorschriften für Frauen und Grundgesetz*, 2003 KRITISCHE JUSTIZ (KJ) 95; Lothar Michael, *Kein "islamisches Kopftuch" im Schuldienst*, 2003 JURISTENZEITUNG 254; Jörn Ipsen, *Karlsruhe locuta, causa non finita – Das BVerfG im so genannten Kopftuchstreit*, 2003 NEUE ZEITSCHRIFT FÜR VERWALTUNGSRECHT (NVwZ) 1210.

99 Christine Langenfeld & Sarah Mohsen, *supra* note 98.
100 *See* Matthias Mahlmann, *supra* note 98; *see also* BVerfG, 2 BvR 1436/02, 24 Sept. 2003, para. 2 (describing the facts of the case well).
101 BVerfGE 108, 284.
102 BVerfGE 108, 285.
103 Verwaltungsgericht (VG) Stuttgart, NEUE ZEITSCHRIFT FÜR VERWALTUNGSRECHT (NVwZ),(2000), 959.
104 Verwaltungsgericht (VG) Mannheim, NEUE JURISTISCHE WOCHENSCHRIFT (NJW), (2001), 2899.
105 Bundesverwaltungsgericht (BVerwG), JURISTENZEITUNG (JZ), (2002), 254.
106 Verwaltungsgericht (VG) Stuttgart, NEUE ZEITSCHRIFT FÜR VERWALTUNGSRECHT (NVwZ), (2000), 959; Verwaltungsgericht (VG) Mannheim, 2001 NEUE JURISTISCHE WOCHENSCHRIFT (NJW), 2899; Bundesverwaltungsgericht (BVerwG), JURISTENZEITUNG (JZ), (2002), 254.

II. The Ruling of the Federal Constitutional Court

The Federal Constitutional Court was asked to rule upon the apparent conflict between the state's right to enforce secular principles in its schools and the teacher's right to freely express his or her religious beliefs. While five of the eight judges held that the denial of civil servant status by local school officials had no legal basis, and thus violated fundamental rights of the complainant, three judges dissented from this finding.

The majority of the Federal Constitutional Court based its ruling on an examination of the impact of art.33 para. 2 of the Basic Law upon this particular case.[108] Art. 33 para. 2 of the Basic Law provides that every German is equally eligible for any public office according to his aptitude, qualifications, and professional achievements. The Court explained that art. 33 para. 2 of the Basic Law did not grant an unconditional right to employment,[109] but that its protections instead boiled down to an aptitude test.[110] Thus, despite the fact that the complainant met the formal qualifications to apply for a teaching position, it remained questionable whether the complainant possessed the aptitude and desired qualification for such a position in a public school both of which were brought into question by insistence on wearing a headscarf.[111]

The school officials and administrative courts had argued that wearing a headscarf in the classroom undermined the neutrality of the state. According to art. 33 para. 5 of the Basic Law, the law governing the civil service is regulated with due regard to the traditional principles of the professional civil service.[112] Therefore, the Federal Constitutional Court examined whether the neutrality of the state could be considered part of the "traditional principles of the professional civil service" in a case like the present one,[113] with the consequence that the complainant's access to a teaching position could be limited. The "traditional principles" require, among other things, that civil servants act with restraint and moderate behaviour.[114] While the administrative courts had deduced that this requirement conflicts with the wearing of a headscarf in the classroom,[115] the Federal Constitutional Court came to the opposite conclusion, referring to religious freedom as guaranteed by art. 4 para. 1 and para. 2 of the Basic Law.[116] Article 4 of the Basic Law provides that freedom of creed, of conscience, and freedom to profess a religious or non-religious faith are inviolable and that the undisturbed practice of religion is guaranteed. To prohibit a devout Muslim from wearing a headscarf, although regarded as a compelling part of the complainant's religious belief,[117] was found by the Federal Constitutional Court to violate the

---

107 (VG) Stuttgart, 2000 Neue Zeitschrift für Verwaltungsrecht (NVwZ), 959; (VG) Mannheim, Neue Juristische Wochenschrift (NJW), (2001), 2899; Bundesverwaltungsgericht (BverwG), Juristenzeitung (JZ), (2002), 254.
108 BVerfGE 108, 295.
109 Id.
110 BVerfGE 108, 296.
111 Id.
112 Hans Jarass & Bodo Pieroth, Grundgesetz Kommentar (7th ed., 2004); GG art. 33, para. 35; 2 Grundgesetz Kommentar (Horst Dreier ed., 1998); GG art. 33 para. 63; Philip Kunig, 2 Grundgesetz-Kommentar (Münch & Kunig eds., 5th ed. 2001); GG art. 33, paras. 59.
113 BVerfGE 108, 296.
114 See BVerwGE 90, 104 (110); BVerfGE 9, 268 (286); BVerfGE 39, 334 (347); BVerfG NVwZ (1994), 474; NVwZ (1994), 474.
115 (VGH) Stuttgart, 2000 Neue Zeitschrift für Verwaltungsrecht (NVwZ), 959; (VGH) Mannheim, Neue Juristische Wochenschrift (NJW), (2001), 2899; Bundesverwaltungsgericht (BverwG), Juristenzeitung (JZ), (2002), 254.
116 BVerfGE 108, 298.
117 The exact religious meaning of headscarves remained contested, see BVerfGE 108, 298.

fundamental right of religious freedom.[118] Moreover, the Court took art. 33 para. 3 of the Basic Law into account. This norm provides that enjoyment of civil and political rights, eligibility for public office, and rights acquired in the public service are independent of religious denomination.[119] Both the fundamental right of religious freedom and art. 33 para. 3 of the Basic law made a case for the complainant's point of view that the refusal to consider her for a job was illegal.[120]

However, adverse effects on religious freedom could be justified, the Federal Constitutional Court noted, if this was indispensable to enforce other fundamental rights or other constitutional principles.[121] The Federal Constitutional Court held that such other constitutional rights, which conflicted with the right of the complainant to wear a headscarf in the classroom,[122] included the public school system (art. 7 para. 1 of the Basic Law),[123] the right of the parents to determine the upbringing of their children (art. 6 para. 2 of the Basic Law),[124] and the religious right of the affected students not to be influenced by other religions in public schools (art. 4 para. 1 of the Basic Law).[125] The religious freedom of the students, the Federal Constitutional Court held, comprised the right not to be influenced or, even bothered by religious symbols attributable to the public school system[126] in particular because of the compulsory nature of education. Unlike the effect of religious symbols in the private sector, students have indeed no chance to escape influential effects exerted on them by the public school system because school education is compulsory.

On a similar basis, the Federal Constitutional Court in an earlier decision ruled in favour of parents and their children who had claimed that a crucifix in a public school room was unconstitutional, and had a detrimental impact on the affected students and the values some parents wanted to instil in their children.[127] However, the Federal Constitutional Court noted that the present case differed from the *Crucifix* case, because it was not the school as such, like in the *Crucifix* case, but an individual teacher who bore the risk of exerting a negative influence on the students.[128] The Court held that the religious message, which the headscarf clearly communicated,[129] could not be attributed to the public school system. On the contrary, the Court said that the headscarf had to be attributed to the individual teacher as an expression of her individual religious conviction.[130] Certainly, the Federal Constitutional Court took into account that a teacher is part of the public school system and that the wearing of a headscarf could have detrimental effects on students and their parents.[131] But the Court emphasized that the public school system was open to religious alterations[132] owing to the fact that, religion is deeply rooted in society as

---

118 BVerfGE 108, 297.
119 BVerfGE 108, 298.
120 *See, e.g.*, Hans Jarass & Bodo Pieroth, GRUNDGESETZ KOMMENTAR (7th ed., 2004); GG art. 3, para. 105; 1 GRUNDGESETZ KOMMENTAR (Horst Dreier ed., 2nd ed., 2004); GG art. 3, para. 116 (moreover, GG art. 3, para. 3 can be added, which states that no person shall be favoured or disfavoured because of his or her religious opinion).
121 BVerfGE 108, 297.
122 BVerfGE 108, 298.
123 BVerfGE 108, 299.
124 BVerfGE 108, 301.
125 BVerfGE 108, 301; Christine Langenfeld & Sarah Mohsen, *supra* note 98; Oliver Gerstenberg, *supra* note 98.
126 BVerfGE 108, 301.
127 *See Crucifix* Decision, *see* BVerfGE 93, 1.
128 BVerfGE 108, 305.
129 *Id.*
130 *Id.*
131 BVerfGE 108, 303.
132 *Id.* (309).

well as in the public sector.[133] However, the Court came to the conclusion that the conflict between the colliding fundamental rights of the complainant, on the one hand, and the fundamental rights of students and their parents, on the other hand, could only be clarified by the parliament.[134] According to its earlier jurisprudence, upon which the *Wesentlichkeitstheorie*[135] was established,[136] the Court deduced that the administrative decision by the school officials lacked a statutory basis. More precisely, the Federal Constitutional Court reasoned that such a fundamental question, which deeply affected fundamental rights, could only be decided by the parliament.[137] Since the competent state parliament of Baden-Württemberg had not passed a law to clarify how to handle such conflicts in public schools, the Federal Constitutional Court came to the conclusion that the school officials, who had banned the complainant from wearing her headscarf, had no legal basis and no legal authority for doing so. As a consequence, the administrative decision, as well as the decisions reached by the administrative courts, were found to violate the complainant's fundamental right of religious freedom.[138] However, this was only a partial victory for the complainant, owing to the Federal Constitutional Court's ruling that the denial of civil servant status was illegal solely because the issue fell within the jurisdiction, not of local school officials but of the parliament, which had not passed a law against headscarves in the classroom. The Federal Constitutional Court clearly stated that the parliament was free to pass a law, which either bans headscarves and other religious symbols from public schools or, allows teachers to wear religious symbols in the classroom.[139] The key factor was solely, one way or another, that any decision by the school officials regarding the wearing of headscarves required a statutory basis. Notwithstanding the apparent objections, state parliaments passed laws banning the wearing of headscarves by teachers in the period following the Federal Constitutional Court's decision.[140]

The three dissenting judges were at severe variance with the Court's majority. The dissenters stated that the denial of civil service status in no way violated fundamental rights of the complainant.[141] They argued that the complainant, who demanded access to a teaching position, could not fall back on the fundamental right of religious freedom.[142] Moreover, the decision of the school officials did not require any additional statutory basis.[143] The dissenters took the view that fundamental rights of teachers take second place to fundamental rights of students and parents.[144] The three dissenting judges emphasized that a teacher, who did not agree to act with restraint and to be neutral in religious and political matters, did not meet the constitution's requirement of aptitude, which the dissenters considered part of the neutrality of the state.[145] Therefore, the dissenting judges concluded that the school officials had acted lawfully and had not violated constitutional rights.

---

133 *See, e.g.*, GG art. 7, para. 3 (religious instruction shall form part of the regular curriculum in public schools).
134 BVerfGE 108, 303–306.
135 This theory provides that all essential and fundamental issues, in particular those, which affect fundamental rights, need to be decided by the legislator.
136 BVerfGE 49, 89 (126); BVerfGE 61, 260 (275); BVerfGE 83, 130 (142).
137 BVerfGE 108, 303 (306, 311).
138 *See* GG art. 33, para. 2, in conjunction with GG art. 4, para. 1, 2, in conjunction with GG art. 33, para. 3.
139 BVerfGE 108, 309.
140 For instance, the government of Baden-Württemberg, among other state governments, decided on Nov. 11, 2003, to give a bill to the vote of the state parliament.
141 BVerfGE 108, 315.
142 BVerfGE 108, 316.
143 BVerfGE 108, 320.
144 BVerfGE 108, 316.
145 BVerfGE 108, 320.

III. Recent Developments

Central to the Federal Constitutional Court's decision was the fact that the state of Baden-Württemberg had failed to issue a specific legislation to address the question of religious dress codes and school dress for teachers in public schools. However, the Court had clearly emphasised that the legislator is free to enact such legislation to balance out the religious freedom of teachers against the religious freedom of pupils and the right to parental education. In the aftermath of the decision, several states deliberated on possible modifications to their present regulations, and in reaction to the Federal Constitutional Court's ruling, passed laws, which prohibit teachers from wearing headscarves.[146] Legalized by such a statutory basis, the Federal Administrative Court in June 2004, upheld a ban on teachers wearing headscarves since the Federal Administrative Court took the view that the requirements made by the Federal Constitutional Court were now met.[147]

Meanwhile, the Islamic headscarf has become one of the most hotly disputed items of clothing in Europe, which led to a comprehensive headscarf-ban in France, comprised of teachers and students, and a considerable debate in Belgium and other European states.[148] Moreover, the European Court of Human Rights addressed the question of general headscarf bans in schools and universities and concluded that such bans were not a form of discrimination, and could be justified as necessary in a democratic society that required the separation of church and state.[149] Although the German headscarf dispute only moots dress codes for teachers without instructing pupils not to wear headscarves in public schools, and is thus not as far-reaching as the debate in France or the decision of the European Court of Human Rights, the question of how to fully integrate Muslim minorities into society remains unanswered. The banning of Muslim symbols, while tolerating others, could signal to Muslims that they are "second-class citizens" thus, putting obstacles to the integration of a continually growing European minority, which still does not win adequate recognition.[150] Developments of recent years have shown that there is a great potential for conflicts arising from religious differences and cultural tensions between Muslim minorities and Christian Majorities.[151] One should call to mind conflicts like the ritual Muslim slaughter or, the participation of female Muslim pupils in sport education or sex education,[152] which had to be handed down by the Federal Constitutional Court because of the inability of the legislator to appropriately deal with these conflicts arising from religious characteristics. Therefore, the headscarf decision takes its place among a line of case law dealing with cultural rights of a Muslim minority in Germany.[153]

---

146 *See* Schulgesetz Baden-Württemberg, v. 1.4.2004 (GBl. § 38 S. 178); Christine Langenfeld & Sarah Mohsen, *supra* note 98.
147 Bundesverwaltungsgericht (BverwG), NEUE JURISTISCHE WOCHENSCHRIFT (NJW), (2004), 3581.
148 Dagmar Schiek, *Just a Piece of Cloth?* 33 INDUS. L. SOC'Y 68 No. 1 (2004); *Chirac Bans Use of Muslim Headscarf in all State Schools*, THE TIMES (London), Dec. 2003, *at* 20.
149 Leyla Şahin v. Turkey, App. No. 44774/98 (Eur. Ct. H.R. June 29, 2004), *at* http://cmiskp.echr.coe.int/tkp197/portal.asp?sessionId=3002773&skin=hudoc-en&action=request; Lucia Dahlab v. Switzerland, App. No. 42393/98 (Eur. Ct. H. R. Feb. 15, 2001), *at* http://cmiskp.echr.coe.int/tkp197/portal.asp?sessionId=3232062&skin=hudoc-en&action=request.
150 Christine Langenfeld & Sarah Mohsen, *supra* note 98, 86; Oliver Gerstenberg, *supra* note 98.
151 Felix Müller, *Report – Bundesverfassungsgericht (Federal Constitutional Court) – 2001/2002*, 1 ANNUAL OF GERMAN AND EUROPEAN LAW 398 (Russell A. Miller & Peer Zumbansen eds., 2004).
152 *Id.*
153 Gabriele Britz, *Kulturelle Rechte und Verfassung*, 60 JUS PUBLICUM (2000).

E. Extradition to the United States of America (BVerfGE 109, 38)

Throughout the course of the "War on Terrorism," the way that potential terrorists were dealt with by the U.S.A. became the subject of ever increasing criticism.[154] In particular, the internment of offenders from Afghanistan and Iraq, in detention camps in Guantanamo Bay (Cuba), and the questionable methods of their treatment, met with disapproval from the public[155] as well as the judiciary.[156] In its November 5, 2003, decision the Federal Constitutional Court determined the legal prerequisites for the extradition of a Yemeni citizen, held by German authorities, to the United States of America for criminal prosecution. The case is unique because it deals with legal relations under international law amongst the Republic of Yemen, as the complainant's state of origin, the United States of America as the requesting state of the forum, and the Federal Republic of Germany as the state of residence.

I. Statement of the Facts

On January 10, 2003, German law enforcement officers arrested the complainant, a Yemeni citizen, in Frankfurt am Main, Germany.[157] The Yemeni was an adviser to the Yemeni Minister for Religious Foundations working as an Undersecretary of State and Imam of the Al-Ishsan Mosque in Sanaa, Yemen.[158] The arrest was motivated by an arrest warrant issued by the United States District Court of the Eastern District of New York, in which the United States authorities charged the Yemeni citizen with having provided money, weapons and communications equipment to terrorist groups, in particular Al-Qaeda and Hamas, and with having recruited new members for these groups.[159]

The reason for the complainant's journey to Germany was a conversation that another Yemeni citizen maintained with the complainant in Yemen. The second Yemeni citizen acted as a confidential informer in an undercover mission organized by the United States investigation and prosecution authorities.[160] In this conversation, the Yemeni confidential informant convinced the complainant that he could bring him into contact with another person abroad that was willing to make a major financial contribution to the various causes allegedly being promoted by the complainant.[161] However, during the complainant's interrogation by the German authorities, following his arrest, the purpose to which the donated money was to be put remained unclear.[162] Never the less, it was unchallenged that the decision to travel to Germany was based on the complainant's voluntary and independent initiative.[163] On January 24, 2003, the embassy of the United States sent to the

---

154 Eyal Benvenisti, *The U.S. and the Use of Force: Double-edged Hegemony and the Management of Global Emergencies*, EUR. J. INT'L L. 677 (2004); Anthea Roberts, *Righting Wrongs or Wronging Rights? The United States and Human Rights Post-September 11*, EUR. J. INT'L L. 721 (2004); Joachim Vogel, *Auslieferung eines durch List aus seinem Heimatstaat Gelockten?* 2004 JURISTENZEITUNG (JZ) 412; Michael Sachs, *Verstoß gegen das Recht auf den gesetzlichen Richter bei Nichtvorlage nach Art. 100 Abs. 2 GG; Grundrechtliche Anforderungen an die Auslieferung von Ausländern*, 2004 JURISTISCHE SCHULUNG (JuS) 620; Philippe Gélie, *Die Verliese von Guantánamo*, FRANKFURTER ALLGEMEINE SONNTAGSZEITUNG, Dec.14, 2003, at 3.
155 Cf. Philippe Gélie, *supra* note 154.
156 Padilla v. Rumsfeld, 352 F.3d 695 (2d Cir. 2003); Gherebi v. Bush, 352 F.3d 1278 (9th Cir. 2003).
157 BVerfGE 109, 39.
158 *Id.*
159 BVerfGE 109, 39.
160 BVerfGE 109, 40.
161 *Id.*
162 *Id.*
163 *Id.*

Bundesregierung (Federal Government) a request for the complainant's extradition for criminal prosecution in the United States.[164] Among others charges, the complainant was charged with membership in a terrorist association.

In the course of the extradition proceedings pending before the *Oberlandesgericht Frankfurt am Main* (Higher Regional Court of Frankfurt am Main), the complainant sought to preclude from the court's consideration of the American extradition request all of the facts stated in the U.S. extradition application, which were attributable to statements by the confidential informant and his influence over the complainant. With the striking of these facts, the complainant was of the opinion that the extradition itself should be declared inadmissible.[165] At the core, the complainant argued that he had been abducted from Yemen and persuaded to travel to Germany, all in violation of international law. This elaborate scheme was necessary, the complainant argued, in order to circumvent Yemeni laws on extradition. Moreover, the complainant asserted that an extradition to the United States violated the minimum standards that international law requires for a state governed by the rule of law. On this point, the complainant argued that the United States, regarding persons who are suspected of terrorism, had fallen back on methods of interrogation that constitute a violation of the ban on torture under Article 3 of the European Convention on Human Rights[166] and Article 1 of the United Nations Convention against Torture.[167] However, the United States Embassy provided assurances to the complainant that he would not be prosecuted by a military tribunal according to the Presidential Military Order of November 13, 2001, or by any other extraordinary court.[168]

At the same time, the embassy of the Republic of Yemen expounded to the Federal Foreign Office of Germany its opinion that the complainant had been persuaded, in violation of international law, to travel from Yemen to Germany in order to circumvent the Yemeni constitution's ban on the extradition of Yemeni citizens.[169] Therefore, the *Bundesregierung* was petitioned to repatriate the complainant to Yemen.

The Higher Regional Court of Frankfurt dismissed both sets of objections, and ascertained that the request for repatriation that had been made by the Republic of Yemen to the *Bundesregierung* did not affect the admissibility of the complainant's extradition to the United States.[170] The court concluded that, even if the deployment of a Yemeni citizen in Yemen as a confidential informant of the United States were to be regarded as a violation of Yemen's sovereignty, and thus an infringement of international law, this would not be contrary to the complainant's criminal prosecution.[171] According to the Higher Regional Court of Frankfurt, no general rule of international law existed that would oblige the state of the forum to withdraw the charge if a person had been induced to commit the offence, and to enter the state of the forum.[172] This was considered valid even under the condition that an agent provocateur who resorted to trickery and violated the territorial sovereignty

---

164 The request for extradition was based on the Extradition Treaty of June 20, 1978, F.R.G.-U.S.; see BUNDESGESETZBLATT (Federal Law Gazette) (BGBI) 1980 BGBI.II, S.646, 1300; *in conjunction with* Supplementary Treaty, Oct. 21 1986, 1988 BGBI.II, S.1086; 1993 BGBI. II, S. 846.
165 BVerfGE 109, 41.
166 MARK JANIS ET AL., EUROPEAN HUMAN RIGHTS LAW 93 (2nd ed., 2000); CLARE OVEY & ROBIN C.A. WHITE, EUROPEAN CONVENTION ON HUMAN RIGHTS 58 (3rd ed. 2002).
167 BVerfGE 109, 41.
168 It is notable that the assurance was given preserving the United States' legal opinion that the military commissions provided in the Presidential Military Order are not extraordinary courts within the meaning of Extradition Treaty, F.R.G.-U.S. art. 13, *see* 66 Fed. Reg. 222,57831 (Nov. 16, 2001) *et seq.*
169 BVerfGE 109, 41.
170 BVerfGE 109, 42.
171 BVerfGE 109, 42 (43).
172 The complainant made himself liable for prosecution in Germany according to the *Strafgesetzbuch* (StGB) (criminal code).

of a foreign state persuaded the complainant.[173] Moreover, the Higher Regional Court of Frankfurt highlighted the fact that the deployment of confidential informants by the U.S.A. did not violate the fundamental principle of the rule of law. To the contrary, the use of undercover investigation was considered a necessary method for the elucidation and prosecution of particularly dangerous offences like terrorism.[174] According to the court, an obstacle to the complainant's extradition to the United States and thus, an absolute impediment to the proceedings, could only be assumed in exceptional cases, e.g. if it became evident that there had been a failure to comply with fundamental principles such as the rule of law and due process. However, the case at hand was not considered such an exceptional case.[175] Finally, the Higher Regional Court stated that the reservations concerning the danger of torture to the complainant had been removed by the assurance given by the United States that the complainant would not be prosecuted by a military tribunal or by any other extraordinary court. According to this assurance, which is binding under international law,[176] it had to be assumed that the complainant would be brought before an ordinary criminal court in the United States. Worrisome reports about inhuman treatment of prisoners suspected of terrorism concerned prisoners, almost without exception, in Guantanamo (Cuba) and Bagram (Afghanistan).[177] The Higher Regional Court emphasized that one could not conclude from existing press reports, on the treatment of persons suspected of terrorism, that ordinary criminal proceedings in the United States of America did not meet the minimum standards of due process or, the rule of law and went so far as to infringe the ban on torture.[178]

The Yemeni citizen lodged an appeal against the Higher Regional Court's order, and challenged the violation of fundamental rights, international law and his right to a fair trial before the Federal Constitutional Court, by means of raising a constitutional complaint.

II. The Ruling of the Federal Constitutional Court

The Federal Constitutional Court dismissed the constitutional complaint as unfounded.[179] After a remark on art.100 para. 2 of the Basic Law,[180] the Court turned its attention to the impact of public international law on the present case.

The Federal Constitutional Court deduced from art. 25 of the Basic Law[181] that the general rules of international law must be respected in the national legislature's organisation of the national legal system, and in the interpretation and application of provisions under national law by the administrative authorities and the courts.[182] From this, the Federal Constitutional Court derived that art. 25 of the Basic Law prevents the administrative authorities, and the courts of the Federal Republic of Germany from interpreting and

---

173 BVerfGE 109, 42 (43).
174 BVerfGE 109, 43 (50).
175 Id.
176 BVerfGE 109, 45.
177 Id.
178 Id.
179 BVerfGE 109, 47.
180 See GG art. 100, para. 2 (stipulating that where, in the course of litigation, doubts exist whether a rule of public international law is an integral part of federal law and whether such rule directly creates rights and duties for the individual, see GG art. 25, the court obtains a decision from the Federal Constitutional Court).
181 See GG art. 25 (providing that the general rules of public international law constitute an integral part of federal law and that they take precedence over statutes and directly create rights and duties for the inhabitants of the federal territory).
182 BVerfGE 23, 288 (300); BVerfGE 31, 145 (177).

applying national law in a manner that violates the general rules of international law.[183] Additionally, the Federal Constitutional Court concluded that all administrative authorities and courts of the Federal Republic of Germany were obliged to refrain from anything that lends effectiveness to acts of non-German organs of state authority, which are performed in violation of general rules of international law in the territorial scope of the Basic Law. They were also prevented from participating in acts of non-German organs of state authority, which are performed in violation of general rules of international law.[184]

The Court addressed the question whether an American act of torture would establish U.S. responsibility under international law *vis-à-vis* Yemen.[185] The Federal Constitutional Court ascertained that in such a case Germany, by extraditing the complainant, ran the risk of supporting a United States action that could possibly be contrary to international law. Under the condition that the U.S. action violated international law, the extradition would make Germany itself responsible under international law *vis-à-vis* Yemen.[186] By resorting to these conclusions, the Federal Constitutional Court held that on the German side, an obstacle precluding the extradition of the complainant could possibly exist assuming that the action of the Yemeni confidential informant, on behalf of the United States investigation authorities, was found to be regarded as a violation of international law.[187] In the eyes of the Court, the territorial sovereignty of a state prohibits sovereign acts by other states or, by organs of state authority on the territory of the state affected.[188] Since it was not a United States official, but rather a Yemeni citizen who convinced the complainant to enter into contact with the donor, the Federal Constitutional Court emphasized that actions taken by private individuals could also be attributed to a state, if such acts were state-controlled.[189]

However, a violation of international law requires, as its basis, the existence of the general rule of international law asserted by the complainant. To determine the existence of a general rule of international law, which prohibits extradition in cases like the one under discussion, the Federal Constitutional Court examined whether there was any customary international law upon which such a claim and remedy could be based.[190]

The Federal Constitutional Court ascertained the existence and scope of general rules within the meaning of art. 25 of the Basic Law by consulting the relevant state practice.[191] The Court's examination of state practice showed that the general rule of international law asserted by the complainant did not exist. The Federal Constitutional Court held that, in this context, it need not be decided whether a national obstacle, which precluded criminal proceedings or extradition, resulted from customary international law if the prosecuted person had been taken from his or her state of origin to the state of the forum or to the requested state by use of force. Admittedly, more recent state practice, in particular the U.S. Supreme Court decision in the *Alvarez-Machain* case,[192] indicated that the principle

---

183 BVerfGE 109, 52.
184 BVerfGE 109, 52; BVerfGE 75, 1 (18–19).
185 BVerfGE 109, 52 (53–56).
186 *See* art. 16 Draft Articles on Responsibility of States for Internationally Wrongful Acts, adopted by International Law Commission at its Fifty-third Session, U.N. GAOR, 56th Sess., Supp. No. 10, UN Doc. A/56/10 (2001) (codifying customary international law in this field); *see* CRAWFORD, THE INTERNATIONAL LAW COMMISSION'S ARTICLES ON STATE RESPONSIBILITY (2002); GG art. 16 at 148 *et seq.* (showing that such state responsibility can under specific preconditions, be established by the support of third parties' action, which is contrary to international law).
187 BVerfGE 109, 52.
188 *Id.*
189 *Id.*
190 *Id.*
191 BVerfGE 109, 54.
192 *See* United States v. Alvarez-Machain, 504 U.S. 655 (1992).

male captus, bene detentus was to be rejected if the state of the forum gained hold over the prosecuted person by committing serious human rights violations, and if the state whose territorial sovereignty was violated protested against such procedure.[193]

However, the Federal Constitutional Court detected distinguishing details in the case at hand, because the complainant's decision to leave Yemen was voluntary.[194] The Court recapitulated that the complainant, in his interrogation by German investigation authorities, had clearly stated that it had been he himself who suggested Frankfurt am Main as the venue of a meeting place that was supposed to be convenient and productive for fund raising, particularly on account of the favourable visa regulations for Yemeni citizens in Germany. Although the complainant was deceived by trickery, such that the motives for which he travelled to Germany were based on deception, the Federal Constitutional Court noted that he was not subjected to direct force aimed at bending his will.[195] Moreover, the complainant was not threatened with the use of force, and the trickery did not facilitate a subsequent forceful abduction.[196] The Court added that the acts of deception were neither performed by German authorities nor attributable to them.[197] Finally, the Federal Constitutional Court held that there were no clues that would allow the assumption that the German authorities cooperated with the United States' criminal prosecution and investigation authorities, in a collusive manner, in order to induce the complainant to travel to Germany.[198]

Additionally, the Federal Constitutional Court emphasized that it must be taken into account that it was doubtful that the luring of a prosecuted person out of his or her state of residence by means of trickery – unlike the use of force – could be regarded as an act contrary to international law at all.[199] The Court added that in the case of the use of trickery, the prosecuted person's intended border crossing was also motivated by his or her own interests, and to the extent that the possibility existed that the prosecuted person decided against departure, the latter could not be considered the object of state coercion.[200] The Federal Constitutional Court noted that certainly the boundary between luring someone out of a state by means of trickery, and breaking someone's will by the use of force, could be a borderline area. For instance, this would be the case when someone was deluded into believing something that in turn had the effect of an irresistible coercion on the person affected.[201] But such circumstances, the Court stated, did not exist in the present case.[202] On the contrary, the complainant travelled to Germany on account of an autonomous decision in order to pursue his specific interests there. After all, the Federal Constitutional Court concluded, no practice has evolved under international law that would make the extradition appear to be an infringement of customary international law.[203]

The Federal Constitutional Court then turned to the complainant's assertion that his rights under art. 2.1, in conjunction with art. 1.1 of the Basic Law and art.19.4 of the Basic

---

193 Cf. Prosecutor v. Dragan Nikolic, ICTY Case No. IT-94-2-AR73, para. 24 *et seq.* (Appeals Chamber 2005), *with reference to* United States v. Toscanino, 500 F.2d 267 (1974); *see also* WILSKE, DIE VÖLKERRECHTLICHE ENTFÜHRUNG UND IHRE RECHTSFOLGEN 272 *et seq.* at 336 (2000).
194 BVerfGE 109, 55.
195 *Id.*
196 *Id.*
197 *Id.*
198 *Id.*
199 BVerfGE 109, 57, cf. Wilske, *supra* note 193, for further references.
200 BVerfGE 109, 57.
201 *Id.*
202 *Id.*
203 BVerfGE 109, 55 (56).

Law, had been violated.[204] The Higher Regional Court had rejected the complainants' submission concerning the methods of interrogation in the United States, with reference to a lack of evidence supportive of the assertions levelled against the United States. The Federal Constitutional Court held that this reasoning was constitutionally unobjectionable.[205] This conclusion was based on the fact that the United States precluded a possible application of the Presidential Military Order of November 13, 2001 in the present case, by their assurance to neither bring the complainant before an extraordinary court after his extradition, nor to apply the procedural law that is provided in the Order of November 13, 2001, nor to take the complainant to an internment camp.[206] Since the assurance given by the United States was considered binding under international law, the Federal Constitutional Court concluded that there were no indications to suggest that the United States would not, upon the complainant's extradition, comply with the assurance given and their obligations vis-à-vis Germany.[207]

In the end, the Federal Constitutional Court dismissed all objections, which were raised by the complainant and declared the extradition to the United States as being consistent with the Basic Law and international law.

III. A Slightly Bitter Taste Remains

Although the U.S. government has given Germany assurances that the suspects will not face a military court or, be confined in an internment camp, there remains a slightly bitter taste taking into account the generally questionable methods of interrogation carried out by U.S. authorities in Guantanamo Bay and other places. Irrespective of the case at hand, one can question whether Germany should extradite suspects to a country, which does not fully respect human rights and applies methods of interrogation and imprisonment, which are partly considered illegal.[208] It would have been desirable if, the Federal Constitutional Court had requested an assurance by the United States to not apply questionable methods of interrogation and imprisonment, as a matter of principal.

---

204 BVerfGE 109, 61.
205 *Id.*
206 BVerfGE 109, 62.
207 *Id.* at (63).
208 Christian Tomuschat, *Menschenrechte – Die Gefangenen in Guantanamo*, 2004 ANWALTSBLATT (AB) 397; Michael E. Kurth, *Der völkerrechtliche Status der Gefangenen von Guantanamo Bay*, 2002 ZEITSCHRIFT FÜR RECHTSPOLITIK (ZRP) 404; Eyal Benvenisti, *The US and the Use of Force: Double-edged Hegemony and the Management of Global Emergencies*, EURO. J. INT'L LAW 677 (2004); Anthea Roberts, *supra* note 154.

Report – *Bundesverwaltungsgericht* (Federal Administrative Court) – 2004

Craig T. Smith*

The final instance of administrative jurisdiction in Germany is the Federal Administrative Court. Located in Leipzig, the Court serves as ultimate interpreter and applier of federal substantive and procedural administrative law. The Court's decisions, primarily appeals from the first-instance Administrative Courts and the appellate Superior Administrative Courts,[1] are subject to review only on constitutional grounds by the Federal Constitutional Court in Karlsruhe.

Among the Court's important decisions in 2004 were three in which the Court confronted religious expression in schools, the balance between personal privacy and public transparency, and the legality of deporting an Islamic extremist to Turkey. These decisions came in the *Islamic Head-Scarf* case,[2] the *Stasi Files* case,[3] and the *Caliph of Cologne Deportation* case.[4]

I. The *Islamic Head-Scarf* Case, BVerwG 2 C 45.03 (24 June 2004)

On 24 June 2004, the Court published another decision in the *Islamic Head-Scarf* case. The Court thereby finally placed a period behind hundreds of lines of text, penned by various state agencies and courts over six years, that considered whether the *Land* Baden-Württemberg had, in 1998, lawfully refused to hire a naturalized German citizen who had been born in Afghanistan. The woman had sought civil-services employment as a teacher. The *Land* determined that she was unfit for the position because she planned to clothe her head, while teaching, in an Islamic head-scarf.[5] Extensive litigation and public debate followed. The litigation progressed through all three levels of administrative jurisdiction until, in mid 2002, the Federal Administrative Court ruled in favor of the *Land*.[6] Soon, however, the Federal Constitutional Court vacated the administrative-court judgment,

---

* Associate Professor, Vanderbilt University Law School, Nashville, Tennessee, U.S.A. Email: craig.smith@law.vanderbilt.edu. This report is the sequel to the report on the Federal Administrative Court's Jurisprudence of 2002–2003, which appeared in the first volume of the Annual of German and European Law. For an introduction to the Court and German administrative law, see that report.
1. Verwaltungsgerichtsordnung [VwGO] [Administrative Court Act], Jan. 21, 1960, BgBl. I at 17, in the newly published version, Mar. 10, 1991, BgBl. I at 86, § 49.
2. Bundesverwaltungsgericht [BVerwG] [Federal Administrative Court], 2 C 45.03, June 24, 2004 (HeadScarf Case).
3. Bundesverwaltungsgericht [BVerwG] [Federal Administrative Court], 3 C 41.03, June 23, 2004 (Stasi Files Case).
4. Bundesverwaltungsgericht [BVerwG] [Federal Administrative Court], 1 C 14.04, December 7, 2004 (Deportation Case).
5. Head-Scarf Case, para. 19.
6. Verwaltungsgerichtshof Baden-Württemberg [VGH] [Administrative Court of Appeals], NEUE JURISTISCHE WOCHENSCHRIFT [NJW] 2899 (2001); BVerwG, NEUE JURISTISCHE WOCHENSCHRIFT [NJW] 3344 (2002); BVerfGE 116, 359.

ruling that the *Land* lacked a sufficient statutory basis for its refusal.[7] The Karlsruhe justices also indicated, however, that the Basic Law would permit a *Land* to enact such a statutory basis. Baden-Württemberg and other *Länder* began enacting statutory provisions that regulate the attire of state-employed teachers. The litigation returned to the Federal Administrative Court.

On 1 April 2004, Baden-Württemberg amended its School Act. The amended Act's § 38 para. 2 stated:

> [Sentence 1:] A teacher in a public school ... may not, within the school, give political, religious, ideological, or similar external manifestations (*Bekundungen*) that have the capacity to endanger or disturb either the neutrality of the *Land* with respect to students or parents or the political, religious, or ideological school peace. ... [Sentence 3:] Fulfillment of the educational task imposed by ... the constitution of the *Land* ... and the corresponding portrayal of Christian or Western developmental and cultural values (*Bildungs- und Kulturwerte*) or traditions do not contradict the conduct-related mandate set forth in Sentence 1.[8]

The amended Act's § 38 para. 3 added that an applicant, to prove his or her suitability for a teaching position, must guarantee compliance with § 38 para. 2 for the applicant's entire foreseeable term of teaching service.[9]

On 24 June 2004, the Federal Administrative Court ruled against the applicant – just as it had done two years earlier. The Court held that the amended School Act complied with both administrative and constitutional law by legitimizing the refusal to hire while respecting the applicant's constitutional rights.

The Court's explanation of this holding proceeded in three major steps. First, the Court explained that under administrative law the amended Act governed the refusal to hire, even though the amendment took effect years after that refusal. This apparent quirk of timing – that a subsequently enacted norm governed a prior act – arose from the teacher's status as an essentially permanent state employee. To review decisions regarding the hiring of such employees, the Court explained, courts must apply subsequently enacted law because such decisions are prognostications concerning an applicant's long-term future employment.[10]

Second, the Court agreed with the *Land* that the applicant's intent to wear an Islamic head-scarf while teaching as a state civil servant rendered her unfit for the job. Wearing the head-scarf is conduct proscribed in § 38 para. 2 of Baden-Württemberg's School Act, the Court reasoned, because it is an unequivocal *Bekundung*: a manifestation of the wearer's religious conviction.[11] Also relevant, the Court added, are other ways that a teacher's wearing of an Islamic head-scarf can be understood, particularly among schoolchildren and parents. They may understand it as an indication that the wearer follows traditions of her society of origin (*Herkunftsgesellschaft*).[12] They also may see the head-scarf as a symbol of Islamic fundamentalism and expression of "distancing from Western society's values."[13]

Third, the Court explained that the amended School Act complies with the Basic Law. On the one hand, the amended Act has sufficient substantive precision.[14] On the other, it satisfies the principle of practical concordance (*praktischer Konkordanz*), which requires practical, proportional balancing of competing fundamental rights.[15]

---

7   BVerfGE 108, 282.
8   Head-Scarf Case, paras. 4, 6, *citing* GBl. Baden-Württemberg (2004) at 178.
9   Head-Scarf Case, para. 7, *citing* GBl. Baden-Württemberg (2004) at 178.
10 Head-Scarf Case, para. 19.
11 Head-Scarf Case, para. 22.
12 Head-Scarf Case, para. 23.
13 *Id.*
14 Head-Scarf Case, para. 29.
15 Head-Scarf Case, para. 32.

The Court rejected the argument that § 38 para. 2 of the amended Act collapsed into contradiction by – just after prohibiting certain religious *Bekundungen* – expressly permitting in schools the "portrayal of Christian or Western developmental and cultural values."[16] Portrayal of these values, the Court reasoned, from a neutral perspective (*von neutraler Warte*) is not an individual religious confession; to the contrary, it is unrelated to "personal, internal *Verbindlichkeit*" (dedication).[17] This lack of such a relationship distinguishes the portrayal from the prohibited *Bekundungen* (manifestations). Consequently, Sentence 3 of § 38 para. 2, the Court insisted, actually clarifies what conduct lies beyond the scope of prohibited *Bekundungen*. Sentence 3 thereby enhances rather than undermines the substantive precision of the School Act.[18]

With respect to practical concordance, the Court ruled that the amended School Act lawfully limited the applicant's religious freedom. The *Land* legislature chose to subordinate a state-employed teacher's rights to those of parents and schoolchildren for the purpose of "securing neutrality and school peace."[19] The legislature thereby chose to *prevent* conflicts rather than merely *react to* them.[20] That preemptive choice, the Court declared, lies within the limits of legislative prerogative.[21] Such a legislative choice is particularly legitimate because maintaining religious peace at school (*religiöse Schulfrieden*) is a compelling purpose.[22] Accordingly, whether teachers' head-scarves or similar *Bekundungen* have already caused specific problems in the schools of the *Land* is irrelevant. The legislature can respond simply to an abstract danger (*abstrakte Gefahr*).[23] In the present case, the abstract danger identified by the *Land* was convincing. A teacher's "infusion of religious or ideological aspects into school and instruction," the Court wrote, can undermine the state's educational task, the parental right to educate their children, and "the negative freedom of belief" of schoolchildren.[24]

II. The *Stasi Files* Case, 3 C 41.03 (23 June 2004)

On 23 June 2004, the Court issued another decision in the long-running *Stasi Files* dispute.[25] This dispute pitted former Chancellor Helmut Kohl against the state agency that administers files created by the German Democratic Republic's secret police popularly known as the "Stasi," an abbreviation of *Staatssicherheitsdienst* (state security service). Kohl sought to prevent the agency from giving to researchers and reporters hundreds of pages of Stasi files that contain information about Kohl.[26] In March 2002 the Court had affirmed a lower administrative court's injunction, issued in 2001, that forbid the agency from releasing the files to which Kohl objected.[27]

---

16 Head-Scarf Case, para. 29.
17 *Id.*
18 *Id.*
19 Head-Scarf Case, para. 31.
20 Head-Scarf Case, para. 33.
21 Head-Scarf Case, para. 32.
22 Head-Scarf Case, para. 38.
23 Head-Scarf Case, para. 33–34.
24 Head-Scarf Case, para. 33.
25 *See* Craig T. Smith, *Report: Bundesverwaltungsgericht (Federal Administrative Court)*, *in* ANNUAL OF GERMAN AND EUROPEAN LAW 422, 424 (2004).
26 *Birthler will Kohl-Akten zum Teil herausgeben*, FRANKFURTER ALLGEMEINE ZEITUNG [FAZ], (June 26, 2004) at 4.
27 BVerwG 116, 104.

In September 2002, however, Germany amended the Stasi Files Act of 1991.[28] This amendment removed a general prohibition against sharing information from Stasi files. The agency emerged with greater power to disseminate such information. The agency again challenged the 2001 injunction against distributing files related to Ex-Chancellor Kohl. Now, the agency argued, no legal basis for the injunction remained. Kohl responded that the amendments violated the Basic Law. The lower administrative court ruled in favor of the agency on 17 September 2003.[29] Before the agency could distribute the files, however, an appeal went directly to the Federal Administrative Court.

Kohl argued, first, that the amended Act unconstitutionally treated victims and perpetrators equally. This argument failed. In most instances no unequal treatment exists, the Court declared, because the amendments retained the general rule: The agency needs the consent of Stasi victims if it wishes to make the victims' files available, whereas the consent of Stasi *collaborators* – perpetrators – is irrelevant.[30] In some instances, however, the amended Act no longer treats all victims equally. Henceforth, victims who are political officials and contemporary historical persons (*Personen der Zeitgeschichte*) cannot, like other victims, *absolutely* prevent dissemination of their Stasi files by withholding consent. Instead, under limited circumstances the agency now may make portions of those files available. Such differential treatment of political officials and contemporary historical persons, however, is a constitutionally permissive legislative choice.[31] The substantial public interest in such persons, the Court reasoned, justifies treating them differently from other victims.[32]

The Court nonetheless handed Kohl a partial victory. Accepting Kohl's arguments relating to personal integrity rather than equality, the Court held that the amended Act left the 2001 injunction significantly – but not entirely – enforceable. Specifically, the Court declared the 2001 injunction's blanket prohibition unenforceable but crafted out of it two lesser restrictions that would continue to bind the agency:

(1) The agency may not make available audiotapes, transcripts of discussions, and files if these contain information about Kohl that concerns his private life.
(2) Without Kohl's consent, the agency may not make available files that contain information about Kohl if "the possibility cannot with certainty be excluded" that the files either:
   a. were collected by violating any person's right to a spatial private sphere (*räumliche Privatsphäre*) or their right of the spoken word (*Recht am gesprochenen Wort*); or
   b. came from files or data collections of German state organs or agencies, political parties, firms, or nongovernmental organizations; or
   c. may have as their basis the above-listed types of information.[33]

The Court based this decision on the general constitutional right of personality.[34] This is a fundamental right derived from Article 2 para. 1 in connection with Article 1 para. 1 of the Basic Law. The former protects "free development of personality," while the latter protects human dignity.[35]

---

28 Fünftes Gesetz zur Änderung des Stasi-Gesetzes [Fifth Act to Amend the Stasi Files Act], Sep. 2, 2002 BgBl. I at 3446.
29 Stasi Files Case, para. 6; Verwaltungsgericht Berlin [VG] [Administrative Court], 1 A 317.02, Sep. 17, 2003.
30 Stasi Files Case, para. 20.
31 *Id.*
32 *Id.*
33 Stasi Files Case. "Order" in the introduction "für Recht erkannt: ..."?
34 Stasi Files Case, para. 23.
35 GRUNDGESETZ [GG] [Constitution] arts. 1 para. 1, 2 para. 1.

Kohl argued that the amended Act violated this general right of personality because it authorized dissemination of some files without consent from affected individuals. The Court responded that the Act properly ensured that dissemination would produce only justifiable impacts on the individual's right of personality.[36] The impacts were acceptable, the Court explained, for several reasons. First, the Act authorized the agency to disseminate personal information regarding political officials and contemporary historical persons only insofar as the information concerns the person's political function or historical role. The Act still barred dissemination of information about his *private* life. Second, the amended Act requires the agency to have balanced the public interest in investigating Stasi activities against the impact on the individual's right of personality and to have determined that the former prevailed.[37] The public interest may be sufficiently weighty, the Court explained, if the dissemination would serve political or historical purposes.[38] By contrast, the public's interest typically would not tip the balance in favor of dissemination if the dissemination would merely serve the media's less scholarly purposes.[39] Third, the amended Act requires the agency to notify the person precisely why and to whom the agency intends to make the files available. Administrative courts may then review the agency's determination. This, the Court concluded, gives the affected person a "realistic possibility" of employing the judiciary to prevent the agency from violating the person's right of personality.[40]

Kohl also objected that the amended Act gave the agency only "very general" standards for case-by-case balancing of the public's interest against the affected individual's right of personality.[41] This lack of specificity, however, did not trouble the Court much. To the contrary, the Court praised the Act's "flexibility" and stated that courts can provide more specific guidelines.[42] The Court did, however, rule that the amended Act's mention of human rights violations required a constitutionally conforming interpretation (*verfassungskonforme Auslegung*). The amended Act requires the agency to take into account (*berücksichtigen*) whether collection of the information in the Stasi files being sought "discernibly rests upon" (*beruht erkennbar auf*) a human rights violation.[43] To this the Court added the following details:

(1) A human rights violation includes entry into an individual's private sphere and violation of an individual's right of the spoken word, even if these occur outside of private areas, for example in offices via unauthorized surveillance of conversations, correspondence, and telecommunication.[44]
(2) The term "rests upon" (*beruht auf*) must be understood broadly. The human rights violation affects not only the information gained through that violation; it also affects all documents that use such information.[45]
(3) The term "discernibly" (*erkennbar*) likewise must be understood broadly. The Stasi frequently violated human rights to gain information. Consequently, such a violation must be discernible whenever any indication of a violation exists, including simply the

---

36 Stasi Files Case, para. 59.
37 Stasi Files Case, para. 38, 42.
38 Stasi Files Case, para. 37.
39 Stasi Files Case, para. 47.
40 Stasi Files Case, para. 59–60.
41 Stasi Files Case, para. 61.
42 *Id.*
43 *Id.*, citing Stasi-Unterlagengesetz [StUG] [Stasi Files Act] 1992, BGBl. I at 2272, § 32, para. 1, sent. 3.
44 Stasi Files Case, para. 63.
45 Stasi Files Case, para. 65.

fact that the information cannot be traced to an unproblematic source and therefore must be presumed to have been collected improperly.[46]

(4) The term "take into account" (*berücksichtigen*) requires the agency to ensure that it not disseminate information collected in violation of human rights. To ensure this, the agency must release such information only for purposes of scientific research. The agency also must impose under conditions that ensure use of the information only for such purposes – and not, for example, for political or media purposes. Finally, the agency may not release audiotapes and transcripts even for research purposes.[47]

With this constitutionally conforming interpretation, required by the general right of personality, the Court concluded, the Act provided a sufficient statutory justification for the Act's substantial impact on the right of personality.[48]

III. The *"Caliph of Cologne" Deportation* Case, BVerwG 1 C 14.04 (7 December 2004)

In December 2004 the Court refused to annul Germany's previously executed deportation of the "Caliph of Cologne" to his native Turkey.[49] This Turkish citizen had lived and worked in Germany for decades as an Islamic cleric. He also had led a fundamentalist organization, widely known as the "Caliph State" (*Kalifatstaat*), that promoted a *jihad* or holy war against Turkey.[50] In 2001 Germany banned the organization, and in 2002 the Court upheld that ban.[51] Also in 2002, Germany revoked the cleric's entitlement to asylum in Germany.[52] Though a constitutional complaint challenging that revocation has remained pending in the Constitutional Court,[53] in September 2002 the Federal Agency for the Recognition of the Foreign Refugees declared that Germany could lawfully deport the man.[54]

An administrative court disagreed.[55] It held that the agency's deportation declaration was unlawful because the cleric could not expect to receive a fair criminal proceeding in Turkey as required by Article 6 para. 1 of the European Convention for the Protection of Human Rights and Fundamental Freedoms (hereinafter "European Human Rights Convention"). Specifically, a Turkish court might, in criminal proceedings against the cleric, rely on testimony extracted from witnesses via torture.[56] A superior administrative court reversed this decision. An appeal then reached the Federal Administrative Court.

The Court affirmed. The agency's deportation declaration was lawful, the Court held, for two reasons. First, no procedural errors were apparent in the superior administrative court's determination that in fact Turkish authorities would not torture the cleric. Administrative law required the Court to accept that determination.[57]

---

46 Stasi Files Case, para. 66.
47 Stasi Files Case, para. 67.
48 Stasi Files Case, para. 23, 62.
49 Deportation Case, para. 2.
50 *Id.*
51 Bundesverwaltungsgericht [BVerwG] [Federal Administrative Court], 6 A 4.02, November 27, 2002.
52 Deportation Case, para. 3.
53 *Id.*
54 Deportation Case, para. 4
55 *Id.*
56 *Id.*
57 Deportation Case, para. 15.

Second, the cleric's fear that Turkey would treat him inhumanely in violation of the European Human Rights Convention was immaterial.[58] The superior administrative court had not erred when it determined that the cleric would not be treated unduly harshly or subject to the death penalty in Turkey.[59] More importantly, Turkey is a member of the Council of Europe and has ratified the Convention.[60] The cleric's arguments, however, rested chiefly on legal principles that govern deportation to a *non*-signatory state. These govern deportation to Turkey, the Court wrote, "only in a limited manner."[61] Specifically, "the deporting state has co-responsibility for respecting minimum human rights standards" in the destination state only if, after the deportation, the alien (1) faces a threat of torture or other severe and irreparable mistreatment and (2) cannot gain timely, effective legal protection through domestic courts and the European Court of Human Rights.[62] In the present case, the deported man could rely on protection from Turkish courts and the Strasbourg court.[63]

---

58 Deportation Case, para. 16.
59 Deportation Case, para. 20–22, 30.
60 Deportation Case, para. 17.
61 Deportation Case, para. 18.
62 *Id.*
63 Deportation Case, para. 19, 25.

Report – *Bundesgerichtshof in Zivilsachen* (Federal Court of Justice, Private Law) – 2003/2004

Jan Stemplewitz*

A. Introduction

This report covers decisions on appeal by the *Bundesgerichtshof*[1] (BGH – Federal Court of Justice) in civil matters from 2003 and 2004. Cases were selected from the areas of contract law, tort law, family law, intellectual property law, company law and securities law.

B. Contract Law

I. Declaration of Guarantee by Employee[2]

The judgment of the BGH in the *Declaration of Guarantee by Employee* case is the latest in a long line of decisions by the BGH on the validity of declarations of guarantee and assumption of joint liability.[3] The respondent was employed by a construction company as a site manager. When the company ran into financial difficulties, it applied for a short term loan of 200,000 DM (approximately 102,250 €) at a savings bank. The bank – claimant in the proceedings – agreed to grant the loan if the company provided sufficient securities in form of personal declarations of guarantee. The respondent and two other employees of the company each signed a standard form guarantee for the loan up to an amount of 200,000 DM plus interest and fees. Three months later, the company went bankrupt. The bank terminated the loan and called in the outstanding sum of approximately 120,000 DM. It sued the respondent as guarantor for a partial amount of 70,000 DM plus interest. The respondent refused payment and claimed that his assumption of joint liability was void pursuant to Section 138(1) *Bürgerliches Gesetzbuch* (BGB – German Civil Code)[4] for violation of *gute Sitten* (*boni mores* – good morals/public policy). The *Landgericht* (LG – Regional Court) *Rostock* dismissed the action accordingly; the *Oberlandesgericht* (OLG – Higher Regional Court) *Rostock* on appeal decided in favor of

---

* Dipl.-Jur. University of Münster (2004); LL.M. (Hons) Victoria University of Wellington (2005). Senior graduate assistant and Ph.D. candidate at the Institute of Public Economic Law, University of Münster. Email: j.stemplewitz@uni-muenster.de
1 For a brief introduction to the *Bundesgerichtshof* and its functions within the German judicial system, *see* Holger Hestermeyer, Report – Bundesgerichtshof-Zivilsachen *(Federal Court of Justice – Private Law)* – 2001/2002, 1 ANNUAL OF GERMAN & EUROPEAN LAW 437 (Russell Miller & Peer Zumbansen eds., 2004).
2 BGHZ 156, 302.
3 *See* Hestermeyer, *supra* note 1, at 449 (*Joint Credit Liability of Relatives* case).
4 "A legal transaction contrary to *boni mores* is void." (translation by author). For a brief elaboration of the jurisprudence relating to § 138 BGB, *see* Peer Zumbansen, *Law of Contracts, in* INTRODUCTION TO GERMAN LAW 179–203 (M. Reimann & J. Zekoll eds., 2005).

the claimant. In partly relying on principles concerning the nullity of guarantees and assumption of joint liability developed in previous decisions, the BGH reversed the ruling of the OLG and held that the respondent's guarantee was void.

With respect to guarantees, the applicability of Section 138(1) BGB requires, on an objective level, that the guarantor assumes liability for a debt that is grossly disproportionate to his or her financial abilities.[5] The test applied by the BGH asks whether the payable interest on the debt exceeds the attachable part of the guarantor's income or assets.[6] With an attachable part of the respondent's income of 546 DM per month, the interest of 17% on the 200,000 DM loan by far exceeded the limit. However, in addition, a violation of *boni mores* requires – as a subjective element – that the guarantor is exploited in a condemnable manner.[7] On this point, the BGH had previously developed a refutable presumption that, in case of a ruinous guarantee for the benefit of a close relative or friend, the guarantee was only taken up because of emotional ties to the debtor and that such emotional attachment was reprehensibly exploited by the creditor.[8] The Court, however, held that the respondent could not avail himself of this presumption since there are generally no emotional ties between employer and employee as, for example, between family members. The BGH deliberately left open the question whether, and if so, under what circumstances, there could also be such a presumption for ruinous declarations of guarantee by employees. Instead, it proceeded to determine whether there had been actual exploitation on part of the claimant bank.

The Court considered that the construction company at which the respondent had been employed was facing a serious liquidity crisis when the guarantee was signed. The respondent could have either signed the guarantee along with his two colleagues or risked the immediate loss of his workplace. The BGH held that in times of high unemployment there is a refutable presumption that an employee who does not hold any share in the profit of the company but nevertheless accepts a potentially ruinous guarantee only does so for fear of losing his or her employment.[9] The bank was aware of the company's situation and must have recognized that the respondent was not making a reasonable decision. The Court therefore found that the bank took advantage of the respondent's predicament and declared the guarantee void pursuant to Section 138(1) BGB.

In addition, the BGH pointed out that a number of provisions in the standard form guarantee unreasonably disadvantaged the respondent within the meaning of (then) Section 9 of the *Gesetz zur Regelung des Rechts der Allgemeinen Geschäftsbedingungen* (AGBG – Standard Business Terms Act).[10] While a breach of Section 9 AGBG was, in itself, insufficient to render the guarantee void pursuant to Section 138(1) BGB, it nevertheless reinforced the impression of a violation of the principles of *boni mores*.

---

5 BGHZ 146, 37 (43); BGH, 24 Zeitschrift für Wirtschaftsrecht (ZIP) 796, 797 (2003).
6 *Id.*
7 *Id.*
8 BGHZ 156, 302; BGHZ 136, 347 (351); BGHZ 151, 34 (37). See Hestermeyer, *supra* note 1, at 449 (*Joint Credit Liability of Relatives* case).
9 BGHZ 156, 302. See Kammergericht (KG – Higher Regional Court of Berlin), 52 Monatsschrift für Deutsches Recht (MDR) 234, 235 (1998).
10 The AGBG was repealed on January 1, 2002. Its substantive provisions were incorporated into the BGB, §§ 305 *et seq*; § 9(1) AGBG (now § 307 BGB) reads: "Provisions in standard business terms are invalid if, contrary to the requirement of good faith, they place the contractual partner of the user at an unreasonable disadvantage." (translation by G. Thomas & G. Dannemann, *available at* http://www.iuscomp.org/gla/statutes).

II. Consumer Right of Revocation for Internet Auction Contracts – eBay Case[11]

The claimant in the *eBay* case was a commercial trader in gold and silver jewelry. He used the internet services of eBay International AG to put up for auction a 15 carat diamond bracelet at a starting price of 1 €. The respondent – a private individual and "consumer" within the meaning of Section 13 BGB[12] – made the winning bid of 252.51 €, but subsequently refused payment and acceptance of the bracelet. He claimed that he validly revoked the distance selling contract pursuant to Sections 312d(1)[13] and 355(1)[14] BGB. The claimant did not dispute the respondent's declaration of revocation but contended that Section 312d(4) No. 5 BGB excluded the right of revocation for internet auction contracts. The action for payment plus interest and shipping costs was dismissed, both by the *Amtsgericht* (AG – District Court) Rosenheim, and on appeal by the *Landgericht* (LG – Regional Court) Traunstein. Leave to appeal to the BGH on points of law was granted.

Section 312d(4) BGB provides that "[s]ubject to any provision to the contrary, the right of revocation does not apply to distance selling contracts [...] – No. 5: that are concluded *by way of auction* (§ 156)" (emphasis added). The key issue for the BGH to resolve was whether this exemption also applied to eBay-type internet "auctions", as Section 156 BGB, to which Section 312d(4) BGB refers, is only applicable to real (live) auctions where an auctioneer actually declares acceptance of the highest bid.[15] Such real auctions – which can, of course, also be run over the internet – require individual authorization under German administrative law,[16] which would be highly impractical for internet "auctions". Consequently, the predominant view under German law, including the jurisprudence of the BGH, does *not* regard eBay-type transactions as auctions within the meaning of Section 156 BGB, but characterizes the highest bid within the prescribed period of time as a contractual acceptance of the seller's binding offer.[17] Along these lines, the BGH held that the execption to the general right of revocation for distant selling contracts in Section 312d(4) No. 5 BGB does not apply where a consumer buys goods from a business at an eBay-type auction.

According to the Court, neither the wording of Section 312d(4) BGB nor its historical, systematical and teleological interpretation warrant an application to "auctions" outside the scope of Section 156 BGB. First, the BGH took the explicit reference to Section 156 BGB as a qualification on the term "auction" rather than a mere example. This, the Court found, was supported by the principle that exceptions – in this case Section 312d(4) BGB – to a general rule (Section 312d(1) BGB setting out the right of revocation) are to be construed narrowly. Second, the legislative history of the provision showed that Parliament had intended a narrow scope for the exclusion of the right of revocation.

---

11 BGH, 58 Neue Juristische Wochenschrift (NJW) 57 (2005). *See* Gerald Spindler, *Internet-Auctions versus Consumer Protection: The case of the Distant Selling Directive*, 6 German Law Journal 725 (2005), at http://www.germanlawjournal.com/pdf/Vol06No03/PDF_Vol_06_No_03_725-733_Developments_Spindler.pdf.
12 "A consumer is any natural person who concludes a legal transaction for a purpose which can neither be attributed to his business nor to his independent vocational activity." (translation by author).
13 § 312d(1).1 BGB provides: "In respect of a distance selling contract, the consumer has a right of revocation in accordance with § 355." (translation by author).
14 § 355(1).1 BGB provides: "Where a consumer is accorded a right of revocation by statute in accordance with this provision, he is no longer bound by his declaration to conclude the contract if he revokes it within the prescribed time." (translation by author).
15 § 156.1 BGB provides: "At an auction, a contract is concluded only upon acceptance of a bid." (translation by author).
16 § 34b *Gewerbeordnung* (GewO – Commerce Act), as amended by Art. 12 of Act from July 20, 2004, BGBl. I at 2014.
17 BGHZ 149, 129 (133). *See* Hestermeyer, *supra* note 1, at 446 (*Contract Formation in Internet Auctions – "Ricardo.de"* case); Spindler, *supra* note 11, at 731 n. 27.

The Committee on Legal Affairs had pointed out in its report[18] on the government's draft of the *Fernabsatzgesetz* (FernAbsG – Distance Selling Act)[19] implementing the EC Distance Selling Directive[20] that most of the so-called "internet auctions" were not auctions in a legal sense as defined by Section 156 BGB. While the Committee expressly recognized that a right of revocation would not be compatible with the typical characteristics of an auction, it emphasized that, even in the area of distance selling, the distinguishing feature of an auction was the actual acceptance of the highest bid.[21] Hence, the reference to Section 156 BGB, which had not been included in the government's draft, was added.

The EC Directive itself does not offer any guidance on the interpretation of the term "auction". It only contains a general exemption for "contracts concluded at an auction,"[22] and allows Member States to "introduce or maintain [...] more stringent provisions compatible with the Treaty, to ensure a higher level of consumer protection."[23] The Court reasoned that the legislature intended such a higher level of consumer protection, since it did not totally exempt distance auction contracts from the provisions of the FernAbsG, but only excluded the right of revocation. According to the BGH, the typical problems consumers face in assessing the quality of goods and the reputation of the seller before concluding a distance selling contract equally apply to eBay-type internet auctions. Therefore, the protective purpose of the right of revocation required a narrow interpretation of the exemption provision. The Court found that neither eBay nor the individual seller would be unduly disadvantaged by such an interpretation of Section 312d(4) No. 5 BGB, since eBay itself imposed in its user agreement a duty to inform a consumer of his or her right of revocation.

C. Tort Law

I. Compensation for Distomo Massacre[24]

In the *Distomo* case Greek nationals sought damages from the Federal Republic of Germany for a massacre committed by a SS-unit integrated into the German army during the German occupation of Greece in 1944. Following an armed conflict with Greek partisans the SS-unit burned down the village of Distomo and shot over 300 innocent inhabitants – amongst them the claimants' parents – as a "retribution measure." The action for compensation in respect of the destruction of the parental home and business as well as disadvantages to the claimants' personal health and professional training was dismissed, both by the *Landgericht* (LG – Regional Court) Bonn, and on appeal by the *Oberlandesgericht* (OLG – Higher Regional Court) Cologne. Leave to appeal to the BGH on points of law was granted.

The BGH first considered whether it was bound by a judgment of the Regional Court of Livadeia in Greece, which, in 1997, had already awarded damages for the massacre to the appellants. The decision was confirmed by the Greek *Areopag* (Supreme Court), however,

---

18 BTDrucks 14/3195, 30, *available at* (in German) http://www.bundestag.de.
19 In 2002, the provisions of the FernAbsG were incorporated into the BGB, §§ 312b *et seq.*
20 Directive of the European Parliament and Council 97/7, 1997 O.J. (L 144) 19 (EC).
21 BTDrucks 14/3195, 30–32.
22 Directive of the European Parliament and Council 97/7, art. 3(1), 1997 O.J. (L 144) 19 (EC).
23 Directive of the European Parliament and Council 97/7, art. 14, 1997 O.J. (L 144) 19 (EC).
24 BGHZ 152, 380. *See* Sabine Pittrof, *Compensation Claims for Human Rights Breaches Committed by German Armed Forces Abroad During the Second World War: Federal Court of Justice Hands Down Decision in* Distomo *Case*, 5 GERMAN LAW JOURNAL 15 (2004), *at* http://www.germanlawjournal.com/pdf/Vol05No01/PDF_Vol05_No01_15-21_Public_Pitroff.pdf.

execution against assets of the Federal Republic of Germany in Greece[25] failed for lack of permission by the Greek government required under Greek law. The BGH reasoned that the principle of *res judicata* only prevents a German court from re-assessing the same factual situation if the foreign decision must be recognized. On this issue the Court held that the Brussels Convention on Jurisdiction and Enforcement of Judgments in Civil and Commercial Matters of 1968 was not applicable to compensation claims against states exercising sovereign powers. Recognition of the Greek judgment, therefore, depended on an application of either the German-Greek Treaty on Mutual Recognition and Execution of Court Decisions, Settlements and Public Documents in Civil and Commercial Matters of 1961 or Section 328 *Zivilprozessordnung* (ZPO – Code of Civil Procedure), which governs the recognition of foreign judgments in general. According to the BGH, both the treaty and Section 328 ZPO required that Greek courts had (international) jurisdiction to hear the case. The Court concluded that this prerequisite was not fulfilled as the principle of sovereign immunity had been breached. Based on this principle of public international law states may claim immunity from another state's jurisdiction for their own acts of sovereign power (*acta iure imperii*). The BGH considered the massacre an act of sovereign power – irrespective of its gravity – since it had been committed by a unit of the German armed forces. While the Court acknowledged recent endeavours not to apply the principle of sovereign immunity to breaches of mandatory rules of public international law (*ius cogens*), it determined that – without doubt[26] – such a restrictive approach was not (yet) generally considered a rule of current public international law. As the judgment of the Livadeia Regional Court therefore could not be recognized, the BGH found it to be non-binding.

On the merits of the case, the Court first decided that specific post-war compensation legislation[27] was not applicable. The massacre as a "retribution measure" did not constitute an act directed against the political belief, race, religious faith or ideology of the Distomo inhabitants as required by the Federal Compensation Act 1953. Instead, the Court treated the claim as a possible liability of the former German Empire for which the Federal Republic of Germany would be liable under principles of state succession.[28] Such reparation claims against the German Empire could generally not be adjudicated as they came under the provisions of the London Debt Agreement[29] of February 27, 1953, which served as a moratorium on claims against Germany until the conclusion of a final peace agreement dealing with reparation.[30] However, the BGH held that the treaty between the former occupying powers and the two German states of September 12, 1990, establishing full sovereignty of a unified Germany,[31] although not a conventional peace agreement, had rendered the London Debt Agreement obsolete. Thus, the moratorium no longer barred the adjudication of reparation claims.

In determining whether the appellants' claims against the German Empire were founded the Court examined them under two possibilities on the basis of the law of 1944.[32] First, the BGH dismissed the claims under public international law, which, at the time, only

---

25 The claimants tried to levy execution, *inter alia*, against the German Goethe Institute in Athens.
26 Otherwise, the BGH would have had to obtain an opinion from the *Bundesverfassungsgericht* (BVerfG – Federal Constitutional Court) first, according to Article 100(2) of the *Grundgesetz* (GG – Basic Law/Constitution). However, the Court relied on decisions by the European Court for Human Rights and the Greek Supreme Special Court, both of which had specifically dealt with this question and had rejected a restrictive approach.
27 *Bundesentschädigungsgesetz* (BEG – Federal Compensation Act), Sep. 18, 1953, BGBl. I at 1387.
28 Articles 134(4), 135a(1) No. 1 GG.
29 London Debt Agreement, Feb. 27, 1953, BGBl. II at 336.
30 London Debt Agreement, *supra* note 29, at Art. 5(2).
31 Zwei-Plus-Vier-Vertrag (Final Agreement with respect to Germany), Sep. 12, 1990, BGBl. II at 1318.
32 Not taking into account, of course, any traces of Nazi ideology in the law of the time.

entitled sovereign states – as opposed to individuals – to claim damages for violations of the laws and customs of war or breaches of human rights.[33] While acknowledging the development of public international law in recent years towards the recognition of (limited) individual rights,[34] the Court pointed out that such a development could not be applied retrospectively.

Second, the BGH considered whether the appellants were entitled to claim damages from the German Empire under domestic state liability provisions for malfeasance in office, Section 839(1) BGB[35] in conjunction with Article 131(1) *Weimarer Reichsverfassung* (WRV – Constitution of the German Empire).[36] It concluded that the massacre constituted a breach of official duty incumbent upon the German armed forces[37] by virtue of the Hague Convention Respecting the Laws and Customs of War on Land of 1907. However, the Court reasoned that, during a state of war, large parts of the domestic legal order were suspended and replaced by the *ius in bello*. As stipulated by Article 131(1) WRV, the state was liable only "in principle" for unlawful acts of its officials. According to the BGH, it was the general understanding at the time that war constituted an exceptional relationship between the belligerent states that excluded liability under domestic law for actions committed by the armed forces of one state towards individuals of the other. In this context, the Court rejected the appellants' proposition that the massacre was not a belligerent act but rather a "police operation" for which state liability would not be barred. The events of June 10, 1944, were directly connected with the foregoing armed conflicts and therefore had to be seen – irrespective of the fact that the massacre was directed against civilians – as a military operation.[38]

II. Photo Composition Case[39]

In the *Photo Composition* case, the respondent published an article in one of its financial news magazines about the apparent difficulties of the Deutsche Telekom AG (German Telecom Corporation) and the responsibility for these problems of the company's (then) chief executive officer Dr. Dr. Ron Sommer. The article included a photo composition which portrayed the CEO sitting on a large crumbling "T" which closely resembled the logo of German Telecom. The CEO's head had been taken from another photograph and merged with someone else's body. In this process, the head photograph had been manipulated to apparently create a greedier impression. The face appeared longer, neck and chin both shorter and thicker, and the skin paler. The CEO sought to enjoin the respondent from disseminating the photo composition in the news magazine. He argued that an average person would not recognize the subliminal negative manipulation and would come to

---

33 In part, the Court based its conclusion on Articles 2 and 3 of the Convention Respecting the Laws and Customs of War on Land (Hague IV) of Oct. 18, 1907, which provide that the Convention only applies "between Contracting Powers" and that "a belligerent party" may be liable to pay compensation to another party.
34 Referring to a judgment of the *Bundesverfassungsgericht* (BVerfG – Federal Constitutional Court). See BVerfGE 94, 315 (329).
35 "If an official wilfully or negligently commits a breach of official duty incumbent upon him towards a third party, he shall compensate said party for any damage arising therefrom." (translation by author).
36 "If an official, in exercising entrusted public powers, commits a breach of official duty incumbent upon him towards a third party, the state or public body in whose employ the official serves shall in principle be liable." (translation by author).
37 "Officials" within the meaning of § 839(1) BGB and Article 131(1) WRV.
38 The decision was upheld by the *Bundesverfassungsgericht* (BVefG – Federal Constitutional Court) on February 15, 2006. BVerfG, 33 EUROPÄISCHE GRUNDRECHTE ZEITSCHRIFT (EuGRZ) 105 (2006).
39 BGHZ 156, 206.

believe that the photo composition was an actual representation of his appearance. The *Landgericht* (LG – Regional Court) Hamburg and, on appeal, the *Oberlandesgericht* (OLG – Higher Regional Court) Hamburg granted injunctive relief based on Section 823(1) BGB[40] in conjunction with Section 1004(1)(2) BGB[41] for a violation of the claimant's personality rights. Upon the respondent's complaint against the OLG's refusal to give leave to appeal, the BGH granted special leave on points of law and reversed the previous decisions.

According to the Court, the claimant had to put up with the photo composition as a satirical expression, which was – contrary to the opinion of the OLG – protected by the constitutionally guaranteed freedom of speech, Article 5(1)(1) *Grundgesetz* (GG – Basic Law/German Constitution).[42] The OLG had reasoned that the photo composition did not enjoy the constitutional protection of Article 5(1) GG, since the subliminal changes in the image of the CEO's head created a false impression of the claimant's actual appearance without having any independent satirical meaning. In response, the BGH remarked that an average person would certainly recognize the photo composition as such, because one would not expect the claimant to actually have his picture taken on a large crumbling "T". Moreover, the Court held that no distinction could be drawn between separate parts of a composite work inasmuch as requiring them to each have an independent satirical character. Otherwise, the actual satirical "coating" which enhances a certain message often through mere exaggeration, distortion or alienation could not be protected by Article 5(1) GG. In addition, the BGH pointed out that a "dissecting approach" in determining whether a satirical portrayal falls within the ambit of Article 5(1) GG was already wrong in principle.[43] Such an interpretation would require that every separable part contained satirical elements in order to trigger the constitutional protection of freedom of opinion for the portrayal as a whole. Instead, the test must be whether there is an overall satirical impression in the light of the context of the composition. Since the portrayal of the claimant did not cross the line of unlawful defamation or libel, the Court held that it was *generally* protected as a satire by Article 5(1) GG.

However, pursuant to Subsection (2) of Article 5 GG, freedom of opinion and expression is not guaranteed in absolute terms, but may be proportionally limited by any "general law", that is, a law that is not directed against any specific opinion or expression, but serves to protect legitimate rights or interests of others. Such general provisions are, for example, Sections 823 and 1004 BGB and Sections 22 and 23 *Kunsturhebergesetz* (KUG – Artistic Works Copyright Act)[44] on which an injunction for violations of personality rights

---

[40] "Anyone who, wilfully or negligently, unlawfully injures the life, body, health, freedom, property or other right of another person shall compensate said person for any damage arising therefrom." (translation by author).

[41] "If further interference is to be apprehended, the owner may sue for an injunction." Although the wording of § 1004(1) BGB only covers interference with ownership, subsection (2) is generally applied to interferences with any absolute right set out in § 823(1) BGB.

[42] "Everyone has the right to freely express and disseminate his opinion in speech, writing, and pictures and to freely inform himself from generally accessible sources." (translation by A. TSCHENTSCHER, THE BASIC LAW (GRUNDGESETZ), *available at* http://www.oefre.unibe.ch/law/the_basic_law.pdf).

[43] Referring to judgments of the *Bundesverfassungsgericht* (BVerfG – Federal Constitutional Court) as well as the BGH. See BVerfGE 86, 1 (12); BGHZ 132, 12 (20); BGHZ 139, 95 (102).

[44] *Kunsturhebergesetz* (KUG – Artistic Works Copyright Act), Jan. 9, 1907, RGBl. at 7.
§ 22 KUG: "A person's image may only be disseminated or displayed publicly with the consent of the person depicted. [...]";
§ 23(1) KUG: "Images of the following may be disseminated or displayed publicly without the consent required under § 22 :
1. Persons of contemporary history;
2. [...]";
§ 23(2) KUG: "Subsection (1) does not apply, if the dissemination or display violates legitimate interests of the person depicted [...]." (translation by author).

can be based. However, in determining whether there has been any unlawful infringement, a court must again weigh the conflicting legitimate interest of free expression as a constitutional right. The fundamental rights and freedoms contained in the Basic Law thereby not only serve as defensive rights against the state, but also provide for an objective set of constitutional values which can have an indirect (horizontal) effect in private litigation.[45] The BGH thus had to balance the respondent's fundamental right to freedom of expression against the claimant's general personality right, which is also protected by the constitution.[46] The Court stressed that the manipulation of the claimant's image was marginal and could probably only be noticed by an average person on closer examination. Furthermore, as a well-known public figure – and thus a "relative"[47] person of contemporary history within the meaning of Section 23(1) No. 1 KUG – he could only avail himself of a limited degree of protection in regard to publications relating to a matter of public interest. Consequently, the BGH found no violation of the claimant's personality rights and allowed the respondent's appeal.

On 14 February 2005, the *Bundesverfassungsgericht* (BVerfG – Federal Constitutional Court) ruled on the claimant's constitutional complaint against this decision of the BGH.[48] The Constitutional Court found that the judgment violated the claimant's general personality right protected by Articles 2(1) and 1(1) GG. While it agreed with the BGH that the respondent was free to portray the CEO on a crumbling "T" as a satirical photo composition, the Court held that the subliminal technical manipulation of the claimant's appearance had an individual significance that required a separate examination. The Federal Constitutional Court remanded the matter back to the BGH for a new determination.

D. Family Law

I. Court Approval for Termination of Life Prolonging Measures[49]

In the *Termination of Life Prolonging Measures* case, the BGH was called upon to decide whether a court could formally approve a request to terminate life prolonging measures based on a patient's living will. The applicant's 72-year-old father had suffered hypoxic cerebral damage as a consequence of a myocardial infarct. The resulting apallic syndrome prevented any form of communication with him and required him to be nourished through a percutaneous endoscopic gastrostomy tube (PEG tube). Two years before, he had drawn up a living will which stipulated, *inter alia*, that he wished no life prolonging measures such as artificial nourishment in case he was terminally ill or had sustained irreversible damage to his brain or other vital organs. The applicant was appointed as *Betreuer* (limited guardian for persons of full age) and requested that the use of the PEG tube be discontinued since a recovery of his father was not to be expected. He sought an order from the guardianship division of the *Amtsgericht* (AG – District Court) Lübeck approving his refusal to consent to further medical treatment. The Lübeck District Court and, on appeal, the *Landgericht*

---

45 *See*, for example, the *Lüth* decision of the *Bundesverfassungsgericht* (BVerfG – Federal Constitutional Court). BVerfGE 7, 198 (English translation *available at* http://www.iuscomp.org/gla/judgments/tgcm/v580115.htm).
46 Developed by the *Bundesverfassungsgericht* (BVerfG – Federal Constitutional Court) from an interpretation of Article 2(1) in conjunction with Article 1(1) of the *Grundgesetz* (GG – Basic Law/Constitution).
47 Unlike "absolute" persons of contemporary history, "relative" persons only form part of contemporary history for limited time or in connection with a specific event.
48 BGH, 57 MONATSSCHRIFT FÜR DEUTSCHES RECHT (MDR) 606 (2005).
49 BGHZ 154, 205.

(LG – Regional Court) Lübeck, rejected the application as they saw no legal basis for the requested order. On further appeal, the *Oberlandesgericht* (OLG – Higher Regional Court) Schleswig referred the case to the BGH, as it intended to dismiss the appeal and thereby deviate from earlier decisions of the *Oberlandesgericht* (OLG – Higher Regional Court) Karlsruhe[50] and the *Oberlandesgericht* (OLG – Higher Regional Court) Frankfurt.[51] Both had held that the consent of a *Betreuer* to the termination of life prolonging measures required approval by the guardianship court under Section 1904 BGB.[52] The three central legal questions at issue before the BGH were: first, whether the omission or refusal of a *Betreuer* to consent to life prolonging measures could be subject to court approval in the first place; second, if so, under what circumstances; and third, whether Section 1904 BGB provided a basis for a court order.

The Court first rejected the proposition that, in general, a refusal of consent – in contrast to the consent itself – could not be approved by the guardianship court because it did not constitute an act but rather an omission. The PEG tube constituted an interference with the physical integrity of the applicant's father and therefore required his consent. Since the patient himself was incapable of giving or refusing his consent, the applicant as his *Betreuer* had to act for him. The BGH did not see any legally relevant difference between the acts of granting or (whether expressly or impliedly) refusing consent.

Second, some legal commentators had argued that a court was generally precluded from approving the termination of life prolonging measures as it represents a strictly personal decision of the patient.[53] However, the BGH reasoned that the refusal to consent to life prolonging measures was not an original decision of the *Betreuer*, but rather an act to enforce the strictly personal desire of the patient which he had previously expressed in the living will.

The BGH also rejected the argument set forth by the Schleswig Higher Regional Court that there were insufficient criteria to determine under what circumstances the decision to end life prolonging measures could be approved. On this issue the Court referred to its criminal law jurisprudence on questions of euthanasia,[54] according to which a doctor could legally cease to continue life prolonging measures if the patient was irreversibly and terminally ill and if the termination of such measures met his or her wishes. The Court stressed that in case the patient had set up a living will, which specifically dealt with the issue of life prolonging measures, such a will was paramount and had to be respected.

Consequently, the BGH saw no reason why the refusal to consent to life prolonging measures should *per se* not be susceptible to judicial approval. On the contrary, the Court argued that there was an imperative need for a possibility to answer legal questions touching on the limits of human life and death by judicial means. However, an approval order could neither be based on a direct nor on an analogous application of Section 1904 BGB. In the Court's opinion, the provision intended to protect a curable patient from injury through hazardous medical treatment, whereas the consent of a *Betreuer* to the termination of life prolonging measures (or the refusal to agree to their continuance) aims at the direct opposite, that is, ending the life of an incurable person. Instead, the Court used its inherent power (and duty) as one of the supreme federal courts to develop the law[55] and

---

50 OLG Karlsruhe, 49 Zeitschrift für Familienrecht (FamRZ) 488 (2002).
51 OLG Frankfurt, 49 Zeitschrift für Familienrecht (FamRZ) 575 (2002).
52 "The consent of the *Betreuer* to a physical examination, medical treatment or operation requires the approval of the guardianship court if there is reasonable apprehension that the person affected may die as a consequence of such measure or suffer severe and long-term health injury. [...]" (translation by author).
53 *See, e.g.*, S. Zimmermann, § *1904*, *in* Bürgerliches Gesetzbuch margin note 42 (H.T. Soergel & W. Siebert eds., 13th ed. 2000).
54 *See, e.g.*, BGHSt 40, 257.
55 *See* BVerfGE 34, 296 (297 *et seq.*); K. Larenz & W. Canaris, Methodenlehre der Rechtswissenschaft 232 (3rd ed. 1995).

thereby create an approval requirement outside the provisions of the Civil Code. While acknowledging that the legislature had contemplated the problem of life prolonging measures without making it subject to an approval requirement, the Court nevertheless held that the absence of such a requirement was not to be understood as a strict prohibition on the development of the written law in this respect.[56]

As regards the requirements of an order by the court, the BGH underlined that an approval of the rejection of life prolonging measures could only be sought if such measures were in fact offered by the attending physicians. Under those circumstances, a *Betreuer* could effectively refuse his or her consent to (further) measures only with the approval of the guardianship court. The court must grant the approval, if the patient has irreversibly entered a terminal phase of his or her illness, and if the continuance of life prolonging measures is against the patient's express (or even presumed) will.

The Court emphasized that the requirement of judicial approval serves both the protection of the patient's fundamental rights to life, self-determination and human dignity, as well as the discharge of the *Betreuer*, who could not be expected to solely carry the burden of a decision against life prolonging measures. The review offers the *Betreuer* a procedure by which he or she can obtain certainty as to the legality of the decision (also from a criminal law point of view). Contrary to concerns raised by the Schleswig Higher Regional Court, the BGH stressed that the guardianship court can only examine the refusal of the *Betreuer* and cannot pass its own judgment on the "life and death" of the patient. The BGH, therefore, allowed the appeal and remanded the case back to the Lübeck District Court to determine whether the requirements for an approval of the applicant's refusal to consent to life prolonging measures were met.

II. Judicial Control of Marital Agreements[57]

The claimant and respondent in the *Judicial Control of Marital Agreements* case had been married to each other from 1985 until 2001. The husband worked as a management consultant with a monthly income of 27,000 DM (approximately 13,800 €), while his wife, a university graduate who had been employed as an archeologist for about a year into their marriage, mainly took care of the household and their two children. Since 1994, she has a pre-tax income of about 550 €. In 1988, two years after their first child had been born and a year before the birth of their second child, they concluded a notarized marital agreement. Therein, both renounced any right to postmarital alimony, other than for childcare,[58] should they divorce.[59] They furthermore excluded equalization and adjustment of pension and annuity rights[60] (*Versorgungsausgleich*) as well as equalization of matrimonial surplus (*Zugewinnausgleich*).[61]

56　The Court expressed the view that it would of course be desirable, if the legislature created an adequate legal basis for a decision by the guardianship court.
57　BGHZ 158, 81.
58　§ 1570 BGB provides that every divorced spouse is entitled to alimony in respect of the upbringing of common children, if, and in as much as, this reasonably prevents him or her from pursuing a professional occupation.
59　§ 1585c BGB *generally* permits individual agreements between the spouses as regards postmarital alimony regimes.
60　Otherwise provided for under §§ 1587 BGB.
61　Pursuant to § 1363(1) BGB, unless otherwise agreed upon as permitted by § 1408 BGB, spouses fall under the statutory matrimonial property regime of the so-called "community of surplus". Despite its name, it is not a true community of property. Each spouse owns and administers independently his or her own property, being (in principle) liable only for debts incurred by himself/herself. Any additional wealth created during the period of the regime (surplus) remains the property of the spouse who created it. It will, however, be equalized on termination of the regime, §§ 1371 BGB.

The agreement also provided, however, that for the duration of the marriage the husband would make payments towards an 80,000 DM (approximately 40,900 €) endowment life insurance for his wife.

In 1999, the couple separated permanently. The two children remained with their mother and received child support from their father. As part of the divorce proceedings, the *Amtsgericht* (AG – District Court) Augsburg, acting as a family court, affirmed the exclusion of both the annuity rights adjustment and the equalization of matrimonial surplus. The Augsburg District Court nonetheless awarded the (ex-)wife 4,752 DM (approximately 2,430 €) in monthly alimony payments. On appeal and cross-appeal, the *Oberlandesgericht* (OLG – Higher Regional Court) Munich not only increased this sum to 3,849 €, but also found that the entire marital agreement was void pursuant to Section 138(1) BGB[62] for violation of *gute Sitten* (*boni mores* – good morals/public policy).[63] Relying on two decisions of the *Bundesverfassungsgericht* (BVerfG – Federal Constitutional Court) on the same subject-matter,[64] the Munich Higher Regional Court concluded that the agreement substantially disadvantaged the wife in a manner that exceeded the limits set by constitutional law. The (ex-)husband as applicant in the original divorce proceedings was, however, granted leave to appeal to the BGH on points of law. The BGH overruled the appellate court's decision and remanded the case back to the Munich Higher Regional Court for a fresh determination in conformity with the following considerations.

In its judgments of 2001, the *Bundesverfassungsgericht* (BVerfG – Federal Constitutional Court) had struck down as unconstitutional decisions of the familiy courts enforcing marital agreements that the Court found severely unbalanced. As in earlier decisions, it ruled that the constitutionally protected private autonomy,[65] which includes freedom of contract, presupposes a relative equilibrium of bargaining positions. Where this equilibrium is fundamentally impaired, for example due to structural inferiority, the weaker party's self-determination is reversed into instrumentalization.[66] The Federal Constitutional Court concluded that the state's enforcement of such agreements constitutes a violation of fundamental rights (especially their positive obligatory dimension) guaranteed under the German Constitution.

The BGH took the present case as an opportunity to revisit and adapt its own position to conform with the requirements set by the BVerfG. According to the BGH, spouses are generally free to contractually exclude the statutory provisions on postmarital alimony as well as the equalization of matrimonial surplus and annuity rights. However, the agreement may not totally undermine the protective purpose of these provisions. A line must be drawn where the agreed distribution of marital encumbrances falls entirely short of the individual circumstances of the marriage, as it appears evidently one-sided and – having due regard to the nature and purpose of marriage – unacceptable for the disadvantaged spouse. This will be the case, the more the agreement modifies core provisions of the statutory postmarital scheme. Hence, the BGH developed an echelon of provisions: the mandatory core primarily comprises the right to maintenace for binging up a common child as

---

62 See *supra* note 4.
63 OLG Munich, 50 ZEITSCHRIFT FÜR FAMILIENRECHT (FamRZ) 35 (2003).
64 BVerfGE 103, 89; BVerfG, 54 NEUE JURISTISCHE WOCHENSCHRIFT (NJW) 2248 (2001). *See* Peer Zumbansen, *Public Values, Private Contracts and the Colliding Worlds of Family and Market*, 11 FEMINIST LEGAL STUDIES 71 (2003); Peer Zumbansen, *Federal Constitutional Court Affirms Horizontal Effect of Constitutional Rights in Private Law Relations and Voids a Marital Agreement on Constitutional Grounds*, 2 GERMAN LAW JOURNAL NO. 6 (April 1, 2001), *at* http://www.germanlawjournal.com/article.php?id=61; Peer Zumbansen, *Constitutional Control of Marital Agreements II: The FCC Affirms Its Path-Breaking Decision*, 2 GERMAN LAW JOURNAL NO. 15 (September 15, 2001), *at* http://www.germanlawjournal.com/article.php?id=86.
65 GRUNDGESETZ (Constitution) art. 2(1).
66 *Compare* Hestermeyer, *supra* note 1, at 449 (*Joint Credit Liability of Relatives* case).

well as maintenance for illness and retirement. These rights take priority over other forms of alimony. The equalization of pension and annuity rights essentially constitutes anticipated retirement alimony and is therefore not subject to the disposition of the spouses without restriction. Finally, the equalization of matrimonial surplus can be freely excluded, since the law itself envisages different matrimonial property regimes.[67]

The Court then outlined how the family courts are to control the adherence of marital agreements to the principles illustrated above. In a first step, the courts must determine the validity of the agreement pursuant to Section 138(1) BGB on the basis of an overall assessment of the individual circumstances *at the time of the conclusion of the agreement*, having special regard to the spouses' respective capital assets and earning capacities as well as their (planned or realized) style of living. An agreement will generally only be contrary to *boni mores*, if it waives core postmarital support consequences without alleviating the negative effects through benefits of some other form. Where the agreement does in fact violate Section 138(1) BGB, the statutory postmarital regime applies. Otherwise, the courts must examine if – and to what extent – one spouse's reliance on the agreement appears contrary to the principles of good faith (Section 242 BGB) in view of the circumstances *at the time of the divorce proceedings*. In such a case, the family court must modify the contractual terms and grant relief that accomodates both parties' legitimate interests in a balanced way.

E. Intellectual Property Law

I. Legality of Deep Links – Paperboy Case[68]

The claimant in the *Paperboy* case publishes various newspapers and magazines in print; a selection of articles is also made freely available on the claimant's websites. The respondent operated an internet search engine ("Paperboy") for online newspaper articles free of charge. After entering a search string, the search engine combed through several online versions of newspapers and other news-related websites, all of which were freely accessible without password protection. The results of the search were delivered as a list of so-called "deep links," that is, hyperlinks that bypassed the homepage of the news website and led the user directly to the specific page where the article containing the search string was located. Apart from the internet address (URL) of each article, the results also contained a reference to the source and short fragments of the respective article. As a special service, Paperboy offered to automatically email the user a list of deep links based on pre-defined keywords every morning as a "personalized daily newspaper". The claimant sued for an injunction alleging that the service infringed its intellectual property rights under the *Urheberrechtsgesetz* (UrhG – Copyright Act) and constituted an act of unfair competition. The decision of the *Landgericht* (LG – Regional Court) Cologne granting the injunction on grounds of unfair competition pursuant to Section 1 *Gesetz gegen den unlauteren Wettbewerb* (UWG – Act Against Unfair Competition)[69] was reversed in part by the *Oberlandesgericht* (OLG – Higher Regional Court) Cologne. The claimant appealed this decision to the BGH seeking restoration of the original judgment. Although the BGH primarily dismissed the appeal for

---

67 §§ 1408 BGB.
68 BGH, 56 Neue Juristische Wochenschrift (NJW) 3406 (2003). *See* Dreier & Nolte, *Liability for Deep Links – Paperboy*, 4 Computer Law Review International 184 (2003).
69 "Any person who, in the course of business activity and for the purpose of competition, commits acts contrary to honest practices may be enjoined from such acts and held liable for damages." (translation by R. Beler, *available at* www.ip-firm.de/uwg_e.pdf). The original Act of 1909 was significantly modified in 2004. The provisions of the old § 1 UWG can now be found in §§ 3, 8 and 9 UWG.

procedural reasons because the complaint against the respondent had been formulated too imprecisely, the Court nevertheless ruled on the merits of the case instead of remanding it back to the Cologne Higher Regional Court.

The Court first considered whether Section 97 UrhG entitled the claimant to enjoin the respondent from offering the Paperboy service. This required a violation of the rights granted by the Copyright Act. As far as the right to reproduction pursuant to Section 16 UrhG was concerned, the Court found that neither the adoption of short fragments of the copyrighted articles nor the setting of the deep links amounted to an infringement. On the one hand, each fragment in itself was too insubstantial to benefit from the protection of literary works and therefore did not constitute a relevant copy of the respective article. On the other hand, the hyperlinks merely consisted of the internet address where the articles were located and contained no part of the articles. Moreover, the Court ruled that the respondent could not be held liable for potential subsequent copyright infringements by the users of the service as it only facilitated access to the articles that were already – without any technical measures of protection – accessible to the public. The BGH rejected the proposition that deep links increased the danger of unlawful copying of the articles by the user who could also access the articles freely through the respective homepage.

For essentially the same reasons, the Court also concluded that the setting of deep links did not infringe the new[70] right to make works available to the public established by Section 15(2) UrhG. The BGH reasoned that the articles had already been made available to the public by the claimant who placed them on the respective websites and could solely decide how long they remained there. While the Paperboy service enabled users to access articles they otherwise might not have otherwise found, its primary function did not go beyond that of a "footnote" or other reference in a printed document.[71]

The Court then turned to the question whether the Paperboy service infringed the *sui generis* rights secured by Section 87b(1) UrhG[72] and accorded to the maker of a database. While assuming that the claimant's newspaper websites were databases within the definition of Section 87a UrhG,[73] and that the respondent had extracted insubstantial parts of the databases in a repeated and systematic manner, the BGH nevertheless held that the respondent's service did not conflict with the normal exploitation of the respective databases or unreasonably prejudiced legitimate interests of the newspaper publishers. In the Court's opinion, the utilization of the short fragments did not replace but rather stimulated the further use of the databases by allowing users to decide whether or not an article was of interest to them. Moreover, the fragments – taken together – did not constitute a substantial part of the database.

Having rejected an injunction based on infringements of rights granted by the Copyright Act, the Court finally considered whether the respondent's service and its use of deep links constituted an act of unfair competition within the meaning of Section 1

---

70 Council Directive 2001/29, Information Society Directive, art. 3, 2001 O.J. (L 167) 10 (EC).
71 In a decision of the U.S. District Court for the Central District of California on the issue of deep links, the court compared the use of deep links to "using a library's card index to get reference to particular items, albeit faster and more efficiently". Ticketmaster Corp. et al. v. Tickets.Com, Inc. 54 U.S.P.Q. 2d 1344 (2000).
72 "The maker of the database has the exclusive right to reproduce, to distribute and to communicate to the public the whole database or a qualitatively or quantitatively substantial part thereof. The repeated or systematical reproduction, distribution or communication to the public of qualitatively and quantitatively insubstantial parts of the database shall be deemed as equivalent to the reproduction, distribution or communication of a qualitatively or quantitatively substantial part of the database provided that these acts run counter to a normal exploitation of the database or unreasonably prejudice the legitimate interests of the maker of the database." (translation by Inter Nationes e.V., *Copyright in the Federal Republic of Germany*, available at http://www.goethe.de/in/download/dengl/urheberrecht-e.pdf); based on Council Directive 1996/98, Database Directive, art. 7, 1996 O.J. (L 77) 20 (EC).
73 *See* Council Directive 1996/98, Database Directive, art. 7 (1), 1996 O.J. (L 77) 20 (EC).

UWG. The claimant had argued that the service illegally exploited the labour of the newspaper websites. The Court disagreed and found that the respondent was instead offering a distinctly separate and useful service, which, of course, built on the existence of publicly available articles on the World Wide Web. By citing the source of the articles, the respondent, in the view of the Court, did not mislead the user as to their true origin.

The BGH also rejected the argument that the use of deep links violated legitimate interests in bypassing advertisements placed on the homepages from which a user would normally begin his or her search. In the Court's opinion, the claimant could neither demand nor expect that a freely available document on the internet was only accessed in a certain, often cumbersome way. While services like Paperboy provided an effective method of retrieving and filtering the tremendous amount of information available on the internet, the Court reasoned that the claimant was free to implement technical measures to prevent access by search engines.

F. Company Law

I. Recognition of Legal Capacity for Companies from the EC – Überseering Decision[74]

In November 1992, the claimant company Überseering BV, incorporated under Netherlands law with limited liability, engaged the respondent Nordic Construction Company Baumanagement GmbH, a company established in Germany, to refurbish a garage and motel that the claimant had previously purchased in the German city of Düsseldorf. The contractual obligations were performed, but Überseering BV claimed that the paint work was defective. In December 1994, two German nationals residing in Düsseldorf acquired all the shares in Überseering BV. The company then unsuccessfully sought compensation from the respondent for the defective work and brought an action before the *Landgericht* (LG – Regional Court) Düsseldorf claiming 1,163,657.77 DM (approximately 595,000 €) plus interest in 1996. The Düsseldorf Regional Court dismissed the action, which was affirmed on appeal by the *Oberlandesgericht* (OLG – Higher Regional Court) Düsseldorf. Both found that the claimant company lacked legal capacity under German law and therefore could not be a party to legal proceedings, Section 50(1) *Zivilprozessordnung* (ZPO – Code of Civil Procedure).[75] The courts reasoned that, according to settled case law of the BGH, a company's legal capacity must be determined by reference to the law applicable in the place of the company's actual centre of administration ("*Sitztheorie*" – company seat principle), as opposed to the law applicable in the state in which the company was incorporated ("*Gründungstheorie*" – incorporation principle). Furthermore, this rule also applied where a company has been validly incorporated in a foreign state and has subsequently transferred its actual centre of administration to Germany. Since, under German law, the centre of administration is the place where the management of a company is active, the Düsseldorf Higher Regional Court found that, by virtue of the transfer of shares to the two German nationals residing in Düsseldorf, the claimant had moved its actual centre of administration to Germany. Consequently, the OLG held that Überseering BV did not enjoy legal capacity unless it was reincorporated under German law.

On the claimant's appeal, the BGH noted that the Court's previous application of the company seat principle had not remained uncontested. Especially in the case where a company's actual centre of administration has been transferred from one Member State of the European Communities to another, the BGH now wondered whether the freedom of establishment guaranteed by Articles 43 and 48 of the Treaty establishing the European

---

74 BGHZ 154, 185.
75 Under Section 50(1) ZPO, any person, including a company, having legal capacity may be a party to legal proceedings; legal capacity being defined as the capacity to be the subject of rights and obligations.

Communities (TEC) precluded connecting the company's legal position with the law of the Member State in which its actual centre of administration is located. While the Court considered it preferable,[76] in view of the current state of Community law and of company law within the European Union, to continue to follow its previous jurisprudence, it also found that an answer could not be clearly deduced from the case law of the ECJ.[77] The BGH, therefore, by order of March 30, 2000, stayed the proceedings and referred the questions on the interpretation of Articles 43 and 48 TEC to the European Court of Justice (ECJ) for a preliminary ruling pursuant to Article 234 TEC.[78]

In its judgment[79] of November 5, 2002, the ECJ ruled that it is incompatible with the freedom of establishment for a member state to deny a company, which was formed in accordance with the law of another member state but has since moved its actual centre of administration, legal capacity and, consequently, capacity to be a party to legal proceedings. Moreover, the ECJ held that, where a company duly formed in one member state exercises its freedom of establishment in another member state, Articles 43 and 48 TEC require the other member state to recognize the company's legal capacity and capacity to be a party to legal proceedings just as it enjoys those rights under the laws of its state of incorporation.[80]

Since the BGH was bound by the decision of the ECJ, the Court had to reverse its own position on the determination of legal capacity of companies that were incorporated in a member state of the European Community but had moved their actual centre of administration to Germany. The Court also had to give up an alternative approach developed in a decision[81] of July 1, 2002, according to which a foreign company could not be recognized in its original corporate form (with limited liability), but as a civil law partnership ("GbR") or general commercial partnership ("OHG") with legal capacity and standing to sue. The BGH held that it would equally violate the freedom of establishment if the foreign company was forced to adopt a non-corporate form (without the possibility of limited liability).

As the claimant enjoyed legal capacity and capacity to be a party to legal proceedings under Netherlands law, the BGH allowed the appeal and remanded the case back to the Düsseldorf Regional Court for consideration of the merits.

G. Securities Law

I. Liability for Wrong Ad Hoc Announcements – Informatec AG Cases[82]

In the *Informatec AG* cases,[83] the BGH delivered one of its most important decisions in

---

76 Mostly for reasons of granting creditors, shareholders and employees the protection of German corporate law, which can be considered fairly strict by international standards.
77 Case C-81/87, The Queen v. Treasury and Commissioners of Inland Revenue, *ex parte* Daily Mail and General Trust, 1988 E.C.R. 5483; Case C-212/97, Centros, 1999 E.C.R. I-1459.
78 BGH, 54 WERTPAPIERMITTEILUNGEN (WM) 1257 (2000); BGH, 21 ZEITSCHRIFT FÜR WIRTSCHAFTSRECHT (ZIP) 967 (2000).
79 Case C-208/00, Überseering BV v. Nordic Construction Company GmbH (NCC), 2002 E.C.R. I-9919, 9943.
80 For a comprehensive discussion of the ECJ's decision, *see* Baelz & Baldwin, *The End of the Real Seat Theory (Sitztheorie): the European Court of Justice Decision in Ueberseering of 5 November 2002 and its Impact on German and European Company Law*, 3 GERMAN LAW JOURNAL NO. 12 (December 1, 2002), at http://www.germanlawjournal.com/past_issues.php? id=214.
81 BGHZ 151, 204. The approach was first advanced by the Advocate General in the *Überseering* case before the ECJ.
82 BGHZ 160, 134; BGHZ 160, 149.
83 The BGH delivered a third judgment (BGH II ZR 217/03) concerning identical claims against the executives of Informatec AG by a third plaintiff. This case, however, was remanded to the trial court for further determination and assessment of questions of fact, especially issues of causation.

the area of securities law in recent years.[84] Informatec AG – a company formerly listed on the NEMAX50® (the index of a former segment of the Frankfurt Stock Exchange for new technology companies) and now insolvent – had issued incorrect *ad hoc* announcements about substantial business deals. The announced contracts were in fact of a far lower scale or had not been concluded at all. The statements had been initiated and approved by the company's CEO and his deputy. Several investors alleged that they had been induced by the announcements to buy shares in Informatec AG, which were later worth only a fraction of a Euro each. In the case of *BGHZ 160, 134*, the investor himself sued the company's executives for damages, whereas in *BGHZ 160, 149*, the investor assigned his claims to a lawyer who, in turn, brought an action against the respondents. This enabled the investor to formally testify as a witness on the question of reliance on the announcements.[85] While the assignee claimant was succesful before the *Landgericht* (LG – Regional Court) Augsburg, the other investor lost his case primarily for lack of proof that he had relied on the anouncements. On appeal, the *Oberlandesgericht* (OLG – Higher Regional Court) Munich dismissed both lawsuits. On further appeal, the BGH reversed the decision of the Munich Higher Regional Court in the case where the investor had testified, and affirmed the dismissal of the other action.

The Court examined the claims against the executives of Informatec AG under several possibilities: First, it had to determine whether an incorrect *ad hoc* announcement could be seen as a "share issue prospectus," potentially triggering liability under a cause of action previously developed by case law.[86] The BGH answered this question in the negative, mainly because it found that an investor can expect a prospectus to accurately and comprehensively convey *all information* relevant for making an investment decision.[87] In contrast, an *ad hoc* announcement generally deals with single events only, informing about new, previously unpublished particulars.

Second, the Court rejected liability of the executives under Section 823(2) BGB[88] in connection with an infrigement of two statutory provisions, Section 15 *Wertpapierhandelsgesetz* (WpHG – Securities Trading Act) and Section 88 *Börsengesetz* (BörsG – Stock Exchange Act), in force at the time the announcements had been made.[89] Since Section 823(2) BGB requires the infringement of a statute *intended to protect the claimant*, either Section 15 WpHG obligating issuers of securities to disclose any new material information without delay, or Section 88 BörsG prohibiting fraudulent acts intended to influence stock prices, had to fulfil this prerequisite. As for Section 15 WpHG, the BGH reasoned that the express exclusion of civil liability for infringements in subsection 6 of the provision showed that the legislature had not intended to protect individual investors but only the

---

84   See Dirk Reidenbach, *Executives' Liability for Wrong Ad Hoc Announcements – A Small Step Forward: A Comment on* In re Informatec AG, *BGH II ZR 217/03, 218/03 and 402/02 of 19 July 2004*, 5 GERMAN LAW JOURNAL 1081 (2004), *at* http://www.germanlawjournal.com/pdf/Vol05/No09/PDF_Vol05_No_09_1081-1093_Private_Reidenbach.pdf.
85   Under German law, parties to a civil lawsuit cannot themselves testify as a witness. However, under §§ 445 et seq. *Zivilprozessordnung* (ZPO – Code of Civil Procedure) interrogation of the parties (*Parteivernehmung*) is another form of admissable evidence. Pursuant to § 447 ZPO, the Court may, on the motion of the party which is under the obligation to furnish proof, interrogate that party, if the opposing party agrees. Where the opposing party disagrees, § 448 ZPO empowers the Court to interrogate *ex officio*, provided that there is an initial likelihood (*Anfangswahscheinlichkeit*) that the fact to be proven is true.
86   See BGHZ 71, 284.
87   BGHZ 123, 106 (109).
88   § 823 BGB provides: "(1) Anyone who, wilfully or negligently, unlawfully injures the life, body, health, freedom, property or other right of another person shall compensate said person for any damage arising therefrom. (2) The same shall apply to anyone who infringes a statutory provision intended for the protection of the aggrieved person. [...]" (translation by author).
89   Now §§ 15, 15a WpHG and §§ 20a, 38 WpHG respectively.

capital market as such. The Court arrived at the same conclusion with regard to Section 88 BörsG, holding that the factual protection enjoyed by investors under this provision was only a reflex to the intended protection of the market.[90] Although three other (criminal offence) provisions, Section 400(1) No. 1 *Aktiengesetz* (AktG – Stock Corporation Act) and Sections 263, 264a *Strafgesetzbuch* (StGB – Criminal Code), that were of relevance to the case would have qualified as protective statutes within the meaning of Section 823(2) BGB, the Court held that neither of them had been violated by the respondents.

Finally, the BGH turned to liability under Section 826 BGB.[91] In both cases the claimants had been able to demonstrate before the trial court that the respondents knew about the falsity of their announcements. As the BGH is, in principle, bound by factual findings of the lower courts,[92] it had to accept these facts as proven. On this basis, the Court held that the appellate court erred in concluding that the facts only supported negligence on the part of the respondents. According to the BGH, it was clear that they had acted wilfully, knowing their announcements to be incorrect and being aware of the impact these may have on potential investors. Furthermore, the Court found that the respondents had acted contrary to *boni mores*, since they had – out of self interest, derived from their ownership of a considerable number of shares – resorted to illegal means for pushing the share price. However, for the plaintiffs to succeed on their claims they still had to prove that they actually relied on the wrong *ad hoc* announcements in making their investment decisions. While the assignee plaintiff had been able to call the assignor as a witness on this point, the other claimant, who bought shares of Informatec AG many months after the announcements had been made, was unable to substantiate his reliance on the statements. The BGH held that the latter could not avail himself of any presumption of reliance as had been previously developed by the Court for share issue prospectuses.[93] Again, the Court stressed the fundamental differences between prospectuses and *ad hoc* announcements. It also found that there was no *prima facie* evidence for investment decisions being primarily based on such announcements, as investors are influenced by a great variety of both rational and irrational factors. Taking into account the rather long period between the announcements and the actual share purchase, the BGH finally concluded that the trial court did not err in holding that there was no initial likelihood of actual reliance, a conclusion tat justified the trial court's denial of requests to examine the claimant pursuant to Section 448 ZPO.[94]

As regards the scope of damages recoverable by the assignee claimant, the BGH awarded full compensation of the initially paid share price. Contrary to the decision of the Augsburg Regional Court, which had only granted the difference between the actual price and the price that would have been paid had the announcements been correct, the BGH found that the claimant was entitled to restitution in kind under Section 249(1) BGB. He could therefore claim from the respondents the entire purchase price in exchange for the (nearly worthless) shares.

---

90 BVerfG, 23 ZEITSCHRIFT FÜR WIRTSCHAFTSRECHT (ZIP) 1986, 1988 (2002); BTDrucks 10/318, 44–46, *available at* http://www.bundestag.de.
91 § 826 BGB provides: "Anyone who wilfully inflicts damage on another person in a manner contrary to boni mores shall be liable to compensate said person for the loss resulting therefrom." (translation by author). Unlike § 823(1) BGB, this provision also allows the recovery of mere economic or financial loss, however, requires that the respondent acted wilfully and not just negligently.
92 § 559(2) ZPO.
93 BGHZ 139, 225 (233). Meanwhile, the legislature has taken up this reversal of the burden of proof in § 45(2) No.1 BörsG, now requiring the issuing company to prove that the investor did not rely on the prospectus. Pursuant to § 44(1).1 BörsG, a claim may only be made for purchases of shares within six months of their issue.
94 *See supra* note 85.

Report – *Bundesgerichtshof in Strafsachen* (Federal Court of Justice, Criminal Law) – 2002/2003

Ralph Grunewald and Christoph J.M. Safferling*

A. Introduction

Choosing a limited number of decisions and judgments from the jurisprudence of the *Bundesgerichtshof* (BGH – Federal Court of Justice) in criminal matters of one year is a delicate matter. Which of the topics are relevant and interesting enough for an international audience? Which of them are important enough or maybe indicate a shift in the Court's reasoning. We report on a series of substantive criminal law issues addressed by the BGH that either carry an international character or seem to us to be paradigmatic for German criminal law, which is often quite different from the Anglo-American legal culture.[1] Unfortunately, space limitations have required us to neglect a number of cases that raised not-insignificant criminal procedure issues. We have chosen eight decisions dealing with substantive criminal law. These pertain to issues of what is called the General Part of criminal law,[2] namely agency (B.I. and B.II. below), self-defense (B.III.1.–3. below), intoxication and diminished responsibility (B.IV. 1 and B.IV.2 below), and inchoate offenses (B.V. below). Even the focus on substantive criminal law did not allow us to avoid leaving aside a number of hot issues, like the so-called *Gubener Hetzjagd*,[3] the question of what

---

* Ralph Grunewald, Dr. jur. (Mainz), LL.M. (University of Wisconsin-Madison) is at present a visiting scholar at the University of Wisconsin, Madison. Christoph Safferling, Dr. iur (Munich), LL.M. (LSE), is Assistant Professor in the Institute for Criminal Law, Criminal Procedural Law and Criminology of the University of Erlangen-Nürnberg, Germany and a member of the editorial board of *German Law Journal*.

1 There is a new, English-language textbook on German Criminal Law. See VOLKER KREY, 1 GERMAN CRIMINAL LAW: BASICS (2002); VOLKER KREY, 2 GERMAN CRIMINAL LAW: LEGAL ELEMENTS OF THE INTENTIONAL OFFENCE COMMITTED BY ACTION (2003). For a review of this publication, *see* Lutz Eidam, *Review Essay – Facilitating a Comparative Analysis of Criminal Law: Volker Krey's Bilingual Textbook on German Criminal Law*, 5 GERMAN LAW JOURNAL 1171 (2004). As often as possible, we will refer to this publication which might be more easily accessible for the international audience than literature in the German language.

2 The differentiation between a "general" and a "special" part of criminal law is widely used in jurisdictions with a codified criminal law. The German *Strafgesetzbuch* (StGB – Criminal Code) is split into the General Part, comprising §§ 1–79b, and the Special Part, consisting of §§ 80–358. This approach is unquestioned in Germany. *See* KREY, 1 GERMAN CRIMINAL LAW, *supra* note 1, at margin numbers 35–40. The differentiation is also known to common law jurisdictions. Compare GLANVILLE WILLIAMS, CRIMINAL LAW. THE GENERAL PART V (2nd ed., 1961). It has been called a tradition by Michael Moor. *See* MICHAEL MOOR, PLACING BLAME 30 (1997). It is also criticized as impracticable. *See, e.g.*, Nicola Lacey, *Contingency, Coherence, and Conceptualism: Reflections on the Encounter between "Critique" and "the Philosophy of the Criminal Law," in* PHILOSOPHY AND THE CRIMINAL LAW 9, 48 (Antony Duff ed., 1998).

3 In this case a number of Neo-Nazis persecuted several foreigners. In the course of the chivvy one of the foreigners died because he cut himself when he was attempting to flee into a house. He acted in sheer panic while his persecutors had long given up their attempts to find him. The skinheads where convicted for "*versuchte Körperverletzung mit Todesfolge*" according to §§ 227, 22, 23 StGB (attempting to inflict bodily injury resulting in the death of the victim). *See* BGHSt 48, 34–39.

the defendant has to do for a withdrawal defense against a charge of an attempted crime,[4] or whether a loaded booby pistol qualifies as a weapon within the meaning of §250 StGB (armed robbery),[5] to name but three. Individual crimes of the Special Part of criminal law are only of marginal interest in this report. Nevertheless, the law of murder (B.III.1. and B.III.3. below) will be an issue. By this we hope to provide an interesting *tour d'horizon* of the activity of the BGH in criminal matters.[6]

B. Substantive Criminal Law

I. SED cases: BGHSt 48, 77

1. Previous Cases

Since the unification of Germany on October 3, 1990 prosecutors and judges have had to deal with political crimes that were perpetrated in the former German Democratic Republic (GDR or East Germany), including a number of judgments concerning border guard incidents along the former East/West German boundary. The *Bundesgerichtshof* issued its latest decision in this regard on November 6, 2002.[7] In the first of these cases the BGH had to deal with those soldiers that pulled the trigger and shot to death citizens of the GDR during attempts to surmount the border fences and reach the Federal Republic of Germany (FRG or West Germany). In a spectacular judgment of November 3, 1992 the BGH declared void GDR legislation that justified the use of all necessary means to prevent border trespassing.[8] In its reasoning the BGH relied mainly on the formula of Gustav Radbruch, which the well-known scholar and pre-Nazi Minister of Justice of the Weimar Republic developed after World War II. "Radbruch's Formula," as the jurisprudential claim has come to be known, holds that a manifestly unjust law is void.[9] Thus, these mostly young soldiers were sentenced to two years probation.[10] The convictions were, however,

---

4 The accused in that case opened two gas taps in his kitchen in a house with 12 apartments in order to commit suicide. He realized that this could also lead to an explosion. He called the fire department but did not close the gas taps. The fire-fighters evacuated about 50 persons and eventually managed to cut the gas line after the accused had lost consciousness. On appeal, the BGH quashed the conviction for attempting to cause an explosion (§§ 308, 22, 23 StGB). The Court held that, according to § 24 StGB, the accused withdrew from the attempt by informing the fire department. See BGHSt 48, 147–152.

5 The question of what qualifies as a weapon has already generated a vast amount of jurisprudence in Germany. The issue is important because in several instances carrying a weapon leads to a much more severe penalty for the defendant. Thus an armed robbery is followed by imprisonment of at least three years (§ 250 (I) StGB), whereas an ordinary robbery has a minimum sentence of one year imprisonment (§ 249 (I) StGB). See HERBERT TRÖNDLE & THOMAS FISCHER, STRAFGESETZBUCH, § 244 margin numbers 3–5 (52nd ed.. 2004). The BGH (in this case the Grand Senate – see below C.I.2.b.) has held that even a loaded booby pistol, by which the pressure of the explosion escapes at the front, qualifies as a weapon. See BGHSt 48, 197–206.

6 A translation of the StGB is provided by the Federal Ministry of Justice *at* http://www.iuscomp.org/gla/statutes/StGB.htm and of the StPO *at* http://www.iuscomp.org/gla/statutes/StPO.htm. Translations and terminology used in this text stem from this "official" translation.

7 BGHSt 48, 77.

8 BGHSt 39, 1.

9 Gustav Radbruch, *Gesetzliches Recht und übergestezliches Unrecht*, SÜDDEUTSCHE JURISTENZEITUNG (SJZ) 105, 107 (1946). A law is unjust if it manifestly disregards fundamental human rights. See BGHSt 39, 1 (16–20). It is interesting to note in this context that international criminal law, as laid down in the Rome Statute of the International Criminal Court, has adopted a similar formula concerning superior orders and prescription of law. According to Art. 33 (I) c of the Rome Statute, orders do not relieve the accused of criminal responsibility if they are "manifestly unlawful."

10 See BGHSt 39, 1; BGHSt 39, 168; BGHSt 40, 218 (231); BGHSt 45, 270 (295).

criticized for neglecting the *Schuldprinzip* (principle of culpability),[11] which would have required the courts to take account of the fact that the soldiers acted in an *unvermeidbarer Verbotsirrtum* (unavoidable error in law).[12] The BGH tried to take heed of this shortcoming by imposing a relatively lenient sentence.[13] This was not meant as a concession by the Court that its reasoning was flawed and the Court has not changed its view since.[14] Indeed, the Court's reasoning in the border guard jurisprudence was upheld by the *Bundesverfassungsgericht* (BVerfG – Federal Constitutional Court).[15]

In the wake of this initial round of transitional justice, the newly unified German justice system did its best not to be confined to the criticism of prosecuting the "little offenders" while turning a blind-eye toward the political leaders of the former GDR.[16] Consequently, there were trials against the military leaders,[17] against members of the *Nationaler Verteidigungsrat* (National Defense Council),[18] and against members of the *Politbüro* (Political Bureau), the SED-party[19] council that was actually responsible for all political decisions in the GDR.[20] The case against *Krenz, Schabowski and Kleiber*[21] (all of them members of both the *Politbüro* and the National Defense Council) was upheld by the European Court on Human Rights.[22] The pursuit of justice for crimes arising out of the GDR regime can be characterized as a "bottom-up" effort; at first those were prosecuted who were the direct actors and only thereafter was the responsible leadership tried.[23]

---

11 The "*Schuldprinzip*" is one of the main principles of German criminal law: "*nulla poena sine culpa.*" It is embedded in Art. 1 (I) of the *Grundgesetz* (GG – Basic Law or Constitution) as decided by the *Bundesverfassungsgericht* (BVerfG – Federal Constitutional Court) in several decisions. See, e.g., BVerfGE 57, 250 (275). The BGH accepted the principle in the early leading case of March 18, 1952, see BGHSt 2, 194 (200) ("Punishment requires culpability. Culpability means blameworthiness. The dishonorable condemnation of culpability denotes that the perpetrator is reproached with having acted unlawfully…, although he could have acted lawfully, i.e. he could have decided in favor of the law.") (translation from KREY, 2 GERMAN CRIMINAL LAW, *supra* note 1, at margin number 221.) The exact content of the principle of culpability and its consequences are heavily debated. See HANS-HEINRICH JESCHECK & THOMAS WEIGEND, LEHRBUCH DES STRAFRECHTS. ALLGEMEINER TEIL 404–430 (5th ed. 1996). The Jescheck and Weigend book is a classical introduction. For an introduction, the Anglo-American reader might find George Fletcher's book valuable: GEORGE FLETCHER, RETHINKING CRIMINAL LAW 737–755 (1978).
12 According to §17 StGB, an unavoidable mistake of law excludes culpability. See CLAUS ROXIN, 1 STRAFRECHT – ALLGEMEINER TEIL §21 margin numbers 66–67 (3rd ed., 1997); Klaus Rogall, *Bewältigung von Systemkriminalität*, in 50 JAHRE BUNDESGERICHTSHOF 428–430 (Claus-Wilhelm Canaris et al., eds., 2000).
13 See Klaus Detter, *Die Bewältigung der Wiedervereinigung durch den BGH in Strafsachen*, in HAGENER UNIVERSITÄTSREDEN 35, 49 (Rektor Fernuni Hagen ed., 2002).
14 See BGHSt 39, 1 (16–20).
15 BVerfGE 95, 96 (133) (referring to the principle of justice and the respect for generally accepted human rights).
16 This was problematic in particular as the trial against the former GDR head of state Erich Honecker could not take place due to alleged sickness. See Berlin Constitutional Court, 100 INTERNATIONAL LAW REPORTS 393 (1995).
17 The leading case is: BGHSt 44, 204.
18 BGHSt 40, 218; BGHSt 45, 270 (286).
19 Sozialistische Einheitspartei – SED (Socialist Unity Party).
20 BGHSt 45, 270 (295).
21 BGHSt 45, 270.
22 Streletz, Kessler and Krenz v. Germany, Eur. Ct. H.R., Application Nos. 34044/96, 35532/97 and 44801/98 (March 22, 2001), *available at* http://cmiskp.echr.coe.int/tkp197/portal.asp?sessionId=3599368&skin=hudoc-en&action=request.
23 In prosecuting NS-crimes the opposite approach, i.e. a "top-down" procedure, had been taken. See Rogall, *supra* note 12, at 418.

2. The *Politbüro* Case

The Court's notable case from November 6, 2002 involved the criminal prosecution of GDR *Politbüro* members. In previous cases involving the *Politbüro* members mentioned above, the crimes implicated included incitement to murder for having voted in favor of granting boarder guards the authority to shoot trespassers to death. The present case involved those *Politbüro* members who did not participate actively in the border policy but did nothing to prevent the shootings at the border. The BGH had to decide whether *Politbüro* members could be held criminally responsible for such an omission.

The peculiarity of criminal proceedings concerned with actions perpetrated under the SED regime in East Germany lies in the fact that the Western judges have to look at the case both from the perspective of former East German law and from the perspective of West German criminal law. This is so because, according to Article 315 Section 1 of the *Einführungsgesetz Strafgesetzbuch* (EGStGB – Introductory Act to the Criminal Code)[24] and §3 (III) of the *Strafgesetzbuch* (StGB – Criminal Code)[25] in the form of the Unification Treaty,[26] the courts must apply the norm which has the least severe consequences for the accused.[27]

The BGH found two different lines of reasoning to support the conclusion that, in both cases before the Court, the accused *Politbüro* members should be held criminally liable for failing to intervene in the GDR's lethal border policy.[28] First, the Court found that, according to former East German criminal law, the accused could have been found guilty of abetting the murder of those seeking to flee across the border.[29] The Court reasoned that by failing to object during the relevant sessions of the *Politbüro*, the accused members supported the fact that the *Politbüro*, as such, ordered the repressive policy at the border. The Court further explained that the accused would have been guilty, under GDR criminal law, of abetting the incitement (on the part of the *Politbüro*) of murder. Abetting a party engaged in inciting a crime, the Court explained, is a position of culpability commensurate with that of abetting the primary actor.[30]

Second, the Court noted that, according to West German law, the *Politbüro* members could not be charged for participating in the criminal act of another (through inciting or abetting the primary actor).[31] Instead, they were being found criminally liable because they

---

24 Einführungsgesetz zum Strafgesetzbuch (EGStGB) (Introductory Act to the Criminal Code) Mar. 2, 1974, BGBl. I at 469.
25 Strafgesetzbuch (StGB) (Criminal Code) Nov. 13, 1998, BGBl. I at 3322.
26 Vertrag zwischen der Bundesrepublik Deutschland und der Deutschen Demokratischen Republik über die Herstellung der Einheit Deutschlands (Unification Treaty), Aug. 31, 1990, BGBl. II at 885.
27 *See* Johannes Wasmuth, *Straf- und Strafverfahrensrecht nach dem Einigungsvertrag*, 11 NEUE ZEITSCHRIFT FÜR STRAFRECHT (NStZ) 160 (1991). *See also* Heinrich Wilhelm Laufhütte, *Strafrechtliche Probleme nach der Wiedervereinigung der beiden deutschen Staaten und ihre Bewältigung durch die Strafsenate des BGH*, ZEITSCHRIFT FÜR VERMÖGENS- UND IMMOBILIENRECHT (VIZ) 521 (2001).
28 BGHSt 48, 77 (79–80).
29 This was the case according to §§9, 22 of the Strafgesetzbuch of the GDR. *See* STRAFRECHT DER DDR, KOMMENTAR ZUM STGB (Staatsverlag der DDR, 5th ed. 1987).
30 BGHSt 48, 77 (81–87).
31 According to West German criminal law criminal responsibility is split into two forms: authorship/perpetration (*Täterschaft*) on the one hand, and participation (*Teilnahme*) on the other hand. Perpetration takes always priority over participation. Therefore criminal courts must first ask whether the accused can be held liable for the commission of the crime. According to §25 StGB, perpetration is divided into three categories: direct authorship, indirect authorship or co-authorship. The relevant provisions are:

§25 Perpetration
(1) Whoever commits the crime himself or through another shall be punished as a perpetrator.
(2) If more than one person commits the crime jointly, each shall be punished as a perpetrator (co-perpetrator).

committed a crime themselves, albeit *through* the soldiers at the border.[32] This remarkable reasoning merits further attention.

First, the BGH needed to establish criminal responsibility for an act of omission, which can only be punished if there is a duty to act.[33] The Court found that, in the case of the "passive" *Politbüro* members, such obligation arose out of Article 30 of the Constitution of the GDR[34] and Articles 6 §1 and 12 §1 and 2 of the International Covenant on Civil and Political Rights (ICCPR),[35] both of which ensured the protection of the right to life and physical integrity in the GDR. The Court reasoned that, as members of the highest political authority in the GDR, the accused were called upon to safeguard the realization of these rights, even at the risk of being discriminated against or expelled themselves.[36]

Second, the Court attributed criminal liability to the *Politbüro* members on the theory of "*Organisationsherrschaft*" (dominance of an organizational structure). Such *Organisationsherrschaft* exists, the Court explained, if a person uses an organizational framework, in which his contribution leads to a certain regular course of events.[37] In the Court's previous decisions in which it considered the criminal liability of "active" *Politbüro* members, the Court held that *Politbüro* members who *actively* voted in favor of a certain policy should be viewed as having contributed to the authorized acts.[38] In the present decision the Court extended the criminal liability to cases of omission.

The concept of "*Organisationsherrschaft*" has a fragile basis and is heavily disputed.[39] Whereas it can be said that the general concept of indirect authorship, i.e. committing a criminal offense through another person, is widely accepted,[40] it is equally true that it usually presupposes that the person who acted directly cannot be held liable. He is considered an "innocent agent." It is exactly this defect of which the accused is aware and manipulates for his criminal intentions. Nevertheless there are cases in which the activity of a high ranking leader almost automatically leads to the commission of a criminal offense by an

---

Only if none of these three forms can be proven may the court continue to ask whether the accused participated in the crime perpetrated by a third person, i.e. incited (§26 StGB) or aided (§27 StGB) the perpetrator. See Wolfgang Joecks, Vor § 25, in 1 MÜNCHENER KOMMENTAR ZUM STGB, margin notes 1–4 (Wolfgang Joecks & Klaus Miebach eds, 2003).

32 BGHSt 48, 77 (89–92).
33 By virtue of §13 StGB which reads:

§13 Commission by Omission
(1) Whoever fails to avert a result, which is an element of a penal norm, shall only be punishable under this law, if he is legally responsible for the fact that the result does not occur, and if the omission is equivalent to the realization of the statutory elements of the crime through action.
(2) The punishment may be mitigated pursuant to §49 (I).

The common law has always been wary of imposing liability for omissions. See ANDREW ASHWORTH, PRINCIPLES OF CRIMINAL LAW 47 (4th ed., 2003). German criminal law, by contrast, accepts that any criminal norm can be fulfilled by omission if there was a duty to act. See JESCHECK & WEIGEND, *supra* note 11, at 605–612.

34 Art. 30 of the Constitution of the GDR embodied the principle that the personality and freedom of each citizen are inviolable and that each citizen could claim protection from state organs.
35 International Covenant on Civil and Political Rights, 19 December 1966, 999 U.N.T.S. 171, ratified by the GDR. The BGH ruled that even before ratification of the ICCPR these human rights were applicable by virtue of the Universal Declaration of Human Rights, G.A. Res. 217A(III), U.N. Doc. A/810 (Dec. 12, 1948). See BGHSt 40, 241.
36 BGHSt 48, 77 (86–88).
37 BGHSt 48, 77 (90–91).
38 BGHSt 40, 218 (236); BGHSt 45, 270 (296).
39 For a summary of the discussion with further references, see CLAUS ROXIN, 2 STRAFRECHT. ALLGEMEINER TEIL §25 margin numbers 105–138 (2003).
40 For further references to the different legal systems, see KAI AMBOS, DER ALLGEMEINE TEIL DES VÖLKERSTRAFRECHTS 568 (2002).

agent who stands on a hierarchically lower level and is ready to unconditionally do as ordered.[41] If the person at the top of this hierarchy knows and uses this structure, it can be said that the offense is also his.[42]

There are critics of this approach in Germany, which has been pioneered mainly by Claus Roxin.[43] A different way to construct criminal liability in these cases is incitement.[44] Nevertheless the German jurisprudence has embarked on a different avenue and in the case at bar this avenue was further corroborated. Any person that uses other persons within an organizational structure as an agent to commit a crime is liable as the author of the crime, even if he is only part of a council that collectively decides to make use of the organization and even if his contribution to this collective decision consists of an omission to prevent the offense. This is a far-reaching interpretation of criminal authorship.[45] We have yet to see how far the BGH is willing to go in applying this concept, not only to political but also to other systems of hierarchically structured power, for example in companies or mafia-like organizations.[46] The "bottom-up" prosecution of individuals who were responsible for human rights violations under the SED regime in the former GDR has come to an end.[47] For the second time in history the (former West but now reunified) German justice system was called upon to deal with systemic crime that took place on German soil. Several enhancements have been achieved – amongst them a rethinking on the strict concept of *nullum crimen* in Art. 103 (II) of the *Grundgesetz* (GG – Basic Law or Constitution).[48] The question of whether justice has been done by judges of reunified German courts, sitting over East German collaborators, will be a question for history to answer.

II. Abetting in Suicide

The following case[49] has a somewhat tragic character both on the side of the victim as well as on the side of the defendant. The overall topic of the case is suicide. To kill oneself is

---

41 The higher ranking person relies only on the proper functioning of the hierarchical structure. These cases are not to be confused with cases of duress. In cases of duress the perpetration of the coercing party is perfectly accepted in German doctrine, pursuant to the principle of *Nötigungsherrschaft* (dominance of necessity). The coercing party is criminally responsible by means of indirect authorship pursuant to §25 (I) StGB. *See* ROXIN, *supra* note 39, at §25 margin numbers 47–60.

42 The BGH has seen such a system in the military command structure of the National People's Army. The superior could rely on the fact that his orders would be automatically followed. *See* BGHSt 40, 218 (236–238) (providing more extensive reasoning).

43 CLAUS ROXIN, TÄTERSCHAFT UND TATHERRSCHAFT 245 (7th ed., 2000). For a summary of the different influential views, *see* Rogall, *supra* note 12, at 418–428; AMBOS, *supra* note 40, at 590–615.

44 Criminal liability for incitement would follow §26 StGB. For a analysis of this solution, *see, e.g.*, JOACHIM RENZIKOWSKI, RESTRIKTIVER TÄTERBEGRIFF UND FAHRLÄSSIGE BETEILIGUNG 87–91 (1997).

45 Although punishment for the inciting party is the same as for the perpetrator (§26 StGB), the stigma of perpetration of a crime is viewed as deserving a much more serious censure than incitement. The aim of the construction is to be in a position to convict armchair culprits as the actual authors of the crime. *See* Joecks, *supra* note 31, at §25 margin numbers 129–132.

46 *See* Christoph Knauer, *Strafbarkeit wegen Totschlags durch Unterlassen bei Nichtherbeiführung eines Beschlusses des SED-Politbüros*, 56 NEUE JURISTISCHE WOCHENSCHRIFT (NJW) 3101, 3103 (2003). Knauer argues that each case must be evaluated individually with regard to what can reasonably be expected from the offender taking into account the legal goods at stake.

47 Detter, *supra* note 13, at 35.

48 Winfried Hassemer, *Staatsverstärkte Kriminalität als Gegenstand der Rechtsprechung*, in 50 JAHRE BUNDESGERICHTSHOF 439 (Claus-Wilhelm Canaris et al., Eds., 2000).

49 Bundesgerichtshof, 56 NEUE JURISTISCHE WOCHENSCHRIFT (NJW) 2326 (2003). *See* Georg Küpper, *Der Täter als "Werkzeug" des Opfers? – BGH, NJW 2003, 2326, und OLG Nürnberg, NJW 2003, 4*, 44 JURISTISCHE SCHULUNG (JuS) 757 (2004); Rolf D. Herzberg, *Vorsätzliche und fahrlässige Tötung bei ernstlichem Sterbebegehren des Opfers*, 24 NEUE ZEITSCHRIFT FÜR STRAFRECHT (NStZ) 1 (2004). A similar case was decided by the *Oberlandesgericht* (OLG – Higher Regional Court) Nürnberg. In that case a suicidal

not an offense in German criminal law.⁵⁰ Therefore neither incitement nor aiding the suicidal person can be punished.⁵¹ On the other hand, §216 StGB punishes homicide upon request.⁵² In the case at hand the person who was weary of life was not in a physical position to commit suicide and needed help from another person.

The accused served his obligatory community service in a nursing home.⁵³ He was given the responsibility of caring for the eventual victim, a 28-year-old man who suffered from dystrophia muscularis (muscle weakness). Due to that illness he was only able to move his mouth and his tongue, with a respiratory capacity of around 10%. The victim had an outstanding intellect, which he used to influence the nurses and care-givers, whom he often manipulated to realize his whims. Beginning in February 2001, he asked the accused to dress him with a plastic bag instead of trousers, claiming to like the feeling of that special material on his skin. The accused did as asked. By the end of February, the victim had asked to be put into a garbage bag and laid into a garbage container on the outside of the building. The victim assured the accused that somebody would retrieve him and take him back into his room after the accused went off-duty; he claimed that he had done this several times before. The accused did as he was asked and did not doubt the assurances of the victim. After putting him into the bags he taped his mouth leaving only a little hole for breathing. He then placed the victim into the container with temperatures around freezing. The next morning the victim was found dead, having suffered from suffocation and hypothermia. The *Landgericht* (Regional Court) of Hamburg discharged the accused.⁵⁴ On the prosecutor's appeal to the BGH, however, the accused was held responsible and a retrial for negligent homicide was ordered.⁵⁵ According to German criminal procedure the

---

person persuaded his wife to shoot at his head with an unloaded gun. She was not told, however, that there was one bullet in the barrel. She shot her husband dead as he intended. The Nürnberg Court held that this behavior fulfills the requirements of §222 (negligent homicide). OLG Nürnberg, 56 NEUE JURISTISCHE WOCHENSCHRIFT (NJW), 4 (2003). See Armin Engländer, *in* 58 JURISTENZEITUNG (JZ) 747 (2003).

50 The statute reads:

§212 (I) StGB – Manslaughter
Whoever kills a human being without being a murderer, shall be punished for manslaughter with imprisonment for not less than five years.

The wording "a human being" is generally understood as referring to other persons and not the actor himself. See, e.g., Albin Eser, *Vorbem §211, in* STRAFGESETZBUCH. KOMMENTAR margin number 33 (Schönke & Schröder eds., 26th ed. 2001).

51 Sections 26 (incitement) and 27 (abetting) StGB both require the intentional commission of an unlawful act by another person. To kill oneself is not an unlawful act, therefore participation is not legally possible. See Herzberg, *supra* note 49, at 1, 2.

52 The statute reads:

§216 Homicide upon Request
(1) If someone is induced to homicide by the express and earnest request of the person killed, then imprisonment from six months to five years shall be imposed.
(2) An attempt shall be punishable.

53 In Germany there (still) exists compulsory military service for all male adults. However, pursuant to the freedom of thought and conscience embodied in Art. 4 (III) of the Basic Law, no one can be forced to be trained with weapons. For this reason, military service can be substituted with what is called *Zivildienst* (social service) in different social institutions, for example, hospitals or nursing homes (as was the case here). Since the end of the so-called Cold War, national service has been a controversial issue. See, FRANKFURTER ALLGEMEINE ZEITUNG, 15 January 2005, at 4.

54 It was a Juvenile Chamber within the Landgericht Hamburg because the defendant was an adolescent of 20 years at the time of the events. According to §§108, 39 *Jugendgerichtsgesetz* (Juvenile Court Act) the Juvenile Chamber is competent to try persons who are under 21 years old.

55 Negligent homicide is punishable according to §222 StGB:

§222 Negligent Homicide
Whoever through negligence causes the death of a human being, shall be punished with imprisonment for not more than five years or a fine.

trial is not terminated until the case is closed on appeal. As a consequence thereof, the accused is not ultimately discharged until the time limit for the appeal has expired or the BGH has quashed the appeal of the prosecutor.[56]

The verdict of the *Landgericht* acquitted the accused, concluding that *both* he and the victim had control over the situation.[57] Although the endangerment was exclusively caused by the accused, the *Landgericht* reasoned that the whole of the criminal situation had to be taken into account, here including the carefully planned strategy of the victim, the excessive demands imposed on the accused, his naivety and his blind confidence. Significantly, the *Landgericht* also noted that the accused was particularly anxious to please the victim. Having considered this broader context of the crime, the *Landgericht* was satisfied that the accused was the instrument of the victim, and therefore not criminally liable for the victim's death.

The BGH reversed that judgment, distinguishing the present case from previous decisions in which the following rule was established and defined: placing oneself in danger cannot be punished if this happens intentionally and without external force. Pursuant to this rule any participation (assistance, causation, enabling) in suicide cannot be penalized. This basic rule, which is almost *communis opinion*,[58] was mainly developed in cases in which the victim swallowed toxin[59] or injected drugs[60] that had been provided by a third person. The Court concluded that this rule does not apply if the participant has a better awareness of the situation and the danger contained therein. In such a case, the Court reasoned, the participant has a better recognition of the risk and the victim does not place himself in danger, but rather, is placed in danger by the participant. Pursuant to this distinction, the aid-providing participant becomes the offender. One of the most relevant criteria, the Court explained, is the question of whether the aid-giving participant had the power to govern the situation by knowing more than the victim or simply by dominating the situation. If so, the Court reasoned that the aid-giving participant had placed the victim in danger and not the victim himself. The Court illustrated this abstract distinction with the facts of the case at hand, which the Court found to show that the accused was in control of the victim. The Court found that he disregarded every-day knowledge of medical causation, although he was trained to care for handicapped people.[61] He exposed the victim to very low temperatures and reduced his breathing conditions. The Court concluded that even the misapprehension that the victim would be rescued later could not argue in favor of the accused being a mere tool of the victim and thus be excluded from criminal responsibility. The Court explained that in cases like these an unassisted, or nearly unassisted, suicide is almost impossible because of the restricted physical abilities of the victim.[62] The BGH did not, however, misconceive that under those circumstances the right to life is transformed into a duty to

---

56 A limited *reformatio in peius* is thus allowed in German law pursuant to §331 (I) *Strafprozessordnung* (StPO – Code of Criminal Procedure), which reads:

(1) The judgment, insofar as it relates to the type and degree of the legal consequences of the offense, shall not be amended to the defendant's detriment only in those cases where the defendant or his statutory representative filed the appeal on fact and law or the public prosecution office appealed on fact and law in his favor.

For further discussion, *see* CHRISTOPH SAFFERLING, TOWARDS AN INTERNATIONAL CRIMINAL PROCEDURE 332–33 (2003).
57 BGH, 56 NEUE JURISTISCHE WOCHENSCHRIFT (NJW)2326, 2327 (2003).
58 *See* Herzberg, *supra* note 49, at 1, 6. Herzberger tried to solve the endangerment problem differently, without focusing on the question who causes the danger finally. He argues that the problem is one of legal causation ("*objektive Zurechnung*").
59 BGH, 53 NEUE JURISTISCHE WOCHENSCHRIFT (NJW) 2286 (2000); BGHSt 46, 279 (288).
60 BGHSt 32, 262 (the leading case in this regard).
61 BGH, 56 NEUE JURISTISCHE WOCHENSCHRIFT (NJW) 2326, 2327 (2003).
62 *Id.* at 2327–28.

live. The Court explained that its ruling could not be given this meaning because there is no right to actively assisted suicide (*aktive Sterbehilfe*) in German law.[63] The question of a right and a duty to live is not limited to Germany. Fairly recently it has also been discussed by the European Court of Human Rights in an English case.[64] In that case, however, the actor was fully aware of the fact that his acts were intended to kill his terminally ill wife. Therefore he would have been guilty of intentional killing. In the Hamburg case, the defendant was tricked by the suicidal person. Because he could have foreseen the death of the person by what he was doing, he is guilty of negligent homicide.

III. Notwehr (Self-defense)

In three major cases the BGH had to deal with potential limitations on the right to *Notwehr* (self-defense). According to §32 StGB, a person who acts in necessary self-defense, is justified in engaging in criminal activity, i.e. the act is not unlawful although it fulfills the elements of the crime.[65] Necessary defense is defined as that defense which is required to avert an imminent unlawful assault against oneself or another person.

The BGH had to decide the following questions related to *Notwehr*. First, whether self-defense in any way relates to the legal characterization of "acting treacherously," which divides manslaughter from murder. The question in the first case below was, whether somebody killing a person *treacherously* will be punished as a murderer with life long imprisonment, although he was in a situation of self-defense (see III.1. below).[66] Second, to what extent the provocation of a self-defense situation limits the rights deriving from §32 StGB (see below III.2.). Third, the applicability of what has come to be known in U.S. criminal law as the "battered wife syndrome" defense; could a case, in which a woman shot her husband while he was sleeping after years of humiliation and physical assault, qualify as self-defense? (see III.3. below).

---

63 *See* Hartmut Schneider, *Vor § 211*, *in* 3 MÜNCHENER KOMMENTAR STGB margin number 89 (Wolfgang Joecks & Klaus Miebach eds, 2003); Albin Eser, *Vorbem. § 211*, *in* STRAFGESETZBUCH. KOMMENTAR, *supra* note 50, at margin number 24. Even "if someone is induced to homicide by the express and earnest request of the person killed" imprisonment will be imposed (§216 StGB), although a more lenient sentence than that imposed for violations of §212 or §211.

64 *Pretty v. United Kingdom*, Eur. Ct. H.R., Application No. 2346/02 (29 April 2002), *available at* http://cmiskp.echr.coe.int/tkp197/portal.asp?sessionId=3600066&skin=hudoc-en&action=request. *See* Susan Millns, *Death, Dignity and Discrimination: The Case of Pretty v. UK*, 3 GERMAN LAW JOURNAL 10 (2002), *at* http://www.germanlawjournal.com/article.php?id=197.

65 The statute reads:

> §32 Necessary Defense
> (1) Whoever commits an act, required as necessary defense, does not act unlawfully.
> (2) Necessary defense is the defense which is required to avert an imminent unlawful assault from oneself or another.

See KREY, 2 GERMAN CRIMINAL LAW: LEGAL ELEMENTS OF THE INTENTIONAL OFFENCE COMMITTED BY ACTION, *supra* note 1, at margin number 217.

66 The statutes read:

> Section 211 Murder
> (1) The murderer shall be punished with imprisonment for life.
> (2) A murderer is, whoever kills a human being out of murderous lust, to satisfy his sexual desires, from greed or otherwise base motives, treacherously or cruelly or with means dangerous to the public or in order to make another crime possible or cover it up.
>
> Section 212 Manslaughter
> (1) Whoever kills a human being without being a murderer, shall be punished for manslaughter with imprisonment for not less than five years.
> (2) In especially serious cases imprisonment for life shall be imposed.

1. BGHSt 48, 207

On the day of the offense the victim met the accused in the accused's apartment.[67] The victim was asking for 5,000 DM, for which he would agree not to tell the police that the accused was dealing in unauthorized copies of music CDs. As the discussion unfolded the victim also threatened to demolish the accused's flat, a threat he promptly began to fulfill by kicking a CD rack. At this point the accused handed over the money. During the following minutes the accused stepped behind the victim, who "did not expect any assault," pulled a knife out of his pocket and quickly cut the throat of the victim, who died immediately.

The *Landgericht* Nürnberg-Fürth convicted the accused of murder and sentenced him to life imprisonment.[68] The Court concluded that the accused had acted treacherously because the victim did not suspect the attack and was defenseless.[69] The accused successfully appealed against the *Landgericht* decision.

Two basic assumptions were central to the consideration of the case by the BGH. First, the Court found that the accused had not acted treacherously, because the victim had to be aware that the accused might defend himself. Second, the Court found that the accused had acted in necessary self-defense.

The criterion "killing a person treacherously" requires that the offender take advantage of a situation where the victim does not expect an attack. That means that the victim must not anticipate any offense or attack concerning life or limb. In this respect, treachery is also a measure of the victim's defenselessness.[70] The Court concluded that in the case at hand, the victim, who was blackmailing the accused, could not be considered free of suspicions of violence simply because the extortion would have found its end after the victim had left the apartment. The Court reasoned that the accused rationally could have been concerned that the victim would continue to demolish the apartment. Characterized in this way, it was the victim who provoked the reaction of the accused and the victim had to be aware that there could be a defensive reaction from the accused. This restrictive interpretation of the criterion "treacherous killing" is also demanded by a normative comparison with the right to necessary self-defense.[71] The Court concluded that the killing could not be regarded as treacherous.

The BGH assumed that the accused was in a situation of necessary self-defense.[72] In contrast to the opinion of the *Landgericht*, the BGH found it significant that the accused was not legally obliged to leave his own flat or to wait until the victim had left the apartment to call the police and report the extortion. The Court explained that §32 StGB entitles anyone who is unlawfully assaulted by somebody to not only protect himself, but also to do anything which would terminate the assault immediately and ultimately. As a basic principle, the least invasive way of defending oneself must be chosen.[73] But the Court emphasized that in the case of doubt, the assaulted party is empowered to take any means necessary to stop the offense. Moreover, the party seeking to invoke the right to self-

---

67 BGH, 56 Neue Juristische Wochenschrift (NJW) 1955 (2003).
68 *See* BGHSt 48, 207 (208).
69 The definition of "*Heimtücke*" is: consciously taking advantage of the guilelessness and defenselessness of the victim in a hostile manner. *See* BGHSt 30, 115; Albin Eser, *Vorbem §211*, *in* Strafgesetzbuch. Kommentar, *supra* note 50, at margin number 24 (with further references).
70 BGHSt 48, 207 (209).
71 BGHSt 48, 207 (211).
72 §32 StGB.
73 *See, e.g.*, BGHSt 24, 358; BGH, 16 Neue Zeitschrift für Strafrecht (NStZ) 29 (1996); BGH, 21 Neue Zeitschrift für Strafrecht (NStZ) 591, 592 (2001); Roxin, *supra* note 12, at §15 margin number 43.

defense will not be held responsible for weighing the conflicting interests; proportionality is not demanded by §32 StGB.[74] In this case, the Court was satisfied that the killing was part of the accused's attempt at protecting his furnishings, end extortion, and secure the return of his 5,000 DM.

The BGH drew a remarkable connection between the criteria "treacherously" and "necessary self-defense," arguing that "treacherously" has a normative implication focusing not only on what the victim expected, but also on what he *ought* to have expected.[75] This part of the Court's decision has been characterized by a commentator as "revolutionary."[76] Without the normative implication, the victim had to be regarded as suspicious that some violence might occur. On this account the further development of the jurisprudence surrounding the criterion "treacherously" is more than interesting because there are many other cases in which unwariness correlates with a right to defend.[77]

On the other hand, the question arises as to whether a "normative implication" was necessary to negate murder in the case. The BGH did not say that this was the only reason. It is more likely that the Court used that term as an additional basis for its holding. The offender of an ongoing extortion loses the especially protected status accorded to the unsuspecting by the "treacherously" criterion merely as a result of his own attack and not as a normative matter.[78] Beyond that point, Hillenkamp has asked if the offender was acting treacherously at all,[79] because he did not take advantage of the situation intentionally, which is a pre-condition of the criterion.[80]

2. BGH, 22 *Neue Zeitschrift für Strafrecht* 425 (2002)

A different problem with the right to self-defense arises in the following case. In the first of this series of cases the attack was considered imminent because the extortion was continuing. The second case provides an example of a situation in which the time limit of the attack is questionable.[81]

The accused had an argument with a third person in a pub. In the course of the argument the accused was hit several times. Eventually the accused fled the scene but lost his shoes in the pub while running away. Having made it safely back home, he decided to

---

74 In contrast thereto, §34 StGB (necessity as justification) warrants proportionality between the protected and the endangered interests. The statute reads:

§34 Necessity as Justification
Whoever, faced with an imminent danger to life, limb, freedom, honor, property or another legal interest which cannot otherwise be averted, commits an act to avert the danger from himself or another, does not act unlawfully, if, upon weighing the conflicting interests, in particular the affected legal interests and the degree of danger threatening them, the protected interest substantially outweighs the one interfered with. This shall apply, however, only to the extent that the act is a proportionate means to avert the danger.

The only social-ethical limit to the right to self-defense is to be *seen* in the term "which is required" (*Gebotenheit*) in §32 StGB (*supra* note 65). Several instances have been developed in the jurisprudence of the BGH in which the right to self-defense is limited. For a summary, see Volker Erb, § *32, in* 1 MÜNCHENER KOMMENTAR ZUM STGB margin numbers 183–212 (Wolfgang Joecks & Klaus Miebach eds, 2003).

75 BGHSt 48, 207 (210) ("The legal order gives to the attacked the right to self-defense. Every attacker must in principle expect the exercise of this right by the attacked in such a situation") (translation CS).
76 Hartmut Schneider, *Anmerkung zu BGH Urteil 1 StR 402/02, in* 23 NEUE ZEITSCHRIFT FÜR STRAFRECHT (NStZ) 428, 429 (2003).
77 Especially in a situation of enduring mistreatment, the denial of murder seems possible.
78 "He is the true aggressor" explained the BGH. BGHSt 48, 207 (210) (translation CS).
79 *See* Thomas Hillenkamp, *BGH, 25.3.2003 – 1 StR 483/02, in* 59 JURISTENZEITUNG 48, 49 (2004).
80 *See* the definition of "treacherously," *supra* note 69.
81 BGH, 22 NEUE ZEITSCHRIFT FÜR STRAFRECHT (NStZ) 425, 426 (2002).

return to the pub to retrieve his shoes. To protect himself he took a "tomato knife" with him. At the pub the accused rattled the door to get in. The landlady opened the door and gave him his shoes, but the accused wanted to get in to the pub to resume his argument with his assailant. The landlady refused to admit the defendant who nonetheless persisted in rattling the door at which point a friend of the landlady appeared and punched the accused twice in the face. The accused fell to the ground but tried to get up again. The victim struck him another time so that the accused tumbled and fell down again. The victim now kept watch over the accused and saw that he tried to stand up again. To avoid any further hassle he stepped towards the accused, who now was afraid of being hit yet again. On this account he drew out the knife and cut the victim seriously.

The *Landgericht* of Stade convicted the accused on charges of dangerous harming pursuant to §224 StGB[82] and sentenced him to three years in prison.[83] This decision was upheld on appeal by the BGH.

The BGH acted on the assumption that the stabbing with the knife could not be justified by *Notwehr*.[84] This is because the accused provoked the conflict by rattling the door. The Court explained that this provocation limits the right to self-defense to a certain degree and that the accused in the present case did not have the full, unlimited right of self-defense.

The Court parsed the relevant facts in the following manner.[85] First, the victim had the right to help the landlady to keep the door shut. The assault on the pub's door was unlawful and the victim was justified in taking measures to aid the landlady in her efforts to prevent the accused from entering the pub.[86] This right to emergency assistance ended, however, when the accused fell down for the final time. Second, the BGH did not decide whether the victim was about to hit the accused again. The Court found it more important that the accused's right to necessary self-defense was limited by his provocation of the defense of the victim at the door. The Court concluded that necessary self-defense is restricted if the underlying situation was provoked by the person who hopes, in turn, to assert the need to defend himself.[87] If the situation is provoked intentionally the would-be defender is considered the offender.[88] If the attacker has been provoked negligently, the

---

82 The statute reads:

§224 Dangerous Bodily Injury
(1) Whoever commits bodily harm:
1. through the administration of poison or other substances dangerous to health;
2. by means of a weapon or other dangerous tool;
3. by means of a sneak attack;
4. jointly with another participant; or
5. by means of a treatment dangerous to life,
shall be punished with imprisonment from six months to ten years, in less serious cases with imprisonment from three months to five years.
(2) An attempt shall be punishable.

83 Landgericht Stade, 22 NEUE ZEITSCHRIFT FÜR STRAFRECHT (NStZ) 425, 426 (2002).
84 Section 32 StGB (necessary self-defense), *supra* note 65.
85 Landgericht Stade, 22 NEUE ZEITSCHRIFT FÜR STRAFRECHT (NStZ) 425, 426 (2002).
86 This right stems from §32 StGB – self-help, *supra* note 65.
87 Landgericht Stade, 22 NEUE ZEITSCHRIFT FÜR STRAFRECHT (NStZ) 425, 426 (2002). *See* SUSANNE RETZKO, DIE ANGRIFFSVERURSACHUNG BEI DER NOTWEHR (2001); JOHANNES WESSELS & WERNER BEULKE, STRAFRECHT – ALLGEMEINER TEIL margin number 346 (33rd ed., 2003).
88 Most scholars and courts deny the right to necessary defense in this situation. *See* Claus Roxin, *Die "sozialethischen Einschränkungen" des Notwehrrechts*, 93 ZEITSCHRIFT FÜR DIE GESAMTE STRAFRECHTS-WISSENSCHAFT (ZStW) 68, 85 (1981); WESSELS & BEULKE, *supra* note 87, at margin number 347; BGH, JURISTISCHE RUNDSCHAU (JR) 205 (1984). Nevertheless, it is the offender who acts unlawfully which must result in a (limited) right to defense. *See* Erb, § 32, *in* 1 MÜNCHENER KOMMENTAR STGB, *supra* note 74, at margin number 201 (with further references).

right to self-defense is limited in three steps: the offended person has to react passively and try to evade the assault; if this does not end the attack the offended person may react more actively to avert the aggression; ultimately, the offended person who provoked the defense situation is allowed to try anything to terminate the assault, at which point his full right to self-defense arises again.[89] In the case at hand the BGH objected that the accused provoked the self-defense scenario negligently and reacted more aggressively than he was allowed to. The Court further reasoned that the accused was obliged to avoid the attack in the first place by saying that he would not try to attack any more. If this was not successful the accused should have given notice that he would use a knife – even if this increased the risk that he would be hit again. The accused had to put up with any bodily injury to that point.[90]

The reasoning of the BGH is problematic because the Court did not expound on how long the right to self-defense is limited in such way that the offended has to tolerate the assault. The Court should have thought about the time elapsed following the incident at the door. In addition, the several kicks and hits the accused had to suffer show that the restriction of the right to necessary self-defense does not last infinitely. In previous cases the Court found that aspects of time and fact end the limitation of the right to self-defense.[91] The BGH did not apply these rules in the present case. Had the Court focused on those aspects it would have had to consider the provocation (here, the rattling of the pub's door) as terminated. The accused was struck badly several times thereafter, which indicates that the provocation had come to an end. As a result the accused should have been found to be justified in using his knife, without any limitations and irrespective of the injuries the accused had to expect.

3. *House-tyrant* case – BGHSt 48, 255

The following case bears also quite a tragic story. It is sad proof of a complete failure of social institutions to encourage battered housewives to stand up against their torturers.[92] The accused shot her husband while he was sleeping. For nearly 15 years the victim repeatedly humiliated, kicked and insulted his wife. The aggression increased over the years and was directed also towards their children. On the day of the offense, the accused did not see any other way to protect herself and the children from being further degraded by the victim. She did not consider herself capable of getting out of the home situation with the help of legal or social institutions and she did not try to contact either of them. The victim had threatened the accused with further violence, especially in the case that she should seek professional help. The accused took that threat very seriously.

The *Landgericht* of Hechingen convicted the accused of treacherously murdering her husband and sentenced her to nine years imprisonment.[93] Due to the exceptional circumstances of the case the *Landgericht* did not impose a life sentence. The BGH upheld the *Landgericht*'s denial of a case of necessary self-defense[94] and necessity as justification.[95] The

---

89 BGHSt 24, 256; BGHSt 26, 143; BGHSt 38, 34; BGH, NEUE ZEITSCHRIFT FÜR STRAFRECHT RECHTSPRECHUNGS-REPORT (NStZ-RR) 194 (1997).
90 Volker Erb, *Aus der Rechtsprechung des BGH zur Notwehr seit 1999*, 24 NEUE ZEITSCHRIFT FÜR STRAFRECHT (NStZ) 369, 375 (2004)
91 BGHSt 26, 256 (257); BGH, 44 NEUE JURISTISCHE WOCHENSCHRIFT (NJW) 503, 505 (1991).
92 BGH, 56 NEUE JURISTISCHE WOCHENSCHRIFT (NJW) 2464 (2003). See BGHSt 48, 255 (256).
93 The *Landgericht*'s decision is reported in BGHSt 48, 255 (256–57).
94 §32 StGB, *supra* note 65. BGHSt 48, 255 (257).
95 §34 StGB, *supra* note 74. BGHSt 48, 255 (257).

Federal Court of Justice also upheld the *Landgericht*'s conclusion that the killing should be considered "treacherous."[96]

In the end, however, the BGH quashed the conviction and ordered a re-trial because the *Landgericht* did not discuss whether a situation of necessity as excuse existed in the case at hand.[97] Under necessity as excuse, anyone faced with an imminent threat to life, limb or freedom, which cannot otherwise be averted, who then commits an unlawful act to avert the danger from himself, a relative, or a person close to him, acts without guilt. A "threat" is a situation in which harm is likely to occur due to the actual circumstances.[98] This also includes a persistent threat in which the harm to life or limb could occur at any time.[99]

In the present case, the terms of necessity as excuse, especially as a result of a persistent threat, seemed to apply.[100] The accused had lived under the threat posed by her husband for many years. There was not a single day that passed without her suffering serious insult from her husband. And the situation became even worse during the days leading up to the offense. An "imminent" danger means that harm can only be avoided by taking immediate action.[101] In the situation of a persistent threat the harm must be very likely to occur at any time.[102] In the case at hand, the threat could have transformed into a severe harm any time. In the past, the victim had awakened and started to abuse his wife without the slightest signal. In this situation of persistent threat, the required degree of "imminence" to satisfy the applicability of necessity as excuse clearly exists. The next element of necessity as excuse, "otherwise be averted,"[103] is less certain under the facts of the case at hand.[104] The *Landgericht* did not discuss that question. For example, the accused could have asked for official help by contacting the police or another social institution. Moreover, she could have attempted to move to a women's shelter.[105] At first, however, she would have had to

---

96 BGHSt 48, 255 (256–57). This finding is truly questionable. Whereas the definition of treacherous has been discussed before (*supra* Section B.III.1.) there is a special tenet, which says that whoever sleeps is guileless. The Court relied exactly on this maxim. However, Hartmut Scheider rightly questions this reasoning. A tyrant, like the one in this case, who starts to abuse his family straight after waking up, cannot be considered innocent when sleeping. Such a violent person must suspect resistance any time. Hartmut Schneider, *supra* note 76.

97 The statute reads:

§35 Necessity as Excuse
(1) Whoever, faced with an imminent danger to life, limb or freedom which cannot otherwise be averted, commits an unlawful act to avert the danger from himself, a relative or person close to him, acts without guilt. This shall not apply to the extent that the perpetrator could be expected under the circumstances to assume the risk, in particular, because he himself caused the danger or stood in a special legal relationship; however the punishment may be mitigated pursuant to Section 49 subsection (1), if the perpetrator was not required to assume the risk with respect to a special legal relationship.
(2) If upon commission of the act the perpetrator mistakenly assumes that circumstances exist, which would excuse him under subsection (1), he will only be punished, if he could have avoided the mistake. The punishment shall be mitigated pursuant to Section 49 (I).

98 BGHSt 48, 255 (258). *See* Theodor Lenckner & Walter Perron, § 34, *in* STRAFGESETZBUCH. KOMMENTAR margin number 12 (Schönke & Schröder eds., 26th ed., 2001); Lenckner & Perron, § 35, *id.* at margin number 11.

99 BGHSt 48, 255 (258).

100 The BGH stated, that according to the facts of the case as established by the *Landgericht* the existence of a protracted danger for wife and children suggested itself. BGHSt 48, 255 (258).

101 BGHSt 48, 255 (259). *See* Bernd Müssig, § 35, *in* 1 MÜNCHENER KOMMENTAR ZUM STGB margin number 22 (Wolfgang Joecks & Klaus Miebach eds., 2003) (with further references).

102 BGHSt 48, 255 (258).

103 *See* text of §35 (I) StGB, *supra* note 97.

104 BGHSt 48, 255 (259–261).

105 In recent years, German legislation has become more supportive in this regard. One of the latest achievements is the so-called *Gewaltschutzgesetz*. Gesetz zum zivilrechtlichen Schutz vor Gewalttaten und Nachstellungen (Protection against Force Act) Dec. 11, 2001, BGBl. I at 3513.

examine whether there were less invasive ways of getting out of the hazardous situation. This is even more true because of the high value attributed to human life in the legal system.[106] A persistent threat can easily be found to be susceptible to alternative solutions, even in tragic and difficult cases like this one.

At the re-trial the *Landgericht* must also evaluate whether the accused mistakenly assumed the existence of the above described threatening situation. §35 (II) StGB: "If upon commission of the act the perpetrator mistakenly assumes that circumstances exist which excuse him under subsection (1), he will only be punished, if he could have avoided the mistake."[107] Thus, in the present case, the accused's assumption that she was confronted with the commission of a crime as a last resort, for herself and her children, would have to be examined. Furthermore it is to ask whether the accused's mistake regarding necessity was avoidable. If it had been avoidable, the new sentence would have to be more lenient.[108]

IV. Schuld(un)fähigkeit (Culpability)

According to §20 StGB,[109] criminal liability is excluded if the offender has consumed alcohol to an extent that he is not in control of himself anymore.[110] If the amount of intoxication does not equal an exogenous psychosis, i.e. comes within the ambit of what is understood by "a pathological emotional disorder" in the sense of §20 StGB, the culpability of such an offender can still be limited such that, pursuant to §21 StGB (diminished responsibility),[111] the accused can, and in principle will, receive a milder sentence.[112] Two questions came before the BGH regarding the *Schuld(un)fähigkeit* (culpability principle)

---

106 BGHSt 48, 255 (262).
107 *Supra* note 97.
108 Pursuant to §35 (II) StGB, *supra* note 97. In English law the battered women's syndrome can also lead to a more lenient sentence, if not to a complete acquittal, by virtue of Sec 2 of the Homicide Act 1957 because of diminished responsibility. *See* JOHN C. SMITH, SMITH & HOGAN: CRIMINAL LAW 235 (10th ed., 2002); ASHWORTH, *supra* note 33, at 284.
109 The statute reads:

§20 Lack of Capacity to be Adjudged Guilty due to Emotional Disorders
Whoever upon commission of the act is incapable of appreciating the wrongfulness of the act or acting in accordance with such appreciation due to a pathological emotional disorder, profound consciousness disorder, mental defect or any other serious emotional abnormality, acts without guilt.

110 The offender can in such a case only be convicted according to §323a StGB, which reads:

Total Intoxication
(1) Whoever intentionally or negligently get intoxicated with alcoholic beverages or other intoxicants, shall be punished with imprisonment for not more than five years or a fine, if he commits an unlawful act while in this condition and may not be punished because of it because he lacked the capacity to be adjudged guilty due to the intoxication, or this cannot be excluded.
(2) The punishment may not be more severe than the punishment provided for the act which was committed while intoxicated.
(3) The act shall only be prosecuted upon complaint, with authorization or upon request for prosecution if the act committed while intoxicated may only be prosecuted upon complaint, with authorization, or upon request for prosecution.

As to the question of when such a level is reached, see Franz Streng, § 20, *in* 1 MÜNCHENER KOMMENTAR StGB margin numbers 68–74 (Wolfgang Joecks & Klaus Miebach eds., 2003).
111 The statute reads:

§21 Diminished Capacity to be Adjudged Guilty
If the capacity of the perpetrator to appreciate the wrongfulness of the act or to act in accordance with such appreciation is substantially diminished upon commission of the act due to one of the reasons indicated in Section 20, then the punishment may be mitigated pursuant to Section 49 subsection (1).

112 The concept of reducing the sentence is laid down in §49 (I) StGB.

during the period under review. First, the Court was asked to consider what happens if the offender *knowingly* drinks and reaches the level of intoxication triggering the mitigation of §21 StGB, which would usually gain him a reduced sentence. Does the offender in such a case still deserve a more lenient sentence? (see 1. below) Second, the Court had to decide what to do with an offender who reaches a level of intoxication triggering the exoneration secured by §20 StGB *during* the commission of the criminal offense (see 2. below).

1. Bundesgerichtshof (BGH), 56 NEUE JURISTISCHE WOCHENSCHRIFT 2394 (2003)

On the day of the offense the accused had several serious arguments with his girlfriend.[113] In the course of these arguments he mistreated her physically, offenses for which he was convicted on the charge of causing physical harm. In the evening he began to drink several bottles of sweet wine, telephoned his girlfriend and threatened to have sexual intercourse with her. He called a taxi, feeling that he was too drunk to be able to drive himself, entered his girlfriend's flat and raped her.

The *Landgericht* of Wuppertal convicted the accused and refused to impose a reduced sentence pursuant to §§21 and 49 StGB because the judges did not believe that the accused drank as much as he claimed.[114] The BGH upheld the findings of the *Landgericht* and then embarked on an immense *obiter dictum*, arguing that, in principle, the sentence is not to be reduced pursuant to §21 StGB when the offender has been intentionally drinking.[115] The case had to be separated from the cases of *actio libera in causa*,[116] where the perpetrator drinks willfully in order to reach a level of excluded culpability according to §20 StGB, and to commit a criminal act under that condition.[117] According to the BGH such actor can be punished for the criminal act with full intent and full culpa.[118]

The BGH saw the difficulty in the conflict between §21 and §323a StGB. In the case where the accused has been drinking to an extent that he is not culpable and cannot be convicted for a willful act (pursuant to §20 StGB), he is to be treated pursuant to §323a StGB,

---

113 BGH, 56 NEUE JURISTISCHE WOCHENSCHRIFT (NJW) 2394 (2003).
114 *See id.*
115 *Id.* at 2395.
116 This is: "an act which is free in its origin."
117 The conflict between "intentional drinking" and "criminal behaviour when heavily intoxicated" is, perhaps, difficult for Anglo-American lawyers to understand. But it is notorious in the German criminal law system. The difficulty lies within the principle of contemporaneity, which is also known to the common law (*see* ASHWORTH, *supra* note 33, at 161–163). In order to overcome the lack of contemporaneity in the case in which the offender commits a criminal act while the fault element is missing, several dogmatic structures have evolved in German criminal law theory. It is not necessary to explain these different views here. *See* MICHAEL HETTINGER, DIE "ACTION LIBERA IN CAUSA": STRAFBARKEIT WEGEN BEGEHUNGSTAT TROTZ SCHULDUNFÄHIGKEIT? (1988); ROXIN, *supra* note 12, at §20 margin numbers 55–73; WESSELS & BEULKE, *supra* note 87, at margin numbers 415–421; JESCHECK & WEIGEND, *supra* note 11, at 445–448. For a different approach, *see* Franz Streng, *Actio libera in causa und verminderte Schuldfähigkeit – BGH NStZ 2000, 584*, 41 JURISTISCHE SCHULUNG (JuS) 540 (2001); Kai Ambos, *Der Anfang vom Ende der actio libera in causa?*, 50 NEUE JURISTISCHE WOCHENSCHRIFT (NJW) 2296 (1997) (comparing other continental legal systems).
118 Despite the dogmatic difficulties, the jurisprudence has always been willing to convict in such cases; *see, e.g.,* BGHSt 17, 333 (335); BGHSt 21, 381; BGHSt 34, 29. Fairly recently, however, it has limited the applicability of the *actio libera in causa*-principle to result crimes; *see* BGHSt 42, 235. *See also* Streng, § 20, *in* 1 MÜNCHENER KOMMENTAR ZUM STGB margin notes 114–150 (Wolfgang Joecks & Klaus Miebach eds., 2003) (with references to the different views and cases). Even though some authors have declared the beginning of the end of the *actio libera in causa*-principle (*see* Ambos, *supra* note 117), it is unlikely that the BGH will abandon the principle entirely. To the contrary, the BGH has applied the principle in more recent decisions. *See* BGH, 19 NEUE ZEITSCHRIFT FÜR STRAFRECHT (NStZ) 448 (1999); BGH, 20 NEUE ZEITSCHRIFT FÜR STRAFRECHT (NStZ) 584 (2000).

which means that he be punished for willful drinking and the consequences thereof. In such cases the sentence may not exceed five years imprisonment.[119] In contrast, an accused who has not been drinking enough to achieve a level of total inculpability, but only a level of diminished responsibility according to §21 StGB, could be sentenced even more leniently, if the rule to reduce the sentence according to §49 StGB is applied. The BGH found this an unacceptable result. The Court held that the (morally) differentiated stages of criminal responsibility must remain as follows: (1) full responsibility leads to full sentence; (2) reduced responsibility for drinking could lead to §21 StGB leniency but must be sanctioned more severely than (3) the case of an absolute lack of criminal responsibility.

Consequently, a person who has been drinking *willfully* cannot be granted the optional sentence reduction available by way of the combination of §§21, 49 StGB.

The decision has been criticized.[120] In particular, the Court's interpretation of §323a StGB has been rebuked as unrealistic. The cause for criminalizing an act is not the actual drinking. This formal starting point was merely chosen by the law to blur the breach of the principle of culpability.[121] In truth, §323a and §21 StGB have the same intention: to reduce the sentence of an offender because of his diminished responsibility resulting from intoxication. They merely stand on different levels of responsibility. §21 StGB therefore has to be harmonized with §323a StGB but not in the sense that no sentence reduction is possible. Instead, the issue of reduced culpability must be integrated into a consideration of a reduction of the sentence.[122]

2. Bundesgerichtshof (BGH), 23 NEUE ZEITSCHRIFT FÜR STRAFRECHT (NStZ) 535 (2003)

The accused and the victim were living together in a single room flat.[123] During an argument that lasted several hours the accused became more and more agitated, in particular as a result of the victim's mockery of the sexual abuse the accused had suffered as a child. The accused responded by taking a machete that had been hanging on the wall and stabbing the victim 33 times. The accused was convicted on a charge of manslaughter and sentenced to a reduced sentence because of reduced criminal responsibility resulting from a deficiency in his ability to control himself.[124] The Federal Court of Justice was confronted with determining whether the deficiency was present all along, including the time preceding the commission of the crime or whether the deficiency came about during the stabbing.

In previous case-law the BGH had to determine whether a conviction would be excluded in a case where the offender's condition could be classified under §20 StGB only after the commencement of the criminal act.[125] In these cases the BGH gave a quite complicated answer: If the acts committed after the defect manifested itself were included in the intent, i.e. were part of the *mens rea*, of the offender, criminal liability would be

---

119 The text of §323, *supra* note 110.
120 See Franz Streng, *Ausschluss der Strafmilderung gem § 21 StGB bei eigenverantwortlicher Berauschung?*, 56 NEUE JURISTISCHE WOCHENSCHRIFT (NJW) 2963 (2003); Eberhardt Foth, *Case-note*, 23 NEUE ZEITSCHRIFT FÜR STRAFRECHT (NStZ) 597 (2003); Helmut Frister, *Case-note*, 58 JURISTENZEITUNG (JZ) 1019 (2003); Günther Neumann, *Case-note*, STRAFVERTEIDIGER (StV) 527 (2003).
121 See supra note 120.
122 In a later case the BGH accepted the criticism. It now applies a general test as to the character of the offender, the situation of the case and the risk of committing a criminal act when intoxicated. See BGH, 57 NEUE JURISTISCHE WOCHENSCHRIFT (NJW) 3350, 3351 (2004).
123 BGH, 23 NEUE ZEITSCHRIFT FÜR STRAFRECHT (NStZ) 535 (2003).
124 By virtue of §§21, 49 StGB, *supra* note 111; BGH, 23 NEUE ZEITSCHRIFT FÜR STRAFRECHT (NStZ)535 (2003).
125 Unlike §21 StGB, which provides for a more lenient sentence, §20 excludes culpability altogether. The leading case in this regard is the so-called *Blutrauschfall* (Bloodlust Case), BGHSt 7, 325.

sustained.¹²⁶ The Court's reasoning can be summarized as follows: the offender may not use himself as an agent in the manifestation of a condition that excludes criminal responsibility. The Court concluded that what is true for §20 StGB and total exclusion of criminal liability must also be true for §21 StGB and the reduction of criminal liability.¹²⁷ Thus, the Court reiterated that although a self-induced manifestation of a deficiency can constitute a deviation from the causal course of events envisaged by the offender, this remains insignificant as long as the activity, as such, was originally intended by the offender.

Abuse of alcohol and criminal conduct often go hand in hand. Every day Courts have to deal with offenders that were limited in their culpability during the commission of a crime because of their intoxication. As drinking is a socially accepted drug, the law is sometimes too lenient with respect to alcohol induced intoxication.¹²⁸ These two decisions show that there is a general tendency of the BGH to a more repressive practice concerning drinking and the mental state of offenders.

V. Criminal Attempt

The law of criminal attempt has much more practical importance in Germany than it has in the Anglo-American legal system. It is not easy to find a precise reason for this fact, but it is quite obvious that there is dramatically less academic writing and there are far fewer cases on the law of attempt.¹²⁹ Maybe one of the reasons why there are more situations in which the accused is charged with criminal attempt could be that the *mens rea* requirements are much more carefully evaluated according to the German criminal law system.¹³⁰ Thus, the offender's foresight of the exact chain of causation is one of the requirements

---

126 *See* BGHSt 7, 325 (329); *See also Jauchegrubefall* (death in the cesspool case), BGHSt 14, 193; ROXIN, *supra* note 12, at §12 margin number 145; WESSELS & BEULKE, *supra* note 87, at margin number 258; KREY, 2 GERMAN CRIMINAL LAW: LEGAL ELEMENTS OF THE INTENTIONAL OFFENCE COMMITTED BY ACTION, *supra* note 1, at margin numbers 385–387. The structure of this case is similar to cases in which the offender is mistaken as to the chain of causation. Generally speaking, the offender acts with the necessary mens rea only if he foresees the chain of causation he has started with his act. He must foresee this not in all its details but in its essential features. *Mens rea* is therefore excluded, if the events develop in a way which was totally unforeseeable or utterly against any normal probability. This is called *wesentliche Abweichung im Kausalverlauf* (essential deviance in the chain of causation).

127 *See* BGH, 23 NEUE ZEITSCHRIFT FÜR STRAFRECHT (NStZ) 535, 536 (2003).

128 In the Anglo-American legal system the practice seems much harder towards alcohol induced crime than in Germany. As Jerome Hale, commenting on US American criminal law, observes: "The case-law also reflects traditional attitudes of marked hostility toward drunken offenders, which renders sound adjudication harder to achieve than in insanity cases." JEROME HALE, GENERAL PRINCIPLES OF CRIMINAL LAW 529 (2nd ed., 1960). For a comparative analysis, *see* JENS WATZEK, RECHTFERTIGUNG UND ENTSCHULDIGUNG IM ENGLISCHEN STRAFRECHT 252–274 (1997). The main difference lies in §20 StGB: the ability to exercise will power to control physical acts in accordance with that rational judgment (*Steuerungsfähigkeit*) is accepted as a total exculpation in German law, whereas in English law it is only acceptable with diminished responsibility. *See* Homicide Act 1957; Lord Parker in R. v. Byrne [1960] 3 All E.R. 1, 4. In cases of drunken offenders, lack of *Steuerungsfähigkeit* is the most common defense.

129 Suffice it to refer to the short chapters on criminal attempt in the textbooks by SMITH & HOGAN, *supra* note 108, at 328–343; WILLIAMS, *supra* note 2, at 614–662. An exception can be found in R.A. DUFF, INTENTION, AGENCY & CRIMINAL LIABILITY (1990). In this publication as well as in his work, CRIMINAL ATTEMPTS (1996), Duff addresses the problem of attempt from a viewpoint of a philosophy of action.

130 The *mens rea* requirements for a criminal attempt are the same, in general terms, as they are for the completed crime. In addition the offender must have an unconditional will to act (*unbedingter Handlungswille*). The relevant norm is §22 StGB, which reads:

    Definition of Terms
    Whoever, in accordance with his understanding of the act (seiner *Vorstellung von der Tat*), takes an immediate step towards the realization of the elements of the offense, attempts to commit a crime.

As to the definitions *see* Eser, *supra* note 50, at margin numbers 12–22.

for *mens rea* as was already an issue in the last of the cases reported above,[131] and it is also the crucial point in this case.

In general a criminal act must correlate with the intent of the offender to commit that crime.[132] But where does the criminal act begin and where is the threshold between (punishable) attempt and a mere act of preparation, which is not punishable?[133] The Federal Court of Justice confronted this question in this rather obscure case.

On the day of the offense the accused tied up his wife after he had numbed her with a sleeping aid during breakfast.[134] He put her into the trunk of his car, drove to another place where he changed to a different car, in which he planned to drive to an apartment owned by both him and the victim. It was his plan to force his wife to sign a general authorization so that he would have full legal power over both his own and his wife's assets.[135] Only after she had signed the documents did the accused plan on killing the victim. But, when he opened the trunk he saw that his wife was already dead. The Landgericht presumed that the victim died of panic and fear or from suffocation in the trunk of the car.[136]

The interesting legal problem in the case lies in the question of whether the accused is responsible for intentionally killing his wife, for an attempt to do so or whether he is only guilty of negligently causing her death. Responsibility for the accomplished killing could be excluded on two grounds. First, according to §22 StGB, whoever, in accordance with his understanding of the act, takes an "immediate step" towards the realization of the elements of the offense, attempts to commit a crime.[137] Because of the intent of the accused the *Landgericht* of Lübeck held that he attempted the homicide by tying and numbing her. The consequence would be that the accused might be punished more leniently than if he could be held responsible for the full completion of the homicide.[138] Second, the accused was not clear about the chain of causation of the events leading up

---

131 *See infra* C.IV.2.
132 The basic condition is not laid down explicitly, but it can be derived from §§8, 16 StGB. §8 StGB: "An act is *committed (begangen)* at the time the perpetrator (...) acted (...)." §16 Abs. 1 S. 1 StGB: "Whoever *upon commission (bei Begehung)* of the act is unaware of a circumstance which is a statutory element of the offense does not act intentionally."
133 In the criminal laws of Anglo-American states the threshold between a mere preparatory act and a criminal attempt is just as heavily debated. In general terms, there is a minimalist theory which requires an act which is "sufficiently proximate" to the result contending with a maximalist approach which is satisfied if the offender has made a "substantial step" towards the realization of the criminal offense; *see, e.g.*, DUFF, CRIMINAL ATTEMPTS, *supra* note 129, at 386; WILLIAMS, *supra* note 2, at 621; FLETCHER, *supra* note 11, at 139–146. The empirical study by Paul H. Robinson and John M. Darley suggests that at least as concerns burglary, the most acceptable theory would be that of dangerous proximity, i.e. to choose a point which is closest possible to the actual violation of the norm. PAUL H. ROBINSON & JOHN M. DARLEY, JUSTICE, LIABILITY, AND BLAME 13–28 (1995)
134 BGH, 55 NEUE JURISTISCHE WOCHENSCHRIFT (NJW) 1057 (2002).
135 *Id.* at 1058. It was difficult for the courts in this case to reconstruct the exact course of events and the plans of the offender. The *Landgericht* gave several alternative settings. According to the principle *in dubio pro reo* the court can base a conviction only on the facts that are the most favorable for the accused. *See generally* LUTZ MEYER-GOßNER, STRAFPROZESSORDNUNG, §261 margin numbers 26–30 (47th ed., 2004); SAFFERLING, *supra* note 56, at 260.
136 *See* BGH, 55 NEUE JURISTISCHE WOCHENSCHRIFT (NJW) 1057 (2002). The determination of the exact cause of death was hampered by the fact that the corpse of the wife has never been found and by the fact that there were no tracks at the scene of the crime that would reveal any details as to the exact cause of death.
137 Section 22 StGB. There are many conflicting theories in this regard; for a summary of the different scholarly theories, *see* ROXIN, *supra* note 39, at §29 margin numbers 97–225. The formula of the BGH for the question is: "[Der Täter muss] subjektiv die Schwelle zum 'Jetzt geht es los' ... überschritten und objektiv zur tatbestandsmäßigen Angriffshandlung angesetzt [haben]." (Subjectively the offender must have crossed the threshold of 'here we go", and objectively he must have set forth the realization of the elements of the offense). *See* the so-called *Tankwart-Fall* (filling station attendant case), BGHSt 26, 201 (203–4).
138 This is so according to §23 (III) StGB.

to his wife's death.¹³⁹ That means that he could have been "unaware of a circumstance which is a statutory element of the effect," with the result that he did not act intentionally and therefore lacked *mens rea* necessary for murder or manslaughter.¹⁴⁰ He could then only be punished for negligence.¹⁴¹ The causal process is an (unwritten) statutory element.¹⁴² Difficulties with this requirement arise above others in situations where the plan of the offender is separated into different stages.¹⁴³ As in this case, the accused thought that he would kill his wife only in the second phase of his plan. Since she died already in the first phase, he was clearly mistaken about the real causal developments. The jurisprudence of the BGH, however, is clear that not every mistake concerning the chain of causation automatically excludes the intent (*mens rea*) of the offender.¹⁴⁴ It only does so, if the difference between the offender's conception of the events and reality is essential.¹⁴⁵ The *Landgericht* opined that the causal process the accused intended does not differ essentially from the process that took place, meaning that the accused acted intentionally. On this basis the *Landgericht* convicted the accused of murder.

This decision was not upheld by the BGH. The Court concluded that the accused had not attempted to kill his wife. The Court explained that, in order to attempt an offense, it is not enough to prepare for it. Rather, the accused must take an "immediate step towards the realization" of the offense.¹⁴⁶ Even a preparatory act can constitute an attempt, provided that this act is intended to lead without obstacle and delay to the completion of the crime.¹⁴⁷ There must not be any intermission or discontinuance in the planned course of events. In the case at hand the BGH based the decision on the assumption that the victim died in the early course of the crime, without the accused realizing or wanting the death at that stage, i.e. he acted unintentionally.¹⁴⁸ According to the plan of the accused several steps remained to be taken (changing the car, driving 100 km to the apartment, forcing the signature) before he wanted to kill her. Thus, binding and drugging the victim were not first steps towards the realization of the murder. He can, as regards the death of his wife, be punished only on the basis of negligence. Moreover, the Court concluded that the question of whether the accused had been mistaken about the situation was irrelevant.¹⁴⁹ It is

---

139 As to the relevance of foresight of the chain of causation for *mens rea* see the case above and the references in note 126.
140 *See* §16 (I) StGB, which reads:

> Mistake about Circumstances of the Act
> (1) Whoever upon commission of the act is unaware of a circumstance which is a statutory element of the offense does not act intentionally. Punishability for negligent commission remains unaffected.
> (2) Whoever upon commission of the act mistakenly assumes the existence of circumstances which would satisfy the elements of a more lenient norm, may only be punished for intentional commission under the more lenient norm.

141 According to §222 StGB, *supra* note 55.
142 It is the absolute prevailing view in German criminal law that the exact chain of causation must be part of the *mens rea* of the offender. *See, e.g.*, ROXIN, *supra* note 12, at §12 margin number 140; KREY, 2 GERMAN CRIMINAL LAW: LEGAL ELEMENTS OF THE INTENTIONAL OFFENCE COMMITTED BY ACTION, *supra* note 1, at 385–387.
143 Leading case in this regard is the so-called *Jauchegrubefall* (death in the cesspool case), BGHSt 14, 193. In the *Jauchegrubefall* the reverse situation was at stake: the offender thought he had already killed the victim in the first stage, whilst death occurred in the second stage, when the offender just wanted to dispose of the would-be corpse.
144 *See* as a leading case the so-called *Blutrauschfall* (bloodlust case), BGHSt 7, 325 (329).
145 BGHSt 7, 325 (329); BGHSt 23, 133 (135); BGHSt 38, 32 (34); Joecks, § *16*, *in* 1 MÜNCHENER KOMMENTAR ZUM STGB margin note 49, *supra* note 31.
146 BGH 55 NEUE JURISTISCHE WOCHENSCHRIFT (NJW) 1056, 1057 (2002).
147 The BGH refers to prior jurisprudence, *supra* note 137.
148 BGH, 55 NEUE JURISTISCHE WOCHENSCHRIFT (NJW) 1056, 1058 (2002).
149 *Id.* at 1057.

only relevant if the offender had acted intentionally, i.e. if there is *mens rea*. If there is not proof that the accused intended the death, there is obviously no defense of mistake of facts (in this case pertaining to the chain of causation) either as there is no substantial will of the offender so that he can actually be mistaken.[150]

D. Conclusion

We have looked at a full variety of critical issues in the jurisprudence of the BGH in the years 2002/2003. It is difficult to give a final comment on the development and carve out major trends in the Court's criminal law decisions. Yet, it is striking that the BGH has a tendency of corroborating established principles in criminal law. Thus, the rigid Germanic right to self-defense has been fortified in a situation where there was not physical attack,[151] at the same time the limits to the right to self-defense in a situation where the accused provoked the attack have been confirmed in a case where the situation had long turned against the accused.[152] The BGH also became more reluctant to accept diminished responsibility for intoxicated offenders.[153]

---

150 As to mistakes of facts pertaining to the chain of causation, *see supra* note 126.
151 *Infra* III.1.
152 *Infra* III.2.
153 *Infra* IV.

Report – *Bundesarbeitsgericht* (Federal Labor Court) – 2002/2003

Anna L. Izzo and Friedemann F. Kiethe[*]

A. Introduction

The official unemployment rate in Germany rose to 10.4% (4.31 million) in December 2003, with a seasonal increase in January and February still to come. The Scientific Advisory Board to the Federal Ministry of Economics and Labor (*Wissenschaftlicher Beirat*) estimated the overall unemployment (both official and unofficial) to number 5.8 million in November 2002.[1] A significant reduction in unemployment was by far the most important concern for voters in the general election in September 2002.

Labor law traditionally tends to protect workers from the risks and perils of their jobs and to favor them as the structurally and socially inferior, the less powerful party in the employment contract.[2] But labor law is also as "political" an area of law as are the classical fields of politics-related law, such as fundamental rights. The overall standard of labor law (including wage levels, additional wage costs, protection against dismissal, etc.) may be perceived in two irreconcilably opposing ways – either as a matter of social improvement or in terms of cost compounding the company's position in a competitive market.[3] Employers in Germany are in fact reluctant to hire staff these days. Are we facing bad times for German labor law?

What measures have been taken in order to encourage employers to hire people? Has the flexibility of employment contracts been enhanced? How can we promote fixed-term employment, since time-limits are always suspected of undermining the protection against wrongful dismissal provided by the Dismissal Protection Act (*Kündigungsschutzgesetz*, KSchG)?[4] Did the Federal Labor Court (*Bundesarbeitsgericht*, BAG) recently award workers with further "luxuries" which effectively destroy employers' confidence in future economic growth and which hinder a reduction in unemployment? Which trends and tendencies can be seen from the latest case law? And what is on the political agenda? What are government and parliament doing to improve the legal framework for increased levels of employment?

---

[*] Anna L. Izzo, LL.M. (EU/International Business Law, Frankfurt 2005), was born in 1977 and passed her First State Examination (J.D. equivalent) in Frankfurt in 2003. She is working on her doctoral thesis. Friedemann F. Kiethe, LL.M. (Vanderbilt, 2005; attorney at law, New York), was born in 1977 and passed his First State Examination in Frankfurt in 2003. He is working on his doctoral thesis.

1 BUNDESMINISTERIUM FÜR WIRTSCHAFT UND ARBEIT, DOKUMENTATION NR. 518, DIE HARTZ REFORMEN – EIN BEITRAG ZUR LÖSUNG DES BESCHÄFTIGUNGSPROBLEMS (2003), *availble at* www.bmwa.bund.de.
2 ZÖLLNER & LORITZ, ARBEITSRECHT 1, 3 (5th ed., 1998).
3 *See* Wolter, *Reformbedarf beim Kündigungsrecht aus Arbeitnehmersicht: Praxiserfahrungen und Schlussfolgerungen*, 20 NEUE ZEITSCHRIFT FÜR ARBEITSRECHT [NZA] 1068, 1069 (2003). *But see* Buchner, Reform des Arbeitsmarkts – Was brauchen und was können wir?, 56 DER BETRIEB [DB] 1510, 1512 (2003).
4 Buchner, *supra* note 3, at 1511; ZÖLLNER & LORITZ, *supra* note 2, at 268f.

B. Case Law

We summarize below the most important cases of those appearing before the Federal Labor Court during 2002/2003.

I. Regarding "On-call" Services as Working Time?

On September 9, 2003, the European Court of Justice (ECJ) issued an important but not surprising ruling on "on-call service" (*Bereitschaftsdienst*). Case C-151/02, *Landeshauptstadt Kiel v. Norbert Jaeger*[5] concerned Norbert Jaeger, who worked as a doctor in the surgical department of a hospital in Kiel, Germany. He regularly performed "on-call" duties during which he had to be present in the hospital and to work (only) when required. He was provided with a bed to enable him to rest when not working. The time spent with "on-call" service was offset in part by the granting of free time and also in part by payment of supplementary remuneration.

The lawsuit dealt with the classification of "on-call" service hours and its consequences for the doctor's maximum working time permitted by law.

Current German law – the Act on Working Time (*Arbeitszeitgesetz*, ArbZG) of June 6, 1994, enacted to transpose Directive 93/104/EC[6] – contains only a very vague statutory definition of "working time" as the period between the beginning and the end of work, with the exception of breaks (§ 2 para. 1 ArbZG). The Act on Working Time mainly fixes the maximum hours of regular working time. It amounts to usually eight hours spread over six days a week, i.e. 48 hours per week. The Act furthermore distinguishes between "readiness for work" (*Arbeitsbereitschaft*), "on-call service" and "stand-by" (*Rufbereitschaft*).[7] However, these three concepts are not defined but stem from case-law.[8] Accordingly, being on-call means that an employee is obliged to be present at a place determined by the employer, on or outside the latter's premises, and to keep himself available to answer his employer's call, but he is authorized to rest or to occupy himself as he sees fit as long as his services are not required.[9] On-call service was categorized as rest time, apart from the periods during which work is actually performed.[10] However, the doctor believed that on-call service constituted working time in its entirety, regardless of the actual proportions of sleeping or working time. In this case, *all* on-call service times would have counted for the maximum working time. Since Dr. Jaeger, as most doctors in hospitals, worked extremely long hours in addition to on-call services, his number of on-call services would have to be reduced dramatically.

He took his case to the regional labor court,[11] which subsequently referred it to the ECJ, asking the Court to interpret a number of provisions of the EC Directive on Working Time (93/104/EC),[12] which is based on the concept of the worker's "health and safety" in his working environment in terms of Article 118a of the EC Treaty (pre-Amsterdam

---

5 *Available at* www.curia.eu.int, or in CELEX document No. 62002J0151.
6 Directive of the European Parliament and Council 93/104 of 23 November 1993, Concerning Certain Aspects of the Organisation of Working Time, 1993 O.J. (L 307) 18 (EC); amended by Directive of the European Parliament and Council 2000/34 of 22 June 2000, Amending Council Directive 93/104 of 23 November 1993, Concerning Certain Aspects of the Organization of Working Time, 2000 O.J. (L 195) 41.
7 Anzinger, § 218, *in* II Münchener Handbuch-Arbeitsrecht – Individualarbeitsrecht (Bd. 2) margin no. 10 (Richardi & Wlotzke eds., 2nd ed., 2000).
8 *Id.*
9 *Id.* at margin no. 18.
10 *Id.* at margin no. 11.
11 Bundesarbeitsgericht, 20 Neue Zeitschrift für Arbeitsrecht [NZA] 742 (2003).
12 Directive of the European Paraliament and Council 93/104 of 23 November 1993, Concerning Certain Aspects of the Organization of Working Time, arts. 1–3, 5–6, 8, 15, 18, 1993 O.J. (L 307) 18 (EC).

version).[13] Three years earlier the ECJ had decided the *SIMAP*[14] case which dealt with Spanish "on-call" service times. This leading case encouraged Norbert Jaeger to file his own lawsuit. The Advocate General[15] and the Court repeated their attitude towards "on-call" service times, based on the concept of working time as defined in Directive 93/104/EC: the need to be present at the place determined by the employer, and to be available in order to provide services immediately, makes it impossible for the doctors concerned to choose where they stay during waiting periods and therefore must be regarded as coming within the ambit of their duties. Being on-call is subject to greater constraints than on "stand-by"; stand-by does not require a worker to be on the premises. Therefore, German law treating periods of on-call duty without activity as "rest periods" is contrary to Community law.

In the aftermath of the *SIMAP* case, German labor courts had tried to interpret the relevant provisions of the ArbZG in accordance with the Working Time Directive. However, after having analyzed the wording of the relevant provisions[16] the Federal Labor Court found an interpretation in accordance with EC law impossible.[17] Thus the Act on Working Time had to be amended. The initial transformation of the Directive into national law did not foresee potential problems related to "on-call" service and did not provide an appropriate regulation. The *Jaeger* case stressed the nonconformity of the relevant passages in the ArbZG and increased the pressure on the German legislator to alter the law.

Meanwhile the legislator undertook the necessary changes in the Law Concerning Reforms on the Labor Market (*Gesetz zu Reformen am Arbeitsmarkt*).[18] The statutory amendment clarified that on-call service is working time. The amendment also tackled the problem of maximum working hours that has become imminent since on-call service is wholly considered working time: annual working hours, including on-call service, may not exceed 48 hours weekly except with the employee's consent. Collective agreements or work or service agreements may extend working hours to more than ten hours daily if the working hours include a considerable amount of time spent on-call.

Now that on-call time is treated as working time, a considerable amount of the savings the German health reform should have generated may be foiled. Estimations of the Doctors' Association *"Marburger Bund"* expect that the 2,000 hospitals in Germany will have to employ around 15,000 additional doctors. The German Hospital Society (*Deutsche Krankenhausgesellschaft*, DKG) even talks of 27,000 doctors. The several associations in the German health system arrogate an additional financial fund up to €1.75 million per annum.[19] Many governments of EU Member States find these consequences of the ECJ's interpretation of the Working Time Directive absolutely impracticable and unrealistic. In their view it not only creates enormous additional costs but also tremendous breaks in supplying patients with health care in general.

As a consequence the European Commission launched consultations on the matter of working time. The Commission is calling for all interested parties to participate. The goal is to revise the EC Working Time Directive. For now, the Commission has three aims:[20]

---

13 Willms, *Art. 118a margin no. 80*, in KOMMENTAR ZUM EU-/EG-VERTRAG (Groeben et al. eds., 5th ed., 1999).
14 Case C-303/98, SIMAP v. Conselleria de Sanidad y Consumo de la Generalidad Valenciana, 2000 E.C.R. I-7963.
15 CELEX 62002C0151.
16 Arbeitszeitgesetz (ArbZG) [Act on Working Time], June 6, 1994, BGBl. I 1994 S. 1170, arts. 2, 5 para. 3, 7 para. 2 sent. 1.
17 Bundesarbeitsgericht, 56 DER BETRIEB [DB] 1387, 1389 (2003).
18 Körner, *Article 4b des Gesetzes zu Reformen am Arbeitsmarkt vom 24. Dezember 2003*, NEUE JURISTISCHE WOCHENSCHRIFT (NJW) 3606, 3608 (2003).
19 *Ärzte-Bereitschaftsdienst in Kliniken ist Arbeitszeit*, FRANKFURTER ALLGEMEINE ZEITUNG, September 9, 2003.
20 Press Release 5 January 2004 *at* http://europa.eu.int/rapid/start/cgi/guesten.ksh?p_action.gettxt= gt&doc=IP/04/1&lg=EN&display= with reference to the consultation http://europa.eu.int/comm/ employment_social/labour_law/documentation_en.htm.

1. Analysis of the implementation of the opt-out[21] and derogations to the period over which working time is calculated ("reference period").
2. Analysis of the impact of recent case law concerning the definition of working time and the qualification of time spent on-call – whether it should be characterized as working time or rest period.
3. Consultation of interested parties on possible future modification of the Directive.

The *Marburger Bund* has reacted with a lack of appreciation and understanding: a revision of the Directive only motivated by economic aspects would endanger the protection of hospital doctors and the security of patients. It would be grotesque, the *Bund* argues, to avoid the working protection, confirmed and attested through many decisions and law suits, by changing the Directive itself.[22]

II. Consumer Protection for Contracts Between Employer and Employee – Employees as Consumers within the Meaning of § 13 German Civil Code?

Having already legally defined the terms "consumer"[23] and "entrepreneur"[24] in the German Civil Code (*Bürgerliches Gesetzbuch*, BGB) in the middle of 2000, the parliament incorporated, with effect from January 1, 2002, various special acts on consumer protection[25] into the Civil Code. At the same time the law of standard business terms was incorporated,[26] having been previously included in the Standard Business Terms Act (*Gesetz zu Allgemeinen Geschäftsbedingungen*, AGBG). Since then a strong controversy about the application of consumer rights and protection laws on the employer–employee relationship has developed. Considering the possible legal consequences it is obvious why the answer to this question is of highest importance.[27]

Should employees be regarded as consumers, they may be entitled to withdrawal within the meaning of § 312 para. 1 BGB.[28] Before 2002, this provision had been the core provision of the Act on the Withdrawal of Doorstep Transactions, implementing the Doorstep Selling Directive 85/577/EEC.[29] Paragraph 312 BGB entitles consumers to withdraw their consent to a contract if the consumer has been induced to conclude the contract as a result of oral negotiations at his place of work or in private residence, on the occasion of a leisure event or subsequent to a surprising approach in a means of transport or in open public space, i.e. in places or venues where a consumer is usually surprised by an offer to conclude a contract and may hence conclude contracts he or she would not have concluded if he or she had had the necessary time to think about it. According to § 13 BGB, a consumer is any natural person who concludes a legal transaction with a purpose that can neither be assigned to his or her commercial nor to his or her self-employed professional activity.

---

21 Allowing Member States not to apply the working hours under certain conditions, e.g. with a prior agreement.
22 *EU korrigiert Arbeitszeitrichtlinie*, FRANKFURTER ALLGEMEINE ZEITUNG, January 6, 2004, at 9.
23 Bürgerliches Gesetzbuch [BGB] [Civil Code] Aug. 18, 1896, § 13.
24 Bürgerliches Gesetzbuch [BGB] [Civil Code] Aug. 18, 1896, § 14.
25 Within the framework of the reform on the law of obligation: Cancellation of Doorstep Transactions (*Haustürgeschäfte*), Distance Contracts (*Fernabsatzgeschäfte*), Consumer Loan Contracts (*Verbraucherdarlehen*).
26 *See* Bürgerliches Gesetzbuch [BGB] [Civil Code] Aug. 18, 1896, §§ 305–310.
27 Reim, Arbeitnehmer und/oder Verbraucher?, 55 DER BETRIEB [DB] 2434 (2002).
28 Previously included in the Act on the Cancellation of Doorstep Transactions and analogous Transactions. According to this provision, a consumer may revoke a contract concerning performance for remuneration which the consumer has been induced to conclude as a result of oral negotiations.
29 Council Directive 85/577 of 20 December 1985, To Protect the Consumer in Respect of Contracts Negotiated Away from Business Premises, 1985 O.J. (L 372) 31 (EEC).

From a formal point of view, the employment contract and any other agreement between employer and employee, e.g. an agreement to terminate the contract, do not serve a self-employed but a dependant professional activity. As a consequence, employees concluding a contract with their employer could fall under the notion of "consumer" in terms of § 13 BGB. The situation in which such contracts are entered into, i.e. usually the employers' premises, may be regarded as comparable to the situation described in § 312 para. 1 BGB.

This also applies to mutual agreements terminating the employment (dissolution contracts) or changing working conditions. According to the further statutory provisions on withdrawal from contracts, §§ 355 to 357 BGB, a consumer may withdraw his or her consent to a contract within two weeks, thus dissolving the contract. But this period of time only commences when the consumer is informed of his or her right to withdrawal by a clearly formulated textual notice. In practice, the employee may be entitled to withdraw months later.

A further change could be caused by the extension of the law of standard business terms onto employment contracts. Employment contracts could be subject to monitoring even if the contract in its actual form has been applied only once, § 310 para. 3 no. 2 BGB. Those general provisions intend to protect the consumer, i.e. a purchaser of goods or services who has to pay remuneration in return. In contrast, labor law is designed to protect the employee as the party to the contract *who renders a service* to a business and *claims* a payment. Furthermore, labor law has developed specific mechanisms of employee protection.

In 2002 and 2003, three judgments of State Labor Courts of Appeal [*Landesarbeitsgerichte*, LAG] dealt with the application of consumer protection norms of the Civil Code to employment contracts.[30] LAG Brandenburg and LAG Hamm concluded that § 312 BGB exclusively concerned a special system of distribution, such as distance contracts and doorstep transactions that required increased levels of consumer protection. The Courts also found an unacceptable collision between the different time limits that operated to preclude the respective remedies: A withdrawal may be declared even six months later (§ 355 para. 3 BGB), whereas lawsuits claiming unfair dismissal of an employee have to be filed within three weeks (§§ 4, 7 Dismissal Protection Act (*Kündigungsschutzgesetz*, KSchG)). The LAG Cologne, in an *obiter dictum*, simply stated that the employee was not in a situation comparable with the consumer's.

In the meantime, the Federal Labor Court decided the first case regarding the right to withdraw under § 312 BGB.[31] In this particular case the Court denied an effective withdrawal by the employee. It found that § 312 BGB is not applicable on dissolution agreements concluded in the employer's offices. The central question, whether or not an employee is to be regarded as a consumer within the meaning of § 13 BGB, was not answered. However, the judges resorted to the history of origin, the legal systematology as well as to the spirit and purpose of § 312 BGB. They clarified that the employer's office is not an atypical environment, rather a typical venue where working conditions are negotiated. From an employee's point of view, the whole situation cannot be perceived as particularly surprising and astonishing. Paragraph 312 BGB relates to "dangerous" distribution systems and surprising situations, and not to contractual negotiations at the same eye level.

Those decisions may serve as first guidelines for the future, but legal uncertainty remains. A possible approach to this problem is returning to the European concept of "consumer," which provided the origin of the German provision. Paragraph 13 BGB has to

---

30 Landesarbeitsgericht Brandenburg [LAG] [Brandenburg Regional Labor Court], 7 Sa 386/02, October 30, 2002; Landesarbeitsgericht Köln [LAG] [Cologne Regional Labor Court], 8 Sa 979/02, December 18, 2002; Landesarbeitsgericht Hamm [LAG] [Hamm Regional Labor Court], 19 Sa 1901/02, April 1, 2003 .
31 Bundesarbeitsgericht [BAG] [Federal Labor Court], 2 AZR 177/03, November 27, 2003.

be interpreted in the context of its European counterpart. European consumer protection law does not provide a uniform definition of the term "consumer." However, the European concept focuses on the consumer's economic role rather than indifferently protecting "the weak."[32] The idea of a prudent and well-informed consumer clearly contradicts an application of the right to withdrawal on employees negotiating contracts with their employer.

III. The Act on Part-Time Work and Fixed-Term Employment Contracts – Current Case Law on Employees' Right to Work Reduced Hours

On January 1, 2001, the German Act on Part-Time Work and Fixed-Term Employment Contracts (*Teilzeit- und Befristungsgesetz*, TzBfG) came into force and replaced existing rules contained in the Act on the Improvement of Employment Opportunities (*Beschäftigungsförderungsgesetz* 1985). By means of the new Act, the government sought to create an adequate legal basis for part-time work and fixed-term employment relationships hoping to meet the needs of present-day employment. At the same time, the Act transposes two EC Directives on part-time and fixed-term work.[33]

Pursuant to the new rules, employees are entitled to reduce their contractual working time provided (1) their employer has more than 15 regular employees and (2) they have worked with that employer for more than six months.[34] An employer must consent to the reduction of working time requested by the employee and allow the employee to work the hours and days he or she wishes unless there are "internal business reasons" for rejecting the request, § 8 para. 4 TzBfG. Those reasons apply if the reduction significantly impairs the organization or the flow of work in the business or significantly impairs the safety of operations or causes disproportionate costs. "Internal business reasons" have not yet been defined in more concrete terms; however, they may be agreed on in a collective agreement.[35] In any case, employers and employees are to discuss the request in order to reach agreement.[36] The butter-soft term "internal business reasons" has given rise to questions: Does it "count" as a reason if the employer cannot find a suitable supplementary co-employee for the remaining working hours? If so, for how long must the employer have tried to find one? How does the employer resource additional employees? Is it only public job centers (*Arbeitsamt*) or must private companies for employment exchange also to be contacted? Are additional costs arising from the introduction of a new employee sufficient "internal business reasons"? What about additional administrative costs in the personnel department? The legislator referred to "rational and comprehensible reasons,"[37] but in fact there is not much legal certainty.

In the period between January 2001 and January 2003, 27% of the employees of all German enterprises exercised their right to reduce working hours. In 17% of the cases the requests were totally rejected, in 13% of the cases the desired working time-tables have not

---

32 Micklitz, §§ 1–240, *in* MÜNCHENER KOMMENTAR – BGB ALLGEMEINER TEIL (Bd. 1) introduction to §§ 13 and 14, margin no. 85 (Säcker ed., 4th ed., 2001).
33 Council Directive 97/81 of 15 December 1997, Concerning the Framework Agreement on Part-time Work Concluded by UNICE, CEEP and the ETUC – Framework Agreement on Part-time Work, 1998 O.J. (L 14) 9 (EC); Council Directive 99/70 of 18 June 1999, Concerning the Framework Agreement on Fixed-term Work Concluded by ETUC, UNICE and CEEP, 1999 O.J. (L 175) 43.
34 Teilzeit- und Befristungsgesetz [TzBfG] [German Act on Part-time Work and Fixed-term Employment Contracts], December 21, 2000, BGBl. I at 1966, § 8.
35 Schüren, § 162, *in* MÜNCHENER-HANDBUCH-ARBEITSRECHT – ERGÄNZUNGSBAND-INDIVIDUALRECHT, margin no. 76 (Richardi & Wlotzke eds., 2nd ed., 2001).
36 Bundesarbeitsgericht, 20 NEUE ZEITSCHRIFT FÜR ARBEITSRECHT (NZA) 742 (2003); Landesarbeitsgericht Düsseldorf, 57 BETRIEBSBERATER (BB) 1541 (2002).
37 Wisskirchen, *Aktuelle Rechtsprechung zum Anspruch auf Teilzeit*, 56 DER BETRIEB DB 277, 278 (2003).

been approved. Two-thirds of the requests have been accepted. But 12% of the interviewed enterprises admitted that they will be more restrained with applicants who will "probably" ask for part-time work in the future.[38] In 2001 87% of all part-time jobs were held by women.[39]

The first labor court decisions concerning the right to reduce working hours were delivered as early as 2001, providing the first guidelines for the practice. A selection of the most recent and most remarkable cases is set out below.

In general, German labor courts assume that the employer bears the burden of proof and has to explain in a comprehensive and concrete way the operational obstacles to the reduction of working hours.[40]

On October 14, 2003, the Federal Labor Court decided that the employer's interest in his concept of operational organization is not disturbed if he is able to employ a *suitable* co-employee.[41] The co-employee is suitable if he or she has the necessary knowledge and skills or at least will be able to obtain knowledge and skills through adequate training by the employer.

In another case the employer denied the reduction of working hours because of a "one-face-to-the-customer" philosophy.[42] But in accordance with the Federal Court this concept constitutes no operational reason if it is not even realizable with full-time employees; in this case the employer would have to take alternative precautions anyway.

On August 19, 2003, the BAG decided a lawsuit dealing with an employee who worked as a teacher and educational specialist in a nursery school for remedial education.[43] The children needed intensive care because of mental handicaps. The Federal Court decided in favor of the employer, who asserted the children's special need for daily continuous care and support by the same person(s). This was regarded an operational reason in the meaning of § 8 para. 4 TzBfG.

Finally, the Federal Labor Court confirmed that a works agreement under § 87 para. 1 no. 2 Works Constitution Act (*Betriebsverfassungsgesetz*, BetrVG) may constitute an operational reason.

Summarizing the case law, German labor courts took their task of concretizing the notion of "internal business reasons" quite seriously.[44] For the employer to deny shorter working hours purely because of displeasure or troublesomeness was found to be insufficient. Neither do courts accept the employers' general argument of increased costs without specific proof. Disruptions of the work flow must be proven by the employer; they only amount to internal business reasons if they cannot be overcome in any reasonable way. If employees express the wish to change to a part-time job, the employer must inform them of any such vacant jobs in the establishment.

IV. Employers' Contributions to Maternity Grants

The protection of the working mother in Germany is governed by the Working Mother Protection Act (*Mutterschutzgesetz*, MuSchG). This Act not only awards working mothers

---

38 According to a survey by the German DIHT (Delegation of German Industry and Trade); *see* Wisskirchen, *supra* note 37, at 277.
39 *See* European Foundation for the Improvement of Living and Working Conditions: www.eiro.eurofound.it; "New law passed on part-time work and fixed-term employment contracts".
40 Arbeitsgericht Arnsberg, 19 NEUE ZEITSCHRIFT FÜR ARBEITSRECHT (NZA) 564 (2002).
41 Bundesarbeitsgericht, 57 Der Betrieb (BB) 986 (2004).
42 Bundesarbeitsgericht, 57 Der Betrieb (BB) 709 (2004).
43 Bundesarbeitsgericht [BAG] [Federal Labor Court], 9 AZR 542/02, August 19, 2003.
44 Wisskirchen, *supra* note 37, at 281.

protection against dismissal during pregnancy and for four months after giving birth, but also places restrictions on the pregnant woman's occupation and maternity benefits.

Usually mothers may not work for a period of time of six weeks before[45] and eight weeks after their child's birth.[46] During this time they are entitled to maternity benefits under § 14 MuSchG amounting to their net income. Maternity benefits are funded by the employer, health insurance and (for women without health insurance) the federal government. The health insurance contributes €13/day, the employer has to finance the difference of the net income.[47] Since 1968 the health insurance contribution has not been increased, therefore the employer's proportion continuously grew with generally rising net incomes. Small businesses with 20 or fewer employees participate in a compensation system[48] according to which the employer's direct contribution is reimbursed by the health insurance, but indirectly paid by all small businesses participating in the compensation system.[49]

In the year 1991/1992 an employer with a staff of 100 employees (50% of them female) refused to pay his part of the pregnant employees' maternity benefit. He argued that his constitutional right to occupational freedom was violated.[50] The Federal Labor Court, however, did not share this opinion.[51] It stated that the provisions on protection of working mothers executed the constitutional command to protection and welfare for mothers[52] and imposed appropriate burdens on the employers. The Court assumed that, in the long term, medium-sized and big businesses would not profit from a compensation system compared to their current direct contributions. The Federal Labor Court recognized a significant increase of employers' maternity costs in relation to health insurance and the federal government, but did not find arbitrary unequal treatment of small businesses (included in a compensation system) on the one hand and medium-sized or big businesses (not being included in a compensation system)[53] on the other hand. The Court also did not find a distortion of competition between German employers (all evenly burdened).[54] Although younger women (who may get pregnant and will be entitled to maternity benefits) might be disadvantaged on the labor market, the Federal Labor Court did not acknowledge that the parliament had exceeded its discretion.[55]

Upon the employer's constitutional complaint against the Federal Labor Court's judgment, the Federal Constitutional Court (*Bundesverfassungsgericht*, BVerfG) held the relevant provisions of the MSchG unconstitutional.[56] In the past, the employers' contributions to maternity grants had been approved by the Federal Constitutional Court twice,[57] but meanwhile the actual and legal context had changed. On one hand, the employers' financial burden had risen to above 50% and, on the other hand, the constitutional principle of gender equality[58] had been fortified to a constitutional command of affirmative action. In principle, the Court reasoned, it was acceptable to place financial burdens of welfare measures

---

45 Mutterschutzgesetz [MuSchG] [Maternity Protection Act], June 20, 2002, BGBl. I at 2318, § 3 (mothers can still waive their maternity leave before giving birth).
46 Mutterschutzgesetz [MuSchG] [Maternity Protection Act], June 20, 2002, BGBl. I at 2318, § 6 para. 1.
47 Mutterschutzgesetz [MuSchG] [Maternity Protection Act], June 20, 2002, BGBl. I at 2318, § 13, § 14 para. 1.
48 Lohnfortzahlungsgesetz [LFZG] [Continued Payment of Wages Act], July 27, 1969, BGBl. I at 946, § 10.
49 Lohnfortzahlungsgesetz [LFZG] [Continued Payment of Wages Act], July 27, 1969, BGBl. I at 946, § 14.
50 GRUNDGESETZ [GG] [Constitution] art. 12.
51 BAGE 81, 222.
52 GRUNDGESETZ [GG] [Constitution] art. 6 para. 1.
53 BAGE 81, 222 (228).
54 *Id.* at 231.
55 *Id.* at 232.
56 Bundesverfassungsgericht, 57 NEUE JURISTISCHE WOCHENSCHRIFT (NJW) 146 (2004).
57 BVerfGE 37, 121ff.; BVerfGE 70, 242.
58 GRUNDGESETZ [GG] [Constitution] art. 3 para. 2.

on the employers, who also bear special responsibility for their employees.[59] But § 14 para. 1 MuSchG disproportionately limits the right to occupational freedom and hence violates the constitutional command to equal gender treatment.[60] Since the compensation system is limited to small businesses, factual discrimination against women working for medium-sized and big businesses is not hindered. Finally the Court stated that the relevant provisions of the MSchG must be replaced before December 31, 2005. The legislator is not obliged to extend the compensation system, but may take other steps to foster equal gender treatment.

V. Wearing Headscarves at Work

For several years now, there have been discussions concerning the issue of muslim women wearing headscarves at work in Germany. One leading case[61] deals with a woman, who immigrated from Afghanistan and wanted to teach as a civil servant. This case went through the system of administrative courts[62] and finally came before the Federal Constitutional Court. The Federal Constitutional Court balanced the right to religious freedom[63] of the prospective teacher and of the pupils concerned, on the one hand, and the concept of civil servants' neutrality,[64] on the other hand. Finally the Court held that any ban on headscarves in German classrooms would have to be authorized by statute. Some German States (*Bundesländer*) are preparing the necessary legislation to keep headscarves out of their classrooms, whilst others have not yet done so.[65]

Another case concerned a Turkish shop assistant who suddenly decided to wear a headscarf at work. The management of the department store did not accept striking clothing in the perfume department, fearing customers might feel affronted and stay away. The dismissed salesperson filed a lawsuit against her employer in the labor court system.[66] Under the Dismissal Protection Act (*Kündigungsschutzgesetz*, KSchG), the employer bears the burden of proof and therefore has to give evidence of a "social justification,"[67] that is, a just cause for the dismissal. The department store was not able to prove any economic disadvantages, neither imminent nor already realized, because of the shop assistant wearing a headscarf. Still, the courts in first and second instance accepted the *abstract* danger of financial loss caused by customers being turned off.[68] However, the Federal Labor Court demanded proof of *specific* economic damages; furthermore it stated that the department store could still employ the shop assistant in a less exposed position somewhere else in the store.[69] The employer's constitutional complaint against the decision of the Federal Labor

---

59 Bundesverfassungsgericht, 57 NEUE JURISTISCHE WOCHENSCHRIFT (NJW) 146, 148 (2004).
60 *Id.* at 149.
61 Bundesverfassungsgericht, 56 NEUE JURISTISCHE WOCHENSCHRIFT (NJW) 3111 (2003).
62 Verwaltungsgericht Stuttgart, 19 NEUE ZEITSCHRIFT FÜR VERWALTUNGSRECHT (NVwZ) 959 (2000); Verwaltungsgerichtshof Mannheim, 54 NEUE JURISTISCHE WOCHENSCHRIFT (NJW) 2899 (2001); Bundesverwaltungsgericht, 55 NEUE JURISTISCHE WOCHENSCHRIFT (NJW) 3344 (2002). *See* Hoevels, *Kopftuch als Kündigungsgrund?*, NEUE ZEITSCHRIFT FÜR ARBEITSRECHT (NZA) 701 (2003).
63 GRUNDGESETZ [GG] [Constitution] art. 4 para. 1.
64 GRUNDGESETZ [GG] [Constitution] art. 33 paras. 2 and 3.
65 The States of Hesse, Bavaria, Berlin, Brandenburg, Lower-Saxony, Saarland and Baden-Württemberg are going to ban headscarves; Hamburg, Schleswig-Holstein and Northrhine-Westphalia will examine each individual case.
66 Landesarbeitsgericht Hessen, 54 NEUE JURISTISCHE WOCHENSCHRIFT (NJW) 3650 (2001); Bundesarbeitsgericht, 56 NEUE JURISTISCHE WOCHENSCHRIFT (NJW) 1685 (2003).
67 Kündigungsschutzgesetz [KSchG] [Dismissal Protection Act]. August 25, 1965, BGBl. I at 1317, § 1 paras. 1 and 2.
68 Landesarbeitsgericht Hessen, 56 NEUE JURISTISCHE WOCHENSCHRIFT (NJW) 3650, 3651 (2003) ("schädliche Entfremdung des Kundenkreises ... nach der Lebenserfahrung nahe liegend und gut nachvollziehbar").
69 Bundesarbeitsgericht, 56 NEUE JURISTISCHE WOCHENSCHRIFT (NJW) 1685, 1687 (2003).

Court was not accepted.[70] The Federal Constitutional Court did not recognize any fundamental constitutional error in the Federal Labor Court's application of the Dismissal Protection Act and in its balancing the salesperson's right to religious freedom and the right of both parties to occupational freedom.[71] The Court concluded that both are inherent in the existing statutory protection against unfair dismissal.

C. Legislation

Amongst countless legislative proposals, we will focus on the most important legislation that either has been passed recently or still is on the political agenda with a realistic chance of being passed sometime soon.

I. "Hartz" Reforms

"Hartz" was undoubtedly the word most frequently used in German politics in 2003. It not only means Dr. Peter Hartz, the person, but also Germany's "dernier crie": reducing unemployment by two million(!) in three years![72]

Dr. Peter Hartz is a member of the governing Social Democratic Party, manager of the Volkswagen company and the board member who is in charge of labor relations. When Volkswagen faced economic difficulties, he introduced a 28-hour/4-day working-week, increased flexibility and thus saved many jobs from being cut. In summer 2002, he was appointed head of a governmental commission on "Reduction of Unemployment and Reorganization of the Federal Employment Office." The commission was staffed by representatives of various groups of society. The Commission's suggestions to "Modern Services on the Labor Market" (*Moderne Dienstleistungen am Arbeitsmarkt*)[73] have not only dominated German politics in 2002, especially during the general election campaign, and in 2003, but they have also met with widespread approval.

In March 2003, the German government announced the so-called "Agenda 2010", a political "to-do list" until 2010. It includes the Hartz reforms as well as a reduction of subsidies and also reforms in related fields of law such as tax law, the Handicrafts Code, the public health care system and the public pension system.[74]

The Hartz reforms consist of three components, (1) deregulation of labor legislation, (2) improved placement of job-seekers, and (3) reformed financial support for the jobless. The various financial measures include (amongst others) a special aid program to combat youth unemployment, unemployment insurance related incentives to employ older unemployed as well as reforms of the unemployment benefits (increased obligations to accept offered jobs, reduced periods for drawing benefits).

The first project was to make employment of the jobless easier. Fixed-term employment and temporary employment are no longer seen as undermining employee protection. Indeed it is revolutionary for traditional German labor law to recognize both forms of employment as a first step out of unemployment.

---

70 Bundesverwaltungsgericht, 56 NEUE JURISTISCHE WOCHENSCHRIFT (NJW) 2815 (2003).
71 GRUNDGESETZ [GG] [Constitution] art. 12 para. 1.
72 MODERNE DIENSTLEISTUNGEN AM ARBEITSMARKT, "HARTZ-BERICHT", part 1, p. 5. (http://www.bmwi.de/Redaktion/Inhalte/Downloads/Homepage_2Fdownload_2FArbeit_2FHartz1.pdf,property=pdf.pdf)
73 http://www.bmwi.de/Redaktion/Inhalte/Downloads/hartzbericht-zusammenfassung-eng-hartz0__e, property=pdf.pdf
74 http://www.bundesregierung.de/artikel,-482917/Die-Massnahmen-der-Agenda-2010.htm

Fixed-term employment has so far been subject to many restrictions such as an objective reason justifying the conclusion of a fixed-term contract as such, and the time limit chosen; without such a justifying reason fixed-term contracts generally could be concluded for a maximum period of two years.[75] If a time limit proved to be void, the rest of the employment contract remained valid, i.e. as a contract of unlimited duration.[76] For newly-formed companies the duration for which fixed-term contracts may be concluded without any justifying reason has been prolonged to four years.[77]

Other measures of the Hartz reforms intend to foster small-sized personal initiative and thus hope to decrease moonlighting. Jobless people who render services in private households and do not earn more than €500 per month, so-called "mini jobs" will only be subject to a flat-rate social security contribution of 10%. The already famous "Me-Inc." (*Ich-AG*) is a preliminary step to self-employment. Me-Inc.s are subsidized with the money that an unemployed person would have been entitled to receive as an unemployment benefit or social insurance contribution. Me-Inc.s earnings up to €25,000 per year only face a flat rate taxation of 10%.

The second project was to improve placement of the unemployed. The employment office is undergoing a major re-branding and will be called "Federal Employment Service" (*Bundesagentur für Arbeit*), (regional) "Competence Center" (*KompetenzCenter*) or (local) "Job Center." Job centers are designed to integrate labor market related counseling and support services such as social and youth welfare, housing, debt-aid and so forth.

Hartz also invented a new tool to make the placement of job-seekers quicker and more effective: Personnel Service Agencies (*Personal Service Agenturen*, PSA). PSA are independent organizational units under private law, either independently founded or arising out of the cooperation between a Job Center and third parties, and operate like any other temporary work agency. The concept is to employ the jobless in the PSA and try to hire them out to an employer – who hopefully will keep this person permanently ("adhesive effect" by means of a placement-oriented temporary job). The interim periods, when somebody employed by the PSA cannot be hired out elsewhere, shall be determined by qualification and training.

In general, the Hartz reforms are welcome to facilitate reducing unemployment. However, particular companies have to be extremely careful. For example contracting a "Me-Inc." can be interpreted as contracting an ordinary employee with full rights to protection against dismissal, to wages pursuant to collective agreements, and so on.[78] The creation of PSA transfers the economic costs of dismissal protection from the original employers via PSA to the taxpayers.[79] Some PSA employed jobless at the end of a month and dismissed them just days later – thus receiving two monthly subsidies, but not granting permanent employment. Is it tantamount to blasphemy to doubt the success of the Hartz reforms; two million jobs within three years!?

---

75   Teilzeit- und Befristungsesetz [TzBfG] [German Act on Part-Time Work and Fixed-term Employment Contracts], December 21, 2000, BGBl. I at 1966, § 14.
76   Teilzeit- und Befristungsesetz [TzBfG] [German Act on Part-Time Work and Fixed-term Employment Contracts], December 21, 2000, BGBl. I at 1966, § 16.
77   Teilzeit- und Befristungsesetz [TzBfG] [German Act on Part-Time Work and Fixed-term Employment Contracts], December 21, 2000, BGBl. I at 1966, § 14 para. 2a.
78   Greiner, *Die Ich-AG als Arbeitnehmer*, 56 DER BETRIEB [DB] 1058, 1062 (2003).
79   Buchner, *supra* note 4, at 1512; BUNDESMINISTERIUM FÜR WIRTSCHAFT UND ARBEIT, DOKUMENTATION NR. 518, *supra* note 1, at 5.

II. Dismissal Protection

The most disputed proposal found in Agenda 2010 reforms was the reform of dismissal protection: Highest levels of dismissal protection perhaps help to keep people in their existing jobs. But at the same time this inflexibility scares employers into not hiring additional staff, because they have to anticipate the potential costs of terminating the employment contract.[80] Invincible entry barriers to the labor market in effect deny the jobless access to employment.[81]

Protection against an ordinary dismissal with notice is governed by the Dismissal Protection Act (*Kündigungsschutzgesetz*, KSchG).[82] Under this Act, applicable to employers employing a certain number of employees and to employees having been employed for more than six months, any dismissal has to be "socially justified".[83] This means, employees may only be dismissed for reasons rooted (1) in the employee's behavior, (2) in the employee's personality, or (3) in the operation of the enterprise (e.g. business process reengineering, redundancies). In the event of operational reasons, the employer has to carry out a "social factor test" (*Sozialauswahl*)[84] and dismiss the employee who is deemed to be least troubled by the dismissal. In the course of the reforms, the social factor test has been narrowed exclusively to the criteria (1) period of employment with the employer, (2) age, (3) obligations to pay maintenance and (4) disabilities. This may lead to an increase in legal certainty if courts strictly limit themselves to those terms and do not return to "undue hardships."[85] Surprisingly, this provision had first been introduced under Helmut Kohl's government in 1996. It was repealed for being deemed "anti-social" as soon as Gerhard Schröder took office in 1998, and finally has been introduced again.

Before 2004, the Act on Dismissal Protection applied to businesses employing more than five persons.[86] Employers with up to five employees hence were very hesitant to hire an additional person and become subject to the limitations of the Dismissal Protection Act. Instead they preferred to make their staff work overtime. This is why companies that, until 31 December 2003, did not fall under the Act on Dismissal Protection because they employed five or less persons are now allowed to hire up to ten employees without being subject to the statutory limitations.[87]

Finally, a new § 1a KSchG awards employees who have been dismissed for operational reasons with the statutory right to choose between statutory dismissal protection or severance payment. The payment shall amount to 0.5 of a monthly salary for each year of employment. The idea itself is far from being revolutionary as, in the past, employers often used compensation payments on a voluntary basis in order to reach amicable settlements with dismissed employees and to avoid potential lawsuits. What really *is* new is the factor of 0.5: whereas voluntary severance payments have frequently been calculated with the

---

80 Buchner, *supra* note 3, at 1512.
81 Buchner, *supra* note 3, at 1511.
82 Bürgerliches Gesetzbuch [BGB] [Civil Code] Aug. 18, 1896, § 626 (governing extraordinary dismissals without notice).
83 Kündigungsschutzgesetz [KSchG] [Dismissal Protection Act], August 25, 1969, BGBl. I at 1317, § 1 paras. 1 and 2.
84 Kündigungsschutzgesetz [KSchG] [Dismissal Protection Act], August 25, 1969, BGBl. I at 1317, § 1 para. 3 sent. 2.
85 Löwisch, *Die kündigungsrechtlichen Vorschläge der „Agenda 2010"*, 20 NEUE ZEITSCHRIFT FÜR ARBEITSRECHT (NZA) 689, 691 (2003); Schnitker & Grau, *Bleibt alles anders? Die Kriterien für die Sozialauswahl bei betriebsbedingter Kündigung nach neuem alten Recht*, 24 ZEITSCHRIFT FÜR WIRTSCHAFTSRECHT [ZIP] 1867 (2003).
86 Kündigungsschutzgesetz [KSchG] [Dismissal Protection Act], August 25, 1969, BGBl. I at 1317, § 23 para 1.
87 Kündigungsschutzgesetz [KSchG] [Dismissal Protection Act], August 25, 1969, BGBl. I at 1317, § 23 para 3, sent. 3.

factor 0.3, the new statutory provision is merely a *minimum* level – which must be observed and which will lead to more expensive redundancy payments schemes.[88]

D. Conclusion

Bad times for Labor Law in Germany? Bad for those who are in a job, or just bad for those in need of a job? While German legislation pretended to tackle unemployment, does the jurisprudence meanwhile thwart all efforts in encouraging employers to hire additional staff?

If a "feel-good" factor might animate business owners to take on more personnel, recent case law does not contribute much to entrepreneurial freedom or promote the impression employers' concerns are taken seriously. Either on-call service substantially effects the safe treatment of hospital patients and the doctors' health or it does not – this is no good example of how the specific effects of legislation have been taken into account *in advance*. The Federal Labor Court's approach to first demand a shortfall in earnings and then allow the dismissal of a saleslady wearing a headscarf might not relax intercultural conflicts, but might generate skepticism of employers emphasizing on a uniform appearance of their staff (e.g. airlines). On the contrary, the Federal Constitutional Court's attitude to maternity grants is a useful step towards tackling the employers' *reasons* for factual discrimination against women.

Recent legislation, especially the Hartz "reforms", is another example of how German politics fail to *substantially* alleviate more and easier employment. The latest reduction of protection against unfair dismissal was all that could be brought down to a common denominator – far from meeting the employers' real needs. The key to economic growth and to more employment is a different public mood – in comprehending work as a common challenge instead of an antagonism. On principle, labor law is one of the crucial local advantages (or disadvantages), just as a competitive taxation system, a lean public administration or reasonable additional wage costs are also.

---

[88] Meinel, *Agenda 2010 – Regierungsentwurf zu Reformen am Arbeitsmarkt*, DER BETRIEB [DB] 1438, 1439 (2003).

Report – *Landesverfassungsgerichte* (State Constitutional Courts) – 2002

Christian von Coelln*

A. Introduction

From the German State Constitutional Courts' point of view, the year of 2002 was highlighted by several anniversaries: The 50th anniversary of the State Constitutional Court of North Rhine-Westfalia was celebrated with a commemorative volume, dealing with almost every relevant subject of state constitutional law and the acts administering the state constitutional courts.[1] Furthermore, the State Constitutional Court of Baden-Wuerttemberg was also able to look back on 50 years of service.[2] The far younger State Constitutional Court of Berlin celebrated its 10th anniversary.[3]

B. Jurisprudence in 2002

I. Law Concerning the Organisation of the State

1. Law of the State Parliaments

Several state constitutional courts had to deal with the right of the members of the state parliament to put questions to their respective state government.

In the federal state Saarland, the State Constitutional Court held that the members of the state parliament have a right to put questions to and obtain information from the government. The Court recognized that this right, although not explicitly mentioned in the state constitution, is part of their constitutional status as parliamentarians.[4] Otherwise, the Court explained, the parliament would not be able to control the

---

* Oberassistent (senior lecturer) at the University of Passau in the Chair for Constitutional and Administrative Law, Administrative Law Concerning Trade and Industry/Media Law.
1 VERFASSUNGSGERICHTSBARKEIT IN NORDRHEIN-WESTFALEN – FESTSCHRIFT ZUM 50-JÄHRIGEN BESTEHEN DES VERFASSUNGSGERICHTSHOFS FÜR DAS LAND NORDRHEIN-WESTFALEN (Michael Bertrams ed., 2002). *See also* Th. Mann, 16 NORDRHEIN-WESTFÄLISCHE VERWALTUNGSBLÄTTER [NWVBl.] 85 (2002) (summarizing the highlights of the Court's jurisdiction arranged by decades).
2 Paul Kirchhof, *Address*, 24 VERWALTUNGSBLÄTTER FÜR BADEN-WÜRTTEMBERG [VBLBW] 137 (2003) (especially Kirchhof's rejection of the idea to invent an individual constitutional complaint to the Court).
3 Press Release, Senatsverwaltung für Justiz, Aus Anlass des 10-jährigen Bestehens des Verfassungsgerichtshofs des Landes Berlin (24 May 2002), *available at* http://www.berlin.de/SenJust/Gerichte/LVerfGH/presse/archiv/05209/index.html.
4 Saarland Constitution art. 66.2(1). *See* VerfGH Bayern, 21 NEUE ZEITSCHRIFT FÜR VERWALTUNGSRECHT [NVwZ] 715 (2002) (for the corresponding jurisdiction of the Constitutional Court of Bavaria). *See also* Christian von Coelln, *Report – Landesverfassungsgerichte (State Constitutional Courts) – 2001, in* 1 ANNUAL OF GERMAN & EUROPEAN LAW (2003) 408 (Russell Miller and Peer Zumbansen eds., 2005).

government. The Court held that the government must answer such questions completely and correctly. This duty is limited such as in cases of governmental incompetence, classified information, colliding basic rights and abuse of the right to question. Moreover, state organs have to show consideration for each other. Therefore, the investigation the government must undertake in order to answer the respective question must not exceed the government's capacities. Finally, the government does not have to *answer* questions that are obviously based on an error. However, the government has *to point out* the error. In the case before the Court, the question (concerning aspects of the Saarland school system) was based on an error, so that the government would, in general, have been allowed to refuse to give an answer. Nevertheless, having chosen to respond, the Court found the government's answer insufficient because the government had based its refusal to answer in detail on the large effort that would have been necessary to answer the question more fully. The Court concluded that this answer had even increased the error.[5]

A second decision of the Saarland State Constitutional Court concerned an investigating committee of the state parliament which had been given the name of a certain person who was considered to be responsible for presumed grievances in waste disposal. The person filed an individual constitutional complaint which was held unfounded. The Court explained that the investigation itself had not touched the presumption of innocence, but, due to the naming, the creation of the investigating committee had interfered with the complainant's right of personality. However, such an infringement may be justified by the parliamentary right of investigation. This includes a right to name a committee in reference to certain affairs or persons, if there is an objective connection to the investigation, which is based on facts, and if the principle of proportionality is observed. These preconditions were fulfilled in the case at hand. A parliamentary investigation, the Court explained, does not interfere with the complainant's rights as much as criminal proceedings do. Furthermore, holders of public offices like the complainant are more likely to endure the described interferences. Giving the investigating committee a different name, the Court held, neither would have been a more moderate measure, as the person's name would inevitably have been mentioned several times, nor would it have been equally efficient. Personification is a common and necessary means of illustrating the object of a parliamentary investigation and of attracting public interest.[6]

This decision of the Saarland Court was cited approvingly by the State Constitutional Court of the federal state Mecklenburg-Western Pomerania, which also had to deal with the right of interrogation of the members of the state parliament and the corresponding duty of the state government to provide answers. One member of the state parliament had asked how often and in which cases law firms from outside the state of Mecklenburg-Western Pomerania had been mandated and how much they were paid. The state government had described the cases only in general and refused to give the names of the out-of-state law firms, asserting data protection concerns and the conclusion that the names of the law firms were not essential to the aim of the question. The Mecklenburg-Western Pomeranian State Constitutional Court regarded both aspects of the government's response to be a violation of the government's duty to answer questions completely, which is laid down explicitly in the Mecklenburg-Western Pomeranian Constitution.[7] There are high demands on a complete answer, the Court pointed out. An answer may only be denied in case of contra-

---

5 VerfGH Saarland, 16 NEUE ZEITSCHRIFT FÜR VERWALTUNGSRECHT – RECHTSPRECHUNGS-REPORT [NVwZ-RR] 81 (2003).
6 VerfGH Saarland, 16 NEUE ZEITSCHRIFT FÜR VERWALTUNGSRECHT – RECHTSPRECHUNGS-REPORT [NVwZ-RR] 393 (2003), *available at* http://www.verfassungsgerichtshof-saarland.de. *See* Sachs, *Annotation*, 43 JURISTISCHE SCHULUNG [JuS] 811 (2003).
7 VERF. MECKLENBURG-VORPOMMERN art. 40.1(1).

dictory third parties' individual interests. Even then, the reason for the denial must be given. The Court also held that the conclusion that some information is not essential for responding to the aim of the question cannot be regarded as a sufficient reason for failing to provide that information because the government may not determine (or change) the aim of the question. Due to the principles of democracy and separation of powers, only the member of the state parliament who posed the question may decide what kind of information he or she needs. Therefore, incomplete answers always have to be justified. The relationship between the duty to give complete answers and the right to deny them is that of rule and exception. The Court concluded that the particular importance of the right of interrogation had not been mentioned sufficiently in the consideration in the case at hand, as only the *professional* sphere of the lawyers would have been affected by a complete answer including their names or the names of their firms. In addition, a law firm that is authorized by a state body has to take into account that this relationship may be subject to parliamentary control.[8]

In the federal state Schleswig-Holstein, members of a committee of the state parliament demanded the production of files from the state government. The government made use of its right of refusal, provided by the state constitution for cases in which a production of files would interfere with the government's ability to function or perform its core responsibility. However, the refusal has to be reasoned before the *Parlamentarischer Einigungsausschuss*, a particular parliamentary board of conciliation. If an agreement cannot be reached between this board and the state government, the files must be presented immediately, unless there is a contradictory decision of the *Bundesverfassungsgericht* (BVerfG – Federal Constitutional Court, acting as Schleswig Holstein's State Constitutional Court). Consequently, the situation before the Court differs from the one in other federal states, where under similiar conditions parliamentarians have to take legal action. In the case before the Court, the state government had successfully applied for an *einstweilige Anordnung* (provisional order). Usually, the standard for granting such a provisional order is high. The Court left open whether it is also required under the particular circumstances in Schleswig-Holstein, as even the high standard was fulfilled in the case at hand. The right to refuse the production of the files pursuant to a provisional order avoided the danger of irreversible damage.[9]

In the federal state Baden-Wuerttemberg, the majority of an investigating committee of the state parliament had refused the minority's demand for a special session in which witnesses would have been examined. The refusal was brought before the Baden-Wuerttemberg State Constitutional Court. As its jurisdiction is limited to alleged violations of the state constitution, the Court left open the question whether there had been a violation of legislation, pursuant to which the minority may enforce a special session. The Court explained that the constitutional right of the parliamentary minority to have an investigating committee established[10] is completed by the constitutional right of the committee's minority to have evidence taken.[11] On the other hand, the Court pointed out, the rights of the minority have to be seen in the context of the principle of majority-rule. Consequently, there is a strained relationship between the majority's and the minority's rights: In general, the majority can determine the committee's course of procedure. However, this possibility is limited by the minority's rights. The majority has to obey the

---

8   VerfG Mecklenburg-Vorpommern, 56 NEUE JURISTISCHE WOCHENSCHRIFT [NJW] 815 (2003). *See* Sachs, *Annotation*, 43 JURISTISCHE SCHULUNG [JuS] 609 (2003).
9   BVerfGE 106, 51 (*Bundesverfassungsgericht* acting as Schleswig Holstein's State Constitutional Court).
10 VERF. BADEN-WÜRTTEMBERG art. 35.1(1).
11 *Id.* at art. 35.2(2).

Prinzip der Verfassungsorgantreue (principle of loyalty of constitutional organs to each other including the duty to show consideration for each other). That means, the Court explained in reference to a decision of the BVerfG,[12] that the majority controls, but with consideration given to the interests of the minority. The minority has to have a certain influence on the procedure, although less than the majority. Therefore, if the minority has a right to have evidence taken, the majority may not refuse the demand (unless the taking of the evidence would be unconstitutional); but the majority may decide on the order in which different matters are dealt with. However, the minority's right must not be undermined such as by postponing the question to the end of the parliamentary term. The Court held that its jurisdiction on this question is restricted to whether the majority's decision is understandable and justifiable. The Court concluded that these requirements were met by the majority's decision in the case at hand.[13]

In the federal state Rhineland-Palatinate advertising material for the chairman of both a political party and a fraction in the state parliament had been paid half-and-half by the party and the fraction. This arrangement gave rise to a problem because the fraction is funded by the state. These state funds could not be used for the party's purposes because the funding of political parties is exclusively subject to federal legislation. Therefore, the public prosecutor instituted investigations. The fraction asked the state parliament to review the appropriation of the funds. The state parliament refused this review as it wanted to wait for the results of the investigations. Finally, the fraction brought an action before the Rhineland-Palatinate State Constitutional Court for a declaratory judgement which would establish the state parliament's duty to confirm the appropriate use of the fraction's funds. This action was partly successful. The Court held that the president of the state parliament would have had the duty to review the appropriation of the funds. On behalf of his organizational power, together with his responsibility for the fractions' possibilities to act effectively in the state parliament and in public, the president has to ensure an unhindered and effective exercise of functions, especially by the opposition. Therefore, the Court explained, the president has to cooperate in the clarification of circumstances like criminal investigations which may hinder a fraction's parliamentary work considerably.

The Court pointed out that a parliamentary fraction may use its funds not only for work in parliament but also for publicity. This appropriation may overlap with party affairs. Nevertheless, the funds are used appropriately as long as a sufficient relationship to the fraction's parliamentary work exists. Thus, a fraction may inform the public about its members, but must not explicitly promote the party itself. As a consequence, the Court held that the use of the funds for advertising posters of the fraction's chairman was legal, whereas the use for advertising prospectuses concerning soccer was not close enough to the fraction's parliamentary work.[14]

The Bavarian State Constitutional Court had to decide on an argument between the majority fraction in the state parliament and an opposition fraction on the constitutionality of provisions concerning the *Parlamentarisches Kontrollgremium* (PKG – parliamentary committee controlling the use of certain technical methods by the state police and by the state office for the protection of the constitution [secret service]). Its limitation to five members had the consequence that the (small) opposition fraction in the state parliament did not get a seat on the committee. The Bavarian State Constitutional Court held that the right of information held by members of parliament generally includes an equal right of access for all fractions to the parliamentary committees. Exceptionally, the size of a committee may be

---

12   BVerfGE 105, 197.
13   StGH Baden-Württemberg, 56 DIE ÖFFENTLICHE VERWALTUNG [DÖV] 201 (2003).
14   VerfGH Rheinland-Pfalz, 22 NEUE ZEITSCHRIFT FÜR VERWALTUNGSRECHT [NVwZ] 75 (2003).

kept so small that not every parliamentary group can be taken into account, especially on behalf of the protection of secrets and of the committee's efficiency of work. The Court concluded that Article 16a, a recent amendment to the Bavarian Constitution, which outlines the rights of the opposition and of the fractions in the state parliament, does not contain a right of every fraction to be represented in all committees. The Court pointed out that the PKG's limitation to five members is constitutional, as the danger of an infringement of the protection of secrets would be enlarged by additional members. With this concern in mind, the Court held that the parliament is allowed to regard other measures such as the exclusion of the public during the committee's sessions as insufficient.

Furthermore, the statutory regulations concerning the election of the PKG's members do not explicitly guarantee the opposition any seats. The Court regarded these regulations as constitutional but stated that it would be an abuse of rights by the majority not to appoint any member of the opposition. On the other hand, only the opposition as a whole has to be represented, not every single fraction. Consequently, the current situation in Bavaria (two out of five seats for the opposition) was held constitutional.

Finally, it was unclear if certain annual reports by two state ministers required by law only have to be given to the PKG or to the plenum of the state parliament as well. The Court pointed out that the regulations have to be interpreted in accordance to the state constitution. The principle of democracy and the fractions' right to participate demand a report to both the PKG and the plenum.[15]

2. Electoral Law

After the 1999 election to the state parliament in the federal state Hesse, the Hessian Election Review Court declared the election to be valid.[16] Thereafter, it became known that the election campaign of the winning party had been partly financed by illegal funds, namely, contributions that had illegally been excluded from the party's statement of account. Based on this information, the Hessian Election Review Court decided to continue its trial. It regarded the use of the unreported funds to be *contra bonos mores*. Article 78.2 of the Hessian Constitution states that actions of bad faith or indecency that influence the results of an election invalidate the election to the degree that the questionable acts are relevant for the result. The Election Review Court intended to examine the 1999 election for a potential violation of this constitutional provision. The state government (formed by the coalition of parties that had initially been declared the winner of the election) regarded the constitutional provision to be contradictory to the *Grundgesetz* (GG – Basic Law) and applied to the Federal Constitutional Court for abstract judicial review of Hesse's election review provisions. The Federal Constitutional Court decided that the election review provisions are compatible with the Basic Law but that they have to be intepreted narrowly. An act of bad faith or violation of common decency may only be assumed if the principles of freedom or of equality of elections have been infringed.[17]

---

15 VerfGH Bayern, 21 NEUE ZEITSCHRIFT FÜR VERWALTUNGSRECHT [NVwZ] 1372 (2002), *available at* www.bayern.verfassungsgerichtshof.de. *See* VerfGH Sachsen, 9 SÄCHSISCHE VERWALTUNGSBLÄTTER [SächsVBl] 185 (2002) (concerning the status of the members of the state parliament and finding a violation of the principle of equal opportunity resulting from an unexpected amendment of the rules of procedure in a parliamentary committee).
16 The Election Review Court is based on Art. 78.1 of the Hessian Constitution. Its task is to examine the election's validity. For an English-language introduction to the Election Review Court and this case in particular, *see* Russell A. Miller, *Lords of Democracy: The Judicialization of "Pure Politics" in the United States and Germany*, 61 WASH. & LEE L. REV. 587 (2004).
17 BVerfGE 103, 111.

Consequently, the Election Review Court terminated its review because it did not find this high standard to be met by the funding scandal allegations leveled against the 1999 state election.

One of the Hessian political parties defeated in the election filed an individual constitutional complaint to the Hessian State Constiutional Court against the terminal decision of the Hessian Election Review Court. The Hessian State Constitutional Court explained that in Hesse the politcal parties' right of equal opportunity is a basic right so that an individual constitutional complaint, not an *Organstreit* (action of one public body against a second one) is the allowable judicial remedy. Nevertheless, the complaint was held inadmissible for a lack of standing to sue. The Court explained that there is a strained relationship between the parliament's democratic legitimation and the protection of its vested rights. Therefore, the reason for challenging an election presupposes a biased interference of state bodies in the will of the electorate, private influence through compulsion or pressure, or similiar interferences. Such circumstances could not be assumed in the case at hand, the Court held. Possible advantages derived from making use of illegal funds could have been balanced in the electoral competition. Moreover, relevant encroachments upon the electoral process by private subjects (including political parties) can only be found to have occurred if the freedom or the equality of the election are as significantly violated as in the case of a punishable infringement of the election. The Court pointed out that the winning party's incomplete statement of account was a violation of the constitutional principle of transparency, but was not so grave as to render the complaint well-founded in this respect.[18]

The Bavarian State Constitutional Court was also called upon to address a matter of election law. Bavarian law excludes adults who are put under complete custody by a court from the right to vote. The Bavarian State Constitutional Court explained that this provision is constitutional, as it is compatible with the principle of equality, with the prohibition of discrimination against disabled persons and with the prohibition of arbitrary legislation. According to the Bavarian State Constitutional Court, the principles of equal and general elections may only be restricted for compelling reasons. Complete custody of persons of the age of majority can be qualified as such a reason, as the custody is only ordered as *ultima ratio*. The parliament may assume typifyingly that the persons concerned do not posses the minimum understanding and capacity necessary to vote. The prohibition of discrimination against disabled persons[19] does not prohibit regulations based on their missing abilities. The Court found that representation of these people by their guardian is impossible in respect of voting which is of the utmost personal character. Furthermore, the Court held that the provision was not arbitrary although it does not exclude all persons lacking the necessary understanding and capacity to vote. The Court explained that the persons concerned do lack those abilities. The Court finally concluded that the distinct treatment of people that cannot read – they are allowed to be supported by another person of their confidence – is justified, as they are nonetheless able to decide on their own.[20]

3. Popular Initiatives and Referendums

In the federal state Saxony, a *Volksantrag* (people's initiative) aiming to change the Saxonian school act was started off. It would have led to increased expenses for teachers of up to 460

---

18 StGH Hessen, 22 NEUE ZEITSCHRIFT FÜR VERWALTUNGSRECHT [NVwZ] 468 (2002), *available at* www.staatsgerichtshof.hessen.de/migration/rechtsp.nsf/bynoteid/78712E6CC038B4A0C1256F 860025A348?Opendocument
19 VERF. BAYERN art. 118a.
20 VerfGH Bayern, 20 BAYERISCHE VERWALTUNGSBLÄTTER [BAYVBL] 44 (2003).

million German marks a year. As the Saxonian Constitution excludes *Abgabengesetze*, *Besoldungsgesetze* and *Haushaltsgesetze* (tax acts, enactments for the remuneration of public officials and budget acts)[21] from popular legislation, the president of the state parliament thought the initiative was contradictory to the constitution and therefore referred it to the State Constitutional Court. In its decision which varies from the jurisprudence of other State Constitutional Courts on this point, the Saxonian State Constitutional Court declared the initiative to be permissible. It explained that in Saxony parliamentary legislation and popular legislation are of equal rank. Unlike the Federal Basic Law, the Saxonian Constiution does not give priority to parliamentary legislation. And unlike the Bavarian Constiution, the Saxony Constitution does not regard popular legislation as a mere supplementary form of law. The Court concluded that the state constitution deliberately takes into consideration that, as a consequence of popular legislation, the majority in the state parliament may not be able to realize its agenda without restriction. Even "intentional decisions bearing budgetary consequences" of the parliament do not enjoy priority. So far, the Saxonian State Constitutional Court objected to the jurisprudence of the State Constitutional Court of Brandenburg.[22] The Court explained that the Saxonian Constiution only prohibits *Haushaltsgesetze* (budget acts) as a subject of popular legislation, not *Gesetze zum Haushalt* (acts concerning the budget). Therefore, the wording of the constitution indicates a narrow understanding which also stands the test of historical and teleological interpretation. The different view of other state constitutional courts, the Saxonian State Constitutional Court explained, is based on the wording and the context of their respective state constitutions. In Saxony, the Court reasoned, a wide interpretation leading to the preclusion of such popular legislation would not make sense, as this would include *Abgabengesetze* and *Besoldungsgesetze* (tax acts and enactments for the remuneration of public officials) which are explicitly and separately named in the state constitution. The parliament's constitutional right to determine the budget is not infringed as long as the parliament may produce a constitutional budget in spite of a popular initiative. Restrictions on the parliamentary majority's priorities are an intended consequence of the equal rank of popular legislation granted by the state constitution. Furthermore, the opposite view would render the limits of popular legislation too indefinite.[23]

4. Communal Self-Administration

In the federal state Saxony, the parliament had concentrated certain functions of local authorities belonging to a *Verwaltungsgemeinschaft* (association of local authorities) in one of the asscociated local authorities. The other local authorities were not allowed to employ personnel for these functions. The Saxonian State Constitutional Court held that these provisions do not violate the right of communal self-administration/communal autonomy. The Court explained that the ban on employing personnel is a mere consequence of the allocation of functions to a different local authority. The Court pointed out that this allocation aims to strengthen communal self-administration by concentrating

---

21 VERF. SACHSEN art. 73(1).
22 VerfG Brandenburg, 12 LANDES- UND KOMMUNALVERWALTUNG [LKV] 77 (2002). Christian von Coelln, *Report – Landesverfassungsgerichte (State Constitutional Courts) – 2001, in* 1 ANNUAL OF GERMAN & EUROPEAN LAW (2003) 408 (Russell Miller and Peer Zumbansen eds., 2005).
23 VerfGH Sachsen, 13 LANDES- UND KOMMUNALVERWALTUNG [LKV] 327 (2003). *See* Sponer, *Summary*, 12 LANDES- UND KOMMUNALVERWALTUNG [LKV] 563, 565 (2002); Sachs, *Annotation*, 43 JURISTISCHE SCHULUNG [JuS] 705 (2003); Junk, *Annotation*, 13 LANDES- UND KOMMUNALVERWALTUNG [LKV] 308 (2003); Zschoch, *Annotation*, 22 NEUE ZEITSCHRIFT FÜR VERWALTUNGSRECHT [NVwZ] 438 (2003); Kertels & Brink, *Annotation*, 22 NEUE ZEITSCHRIFT FÜR VERWALTUNGSRECHT [NVwZ] 435 (2003).

the administrative abilities in one capable local authority; this, the Court concluded, is not disproportionate.[24]

In all federal states, local authorities are enabled by the respective *Kommunalabgabengesetz* (local tax act) to establish an obligation to pay contributions for road construction by way of by-laws. In Saxony-Anhalt, the competent *Oberverwaltungsgericht* (Higher Administrative Court) decided that the local tax act even permits demands for contributions for roads the construction of which was finished before the relevant by-law was enacted. The Saxony-Anhalt state parliament regarded this interpretation as wrong and retroactively abolished the possibility of such an interpretation by establishing what the parliament called an "authentic interpretation" of the local tax act. This amendment was held unconstitutional by the Saxony-Anhalt State Constitutional Court. The Court explained that it was a violation of the local legislative and financial authority because the preconditions of a retroactive act were not given. There is no constitutional obligation for the parliament to enable local authorities to collect contributions. However, if the local authorities have been so empowered, the execution of their right of collection becomes part of their communal self-administration. The Court concluded that, although an "authentic interpretation" by the parliament is, in principle, possible, the prohibition of retroactivity based on the principle of the rule of law must nonetheless be observed. In contrast to the relationship between the state and its citizens, the protection of public confidence is irrelevant between the state and local authorities. The lawful enactment of by-laws merits protection and the unlawful does not. The by-law in the case at hand had been lawful, as it had been accepted by the Higher Administrative Court. The State Constitutional Court held that none of the preconditions for an exceptionally retroactive act (nullity of the old act, confused legal situation, reasons of common weal prior to legal security) were fulfilled. At least, the local authorities' interest to furnish themselves with finances predominated the citizens' advantage of the new act.[25]

The State Constitutional Court of Brandenburg declared an act of parliament void that relocated the establishment of municipal development plans from the local authorities to the *Amt* (association of local authorities). The Court explained that the relocation of competences was within the scope of the *Baugesetzbuch* (federal building code). Nevertheless, the right of communal self-administration[26] gives local authorities priority to fulfill tasks of local relevance, the Court held. The suspension of these tasks presupposes that the reasons for the suspension are prior to the constitutional principle of the distribution of tasks, e.g. if the fulfillment of the tasks is not ensured by the local authorities. This was not the case in the decision at hand.[27]

In a second decision, the State Constitutional Court of Brandenburg found that the legislative establishment of a minimum size for local authorities belonging to an *Amt* does not violate the right of self-administration of smaller local authorities. A minimum size is required to provide the necessary institutions. Nevertheless, the Court explained, dissolution of a local authority must not be the obligatory consequence of falling short of the requisite minimum number of inhabitants. The regulation has to be flexible enough to take particular circumstances into account. In the case at hand, this precondition was fulfilled as the local authorities "should" only "regularly" have the minimum size. On the other

---

24 VerfGH Sachsen, 9 SÄCHSISCHE VERWALTUNGSBLÄTTER [SÄCHSVBL] 187 (2002). *See* Sponer, *Summary*, 12 LANDES- UND KOMMUNALVERWALTUNG [LKV] 563, 565 (2002).
25 VerfG Sachsen-Anhalt, 12 LANDES- UND KOMMUNALVERWALTUNG [LKV] 328 (2002).
26 VERF. BRANDENBURG art. 97.
27 VerfG Brandenburg, 12 LANDES- UND KOMMUNALVERWALTUNG [LKV] 516 (2002), *available at* http://www.verfassungsgericht.brandenburg.de. *See* Rademacher & Janz, *Annotation*, 12 LANDES- UND KOMMUNALVERWALTUNG [LKV] 506 (2002).

hand, the Court held that a varying financial support by the state aiming to persuade local authorities to associate on a voluntary basis is constitutional.[28]

In the federal state Northrhine-Westfalia local authorities with a certain number of inhabitants principally had to appoint *hauptamtliche Gleichstellungsbeauftragte* (gender discrimination omsbudspersons who do not fulfill this task on an honorary basis). A new act of the state parliament turned this condition into a strict obligation. The State Constitutional Court decided that the reversal of the exceptional possibility to appoint honorary ombudspersons affects the local authorities' organizational autonomy, but is no violation of the right of communal self-administration. The Court explained that the new provision is proportionate, as *hauptamtlich* neither means "full-time employed" (as it would usually be explained and translated) nor does it prescribe the extent of the ombudspersons' work.[29]

In 1999, the *Konnexitätsprinzip* (principle of coherence) had been established in the Brandenburgian Constiution.[30] The principle obliges the state to set up provisions on the covering of costs when delegating new functions to the local authorities. If these functions lead to an additional financial burden for the local authorities, compensation has to be guaranteed. The State Constitutional Court of Brandenburg held that a pre-existing function can also be characterized as "new" and therefore necessitating the required compensation, if a right to give instructions concerning the manner of fulfilling the function is newly granted to the state. The Court explained that in Brandenburg the *Konnexitätsprinzip* is strict, not relative,[31] which means that the additional financial burden basically has to be complete and is independent of the financial capacity of the local authorities. On the other hand, the constitution does not demand a reimbursement. Therefore, the compensation does not have to cover the costs cent by cent. Typifying and generalising provisions are constitutional methods for satisfying the obligations arising from the *Konnexitätsprinzip*. The parliament may also provide incentives for an economical execution of the law. However, every single local authority has to have a realistic chance for complete compensation. Furthermore, the Court explained that the provisions for the compensation must be based on a consolidated prognosis. The Court left undecided the question how intensive the judicial review on this aspect may be. In the case at hand the prognosis was held unacceptable. Additionally, the Court found fault with the act under review in that it did not ensure a sufficient financial security to the local authorities and that the question of a complete compensation was not provided in the act but was left to the executive.[32]

---

28 VerfG Brandenburg, 12 LANDES- UND KOMMUNALVERWALTUNG [LKV] 573 (2002), *available at* http://www.verfassungsgericht.brandenburg.de. In a point not reported above the decision refers to VerfG Brandenburg, case number VfGBbg 40/01, of May 16, 2002, *available at* www.verfassungsgericht.brandenburg.de. (In this decision, the Court had held that a local authority only has a right to have an *Amts*-administration at its disposal and that the local authority cannot demand that this administration be organized in a particular way.)
29 VerfGH Nordrhein-Westfalen, 21 NEUE ZEITSCHRIFT FÜR VERWALTUNGSRECHT [NVwZ] 1502 (2002).
30 VERF. BRANDENBURG art. 97.3.
31 The Court explicitly refers to VerfG Brandenburg, 12 LANDES- UND KOMMUNALVERWALTUNG [LKV] 77 (2002) (in which this question had not been answered). *See* Christian von Coelln, *Report – Landesverfassungsgerichte (State Constitutional Courts) – 2001*, *in* 1 ANNUAL OF GERMAN & EUROPEAN LAW (2003) 408 (Russell Miller and Peer Zumbansen eds., 2005).
32 VerfG Brandenburg, 12 LANDES- UND KOMMUNALVERWALTUNG [LKV] 323 (2002), *available at* http://www.verfassungsgericht.brandenburg.de.

5. Miscellaneous

The State Constitutional Court of Bremen had to decide on the constitutionality of the *Beleihungsgesetz* (act concerning the fulfillment of state functions by private persons or by legal persons under private law). The Court explained that although the conferring of functions to these persons is only possible on the basis of an act of parliament, not every single delegation demands a particular act. One global act is sufficient if its regulations are detailed enough. Furthermore, the principle of democracy requires that the state remains responsible for the delegated functions. Therefore, substantive supervision by the state which must employ enough supervisory personnel and use its supervisory powers efficiently, is necessary. The Court explained that the necessity of parliamentary control demands that the legal relationship between the state and legal persons under private law must ensure that shareholders' rights do not interfere with the state's influence. The state parliament's right of control was not violated because the parliament kept its right to demand information from the competent minister (in Bremen, the competent minister being a state senator). Finally, the Court explained that Article 33.4 of the Basic Law is incorporated into its standard of review. According to this provision, the exercise of state authority as a permanent function is, as a rule, entrusted to members of the public service whose status, service and loyalty are governed by public law. The Court explained that Article 33.4 of the Basic Law is a part of the state constitution as far as the provision is binding for the state, but that it had not been violated by the state act. The delegation of state authority to private persons or legal persons under private law is not strictly prohibited, but only "as a rule." Based on this analysis, the state act was deemed constitutional.[33]

II. Law of Constitutional Procedure

1. Conflicting Actions of Public Organs

In the federal state Northrhine-Westfalia, a political party raised an unsuccessful petition aiming to abolish the need of certain supporting signatures prior to elections. In its action to the State Constitutional Court the party criticized the parliament's inactivity on the issue. The Court explained that legislative inactivity may, in general, violate the principles of equality of elections and of equal political opportunity and may therefore be referred to by a political party as a constitutional organ.[34] Nevertheless, the parliament cannot be obliged by a petition to review or change the legal situation. When raising a petition, a political party does not act as a constitutional organ but as *Jedermann* (Everyman). Therefore, the action was held inadmissible.[35]

---

33 StGH Bremen, 22 NEUE ZEITSCHRIFT FÜR VERWALTUNGSRECHT [NVwZ] 81 (2003), *available at* http://www.bremen.de/info/presse/beleihungsgesetzurteil.pdf.
34 This question was left open by the *Bundesverfassungsgericht* (acting as Schleswig Holstein's State Constitutional Court), BVerfGE 103, 164 (170).
35 VerfGH Nordrhein-Westfalen, 16 NEUE ZEITSCHRIFT FÜR VERWALTUNGSRECHT – RECHTSPRECHUNGS-REPORT [NVwZ-RR] 83 (2003).

2. Basic Rights in the State Constitutions and Application of Federal Law

The Saxonian State Constitutional Court held in 2001[36] that its jurisdiction to review the application of federal law by a state court in order to determine, whether the state court observes the basic rights of the state constitution is not limited to procedural law and basic rights. The Court pointed out that it might also review, whether the application of substantive federal law observes the state constitution's substantive basic rights.[37] Although this decision deviated from the jurisprudence of the Hessian State Constitutional Court, the Saxonian Court did not recognize a duty first to obtain a decision from the Federal Constitutional Court according to Article 100.3 Basic Law on these matters. The Saxonian State Constitutional Court concluded that the constitutional complaint in the case at hand was unfounded. Therefore, the claimed jurisdiction did not become practically relevant.[38]

The Hessian State Constitutional Court left open, whether a decision of a federal court automatically renders a constitutional complaint to the State Constitutional Court against the preceding decision of the highest state court inadmissible.[39]

3. Constitutional Complaints of Local Authorities

The State Constitutional Court of Northrhine-Westfalia decided that a local authority is not immediately affected by (and therefore cannot bring in a constitutional complaint against) an act of parliament that has to be concretized by additional legislation, even if the latter may in turn be subject to a constitutional complaint.[40]

In Brandenburg, the State Constitutional Court regarded a constitutional complaint of a local authority as inadmissible. The complaint referred to the establishment of a minimum size for local authorities to belong to an *Amt* by an act of the state parliament.[41] The Court found that the complaint was not based on an alleged violation of constitutional provisions linked with the right of communal self-administration. The complaining local authority reasoned that, in the state parliament, the right of the fractions to take part in the parliamentary work and the opposition's rights granted by the principle of democracy had been infringed. The Court explained that the situation might be different if the act of the state parliament had been obviously formally unconstitutional. Furthermore, the Court held that the failure to set up a legislative model for the reform of local authorities cannot be subject to a constitutional complaint. The Court left open, whether a constitutional complaint by a local authority may ever be based on an alleged omission of the parliament. At least, the Court explained, there must be an obligation for the parliament to act, which was not the case in the complaint before Court.[42]

---

36 The decision actually belongs to the report on the state constitutional courts from the first volume of this series, but had not been published early enough to receive mention. See Christian von Coelln, *Report – Landesverfassungsgerichte (State Constitutional Courts) – 2001, in* 1 ANNUAL OF GERMAN & EUROPEAN LAW (2003) 408 (Russell Miller and Peer Zumbansen eds., 2005).
37 See Christian von Coelln, *Report – Landesverfassungsgerichte (State Constitutional Courts) – 2001, in* 1 ANNUAL OF GERMAN & EUROPEAN LAW (2003) 408 (Russell Miller and Peer Zumbansen eds., 2005). See also VerfG Brandenburg, case number VfGBbg 99/02, of November 21, 2002, *available at* www.verfassungsgericht.brandenburg.de (leaving the question open).
38 VerfGH Sachsen, 10 SÄCHSISCHE VERWALTUNGSBLÄTTER [SächsVBl] 165 (2003).
39 StGH Hessen, 16 NEUE ZEITSCHRIFT FÜR VERWALTUNGSRECHT – RECHTSPRECHUNGS-REPORT [NVwZ-RR] 1 (2003), *available at* http://www.staatsgerichtshof.hessen.de/migration/rechtsp.nsf/bynoteid/45D3002DB60AB1CFC1256F8600259FD5?Opendocument.
40 VerfGH Nordrhein-Westfalen, 118 DEUTSCHES VERWALTUNGSBLATT [DVBL] 394 (2003).
41 See *infra* B.I.4.
42 VerfG Brandenburg, 12 LANDES- UND KOMMUNALVERWALTUNG [LKV] 576 (2002), *available at* http://www.verfassungsgericht.brandenburg.de.

4. Admission of Individual Constitutional Complaints

In the year 2000, the *Hessisches Staatsgerichtshofgesetz* (HessStGHG – Hessian State Constitutional Court Act) was supplemented by two provisions. First, pursuant to new Article 43.1(2), an individual constitutional complaint to the state constitutional court is inadmissible, if an individual constitutional complaint on the same subject is filed to the Federal Constitutional Court, unless the state constitution's basic rights exceed the standard of protection provided by the Federal Basic Law. Second, Article 43 a permits the Court to refuse the admission of individual constitutional complaints by a unanimous decision, if a complaint is obviously inadmissible or unfounded, in case of a lack of constitutional importance or due to a missing serious disadvantage for the complainant. The Court does not have to give reasons for the decision.

An individual constitutional complaint was filed against these provisions in the Hessian State Constitutional Court. The complaint was based on an alleged violation of Article 131 of the Hessian Constitution which provides the State Constitutional Court's jurisdiction for individual constitutional complaints. As this provision is not a basic right, the Court dismissed the complaint. Nevertheless, the Court made some remarks on the role of the state constitutional jurisdiction by way of an *obiter dictum*. The Court explained that the new provisions are compatible with Article 131 of the state constitution. The provisions lie within the parliament's scope of authority. Article 43.1(2) HessStGHG does not exclude individual constitutional complaints, but merely removes a dualism of judicial remedies that is not required by the state constitution. The constitution only demands that the protection of the individual's basic rights does not run idle. The Court held that the new provision stands this test as a complaint to the State Constitutional Court remains possible in the case that the implicated protections secured by the state constitution exceed the protections provided by the Basic Law. Article 43a HessStGHG was qualified as a mere simplification of the Court's procedure. The Court pointed out that legislative intent expressly explains that a huge number of complaints may be handled by a procedure similiar to the American "system of certiorari." Furthermore, the partly objective function of an individual constitutional complaint is an argument for excluding irrelevant complaints. Finally, the Court held that the constitution does not contain an obligation to give reasons for a decision. Although the complainant is certainly interested in getting such information, the limited ressources of the Court must also be taken into account.[43]

Soon after this decision, the Court had to apply Article 43.1(2) HessStGHG. It held that an individual constitutional complaint to the State Constitutional Court becomes inadmissible because of a parallel complaint to the Federal Constitutional Court even if the latter is withdrawn. Due to the unequivocal wording and to the telos of the provision, it does not matter if the Federal Constitutional Court has already dealt with the complaint.[44]

III. Basic Rights

In the federal state Brandenburg, a civil servant filed an individual constitutional complaint against the search of his private home and his official premises. The complaint was

---

43 StGH Hessen, 57 JURISTENZEITUNG [JZ] 939 (2002), *available at* http://www.staatsgerichtshof.hessen.de/migration/rechtsp.nsf/bynoteid/045C04F30B99D544C1256F860025A37D?Opendocument. *See* Uerpmann, *Annotation*, 57 JURISTENZEITUNG [JZ] 942 (2002).
44 StGH Hessen, 16 NEUE ZEITSCHRIFT FÜR VERWALTUNGSRECHT – RECHTSPRECHUNGS-REPORT [NVwZ-RR] 2 (2003), *available at* http://www.staatsgerichtshof.hessen.de/migration/rechtsp.nsf/bynoteid/3948727344AB6249C1256F860025A0B5?Opendocument.

unfounded. The State Constitutional Court explained that, contrary to the corresponding basic right in the Federal Basic Law,[45] official premises are not protected by the state constitution's guarantee of the inviolability of the home.[46] However, they are protected by the state constitution's right of free development of one's personality.[47] Furthermore, the Court held that the right of data protection,[48] like the federal basic right of *informationelle Selbstbestimmung* (right of self-determination over personal data), protects against any attachment of personal data by the state, but is not affected by the mere search of rooms, rather only by a seizure. The Court regarded this case as a part of its permanent jurisdiction: An invidual constitutional complaint against measures regulated by federal law (as the search of rooms) may be based on basic rights that are equal in content to basic rights provided by the Basic Law.[49] This seems to be contradictory to the different scope given to the guarantee of the inviolability of the home in the two constitutions. However, the Court obviously assumes that it is sufficient that several basic rights of the state constitution grant the same protection as one single federal basic right.

In a second decision involving the search of rooms the Court dealt with a case in which a private home had been searched without a search warrant ordered by a judge. The Court pointed out that the police must try to contact a judge even if the search takes place out of usual office hours, unless the success of the search is endangered by this delay.[50]

Furthermore, the Court held that the right to consult a lawyer prior to measures of detention is violated, if a judge starts with an interrogation although a lawyer (whose wish to participate was obvious) had not yet arrived.[51]

The Bavarian State Constitutional Court decided that the prohibition of keeping corpses anywhere but in municipal mortuaries is disproportionate, as it is not necessary. Keeping the corpses in private mortuaries owned by funeral directors is equally suitable, but less affecting to the funeral directors' basic rights.[52]

In the federal state Saxony-Anhalt, the school act provides that children regularly have to attend primary schools 5.5 hours a day. During this period of time they are partly taught in lessons and they are partly cared for pedagogically. Some parents and one pupil regarded this act as a violation of their basic rights (right of care and custody, protection of the family and the right of personality). The Saxony-Anhalt State Constitutional Court did not share this view. On the basis of a comprehensive examination of the parents' rights on the one hand and the state's educational mandate on the other hand the Court explained that both positions are equivalent. The state only has to take the families' interests into consideration, but does not have to make allowances for every parental request. Therefore, the pedagogical care does not have to be offered on a voluntary basis. Even apart from the mere lessons, there is no absolute priority of parental rights which are not strengthened by the constitutional guarantee provided for the institution "family." The Court finally pointed out that the school act is not disproportionate. A voluntary presence would not

---

45 GRUNDGESETZ [GG] [Constitution/Basic Law] art. 13.1.
46 VERF. BRANDENBURG art. 15.1.
47 VERF. BRANDENBURG art. 10.1.
48 VERF. BRANDENBURG art. 11.1.
49 VerfG Brandenburg, 57 JURISTISCHE RUNDSCHAU [JR] 59 (2003), *available at* http://www.verfassungsgericht.brandenburg.de.
50 VerfG Brandenburg, 13 LANDES- UND KOMMUNALVERWALTUNG [LKV] 27 (2003), *available at* http://www.verfassungsgericht.brandenburg.de.
51 VerfG Brandenburg, 57 JURISTISCHE RUNDSCHAU [JR] 192 (2003), *available at* http://www.verfassungsgericht.brandenburg.de). *See also* VerfG Brandenburg, case number VfGBbg 87/02, of October 25, 2002, *available at* http://www.verfassungsgericht.brandenburg.de.
52 VerfGH Bayern, 133 BAYERISCHE VERWALTUNGSBLÄTTER [BayVBl] 558 (2002).

be of equal efficiency as it would not ensure the presence of all pupils, which was intended by the parliament.[53]

The relationship between parental and state educational rights was also dealt with in a decision of the Bavarian State Constitutional Court. For religious reasons, two American baptists living in the federal state Bavaria did not want their daughter to be subject to general compulsory education. They argued that she was taking correspondence courses of the American Roanoke Baptist School. Therefore, they complained that their parental right to determine the education of their child was violated by the state's insistence that the child attend public school. The Court found that this right is permissibly restricted by the state's interest in general compulsory education. The right of education does not grant the parents an exclusive claim to educate their children. The Court found that the state has an equivalent interest, though only as far as scholastic education is concerned. The Court explained that compulsory education is a useful institution, but that it has to take into consideration the parents' freedom of religion which includes the right to teach their children in religion and philosophy of life. The Court acknowledged that the value system taught by scholastic education may differ from the parents'. However, the school only has to refrain from being evangelical; it must leave room for parental ideas. In detail, the Court concluded that several teaching methods and some teaching material rejected by the parents (e.g. painting mandalas, sex education, theory of evolution) are constitutional. Reliance upon correspondence courses, the Court held, do not oblige the state to make exceptions from general compulsory education as such courses cannot compensate for the holisitic content of scholastic education.[54]

In the federal state Bavaria, certain private hospitals, retirement homes, old people's homes and geriatric care centres are exempted from the duty to pay radio and TV licence fees, whereas equivalent private institutions for the disabled are not. The Bavarian State Constitutional Court held this provision to be compatible with the constitutional principle of equality.[55] The Court explained that exemptions are exceptional and can only be granted within a narrow range. On the other hand, there is a wide range of discretion to refrain from granting further exemptions. In the case at hand, the Court affirmed a sufficient reason for the inequal treatment: disabled persons are usually personally exempted from radio and TV licence fees, whereas old and ill people are not. Therefore, the Court concluded that the provision does not violate the prohibition on the discrimination of disabled persons.[56]

---

53 VerfG Sachsen-Anhalt, 13 LANDES- UND KOMMUNALVERWALTUNG [LKV] 131 (2003) (see the dissenting opinion of one of the judges).
54 VerfGH Bayern, 134 BAYERISCHE VERWALTUNGSBLÄTTER [BayVBl] 236 (2003), *available at* http://www.bayern.verfassungsgerichtshof.de/).
55 VERF. BAYERN art. 118.1.
56 VerfGH Bayern, 134 BAYERISCHE VERWALTUNGSBLÄTTER [BayVBl] 333 (2003).

Report – European Court of Justice – 2003/2004

Kai Peter Ziegler[*]

A. Introduction: Summaries of Cases Impacting Germany

During the period under review the European Court of Justice (ECJ) handed down several decisions either of particular significance to Germany or presenting special interest for the German legal order. Obviously, not all of these cases can be addressed here. However, a selection of high-impact rulings has been outlined and three important cases are examined in detail.

In the case of *Kühne & Heitz*,[1] the Court required national administrations under certain conditions to *review final administrative decisions*, even when they have been confirmed by final national judgments, where a subsequent decision of the ECJ interprets a Community law provision differently. That is seen partially to be at odds with the German notions of *Bestandskraft* (binding effect of an administrative decision) and *Rechtskraft* (*res judicata*) of judgments.

The ECJ's interpretation of the so-called Stability and Growth Pact,[2] designed to avoid excessive government deficits for members of the Euro Zone,[3] led to the annulment of a document that was designed to allow Germany and France to escape sanctions for their budget deficits.[4] However, the European Commission subsequently agreed to a "more flexible" application of the Pact.[5]

In the field of taxation several important judgments were issued. The ECJ ruled that a taxpayer who invests in companies established in other Member States is entitled to the same tax credits from which he or she would have benefited had the investment been in companies established in the Member State of his or her residence.[6] The ECJ went on to clarify that taxpayers receiving a small part of their income in one Member State when residing in another Member State have a right to benefit from income tax allowances or

---

[*] Legal Assistant to Advocate General Juliane Kokott at the European Court of Justice.
1 Case C-453/00, Kühne & Heitz NV v. Produktschap voor Pluimvee en Eieren, 2004 E.C.R. I-837.
2 At the time of the creation of the Euro, Germany pressed other Member States to accept a so-called "Stability and Growth Pact," which was intended to safeguard monetary stability. Its central provision is Article 104 EC on the avoidance of excessive budget deficits.
3 *See generally* SELECT COMMITTEE ON THE EUROPEAN UNION, REPORT – THE STABILITY AND GROWTH PACT, 2002–3, H.L. 72. *See also* Imelda Maher, *Economic Policy Coordination and the European Court: Excessive Deficits and ECOFIN Discretion*, 29 EUROPEAN LAW REVIEW 831–841 (2005).
4 Case C-27/04, Commission of the European Communities v. Council of the European Union, (ECJ July 13, 2004), *at* http://europa.eu.int/eur-lex/lex/LexUriServ/LexUriServ.do?uri=CELEX:62004J0027:EN:HTML.
5 *See* Council Regulation 1056/2005, Amending Regulation (EC) 146/97 On Speeding Up and Clarifying the Implementation of the Excessive Deficit Procedure, 2005 O.J. (L 174) 5; *Kommission reformiert den Stabilitätspakt*, SUEDDEUTSCHE.DE, Sept. 3, 2004, *at* http://www.sueddeutsche.de/ausland/artikel/577/38539/.
6 Case C-319/02, Petri Manninen, (ECJ Sept. 7, 2004), http://europa.eu.int/eur-lex/lex/LexUriServ/LexUriServ.do?uri=CELEX:62002J0319:EN:HTML.

deductions in the Member State of employment.[7] Furthermore, the ECJ held that Article 43 EC precludes a Member State from taxing increases in the value of assets when a taxpayer transfers his or her tax residence to another Member State but has not yet realized an increase in the value of those assets.[8] The prohibited tax policy was meant to prevent tax evasion. The ECJ also ruled that the assessment of the value of immovable property for the purpose of inheritance tax may not vary according to the last residence of the deceased.[9] Such judgments to the benefit of taxpayers obviously have a significant impact on national budgets. Not surprisingly, the ECJ recently came under political pressure to modify its tax jurisprudence, not least by the German minister of finance.[10]

In the realm of business, the ECJ delighted consumers with a ruling that the conversion rules on the introduction of the Euro do not allow mobile phone operators to round-up calculation units on per-minute tariffs to the next cent; rather, the rounding-up may only occur with respect to the final amount of the bill.[11] In the aggregate, the ruling saved consumers millions, if not billions of Euro. Mobile phone operators and other calculation businesses may be presumed to be less delighted.[12]

The pharmaceutical industry argued that the German health care system was incompatible with EC competition law because it allowed groups of sickness funds to determine fixed maximum prices for medicinal products.[13] The ECJ declared those funds, under these circumstances, to be exempt from the terms of Article 81 EC, which applies to "undertakings" or "associations of undertakings."[14] However, anticipating that the German prohibition of advertisement and sale of medicinal products by mail order over the Internet would be found incompatible with Community law, the German parliament revised the law ahead of the *Doc Morris* decision.[15] Unexpectedly, the ECJ found the prohibitions to be

---

7 Case C-169/03, Wallentin v. Riksskatteverket, (ECJ July 1, 2004), http://europa.eu.int/eur-lex/lex/LexUriServ/LexUriServ.do?uri=CELEX:62003J0169:EN:HTML .
8 Case C-9/02, de Lasteyrie du Saillant v. Ministère de l'Économie, des Finances et de l'Industrie, 2004 E.C.R. I-2409.
9 Case C-364/01, Heirs of H. Barbier v. Inspecteur van de Belastingdienst Particulieren/Ondernemingen buitenland te Heerlen, 2003 E.C.R. I-15013.
10 See Karl Doemens & Andreas Rinke, *"Finanzpolitik ist nicht jusitziabel" – Der Bundesfinanzminister über die Reform des Stabilitätspakts, seine Rolle im Kabinett und die unkalkulierbaren Risiken von EuGH-Urteilen*, HANDELSBLATT, Feb. 14, 2005, at 2.
11 Case C-19/03, Verbraucher-Zentrale Hamburg eV v. O2 (Germany) GmbH & Co. OHG, (ECJ Sept. 14, 2004), http://europa.eu.int/eur-lex/lex/LexUriServ/LexUriServ.do?uri=CELEX:62003J0019:EN:HTML.
12 See Jean-Marc Belorgey et al., *Comment arrondir les sommes d'argent lors du passage à l'euro?*, 41 AJDA – ACTUALITÉ JURIDIQUE – DROIT ADMINISTRATIF 2267 (2004).
13 See Daniel Riedel, *Krankenkassen keine Unternehmen i. S. des Wettbewerbsrechts – Arzneimittelfestbeträge zulässig*, 16 EUROPÄISCHE ZEITSCHRIFT FÜR WIRTSCHAFTSRECHT 245 (2004); K.P.E. Lasok, *When is an Undertaking not an Undertaking?*, 25 EUROPEAN COMPETITION LAW REVIEW 383 (2004); Christian Koenig & Christina Engelmann, *Das Festbetrags-Urteil des EuGH: Endlich Klarheit über den gemeinschaftsrechtlichen Unternehmensbegriff im Bereich der Sozialversicherung?*, 16 EUROPÄISCHE ZEITSCHRIFT FÜR WIRTSCHAFTSRECHT 682 (2004).
14 Joined cases C-264/01, C-306/01, C-354/01 and C-355/01, AOK Bundesverband, Bundesverband der Betriebskrankenkassen (BKK), Bundesverband der Innungskrankenkassen, Bundesverband der landwirtschaftlichen Krankenkassen, Verband der Angestelltenkrankenkassen eV, Verband der Arbeiter-Ersatzkassen, Bundesknappschaft and See-Krankenkasse v. Ichthyol-Gesellschaft Cordes, Hermani & Co. (C-264/01), Mundipharma GmbH (C-306/01), Gödecke GmbH (C-354/01) and Intersan, Institut für pharmazeutische und klinische Forschung GmbH (C-355/01), 2004 E.C.R. I-2493.
15 See Case C-322/01, Deutscher Apothekerverband eV v. 0800 DocMorris NV and Jacques Waterval, 2003 E.C.R. I-14887. See also Gesetz zur Modernisierung der gesetzlichen Krankenversicherung, Nov. 14, 2003, BGBl. I at 2190; Benjamin Koch, *Eine erste Bewertung der Entscheidung "DocMorris" des EuGH*, 16 EUROPÄISCHE ZEITSCHRIFT FÜR WIRTSCHAFTSRECHT 50 (2004); Christopher Lenz, *Warenverkehrsfreiheit nach der DocMorris-Entscheidung zum Versand von Arzneimitteln*, 57 NEUE JURISTISCHE WOCHENSCHRIFT 332 (2004); Christian Koenig, *Das Urteil des EuGH in der Rechtssache Deutscher Apothekerverband/Doc Morris*, in GEDÄCHTNISSCHRIFT FÜR MEINHARD HEINZE 501 (Wolfgang Giter et al. eds., 2005); Richard

incompatible only with regard to non-prescription drugs, while finding the legislation for prescription drugs to be in conformity with Community law. Germany appears prepared to retain its more expansive reform which permits Internet sales of both non-prescription and prescription drugs.

In environmental matters, the ECJ found the revised German deposit and return system for cans incompatible with Community law because it put providers of beverages from other Member States at a disadvantage.[16] In another case, the ECJ provided a definition of the term "waste" which is at odds with the definition in German law and requires a thorough rethinking of the matter.[17]

Many argued that public order in Germany was at stake when the ECJ required the recognition of driver's licenses issued by other Member States even where the holder of a non-German license resided in Germany and had had his or her German license withdrawn and the renewal thereof temporarily suspended.[18] Can there be anything more important to a German than driving privileges? And, under such circumstances, could the German bureaucracy possibly believe that *alles ist in Ordnung*?[19]

B. Significant Cases

The first of the three cases addressed here in more detail touched upon values deemed fundamental to the German constitutional order and addressed their recognition by the Community legal order. The second case required changes to German administrative organization and procedure and to the way judicial control over administrative decisions is exercised. The third case expanded national court's duties to interpret national law in conformity with Community Directives.

I. The Omega Case[20]

1. The Facts

Omega, a German company, had been operating a "laserdrome." The equipment was supplied by a British company under a franchising contract and included laser targeting devices and sensory tags fixed either in firing corridors or to jackets worn by players.

The Bonn police authority issued an order against Omega, prohibiting games with the object of firing laser beams at human targets, in essence a game in which the participants

---

Lang, *Comment on* Deutscher Apothekerverband eV v. 0800 DocMorris NV and Jacques Waterval, 42 COMMON MARKET LAW REVIEW 189 (2005).

16 Case C-463/01, Commission of the European Union v. Germany, (ECJ Dec. 14, 2004), http://europa.eu.int/eur-lex/lex/LexUriServ/LexUriServ.do?uri=CELEX:62001J0463:EN:HTML; Case C-309/02, Radlberger Getränkegesellschaft mbH & Co. and S. Spitz KG v. Land Baden-Württemberg, (ECJ Dec. 14, 2004), http://europa.eu.int/eur-lex/lex/LexUriServ/LexUriServ.do?uri=CELEX:62002J0309:EN:HTML.
17 Case C-1/03, Van de Walle, 2004 E.C.R. I-7613.
18 Case C-476/01, Kapper, 2004 E.C.R. I-5205.
19 Perhaps the fuss in Germany over the Community's control over driving is a good example of the German "character" satired by Professor Weiler in his foreword to the first edition of this series? *See* J.H.H. Weiler, *Foreword, in* I ANNUAL OF GERMAN & EUROPEAN LAW – 2003 xi (Russell Miller & Peer Zumbansen eds., 2005).
20 Case C-36/02, Omega Spielhallen- und Automatenaufstellungs-GmbH v. Oberbürgermeisterin der Bundesstadt Bonn, (ECJ Oct. 14, 2004), http://europa.eu.int/eur-lex/lex/LexUriServ/LexUriServ.do?uri=CELEX:62002J0036:EN:HTML [hereinafter "Omega"].

played "at killing people." The order was issued under Paragraph 14 (1) of the *Ordnungsbehördengesetz Nordrhein-Westfalen* (Law governing the North Rhine-Westphalia Police authorities), which provides: "The police authorities may take measures necessary to avert a risk to public order or safety in an individual case."[21] The Bonn Police authority asserted that the games constituted a danger to public order. Acts of simulated homicide and the engendered trivialisation of violence were considered contrary to fundamental values prevailing in public opinion.

That view was ultimately confirmed by Germany's *Bundesverwaltungsgericht* (BVerwG – Federal Administrative Court), which held that the commercial exploitation of a "killing game" constituted an affront to human dignity.[22] Human dignity is the most fundamental concept of the German constitution, the BVerwG noted, established in the first sentence of Article 1 (1) of the *Grundgesetz* (GG – Basic Law or Constitution).[23] The BVerwG held that the constitutional principle of human dignity may be infringed by the awakening or strengthening in the players of an attitude degrading of the fundamental right of each person to be acknowledged and respected. In the present case, this would occur via the representation of fictitious acts of violence for the purposes of a game. A cardinal constitutional principle such as human dignity, the BVerwG reasoned, could not be waived in the context of entertainment, and, in national law, the fundamental rights invoked by Omega could not alter that assessment.[24]

However, since the equipment was provided by a British company and Omega was operating under a franchise agreement, the BVerwG was concerned that the ordered prohibition might infringe the freedom to provide services under Article 49 EC and the free movement of goods under Article 28. It therefore asked the ECJ whether: (a) a prohibition such as the one at hand, arising from fundamental values of the national constitution like human dignity, is compatible with Community law; and (b) the Member States' power to restrict fundamental freedoms guaranteed by the EC Treaty is subject to the condition that the restricting legal concept is common to all Member States.[25]

2. The Holding

The ECJ first determined that the freedom to provide services was the applicable fundamental freedom and then founded its reply on Article 46 EC, which applied by virtue of Article 55 EC.[26] Article 46 EC allows for restrictions to be justified for reasons, *inter alia*, of public policy. The ECJ found that the Bonn police authority had relied on considerations of public policy in issuing the order.[27]

The ECJ emphasized, however, that, according to settled case-law, a derogation from a

---

21 *See* Gesetz über Aufbau und Befugnisse der Ordnungsbehörden – Ordnungsbehördengesetz (OBG), May 13, 1980, GVBl. NRW at 528, para. 14 (last modified by law of Dec. 20, 1994, GVBl. NRW at 1115).
22 Case C-36/02, Omega, *supra* note 20, at para. 11. *See* Craig T. Smith & Irene Schlünder, *Report – Bundesverwaltungsgericht (Federal Administrative Court) – 2001/2002*, *in* I ANNUAL OF GERMAN & EUROPEAN LAW – 2003 422, 434 (Russell Miller & Peer Zumbansen eds., 2005).
23 GRUNDGESETZ [GG] [Constitution] art. 1.1 (F.R.G.).
24 Case C-36/02, Omega, *supra* note 20, at para. 12.
25 Preliminary references are governed by Article 234 EC. Where, in a case before a national court, provisions of EC law or of EU law prove decisive for the case and the interpretation of these provisions is not clear, the national court refers a question to the ECJ. Upon receiving the answer, the national court decides the case before it.
26 Case C-36/02, Omega, *supra* note 20, at paras. 24 to 27.
27 *Id.* at para. 28.

fundamental freedom based on the concept of public policy must be interpreted strictly.[28] The scope of such public policy exceptions cannot be determined unilaterally by each Member State and its invocation is subject to control by the Community institutions. Public policy, the ECJ explained, may be relied on only if there is a genuine and sufficiently serious threat to a fundamental interest of society.[29]

The ECJ further held that, in spite of the strict application of the public policy exception, national authorities must be granted a margin of discretion within the limits of the EC Treaty because the specific circumstances which may justify recourse to the concept of public policy may vary from one country to another and from one era to another.[30]

The ECJ further recalled that fundamental rights form an integral part of the general principles of EC law and that in defining these rights it draws inspiration from the constitutional traditions common to the Member States, as well as from international human rights treaties, in particular from the European Convention on Human Rights (ECHR).[31] The Community legal order, the ECJ declared, strives to ensure respect for human dignity as a general principle of law. It follows from this, the ECJ concluded, that the objective of protecting human dignity is compatible with Community law, regardless of the principle's particular status in German law.[32]

However, the ECJ explained that under EC law, specific measures restricting fundamental freedoms may be justified on public policy grounds only if they pass a proportionality test. They must be necessary for the protection of the interests they are intended to guarantee and no less restrictive measures may be available to attain those objectives.[33]

The ECJ emphasized that a restrictive measure does not necessarily have to correspond to a conception shared by all Member States, in the sense of a precise way in which the fundamental right or legitimate interest in question is to be protected. On the contrary, the need for, and proportionality of, the provisions adopted are not excluded merely because one Member State has chosen a system of protection different from that adopted by another State.[34]

The ECJ then applied the test by stating that, according to the referring court (here the BVerwG), the prohibition, in particular of the representation of acts of homicide, corresponds to the level of protection of human dignity which the national constitution seeks to guarantee in Germany. The ECJ also considered that, by prohibiting only the variant of the game in which the aim is to fire at human targets and thus to play at killing people, the order did not exceed the measures necessary to attain the objective pursued by the competent national authorities.[35]

---

28 *Id.* at para. 30. The cases to which the ECJ referred as "settled case law" include Case 41/74, Van Duyn, 1974 E.C.R. 1337, para. 18; Case 30/77, Bouchereau, 1977 E.C.R. 1999, para. 33.
29 Case C-36/02, Omega, *supra* note 20, para. 30. The ECJ referred to Case C-54/99, Église de Scientologie, 2000 E.C.R. I-1335, para. 17.
30 *Id.* at para. 31 (*citing* Case 41/74, Van Duyn, 1974 E.C.R. 1337, para. 34).
31 *Id.* at para. 33 (*citing* Case C-260/89, ERT, 1991 E.C.R. I-2925, para. 41; Case C-274/99 P, Connolly v. Commission of the European Union, 2001 E.C.R. I-1611, para. 37; Case C-94/00, Roquette Frères, 2002 E.C.R. I-9011, para. 25; Case C-112/00, Schmidberger, 2003 E.C.R. I-5659, para. 71).
32 *Id.* at para. 34 (*citing* Opinion of Advocate General Stix-Hackl delivered on March 18, 2004, in Case C-36/02, Omega, at paras. 82–91, http://europa.eu.int/eur-lex/lex/LexUriServ/LexUriServ.do?uri=CELEX:62002C0036:EN:HTML).
33 *Id.* at para. 36 (*citing* Case C-54/99, Église de Scientologie, 2000 E.C.R. I-1335, para. 18).
34 *Id.* at paras. 37 and 38 (citing Case C-124/97, Läärä and Others, 1999 E.C.R. I-6067, para. 36; Case C-67/98, Zenatti, 1999 E.C.R. I-7289, para. 34; Case C-6/01, Anomar and Others, (ECJ Sept. 11, 2003) para. 80, http://europa.eu.int/eur-lex/lex/LexUriServ/LexUriServ.do?uri=CELEX:62001J0006:EN:HTML).
35 *Id.* at para. 39.

The ECJ concluded that in these circumstances the order could not be regarded as a measure unjustifiably undermining the freedom to provide services.

3. Commentary

German sensitivity has increased in recent years with respect to the ECJ's "grip" on fundamental rights in "Community law situations." More than once, the fear has been voiced that an ever expanding applicability of community law would lead to national guarantees being set aside by fundamental rights guaranteed at the Community level, thereby supplanting mature national protection systems.[36] A "zoning up" to Community level of all fundamental rights questions and a uniform standard throughout the Community, developed and applied by the ECJ, is at the center of this concern.

No wonder these fears ran high ahead of the *Omega* decision. What, indeed, if the Court had decided otherwise? A contradiction between a fundamental freedom of the EC treaty and the central value of the German constitution would have been the result. From an EC law perspective, its fundamental freedom would have had to prevail over the national constitution. From a German law perspective, such compliance would, to say the least, have been "difficult." According to almost universal agreement in both German legal scholarship and practice, restrictions to human dignity cannot be justified.[37] The only way, then, would have been to reinterpret the concept and conclude that human dignity is not affected in such situations.

But why hasn't this dramatic conflict arisen? First, the ECJ was obviously well aware of the situation and had earlier recognized human dignity as a general principle of Community law.[38] Second, the manner in which the ECJ chose to resolve the potential conflict had been previously tested in the *Schmidberger* decision.[39] In *Omega*, the ECJ followed the same lines of reasoning, illustrating its concept for the interplay of fundamental rights protection at the Community level and at the national level. It is, after all, nothing but a variant of the ECJ's general test of justifications for restrictions.[40]

Measures restricting fundamental freedoms of the EC treaty can only be justified where they pursue aims recognized by Community law at the same primary law level. Thus, if the justification is to be a fundamental right, it has to be one of Community law. A national fundamental right cannot justify a restriction. The ECJ has consistently held that the preservation of fundamental freedoms requires a narrow interpretation of restrictive justifications. By these standards, justifying a restrictive measure appears to be a hard task.

Yet, the ECJ allows the justification concepts at Community level to be filled with varying content, according to place and time, which is to say, according to national circumstances. The ECJ leaves national authorities a margin of discretion to assess the importance of certain values to society even where they compete with a fundamental freedom. For instance, the ECJ consistently held that the protection of consumer health is an aim recognized at the Community level (for instance in Article 30 EC) and that the level

---

36 *See, e.g.*, Frank Schorkopf, *Nationale Grundrechte in der Dogmatik der Grundfreiheiten : Präzisierungen des unionsverfassungsrechtlichen Verhältnisses von Europäischer Union und Mitgliedstaaten durch den EuGH?*, 64 ZEITSCHRIFT FÜR AUSLÄNDISCHES ÖFFENTLICHES RECHT UND VÖLKERRECHT 125 (2004).
37 *See* Wolfram Höfling, *Art. 1 GG, in* GRUNDGESETZ – KOMMENTAR margin number 10 (Michael Sachs ed., 1996); BVerfGE 75, 369 (380).
38 *See* Case C-377/98, Netherlands v. Parliament and Council, 2001 E.C.R. I-7079, paras. 70 and 77.
39 *See* Case C-112/00, Schmidberger v. Austria, 2003 E.C.R., I-5659, paras. 69 to 94.
40 *See, e.g.*, Case C-41/02, Commission v. Netherlands, (ECJ Dec. 2, 2004) paras. 42 to 70, http://europa.eu.int/eur-lex/lex/LexUriServ/LexUriServ.do?uri=CELEX:62002J0041:EN:HTML.

of protection sought is a matter to be defined by national authorities.[41] The ECJ usually restricts its check of such justifications to verifying whether a measure taken is proportionate in relationship to the protection sought.[42]

The same now applies where fundamental rights are invoked as a justification. While the fundamental right must be recognized at the Community level (it is hard to see one that the ECJ has not or would not recognize), the level of protection it requires is largely determined by the protection the reciprocal fundamental right at the national level affords. The Community justification system and its fundamental rights may be seen as containers of mostly procedural rules with some, but little substantive content, the remainder of which can be filled through an opening towards the national fundamental rights and their content.[43]

This allows the ECJ to take into account the differences among the social and legal concepts and sensitivities in the Member States. A Community concept of human dignity formed by national content on a case-by-case basis allows, for instance, for a justification of a prohibition of games "playing at killing" in Germany while the United Kingdom can freely continue to allow its residents to play these games. National concepts of fundamental rights are clearly not supplanted, but recognized and taken into account at the Community level.

On the other hand, the ECJ does not surrender the fundamental freedoms to national fundamental rights, because the balancing in the proportionality test takes place between the fundamental freedom and the fundamental right (container) at the Community level. In this case, for instance, had the national fundamental right been the relevant standard, the balancing in which the ECJ engaged could not have taken place because such balancing would be impossible under German law.

In essence, the ECJ's proportionality test amounts to a check of whether outer limits are respected. To compare it to U.S. categories, the Court's test, where fundamental rights are invoked to justify a restriction of a fundamental freedom, is not one of "strict scrutiny," but rather of "rational relationship scrutiny," or at most one of "intermediate scrutiny."[44] Under a stricter test the ECJ could have, for instance, considered whether it was really necessary to afford adults that sort of protection, or whether restrictions for adolescents would have been sufficient.

Such "soft scrutiny" seems to be in contradiction to what was said at the outset. Indeed, what is left, in these cases, of the "narrow interpretation" of restriction justifications? Clearly very little. Rather, where fundamental rights are invoked as the public policy justification for a departure from Community mandates they may be expected to mostly carry the day. This is why some propose taking such situations out of the justification process altogether and to engage in a direct balancing of the fundamental freedom and the fundamental right,[45] while others urge the ECJ to refer to Article 6 (3) EU as a mandate to respect decisions regarding fundamental values and identity taken by the Member States.[46]

If, in *Omega*, the ECJ has kept within the traditional structures of assessing restrictions and justifications, this was of no detriment to either of the balancing elements. It is,

---

41 *Id.* at paras. 42 to 44.
42 *Id.* at paras. 46 to 69.
43 Of course, this applies to national measures only. Community measures are checked against a substantive standard that the Court infers from common constitutional traditions of the Member States and international human rights agreements, most prominently the ECHR.
44 *See* JOHN E. NOWAK & RONALD D. ROTUNDA, CONSTITUTIONAL LAW 685 (7th ed, 2004).
45 *See* Alberto Alemanno, *À la recherche d'un juste équilibre entre libertés fondamentales et droits fondamentaux dans le cadre du marché intérieur*, REVUE DU DROIT DE L'UNION EUROPÉENNE 70 (2004).
46 *See* Gabriel Toggenburg, *Grundrechte, Grundfreiheiten, Grund zum Nachfragen anlässlich der Rechtssache Omega*, EUROPEAN LAW REPORTER 2 (2005).

perhaps, even better suited to such situations because it may allow more easily the opening of a window to national valuations than a direct balancing of fundamental freedoms and fundamental rights, which might then assert more Community content. Should the ECJ stick with that approach, which is rather likely, it would be beneficial in terms of clarity and predictability should the Court openly address its scrutiny approach. In that regard, it is submitted that the currently applied standard of less than strict scrutiny seems generally well suited where fundamental rights are invoked.

However, the fact that fundamental rights, and concepts like human dignity in particular,[47] can be construed quite broadly, as illustrated by the *Omega* case, begs for some vigilance and, at least in some instances, for intermediate scrutiny to be applied to the proportionality test. For example, some justly raise questions about the compatibility with human dignity, as construed by German authorities in this case, of certain late-night TV programs, freely available DVD movies and computer games.[48] Taken seriously, this domestic view of human dignity could result in broad limitations on the free movement of these goods.

A last reproach of the *Omega* judgment from German academics is that the content of human dignity as a Community concept remains undefined.[49] The animal is out there, but no one knows what it looks like. Based on the foregoing argument, however, that was precisely the purpose of the exercise, and rightly so. The ECJ did not have to define the exact extent of human dignity at the Community level, because it was addressing a national measure. In these cases national values have to be weighed against Community interests and some discretion must be accorded to national authorities in order not to impose a single standard supplanting national protection systems.[50]

The silhouette of the Community notion of human dignity will emerge, it is submitted, when the ECJ addresses Community measures that raise questions to that effect.

II. The Orfanopoulos *and* Oliveri Cases[51]

In the *Orfanopoulos* and *Oliveri* cases German administrative organization and procedure as well as the extent of administrative courts' judicial review of administrative decisions was at issue.

1. The Facts

Mr. Orfanopoulos, a Greek national born in 1959, joined his parents in Germany in 1972, at the age of 13. He married a German national in 1981 and had three children with his wife. Mr. Orfanopoulos had no professional training qualifications and was mostly unemployed. He was a drug addict and had been convicted on nine occasions of narcotics offences and for committing acts of violence. Attempts at detoxification ended in

---

47 For example, the Israeli Supreme Court, in absence of a fundamental rights catalogue, had derived all fundamental rights from that concept.
48 *See* Jürgen Bröhmer, *Zulässige Untersagung eines Tötungsspiels*, 16 EUROPÄISCHE ZEITSCHRIFT FÜR WIRTSCHAFTSRECHT 755 (2004).
49 *Id.*
50 For instance, had the ECJ taken this route to defining human dignity as a Community norm, and then opted for the German model, the United Kingdom would have been under a positive obligation to prohibit the games at issue also.
51 Joined cases C-482/01 and C-493/01, Georgios Orfanopoulos and Others (C-482/01) and Raffaele Oliveri (C-493/01) v. Land Baden-Württemberg, 2004 E.C.R. I-5257.

discharges from the establishments for disciplinary reasons. In 1999, he was imprisoned for six months, and since September 2000 he had been serving another sentence.[52]

He had residence permits until 1999 and applied for an extension. In February 2001, the *Regierungspräsidium*[53] rejected his application for extension, ordered his expulsion and informed him that he would be deported on his release from prison. The expulsion decision was based on the number and seriousness of the offences committed and on the risk of future offences related to his dependency on drugs and alcohol. Between 1992 and 1998, Mr. Orfanopoulos had received several warnings as to the possible consequences of his conduct with respect to his immigration status.[54]

Indeed, paragraph 47 (1) (2) of the German Law on Aliens provides that an alien is to be expelled if he or she has been finally sentenced to a term of imprisonment without suspension under the Law on Narcotics or for a breach of the public peace.[55] However, paragraph 48 (1) (4) of the Law on Aliens affords special protection to aliens who live in a family relationship with a German national.[56] Under these provisions, aliens may be expelled only on serious grounds of public security and public policy. Special protection status therefore hinders mandatory expulsion. Yet, according to paragraph 47 (3) of the Law on Aliens, the effect of such special protection does not to hinder expulsion altogether, but is simply meant to reduce the mandatory expulsion to expulsion as a general rule.[57] That is to say, expulsion will take place unless compelling reasons recommend against it; a refutable presumption for expulsion applies.

This scheme is a longstanding and fundamental pillar of the German Law on Aliens.[58] It is completed by the Law on the Residence of Nationals of the Member States of the European Community, which provides that expulsion or deportation of Community nationals shall be permitted only where the personal conduct gives rise to (serious) grounds of public policy, public security or public health. In other words, no presumptions as to expulsion apply.[59]

However, the *Regierungspräsidium* did not apply these special rules for Community nationals to Mr. Orfanopoulos, but instead applied the general rules for such situations from the Law on Aliens. Under these rules, the *Regierungspräsidium* concluded that, taking into account the personal circumstances of Mr. Orfanopoulos, the general interest in public security and public policy should prevail over his individual interest in continuing to reside in Germany.[60]

Mr. Orfanopoulos considered that decision, which was based on provisions of the Law on Aliens, to be incompatible with Community law and brought a challenge against that decision before the administrative court of Stuttgart.[61]

The facts of the second case are very similar. Mr. Oliveri, an Italian national, was born in Germany in 1977 and continuously resided in Germany. He never obtained a certificate of completion of studies. A drug addict as well, he became infected with HIV and chronic

---

52 *Id.* at paras. 22 to 25.
53 An institution at the second level of the administrative hierarchy in the state of Baden-Württemberg.
54 Joined cases C-482/01 and C-493/01, Orfanopoulos and Oliveri, *supra* note 51, at paras. 26 and 27.
55 Ausländergesetz (AuslG – German Law on Aliens), Feb. 16, 2001, BGBl. I, at 266, para. 47 (1) (2)).
56 *Id.* at para. 48 (1) (4).
57 *Id.* at para. 47 (3).
58 *See* ARNO KLOESEL ET AL., DEUTSCHES AUFENTHALTS- UND AUSLÄNDERRECHT – KOMMENTAR § 101 IV 12 (5th ed. 2005).
59 *See* Gesetz über Einreise und Aufenthalt von Staatsangehörigen der Mitgliedstaaten der Europäischen Wirtschaftsgemeinschaft (AufenthG/EWG – Law on the Residence of Nationals of the Member States of the European Community), Dec. 27, 2000, BGBl. I at 2042.
60 Joined cases C-482/01 and C-493/01, Orfanopoulos and Oliveri, *supra* note 51, at paras. 27 and 28.
61 *Id.* at para. 29.

hepatitis C. Two attempts at detoxification failed. Mr. Oliveri had committed numerous offences and had been criminally sanctioned for theft and the illegal sale of narcotics. He was first imprisoned in November 1999, and thereafter since April 2000.[62]

In 1999, Mr. Oliveri received a warning as to the possible consequences of his conduct under the German Law on Aliens and in 2000, the *Regierungspräsidium* ordered his expulsion, threatening deportation to Italy. The decision was based on the frequency and seriousness of the offences, and on the risk of further offence because of his dependency on drugs. The failed detoxification was taken as evidence that he was neither willing nor able successfully to complete such treatment, which would have fostered prospects for reintegration into German society. The *Regierungspräsidium* thus considered the requirements in Paragraph 47 (1) (2) of the Law on Aliens for mandatory expulsion to be met.[63]

Special protection under paragraph 48 (1) of that law was not afforded to Mr. Oliveri. While he had lived with his parents until his arrest, his criminal conduct was seen as proof of loosened ties and his HIV infection did not imply, in the view of the *Regierungspräsidium*, that he was completely dependent on his parents' assistance.[64]

Mr. Oliveri brought an action before the administrative court of Stuttgart against the expulsion decision and claimed that risks of further offences had receded, because he had matured while in prison and now wished to undergo detoxification. The prison medical service later informed the referring court that Mr. Oliveri had fallen very seriously ill, that he was likely soon to die, and that it was to be feared that he would not receive the necessary medical care in Italy.[65]

Under the law of Baden-Württemberg, the second administrative level, the *Regierungspräsidium*, is competent for expulsion decisions concerning prisoners.[66] Usually, however, that body's task is to rule on objections to decisions of the first administrative level. As a consequence, no administrative review is available for decisions handed down directly by the *Regierungspräsidium*. The individual can only take the case to court. Yet, under the code of procedure for administrative courts, these courts cannot take subsequent developments into account. They have to decide on the basis of the facts established on the day the administration took its decision.[67] And, unlike the *Regierungspräsidium* when ruling on an objection, the administrative court cannot assess the expediency of an expulsion.[68]

Under these circumstances, the administrative court of Stuttgart asked the ECJ, *inter alia*, whether: (a) Community law precludes national legislation providing for mandatory expulsion of nationals of other Member States who have been sentenced to imprisonment without suspension; (b) developments subsequent to decisions of the administrative authority had to be taken into account by the national courts; and (c) whether the absence of a review process allowing for an examination of the expediency of an administrative expulsion decision is in conformity Community law.

---

62 *Id.* at paras. 32 to 34.
63 *Id.* at para. 35.
64 *Id.* at para. 36.
65 *Id.* at paras. 37 and 38.
66 *See* Verordnung der Landesregierung und des Innenministeriums über Zuständigkeiten nach dem Ausländergesetz und dem Asylverfahrensgesetz (Ausländer- und Asyl-Zuständigkeitsverordnung-AAZuVO – Regulation on jurisdiction over proceedings relating to aliens and asylum), July 19, 1995, Gbl. at 586, consolidated at 771, para. 7 (1) (1) (last modified by Article 2 ÄndVO of March 23, 1998, GBl. at 187).
67 *See* ERICH EYERMANN & LUDWIG FRÖHLER, VERWALTUNGSGERICHTSORDNUNG – KOMMENTAR § 113 margin number 45 (11th ed. 2000); FERDINAND KOPP & WOLF-RÜDIGER SCHENKE, VERWALTUNGSGERICHTSORDNUNG – KOMMENTAR § 113 margin number 29 (13th ed. 2003).
68 *See* ERICH EYERMANN & LUDWIG FRÖHLER, VERWALTUNGSGERICHTSORDNUNG – KOMMENTAR § 114 (11th ed. 2000); FERDINAND KOPP & WOLF-RÜDIGER SCHENKE, VERWALTUNGSGERICHTSORDNUNG – KOMMENTAR § 114 (13th ed. 2003).

2. The Holding

a) Question One

The ECJ began by recalling that the principle of freedom of movement for workers in Article 39 EC must be given a broad interpretation, and that an expulsion of nationals of other Member States is an obstacle to the exercise of that freedom. While such an obstacle may be justified under Article 39 (3) of Directive 64/221[69] on grounds of public policy, derogations from that principle must be interpreted strictly. The ECJ added that, by virtue of the new Union citizenship status (Article 17 EC), which is destined to be the fundamental status of nationals of the Member States, a particularly restrictive interpretation of derogations from that freedom is required.[70]

By that standard, measures of public policy under Article 3 of the Directive must be based exclusively on the personal conduct of the individual concerned. Community law precludes the deportation of a national of a Member State based on reasons of a general preventive nature, that is to say, for the purpose of deterring others. Article 3 of the Directive further directs that previous criminal convictions alone cannot justify such measures; rather, the ECJ recalled, the concept of public policy additionally requires a genuine and sufficiently serious threat to public policy, affecting a fundamental interest of society.[71]

With respect to Mr. Oliveri, the ECJ observed that, under the German Law on Aliens, a mandatory expulsion automatically follows specific criminal convictions, without any account being taken of the personal conduct of the offender or of the danger which that person represents for the requirements of public policy. Unsurprisingly then, the Court concluded that such national legislation is precluded by Community law.[72]

Regarding Mr. Orfanopoulos, the situation was a little more complicated because, as the ECJ acknowledged, the expulsion order took account of Mr. Orfanopoulos' personal conduct and his family circumstances, and because expulsion was not mandatory, but a presumption only applied on the basis of his conviction. Yet, that presumption, the ECJ held, still contained an element of automatism towards expulsion: While paragraph 48 (1) of the Law on Aliens allows for expulsion of specially protected persons only on serious grounds of public security and public policy, such grounds are deemed to exist in cases of criminal convictions without suspension, just as in the case of a mandatory expulsion. Where the effect of such a presumption is expulsion, without proper account being taken of the deportee's personal conduct or of the danger he or she represents for the requirements of public policy, the ECJ found the presumption to be contrary to Article 39 EC and Article 3 of the Directive.[73]

The ECJ then went on to explain what exactly was required to satisfy Community law standards. In the view of the ECJ, a case-by-case examination is necessary, which assesses personal conduct, weighs its impact on public policy considerations, and balances the public interests involved against the principle of the free movement of persons and the funda-

---

69 Council Directive 64/221, Co-ordination of Special Measures Concerning the Movement and Residence of Foreign Nationals which are Justified on Grounds of Public Policy, Public Security or Public Health, O.J., English special edition, Series I, Chapter 1963–1964, at 117.
70 Joined cases C-482/01 and C-493/01, Orfanopoulos and Oliveri, *supra* note 51, at paras. 64 and 65. Regarding Union citizenship, the ECJ referred to the Case C-184/99, Grzelczyk, 2001 E.C.R. I-6193, para. 31 and Case C-138/02, Collins, (ECJ March 23, 2004) para. 61, http://europa.eu.int/eur-lex/lex/LexUriServ/LexUriServ.do?uri=CELEX:62002J0138:EN:HTML.
71 Joined cases C-482/01 and C-493/01, Orfanopoulos and Oliveri, *supra* note 51, at paras. 66 and 68 (citing Case 30/77, Bouchereau, 1977 E.C.R. 1999, para. 35).
72 *Id.* at paras. 69 and 70.
73 *Id.* at paras. 92 to 94.

mental rights of the individual. In that last respect, the ECJ pointed specifically to the importance of ensuring the protection of the family life of Community nationals as guaranteed by Article 8 of the ECHR and further supported by the principle of proportionality. In situations such as the present cases, the ECJ held that account had to be taken particularly of the nature and seriousness of the offences, of the duration of residence, of the period elapsed since the commission of the offence, of the family circumstances, and of the seriousness of the difficulties which the spouse and any of their children risk facing in the country of origin of the person concerned.[74]

b) Question Two

The second question, whether developments subsequent to decisions of the administrative authority had to be taken into account by the national courts, was relevant for Mr. Oliveri's situation, because, on the one hand, Mr. Oliveri claimed positive developments in personal attitude after the expulsion order and, on the other hand, his HIV infection had, in the meantime, reached the state of AIDS.

The ECJ first stated the obvious, namely that, between the date of an expulsion order and the date of its judicial review, a threat to public policy, resulting from the conduct of the person to be expelled, may cease or be substantially reduced by circumstances, especially if a lengthy period elapses between the date of the expulsion order and that of the review of that decision by the competent court.[75]

The ECJ then inferred from the principle that derogations must be interpreted strictly, that the requirement of a present threat must in general be satisfied at the time of the expulsion. Recognizing that it is for the domestic legal system of each Member State to lay down the procedural rules governing court actions, the ECJ resorted to the principle of *effet utile* of Community law to justify this intrusion. The principle states that national rules may not render virtually impossible or excessively difficult the exercise of rights conferred by Community law.[76]

Consequently, the ECJ held that a national practice that does not allow for the taking into account of developments subsequent to an administrative decision is liable to adversely affect the right to freedom of movement to which nationals of the Member States.[77]

c) Question Three

The third question, whether the absence of an objection proceeding allowing for an examination of the expediency of an administrative expulsion decision is in conformity with Community law, related to both applicants. In both cases no additional administrative review of the expulsion orders was available.

The ECJ held that Article 9 (1) of Directive 64/221 is designed to afford minimal procedural safeguards to persons affected by expulsion orders. It applies where an appeal to a court of law is not available, where such an appeal is limited to the legal validity of the decision, or where the appeal has no suspensory effect. In these situations, it requires the intervention of an authority other than the one that took the expulsion decision.[78] The ECJ had already decided that the intervention of that second authority had to encompass an

---

74 *Id.* at paras. 95 to 99.
75 *Id.* at paras. 78 and 81.
76 *Id.* at paras. 79 to 81. The principle of *effet utile* was, for instance, the central argument for direct applicability of directives. *See* Case 148/78, Ratti, 1979 E.C.R. 1629.
77 *Id.* at para. 81.
78 *Id.* at para. 105.

exhaustive examination of all facts and circumstances, including the expediency of the measure in question.[79]

It was undisputed that the review of a *Regierungspräsidium*'s expulsion order by administrative courts did not allow for an exhaustive examination of the expediency of an expulsion order. Rather, administrative courts can only check for errors, such as complete lack of expediency considerations, an erroneous factual basis, or the taking into account of non-pertinent aspects.[80] The German Government unsuccessfully argued that this was sufficient under Article 9 (1) of the Directive. Instead, the ECJ concluded that only an exhaustive examination of the expediency could meet the requirements of a sufficiently effective protection and of the *effet utile* of the provision.[81]

3. Commentary

The judgment was not surprising because it brought nothing new. The major questions of the case had been similarly decided in previous cases involving other member states.[82] Germany had nonetheless failed to draw the consequences from these rulings, and there are consequences to be drawn. In light of the established precedent that informed the ECJ's decisions in these cases, one can fairly wonder why the rulings were greeted with disdain from some parts of German academia.[83]

Two reasons explain this reaction. First, on the face of it, the judgments require fundamental changes in the Law on Aliens, in administrative organization, and in the way judicial review functions are carried out in German administrative courts. Second, regarding the first question, the wrong legal basis was challenged: the Law on Aliens should not have been applied in the way the administration applied it. Rather, the specific law for Union citizens should have been taken into account and its application would, in all likelihood, have met the ECJ's balancing requirements. However, the ECJ must reply to preliminary references on the basis of the law as presented to it by the referring court.[84] So, despite demands of the German government that the ECJ should consider the better suited specific law on Union citizens, the ECJ was obliged to consider only the Law on Aliens under the terms of the reference.

This line of criticism indicates that the reply to the first question did not actually require major changes to the existing law. And yet, the ruling was taken into account by the German parliament when recently enacting the *Zuwanderungsgesetz* (Law on

---

79 *Id.* at para. 106 (*citing* Case C-131/79, Santillo, 1980 E.C.R. 1585, para. 12; joined Cases 115/81 and 116/81, Adoui and Cornuaille, 1982 E.C.R. 1665, para. 15).

80 *See* Verwaltungsgerichtsordnung (VwGO – code of procedure for administrative courts), March 19, 1991, BGBl. I S. 686, para. 114 (last modified by Article 15 Zweites ZuständigkeislockerungsG of May 3, 2000, BGBl. K S. 632).

81 *Id.* at paras. 109 and 110 (*citing* Case 222/84, Johnston, 1986 E.C.R. 1651, para. 17; Case 222/86, Heylens and Others, 1987 E.C.R. 4097, paras. 14 and 15).

82 Question 1 had been previously decided. *See* Case C-30/77, Bouchereau, 1977 E.C.R. 1999, para. 35; C-348/96, Calfa, 1999 E.C.R. I-11, paras. 22 to 24. Question 2 had not actually been decided, but the decision could be easily expected on the basis of prior rulings on Article 3 of the directive. *See* Case C-348/96, Calfa, 1999 E.C.R. I-11, paras. 23 and 24. Question 3 had previously been considered by the ECJ as well. *See* Case C-131/79, Santillo, 1980 E.C.R. 1585, para. 12; Joined Cases 115/81 and 116/81, Adoui and Cornuaille, 1982 E.C.R. 1665, 15; Case 222/84, Johnston, 1986 E.C.R. 1651, para. 17; Case 222/86, Heylens and Others, 1987 E.C.R. 4097, paras. 14 and 15.

83 Others, however, rather blamed the hierarchical structure of the German court system for a perceived failure of German courts to refer questions in time to the ECJ. *See* Rolf Gutmann, *Fehlender Mut zum gesetzlichen Richter*, 57 NEUE JURISTISCHE WOCHENSCHRIFT 28 at III (2004).

84 *See* joined cases C-482/01 and C-493/01, Orfanopoulos and Oliveri, *supra* note 51, at para. 42 (citing Case C-58/98 Corsten, 2000 E.C.R. I-7919, para. 24; Case C-475/99, Ambulanz Glöckner, 2001 E.C.R. I-8089, para. 10; Case C-153/02, Neri, 2003 E.C.R. I-13555, paras. 34 and 35).

Immigration), which revised and modernized the laws on aliens, on asylum seekers, and on immigration.[85] While the traditional expulsion system was maintained for third country nationals, it no longer applies to Union citizens.[86]

Regarding the reply to the third question, the state of Baden-Württemberg and other states in a similar situation will have to make changes in their administrative organization. But again, they will probably not prove to be major changes, because the requirements for an expediency review of initial administrative decisions can be met in four ways. Least likely is the option to hand more extensive expediency review powers to the administrative courts, because that would be inconsistent with the German concept of judicial functions.[87] Quite unlikely, too, would be the creation of a *Rechtsausschuss* (independent review board), though they exist in other states, such as Rheinland-Pfalz (*Kreisrechtsausschüsse*). Instead, the affected states will probably either create review powers at the third administrative level, the ministry, or, most likely, hand the competence for initial decisions down to first administrative level, local administration. That is the rule for all aliens other than prisoners and it is hard to see why it could not be done for imprisoned aliens, too. The *Regierungspräsidium* would then be the review level, as usual.

Changes to legal review of administrative decisions will also have to come about, but they will probably be limited to actions brought by Union citizens. At least, no major review of jurisprudence is in sight. The ruling is unlikely, then, to have an effect on either the status of third country nationals – except, perhaps for Turkish citizens, under the associations agreement – or on German judicial review in general. And the changes brought about appear well justified under Community law.

Little reason, one may conclude, for academic disdain.

III. The Pfeiffer Case[88]

The last case addressed the recurring question of a horizontal direct application of Directives between individuals in proceedings before national courts. While upholding its long standing jurisprudence, the ECJ added a "twist" that may well have a major impact on national legal orders.

1. The Facts

The *Deutsches Rotes Kreuz* (DRK – German Red Cross) operates a land-based emergency service, mostly manned around the clock, that is carried out by means of ambulances and emergency medical vehicles. An ambulance crew consists of two paramedics, whilst an

---

85 Gesetz zur Steuerung und Begrenzung der Zuwanderung und zur Regelung des Aufenthalts und der Integration von Unionsbürgern und Ausländern (Zuwanderungsgesetz), July 30, 2004, BGBl. I at 1950.
86 *See* Gesetz über den Aufenthalt, die Erwerbstätigkeit und die Integration von Ausländern im Bundesgebiet (Aufenthaltsgesetz – AufenthG), July 30, 2004, BGBl. I at 1950, paragraph 1 (2) (1) (enacted by the Zuwanderungsgesetz, this law exempts Union citizens from its rules and refers to the Gesetz über die allgemeine Freizügigkeit von Unionsbürgern (FreizügG/EU – Freizügigkeitsgesetz/EU), July 30, 2004, BGBl. I at 1950, which was also enacted by the Zuwanderungsgesetz).
87 *See* ERICH EYERMANN & LUDWIG FRÖHLER, VERWALTUNGSGERICHTSORDNUNG – KOMMENTAR § 114 (11th ed. 2000); FERDINAND KOPP & WOLF-RÜDIGER SCHENKE, VERWALTUNGSGERICHTSORDNUNG – KOMMENTAR § 114 (13th ed. 2003).
88 Joined cases C-397/01 to C-403/01, Bernhard Pfeiffer (C-397/01), Wilhelm Roith (C-398/01), Albert Süß (C-399/01), Michael Winter (C-400/01), Klaus Nestvogel (C-401/01), Roswitha Zeller (C-402/01) and Matthias Döbele (C-403/01) v. Deutsches Rotes Kreuz, Kreisverband Waldshut eV, (ECJ Oct. 5, 2004), http://europa.eu.int/eur-lex/lex/LexUriServ/LexUriServ.do?uri=CELEX:62001J0397:EN:HTML.

emergency medical vehicle consists of an emergency worker and a doctor. When they are alerted of an emergency, these vehicles respond in order to provide medical assistance to patients. Subsequently, patients are usually taken to a hospital.[89]

Mr. Pfeiffer had been employed by the DRK as an emergency worker. He contended that he was wrongly required to work more than 48 hours per week on average from June 2000 to March 2001 and claimed payment for the extra hours. As part of the same legal actions, former colleagues of Mr. Pfeiffer who still worked for the DRK sought a determination of the maximum period which they must work per week.[90]

Paragraph 3 of the German Law on Working Time provides, as the general rule, that employees' daily working time must not exceed an average eight hours per working day over 6 calendar months or 24 weeks, with a daily maximum of 10 hours.[91] However, paragraph 7 of the law allows for collective agreements to extend working time beyond 10 hours per day where working time regularly includes significant periods of *Arbeitsbereitschaft* ("duty time"). During duty time, the employee must be available at the place of employment and has to remain continuously attentive in order to be able to act immediately, should the need arise.

Paragraph 14 (2) (b) of the collective agreement on working conditions for German Red Cross employees allows for an extension of normal working time to 11 hours per day where it includes duty time of at least 3 hours per day.[92]

The competent German labor court found that weekly working time in the DRK emergency service was, on average, 49 hours and that duty time was at least 3 hours per day on average.[93]

In Mr. Pfeiffer's view, a weekly working time of 49 hours contradicted Article 6 of Directive 93/104,[94] which provides that, for the need to protect the safety and health of workers, Member States must ensure that the average working time for each seven-day period, including overtime, does not exceed 48 hours. The Directive defines working time in Article 2 as "any period during which the worker is working, at the employer's disposal and carrying out his activity or duties, in accordance with national laws and/or practice" and rest periods as "any period which is not working time." However, Article 18 (1) (b) (i) of the Directive allows for a derogation from these limits where the employee has given his prior consent.

Under these circumstances, the labor court asked the ECJ, *inter alia*, whether: (a) Article 18 (1) (b) (i) of Directive 93/104 requires the consent to be given individually by a worker and to expressly refer to the extension of working time beyond 48 hours, or whether such consent may also reside in a contract of employment, when it provides that working conditions are to be governed by a collective agreement which allows for such an extension; and (b) Article 6 of Directive 93/104 could be relied on by individuals before national courts where a Member state has not properly transposed the Directive into national law.

---

89 *Id.* at para. 29.
90 *Id.* at paras. 31 to 33.
91 Arbeitszeitgesetz (ArbZG – Law on Working Time), June 6, 1994, BGBl. I at 1170, para. 3.
92 *See* joined cases C-397/01 to C-403/01, Pfeiffer and others, *supra* note 86, at para. 25.
93 *Id.* at para. 35.
94 Council Directive 93/104, Concerning Certain Aspects of the Organization of Working Time, 1993 O.J. (L 307) 18.

2. The Holding

a) Question One

With regard to the first question, the ECJ underscored that the objective of the Directive is to protect the safety and health of workers by affording them minimum rest periods and adequate breaks, through an upper limit on weekly working time. While allowing for derogations, their implementation is subject to strict conditions intended to secure effective protection.

The ECJ recalled previous decisions in which it concluded that the consent given by trade-union representatives in collective agreements is not equivalent to the consent given by the worker him- or herself.[95] In the light of the safety and health objectives, any relinquishment of the minimum rest periods which the Directive conferred upon workers as a social right must be agreed to freely and with full knowledge of all facts. Those conditions, the ECJ concluded, are not met where the worker's employment contract merely refers to a collective agreement authorizing an extension of maximum weekly working time, because it is by no means certain that the worker knew of the restriction of the rights.[96]

b) Question Two

As to the second question – whether Article 6 (2) of the Directive may be taken to have direct effect – the ECJ first interpreted the provision to allow for an assessment by the national court of whether the national law is compatible with the Directive's requirements. In a second step, the ECJ examined whether the provision satisfies the conditions which enable individuals to rely on it before the national courts.[97]

The ECJ noted that Article 6 (2) of the Directive imposes, for the protection of workers' safety and health, a 48-hour limit for the average working week, which is expressly stated to include overtime. The ECJ recalled that it had already held that *Bereitschaftsdienst* ("on-call time"), where the worker is required to be physically present at a place specified by his employer, ready to take up his duties, but where he is authorized to rest as he sees fit, as long as his services are not required, must be regarded as working time. With duty time in emergency services requiring higher readiness to resume one's duties than on-call time, duty time has to be considered working time, too. Accordingly, periods of duty time have to be taken into account for calculating working time.[98]

The ECJ concluded that under Article 6 (2) and the purpose and scheme of the Directive, the 48-hour upper limit on average weekly working time constitutes a rule of Community social law of particular importance from which every worker must benefit, since it is necessary to protect his or her safety and health, and that therefore national legislation, such as the German law at issue, is not compatible with the requirements of Article 6 (2) of the Directive.[99]

Regarding the direct effect, the ECJ found that the wording of Article 6 (2) of the Directive was unconditional and sufficiently precise to satisfy the criteria of direct applicability: indeed, devoid of any condition, it imposes on Member States in unequivocal terms the precise obligation to provide for a 48-hour maximum of average weekly working

---

[95] See joined cases C-397/01 to C-403/01, Pfeiffer and others, *supra* note 86, at para. 81 (citing Case C-303/98, Simap, 2000 E.C.R. I-7963, para. 74).
[96] *Id.* at paras. 82 to 85.
[97] *Id.* at paras. 88 and 89.
[98] *Id.* at paras. 90 to 95 (*citing* Case C-151/02, Jaeger, 2003 E.C.R. I-8389, paras. 71, 75 and 103).
[99] *Id.* at paras. 100 and 101.

time.[100] However, the labor court's question targeted a direct application of the Directive between private parties: Mr. Pfeiffer, an individual, and the DRK, which has a private status and is not a state entity. In that regard, the ECJ has consistently held that a Directive can only impose obligations on the Member states, not on individuals or private entities and cannot therefore be relied upon against private parties. A direct application in proceedings exclusively between private parties is therefore excluded.[101]

The ECJ went on to refer to its prior case-law on the Member States' duties under Article 10 EC and Article 249 EC.[102] These duties require Member States to take all appropriate measures to achieve the results envisaged by a Directive, and that this obligation is binding on all the authorities of Member States including, for matters within their jurisdiction, the courts. It is indeed the responsibility of the national courts to provide the legal protection which individuals derive from the rules of Community law and to ensure that those rules are fully effective.[103]

The ECJ considered this to be *a fortiori* the case where, as here, the national court has to apply domestic provisions which have been specifically enacted as a transposition of a Directive. In such cases, the ECJ requires the national court to presume that the Member State had the intention of fulfilling entirely the obligations arising from the Directive concerned. Thus, the national court is bound to interpret national law, as far as possible, in the light of the wording and the purpose of the Directive concerned, in order to achieve the result sought by the Directive.[104]

However, if the obligation to interpret domestic law in conformity with Community law chiefly concerns provisions implementing the Directive, the ECJ has also required the national court to consider national law as a whole in order to assess the extent to which it may be applied so as to avoid a result contrary to that sought by the Directive.[105] This is the case where "the application of interpretative methods recognized by national law enables a provision of domestic law to be construed in such a way as to avoid conflict with another rule of domestic law or the scope of that provision to be restricted to that end by applying it only in so far as it is compatible with the rule concerned, the national court is bound to use those methods in order to achieve the result sought by the Directive."[106]

Accordingly, "when hearing a case between individuals, a national court is required, when applying the provisions of domestic law adopted for the purpose of transposing obligations laid down by a Directive, to consider the whole body of rules of national law and to interpret them, so far as possible, in the light of the wording and purpose of the Directive in order to achieve an outcome consistent with the objective pursued by the Directive."[107] The "national court must thus do whatever lies within its jurisdiction to ensure that the maximum period of weekly working time, which is set at 48 hours by Article 6(2) of Directive 93/104, is not exceeded."[108]

---

100 *Id.* at paras. 103 to 106.
101 *Id.* at paras. 108 and 109 (*citing* Case 152/84, Marshall, 1986 E.C.R. 723, para. 48; Case C-91/92, Faccini Dori, 1994 E.C.R. I-3325, para. 20; Case C-201/02, Wells, (ECJ Dec. 10, 2003) para. 56, http://europa.eu.int/eur-lex/lex/LexUriServ/LexUriServ.do?uri=CELEX:62002O0204(01):EN:HTML).
102 *Id.* at paras. 110 to 113 (citing Case 14/83, Von Colson and Kamann, 1984 E.C.R. 1891, para. 26; Case C-106/89, Marleasing, 1990 E.C.R. I-4135, para. 8; Case C-91/92, Faccini Dori, 1994 E.C.R. I-3325, para. 26; Case C-126/96, Inter-Environnement Wallonie, 1997 E.C.R. I-7411, para. 40; Case C-131/97, Carbonari and Others, 1999 E.C.R. I-1103, para. 48; Case C-334/92, Wagner Miret, 1993 E.C.R. I-6911, para. 20).
103 *Id.* at paras. 110 and 111.
104 *Id.* at paras. 112 and 113.
105 *Id.* at paras. 115 (*citing* Case C-131/97, Carbonari and Others, 1999 E.C.R. I-1103, paras. 49 and 50).
106 *Id.* at para. 116.
107 *Id.* at para. 119.
108 *Id.* at para. 120

3. Commentary

With regard to Directives, the primary task of Member States, one should remember, is to correctly transpose them into national law. Where a Member State fails to do so, Community law provides three "sanctions," namely direct applicability of the Directive, liability of the Member State for damages and losses suffered by individuals because of the failure to transpose correctly, and infringement procedures initiated by the Commission, opening the way to sanctions under Article 228 EC.[109]

In the ECJ's jurisprudence, direct applicability has always been limited to "vertical situations."[110] That is to say that, where the conditions for direct applicability are met, individuals can rely on a Directive when making claims against the Member State. On the other hand, the ECJ always ruled out a direct "horizontal" applicability of Directives among private parties, chiefly because, by virtue of Article 249 EC, Directives create obligations for Member States only, and because the citizens' confidence into their legal order has to be protected.

On the face of it, then, the ruling brings "nothing new." Where horizontal direct applicability is at issue, Directives still cannot set aside national law. In his opinion on the case, Advocate General Ruiz-Jarabo Colomer had proposed abandoning this traditional jurisprudence in favor of direct horizontal applicability.[111] It follows clearly from the judgment that the ECJ is not (yet) prepared to make that leap.

Consequently, the task for national courts remains "simply" to interpret the national law, to the extent possible, in accordance with the aims of Directives. In detailing that duty, however, the ECJ has given an important "clarification" that is likely to prove a substantial step towards results akin to a direct horizontal applicability.

This "clarification" consists of two elements. First, the ECJ underscored the duty of national courts to look beyond transposition provisions and into the entire national legal order, to find a means to reach the Directive's desired result. While the ECJ stated this duty before, and it has been clear for a while, that, for instance, where specific transposition provisions fell short, blanket clauses of general law had to be resorted to where possible, the emphasis that the ECJ placed on looking for alternative means is new, and the ECJ added a new "twist" regarding methods of interpretation.

The ECJ expressly required national courts to make use of all interpretation methods available under national law. That encompasses, it is submitted, not only the interpretive methods usually applied to the legal matter, but all others, too. In that regard, German methodology offers a rich choice. One might, for instance, think of the constitutionally

---

109 *See* PAUL CRAIG & GRÁINNE DE BÚRCA, EU LAW: TEXT, CASES, AND MATERIALS 114, 202 (3rd ed. 2003); ANTHONY ARNULL ET AL., WYATT AND DASHWOOD'S EUROPEAN UNION LAW 89 (4th ed. 2000); K.P.E. LASOK & D. LASOK, LAW AND INSTITUTIONS OF THE EUROPEAN UNION 142 (7th ed. 2001).
110 *See* Case 148/78, Ratti, 1979 E.C.R. 1629; Case 80/86, Kolpinghuis Nijmegen, 1987 E.C.R. 3969; Case 152/84, Marshall, 1986 E.C.R. 723; Case C-106/89, Marleasing, 1990 E.C.R. I-4135; Case C-91/92, Faccini Dori, 1994 E.C.R. I-3325.
111 *See* Opinion of Advocate General Ruiz-Jarabo Colomer delivered on May 6, 2003, in joined Cases C-397/01 to C-403/01, Bernhard Pfeiffer and Others, at paras. 56 to 59, http://europa.eu.int/eur-lex/lex/LexUriServ/LexUriServ.do?uri=CELEX:62001C0397:EN:HTML. In an unusual second opinion on the case, which had become necessary because of a reattribution of the case to the Grand Chamber and a reopening of the oral procedure, and which was delivered on 24 April 2004, the Advocate General nuanced his approach, but reached essentially the same result. *See* Opinion of Advocate General Ruiz-Jarabo Colomer delivered on April 27, 2004, in joined Cases C-397/01 to C-403/01, Bernhard Pfeiffer and Others, at paras. 17 to 48, http://curia.eu.int/jurisp/cgi-bin/form.pl?lang=en&Submit=Submit&alldocs=alldocs&docj=docj&docop=docop&docor=docor&docjo=docjo&numaff=C-397%2F01&datefs=&datefe=&nomusuel=&domaine=&mots=&resmax=100.

based concepts of *vertragskonforme Auslegung*,[112] or of *praktische Konkordanz*,[113] which would not usually apply to the interpretation of German civil law.

The second aspect resides in the examples that the ECJ provided and is intimately linked to the choice of interpretive methods, because interpretive methods vary according to the challenge to be dealt with. The challenge which the ECJ poses to the national courts involves the resolution of a collision of norms of equal status, as some have correctly identified.[114] This implies that national courts, for purposes of interpreting national law, have to consider conflicting provisions of a Directive to have the same legal status as the national norm. That is a proposition entirely different from merely providing an aim that should be reached, if an interpretation of the norm so allows. In addition, choice among the available interpretation methods has to be made so as to let the Directive prevail in that conflict, wherever possible.

Clearly that standard now proves much closer to a direct horizontal applicability than that which was in place before this judgment. But it stops just short of it. The limitations are that national law ultimately must be the source of any obligation for individuals and that courts are not required to go beyond the limits set by national law for their competence. They only have to apply interpretation methods available under national law. Where all else fails, the conflicting national law will prevail. Yet, there is a long way to go before that result can be reached. Some even suggest that courts will, in the future, have to consider interpretations *contra legem*.[115]

Why has the ECJ gone so much farther in this case? There may be several reasons. First, the *effet utile* of Community law was at stake. The Directive was incorrectly transposed, yet, at the time of the enactment of the German transposition law, that error was not obvious enough to allow Mr. Pfeiffer to successfully seek compensation from the German state; and, an infringement procedure looked both unlikely and would not have helped Mr. Pfeiffer. Second, benefiting from the *Jaeger* decision,[116] state employees in similar situations could already invoke the direct applicability of the Directive; leaving Mr. Pfeiffer and his colleagues with nothing at all to show would simply have seemed unjust. Third, the ECJ had often been ready to extended Community law obligations more easily to worker-employer situations than elsewhere,[117] because the characteristic subordination situation is akin to the one in a state-citizen situation. Finally, under these circumstances, the Advocate General's opinion may have pushed the ECJ to look for further means.

In the meantime, the Commission has announced plans to submit a proposal to revise the Directive, so as to exclude "duty time" from the ECJ's definition of "working time." The substantive part of the judgment may, therefore, not endure. The new procedural duties for national courts, however, look set to stay, and may change German legal methodology more profoundly than many expect.

---

112 "Vertragskonforme Auslegung" applies where a new law is at odds with obligations arising under an earlier international treaty which has the status of a law. Usually, the *lex posterior derogat legi priori* rule would set aside the treaty, but the *Bundesverfassungsgericht* (BVerfG – German Federal Constitutional Court) consistently ruled that, unless express intent to the contrary can be shown, the German legislator did not want to breach its international obligations. The treaty then usually prevails.
113 "Praktische Konkordanz" means that, where to fundamental rights collide, both have to be interpreted so as to allow each other the maximal, mutually compatible protective effect.
114 *See* Karl Riesenhuber & Ronny Domröse, *Richtlinienkonforme Rechtsfindung und nationale Methodenlehre*, 51 Recht der internationalen Wirtschaft 47 (2005).
115 *Id.*
116 *See* Case C-151/02, Jaeger, 2003 E.C.R. I-8389.
117 *See* Case 36-74, Walrave and Koch, 1974 E.C.R. 1405, paras. 16/19 to 25; Case C-415/93, Bosman, 1995 E.C.R. I-4921; Case 43-75, Defrenne, 1976 E.C.R. 455.

Report – European Court of Human Rights – 2003/2004

Florian F. Hoffmann*

A. Introduction

The trend of previous years, specifically the expansion of quantity and consolidation of quality in the European human rights system, has continued during the period under review. The total number of applications lodged with the unified Court continues to rise steadily and in 2003 was up by approximately eleven percent (from 34,508 to 38,435[1]) from 2002, which saw a rise of roughly ten percent in the number of applications.[2] The percentage of applications declared admissible in relation to the total number of applications lodged (irrespective of whether there was a subsequent finding of a violation in the admitted cases) continued to climb towards two percent.[3] Finally, the number of judgements rendered by the Court in 2003 is, with 753, roughly in line with that of previous years, with 2000 and 2002 counting as exceptions to that confirmed trend.[4]

This simultaneous expansion of the number of individuals seeking redress on the supra-national (European) level, and the gradual consolidation of the Court's case-load can be said to be owed to two principal factors. The first is the impressive rise in applications from Central and Eastern European (CEE) countries.[5] At sixty-one percent of all applications lodged in 2003, the number of applications from the CEE countries increased twenty-five percent on the previous year. This is a clear indication that the perception of the European system as a viable mechanism for redress beyond domestic remedies has taken a firm hold within that region.[6] This perception seems not to be influenced by the

---

* Florian Hoffmann is currently an Assistant Professor of Law at the Pontificia Universidade Catolica do Rio de Janeiro (PUC-Rio) and the Deputy Director of the Law Department's human rights center, the Nucleo de Direitos Humanos. He has recently completed a PhD thesis at the European University Institute, entitled *Can Human Rights Be Transplanted: reflections on a pragmatic theory of human rights under conditions of globalization*; he has also published on international accountability, and international legal theory; he is currently an international law editor for the *German Law Journal*.

1 Figures for 2003 are provisional only; *see* COUNCIL OF EUROPE/EUROPEAN COURT OF HUMAN RIGHTS, SURVEY OF ACTIVITIES FOR 2003 34 (2003), *available at* http://www.echr.coe.int/Eng/EDocs/2003SURVEYCOURT.pdf.
2 *See* COUNCIL OF EUROPE, SURVEY OF ACTIVITIES FOR 2003, *supra* note 1; COUNCIL OF EUROPE/EUROPEAN COURT OF HUMAN RIGHTS, SURVEY OF ACTIVITIES FOR 2002 34 (2002) *available at* http://www.echr.coe.int/Eng/EDocs/2002SURVEYCOURT.pdf; COUNCIL OF EUROPE/EUROPEAN COURT OF HUMAN RIGHTS, SURVEY OF ACTIVITIES FOR 2001 34 (2001), *available at* http://www.echr.coe.int/Eng/EDocs/2001SURVEYCOURT.pdf.
3 *See* COUNCIL OF EUROPE, SURVEY OF ACTIVITIES FOR 2003, *supra* note 1; COUNCIL OF EUROPE, SURVEY OF ACTIVITIES FOR 2002, *supra* note 2; COUNCIL OF EUROPE, SURVEY OF ACTIVITIES FOR 2001, *supra* note 2.
4 *See* COUNCIL OF EUROPE, SURVEY OF ACTIVITIES FOR 2003, *supra* note 1; COUNCIL OF EUROPE, SURVEY OF ACTIVITIES FOR 2002, *supra* note 2; COUNCIL OF EUROPE, SURVEY OF ACTIVITIES FOR 2001, *supra* note 2.
5 Excluding Turkey, but including Russia, as well as all other Council of Europe Member States previously part of the Warsaw Pact, or of the former Yugoslavia.
6 *But see* István Pogány's thought-provoking essay *Refashioning Rights in Central and Eastern Europe: Some Implications for the Region's Roma*, 10 EUR. PUB. L. 85–106 (2004) (showing that not all population groups in that region have so far been able to benefit from the 'rights revolution' there).

number of violations actually found by the Court.[7] The second factor is the increasing functionality of the Court's procedure in relation to maintaining a manageable workload and an adequate output of decisions. Despite the still significant need for further reform on account of the growing number of applications,[8] the various filters which have gradually come to be incorporated into the Court's process seem to be beginning to have an effect.

A sense of the Court's long-term vision of itself emerges from its relatively low application-to-decision ratio, as well as an increasing differentiation of applications into two classes. One class involves "lead cases," which merit greater scrutiny, whereas the other involves "repeat" or "clone" violations, which result from "structural" deficiencies in specific Member States and which the Court deals with in an ever more summary fashion.[9] In general, the Court does not understand itself to be *a certiorari*-empowered Supreme Court selecting only a handful of lead cases each year,[10] but neither does it intend to serve as a supranational last instance in those (many) cases where Member States' domestic systems fail. Instead, it would seem that the Court is increasingly striving to again bring its standard-setting and standard-maintaining role to the fore. The latter has been partially obscured by a symptom of its success, namely the large influx of applications concerning standard "structural" violations, such as the notorious length of civil proceedings in Italy.[11]

B. Selected Jurisprudence Concerning Germany

In terms of overall statistics, the Court's dealings with Germany have, in line with the general trend, seen a further increase in applications lodged against Germany in 2003. At roughly a seven-and-a-half percent increase in relation to 2002, the increase in German applications was smaller than in the preceding year.[12] Twenty-four percent of German

---

[7] It is difficult to calculate on the basis of the available figures whether the ratio of applications lodged and violations found is higher in CEE countries than in the rest of the Council's member states; to do this, the application histories for each "heap" of lodged application would need to be tracked across several years, as the different stages of the process are spread out in time; an interesting research project, but not one possible within the confines of the present Report.

[8] *See* the various reform proposals that have emerged from the reflection process that was initiated by the European Ministerial Conference on Human Rights in 2000, and which was concluded with the adoption of the 14th Protocol of the Convention and the Declaration on "Ensuring the effectiveness of the implementation of the European Convention on Human Rights at national and European level" by the Council's Committee of Ministers in May 2004. *See Draft Declaration of the Committee of Ministers*, Steering Committee for Human Rights, 57th Meeting, Doc. No. CDDH(2004)004 (2004), *available at* http://www.coe.int/T/F/Droits_de_l'Homme/CDDH(2004)004%20E%20Final%20Addendum%20III-Declaration.asp; *see also* Paul Mahoney, *New Challenges for the European Court of Human Rights Resulting from the Expanding Case Load and Membership*, 21 PENN STATE INTERNATIONAL LAW REVIEW 101 (2002); Alastair Mowbray, *Proposals for Reform of the European Court of Human Rights*, 2000 PUB. L. 252 (2002); and Robin C. A. White, *The Report of the Evaluation Group on the Court of Human Rights*, 27 EUR. L. REV. 1 (2002).

[9] *See* especially *Recommendation Rec(2004)6 of the Committee of Ministers to member states on the improvement of domestic remedies*, Comm. of Ministers, 114 Sess., (2004), *at* https://wcm.coe.int/ViewDoc.jsp?id=743317&Lang=en.

[10] *See* the discussion of this point in the Evaluation Group's 2001 Report 91 (2001) *available at* http://cm.coe.int/stat/E/Public/2001/rapporteur/clcedh/2001egcourt1.htm; *see generally* the discussion of the Court's reform efforts in the previous Annual – notably Florian Hoffmann, *Report – European Court of Human Rights – 2001/2002*, *in* THE ANNUAL OF GERMAN & EUROPEAN LAW (AGEL) (Russell A. Miller and Peer C. Zumbansen eds., 2003).

[11] *See also*, MARC-ANDRE EISSEN, THE LENGTH OF CIVIL AND CRIMINAL PROCEEDINGS IN THE CASE-LAW OF THE EUROPEAN COURT OF HUMAN RIGHTS (1996).

[12] The increase of applications lodged was 9.5 percent between 2001 and 2002, though it was only approximately four percent between 2000 and 2001, revealing no definite pattern in the rate of increase.

applications lodged were declared inadmissible. Only approximately half of one percent of the remaining German applications were declared admissible and went to judgement.[13] The ratio of German cases-lodged to cases-declared-admissible is, hence, considerably lower than the two-percent average. In 2003, Germany occupied seventh place (of forty-four) in terms of lodged, and tenth place in terms of admissible applications. In terms of total population, this ranking seems appropriate; after the Russian Federation, Germany has the second-largest population in the Convention area.

Despite the relatively large (absolute) number of applications, the cases declared admissible or ultimately decided by the Court in the period under review concerned only a handful of issues: the length of court proceedings (falling under Art. 6.1); parental visitation rights (by and large falling, *inter alia*, under either Arts. 8 or 14, or both); and the treatment or status of "aliens" (Art. 14 read in conjunction with Art. 8). Next to these applications, which can be said to be emanating from "structural" defects in German legislation or the legal system, there have, of course, also been a number of idiosyncratic complaints, some of which link up with important precedents in others member states, such as decisions regarding transsexuality (Arts. 6(1), 8, and 14 – read in conjunction with Art. 8).

Generally, of the thirty-four German judgements and admissibility decisions rendered by the Court in 2003 and the first quarter of 2004,[14] roughly twenty-five involved disputes that had been appealed to the Federal Constitutional Court. Of these cases, only slightly more than a fifth actually had been heard by that tribunal. This, again, confirms the already indicated trend of the Court serving as a last appeal in cases in which final domestic recourse is denied. However, the relatively large number of cases rejected by the Federal Constitutional Court, which nonetheless survive admissibility scrutiny in the European system is noteworthy; it may either point to another "structural" fault line in the German legal system, or, inversely, to the Court's inability to properly identify the kind of paradigmatic cases on which it would like to concentrate. That said, many of the cases had been rejected by the Federal Constitutional Court on account of not raising a constitutionally relevant question, though they may still very well raise a Convention-relevant issue. In these cases, the Court could be said to function as a complementary review mechanism, rather than as a last – and purportedly superior – instance.

In the following pages a selection of the German jurisprudence of the European Court of Human Rights will be reviewed.

I. Parental Access Rights

One of the main areas in recent years in which the Federal Republic has been scrutinized in Strasbourg has been with respect to family law,[15] and, more precisely, the issue of parental access rights falling, *inter alia*, under Art. 8. The period under review was no different in that respect. The Court had previously decided two important, precedent-setting cases on the matter, notably *Elsholz v. Germany*[16] in 2000, and *Hoffmann v. Germany*[17] in

---

13 *See* COUNCIL OF EUROPE, SURVEY OF ACTIVITIES FOR 2003, *supra* note 1.
14 The Court rendered seventeen judgements and seventeen admissibility decisions on Germany during the period under review; admissibility decisions on applications on which judgements were also rendered during this period are only counted as judgements.
15 On this general theme, *see also* Katja Schweppe, *Child Protection in Europe: Different Systems – Common Challenges*, 3 GERMAN LAW JOURNAL NO. 10 (2002).
16 Elsholz v. Germany, App. No. 25735/94 (Eur. Ct. of H.R., 2000), *at* http://cmiskp.echr.coe.int/tkp197/portal.asp?sessionId=3060047&skin=hudoc-en&action=request.
17 Hoffman v. Germany, App. No. 34045/96 (Eur. Ct. of H.R., 2001), *at* http://cmiskp.echr.coe.int/tkp197/portal.asp?sessionId=3060053&skin=hudoc-en&action=request.

2002, and in 2003, the Court rendered no less than four final and three admissibility decisions on applications broadly falling under this thematic heading (all of which are reviewed here).

Of these family law cases, the most widely noted are two cases decided in tandem by the Court, namely *Sommerfeld v. Germany*,[18] and *Sahin v. Germany*,[19] both concerning the visiting rights by fathers of children born out of wedlock. Both applications, and, indeed, their immediate precedent, *Hoffmann*, alleged violations of their right to family life (Art. 8), in conjunction with allegations of undue discrimination (Art. 14).[20] In addition, *Sommerfeld* also complained of an infringement of his rights to a fair trial under Art. 6.1.[21] The cases' noteworthiness stems, among other reasons, from the fact that the cases were reviews of judgements rendered by the Fourth Section of the Court in 2001.[22] The Grand Chamber review of the Section's finding of violations of Arts. 8 and 14 had been requested by the German government pursuant to Art. 43 of the Convention and Rule 73 of the Court's Rules of Procedure.[23] It should be noted that what in effect amounts to an appeal procedure within the new, post-Protocol 11 Court, is still a very rare occurrence, leave for which is only granted in exceptional circumstances.[24]

---

18 Sommerfeld v. Germany, App. No. 31871/96 (Eur. Ct. of H.R., 2003), at http://cmiskp.echr.coe.int/tkp197/portal.asp?sessionId=3060067&skin=hudoc-en&action=request
19 Sahin v. Germany, App. No. 30943/96 (Eur. Ct. of H.R., 2003), at http://cmiskp.echr.coe.int/tkp197/portal.asp?sessionId=3060064&skin=hudoc-en&action=request
20 *See* Sommerfeld v. Germany App. No. 31871/96, paras 29 and 46 (Eur. Ct. of H.R., 2001), at http://cmiskp.echr.coe.int/tkp197/portal.asp?sessionId=3060067&skin=hudoc-en&action=request; and Sahin v. Germany, App. No. 30943/96, paras. 31 and 50 (Eur. Ct. of H.R., 2001), at http://cmiskp.echr.coe.int/tkp197/portal.asp?sessionId=3060064&skin=hudoc-en&action=request; as well as *Hoffmann*, App. No. 34045/96, at paras. 31 and 46 (2001).
21 *Sommerfeld*, App. No. 31871/96, para. 59 (2003).
22 *Sahin*, App. No. 30943/96, (2001); and *Sommerfeld*, App. No. 31871/96, (2001).
23 Art. 43 of the Convention provides that

> (1) within a period of three months from the date of the judgment of the Chamber, any party to the case may, in exceptional cases, request that the case be referred to the Grand Chamber.
> (2) a panel of five judges of the Grand Chamber shall accept the request if the case raises a serious question affecting the interpretation or application of the Convention or the protocols thereto, or serious issue of general importance.
> (3) if the panel accepts the request, the Grand Chamber shall decide the case by means of a judgment.

Rule 73 of the Court's Rules of Procedure provides that

> In accordance with Article 43 of the Convention, any party to a case may exceptionally, within a period of three months from the date of delivery of the judgment of a Chamber, file in writing at the Registry a request that the case be referred to the Grand Chamber. The party shall specify in its request the serious question affecting the interpretation or application of the Convention or the Protocols thereto, or the serious issue of general importance, which in its view warrants consideration by the Grand Chamber.
> (2) A panel of five judges of the Grand Chamber constituted in accordance with Rule 24 § 5 shall examine the request solely on the basis of the existing case file. It shall accept the request only considers that the case does raise such a question or issue. Reasons need not be given for a refusal of the request.
> (3) If the panel accepts the request, the Grand Chamber shall decide the case by means of a judgment.

24 In 2002, when Germany's rehearing request was lodged, a total of sixty-four such requests were received by the Panel of the Grand-Chamber, nineteen of which emanated from defending governments, and only eight of which were granted – six having been lodged by defendant governments, two by applicants; by comparison, in 2003, eighty-seven requests were lodged, thirteen of which came from defending governments; of these, nine were granted by the Panel, with four of these stemming from governments. The ratio of re-examination requests and grants is, hence, in both periods, within the ten to fifteen percent margin, which corresponds to the Court's stated objective of making re-examinations a highly exceptional feature of its procedure.

The main issue raised by the Government in the re-hearing was that the Fourth Section had, in its view, improperly restricted the Member States' margin of appreciation and substituted its own reading of the facts with those of the competent domestic tribunals.[25] The facts in both cases are similar. Sahin and Sommerfeld are fathers of children born out of wedlock, who had regular contact with their children for the first two and five years respectively and up to the termination of the parents' relationship, whereupon contact was prohibited by the mothers of the children.[26] Both applicants thereupon sought court orders granting them visiting rights, which were refused by both the relevant *Amtsgerichte* (district courts) and, on appeal, *Landgerichte* (regional courts).[27] The Federal Constitutional Court refused to entertain the fathers' complaints.[28]

The domestic courts' reasoning hinged on the subsequently repealed sections 1634 and 1705 of the *Bürgerliches Gesetzbuch* (German Civil Code),[29] which stipulated a differentiated parental access regime for children born in and out of wedlock. For children born out of wedlock, Section 1705 established a general presumption that custody rested with the mother and allocated visiting rights for natural fathers only when, according to expert opinion and by determination of the family court, it was in the best interest of the child. Importantly, the Fourth Section's judgement was based, in part, on the particular way in which the child's best interest had been determined by the domestic courts. Curiously, in *Sahin*, the Chamber had found the domestic process inadequate for having exclusively relied on expert opinion, without hearing from the child,[30] whereas in *Sommerfeld*, the inadequacy was the domestic court's exclusive reliance on the testimony of the child, without the benefit of an expert's opinion.[31] In the Chamber's view, neither process sufficiently protected the applicant's interest in full access to the proceedings. Thus, it found a violation of Art. 8 in both cases on account of the flawed domestic proceedings.[32] It also found, in both cases, a violation of Art. 14, in conjunction with Art. 8, because the legislation placed different burdens of proof on fathers of children born in and out of wedlock in the determination of the child's best interest.[33] On this point the Chamber had specifically taken into account the fact that the legislation was, at the time of its hearing on the matters, already in the process of repeal, with a number of leading Federal Constitutional Court decisions regarding its constitutionality pending.[34] In *Sommerfeld*, the Chamber also

---

25 See Sommerfeld v. Germany, App. No. 31871/96, para. 7 (Eur. Ct. of H.R., 2003), at http://cmiskp.echr.coe.int/tkp197/portal.asp?sessionId=3060067&skin=hudoc-en&action=request; and Sahin v. Germany, App. No. 30943/96, para. 7 (Eur. Ct. of H.R., 2003), at http://cmiskp.echr.coe.int/tkp197/portal.asp?sessionId=3060064&skin=hudoc-en&action=request.
26 See *Sommerfeld*, App. No. 31871/96, paras. 11–26 (2003); and *Sahin*, App. No. 30943/96, paras. 11–29 (2003).
27 In the case of *Sommerfeld v. Germany*, refer to the decisions of June 1, 1994, by the Rostock District Court, and of June 17, 1994, by the Rostock Regional Court; and in the case of *Sahin*, refer to the decisions of September 5, 1991, by the Wiesbaden District Court, and of December 23, 1992, and August 25 1993 (on appeal) by the Wiesbaden Regional Court.
28 See the decisions by three-judge panel the German Constitutional Court of January 19, 1996 (*Sommerfeld*) and of December 1, 1998 (*Sahin*).
29 § 1634 section 1 of the Civil Code states that "1. A parent not having custody has the right to personal contact with the child. The parent not having custody and the person having custody must not do anything that would harm the child's relationship with others or seriously interfere with the child's upbringing ..."; § 1795 stipulated, *inter alia*, that "Custody over a minor child born out of wedlock is exercised by the child's mother ..."; as cited in both judgements.
30 Sahin v. Germany, App. No. 30943/96, para. 54 (Eur. Ct. of H.R., 2003), at http://cmiskp.echr.coe.int/tkp197/portal.asp?sessionId=3060064&skin=hudoc-en&action=request.
31 Sommerfeld v. Germany, App. No. 31871/96, para. 49 (Eur. Ct. of H.R., 2003), at http://cmiskp.echr.coe.int/tkp197/portal.asp?sessionId=3060067&skin=hudoc-en&action=request.
32 *Sommerfeld*, App. No. 31871/96, para. 45 (2003); and *Sahin*, App. No. 30943/96, para. 49.
33 *Sommerfeld*, App. No. 31871/96, para. 94 (2003); and *Sahin*, App. No. 30943/96, para. 61.
34 *Sommerfeld*, App. No. 31871/96, para. 57 (2003); and *Sahin*, App. No. 30943/96, para. 60.

found a violation of Art. 6.1 as the application of section 63 of the domestic Act on Non-Contentious Proceedings, which governed access to proceedings, deprived the applicant of a right to appeal the access to decision of the court of first instance.[35]

The Grand Chamber reversed the Chamber's finding of a violation of Art. 8, but upheld the finding of a violation of Art. 14 in conjunction with Art. 8.[36] The Grand Chamber further held that, in light of its decision to uphold the Section's finding of a violation of Art. 14, it did not need to separately examine the alleged violation of Art. 6.1 in *Sommerfeld*. The important distinction which the Grand Chamber made *vis-à-vis* the Chamber's judgement concerned, in line with the Government's submission, two issues: (1) the conduct of the German tribunals; and (2) the quality of the legislation on which the former was based. The Chamber had found the relevant section of the German Civil Code discriminatory *and* also impugned the domestic tribunals for their substantive determination of the child's best interest, which it alleged to have been insufficiently protective of the fathers' interests. The Grand Chamber, on the other hand, found that in the given circumstances the domestic tribunals had both acted reasonably and within their margin of appreciation.[37] The Grand Chamber explained that the margin of appreciation enjoyed by the domestic courts was wide with regard to the general determination of access rights (implicated in the present cases) but narrow with regard to the imposition of any further restrictions of parental rights.[38] The Grand Chamber did, however, uphold the Chamber's finding of unjustified discrimination on account of the legislation in force at the time of the domestic decision.[39] Thus, it effectively vindicated the government's request for re-examination, as the latter's main claim had been that the margin of appreciation had not been overstepped by the domestic tribunals and that the interest of both fathers and children had been adequately protected by the tribunals' substantive determination.

Ultimately, *Sahin* and *Sommerfeld* are probably more important in relation to the Court's evolving margin of appreciation doctrine than with regard to setting out a general standard for parental access rights under Art. 8.[40] This is so, given that the German legislation in question, which was found to constitute undue discrimination, has since been repealed by the *Reform zum Kindschaftsrecht* (Law on Family Matters), which entered into force on June 1, 1998, following a political process that was only marginally influenced by the proceedings before the European Court. That said, the emphasis placed by both the Fourth Section and the Grand Chamber on the discriminatory character of access regimes differentiating between parents, and specifically fathers, of children born within and out of wedlock represents an important confirmation of earlier precedent.[41]

---

35 *Sommerfeld*, App. No. 31871/96, paras. 59–66 (2003).
36 *Sommerfeld*, App. No. 31871/96, para. 74 (2003); and *Sahin*, App. No. 30943/96, para. 75.
37 *Sommerfeld*, App. No. 31871/96, paras. 75 and 78 (2003); and *Sahin*, App. No. 30943/96, paras. 78 and 95.
38 See *Sommerfeld*, App. No. 31871/96, para. 39 (2003).
39 See *Sommerfeld*, App. No. 31871/96, para. 63 (2003); and *Sahin*, App. No. 30943/96, para. 65.
40 On the margin of appreciation doctrine, *see, inter alia*, Eyal Benvenisti, *Margin of Appreciation, Consensus, and Universal Standards*, 31 N.Y.U. J. INT'L L. & POL. 843 (1999); Douglas Lee Donoho, *Autonomy, Self-Governance, and the Margin of Appreciation: Developing a Jurisprudence of Diversity Within Universal Human Rights*, 15 EMORY INTERNATIONAL LAW REVIEW 391 (2001); and Michael R. Hutchinson, *The Margin of Appreciation Doctrine in the European Court of Human Rights*, 48 INT'L & COMP. L. Q. 638 (1999).
41 *See, inter alia*, Elsholz v. Germany, App. No. 25735/94, note 15 (Eur. Ct. of H.R., 2000), at http://cmiskp.echr.coe.int/tkp197/portal.asp?sessionId=3060047&skin=hudoc-en&action=request; as well as Camp and Bourimi v. the Netherlands, App. No. 28369/95 (Eur. Ct. of H.R., 2001), at http://cmiskp.echr.coe.int/tkp197/portal.asp?sessionId=3060130&skin=hudoc-en&action=request; and Inze v. Austria, App. No. 8695/79 (Eur. Ct. H.R., 1987), at http://cmiskp.echr.coe.int/tkp197/portal.asp?sessionId=3060133&skin=hudoc-en&action=request.

In two other paternal access applications, *Nekvedavicius v. Germany*[42] and *Stenzel v. Gemany and Poland*,[43] the Court dismissed and adjourned its decision, respectively.

In *Nekvedavicius*, the father of a child born out of wedlock had instituted two rounds of unsuccessful access proceedings in the domestic courts. The first attempt was made before the legislative reforms brought on by the *Reform zum Kindschaftsrecht* in 1998. The second attempt was made after those reforms. As is common in these applications, the father complained of an Art. 8 violation in regard to both the early and later rounds of proceedings.[44] With regard to the first round of proceedings, the father also complained of a violation of Art. 14 in conjunction with Art.8.[45] In a somewhat innovative turn, the father also complained of a violation of his right to fair trial under Art. 6.1, of degrading and cruel treatment under Art. 3 (on account of the psychological suffering allegedly inflicted on him by the lengthy and unsuccessful court proceedings), and of a denial of his right to an effective remedy under Art. 13 (on account of the allegedly unduly high refusal rate of a review of paternal access decisions on part of the Federal Constitutional Court).[46] The Court, in turn, found that the domestic tribunals' decisions to deny access with a view to protecting the child's best interest, and in light of the strong animosity between the child's parents, was justified under both the previous and the reformed legislation, and it confirmed its *dictum* in *Sommerfeld* and *Sahin* that the margin of appreciation was wide in relation to access decisions.[47] The Court thus dismissed the application with regard to Art. 8, as well as to Art. 14, as manifestly ill-founded. Neither of these claims was subject to the Court's review on account of the repeal of the earlier, discriminatory provisions of the law.[48] The Court also dismissed the alleged violations of Arts. 3, 6.1, and 13 as manifestly ill founded. The Court reasoned that that the absence of an Art. 8 violation precluded any claim that the denial of access constituted cruel or degrading treatment under Art. 3 or that the access proceedings amounted to a denial of access to a court or a legal remedy under Art. 6.1.[49]

The pending case of *Stenzel*, in turn, concerned a complaint against a denial of custody and (paternal) access involving both Poland and Germany.[50] The applicant, a Polish national whose estranged former spouse had settled and remarried in Germany together with their daughter, alleged that his right to family life under Art. 8 had been violated by the Polish courts on account of their alleged failure to enforce a positive access decision, and by a German court of first-instance for having modified the (Polish) divorce judgement to grant exclusive custody to the mother.[51] The application deals with what could be termed "transnational access proceedings," or rather, lack thereof, as part of the complaint stems from the failure of the Polish and German tribunals to coordinate their judgements on the matter. The Court, however, found the complaint against Germany inadmissible for non-exhaustion of local remedies; the applicant had never appealed the German decision. The Court also adjourned the admissibility decision on the complaint against Poland until receipt of a response from the government.[52]

---

42 Nekvedavicius v. Germany App. No. 46165/99 (Eur. Ct. H.R. 2003).
43 Stenzel v. Germany and Poland, App. No. 63896/00 (Eur. Ct. H.R.).
44 *Nekvedavicius*, App. No. 46165/99, at 7.
45 *Id.*
46 *Nekvedavicius*, App. No. 46165/99, at 7–8.
47 *Nekvedavicius*, App. No. 46165/99, at 10.
48 Nekvedavicius v. Germany, App. No. 46165/99 11–12 (Eur. Ct. H.R. 2003).
49 *Nekvedavicius*, App. No. 46165/99, at 14–15.
50 Stenzel v. Germany and Poland, App. No. 63896/00 (Eur. Ct. H.R.).
51 *Stenzel*, App. No. 63896/00 at 11.
52 *Stenzel*, App. No. 63896/00 at 11–12.

II. Child Custody Rights

Custody proceedings constitute a second family-related area with which the Court has repeatedly had to deal *vis-à-vis* Germany. In its noteworthy decision in *Görgülü v. Germany*,[53] the Court established the right of biological fathers to be reunited with their children even against the wishes of foster parents. The applicant had complained of violations of Arts. 6.1 and 8 after a German court, in appeal proceedings, failed to grant him custody and access.[54] The complainant is the biological father of the child, who was born out of wedlock and was given up for adoption by the child's mother without the father's knowledge or consent. The child had since been raised by foster parents and the court of appeals reversed an initially positive custody and access decision by the first-instance district court,[55] reasoning, *inter alia*, that separation from the foster parents would not be in the best interest of the child.

In its decision, the European Court began by reiterating both the subsidiary character of its review in relation to domestic jurisprudence and the wide margin of appreciation enjoyed by domestic authorities with regard to custody matters, a wide margin that is narrowed somewhat with regard to access rights and other limitations placed upon a parent's contact with his/her child.[56] It then went on to find that the court of appeals' denial of the custody request, while mindful of the potentially detrimental effects an instant separation from the foster parents would have on the child, had, nonetheless, violated the applicant's rights under Art. 8.[57] The European Court explained that the domestic court of appeals had not sufficiently taken into account the importance of the relationship of a child with its biological father. Indeed, the Court interpreted its earlier custody and access jurisprudence in such way as to establish an obligation by State parties to help reunite natural parents with their children.[58] There is, according to the Court, a positive duty on the part of the state to help enable ties between children and their natural parents, subject to what could be termed the "best interest of the child" test. In the present case, the court of appeals had not explored all possible means of helping to re-establish ties between the biological father and the child, and had interpreted the "best interest" test too narrowly and with too great a concern for the short term. The Court concluded that the court of appeals had, there-

---

53 Görgülü v. Germany, App. No. 74969/01 (Eur. Ct. H.R., 2004), *at* http://cmiskp.echr.coe.int/tkp197/portal.asp?sessionId=3060141&skin=hudoc-en&action=request.
54 *Görgülü*, App. No. 74969/01, para. 33 (2004).
55 *See* the decisions by the district court in Wittenberg (March 9, 2001), and the appellate court in Naumburg (April 10 and April 27, 2001).
56 *Görgülü*, App. No. 74969/01, para. 41 (2004); the lead reference here being Elsholz v. Germany, App. No. 25735/94, note 16 (Eur. Ct. of H.R., 2000), *at* http://cmiskp.echr.coe.int/tkp197/portal.asp?sessionId=3060047&skin=hudoc-en&action=request,.
57 *Görgülü*, App. No. 74969/01 at para. 47.
58 *Görgülü*, App. No. 74969/01 at para. 45; citing, in particular, Keegan, Kroon and Others v. the Netherlands, App. No. 16969/90 (Eur. Ct. H.R., 1994), *at* http://cmiskp.echr.coe.int/tkp197/portal.asp?sessionId=3060141&skin=hudoc-en&action=request; K. and T. v. Finland, App. No. 25702/94 (Eur. Ct. H.R., 2001), *at* http://cmiskp.echr.coe.int/tkp197/portal.asp?sessionId= 3060141&skin=hudoc-en&action=request; Johansen v. Norway, App. No. 17383/90 (Eur. Ct. H.R., 1996), *at* http://cmiskp.echr.coe.int/tkp197/portal.asp?sessionId=3060141&skin=hudoc-en&action=request; Olsson v. Sweden (I), App. No. 10465/83 (Eur. Ct. H.R., 1988), *at* http://cmiskp.echr.coe.int/tkp197/portal.asp?sessionId=3060141&skin=hudoc-en&action=request; Sylvester v. Austria, App. Nos. 36812/97 (Eur. Ct. H.R., 2004), *at* http://cmiskp.echr.coe.int/tkp197/portal.asp?sessionId=3060141&skin=hudoc-en&action=request; and Sylvester v Austria 40104/98 (Eur. Ct. H.R., 2003), *at* http://cmiskp.echr.coe.int/tkp197/portal.asp?sessionId=3060141&skin=hudoc-en&action=request; and W. v. the United Kingdom App. No. 9749/82 (Eur. Ct. H.R., 1987), *at* http://cmiskp.echr.coe.int/tkp197/portal.asp?sessionId=3060141&skin=hudoc-en&action=request.

fore, violated Art. 8 in its custody decision.[59] In the same vein, the court of appeals' (equally negative) access decision disrespected, in the Court's view, the principle that children must, where possible, not be separated from heir (biological) parents, as this meant "cutting them off from their roots."[60] Consequently, the Court found a violation of Art. 8 in relation to the access decision as well.[61] The Court then rejected the applicant's further allegation of a due process violation under Art. 6.1.[62]

It is noteworthy that, despite formally recognizing a wide margin of appreciation in custody matters, the Court, in effect, rendered a highly substantive decision, not merely reviewing the procedural fairness of the domestic proceedings, or the due balancing of the child's and the parents' interests, but defining the Convention regime as favouring biological over foster parents.[63]

Interestingly, this decision triggered further proceedings in Germany. The notorious 14th Senate of the Naumburg Court of Appeal, which had been responsible for the decisions impugned before the European Court, set aside a decision by the Wittenberg District Court, which gave effect to the European Court's judgment by awarding exclusive custody to the biological father.[64] The Court of Appeal's main justification was that it was not bound by the European Court's decision, as the latter had no direct effect upon judicial organs of the Federal Republic. The applicant appealed this decision to the Federal Constitutional Court, which, in turn, set aside the Appeal Court's decision and sent the case back to a different chamber of that Court.[65] The Federal Constitutional Court's decision is particularly noteworthy because it set out in principle the legal status of European Court of Human Rights decisions in German (constitutional) law.[66] Astonishingly, even this decision by the Federal Republic's highest tribunal did not preclude the Naumburg Court of Appeal from again suspending the biological father's visiting rights. Again the Naumburg Court of Appeal reasoned that contact between father and child would be detrimental to the child's interest.[67]

---

59 Görgülü v. Germany, App. No. 74969/01, paras 46–7 (Eur. Ct. H.R., 2004), at http://cmiskp.echr.coe.int/tkp197/portal.asp?sessionId=3060141&skin=hudoc-en&action=request.

60 *Görgülü*, App. No. 74969/01, at para. 47; here the Court cited Gnahoré v. France, App. No. 40031/98 (Eur. Ct. H.R., 2000), at http://cmiskp.echr.coe.int/tkp197/portal.asp?sessionId=3060141&skin=hudoc-en&action=request; P., C. and S. v. United Kingdom App. No. 56547/00 (Eur. Ct. H.R., 2002), at http://cmiskp.echr.coe.int/tkp197/portal.asp?sessionId=3060141&skin=hudoc-en&action=request; and again Johansen v. Norway, App. No. 17383/90, note 30 (Eur. Ct. H.R., 1996), at http://cmiskp.echr.coe.int/tkp197/portal.asp?sessionId=3060141&skin=hudoc-en&action=request.

61 *Görgülü*, App. No. 74969/01, at paras. 48–51.

62 *Görgülü*, App. No. 74969/01, at paras. 56–60.

63 *See* EGMR: BIOLOGISCHER VATER WICHTIGER ALS ADOPTIVELTERN, *at* http://rsw.beck.de/rsw/shop/default.asp?docid=113157&highlight=g%D6RG%DCL%DC

64 *See* the decisions by the trial court of Wittenberg (Mar. 19, 2004) and the appellate court of Naumburg (Mar. 30, and Jun. 30, 2004).

65 *See* BVerfG, 2 BvR 1481/04, *available at* http://www.bundesverfassungsgericht.de/cgi-bin/link.pl?entscheidungen.

66 For reasons of space, the decision cannot here be discussed in detail, but, in essence, the Court found that German tribunals are not directly bound by ECHR decisions, but must take them into consideration, which, in the Court's view, the Naumburg Appeals Court had not done; the general part of this decision attracted much comment, not least from the President of the ECHR, Luzius Wildhaber, who expressed concern that the FCC's decision might set the wrong precedent (*see* interview in *Das tüt mir weh: Der Präsident des Europäischen Gerichtshofs für Menschenrechte, Luzius Wildhaber, über das umstrittene "Caroline-Urteil", das schwierige Verhältnis zum Bundesverfassungsgericht und die vorbildliche Lernfähigkeit der Türkei*, DER SPIEGEL, Nov. 15, 2004); the decision was, however, defended by the FCC's President, Hans-Jügen Papier, in a reply in the FRANKFURTER ALLGEMEINE ZEITUNG, Dec. 9, 2004 at 5; *see generally* the extensive discussion of the decision in Matthias Hartwig, *Much Ado About Human Rights: The Federal Constitutional Court Confronts the European Court of Human Rights*, Parts I–IV, 6 GERMAN LAW JOURNAL 869 (2005) at http://www.germanlawjournal.com/article.php?id=600.

67 *See* the decision by the trial court of Wittenberg (Dec. 2, 2004), and the appellate court of Naumburg (Dec. 8. and Dec. 20, 2004).

The applicant again appealed against this renewed suspension of visiting rights to the Federal Constitutional Court, which, first issued a preliminary injunction reinstating the applicant's visiting rights, and then confirmed that reinstatement in its subsequent decision on the merits.[68] Particularly in its decision on preliminary measures, the Court strongly criticized the 14th Senate of the Naumburg Court of Appeal, charging it, *inter alia*, with arbitrariness and with partly deciding on grounds immaterial to the object of the case.[69]

Another custody-related application, *Paradis v. Germany*,[70] was declared inadmissible, even though it concerned the return, potentially by force, of two siblings to their Canadian father, who had been allocated custody by a Canadian tribunal. Like *Stenzel*, the case involved transnational proceedings, as both Canadian and German tribunals were involved, though, unlike *Stelzel*, there was direct interaction between the tribunals on account of the Hague Convention on the Civil Aspects of International Child Abduction of 1980.[71] As the children had been brought to Germany by their (German) mother in violation of a Canadian court order (as a consequence of which she lost her original (Canadian) custody rights), the German tribunals had to take the Hague Convention, as well as the Canadian tribunal's judgement, into account in their custody and return decisions. The German court of first instance allocated (German) custody to the mother, reasoning, *inter alia*, that Art. 3 of the Hague Convention[72] did not apply because she had been in sole custody at the time the child was removed.[73] That decision was reversed on appeal, with the court of appeals applying the Hague Convention and ordering the return of the children, by force if necessary.[74] The European Court, in turn, found that, as the Hague Convention had the best interest of the child as its main objective, its application had to be considered as, in principle, compatible with that purpose.[75] Given that Ms. Paradis had enjoyed all relevant procedural safeguards in the German proceedings, and retained legal remedies in the Canadian proceedings, the German tribunals' decision to fulfil the international obligation of returning the wrongfully removed children to Canada could not amount to a violation of Art. 8, even if its implementation potentially involved the use of force as a last resort.[76]

Another, custody case, *Haase v. Germany*,[77] concerned the withdrawal of custody from the parents, and the placement of seven siblings into public care. In particular, the measures taken by the German authorities had included the removal of the applicant's youngest daughter from the hospital seven days after her birth and without the knowledge of the mother.[78] The withdrawal of parental responsibility had resulted from a series of first- and

---

68 See the decisions by the Federal Constitutional Court of Dec., 28, 2004 and of Apr. 5, 2005; after the first decision, on preliminary measures, the Court also rejected, Feb. 1, 2005, formal objections to the preliminary measures by the Wittenberg Youth Office, the foster parents, and the legal guardian.
69 See especially paras. 21 and 22 of the 28 December 2004 decision mentioned above.
70 Paradis v. Germany, App. No. 4783/03 (Eur. Ct. H.R., 2003)
71 Convention on the Civil Aspects of International Child Abduction, Oct. 25, 1980, at http://www.hcch.net/e/conventions/text28e.html.
72 Art. 3.a. stipulates that "the removal or the retention of a child is to be considered wrongful where: (a) it is in breach of rights of custody attributed to a person, an institution or any other body, either jointly or alone, under the law of the State in which the child was habitually resident immediately before the removal or retention; [...] the rights of custody mentioned in sub-paragraph (a) above may arise in particular by operation of law or by reason of a judicial or administrative decision, or by reason of an agreement having legal effect under the law of that State."
73 See the decision of the Zweibrücken District Court (Sept. 28, 2001).
74 See the decision by Zweibücken Court of Appeal (Jun. 26, 2002).
75 See Paradis v. Germany, App. No. 4783/03 11 (Eur. Ct. H.R., 2003).
76 See id. at 13; (the Court citing Ignaccolo-Zenide v. Romania, App. no. 31679/96 (Feb. 1, 2000)).
77 Haase v. Germany, App. No. 11057/02 (Eur. Ct. H.R., 2004), at http://cmiskp.echr.coe.int/tkp197/portal.asp?sessionId=3259300&skin=hudoc-en&action=request
78 *Haase*, App. No. 11057/02 at para. 16.

second-instance decisions, which had at first been initiated as a result of a basic review process undertaken by the relevant youth authority following the applicant's submission of a family benefits request.[79] After implementation of the decision to withdrawal the children, the Federal Constitutional Court declared admissible the applicant's constitutional complaint regarding the court proceedings. In spite of this admissibility decision, the Federal Constitutional Court refused to grant the provisional measures requested by the applicant, which would have immediately reunified her with her children.[80] In its decision on the merits of the case, the Federal Constitutional Court found the court proceedings to have been deficient largely because they relied too heavily on the initial opinion of the youth office and one expert witness, without having made sufficient efforts to substantiate the latter's recommendation of a separation of the children from their parents.[81] The Federal Constitutional Court ordered the relevant district court to make a fresh determination as to whether the grave measure of separation should be continued and, if that was the case, whether access rights nonetheless should be granted to the parents.[82] The district court, as a consequence, engaged in a series of hearings at which the children provided testimony and new expert opinions were commissioned. The district court ultimately came to the conclusion that the withdrawal of parental rights should be continued, and that access needed to be severely limited. The Federal Constitutional Court refused to entertain a complaint against this new decision.

In the proceedings before the European Court of Human Rights, the Government raised two preliminary objections. First, the Government alleged non-exhaustion of domestic remedies, on account of the access proceedings, which had not been appealed by the applicants.[83] Second, the Government asserted an objection to standing and mootness due to the loss of "victim" status, on account of the allegedly favourable decision by the Federal Constitutional Court.[84] As to the first of these issues the European Court of Human Rights agreed that domestic remedies had not been exhausted, noting that the merits involved merely the custody decisions, which had resulted in Federal Constitutional Court review.[85] As to the second of these issues, the European Court of Human Rights held that the constitutional court's decision could not be counted as a remedy for the complaint in question, as it evidently did not result in the desired reunion of parents and children, but merely in the consideration of new evidence.[86]

With these jurisdictional and justiciability issues resolved, the Court then went on to consider whether the withdrawal decision constituted a violation of Art. 8. It began by setting out the general principles which guide its Art. 8 jurisprudence in custody and access cases, notably: the strictly subsidiary character of the Convention system *vis-à-vis* national authorities;[87] the wide margin of appreciation in relation to custody proceedings with a stricter margin in relation to access limitations in the context of custody decisions;[88] the

---

79 *Haase*, App. No. 11057/02 at paras. 10–15.
80 *Haase*, App. No. 11057/02 at para. 24.
81 See BVerfG, 1 BvR 605/02 of March 4, 2002, paras. 1–5, *available at* http://www.bverfg.de/entscheidungen/rk20020404_1bvr060502.html.
82 Haase v. Germany, App. No. 11057/02 para 28, 31 (Eur. Ct. H.R., 2004), *at* http://cmiskp.echr.coe.int/tkp197/portal.asp?sessionId=3259300&skin=hudoc-en&action=request.
83 *Haase*, App. No. 11057/02 at para. 59.
84 *Haase*, App. No. 11057/02 at para. 67.
85 *Haase*, App. No. 11057/02 at paras. 61–66.
86 *Haase*, App. No. 11057/02 at para. 69 (the Court citing here Dalban v. Romania, App. No. 28114/95 (Eur. Ct. H.R., 1999)).
87 Haase v. Germany, App. No. 11057/02 para 89 (Eur. Ct. H.R. 2004), *at* http://cmiskp.echr.coe.int/tkp197/portal.asp?sessionId=3259300&skin=hudoc-en&action=request.
88 *Haase*, App. No. 11057/02 at para. 90.

substantive priority of natural parents over foster parents or public authorities with respect to custody and access;[89] and, in relation to the priority given to biological parents, the preferred temporary character of withdrawal decisions, which are to be taken only if the parents enjoyed the right to be heard and were involved in the proceedings.[90] In the present case, the Court found that the severity of the measures adopted by the district court, and in particular, the separation of the seven-day-old infant from his mother, were not warranted by the level of evidence on which the district court had based its decision.[91] In other words, the strict standards applicable to the type of decision in question were not met. In the Court's view, it had not been sufficiently established that the children's best interest could only and exclusively be maintained through immediate, complete and permanent separation. The Court, therefore, found a violation of Art. 8 and awarded damages.[92]

III. Rights of Legal Aliens

In three decisions, the Court dealt with the treatment of foreigners, a notorious topic in which the Federal Republic has been finding itself more often before the Court than it can wish for. Two of those decisions, notably *Okpisz v. Germany*[93] and *Niedzwiecki v. Germany*,[94] are, as yet, merely at the admissibility stage of review. The cases concerned Polish nationals who had entered Germany as recognised refugees under a policy concerned with nationals of countries of the former Eastern Block.[95] Ironically, these "foreigners" became, as of May 1, 2004, nationals of a member state of the European Union, and can, as such, hardly be considered to be foreigners in the ordinary sense.[96] The complaints at issue do, however, concern the rights of certain types of non-nationals as such, irrespective of the specific nationality of the applicants. Both cases concerned the withdrawal of child benefits from the applicants as a result of legislative reform.[97] The point at issue was the withdrawal of child benefits only from persons in possession of a temporary residence permit, even if there had been a well-established practice of routinely

---

89 *Haase*, App. No. 11057/02 at para. 93.
90 *Haase*, App. No. 11057/02 at para. 95 (the Court citing Hokkanen v. Finland, App. No. 19823/92 (Eur. Ct. H.R. 1994), Kutzner v. Germany, App. No. 46544/99 (Eur. Ct. H.R. 2002), as well as K. and T. v. Finland App. No. 25702/94 note 30 (Eur. Ct. H.R. 2000), and P., C., and S. v. United Kingdom App. No. 56547/00 note 30 (Eur. Ct. H.R. 2002), and Sahin v. Germany, App. No. 30943/96 note 21 (Eur. Ct. of H.R., 2003) and Sommerfeld v. Germany, App. No. 31871/96, note 21 (Eur. Ct. of H.R., 2003).
91 *See* especially *Haase*, App. No. 11057/02 at paras. 101–105.
92 *Haase*, App. No. 11057/02 at paras. 105 and 112–121.
93 Okpisz v Germany, App. No. 59140/00 (Eur. Ct. H.R. 2003), *at* http://cmiskp.echr.coe.int/tkp197/portal.asp?sessionId=3259345&skin=hudoc-en&action=request
94 Niedzwiecki v Germany, App. No. 58453/00 (Eur. Ct. H.R. 2003), http://cmiskp.echr.coe.int/tkp197/portal.asp?sessionId=3259356&skin=hudoc-en&action=request
95 The so-called *Ostblockbeschlüsse der Innenminister der Länder*.
96 As of the Maastricht Treaty of 1993, there is a genuine European citizenship (Art. 18) which grants the right to free movement and residence within the European Union (Art. 14 EC Treaty); furthermore, social security measures cocerning employed persons and their families moving within the Community are set out in Council Regulation 1408/71, 1971 O.J. (L 149) – updated and amended in Council Regulation 118/97, 1996 O.J. (L 28), as well as several subsequent amendments to the latter Regulation *see* http://europa.eu.int/scadplus/leg/en/cha/c10516.htm; accession of ten new EU member states, of which the Republic of Poland is one, occurred through the Treaty of Accession of Apr. 16, 2003, with accession becoming effective on May 1, 2004. The fact that the fifeteen old memeber states may, for a transitionary period (until 2009), impose cerain restrictions or safeguard conditions on freedom of movement and residence *vis-à-vis* the new member states is merely of academic importance in the present context.
97 Notably of the Federal Child Benefits Act (*Bundeskindergeldgesetz*), v. 1 Jan. 1994 (BGBl. I S. 714), as well as an equivalent stipulation in the Income Tax Act (*Einkommensteuergesetz*), v. 1 Jan. 1996 (RBBl. S. 1934).

renewing the benefits. By contrast, persons holding permanent residence permits continued to be entitled to such benefits. Both applications asserted undue discrimination, which the Court took to amount to an allegation of a violation of Art. 14 read in conjunction with Art. 8.[98] The Government argued, *inter alia*, that the applications were manifestly ill-founded. First, the Government urged that the payment of child benefits was not implied in the abstract protection set out in Art. 8.[99] Second, the Government argued that the decision to withdraw such payments from non-permanent residents did not overstep its margin of appreciation because the decision was both justified and proportional.[100] The applicants, in turn, argued that their precise status as temporary residents was not pertinent to the allocation of child benefits, particularly in light of the fact that they had maintained their permanent residence in Germany, that they were in possession of work permits, and that they had paid taxes.[101] The Court declared the Art. 14 (in conjunction with Art. 8) claims to be admissible in both cases, with a decision on the merits pending as of the time of writing.[102]

IV. Length of Legal Proceedings

It is by now commonplace that one of the most frequent types of Convention violation is the excessive duration of civil proceedings as proscribed by Art. 6.1. Indeed, as was already pointed out, the Court has adopted what almost amounts to a summary procedure for Art. 6.1 applications for those member states where such violations are of a structural, and hence, continuous nature.[103] Generally the Federal Republic has not been counted among the latter group, though it, too, has been facing repeated challenges on account of the length of its civil proceedings, especially in relation to cases before the Federal Constitutional Court.

One case, *Herbolzheimer v. Germany*,[104] stands out not on account of the legal issues involved, which concern a standard length-of-time violation, but because of its facts. The case concerns the drawn out legal dispute between two well-known composers and producers of jazz and popular music, notably Peter Herbolzheimer and Frank Farian. Romanian-born Herbolzheimer, 69, began his distinguished career as a musician, composer, and band leader in the early 1950s in Germany and went on to become an established and highly respected name in international jazz. Herbolzheimer wrote, among many other well-known pieces, the official hymn for the opening of the 1972 Olympic Games in Munich, and founded, in 1980, the German National Youth Jazz Orchestra

---

98 See Okpisz v. Germany, App. No. 5914/00 4 (Eur. Ct. H.R. 2003), *at* http://cmiskp.echr.coe.int/tkp197/portal.asp?sessionId=3269929&skin=hudoc-en&action=request; and Niedzwiecki v Germany, App. No. 58453/00 6 (Eur. Ct. H.R. 2003), *at* http://cmiskp.echr.coe.int/tkp197/ portal.asp?sessionId=3259356&skin=hudoc-en&action=request Niedzwiecki; in Niedzwiecki, the applicant had, in fact, complained against cruel and degrading treatment and racism under Arts. 3 and 2.2. (Protocol No. 4), as well as collateral violations of Arts. 6 and 13; the Court, however, reiterated its right to attribute to a set of facts the characterizations in law it deems most fitting, even if different from those alleged in the applications –here citing Rehbock v. Slovenia, App. No. 29462/95 (Eur. Ct. H.R. 1998), *at* http://cmiskp.echr.coe.int/tkp197/portal.asp?sessionId=3269936&skin=hudoc-en&action= request, and it promptly re-characterised the facts of alleged Art. 14-cum-Art. 8 violations.
99 *Okpisz*, App. No. 5914/00 at 6, and *Niedzwiecki*, App. No. 58453/00 at 6–7.
100 See *Okpisz*, App. No. 5914/00 at 6–7, and *Niedzwiecki*, App. No. 58453/00 at 7.
101 See *Okpisz*, App. No. 5914/00 at 7, and *Niedzwiecki*, App. No. 58453/00 at 7.
102 *Okpisz*, App. No. 5914/00 at 7, and *Niedzwiecki*, App. No. 58453/00 at 9.
103 The most notorious example being, of course, Italy.
104 Herbolzheimer v. Germany, App. No. 57249/00 (Eur. Ct. H.R., 2003), *at* http://cmiskp.echr.coe.int/tkp197/portal.asp?sessionId=3269950&skin=hudoc-en&action=request.

(*Bundesjugendjazzorchester* [BuJazzO]), which he has led since.[105] Frank Farian, 63, born as Franz Reuther in the state of Saarland, is one of Germany's best-known international pop music composers. He is the creator, *inter alia*, of the highly successful groups *Boney M* and *Milli Vanilli*. Indeed, the dispute at issue arose from *Boney M*'s hit "Brown Girl in the Ring," which, released in 1978, became the second-biggest selling single in UK chart history.[106] One year after the song's release, Peter Herbolzheimer entered into civil proceedings against Farian at the Hamburg District Court, alleging that "Brown Girl in the Ring" was, in fact, an unacknowledged replica of an earlier song he had written, entitled "Brown Girl." The first phase of the civil proceedings was concluded in 1989 with a ruling in favour of Herbolzheimer from the appellate court, though only in relation to the merits of the claim and not in relation to damages.[107] Damages were to be determined in the second phase of the proceedings, which became exceedingly complex: a second defendant, Malcolm Maragon,[108] joined the proceedings; two lengthy and much delayed expert opinions were presented to the court; Herbolzheimer's team weathered a change of counsel; the presiding judge became ill and eventually passed away; and finally, Herbolzheimer rejected a settlement offer made by the defendants.

In December 2000, the Hamburg District Court finally rejected Herbolzheimer's request for payment of his share of profits, a decision confirmed by the Hanseatic Regional Court in 2002.[109] As of 1998, Herbolzheimer had repeatedly inquired with the District Court as to the apparently extraordinary length of the proceedings; later he also lodged complaints with the Attorney-General of the State of Hamburg,[110] and with the Federal Constitutional Court; the latter subsequently refused to entertain Herbolzheimer's complaint, arguing that the delay could not be imputed to the District Court.[111] This became the main question in relation to the applicant's complaint of a Convention violation: the imputability of the length of proceedings to the government. The government argued not only that the determination of the income derived from the musical part of the song was, in itself, complex and time-consuming, but also that factors beyond its control significantly contributed to the delay, most notably the challenge by the applicant of the first expert opinion, which led to the commissioning of a second opinion, as well as the entry of a third party, Mr. Maragon, in the proceedings.[112]

The European Court of Human Rights conceded that the proceedings were both complex and owed their excessive length in part to conduct attributable to the applicant, though it did not consider this to have been the decisive cause of the civil suit's long duration.[113] Indeed, the Court reiterated its own earlier *dicta* to the effect that even in civil proceedings organised in an adversary manner (i.e. corresponding to the German *Parteienprinzip* (party principle)), the presiding judge was still to be considered responsible for the

---

105 *See* http://www.jazzpages.com/PeterHerbolzheimer/.
106 *See* http://www.groovecave.com/boneym/bio/bm_bio.htm.
107 *See* the decisions by the Hamburg District Court of Aug. 28, 1987 and by the Hanseatic Regional Court of Feb. 23, 1989.
109 Maragon was implicated by Farian as allegedly being responsible for the *Brown Girl in the Ring* arrangement, whereupon he joined the domestic proceedings as a co-defendant. Curiously, Maragon had earlier been romantically engaged with Liz Mitchell, *Boney M*'s lead singer, with whom he had earlier formed a small ensemble called Malcolm's Locks, prior to *Boney M*'s creation; *see* http://www.lizmitchellfanclub.com/malcolm.html.
109 *See* the decisions by the Hamburg District Court of Dec. 1, 2000 and by the Hanseatic Regional Court of Apr. 18, 2002.
110 *See* Response Letter from the Attorney-General of the State of Hamburg (Jul. 30, 1998).
111 *See* the decision by a three-judge panel of the Federal Constitutional Court, BVerfGE 101, 397.
112 *See* Herbolzheimer v. Germany, App. No. 57249/00 para. 43 (Eur. Ct. H.R., 2003), *at* http://cmiskp.echr.coe.int/tkp197/portal.asp?sessionId=3269950&skin=hudoc-en&action=request.Herbolzheimer.
113 *Herbolzheimer*, App. No. 57249/00 at paras. 46–47.

prompt and reasonably quick running of the proceedings. Member states in turn had a duty under the Convention to organise their administration of justice so as to fulfil Convention obligations such as a "prompt trial."[114] The Court, consequently, found a violation of Art. 6.1, and awarded costs and a small amount of damages, which, however, were far below the sum originally involved in Peter Herbolzheimer's suit against Frank Farian.[115]

Another length of time issue was raised in *Voggenreiter v. Germany*,[116] a complex decision on the question of whether a nearly seven-year period for an ultimately negative admissibility decision by the Federal Constitutional Court constituted a violation of Art. 6.1. Curiously, the case's complexity arose not so much from the length of time issue, but from the government's contention that it fell outside of Art. 6.1 altogether.

The facts concerned domestic legislation – notably the Disestablishment of Freight Tariffs Act of 1993, which, in implementation of Art. 13 of the Single European Act of 1986, ended the national determination and supervision of freight tariffs. One result of this liberalization measure was to render obsolete those private undertakings (known as *tarifeurs*) that had, in part, carried out tariff supervision as sub-contractors of the then Federal Agency for Freight Traffic. The plaintiff had been one such *tarifeur*, who, as a consequence of the entry into force of the Act, had been forced to close down her business. Just before entry into force of the Act, the applicant lodged a complaint at the Federal Constitutional Court, alleging that the Act violated her constitutional rights to professional liberty and property.[117] After approximately six months, the Federal Constitutional Court rejected her request for preliminary measures,[118] but stated that, *prima facie*, her complaint was both admissible and well founded. Yet, it was only in 2000 that that court finally declared the application inadmissible, finding that the challenged Act did not directly concern the regulation of the applicant's profession, and that, therefore, no civil claim as to professional liberty or loss of future income could result therefrom.[119]

The complainant thereupon applied to the European Court of Human Rights, asserting a violation of Art. 6.1.[120] Although the length of time in question would almost certainly fall outside any acceptable limit, the government argued that the Art. 6.1 simply did not apply, as, in line with the Federal Constitutional Court's decision, no civil claim could stand against the government.[121] However, the European Court of Human Rights found, *inter alia*, that the Federal Constitutional Court's initial declaration that the applicant's complaint was *prima facie* well-founded indicated that the German court did not, in principle, exclude the possibility of a civil claim by the applicant against the government.[122]

---

114 *Herbolzheimer*, App. No. 57249/00 at paras. 48–49.
115 *See Herbolzheimer*, App. No. 57249/00 at paras. 52–58, the Court awarded seven-thousand Euros in damages, whereas Herbolzheimer had demanded twenty-thousand Euros in his application; however, in the course of domestic proceedings, Herbolzheimer's share of profits derived from *Brown Girl in The Ring* was estimated to be up to two-million Deutschmarks, or roughly one-million Euros.
116 Voggenreiter v. Germany, App. No. 47169/99 (Eur. Ct. H.R., 2004), *at* http://cmiskp.echr.coe.int/tkp197/portal.asp?sessionId=3269953&skin=hudoc-en&action=request.
117 *See Voggenreiter*, App. No. 47169/99 at para. 14, *see also* GRUNDGESETZ [GG] [Constitution] arts. 12.1 and 14.1.
118 *See* BVerfGE 81, 93; the legal basis for provisional measures is Art. 32 of the Law of the Federal Constitutional Court; *see* Andreas Maurer, *Public Law The Federal Constitutional Court's Emergency Power to Intervene: Provisional Measures Pursuant to Article 32 of the Federal Constitutional Court Act*, 2 GERMAN LAW JOURNAL 13 (2001) (discussion of provisional measures in the Federal Constitutional Court).
119 *See* the decision by the Federal Constitutional Court of November 29, 2000.
120 *Voggenreiter*, App. No. 47169/99 at para. 27.
121 *Voggenreiter*, App. No. 47169/99 at para. 28.
122 Voggenreiter v. Germany, App. No. 47169/99 paras. 36–37 (Eur. Ct. H.R., 2004), *at* http://cmiskp.echr.coe.int/tkp197/portal.asp?sessionId=3269953&skin=hudoc-en&action=request.

Furthermore, the Court found that, insofar as the Federal Constitutional Court's decision directly impacted on the applicant's situation by, for example, not mandating a longer transition period, a civil claim did lie against the government, if only in relation to the applicant's right to professional liberty, and not in relation to her right to property.[123] Having thus established that the applicant's claim fell within Art. 6.1, the Court went on to find, as would be expected, that a nearly seven-year period for rendering a decision was excessive.[124] The Court, therefore, awarded costs and modest damages.[125]

V. Miscellaneous Cases

Finally, the Court also rendered judgements in a few cases that raise new or singular issues, and which cannot, hence, be easily classified. In one such case, *Wendenburg and Others v. Germany*,[126] the legal profession itself was at issue, notably in relation to the potential tension between the state's right to regulate professional activities in the common interest, and the individual's right to a livelihood based on legitimate expectations. The applicants, eighteen barristers practicing in various German *Länder*, complained that a decision by the Federal Constitutional Court, as well as subsequent federal legislation, deprived them of their livelihood by disestablishing their previously held exclusive right of representation before appeals chambers (*Singularzulassung*). The issue had originally arisen on account of the mixed regime of certification in which exclusive rights of audience had only been in place in seven of the sixteen *Länder*, whereas in the rest, barristers had enjoyed combined rights of audience (*Simultanzulassung*). In December 2000, the Federal Constitutional Court, in the case of a barrister certified for the lower courts whose application for exclusive rights of audience in appeal proceedings had been refused, declared the granting of exclusive rights of audience in the seven states where it was applicable at the time to be unconstitutional.[127] It rejected the main rationale of exclusive rights of audience, notably the alleged benefits for the client derived from a division of labour and specialisation of barristers as to judicial instance,[128] as no longer justifying a common interest restriction on professional liberty. The Federal Constitutional Court then went on to establish a two-year transitional period so that specialised appeals barristers, who did, in general, not dispose of their own client-base but relied on referrals from first-instance colleagues, could adapt to the new circumstances; in doing so, it remained far below the ten-year transition period requested by the applicants and a number of lawyers' associations.

The barristers then turned to the Court, alleging a violation of their right to property under Art. 1 Prot. 1; of their right to family life under Art. 8; and of their right to a remedy

---

123 *Voggenreiter*, App. No. 47169/99 at para. 45; in relation to civil claims for professional liberty, the Court cited König v. Germany, App. No. 6232/73 (Eur. Ct. H.R., 1978), at http://cmiskp.echr.coe.int/tkp197/portal.asp?sessionId=3269975&skin=hudoc-en&action=request, Le Compte, Van Leuven und De Meyere, v. Belgium, Appl. Nos. 6878/75 and 7238/75 (Eur. Ct. H.R., 1981), at http://cmiskp.echr.coe.int/tkp197/portal.asp?sessionId=3270032&skin=hudoc-en&action=request, Kraska v. Switzerland, App. No. 13942/88 (Eur. Ct. H.R., 1993), at http://cmiskp.echr.coe.int/tkp197/portal.asp?sessionId=3270040&skin=hudoc-en&action=request; and Ferrazzini v. Italy [Grand Chamber], Application No. 44759/98 (Eur. Ct. H.R., 2001), at http://cmiskp.echr.coe.int/tkp197/portal.asp?sessionId=3270046&skin=hudoc-en&action=request.
124 Voggenreiter v. Germany, App. No. 47169/99 paras. 52–53 (Eur. Ct. H.R., 2004), at http://cmiskp.echr.coe.int/tkp197/portal.asp?sessionId=3269953&skin=hudoc-en&action=request.
125 *Voggenreiter*, App. No. 47169/99 at paras. 55–60.
126 Wendenburg and Others v. Germany, App. No. 71630/01 (Eur. Ct. H.R., 2003), at http://cmiskp.echr.coe.int/tkp197/portal.asp?sessionId=3270049&skin=hudoc-en&action=request.
127 *See* BVerfGE 103, 1.
128 Known in German commentary as the "Four-Eyes Principle" (*Vier-Augen-Prinzip*).

as provided by Arts. 6 and 13.[129] The reasoning behind the first two complaints was that the disestablishment of exclusive rights of audience allegedly deprived them of the basis upon which they had legitimately relied for their livelihood, constituting in the applicants' eyes, both an infringement of their property rights and, on account of the difficulties caused by the former, of their family life.[130] As for the first allegation, the Court, while reaffirming its own subsidiarity and the wide margin of appreciation enjoyed by national authorities in determining the necessity of a measure of control, nonetheless did review the merits of the decision of the Federal Constitutional Court. It confirmed the government's affirmation that the loss of future income fell, according to the Court's jurisprudence, outside the scope of Art. 1, Prot. 1,[131] but rejected the government's related claim that a lawyer's clients could not amount to a possession within the meaning of the article.[132] Indeed, the very privileges that underlay the applicants' claim did give rise to the legitimate expectation of acquiring certain possessions.[133] However, the Court then found that the Federal Constitutional Court's decision served the common interest, as it was founded on evidence that technological change had rendered any exclusive audience system largely obsolete.[134] The Court, through its questionnaire to the government, verified that between eighty and ninety percent of all barristers affected by the Federal Constitutional Court's decision had, within the given transition period, moved to so-called mixed partnerships that deal with all jurisdictional levels. It took this to indicate that an adaptation of the concerned barristers' practice was, in fact, possible within the given time period. This rendered the Federal Constitutional Court's decision not merely a justifiable determination of the public interest, but also plainly proportional in relation to the aim pursued.[135] The aforementioned wide margin of appreciation in such cases meant that national determinations would be accepted unless manifestly arbitrary or unreasonable, which, in the Court's view, was not the case here.[136] It therefore dismissed this first part of the application as manifestly ill founded, as it did the related Art. 8 claim, which, in the Court's view, did not raise any new issues.[137] Likewise, the Court found that the applicants' allegation of a judicial due process violation under Arts. 6 and 13 was inadmissible; the lack of an individual hearing of the plaintiffs, which resulted from the nature of the Federal Constitutional Court's case,[138] could not as such constitute a violation of

---

129 *Wendenburg*, App. No. 71630/01 at 19.
130 *Wendenburg*, App. No. 71630/01 at 19–23.
131 *See Wendenburg*, App. No. 71630/01 at 23; the Court citing Denmark v. the United Kingdom, App. No. 37660/97 (Eur. Ct. H.R., 2000), *at* http://cmiskp.echr.coe.int/tkp197/portal.asp?sessionId= 3270057&skin=hudoc-en&action=request; Ian Edgar (Liverpool) Ltd. v. the United Kingdom, App. No. 37683/97 (Eur. Ct. H.R., 2000), *at* http://cmiskp.echr.coe.int/tkp197/portal.asp?sessionId= 3270063&skin=hudoc-en&action=request; and Van Marle and Others v. the Netherlands, App. Nos 8543/7, 8674/79, 8675/79, 8685/79 (Eur. Ct. H.R., 1986), *at* http://cmiskp.echr.coe.int/tkp197/ portal.asp?sessionId=3270069&skin=hudoc-en&action=request.
132 *See* Wendenburg and Others v. Germany, App. No. 71630/01 23 (Eur. Ct. H.R., 2003), *at* http:// cmiskp.echr.coe.int/tkp197/portal.asp?sessionId=3270049&skin=hudoc-en&action=request; the Court citing Olbertz v. Germany, App. No. 37592/97 (Eur. Ct. H.R., 1986), *at* http://cmiskp.echr.coe.int/ tkp197/portal.asp?sessionId=3270069&skin=hudoc-en&action=request, and Döring v. Germany, App. No. 67595/97 (Eur. Ct. H.R., 1999).
133 *Wendenburg*, App. No. 71630/01 at 23.
134 *Wendenburg*, App. No. 71630/01 at 24–25
135 *See Wendenburg*, App. No. 71630/01 at 24.
136 *Wendenburg*, App. No. 71630/01 at. 25–26.
137 *See Wendenburg*, App. No. 71630/01 at 26.
138 The Federal Constitutional Court heard evidence from a number of legal and barristers associations, but not from the plaintiffs individually, as the case did not concern them but the barrister who had lodged the concrete review proceedings upon the rejection of his application for rights of audience in the court of appeal.

Art. 6,[139] nor did the non-justiciability of that tribunal's decisions represent a lack of legal remedy as defined by Art. 13.[140] The Court equally rejected the applicants' further submissions concerning subsequent legislation meant to implement the Federal Constitutional Court's *dictum*, and which, in the applicants' view, exceeded the regime established by that decision, and which, hence, augmented the violations complained of. Apart from the potential non-exhaustion of domestic remedies in relation to the implementation legislation, the Court found the additional claims to be unsubstantiated.[141]

In rejecting the complaint by some of the formerly specialised appeal barristers, the Court saved the Federal Republic from having to reconcile a decision by the Court with a divergent decision of the Federal Constitutional Court which has, of course, the force of law according to section 31 of the Federal Constitutional Court Act. Even if the Court had merely mandated the Federal Republic to increase the transition period to the ten years demanded by the applicants, it would have effectively asked the government to prolong by another eight years a situation which, from a domestic perspective, would be considered unconstitutional. Furthermore, had the Court found in favour of the applicants, it might also have awarded damages for loss of income, which, given the ordinarily rather high remunerations formerly received for exclusive appeal work, would have represented a significant expense for what in the end is a rather small group of barristers.[142]

Finally, the Court also had the opportunity to pronounce itself on one of the perennial issues before it, notably on the concept and (legal) consequences of transsexuality.[143] *Van Kück v. Germany*[144] concerned a male-to-female transsexual who had unsuccessfully sued a private health insurance company for partial restitution of costs incurred from her gender reassignment operation. Although the applicant had been granted a name change in recognition of her condition by a district court in 1990,[145] the proceedings against the insurance company before the Berlin Regional Court two years later re-opened the question of the nature of her transsexuality. In order to establish whether the company was liable to pay half of the costs of the operation,[146] that tribunal undertook to determine whether the applicant was, in fact, a transsexual, whether her kind of transsexuality amounted to a disease, and whether gender re-assignment was the necessary treatment.

To this end, the Regional Court obtained an expert opinion, which pointed out that, in general, the effect of gender re-assignment surgery was disputed and that it was only one

---

139 *Wendenburg*, App. No. 71630/01 at 28, the Court citing here its own precedent in Lithgow and others v. United Kingdom, App. Nos. 9006/80; 9262/81; 9263/81; 9265/81; 9266/81; 9313/81; 9405/81 (Eur. Ct. H.R., 1986), *at* http://cmiskp.echr.coe.int/tkp197/portal.asp?sessionId=3270080&skin=hudoc-en&action=request.
140 Wendenburg and Others v. Germany, App. No. 71630/01 28 (Eur. Ct. H.R., 2003), *at* http://cmiskp.echr.coe.int/tkp197/portal.asp?sessionId=3270049&skin=hudoc-en&action=request.
141 *See Wendenburg*, App. No. 71630/01 at 28.
142 *See* Hermann Schünemann, *Roma locuta. ... Vier Augen-Prinzip bleibt aktuell*, 4 ANWALT (2001), *at* http://rsw.beck.de/rsw/shop/default.asp?sessionid=C63B1E3B8DCB4D528022784C14917494&docid=18000&highlight=Wendenburg; Volker Römermann, *EGMR versus BVerfG: Nachspiel zur OLG-Simultanzulassung*, 7 ANWALT (2002) *at* http://rsw.beck.de/rsw/shop/default.asp?sessionid=C63B1E3B8DCB4D528022784C14917494&docid=68439&highlight=Wendenburg.
143 *See, inter alia*, Urfan Khaliq, *Transsexuals in the European Court of Human Rights: X, Y and Z v UK*, 49 N. IR. LEGAL Q. 191 (1998), for a general analysis of the Court's reasoning which uses its transexuality jurisprudence as one example. *See* Oreste Pollicino, *Legal Reasoning of the Court of Justice in the Context of the Principle of Equality Between Judicial Activism and Self-restraint*, 5 GERMAN LAW JOURNAL 3 (2004).
144 Van Kück v. Germany, App. No. 35968/97 (Eur. Ct. H.R., 2003), *at* http://cmiskp.echr.coe.int/tkp197/portal.asp?sessionId=3270086&skin=hudoc-en&action=request.
145 *See* the decision by the Schöneberg District Court of Dec. 20, 1991.
146 The other half were, in accordance with the applicants insurance policy, paid for the her public authority employer.

of several therapeutic alternatives. The expert opinion nevertheless recommended the operation in this particular case, as the most suitable therapy. The Regional Court rejected the applicant's claim, arguing that gender reassignment surgery could not reasonably be considered a necessary therapy.[147] While the applicant appealed the decision, she went ahead with the scheduled operation. The Court of Appeal confirmed the Regional Court's decision, pointing out that the cautiousness of the expert's advice indicated the lack of a firm ground for the applicant's claim.[148] Furthermore, it reasoned that the applicant did not have a claim against the insurance company on account of her allegedly having brought about her condition herself by having earlier commenced hormone treatment without a physician's guidance.

The applicant thereupon brought the case before this Court, complaining against violations of Arts. 6(1), 8, and 14 – read in conjunction with Art. 8.[149] In relation to the first claim, she argued that the German courts had determined the necessity of her treatment in an arbitrarily narrow way, and that the Court of Appeal had only relied on a previous expert opinion and drawn arbitrary conclusions from it.[150] The Court, in turn, first outlined its general approach to transsexualism as it has evolved in its considerable case law on the issue;[151] it cited *Rees v. United Kingdom*,[152] *Cossey v. United Kingdom*,[153] and *B. v. France*[154] as illustrations of its initial approach, which viewed transsexualism as a condition that had not yet hardened into an undisputed scientific concept. Yet, the Court had modified this approach in its more recent decisions, notably *I. v. the United Kingdom*,[155] and, most importantly, *Christine Goodwin v. the United Kingdom*,[156] in which it held that transsexualism had become widely recognized as a medical condition – namely "gender identity disorder," that good faith and non-arbitrariness had to be presumed with regard to the transsexual's undertaking of gender-reassignment surgery, and that the chromosomal element of gender, which is the only unchangeable biological aspect of gender, could not be taken to be decisive.

The Court, therefore, found that the Regional and Appeal Court's decisions regarding the "medical necessity" of the operation had not been reasonable, as their exclusive reliance on one general expert opinion could not be sufficient to make such a complex determination.[157] Similarly, the domestic tribunals' affirmation of the applicant's co-responsibility for his medical condition was not, in the Court's view, based on a careful

---

147 See the decision by the Berlin Regional Court of Aug. 3, 1993.
148 See the decision by the Berlin Court of Appeal of Jan. 27, 1995.
149 *Van Kück*, App. No. 35968/97 at paras. 38, 66, 87
150 Van Kück v. Germany, App. No. 35968/97 para 39–40 (Eur. Ct. H.R., 2003), *at* http://cmiskp.echr.coe.int/tkp197/portal.asp?sessionId=3270086&skin=hudoc-en&action=request.
151 *Van Kück*, App. No. 35968/97 at paras. 46–52.
152 Rees v. United Kingdom, App. No. 9532/81 (Eur. Ct. H.R., 1986), *at* http://cmiskp.echr.coe.int/tkp197/portal.asp?sessionId=3270089&skin=hudoc-en&action=request.
153 Cossey v. United Kingdom, App. No. 10843/84 (Eur. Ct. H.R., 1990), *at* http://cmiskp.echr.coe.int/tkp197/portal.asp?sessionId=3270092&skin=hudoc-en&action=request
154 B.B. v. France, App. No. 30930/96 (Eur. Ct. H.R., 1998), *at* http://cmiskp.echr.coe.int/tkp197/portal.asp?sessionId=3270095&skin=hudoc-en&action=request.
155 I. v. Untied Kingdom, App. No. 25680/94 (Eur. Ct. H.R., 2002), *at* http://cmiskp.echr.coe.int/tkp197/portal.asp?sessionId=3270098&skin=hudoc-en&action=request.
156 Christine Goodwin v. United Kingdom, App. No. 28957/95 (Eur. Ct. H.R., 2002), *at* http://cmiskp.echr.coe.int/tkp197/portal.asp?sessionId=3270101&skin=hudoc-en&action=request; on Christine Goodwin and I. *See* Ralph Sandland, *Crossing and not Crossing: gender, sexuality and melancholy in the European Court of Human Rights*, 11 FEMINIST LEGAL STUDIES 191 (2003); Eugene Macnamee, *Girls and Boys*, 15 LAW AND CRITIQUE 25 (2004); and Sharon Cowan, *That Woman is a Woman: the Case of Bellinger v. Bellinger and the mysterious (dis)appearance of sex*, 12 FEMINIST LEGAL STUDIES 79 (2004).
157 Van Kück v. Germany, App. No. 35968/97 paras. 53–57 (Eur. Ct. H.R., 2003), *at* http://cmiskp.echr.coe.int/tkp197/portal.asp?sessionId=3270086&skin=hudoc-en&action=request.

enough evaluation of existing scientific evidence; it consequently found that the domestic courts' decisions regarding the "medical necessity" of the operation had not been reasonable, as their exclusive reliance on one general expert opinion could not be sufficient to make such a complex determination. Similarly, the domestic tribunals' affirmation of the applicant's co-responsibility for his medical condition was not, in the Court's view, based on a careful enough evaluation of existing scientific evidence; it consequently found the applicant's right to a fair trial violated.[158] It then considered the applicant's claim that her right to private and family life had also been violated by the domestic decisions, notably by depriving her of the possibility to live according to her gender preference. Here the Court again pointed to its jurisprudence which had, *inter alia*, interpreted "private life" as potentially including aspects of a person's physical or social identity, and which generally contained, to differing degrees, the notion of personal autonomy.[159] It also cited again its decision in the *Christine Goodwin* case, which affirmed that transsexualism in general was protected by the Convention. It then went on to find the government's contention that the case concerned merely the applicant's entitlement to a (private) insurance reimbursement and not her transsexuality as such to be irrelevant; rather, what was at stake, in the Court's view, was the consequences the domestic tribunals' decisions had on the applicant's right to respect for her private and family life and all that that entailed. It consequently found the burden of proof placed on the applicant by the German courts as regards the medical necessity of the operation to be disproportionate, and Art. 8, therefore, violated. Furthermore, it found no separate violation to have arisen in relation to Art. 14, and it awarded damages and costs, the former corresponding to the value at issue in the domestic proceedings.[160]

This decision produced a dissent by the Chamber's President, Judge Cabral Barreto, and Judges Hedigan and Greve, as well as a concurring opinion by the German Judge Ress.[161] The dissent is interesting in that it concerns the effect of Convention rights on relations between private parties; a phenomenon commonly referred to as horizontal effect.[162] Hence, the dissenting judges fully accepted the Court's approach to transsexuality as articulated in *Christine Goodwin*, but did not, unlike the majority and the applicant, see the present case as one concerning the nature and legal consequences of transsexuality, but as one essentially concerning the liability of a third-party insurance company in relation to gender reassignment surgery. In the view of the dissenting judges, the German courts' determination of medical necessity in the context of their adjudication of a civil claim against a third-party was reasonable, as was their attempt to establish the applicant's co-responsibility for his condition on the basis of the evidence before them. Otherwise, the third-party's right to freely negotiate and to litigate the contracts it enters would be unduly restricted.

Judge Ress' concurring opinion directly responded to the latter contention, arguing that German constitutional law, as well as Convention jurisprudence assumed the horizontal

---

158 *Van Kück*, App. No. 35968/97 at paras. 58–65.
159 *Van Kück*, App. No. 35968/97 at paras. 69–86; the Court referring here, interestingly, to Pretty v. the United Kingdom, App. No. 2346/02 (Eur. Ct. H.R.).
160 *Van Kück*, App. No. 35968/97 at paras. 87–102.
161 *Van Kück (dissent)*, App. No. 35968/97 at 23–28.
162 *See, inter alia,* Vaios Karavas and Gunther Teubner, *http://www.CompanyNameSucks.com: The Horizontal Effect of Fundamental Rights on 'Private Parties' within Autonomous Internet Law*, 4 GERMAN LAW JOURNAL 12 (2003) at http://www.germanlawjournal.com/article.php?id=356; and *Federal Constitutional Court Affirms Horizontal Effect of Constitutional Rights in Private Law Relations and Voids a Marital Agreement on Constitutional Grounds*, 2 GERMAN LAW JOURNAL No. 6 (2001); *see also* the Court's decision in *Young, James, and Webster v. United Kingdom*, App. Nos. 7601/76 and 7806/77 (Eur. Ct. H.R., 1981), at http://cmiskp.echr.coe.int/tkp197/portal.asp?sessionId=3270111&skin=hudoc-en&action=request.

effect of the rights guaranteed in either document, and that this was particularly so in the present case, as the relationship between private and public health insurance schemes was complementary in Germany. The rights guaranteed under Art. 8 did, hence, have to be fully considered in any determination of the civil claim, which had not occurred in the present case.

C. Outlook

There is no coherent thread to these reviewed cases. Although in five out of eight judgements discussed[163] Convention violations were found, their particular significance both in relation to the general state of (Convention) human rights in Germany, and to the overall Convention system varies. As to the former, it is probably only the transsexuality problematique that results from embedded structural problems, with complaints of access to and the length of proceedings of the Federal Constitutional Court appearing on the margins of the majority of applications against Germany. Article 8 violations related to parental custody and access rights also appear with a certain regularity, though part of the problem seems to have been solved with the long-overdue change in legislation on the status of fathers of children born out of wedlock. As regards the Convention system dimension of the cases reviewed, it is again *Van Kück* and possibly the very strong substantive determination of the precedence of biological parenthood in *Görgülü* that may turn out to be significant precedents in the Court's jurisprudence.

With the 14th Protocol of the Convention up for signature and entry into force, and the four-year consultation process on the further reform of the Convention system finalized, thus bringing to a conclusion a ten-year reconstruction period, the Court's future looks more consolidated than ever. And if one also assumes that the upheavals caused by the Convention area's grand expansion now nearly a generation ago have emerged toward a new level of Convention normality, the Court appears well set to deal with the post-millennial Europe. Yet, new potential dangers are lurking in many shadowy corners, for many people currently within the Convention area may only now be learning how to describe their trials and tribulations in rights terms, and how to effectively take their country to the Court. Yet, the greatest threat to the Convention system, and the Court's ability to maintain it at internationally recognised high standards, may not lie in the further expansion of applications, but rather in changing practices in some of the oldest member states. The so-called "war on terror," which is fought by many Council of Europe member states as fervently as it is by the United States, is fast undermining standards already taken for granted, and reintroducing treatments long thought to have been banned from the repertoire of "civilised nations." It is this challenge which will require a more seasoned and sustained response from the Court than, say, any further increase in length of time of civil proceedings cases. Or, to borrow from *Boney M*'s contested hit: "show me your motion," European Court of Human Rights.[164]

---

163 In total, of the seventeen judgements rendered by the Court in the period under review, only two non-violations were found.
164 © 1978 by Far-Musikverlag GmbH.

SECTION IV:
BOOK REVIEWS

Basil Markesinis and Hannes Unberath: *The German Law of Torts: A Comparative Treatise*, 4th edition (Oxford and Portland, OR: Hart Publishing, 2002, 1050 pp., ISBN 1-84113-297-7, $75.00)

Bernhard Grossfeld[*]

Within sixteen years, this treatise has reached its fourth edition and, therefore, rightly attained the stature of a classic of comparative tort law. It is especially fortunate that this effort has concentrated on German tort law and thus contributed to bringing English law within the gravitational force of European law. The references to German law remain up-to-date, which is, no doubt, thanks to the fact that Hannes Unberath joined the project as co-author.

The book presents the English/American reader with German law in context. For this reason, it begins with a description of the organization of the German judicial system, beginning with the *Reichskammergericht* (Imperial Chamber of Justice – est. 1495) and moving on to the *Reichsgericht* (RG – Supreme Court of the German Reich) and its successor, the *Bundesgerichtshof* (BGH – Federal Court of Justice). The hierarchy of courts and stages of appeal are also presented. From this organizational introduction, the book moves on to consider the style and method of reasoning in decisions of the Federal Court of Justice. The authors note that the method of reasoning is brought forward in an "abstract manner," leaving very little room for fantasy. However, the constant stock-taking in legal policy arguments should alleviate some of the court texts' occasional dryness.

Only after these introductory efforts does tort law enter on the scene: the essential rules are provided in English translation. Still, the reader is not confronted with the details. First, consideration is given to the *Bürgerliches Gesetzbuch* (BGB – German Civil Code) in general, its roots in the system of the *Pandects*[1] and the influence of French law. The foreign reader receives much more exposure to German legal history than most German law students. Since comparative law without legal history is not possible, this extensive background is necessary. Thereafter, the authors inform the reader specifically of the impact of constitutional law on civil law. The constitutional provisions concerned with fundamental rights are also provided in English translation. The introductory section concludes with a discussion of the place of the ordinary law in the framework of the constitution.

---

[*] Professor emeritus, University of Münster. Professor, Southern Methodist University, Dallas, Texas. This review was previously published in 5 GERMAN LAW JOURNAL 511 (2003).

1 The Roman Kaiser Justinian (527–565) collected and codified the existing Roman law in a four-part treatise, the second part of which is entitled *Digesten* (also called "*Pandekten*") and the other three being entitled *Institutionen* (Part I), *Codex* (Part III), and *Novellen* (Part IV). The *Digesten* (*Pandekten*) grew out of the compilation work of case materials and interpretations of some forty Roman jurists between 100 A.D. and 250 A.D. *See* STEPHAN MEDER, RECHTSGESCHICHTE 794–5 (2nd ed., 2005). [The Editors]

The presentation of tort law revolves around Sections 823, 826 and 831 of the BGB and *Gefährdungshaftung* (strict liability) in general. The construction of the book is uniform. It begins with a comprehensive introduction followed by decisions, most frequently from the case law of the Federal Court of Justice, but also from the *Bundesverfassungsgericht* (BVerfG – Federal Constitutional Court) and occasionally other courts. The decisions are often enhanced with commentary. In these comments, the reader finds comparative law observations wherein the authors fill out the framework of the subject matter with details. The reader will find 151 decisions in English translation that make up more than half of the book. Germans are likely to learn much that is unexpected about themselves from the perspective of the foreign observer. It is understandable that the former president of the Federal Court of Justice, Walter Odersky, wrote such an appreciative, even grateful, foreword to the book. Where else does German law find a platform with such a far-reaching, international impact? Contributing to this effect is the elegant language used by the authors, which is characterized by a lightness and vividness that Germans should strive towards as an ideal.

The book offers yet another surprise. At the beginning of the last third of the book, the authors have published a legal and judicial map of Germany (from the period preceding the development of the BGB) and a map of the Federal Republic of Germany. Following the maps are brief introductions to a number of German jurists, including some who are still alive. The authors explain that focusing only on the past "would imply that the present offers unworthy successors." Relatively detailed treatment is given to Carl von Savigny and Rudolf von Ihering. Shorter treatment is given to Otto von Gierke, Hans Carl Nipperdey, Werner Flume, Ernst von Caemmerer, Robert Fischer, Bruno Heusinger, Fritz Hauss and Walther Stimpel.

The portion of the book (nearly half) concerned with Section 823 Para. 1 of the BGB warrants a somewhat closer examination. In keeping with the above format, it begins with a "Commentary" of some 70 pages where the authors explain such concepts as "life," "body and health," "property," "other rights," unlawfulness," and "fault." The concepts of "duties of care" and "causation" receive wide-ranging consideration thereafter. Contracts creating a duty of care towards third parties and third party liability are mentioned at various points. Ninety-four decisions follow. Among them is the "Nervous Shock" Case, which is placed in a broad context alongside English and American cases. The "Prenatal Injuries" Case leads to the discussion of the concepts of "wrongful life" and "wrongful death." The authors understand what issues and concepts to stress. Among other issues, there are decisions dealing with "economic loss" and "established operating business." The authors examine the "constitutionalization of private law", or the 'horizontal effect of fundamental rights' (*Drittwirkung der Grundrechte*) and discuss "personality and privacy rights." Unlawfulness and fault, the duties of care, product liability and damage to the product, and causation are all treated with concern for comparative law. The authors understand their subject and they present it in a sophisticated manner.

This marvelous book is an ambassador for German legal culture for which we should be very grateful.

Translated by Russell Miller

Peter L. Murray and Rolf Stürner: *German Civil Justice* (Durham, NC: Carolina Academic Press, 2004, 670 pp., ISBN 1-59460-003-1, $65.00)

Giesela Rühl*

The modern German system of civil justice is one of the most respected in the world. It has a reputation for being efficient and relatively successful. For these reasons it has been described and analyzed in numerous treatises, commentaries, texts and articles. However, as almost all of these works are written and published in German, they are not accessible to persons who are unfamiliar with the German language. In *German Civil Justice*, Peter L. Murray and Rolf Stürner address this perceived drawback by presenting a comprehensive description of the German system of civil justice in the English language.

The authors are perfectly prepared for the task. They have both studied and taught civil procedure for many years – Murray in the United States (Harvard Law School) and Stürner in Germany (University of Freiburg). In addition, they have both published numerous books and articles dealing with various topics related to the themes in *German Civil Justice*, and both have conducted comparative legal research and studied the civil justice systems of other countries. However, what distinguishes Murray and Stürner from most scholars in their field is that they have long lasting practical experience in their respective civil justice systems – Murray as a litigator and Stürner as a judge. It is the combination of scholastic and practical perspective that makes *German Civil Justice* a remarkable treatise about the theory of German civil procedure law and the realities of litigation in modern Germany.

German Civil Justice is divided into 13 Chapters, which can be structured into five parts. The first part comprises Chapters 1 through 4 and is introductory in character. Murray and Stürner begin with a short overview of the German civil justice system and a brief summary of the history and development of German civil procedure. They continue with a description of the organization and structure of the German judicial system followed by an overview of the institutional framework of civil justice in Germany, including education of lawyers and judges, structure and regulation of the German bar, lawyers' organizations, fees and compensation, legal aid and access to justice.

The second part consists of Chapters 5 and 6 and is preparatory in nature. It lays the foundation for the upcoming detailed description of German court proceedings by addressing subject matter jurisdiction and venue in civil cases as well as other fundamental issues of German civil justice, notably the nature and purpose of a civil lawsuit, the role of the parties and the counsels and the role of the judge. Careful attention is also paid to a number of abstract principles, which underlie the more specific statutory rules without being expressly stated and which are intended to implement fundamental rights and values. Out of these numerous principles the authors focus in some detail on the principle of party control over the initiation, the scope and the termination of a claim (*Dispositionsgrundsatz*), the principle of party control over the specification of facts and the means of proof (*Verhandlungsgrundsatz*), the principle of oral presentation of factual assertions and legal arguments (*Mündlichkeitsgrundsatz*), and finally, the principle of open access of the public to plenary proceedings (*Öffentlichkeitsgrundsatz*).

The third part of *German Civil Justice* extends from Chapters 7 through 10 and concentrates on what the authors call the core of the book: the description and analysis of

---

* Senior Research Fellow at the Max-Planck-Institute for Foreign Private and Private International Law, Hamburg, Germany. Since 2005, she has been a member of the editorial board of the GERMAN LAW JOURNAL. This review was previously published in 6 GERMAN LAW JOURNAL 735 (2005).

German civil proceedings in their various instances. Murray and Stürner distinguish three main phases of a civil lawsuit – namely, the initial preparatory phase, the oral plenary phase, and the appellate phase – and address each of them in chronological order. Accordingly they start with a portrayal of the preparatory phase of a lawsuit, specifically covering initiation of a complaint, service of process, service of responsive pleadings and preparation of the oral plenary proceedings. They point out that the various steps that have to be taken at this stage of a lawsuit may lead to protraction of the proceedings, and that in practice, however, courts shorten the preparatory phase by setting strict limits and enforcing evidentiary and issue preclusions. They also note that although the focus of the preparatory phase is – as the name suggests – the preparation of the case for plenary disposition, in practice many cases are disposed of during this phase by procedural dismissal or settlement.

Following these remarks regarding the first phase of a lawsuit, Murray and Stürner focus on the second phase, the so called plenary and evidentiary proceedings (*Hauptverhandlung*); the heart of German civil lawsuits during which the court and the parties discuss the issues of law as well as disputed facts. Heavily relying on their practical experience, they explain the purpose and scope of the plenary hearing, its conceptual structure as well as the gathering and evaluation of evidence by the court. In doing so they specifically focus on the means of proof, which are statutorily limited to observation and inspection of person and things (*Augenschein*), documents (*Urkunden*), witness testimony (*Zeugen*), expert testimony (*Sachverständige*), and party testimony (*Parteivernehmung*). The authors terminate their description of the second phase by looking to different types of judgments, their necessary content and their res adjudicata effect. Emphasis is placed on so-called uncontested judgments such as default judgments (*Versäumnisurteile*), judgments by which the defendant voluntarily recognizes the validity of the claim (*Anerkenntnisurteile*), and judgments by which the plaintiff waives the claim (*Verzichtsurteile*).

With these remarks on judgments, the stage is set for the discussion of the appellate phase of a civil lawsuit. Murray and Stürner begin with a brief description of the purpose of appellate justice in Germany, pointing to three different functions: reexamination of the facts relevant to the underlying dispute, correction of errors in the interpretation and application of the law, maintenance and enforcement of correct procedure. Against this background Murray and Stürner give a brief overview of the large number of appellate remedies designed to serve these functions. However, in the following detailed description they confine themselves to the three most important ones: the second instance appeal of facts and law (*Berufung*), the review appeal of law and procedure (*Revision*) and the miscellaneous appeal (*Beschwerde*). They outline the requirements for the initiation of an appeal, the scope of review, the procedure and the judgment following an appeal. In doing so Murray and Stürner take into account the most recent structural changes of German civil procedure that became effective on January 1, 2002 and that restrict the review of first instance fact finding. They also account for the ongoing debate about cutting back the number and the scope of appellate remedies.

The fourth part of *German Civil Justice* comprises Chapters 11 and 12 and is best seen as an annex to Chapters 7 through 10. It covers various special proceedings, which serve different purposes, beginning with modified forms of first instance proceedings and moving to so-called civil warning proceedings for collecting claims likely to remain uncontested (*Mahnverfahren*), security proceedings for obtaining prejudgment attachments (*Arrest*) or provisional measures (*Einstweilige Verfügungen*), non-contentious proceedings for dealing with more or less non-adversarial matters such as guardianship, probate and registration of real estate (*Freiwillige Gerichtsbarkeit*), proceedings for the execution of judgments (*Zwangsvollstreckung*), bankruptcy proceedings (*Insolvenzverfahren*), arbitration proceedings (*Schiedsverfahren*), and finally, proceedings for case settlements and alternative dispute resolution. The fourth part also addresses international matters, notably international jurisdiction, recognition and enforcement of foreign judgments, service of foreign process, provisional measures to secure claims in foreign courts and taking of evidence for use in foreign proceedings. However, due to the complexity of the subject the authors do not go into much depth and concentrate on the most important doctrines governing German international civil procedure.

The last part of *German Civil Justice*, consisting only of Chapter 13, is devoted to a comparison and evaluation of the German and Anglo-American civil justice system and can be seen as the real core of the work. Along the lines of seven main functions of civil litigation Murray and Stürner contrast purposes of civil justice in Germany and the United States, institutional independence and credibility, quality of fact finding and application of law, cost of litigation, duration of proceedings, access to justice as well as confidence of the public in the system of civil justice. They conclude that, despite persisting differences, signs of convergence can be observed between Germany and the civil law world on the one hand and the United States and the common law world on the other hand.

All in all, this book is an outstanding treatise on the German system of civil justice. It fills a long-lasting gap in the judicial literature market because it is the first book in the English language to give a detailed description of the historical, cultural, institutional, and legal framework of civil litigation in Germany, and is the first book in the English language to give a comprehensive overview of the German law of civil procedure. However, the truly remarkable feature of *German Civil Justice* is that Murray and Stürner go beyond a mere description of the development and the current state of German law. They compare the German and the Anglo-American civil justice system against the background of cultural, economic, historical and social differences and thereby enhance the mutual understanding of law and legal institutions in both countries. By evaluating both systems they also contribute to the ongoing global debate about efficiency of legal systems.

On a technical level one might add that the book is exceptionally well written and structured in a way that is easily understandable for English-speaking lawyers, especially for those with a common law background. Furthermore, the large number of references to source materials, commentaries, treatises, and articles throughout the text, as well as the bibliography at the very end allow for further research into specific areas. The only thing that curtails the practical use of the book is the index, which is too short for a work of more than 600 pages and therefore does not facilitate systematic research. However, despite this rather small drawback, *German Civil Justice* can only be highly recommended to everybody with an interest in German civil procedure.

Two concluding remarks need to be made. First, Murray and Stürner do not cover some aspects – such as administrative proceedings, labor proceedings, social welfare proceedings and tax proceedings – that American lawyers would usually expect to be included in a comprehensive book on civil justice. As the authors point out, tackling these issues would have gone beyond the scope of the book and would have required cutbacks in the description of other, more fundamental issues of German law. One might add that according to the narrow notion of civil procedure usually applied in Germany the above-mentioned proceedings do not even belong to civil procedure. Therefore, from a German perspective the authors indeed provide a comprehensive guide to German civil justice.

Second, although Murray and Stürner take into account all law reforms and changes effective by the time of publication they were not able to keep up with the pace of the German legislature. On September 1, 2004 the Modernization of Justice Law (*Justizmodernisierungsgesetz*) of July 1, 2004 became effective. Enacted with the aim of making German civil proceedings more efficient, the most important changes affect the requirements for disposition of cases other than through judgment, the requirements for recusing judges and the consideration of written expert testimony. Additionally, on July 1, 2004 the Modernization of Costs Law (*Kostenrechtsmodernisierungsgesetz*) of May 5, 2004 came into effect. It has replaced the Federal Attorneys Fee Law (*Bundesgebührenordnung für Rechtsanwälte*) by the Attorneys Compensation Law (*Rechtsanwaltsvergütungsgesetz*) and restructured the Court Costs Law (*Gerichtskostengesetz*). However, neither the Modernization of Justice Law nor the Modernization of Costs Law touches on the basic principles of the German system of civil litigation. They certainly do not impair the significance of *German Civil Justice* and its usefulness for the English-speaking world.

Marcel Storme (ed.): *Procedural Laws in Europe. Towards Harmonisation* (Antwerpen/Apeldoorn: Maklu, 2003, 472 pp., ISBN 90-6215-881-1, €85)

Jan Bolt*

The ongoing Europeanization of substantive private law is highly visible. Since the 1980s, numerous EC Directives have greatly influenced the Member States' laws of obligations.[1] The European Commission is currently even considering a major step towards unification: the drafting of optional EU-wide contract law rules.[2] Also, for quite some time now several privately organized groups of legal scholars have contemplated reasons for and the means to harmonize or unify private law in Europe.[3]

By contrast, efforts aimed at harmonizing the Member States' procedural laws have lagged behind until recently. Even though the necessities of international litigation led the Member States to adopt various conventions addressing certain problems of international private law[4] and international procedural law (most notably the Brussels Convention[5]),

---

* Institute for Comparative Law, Johann Wolfgang Goethe-Universität Frankfurt am Main, Germany.
1 For a compilation of the most important Directives *see* EUROPÄISCHES SCHULDRECHT/EUROPEAN LAW OF OBLIGATIONS (Magnus ed., 2002) (in German, English and French). A very important recent example is the Directive 1999/44/EC of the European Parliament and of the Council of 25 May 1999 on certain aspects of the sale of consumer goods and associated guarantees. This Directive led to a major reform of German contract law ("Schuldrechtsmodernisierung"), *see* Peter Rott, *German Sales Law Two Years After the Implementation of Directive 1999/44/EC*, 5 GERMAN LAW JOURNAL 237 (2004), *available at* http://www.germanlawjournal.com/article.php?id=386.
2 For the current debate about the Commission's action plan "A more coherent European contract law" – COM(2003) 68 final – envisioning, *inter alia*, optional EU-wide contract law rules *see* Staudenmayer, EUROPÄISCHE ZEITSCHRIFT FÜR WIRTSCHAFTSRECHT (EuZW) 165 (2003); Staudenmayer, ZEITSCHRIFT FÜR EUROPÄISCHES PRIVATRECHT (ZEuP) 828 (2003); Basedow, ZEITSCHRIFT FÜR EUROPÄISCHES PRIVATRECHT (ZEuP) 1 (2004).
3 E.g., the Commission on European Contract Law (the so-called Lando Commission) was already established in 1980. The Lando Commission has devised Principles of European Contract Law, *see* PRINCIPLES OF EUROPEAN CONTRACT LAW, PARTS I AND II (Lando & Beale eds., 2000); PRINCIPLES OF EUROPEAN CONTRACT LAW, PART III (Lando, Clive, Prüm & Zimmermann, eds., 2003). Wurmnest, ZEITSCHRIFT FÜR EUROPÄISCHES PRIVATRECHT (ZEuP) 714 (2003), provides an extensive survey of other important scholarly efforts.
4 Convention on the Law Applicable to Contractual Obligations, June 19, 1980, 1980 O.J. (L 266) (Rome Convention).
5 Convention on Jurisdiction and the Enforcement of Judgments in Civil and Commercial Matters, Sept. 27, 1968, 1998 O.J. (C27) 1. The Convention is now replaced by the Brussels I Regulation, *see infra* note 17. Also, in the area of judicial assistance, most Member States are part to the Hague Convention Relating to Civil Procedure of 1 March 1954 (dealing also with security for costs and with proceedings in forma pauperis), to the Hague Convention on the Service Abroad of Judicial and Extrajudicial Documents in Civil or Commercial Matters of 15 November 1965, and to the Hague Convention on the Taking of Evidence Abroad in Civil or Commercial Matters of 18 March 1970.

none of these measures had a great influence on core areas of the respective national procedures.[6] However, a significant harmonizing effect can be attributed to the preliminary rulings of the European Court of Justice (ECJ).[7] The ECJ occasionally even invalidated national provisions infringing upon the freedoms of the internal market[8] or violating the general prohibition against discrimination on grounds of nationality (now Art. 12 EC).[9]

In 1990, the European Commission requested a group of experts chaired by Prof. Marcel Storme to draft an EC Directive containing a European model code of civil procedure. The purposefully fragmentary result – covering 16 select topics which were found to be amenable to harmonization – was presented to the European Commission in 1993.[10] In Germany, the proposed model code drew some heavy criticism by procedural scholars.[11] Some questioned a current need for or even the desirability of unified national procedural rules in the European Union.[12] Also, the project was perceived as having been undertaken without sufficient comparative preparatory work.[13] Although the European Commission did not pursue the matter further, it can nevertheless be said that the efforts of the Storme working group provided the starting point for an intensive debate about the scope and the means of harmonizing the national procedural rules.

In October 1997, the Treaty of Amsterdam brought drastic changes.[14] The Community was given the task of establishing progressively an area of freedom, security and justice (Art. 61 EC).[15] The new Arts. 61, 65 EC empower the Council to adopt measures in the field of judicial cooperation in civil matters having cross-border implications in so far as necessary for the proper functioning of the internal market. These measures are not limited to the traditional areas of international civil procedure like jurisdiction, recognition and enforcement or judicial assistance. Art. 65(c) EC explicitly allows eliminating obstacles to the good functioning of civil proceedings, if necessary by promoting the compatibility of the rules on civil procedure applicable in the Member States. Furthermore, the political leaders of the Member States have made it clear that they view the development of the envisaged European area of freedom, security and

---

6   Kerameus, 66 RABELS ZEITSCHRIFT FÜR AUSLÄNDISCHES UND INTERNATIONALES PRIVATRECHT 1, 2 (2002).
7   In 1971, the signatory states conferred on the ECJ jurisdiction to interpret the Brussels Convention via preliminary rulings. These rulings have a harmonizing effect, because the ECJ interprets the provisions of the Convention – among them key concepts of procedure like lis pendens – autonomously, Hess, NEUE JURISTISCHE WOCHENSCHRIFT (NJW) 23, 24 (2000); Kerameus, 66 RABELS ZEITSCHRIFT FÜR AUSLÄNDISCHES UND INTERNATIONALES PRIVATRECHT 1, 12 (2002); see also Stürner, Der deutsche Prozeßrechtslehrer am Ende des 20. Jahrhunderts, in FESTSCHRIFT FÜR GERHARD LÜKE 829, 835 (Hanns Prütting ed., 1997).
8   Case C-20/92, Hubbard v. Hamburger, 1993 E.C.R. I-3777: obligation of a foreign plaintiff to provide security for costs, § 110 para. 1 German Code of Civil Procedure.
9   Case C-398/92, Mund & Fester v. Hatrex, 1994 E.C.R. I-467, with comment by Schlosser, ZEITSCHRIFT FÜR EUROPÄISCHES PRIVATRECHT (ZEuP) 253 (1995): permission to attach a debtor's assets (dinglicher Arrest) solely on the ground that a subsequent judgment will have to be enforced abroad, § 917 para. 2 German Code of Civil Procedure.
10 RAPPROCHEMENT DU DROIT JUDICIAIRE DE L'UNION EUROPÉENNE – APPROXIMATION OF JUDICIARY LAW IN THE EUROPEAN UNION (Marcel Storme ed., 1994). For a presentation of the project see also Kerameus, 43 AM. J. COMP. L. 401, 410 (1995).
11 H. Roth, 109 ZEITSCHRIFT FÜR ZIVILPROZEß 271, 308 (1996) Schilken, 109 ZEITSCHRIFT FÜR ZIVILPROZEß 315, 330 (1996) (concerning enforcement).
12 See especially Stürner, Das Europäische Zivilprozeßrecht – Einheit oder Vielfalt?, in WEGE ZU EINEM EUROPÄISCHEN ZIVILPROZEßRECHT 1, 9 (Wolfgang Grunsky ed., 1992); id. at 17: irrational urge towards uniformity.
13 H. Roth, 109 ZEITSCHRIFT FÜR ZIVILPROZEß 271, 313 (1996).
14 Treaty of Amsterdam, 2 October 1997, 1997 O.J. (C 340) 1, came into force on May 1, 1999.
15 See the latest update of the European Commission's scoreboard to review progress on the creation of an "area of freedom, security and justice" in the European Union, at 40, COM (2003) 812 final. The Commission has set up a website as well. The address is http://europa.eu.int/comm/justice_home/index_en.htm.

justice as a top priority.[16] As a result, the Community has already passed a large number of acts with remarkable speed, most of them in the form of Regulations.[17] The Commission and the Council are currently pursuing a strategy of sectoral harmonization or even unification of all aspects of procedural law concerning cross-border litigation between the Member States.[18] It is therefore no exaggeration to speak of a rapidly emerging law of European or internal market civil procedure that is settled between the national and the international procedural laws.[19] Also, even though there are no plans to approximate or unify the Member States' procedural laws outside the area of international litigation, the national laws will nonetheless be affected by some of the European Commission's projects.[20]

Against this background Prof. Storme organized a colloquium on "The Coming Together of Procedural Laws in Europe" in Brussels on October 26–27, 2001 which stood under the auspices of the European Commission and of the Belgian Ministry of Justice. The participants, who came from all of the European Union's current and from most of the prospective Member States, ventured to take a look at the possible future of European-style litigation. The book containing the proceedings is structured along the three great questions of harmonization: Why?, What? and How? The 24 contributions are mostly in English (10) or German (8). There are some French (3) and some Dutch (3) articles as well. Because of the large number of contributions, only some of them can be presented in this review.

16 See the introduction to the Presidency Conclusions of the European Council meeting in Tampere in October 1999: "The European Council is determined to develop the Union as an area of freedom, security and justice by making full use of the possibilities offered by the Treaty of Amsterdam. ... The European Council will place and maintain this objective at the very top of the political agenda." See also the Council's Draft Programme of Measures for Implementation of the Principle of Mutual Recognition of Decisions in Civil and Commercial Matters, 2001 O.J. (C 12/1).
17 Council Regulation (EC) No 44/2001 of 22 December 2000 on jurisdiction and the recognition and enforcement of judgments in civil and commercial matters (Brussels I), replacing the Brussels Convention; Council Regulation (EC) No 1347/2000 of 29 May 2000 on jurisdiction and the recognition and enforcement of judgments in matrimonial matters and in matters of parental responsibility for children of both spouses (Brussels II); Council Regulation (EC) No 1346/2000 of 29 May 2000 on insolvency proceedings; Council Regulation (EC) No 1348/2000 of 29 May 2000 on the service in the Member States of judicial and extrajudicial documents in civil and commercial matters; Council Regulation (EC) No 1206/2001 of 28 May 2001 on cooperation between the courts of the Member States in the taking of evidence in civil or commercial matters; see also the Council Directive No 2002/8/EC of 27 January 2003 to improve access to justice in cross-border disputes by establishing minimum common rules relating to legal aid for such disputes, and the Council decision of 28 May 2001, 2001/470/EC, establishing a European Judicial Network in civil and commercial matters. Also, Community acts included procedural rules to further substantive issues, see, e.g., the Directive 1998/27/EC of the European Parliament and of the Council of 19 May 1998 on injunctions for the protection of consumers' interests. Notable legislative competences are Art. 95 EC (establishment and functioning of the internal market) and Art. 153 EC (consumer protection).
18 See the European Commission's scoreboard, supra note 15, at 39; R. Wagner, NEUE JURISTISCHE WOCHENSCHRIFT 2344, 2346 (2003); Hess, JURISTENZEITUNG 573, 578 (2001).
19 Hess, PRAXIS DES INTERNATIONALEN PRIVAT- UND VERFAHRENSRECHTS 389, 390 (2001); Stadler, PRAXIS DES INTERNATIONALEN PRIVAT- UND VERFAHRENSRECHTS 2, 3 (2004).
20 See, e.g., Commission Proposal for a Regulation Creating a European Enforcement Order for Uncontested Claims, COM (2002), 159 final – 2002/0090 (COD), the approval with amendments by the European Parliament, A5-0108/2003, and the amended Commission proposal COM(2003), 341 final. In order to facilitate cross-border enforcement, the European enforcement order would eliminate the recognition procedure (Art. 38 Brussels I Regulation) for certain types of judgments. The national proceedings, in turn, will have to adhere to certain minimum standards, especially with regard to the service of documents, Arts. 11–15 of the amended Commission proposal. The European enforcement order will be the first step to extend the principle of mutual recognition, originally relating to the free movement of goods, to the area of civil procedure, compare the Tampere Presidency Conclusions, paras. 33–34, 37. See the critical remarks by Stadler, PRAXIS DES INTERNATIONALEN PRIVAT- UND VERFAHRENSRECHTS 2, 5 (2004); see also Hess, PRAXIS DES INTERNATIONALEN PRIVAT- UND VERFAHRENSRECHTS 389, 391 (2001).

1. Harmonization: Why ?

Torbjörn Andersson presents a model to roughly evaluate the present level of approximation in a certain area of law by using the dichotomy of European approximation and Member State discretion. He points out that the model is only thought to be understood as a means of understanding the levels of approximation, and that it would be impossible to conclusively assess a level. The approximation level of civil procedure is described to be between "low" and "rather low". This means that the Member States have very large or at least considerable discretion in this area of law. The dynamics, however, would work solely in the direction of further approximation. The purpose of approximation is dealt with rather briefly. Andersson doubts whether the scope of any analysis is wide enough to discuss the connection between general objectives and approximation in a meaningful way. But he states that the European political ambition to integrate substantive law and political policy in various fields has created a practical need for the approximation of civil procedure, because court procedure determines the pratical results of substantive law reforms, and variations in procedure impair the uniform treatment in substance between the citizens of the Member States.

The article by Gerhard Walter deals with the current process of unifying procedural law in Switzerland through a new federal code of civil procedure replacing the 26 cantonal codes and the existing federal code.[21] He points out that the Swiss experience is particularly interesting for the approximation efforts of the European Union, because Switzerland with its four official languages is by no means a homogenous country. The fact that the Swiss are nevertheless striving for a unified civil procedure – excluding only the organization of the judiciary – is explained with the uniformity of the economic area Switzerland, the approximation of living conditions, the problem to ensure a fair, equal and efficient enforcement of uniform substantive law, and with the foregoing piecemeal approximation via federal laws. Walter goes on to present some lessons that can be learned by the European reformers from the Swiss experience. For instance, he points out the need for a well-balanced mixture of academics and practitioners devising the new procedural rules.

2. Harmonization: What?

This section of the book contains articles dealing with the harmonization of certain areas from the "fringes" of civil procedure. Wendy Kennett discusses the particularly difficult harmonization of the enforcement of civil judgments. She addresses several obstacles to improving cross-border enforcement in the EU such as the differences in the types of enforceable instruments, particularly the highly differing regulations concerning enforcement. Kennett distinguishes between jurisdictions in which enforcement is entrusted solely to agents who specialize in that function (like the French huissier de justice) and other jurisdictions in which control over enforcement is more diffuse, though the process is channelled to a greater or lesser extent through the courts (as is the case in Germany). Also, she points to the big differences in powers Member States have conferred on enforcement agents in the search for information and assets. Critical points include the right to enter the debtor's premises and data privacy considerations. In conclusion, Kennett cautions that enforcement laws are deeply embedded in national histories and

---

21 For a presentation of the preliminary draft *see* Sutter-Somm, 7 ZEITSCHRIFT FÜR ZIVILPROZEß INTERNATIONAL 369 (2002).

cultures, making them potentially resistant to change. She argues nevertheless that in the light of the free movement of debtors and their assets common targets should be set for the Member States' enforcement systems.

Rolf Stürner's general report on summary proceedings covers a wide range of procedural instruments aimed at expediting protection and enforcement of substantive rights. At first, Stürner turns to the common European constitutional and historical background of the matter. He puts forward that the provision of a minimum standard of summary proceedings is required by Art. 6(1) of the European Convention on Human Rights and by the constitutional traditions of the EU Member States. Also, he points out the common historical roots of summary proceedings across the EU. It is therefore not surprising that the following comparative evaluation yields more similarities than differences between the Member States' regulations. All Member States provide provisional measures as well as expedited proceedings to obtain a regular judgment. Stürner discusses significant national and regional peculiarities in-depth. Finally, from these comparative observations conclusions are drawn whether harmonization in a certain area is needed, and which solution should be preferred. Stürner recommends, inter alia, to introduce uniform orders for payment on application by the creditor without special requirements. Also, EU-wide preliminary attachment of assets (rather than English-style freezing injunctions) should be granted by courts in all Member States when necessary for the protection of the execution of money judgments.

Neil Andrews presents a model for a uniform European protective order that would be recognized and enforced by courts across the EU. The enivsaged order is of a drastic nature. The respondent is prevented from dissipating his assets, regardless of the jurisdiction in which they are located. He is also forced to disclose such assets. Furthermore, Andrews puts forward an ancillary search order for the preservation of vital evidence. These orders can be granted ex parte and before the commencement of the main civil proceedings. Their effects are solely in personam; no proprietary or possessory interests in the respondent's assets are conferred. Also, informed non-parties (mostly banks) must refrain from acting inconsistently with the order. In his concluding remarks, Andrews concedes that his model is much influenced by the English freezing injunctions and civil search orders. He argues, however, that the (continental) solution proposed by Stürner in his general report, which gives the creditor real security over specified assets,[22] would interfere with the order of security rights in commercial dealings and confer unwarranted benefits on the applicant creditor. Unfortunately, further comparative observations are lacking.

The article by Burkhard Hess deals with fast-track debt collection, i.e., expedited procedures that enable a creditor to quickly obtain an enforceable title. The court, on application of the creditor, orders the debtor ex parte to either dispute the claim or pay the sum of money fixed in the order. The creditor receives an enforceable title unless the debtor objects within a certain amount of time. Hess points out that regulations across the EU differ widely, even though Member States are required by European legislation to ensure the possibility of obtaining an enforceable title within a period of 90 days.[23] For instance,

---

22 E.g., the German Arrest and subsequent attachment of specified assets, §§ 916–934 German Code of Civil Procedure.

23 Directive 2000/35/EC of the European Parliament and of the Council of 29 June 2000 on combating late payment in commercial transactions, Art. 5: "Member States shall ensure that an enforceable title can be obtained, irrespective of the amount of the debt, normally within 90 calendar days of the lodging of the creditor's action or application ..., provided that the debt or aspects of the procedure are not disputed. ...". Further Community action is foreseeable, compare the *Commission Green Paper on a European Order for Payment Procedure and on Measures to Simplify and Speed Up Small Claims Litigation*, COM (2002) 746 final.

specific proceedings resulting in an order for payment are not available in all Member States. In some jurisdictions, but not in others, the applicant is required to substantiate the claim or supply supporting documentary evidence. Hess therefore argues that a practical need exists for a uniform procedure to easily collect money debts. He goes on to examine the scope of the Community competences. He explains that Art. 95 EC allows only the setting of minimum standards, while Art. 65(c) EC requires cross-border implications, so that purely national proceedings are not covered. Hess also evaluates the order for payment procedure (Art. 11) of the Storme working group's model code of civil procedure.[24] While affirming the general viability of the proposed rules, he criticizes that the applicant needs to supply supporting documents. This obligation would make it impossible to streamline the procedure via electronic data processing.

Harald Koch discusses the prospects of harmonizing complex litigation in the European Union. He puts forward two reasons for pursuing harmonization: prevention of forum shopping and effective realization of certain important substantive Community policies like environmental and consumer protection (Art. 3(l) and (t) EC). Koch makes a basic distinction between suits brought by associations in the public interest, which are the prevailing type of suits in Continental Europe, and group actions in the interest of the group members. He goes on to point out that the availability of complex and collective procedures is generally desirable, because they increase the efficiency of the judicial system and serve as a means to effectively enforce substantive law. Potential for misuse – especially in the case of group actions – would have to be countered by judicial supervision of the proceedings. Finally, Koch proposes certain steps towards harmonization. The first step would be to supplement the existing EC Directive on injunctions for the protection of consumers' interests[25] by making infringements upon all legal norms of European origin actionable, and by allowing associations and other collective interest representatives to not only seek injunctive relief, but to sue for damages, too.

3. Harmonization: How?

Peter Gilles presents ten theses on the process called Europeanization of procedural law.[26] At first, he points out the difficulty of the subject by noting that no theory of Europeanization exists, and that the meaning of terms like harmonization or approximation remains unclear. He also criticizes a widespread tendency to address procedural details rather than fundamental issues of civil procedure.[27] Instead, he advocates to focus on fundamental procedural principles and common European constitutional requirements first, in order to gain a general framework for procedural approximation or unification. Furthermore, Gilles expresses strong reservations concerning the general feasibility of harmonizing or approximating the national laws. Unification, on the other hand, would enable a search for the best solution instead of choosing some sort of middle course that is somehow perceived to be agreeable, because it does not deviate too much from the Member States' current rules.

---

24 See RAPPROCHEMENT, *supra* note 10.
25 Directive 1998/27/EC of the European Parliament and of the Council of 19 May 1998 on injunctions for the protection of consumers' interests.
26 See also Gilles, 7 ZEITSCHRIFT FÜR ZIVILPROZEß INTERNATIONAL 3 (2002).
27 *Compare* the huge international joint project by the American Law Institute and Unidroit on transnational procedure: in the beginning, the participants only endeavored to devise detailed rules, but the scope was later extended to include principles as well; for the current version *see* ALI/Unidroit, Principles and Rules of Transnational Civil Procedure, Council Draft No. 2 of 29 September 2003, available at http://www.ali.org/ali/TransCP-CD2.pdf. For a detailed presentation of the project *see* the contributions to the UNIFORM LAW REVIEW 739–1033 (2001–4).

In sum, the book contains the views of some of Europe's leading proceduralists on the ongoing Europeanization of civil procedure. Their works demonstrate the willingness to participate in the creation of the European area of freedom, security and justice rather than leaving everything up to the European Commission. This makes one hope that the process will lead to an overall improvement of civil procedure in Europe. Also, civil procedure might be spared from the Community legislation-induced chaos that has ensued in certain areas of private and public substantive law.[28]

European Corporate Law and National Divergences: The Case of Takeover Regulation[*]

Joseph A. McCahery et al. (eds.): *Corporate Governance Regimes: Convergence and Diversity* (Oxford, New York: Oxford University Press, 2002, 696 pp.)
Christin M. Forstinger: *Takeover Law in the EU and the USA: A Comparative Analysis* (European Monographs 41) (The Hague, London, New York: Kluwer Law International, 2002, 182 pp.)
Jennifer Payne (ed.): *Takeovers in English and German Law* (Oxford, Portland, OR: Hart Publishing, 2002, 183 pp.)

Peer Zumbansen[**]

A. Introduction

When the European Parliament ("EP") failed to pass the carefully drafted thirteenth Directive related to Corporate Takeovers in Europe ("Takeover Directive")[1] in July 2001,[2]

---

28 *See* the Commission's Action Plan "A More Coherent European Contract Law" at 8, COM (2003) 68 final.

[*] This review was previously published in 3 WASH. U. GLOBAL STUD. L. REV. 867 (2004). The reviewer is grateful to the *Washington University Global Studies Law Review* for the permission to reprint this review.
[**] Osgoode Hall Law School, York University, Toronto, Canada. Canada Research Chair in the Transnational and Comparative Law of Corporate Governance. Director of the Comparative Research in Law & Political Economy Network (CLPE). Dr. Peer Zumbansen was a post-doctoral lecturer at the University of Frankfurt Law School. He holds degrees in law from the University of Frankfurt, the Université de Paris X Nanterre, and Harvard Law School, as well as a Ph.D. from Frankfurt. After a year-long research fellowship as a Jean Monnet Fellow at the European University Institute in Florence (2001–2002), he was a visiting professor at the University of Idaho College of Law in the Fall of 2003 and at Osgoode Hall Law School, York University, Toronto in Spring 2004. In April 2004, Dr. Zumbansen passed the Habilitation (full-professor qualification) at the University of Frankfurt Law School and took a Canada Research Chair for the Transnational and Comparative Law of Corporate Governance at Osgoode Hall Law School, York University, Toronto, Canada in the Fall of 2004. He is the co-founder and co-editor in chief of GERMAN LAW JOURNAL, at http://www.germanlawjournal.com.
1 *See* Christian Kirchner & Richard W. Painter, *Takeover Defenses under Delaware Law, the Proposed Thirteenth EU Directive and the New German Takeover Law: Comparison and Recommendations for Reform*, 50 AM. J. COMP. L. 451, 455–56 (2002) (a concise account of the legislative history of the Directive dating back to the 1974 "Pennington Report" (Doc XI/56/74) and the first Commission Proposal of 1989).
2 *See* Press Release, European Commission, Commission Regrets Rejection of Takeovers Directive by the European Parliament (July 4, 2001), *available at* http://europa.eu.int/comm/internal_market/en/company/company/news/01-943.htm (last visited Mar. 27, 2004). In this communication, the EU Internal Market Commissioner, Frits Bolkestein, said,

> I am very disappointed that the European Parliament has not been able to ratify the agreement approved by its delegation last month, despite the tremendous efforts made by the Commission

the European Commission ("Commission") immediately set out to overcome the obstacles that had ultimately prevented the Directive from passing.[3] On September 4, 2001, precisely two months after the Directive was defeated in the EP,[4] the Commission established the High Level Group of Company Law Experts ("Expert Group"). The Expert Group was charged with recording and synthesizing the divergent takeover regimes and regulatory approaches of the Member States as a first step[5] in the preparaton of a new proposal.[6] In light of the exhaustive diplomatic and legislative struggles leading up to the 2001 vote in the EP, in particular with regard to the question of how a European takeover

> and the Council to meet the Parliament's concerns. Twelve years of work have been wasted by today's decision. This vote represents an important setback for achieving the targets agreed by the EU's Heads of State and Government in Lisbon of realising an integrated European capital market by 2005 and making Europe the most competitive economy in the world by 2010. ... It is tragic to see how Europe's broader interests can be frustrated by certain narrow interests.

Id.

3 See Janet Dine, *The Framework Thirteenth Directive on Takeovers – The Protection of Shareholders and the Basis of Judicial Review of the Panel*, in DEVELOPMENTS IN EUROPEAN COMPANY LAW 201 (Barry A.K. Rider & Mads Andenas eds., 1996); Klaus-Heiner Lehne, *Die 13. Richtlinie auf dem Gebiet des Gesellschaftsrechts betreffend Übernahmeangebote – gescheitert, aber dennoch richtungweisend für das künftige europäische Übernahmerecht [The Thirteenth Directive in the Field of Corporate Law concerning Acceptance Failed, but leads in the right direction for the future of European Acceptance]*, in WpÜG: DAS WERTPAPIERERWERBS- UND ÜBERNAHMEGESETZ MIT ÜBERNAHMEKODEX UND CITY CODE [GERMAN TAKEOVER STATUTE WITH TAKEOVER CODE AND CITY CODE] 33 (Heribert Hirte ed., 2002) [hereinafter WpÜG] (detailing the legislative history); Sorika Pluskat, *Das Scheitern der europäischen Übernahmerichtlinie [The Failure of the European Takeover Directive]*, 55 WERTPAPIERMITTEILUNGEN 1937 (2001).

4 This failure attains almost tragic dimensions when considered in light of speculation that, had it not been for the late arrival of two British European parliamentarians, the Directive might actually have been passed on that occasion. See, e.g., Helen J. Callaghan, *Paper for the 15th Annual Meeting of the Society for the Advancement of Socio-Economics, Aix-en-Provence, Battle of the Systems of Multi-Level Game? Domestic Sources of Anglo-German Quarrels over EU Takeover Law and Worker Consultation* (June 26–28, 2003), available at http://www.sase.org/conf2003/papers/callaghan_helen.pdf (last visited Feb. 1, 2004) (describing the effect that the Directive would have had on Germany's takeover law, an effect that Germany had tried to avoid at all costs). But see Kirchner & Painter, *supra* note 1, at 461. The authors argue that, had it not been for the European Court of Justice (ECJ) Advocate General's (AG) statement made two days before the vote in the EP, the Directive would have passed the EP. Id. The AG's role is to assess the legal merits of a case before the ECJ; the ECJ often then follows his assessment. The statement was made with regard to the pending case against Spain, Portugal and France concerning so-called "Golden Shares." The AG criticized Golden Shares because he claimed that they would give the prior government owner of recently privatized state enterprises, in which the government continues to hold securities, veto rights in the event of a takeover attempt. Id. This announcement reinforced concerns that some Member States, including Germany, would be at a competitive disadvantage against France and the other Member States that permit Golden Shares. "The timing of this announcement, perhaps more than anything, sealed the fate of the Thirteenth Directive in Parliament." Id. For an insightful assessment of the Court's three "Golden Shares" decisions of June 4, 2003, see Johannes Adolff, *Turn of the Tide? The "Golden Share" Judgments of the European Court of Justice and the Liberalization of the European Capital Markets*, 3 GERMAN LAW JOURNAL NO. 8 (Aug. 1, 2002), available at http:// www.germanlawjournal.com/article.php?id=170 (last visited Mar. 27, 2004). The ECJ ruled in two other cases involving "Golden Shares." See Case C-463-00, Commission v. Kingdom of Spain, 2003 O.J. (C 158) 3; Case C-98/01, Commission v. United Kingdom of Great Britain and N. Ireland, 2003 O.J. (C 158) 4. Previously, the Commission had sent a formal request to the German government to "provide certain justifications" for its "Volkswagen law," which gives Volkswagen's home state of Lower Saxony favorable share voting rights in the publicly held Volkswagen AG (Mar. 19, 2003).

5 See Report of the High Level Group of Company Law Experts on Issues Related to Takeovers, (Jan. 10, 2002), available at http:// europa.eu.int/comm/internal_market/en/company/company/news/hlg01-2002.pdf (last visited Mar. 27, 2004).

6 In addition, the Expert Group, under its chairman, Jaap Winter, was asked to provide the Commission with "independent advice ... on key priorities for modernizing company law in the European Union." Id. at 1. See *The High Level Group of Company Law Experts, A Modern Regulatory Approach for Company Law in Europe* (Nov. 4, 2002), available at http://europa.eu.int/comm/internal_ market/en/company/company/modern/consult/report_en.pdf (last visited Mar. 27, 2004).

regime could ensure a level playing field among Member States with very different corporate law and securities regulation systems,[7] the Expert Group's report on takeover law was greatly anticipated. Shortly after its presentation on January 10, 2002, the Expert Group initiated a public consultation procedure regarding the Group's second task. This procedure was designed to foster well-informed discussion among interested parties from all Member States regarding a wide range of corporate law issues. The discussions would not be limited exclusively to takeover regulation.[8]

The Commission presented its second draft of the Takeover Directive on October 2, 2002.[9] The second draft adopted many of the Expert Group's proposals, including a prohibition against any defensive measures[10] taken by management without prior shareholder approval,[11] and regulation of mandatory bids to make all shareholders a bid at an equitable price after the bidders have obtained a qualifying amount of shares.[12] The latter regulation reflects a central point of divergence between Continental and Anglo-American approaches to takeover regulation.[13] In addition, the Commission adopted the proposals made by both the Expert Group and the European Parliament with regard to including an "equitable price" requirement[14] and regulating "squeeze-out"[15] and "sell-out" procedures.[16] Finally, the draft proposal established an obligation upon the management of both the bidder and the target corporation to inform employees about a bid. The draft proposal explicitly referred to Member State laws and previous EC Directives regarding worker participation and involvement.[17] It invoked these rules

---

7 Other issues of great concern included the controversial requirement of a mandatory offer by the control-acquiring bidder to all shareholders, the disclosure of all conditions of the bid, the right of corporate management to adopt defensive measures against a hostile bid ("neutrality rule"), the participation of non-shareholder stakeholders in the decision-making process in a takeover situation, and squeeze-out and sell-out rights in situations where the bidder or those acting in concert therewith have acquired the controlling percentage of voting rights in the company. For a list of disputed issues, *see* Kirchner & Painter, *supra* note 1, at 458. For a comprehensive history and discussion of the Commission's attempts to develop a European takeover regime, *see* Theodor Baums, *Zur Harmonisierung des Rechts der Unternehmensübernahmen in der EG [Harmonizing Takeover Law in the EU]*, Universität Osnabrück, Institut für Handels- und Wirtschaftsrecht, Working Papers 03/95 (1995), *available at* http://www.jura.uni-osnabrueck.de/institut/hwr/PDF/a0395.pdf (last visited Feb. 1, 2004) [hereafter Baums, *Zur Harmonisierung*].

8 *See* Press Release, European Commission, *A Modern Regulatory Framework for Company Law in Europe: A Consultative Document of the High Level Group of Company Law Experts* (Apr. 25, 2002), *available at* http://europa.eu.int/rapid/start/cgi/guesten.ksh?p_action.gettxt=gt&doc=IP/02/625|0|RAPID&lg=EN&display= (last visited Feb. 1, 2004).

9 *See Commission Proposal for a Directive of the European Parliament and Council on Takeover Bids*, COM (2002) 534 final (Oct. 2, 2002), *available at* http://europa.eu.int/eur-lex/en/com/pdf/2002/com2002_0534en01.pdf (last visited Mar. 27, 2004) [hereinafter Draft Proposal].

10 For a brief description of the most common anti-takeover defensive measures, *see* Kirchner & Painter, *supra* note 1, at 452.

11 *See* Draft Proposal, *supra* note 9, at art. 9.

12 *See* Draft Proposal, *supra* note 9, at art. 5.

13 *See* Paul Davies, *The Notion of Equality in European Takeover Regulation*, *in* TAKEOVERS IN ENGLISH AND GERMAN LAW 9 (Jennifer Payne ed., 2002).

14 In the event that the bidder and those acting in concert with him acquire a controlling percentage of the Corporation's voting shares, the minority shareholders must be offered an equitable price for their shares. Draft Proposal, *supra* note 9, art.5(1). The equitable price of a share is defined as the highest price paid for such a share by the same offeror (or those acting in concert with him) over a period between six and twelve months prior to the bid. *Id.* art. 5(4).

15 A squeeze-out right is the bidder's right, after having made a bid to all holders of the target company for all of their securities, to require the holders of the remaining securities to sell the bidder those shares at a fair price. *Id.* art. 14.

16 A sell-out right is the right of a minority shareholder to require the bidder, after a bid to all shareholders, to buy the remaining securities from the minority shareholder at a fair price. *Id.* art. 15.

17 *See* Council Directive 94/45/EC, 1994 O.J. (L 254) 64 (Works Councils); Council Directive 98/59/EC, 1998 (L 225) 16 (Collective Redundancies); Directive 2002/14/EC, 2002 O.J. (L 80) 29 (Employee Information and Consultation), *available at* http://europa.eu.int/eur-lex/en/search/search_lif.html (last visited Feb. 1, 2004).

by requiring employee involvement in deliberations regarding the possible consequences of a takeover.[18]

Altogether, however, the new draft, while clearly influenced by the Expert Group report, did not embrace all of its recommendations.[19] This is particularly true of the "breakthrough rule" that the report suggested as a means for overcoming the obstacles that previously prevented the Directive from passing.[20] The breakthrough rule,[21] which was a central and defining feature of the Expert Group's proposal, was intended to allow a bidder, upon acquiring a qualifying majority of the target company's stock, to override all existing defensive measures by the target's management, including any differentiation of voting rights. All Member States voiced intense criticism against this rule, which led the Commission to exclude this instrument from its latest draft proposal.[22] The Commission instead adopted a "mini," or "limited" breakthrough rule[23] that blocked the transfer of certain classes of stock and prohibited voting restrictions.[24] In light of the emerging conflict between the Commission and the Expert Group, the EP commissioned Professors Barbara Dauner-Lieb and Marco Lamandini to provide an independent assessment of these regulatory issues in June of 2002. In this assessment, particular emphasis was placed on establishing a level playing field among participating states, despite the diversity of takeover regimes in Europe and differences between Europe and the United States. The report by Dauner-Lieb and Lamandini[25] largely embraced the Expert Group's recommendations. In particular, the report offered a critique of the draft proposal's exclusion of multiple voting rights in the regulatory context of the mini-breakthrough rule.[26]

The last chapter of this exhausting law-making enterprise is the EP's positive vote on the new Directive proposal on December 16, 2003 and the Council's formal vote on the Directive's passage on March 30, 2004. The revised proposal, which was presented on November 27, 2003, surely signified the final attempt for the successful adoption of a Europe-wide takeover regime.[27] The Directive[28] that was signed by the Council and the EP on April 21, 2004, must be adopted by the Member States by 2006. In response to the intensive debates that have gone on over the past few years, the present Directive – in its newly inserted art. 11A – embraces an optional scheme for defensive measures that delegates a number of strategic choices back to the corporate actors themselves.[29] At the same

---

18 See Draft Proposal, *supra* note 9, at 10.
19 A concise outline of the Commission's approach for its new proposal can be found in its "Explanatory Memorandum." *Id.* at 3–5.
20 See Report of the High Level Group of Company Law Experts on Issues Related to Takeover Bids, *supra* note 5, at 4.
21 *Id.*
22 See Erik Berglöf & Mike Burkart, *European Takeover Regulation*, ECON. POL'Y 171, 174 (2003).
23 See Barbara Dauner-Lieb, *Das Tauziehen um die Übernahmerichtlinie – eine Momentaufnahme [The Struggle over the Takeover Directive – A Snapshot]*, DEUTSCHES STEUERRECHT [GERMAN TAX LAW] 555, 556 (2003). See also Dauner-Lieb & Lamandini, *Report to the European Parliament on the Commission's new proposal of a Directive on company law concerning takeover bids*, Study No. IV/2002/06/01 at 7, available at http://www.uni-koeln.de/jur-fak/lbrah/pdf_docs/gutachten_ daunerlieb_lamandini_en.pdf (last visited Mar. 27, 2004) [hereinafter Report to the European Parliament].
24 See Draft Proposal, *supra* note 9, art. 11.
25 See Report to the European Parliament, *supra* note 23.
26 See *id.* at 42–46.
27 Proposal for a Directive of the European Parliament and of the Council on Takeover Bids, available at http://www.jura.uni-duesseldorf.de/dozenten/noack/Texte/Sonstige/TO2003.htm (last visited May 7, 2004).
28 The Directive's text is available at http:// register.consilium.eu.int/pdf/en/03/st15/st15476.en03.pdf (last visited May 7, 2004).
29 See Silja Maul & Danièle Muffat-Jeandet, *Die Übernahmerichtlinie – Inhalt und Umsetzuung in nationales Recht (Teil I), [The Takeover Directive – Contents and Transformation into National Law (Part I)]*, 49 AKTIENGESELLSCHAFT 221, 222 (2004); Silja Maul & Athanasios Kouloridas, *The Takeover Bids Directive*,

time, the Member State can choose to adopt or to reject the much-disputed neutrality rule (art. 9) and the breakthrough rule (art. 11). Companies, it should be noted, are given the freedom to opt into this regime.[30] In light of the quarrels that have accompanied the passage of the Directive, it is still too early to predict exactly how the Member States will react to the Directive in their transformation process.[31] At the same time, its recent adoption appears to give testimony to what insightful observers of the European Integration have coined "reflexive harmonization."[32] Future discussion regarding the implementation of the Directive will reveal the extent to which Member States, as well as political and corporate actors, will take advantage of the potential for creative interpretation and engage in mutual learning throughout the process of transposing the Directive into national law. A brief retrospective into the history of Europe's harmonization program will allow us to better situate the challenges and intricacies that unfolded in the context of the Takeover Directive.

II. The Aspirations and Frustrations of Europe's Harmonization Program

New attempts by the European Commission to pass a European takeover directive must be examined within the context of the instrument's extensive legislative history. In 1974, the Commission requested a report from Robert Pennington[33] that was intended to "review the European takeover landscape and to prepare a first draft of a proposal in respect to takeover bids."[34] Fifteen years later, in 1989, the Commission presented its first draft proposal.[35] Although the Pennington Report failed to cull sufficient Member State support to pursue a Europe-wide installment of takeover rules at that time, the Commission's landmark White Paper of 1985, concerning the completion of the internal market, changed this attitude.[36] The Commission outlined, inter alia, an agenda for the creation of "conditions likely to favour the development of cooperation between undertakings."[37] In the White Paper, the

---

5 GERMAN LAW JOURNAL 355 (2004), *available at* http:// www.germanlawjournal.com/pdf/Vol05No04/ PDF_Vol_05_No_04_355-366_Private_Maul_ Kouloridas.pdf (last visited May 7, 2004).

30 For a concise description of the optional regime, *see* Maul & Kouloridas, *supra* note 29, at 356–59.

31 For an assessment of the need for legislative adaptation of the German Takeover Law, *see* Peter M. Wiesner, *Die neue Übernahmerichtlinie und die Folgen, [The New Takeover Directive and the Consequences]*, ZEITSCHRIFT FÜR WIRTSCHAFTSRECHT (ZIP) 343 (2004); Hartmut Krause, *Die EU-Übernahmerichtlinie – Anpassungsbedarf im Wertpapiererwerbs- und Übernahmegesetz [The EU Takeover Directive – Need for Adaptation in the WpÜG (German Takeover Statute)]*, 59 BETRIEBSBERATER [BB] 113 (2004).

32 *See* Simon Deakin, *Regulatory Competition versus Reflexive Harmonisation in European Company Law*, in REGULATORY COMPETITION AND ECONOMIC INTEGRATION: COMPARATIVE PERSPECTIVES 209 (Daniel C. Esty & Damien Geradin eds., 2001).

33 EC-Commission Doc. XI/56/74. *See* Klaus J. Hopt, *Università degli Studi di Roma – La Sapienza, Centro di studi e ricerche di diritto comparato e straniero [University of Rome – La Sapienza, Center for the Study and Research of Domestic and International]*, COMPANY LAW IN THE EUROPEAN UNION: HARMONIZATION OR SUBSIDIARITY 7 (1998), *available at* http:// w3.uniroma1.it/idc/centro/publications/31hopt.pdf (last visited Mar. 28, 2004).

34 CHRISTIN M. FORSTINGER, TAKEOVER LAW IN THE EU AND THE USA: A COMPARATIVE ANALYSIS 99 (2002).

35 *See* Proposal for a Thirteenth Council Directive on Company Law Concerning Takeover and Other General Bids, 1989 O.J. (C 64) 8.

36 *See Competing in the Internal Market: White Paper from the Commission to the Council of Europe*, COM (1985) 310 final, *available at* http:// europa.eu.int/comm/off/pdf/1985_0310_f_en.pdf (last visited Mar. 28, 2004).

37 *Id.* at 34. The document largely established the legislative approach eventually adopted by the Commission in its 1996 draft proposal. Proposal for a 13th European Parliament and Council Directive on Takeover Bids, 1996 O.J. (C 162) 6. This draft signified a distinctive step away from the full harmonization approach of the takeover regimes in various member states at the European level in favor of the "framework" approach of the Commission. *See* FORSTINGER, *supra* note 34, at 103–08 (providing a careful description of the framework approach taken in the Commission's draft proposal).

Commission alluded to the wide variety of corporate law regimes pertaining to the regulation of takeovers among the Member States. Above all, it envisioned the creation of equal standards with regard to "the information to be given to those concerned, while it would be left to the Member State to devise procedures for monitoring such operations and to designate the authorities to which the powers of supervision were to be assigned."[38] This principled approach, however, was sacrificed in part during the ensuing discussions and proposals for the directive in the years following the White Paper. The Commission, having finally presented its first draft directive in 1989, recognized the need to present a revised proposal as early as 1990,[39] after it received substantial criticism and numerous recommendations from both the European Community's Economic and Social Committee (ECOSOC) and the EP.[40] In response to growing economic pressure felt by Member States during the mid- to late 1980s and the addition of the subsidiarity principle to the EC Treaty via the Maastricht Treaty of 1992 (according to which regulatory competence was deemed to rest with Member States in all fields where regulation had not explicitly been assigned to the European Community[41]), the Commission announced that it would prepare a revised draft proposal for a takeover directive. After numerous delays, this proposal was finally presented to the Council and the EP on February 8, 1996.[42] This revised proposal signified a decisive turning point in what had previously been little more than a tedious and exhausting process for lawmakers and negotiators. The "framework" approach adopted by the Commission in its 1996 proposal contained general principles for a Europe-wide takeover regime that left the Member States substantial latitude for interpretation when converting the Directive into national law. Upon further recommendations from both the ECOSOC and the EP, the Commission adopted an amended proposal in November of 1997.[43] This amended proposal led to a common position that was unanimously accepted by the Council on June 19, 2000[44] and by the Commission on July 26, 2000. This version was a source of furious debate among Member States until it was ultimately defeated in July of 2001.[45]

Until as recently as the autumn of 2003, it was difficult to predict whether and when a new directive would come to pass. The greater economic and socio-political factors, which hardly seem to be captured by the "level playing field" terminology, appeared to have suc-

---

38 *White Paper*, COM (1985) 310 final, *supra* note 36, at 35.
39 *See* 1990 O.J. (C 240); COM (1990) 416 final (explanatory memorandum thereto).
40 *See* Draft proposal, *supra* note 9, at 2 (explanatory memorandum).
41 For a description and critique of the use of the subsidiarity principle with regard to the takeover Directive, *see* Hopt, *supra* note 33, at 9–12 (arguing that both the subsidiarity principle and the framework conception of the Commission's Directive proposals remained too vague and could not, therefore, delineate the boundaries for Community competences); George Bermann, *Taking Subsidiarity Seriously: Federalism the European Community and the United States*, 94 COLUM. L. REV. 331 (1994) (providing a canonical comparative analysis of EU and US federalism and the role played by the subsidiarity principle herein); Patrick R Hugg, *Transnational Convergence: European Union and American Federalism*, 32 CORNELL INT'L L.J. 43, 101 (1998) (asserting that, in spite of the subsidiarity principle, the EU deepened its competences pursuant to the 1997 Amsterdam Treaty); Ernest A. Young, *Protecting Member State Autonomy in the European Union: Some Cautionary Tales from American Federalism*, 77 N.Y.U. L. REV. 1612, 1636 (2002) (describing the introduction of the subsidiarity principle in the Maastricht Treaty as a response to the expansion of community competences and the ECJ's "aggressive promotion of community law").
42 *See* Proposal for a 13th European Parliament, *supra* note 37; COM (1995) 655 final (explanatory memorandum thereto).
43 *See* Amended Proposal for a Thirteenth European Parliament and Council Directive on Company Law Concerning Takeover Bids, 1997 O.J. (C 378); FORTSINGER, *supra* note 34, at 101.
44 2001 O.J. (C 23).
45 *See* Kirchner & Painter, *supra* note 1, at 456. Before the Draft Directive failed to gain parliamentary approval on July 4, 2001, the Conciliation Committee had carefully, and with much devotion, crafted an agreement on June 6, 2001, that led to the previously mentioned Common Position of June 19, 2000.

cessfully delayed, or even buried, all further attempts at a takeover directive that would pursue an agenda as ambitious as the Commission's latest Proposal. Now, in May 2004, it has become obvious that the Italian proposal for an option model,[46] while immediately and sternly criticized by Internal Market Commissioner Frits Bolkestein,[47] did eventually open new avenues for passing a takeover directive. With the Directive finally passed by the EP, and adopted and signed by the Council in April 2004, the debate over its merits, nevertheless, appears to be far from closed. Against this background, to write or edit a book on takeover law is truly a courageous undertaking. It is also this background, however, against which we can assess a number of recent publications dealing with takeover law in particular, and with European regulatory competition in general.

III. Writing on a Moving Target

Of the three books herein reviewed,[48] two present comparative assessments, one between the UK and Germany, and the other between the US and the EU. The third book assembles what is bound to become a classical collection of major writings on the continuing debate over the convergence or divergence of corporate governance systems.[49] All three volumes appeared shortly after the directive was defeated in the EP. Unfortunately, there was too little temporal distance to include all ensuing and ongoing discussions sparked by that event. Allowing more time to lapse between the directive's defeat and the publication of these volumes, however, would have had little, if any, influence on the texts. These works, particularly the volumes by Payne and Forstinger, attempt to provide a greater picture of takeover regulation by including domestic, international, and comparative perspec-

---

46 See Gerard Hertig & Joseph McCahery, *Towards a Pro-Choice EU-Takeover Bids Directive*, Ctr. for Eur. Pol'y Stud. (Jan. 2004), *available at* http://www.ceps.be/Article.php?article_id=131& (last visited Mar. 28, 2004).

47 "A particular source of disappointment is the way in which the takeovers Directive has fallen victim to horsetrading and unholy alliances of convenience related to totally extraneous issues." Furthermore,

> The Competitiveness Council says that it wants to be seen to be taking decisions. In all sincerity, I have to say that if the Council continues to take decisions like this one, the European Union will never reach its target of becoming the most competitive economy in the world by 2010. On this issue, we have actually gone a long way in reverse gear since the Council endorsed the previous takeovers Directive in June 2001, with 14 Member States in favour.

Memo/03/245, European Commission, Results of the Competitiveness Council of Ministers, (Nov. 28, 2003), *available at* http:// www.europa.eu.int/rapid/start/cgi/guesten.ksh?p_ action.gettxt=gt&doc= MEMO/03/245|0|AGED&lg=EN&display= (last visited Mar. 30, 2004).

48 CORPORATE GOVERNANCE REGIMES: CONVERGENCE AND DIVERSITY (Joseph A. McCahery et al. eds., 2002); FORSTINGER, *supra* note 34; TAKEOVERS IN ENGLISH AND GERMAN LAW, *supra* note 13.

49 See CORPORATE GOVERNANCE REGIMES, *supra* note 48, at Pt. I. For an earlier landmark collection of papers in this relatively young debate, *see* COMPARATIVE CORPORATE GOVERNANCE – STATE OF THE ART AND EMERGING RESEARCH (Klaus J. Hopt et al. eds., 1998); Brian R. Cheffins, *Current Trends in Corporate Governance: Going from London to Milan via Toronto*, 10 DUKE J. COMP. & INT'L L. 5 (1999) [hereinafter Cheffins, Current Trends]; Ronald J. Gilson, *Globalizing Corporate Governance: Convergence of Form or Function?*, 49 AM. J. COMP. L. 329 (2001); Jeffrey N. Gordon, *Pathways to Corporate Governance? Two Steps on the Road to Shareholder Capitalism in Germany*, 5 COLUM. J. EUR. L. 219 (1999) [hereinafter Gordon, *Pathways*]; Jennifer Hill, *Introduction: Comparative Corporate Governance and Takeovers*, 24 SYDNEY L. REV. 319 (2002); Katharina Pistor et al., *The Evolution of Corporate Law: A Cross Country Comparison*, 23 U. PA. J. INT'L ECON. L. 791 (2002); Edward Rock, *America's Shifting Fascination with Comparative Corporate Governance*, 74 WASH. U. L.Q. 367 (1996); Mark J. Roe, *Some Differences in Corporate Structure in Germany, Japan, and the United States*, 102 YALE L.J. 1927 (1993) [hereinafter Roe, *Some Differences*]; Detlev Vagts, *Reforming the "Modern Corporation": Perspectives from the German*, 80 HARV. L. REV. 23 (1966); Mark D. West, *The Puzzling Divergence of Corporate Law: Evidence and Explanations from Japan and the United States*, 150 U. PA. L. REV. 527 (2001).

tives. The juxtaposition of these dimensions has proven pivotal to the discussions and inquiries of both the last decade and previous decades.[50] Amidst the overwhelming amount of recent scholarship on comparative corporate governance in general,[51] and takeovers in particular,[52] these three volumes neither claim nor assume a position as proverbial leader of the pack. The host of regulatory, economic, political, historical, and cultural issues connected in one way or another with takeover regulation is so diverse that a single publication could rarely leave a reader completely satisfied.[53] The books under review, however, do provide us with a wide array of valuable insights into the pressing issues related to takeovers. This ultimately makes all of them very timely, interesting, and inspiring reading.

The comparative perspective on English and German takeover laws, originally assembled by Jennifer Payne for a workshop in Oxford in September of 2001, unfolds in a particularly useful manner. Despite the drastic differences between the structural economic foundations of the two countries, hardly any other country's takeover laws have left as significant an imprint on Germany's takeover legislation over the years as those of the United Kingdom.[54] Germany has recently undergone a veritable tour de force with regard to adapting both its securities and corporate law to the radical pressures of globalized capital markets.[55] Germany continues to find itself under conflicting pressures, as market players and the government undertake substantial efforts to bring into line Germany's notoriously dense network of closely-held corporations, strong cross-holdings among major industrial players and financial institutions. German stock corporations' two-tiered board of managers and supervisors are also to be brought in line with the capital market demands of international investors.[56] The conversion from bank-centered, long-term financing

---

50 See RICHARD BUXBAUM & KLAUS J. HOPT, LEGAL HARMONIZATION AND THE BUSINESS ENTERPRISE (1988).
51 See Bolkstein, *supra* note 47; John W. Cioffi, *State of the Art: A Review Essay on Comparative Corporate Governance: The State of the Art and Emerging Research*, 48 AM. J. COMP. L. 501 (2000). Another insightful analysis with comparative views on France and Germany is provided in Mary O'Sullivan, *The Political Economy of Comparative Corporate Governance*, 10 REV. INT'L POL. ECON. 23 (2003).
52 See John W. Cioffi, *Restructuring "Germany Inc.": The Politics of Corporate Governance Reform in Germany and the European Union*, 24 L. & POL'Y 355 (2002) [hereinafter Cioffi, *Restructuring "Germany Inc."*]; Simon Deakin & Giles Slinger, *Hostile Takeovers, Corporate Law, and the Theory of the Firm*, 24 J. L. & SOC'Y 124 (1997) (concise analysis and comparative approach to takeover law in Europe, with particular emphasis on the United Kingdom, the United States, and Germany).
53 For different methods for exploring these backgrounds, *see* MARK J. ROE, POLITICAL DETERMINANTS OF CORPORATE GOVERNANCE: POLITICAL CONTEXT, CORPORATE IMPACT (2003); Roe, *Some Differences, supra* note 49. Much of the "Varieties of Capitalism" literature has been devoted to the exploration of comparative corporate governance systems, with particular emphasis on the historical trajectories and structural conditions of corporate governance systems. *See* Sigurt Vitols, *Varieties of Corporate Governance: Comparing Germany and the UK*, *in* VARIETIES OF CAPITALISM: THE INSTITUTIONAL FOUNDATIONS OF COMPARATIVE ADVANTAGE 337 (Peter A. Hall & David Soskice eds., 2001). For insightful approaches that reach beyond the "Varieties of Capitalism" perspectives on "comparative institutional advantages," *see* Callaghan, *supra*, note 4; Cioffi, *Restructuring "Germany Inc."*, *supra* note 52.
54 A good comparative view on Germany and the UK is given by Paul L. Davies, *Shareholder Value, Company Law, and Securities Markets Law: A British View*, *in* CAPITAL MARKETS AND COMPANY LAW 261 (Klaus J. Hopt & Eddy Wymeersch eds., 2003); Paul L. Davies, *Struktur der Unternehmensführung in Großbritannien und in Deutschland: Konvergenz oder fortbestehende Divergenz?* [*Structure of Corporate Governance in the UK and Germany: Convergence or Persisting Divergence?*], 30 ZEITSCHRIFT FÜR UNTERNEHMENS- UND GESELLSCHAFTSRECHT 269 (2001); Gregory Jackson, *Comparative Corporate Governance: Sociological Perspectives*, *in* THE POLITICAL ECONOMY OF THE COMPANY 265 (John Parkinson et al. eds, 2000); Vitols, *supra* note 53.
55 *See* Theodor Baums, *Company Law Reform in Germany*, 3 J. CORP. STUD. 181 (2003) [hereinafter Baums, *Company Law Reform*].
56 *See, e.g.*, Klaus J. Hopt, *Takeovers, Secrecy, and Conflicts of Interest: Problems for Boards and Banks*, *in* TAKEOVERS IN ENGLISH AND GERMAN LAW, *supra* note 13, at 33; Thorsten Pötzsch, *Regulatory Structures*, *in* TAKEOVERS IN ENGLISH AND GERMAN LAW, *supra* note 13, at 75; *see also* Klaus J. Hopt, *Common Principles of Corporate Governance in Europe*, *in* CORPORATE GOVERNANCE REGIMES, *supra* note 48, at 176–81 (describing the differences between the one-tiered and two-tiered board systems in Great Britain, the United States, and Germany).

relationships between large German firms and financial institutions to conditions that make Germany attractive to foreign investment has been a lengthy, ongoing struggle. This process has ultimately spurred a fundamental debate over the merits of historically-grown corporate law structures. The British-German comparison taken up by the authors in Payne's collection is remarkably helpful for addressing the structural elements that naturally came under pressure when Germany tackled its system of Rhenish capitalism,[57] most notably through the passage of the Transparency Act in 1998.[58] In light of the ensuing European developments concerning a takeover directive that would eliminate managerial discretion when launching defensive measures against hostile bids and would work toward a European market for corporate control, the passage of the Act now seems like a watershed moment. Meanwhile, it has become clear that the Act exposed German companies to dangers that had not been fully anticipated,[59] by weakening German companies' defenses against takeover bids. Takeover bids were largely unknown in Germany until recently. The headline-making takeover of the German industrial giant Mannesmann by the British Telecommunications firm Vodafone in 1999–2000[60] was a wake-up call for German lawmakers, which forced them to seriously reconsider the future avenues they would utilize to restructure German corporate and securities law. Realistic methods had to be assessed in light of both an increased demand by German companies for foreign capital, as well as widespread fear surrounding the replacement of Germany's long-tested forms of internal control of company boards through the supervisory board complemented with various, market-based forms of outside control through the stock market.[61] An intimate American observer of German corporate governance, Jeffrey Gordon, recently observed:

> In the years that the 13th Directive was debated, Germany moved from a closed to a more open system of corporate control; many of its extra-board barriers came down. This took place through significant corporate law changes, for example, the end of capped voting and new limitations on bank exercise of customer proxies. Also important was a tax law change, the phase out in January 2002 of the capital gains tax on the sale of corporate shareholdings, that would eliminate the financial lock-in of corporate cross-shareholdings. There were also ownership structure changes that produced over the 1990s a significant increase in the number of firms with dispersed ownership without a large blockholder. … Germany had opened itself to the market for corporate control to a much greater extent than its EU partners, except for the UK, and, not unreasonably in my view, was concerned about potential harms from economic nationalism potentiated by an incompletely liberalized cross-border regime.[62]

---

57 *See* MICHEL ALBERT, CAPITALISME CONTRE CAPITALISME [CAPITALISM VS. CAPITALISM] (1991) (classical assessment of so-called "Rhenish capitalism").
58 Gesetz zur Kontrolle und Transparenz im Unternehmensbereich [Law Regarding Corporate Control and Transparency] Apr. 27, 1998, BGBl. I at 786.
59 *See* Cioffi, *Restructuring "Germany, Inc."*, *supra* note 52 (careful reconstruction of the political process leading up to the Transparency Act and the German government's attempts to re-establish protective walls in negotiating the European Takeover Directive).
60 *See* Martin Höpner & Gregory Jackson, *Entsteht ein Markt für Unternehmenskontrolle? Der Fall Mannesmann [Is There a Market for Corporate Control? The Case of Mannesmann]*, *in* ALLE MACHT DEM MARKT? STUDIEN ZUR ABWICKLUNG DER DEUTSCHLAND AG [ALL POWER TO THE MARKET? STUDIES OF GROWTH IN GERMAN CORPORATIONS] 147 (Wolfgang Streeck & Martin Höpner eds., 2003),
61 *See* Jeffrey N. Gordon, *An American Perspective on the New German Anti-Takeover Law*, 12 DIE AKTIENGESELLSCHAFT, at 4 (Dec. 2002), *available at* http://ssrn.com/abstract=336420 [hereinafter Gordon, *An American Perspective*]. The different ownership and control structures of American, English, German, and other European companies is described in great detail in FORSTINGER, *supra* note 34, at 48–56.
62 Gordon, *An American Perspective*, *supra* note 61, at 4. For an assessment of the changed conditions of the role of banks in German companies, *see* Hopt, *Common Principles of Corporate Governance in Europe?*, *in* CORPORATE GOVERNANCE REGIMES, *supra* note 48, at 186–88; Peter O. Mülbert, *Bank Equity Holdings in Non-Financial Firms and Corporate Governance: The Case of German Universal Banks*, *in* COMPARATIVE CORPORATE GOVERNANCE, *supra* note 48, at 445.

IV. Comparative Perspectives on Lawmaking

These events clearly show that an ongoing comparative dialogue is needed.[63] At the beginning of his presentation at the 2001 workshop in Oxford, Klaus Hopt remarked on the irony of a German corporate law scholar speaking in England about takeover law.[64] While Germany had not historically experienced many takeovers, England's experience with both takeovers and takeover regulation was very rich. The City Code on Takeovers and Mergers, adopted as a self-regulatory instrument in 1992, served as a primary model for Germany's first attempt to create a takeover code in 1996: the *Übernahmekodex*.[65] Unfortunately, the Code's full regulatory potential was never realized because many large companies did not adhere to it. A remarkable development later ensued: German lawmakers prepared a legislative takeover statute in a climate characterized by both a widespread belief that such a statute was indeed needed and a deep-rooted skepticism about its possible regulatory scope. This development is concisely depicted in Hopt's chapter in Payne's collection.[66] Corporations in Germany had come under pressure as a result of the developments described above and, in the meanwhile, the legislature resumed active engagement in conceptualizing and preparing a federal takeover statute in 1997, twenty-two years after its first attempts in 1975.[67] One of the most striking developments that followed the European Takeover Directive's defeat in the summer of 2001 was the passage of a national takeover statute by the German parliament during December of that year, taking effect on January 1, 2002.[68] This statute, the scope of which is well worth a number of subsequent discussions among the authors of the volumes considered here, has inspired substantial commentary, both critical and affirmative.[69] Rendering the story of European takeover law

---

63 See Cheffins, *Current Trends*, supra note 49, at 5–6.

> The topic should not be studied in isolation within any one country. Instead, corporate governance is becoming an important issue in all industrial economies, and students of the topic need to be aware of what is occurring outside their respective countries. As trade barriers fall, markets expand, information flows improve, and restrictions on investment disappear, it will become progressively easier for investors of one country to invest in corporations in another. Movement towards a worldwide capital market could in turn have a substantial impact on corporate governance in individual countries. In a world with intense competition for global savings, sophisticated investors will be attracted to jurisdictions in which investment structures serve shareholders' interests. Since the attractiveness of a particular locality will depend on its system of corporate governance, local norms may be adjusted to make domestic markets more accommodating to global trends.

Id. (footnotes omitted).

64 TAKEOVERS IN ENGLISH AND GERMAN LAW, supra note 13, at 3. "To talk in England about takeovers and takeover regulation is, to quote the Romans, 'carrying owls to Athens.'" *Id.*

65 See Patrick Drayton, *Regulatory Structures*, in TAKEOVERS IN ENGLISH AND GERMAN LAW, supra note 13, at 65 (concise assessment of the Takeover Code and its application to the Takeover Panel, the Financial Services Authority, and the courts); Tobias A. Heinrich, *Bedeutung und Regelungsprogramm des englischen City Code und der Rules Governing Substantial Acquisitions of Shares [Meaning and Regulations of the English City Code and the Rules Governing Substantial Acquisitions of Shares]*, in WPÜG, supra note 3, at 45.

66 TAKEOVERS IN ENGLISH AND GERMAN LAW, supra note 13, at 33.

67 See Theodor Baums, *Vorschlag eines Gesetzes zu öffentlichen Übernahmeangeboten [Proposal for a Public Take-Over Bids Law]*, ZEITSCHRIFT FÜR WIRTSCHAFTSRECHT (ZIP) 1310 (1997).

68 Gesetz zur Regelung von öffentlichen Angeboten zum Erwerb von Wertpapieren und Unternehmensübernahmen [Law to Regulate Public Takeover Offers Through Securities Acquisition and Takeovers], Dec. 20, 2001 (BGBl. I p.3822).

69 See Cioffi, *Restructuring "Germany Inc."*, supra note 52; Gordon, *An American Perspective*, supra note 61; Kirchner & Painter, supra note 1; Frank Wooldridge, *The New German Takeover Act*, 14 EUR. BUS. L. REV. 75 (2003). For comprehensive, practice-oriented commentary published since the Statute's passage, see GERMAN TAKEOVER LAW – A COMMENTARY (Gabriele Apfelbacher et al. eds., 2002); JOHANNES ADOLFF ET AL., PUBLIC COMPANY TAKEOVERS IN GERMANY (2002); WPÜG, supra note 3; RUDOLF NÖRR & ALFRED STIEFENHOFER, TAKEOVER LAW IN GERMANY (2003).

even more open-ended, the German legislature granted the management of target companies the right to adopt defensive measures against hostile bids without prior approval from the general shareholder assembly.[70] This formula reflects the legislature's belief in the competence of management to decide on takeover bids, without the need for authorization from the shareholder assembly.[71]

While the discussion on takeover regulation continues,[72] it is important to bear in mind that an adequate assessment of the regulatory context and the political economy, from which any takeover regulation arises, must be built upon careful consideration of the different historical developments and political decisions that have shaped various regulatory regimes.[73] The works herein reviewed clearly reflect this awareness. This is particularly important in light of the fact that the international debate over convergence and divergence of corporate governance regimes, to which the volume edited by McCahery et al., provides an excellent contribution, develops in at least two other critical dimensions that have yet to achieve sufficient recognition within mainstream scholarship on corporate law. These dimensions concern the changes taking place with regard to the evolution of corporate law through a combination of private norm-generation through different methods of self-regulation and formal legislation.[74] The radical changes to the process of lawmaking, through the emergence of corporate governance codes, codes of conduct, and recommendations of best practice that have recently evolved in Germany[75] and in many other countries,[76] as well

---

70 Takeover Code § 33(1) reads

> After publication of the decision to make a bid until the publication of the result in accordance with § 23 para. 1 sentence 1 no. 2, the management board of the target company may not take any action which could prevent the bid being successful. This does not apply to actions which would also have been taken in the course of due and diligent management of a company which is not affected by a takeover bid, seeking a competitive bid or to actions to which the supervisory board of the target company has agreed.

Takeover Code § 33(1), translated in NÖRR & STIEFENHOFER, *supra* note 69, at 176.

71 *See* Takeover Act § 33(1), translated in NÖRR & STIEFENHOFER, *supra* note 69, at 176 (emphasis added). While a board "may not take any action which could prevent the bid being successful," those actions "which would also have been taken in the course of due and diligent management of a company which is not affected by a takeover bid, seeking a competitive bid" or "which the supervisory board of the target company has agreed" are excluded. *Id.*

72 *See* Gordon, *An American Perspective*, *supra* note 61; Kirchner & Painter, *supra* note 1.

73 *See* Lucian Ayre Bebchuk & Mark J. Roe, *A Theory of Path Dependence in Corporate Governance and Ownership*, 52 STAN. L. REV. 127 (1999); Helmut Kohl, *Path Dependence and German Corporate Law: Some Skeptical Remarks from the Sidelines*, 5 COLUM. J. EUR. L. 189 (1999); Mark J. Roe, *Path Dependence, Political Options and Governance Systems*, in COMPARATIVE CORPORATE GOVERNANCE: ESSAYS AND MATERIALS 165 (Klaus J. Hopt & Eddy Wymeersch eds., 1997).

74 An important example is the German Corporate Governance Code, which was conceptualized and prepared by two government commissions between 2000 and 2002. This code provides corporate actors with a concise account and description of German corporate governance and offers recommendations for corporate behavior. German Corporate Governance Code, http://www.corporate-governance-code.de/index-e.html (last visited Mar. 28, 2004); *see* Theodor Baums, *Interview: Reforming German Corporate Governance: Inside a Law Making Process of a very new nature*, 2 GERMAN LAW JOURNAL NO. 12 (2001), available at http://www.germanlawjournal.com/past_issues.php?id=43 [hereinafter Baums, *Interview*]; Baums, *Company Law Reform*, *supra* note 55.

75 *See* Baums, *Interview*, *supra* note 74; Bericht der Regierungskommission Corporate Governance – Unternehmensführung, Unternehmenskontrolle, Modernisierung des Aktienrechts [*Report of the Government Commission Corporate Governance – Management of Enterprises – Modernization of the Stock Corporation Law*], BRDrucks 14/7515, Aug. 14, 2001; Peer Zumbansen, *The Privatization of Corporate Law? Corporate Governance Codes and Commercial Self-Regulation*, JURIDIKUM 136 (2002).

76 An instructive assessment of the UK is provided in BRIAN R. CHEFFINS, COMPANY LAW, THEORY, STRUCTURE AND OPERATION 346 (1997). For theoretical background, *see* Rob Baggott, *Regulatory Reform in Britain: The Changing Face of Self-Regulation*, 67 PUB. ADMIN. 435 (1989); Julia Black, *Constitutionalising Self-Regulation*, 59 MOD. L. REV. 24 (1996).

as in international institutions,[77] have an important bearing on our future assessment of corporate law from a comparative perspective. The constant and increasing export of established, albeit constantly evolving,[78] systems of law into the unstable and developing markets of post-crisis regions or transformation states[79] sounds an urgent call for reflection. Conducting comparative assessments of the conditions under which export or transplantation of substantive law takes place, as well as of how our law making procedures continue to change and unfold, can provide a valuable insight into how certain models have formed and into their resulting consequences. This contemplative process is particularly important with regard to the export of widespread corporate governance codes, best practice recommendations,[80] and other market-based, self-regulatory frameworks into countries undergoing dramatic restructuring of formerly state-run industries and economic infrastructures.[81]

The second, crucial dimension, ripe for review by contemporary corporate governance scholars, deals with the economic pressure experienced by mature industrial and post-industrial states to develop innovative means for economic and corporate growth. While this need may seem almost painfully commonplace,[82] its realization, in the context of radically interconnected markets and immense pressure on local and transnational spheres of production,[83] constitutes a pivotal issue for contemporary comparative scholars working with corparate governance.[84]

V. Toward a New Paradigm in European Corporate Law

Against this background, this review develops an assessment of the comparative dialogues presented in Payne's collection, as well as the books by Forstinger and the McCahery

---

77 See, e.g., the Corporate Governance Principles issued by the OECD, available at http://www.oecd.org; see also Carolin F. Hillemanns, *UN Norms on the Responsibilities of Transnational Corporations and other Business Enterprises with regard to Human Rights*, 4 GERMAN LAW JOURNAL 1065 (2003) (for a development in international corporate social responsibility), available at http://www.germanlawjournal.com/pdf/Vol04No10/PDF_Vol_04_No_10_1065-1080_European_Hillemanns.pdf (last visited Oct. 4, 2003).
78 See Pistor et al., *supra* note 49.
79 See, e.g., Katharina Pistor, *Of Legal Transplants, Legal Irritants, and Economic Development*, in CORPORATE GOVERNANCE AND CAPITAL FLOWS IN A GLOBAL ECONOMY 347 (Peter Cornelius & Bruce Kogut eds., 2003); Erich Schanze, *Legislating for System Change: The Russian Company Acts of 1995 and 1998*, 156 J. INST. & THEORETICAL ECON. 19 (2000); Frederick Schauer, *Legal Development and the Problem of Systemic Transition*, 13 J. CONTEMP. LEGAL ISSUES 261 (2003).
80 See Country List, European Corporate Governance Institute, at http://www.ecgi.org/codes/all_codes.htm (last visited Mar. 28, 2004).
81 See KERRY RITTICH, RECHARACTERIZING RESTRUCTURING. LAW, DISTRIBUTION AND GENDER IN MARKET REFORM (2002).
82 See *Reinventing Europe: Innovation: With so much of its Industrial Base Aging and Resistant to Change, how can Europe Close the Research and Development Gap with America?*, THE ECONOMIST TECHNOLOGY QUARTERLY, Sept. 6, 2003, at 28, available at 2003 WL 58583964.
83 See J. Rogers Hollingsworth, *New Perspectives on the Spatial Dimensions of Economic Coordination: Tensions Between Globalization and Social Systems of Production*, 5 REV. INT'L POL. ECON. 482 (1998); Kathryn Ibata-Arens, *The Comparative Political Economy of Innovation*, 10 REV. INT'L POL. ECON. 147 (2003).
84 See Mary O'Sullivan, *The Innovative Enterprise and Corporate Governance*, 24 CAMBRIDGE J. ECON. 393 (2000); Walter W. Powell, *The Capitalist Firm in the Twenty-First Century: Emerging Patterns in Western Enterprise*, in THE TWENTY-FIRST-CENTURY FIRM: CHANGING ECONOMIC ORGANIZATION IN INTERNATIONAL PERSPECTIVE 33 (Paul Dimaggio ed., 2001); PEER ZUMBANSEN, INNOVATION UND PFADABHÄNGIGKEIT. DAS RECHT DER UNTERNEHMENSVERFASSUNG IN DER WISSENSGESELLSCHAFT [INNOVATION & PATH-DEPENDENCE. THE CONSTITUTION OF THE FIRM IN THE KNOWLEDGE SOCIETY] (completed book manuscript, University of Frankfurt, forthcoming 2004/2005).

volume. Forstinger presents us with a detailed reconstruction of state-based regulation of corporate law and federal securities regulation in the United States as a means for comparing the American conditions for a market for corporate control with those existing in Europe.[85] Meanwhile, the contributions in the volume edited by McCahery et al. supply a rich collection of insightful, often critical, assessments of the arguments made in the course of international debate over corporate governance. Forstinger's work is well-structured, and her comparative assessment of the development of a market for corporate control and the contrastingly few opportunities for creating an equivalent market in the European Union is quite informative. At the same time, Forstinger does not limit herself to an extensive treatment of the legislative and jurisprudential elements that mark the evolution of both markets. Instead, while descriptive in her treatment of the material used for her study, she leads the reader toward an inspiring outlook on the future development of European takeover regulation. Although Forstinger does not speculate regarding successful passage of the Commission's badly wounded takeover directive in the near future,[86] she has a sound basis for rejection of the notion that "full regulatory competition" will overcome the deadlock.[87]

While conditions ripe for competitive federalism in Europe might still seem unattainable, the European Court of Justice's recent *Inspire Art* ruling on September 30, 2003,[88] as well as those preceding it, namely *Centros* and *Überseering*, might have dramatically altered this situation.[89] These cases go a long way toward resolving the struggle[90] between those

---

85 FORSTINGER, *supra* note 34, at 1 n. 1. *See* William L. Cary, *Federalism and Corporate Law: Reflections Upon Delaware*, 83 YALE L.J. 663 (1974); *contra* ROBERTA ROMANO, THE GENIUS OF AMERICAN CORPORATE LAW (1993); Lucian Ayre Bebchuk, *Federalism and the Corporation: The Desirable Limits on State Competition in Corporate Law*, 105 HARV. L. REV. 1437 (1982); Lucian Ayre Bebchuk & Allen Ferrell, *Federalism and Corporate Law: The Race to Protect Managers from Takeovers*, 99 COLUM L. REV. 1168 (1999); Lucian Ayre Bebchuk & Allen Ferrell, *On Takeover Law and Regulatory Competition*, 57 BUS. LAW. 1047 (2002); David Charny, *Competition among Jurisdictions in Formulating Corporate Rules: An American Perspective on the "Race to the Bottom" in the European Communities*, 32 HARV. INT'L L.J. 423 (1991).

86 *See* FORSTINGER, *supra* note 34, at 154: "The rejection of the amended proposed takeover Directive has diminished a European framework for the regulation of takeovers, at least for the very near future." *Id.*

87 *Id.* at 156. *See also* Baums, *Zur Harmonisierung*, *supra* note 7, at 14; Theodor Baums, *Das Ende der Deutschland AG? Unternehmensrechtsreform in Deutschland [The End of Germany Inc.? Corporate Law Reform in Germany]*, *in* KAPITALMARKT DEUTSCHLAND: ERFOLGE UND ENTWICKLUNGEN [GERMAN CAPITAL MARKET: RESULTS AND CHANGES], White Paper 39 (Deutsche Börse Group ed., 2003).

88 Case C-167/01, Kamer van Koophandel en Fabriken voor Amsterdam v. Inspire Art Ltd., 2003 O.J. (C 275) 10, *available at* http:// europa.eu.int/smartapi/cgi/sga_doc?smartapi!celexapi!prod! CELEXnumdoc&lg= EN&numdoc=62001J0167&model=guichett (last visited Mar. 31, 2004); *see* Kersting & Schindler, *The ECJ's Inspire Art Decision of 30 September and Its Effects on Practice*, *in* 4 GERMAN LAW JOURNAL NO. 12, 1277 (2003), *available at* http://www.germanlawjournal.com/article.php?id=344 (last visited Mar. 31, 2004).

89 *See* Kilian Baelz & Teresa Baldwin, *The End of the Real Seat Theory (Sitztheorie): The European Court of Justice Decision in Ueberseering of 5 November 2002 and its Impact on German and European Company Law*, *in* 3 GERMAN LAW JOURNAL NO. 12 (2002), *available at* http://www.germanlawjournal.com/current_issue.php?id=214 (discussing the Court's later ruling in Überseerung and the subsequent decisions on the development of regulatory competition in Europe); Simon Deakin, *Regulatory Competition versus Reflexive Harmonisation in European Company Law*, *in* REGULATORY COMPETITION AND ECONOMIC INTEGRATION: COMPARATIVE PERSPECTIVES 190 (Daniel C. Esty & Damien Geradin eds., 2001) (assessing the European corporate law scene after the court's 1999 *Centros* judgment); Sebastian Mock, *Harmonization, Regulation and Legislative Competition in European Corporate Law*, 3 GERMAN LAW JOURNAL NO. 12 (2002), *available at* http://www.germanlawjournal.com/current_issue.php?id=216 (last visited Oct. 3, 2003) (dealing with regulatory competition in the field of European Corporate law); Frank Wooldridge, *Überseering: Freedom of Establishment of Companies Affirmed*, 14 EUR. BUS. L. REV. 227 (2003).

90 For an analysis of Case C-212/97, Centros Ltd. v. Erhvervs-Org., 1999 O.J. (C 136) 3, *see* FORSTINGER, *supra* note 34, at 41 (providing an extensive discussion of the doctrinal conflict over this issue); Daniel Zimmer, *Mysterium Centros – Von der schwierigen Suche nach der Bedeutung eines Urteils des Europäischen Gerichtshofes [The Mystery of Centros: The Difficult Search for the Meaning of the ECJ's Decision]*, 164 ZEITSCHRIFT FÜR DAS GESAMTE HANDELSRECHT UND WIRTSCHAFTSRECHT (ZHR) 23 (2000).

European corporate law regimes applying domestic law to corporations based in these countries (the "siege reel," or "real seat" doctrine), and those embracing the dominant US model of state competition for incorporation ("incorporation doctrine").[91] Forstinger concludes her study with an intriguing reconsideration of the aforementioned 1985 White Paper that accommodated different interests within the framework of a single legal measure.[92] In light of the persisting differences among EU Member States' systems of corporate law, Forstinger takes up the recent and far-reaching observations of Simon Deakin[93] and argues that "[m]inimum standards are seeking to promote diverse, local-level approaches to regulatory problems by creating a space for autonomous solutions to emerge."[94] Beyond this assessment, which is reflected in parallel discussions regarding future prospects of European harmonization programs,[95] lies a subtle theoretical appraisal of the harmonization processes that ties this debate back to issues of legal transplantation and system change. The paradigm of reflexive law, originally developed in response to regulatory deadlock resulting from political pressure against juridification in the 1970s and early 1980s,[96] has received increased recognition in present international debates. This recognition has occurred in the context of European integration[97] and corporate law regulation,[98] as well as that of international environmental protection and sustainable development.[99] At present, reflexive law unfolds in an even more intricate manner, as comparative views on legal transplantation often fail to capture the co-evolutionary processes that unfold in a given legal, social, and political order when legal transplantation takes place. Rather than a mere integration into another legal order, what actually takes place is a sophisticated process of interaction and confrontation between the imported instrument and other areas and regulatory spheres within the receiving system. As an imported legal standard is introduced into the receiving legal order, the connected social systems (including industrial relations, insurance, financing, and production regimes), each with its own

---

91 *See* FORSTINGER, *supra* note 34, at 41–48; Werner F. Ebke, *Centros – Some Realities and Some Mysteries*, 48 AM. J. COMP. L. 623 (2000).
92 FORSTINGER, *supra* note 34, at 158.
93 Deakin, *supra* note 89, at 211.
94 FORSTINGER, *supra* note 34, at 159.
95 Michael Dougan, *Minimum Harmonization and the Internal Market*, 37 COMMON MKT. L. REV. 853, 858 (2000) (describing the move from Single Market harmonization policy to the integration of more policy objectives through consecutive treaties since 1986).
96 *See* Klaus Günther, *Der Wandel der Staatsaufgaben und die Krise des regulativen Rechts [Changing State Functions and the Crisis of Regulatory Law]*, in WACHSENDE STAATSAUFGABEN – SINKENDE STEUERUNGSFÄHIGKEIT DES RECHTS [INCREASING STATE FUNCTIONS – SINKING REGULATORY ABILITY OF THE LAW] 51 (Dieter Grimm ed., 1990); Gunther Teubner, *Juridification – Concepts, Aspects, Limits, Solutions*, in JURIDIFICATION OF SOCIAL SPHERES 3 (Gunther Teubner ed., 1987); Gunther Teubner, *Reflexives Recht*, 68 ARCHIV FÜR RECHTS UND SOZIALPHILOSOPHIE 13 (1982); Rudolf Wiethölter, *Materialization and Proceduralization in Modern Law*, in DILEMMAS OF LAW IN THE WELFARE STATE 221 (Gunther Teubner ed., 1986).
97 *See* Michael Dougan, *Vive la Différence? Exploring the Legal Framework for Reflexive Harmonisation Within the Single European Market*, in 1 ANNUAL OF GERMAN AND EUROPEAN LAW 2003 (Russell Miller & Peer Zumbansen eds., 2004).
98 Deakin, *supra* note 89, at 211–13; FORSTINGER, *supra* note 34, at 158–69. Forstinger states: "This approach uses both centralized regulation of minimum standards to overcome market failures, existing specifically in the area of takeovers, and some degree of self-regulation to preserve space for autonomous governance at member state level." *Id.* at 158. He continues, "The aim of reflexive harmonization is to protect the diversity of national legal systems, while at the same time seeking to channel the process of evolutionary adaption of rules at state level." *Id.* at 160.
99 *See* Peter Cornelius & Bruce Kogut, *Creating the Responsible Firm: In Search for a New Corporate Governance Paradigm*, 4 GERMAN LAW JOURNAL 45 (2003), *available at* http://www.germanlawjournal.com/pdf/Vol04No01/PDF_Vol_04_No_01_45-52_Private_Cornelius_Kogut.pdf (last visited Oct. 5, 2003).

internal dynamics, will likely be aggravated by this import.[100] This perspective ultimately illuminates the tenacity displayed by different systems during the process of European integration while, at the same time, helping us better understand the complex interplay of legal reform, political decisions, and embedded cultural and social systems. Regarding the earlier allusion to widespread emergence of self-regulation in the context of corporate law and other fields,[101] a reflexive law approach that considers the co-evolutionary processes of minimum harmonization and ongoing processes of self-regulation and adaptation in the Member States might prove particularly helpful because it facilitates ongoing deliberation and mutual education.[102] In this respect, the legislative aftermath of the Takeover Directive, along with the passage of a German Takeover Act, might prove enormously helpful to the continuing search for an adequate European takeover regime, a search that will ultimately be a learning process.

---

100 Gunther Teubner, *Legal Irritants: How Unifying Law Ends Up In New Divergences*, in VARIETIES OF CAPITALISM: THE INSTITUTIONAL FOUNDATIONS OF COMPARATIVE ADVANTAGE 417 (Peter A. Hall & David Soskice eds., 2001).

101 *See* Mark Bevir & R.A.W. Rhodes, *Searching for Civil Society: Changing Patterns of Governance in Britain*, 81 PUB. ADMIN. 41 (2003); Robert Elgie, *Governance Traditions and Narratives in Public Sector Reform in Contemporary France*, 81 PUB. ADMIN. 141 (2003); Richard J. Stillman II, *Twenty-First Century United States Governance: Statecraft and the Peculiar Governing Paradox it Perpetuates*, 81 PUB. ADMIN. 19 (2003).

102 This point is adequately stressed by FORSTINGER, *supra* note 34, at 155, 160–62; *compare* Baums, *Zur Harmonisierung*, *supra* note 7, at 14. The conceptual background for the establishment of governance schemes on the European level that allow for mutual learning among the different Member States, developed by means of the Open Method of Coordination ('OMC'), was presented at the EU's Lisbon Council in 2000. *See* Joanne Scott & David Trubek, *Mind the Gap: Law and New Approaches to Governance in the European Union*, 8 EUR. L.J. 1 (2002) (assessing the OMC). "Unlike the [classical community method], which is designed to create law at the Union level, the OMC aims to coordinate the actions of the several Member States in a given policy domain and to create conditions for mutual learning that hopefully will induce some degree of voluntary policy convergence." *Id.* at 4 (emphasis added). *See also* DIAMOND ASHIAGBOR, SOFT HARMONISATION: LABOUR LAW, ECONOMIC THEORY AND THE EUROPEAN EMPLOYMENT STRATEGY 226 (2002); PHIL SYRPIS, LEGITIMISING EUROPEAN GOVERNANCE: TAKING SUBSIDIARITY SERIOUSLY WITHIN THE OPEN METHOD OF COORDINATION (2002); Dougan, *Vive la Différence?*, *supra* note 97; Dermot Hodson & Imelda Maher, *The Open Method as a New Mode of Governance: The Case of Soft Economic Policy*, 39 JOURNAL OF COMMON MARKET SUDIES 719 (2001).

Klaus König (ed.): *Deutsche Verwaltung an der Grenze zum 21. Jahrhundert*
(Baden-Baden: Nomos Verlagsgesellschaft, 2002, 636 pp., €82.00, ISBN 3-7890-8170-1)

Markus Pöcker[*]

A. Introduction

In the current German discussion of administrative law, the theory of public administration and the theory of public/administrative law must be considered as two separate discourses. They tend to describe their common subject of public administration in quite different ways. While the theory of administrative law still sees administrative action as almost completely determined by parliamentary acts of legislation, the theory of public administration tends to view such determinism as outmoded and overruled by new rationalities of action. Public management and governance are the current keywords to describe these new rationalities.

B. The Theory of Public Administration's View on Public Administration

Describing German public administration and its current rationality of action was one of the fields of attention of Klaus König's[1] project *"Deutsche Verwaltung an der Grenze zum 21. Jahrhundert"* (German public administration at the threshold of the 21st century), which took place in several discussions from 1999 to 2001. The participants' papers have now been collected and published.[2] The different perspectives of both theories – administration and administrative law – can be studied quite well in this volume. For example, Werner Jann's paper "Der Wandel verwaltungspolitischer Leitbilder: Von Management zu Governance" deals with the current and past rationalities of public administration from an administrative theory position. He considers whether or not there is currently a change in what he calls the *"Leitbild"* of German public administration; Jann uses this term to describe "systems of ideas"[3] regarding the most important constituents of administration, like fundamental relations of cause and effect, and who is operating them. He sees four different *"Leitbilder"* at work in the post-World War II history of German public administration, which he classifies according to the role advised to the state in each *"Leitbild"*. Accordingly, there is the "democratic" state (from the beginning of the 1950s onwards), the "active" state (from the mid-1960s onwards), the "slim" state (from the end of the 1970s onwards), and the "enabling/activating" state (since the mid-1990s). Jann claims that only one of these *"Leitbilder"*, the democratic state of the 1950s, relates to the parliamentary act of legislation as a fundamental component, such that it describes the relation between politics and public administration as an issue of legislative programs matched by fundamental keywords like "hierarchy", "legislative acts" and "rule of law". In Jann's opinion, the *"Leitbilder"* that followed the democratic state do not bear any relation to the parliamentary legislative act. While he describes the active state as centred around the idea of

---

[*] Dr. Iur., academic assistant and lecturer, Institute for Public Law, University of Frankfurt, poecker@jur.uni-frankfurt.de.
[1] Dr. Iur., Dr. rer. pol., professor of public law, Deutsche Hochschule für Verwaltungswissenschaften Speyer.
[2] DEUTSCHE VERWALTUNG AN DER GRENZE ZUM 21. JAHRHUNDERT (Klaus König, ed., 2002).
[3] Werner Jann, *Der Wandel verwaltungspolitischer Leitbilder: Von Management zu Governance*, in DEUTSCHE VERWALTUNG AN DER GRENZE ZUM 21. JAHRHUNDERT 282 (Klaus König, ed., 2002).

planning, with politics and administration functionally intertwined, the "slim" state is identified by the idea of managerialism, with politics and administration relating to each other by means of contracts. The current activating/enabling state is described by him as the state of governance and responsibilities shared between politics and administration. According to these descriptions, the parliamentary act of legislation lost its paradigmatic quality for public administration in the mid-1960s.

Werner Jann's view represents a common opinion among those writers in König's collection who give a current description of public administration from the point of view of the theory of administration. Christoph Reichard's paper "Verwaltung als öffentliches Manageme" (administration as public management), for example, observes a turn to the concept of New Public Management and describes this as a result of the profound inefficiency of "classic" means of predetermining administrative action, among which he counts hierarchical organisation and the parliamentary act of legislation,[4] while Carl Böhret speaks of a "transindustrial society", which has long outmoded the old "Max Weber-world" of a strictly legalistic administration.[5]

C. The Theory of Public Law and its View on Public Administration

Writers with backgrounds in the theory of administrative law take a diametrically opposite approach. For example, Karl-Peter Sommermann views the concept of public administration ruled strictly by law (i. e. mainly parliamentary acts of legislation) as fit to master both the current and future tasks that might face public administration. In his opinion, it is the only way to make state action calculable.[6] Hans Peter Bull is somewhat less outspoken and uses phrases we know from the current German discussion about governance. Bull argues that the parliamentary act of legislation did not lose its ability to predetermine administrative action in recent times, but claims it may never have had this ability "completely".[7] The depth of his allegiance to the notion of legislative predetermination of administrative acts becomes apparent in his belief that the fundamental duties and responsibilities of the state can be defined by analysing the German Basic Law (*Grundgesetz*, GG): "Even if constitutional law and parliamentary acts of legislation may be seen as quite irrelevant at the moment, they will be re-installed in their old position when the current trend for privatisation is over."[8] It is no wonder that this point of view does not consider itself put into question, let alone overtaken, by concepts like the "slim" or "activating/enabling" state. Such *"Leitbilder"* are criticized for their lack of clarity about the concept of state and administrative duties they purportedly represent. Bull thinks the "simple fact" that former state competences were transferred to separate organizational units outside the state cannot be seen as a move in the direction of a "slim" or "activating/enabling state". Even in a civil society, he sees the state in a key role of responsibility.[9] Sommermann's summary is quite similar. In his opinion, the concept wherein legislative acts predetermine administrative action should be kept as the basic idea for modern society. He is certain that this

---

4 Christoph Reichard, *Verwaltung als öffentliches Management*, in DEUTSCHE VERWALTUNG AN DER GRENZE ZUM 21. JAHRHUNDERT 255 (Klaus König, ed., 2002).
5 Carl Böhret, *in* DEUTSCHE VERWALTUNG AN DER GRENZE ZUM 21. JAHRHUNDERT 59, 64 (Klaus König, ed., 2002).
6 Karl-Peter Sommermann, *in* DEUTSCHE VERWALTUNG AN DER GRENZE ZUM 21. JAHRHUNDERT 101 (Klaus König, ed., 2002).
7 Hans Peter Bull, *in* DEUTSCHE VERWALTUNG AN DER GRENZE ZUM 21. JAHRHUNDERT 77 (Klaus König, ed., 2002).
8 *Id.*, 85.
9 *Id.*, 95.

concept will become even more important if the process of organizational disintegration should continue,[10] and that singular problems in practical circumstances of predetermining administrative action by legislative acts cannot put the whole concept into question. On the contrary, the concept's unchanged relevance for both present and future is supposed to be rooted in its idea of individual freedom.[11]

These statements must be set against the backdrop of the "Schriften zur Reform des Verwaltungsrecht". This forum has been the only institutionalized forum for administrative law and theory scholars where problems of administrative innovation have thoroughly been addressed over the past years. Its concept, which shaped the whole German discussion on administrative law theory in past years, was developed by Wolfgang Hoffmann-Riem[12] and Eberhard Schmidt-Aßmann.[13] They defined the forum's prime topic of interest – how administrative law can still be used today as a means of causing social effects in complex and fragmented society – and its methodical approach, which is meant to combine normative ways of thinking with empirical social sciences (politology, sociology). The forum's organisational frame was a symposium, taking place once a year between 1993 and 2003, with the participants' papers being collected in a series of 10 volumes.[14] In their introduction to the first volume of this series, Schmidt-Aßmann and Hoffmann-Riem, as the founders of this discourse, very clearly state that "German administrative law is rooted in a 19th century liberal concept which is centred around the parliamentary act of legislation as the pre-eminent means to predetermine administrative action. This concept is expressed in the figures of rule of law and administrative execution of law. This concept is important and indispensable for our time, too,"[15] thus centering their whole approach on the idea of public administration as ruled by the parliamentary act of legislation.

D. A possible explanation for the different points of view

Sommermann thinks the obvious differences between administration theory and administrative law theory may simply have something to do with misunderstandings. The concept of predetermining administrative action by legislative acts does not imply some kind of "pure legalism", as he puts it. Sommermann readily admits that the concept might create a "hypertrophical dogmatism", but qualifies this outcome as a mere side effect that only blurs the "real" image of the liberal concept.[16] But what if these were not misunderstandings? What if the new "*Leitbilder*" (as given by Jann) were appropriate descriptions of today's public administration? This possibility cannot be easily disregarded. On the contrary, the strong belief in parliamentary acts of legislation needs to be justified as well. The fact that such justification is not even attempted shows that this belief might not be the result of conceptual argumentation and reasoning. Rather, it could also be rooted in some kind of unconscious limitation of the mind that inhibits the

10   Karl-Peter Sommermann, *supra* note 6, at 100.
11   *Id.*, 107.
12   Dr. Iur., professor of public law, University of Hamburg, and judge of the Bundesverfassungsgericht.
13   Dr. Iur., professor of public law, University of Heidelberg.
14   REFORM DES ALLGEMEINEN VERWALTUNGSRECHTS (Hoffmann-Riem et al. eds., 1993).
15   "Das deutsche Verwaltungsrecht fußt, das ist immer wieder festgestellt worden, auf einem im 19. Jahrhundert ausgebildeten liberal-rechtsstaatlichen Konzept, das im parlamentarischen Gesetz das zentrale Steuerungsmittel sah und seine spezifischen Steuerungsleistungen in den Dogmen der Gesetzesbindung und des hoheitlichen Gesetzesvollzugs ausdrückte. Dies alles sind wichtige und unverzichtbare Grundannahmen auch für unsere Zeit." Hoffmann-Riem & Schmidt-Aßmann, *in* REFORM DES ALLGEMEINEN VERWALTUNGS-RECHTS 7 (Hoffmann-Riem et al. eds., 1993) (translation by the author).
16   Karl-Peter Sommermann, *supra* note 6, at 100.

possibility of imagining and conceiving different ideas of how administration could also work in a new "*Leitbild*".

A possible explanation for the unconscious limitation that causes this conceptual inhibition can only be sketched roughly here. There are at least a few indications as to why and how such a limitation might have developed. In Germany, academic studies of law and its teaching form a social environment, wherein the law student is permanently exposed to communication based on a strict distinction between the parliamentary act of legislation on the one hand and its execution on the other hand. This form of communication continues after university in almost every profession the young lawyer might choose. Of course, this distinction refers directly to the 19th century liberal (and rationalist) concept of the parliamentary act of legislation as the sole source for solving all cases by means of its execution; indeed, this is the same concept that Schmidt-Aßmann and Hoffman-Riem proclaim as "important and indispensable for our time, too".

It could prove interesting and useful to explore if this specific form of rule-based communication, which is today effectively a routine of communication, might be the reason behind the current limited ability to conceive of a different "*Leitbild*" or a new rationality of action for public government. It might be more useful to see whether this seemingly closed conceptual circuit can curb the possibilities of conceiving new rationalities of action for public government. In order to answer this question, one would have to distinguish between the liberal concept of predetermining administrative action by parliamentary legislative acts and their execution versus the routine of communication in the studies, teachings and practice of law based upon this liberal concept. The need to communicate the results and reasons of the legislative act's execution would lead to the effect of this liberal concept structuring the communication itself. As long as the liberal concept structures the studies, teachings and practice of law, it is indispensable that the result of the legislative act's execution be related, in the communication, to the supposedly causal legislative act. Otherwise, communication would not be possible and operable. In this way, the liberal concept would structure the conditions for comprehending an act of communication as law-related. The reverse relation between communication and the conceptual aspect could be imagined as an effect of recall and renewal. Every communicative act would not only be founded in the liberal concept, but at the same time recall and renew this concept in the communicator's mind. Ultimately, both aspects would have to be imagined as interdependent. This relation of interdependency could be imagined as getting tighter with time and exercise, as long-term exercise would lead to one aspect being influenced by the other in a more intense way. The growing strength of this interdependency would suppress as irrelevant every form of communication that did not refer to the liberal concept of law dominated by the parliamentary legislative act. This brief intellectual history could help explain why writers with a background in administrative law seem limited in their ability to conceive different rationalities of action for public administration.

If these thoughts were true, many discussions would have to be restructured in the future, including the German debate between administrative theory and the theory of administrative law. The possibility of a substantial exchange between both sides would depend on the way one dealt with these specific limitations in conceptual thinking. New strategies of communication would have to be developed in order to both break up these limitations and point in new directions. The particulars of such a progression cannot be detailed in this paper. But the direction seems quite clear: these strategies would have to demonstrate how to both put into question and overcome the current ubiquitous relevance of the liberal concept.

Giovanna Borradori (ed.): *Philosophy in a Time of Terror. Dialogues with Jürgen Habermas and Jacques Derrida* (Chicago and London, University of Chicago Press, 2003, 224 pp., ISBN 0-226-06664-9)

Martti Koskenniemi[*]

An international lawyer is in part pleased, in part embarrassed when philosophers contemplating the international order put their hope in international law. True, such declarations of faith are not normally for the law as it is but as a reformed ideal. But they do enact a routine move international lawyers have made since the late nineteenth century: one's faith is never to present law, but always to present how it will be in a desired future.[1] Messianism may perhaps be interpreted as a defence to excessive expectations loaded on experts of a technical craft. But it must surely be taken seriously when manifested in dialogues with Jürgen Habermas and Jacques Derrida, two of Europe's most influential public intellectuals.

This book is not a discussion between Habermas and Derrida but between each and the editor, Giovanna Borradori, Professor of Philosophy at Vassar College. Each is invited to approach the significance of the terrorist attacks on the World Trade Center in 2001 from his own standpoint. The book does not develop into an encounter: perhaps this would have been too much to hope. But it does show the striking similarity of the political conclusions drawn by two philosophers, often seen as adversaries, from the attacks and their aftermath. The dialogues are framed by the editor in two lengthy exposés of the thought of each philosopher plus a commentary on each dialogue. These glosses usefully link the debate to larger themes though to suggest, as Borradori does, that the dialogues are about "the legacy of the Enlightenment in a globalized world" and that Habermas and Derrida "share an allegiance to the Enlightenment" is to have that word do too much work, a reflection of the editor's own project instead of her interlocutors'. To suggest that their agreement is about "the Enlightenment" depoliticizes their positions in a way that is faithful to neither, nor to the interest of situating them as participants in an on-going public debate about the transformation of international order.

The invocation by Habermas of the Kantian ideal of cosmopolitan law against American unilateralism after "September 11" follows from his discursive theory of politics: the dark (power) politics of the United States, understood as hegemony, against the (weak and uncertain) legalism of Europe.[2] Habermas joins most "old European" intellectuals in seeing the world endangered less by terrorism than by the US response and in complaining about Europe's failure to oppose "the self-centered course of a callous superpower".[3] Though the International Criminal Court, the ABM Treaty or the Biological Weapons

---

[*] Professor of International Law, Director, Erik Castren Institute, Helsinki. This review essay was previously published in 4 GERMAN LAW JOURNAL 1087 (2003).

1 Martti Koskenniemi, *Legal Cosmopolitanism: Tom Franck's Messianic World*, 35 N.Y.U. J. INT'L L. & POL., 471–486, (2003).

2 The views of Habermas on the nature of the conflict between the morally inspired hegemonic unilateralism of the United States and the pluralistic universalism of (Kantian) international law is laid out with great clarity and force in Jürgen Habermas, *Interpreting the Fall of a Monument*, 4 GERMAN LAW JOURNAL 701–708 (2003), available at http://www.germanlawjournal.com/pdf/Vol04No07/PDF_Vol_04_No_07_701-708_European_Habermas.pdf. The article was originally published in German in the FRANKFURTER ALLGEMEINE ZEITUNG on 17 April 2003.

3 GIOVANNA BORRADORI, PHILOSOPHY IN A TIME OF TERROR. DIALOGUES WITH JÜRGEN HABERMAS AND JACQUES DERRIDA 27 (Giovanna Borradori ed., 2003). A representative view would be: "[C]'est la véritable victoire du terrorisme que d'avoir plongé tout l'occident dans l'obsession sécuritaire, c'est à dire dans une forme voilée du terreur perpétuelle", JEAN BAUDRILLARD, POWER INFERNO. REQUIEM POUR LES TWIN TOWERS. HYPOTHÈSES SUR LE TERRORISME. LA VIOLENCE DU MONDIAL 59 (2003).

convention, all of which were rejected by the United States, are aspects of an old law, Habermas situates them firmly in a Kantian historical trajectory: "we have long found ourselves in the transition from classical international law to what Kant had anticipated as a state of world citizenry."[4] This is why there is need for American compliance, and why Europe will need to take on "the civilizing role."[5] The view of the tasks of international law, present and future, in the 18-page dialogue that Borradori conducts with Habermas is thoroughly familiar: a fragile voice of an integrating civilization against the selfish egotism of the powerful.

But when Jacques Derrida confesses that he, too, will "take the side of the camp that, in principle, by right of law, leaves a perspective open for perfectibility in the name of the 'political', 'democracy', 'international law', international institutions, and so on,"[6] it may be more difficult to situate this in the context of his philosophy of deconstruction. In this 51-page dialogue, international law appears both as a somewhat ineffective and ambivalent – yet necessary – set of present constraints and as the promise of a cosmopolitan future. Again, the main danger is not from isolated "terrorists" but from the technological modernity that helped bring terrorism about and receives legitimacy from the victimhood now offered to the world's most powerful political entity. Again, the promise of resistance and progress are embodied in a Europe conceived as the representative of law: "Without forsaking its own memory, by drawing upon it, in fact, as an indispensable resource, Europe could make an essential contribution to the future of international law …".[7]

To be sure, neither thinker believes that politics could be replaced by international law, even in the future. In addition to Kant, both take up the name of Carl Schmitt. Habermas accepts that invoking universal law may also sometimes work as an apology of hegemony. To counter the Schmittian reduction of universalism into a smokescreen over particular interests, he insists on democracy's self-correcting character, its nature as Bildung. Habermas accepts that the model of discursive democracy, coupled with loyalty to basic constitutional principles, works internationally in a more fragmented, distanced environment than the domestic order. The difference is one of degree, however, not of principle, and recent developments towards the legalization of some aspects of international politics have worked to diminish it.[8] In any case, for Habermas, the hegemonic danger is checked by a logical fiat embedded in a truly democratic international public realm: "any deconstructive unmasking of the ideologically concealing use of universalistic discourses actually presupposes the critical viewpoints advanced by these same discourses. Moral and legal universalism is, thus, self-reflexively closed in the sense that its imperfect practices can only be criticized on the basis of its own standards."[9]

Derrida, too, is conscious of the limits of law. He accepts Schmitt's view of the irreducibility of the (political) decision to any anterior structure but turns decisionism on its head. Deconstruction reveals that a universal democracy is always unfulfilled, always a

---

4   BORRADORI, *supra* note 3, at 38.
5   BORRADORI, *supra* note 3, at 27.
6   BORRADORI, *supra* note 3, at 114.
7   BORRADORI, *supra* note 3, at 116.
8   Earlier, Habermas had accepted Schmitt's critique as it concerned the unmediated moralisation of politics and offered against this what he calls the "decisive moment" of mediation by "an authority that judges impartially and fulfills the conditions of neutral criminal punishment", Jürgen Habermas, *Kant's Idea of Perpetual Peace with the Benefit of Two Hundred Years' Hindshight*, in PERPETUAL PEACE. ESSAYS ON KANT'S COSMOPOLITAN IDEAL 147 (James Bohman & Matthias Lutz-Bachmann eds., 1997). Habermas is surely right when he observes that drawing attention to the danger of moralisation provides no reason to discard attempts towards institutional regulation. Whether today's multilateral institutions effectively exemplify such authority, may however be debated.
9   BORRADORI, *supra* note 3, at 42.

democracy to-come. There is no closed system of ready-made responses that could only be "applied". Every decision, every political, legal, or administrative act will thus raise the question of justice in terms of the personal responsibility of the one who decides. As Derrida has often argued, justice does not end with but only begins with law. The fact that the universal is always also particular, the legal also more than just "legal", does not open the way to the Schmittian nightmare: it is the precondition for there to be something like a realm of politics in which issues of right, good and just can be meaningfully debated and approached. There is no closure. The universal is always a horizon that recedes as it is approached.[10] This seems to be not too far from the Kantianism of Habermas – despite Derrida's reservations about the use of the notion of "regulative idea" to characterize such openness.[11]

Habermas and Derrida share an image of international law that is very familiar for international lawyers because of the juxtaposition with "politics" it entails, because of the gradual dissolution of that juxtaposition the more concrete one's argument becomes, and because the threatening collapse of law into politics is checked by the displacement of present imperfection by future promise. The problem, however, lies in the initial juxtaposition, a certain unwillingness to see how international law is always already meshed with present politics. The law is not – or is not only – the fragile European humanitarianism that is timidly opposing American empire. It is also that empire, its wars and its violence, and the conditions that make something like "September 11" possible. Sovereign statehood and globalisation, non-intervention and intervention are all parts of a ubiquitous framework of legal norms and structures which creates some good, and some bad, consequences. As Anne Orford has recently shown, international law is not a white knight waiting in some (European) capital to intervene when politics goes wrong. It is always *already* there structuring the private and public relations within which material and spiritual resources are distributed in the world.[12] In this regard, international law is both the disease and the cure and merely putting one's hopes in it makes no sense as a political program.

Much of what the two philosophers say – when they do not seek to enlist international law tout court for their cause – indirectly underwrites this. When Borradori asks both interlocutors about whether "September 11" should be seen as an event of world-historical significance, neither provides a straight answer. For Habermas as well as Derrida, an obsessive concentration on that date directs attention away from what made it possible and from what it legitimized as a reaction. As Habermas points out, "fundamentalism" is thoroughly conditioned by the modernity it opposes. Yet its desperate protest against secularism fails as a serious political claim: it cannot overcome the enemy it attacks. But as it leads to an "overreaction" and a "playing of the terrorists' game" by the US Government, it calls for a defence of political modernity. And that defence takes up most of the contribution by Habermas. This seems fine, with one reservation, however. Surely one aspect of that modernity is also the fact of governance through secular legal rules, and one aspect of "September 11" is a challenge to the way these rules uphold the North/South opposition that Habermas agrees provides the context within which Muslim fundamentalism must be understood. Instead of an appeal to law, why not a critique of law?

Derrida, too, refuses to focus on "9/11". Far from being an "event" in the philosophi-

---

10 I have tried to articulate something like this as part of international law's political project in Martti Koskenniemi, *What is International Law For?*, in INTERNATIONAL LAW 105–111 (Malcolm Evans ed., 2003).
11 BORRADORI, *supra* note 3, at 133–135.
12 ANNE ORFORD, READING HUMANITARIAN INTERVENTION. HUMAN RIGHTS AND THE USE OF FORCE IN INTERNATIONAL LAW (2003).

cal sense that juxtaposes it with (mere) "being",[13] that signifier has now become part of a political discourse appropriated for varying purposes. Approaching it through deconstruction, Derrida's discussion of the 9/11 "event" is, like that of Habermas, ideology criticism. Terrorism now becomes an "autoimmunity disorder": produced by the United States during the Cold War and after, a kind of "suicide of those who welcomed, armed and trained [the terrorists]"[14] – a product of that which it rejects, mirror-image of its target.[15] The prognosis is sombre: product of the violence that seeks to suppress it, terrorism created a trauma that cannot be relieved by mourning because the heart of the trauma is not the *past event* but the fear for the *future event* whose catastrophic nature can only be guessed. Imagination is here fed by a media without which there would have been no "world-historical event" in the first place. The circle is almost unbreakable: terrorism and that which it is against are locked in a reciprocal game of destruction where causes may no longer be distinguished from consequences.

Both philosophers discuss terrorism in the context of globalisation, or as Derrida insists, *mondialisation*. For Habermas, this provides an occasion to indict the injustice of the global system. Reconfiguring the international as a democratic political community must begin "through the improvement of living conditions, through a sensible relief from oppression and fear".[16] This is absolutely necessary as a precondition of an atmosphere of trust and truthfulness within which discursive democracy may emerge. If the West is to have a "civilizing impact,"[17] it will have to renounce a politics (of identity) that allows inclusion only by assimilation or conversion. However difficult this may be in the international context, one should aim for shared understandings, the hermeneutic moment of a fusion of horizons between that which is and that which is not "the West".

Derrida accepts that it may be impossible to capture the present conflict in traditional categories of war, civil war, and even "partisan war." The events are situated in an environment of semantic instability. "Terrorism" cannot be fixed in a definition. And yet, he points out, following Schmitt, this is one aspect of the politics of law: the attempt by the dominant power "to impose and, thus, to legitimate, indeed to legalize (for it is always a question of law) on a national or world stage, the terminology and the thus the interpretation that best suits it in a given situation."[18] The moment is, clearly, one of re-interpretations, of novel and deterritorialized ideas and concepts: "…radical changes in international law are necessary, but they might take place in one generation or twenty."[19] What is needed, Derrida now suggests, is "accountability from those in charge of public discourse, those responsible for the language and institutions of international law."[20]

Such conventional cosmopolitanism must, however, recognize the ambivalence of legal concepts and institutions, including the Janus-sided nature of territorial sovereignty and

---

13 The opposition between the radical break of "l'événement" to the bourgeois tranquillity of "l'être" which derives from Heidegger is a much-debated theme of recent continental philosophy. *See, e.g.*, ALAIN BADIOU, L'ÊTRE ET L'ÉVÉNEMENT (1988). *See also* the book review, Martti Koskenniemi, *Alain Badiou D'Un désastre obscur: sur la fin de la verité de l'état* (1998) and *Ethics: An Essay on the Understanding of Evil* (2001), *in* XI FINNISH YEARBOOK OF INTERNATIONAL LAW 430–442 (2000).
14 BORRADORI, *supra* note 3, at 95.
15 Likewise, BAUDRILLARD, *supra* note 3, at 14–18, 38.
16 BORRADORI, *supra* note 3, at 36.
17 *Id.*
18 *Id.*, 105. Baudrillard suggests that an event can be an event only outside discourse and that it ceases to be one when captured by discourse, BAUDRILLARD, *supra* note 3, at 21–25, 35. As discourse gives meaning, an "event" (in the heavy, Heideggerian sense also employed by Badiou) can only be meaningless. Derrida does not go that far. The event may be represented in discourse, even if it may be only revealed in deconstruction, through a glimpse at the "trace" it has left on the conceptual surface.
19 BORRADORI, *supra* note 3, at 106.
20 *Id.*

its *mondialized* counterpart. In the first place, "wherever it is believed globalization is taking place, it is for better and for worse".[21] And then "[i]n many contexts, the state might be the best protection for certain forces and dangers".[22] This is surely right. As Roberto Unger and others have shown, institutions (including institutions such as the State or an international system of governance) do not have fixed social consequences but may be used for many different purposes.[23] Derrida is right to stress the semantic openness of the categories through which the international world is now perceived. But it is uncertain if this underwrites the (Kantian?) view that we live in transition from one type of relative fixedness to another, and even less certain that it is possible to distinguish "opportunistic"[24] semantic policies from those that are not. If politics is about the projection of meaning-contents to disputed words in an (agonistic) environment where institutional alternatives can only be contextually assessed, everyone is always an "opportunist".

Derrida views the clash of Muslim fundamentalism and the United States as a clash between two political theologies in fashion that forces Europe into the position of the gentle civilizer: a position in which Europe has, for both Habermas and Derrida, so far failed. For Habermas, too, the clash is between two closed systems between which no dialogue presently seems possible. Both invoke Europe's role as a mediator, insisting on the need for the dialogue to open by addressing the world's social and economic injustices, and both argue towards the cosmopolitan vision of world citizenship.[25] To get there, Habermas invokes the notion of tolerance, but Derrida rejects it.

Derrida is critical of tolerance as an offshoot of a religious, authoritarian world-view: "tolerance is first of all a form of charity ... the good face of sovereignty, which says to the other from its elevated position, I am letting you be ...".[26] Derrida invokes the (Kantian) notion of hospitality, a pure hospitality that is not based on invitation, that opens itself "to someone who is neither expected not invited. To whomever arrives as an absolutely foreign visitor, as a new arrival, nonidentifiable and unforeseeable, in short, wholly other".[27] Such hospitality has something of political theology about it: it cannot be realized on this earth. For every act would always already positivize it, re-inscribe hospitality under certain conditions (an invitation, a membership, a victimization, etc.). The interesting question is the relationship between the way Derrida arrives at the transcendental through the idea of "pure and unconditional hospitality" and his legal reformism that seems otherwise without direction (for neither sovereignty nor globalization provided it, unconditionally). The temptation is to see Derrida advocating – as he almost did in his famous essay on legal theory[28] – an ethically founded view of law whose focus was always on the (indeterminable) moment of decision at which crystallize both the justice of the institution whose decision it is, and the decision-maker's accountability to those the decision concerns.

Habermas refuses the turn to the transcendental. "Tolerance" may indeed possess the paternalistic overtones for which Derrida rejects it. But this is precisely why tolerance must be situated in a dialogic framework of rules and procedures. "Within a democratic

---

21 *Id.*, at 123.
22 *Id.*, at 131.
23 ROBERTO UNGER, FALSE NECESSITY. ANTI-NECESSITARIAN SOCIAL THEORY IN THE SERVICE OF RADICAL DEMOCRACY (1987).
24 BORRADORI, *supra* note 3, at 102.
25 Europe's role as the "vanishing mediator" or the translator between the US and the East, itself transforming in the course of such mediation, is interestingly discussed in ÉTIENNE BALIBAR, L'EUROPE, L'AMERIQUE, LA GUERRE 35–61 (2003).
26 BORRADORI, *supra* note 3, at 127.
27 *Id.*, at 128–129.
28 Jacques Derrida, *Force of Law: The Mystical Foundation of Authority*, in DECONSTRUCTION AND THE POSSIBILITY OF JUSTICE 3–29 (Drucilla Cornell, Michael Rosenfeld & David Gray Carlson eds., 1992).

community whose citizens reciprocally grant one another equal rights, no room is left for an authority allowed to one-sidedly determine the boundaries of what is to be tolerated".[29] To work acceptably, toleration requires a system of rights embedded in a constitution, understood as a self-correcting learning process.

* * * * *

Neither Habermas nor Derrida fully play the interviewer's game. Both embark on trajectories of thought that do not always address the questions Borradori poses to them. The questions work more as spring-boards for general reflection. Apart from the question of tolerance vs. hospitality, there is little direct engagement between them. The styles of argument of the two philosophers differ, as was to be expected, and it is quite fascinating to follow their different economies of expression in articulating parallel interpretations of September 11 and of what a desirable future might look like. Both see the main danger coming not from "terrorists" but from the West's response. Both appeal to law and multilateralism against American hegemony. Each sketches his utopia less in terms of positive principles than as an open-ended future. As the editor points out, despite the often stark juxtaposition between the supporters of Critical Theory and Deconstruction in the academy, the main protagonists of those two strands of thought appear to be much closer in political intuition than one might assume. Or perhaps this is only because they are both distinctly European thinkers whose shared identity as such is revealed immediately as they are made to face the awesome face of American hegemony – a conjecture whose implications for any study of philosophy as a social force would be interesting to pursue.

Catherine Dupré, *Importing the Law in Post-Communist Transitions: The Hungarian Constitutional Court and the Right to Human Dignity* (Oxford and Portland, OR: Hart Publishing, 2003, 224 pp., ISBN: 1-841-13131-8)

Renáta Uitz[*]

A. Human Dignity as an International Legal Norm

In 1948, a document adopted by unprecedented international consensus declared that the "recognition of the inherent dignity and of the equal and inalienable rights of all members of the human family is the foundation of freedom, justice and peace in the world".[1] In its 30 articles, the Universal Declaration of Human Rights (UDHR) calls for a wide range of rights to respect and protect human dignity. "Maritain said it best: whether the music played on the Declaration's thirty strings will be 'in tune with, or harmful to, human dignity, will depend primarily on the extent to which a 'culture of human dignity' develops."[2]

---

29 BORRADORI, *supra* note 3, at 41.

[*] Associate professor of comparative constitutional law, Legal Studies, Central European University, Budapest.
1 G.A. Res. 217A (III), U.N. Doc. A/810 (Dec. 10, 1948). [Hereinafter Universal Declaration of Human Rights (UDHR)].
2 Mary Ann Glendon, *Knowing the Universal Declaration of Human Rights*, 73 NOTRE DAME L. REV. 1153, 1173 (1998).

B. A Brief Comparative Analysis of Human Dignity in Various Jurisdictions

Since the enactment of the UDHR, numerous constitutions have sought to provide for the protection of human dignity in express terms. Among these documents, which frame rather different constitutional and legal cultures, are the *Grundgesetz* (German Basic Law), the Israeli Basic Law of 1992 on Human Dignity and Liberty and the post-apartheid interim and final constitutions of South Africa. These dignity provisions did not remain empty declarations; instead, they came to attain special status in constitutional adjudication.

Respect for and protection of human dignity in Art. 1 of the German Basic Law was meant as a guiding principle for all times[3] and it did spectacularly enrich rights jurisprudence in Germany. In the *Lüth* case, the German Constitutional Court stated that the Basic Law is not a value-neutral document; that the provisions on basic rights protect a set of values which form an objective order; that while this is not a fixed hierarchy, it "centers upon dignity of the human personality freely developing within the social community".[4] However, the German Constitutional Court's understanding of human dignity is not of timeless validity and may change in concrete cases.[5]

A rich understanding of human dignity has permeated South African rights jurisprudence. When abolishing capital punishment in *S. v. Makwanyane*,[6] the justices of the South African Constitutional Court relied on human dignity. Interestingly, however, they did not adhere to only one understanding of human dignity. Justice Chaskalson's lead opinion took advantage of a comparative analysis of dignity-based arguments in international and foreign jurisprudence. In addition to this analysis, other justices, including Justice Mokgoro, added their observations on ubuntu, which is a concept named in Zulu and well-known in many African languages that has no simple English translation.[7]

> Generally, *ubuntu* translates as *humaneness*. In its most fundamental sense, it translates as *personhood* and *morality*. Metaphorically, it expresses itself in *umuntu ngumuntu ngabantu*, describing the significance of group solidarity on survival issues so central to the survival of communities. While it envelops the key values of group solidarity, compassion, respect, human dignity, conformity to basic norms and collective unity, in its fundamental sense it denotes humanity and morality. ...[8]

While the reference to *ubuntu* was omitted from the South African final Constitution, the South African Constitutional Court preserved this concept in its jurisprudence.[9] With respect to the concern for human dignity in South African constitutional jurisprudence, *ubuntu* is regarded as a "guiding value," which reflects a set of value choices informing the interpretation of various constitutional provisions in a truly multiethnic and multicultural society.[10]

---

3   Ernst Benda, *The Protection of Human Dignity (Article 1 of the Basic Law)*, 53 SMU L. REV. 443, 445 (2000).
4   BVerfGE 7, 198. Available in English *in* DONALD P. KOMMERS, THE CONSTITUTIONAL JURISPRUDENCE OF THE FEDERAL REPUBLIC OF GERMANY 361-368 (2nd ed, 1997).
5   BVerfGE 45, 187 *in* DAVID P. CURRIE, THE CONSTITUTION OF THE FEDERAL REPUBLIC OF GERMANY 315 (1994), at note 287.
6   *S. v. Makwanyane and Another*, 1995 (3) SA 391 (CC).
7   Peter Norbert Bouckaert, *Shutting Down the Death Factory: The Abolition of Capital Punishment in South Africa*, 32 STAN. J. INT'L L. 287, 310 (1996).
8   *S. v. Makwanyane and Another*, 1995 (3) SA 391 (CC).
9   *Hoffmann v. South African Airways*, 2001 (1) SA 1 (CC).
10 Lourens M. du Plessis, *The Evolution of Constitutionalism and the Emergence of a Constitutional Jurisprudence in South Africa, An Evaluation of the South African Constitutional Court's Approach to Constitutional Interpretation*, 62 SASK. L. REV. 299, 315 (1999).

The constitutions of Canada, France or the United States do not contain any references to human dignity. Nonetheless, the constitutional review process has made us mindful of the dignitary aspect of constitutional rights and equal protection over the past few decades. In *Law v. Canada (Minister of Employment and Immigration)*, Justice Iacobucci of the Supreme Court of Canada stated that the purpose of the equality clause [s.15(1)] of the Canadian Charter of Rights and Freedoms is to

> prevent the violation of essential human dignity and freedom through the imposition of disadvantage, stereotyping, or political or social prejudice, and to promote a society in which all persons enjoy equal recognition at law as human beings or as members of Canadian society, equally capable and equally deserving of concern, respect and consideration.[11]

Similarly, without any explicit textual backing, the French Constitutional Council found, in the *Bioethics* decision,[12] that the preamble of the 1946 French Constitution protects human dignity from subjugation and degrading treatment as a principle of constitutional value.[13] Most recently, in *Lawrence v. Texas* – overruling precedent – the majority of the U.S. Supreme Court clearly acknowledged that, under the U.S. Constitution, "adults may choose to enter upon [a homosexual] relationship in the confines of their homes and their own private lives and still retain their dignity as free persons."[14]

Concern for human dignity is also infusing the jurisprudence of the European Court of Human Rights (ECHR). Traditionally, invasion of human dignity was considered by the ECHR in the context of the prohibition of torture [Art. 3 of the European Convention on Human Rights].[15] Following scattered references[16] in the *Pretty* case, the ECHR recently made a similar declaration as a main premise for its privacy analysis [Art. 8].[17] Since then the ECHR has consistently reaffirmed and refined this finding in the context of Art. 8, holding that

> ... the very essence of the Convention is respect for human dignity and human freedom. Under Article 8 of the Convention in particular, where the notion of personal autonomy is an important principle underlying the interpretation of its guarantees, protection is given to the personal sphere of each individual, ...[18]

---

11 *Law v. Canada (Minister of Employment and Immigration)*, [1999] 1 S.C.R. 497, para 51.
12 CC Decision No. 94-343/344 DC, July 27, 1994.
13 *Reaffirmed in* CC Decision No. 96-377 DC, July 16, 1996.
14 Lawrence v. Texas, 539 U.S. 558, 567 (2003).
15 Mark Janis, Richard Kay & Anthony Bradley, European Human Rights Law, Text and Materials 102 (2nd ed., 2000).
16 *See* Eur. Court H.R., C.R. v. United Kingdom, App. No. 20190/92, at para. 42 (Nov. 22, 1995), http://cmiskp.echr.coe.int/tkp197/view.asp?item=1&portal=hbkm&action=html&highlight=20190/92&sessionid=6794571&skin=hudoc-en, *also* Eur. Court H.R., Kokkinakis v. Greece, App. No. 14307/88, at para. 14 (May 25, 1993), http://cmiskp.echr.coe.int/tkp197/view.asp?item=1&portal=hbkm&action=html&highlight=kokkinakis&sessionid=6794647&skin=hudoc-en and Eur. Court H.R., Cossey v. United Kingdom, App. No. 10843/84, at para. 27 (Sept. 27, 1990), http://cmiskp.echr.coe.int/tkp197/view.asp?item=1&portal=hbkm&action=html&highlight=10843/84&sessionid=6794647&skin=hudoc-en.
17 Eur. Court H.R., Pretty v. United Kingdom, App. No. 2346/02, at para. 85 (Apr. 29, 2002), http://cmiskp.echr.coe.int/tkp197/view.asp?item=1&portal=hbkm&action=html&highlight=2346/02&sessionid=6794647&skin=hudoc-en.
18 Eur. Court H.R., I. v. United Kingdom, App. No. 25680/94, at para. 70 (July 11, 2002), http://cmiskp.echr.coe.int/tkp197/view.asp?item=1&portal=hbkm&action=html&highlight=25680/94&sessionid=6794647&skin=hudoc-en. *See also* Eur. Court H.R., Goodwin v. United Kingdom, App. No. 28957/95, at para. 90 (July 11, 2002) http://cmiskp.echr.coe.int/tkp197/view.asp?item=1&portal=hbkm&action=html&highlight=28957/95&sessionid=6794647&skin=hudoc-en and Eur. Court H.R.,Van Kück v. Germany, App. No. 35968/97, at para. 69 (June 2, 2003) http://cmiskp.echr.coe.int/tkp197/view.asp?item=1&portal=hbkm&action=html&highlight=35968/97&sessionid=6794647&skin=hudoc-en.

C. Human Dignity and the Law in Transition in Post-communist Hungary

By analyzing the role of human dignity in constitutional jurisprudence amidst democratic transition, Catherine Dupré offers insight into an important segment of this flourishing culture of human dignity in *Importing the Law in Post-communist Transitions: The Hungarian Constitutional Court and the Right to Human Dignity* (2003). Dupré notes that the right to human dignity in post-communist constitutions is not simply one of many constitutional rights; rather, it is a symbolic statement about the type of society these constitutions sought to bring about.[19] However, such a programmatic understanding of the constitutional protection of human dignity can itself be seen as a reflex preserved from communism. After all, instead of establishing working governments, communist constitutions placed societies at the whims of a party-dominated state acting in the name of 'hallucinatory visions of the future'. As Sajó cautions: "Constitutions that serve constitutionalism are not born to foster illusions ... Instead, they reflect the fears originating in, and related to, the previous political regime."[20]

When discussing the Hungarian Constitutional Court's jurisprudence on human dignity, Dupré explains the Court's approach as importing foreign law and adapting it to the Hungarian context. It is argued that the Hungarian Constitutional Court imported German dignity jurisprudence in a selective manner[21] and transformed German jurisprudence as if the justices had used natural law arguments. In this process, Hungarian constitutional justices infused the constitutional text with values that they derived from an exterior, anterior source that they detached from its original temporal or national context.[22] Dupré devotes an entire chapter to how this concept of human dignity then played a central role in undoing the remnants of the communist legal heritage.[23]

The task undertaken by Dupré is a challenging one for a number of reasons. First, the Hungarian Constitutional Court established in 1989 was one of the most active post-communist constitutional courts. As is widely known, democratic transition did not arrive with a new constitution to Hungary. The text of the Hungarian Constitution itself is far from being a coherent normative edifice. Some sections applicable to rights are transformed versions of rules enacted during the communist regime, while other provisions are but translations of international or foreign instruments of rights protection. Furthermore, apart from its chapter on fundamental rights, the Hungarian Constitution has crucial rights-related provisions scattered throughout its text. Handling such a patchwork of constitutional provisions is an intricate task for the constitutional interpreter who is expected to decide in a principled manner. While being a creation of democratic transition itself from the very first day of its operation, the Hungarian Constitutional Court became a most influential participant in building constitutionalism 'from scratch'. Consequently, the justices were faced with the dilemma of fashioning a jurisprudence that was flexible enough to fit the constitution of the day and yet withstand any major constitutional overhauls. Although the Hungarian constitution-making process never got beyond crafting partial amendments to the 1949 law, these particular considerations cannot be ignored when analyzing one of the central concepts of Hungarian constitutional jurisprudence.

Dupré is aware of the difficulties of constitution-building from the bench of a new constitutional court. In such circumstances, consulting foreign constitutional jurisprudence

---

19 CATHERINE DUPRÉ, IMPORTING THE LAW IN POST-COMMUNIST TRANSITIONS: THE HUNGARIAN CONSTITUTIONAL COURT AND THE RIGHT TO HUMAN DIGNITY 7, 25–26 (2003).
20 ANDRÁS SAJÓ, LIMITING GOVERNMENT: AN INTRODUCTION TO CONSTITUTIONALISM 1–2 (1999).
21 SAJÓ, *supra* note 20, at 154.
22 *Id.* at 11–12, 157–161.
23 *Id.* at chapter 6.

offers a relatively safe path. As Dupré argues, when the Hungarian Constitutional Court referred to 'modern constitutions' in the course of this exercise, the justices essentially imported German constitutional jurisprudence.[24] This choice can be explained by the prestige and success of German constitutional jurisprudence, the justices' knowledge of German constitutional law[25] and the fact that the German experience did fit certain cases before the Hungarian Court.[26] Dupré's analysis reveals textual allusions to German jurisprudence[27] and points out matches in narratives.[28] Unfortunately, the exploration halts at this point and does not investigate whether any of these matches could be due, at least in part, to deeper connections between the German and Hungarian legal traditions. For instance, it might have been interesting to learn how these examples could be seen in the light of familiar correspondences in legal fields other than constitutional law, dating back to the times of the Austro-Hungarian Empire.

The book's central analysis seeks to reveal the extent and manner in which the imported German concept of human dignity contributed to building constitutionalism in post-communist Hungary. A comparative analysis of German and Hungarian abortion cases does point out significant differences and reveals that, although the conception of dignity as applied by the Hungarian Constitutional Court resonates with German jurisprudence, the internal logic of the approaches followed by the two courts is radically different.[29] Contrasting Hungarian and German dignity jurisprudence, Dupré concludes that the Hungarian concept is a liberal understanding of human dignity, which centers on the individual and human autonomy and is divested of human dignity's implications and impact on the community and society.[30] This finding leads to a sharp conclusion in the analysis of the Hungarian capital punishment[31] case, where the Constitutional Court is criticized for focusing on the individual's dignity, while failing to mention society's need for retribution and protection against criminal deeds.[32] This conclusion results from an approach that differs radically from the standard account of the Court's dignity jurisprudence that prevails in domestic scholarship.

As Dupré also indicates,[33] both Hungarian legal scholarship and the Hungarian Court tend to distinguish between various conceptions of human dignity in the Court's jurisprudence,[34] which itself evolved over a longer period of time in a line of cases that was, at times, invisible to the non-Hungarian audience. Accordingly, in certain cases, the Constitutional Court reads the right to human dignity in connection with the right to life and does not allow any limitations on it. The most prominent example of this connection is the Court's decision abolishing capital punishment. Since the Constitutional Court saw the unity of the individual's human dignity and right to life as an absolute limitation on the state's criminal jurisdiction, there was no room for further justification. Although concurring justices offered alternative conceptions of dignity, the Court's judgment relies upon an absolute that was created by this entanglement of the right to human dignity with the right to life.

Far from the language of absolutes, the Hungarian Constitutional Court also invokes a dignity-based narrative when it offers constitutional protection to such rights, interests

---

24 *Id.* at 89–95.
25 *Id.* at 95–101.
26 *Id.* at 10–104.
27 *Id.* at 92–94.
28 *Id.* at 66–68, 96–97.
29 *Id.* at 114–117.
30 *Id.* at 149.
31 *Id.* at 108 and 110.
32 *Id.* at 124.
33 Dupré, *supra* note 19, at 70 *et seq.*
34 László Sólyom, Az alkotmánybíráskodás kezdetei Magyarországon [The beginnings of constitutional adjudication in Hungary] 442–463 (2001).

and subjects that are not expressly mentioned in the Constitution. According to the Court, where a classification does not discriminate on the basis of fundamental rights or on grounds listed in the Constitution's non-discrimination clause [Art. 70/A], the requirement of "treatment of persons as subjects with equal dignity" is controlling. In such cases, the justices apply a reasonableness test that is more permissive than the requirement of necessity-proportionality applied in rights cases. The reason for deference is simple: as the Constitution does not offer any explicit guidance, the Constitutional Court cannot be more demanding. This aspect of dignity jurisprudence is probably the most difficult to capture due to the variety and complexity of issues raised in the cases where the Constitutional Court resorts to this ground of review.

This complexity is especially obvious in the case concerning compensation for moral harms caused by illegal governmental action. In one particular case, the justices had to decide whether it was constitutional for the legislature to distinguish between victims of Nazi concentration camps and of Soviet Gulag.[35] While the judgment unquestionably touches upon the dignity of deceased victims, additional considerations guiding the Constitutional Court's decision present the dignity argument in a different light. Belonging with other cases on restitution and compensation, in which the Constitutional Court consistently held that restitution takes place *ex gratia* and not as of right, this decision affirms both the government's wide discretion in legislating and that the standard of constitutionality of governmental action is "treatment of persons as subjects with equal dignity."[36] If one were seeking substantive components of dignity jurisprudence in the case, this technicality might explain, in part, the awkwardness of the Hungarian Constitutional Court's reasoning.

At the core of Hungarian dignity jurisprudence are the cases where the Constitutional Court takes the right to human dignity as a 'mother right', construing it as a right to self-determination (autonomy).[37] In such cases, as with any other fundamental rights, the right to dignity and subsidiary rights derived there from are subject to a limitation analysis under a necessity-proportionality test. The bulk of the cases examined by Dupré fall within this category and, correspondingly, this section is where her analysis is the most compelling.[38] As identified with a sharp eye, a characteristic feature of this jurisprudence is that rights derived from human dignity are transformed into instruments for warding off governmental intrusion. These derivatives of human dignity and self-determination (autonomy) are then used by the Court to displace certain alternative constitutional provisions with a communist flair.[39] Dupré's most critical observation recognizes that, in doing so, the Constitutional Court undid the remnants of the communist constitution without confronting its communist past.[40]

This conclusion seems to validate Arendt's observation on the role of human rights and human dignity in *The Origins of Totalitarianism*[41] and also corresponds with the self-proclaimed mission of the Constitutional Court concerning the communist past. Although Arendt does not offer a comprehensive theory of constitutionalism and human rights, she does see political institutions of constitutional government as safeguards against the tendencies of totalitarian governments aiming to eradicate liberty and its preconditions.[42] In

---

35 22/1996 (VI. 26.) AB decision.
36 21/1990 (X . 4.) AB decision, 8/1991 (VI. 3.) AB decision and 16/1991 (IV. 20.) AB decision.
37 SAJÓ, *supra* note 20, at 66–68.
38 *Id.* at 75–86, 109–112.
39 *Id.* at 134–154.
40 *Id.* at 191.
41 HANNAH ARENDT, THE ORIGINS OF TOTALITARIANISM 290–299 (1973).
42 Jeffrey Isaac, *A New Guarantee on Earth, Hannah Arendt on Human Dignity and the Politics of Human Rights*, 90 AM. POL. SCI. REV. 61 (1996).

some way, this consideration might excuse the Constitutional Court's emphasis on the individualistic aspect of human dignity.

For the Constitutional Court, the task of clearing the legal system of the sediments of the previous regime did not focus on passing judgment over the past, but instead concentrated on building the foundations of the polity's future. For the Hungarian Court, rights protection soon became a prominent means of eliminating the heritage of the communist past and building new, democratic institutions. As the Constitutional Court clearly stated in the retroactive criminal justice case[43]

> The old law remains in force. As for validity, there is no difference between norms "from before" and "from after" the Constitution. The legitimacy of the various regimes of the past 50 years is irrelevant in this respect, more precisely, it has no significance in constitutional analysis.[44]

As Chief Justice Sólyom, the first chief justice of the Constitutional Court, explained: the Hungarian Constitutional Court developed its jurisprudence on the premise of legal continuity and the rule of law, while at the same time placing judicial activism in the protection of constitutional rights at the top of its agenda.[45] In the broader context of transition to democracy, as described by Teitel, "the turn to legalism, however contingent, is emblematic of the liberal state, with transitional justice reconstructing political identity on a juridical basis by deploying the discourse of rights and responsibilities."[46] Thus, while the Hungarian Court clearly departed from the German conception of human dignity, Hungarian jurisprudence, as reconstructed by Dupré, seems to fit a broader paradigm of rights and constitutionalism in democratic transition.

D. Contextualizing Human Dignity and the Human Rights Agenda

In the age of the UDHR in the Western hemisphere, respect for human dignity has been intrinsically linked with the protection of human rights. Any culture or society that offers an alternative understanding of human rights or human dignity comes under scrupulous scrutiny from the advocates of a Western canon.[47] Asian values, the teachings of Islam or lessons from democratic transition are usually seen as justifications for departure from a settled concept. Some of these points, however, may also be perceived as legitimate alternative understandings from which all participants of the contemporary human rights discourse might benefit. As the above overview suggests, human dignity is not a homogeneous concept with a fixed meaning: constitution-makers and interpreters of constitutions informed by the experiences of various differing cultures, traditions and circumstances give different interpretations to the concept. In order to understand the conceptions and potential implications of dignity jurisprudence, it is essential to explore the development of particular understandings of human dignity in their broader historical, political and legal context. In the reality of an ever-expanding range of issues, from the demands of biotechnology to building stable democracies in newly liberated, fragmented societies, there remains both room and need for broadening the discourse. Catherine Dupré's book presents the community concerned with understanding human rights a nuanced conception of human dignity in democratic transition, which ultimately provides an exciting opportunity to revisit one of the central concepts of this discourse.

---

43 11/1992 (III. 5.) AB decision.
44 11/1992 (III. 5.) AB decision, ABH 1992, 81.
45 See SÓLYOM, *supra* note 33, at 113, 117–118.
46 RUTI TEITEL, TRANSITIONAL JUSTICE 225 (2000).
47 Jack Donnelly, *Human Rights and Human Dignity, An Analytic Critique of Non-Western Conceptions of Human Rights*, 76 AM. POL. SCI. REV. 303 (1982).

Andreas Fahrmeir: *Citizens and Aliens – Foreigners and the Law in Britain and the German States, 1789–1870* (New York, Oxford: Berghahn Books, 2000, ISBN 1-57181-717-4)

*Helene Oger**

Andreas Fahrmeir's original and captivating book studies nationality laws during a period for which very few studies exist. It demonstrates the extent to which the 19th century indicates how attempts to characterize starkly contrasting models of nationhood will fail.

Indeed, by contrast to the traditional division[1] between three main models of citizenship, i.e. the German ethnic citizenship model, the French civic Republican model and the British multicultural model, Fahrmeir, focusing on a comparison between the German and the British models, demonstrates that there is no such antagonistic difference. He shows that this lack of antagonism arises for different reasons, such as the importance of the general context (general approach of states regarding nationality and immigration, economic and political situation at a precise time) and the inner evolution and paradoxes of each system.

Beyond merely recalling contrasted histories, Fahrmeir implicitly teaches us that nationality and immigration policies are contingent, pragmatic, and evolve according to states' needs. Indeed, Fahrmeir questions the relevance of the traditional classification itself.[2]

It is also important to highlight the well-documented quality of Fahrmeir's bibliography and endnotes. However, he sometimes undermines important facts and lacks some logical links between several arguments.

According to Brubaker, the French conception of nationhood would be universalist, assimilationist, and state-centred, whereas the German conception would be particularist, organic and *Volk*-centred. Ethnic or cultural unity would be primary and constitutive of this conception of German nationhood. Consequently, the French conception of citizenship would be more accessible to immigrants than the German one. By this logic, the multicultural British model would be the one most open to immigrants. However, according to Brubaker, this classification would have been relatively questioned by the post-war migrations. According to Fahrmeir, things have never been that clear-cut.

In the first chapter, entitled "definitions of citizenship," Fahrmeir acknowledges that a strong emphasis on culture and descent did exist to some extent in Germany. However, he makes several relevant objections to drawing conclusions about immigration policy on the basis of such superficially clear-cut distinctions.

First, he recalls both that the German jurists of the time were unaware of the rule of *ius sanguinis* and that the influence of French law (based on *ius sanguinis*) had been great at that time. Second, the rule that citizens could not be forced to leave their fatherland had an important impact. Third, in fact, as well as in theory, citizenship law remained within the jurisdiction of the individual states. Significantly, since citizenship was lost by emigration, *ius sanguinis* could not be the unique leading rule. Instead, citizenship had to be acquired by means other than *ius sanguinis*, namely by *ius soli*. Indeed, the treaties regulating deportation of foreigners between the different German states acknowledged that loss of citizenship after some time of residence in another state would correspond to

---

* PhD candidate, European University Institute, Florence. Email: helene.oger@iue.it
1 This traditional division is derived from the original work of Rogers Brubaker who clearly opposed for the first time the French and German models of citizenship. *See* ROGERS BRUBAKER, CITIZENSHIP AND NATIONHOOD IN FRANCE AND GERMANY (1992).
2 A similar conclusion has been reached by Dieter Gosewinkel. *See* DIETER GOSEWINKEL, EINBUERGERN UND AUSSCHLIESSEN. DIE NATIONALISEIRUNG DER STAATSANGEHOERIGKEIT VOM DEUTSCHEN BUND BIS ZUR BUNDESREPUBLIK DEUTSCHLAND (2001).

the acquisition of another nationality. Fahrmeir argues somewhat less persuasively that, if the principle of descent was reinforced after 1848 and before 1913, then it was still not the unique principle of the time. He thus explains that the uniqueness of the law of descent has been a gradually developed principle. Not only has this uniqueness developed gradually, I would further argue that it has also depended on its context.

The exaggeration by the mainstream of the German system is mostly based on the system between 1913 and 1949. After 1949, the unique principle was still ius soli; however, in practice, there were many infringements leading up to the first reform of 1990 and the great reform of 1999. In other words, Fahrmeir replicates the general understanding method of analysis to highlight its lack of coherence. This conclusion clearly questions his own reasoning. Conversely, the argument of contradiction, between an always evolving society, in which states make strategic choices regarding their nationality policies, and a fixed theoretical model, would have been much more powerful.

Nevertheless, Fahrmeir significantly shows the inconsistency of the British definition of nationality based on the liberal principle of common law, namely residence (by opposition to nationality) consequently conflicting with other laws, particularly tax and succession laws. Indeed, with the common law rule of nationality, children born abroad from British parents (thus foreigners) would not have been able to inherit their parents' properties in Great Britain. Moreover, until 1844, and in contrast to German laws, naturalized people did not have equal rights and could not use their British nationality outside British territory from 1849 onwards. Additionally, in 1922, British nationality became a true imperialistic nationality, thereby extending the acquisition of nationality for all British descendants. Thus, British nationality has always been quite broad. However, rather than simply responding to a much more liberal spirit, British nationality has clearly corresponded to specific needs at specific periods, such as imperial strategies of conquest.

In the second chapter Fahrmeir continues with his critical comparison by explaining the naturalisation process in both countries.

In Germany, as all citizens of a state had to be settled in a specific municipality, foreigners desirous of naturalisation had to acquire municipal as well as state citizenship. This process of acquiring both forms of citizenship was extremely expensive. While previous residence was not a condition for naturalisation in German states, religious beliefs were held to be as important as 'correct' political opinions. In this respect, we can reproach Fahrmeir for understating the extremely negative consequences of such a policy for Jews. However, and in contrast to Great Britain, once a certificate of naturalisation had been issued, naturalized foreigners possessed all the rights of citizens. In this way, Germany's policy was generally a generous one. In Great Britain, acquiring citizenship was also extremely expensive. In contrast to Germany, Great Britain's procedures stipulated that applicants had to state a reason for seeking naturalisation, express their intention to reside permanently in the UK, be 'respectable' persons, and reside in the UK for three years. This process looks somewhat more demanding than its German counterpart; in practice, Germany granted naturalisation much more generously than the UK or France at that time. This higher German naturalisation rate is explained, in part, because *ius soli* was much more developed in Great Britain than in Germany.

In chapter 4 Fahrmeir shows that foreigners living in Germany had much more limited rights (especially regarding employment) than their counterparts residing in Great Britain, where very few occupations were closed to foreigners because of their nationality. Finally, deportation was also much more developed in Germany than in Great Britain.

Yet, as Fahrmeir explains in chapter 5, the reasons for these discrepancies, not as important as we normally hold them to be, are not the result of the liberal British philosophy and the racist German attitude. Such polarizations are much too clear-cut. Instead, these discrepancies can be explained, in part, by the economic success of the UK at that time as well as the mass migration to Germany, which Great Britain experienced in a much more limited way.

Although he does not describe it explicitly, Fahrmeir ultimately implies that such citizenship policy choices are based on contingencies within a general situation and context at a precise time in a studied country, which, in principle, recalls the traditional classification.

Fiona Cownie: Legal Academics. Culture and Identities (Oxford and Portland, OR: Hart Publishing, 2004, 227 pp., ISBN 1-84113-061-3, £30)

Alexandra Kemmerer*

Law seems to have a special status among social phenomena by reason of its forms, its rituals, its specialised language, its special rationality even, and its specific social effects. But, on the other hand, law is clearly embedded in the totality of the social process which is its cause, and on which it has a substantial determinative effect, not least in providing the continuing structure of society, its hardware programme.[1]

The phenomenon of law is always situated in a broader context.[2] This is also true for its teachers. But what do we know about the "social embedding" of legal academics? To what extent does the study of law permeate their life? How does their social background, their gender, their intellectual self-perception, affect the construction of their professional identities and thereby affect legal tradition, legal traditio, in the true sense of the word?

While legal history unveils the "lived experience" of late members of the profession often without hesitation,[3] contemporary legal academics sharing their personal learning experiences in and with the law are still rare exceptions. Admittedly, it has been one of the defining characteristics of the Critical Legal Studies (CLS) movement to shed light on the individual lawyer, on his or her private and political life.[4] The growth and influence of the

---

* Alexandra Kemmerer is Ph. D. candidate and research assistant at the Institute for International Law, European Law, and European Private Law, University of Würzburg (akemmerer@jura.uni-wuerzburg.de). In 2004, she was a visiting researcher at the European University Institute, Florence. Her writing on, *inter alia*, European and international legal culture regularly appears in the FRANKFURTER ALLGEMEINE ZEITUNG (FAZ). Since 2003, she has been a member of the editorial board of the GERMAN LAW JOURNAL. This review was previously published in 5 GERMAN LAW JOURNAL 1003 (2004).

1 P. ALLOTT, THE HEALTH OF NATIONS: SOCIETY AND LAW BEYOND THE STATE 36 (2002).
2 *See, e.g.*, for the "law in context" approach of the "Frankfurter Schule der Privatrechtstheorie" ("Frankfurt School of Private Law Theory") inspired by RUDOLF WIETHÖLTER, RECHTSVERFASSUNGSRECHT. RECHTFERTIGUNG ZWISCHEN PRIVATRECHTSDOGMATIK UND GESELLSCHAFTSTHEORIE (C. Joerges & G. Teubner eds., 2003). As books are always placed next to other books, this review of Fiona Cownie's monograph is also a reflection on Peer Zumbansen, *Das soziale Gedächtnis des Rechts, oder: Juristische Dogmatik als Standeskunst, in* RECHTSVERFASSUNGSRECHT, 151–179.
3 For a rich collection of legal biographies, *see* M. STOLLEIS ED., JURISTEN. EIN BIOGRAPHISCHES LEXIKON. VON DER ANTIKE BIS ZUM 20. JAHRHUNDERT (2nd ed. 2001). However, sometimes special efforts have to be made to overcome historiographic reluctance, *see* M. Stolleis, *Reluctance to glance in the mirror: The Changing Face of German Jurisprudence after 1933 and post-1945, in* DARKER LEGACIES OF LAW IN EUROPE. THE SHADOW OF NATIONAL SOCIALISM AND FASCISM OVER EUROPE AND ITS LEGAL TRADITIONS 1 (C. Joerges & N. S. Ghaleigh eds., 2003). An example for a closer look on one of the most ambiguous legal-academic biographies, picked from the ever-growing piles of literature on Carl Schmitt, is B. Rüthers, *Die Tagebücher Carl Schmitts – ein frühes Selbstporträt?*, JURISTENZEITUNG 445, 448 (2004).
4 An interesting strand of the 'critical' movement are, not only in this regard, the 'New Approaches to International Law' (NAIL), *see* D. Kennedy, *A New Stream of International Legal Scholarship*, 7 WIS. INT'L

"critical" school have been considerable in the United States and, to a lesser extent, in other parts of the Anglo-American legal system. Apart from these legal cultures, however, CLS has been less influential. Furthermore, the "critical" movement often confines itself to a critical approach to teaching, leaving aside the teacher as a multi-faceted individual. In the *Curriculum Vitae* of today's legal academic, all personal footnotes, all references to a social *Lebenswelt* are missing.[5] And while the ever-changing landscape of legal education remains a challenging laboratory for reforms, we do not know much about the real everyday-life inside the law. Apart from our personal experience as students or teachers, apart from anecdotical references in *Festschrift* literature rarely read by students or even a wider academic public, the professional socialisation and identity of legal academics, at first glance so familiar to us, remains in the dark.

Therefore, it does not come as a surprise that Fiona Cownie's study of the lived experience of legal academics at first required from the author the skill to "exotize the domestic."[6] Being a Professor of Law at the University of Hull and Chair of the Legal Education Committee of the Society of Legal Scholars, Cownie is by no means an outsider in her field of research. Yet, the author emphasizes that – as already Pierre Bourdieu showed in his classical study of French academia – an authoritative account can best be produced by a reflexive encounter with the "known," the apparently familiar. "It is a process of 'participant objectification,' which seeks to avoid the false choice between the unreal intimacy of a subjectivist position and the equally misleading superiority of objectivism." (25)

Operating from a "socio-legal" perspective, the author sets out to explore the culture of legal academia in the United Kingdom as it is experienced by academic lawyers. Key to her understanding of legal academia is "the interplay between the culture of the discipline as a whole, and the individual academic identities forged within that culture." Familiarity with approaches such as CLS or "Feminist Perspectives on Law," according to Cownie, enables the researcher to find out "what goes on in the law school." They do, however, "not allow you to see beyond the public face of law teaching, to find out how much law teachers enjoy teaching, whether they think they are good at it, to what extent they adopt any of these different approaches, or what they think they are trying to do when they are teaching their students." Maybe Fiona Cownie should have had a closer look to works from the other side of the Atlantic before coming to her somewhat surprising general evaluation of the "critical" movement. David Kennedy's essays, for example, would have been a good pick.[7]

L. J. 1 (1988), and D. Kennedy & C. Tennant, *New Approaches to International Law: A Bibliography*, 35 HARV. INT'L L. J. 417 (1994). Although NAIL has been completed at a conference at Harvard Law School in 1997, the process of a critical examination of international law starting from its protagonists goes on, *see* D. KENNEDY, THE DARK SIDES OF VIRTUE: REASSESSING INTERNATIONAL HUMANITARIANISM (2004). The book explores, rooted in David Kennedy's own experiences in numerous humanitarian efforts as well as in legal academia, the satisfactions of international humanitarian engagement – but also the disappointments of idealism. Kennedy takes his readers from Harvard Law School to the jails of Uruguay, from the corridors of the United Nations to the founding of an NGO dedicated to the liberation of East Timor in a Lissabon kindergarten, from opposing the war in Vietnam to discussing international law aboard an U.S. aircraft carrier in the Persian Gulf.

5 See P. Zumbansen, *Innen- und Außenansichten des Rechts in der Globalisierung*, Habilitationsvortrag an der Johann Wolfgang Goethe Universität Frankfurt, June 9, 2004, on file with the author): "Jedenfalls fehlen auch in einem stringent wirkenden Lebenslauf regelmäßig die Fussnoten und Verweise auf die soziale Lebenswelt, in deren Fürsorge, Ironisierung und Ermahnung die einen oder anderen Ereignisse überhaupt zu Ereignissen werden konnten. Es fehlen auch die Verweise auf die wunderbaren Zufälle und Glücksfälle, die in professioneller Hinsicht Pfadabhängigkeiten zu begründen halfen und damit auch Mut zur Innovation gaben, die aber auch dabei halfen, die Relativität des täglichen Raschelns mit Papieren zu erkennen."

6 P. BOURDIEU, HOMO ACADEMICUS (1984).

7 *See, inter alia*, D. Kennedy, *International Legal Education*, 26 HARVARD INT'L L.J. 361 (1985).

Setting out to use a "cultural approach" to study academic law, Cownie soon had to realize that culture is not an easy thing to deal with; a slippery concept even for anthropologists. After introducing different definitions of culture, the author simply states that "culture, then, is about beliefs, values and customs. In terms of studying legal academics, it involves paying attention to the way people live their lives in law schools, focusing on norms and values which they share because they are legal academics." Dealing with identity, however, turned out to be no easier task: "Just as 'culture' is a complex and contentious concept, so is 'identity.'" "Identity," in Cownie's interpretation, refers to the ways in which individuals and collectives are distinguished in their social relations with other individuals and collectivities: "In relation to individuals, identity is our understanding of who we are and who other people are, as well as other people's understanding of themselves and others."

Certainly, as in most European legal cultures, much has been written on various aspects of legal education in the United Kingdom. There is a wide variety of literature on legal pedagogy, ranging from lamentations about the lack of theoretical knowledge of education among law teachers to debates about the introduction of legal skills and clinical legal education and the place of legal ethics in the academic legal curriculum. Another major area of writing about the legal academy, strongly influenced by the Critical Legal Studies movement (CLS) and, to a lesser extent, by feminist perspectives, explores the approach which should be taken to the researching and teaching of law. But all these works belong to the "public life" of academia which is for the author only a starting point to venture into the "more private aspects of legal academia." It is the "everyday life" of legal academics in Britain that Cownie sets out to examine comprehensively – including their approach to legal analysis, their personal career choices, their joys and labours with teaching and research, their self-perceptions and their attitudes towards administration, networking and Higher Education Policy. The "public," however, is absent even in private: none of the respondents expressed the intention to "contribute something to society" as a reason for being a lawyer.

Out of the sixty-seven university law schools in England which offer "qualifying law degrees" (i.e. degrees which are accepted by the legal profession as the "academic stage" of legal training), Cownie chose seven research sites and thereby respondents which reflected variations in institution, status, experience and gender. The institutions were selected so that they included an elite law school in the "golden triangle" of Oxford, Cambridge and London, an old-established civic, a new civic, and three former polytechnics, all located in cities of varying sizes. Between June 2001 and December 2002, fifty-four interviews were conducted. The group of interviewees included thirty-five men and nineteen women, and individual academics were selected so as to include varying levels of status and experience.

Examining the habits of law's inhabitants, Fiona Cownie found the discipline in flux. This is, according to her, particularly true for legal academics' approach to law. While almost all the respondents were clear that being an intellectual is not a necessary quality to be a successful academic lawyer, a majority pointed out that the legal academics producing the best work *are* intellectuals.[8] "With half of my respondents describing themselves as adopting a socio-legal or critical-legal approach, and feminism routinely used in teaching a wide variety of subjects," the author states a well advanced "movement from an exclusively

---

8   It should be noted that Cownie, despite her rather positive assessment of the "intellectual drift" occurring in British legal academia, does not even mention the role of the academic lawyer as public intellectual which has a long tradition in many legal cultures. *See, e.g.*, R. POSNER, PUBLIC INTELLECTUALS: A STUDY OF DECLINE 359–386 (2001). For a witty contribution to the well-worn debate on whether there is something such as a "British Intellectual" at all, *see* S. Collini, *"Every Fruit-juice Drinker, Nudist, Sandal-wearer ...": Intellectuals as Other People, in* THE PUBLIC INTELLECTUAL 203, 214 (H. Small ed., 2002).

black-letter culture to a pluralistic one, peopled by lawyers adopting very different approaches to the study of law." Cownie does not hold back her enthusiasm about the British turn to scholarship: "Doctrinal law is not what it used to be, with the majority of black-letter lawyers regarding the introduction of various policy related matters as crucial to their analysis of legal phenomena."

Shedding light on various aspects of the legal academic career, from the initial decision to study law at university to the qualities and skills which contemporary legal academics think are necessary to be a good legal academic (and those which make it likely that someone will become a professor), Fiona Cownie presents rather sobering conclusions. Only one person described her interest in law as "passionate." Another principal lecturer choose to read law rather randomly – because he did not want to end up as a teacher after studying history or languages. Talking about the qualities of a good academic lawyer, analytical and communication skills were ranked on top, while imagination did not seem a highly valuable element of legal analysis. Nearly half of the respondents regarded ruthlessness or ambition as necessary qualities for those who want to go on for a Chair.

Even if there seems to be no room for the "good citizens" on the ladder to academic fame, legal academics are overall very positive about their career choice. They are proud to be doing this job and often perceive themselves as belonging to a high-status profession.[9] For some, being a legal academic is a vocation – badly paid, but for the most part, hugely rewarding. *To speak as truth to power* is a professional ideal as tempting for the academic lawyer as for the humanitarian activist in general or, occasionally, for the writer educated in law.[10] When asked what they liked most about being a legal academic, the factor identified most often, besides the variety of tasks, was autonomy, or the freedom to organize one's own working life.[11] The flip side of flexibility, however, is sometimes the inability to maintain an appropriate balance between work and other activities: "You never really leave your work behind," stated a professor in his mid-career at an old university. But the most disliked parts of the experience to be an academic lawyer are increased accountability measures such as the Research Assessment Exercise (RAE)[12] and the Quality Assessment Exercise (QAE),[13] and the pressure to publish a certain number of pieces per year.

Academic lawyers enjoy teaching; they enjoy helping students to learn. Overwhelmingly, they regard lecturing as a "performance," and are quite skillful in "dramatizing" their lectures. Research has come to play an increasingly important part in the life of

---

9 "Yes, I am proud. If you have been a historian, and then you go into law, there's a great difference in the way you're received. Anyone can do history, but law gets respect – often misplaced, I'm sure, but it does get respect …" (principal lecturer, experienced, female, new university) (99).

10 *See* D. Kennedy, The Dark Sides of Virtue: Reassessing International Humanitarianism, at XVI (2004); *see also* J. Zeh, *Wir trauen uns nicht: Viele Schriftsteller halten Politik für Expertenkram – und vor allem für Privatsache*, 11 Die Zeit 53 (2004) "Nach meiner politischen Einstellung befragt, würde ich antworten, dass ich meinen Kinderglauben an die Gerechtigkeit noch nicht verloren habe. Ich würde anführen, dass ich meine juristischen Kenntnisse bislang ausschliesslich darauf verwende, ehrenamtlich gegen demokratischen Kolonialismus auf dem Balkan, gegen ugandische Kriegsverbrecher und gegen die Telekom zu kämpfen."

11 "I suppose what I really like is the individual freedom. It's a job where you can, to a large extent, do what you want, work on questions that interest you. You can spend a lot of time reading books – I like reading books, and at times, certainly not all the time, but at times it can just seem like one of the best jobs in the world, because you can be sitting in the garden in the summer reading what I think are very interesting books, and being paid for it – it's a pretty good deal. It's not always like that, but that's what's really good." (lecturer, early career, male, old university) (104).

12 The Research Assessment Exercise (RAE) is an exercise conducted nationally to assess the quality of UK research and to inform the selective distribution of public funds for research by the four UK higher education funding bodies, see www.rae.ac.uk (last visited on 12 July 2004).

13 The Quality Assessment Exercise (QAE), an assessment of the quality of teaching, takes place every four years and every department at every university in the UK is subjected to it.

academic lawyers; RAE and other forms of "managerialism" are also often seen as making the profession more stressful. The rigid external timetable imposed on the production of research, the almost constant review of personal research agendas, and a new culture of competition are only a few negative effects noted by Cownie's respondents. The negative attitudes expressed to administration in general are unsurprising. Administration is a necessary evil whose burdens are unevenly distributed among academic staff, because some people are very good at getting out of it. The attitudes of the respondents towards the increasing amounts of bureaucracy and "audit" now found in academic life reflect the feelings of the rest of the academy, constituting "one of the less attractive features of the culture of academic law."

Another particular feature of law's academic culture is networking. Three-quarters of Cownie's respondents had a network of academic contacts, were connected to "significant others." Apart from their importance for research-related exchange, Cownie emphasizes, networks may be helpful in overcoming the "politics" of legal academia. But she also highlights gossip as a particular feature of the culture of academic law.

"Identity matters," states Fiona Cownie, and it does not come as a surprise that gender, class, race, ethnicity and sexual orientation affect the culture of legal academia as much as other social environments. However, her reflections on the "hegemonic masculine heterosexuality of the law school" are not entirely convincing. But as there is still much work to be done "on the ways in which gender plays out in the law school," it is to be seen whether the so far "somewhat superficial" awareness of gender issues among legal academics is a result of a lack of attention towards these issues or simply an effect of a minor importance of these questions for contemporary legal identities.

"While academic lawyers have many things in common, the lived experience of being an academic lawyer differs significantly in different countries; one should not assume that experiences as legal academic in one jurisdiction can automatically be transferred to another jurisdiction." But, as Peer Zumbansen recently emphasized in Johann Wolfgang von Goethe's words, we should learn from the "merits of foreign nations,"[14] not only as far as legal education in the narrow sense is concerned, but also when we think about *Bildung* in a broader context. Stressing the limited scope of her research, Fiona Cownie expresses the hope that the ideas and theories discussed in her book will stimulate others to question the culture of their own law schools, and to think further about a number of issues she raises. And indeed, it is to be hoped that similar research will be conducted in other legal cultures. Having in mind the ever-increasing importance of lawyers in the legal and political structures of the European Union,[15] an extensive comparative study of the culture and identity of European legal academics would be a desirable further step.

For now, we may for a moment listen to Fiona Cownie's slightly optimistic conclusions, offering special comfort to legal academics in the less and less attractive academic cultures[16] of some European countries:

---

14 See P. Zumbansen, *Das soziale Gedächtnis des Rechts, oder: Juristische Dogmatik als Standeskunst*, in RECHTSVERFASSUNGSRECHT. RECHT-FERTIGUNG ZWISCHEN PRIVATRECHTSDOGMATIK UND GESELLSCHAFTSTHEORIE 151, 173 (C. Joerges & G. Teubner eds., 2003).

15 See L. SIEDENTOP, DEMOCRACY IN EUROPE (2001). For a critical assessment of law's function in the process of European integration, see U. HALTERN, DER EUROPARECHTLICHE BEGRIFF DES POLITISCHEN HABILITATIONSSCHRIFT 252 (2003).

16 See P. Zumbansen, *supra* note 14, at 174, for an account of the everyday-life of legal academia in a major German university: "In Deutschland erreicht der Professor die Studenten nur per Mikrophon, und die Studenten erreichen den Professor gar nicht, schon gar nicht in seinem Büro. Macht nichts, weil sie ihn oft nicht einmal dem Namen nach kennen. Dass die Veranstaltungen überfüllt sind, macht auch nichts, weil weder die Studenten noch der Professor die riesigen Veranstaltungen mögen und sie deshalb eher in einer Mischung aus Resignation und Zynismus ertragen."

I would argue that in this study of legal academics, I have found considerable evidence of the enduring nature of certain core aspects of the culture of academic law, which suggest that the professional identities of legal academics may be more resistant to pressure than some commentators have acknowledged. Their prime objective as teachers was to teach students to think; despite benchmarks, audit and other forms of quality assessment, they did not talk in terms of 'transferable skills' or increasing the employability of their students. When asked about their personal view of success, their aim was to establish themselves as an expert in their field, who would be respected by other academics; other than in highly specialized fields, they did not look outside academia for peer approval. The qualities they identified as being desirable in a legal academic, such as powers of analysis and communication, where those which have been traditionally valued in the academy. Academic lawyers are subject to the changes taking place in higher education just as much as members of other 'academic tribes'. They teach more students, they are subject to almost constant surveillance, and not surprisingly, they feel under pressure, especially the women. However, overall, the culture of academic law and the professional identities constructed within it display a great deal of resilience, both retaining a fundamentally academic orientation.

We may then, for a moment, contemplate a merger between two traditional features of academic culture: "Professor und Künstler,"[17] professor and artist. If legal academia is truly a "site of power," as Fiona Cownie argues with Pierre Bourdieu's famous metaphor,[18] it may not limit itself to ambition without passion, to reading the law without critical theoretical reflection. After all, creative intellectual imagination might be a more important professional quality than analysis and communication have so skillfully taught us.

Andreas Müller-Driver: *Grenzüberschreitende Restrukturierungen von Kapitalgesellschaften zwischen Deutschland und England* (European University Studies, Vol. 3456) (Washington, D.C.: Peter Lang, 2002, 240, pp., ISBN 3-631-38653-2)

Anna L. Izzo

Within the framework of increasing economic globalisation, cross-border acquisitions of companies, transnational reorganisations, and the possibility for companies to transfer their registered office from one Member State of the EU to another, have all become of utmost importance. European Corporate Law has been, and still is, both a cause and a consequence of this. It influences and affects the national legal systems of the Member States to an increasing extent. A main aspect and a matter of great practical importance is the fate of the legal entity in those cases and to which extent those transactions allow the perpetuation of the legal personality. The case law rendered by the European Court of Justice (ECJ) is central to the recent developments in this area.

Müller-Driver delivered his doctoral thesis on transnational reorganisations of companies in 2002 putting the main emphasis on reorganisations between Germany and England. He begins with a detailed and clearly structured description of the national systems and legal possibilities of reorganisations of companies in Germany and England. He presents

---

17 *Id.* at 178.
18 FIONA COWNIE, LEGAL ACADEMICS: CULTURE AND IDENTITIES 3 (2004).

* Anna L. Izzo, LL.M. (EU/International Law, Frankfurt 2005), was born in 1977 and passed her First State Examination (J.D. equivalent) in Frankfurt in 2003.

the most important forms of reorganisations in both countries. German law recognizes (1) "Verschmelzung" (Merger), (2) "Spaltung" (Demerger) in its subdivision (2a) "Aufspaltung" (Division), (2b) "Abspaltung" (Spin-off) and (2c) "Ausgliederung" (very similar to the demerger – used for the formation of combines), (3) the asset-transfer and finally (4) the change of a company's status. The author precedes the reorganization forms in England with a particularly noteworthy synopsis of the English legal statutes of companies. The reader learns about partnerships and companies as well as other subdivisions, public, limited, and unlimited companies. Additional details are provided about the minimum capitalization, the incorporation, the taking up of business, the memorandum and articles of association, and the organs of the company, respectively the general meeting, board of directors, the Secretary and Auditor. With regard to the reorganizations, Andreas Müller-Driver examines the merger/amalgamation, division and the re-registration, always pointing out the different (or similar) terminology and usage in English and German language, while showing similarities or disparities on this occasion. Readers will learn in great detail about the re-registration of a Private Company (Ltd.) into a Public Company (Plc.) and vice versa, of a Limited Company into an Unlimited Company, about the Reconstruction within the Voluntary Winding-up under section 110 Insolvency Act 1986 and finally about the Schemes of Arrangements under section 425 Company Act 1985, which conceptionally corresponds to enforced settlements between dissenting members.

In part 3, Müller-Driver compiled an extensive depiction of the relevant international company law as a part of the conflict of law. It is worth mentioning at the outset that there were (and still are) two competing theories in the frame of conflict of law:[1] according to the Real Seat Theory, the legal capacity of a company was determined by reference to the law applicable in the place where its actual centre of administration is established. In contrast, pursuant to the incorporation theory, legal capacity is determined in accordance with the law of the state in which the company was incorporated. English and American legal theory has always followed the incorporation principle. In continental Europe, the Netherlands, Switzerland and Denmark have followed the incorporation principle whereas Germany, France, Belgium and Luxembourg previously adopted the company seat principle.

First, Müller-Driver points out the different possible seats of a company both in Germany and England: the Domicile, the Registered Office, the Place of Business or Branch and seats according to the spirit of tax law. He then makes up an exemplary survey of the above-mentioned theories with all variations and subdivisions and even the historical background and developments in the two countries. As is logically necessary, he relates these theories to European law and especially to European case law.

Due to the comparatively restrictive corporate laws in many of the individual states in the USA and the exceptional freedom to change the legal status of corporations in the State of Delaware, the corporation of the State of Delaware has become the universal institute in terms of corporate law within America. In European jurisdiction a similar trend is in the offing. The four most important cases that have been rendered by the ECJ *up to now* – and therefore partly after Müller-Driver's thesis – are referred to as *Daily Mail*,[2] *Centros*,[3] *Überseering*[4] and *Inspire Art*.[5]

---

1 *See* Münchener Kommentar, *Kindler*, 3 INTERNATIONALES GESELLSCHAFTSRECHT (1999) at para. 258 and SCHWARZ, EUROPÄISCHES GESELLSCHAFTSRECHT, para. 159, 164.
2 Case C-81/87, The Queen v. Treasury and Commissioners of Inland Revenue, *ex parte* Daily Mail and General Trust, 1988 E.C.R. I-5483.
3 Case C-212/97, Centros, 1999 E.C.R. I-1459.
4 Case C-208/00, Überseering BV v. Nordic Construction Company GmbH (NCC), 2002 E.C.R. I-9919, 9943.
5 Case C-167/01, Inspire Art, 2003 E.C.R. I-10155.

In *Daily Mail* the Court had to decide, in light of the articles on freedom of establishment,[6] to what extent a UK company could be refused the transfer of its central management and control to another state. The case did not involve the transfer of seat. On the basis of a very elaborate reasoning, the Court decided that the cited Treaty articles confer no such right. It held that "the Treaty regards the difference in national legislation concerning the required connecting factor and whether the registered office or real head office ... may be transferred ... as problems which are not resolved by the rules of establishment but must dealt with by future legislation or conventions." Later the Court restated its opinion declaring that the treaty rules did not affect the relationship between a state and its corporate entities, formed under its jurisdiction, and that this matter did not concern freedom of establishment. Indeed any legislation is free to deal with its own legal entities and to determine the conditions on which it grants or refuses legal personality.

In the well-known ECJ *Centros* decision of March 9, 1999 a Danish commercial register refused to register a branch of a British private limited company on the grounds that the foundation of the company in England had not complied with the Danish law regarding minimum capitalisation. Using the same argument foreign corporations were denied registration in the commercial register also in Germany at that time. The ECJ considered this a violation of the European freedom of establishment and that therefore the company should be allowed to register and trade in Denmark. The court analysed on what grounds the Danish registrar could have refused. Fraud and circumvention, or the "general good" exception were identified as the grounds on which national legislation could validly have imposed additional requirements. The case was considered in legal writing as the first significant step towards the Courts preference for the incorporation doctrine within the frame of conflict of law.

In the following and especially in its most recent judicature, the ECJ's continued its tendency of deciding in favour of the freedom of establishment by holding that rules submitting pseudo-foreign companies to the corporate law of the host state were inadmissible.

In the *Überseering* decision a Dutch company sued a German contractor in payment for deficient building works. The company had transferred its centre of business to Germany and its shares had been bought by German citizens. The German Court refused the company access to court, because it held that the company, having its seat in Germany, should have reincorporated according to German Law, and in the absence of such re-incorporation, being a Dutch company, German law considers it inexistent. The ECJ held the German theory, based on the strictest reading of the real seat doctrine, contrary to the Treaty as it would have resulted in the negation of the existence of a company, although this company had been validly formed in another Member State. Although there was some discussion in Germany about the possibility that the German legal order could have downgraded it to another, much weaker company form, it should be noted that the Court expressly held that the company that the German legal order should have accepted to act in its legal system was in fact a company of Dutch origin, with all its characteristics under Dutch Law.

The *Inspire Art* decision of September 30, 2003 moved the subject one step further as it raised the question as to what extent a national legislator can impose additional requirements on companies that have been formed under the jurisdiction of a Member State where its registered office is located, but without having developed any business activity there. The case related once more to a UK private limited company that had applied for registration with the Dutch commercial Registry where it intended to start its business

---

6 Treaty Establishing the European Economic Community, Aug. 31, 1992, 1992 O.J. (C 224) Arts. 52 and 58.

activity. It did not conduct business in the UK. According to a Dutch "Law on Formally Foreign Companies", these companies must add a suffix to their name to indicate their status as pseudo-foreign-companies. The Court held that a corporate entity validly established in one member state may transfer its administrative seat to another member state without having to comply with the second member state's stricter corporate legislation. In the absence of abuse – established on a case-by-case basis – the fact that the company has been formed in the other state or carries on its activities (almost) exclusively in the state of establishment does not deprive the company of its right of free establishment under the Treaty. The decision is expected to increase competition between legal types of companies throughout Europe and puts further strain on the minimum capitalisation and strict capital maintenance rules of German corporate law.

As already mentioned, the author delivered his thesis in 2002, and therefore he could not take into consideration the decisions *Überseering* and *Inspire Art*, only *Daily Mail*, *Centros* and the less well-known *Segers*[7] decision in 1986 and *Gebhard*[8] decision in 1995. But *Überseering* was in preparation: the German *Bundesgerichtshof* (BGH) had submitted its case with resolution of March 30, 2000[9] to the ECJ. Müller-Driver also tackled this issue. Through interpretation of the previous European decisions he draws the conclusion that the ECJ would not find a violation of the Art. 43, 48 of the Treaty. According to Müller-Driver, the *Centros* decisions did not implicate a renunciation of the previous jurisdiction (especially *Daily Mail*), and consequently no unlawfulness of the real-seat-theory. He argued that the real-seat-theory should not be judged under the right of settlement because this right would not find any application from the beginning. Articles 43 and 48 of the Treaty would only guarantee the secondary right of settlement, not the primary right and therefore the Treaty would be indifferent to the regulations of legal conflicts. Since the ECJ's *Inspire Art* decision, we know that on this analysis he was wrong.

As a further milestone, the European Court of Justice ruled on March 11, 2004 that the French legislation taxing unrealized capital gains simply because a taxpayer moves to another EU member state infringes the freedom of establishment (case C-9/02 Hughes de Lasteyrie du Saillant[10]). The case involved an individual who moved from France to Belgium for professional reasons. Upon the move, he was required by French law to pay taxes immediately on unrealized capital gains on qualifying participations he and his family had held during the preceding five years. Suspension of payment of the tax was subject to application, provision of guarantees, and the designation of a representative in France. The ECJ held that these laws restrict the freedom of workers to move within the EU and cannot be justified because they imply a tax evasion motive as a result of a mere change in residence and also because the rules are disproportionate. The decision follows the opinion of Advocate General Mischo and means that all countries that have similar exit tax rules (Germany for example: § 6 Außensteuergesetz – code for external law of taxation) must revise their relevant laws. The ruling could also be important for companies that want to transfer their registered office or place of management and sheds new light on the 1988 *Daily Mail* decision – so far a very broad and controversial discussion has taken place.

The author also goes into law already existing and law in the development stage at that moment, especially European Directives and Decrees.

After two public consultations in 1997 and 2002, the need for legislation allowing companies to transfer their registered office from one Member State to another without first

---

7   Case C-79/85, Segers v. Bestuur van de Bedrijfsvereniging voor Bank- en Verzekeringswezen, 1986 E.C.R. I-2375.
8   Case C-55/94, Gebhard v. Consiglio dell'Ordine degli Avvocati e Procuratori di Milano, 1995 E.C.R. I-4165.
9   Bundesgerichtshof (BGH), DER BETRIEB (DB) 1114, 1115 (2000) (Überseering Case).
10 Case C-9/02, Hughes de Lasteyrie du Saillant, GMBHRUNDSCHAU (GMBHR) 504 (2004).

having to be wound up in their home Member State was highlighted. "The advantage by a company from transferring its registered office on these terms from one Member State to another stems from the twofold need for the company (1) to be able to adapt its location or organisational structure both to market changes and to changes in its position on those markets by choosing the national law which, in its view, best meets its requirements and (2) to be relieved of the obligation, when carrying out such adaption, to go through liquidation proceedings."[11] The Commission in its Action Plan of May 21, 2003, undertook to adopt a proposal for a Directive in near future. The present observations actually have as their objective the change of the registered office based on the concepts developed for the Societas Europeae (SE).

On October 8, 2004 the Statute for the European Company came into force.[12] The concept of Societas Europeae is a compromise between harmonisation and the principle of subsidiarity. The European Company Statute (ECS) has created a common set of rules for the companies operating throughout the EU, with an adaptive structure.[13] The SE will also facilitate cross-border operations instead of a costly and complex network of subsidiaries. The jurisprudence of the ECJ had already recognized a limited freedom of movement (see above), but there is now a new main contribution to establishment of freedom of movement of companies in Article 8 combined with the other articles of the Statute. Nevertheless the ECS is not homogenous as it contains some structural constraints to the freedom of movement and therefore alternatives could and should be developed in future. Article 8 of the ECS establishes the freedom of movement of the SE by authorizing the transfer of the registered office within the EU, Section 1. But this freedom is strictly defined, both by article 7 recognizing in appearance the real seat theory, Section 2, and also by the proceeding of transfer, Section 3. According to article 8 section 1: "The registered office on an SE may be transferred to another Member State in accordance with paragraphs 2 to 13 (about the proceeding of the transfer). Such a transfer shall not result in the winding up of the SE or in the creation of a new legal person". This article authorizes the cross-border establishment of the SE. Consequently, an SE could choose its applicable law by transfer of its registered office and by cross-border merger, even in a Member State in which it does not have a domicile. Underlying is a flexible scope within which companies will be able to transfer their registered office from one Member State to another without having to undergo liquidation. As mentioned above, the SE could so choose the applicable company law. Article 9 of the regulation determines the law applicable for the SE. Article 7 establishes that: "The registered office of an SE shall be located within the Community, in the same Member State as its head office. A Member State may in addition impose on SEs registered in its territory the obligation of locating their head office and their registered office in the same place". Clearly the Regulation admits the real seat theory. This recognition of the real seat theory has two consequences: (1) The SE is free to change its registered office, but the head office has to be on the same place. (2) This Article raises a contradiction with the *Überseering* case. It seems absurd that – according to the *Überseering* case – national companies benefit from a larger freedom of movement by the adoption

---

11 See Action Plan of May 21, 2003, COM (2003) 284 final, *in* ZEITSCHRIFT FÜR WIRTSCHAFTSRECHT (ZIP) 172 (1997), concerning the public consultation *available at* http://europa.eu.int/comm/internal_market/company/seat-transfer/2004-consult_de.htm; Eidenmüller, *Mobilität und Restrukturierung von Unternehmen im Binnenmarkt*, JURISTENZEITUNG (JZ) 24 (2004).
12 Regulation No. 2157/2001/EC of 8 October 2001, Nr. L 294/1.
13 See Herzig & Griemla, *Steuerliche Aspekte der Europäischen Aktiengesellschaft/Societas Europaea (SE)*, STEUER UND WIRTSCHAFT (StuW) 55 (2002) and Kallmeyer, *Europa-AG – Strategische Optionen für deutsche Unternehmen*, DIE AKTIENGESELLSCHAFT (AG) 197 (2003) and Kessler, Achilles & Huck, *Die Europäische Aktiengesellschaft im Spannungsfeld zwischen nationalem Steuergesetzgeber und EuGH*, INTERNATIONALES STEUERRECHT (IStR) 715 (2003).

of an "apparent formation theory;" in fact, it comes very close to an absolute mutual recognition, more than to a "simple" freedom of movement. It seems that the SE is not conceived to be a simple vehicle between the different public limited liability companies.

With regard to the acceptance on the part of the economic "reality" it is noteworthy to mention a very recent statement by General Motors (and the Opel AG): they are planning the foundation of a SE (with seat in Brussels) "absorbing" the Opel AG and hundred subsidiaries in order to become more efficient and reduce bureaucracy.[14] Generally Müller-Driver's scepticism as regards the success of the SE is far from rare in literature and practice.

In 2003 the European Commission also presented a proposal for a Directive to make cross-border mergers easier by overcoming obstacles caused by different national laws.[15] It would make such mergers simpler for all companies with share capital. The proposed Directive would set up a cross-border merger procedure whereby mergers would be governed in each Member State by the principles and rules applicable to domestic mergers. The current proposal differs from the original proposal of 1984 mainly in scope and in the way it deals with the participation of employees in the decision-making bodies of the acquiring company or of the new company created by the cross-border merger. In that respect, it takes into account the principles and solutions incorporated in the European Company Statute Regulation and the accompanying Directive on worker involvement. The original proposal covered only public limited liability companies. The new one extends that scope to include all companies with share capital, which may be defined as companies having a legal personality and separate assets which alone serve to cover their debts. It is aimed primarily at companies which are not interested in forming a European Company (for the most part small and medium-sized enterprises).

Though the contemplations and reflections of the work are on the assumption that the real-seat-theory in Germany will continue to be valid and applicable, the thesis is still of interest for everyone dealing with this matter. It shows the difficulty of interaction between different conflicts of law. Müller-Driver not only makes precise distinctions between different constellations and facts (e.g. the move in and move out of companies), but also touches most of the problematic points and increases the reader's awareness of those aspects. Even after the latest case law of the ECJ and newly passed European laws, there are still unsolved questions about how to treat companies moving out of a country as well as which forms of transformations are subject to the freedom of settlement. Much has been set in motion in Europe and still is in development. In any case one can get a very good overview of the relevant English law and the possibilities of reorganisations in and from England.

---

14 SUEDDEUTSCHE ZEITUNG, October 25, 2004, at 23.
15 *Commission Communication Integrating Migration Issues in the European Union's Relations with Third Countries*, COM (2003) 703 final–2003/0277 (COD) *available at* http://europa.eu.int/comm/internal_market/en/company/company/mergers/docs/crossbordermergers-comm_de.dpf; Rogall, *Die grenzüberschreitende Abspaltung nach der geplanten Änderung der steuerlichen Fusionsrichtlinie*, RECHT DER INTERNATIONALEN WIRTSCHAFT (RIW) 271 (2004).

Jan Pieter Krahnen and Reinhard H. Schmidt (eds.): *The German Financial System* (Oxford, U.K.: Oxford University Press, 2004, ISBN 0-19-925316-1, 550 pp., £79.00. Also available at Oxford Scholarship Online)

David C. Donald*

The *German Financial System* presents a detailed, economic analysis of the German banking and securities sectors as at mid-2003 and should be read by anyone who is serious about understanding German finance. The book is edited by Prof. Jan Pieter Krahnen, who is the director for Frankfurt's Center for Financial Studies,[1] and Prof. Reinhard H. Schmidt, who is a member of the Faculty of Economics and Business Administration of the Johann Wolfgang Goethe-Universität in Frankfurt.[2] Professors Krahnen and Schmidt also contribute individual chapters as well as introductory and concluding chapters that serve to frame the text. The remainder of the book is written by a team predominantly composed of German economists, with the support of a couple legal scholars.

The *German Financial System* (hereinafter referred to as the "book" or the "text") is written in a very readable English for international consumption (including electronically over the internet). Although it is an anthology of articles authored by separate experts in various fields of research, each chapter was prepared with an eye on the book's overall design. It presents the German banking and securities sectors as they stood in early 2003, half way through an extensive program of legislative reform and beset by self-doubt after the collapse of the 90's bull market in which the reform movement had found support. The book focuses on the German banking and securities sectors in their functions of financing the other sectors of the economy, asks whether the German economy is really "bank dominated" with "underdeveloped" capital markets, and – finding this to be the case – whether it is a good thing to push toward a more "market-oriented" system. The text carefully evaluates the leading economic studies of the German financial, securities and corporate sectors, and analyzes much studied topics like the "*Hausbank*" relationship and the application of the "path dependence" theory formulated by Professors Lucian Arye Bebchuk and Mark Roe[3] to Germany's corporate and financial systems. My review will only touch some of the obvious highlights of this dense, 514-page work.

A carefully written text by German scholars in English is a welcome event. Twentieth-century Germany is a fascinating object for scholarly study in numerous disciplines. For example, during a mere thirty years from 1919 to 1949, the German state abruptly jolted through five forms of government: from a monarchy to a democracy to a Nazi dictatorship,[4] and then into two separate governments, one democratic and the other communist.[5]

---

*Research Associate and doctoral candidate, Institute for Law and Finance, Johann Wolfgang Goethe-Universität, Frankfurt am Main. Email donald@ilf.uni-frankfurt.de. Previously published in 6 GERMAN LAW JOURNAL 833 (2005).

1 Information on the Center for Financial Studies and its activities is available at http://www.ifk-cfs.de/English/homepages/h-wiruberuns.htm.
2 Information on the Faculty of Economics and Business Administration is available at http://www.wiwi.uni-frankfurt.de/1.0.html?&L=3.
3 *See* Lucian Arye Bebchuk & Mark Roe, *Path Dependence in Corporate Ownership and Governance*, in CONVERGENCE AND PERSISTENCE IN CORPORATE GOVERNANCE 69 (Jeffrey N. Gordon & Mark Roe eds., 2004). The essay was originally published in 52 STAN L. REV. 127 (1999). The 2004 version contains references to newer empirical research.
4 *See e.g.*, MICHAEL STOLLEIS, GESCHICHTE DES ÖFFENTLICHEN RECHTS IN DEUTSCHLAND: WEIMARER REPUBLIK UND NATIONALSOZIALISMUS 74, 316 (2002).
5 *See* GOLO MANN, DEUTSCHE GESCHICHTE DES 19. UND 20. JAHRHUNDERTS 981 (1992).

In 2005, Germany presents the intriguing feature of a country with a culturally homogeneous history, but whose population was for an entire generation separated into two groups, isolated from one another, and educated in different political philosophies that were nearly diametrically opposed. If "irrational exuberance" caused serious whiplash among U.S. investors between 1996 and 2002, one can only attempt to imagine the psychological impact of a "newly liberated" German stepping out of communism to invest in Germany's late 1990's IPO boom only then to lose her entire savings by 2002. The authors wrote their contributions to the text shortly after this significant collapse of the equity markets.

Further, it is always difficult to understand the inner workings of any country from the outside. The English-speaking world has been fortunate to often receive the expert knowledge of ex-patriot Germans. The United States received a first large wave of Germany's best and brightest in the mid-nineteenth century when their attempts to form a German nation with a constitutional, democratic government came up against the Prussian military.[6] Toward the middle of the twentieth century, the United States then received a second wave of highly talented Germans who fled the horrors of Nazi Germany. Such ex-patriot Germans brought an intimate knowledge of Germany to U.S. universities and shared their insights with a generation of students. The reasons for such emigration have of course long disappeared, and the trickle of younger German scholars into North America – such, for example, as Peer Zumbansen in Toronto, Katarina Pistor at Columbia, and two of the contributors to the book, Christian Leuz at Wharton and Frank Schmid at the Federal Reserve Bank – no longer completely fills the demand for information about Germany. U.S. legal scholarship has thus in recent years come to depend more and more on the studies and observations of talented Americans who do not necessarily bring a "native" understanding of Germany, its language and culture, to their work. One thinks in particular of Mark Roe's various analyses of German bank holdings and "social democracy" as determinants of German corporate governance.[7]

While this American-based scholarship on Germany is valuable, it tends to use Germany as one of a number of exterior controls to prove or disprove a theory formulated primarily for use in the United States. The scholarship asks: "Why isn't Germany like us?" and "What is the social cost or (even) benefit of this deformation?" Indeed, even if the analysis is not burdened with a specific agenda, the starting point of any comparison will already tend to stencil out a caricature: the second object compared usually looks quite different exactly because it is the second object. If you start with a chair and compare a table to it, the table will be characterized as extremely broad, high and missing a backrest. If you begin, say, with German corporate law and compare U.S. corporate law to it, the U.S. law will be characterized as lacking detailed appraisal procedures to guarantee accurate valuation of in-kind capital contributions and bereft of rules for the treatment of shareholder loans in the case of insolvency, not to mention totally lacking any provision for independent, supervisory directors. These are major topics in any text on German corporate law, while the first two are hardly addressed in a similar, U.S. text, and the third falls into the realm of securities regulation. In this way, even a completely neutral starting point for a comparison removes from view many of the subjects that a U.S. scholar would traditionally focus on and highlights absences as potential deformities.

In the field of law – in addition to the fine contribution of the *German Law Journal* – there is a growing supply of high-quality work in English on Germany by some of

---

6   *Id.* at 248.
7   *See* MARK ROE, THE POLITICAL DETERMINANTS OF CORPORATE GOVERNANCE (2003) and STRONG MANAGERS WEAK OWNERS: THE POLITICAL ROOTS OF AMERICAN CORPORATE FINANCE (1994).

Germany's best legal scholars. These include works by Klaus Hopt (based in Hamburg)[8] and Theodor Baums (based in Frankfurt)[9] on corporate law, by Michael Gruson (based in New York and Frankfurt)[10] and Norbert Horn (based in Cologne)[11] on banking law, and by Michael Stolleis (based in Frankfurt)[12] on legal history. The *German Financial System* fits in this newer line of work and would be valuable – if for nothing else – exactly because it gives the foreign reader an understanding of the German financial system as it is currently understood by leading scholars within Germany.

The book is organized as a tightly knit anthology. Analyses of individual sub-sectors of the economy and related topics are sandwiched between introductory and concluding chapters that serve to guide the reader's focus and interpret the book's content, without forcing the reader to reach a specific conclusion. The first chapter, which is available on the internet,[13] is aptly entitled "The Purpose and Structure of the Book" and explains the book's main goal. Professors Krahnen and Schmidt explain that the book is a "country study" that aims to set forth the political determinants behind the evolution and shape of the German financial system: "The individual chapters of this book are, therefore, meant not only to provide information and analysis, but also to shed light on a number of myths surrounding the German financial system. Perhaps the most obvious myth about the German financial system is the controversy concerning relationship lending."[14] Various chapters of the book offer evidence from a number of angles to prove that the German financial system is indeed "bank-based" rather than "market-based." Yet this only tells half the story about the book's purpose. Chapter 2, entitled, "What Constitutes a Financial System in General and the German Financial System in Particular?" sets forth the theoretical framework for the text. The chapter describes a number of increasingly sophisticated models through which a "system" can be understood, ascending from a mere descriptive enumeration of the institutions in an economy (the reader is certainly familiar with this approach, which is used in many overview texts), through an analysis of the roles that particular institutions play in an economy or sector (this functional approach is a standard practice in comparative studies), to an analysis of the complementary and consistent links between individual elements that cause such elements to constitute a system. The authors build on this last model, which they draw primarily from the work of Paul Milgrom and John Roberts, who in turn base their work on a branch of mathematics

---

8   *See, e.g.*, REINER R. KRAAKMAN, PAUL DAVIES, HENRY HANSMANN, GÉRARD HERTIG, KLAUS J. HOPT, HIDEKI KANDA & EDWARD B. ROCK, THE ANATOMY OF CORPORATE LAW A COMPARATIVE AND FUNCTIONAL APPROACH (2004), and KLAUS HOPT & EDDY WYMEERSCH, EDS., COMPARATIVE CORPORATE GOVERNANCE (1997).

9   *See, e.g.*, Theodor Baums & Kenneth Scott, *Taking Shareholder Protection Seriously? Corporate Governance in the United States and Germany.* Johann Wolfgang Goethe-Universität, INSTITUTE FOR BANKING LAW, WORKING PAPER NO. 119 (2003), *available at* http://www.jura.uni-frankfurt.de/baums/; Baums, *Changing Patterns of Corporate Disclosure in Continental Europe: The Example of Germany, in* GIRURISPRUDENZA COMMERCIALE (2003); Baums, *Chapter on Germany, in* SHAREHOLDER VOTING RIGHTS AND PRACTICES IN EUROPE AND THE UNITED STATES 109 (Theodor Baums & Eddy Wymeersch eds., 1999); Baums, *The German Banking System and its Impact on Corporate Finance and Governance, in* THE JAPANESE MAIN BANK SYSTEM 409 (Masahiko Aoki & Hugh Patrick eds., 1995); and Baums, *Takeovers versus Institutions in Corporate Governance in Germany, in* CONTEMPORARY ISSUES IN CORPORATE GOVERNANCE 151 (D.D. Prentice & P.R.J. Holland eds., 1993).

10 Michael Gruson, *Banking Regulation and Treatment of Foreign Banks in Germany, in* REGULATION OF FOREIGN BANKS 339 (Michael Gruson & Ralph Reisner eds., 3rd ed. 2000).

11 NORBERT HORN, ED., GERMAN BANKING LAW AND PRACTICE IN INTERNATIONAL PERSPECTIVE (1999).

12 *See, e.g.*, MICHAEL STOLLEIS, A HISTORY OF PUBLIC LAW IN GERMANY 1914–1945 (Thomas Dunlap, trans., 2004). The German edition of this work is cited in footnote 4.

13 The chapter is available free of charge in PDF format on the Oxford University Press website *at* http://www.oup.co.uk/pdf/0-19-925316-1.pdf.

known as "lattice theory".[15] However, as Chapter 2 explains, the book applies the theory somewhat intuitively and analogically:

> Unfortunately, a formal proof of complementarity and consistency based on the mathematical theory which underlies the theory of complementarity cannot be performed in practice because it would require much more information than is available. However, one can attempt to describe a given financial system informally in such a way that complementarities which are presumed to exist become visible. If one can show that different key elements of the financial system in question fit together in a specific way, then this system is also likely to be consistent ...[16]

> [Moreover,] we assume that the consistency of a financial system, or a good fit of its main elements, creates economic benefits.[17]

As a consequence, the text places its discussion of the "bank-based" nature of the German financial system within a framework of presumed (unproved) complementarities that are also not really proven to be consistent, and this assumed systematic network is then further assumed to be efficient. The overall structure looks like the arguments sometimes promoted in the modern theory of science, in which a theory might be evaluated by internal consistency rather than external verifiability. As said, this theory is introduced in the first and last chapters as a framework within which the text may be interpreted, and does not really affect the content of the other chapters with the exception of Prof. Schmidt's economic analysis of German corporate governance in Chapter 12.

The book offers information and insights on most aspects of German finance. The text contains three excellent chapters detailing the types of German banks, how they are regulated and the costs and benefits of their typical relationships, in particular the *Hausbank* relationship, with client firms. In another chapter, Dr. Andreas Worms, Deputy Head of Money and Capital Markets at the Deutsche Bundesbank, explains in detail the roles played by banks in channeling monetary policy from the European Central Bank to the non-financial sectors of the German economy. An otherwise very useful chapter – authored by Prof. Raimon Maurer – describes the types of institutional investors that are active in the German market, the economics of their growth, and their regulation. It must, however, have gone to press just before Germany's Investment Modernisation Act went into final form in 2003, which makes the chapter in part somewhat out-of-date.[18] Two chapters present a competent outline of the German equity markets and existing measures for investor protection, although the authors' good work has, again, partly been out-paced by the rapid change that the German markets have experienced in recent years.[19] A related chapter presents valuable insight into the trends in initial public offerings and venture cap-

---

14 JAN PIETER KRAHNEN & REINHARD H. SCHMIDT, THE GERMAN FINANCIAL SYSTEM 4 (Krahnen & Schmidt eds., 2004).
15 *See* Paul Milgrom & John Roberts, *Complimentarities and Fit: Strategy, Structure and Organizational Change in Manufacturing*, 19 JOURNAL OF ACCOUNTING AND ECONOMICS 180, 181 (1995).
16 KRAHNEN & SCHMIDT, *supra* note 14, at 29.
17 *Id.* at 62.
18 On the Investment Modernisation Act, *see* Edgar Wallach, *Hedge Funds Regulation in Germany*, *in* HEDGE FUNDS: RISKS AND REGULATION 119 (Theodor Baums & Andreas Cahn eds., 2004).
19 Since the book was published, Germany has adopted the Investor Protection Improvement Act of 28 October 2004 (*Das Gesetz zur Verbesserung des Anlegerschutzes vom 28.10.2004*), which significantly amended the Securities Trading Act (*Wertpapierhandelsgesetz*) to bring German rules on insider dealing and market manipulation into conformance with EU rules, a Business Integrity and Modernization of Shareholder Actions Act (*Gesetzes zur Unternehmensintegrität und Modernisierung des Anfechtungsrechts*, or "*UMAG*"), which facilitates shareholder suits against management, and the Securities Suit Joinder Act (*Gesetzes zur Einführung von Kapitalanleger-Musterverfahren*), which allows a number of related securities complaints to be joined together for streamlined proceedings.

ital over the years and investigates why the volumes of such activity differ from that found in the United States and the United Kingdom. In another chapter, two professors of accounting (Jens Wüstermann at Mannheim and Christian Leuz at Wharton) view German accounting rules in light of the accusation that they provide less information than their U.S. and U.K. counterparts, and conclude that German accounting principles were indeed designed for a system of insiders. Three other chapters address corporate governance and the market for corporate control in Germany.[20]

The reader comes away from the book with an excellent overview of the German banking system, a good idea of the types and position of institutional investors active in Germany and an understanding of how the German equity markets are structured. However, the book's particular focus on the relationship between banking and industry, and on the effects of this relationship on the development of the equity markets and corporate governance has led to the exclusion of two of the more significant elements of German finance. First, the active German debt market, and its peculiar institution of the *Pfandbrief* are hardly discussed.[21] Nowhere in its discussion of organized equity markets does the book give more than a passing reference to Eurex, which is the world's largest futures and options exchange, and is jointly operated by Deutsche Börse AG and SWX Swiss Exchange.[22] Eurex eclipsed the London futures market not long after its creation and has quickly grown into one of the world's premier markets.[23]

The book's strength is its analysis of the role of banks in Germany. Chapters 2 and 3 present convincing evidence that Germany indeed has a bank-based financial sector and that intermediation through banks is still strong in the German economy, and Chapter 7 provides a careful analysis of the *Hausbank* relationship and its potential advantages.

In Chapter 2, Schmidt and Tyrell explain that influential studies published during the 1990's appeared to prove that the German economy was no more bank based than, say, the United Kingdom.[24] Yet this chapter cites work by Hackethal (one of the co-authors of the text) and Schmidt[25] that demonstrates that these studies rested on the following erroneous assumption: "all financing that flows from one type of source, such as the funds flowing

---

20 For a summary of the German government's program to reform corporate governance and the measures taken up through 2002, *see* Theodor Baums, *Company Law Reform in Germany*, JOURNAL OF CORPORATE STUDIES 181 (2003). Professor Baums chaired the government's special Commission that studied German corporate and securities law and produced a report containing recommendations in 2001. For an inside account of the Commission's work, *see* Baums, *Reforming German Corporate Governance, Interview*, 2 GERMAN LAW JOURNAL NO. 12 (2001), *at* http://www.germanlawjournal.com/article.php?id=43. Most of the Government Commission's recommendations have been enacted. *See* preceding note for a partial list of laws enacted. An English translation of the Commission's recommendations is available as an annex to Theodor Baums, "Company Law Reform in Germany," Institut für Bankrecht Arbeitspapier No. 100 (2003), *available at* http://www.jura.uni-frankfurt.de/ifawz1/baums/Bilder_und_Daten/Arbeitspapiere/.
21 For an in-depth analysis (in German) of the German regulation of debt issues and reforms that are being contemplated, *see* THEODOR BAUMS & ANDREAS CAHN, DIE REFORM DES SCHULDVERSCHREIBUNGSRECHTS (Baums & Cahn eds., 2004).
22 For information on the establishment of Eurex, *see* SIEGFRIED KÜMPEL, BANK- UND KAPITALMARKTRECHT 2085 *et seq.* (2nd ed., 2000). Current information on Eurex, including a link to information on its Chicago-based subsidiary, eurex US, is *available at* http://www.eurexchange.com/index.html
23 As Pagano and von Thadden note, "The volume of trade on EUREX has increased almost tenfold between 1996 and mid-2001, from €172.4 billion to €1,639.1 billion. ... In the process it killed off Bund futures trading on London's LIFFE. Also futures trading in French, Italian, and Spanish bonds dwindled into disappearance by 2001." Marco Pagano & Ernst-Ludwig von Thadden, *The European Bond Markets under EMU* 16 (Working Paper, November 2004), Forthcoming in the OXFORD REVIEW OF ECONOMIC POLICY.
24 *See* KRAHNEN & SCHMIDT, *supra* note 14, at 44.
25 Andreas Hackethal & Reinhard H. Schmidt, *Financing Patterns: Measurement Concepts and Empirical Results*, WORKING PAPER NO. 33, Finance and Accounting Series, University of Frankfurt (2003), a revised version (WP 125) is *available at* http://www.wiwi.uni-frankfurt.de/schwerpunkte/accounting/index.php?men=4&lg=0&case=wp.

from the banking sector to the non-financial sector, are first used to fund the reverse flow of the same type, such as debt repayment from corporations to banks. By implication, it is assumed that only what remains after this netting is used for investment purposes."[26] Since loans must be paid back, this assumption resulted in a net flow of zero funds from the banking sector to the non-financial sectors, leaving internal financing as the dominant source of funds for the non-financial sectors. Instead of netting out fund flows, Hackethal and Schmidt look at "gross financial flows, without specifying ex ante how any of the inflowing funds are used."[27] The results show that "German banks provide a far larger share of external corporate financing than American banks, whereas securities financing ... is virtually insignificant."[28]

In Chapter 3, after outlining the types, sizes, numbers and market shares of the various types of banks in Germany, Professor Andreas Hackethal uses intermediation ratios[29] and securitization ratios[30] to analyze the role of banks in Germany as compared to the economies of the United States, the United Kingdom, France and Japan. His results show that in the United States and the United Kingdom, "[b]ank loans, commercial paper, corporate bonds, and corporate equity held by banks constituted only about 10 per cent of enterprises' total inter-sector liabilities at the end of the observation period [1998]. ... In sharp contrast ... [in Germany] [t]he ratio has remained roughly constant at 60 per cent."[31] Hackethal concludes that "the immense stability in intermediation ratios and financing patterns of firms between 1970 and 2000 ... [is] strong evidence for our view that the way in which and the extent to which German banks fulfil the central functions for the financial system are still consistent with the overall logic of the financial system."[32]

Chapter 7 is perhaps the most interesting in the book. In it, Elas and Krahnen provide a very insightful analysis of the *Hausbank* relationship. The results of a 1997 study questioning banks about their relationships with clients showed that a *Hausbank* typically has:

- a high share of the client's debt financing,
- a high share of the client's payment transactions,
- a high share of the client's long-term or short-term financing,
- a special, intense or exclusive business relationship with the client,
- a long-term relationship with the client firm, and
- influence over the client firm's management.[33]

The chapter then performs a careful evaluation of the empirical studies testing the potential benefits of the *Hausbank* relationship. The chapter concludes that *Hausbanks* typically have access to non-public information from their borrowers, especially in the case of mid-sized firms, that the relationship tends to facilitate financing after rating downgrades, and that *Hausbanks* are more likely to take part in workouts of distressed client firms.[34] The authors do not examine the relationship between the possession of non-pub-

---

26 KRAHNEN & SCHMIDT, *supra* note 14, at 46, *see also id.* at 94.
27 *Id.* at 46.
28 *Id.*
29 "Intermediation ratios measure the proportion of sectors' total financial assets and liabilities, respectively, that constitute claims on financial institutions (asset intermediation ratios) or liabilities vis-à-vis financial institutions (liability intermediation ratios)." *Id.* at 90–91).
30 "Securitization ratios take an instrumental perspective and measure the proportion of total claims and liabilities, respectively, that take the form of securities." *Id.* at 91.
31 *Id.* at 93–94.
32 *Id.* at 100–101.
33 *Id.* at 211–212.
34 *Id.* at 227.

lic information and the rules on insider dealing, market manipulation, and required current reports.

The only disappointment in Chapter 7 is a discussion of custodian banks' exercise of the voting rights from their customers' shares. Surprisingly, the chapter fails to acknowledge the significant reforms of proxy voting that the German government found necessary to enact in 1998[35] and 2000,[36] and also appears to equate collective action problems that may stand in the way of coordinated action by custodian banks with the outright exclusion of such action.[37] Oddly enough, the authors ignore the findings of the German government when preparing the 1998 and 2000 legislation, fail to consider newer figures on bank equity and proxy votes,[38] apparently fail to grasp the problem of custody account votes being used to "rubber-stamp" management positions, and then without offering anything more, assert in summing up the chapter that "contrary to the common presumption in the literature, the available evidence does not suggest that banks use proxy-voting rights in a systematic way to influence management decisions."[39] Regretfully, this does not match the rigor found in the rest of the chapter.

The text presents a theory of the German financial system's complementary "inner logic". As said above, the text not only describes the institutions of the German banking and securities sectors and attempts to pin down the true functions of individual institutions and relationships, but also seeks to present (at least intuitively) the inner complementariness and consistency of the system's components, as well as relate such systemic feature to the process of evolution and reform taking place at the time the book went to print. The theoretical framework is to be understood in the context of the "path dependence" theory of Bebchuk and Roe, as a related publication by Schmidt and Spindler makes clear,[40] and it seeks to find confirmation in the various conclusions presented in the book. The theory is discussed at varying levels of abstraction and with somewhat varying conclusions in Chapters 2, 12 and 15. The text posits an insider system of "three groups of powerful and 'influential' stakeholders – blockholders, employee and/or union representatives, and banks,"[41] and finds that the monitoring activity they perform is "made relatively easy by the fact that the groups which form what we have called the governing coalition have a largely similar long-term goal. It does not consist in the maximization of shareholder value, but rather in ensuring stability and growth."[42] The goal of the business corporation is thus complementary and consistent with the interests of its governing coalition. Moreover, the nature of the coalition and the goal of the corporation are consistent with other characteristics of the German financial system: "Its functioning rests on internal, non-public information as opposed to public information,"[43] and corporate finance comes largely from relationships with a small number of banks.[44]

---

35 *See* Gesetz zur Kontrolle und Transparenz im Unternehmensbereich (Law for Monitoring and Transparency in Business Undertakings) (KonTraG), Apr. 27, 1998, BGBl. I-786.
36 *See* Gesetz zur Namensaktie und zur Erleichterung der Stimmrechtsausübung (Law Concerning Registered Shares and to Facilitate the Exercise of Voting Rights), Sept. 6, 1995, BGBl. I at 1089.
37 *See* KRAHNEN & SCHMIDT, *supra* note 14, at 200–202.
38 *See* FARIZIO BARCA & MARCO BECHT, THE CONTROL OF CORPORATE EUROPE (2001).
39 *See* KRAHNEN & SCHMIDT, *supra* note 14, at 227.
40 *See* Reinhard H. Schmidt & Gerald Spindler, *Path dependence and complementarity in corporate governance*, in CONVERGENCE AND PERSISTENCE IN CORPORATE GOVERNANCE, *supra* note 3, at 114.
41 *See* KRAHNEN & SCHMIDT, *supra* note 14, at 395. For a similar finding of complementary between at least two of these elements, *see also* ROE, DETERMINANTS, *supra* note 7, at 81 ("Codetermination and block ownership are complementary, and it is hard for one to exit without the other also existing, irrespective of which one came first.")
42 KRAHNEN & SCHMIDT, *supra* note 14, at 396.
43 *Id.* at 397.
44 *Id.*

One result of constructing a constellation in mutually dependent balance is, however, that change is made very difficult. If a policy maker sets the goal of constructing a harmonious model reflecting an accepted paradigm, individual elements like protecting the rights of a given group or achieving a certain economic result will become less relevant than the overall design. This systemic perspective can be seen in the text's discussion of Germany's efforts to reform its corporate governance system. The text admits that the German system of insider control may benefit by extracting rents from disenfranchised outsiders:

> Where does this compensation [for active participants in monitoring] come from? In part ... it may also come from the "exploitation" of those shareholders who are not insiders, that is, the small shareholders and possibly also some institutional investors. There is no doubt that shareholder protection has been weak in Germany for a long time. ... However, in functional terms, it may have been necessary since with a very high level of investor protection in place it might not have been possible to compensate the active stakeholders for their monitoring effort, and thereby to provide them with incentives to monitor management.[45]

The fact that "shareholder protection has been weak in Germany for a long time" led the German Government Commission on Corporate Governance in 2001 to recommend certain actions to strengthen shareholders' rights.[46] Some of the Government Commission's recommendations on investor protection were enacted before the book was published and others have been enacted since.[47] Following the theory emphasizing complementariness and consistency, the book does not take issue with the Government Commission's efforts to empower the disenfranchised or increase the attractiveness of the German market for international investors, but rather with its failure to choose "the best model of corporate governance for Germany."[48] In the delicate world of complementary and consistent systems, a policy maker cannot simply help one group exercise its rights or discipline the abuse of another, but must choose an entire model and replace the old one all at once. In order to avoid imbalance, changes may well be "abrupt and far-reaching."[49] In this way, the theory of complementary constellations runs into a dead end: change might be reasonable, but it creates inconsistency, and yet it is politically impossible to replace an entire financial system simultaneously.

As said, however, the book does not press this theory to the end, but swerves away from its ramifications with a pragmatic wisdom that may be *inconsistent*, but is welcome. In the book's last chapter, Professors Krahnen and Schmidt take a position that no longer posits complementariness and consistency as the measure of German finance, but offers an agnostic assortment of three stylized views: (i) a market-based system is better, and evolution towards it increases welfare, (ii) consistency is the key, and use of either a pure bank-based or a pure market-based model increases welfare, or (iii) a system combining the advantages of bank-based and market-based systems increases welfare.[50] As the "best of both worlds" solution, the authors seem to prefer the last view without first subjecting it to a complementary litmus test. Indeed, the book then offers a refreshingly lawyer-like mechanism that could allow the value of corporate loans containing a valuable element of

---

45   *Id.* at 403. The economic consideration that controlling shareholders may have to be compensated for monitoring activities has also been raised by thoughtful commentators with regard to U.S. corporate law. *See* Ronald J. Gilson & Jeffrey N. Gordon, *Controlling Controlling Shareholders*, 152 U. PA. L. REV. 785 (2003).
46   *See* BERICHT DER REGIERUNGSKOMMISSION "CORPORATE GOVERNANCE" (Theodor Baums, ed., 2001).
47   *See supra* note 19.
48   KRAHNEN & SCHMIDT, *supra* note 14, at 406, emphasis added.
49   *See id.* at 389.
50   *See id.* at 498–513.

private, "relationship specificity" to be given an accurate value even under fair value accounting rules by permitting firms to "carry the difference between the nominal value of a claim [i.e., considering the benefits of private relationship] and its fair market value as an asset (i.e., to activate the wedge as a special goodwill asset)."[51] Thus, the book ends as it begins, with plenty of creative energy and valuable insights.

Jörg Menzel: *Landesverfassungsrecht* (Richard Boorberg Verlag, 2002, 644 pp., ISBN 3-415-02987-5)

Christian von Coelln[*]

A.

Jörg Menzel's book on the constitutional law of the German federal states is based on his doctoral thesis originally finished in 1995. In the following years, Menzel continued to work on the subject. His efforts have resulted in a fine work that documents the current dynamic developments in the constitutional law of the federal states. The remarkable book is – quite exceptional for a doctoral thesis – solidly hard-covered. As far as its content is concerned, it fills a significant gap in German legal literature. Recently, different studies of the constitutional *procedural* law of the German federal states – an aspect of the law that had been interpreted extensively years ago[1] – have been published. Constitutional law of the states had also been a part of the respective research, as it belongs to the standard of review of the state constitutional courts. However, it was only touched upon indirectly in these studies. Furthermore, all studies gave special emphasis to the basic rights. Consequently, a comprehensive work that examines the constitutional law of the German federal states had been missing until Menzel's volume was published.

B.

Menzel's work is divided into five parts. In the first part, Menzel describes the strained relationship between the sovereignty of the constitution and homogeneity as the fundamental problem of every federal state by referring to the history of the constitutions, to the theory of states and to the comparative law. Within his description, he rightly does not try to subordinate the different ways of organization to one common idea: General statements on "the" federal state are impossible. Nevertheless, an independently legitimated political government, as well as a constitutional autonomy of the federal states limited by an all-state requirement of homogeneity, can be regarded as constant factors of a federal structure of government. However, Menzel correctly points out that the phenomena of organizational autonomy and the obligation to preserve homogeneity do not occur in federal states only. On the contrary, they can also be noticed in other forms of government, such as decentralized states (e.g. different forms of organizational autonomy in Belgium,

---

51 *Id.* at 512.

[*] *Oberassistent* (senior lecturer) at the University of Passau, Chair for Constitutional and Administrative Law, Administrative Law Concerning Trade and Industry/Media Law.
1 STARCK & STERN, LANDESVERFASSUNGSGERICHTSBARKEIT, VOLS. 1–3 (1983).

Italy and Spain) or supranational organizations (elements of homogeneity can be found for example in the UN, in the Commonwealth of Nations and in the European Union).

The second and largest part looks into the Basic Law's dogmatic concept of federal states, which is characterized by elements of diversity as well as by unity. Those features usually stand in contrast to each other. Menzel therefore talks about a state constitution as *"einem Element pluralistisch verfasster Bundesstaatlichkeit"* (i.e. an element of pluralistically composed federal states). Subsequently, he takes into consideration the legislative power of the state constitutions. He convincingly dismisses the disputed view that the federal states are bound to the rules of the Basic Law concerning the allocation of legislative competences when enacting a constitution. Moreover, he explains that the right of the states to enact a constitution can result in banning the competences of the Federal legislator. Menzel also points out that the right of the federal states to enact their own constitution is accompanied by a corresponding duty. Constitutional concepts differing from the Basic Law may be desirable within the scope of the demanded homogeneity; however, in the legal sense, nothing can be objected to a so-called "Xerox-federalism"[2] either, i.e. the adoption of the structures of the Basic Law.

As the federal states are not bound to the allocations of legislative competences when enacting a constitution, they may regulate certain legal questions for which the Federal legislator is competent as far as simple law is concerned. Therefore, it is possible that a provision of a state constitution may collide in content with a provision of the simple Federal law. Menzel supports the increasingly popular view that, in such cases, the provision of the state constitution is not – like provisions of the states' simple law – derogated by Art. 31 Basic Law (*Bundesrecht bricht Landesrecht*/Federal law takes precedence over state law). Instead, the provision only must not be applied in the relevant case. Apart from the conflict between the two laws, the provision of the respective state constitution remains valid and applicable. These considerations are well-rounded by comments on the demands that the duty of homogeneity (enshrined in the Basic Law in Article 28.1) makes on the state constitutions.

Afterwards, Menzel turns his attention to the procedural updating of state constitutional law as "law in action" by the state constitutional courts. He correctly emphasizes the revaluation the state constitutional courts' jurisdiction has experienced during the last few years.

In the third part of the book, the reader is given a general outline of the constitutions of all federal states, arranged in the order of their historical development. Some constitutions had been enacted before the Basic Law was drafted, some were enacted shortly afterwards, and others were enacted just after the German reunification. Menzel succeeds in clarifying the considerable differences between the structures of these constitutions.

Part four is especially relevant, given that Menzel systematically compares the 16 German state constitutions. He focuses on the rules of the law concerning the organisation of the state, the basic rights and the constitutional jurisdiction. In this context, the ensuing discovery of a variety of regulations quickly dispels the impression of an exaggerated unity. The "new states" had been especially open to experimentation and had shown themselves to be quite inventive when enacting their constitutions, particularly with respect to the basic rights.

In the fifth and final part, Menzel analyses the function of the state constitutions in the Federal State of the Basic Law and summarizes the results of the book. He correctly points out that the state constitutions can be very helpful as a standard of comparison for the interpretation of the Basic Law. The state constitutions also underline the federal states' quality as states in the legal sense and play an important role as a symbol of the pluralistic Federal State. These functions go beyond the role of a mere provision that must be observed.

---

2 JÖRG MENZEL, LANDESVERFASSUNGSRECHT 179 (2002).

C.

Not many doctoral theses become standard works shortly after their publication. Menzel's thesis is one of the rare exceptions. Anyone intending to work in the field of state constitutional law is obliged to read it. Even today, not many essays on the subject exist that do not cite Menzel's work.

Not all of Menzel's results are uncontestable, however. For instance, one might debate whether an infringement of Article 28.1 [1] Basic Law really leads to a legal consequence that differs from the one caused by an infringement of Art. 28.1 [2, 3, 4] Basic Law (p. 248 ff.). Alternatively, one might also discuss whether the state constitutional courts are released from the duty of presentation prescribed in Article 100.1 Basic Law (p. 292 ff.).

For the rating of a work whose second and fourth part are especially suitable for a handbook of German federalism, these differences of opinion do not play an important role. Due to an arguably disproportionate focus on the Federal constitutional law, many interpretations the federal variety offers remain underutilized. As the book makes literary access to many aspects of federalism far easier, it will considerably contribute to the realization of state constitutional law and, consequently, further the acknowledgement of such law in legal praxis.

SECTION V:
GERMAN FEDERAL CONSTITUTIONAL COURT
Teacher's Headscarf Case (BVerfGE 108, 282)*

Judgment of the Second Senate of 24 September 2003
on the basis of the oral hearing of 3 June 2003
– 2 BvR 1436/02 –

Editors' Summary of Facts and Procedure

The complainant sought to be appointed to the teaching profession in the *Land* (state) Baden-Württemberg. The administrative authorities denied her application on the grounds that, as a Muslim, she would insist upon wearing a headscarf while teaching. The decision was justified with the argument that the headscarf is to be interpreted, *inter alia*, as a political symbol of cultural delimitation, and thus, wearing it when teaching would not be compatible with the requirement of state neutrality. In her challenge to the administrative decision the complainant argued that wearing the headscarf not only serves as a feature of her personality, but also the expression of her religious conviction; under the precepts of Islam, wearing a headscarf is part of her Islamic identity. The complainant conceded that the state has an obligation to preserve neutrality in questions of religion. However, she argued that when the state fulfils its duty to provide education under Article 7.1 of the *Grundgesetz* (GG – Basic Law or Constitution) it is not obliged to do away with *all* religious and ideological references, but instead the state has to achieve a balance between conflicting interests.

The complainant's challenge to the decision to reject her application was unsuccessful in the subsequent administrative proceedings and administrative courts of various instances. The courts held that wearing a headscarf for religious reasons indicated a lack of "aptitude," as that term is used in Baden-Württemberg's Civil Service Act (*Landesbeamtengesetz Baden-Württemberg*). In reaching this conclusion the courts reasoned that the complainant's freedom of religion conflicted with both the state's duty of neutrality and the rights of students and their parents. This was especially the case when viewed from the perspective that the headscarf demonstrated the complainant's profession of Islamic faith. General compulsory school attendance and the students' lack of influence in the selection of their teachers aggravated the matter, the courts explained, because students would have no possibility of avoiding exposure to this expression of

---

* Permission for publication of the translation of this opinion has been granted by the Bundesverfassungsgericht, Schloßbezirk 3, 76131 Karlsruhe, Bundesrepublik Deutschland. All rights to the translation are reserved by the Bundesverfassungsgericht (2004).

faith. This, the courts reasoned, gave rise to the risk of influence, including unintended influence, by the teacher, who would be viewed as a person of authority by her students. The teacher's right to conduct herself in accordance with her religious conviction, the courts reasoned, must have lower priority than the conflicting freedom of religion enjoyed by the students and their parents. Furthermore, the courts noted that under Article 33.5 of the Basic Law teachers were obliged to accept restrictions of their positive freedom of religion. This sacrifice, the courts explained, is necessary in order to guarantee that school lessons take place in an environment of religious neutrality.

In her complaint to the *Bundesverfassungsgericht* (BVerfG – Federal Constitutional Court) the complainant asserted a violation of Articles 1.1, 2.1, 3.1, 3.3.1, 4.1 and 4.2 and 33.2 and 33.3 of the Basic Law.

Headnotes

1. There is no sufficiently definite statutory basis in the current law of the Land (state) Baden-Württemberg for a prohibition on teachers wearing a headscarf at school and in lessons.
2. Social change, which is associated with increasing religious plurality, may be the occasion for the legislature to redefine the admissible degree of religious references permitted at school.

Ruling

1. The judgment of the Federal Administrative Court (*Bundesverwaltungsgericht*) of 4 July 2002 – BVerwG 2 C 21.01 –, the judgment of the Baden-Württemberg Higher Administrative Court (*Verwaltungsgerichtshof Baden-Württemberg*) of 26 June 2001 – 4 S 1439/00 –, the judgment of the Stuttgart Administrative Court (*Verwaltungsgericht Stuttgart*) of 24 March 2000 – 15 K 532/99 – and the ruling of the Stuttgart Higher School Authority (*Oberschulamt Stuttgart*) of 10 July 1998 in the form of the ruling on an objection of 3 February 1999 – 1 P L., F./13 – infringe the complainant's rights under Article 33.2 in conjunction with Article 4.1 and 4.2 and with Article 33.3 of the Basic Law. The judgment of the Federal Administrative Court is overturned. The matter is referred back to the Federal Administrative Court.

2. The Federal Republic of Germany and the *Land* Baden-Württemberg are ordered each to pay half the complainant's necessary costs for the constitutional complaint proceedings.

Grounds

* * *

B.
The constitutional complaint is admissible and is well-founded. The decisions challenged violate Article 33.2 of the Basic Law in conjunction with Article 4.1 and 4.2 of the Basic Law and with Article 33.3 of the Basic Law.

* * *

II.

* * *

2. If a duty is imposed on the civil servant that, at school and in lessons, teachers may not outwardly show their affiliation to a religious group by observing dress rules with a religious basis, this duty encroaches upon the individual freedom of faith guaranteed by Article 4.1 and 4.2 of the Basic Law. It confronts those affected with the choice either to exercise the public office they are applying for or obeying the religious requirements as to dress, which they regard as binding.

Article 4.1 of the Basic Law guarantees freedom of faith, conscience and religious and ideological belief; Article 4.2 guarantees the right of undisturbed practice of religion. The two subsections of Article 4 of the Basic Law contain a uniform fundamental right which is to be understood comprehensively (cf. BVerfGE 24, 236 (245–246); 32, 98 (106); 44, 37 (49); 83, 341 (354)). It extends not only to the inner freedom to believe or not to believe, but also to the outer freedom to express and disseminate the belief (cf. BVerfGE 24, 236 (245)). This includes the individual's right to orientate his or her whole conduct to the teachings of his or her faith and to act in accordance with his or her inner religious convictions. This relates not only to imperative religious doctrines, but also to religious convictions according to which a way of behaviour is the correct one to deal with a situation in life (cf. BVerfGE 32, 98 (106–107); 33, 23 (28); 41, 29 (p 49)).

The freedom of faith guaranteed in Article 4.1 and 4.2 of the Basic Law is guaranteed unconditionally. Restrictions must therefore be contained in the constitution itself. This includes the fundamental rights of third parties and community values of constitutional status (cf. BVerfGE 28, 243 (260–261); 41, 29 (50–51); 41, 88 (107); 44, 37 (49–50, 53); 52, 223 (247); 93, 1 (21)). Moreover, restricting the freedom of faith, which is unconditionally guaranteed, requires a sufficiently definite statutory basis (cf. BVerfGE 83, 130 (142)).

3. Article 33.3 of the Basic Law is also affected. It provides that admission to public offices is independent of religious belief (sentence 1); no-one may suffer a disadvantage by reason of belonging or not belonging to a faith or to an ideology (sentence 2). Consequently, a connection between admission to public offices and religious belief is out of the question. Article 33.3 of the Basic Law is directed in the first instance against unequal treatment directly linked to the profession of a particular religion. In addition, the provision at all events also prohibits refusing admission to public offices for reasons that are incompatible with the freedom of faith protected by Article 4.1 and 4.2 of the Basic Law (cf. BVerfGE 79, 69 (75)). This does not exclude creating official duties that encroach upon the freedom of faith of office-holders and applicants for official offices, and that thus make it harder or impossible for religious applicants to enter the civil service, but it does subject these to the strict requirements of justification that apply to restrictions of freedom of faith, which is guaranteed unconditionally; in addition, the requirements of strictly equal treatment of the various religions must be observed, both in creating and in the practice of enforcing such official duties.

4. a) The wearing of a headscarf by the complainant at school as well as outside school is protected by the freedom of faith, which is guaranteed in Article 4.1 and 4.2 of the Basic Law. According to the findings of fact made by the non-constitutional courts and not disputed in the proceedings relating to the constitutional complaint, the complainant regards the wearing of a headscarf as bindingly imposed on her by the rules of her religion; observing this dress rule is, for her, the expression of her religious belief. The answer to the controversial question as to whether and how far covering the head is prescribed for women by rules of the Islamic faith is not relevant. It is true that not every form of conduct of a

person can be regarded as an expression of freedom of faith, which enjoys special protection, purely according to its subjective intention; instead, when conduct by an individual that has been claimed to be an expression of the individual's freedom of faith is assessed, that his or her particular religious group's concept of itself may not be overlooked (cf. BVerfGE 24, 236 (247–248)). A duty of women to wear a headscarf in public may, by its content and appearance, as a rule of faith founded in the Islamic religion, be attributed with sufficient plausibility to the area protected by Article 4.1 and 4.2 of the Basic Law (on this, see also BVerfGE 83, 341 (353)); this was done by the non-constitutional courts in a manner that cannot be constitutionally objected to.

b) The assumption that the complainant lacks the necessary aptitude to fulfil the duties of a teacher at the primary school und non-selective secondary school, because, contrary to an existing official duty, she wanted to wear a headscarf at school and in lessons, and this headscarf showed clearly that she was a member of the Islamic religious groupus community, and the refusal to admit her to a public office, which was based on this, would be compatible with Article 4.1 and 4.2 of the Basic Law if the intended exercise of freedom of faith conflicted with objects of legal protection of constitutional status and this restriction of the free exercise of religion could be based on a sufficiently definite statutory foundation. Interests that are protected by the constitution that conflict with freedom of faith here may be the state's duty to provide education (Article 7.1 of the Basic Law), which is to be carried out having regard to the duty of ideological and religious neutrality, the parents' right of education (Article 6.2 of the Basic Law) and the negative freedom of faith of schoolchildren (Article 4.1 of the Basic Law).

aa) In Article 4.1, Article 3.3 sentence 1 and Article 33.3 of the Basic Law, and in Article 136.1, Article 136.4 and Article 137.1 of the Weimar Constitution (*Weimarer Reichsverfassung*) in conjunction with Article 140 of the Basic Law, the Basic Law lays down for the state as the home of all citizens the duty of religious and ideological neutrality. It bars the introduction of legal structures in the nature of a state church and forbids giving privileged treatment to particular faiths and excluding those of a different belief (cf. BVerfGE 19, 206 (216); 24, 236 (246); 33, 23 (28); 93, 1 (17)). The state must be careful to treat the various religious and ideological communities with regard to the principle of equality (cf. BVerfGE 19, 1 (8); 19, 206 (216); 24, 236 (246); 93, 1 (17)) and may not identify with a particular religious community (cf. BVerfGE 30, 415 (422); 93, 1 (17)). The free state of the Basic Law is characterised by openness towards the variety of ideological and religious convictions and bases this on an image of humanity that is marked by the dignity of humans and the free development of personality in self-determination and personal responsibility (cf. BVerfGE 41, 29 (50)).

However, the religious and ideological neutrality required of the state is not to be understood as a distancing attitude in the sense of a strict separation of state and church, but as an open and comprehensive one, encouraging freedom of faith equally for all beliefs. Article 4.1 and 4.2 of the Basic Law also contain a positive requirement to safeguard the space for active exercise of religious conviction and the realisation of autonomous personality in the area of ideology and religion (cf. BVerfGE 41, 29 (49); 93, 1 (16)). The state is prohibited only from exercising deliberate influence in the service of a particular political or ideological tendency or expressly or impliedly identifying itself by way of measures originated by it or attributable to it with a particular belief or a particular ideology and in this way itself endangering religious peace in a society (cf. BVerfGE 93, 1 (16–17)) The principle of religious and ideological neutrality also bars the state from evaluating the faith and doctrine of a religious community group as such (cf. BVerfGE 33, 23 (29)).

Under the understanding until now of the relationship between state and religion, as it is reflected in the case-law of the Federal Constitutional Court, this applies above all to the area of the compulsory school, for which the state has taken responsibility, and for which, by its nature, religious and ideological ideas have always been relevant (cf. BVerfGE 41, 29 (49); 52, 223 (241)). In this view, Christian references are not absolutely forbidden in the organisation of state schools; however, school must also be open to other ideological and religious content and values (cf. BVerfGE 41, 29 (51); 52, 223 (236–237)). In this openness, the free state of the Basic Law preserves its religious and ideological neutrality (cf. BVerfGE 41, 29 (50)). For the tensions that are unavoidable when children of different ideological and religious beliefs are taught together, it is necessary, giving consideration to the requirement of tolerance as the expression of human dignity (Article 1.1 of the Basic Law) to seek a balance (cf. BVerfGE 41, 29 (63); 52, 223 (247, 251); 93, 1 (21 ff.); for more detail, see dd) below).

bb) Article 6.2 sentence 1 of the Basic Law guarantees to parents the care and education of their children as a natural right, and together with Article 4.1 of the Basic Law it also includes the right to educate children in religious and ideological respects; it is therefore above all the responsibility of the parents to convey to their children the convictions in religious and ideological matters that they regard as right (cf. BVerfGE 41, 29 (44, 47–48); 52, 223 (236); 93, 1 (17)). Corresponding to this is the right to keep the children away from religious convictions that appear to the parents to be wrong or harmful (cf. BVerfGE 93, 1 (17)). However, Article 6.2 of the Basic law does not contain an exclusive right of education for the parents. Separately and in its sphere given equal rights beside the parents, the state, to which under Article 7.1 of the Basic Law the supervision of all education is delegated, exercises its own duty to provide education (cf. BVerfGE 34, 165 (183); 41, 29 (44)). How this duty is to be carried out in detail, and in particular to what extent religious references are to have their place at school, is subject within the limits laid down by the Basic Law, above all in Article 4.1 and 4.2 of the Basic Law, to the freedom of organisation of the *Länder* (cf. BVerfGE 41, 29 (44, 47–48); 52, 223 (242–243); for details, see dd) below).

cc) Finally, the freedom to exercise religious conviction relied on by the complainant conflicts with the negative freedom of faith of the pupils in her wearing of a headscarf at school and in lessons. Article 4.1 and 4.2 of the Basic Law, which protects equally the negative and the position manifestations of freedom of faith, also guarantees the freedom to stay away from cultic acts of a religion that is not shared; this also applies to cults and symbols in which a belief or a religion represents itself. Article 4 of the Basic Law leaves it to the individual to decide what religious symbols he or she recognises and reveres and which he or she rejects. Admittedly, in a society that affords space to differing religious convictions, he or she has no right to be spared cultic acts, religious symbols and professions of other faiths. But this must be distinguished from a situation created by the state in which the individual is exposed without an alternative to the influence of a particular faith, to the actions in which this manifests itself and the symbols through which it presents itself (cf. BVerfGE 93, 1 (15–16)). In this respect, Article 4.1 and 4.2 of the Basic Law have the effect of securing freedom precisely in areas of life that are not left to be organised by society itself but that the state has taken responsibility for (cf. BVerfGE 41, 29 (49)); this is affirmed by Article 140 of the Basic Law in conjunction with Article 136.4 of the Weimar Constitution, which prohibits forcing anyone to take part in religious exercises.

dd) The Basic Law gives the *Länder* a broad freedom of organisation in education; in relation to the ideological and religious character of state schools too, Article 7 of the Basic Law takes account of the fact that the *Länder* are to a large extent independent and within the limits of their sovereignty in education matters may in principle organise compulsory schools freely (cf. BVerfGE 41, 29 (44–45); 52, 223 (242–243)). The relationship between the positive freedom of faith of a teacher on the one hand and the state's duty of religious and ideological neutrality, the parents' right of education and the negative freedom of faith of the pupils on the other hand, taking into account the requirement of tolerance, is inevitably sometimes strained, and it is the duty of the democratic *Land* legislature to resolve this tension; in the public process of developing an informed opinion, the legislature must seek a compromise that is reasonably acceptable to everyone. When legislating, the legislature must orientate itself to the fact that on the one hand Article 7 of the Basic Law permits ideological and religious influences in the area of education, provided the parents' right of education is preserved, and on the other hand Article 4 of the Basic Law requires that ideological and religious constraints are excluded as far as at all possible when the decision is made in favour of a particular form of school. The provisions must be seen together, and their interpretation and their area of influence must be coordinated with each other. This includes the possibility that the individual *Länder* may make different provisions, because the middle course that needs to be found may also take into account school traditions, the composition of the population by religion, and whether it is more or less strongly rooted in religion (cf. BVerfGE 41, 29 (50–51); 93, 1 (22–23)).

These principles also apply to the answer to the question as to the extent to which teachers may be subjected to duties as to their appearance and conduct at school, restricting their individual fundamental right of freedom of faith, in connection with the preservation of the ideological and religious neutrality of the state.

5. a) In considering the question of whether a specific form of dress or other outward sign has a religious or ideological significance in the nature of a symbol, attention must be paid to the effect of the means of expression used and to all possibilities of interpretation that are possible. Unlike the Christian cross (on this, see BVerfGE 93, 1 (19–20)), the headscarf is not in itself a religious symbol. Only in connection with the person who wears it and with the conduct of that person in other respects can it have such an effect. The headscarf worn by Muslim women is perceived as a reference to greatly differing statements and moral concepts:

As well as showing the desire to observe dress rules that are felt to be binding and have a religious basis, it can also be interpreted as a symbol for upholding traditions of the society of the wearer's origin. In the most recent times, it is seen increasingly as a political symbol of Islamic fundamentalism that expresses the separation from values of western society, such as individual self-determination and in particular the emancipation of women. However, according to the findings of fact in the non-constitutional courts, which were also confirmed in the oral hearing, this is not the message that the complainant wishes to convey by wearing the headscarf.

The expert witness Dr. Karakaşoğlu, who was heard in the oral hearing, carried out a survey of about 25 Muslim students at colleges of education, twelve of whom wore a headscarf, and on the basis of this survey she showed that the headscarf is also worn by young women in order to preserve their own identity and at the same time to show consideration for the traditions of their parents in a diaspora situation; in addition, another reason for wearing the headscarf that had been named was the desire to obtain more independent protection by signalling that they were not sexually available and integrating themselves into society in a self-determined way. Admittedly, the wearing of the headscarf was intended to document in public the value one placed on religious orientation in one's own life, but it was understood as the expression of an individual decision and did not conflict with a modern lifestyle. As understood by the women questioned, preserving their difference is a precondition for their integration. It is not possible to make any statements that are representative of all Muslim women living in Germany on the basis of the interviews conducted and evaluated by the expert witness, but the results of the research show that in view of the variety of motive, the interpretation of the headscarf may not be reduced to a symbol of the social repression of women. Rather, the headscarf can for young Muslim women also be a freely chosen means to conduct a self-determined life without breaking with their culture of origin. Against this background, there is no evidence that the complainant, merely because she wears a headscarf, might for example make it more difficult for Muslim girls who are her pupils to develop an image of woman that corresponds to the values of the Basic Law or to put it into effect in their own lives.

To assess whether the intention of a teacher to wear a headscarf at school and in lessons constitutes a lack of aptitude, the decisive question is what effect a headscarf can have on someone who sees it (the objective standpoint of the onlooker); therefore all conceivable possibilities as to how the wearing of a headscarf might be regarded must be taken into account in the assessment. However, this has no effect on the fact that the complainant, who plausibly stated that she had religiously motivated reasons for her decision always to wear a headscarf in public, can rely for this conduct on the protection of Article 4.1 and 4.2 of the Basic Law, which is closely related to the paramount constitutional value of human dignity (Article 1.1 of the Basic Law; cf. BVerfGE 52, 223 (247)).

b) With regard to the effect of religious means of expression, it is necessary to distinguish whether the symbol in question is used at the instigation of the school authority or on the basis of one single teacher's personal decision; such a teacher may rely on the individual right of freedom in Article 4.1 and 4.2 of the Basic Law. If the state tolerates teachers wearing dress at school that they wear by reason of a personal decision and that can be interpreted as religious, this cannot be treated in the same way as a state order to attach religious symbols at school (on this, cf. BVerfGE 93, 1 (18)). The state that accepts the religious statement of an individual teacher associated with wearing a headscarf does not in so doing make this statement its own and is not obliged to have this statement attributed to it as intended by it. The effect of a headscarf worn by the teacher for religious reasons may, however, become particularly intense because the pupils are confronted with the teacher, who is the focal point of lessons, for the whole time when they are at school without a possibility of escape. On the other hand, the teacher may differentiate when explaining to the pupils the religious statement made by a garment, and in this way she may weaken its effect.

c) There is no confirmed empirical foundation for the assumption that the complainant would commit an infringement of her official duty because of the feared controlling influence of her headscarf on the religious orientation of the schoolchildren.

In the oral hearing, the expert witness Professor Dr. Bliesener was heard on this point; he stated that from the point of view of developmental psychology there is at present no confirmed knowledge that proves that children are influenced solely because every day they meet a teacher who wears a headscarf at school and in lessons. Only if there were also conflicts between parents and teacher that might arise in connection with the teacher's headscarf were onerous effects to be expected, in particular on younger pupils. The two other expert witnesses heard by the Senate, Ms Leinenbach, Director of the Psychology Department, and Professor Dr. Riedesser, presented no information that contradicted this. Such an unconfirmed state of knowledge is not sufficient as the basis of an official application of the indeterminate legal concept of aptitude, which encroaches substantially upon the complainant's fundamental right under Article 4.1 and 4.2 of the Basic Law.

d) At all events, there was not a sufficiently definite statutory basis for rejecting the complainant for lack of aptitude as a result of her refusal to remove the headscarf at school and in lessons.

The school authority and the nonconstitutional courts present the view that the complainant's intention to wear a headscarf as a teacher constitutes a lack of aptitude because pre-emptive action should be taken against possible influence on the pupils, and conflicts, which cannot be ruled out, between teachers and pupils or their parents should be avoided in advance; at present this view does not justify encroaching upon the complainant's right under Article 33.2 of the Basic Law, which is equivalent to a fundamental right, nor the accompanying restriction of her freedom of faith. No tangible evidence could be seen in the proceedings before the nonconstitutional courts that the complainant's appearance when wearing a headscarf created a concrete endangerment of the peace at school. The fear that conflicts might arise with parents who object to their children being taught by a teacher wearing a headscarf cannot be substantiated by experience of the complainant's previous teaching as a trainee. The current civil service and school legislation in the *Land* Baden-Württemberg is not adequate to permit a prohibition on teachers wearing a headscarf at school and in lessons on the grounds of abstract endangerment. The mere fact that conflicts cannot be ruled out in future does not, in the absence of a legal basis designed for this purpose, justify deriving from the general civil-service-law requirement of aptitude an official duty on the part of the complainant to give up exercising her religious conviction by wearing a headscarf.

Under civil service law, in view of the state's duty of religious and ideological neutrality at school described above under B. II 4. b) aa), neither the concept of aptitude contained in § 11.1 of the Baden-Württemberg Civil Service Act nor the duties for civil servants laid down in §§ 70 *et seq.* of the Baden-Württemberg Civil Service Act, which are to be taken into consideration as orientation in assessing the aptitude of an applicant for a public office, can serve as the basis for a duty of teachers not to permit their affiliation to a particular religion or ideology to be outwardly discernible, in order in this way to pre-emptively counter potential dangers.

Under § 70.1 sentence 1 of the Baden-Württemberg Civil Service Act, the civil servant serves all the people, and under § 70.1 sentence 2 the civil servant must fulfil his or her duties impartially and fairly, and must take account of the welfare of the public in carrying out his or her duties. Under § 70.2 of the Baden-Württemberg Civil Service Act, the civil servant must acknowledge the free democratic fundamental order of the Basic Law and stand up for its preservation in all his or her conduct. It is not apparent that the complainant would be prevented from doing this by wearing a headscarf. Nor does the requirement of moderation in § 72 of the Baden-Württemberg Civil Service Act, which provides that a civil servant who is involved in politics shall observe the moderation and restraint that follow from his or her position *vis-à-vis* the whole of society and from the consideration for the duties of his or her office, cover the case of wearing a headscarf for religious reasons. The same applies to the duty of civil servants to devote themselves with full dedication to their office (§ 73.1 of the Baden-Württemberg Civil Service Act), to exercise their office unselfishly to the best of their belief (§ 73.2 of the Baden-Württemberg Civil Service Act) and to base their conduct both on duty and off duty on doing justice to the respect and the confidence demanded by their profession (§ 73.3 of the Baden-Württemberg Civil Service Act). A prohibition preventing teachers at a state primary school and non-selective secondary school from wearing a headscarf for religious reasons and that restricts fundamental rights cannot be derived from these general duties under civil-service law. Finally, § 94 of the Baden-Württemberg Civil Service Act contains no regulations on a particular form of working dress for teachers.

Nor do the provisions in Articles 11 to 22 of the Constitution of the *Land* Baden-Württemberg of 11 November 1953 (Baden-Württemberg Law Gazette p. 173) on education and teaching and the Baden-Württemberg Education Act (*Schulgesetz für Baden-Württemberg* – SchG) as amended on 1 August 1983 (Baden-Württemberg Law Gazette, p. 397), in particular §§ 1 and 38 thereof, contain any provision under which the general civil service law duties of moderation and restraint for teachers could be interpreted in concrete terms to mean that they were not permitted at school to wear any dress or other symbols that show that they belong to a particular religious group community. At present, therefore, the necessary sufficiently definite statutory basis does not exist to decide that teachers of the Islamic faith, by reason of their declared intention to wear a headscarf at school, lack aptitude for service at the primary school and non-selective secondary school and thus to restrict their fundamental right under Article 4.1 and 4.2 of the Basic Law.

6. However, the *Land* legislature responsible is at liberty to create the statutory basis that until now has been lacking, for example by newly laying down the permissible degree of religious references in schools within the limits of the constitutional requirements. In doing this, the legislature must take into reasonable account the freedom of faith of the teachers and of the pupils affected, the parents' right of education and the state's duty of ideological and religious neutrality.

a) The Federal Administrative Court, in the judgment challenged, emphasised, *inter alia*, that with growing cultural and religious variety, where an increasing proportion of schoolchildren were uncommitted to any religious denomination, the requirement of neutrality was becoming more and more important, and it should not, for example, be relaxed on the basis that the cultural, ethnic and religious variety in Germany now characterised life at school too. In the oral hearing, the representative of the Stuttgart Higher Education Authority, Professor Dr. F. Kirchhof, argued that the state's duty of ideological and religious neutrality in schools must now be treated more strictly, in view of the changed circumstances.

Social change, which is associated with increasing religious plurality, may be the occasion for redefining the admissible degree of religious references permitted at school. A provision to this effect in the Education Acts may then give rise to concrete definitions of teachers' general duties under civil service law, including duties with regard to their appearance, to the extent that the latter shows their affiliation to particular religious convictions or ideologies. It is therefore conceivable that there could also be statutory restrictions of the freedom of faith, in compliance with the constitutional requirements. If it is apparent from the outset that an applicant will not comply with such rules of conduct, this can be stated to the applicant as a lack of aptitude.

A provision prohibiting teachers from continuously showing their membership in a particular religious group or belief by external signs is part of the law determining the relationship between state and religion in schools. The religious diversity in society, which has evolved gradually, is reflected here particularly clearly. School is the place where differing religious views inevitably collide and where this juxtaposition has particularly great effects. Tolerant coexistence with people of other beliefs could be practised here with most lasting effect through education. This need not mean denying one's own convictions; instead, it would give a chance for insight and to strengthen one's own point of view, and for mutual tolerance that does not see itself as reducing all beliefs to the same level (cf. BVerfGE 41, 29 (64)). Reasons could therefore be given for accepting the increasing variety of religions at school and using it as a means for practising mutual tolerance and in this way making a contribution to the attempt to achieve integration. On the other hand, the development described above is also associated with a greater potential for possible conflicts at school. There may therefore also be good reasons to accord the state duty of neutrality in schools a stricter importance that is more distanced than it has been previously, and thus, as a matter of principle, to keep religious references conveyed by a teacher's outward appearance away from the pupils in order to avoid conflicts with pupils, parents or other teachers.

b) It is not the duty of the executive to decide how to react to the changed circumstances, and in particular what rules of conduct with regard to dress and other aspects of behaviour towards schoolchildren should be imposed on teachers to define more specifically their general obligations under civil service law and to preserve religious peace at school, and what requirements therefore are part of aptitude for a teaching post. Rather, it is necessary for the democratically legitimated *Land* legislature to make provisions in this respect. Only the legislature has a prerogative of evaluation to assess the actual developments; it depends on this assessment whether conflicting fundamental rights of pupils and parents or other values of constitutional status justify legislation that imposes on teachers of all religions extreme restraint in the use of symbols with religious reference; authorities and courts cannot exercise this prerogative of evaluation themselves (cf. BVerfGE 50, 290 (332–333); 99, 367 (389–390)). The assumption that a prohibition of wearing headscarves in state schools may be a permissible restriction of freedom of faith as an element of a legislative decision about the relation between state and religion in the education system is also in harmony with Article 9 of the European Convention for the Protection of Human Rights and Fundamental Freedoms (cf. European Court of Human Rights, decision of 15 February 2001, *Neue Juristische Wochenschrift* 2001, pp. 2871 ff.).

aa) The constitutional necessity of legislation follows from the principle of the requirement of parliamentary approval. The principle of a constitutional state and the requirement of democracy oblige the legislature to pass the provisions essential for the realisation of fundamental rights itself (cf. BVerfGE 49, 89 (126); 61, 260 (275); 83, 130 (142)). How far the legislature must itself determine the guidelines necessary for the area of life in question depends on its relation to fundamental rights. The legislature does have such an obligation if conflicting fundamental civil rights collide with each other and the limits of each are fluid and can be determined only with difficulty. This applies above all if the fundamental rights affected, like positive and negative freedom of faith in the present case and the parents' right of education are, by the wording of the constitution, guaranteed without a constitutional requirement of the specific enactment of a statute and a provision intended to organise this area of life is necessarily obliged to determine and specify their limits inherent in the Basic Law. Here, the legislature has a duty at all events to determine the limits of the conflicting guarantees of freedom at least to the extent that such a determination is essential to the exercise of these civil rights and liberties (cf. BVerfGE 83, 130 (142)).

When it is necessary for parliament to pass legislation can be decided only in view of the subject area and the nature of the object of constitutional definition involved. The constitutional criteria of evaluation here are to be derived from the fundamental principles of the Basic Law, in particular the fundamental rights guaranteed there (cf. BVerfGE 98, 218 (251)). Admittedly, the mere fact that a provision is politically controversial does not mean that it would have to be seen as essential (cf. BVerfGE 98, 218 (251)). Under the constitution, however, the restriction of fundamental freedoms and the balancing of conflicting fundamental rights are reserved to parliament, in order to ensure that decisions with such repercussions result from a procedure that gives the public the opportunity to develop and express its opinions, and that requires parliament to clarify the necessity and extent of encroachments upon fundamental rights in public debate (cf. BVerfGE 85, 386 (403–404)).

In the education system in particular, the requirements of a constitutional state and the principle of democracy of the Basic Law oblige the legislature to make the essential decisions itself and not to leave them to the school board (cf. BVerfGE 40, 237 (249); 58, 257 (268–269)). This also applies, and applies in particular, if and to the extent that, in reaction to changed social circumstances and increasing ideological and religious variety at school it is intended to respond with a stricter restraining of all religious references and thus to newly define the state's duty of neutrality within the boundaries laid down by the constitution. Such a division is of considerable significance for the realisation of fundamental rights in the relationship between teachers, parents and children, and also the state.

bb) A provision that one of the duties of a teacher is to refrain in class from wearing a headscarf or any other indications of religious conviction is a material (*wesentlich*) provision in the meaning of the case-law on the requirement of parliamentary approval. It encroaches substantially upon the freedom of faith of the person affected. It also affects people belonging to various religions with varying intensity, depending on whether they regard the observance of particular dress customs as part of the exercise of their religion or not. As a result, it has special effects of exclusion for particular groups. Because of this relation to groups, the creation of such an official duty for teachers is of material significance, over and above its significance for the exercise of the individual fundamental right, for the function of social organisation inherent in the freedom of faith.

Finally, the introduction of an official duty that prohibits teachers from allowing their outward appearance to show their religion must be expressly laid down by statute, for one reason because such an official duty can only be justified and enforced in a constitutional manner – *inter alia* compatible with Article 33.3 of the Basic Law – if members of different religious communities groups are treated equally by it. This is not guaranteed to the same extent if it is left to authorities and courts to decide from case to case whether such an official duty exists and what its scope is, depending on their predictions as to the potential for influence and conflict of identifying characteristics of religious affiliation in the appearance of the teacher in question.

III.

As long as there is no statutory basis that indicates specifically enough that teachers at the primary school and non-selective secondary school have an official duty to refrain from identifying characteristics of their religious affiliation at school and in lessons, then on the basis of prevailing law it is incompatible with Article 33.2 in conjunction with Article 4.1 and 4.2 of the Basic Law and Article 33.3 of the Basic Law to assume that the complainant lacks aptitude. The decisions challenged by the constitutional complaint therefore infringe the legal position of the complainant guaranteed in these provisions. The judgment of the Federal Administrative Court is overturned and the matter is referred back to the Federal Administrative Court (§ 95.2 of the Federal Constitutional Court Act, *Bundesverfassungsgerichtsgesetz*). It is to be expected that the proceedings can be concluded there on the basis of § 11.1 of the Baden-Württemberg *Land* Civil Service Act, which under § 127 number 2 of the Civil Service Law Framework Act admits an appeal on a point of law; in these proceedings, the decisive concept of aptitude must be interpreted and applied in accordance with the provisions – amended if applicable – of the law of school education of the *Land*.

The decision on the reimbursement of necessary expenses is based on § 34a.2 of the Federal Constitutional Court Act.

C.

This decision was passed by five votes to three.

(signed)   Hassemer   Sommer   Jentsch

Broß   Osterloh   Di Fabio

Mellinghoff   Lübbe-Wolff

Dissenting opinion
of the judges Jentsch, Di Fabio and Mellinghoff
on the judgment of the Second Senate of 24 September 2003
– 2 BvR 1436/02 –

The majority of the Senate assume that particular official duties of a civil servant, if they are connected to the civil servant's freedom of religion or ideology, may be created only by a law passed by parliament. Until now, this view has been stated neither in case law nor literature, nor by the complainant herself. If this point of view is adopted, not only does the fundamental constitutional question submitted to the court as to the state's neutrality in the school's sphere of training and education remain undecided; the view also results in an erroneous weighting, not based on the Basic Law, in the system of the separation of powers and in the understanding of the normative power of fundamental rights in connection with access to public offices. The decision disregards the expressly stated intention of the Baden-Württemberg *Land* parliament that it would not pass a formal statute by reason of the complainant's case; in addition, it leaves the parliament uncertain as to how a constitutional provision can be made. Finally, the majority of the Senate give the *Land* legislature no possibility of preparing itself for the new situation under constitutional law that the Senate assumes will exist, and neglects to inform the judiciary and the administration how they are to proceed until a *Land* statute is passed.

I.

In order to justify the constitutional requirement that a statute must be specifically enacted, the majority of the Senate wrongly assume that there was a serious encroachment upon the complainant's freedom of religion and ideology. In this they fail to appreciate the functional restriction, with regard to civil servants, of the protection of fundamental rights. In the case of access to a public office, there is no open situation where legal interests of equal value are weighed up; the legal relationship that is essential to the realisation of fundamental rights at school is shaped in the first instance by the protection of the fundamental rights of pupils and parents.

1. Those who become civil servants place themselves by a free act of will on the side of the state. A civil servant can therefore not rely on the effect of the fundamental rights to guarantee freedom in the same way as someone who is not part of the state organisation. In exercise of their public office, therefore, civil servants are protected by the promise of freedom as against the state guaranteed by fundamental rights only to the extent that no restrictions arise from the special reservation to civil servants of the exercise of sovereign powers. Teachers with the status of civil servants, even within the scope of their personal pedagogical responsibility, do not teach in exercise of their own freedom, but on the instructions of the general public and with responsibility to the state. Teachers who are civil servants therefore from the outset do not enjoy the same protection by fundamental rights as parents and pupils: instead, the teachers are bound by the fundamental rights because they share in the exercise of state authority.

In formulating official duties for the civil servants, the state administrative authority also fulfils the requirements of its obligation under Article 1.3 of the Basic Law; the civil servant's official duty is the reverse side of the freedom of the citizen who is confronted by state authority in the person of the official. If official duties are imposed on the teacher for the exercise of his or her office, therefore, this is not a matter of encroachments upon society outside the state-controlled sphere or an occasion for the ensuing call for law passed by parliament to protect the citizen. The state relies on official duties to ensure in its internal sphere uniform administration complying with statute and the constitution.

The majority of the Senate did not take this difference in structure adequately into account. As a result, the situation of the teacher on the one hand and of the pupils and parents on the other hand, which differ with regard to fundamental rights, are not correctly understood. In particular the legal position of the applicant, who has no legal claim to enter the sphere of state control as he or she desires, may not be seen under the aspect of a subject of fundamental rights defending himself or herself against the state. Voluntary entry into the status of a civil servant is a decision made by the applicant in freedom, choosing obligation to the public interest and loyalty to an employer that, in a democracy, acts for the people and is monitored by the people. A person who wishes to become a civil servant may therefore not reject the requirement of moderation and of occupational neutrality, neither in general nor with reference to specific official or private constellations that can be recognised in advance. At all events it cannot be reconciled with these duties if the civil servant plainly uses his or her employment, within the sphere of that civil service, as a space to profess beliefs, and thus effectively as a stage on which to develop the civil servant's own fundamental rights. The duty conferred on the civil servant consists in expertly, objectively, dispassionately and neutrally assisting in giving effect to democratic intention, that is, the intention of legislation and of the responsible government, and in taking second place as an individual where the civil servant's claims to realisation of his or her personality are likely to create conflicts in his or her employment and thus obstacles to the realisation of democratically formed will.

2. Civil servants are fundamentally different from those citizens who are subjected to a special status relationship by measures of public authority but do not in this connection enter the sphere of the state, merely a special legal relationship, such as pupils and their parents, who have the right to educate them, in the compulsory state school (BVerfGE 34, 165 (192–193); 41, 251 (259–260); 45, 400 (417–418); 47, 46 (78 ff.)) or prisoners in prison (BVerfGE 33, 1 (11)). It is therefore an error to believe that it is possible to fight another battle for the Basic Law's idea of freedom, following the struggle against the institution of the special relationship of subordination (*besonderes Gewaltverhältnis*), by emphasising fundamental rights positions in the internal sphere of the civil service. The opposite is the case. If one sees teachers, who are bound by fundamental rights, primarily as subjects of fundamental rights, and thus sees the teacher's personal liberty rights in opposition to those of pupils and parents, one reduces the freedom of those for whose sake the theory of materiality (*Wesentlichkeitstheorie*, the theory that material decisions must be laid down by the legislature rather than decided by the executive), broadened the constitutional requirement in school education law that matters should be specifically enacted in statutes.

The relationship of the civil servant to the state is a particular relationship of proximity with its own inherent rules, which are recognised by the constitution and regarded as worth preserving. Under the balanced concept of the Basic Law, civil servants are certainly intended to be freedom-conscious citizens – if not, loyalty to the free constitution would only be lip service – but at the same time they are to observe the fundamental priority of official duties and the intention of the democratic institutions embodied in it. As a personality, the civil servant is not a mere "instrument of execution", even if he or she decides to work for the public good. Those who wish to become civil servants, however, must loyally identify themselves with the constitutional state in important fundamental questions and when observing their official duties, because the state, conversely, is represented by its civil service and is identified with the concrete civil servant. All the principles of the permanent civil service are dominated by this idea of reciprocity and proximity.

***

3. The evaluation of aptitude in connection with the special right of equality under Article 33.2 of the Basic Law must not be mistaken for an encroachment upon the freedom under Article 4.1 of the Basic Law.

The requirement and, as it were, the normal case of classical civil rights and liberties is an intrusion by state authority into the sphere of the citizen. The constellations in which the citizen approaches the state, claims benefits from the general public or offers his or her services to the general public deviate from this normal case. Here, state authority does not intrude on society, but subjects of fundamental rights seek proximity to the state organisation, desire the state to act, seek a legal relationship.

The constitutional complaint challenges the violation of Article 33.2 in conjunction with Article 33.3 of the Basic Law and therefore relies on a special right of equality. If rights of equality are asserted in isolation or connection with a claim for performance, however, the constitutional requirement of the specific enactment of a statute cannot be relied on. The infringement of equality does not give rise to an encroachment upon a right of freedom that could trigger the requirement of the specific enactment of a statute. The constellation surrounding the encroachment is different: the appointment of a teacher whose person does not offer a guarantee that he or she will carry out his or her duties neutrally in class indirectly affects fundamental rights of the pupils and their parents; as a result, at best there could be a discussion as to whether a statute is necessary with regard to protecting the freedom of the pupils and parents.

***

4. Finally, another reason for which there is no need for a statute is that the evaluation of the aptitude of a civil servant has indirect effects in a legal relationship that is material for fundamental rights. Admittedly, in the past the application of the constitutional requirement in education law that a statute be specifically enacted was extended for the sake of the parents and pupils, but not to protect the teachers who were civil servants. The situation of civil servants, as a relationship of particular proximity between citizen and state, was, unlike education law with its character of a benefit directed outwards and affecting the rights of parents, specifically not understood as a legal relationship shaped by the civil servant's claim to fundamental rights (cf. Oppermann, *Verhandlungen des 51. Deutschen Juristentages* (Proceedings of the 51st German Lawyers' Conference) 1976, vol. I, part C, reports, *Nach welchen rechtlichen Grundsätzen sind das öffentliche Schulwesen und die Stellung der an ihm Beteiligten zu ordnen?* (By what legal principles are the state school system and the position of those involved in it to be categorised?), C 46–47).

***

II.

The civil servant's duty of neutrality follows from the constitution itself; it does not need to be further supported by *Land* statutes. Civil servants who give no guarantee that in their conduct as a whole they will carry out their duties neutrally and in a way appropriate to the requirements of the particular employment lack aptitude in the meaning of Article 33.2 of the Basic Law (cf. BVerfGE 92, 140 (151); 96, 189 (197)).

The grounds given by the majority of the Senate push the constitutional personal liberty rights a long way into civil service law without giving appropriate weight to the structural decision made by the Basic Law in Article 33 of the Basic Law. These grounds can therefore not be brought into accord with fundamental statements of the constitution on the relationship between society and state. In particular, they misjudge the position of the civil service in realising democratic will.

1. Those who aspire to a public office seek in the status activus (rights to take part in a democratic state) proximity to public authority and, like the complainant, wish to create a particular relationship of service and loyalty to the state. This particular position of duty, which is constitutionally protected by Article 33.5 of the Basic Law, takes precedence over the protection of the fundamental rights (cf. BVerfGE 39, 334 (366–367)), which in principle applies to civil servants too, to the extent that the duty and purpose of the public office so require. Accordingly, the citizen's right arising under Article 33.2 of the Basic Law grants equal access to public offices only if the applicant fulfils the factual requirements of the right, which is equivalent to a fundamental right – aptitude, qualifications and professional achievement. The employer is authorised and constitutionally obliged to determine that an applicant is fit for a public office (Article 33.2 of the Basic Law).

* * *

2. The state whose constitution is the Basic Law needs the civil service in order that the will of the people may take effect in practice. The civil service realises the decisions of parliament and of the responsible government; it puts the principle of democracy and the constitutional state into a concrete form (Article 20.1 of the Basic Law). The design of the constitution aims at democratic rule in a legally constituted form. Both the legislation passed by parliament and the political leadership given by the government therefore require the neutral civil service with its expert knowledge (cf. BVerfGE 7, 155 (163)). Statute and law are a promise for the citizen who is subject to state authority that the form in which a fact situation will be legislated on will be abstract and general and without respect of person. In conformity with this, the civil servant too, who is called to implement the law and to realise the political will of the government in a legal form, acts as a neutral fiduciary *vis-à-vis* the citizen.

* * *

3. The requirement of neutrality and moderation for civil servants that follows from this is one of the tradition fundamental principles of the permanent civil service (Article 33.5 of the Basic Law); it has been enacted in non-constitutional law in sections 35.1, 35.2 and 36 of the Civil Service Law Framework Act and in the civil service Acts of the Länder (cf. § 72 of the Baden-Württemberg *Land* Civil Service Act: cf. BVerfGE 7, 155 (162); Battis in: Sachs, *Grundgesetz*, 3rd ed., Article 33, marginal number 71; Lübbe-Wolff in: Dreier, *Grundgesetz*, vol. II, 1998, Article 33, marginal number 78). This corresponds to the basic duty of neutrality of the state, which also applies in the sphere of religion and ideology, which is derived precisely from the freedom of faith of Article 4 of the Basic Law in conjunction with Article 3.3, Article 33.3 of the Basic Law and from Article 140 of the Basic Law in conjunction with Article 136.1, 136.4 and Article 137.1 of the Weimar Constitution (cf. BVerfGE 19, 206 (216); 93, 1 (16–17); 105, 279 (294)). To this extent, the principles of the permanent civil service under Article 33.5 of the Basic Law create a direct constitutional reservation that in advance restricts the scope for civil servants to exercise their fundamental rights: to protect the fundamental rights of those who are not integrated into the state organisation.

* * *

III.

A teacher at a primary school or non-selective secondary school violates official duties if, in lessons, she uses symbols as part of her dress that are objectively likely to result in obstacles at school or even constitutionally significant conflicts in relation to school. The uncompromising wearing of the headscarf in class that the complainant seeks is incompatible with the requirement for a civil servant to be moderate and neutral.

1. When civil servants exercise a public office, even if they are modern, open and courageous, fundamental rights are guaranteed by the constitution only if there is no suspicion that there will be a marked conflict with the employer's development of informed political opinion and no obstacle to the exercise of the public office conferred. When the majority of the Senate assume that only the existence of tangible evidence of a "concrete endangerment of the peace of the school" is sufficient to deny the aptitude of an applicant for a civil service post, they misjudge the standard for the assessment of aptitude.

The Senate majority themselves also admit that religiously motivated dress of teachers may influence schoolchildren, lead to conflicts with parents and in this way disrupt the peace of the school. In the case of conflict in particular, they state, it must also be expected that there will be onerous effects on younger pupils. This potential situation of danger, however, cannot be cited in response to a prospective teacher at the stage of "abstract danger", but only when tangible evidence of the endangerment of the peace of the school has materialised. In this view, if conflicts have not crystallised, the authority making the appointment can no longer find there is a lack of aptitude.

In this view, the majority of the Senate misjudge the standard of evaluation for the assessment of aptitude under Article 33.2 of the Basic Law. For because the removal from office of a person retaining civil service status for life on account of violation of his or her official duties is possible under the traditional principles of permanent civil service only to a restricted extent and by way of formal disciplinary proceedings, the employer must in advance see to it that no-one becomes a civil servant who cannot be guaranteed to observe the official duties under Article 33.5 of the Basic Law. The constitutionally legitimate means for this is the consideration and decision of whether the applicant has the necessary aptitude for the office applied for. Doubts as to this that cannot be removed permit the appointing authority to make a negative prediction, since here it is not possible to establish aptitude positively (cf. BVerfGE 39, 334 (352–353)). Preventive measures to protect children and the parents' right of education, moreover, do not in principle require that a situation of danger be scientifically and empirically proved (cf. BVerfGE 83, 130 (140)).

Reference to the concept of "abstract danger", which is taken from police law, cannot therefore appropriately solve the conflicts in the assessment of aptitude. On the contrary: the free constitutional state is prohibited from postponing denying that civil servants have the necessary aptitude until it becomes probable that their foreseeable conduct in office will cause damage to particular objects of legal protection, as the concept of danger implies. The distinction between concrete and abstract danger may therefore be used to describe the classical threshold of interference in the relationship between the citizen and the state, but not to describe the standard for the discretion in appointment incumbent on state administration. It cannot accord with the civil service law reservation to civil servants of the exercise of sovereign powers if the constitutional state would have to rely on the threshold of danger under police law against its own civil servants who represent the state and through whom the state acts in order to control their conduct in office. This applies all the more in that the complainant wishes to teach primary school and non-selective secondary school pupils in a state compulsory school, that is, in an area that is sensitive for pupils and parents from the point of view of fundamental rights. In this respect it is therefore not a question of potential dangers or modalities of danger under police law, but merely whether the school authority, in putting into specific terms not only provisions of *Land* law, but also the constitutionally valid principles of permanent civil servants in the meaning of Article 33.5 of the Basic Law assumed on a basis that can be followed that there was a risk of a violation of duty. This is clearly the case.

2. The school board, on the evidence of the record of the conversations relating to aptitude and according to the statements in the oral hearing before the Federal Constitutional Court, certainly showed understanding of the complainant's religious convictions; conversely, however, the complainant clearly showed no understanding for the employer's desire to show neutrality. Except in extreme cases such as the immediate threat of violence, she found she would not be capable of refraining from wearing a symbol of strong religious and ideological expressiveness while teaching. Apart from the fact that this rigidity gives rise to doubts as to the complainant's prior loyalty to the political aims of her employer and the order of values in the Basic Law, *inter alia* in a possible conflict with religious convictions of Islam, in this way, even at the early stage of evaluation of aptitude, circumstances became known that would make it substantially more difficult to use the applicant in every function at school and that would bring the *Land* authority of the state into conflicts with pupils and their parents, but possibly also with other teachers, that can be predicted even today.

* * *

4. The assumption of the majority of the Senate that the cross on a classroom door and the headscarf of a teacher in class are not comparable, a comparison decided in favour of the complainant, misjudges the fundamental rights position of the pupils and parents affected. The decisive factor here is the influence to which the individual pupil in a compulsory state school and under state responsibility is subjected. If, in surroundings with a Christian influence, a cross hangs above the school door – not a large crucifix behind the teacher (cf. BVerfGE 93, 1 (18)) – this can scarcely any longer be regarded as an encroachment upon the negative freedom of religion or the parents' right of education. Children have too few associations with a mere everyday object on the wall that has no immediate relation to a concrete person or real-world fact situation. The cross, over and above its religious significance, is too much a general cultural symbol for a culture, fed by Jewish and Christian sources, bound by values but open, that has become tolerant as a result of wide historical experience, some of it painful.

In contrast, teachers, as persons and as personalities, have a material moulding effect on the children, especially at primary school and in the function of class teachers. If a teacher wears striking dress, this creates impressions, gives rise to questions and encourages imitation. In the oral hearing, the expert witness Professor Dr. Bliesener stated on this point that the conduct of the teacher encourages the pupils to imitate it: this happens because the pupils at a primary school often have a close emotional relationship, and the teacher is also expect to aim for this, for pedagogical reasons, and because the attention of children is clearly directed at the teacher and the teacher's authority is also perceived in the context of the school.

The complainant's statement that if there were questions about the headscarf she would answer these untruthfully and in contradiction to her religious conviction, saying it was only a fashion accessory, is not appropriate to avoid a conflict of fundamental rights. For children too are aware of the religious significance of wearing a headscarf permanently, that is, even indoors. In addition, schoolchildren interact not only with the teacher, but also with their parents and wider social surroundings. Parents who answer their children's questions truthfully within their own understanding of education will not be able to avoid explaining that the teacher wears the headscarf because only in this way can she preserve in public her dignity as a woman. But here there are the seeds of a conflict with the moral concepts of children with non-Islamic parents, and possibly even with Islamic parents who do not believe in a requirement that women cover themselves in public. The objective irritation effect of a symbol that is also political and cultural may easily reach the child, by way of reactions in its social surroundings, and lead the child to ask whether, in a conflict of values that it cannot judge, it should take the side of the teacher or the side of its social surroundings, which decidedly reject the headscarf, and which may include its parents. In the oral hearing, the expert witness Professor Dr. Bliesener in this connection referred to the possibility that children of primary school age might be emotionally overtaxed if a permanent conflict developed between the teacher on the one hand and the parents or individual parents on the other hand.

5. In order that an official duty, directed towards moderation in the civil servant's dress, can lawfully be put into concrete terms by the employer, no empirical proof of "dangerous situations" is needed, and still less is it necessary for the *Land* legislature to carry out scientific surveys in order to establish the "endangerment". A constitutional requirement of the specific enactment of a statute with a duty for the legislature to offer proof, for the mere purpose of putting official duties into concrete terms and ordering them to be applied, is not merely foreign to the system, but also takes the free constitutional state further into an immobility that obstructs its effectiveness. It is quite adequate for the assessment of aptitude that the use of meaningful symbols as part of dress a conflict appears reasonably possible or even likely.

This is the case, because the headscarf clearly, at least in part, carries a heavy symbolic meaning as a symbol of political Islamism – this is shown even by the public reactions to the court proceedings instigated by the complainant – and corresponding defensive reactions are to be expected. This objective content also includes the emphasis of a moral distinction between women and men that is likely to lead to conflicts with those who in turn support equality, equal value and equal treatment in society of women and men (Article 3.2 of the Basic Law) as a high ethical value.

* * *

6. The complainant stated that she felt her dignity was violated if she appeared in public with her hair uncovered. Even if the complainant did not expressly state it in so many words, this suggests the converse conclusion that a woman who does not cover her head gives up her dignity. Such a distinction is objectively qualified to give rise to values conflicts at school. This applies even in the relationship between the teachers, but particularly in relation to parents; their children, experience shows, develop a special relationship to their teacher in the primary school in particular.

Whether it is politically or pedagogically right or wrong to confront children as soon as possible with other standards of value or a lives based on a different understanding of the dignity of women than that of their parents is legally immaterial. The only significant factor is whether the appointing authority's assessment is understandable when it argues that there is a possibility of conflicts at school that could perfectly well have been avoided if the teacher had shown moderation in this respect. The responsible school board assumed without error that this was the case.

The headscarf, worn as the uncompromising compliance with an Islamic requirement that the complainant assumed existed for women to cover themselves, at present represents for many people inside and outside the Islamic religious community group for a cultural and political statement with a religious foundation, relating in particular to the relationship of the sexes to each other (cf. e.g. Nilüfer Göle, *Republik und Schleier*, 1995, pp. 104 ff.; Erdmute Heller & Hassouna Mosbahi, *Hinter den Schleiern des Islam*, 1993, pp. 108 ff.; Rita Breuer, *Familienleben im Islam*, 2nd ed. 1998, pp. 81 ff.; Tariq Ali, *Fundamentalismus im Kampf um die Weltordnung*, 2002, pp. 97ff.). The majority of the Senate did not attach enough significance to this circumstance. As a result, they also did not consider the question as to whether, among the adherents of the Islam faith in Germany, there was a not insignificant or even growing number of people who regard the headscarf and the veil as a cultural challenge made to a society whose value system they reject, and above all, whether defensive reactions are to be expected from among the majority of the citizens of different faiths, and if so, what form these reactions might take. At all events, important commentators on the Koran are also of the opinion that the requirement that women cover their heads is based on the necessity of keeping women in their role of serving men, independently of the question as to whether a strict requirement to this effect even exists. This distinction between men and women is far removed from the values of Article 3.2 of the Basic Law.

* * *

IV.

The majority of the Senate extend the constitutional requirement of the specific enactment of a statute to an area which, because it is dependent on the individual case and because it is subject to existing constitutional obligations, is in practice not accessible to control by statute (cf. BVerfGE 105, 279 (304)).

1. The parliament of the *Land* Baden-Württemberg expressly and with good reasons refused to pass a formal statutory provision occasioned by the assessment of aptitude in the present case. In the period relevant for this litigation, the *Land* parliament twice dealt with the problem of teachers who wish to wear a headscarf in class (Minutes of plenary proceedings (*PlenarProt.*) 12/23 of 20 March 1997, pp. 1629 ff.; Minutes of plenary proceedings 12/51 of 15 July 1998, pp. 3977 ff.). The concrete case of the complainant was debated in detail in the plenary debate of 15 July 1998 (Minutes of plenary proceedings 12/51 of 15 July 1998) and a resolution was passed on a motion by the parliamentary *Republikaner* party; the motion was for legislation to be passed (*Land* parliament document, LTDrucks, 12/2931 of 9 June 1998). By a large majority, with only the votes of the *Republikaner* party opposing, the parliament voted not to pass legislation on the question of assessment of aptitude with regard to the wearing of religious symbols in class. The decision was stated to have been made because broader and more detailed legislation was not necessary; statutory provision would make it more difficult to make the appropriate assessment of aptitude based on the individual case and thus also to exercise the scope for interpretation in awarding public offices and at the same to do justice to personal liberties.

* * *

2. The majority of the Senate require the *Land* legislature to put constitutional restrictions inherent in the Basic Law into concrete terms, although they can be determined concretely enough from the Basic Law. It is therefore doubtful whether the *Land* legislature is even authorised to put these inherent restrictions into concrete terms, beyond making a declaration confirming them or clarifying them.

* * *

3. The Senate did not do justice to the task of answering a fundamental constitutional question, although the case is ripe for a decision. As a result, the *Land* legislature must now pass a statute, which according to the dissenting opinion is not even necessary, and this without being granted a transitional period for this surprising necessity. In addition, it would scarcely be compatible with the principle of equality to incorporate a statutory basis for a general prohibition of significant religious or ideological symbols in office, as suggested by the majority of the Senate, only in the Education Act and not generally in the *Land* Civil Service Act; the relevant conflict situations may occur in other areas of the civil service too, for example in connection with the youth welfare service, social work, public safety or the administration of justice.

* * *

(signed)   Jentsch   Di Fabio   Mellinghoff

INDEX

A
Action Plan on the Free Movement of Workers 225–6
administrative agencies in USA
  executive review 63–4
  judicial review 64–9
administrative law
  in Germany and USA 60–88
  judicial review in Germany 71–6
  rising volume in USA 69–71
Adoui and Cornaille case (ECJ) 246
agency rulemaking power in Germany 71–2
Aka v. Turkey (Eur. Ct. H.R.) 163
Akrich case (ECJ) 265, 272
Akus v. Turkey (Eur. Ct. H.R.) 163
Albert Haidn case 93, 94
allgemeine Handlungsfreiheit (general freedom to act) 50
America *see* USA
American Depression and New Deal 62–3
Anglo-Saxon legal tradition 160, 162
Angonese case (ECJ) 265, 267, 277, 282
anti-extremism 52–4, 55
anti-National-Socialism 55–7
Antonisson case (ECJ) 247
Arbeitsbereitschaft (readiness for work) 400
AWACS Mission decision (FCC) 339–42

B
Baden-Württemberg, State Constitutional Court 414–15
Baha'i 3–4, 21
Baumbast case (ECJ) 254–5, 259, 261, 271, 278, 302, 314
Bavaria, State Constitutional Court 415–16, 417, 424, 425
Benda, Ernst 60
Bereitschaftsdienst (on-call service) 400–2
Bestandskraft (binding effect of administrative decision) 426
BGHSt *see* Bundesgerichtshof Strafsachen
BGHZ *see* Bundesgerichtshof-Zivilsachen
Bickel and Franz case (ECJ) 304, 321, 322–3

Bolt, Jan 472–8
Bonsignore case (ECJ) 246
Borradori, Giovanna 497
Bouchereau case (ECJ) 246
Brack case (EJC) 220–1
Brandenburg, State Constitutional Court 419–20, 422, 423–4
Bremen, State Constitutional Court 421
Brokdorf decision (FCC) 45
Bundesarbeitsgericht (Federal Labor Court) 399–411
Bundesgerichtshof Strafsachen (BGHSt) (Federal Court of Justice, Criminal Law) 378–98
Bundesgerichtshof-Zivilsachen (BGHZ) (Federal Court of Justice, Civil Law) 361–77
Bundesverfassungsgericht (Federal Constitutional Court) (FCC) 23–44, 333–53
Bundesverwaltungsgericht (Federal Administrative Court) (FAC) 354–60
bylaws and statutory orders 71

C
Caliph of Cologne Deportation case (FAC) 359–60
Carpenter case (ECJ) 264, 267, 276, 277, 282
Carter v. Carter Coal Company 62
Castelli v. ONPTS case (ECJ) 249
Centros judgment (EJC) 135, 137–8, 143, 145, 146, 153–5
Charter of Fundamental Rights of the European Union 177, 181–2, 211, 327–8, 330
Chen case (ECJ) 260–2, 272, 275, 278, 280, 281, *see also Zhu and Chen* case
Chevron deference rule 64–9
Chevron U.S.A. Inc. v. Natural Resources Defense Council 65–9
Christians, evangelical 21
church and state 1, 2
Citizens and Aliens – Foreigners and the Law in Britain and the German States 509–11
Coelln, Christian von 412–25, 530–2

Collins case (ECJ) 260–2, 262, 267, 274, 277, 281, 282
Commission
   European constitutionalism 176, 188, 189, 198, 199–200
   Regulation 1408/71, personal scope 218, 224–30, 338
Commission v. German (Lawyers) case (ECJ) 263
Communist Party (KDP) 53–4
Community Protection Act, Washington State 99–100
company formation
   under Delaware law 153–4
   under German law 148–9
company law, German Federal Court of Justice 374–5
conflict of laws in Germany 132–55
Constitutional Courts of the Länder 412–25
Constitutional Treaty, The 179, 180–201, 206–10, 211–15, 271, 282, 284, 328–30
consumer protection, for contracts between employer and employee 402–4
Consumer Sales Directive 1999/44/EC, implementation in Germany 116, 118–30
   conformity 123–5
   consumer guarantees 130
   consumer sales/other sales 120–2
   limitation periods 128–9
   redress 129–30
   remedies 125–8
Continental legal reasoning 160
contract law, German Federal Court of Justice 361–4
Convention on the Future of Europe 198–201
Corporate Governance Regimes: Convergence and Diversity 478–92
corporate law, German 132–55
Council of Europe
   European constitutionalism 180, 186, 188, 191–2, 200–1, 206–9
   Regulation 1408/71, personal scope 218, 330–6, 338
Council of Ministers *see* Council of Europe
Court Approval for Termination of Life-prolonging Measures case (BGHZ) 368–70
Cownie, Fiona 511–16
criminal law in Germany 378–98
   agency 379–86
   criminal attempt 395–8
   diminished responsibility 392–5
   inchoate offences 395–8
   intoxication 392–5
   preventive detention 105–6
   self-defense 386–92
Criminal Proceedings v. Bickel & Franz case (ECJ) 257, *see also* Bickel and Franz case
Criminal Proceedings v. Florus Wijsenbeek case (ECJ) 257, *see also* Wijsenbeek case
cross-border corporate issues 132–4

D
Daily Mail decision (ECJ) 141
Declaration of Guarantee by Employee case (BGHZ) 361–2
Dellavalle, Sergio 171–215
democracy 45–59
   a civil society 57–9
   in European Union 173–9
   libertarian and protectionist 48–52
   militant 51–2, 55
   restrained and unrestrained 47–8
Denmark 137–8
detention, preventive *see* Germany, preventive detention
Deutsche Verwaltung an der Grenze zum 21. Jahrhundert 493–6
D'Hoop case (ECJ) 258, 261, 274, 320, 321, 324
Diatta v. Land Berlin case (ECJ) 250, 271
Directive 1999/44/EC see Consumer Sales Directive 1999/44/EC, implementation in Germany
Directive 2004/38 251–3
dismissal protection 409–10
Dismissal Protection Act 399, 403, 407, 409–10
Distomo case (BGHZ) 364–6
Donald, David C. 522–9
Donatella Calfa case (ECJ) 246
Drittwirkungssituationen (third party effect) 50
driver's licenses, ECJ judgment 428
Dupré, Catherine 502–8
Durchgriffshaftung (piercing the corporate veil) 132, 149–51

E
eBay case (BGH) 363–4
EC Treaty 255–66, 273–82, 283–4, 286–331
Economic Miracle 2
Edinburgh Council 230–1
electoral law, German states 416–17
Elsen case (ECJ) 301, 304, 320, 321, 324
employees as consumers 402–4
Entsorgung der Vergangenheit (disposal of the past) 53
environment, ECJ judgments 428
Equalization of Tax Liability case (FCC) 72

equivalence principle 30–1
Euro, ECJ judgment on introduction of 427
Eurojust 177
European Charter of Fundamental Rights 271, 284
European citizenry, bringing closer to Institutions 205–12
European citizenship 239–40, 255–62
    freedom of movement 283–332
    meaning of concept 255–62
    origin of concept 239–40
    Regulation 1408/71 225–7
European Community Treaty see EC Treaty
European Constitutionalism 171–215
European Convention on Human Rights 47, 158–9, 170, 284
European Convention on Social and Medical Assistance 310–11
European Council *see* Council of Europe
European Court of Human Rights
    2003–2004 report 445–65
    concerning Germany *see* Germany, decisions of European Court of Human Rights
    establishment 158
    interpretation of judgments 156–70
European Court of Justice (ECJ) 176
    concerning Germany 132–55, 426–44
European Defence Agency 190
European Parliament 176, 183, 186, 188, 189, 191–8, 205–10
European people (community of the citizens of the Union) 179–205
European Union
    judicial cooperation 186–7
    the *people* concept interpreted 202–5
    public power 171–215
    Treaty on 255–6, *see also* Maastricht Treaty
Europol 177
Extradition to USA decision (FCC) 348–53

F
FAC *see* Federal Administrative Court
Fahrmeir, Andreas 509–11
family insurance 31–2
family law, German Federal Court of Justice 368–72
FCC *see* German Federal Constitutional Court
Federal Administrative Court *see* Bundesverwaltungsgericht; German Federal Administrative Court
federal agencies in USA 61–2
Federal Constitutional Court *see* Bundesverfassungsgericht; German Federal Constitutional Court

Federal Court of Justice *see* Bundesgerichtshof Strafsachen; Bundesgreichtshof Zivilsachen; German Federal Court of Justice
Federal Labour Court *see* Bundesarbeitsgericht
Fiorini aka Christini v. SNCF case (ECJ) 249
fixed-term employment contracts 404–5
Forstinger, Christin M. 478–92
Foster, Nigel 239–82
four fundamental freedoms, the 204, 225, *see also* free movement of persons in European Union
Frankenberg, Günter 45–59
free movement of persons in European Union 239–332
    contribution of European Court of Justice 248–51
    definitions 284
    Directive 2004/38 251–3
    European citizenship 239–40, 255–62
    expansion of rights 244–8
    further developments 327–32
    general Directives 255
    general right 294–327
    market-related rights 285–94
    original legal basis 240–4
    third country nationals 240, 262, 263, 267–73
    Treaty on European Union 255–6
    as a Union citizen's right 283–332
    welfare and family rights 273–80
freedom of establishment 132–55
Fremdvölkische (aliens) 57
French Revolution 173–4

G
Gaal case (ECJ) 250–1
Garcia Avello case (ECJ) 321
Gebhard case (ECJ) 143
German Civil Justice 469–72
German Federal Administrative Court 354–60
    see also Bundesverwaltungsgericht
German Federal Constitutional Court
    preventive detention 94–7
    religious and ideological protections of the Basic Law 3–4
    see also Bundesverfassungsgericht
German Federal Constitutional Court (FCC) 45–6, 333–53, *see also* individual (FCC) cases and decisions
German Federal Court of Justice
    company law 374–5
    contract law 361–4
    criminal law 378–98
    family law 368–72

intellectual property law 372–4
private law 361–77
securities law 375–7
tort law 364–8
see also Bundesgerichtshof Strafsachen;
    Bundesgreichtshof Zivilsachen
German Financial System, The 522–9
German law
    administrative law 71–88
    company formation law 148–9
    conflict of laws 132–55
    corporate law 132–55
    criminal law *see* criminal law in Germany
    labor law 399–411
    partnerships 135–7
    sales law 116–31, *see also* Consumer Sales
        Directive 1999/44/EC
*German Law of Torts, The: A Comparative
    Treatise* 467–8
German states
    communal self-administration 418–20
    electoral law 416–17
    jurisprudence 412–25
    law of constitutional procedure 421–5
    law on organisation of the State 412–21
    law of parliament 412–16
German statutory social welfare system 23–44
Germany
    breakdown of population 2–3
    Constitution 174, 184
    decisions of European Court of Human
        Rights
        barristers' rights of audience 460–2
        child custody 452–6
        legal aliens 456–7
        length of legal proceedings 457–60
        parental access 447–51
        transsexuality 462–5
        see also individual (Eur. Ct. of H.R.) cases
    decisions of European Court of Justice
        132–55, 426–44, *see also* individual (ECJ)
        cases
    partnerships 135–7
    preventive detention 89–115
        Bavarian State law 91–2
        comparison with USA 105–13
        Federal Constitutional Court rules 94–7
        Federal Government position 97–8
        reaction of scholars 93–8
    religious freedoms 1–22
    statutory social welfare system reform
        23–44
Gesellschaft bürgerlichen Rechts (GbR)
    (private law partnership) 132, 135–7

*Gesetz zur Unterbringung von besonders
    rückfallgefährdeten hochgefährlichen
    Straftätern* (Law for the Treatment of
    Especially Recidivism-prone Dangerous
    Criminals) 91–2
Gewährleistungstheorie (warranty theory) 117
Gewaltverbot (prohibition of violence) 50
Giagounidis case (ECJ) 279–80
Gillette, Justice W. Michael, Oregon Supreme
    Court 68
*Grenzüberschreitende Restrukturierung von
    Kapitalgesellschaften zwischen Deutschland
    und England* 516–21
Grimm, Justice Dieter, FCC 60
Grossfeld, Bernhard 467–8
Gründungstheorie (*incorporation* theory) 134
Grunewald, Ralph 378–98
Grzelczyk case (ECJ) 254, 257–8, 274–6, 301–2,
    304, 311, 313, 316–18, 321, 322–3, 326

H
Haidn, Albert case 93, 94
Hammel, Andrew 89–115
Hart, H.L.A. 115
Hartz, Dr. Peter 408–9
Hartz reforms 408–9, 411
Headscarf case *see Islamic Head-scarf* case
    (FAC); *Teacher's Headscarf* case (FCC)
headscarves, wearing at work 407
health insurance 25
    pensioners' 35–8
    third parties 38–44
Herrenchiemsee Convention 52–3
Hesse, State Constitutional Court 416–17, 422,
    423
Hinckley, John, Jr. 107
Hoekstra case (EJC) 219
Hoffmann, Florian F. 445–65
House-tyrant case (BGHSt) 390–2
Hughes de Lasteyrie du Saillant judgment (ECJ)
    146
human dignity and human rights 1

I
ideological protection under the Basic Law 3–4
immigration of foreigners to Germany 2
*Importing the Law in Post-communist Transitions:
    The Hungarian Constitutional Court and the
    Right to Human Dignity* 502–8
Informatec cases (BGHZ) 375–7
Inspire Art judgment (ECJ) 143, 144–5, 146,
    147, 149, 152–5
insurance
    family 31–2

health *see* health insurance
long-term care 26, 31, 32–5
pension 24–5
private contrasted with statutory social insurance 26–7, 32–5
intellectual property law, German Federal Court of Justice 372–4
intra-European social security 216–38
Islamic Head-Scarf case (FAC) 354–6, *see also Teacher's Headscarf* case (FFC)
Italian Constitution (1947) 55
Izzo, Anna L. 399–411, 516–21

J
Jaeger, Renate 23–44
Jehovah's Witness case (FCC) 15–17, 18, 21
Jehovah's Witnesses 3–4, 15–17, 21
Jews 21, 57
judgments of the European Court of Human Rights
defined 156
how to read and interpret 165–8
Judicial Control of Marital Agreements case (BGHZ) 370–2
Justizvollzugsamt (correction facility) 91

K
Kaba I case (ECJ) 301
Kalac v. Turkey (Eur. Ct. H.R.) 163–4
Kansas Supreme Court 103–5
Kansas v. Crane 103–5, 113
Kansas v. Hendricks 103–5, 113
KPD (Communist Party of Germany) 53–4
Kelsen, Hans 157
Kemmerer, Alexandra 511–16
Khalil judgment (ECJ) 230, 233–7
Kiethe, Friedemann F. 399–411
Kinzig, Dr. Jörg 97–8
Kohl, Helmut 356–9
König, Klaus 493
Kopftuchentscheidung see Islamic Head-scarf case (FAC); *Teacher's Headscarf* case (FCC)
Koskenniemi, Martti 497–502
Krahnen, Jan Pieter 522
Krankenhausfinanzierungsgesetz (Hospital Funding Act) 42
Kühne & Heitz case (ECJ) 426

L
labor law in Germany 399–411
Lamassoure Report 183–4
Landeshauptstadt Kiel v. Norbert Jaeger (ECJ) 400–1

Landesverfassungsgerichte (Constitutional Courts of the Länder) 412–25
Landverfassungsrecht 530–2
Learning Sovereign, The 45–59
Legal Academics: Culture and Identities 511–16
legal precedents, interpretation of 156–70
life-prolonging measures *see Court Approval for Termination of Life-prolonging Measures* case (BGHZ)
Lüth decision (FCC) 45
Luxembourg Accord 191

M
Maastricht Treaty 176–7, 206, 210–11, 255–6, 316, 327
McAllister, Marc Chase 60–88
McCahery, Joseph A. 478
Manjit Kaur case (EJC) 256
Mantelgesellschaften (shelf companies) 132, 147–9
Marburger Bund (German Doctors' Association) 401–2
María Martínez Sala v. Freistaat Bayern case (ECJ) 257, 273, 275, 300, 301, 311, 312, 321–2, 323
marital agreements *see Judicial Control of Marital Agreements* case (BGHZ)
Markesinis, Basil 70, 467–8
Martínez Sala case *see María Martínez Sala v. Freistaat Bayern* case
Martinsen, Dorte Sindbjerg 216–38
Massregel der Besserung und Sicherung (Reform and Preventive Measures) 92, 109
maternity grants, employers' contributions 405–7
Mecklenburg-Western Pomerania, State Constitutional Court 413–14
Menzel, Jörg 530–2
Morson and Jhanjan case (ECJ) 263
Mothers Judgment case (FCC) 27
Mr and Mrs Richard Meade case (ECJ) 268
MRAX case (ECJ) 279
Müller, Felix 333–53
Müller-Driver, Andreas 516–21
Müller-Metz, Judge Dr. Reinhard 94
Murray, Peter L. 469–72
Muslim Teacher's Headscarf case *see Islamic Head-scarf* case (FAC); *Teacher's Headscarf* case (FCC)
Muslims' rights under the Basic Law 4
Mutsch case (ECJ) 249
Mutterschutzgesetz (Working Mother Protection Act) 405–7

N

Nachträgliche Anordnung der Unterbringung in der Sicherungsverwahrung (Subsequent Ordering of Treatment in Preventive Detention) 97
national parliaments and European Union 198–201
Nationaldemokratische Partei Deutschlands (NPD National Democratic Party of Germany) 334–9
NATO 189, 339–42
Nazi regime 48–9
Nazi-SRP 53–4, 55
negative republicanism 55–7
neo-Nazism 49, 55–6, 57
Netherlands, The 139, 141, 144–5
Netherlands v. Reed (ECJ) 249–50, 271
New Deal and American Depression 62–3
Nichteinmischung (non-interference) 49
no demos thesis 202
Nordrhein-Westfalen v. Uecker and Jacquet case (ECJ) 263–4
Northrhine-Westfalia, State Constitutional Court 420, 421, 422
Notwehr *see* criminal law in Germany, self-defense
NPD Party Ban case (FCC) 334–9

O

Odievre v. France (Eur. Ct. H.R.) 164–5
O'Flynn case (ECJ) 249
Oger, Helene 509–11
Oliveri case (ECJ) 309, 433–9
Omega case (ECJ) 428–33
on-call service as working time 400–2
O.N.E. v. Deak case (ECJ) 249
Orfanopoulos case (ECJ) 309, 433–9
OSHO case (FCC) 17–20, 21

P

Paperboy case (BGH) 372–4
part-time work 404–5
Parteienprivileg (party privilege) 47
partnerships in Germany 135–7
Payne, Jennifer 478
pension insurance 24–5
pensioners' health insurance 35–8
People of the Citizens of the Union 201–5
Perlin, Professor Michael 107
Pfeiffer case (ECJ) 439–44
pharmaceutical industry, ECJ judgments 427–8
Philosophy in a Time of Terror. Dialogues with Jürgen Habermas and Jacques Derrida 497–502

Photo Composition case (BGHZ) 366–8
Pöcker, Markus 493–6
Politbüro case (BGHSt) 381–3
political parties, banning of 46, 49, 51, 52–7, 58
Posner, Chief Justice Richard, Seventh Circuit 69
precedents, doctrine of 160–5
Pretty v. United Kingdom (Eur. Ct. H.R.) 164
preventive detention *see* Germany, preventive detention
private law, German Federal Court of Justice 361–77
Procedural Laws in Europe. Towards Harmonisation 472–8
property, protection of 27, 29–32
public power, in European Union 171–215
Pusa case (ECJ) 320, 321, 324

R

R. v. Saunders case (ECJ) 263, 281
racism 228
Radbruch's Formula 379–80
Raulin case (ECJ) 304
real seat theory 132–44, 145–7, 151–5
Rechtskraft (*res judicata*) 426
Rechtsstaat (the rule of law) 48
Reed case *see Netherlands v. Reed*
Reform and Prevention Measures 92, 109
Regulation 1408/71, personal scope 218–38
rehabilitation, in Germany and USA 106–13
religious freedoms in Germany 1–22
religious protection under the Basic Law 3–4
Rhineland-Palatinate, State Constitutional Court 415
Riester pension 24
Ritual Slaughter case (FCC) 4, 5–11, 12, 14, 21
Roman law 158, 159
Roosevelt, President Franklin D. 62–3
Rott, Peter 116–31
Rufbereitschaft (stand-by) 400
Rühl, Gisela 469–72
Ruhl, J.B. 69–70
Rutili v. France case (ECJ) 263

S

Saarland, State Constitutional Court 412–13
Sabasch case 89–90
Safferling, Christoph J. M. 378–98
Sala case *see Maria Martínez Sala v. Freistaat Bayern* case
sales law, German 116–31, *see also* Consumer Sales Directive 1999/44/EC
Salvia, Michele de 166
Saxony, State Constitutional Court 417–19, 422

Saxony-Anhalt, State Constitutional Court 419, 424
Schechter Poultry Corp. v. United States 62
Scheuing, Dieter H. 283–332
Schleswig-Holstein, State Constitutional Court 414
Schmidt, Reinhard H. 522
Scholz case (ECJ) 264
Schuld(un)fähigkeit (culpability) 392–5
Schulz, Martin 132–55
Scozzari and Giunta v. Italy (Eur. Ct. H.R.) 164
securities law, German Federal Court of Justice 375–7
SED cases (BGHSt) 379–83
Selmouni v. France (Eur. Ct. H.R.) 164
separation of powers 158–9
sexual predator laws 90–1, 109
sexually violent predator (SVP) *see* SVP laws
sickness benefit payments, duration of 29–30
SIMAP case (ECJ) 401
Single European Act (1987) 176, 191, 192, 206
Sitztheorie (*real seat* theory) 132–44, 145–7, 151–5
Skanavi and Chyssanthakopoulos case (ECJ) 256–7
Smith, Craig T. 354–60
social justice principle 29
social security, intra-European 216–38
sovereignty 45–59, 173–9
Stability and Growth Pact 426
Stasi Files case (FAC) 356–9
statutory orders and bylaws 71
Stemplewitz, Jan 361–77
Storme, Marcel 472
students, maintenance grants 315–18
Stürner, Rolf 469–72
suicide, abetting in 383–6
Surinder Singh case (ECJ) 264, 265
SVP laws
 Kansas State 103–5
 Washington State 100–3

T
Takeover Law in the EU and the USA: A Comparative Analysis 478–92
Takeovers in English and German Law 478–92
taxation, ECJ judgments 426–7
Teacher's Headscarf case (FCC) 11–15, 19–20, 21, 342–7, 531–50
terrorism 348–53
third country nationals 240, 262, 263, 267–73, *see also* social security, intra-European

tort law, German Federal Court of Justice 364–8
Treaty of Amsterdam 193, 197, 198, 206
 free movement of persons 232–3
Treaty Establishing a Constitution for Europe see Constitutional Treaty, The
Treaty on European Union 255–6
Treaty of the European Union 255–6, *see also Maastricht Treaty*
Treaty of Maastricht see Maastricht Treaty
Treaty of Nice 175, 179, 193–5, 197–8, 202, 206, 215
Treaty of Rome 191, 216
 free movement of workers 216, 228–30, 231
Trojani case (ECJ) 259, 275, 302, 311, 314, 321, 323, 326

U
Überseering
 decision (BGHZ) 374–5
 judgment (EJC) 139–44, 145, 146–7, 149, 151, 153–5
Uitz, Renata 502–8
Unberath, Hannes 467–8
United Kingdom (UK) 137–8, 141, 144–5
Untermassverbot 96
US Supreme Court, preventive detention 103–5
USA 348–53
 administrative law system 61–71
 comparison with Germany 76–88
 Constitution 173
 preventive detention
 comparison with Germany 105–13
 Kansas State 103–5
 Supreme Court rules 103–5
 Washington State 99–103

V
Vander Elst case (ECJ) 268
Verfassungsmässigkeit des Wegfalls der Höchstdauer der erstmaligen Sicherungsverwahrung (Constitutionality of Abolition of Maximum Time Limit on First-time Preventive Detention) case (FCC) 112–13
versicherungsfremde Leistungen (out-of-insurance benefits) 27
Volksgemeinschaft (people's community) 55, 57
Vollzugsziel (goal of confinement) 110
Vorratsgesellschaften (shelf companies) 132, 147–9

W
welfare and family rights in EU 273–80
Weltanschauung (philosophical creed) 1
Wesenverwandtschaft (essential likeness) 55–6
wholly internal rule 263–7
Wijsenbeek case (ECJ) 301, 318–20
Wirtschaftswunder 2
working time 400–2

Y
Yiadom case (ECJ) 301, 308–9

Z
Zhu and Chen case (ECJ) 302–3, 314–15
Ziegler, Kai Peter 426–44
Zumbansen, Peer 478–92
Zupančič, Boštjan M. 156–70